Apollos Old Testament Commentary

14

PSALMS

TITLES IN THIS SERIES

EXODUS, T. Desmond Alexander
LEVITICUS, Nobuyoshi Kiuchi
NUMBERS 1 – 19, L. Michael Morales
NUMBERS 20 – 36, L. Michael Morales
DEUTERONOMY, J. G. McConville
JOSHUA, Pekka M. A. Pitkanen
RUTH, L. Daniel Hawk
1 & 2 SAMUEL, David G. Firth
1 & 2 KINGS, Lissa Wray Beal
PSALMS, David G. Firth
PROVERBS, Paul Overland
ECCLESIASTES & THE SONG OF SONGS, Daniel C. Fredericks and Daniel J. Estes
DANIEL, Ernest C. Lucas
HOSEA, Joshua N. Moon
OBADIAH, JONAH & MICAH, Elaine A. Phillips
HAGGAI, ZECHARIAH & MALACHI, Anthony R. Petterson

SERIES EDITORS

Gordon J. Wenham, 2002–23
David W. Baker, 2002–
Beth M. Stovell, 2023–

APOLLOS OLD TESTAMENT
COMMENTARY

14

PSALMS

Series Editors
David W. Baker and Beth M. Stovell

DAVID G. FIRTH

Apollos,
London, England

First published in Great Britain in 2025

Apollos
Studio 101, The Record Hall, 16–16A Baldwin's Gardens, London EC1N 7RJ
ivpbooks.com

EU GPSR Authorised Representative
LOGOS EUROPE, 9 rue Nicolas Poussin, 17000, La Rochelle, France
Email: Contact@logoseurope.eu

British Library Cataloguing-in-Publication Data
A catalogue record for this book is available from the British Library

ISBN 978–1–78974–485–9
eBook ISBN 978–1–78974–486–6

10 9 8 7 6 5 4 3 2 1

Typeset by Fakenham Prepress Solutions, Fakenham, Norfolk NR21 8NL
First printed in Great Britain by Clays Ltd

eBook by Fakenham Prepress Solutions, Fakenham, Norfolk NR21 8NL

Produced on paper from sustainable sources

Inter-Varsity Press publishes Christian books that are true to the Bible and that communicate the gospel, develop discipleship and strengthen the church for its mission in the world.

IVP originated within the Inter-Varsity Fellowship, now the Universities and Colleges Christian Fellowship, a student movement connecting Christian Unions in universities and colleges throughout Great Britain, and a member movement of the International Fellowship of Evangelical Students. Website: www.uccf.org.uk. That historic association is maintained, and all senior IVP staff and committee members subscribe to the UCCF Basis of Faith.

In memory of
W. S. Prinsloo

CONTENTS

TABLES

EDITORS' PREFACE

The Apollos Old Testament Commentary takes its name from the Alexandrian Jewish Christian who was able to impart his great learning fervently and powerfully through his teaching (Acts 18:24–25). He ably applied his understanding of past events to his contemporary society. This series seeks to do the same, keeping one foot firmly planted in the universe of the original text and the other in that of the target audience, which is preachers, teachers and students of the Bible. The series editors have selected scholars who are adept in both areas, exhibiting scholarly excellence along with practical insight for application.

Translators need to be at home with the linguistic practices and semantic nuances of both the original and target languages in order to be able to transfer the full impact of the one into the other. Commentators, however, serve as interpreters of the text rather than simply its translators. They also need to adopt a dual stance, though theirs needs to be even more solid and diversely anchored than that of translators. While they also must have the linguistic competence to produce their own excellent translations, they must moreover be fully conversant with the literary conventions, sociological and cultural practices, historical background and understanding, and theological perspectives of those who produced the text as well as those whom it concerned. On the other side, they must also understand their own times and culture, able to see where relevance for the original audience is transferable to that of current readers. For this to be accomplished, it is not only necessary to interpret the text; one must also interpret the audience.

Traditionally, commentators have been content to highlight and expound the ancient text. More recently, the need for an anchor in the present day has also become more evident, and this series self-consciously adopts this approach, combining both. Each author analyses the original text through a new translation, textual notes, a discussion of the literary form, structure and background of the passage, as well as commenting on elements of its exegesis. A study of the passage's interpretational development in Scripture and the church concludes each section, serving to bring the passage home to the modern reader. What we intend, therefore, is to provide not only tools of excellence for the academy, but also tools of function for the pulpit.

David W. Baker
Beth M. Stovell

AUTHOR'S PREFACE

This is not a commentary I expected to write. As one of the original series editors, Professor Gordon Wenham had initially assigned this volume to himself, the first fruit of which is evident in some preliminary works he published. Unfortunately, problems with his health meant he was unable to undertake its writing, but he was gracious enough to pass the assignment to me. I want to begin, therefore, by noting the immense contribution Gordon has made and to express my sorrow that we will not see the full benefit of that work in a commentary on Psalms. At the same time, I need to thank him for his support for me as I undertook this work.

My own journey in the study of the Psalms can be traced back to my doctoral work. It was my privilege to attend the Old Testament Society of South Africa's annual meeting at the University of the Free State in 1992. Having travelled down from Zimbabwe where we were then working, I received a lift from Pretoria to Bloemfontein with a group going there from the University of Pretoria. The only non-Afrikaans speaker in a minibus, it was my privilege to meet Professor W. S. Prinsloo and a group of other scholars who were all part of the Psalms research project he had established there – Professors Phil Botha, Gert Prinsloo, Dirk Human and Henk Potgieter. All were gracious enough to accept the limitations of an English speaker in the vehicle, making me welcome among them. Moreover, the journey down was like an extended seminar on Psalms, one that continued when I met Professor Fanie Snyman from the University of the Free State, someone who had also studied with Professor Prinsloo. My interest in the study of the Psalms existed before this, but the possibilities of formal research on the Psalms were opened up to me as never before, and when seeking an appropriate direction for doctoral research I found a congenial yet rigorous supervisor in Professor Prinsloo. He modelled careful attention to the text and its theological significance while supporting me as a student. He was at the time working on a short commentary in English, though much of his other work is in Afrikaans. Although that commentary was published, his death in 1997, a little over a year after I completed my dissertation, meant that we lost a pioneering scholar when his most productive work remained ahead of him. It has been my privilege, though, to continue working in various ways with the South African colleagues I met then, even after returning to Australia and then moving to the United Kingdom. Although we have all varied Professor Prinsloo's work in different ways, we can all acknowledge having learned much from him. One area of great importance in his model was attention to the structure of a poem, and though it is presented in less detail here, it is a feature that continues to inform my work. Because of his formative influence on me, it is only right that this book be dedicated to his memory.

Alongside those in South Africa it has been my privilege to share the study of Psalms with colleagues from across the world. Across the Atlantic, I have long valued discussing psalms with Tremper Longman III, David Howard, Dan Estes, Mark Boda and Brittany Melton. Here in Britain, people like Jamie Grant, Philip Johnston, Sue Gillingham, Samuel Hildebrandt and Megan Daffern have all shaped my reading of Psalms, as have Lindsay Wilson and Kit Barker back in Australia. No doubt there are some I have forgotten (and to whom I apologize!), but the important point is that my own study of Psalms has been greatly enriched by sharing them with others. Studying these wonderful poems within such a community of international scholarship is an immense privilege from which I have benefited greatly. It has also been my privilege to supervise several students who have worked on Psalms from whom I have also learned much, so it is appropriate also to thank Simon Stocks, Matt Ayars, Cheryl Eaton, Michelle Stinson, Erica Mongé-Greer, Matthew Montgomery and Liz Grier.

As well as the wider community of Psalms scholarship, it has also been my privilege to write this commentary as a member of the faculty at Trinity College, Bristol. This has been a convivial place in which to write, and I wish to thank our principal, Reverend Dr Sean Doherty for his support in its writing. Thanks are also due to my other colleagues who have heard me speak on Psalms in a range of settings and who have continually encouraged me in my work. Alongside Trinity, I am privileged to be a Research Associate of the University of the Free State, and want to thank Professor Lodewyk Sutton and Mrs Marina van Biljon for various ways they have supported and enabled my work.

A great deal happens between the submission of a manuscript and its publication. Thanks are due to both David Baker and Beth Stovell as series editors for their careful reading of the manuscript. Eldo Barkhuizen and Rima Devereaux have worked wonders in their editorial work. Thanks are also due to Tom Creedy for overseeing the whole process.

Finally, I need to acknowledge the support and prayer of my family as I have completed this work. In particular, my wife Lynne continues to go above and beyond in providing encouragement and support for my work. It is a joy to continue this work with her.

David G. Firth

ABBREVIATIONS

TEXTUAL

4Q522	Manuscript from cave 4, Qumran with a non-canonical text and Psalm 122
4QPs[a]	First Psalms scroll, cave 4, Qumran
4QPs[b]	Second Psalms scroll, cave 4, Qumran
11QMelch	Melchizedek scroll, cave 11, Qumran
11QPs[a]	First Psalms scroll, cave 11, Qumran
11QPsAp[a]	Manuscript of Apocryphal Psalms, cave 11, Qumran
11QPs[b]	Second Psalms scroll, cave 4, Qumran
A	Aleppo Codex
Aram.	Aramaic
b.	Babylonian Talmud
Gk	Greek
Hebr.	Hebrew
K	Kethib
L	Leningrad Codex of Masoretic Text
LXX	Septuagint
MS(S)	manuscript(s)
MT	MasoreticText
Q	Qere (the Hebrew text to be read out)
Sop.	*Sophrim* (Mishnah)
Sym	Symmachus
Syr.	Syriac Peshitta
Tg	Targum
Ugar.	Ugaritic
Vg	Vulgate

HEBREW GRAMMAR

abs.	absolute
act.	active
cohort(s).	cohortative(s)
conj.	conjunction
const.	construct
f.	feminine
gen.	genitive

hiph(s).	hiphil(s)
hithpol.	hithpolel
hoph.	hophal
imp.	imperative
impf(s).	imperfect(s)
infin(s).	infinitive(s)
juss.	jussive
m.	masculine
mg.	margin
niph.	niphal
pass.	passive
pf(s).	perfect(s)
pi.	piel
pl.	plural
pr.	pronoun/pronominal
prec.	precative
prep.	preposition
ptc(s).	participle(s)
pu.	pual
qat.	qatal
sg.	singular
suff.	suffix
voc(s).	vocative(s)

MISCELLANEOUS

ANE	Ancient Near East(ern)
BC	Before Christ
CSB	Christian Standard Bible
esp.	especially
ESV	English Standard Version
ET	English Translation(s)
EVV	English versions
GNB	Good News Bible
km	kilometres
LEB	Lexham English Bible
lit.	literally
NASB	New American Standard Bible
NEB	New English Bible
NET	New English Translation
NIV	New English Version
NJPS	New Jewish Publication Society translation
NLT	New Living Translation
NRSV	New Revised Standard Version

NT New Testament
OT Old Testament
REB Revised English Bible
RSV Revised Standard Version

JOURNALS, REFERENCE WORKS, SERIES

AcT *Acta theologica*
AcT Supp *AcT Supplement*
ANES *Ancient Near Eastern Studies*
BASOR *Bulletin of the American Society of Overseas Research*
BBR *Bulletin of Biblical Research*
BDB F. Brown, S. R. Driver and C. A. Briggs, *A Hebrew and English Lexicon of the Old Testament*, Oxford: Clarendon, 1907; repr. Peabody: Hendrickson, 2005
BHQ A. Schenker et al. (eds.), *Biblia Hebraica Quinta*, Stuttgart: Deutsche Bibelgesellschaft, 2004–
BHS K. Elliger and W. Rudoph (eds.), *Biblia Hebraica Stuttgartensia*, Stuttgart: Deutsche Bibelgesellschaft, 1967–77
Bib *Biblica*
BibInt *Biblical Interpretation*
BSac *Bibliotheca sacra*
BTB *Biblical Theology Bulletin*
BZ *Biblische Zeitschrift*
C&C *Canon & Culture*
CBQ *Catholic Biblical Quarterly*
CJ *Concordia Journal*
CTJ *Calvin Theological Journal*
CTQ *Concordia Theological Quarterly*
CurrTM *Currents in Theology and Mission*
DCH *Dictionary of Classical Hebrew*, Sheffield: Sheffield Phoenix, 8 vols, 1993–2016
ETL *Ephemerides Theologicae Lovanienses*
EvQ *Evangelical Quarterly*
GKC E. Kautzsch (ed.), A. E. Cowley (tr.), *Gesenius' Hebrew Grammar*, 2nd edn, Oxford: Clarendon, 1910
GTJ *Grace Theological Journal*
HALOT L. Köhler and W. Baumgartner, *A Hebrew and Aramaic Lexicon of the Old Testament*, Leiden: Brill, 1994–2000
HBT *Horizons in Biblical Theology*
HeBAI *Hebrew Bible and Ancient Israel*
HS *Hebrew Studies*
HTR *Harvard Theological Review*

HTS	*Hervormde Teologiese Studies*
HUCA	*Hebrew Union College Annual*
IdS	*In die Skriflig*
Int	*Interpretation*
J-M	Paul Joüon and T. Muraoka, *A Grammar of Biblical Hebrew*, Rome: Pontifical Biblical Institute, 2006
JANES	*Journal of Ancient Near Eastern Studies*
JBL	*Journal of Biblical Literature*
JETS	*Journal of the Evangelical Theological Society*
JHS	*Journal of the Hebrew Scriptures*
JNSL	*Journal of Northwest Semitic Languages*
JPT	*Journal of Pentecostal Theology*
JQR	*Jewish Quarterly Review*
JRT	*Journal of Religious Thought*
JSem	*Journal of Semitics*
JSOT	*Journal for Study of the Old Testament*
JTI	*Journal of Theological Interpretation*
JTS	*Journal of Theological Studies*
LTQ	*Lexington Theological Quarterly*
NTT	*Nederduitse Teologise Tydskrif*
OTE	*Old Testament Essays*
PP	*Psalmody and Poetry*
Proof	*Prooftexts: A Journal of Jewish Literary History*
PRS	*Perspectives in Religious Studies*
PRSt	*Perspectives in Religious Studies*
RB	*Revue Biblique*
ResQ	*Restoration Quarterly*
RevExp	*Review and Expositor*
RS	*Religious Studies*
ScEs	*Science et esprit*
Scrip	*Scriptura*
SJOT	*Scandinavian Journal of the Old Testament*
SK	*Skrif en Kerk*
STJ	*Stellenbosch Theological Journal*
Them	*Themelios*
ThTo	*Theology Today*
TJ	*Trinity Journal*
TynB	*Tyndale Bulletin*
VE	*Vox evangelica*
VeE	*Verbum et Ecclesia*
VT	*Vetus Testamentum*
W-O	B. K. Waltke and M. O'Connor, *An Introduction to Biblical Hebrew Syntax*, Winona Lake: Eisenbrauns, 1990
WHS	R. J. Williams (ed.), 3rd edn rev. and expanded by J. C.

	Beckman, *Williams Hebrew Syntax*, Toronto: University of Toronto Press, 2007
WW	*Word & World*
ZAW	*Zeitschrift für die alttestamentliche Wissenschaft*

INTRODUCTION

Introductions to commentaries tend to move in one of two directions – they are either a comprehensive introduction to the book on which the commentary is written, or they are a shorter work that provides an orientation to the decisions lying behind the commentary that follows. Since there is no shortage of excellent introductions to the Psalms (e.g. Futato 2007; Jacobson and Jacobson 2012; or Creach 2020), this introduction takes the second path. Where appropriate, reference is made to more detailed works that would support the work done here, but the goal is to provide a hermeneutical orientation to the commentary that follows.

1. NAME

There is a fundamental ambiguity in the English title of the book 'The Psalms'. As a title, it could refer either to the individual poems (which we call 'the psalms') that comprise the book, or it could refer to the book itself, since both can be called 'The Psalms'. At other points we may see the book called 'The Psalter', a title that always focuses attention on the book as a whole. How we understand the book's title has hermeneutical implications for how we read it, focused on either the discrete poems or the whole book – though of course doing one does not prevent us from doing the other. At this point, perhaps, it is enough to note that what we call a biblical book is not hermeneutically neutral.

We may also note that the term 'Psalms' is itself an unusual word. English does not generally begin words with 'Ps', which is perhaps why we leave the initial 'P' silent, something not necessarily true in other languages. In my experience, children who are introduced to the Bible and come across the word invariably attempt to pronounce the initial 'P' since that is what we normally do in English. But even apart from the curiosities of pronunciation, what exactly is a 'psalm'? And slightly more curiously, why is it that in most English translations there is a note in the titles that marks out some fifty-seven of the psalms as 'A Psalm' (e.g. Pss 3, 5, 6), while others lack this designation? Does this mean the others are not actually psalms? Put differently, why might some psalms need to be designated as such while others do not?

Here we need to pause and note that we are in fact dealing with a range of factors that have emerged from the history of interpretation, starting with the issue of translation. Our English title 'Psalms' is effectively a transliteration of the title from when the book was translated into Greek in the LXX (*Psalmoi*), possibly in the second century BC. In English we have adopted a Greek word into our own language (hence, the slightly awkward initial 'Ps'), though as is common with loanwords it has come to have a more technical sense than in its original setting. The Greek *psalmos* (the singular for *psalmoi*) means a praise song. By the time of the NT, we can already see two main uses for the term, so that in Luke 24:44 it is used in a technical sense to refer to the Book of Psalms (and perhaps through it to the whole third division of the Hebrew canon known as the Writings), whereas in 1 Corinthians 14:26 it still has the more general sense of a praise song. By calling the book *Psalmoi*, those responsible for its formation in LXX have called it 'Songs of Praise'. In this, the book's title is derived from the most common element in the titles (*psalmos*), which in some way describe the poem (see below on 'Psalm titles').

However, a quick glance at psalms that include *psalmos* in the title in LXX may give pause for thought. The first psalm to use this title is Psalm 3, a psalm where the speaker complains to Yahweh about the actions of various enemies, though also expressing confidence in Yahweh. We may not expect it in English since the next psalm to include 'A Psalm' in the title is Psalm 5, but the term also occurs in LXX's title of Psalm 4, though here it is equivalent to 'with stringed instruments' in many English titles. But apart from the change of case (dative rather than nominative) it is the same word, highlighting a further nuance to the word in terms of its musical associations. But if we are looking for praise, we may note that although there is some confidence (vv. 7–8), it too may be better described as a song of complaint. The same is true of Psalm 5. The Greek tradition that has been formative for the English thus labels the whole book as 'Songs of Praise', a label it also gives to various individual psalms, but it quickly becomes clear that the praise offered here is not simply equated with times of feeling good and comfortable. As Dennis Tucker observes, when we praise, 'We are declaring that the God who is worthy of praise is the God who will redeem the brokenness of our lamenting world' (Tucker and Grant 2018: 1045). In labelling psalms that may otherwise seem to be words of complaint rather than praise as a song of praise, the Greek tradition has grasped an important theological point about the nature of praise. Praise is something that must include proper recognition of the fact that we live in a disordered world that needs to be put to right. Each song of praise, and indeed these Songs of Praise, are an important pointer to this.

But in calling the book *Psalmoi*, the Greek tradition has chosen to minimize other dimensions of the book. Admittedly, we are not always sure how best to translate parts of some psalm titles (and LXX was clearly guessing at points), but by focusing on those with *psalmos* in the title, we give less emphasis to other elements in the titles. For instance, Psalm 17 is said to be a 'prayer' (LXX gives a fairly literal translation). This term is less common in titles (elsewhere only Pss 86, 90, 102, 143), but it does occur a further twenty-eight times in the psalms themselves, unlike the term translated *psalmos*, which does not occur outside the titles. This is not to suggest that a song of praise may not also be a prayer, but rather to note that the title *Psalmoi* encourages a stronger focus on sung praise than prayer. This demonstrates that every summary title will highlight some features while omitting others.

When we think of the title in English, however, it is probable that understanding a psalm as a 'song of praise' does not represent the most prominent sense given to it. In many Christian traditions, various psalms are chanted rather than sung, meaning that the element of music is given less prominence. They are also often read (perhaps as a call to worship) and so presented to congregations in much the same way as other parts of the Bible. If a full psalm is sung, it is more likely to be a choral piece (perhaps still in Latin) in more traditionally liturgical churches, whereas the charismatic tradition is more likely to build a worship song around one or two verses from a psalm, but seldom the whole psalm. The English language tradition therefore tends to regard a 'psalm' as one of the (more or less!) one hundred and fifty poems found in the Masoretic book of Psalms. The wider sense from the Greek tradition has not completely fallen away, but the focus on one particular set of poems, rather than on understanding 'psalms' as a more general word (as the Greek is), means our hermeneutical stance has tended to be much narrower.

The Greek tradition, however, was also trying to capture something inherent to the Masoretic (MT) book. The title there is *Sepher Tehellim*, or 'book of praises'. Although it uses a term more specifically associated with music, the Greek title captures this element, whereas it exists only in a more vestigial form in English usage. The Hebrew does not have to include music, though it can do so. Yet, although the book uses this title, it occurs as a title only in Psalm 145. It does, however, occur in a further twenty-nine instances in the book, along with the cognate verb *hll* ('praise' – found in the form 'Hallelujah' or 'Praise Yah'). It could therefore be representative of the book's content, provided we understand praise in the terms that Tucker has noted. The Hebrew tradition uses a different term (*mizmôr*) in those titles that English versions typically render as 'a Psalm', though we might better translate it as 'a melody' and so recognize the musical dimension. Within the psalms, there is a gradual movement from complaint to praise as the dominant motif (Brueggemann 1991b), so the Hebrew title captures this element. This reaches its climax in the Final Hallel, Psalms 146–150, each of which is framed by the cry 'Hallelujah' – a cry that is simultaneously an act of praise and a summoning of others to join that praise. The praise offered within the Psalter is frequently musical, but it is not only musical, for it includes dance elements (e.g. Pss 149:3; 150:4) and other forms of bodily movement such as washing hands and walking around the altar while proclaiming Yahweh's great deeds (Ps. 26:6–7) or raising a cup in thanksgiving (Ps. 116:13). Praise is not only musical, though, to judge by the band put together in Psalm 150:3–5, it can certainly include it.

As with the Greek title, the Hebrew tradition cannot encompass everything about the book in a single title. However, when the title is read in the light of the book's content, we are given reason to understand praise as much more than happy words we speak when things are going well. Praise is a reminder of who God is and why we need him in a broken world, one where we also hold to the pain that is presented in complaint poems as an element of our praise. Moreover, where the Greek title encourages an emphasis on musical praise, the Hebrew title allows for a wider understanding of praise, one that can be developed through the content of some of the psalms in a way that the Greek title does not. Each title is a hermeneutical signal that highlights at least some aspects of how this book is to be read.

As well as 'Psalms', English readers may also be familiar with 'Psalter'. This too derives from the Greek translation, this time using the word for the 'lyre', an instrument mentioned at various points in the book (e.g. Ps. 149:3). This title also highlights the musical dimension, though English usage has now moved away from this, with 'Psalter' more commonly used as a term for the whole book, a means of resolving the ambiguity of whether 'Psalms' means particular psalms or the book itself. Those familiar with a psaltery (a plucked-string instrument with a flat sound board, though it is not a lyre) may still recognize the musical background in the term, but current English usage tends to move away from both the elements of praise and music, so discussion of the Psalter is now concerned with a book that is a collection of Psalms, the best known of which remains the book of Psalms. Again, the title used signals a hermeneutical stance towards the book, this time one that signals (at least to some extent) the possibility of reading the individual psalms in a more collective manner. But then, whichever title is used signals (to some extent) a hermeneutical choice.

2. TEXT

As seen above, the Psalter has come down to us in several forms, the best known of which are the MT and LXX, though there is also the important variation of 11QPs[a]. This is a fragmentary manuscript from Qumran, also known as 11Q5 as a means of not closing off discussion of whether it is a Psalter. It includes approximately forty psalms (mostly incomplete) plus about ten other poetic compositions, including Psalm 151, itself otherwise known from LXX. It also presents the psalms in a different order from that familiar from MT; for example scattering the Songs of the Ascents rather than presenting them as a collection. In that our concern is with the MT Psalter, we do need to consider here its particular shape, but rather note that it provides an important witness to many psalms from a much earlier period than our main Masoretic manuscripts. In fact, Psalms are well attested from the Qumran manuscripts, all of which have been helpfully collated by Flint (2014), who notes which passages are recorded in the various manuscripts that have been recovered. Electronic editions of these manuscripts are now available, making them much more accessible to researchers, and these can resolve some of the difficulties in the manuscripts. So, at points it remains important to examine photographs of the manuscripts, many of which are now available free online. Many of these manuscripts are only small fragments, but are enough to demonstrate that (in whatever form) Psalms were highly valued at Qumran (see Flint 2013), even if these manuscripts also raise important questions about the form of the text of Psalms.

Important questions now exist around the shape of the text of every part of the OT, a significant shift from the situation only a few decades back. The Qumran material has provided textual evidence in Hebrew that is considerably older (often over a thousand years) than Codex L, the manuscript which is the oldest complete available Masoretic manuscript. Codex A (the basis of the Hebrew University project of a new edition of the Hebrew Bible) is older but was damaged in the mid-twentieth century and is now incomplete. The main printed edition (*BHS*) remains a diplomatic presentation of Codex L, though with variants noted by the editors. It is currently being replaced by *BHQ*, but the fascicle for Psalms has not appeared at the time of writing. Although it will present the text-critical information differently, it will still be based on Codex L. Codex L is also the basis for most electronic versions of MT. By contrast, the Oxford Hebrew Bible is intended to provide an eclectic text prepared by an editor, following the pattern familiar from editions of the Greek

New Testament. As with the other projects, the Psalms volume has not yet appeared, so *BHS* remains our main resource. It is important to stress that although *BHS* presents a Masoretic manuscript, and these manuscripts do not show huge variance, it is not itself equivalent to MT. There are points where it seems to contain errors when compared to other manuscripts (cf. 'Notes' on Ps. 149:7). As such, MT must still be reconstructed to some extent, though the main evidence for this is found in the apparatus of *BHS*.

Despite the new questions that have emerged and the important consideration of the evidence from Qumran, along with the fact that at some points Gk (mostly LXX, though other recensions can be significant) can provide a better reading, MT remains the primary vehicle for recovery of the canonical text (with Childs 1979: 10–106). As such, while recognizing that MT as we have it now is not identical with the canonical text, there is still good reason to use it as the basis for exegesis and reflection, and that approach is followed throughout this commentary.

3. PSALMS AND PSALTER

If the title we give to this book signals a hermeneutical stance towards it, so too does the question of whether we are discussing the 'Psalms' or the 'Psalter'. As noted above, 'Psalms' is potentially ambiguous in referring either to the individual poems (or groups of them) or to the book. But 'Psalter' refers to the book. While allowing that 'Psalms' and 'Psalter' can be fairly exact synonyms, at this point it will be useful to use 'Psalms' in the more limited sense of referring to the poems collected in the book, and 'Psalter' as the book itself. The question to ask, then, is are we seeking to interpret the psalms or the Psalter? In asking this, we are concerned with identifying the primary focus of the interpretative task – is it the psalms or the Psalter? Of course, even if we conclude that the Psalter is the main focus, we can interpret it only through the psalms.

3.1. Interpreting the Psalms

It is not unreasonable to suggest that the dominant focus of interpretation has been the Psalms themselves. Indeed, an often-raised criticism of making the Psalter the focus of attention has been that this is only a reasonably recent development, not something that has featured strongly in the history of research. Although Jenkins (2020a) has shown that there have been those through history who have attended to the shape of the Psalter, it remains the case that his examples are to some extent outliers, and the dominant focus has been on the Psalms rather than the Psalter. Of course, even before the emphasis on the interpretation of the

Psalter developed there were points where interpreters noted that certain psalms (e.g. the Songs of the Ascents, Pss 120–134) were clearly gathered for a reason, but the focus remained the psalms themselves. We can note three main features of this hermeneutical stance – poetic features, standard forms and the place of psalms in Israel's worship.

3.1.1. Psalms as poetry

All modern English versions present the psalms as poetry. This recognizes the fact that, even if their form of poetry is different from that common in Western culture, they need to be read differently from prose. Yet, it is not always clear that the dimension of the psalms as poetry has necessarily had a great impact on how they are interpreted. That is, the fact that poems do not express themselves in the same ways, as prose is not always appreciated, with verses cited from Psalms cited to support certain theological points as if they were expressed in prose. As a starting point, we can therefore note that poetry often expresses itself in non-literal ways, and that its mode of constructing meaning does not refer to the world in the same manner as at least some forms of prose may. For example, in Psalm 22:6 the psalmist claims to be a grub and not a human. It does not take much reflection to realize that this cannot be meant in any literalistic manner, not least because the psalmist's adversaries in the following verses act as those who address a human. We are led to conclude that the speaker here is, in fact, a human and not a grub. None of this makes the claim of the verse any less important, and neither does it make it false. Rather, we are forced to ask about how the speaker can be understood as a grub and how human status may be denied. As becomes clear through the poem, this is about relative social status and power, all of which the psalmist lacks. The affirmation is true, but in a particular way. A prose text may move in this direction, but it is much more frequent in poetry.

No precise definition of poetry can be given because we recognize poetry relative only to other types of text, and there are numerous points in the OT where it is not clear if a particular text should be regarded as poetry or prose. However, in general poetry is an elevated use of language that represents an intentional variation on what may be called 'standard language', most obviously by placing it into something that can be recognized as verse (Goh 2017: 1–2). The use of non-literal language is not unique to poems (metaphors can exist in any genre), but in poetry it is more common. However, it is the 'versification' (Goh 2017: 1) that most obviously marks out a poem.

When we turn from poetry as a general concept to the specifics of the OT, we recognize that Hebrew poets created verse within the constraints of their language and culture. It is important to stress that the processes by which poets move from standard language to versified language is relative to the constraints of their own language. Features that may be relatively common in one language, and thus not a feature of verse, may be comparatively rare in another and so something that poets explore. In Hebrew, it has been recognized for some time that parallelism (a repetition of some element – whether semantic or grammatical [see Ayars 2019] – within a grammatical segment) forms the most commonly employed poetic feature. When we are aware of it, we can easily see it in most psalms. As numerous excellent works on Hebrew poetry are available (e.g. Alter 1985; Berlin 1985; W. G. E. Watson 1986; Goh 2017), there is no need to discuss either the various forms of parallelism or the main modes of poetic adornment here beyond noting that, for the most part, an attempt has been made in the commentary to avoid the technical language of poetry as much as possible in order to make the volume more accessible. However, in line with the more recent work on parallelism, the Lowthian distinction between synonymous, antithetic and synonymous parallelism has not generally been followed, though at points it retains some heuristic value. Rather, following the major work of James Kugel (1981), all parallelism has been understood on the pattern of 'A and, what's more, B'. The question is then to determine how 'B' develops 'A' and thus whether it primarily echoes or extends the previous-part line (following Jacobson and Jacobson 2012: 17–20).

A great deal of helpful attention has been given to the study of parallelism within the poetic line (e.g. Stocks 2012), but it is also clear that parallelism can occur at different levels of any one poem, and that our goal must be to interpret an entire poem, a process that attends to a range of semantic, semiotic and structural features (with W. S. Prinsloo 1994a). Hence, our goal must always be to interpret an entire poem. At one level, this is a thankless task because poetry almost always creates a surplus of meaning (not least in its emotional impact), and so no interpretation can really be comprehensive. But this does not mean the attempt should not be made. Rather, we need to attend to the presence of poetic features such as parallelism at the level of the individual poetic line and then at all levels of the poem above that. That is, we attend to the main building blocks of a poem, exploring how they interrelate in seeking to understand it as a whole. Such an understanding must be the goal of the poetic analysis.

Unfortunately, the language employed in providing this analysis is complex and not always agreed upon – for example, do we speak of a bicolon or a distich? Complicating this, it is not possible to use 'verse' to describe a particular segment of a psalm because in the Bible 'verse' refers to the referencing system that is used to identify a particular piece of text within it. Since some choices have to be made, the following are used in this commentary:

- 'Line' or 'poetic line' is used to describe the basic unit of sense within a poem. This is commonly but not always equivalent to a verse in English Bibles. The line can be analysed into various segments which are here called a 'part line'. Poetic lines typically come in two or three parts (others are possible), with a line made up of two parts called a 'bicolon' and three parts a 'tricolon'. A monocolon occurs when there is no parallel unit in the grammatical segment.
- The psalms are more than a collection of individual lines, and build meaning through the relationship of the various parts within them. Since poetry is structured language, attention is therefore paid to how the various lines are placed relative to one another. This leads to the segmentation of each poem into larger segments marked by grammatical or semantic shifts within the psalm. Not all segment divisions operate at the same level (like the subheadings in this introduction). The principal divisions in each psalm are here called 'stanzas'. Usually, these are more than a single poetic line, but this is not necessary. The stanzas themselves may contain smaller changes, and these too should be recognized. Accordingly, the segments within each stanza are here called 'strophes'. A structure for each psalm is provided that analyses it on this system. It should be noted that although every psalm can be analysed in terms of its stanzas, it is not always necessary that there should be strophes.

3.1.2. Standard forms of Psalms

A major development in the study of the Psalms in the twentieth century was recognition of the fact that many of them showed significant formal patterns. The pioneer of this work was Herman Gunkel (1998) whose significant work was completed early in the twentieth century even if the English translation came only many years later. Gunkel recognized that certain life settings (what he called *Sitz im Leben*) led to certain types of poems. Such language can be described as stereotypical (though not in a pejorative sense) in that a community learns to use particular types of language in certain circumstances. To use a modern example, even extempore prayers at a wedding follow a recognizable pattern that is immediately different from those spoken at a funeral. None of this prevents genuine creativity on the part of those who pray, but it is creativity within a form rather than something new that is created every time. Such language patterns also allow the congregation to respond to a prayer with their own 'amen' – and indeed, a response of 'amen' to something is commonly an indicator that what has come before is a prayer. The life setting (*Sitz im Leben*) has led to the use of particular language, something that is especially true in formal contexts such as worship.

Gunkel's insights were challenged, reformed and modified through much of the twentieth century, but the types that he established have remained the dominant ones. The main categories (known as a *Gattung*) are as follows:

- Individual complaint (or lament)
- Communal complaint
- Hymn
- Thanksgiving song
- Royal psalm

In addition, we can note some less-common types:

- Song of trust
- Wisdom

One major problem with this system is that some psalms are defined on the basis of the poem's formal structure (e.g. the individual complaint), whereas others are defined on the basis of some of their content (royal, wisdom). Indeed, a royal psalm may also be one of the other categories since its defining feature was reference to the king, and the king may reasonably offer a complaint or express thanksgiving. Gunkel identified only a small number of psalms as royal, whereas Eaton (1976) reckoned that the majority of poems where an individual spoke were royal. Likewise, recognizing 'wisdom' has long proved challenging (see Cheung 2015; Stocks 2016), even if most scholars were content that wisdom was present. Recent questions about whether or not wisdom is even a recognizable genre (Kynes 2018) have complicated matters, though in fact Kynes's proposals probably make it easier to recognize wisdom as a feature within various psalms even if it makes it less likely that we can continue to speak of 'wisdom' as a particular type of psalm (though see Cheung 2022).

A second problem with Gunkel's model is that it is not always possible to identify a *Sitz im Leben* for any given psalm beyond something quite general. This is not always the case, and in some psalms a *Sitz im Leben* remains at least reasonably transparent (see comments on Ps. 7). But often we cannot say much more than that a particular psalm probably had a role in Israel's worship in the temple. The difficulty is that the model requires us to work backwards from the text that we now have to a hypothetical situation that preceded it (for examples, see below 'The Psalms and Israel's worship'). This can be problematic when the hypothesized *Sitz im Leben* controls the reading of the text, meaning that it has greater control over the interpretation than the text itself. We have to allow for the possibility that various psalms were edited over time so that they could be used in a range of settings, meaning that an original *Sitz im Leben* may be only one of a number of settings that could be relevant for a psalm's interpretation. Indeed, we have evidence of some psalms being edited. For example, Psalms 14 and 53 are very similar to one another and often treated as replicas. But Botha (2013b) has shown that each has been edited in different ways that are relevant to their present literary context. These psalms demonstrate that there was a concern to adapt and update earlier poems, even if in small ways, to make them applicable to a range of settings.

Finally, Gunkel was suspicious of psalms that used elements of varying types, seeing this as a decline in Israel's psalmody. Not all who followed him remained as suspicious about these psalms as him, but the fact that he was forced to acknowledge the presence of 'mixed types' shows that although introductions to the Psalms still list his categories, many psalms integrate elements, making it difficult to assign them to one category or another. For instance, Psalm 145 could be understood as a hymn – it certainly provides reasons for praise. But it also integrates elements that may be thought to belong more in the realm of wisdom, such as its use of the acrostic structure and use of words of encouragement to its audience (e.g. vv. 17–20). Likewise, Psalm 146 is a hymn, notable from its use of 'Hallelujah' to frame for the poem. But its admonition against trusting in human leaders (vv. 3–4) sounds more like a wisdom statement. If there are features of multiple psalm types, then presumably there is also a range of life settings in which these psalms could be used.

The various psalm types remain a useful guide to the main types of poems found in Psalms, and Gunkel's (1998) basic insight into the ways in which certain human experiences lead to stereotypical language remains helpful. Nevertheless, the categories work better as a guide to the types of experience they may address than as a specific guide to their *Sitz im Leben* (Firth 2005b: 165). That is, we can helpfully use the categories descriptively rather than prescriptively. They help us become aware of the life settings that could give rise to a particular type, but we also accept that the creativity of the poets (both originators and revisers) means that while the categories remain a helpful way of seeing compositional patterns, we cannot allow a reconstructed life setting to control interpretation. Such an approach prioritizes the text itself rather than a proposed background while also accepting that not all psalms comfortably fit into any one category.

3.1.3. The Psalms and Israel's worship

Not all the psalms show obvious connections with Israel's worship. Psalm 1, for example could have been used in public worship, but there is nothing in the psalm that would necessarily lead us to expect that it would (or that it wouldn't!). Other psalms show numerous features that lead us to associate them with Israel's worship, especially in the temple. Discussion of such matters is often expressed in terms of the 'cult', with factors in this worship described as 'cultic'. This is a technical sense of the term that should be distinguished from the modern sense of a cult as a sectarian (and often deviant) religious group. Some of these cultic features may be less evident to modern readers than they were to ancient ones, but familiarity with the different psalms usually makes these cultic acts relatively transparent, though some remain uncertain. For instance, in Psalm 3:5 the psalmist reports on lying down and sleeping and then awaking before expressing confidence in Yahweh's protective power. This could simply refer to the normal routines of life that all experience, sleeping and then awaking, but it could also refer to an act where a supplicant spent the night in the temple before God. Some choices about the psalm's *Sitz im Leben* could lead to us concluding that this refers to a cultic act, but it is not a necessary reading.

At other points, though, the cultic elements in a psalm are difficult to miss. For example, in Psalm 5:7, the psalmist reports entering the temple and bowing down. The psalm clearly describes a cultic act that an individual enacts, a moment of worship. This does not have to mean that the speaker is acting out what is described as it happens in the poem, but this would theoretically be possible. Other psalms find a speaker addressing a congregation, as for example in Psalm 30:4–5. In the immediately preceding verses, the speaker introduces a moment of personal thanksgiving for deliverance Yahweh has wrought, words that are addressed to God. But a congregation is then addressed, a group who are summoned to offer their own praise to God. The psalmist's experience becomes a model for the rest of the faithful, and they can be called to offer their own praise. Some psalms also refer to what may be called more formal moments of Israel's worship. For example, Psalm 81 not only summons a congregation to worship; it also specifically ties the worship described (including various musical instruments, several of which recur in the band in Ps. 150:3–5) to the announcement of a festal day (Ps. 80:3). Unfortunately, it does not tell us exactly which festival is in mind, and a range of possibilities remain. Nevertheless, a cultic background is expressly present here. Similarly, Psalm 68 describes a parade of worshippers involved in joyful worship, even if once again it is not possible to identify a particular cultic event from the details of the psalm. But overall, we gain a picture of worship across the Psalms that is joyful and fully embodied, worship that was often loud and musical. But we also find silence (Ps. 65:1) in a psalm that clearly associates itself with the temple, so we should not imagine that all worship took a similar form. Rather, the worship expressed in Psalms takes on a multitude of forms, reflecting the fact that worship is not tied to any one mode and that complaint is as much an act of worship as is praise.

Although many psalms clearly refer to cultic acts, some research has tried to go further, attempting to identify festivals and other cultic acts that we may not otherwise recognize by integrating features of various psalms. Some of these studies attempted to identify particular processes that might have occurred, as for example the attempt by van der Toorn (1988) to identify some cultic practices that lay behind prayers offered by those accused of serious crimes at the temple. Since some of those prayers may well be preserved in Psalms (see on Ps. 7), it is highly likely that there were recognized processes by which supplicants could be declared innocent or guilty. None of the prayers possibly associated with this directly indicate what the process might have been, so van der Toorn's work is an attempt to piece together various fragments in Psalms to identify it. The difficulty with work such as this is when it attempts to identify a *Sitz im Leben* that is not transparent in the psalm and then uses this reconstructed setting to interpret various passages. In doing so, the reconstruction controls the interpretation of the text, but the reconstruction is a scholarly construct. Staying with the example of van der Toorn, it should be said that there is nothing fundamentally implausible in his proposal, but neither is there direct evidence that supports it, and most of his points can be interpreted differently.

Something similar must be said about more detailed attempts at the reconstruction of various festivals through the Psalms, an approach that was particularly prominent in the last century, and which remains important for some readings now. Here, the driving force was Gunkel's student Sigmund Mowinckel. Mowinckel (1962, 1: 106–192), setting Psalms in a wider ANE setting, argued for the existence of a New Year's festival that he then reconstructed in some detail. We cannot here note all the details of his proposal but should instead note that both alternative festivals and variations on the rituals in Mowinckel's argument were reconstructed by scholars such as Weiser (1962: 35–52), J. H. Eaton (1976: 134–197) and Croft (1987: 89–113). Although they emphasize different matters, and those of Eaton and Croft focus more on a royal ritual rather than the new year as such, they sometimes draw on the same texts but reach different conclusions about them. The possibility of such reconstructions seems to depend on the flexibility of the language found in Psalms, language that is open to a range of reconstructions, and so capable of being read in support of a range of different proposals (cf. Creach 2020: 96). Moreover, we have to accept that the psalms we have are a selection from what was undoubtedly a larger body of material, meaning that elements of these festivals (assuming they existed) have probably not been passed down to us. As such, we are better to recognize that each of these is a reconstruction, one that requires the scholar to identify the clues and then decide how the proposed festival might have functioned. It should also be noted that there is no direct evidence from elsewhere in the OT to support their existence. Although the possibility of these festivals can be retained, we should recognize that they are reconstructions that should not take priority over the text itself.

There is therefore much that we can identify about Israel's worship in and through the Psalms. But we must also recognize that there is much that we simply cannot know. Reconstructions are interesting, and some are plausible, but, because so much involves informed guesses, they should not control the reading of the Psalms.

3.1.4. Reading Psalms

Some hermeneutical observations need to be drawn from the discussion to this point. The following seem most relevant:

1. In interpretation, the psalm itself remains the primary object. This must involve attention to its language, poetic devices and structure, as these are inherent to the text.
2. Each psalm needs to be interpreted on its own merits rather than being controlled by reconstructions. This is because a poem is a complete literary work, and thus needs to be interpreted as a unit. Where a poem is divided into multiple psalms (as in Pss 9–10; 42–43) we still need to interpret the whole poem while recognizing that they are now presented as two psalms, since this would be transparent to an ancient audience.
3. Factors such as formal classification can be relevant when they are transparent in the text, but the freedom of poets to transcend categories should be recognized.
4. Factors such as *Sitz im Leben* can also be important, but only to the extent that they are directly evident in the text.
5. Humility in interpretation is essential, since there remains much that we do not know and probably can never know.
6. Interpretation of the Psalms will not end, and the last word is unlikely to be spoken.

3.2. Interpreting the Psalter

Where the dominant mode of interpretation has focused on the Psalms, a more recent trend has seen attention shift to the Psalter, understanding Psalms as a coherent book which has an identifiable form and message. This is sometimes referred to as a 'canonical' interpretation, but it is better to speak of a Psalter interpretation as it would be possible to interpret the book without feeling constrained by its status as canon, and numerous scholars who follow a Psalms level interpretation affirm their status as canon. As noted above, this is not entirely novel, but the attention given to it does represent a significant shift. Significant impetus towards this mode of reading was provided by Brevard Childs. In his *Introduction to the Old Testament as Scripture* (1979) he consistently argued for the importance of reading biblical texts as whole units, developing themes from some of his earlier work. His chapter on Psalms (1979: 504–524) outlined a case for reading Psalms as a whole, with Psalm 1 as an intentional introduction to the book, and a greater eschatological focus than earlier cultic approaches had recognized. Childs's work laid the foundations for a focus on the Psalter, but it was the published doctoral thesis of his student Gerald Wilson (1985a) that would foster growing attention to the Psalter as a consciously edited work. Wilson's work should be read alongside that of Clinton McCann, which was independently reaching similar conclusions. Although McCann's doctoral thesis (on Ps. 73) has unfortunately not been published, his *Theological Introduction* (1993) was an important work that brought together the main elements of a Psalter-based approach to interpretation. Where Wilson's work was well outside the mainstream of interpretation when it appeared, and some remain unconvinced by the approach (e.g. Whybray 1996), Psalter-based interpretation is now relatively widespread (see the sketch of this movement by Zenger 2010b).

In terms of Psalter interpretation, we need to consider three relevant issues – formation of the Psalter, its structure and how we determine relationships between individual and groups of psalms.

3.2.1. Formation of the Psalter

Most readers of this volume will probably assume that there are 150 psalms in the Psalter. This is, after all, the standard form and faithfully represents the Psalter as we know it from MT. The main form of LXX Psalter also contains 150 psalms, though some know an additional psalm (Ps. 151), and some Syriac traditions also take the count to 155. Depending on how we understand a manuscript from the Cairo Genizah, the number could even rise to 156 (Charlesworth 2018). If nothing else, this provides evidence for something that may otherwise be deemed self-evident, which is that the psalms in the Psalter represent a selection from a wider body of psalmody in Israel. Outside Psalms, we may note the prayers of Hannah (1 Sam. 2:1–10) or Jonah (Jon. 2:1–9) as examples of texts that would otherwise have seemed quite at home in the Psalter. It is, however, important to stress that the Psalter is a selection of poems that have been brought together. Other poems could have been included, but these are the ones that the Masoretic tradition deemed appropriate. Even when we stay with the 150 psalms, comparison with LXX quickly makes clear that these psalms could be arranged differently. MT and LXX are only the same to the end of Psalm 8. Using MT numbering as standard, we can then note that LXX treats Psalms 9–10 as a single psalm. The numbering of the two then varies by one until Psalms 114–115 which LXX also presents as a single psalm. The variation in numbering quickly returns to one as LXX presents Psalm 116 as two psalms. The numbering between these two traditions realigns only when LXX presents Psalm 147 as two psalms. One can debate the virtues of how each tradition represents these psalms, but the point to note here is that this points to differing models of how this material is brought together and presented, even if it is essentially the same material. Those responsible for LXX have made different decisions about how to present this material from what we have in MT, so even though both are the Psalms, they are not the same Psalter. Since this volume is concerned with the MT Psalter, as the form generally recognized as canon, I will not trace the differences further. We could, however, also note what could be a very different Psalter at Qumran, if 11QPs[a] is in fact a Psalter (cf. Willgren 2016a: 121–129). Here, it suffices to note that this manuscript, the main Psalms manuscript from Qumran, presents a mixture of biblical psalms with a range of other liturgical texts, frequently organizing the biblical psalms in a very different order from that familiar from MT. The variations between 11QPs[a] and MT all point to the fact that Psalms could be grouped and arranged in a range of ways, and these variances would presumably point to different editorial goals.

The MT Psalter also shows internal evidence of editing. Some of this is clearly visible and suggests that its editorial choices were not necessarily all made at the same time. The most easily recognized evidence for editing is the presence of titles on many psalms (see below, 'Psalm titles'). Even if the function of these titles is open to debate, they stand outside the poems to which they are attached, making them clear evidence of editorial work. We should also consider the note found at Psalm 72:20 about the end of the 'prayers of David'. The exact function of this note is open to a range of possibilities (see 'Comment' there), but it is clearly something that stands outside the body of the poem, representing an editorial comment of some sort. Although most Davidic psalms have come before this point, there are still Davidic psalms after it, and in any case Psalm 72's title indicates it is 'Solomonic'. Beyond this, we can note that the Psalter is arranged into five books (see below, 'Structure of the Psalter'), with the first four ending with a similar but not identical doxology (Pss 41:13; 72:19 (in this case immediately before the note in v. 20), 89:52 and 106:48. Book 5 differs from the rest in lacking such a doxology, but Psalms 146–150 (or perhaps Pss 145–150) now fulfil this function. The variations in the form of the doxologies (see Willgren 2016a: 205–211), plus the clear shift in Book 5, all suggest that even if there was a pressure towards general conformity in the Psalter's formation, it is unlikely to have come together at one point.

As a second point, we should note the presence of repeated psalms. Although there are small changes, which means each needs to be interpreted in its own right, Psalms 14 and 53 are clearly the same basic poem. The same is true of Psalms 40:13–17 and 70, while Psalm 108 is for the most part the result of joining Psalms 57:7–11 and 60:5–12. Although the Psalter now makes slightly different use of each of these texts, it would be surprising if a single editorial process retained these duplicates. Rather, it seems likely that the final edition of the Psalter has received these texts in a form that had been passed on to them.

Finally, we can note the presence of what is known as the 'Elohistic Psalter' (Pss 42–83; see 'Form and structure' at Ps. 42). These psalms are notable for their preference for Elohim as the divine name rather than Yahweh, even though the rest of the Psalter has a strong preference for Yahweh. Strikingly, some of the repeated psalms occur across the division between the Yahwistic and Elohistic Psalter, so that Psalm 14 uses 'Yahweh' while Psalm 53 uses 'Elohim'. The same is generally true of Psalms 40:13–17 and 70, though the shift between names is less consistent there (cf. Firth 2022). It is not really possible to determine which is the original poem in either case and therefore which way the divine name was adjusted. But we can say with confidence that this points to editorial work, editorial work that almost certainly preceded the form of the Psalter as we now have it.

Any attempt to understand the Psalter as a complete unit must therefore take into account its anthological character, accepting that, to at least some extent, the final editors were working with pre-formed material. None of this is enough to prevent coherence in the final edition, but it does indicate that any reading of the Psalter needs to accept that it was brought together with some constraints already in place. If 11QPs[a] is a Psalter, then it suggests that it was possible to form a Psalter with considerable freedom relative to source material, but it seems likely that the compilers of MT Psalter took a more conservative approach, often keeping material together in the form in which they received it. This would include not only the Elohistic material, but also groups like the Songs of the Ascents (Pss 120–134). Their editing remains visible, but it is editing of an anthology that accepted some material as already formed and thus not subject to further work.

3.2.2. Structure of the Psalter

Despite the constraints with which they worked, it is also possible to see a structure to the Psalter, a structure that suggests it is not a random collection of 150 poems. Rather, allowing for the constraints imposed by the presence of the existing material, the editors have created a coherent collection, one for which a comprehensive understanding is possible.

Recognition of the constraints caused by the presence of existing material means that we are working towards what Grant (2024: 236) has characterized as a more 'minimalist' model for reading the Psalter. As such, although some readings of the Psalter have argued for a narrative structure for the whole (e.g. Wilson 1985a; Mitchell 1997), we here face a similar problem to that noted above for the proposed festivals in that these proposals move in contradictory directions (is it the failure of the Davidic covenant or a strongly Davidic messianic text?). Goldingay (2016: 289) has quipped that such approaches (which would be Grant's 'maximalists') involve an 'overly speculative connecting of dots'. When this involves the construction of a narrative that runs through the book, then Goldingay's view seems a safe position to adopt.

Despite this, there are factors in the Psalter that, pointing to its coherence, can be understood as supporting a narrative structure. Koorevaar (2010) expresses this simply when he adapts Aristotle's description of a narrative as a text with a beginning, middle and end. Although the earlier approaches to the Psalter took its introduction only as Psalm 1, the more common approach has been to see it as Psalms 1–2 (with some links into Ps. 3; see Cole 2012). Psalms 146–150 form a clear conclusion, with each psalm marked by its Hallelujah frame, and so the balance of the book constitutes the middle. Koorevaar's model is more sophisticated than this summary may suggest, and there is still enough to highlight some difficulties with it. Most importantly, Aristotle (in the *Poetics*) is describing texts that are recognized as narratives and highlighting their structure, but it is not clear that we can work in reverse and say that the presence of this structure is evidence that the text is a narrative. After all, every psalm has a beginning, middle and end, and although some can reasonably be described as a story, not all can. However, Koorevaar is correct to build on research that points to an overall structure for the Psalter, something that has since been developed on a much larger scale by Peter Ho (2019). But before Ho, we can also note Janowski's (2010) argument that the Psalter can be understood as the equivalent of a temple of words, one that we enter through Psalms 1–2, inhabit through the rest, and then leave through the Final Hallel (Pss 146–150). Janowski's approach is, in effect, an extended metaphor that reflects on the structure of the Psalter, but also one that at least points to the major elements of its structure.

However, it is Peter Ho who has provided the most substantial recent study on the Psalter and its overall shape, attending to how a range of factors function in the Psalter (2019: 41). Ho is sensitive to criticisms that have been levelled against attempts to force a unity on to the Psalter, and so seeks to construct a model for the macrostructure that can be recognized by readers while taking seriously elements that hold the book together. His strongly Davidic reading could be criticized in the same way as many other maximalist approaches to the Psalter, but his attention to the presence of numerous linking features that hold the Psalter together means he avoids some of the pitfalls of requiring readers to connect too many speculative dots. However, the complexity of his model is itself problematic, including thirteen explicit factors that hold the Psalter together and a further nineteen tacit ones (see P. C. W. Ho 2019: 35–37). Longman (2024: 173) wonders if the sheer number of elements Ho requires readers to recognize may itself be evidence that it is too complex to work, a conclusion that becomes more persuasive when we recognize that these elements contribute to three overarching narratives (2019: 6). The maximalist reading Ho offers thus seems to collapse under the weight of its own complexity. But if we remove the overarching narrative and accept that the Psalter's compilers were often working with pre-formed material, then a minimalist reading of his approach becomes possible. In this case, we need to accept that many of his linking factors might have been primarily relevant for material that has come pre-formed into the Psalter. However, it does show that the idea of editing material into a coherent form was not simply an innovation in the Psalter's final form but rather built into all the stages by which it emerged.

In the light of this, it seems wise to adopt a minimalist approach to the Psalter, one that recognizes the major structural elements that form the Psalter, while also allowing that different levels of editing remain. We can, however, note that some elements of the Psalter's structure broadly agree:

1. It contains five books, a division recognized in the rabbinic literature; the first four are marked by a concluding doxology. The five books are Psalms 1–41, 42–72, 73–89, 90–106 and 107–150.
2. It contains a Yahwistic Psalter (Pss 1–41, 84–150) and an Elohistic Psalter (42–83).
3. It contains an introduction (Pss 1–2).
4. It contains a conclusion (Pss 146–150).

Certain of these factors overlap, meaning that some psalms may have multiple functions within the book. This is most obviously evident with the introduction and conclusion, both of which are now part of their respective books. It is entirely plausible that these were added when the Psalter reached its conclusion, but are now integrated into its final form and need to be read in that context. Likewise, the Elohistic Psalter moves across the boundary between Books 2 and 3, creating a 'soft break' between those books. Although not obvious from what has been noted above, there is also a 'soft break' between Books 4 and 5, as the historical recitals of Psalms 105–106 that close Book 4 are also closely linked to Psalm 107 as it opens Book 5. On the other hand, the break between Books 1 and 2 can be understood as a 'hard break' since it also is the point where the Elohistic Psalter begins. Likewise, there is a hard break between Books 3 and 4. The structural components thus interact with one another, enabling the five books to operate like chapters within a modern book rather than as wholly discrete elements, though there is some variability in how they interact. At the same time, each Book has its own form, which can be traced briefly.

3.2.2.1. Book 1

Book 1 sets out the Psalter's main themes. Psalms 1–2, marked as a pair by the absence of a title, introduce it and the Psalter. In Book 1, the absence of a title links a psalm to its predecessor – note that Psalm 10 continues the same poem as Psalm 9 while Psalm 33 opens by summoning the sung praise with which Psalm 32 closed. Psalms 1–2 are also marked by shared vocabulary and use of a beatitude as an inclusion. They set out the position of the righteous in contrast to the wicked, as those devoted to Yahweh, and who express that devotion through reflection on Torah and submission to Yahweh's king. Together, these forms of devotion represent a state of blessedness that all should desire. The rest of the Psalter works out what this looks like in a world where both the wicked and those who rebel against Yahweh's king seem to thrive, pausing from time to time to provide further reassurances. These reassurances are needed because most psalms in Book 1 can be classified as complaints, prayers where the faithful ask Yahweh to bring his justice into the world.

Book 1 is also strongly Davidic (see below, 'Psalm titles'). Apart from Psalms 1–2, 10, 33, every psalm has a Davidic element in the title. No other book is so strongly Davidic. The consistency of this feature means that the titles are less important for marking major sections than the other books. Instead, there are variations in content that provide the major markers for structure, along with acrostic psalms. Attending to these features leads to the following structure, though it should be noted that the boundaries between the sections are 'soft' and that the outer psalm in each section is also joined to the other sections:

1. Introduction (1–2)
2. Prayers for protection (3–7)
3. Celebration of creation (8)
4. Prayers for protection (9–14)
5. Chiasm centred on Torah and kingship (15–24)
6. Confession of trust and more prayers for help (25–34)
7. Yahweh as deliverer (35–41)

3.2.2.2. Book 2

Book 2 immediately differentiates itself from Book 1 by commencing with a collection of Korahite psalms before an Asaphic one, and then a further Davidic collection before closing with a Solomonic one. Only two psalms lack a title (Pss 43, 71), and in both cases this points to a strong connection to the preceding psalm, with Psalm 43 continuing the same poem as Psalm 42 and Psalm 71 taking up the closing prayer of Psalm 70. A further difference is that Book 2 commences the Elohistic Psalter. Unlike the variations in titles, this strong preference for the Elohim as the divine name runs throughout the book.

Although other factors can be noted, and again the breaks are not 'hard', Book 2 is most obviously structured through its titles (on the technical terms, see below, 'Psalm titles'), leading to the following structure:

1. First Korahite collection (42–49)
2. First Asaphic psalm (50)
3. Prayers of David (51–72)
   a. Nathan's visit (51)
   b. 'Maskil' (52–55)
   c. 'Miktam' (56–60)
   d. Calls to be heard (61–64)
   e. Songs (66–68)
   f. Petitions (69–71)
   g. Solomonic psalm (72)

3.2.2.3. Book 3

Book 3 continues the Elohistic Psalter through to Psalm 83. All the Elohistic psalms in this book are also Asaphic. From Psalm 84 the Psalter reverts to Yahweh as the preferred divine name, and at this point a second group of Korahite psalms are included. It is notable that whereas the first Korahite collection is Elohistic, the second is Yahwistic. The second Korahite collection is interrupted by a Davidic psalm before resuming in Psalm 87. Psalm 88 is then a bridging psalm as it is both Korahite and associated with an 'Ezrahite', which links it with Psalm 89. Psalms 88–89 are thus joined to each other and the rest of the book, bringing the book to a close with two notably downbeat texts. The titles are thus the most obvious editorial technique in Book 3, with every psalm having a title. This leads to the following structure:

1. Second Asaphic collection (73–83)
2. Second Korahite collection, Part 1 (84–85)
3. A Davidic psalm (86)
4. Second Korahite collection, Part 2 (86–87/88)
5. 'Ezrahite' complaints (88–89)

3.2.2.4. Book 4

Where titles are a dominant feature of Books 1–3, that is not the case in Book 4, where only Psalms 90, 92, 98 and 100–103 are titled. The titles do play some part in structuring the book, most obviously in that Psalms 100–103 are Davidic, though there is good reason to think of Psalm 100 as finishing a section (Pss 93–100; cf. Howard 1997). However, as is commonly the case, certain psalms can act as a hinge, joining one part of the book to another, and that seems to be the case with Psalm 100. The introduction of Moses into the title of Psalm 90 is vital, since he is mentioned a further six times (Pss 99:6; 103:7; 105:26; 106:16, 23, 32), making him a pivotal figure for the book. Given the concentration on him in Psalm 106, when combined with the title of Psalm 90, we can recognize Moses as a pivotal figure for Book 4, especially when we note that he is mentioned only one other time in the whole Psalter (Ps. 77:20). Since titles play a lesser role, we instead attend more to repeating features in adjacent psalms that point to groups, such as the interchange of 'Yahweh reigns' and 'Sing a new song' in Psalms 93, 96–99. Taking these into account, we can analyse this book in three major segments:

1. Historical and wisdom introduction (90–92)
2. Yahweh's reign (93–100)
3. Yahweh's faithfulness through time (101–106)

3.2.2.5. Book 5

The Psalter's closing book brings together the main themes of the Psalter, so that it is both a discrete book within the Psalter and its close. In doing so, its final elements also point back to Psalms 1–2, especially Psalms 148–149, which Vesco (2006, 2: 1371) has noted have important links to one another, preparing for the final summons to praise in Psalm 150. Titles are scarcer here than in Books 1–3, but more plentiful than in Book 4, and clearly form at least one element in the book's structure. However, there are also extended sections without titles, meaning that Book 5 operates with structuring models that draw on each of the preceding books. Just as Book 1 has a clear introduction (both to it and the Psalter), so also the Final Hallel (Pss 146–150) forms a clear conclusion to Book 5 and the Psalter. Within Book 5, these psalms are untitled, but emerge directly from the vow of praise in Psalm 145:21, thus drawing on the structural role of the absence of titles in Books 1–2. It also opens with an untitled psalm (Ps. 107), one that in this case is also closely linked to Psalms 105–106 at the end of Book 4 through its repetition of the opening 'Give thanks to Yahweh' (Pss 105:1; 106:1; 107:1). After this, there is a small Davidic collection before another group of untitled psalms (Pss 111–119). Here, we can note that Psalms

111–112 are acrostics that celebrate Torah, as is Psalm 119. The acrostics Psalms 25, 34 provided structural foundations in Book 1, providing the boundaries for sections in that Book, and the same model is employed here, with these psalms providing an inclusion around Psalms 113–118, a group of praise psalms. This is then followed by the Songs of the Ascents (Pss 120–134), poems which are linked by their title and shared content and poetic devices. Psalms 135–137 are untitled but are linked by a concern with Israel's story. The structuring of the Songs of the Ascents and these three poems thus draw on patterns in Book 4. Following these, there is the final Davidic collection (Pss 138–143) which shares a common title before the Final Hallel. Book 5 is therefore the most complex of the Books, possibly because it draws on several largely pre-formed elements. Nevertheless, its general structure can be seen clearly:

1. Giving thanks (Ps. 107)
2. Davidic collection (108–110)
3. Torah and praise (111–119)
    a. Torah acrostics (111–112)
    b. Egyptian Hallel (113–118)
    c. Torah acrostic (119)
4. Songs of the Ascents (120–134)
5. Israel's story (135–137)
6. Final Davidic collection (138–145)
7. Final Hallel (146–150)

3.2.3. Grouping psalms

Attention to the Psalter's shape makes clear that it has been edited into a whole, though it is also a work for which editing has occurred at different levels and it is not always possible to say with confidence whether one piece of editing was performed by the final editors or was part of the previously formed material that they felt constrained to retain. What we have noted above about LXX Psalter or 11QPs[a] would suggest that not all editors felt as strongly constrained by the traditions they had received as we find in MT, so clearly different decisions could have been made. Nevertheless, MT Psalter shows signs of both being a work that was edited to some extent but also one where the editors adopted a fairly conservative approach to the material they had received. However, as can be seen from the structure of both the whole Psalter and its five books, there is strong evidence that psalms were grouped. Such grouping suggests that the setting in which we find the individual psalms is potentially significant for the interpretation of an individual psalm. That is, although we often cannot determine a psalm's *Sitz im Leben*, we can confidently observe its placement in the

Psalter (*Sitz im Buch*) and consider the possibility that the *Sitz im Buch* represents the information that the Psalter's compilers intended for those who read it. To take only one example, a great deal of effort has gone into discussion of how to translate *yhwh mālak* in Psalms 93:1, 97:1, 99:1 – is it 'Yahweh is king', 'Yahweh has become king' or 'Yahweh reigns'? Each is a plausible option when we consider the grammar and syntax (cf. Brettler 1989: 125–158), but discussion about the exact nuance that was most appropriate for translation was largely tied to an attempt to identify the *Sitz im Leben*, usually in a proposed festival. But there is nothing in the Psalter itself, or in Book 4 (cf. Ps. 47:8) that definitely resolves this for us. Rather, these psalms now take on a more eschatological colour precisely because they are presented without *Sitz im Leben*. Whatever function they may have had in Israel's worship can only be guessed at (even if some of those guesses are well informed) but the *Sitz im Buch* is clear, especially because of the effect of grouping together psalms with this particular language. This effect is heightened through the links to 'Sing a new song' (Pss 96:1; 98:1), language that seems to refer to a victory Yahweh has won, and the anticipation of Yahweh's reign being expressed over all the nations (Pss 96:10), with his salvation being seen by the ends of the earth (Ps. 98:3). Indeed, Psalm 100 now invites all the earth to come and worship Yahweh, worship that anticipates his final victory where his reign is seen over all creation. There is thus strong evidence that the Psalter has been shaped, and that various psalms have been grouped to provide it with an overall theological shape (cf. Creach 2024).

An important component in this shaping is the grouping of psalms, a mechanism that suggests they should (at least to some extent) be read in the light of each other. As an anthology, the primary focus of interpretation is the individual psalm, but, as shown above, the *Sitz im Buch* can also be interpretatively significant. Given P. C. W. Ho's detailed work (2019: 35–37), there is no need here to list all the possible ways in which the Psalter provides links between individual psalms. As noted, there are important variations in how those links are provided in each book, so care must be taken not to impose a mechanism for grouping psalms from one book to another unless there is also evidence in that book that it employs that system. For instance, although the lack of a title points to a strong connection to the immediately preceding psalm in Books 1–2, Book 4 does not use this as a linking device, and the evidence for its use in Book 5 is uneven. Are there then criteria by which we may determine that a particular set of psalms is to be read as a group?

Unfortunately, there is no one answer to this, precisely because of the variations across the books. Rather, attention must be given to the devices used in each book, if only to ensure that inappropriate criteria are not applied. Within Book 2, for instance, the repeated use of the technical term 'Miktam' in the headings of Psalms 56–60 is a strong indicator that these psalms are to be read in the light of each other, a connection that is strengthened by the mention of what seems to be tunes (in the case of Pss 57–58, the same one) across this group, something not present in either Psalm 55 or 61 which also lack 'Miktam'. Since the use of technical terms in the titles to group psalms does not seem to be used in other books, but can be demonstrated elsewhere in Book 2, we have strong evidence that these psalms form a coherent group. However, one consistent device is used across the Psalter, which is the presence of catchwords that join particular psalms. The presence of such terms has long been recognized – for instance, Delitzsch's (1996, repr.) classic nineteenth-century commentary frequently comments on the presence of such features, though it tends not to explore this in great deal. However, some words are so common (e.g. *ḥesed*, 'kindness') that finding them in successive psalms is unlikely to have much significance. But rarer terms or repeated phrases can be a significant contributor in determining whether or not certain psalms are placed within the book or the Psalter overall in a way that is significant for interpretation.

Thematic links are also potentially significant, though thematic similarity is more difficult to demonstrate than repeated lexemes or phrases. Quinn (2023: 17–35) has attempted to develop a statistical system for determining this. Whether or not the statistics she presents are themselves sufficiently robust to support all her conclusions, the factors that she brings together do represent a valid set of criteria that can be weighed in asking whether a given grouping of psalms forms a collection for which the connections are interpretatively significant. Returning to Psalms 56–60, we can note that Psalms 56–57, 59 each include refrain-like material (comparatively rare in the Psalter), while both Psalms 58, 60 include material citing other speakers (58:11; 60:6–8). These repetitions in the titles and form of the poems also mean that the various ways in which the motif of trust is repeated through them could be regarded as interpretatively significant. On its own, trust is commonly enough expressed (esp. in the Songs of the Ascents), but, when combined with the other factors, there is reason to think it is central to these psalms.

Ultimately, the evidence for reading psalms within groups is cumulative, and must be assessed on the weight of evidence rather than simply adding up the total number of connections. However, to aid readers in identifying points where this is potentially significant the 'Form and structure' section for each psalm includes a brief reflection on these sorts of links. There, points where the connections are stronger are noted, and also points where the connections with previous psalms may be weaker. The evidence there suggests that certain psalms may be regarded as introducing new segments within each book or within the Psalter overall. At key points, this is also taken up in the 'Explanation' section, though for reasons of space this has not always been possible.

3.2.4. Reading the Psalter

As with 'Reading Psalms' (see above), some hermeneutical reflections should be drawn at this point. The following seem most pertinent:

1. The Psalter has an overall shape, which is significant for interpretation, moving from the introduction (Pss 1–2) to the conclusion (Pss 146–150).
2. The five-book structure is built into the Psalter and is an important consideration in its interpretation.
3. The individual psalm remains the key point of interpretation. Formation of the Psalter has not resulted in a situation whereby the meaning of a psalm is subsumed by its place in the Psalter, though certain options may be prioritized.
4. Because the Psalter is a literary work, attention should be given to the possibility that certain psalms have been grouped in ways that could be interpretatively significant. *Sitz im Leben* may not always be significant, but *Sitz im Buch* can be.
5. Possible interpretative significance needs to be weighed to determine whether connections are meaningful, taking into account the sort of criteria noted above.

4. PSALM TITLES

In the light of all that has been said about reading both individual psalms and the Psalter, it is clear that the titles of the psalms provide an important component for interpretation. It should be stressed that, within MT, the title is always presented as part of the psalm and is often the first verse and sometimes the first two verses of the psalm. As such, the pattern seen in some English translations of removing the titles to a footnote (e.g. GNB, NEB) is to be resisted since the titles are themselves part of the canonical text. At the same time, since they are clearly not a part of the poem (and so at some level are an editorial addition), it is appropriate to show them separately, though there is much to be said for the pattern in some European languages (e.g. Dutch, French, German) of retaining the versification of the Hebrew so that the title is more clearly seen as integrated with the poem itself. However, consistent with the normal English pattern, throughout this volume the title is not included in the versification, though each psalm can be thought of as a combination of the title and the poem. That is, the interpretation of the psalm is a combination of reflection on the title (where present – though its absence can be significant) and the poem, while recognizing that the titles can fulfil a range of different functions. This is because many titles contain multiple pieces of information, and consideration of the titles must attend to all the elements in any given title. Attention here is paid only to MT titles – LXX adds a number of Davidic titles while also associating much of the Final Hallel with Haggai and Zechariah. 11QPs[a] (where available) generally follows MT closely, but with one additional Davidic psalm (Ps. 123) and a small variant at Psalm 145.

The titles contain five basic types of information – collection membership, genre, historical notes, performative guidance, and characterizing notes – though these divisions are not absolute. Because the titles are so terse, we are often left with elements for which no clear interpretation can be given. For instance, in Psalm 7 we do not know what a 'Shiggaion' is, nor anything more about 'Cush the Benjaminite'. It is reasonable to assume that these notes were significant for the Psalter's editors (whether final editors or those of the book or even particular section of Book 1, where Ps. 7 is found cannot be determined with confidence), but the most we can do now is make informed guesses about them. Indeed, the meaning assigned to most elements in the titles can best be described as informed guesses. However, as noted, even though we often do not know what the various terms mean, we can see that they are often used as a mechanism for grouping psalms; so, attending to the titles is interpretatively important.

4.1. Collection membership

By far the most common item in the titles is a note indicating the psalm's membership in a particular collection. Where relevant, these are marked by the preposition *lĕ* before either a name or mention of the director. As it is possible to be listed as belonging both to the director and a specific name, we have to reckon with the possibility that a given psalm could belong to multiple collections. In that Psalm 88's title links it to both the Korahites and Heman the Ezrahite as well as the director, we see that even a name link does not mean that the psalm belongs only to the one collection, though the most common combination is only one name and the director.

The collections are of varying size, with the following occurring:

1. 'Davidic' occurs seventy-four times. The vast majority of these are in Books 1 (37 times) and 2 (19 times), with the rest scattered across the remaining Books: Book 3 (once), Book 4 (twice), Book 5 (15 times). Often translated as '[a psalm] of David', it is understood to mean that David is the author. The OT knows of David as a musician and composer (2 Sam. 23:1), so there is no reason to dispute that David composed psalms, especially as a note near the end of 11QPs[a] also points to him as a composer of psalms. But whether this note is intended to indicate that David was their

composer is another matter. Certainly, the preposition can be used to indicate authorship (*WHS* §270), but it could also be used to indicate possession in other ways, and we can determine the nuance of a preposition only where we have a complete sentence, something lacking for the titles, though in Psalm 89:3 we do find the same expression used where authorship is clearly not intended. However, there is also evidence in the Psalter that suggests it does not view David as the author. Most importantly, in some 'Davidic' psalms we find mention of David as a figure separate from the authorial voice (Pss 18:51; 122:5; 144:10; cf. Mays 1994a: 87–98). If these psalms are 'Davidic' but speak of David separately, then there is good reason to think that in these cases the phrase does not mean 'written by David'. If so, then all cases are open to debate. Various references within psalms are potentially difficult to reconcile with Davidic authorship, but these are significant only if we need to defend the phrase as meaning 'written by David'. David may well be the author of some, but the phrase does not necessarily mean that, and so the less specific 'Davidic' is used in the translation.

2. 'The director's' occurs fifty-five times. All but three of these instances occur in Books 1–3 (the exceptions are Pss 109, 139 and 140). Based on occurrence of the same term in 1 Chronicles 15:21, it probably refers to a musical leader, though LXX derives it differently, understanding it as 'eternity'.
3. 'A Song of the Ascents' occurs in the titles of fourteen psalms, with a small variation in Psalm 121. These poems (except for Ps. 132) are very brief and include similar poetic patterns.
4. 'Asaphic' occurs in twelve psalms, all in the Elohistic Psalter, once in Book 2 and otherwise in Book 3. The name Asaph should be traced back to 1 Chr. 6:24, where an Abiasaph is mentioned as among temple singers. Asaph is a musician in 1 Chronicles 15:17, 19, and was a worship leader in 1 Chr. 16:5. The form of the title is otherwise the same as for David, so 'Asaphic' is used to leave open the ways in which these psalms are associated with Asaph.
5. 'Korahite' occurs in eleven psalms, spread across Books 2 (7 times) and 3 (4 times). The name refers to a Levitical guild first alluded to in 1 Chronicles 6:22 who are associated with a group of Kohathites (2 Chr. 20:19). Korahites were also gatekeepers at the temple (1 Chr. 26:19). The grammatical form is the same as for the Davidic psalms, and so the title is understood as referring to the collection; hence, the more general 'Korahite' is used to leave open questions of authorship.
6. 'Jeduthun's' occurs three times (Pss 39, 62, 77). A Jeduthun is mentioned in 1 Chronicles 25:1–6 as a Levitical musician. 'Jeduthun' always occurs with another collection.

7. ‘Solomonic’ occurs in two psalms (Pss 72, 127). The same issues arise as with Davidic. Plus, we have the curious fact that Psalm72:20, a Solomonic psalm, includes the note that the prayers of David had ended; so, the psalm was also associated with him in some way. Again, the more general ‘Solomonic’ is used to leave questions of authorship open.
8. ‘Heman the Ezrahite’ and ‘Ethan the Ezrahite’ are mentioned once each, in Psalms 88 and 89.
9. ‘Mosaic’ occurs once (Ps. 90). Again, the form is unclear, so the more open form is used.

4.2. Genre

Along with the collection information, several psalms also include information about the poem, probably pointing to the genre, though in many cases we cannot be sure about what the term means or how it may differ from other psalms that may have a similar title:

1. ‘A melody’ (*mizmôr*). Traditionally translated as ‘a psalm’, but this creates confusion with the title of the book and also the fact that all the poems in the book can be called a psalm. Derives from a root relating to music; hence, ‘a melody’. The term occurs fifty-seven times and is spread across all five books.
2. ‘A song’ occurs in the titles of thirty-three psalms, including all the Songs of the Ascents. It is not clear how this is distinguished from ‘a melody’ since these also seem to imply singing. Psalm 45 is specifically described as a love song.
3. ‘Maskil’ could associate the psalm with a wisdom tradition. It occurs in the titles of thirteen psalms, spread across Books 1, 2, 3 and 5, and once in Psalm 47:7.
4. ‘Miktam’ could mean ‘written on a tablet’, though this is uncertain. It occurs in six psalms, one in Book 1 (Ps. 16) and the others in Book 2 (Pss 56–60).
5. ‘Prayer’ occurs in four titles (Pss 17, 86, 90, 102), though the word occurs a further twenty-six times in various psalms, and in Psalms 86 and 102 it occurs in both the title and the body of the psalm.
6. ‘Shiggaion’ is a word of unknown meaning (cf. Hab. 3:1), occurring only at Psalm 7.
7. Psalm 100’s title notes it is ‘for thanksgiving’.
8. ‘An anthem’ renders *tĕhillâ*. Often translated as ‘praise’ when it occurs in the body of a poem, in Psalm 145 it occurs as a genre marker in the title, marking it as a praise song.

4.3. Historical notes

Historical notes that link psalms with an event in David's life (always events from Samuel, not Chronicles) are found in thirteen psalms (Pss 3, 7, 18, 34, 51, 52, 54, 56, 57, 59, 60, 63, 142). The significance of these notes depends in part on how we understand 'Davidic' in these psalms. It is plausible that these psalms are presented as poems David composed at the time mentioned, and certainly this would be the case if we understand 'Davidic' in terms of authorship. But we can understand Davidic here as indicating a collection, albeit one that is read through the figure of David. In this case, David becomes a clear historical exemplar of how this prayer could have been prayed, while still making them available to all worshippers to use as their own.

4.4. Performative guidance

A range of notes are attached that seem to provide some guidance as to how a given psalm might have been performed. Many of these appear to have been musical, indicating a setting, such as instrumentation or a tune. Tunes are typically indicated by using the preposition *ʿal* (here, 'according to'). The following can be noted:

1. 'With stringed instruments' occurs in the titles of seven psalms, spread across Books 1–3, and always part of the director's collection.
2. 'According to Lilies' is probably a tune, occurring at Psalms 45, 60, 69, 80. These are all part of the Elohistic Psalter, so this may be a tune distinctive to the group initially responsible for it.
3. 'According to Do Not Destroy' occurs at Psalms 57, 58, 59, 75, and probably indicates a tune.
4. 'According to Gittith' is obscure, occurring only at Psalms 8, 81, 84.
5. 'Upon the eighth' occurs twice: Psalms 6, 12. It is possibly a reference to an octave and hence to tuning, but this is uncertain.
6. 'For commemoration' occurs at Psalms 38, 70.
7. 'According to Mahalath' is obscure, possibly a tune. It occurs at Psalms 53, 88 (though there it is 'Mahalath Leannoth').
8. 'For the flutes' occurs in Psalm 5.
9. 'According to Muth-labben' is obscure, occurring only at Psalm 9.
10. 'According to the doe of the morning', occurring only at Psalm 22, is possibly a tune.
11. 'A Song at the dedication of the house' occurs at Psalm 30. It seems to point to an adaptive use of a psalm about healing from illness for the dedication of the temple, probably the second temple.

12. 'For commemoration' occurs at Psalms 38, 70. Both are urgent appeals, so it could be a genre label, though reference to the memorial offering is possible.
13. 'According to maidens' is unique to Psalm 46, possibly indicating the tune (cf. 1 Chr. 15:20).
14. 'According to the silent dove of the distant ones' is possibly a tune, occurring at Psalm 56.
15. Psalm 92 is 'A Song for the Sabbath'.

4.5. Characterizing notes

These notes provide a brief observation about someone who is mentioned in the title.

1. 'Yahweh's servant' characterizes David at Psalms 18 and 36.
2. 'Man of God' characterizes Moses at Psalm 90.
3. 'For a needy one when faint and pouring out one's complaint before Yahweh' characterizes the petitioner at Psalm 102.

5. THE PSALTER AS A THEOLOGICAL COMPILATION: A READING

Reflecting on the theology of Psalms remains an important task. Where earlier approaches tended to be dismissive of the idea of there being a theology of the psalms, thinking instead only of the theology of the individual texts, more recent works (e.g. Howard and Schmutzer 2023; Creach 2024) have built on McCann's pioneering work (1993; though cf. Creach 1996) to understand the Psalter itself as a work with a theological agenda. This is in addition to works on the theology of the Psalms that have tended to work by aggregating information from individual psalms (e.g. Kraus 1992; Grogan 2001; though Grogan's volume does integrate this with Psalter studies). At this point, the distinction between Psalms and Psalter does break down to some extent since the Psalter is made up of the psalms. However, if our focus is on the shape of the Psalter itself then we can see that it presents itself as a theological work, a work that certainly includes the themes found in its component parts, but also something that is more than just its parts. In particular, it can be argued that the whole Psalter is a work that wrestles with the question of divine faithfulness in a world where the wicked often seem to triumph. We could make this the question of theodicy, though so labelling it may mean that we attempt to domesticate an always-challenging issue, making it an intellectual challenge to be solved rather than something to be lived, prayed and praised. Although at points the Psalter does address this more as an intellectual issue (e.g. Pss 37, 49, 73), even these texts maintain a close link to the life that is lived, prayed and praised. So, we may say that there are points where the intellectual dimension of the issue is allowed greater prominence, showing that experience and reflection properly belong together, but that the experiential dimension always remains. Hence, I offer here a brief sketch of how the Psalter explores this theme, moving from the hermeneutical orientation adopted in reading it to a summary of its central themes.

Fundamental to the Psalter is the issue of the righteous and the wicked, and how it is that the righteous know that Yahweh watches over them. This issue is established in Psalms 1–2. With their beatitudes forming an inclusion for the pair, they establish that the desirable life is one centred on constant engagement with Yahweh's Torah and submission to his king. That is, there are two principal mechanisms by which Yahweh's reign is known – Torah and king. The one who lives in the state of blessedness is, for both the individual and the nation, one who accepts these two mechanisms, and whose life is shaped by them. Psalm 1 also introduces the righteous and the wicked, a pair who are central to the rest of the book. The righteous are those who orient themselves in terms of Yahweh's Torah and king, while the wicked are those who do not. That is, these are not moral labels (as is typically the case in modern Western discussion) but relational ones. Through these mechanisms, Yahweh's reign is made evident, and the desirable life accepts them. At the Psalter's close, Psalm 149 returns to these issues, leaving Psalm 150 as the closing response. There, we see the hope of Yahweh's victory over the nations as the praise of his people becomes the weapon that overcomes the kings who have refused to acknowledge his reign. Indeed, the whole of the Final Hallel (Pss 146–150) can in part be seen as gathering up themes from Psalms 1–2. It emphasizes the importance of trusting Yahweh rather than human leaders (Ps. 146:3–4), proclaiming a beatitude (Ps. 146:5–7) on those whose hope is in him. Yahweh's power as creator, only hinted at in Psalms 1–2, is especially prominent in the Final Hallel, as this helps explain how his justice is worked out in creation. Both Psalms 147 and 148 also reflect in different ways on the power of Yahweh's word in creation, so that by the time we reach Psalm149:4 we understand how he can work in and through his people, taking pleasure in them and adorning them with salvation. The promise of Yahweh's concern for the righteous, and thus his care for them, reaches its climax as the Psalter closes.

We cannot fully trace the motif of the righteous and the wicked throughout the Psalter here, but it is also notable that Psalm 145:20 also evokes the promise of Psalm 1:6 immediately before its closing vow of praise leads into the Final Hallel. However, within the boundaries of the Psalter we do note that the problem of the wicked and how the righteous may be regarded as living a life of blessedness is never far from the surface. As soon as we turn from Psalms 1–2 to Psalm 3, we discover a psalmist beset by adversaries, those who claim there is no salvation in God for the speaker (Ps. 3:2). There may be some significance in the fact that Psalm 149:4 celebrates Yahweh's provision of salvation for the afflicted, especially if Psalm 3 is an intentional point of movement into the body of the Psalter. Here, we see that what is denied to the righteous in their affliction in Psalm 3 can be celebrated as Yahweh's provision for them in Psalm 149, though since the language of salvation occurs some forty-five times across the Psalter this may be more of a happy coincidence. Nevertheless, the whole of Psalms 3–7 seems to be an intentional introduction to the prayers that dominate Books 1–2, prayers that are often complaints that cry out for Yahweh's justice to be enacted. These prayers show a range of elements that link them both to Psalms 1–2 and 8–14 (Firth and Melton 2022: 101–105), but a consistent feature is that the psalmist is under threat from those who do not recognize Yahweh's authority. Even where the specific language of 'righteous' and 'wicked' is not used, this clearly lies conceptually in the background. How is it that we can affirm the reality of Yahweh's commitment to the righteous, to those who take refuge in him, when so many seem content to deny the possibility of Yahweh's acting? Indeed, by the time we reach Psalm 10:4 we find the wicked mentioned and defined by their thought that 'there is no God'. In Psalm 10:11 this statement is clarified so we understand it as a form of practical atheism, a world in which Yahweh is thought not to act. But if that is so, then what is the hope of the righteous? A partial resolution of this is offered in Psalm 14, which makes clear that those who think there is no God are fools. Wickedness and folly are one and the same, because both deny the reality of Yahweh's reign.

Although the identity of the righteous and wicked may seem straightforward to this point, there have already been points that complexify this. In Psalm 7, for instance, the petitioner asks to be judged by Yahweh, probably with reference to a crime, though that is no longer explicit in the psalm. But the nature of this prayer, and Psalm 139 at a similar point near the Psalter's end, recognizes that the identification of these people is not necessarily straightforward. Other psalms are scattered through the Psalter that reflect a similar reality – that some may well need Yahweh to show them that they are in fact among the righteous or condemn them if they are among the wicked. This is because the wicked are not necessarily others – they could well be those who pray. If Psalms 7 and 139 allow that those who pray may in fact be among the wicked (while hoping they are righteous), then Psalm 51 is the clearest example of all that the one who prays may be wicked and not righteous. Read against the background of David's adultery with Bathsheba and murder of Uriah (2 Sam. 11), it is a prayer of one who knows he is guilty. The background of David's crimes means that the confession of sin here is as dark as could be imagined. But it is also a prayer that appeals to Yahweh to be made right once more, an act of mercy that would restore the petitioner to the joy of Yahweh's salvation (Ps. 51:12). This prayer establishes a contrast between this petitioner and the one who boasts in Psalm 52, failing to see that it is the righteous who shall finally be glad (Ps. 52:6). One who boasts in this way and does not understand God's enduring kindness (Ps. 52:1) can be classified with the fool who denies the reality of God (Ps. 53:1). Nevertheless, Psalm 51's plea for forgiveness, especially given the celebration of forgiveness in Psalm 32, is an important reminder of the possibility of the wicked becoming righteous through God's mercy.

We have needed to pass over several psalms to reach this point, not because they are irrelevant but because only a small amount can be covered here. But if we backtrack briefly, we can note that the problem of the righteous and the wicked is predominantly an individual problem in Books 1–2. There are points where a communal dimension becomes evident, especially when the place of the king is expressly considered (esp. Pss 18, 20–21), and at such points the question of Torah becomes important through their connections with Psalm 19 (with Grant 2004). But the weight of interest in this issue is focused on the individual. This becomes especially clear in Psalm 37, which admonishes its listener (framed as an individual, even if a representative one) not to fret over the apparent prosperity of the wicked and instead to commit to Yahweh. In effect, this becomes a restatement of Psalms 1–2, even if the psalm is more than this. But Psalm 49 then reflects on this issue at a communal level, though it now addresses the nations, the very people Psalm 2 had admonished to take refuge in Yahweh's king. But the bulk of the psalm reflects on the decision an individual needs to take when faced with the prosperity of evildoers. The nations need to hear this, because it provides yet more reason for them to take refuge in Yahweh's king, but the issue itself is still presented through the experience of an individual. Psalm 50, providing a bridge between the first Korahite collection (Pss 42–49) and the Prayers of David (Pss 51–72), challenges the wicked about claiming Yahweh's statutes and covenant (Ps. 50:16) before asserting (with God's speaking) that the wicked do not escape God's judgement, and that God should be glorified with thanksgiving (Ps. 50:22–23), itself also anticipating the restoration of sacrifice in Psalm 51:18–19. This emphasis on the individual receives an important counterpoint at the end of the Prayers of David (Pss 51–72), prayers that in Psalm 72 have a particular focus on the coming of the nations to God (Pss 65–68). This royal psalm again provides important links to Psalms 1–2, as the king here becomes the exemplar of Torah righteousness in Psalm 1 for the good of the community, and also the one to whom the nations should come. The king is to embody the righteousness of Psalm 1, and so be the one through whom the blessings of Psalms 1–2 are worked out.

Psalm 73 then introduces Book 3 with a further reflection on the issues of the prosperity of the wicked from the perspective of an individual, though it has several strong links to Psalm 72 as well as to the Asaphic psalms that follow. Here, the individual's personal resolution of this issue (even if the resolution itself is not explained beyond the experience of worship) is presented to the community, a fact that is evident from the opening affirmation of God's goodness to Israel (cf. 'Notes' on Ps. 73:1). What this individual has discovered is shared so that the community may also discover its truth. This then becomes important in the rest of Book 3, where the challenges faced by the community (possibly in the exile, but this is not explicit) become especially evident. Indeed, if we read Psalm 73 as Book 3's introduction we may note that Psalm 74 opens by asking if God has cast off his people for ever (Ps. 74:1) and ends by asking if his kindness sworn to David is something that can still be trusted given the afflictions of his servants along with those of the king (Ps. 89:49–51). The problem of the success of nations who seem to deny Israel's God is thus pivotal for Book 3. Psalm 73 has shown that a means of resolving this may be seen in worship, but if the sanctuary has been destroyed and the king no longer reigns, then what hope is there? This is perhaps why there is such a strong desire to be at the sanctuary in Psalm 84 and to anticipate the final triumph of Zion in Psalm 87. The issue of the prosperity of the wicked and the blessedness of the righteous (those loyal to Yahweh) thus takes on a decidedly communal cast in Book 3, even if the individual element does not disappear.

Book 4 follows the more communal concerns of Book 3 with a strongly communal focus. A significant function of Book 4 is to respond to the sense of crisis with which Book 3 ends, and the introduction of a Mosaic psalm at its head is an important contributor to this, asking the community to reflect on a much longer period of time than their immediate experience may suggest. In this, Psalms 90–92 remind them of how Yahweh can be their dwelling place, providing security and reminding them that in Yahweh's span of time the flourishing of the wicked is really like the time it takes for grass to flourish before it is destroyed (Ps. 92:5–7). It is in the light of this that Yahweh's reign can be proclaimed in Psalms 93–99, a reign that anticipates the time when all the nations will enter the temple and worship him, fulfilling the hope of Psalm 2. In this setting, it is still important to ask Yahweh to act against the wicked (Ps. 94:3–7), with the wicked again being those who work on the assumption that Yahweh does not act. There is thus an important tension that is held through these psalms, even as they become progressively more exultant in the hope of Yahweh's reign. There are also reminders that they too can become the problem if they do not remain faithful (Ps. 95:7c–11), but Yahweh's revealing of salvation before the nations, a demonstration of his covenant faithfulness (Ps. 98:2–3) continues to provide hope. Book 4 does not ignore the individual. The speaker in Psalm 101 may be the king making vows to promote justice and silence the wicked, but the text is sufficiently open that others can hear in this vow a pattern for their own life. Likewise, the speaker of Psalm 102 is an individual who needs to see evidence of Yahweh's reign, but whose life is also situated in the need for Zion and the nations to experience Yahweh's compassion. Likewise, Psalm 103 has an individual speaker, but the voice is a representative one that celebrates Yahweh's compassion and forgiveness for all before calling all the heavens to join in praise. Mention of forgiveness here, especially through an allusion to Exodus 34:6–8, prepares for Psalms 104–106, which celebrate Yahweh's work in creation and sustenance of Israel through its history. In Psalm 106:6 this leads to a confession of sin, a reminder that Yahweh's dealing with wickedness may need to start with the community. The wicked are not simply the other, but any who live without regard for Yahweh's concerns. The good news in this psalm is that Yahweh does relent, even on those in captivity, because of his kindness (Ps. 106:44–46). As such, because they have turned to him and confessed their sin, he can save even those who have not been righteous. From this, Book 4's close also introduces the key term 'Hallelujah' (Pss 104:35; 105:4; 106:1, 48), something that is simultaneously a summons to praise and an act of praise, thus anticipating the role praise will have in demonstrating Yahweh's reign in Psalm 149:6.

Although the wicked are perhaps less prominent in Book 5, the problem they pose does not evaporate and important elements in Book 5 (esp. the final Davidic collection, Pss 138–145) take up this theme. Book 5 is perhaps the most difficult book to trace a theme through, though it does make use of the refrain 'Give thanks to Yahweh because he is good' at key points, opening with this phrasing (Ps. 107:1; cf. Pss 118:1; 136:1), which it has also taken up from Psalm 106:1. Yahweh's goodness is a fundamental datum for Book 5, one that reaches to all those Yahweh has redeemed. There remain adversaries to be overcome (Pss 108–110), though victory over them can be seen as simultaneously an act of Yahweh and his king. This prepares for a pair of Torah acrostics (Pss 111–112) that have important links to Psalm 1, and assure the righteous of their security (Ps. 112:6). These psalms also anticipate Psalm 119, a poem that by its sheer length dominates Book 5 with its emphasis on Torah as central to the faithful life, albeit a life that also needs Yahweh to act and provide salvation for someone who has strayed from the way like a sheep (Ps. 119:174–176). Again, the possibility is raised that the wicked may actually be those who otherwise seem to be righteous but have lost sight of Yahweh's purposes. These Torah psalms surround a collection known as the 'Egyptian Hallel' (Pss 113–118), poems that celebrate Yahweh's actions for his people and thus affirm that the declarations of his saving acts in Psalm 107 have been experienced by the community in their past. The community who celebrates Yahweh in the Songs of the Ascents (Pss 120–134) also acknowledges this, knowing that Yahweh is the one who needs to save (Ps. 120) but also the one who watches over his people (Ps.

121). The tension that exists between Psalms 1–2 and 3 continues here, though there are hints that this community has also known Yahweh's mighty acts on its part (Pss 124, 126). The strongly sapiential tone that emerges as we move through this collection encourages greater faithfulness, especially as it echoes Psalms 1–2 with its own beatitudes in Psalms 127–128. The community still needs to see Yahweh deal with the wicked, and its hope for this has a Davidic shape in Psalm 132, but it is also shaped through communal relations that promote peace and worship (Pss 133–134). Yahweh's actions for Israel can then be celebrated in Psalms 135–136, noting Yahweh's compassion on his people (Ps. 135:14) as a reason to believe he will vindicate his people. The stories of the past are thus a reason to continue trusting Yahweh, with the praise of these poems also shaping a community of trust as the one who has remembered it in its time of weakness (Ps. 136:23–25). Psalm 137 may represent a point where the community wrestles with the continued existence of the wicked in Babylon but has to trust Yahweh to resolve that challenge. From this, the final Davidic collection provides an example of thanksgiving (Ps. 138) and a further warning of the possibility that wickedness may remain within the community (Ps. 139). Each of Psalms 140–143 is a prayer of a faithful individual, each asking Yahweh to effect rescue in some way, even confessing that no one is righteous before Yahweh (Ps. 143:2). Here, 'righteousness' is expressed in absolute terms, but it is clear within the poem that the psalmist remains among the righteous in the sense of those committed to Yahweh. Psalm 144 is the final royal psalm, and thus a close partner to Psalm 2, though it also makes clear that a king is a limited help – it is Yahweh who must finally win. The image of the community after the victory Yahweh wins (Ps. 144:8) echoes the flourishing life of Psalm 1:3, except that it is here applied to the community and not just the individual. Yahweh's kingdom and the coming of his reign is thus the community's hope in Psalm 145, a hope that leads to the Final Hallel (Pss 146–150) in which the hope of Yahweh's reign can be celebrated across both the community and the whole of creation. The tension established at the start of Book 1 between the presence of the righteous and the wicked is finally resolved through the praise of those faithful to Yahweh. This is the hope to which the Psalter points, an eschatological image of final victory and praise, a hope that is resolute in insisting that, until that victory is finally seen, both the individual and the community must continue to trust in Yahweh and the hope of his kindness (*ḥesed*) in the midst of struggle and uncertainty. The righteous will triumph because Yahweh triumphs, and then praise will be all in all. We are not there yet, but we know where we shall be.

TEXT AND COMMENTARY BOOK 1

PSALM 1

Translation

1Oh the blessedness of the one who does not walk by the advice of the wicked,
nor stand on the path of sinners
nor sit in the assembly of scorners.
2whose delight is in the Torah of Yahweh,
meditating on his Torah day and night.
3This one is like a tree
planted by waters of the canals
which gives its fruit in season
and whose leaf does not wither,
everything this one does prospers.

4Not so the wicked,
they are like the chaff driven before the wind.
5Therefore, the wicked shall not rise in the judgement,
nor sinners in the congregation of the righteous.

6Because Yahweh knows the way of the righteous,
but the way of the wicked shall perish.

Notes on the text

3. Hebr. *plg* refers to something cut; hence, a canal rather than a natural stream. *BHS* suggests deleting the closing line as a gloss from Joshua 1:8. There is no manuscript support for this and the present text shows that both the Prophets and Writings commence with reference to life shaped by Torah.

Form and structure

Having been largely ignored under the influence of Gunkel's form-critical model, this psalm was moved to the centre of discussions about the Psalter by Wilson's influential study (1985b). This is because its position as the entrance to the Psalter means it is now commonly treated as the book's introduction, either on its own or in conjunction with Psalm 2 (cf. Cole 2012; Willgren 2016a: 136–171). But even those who are concerned with the whole Psalter still need to treat this psalm on its own terms, because only then can its relationship to the poems that follow be assessed. There are numerous lexical similarities between Psalms 1 and 2 (cf. Botha 2005a: 201), but these are most important for understanding why they have been juxtaposed at the beginning of the Psalter. Even when the juxtaposition of these psalms is recognized, Psalm 1's placement means it is the primary introduction (Weber 2006). That is, Psalm 1 guides readers of the Psalms about the basic orientation they need as they engage with the Psalter, though its brevity means it cannot engage with the issues that follow.

Form-critically, Psalm 1 is a 'Torah psalm'. However, this is a less helpful classification because it depends on one element rather than treating the whole text. The word 'Torah' is clearly important, though the psalm never takes time to define it. This is because it is already extending the meaning of the term in earlier OT texts (S. C. Jones 2016: 538). The term is rooted in the Pentateuch (Botha 2005b), but it now sees Yahweh's instruction as moving beyond that point. It is unlikely that the term now covers the Psalter as a primary reference (cf. Lefebvre 2016: 440–444), though the editor who placed this psalm at the beginning of the book could well intend this. The psalm also explores motifs more typically associated with wisdom (e.g. the 'two-ways' metaphor), but unlike that tradition's focus on the wise and the foolish, the psalm concentrates on the righteous and the wicked (Longman 2014: 55). These elements create close links with Joshua 1:8 and Jeremiah 17:7–8 (cf. Emanuel 2022: 22–25) and are thus part of the process by which Yahweh's instruction from the wider canon is drawn into the psalm.

Although Psalm 1 is sometimes regarded as being somewhat prosaic, Seow (2013) has demonstrated that it is properly treated as a carefully composed poem. Structurally, it can be divided into three stanzas, though each is folded into the other:

1. The blessed life (1–3)
2. The wicked life (4–5)
3. The two results (6)

Structured this way, it is notable that the psalm focuses more on the life of the righteous, since this is the way that is commended. Its poetry is a commendation of righteousness while acknowledging that not all will choose this path. This becomes even more notable when we note that the poetic lines in the second strophe are briefer than those of the first. As well as this strophic form, the psalm is also shaped by the alphabet, its opening word commencing with aleph and its last with taw, the first and last letters of the Hebrew alphabet. The psalm is brief, but through this device shows it has said all that is needed.

Comment

1. In commending the way of righteousness through a beatitude, the psalm opens by pointing to its opposite – indeed the word 'righteous' will not appear until verse 5. The one who lives in blessedness does not take advice from the wicked, stand with sinners nor sit with scorners. Inclusive language translations often make this whole verse pl. (e.g. NRSV, 'Happy are those'), but this loses the contrast between the many who take the wrong path and the individual who does not follow this way (deClaissé-Walford et al. 2014: 60). These are paths many will find attractive, but the individual here has not turned to them. The identity of this person is not specified here, but as *'îš* is most commonly 'a man' it is best to leave the identity open to cover any person. There may be an association with the king since he was meant to exemplify this pattern (and read in the light of Ps. 2 this becomes possible), but the association with Joshua points to the fact that non-royal figures can also live this life of blessedness. The word *'ašrê* (oh the blessedness), used to introduce a beatitude, describes a life that is in a state of blessedness, unlike words built on the root *brk* (bless), where a blessing refers to granting something extra. It is often used to present something as a desirable choice, which is its function here. The desirable choice is not to go with the many.

2–3. Where v. 1 described the desirable life in terms of what it is not, the focus now is on its content. Rather than wickedness, this one's delight is in Yahweh's Torah, the importance of which is evident from its mention in both parts of verse 2. 'Torah' here covers Yahweh's teaching in a broad sense, though it is certainly rooted in earlier parts of the OT. Torah is not simply known – it is a source of delight. As instruction, it contrasts strongly with the advice offered in verse 1 that is contrary to the blessed way. Delight in Torah is a life centred on it. The most obvious expression of this delight is regular meditation on it. The verb *hgh* (meditate) does not refer to a silent activity but often means 'murmur'. Delight is expressed in continued discussion of Yahweh's teaching. The life shaped this way is productive, as the person with this delight is compared to a tree planted by a regular flow of water (not always a given in Israel). Such a tree would produce its fruit and remain healthy, unlike those without regular nutrients. The last line of verse 3 could refer to the tree of the person, though what is true of the tree is also true of the person centred on Torah meditation. Much of the Psalter will describe those assailed by various enemies, so this is an important point of orientation. The path to flourishing is shaped by delight in Yahweh's Torah, not the option of going with the many.

4–5. After the extended reflection on the blessed life, verse 4 is notably terse. The contrast between the one and the many is continued here as 'the wicked' is pl. There are many who will not flourish, and this is asserted with simplicity. Once more, arboreal images are used (W. P. Brown 2002: 56–57), but here everything is insubstantial. Chaff, the husk of the grain separated in winnowing, was driven by the wind, contrasting with the firmly planted tree. Other texts express concern that the wicked are not always treated this way (Job 21:18; Ps. 35:5), but such complaints can be raised only when a general orientation is expected. The insubstantial nature of the wicked means they do not rise in the judgement. The nature of the judgement is not defined, and it could be eschatological (so Anderson 1972, 1: 62) or more immediate (Broyles 1999: 43). If we place more weight on the second half of verse 5, the reference could be to continued presence among the worshipping community, the congregation of the righteous. But the text may not require a specific choice.

6. The closing verse emerges directly from the two before, but is also connected to verse 1 through the poem's alphabetic structure. Reference to the righteous in verse 5 is now developed by pointing to Yahweh's continued 'awareness' (*yôdēʿa*) of them, the ptc. indicating that Yahweh's knowledge of the righteous is not temporary. Mention of the way of the wicked not only joins this comment to verse 5, but also points back to verse 1 where the wicked and their way was introduced. This way will perish, though how or when is not stated. It is the way not to be followed, and that it perishes proves its insubstantial nature.

Explanation

As the entrance point to the Psalter, this psalm provides readers with a basic orientation. It will be challenged by many of the psalms that follow, which will dialogue with it in various ways as the challenges posed by the wicked become more complex. But although its message will be nuanced, it is not rejected. This is because it understands that the choice of following the way of blessedness is made in full awareness of the alternative suggested by the crowd. The way it proposes is a life that finds its fulfilment in being shaped by Yahweh's Torah. This is not the popular way, and as we progress through the Psalter will prove to be a hard one (cf. Matt. 7:13–14). But it is the way of blessedness because being shaped by Yahweh's Torah is the way of flourishing.

PSALM 2

Translation

1Why are the nations restless,
  the peoples mumbling what is futile?
2The kings of the earth take their stand
  and the rulers take counsel together
  against Yahweh and his anointed.
3'Let us tear off their bonds
  and throw away their cords.'

4He who is seated in the heavens laughs
  the Lord derides them.
5Then he will speak to them with anger
  terrify them in his wrath.
6'But I, I have installed my king,
  upon Mount Zion, my holy mountain.'

7I will recount the decree,
  Yahweh said to me 'You are my son,
  I have begotten you today.
8Ask of me and I will give nations as your inheritance
  the ends of the earth as your possession.
9You may break them with a sceptre of iron,
  you may shatter them like a potter's vessel.'

10Now, be wise kings!
  Be warned, judges of the earth!
11Serve Yahweh with fear,
  and rejoice with trembling.
12Deal sincerely,
  lest he be angry, and you perish on the way,
  because his anger will burn quickly.
Oh, the blessedness of all taking refuge in him!

Notes on the text

5. Lam (2014) argues that Ugar. background suggests that *yĕbahălēmô* is 'disinherit' rather than 'terrify' them. This is plausible, and the archaic suffix here supports the possibility, but the evidence needs supplementing, and the intensification within the parallelism still supports the more traditional rendering.

9. LXX derives *tĕrō'ēm* from *r'h*; hence, 'shepherd'. But an Aramaism, from *r''* is more likely. See Tournay 1991: 219.

12. MT *bar* is an often-emended crux (cf. NRSV). Normally understood as Aramaic 'son', it is odd in a Hebrew text that has already used the Hebrew *bēn* (son) in verse 7. There are other Aramaisms in the psalm, so the word is not impossible. But *bar* in Hebrew can mean 'pure' and a Hebrew word is preferable. Although the verb *nšq* most commonly means 'kiss', *nšq* II may mean 'to handle' (Ps. 78:9) or even 'submit' (Gen. 41:40). These meanings are not established but, as Goldingay (2006a: 93) notes, there are several points where the verb's meaning is unclear, and the above is plausible given these possibilities. See also Sabottka 2006, though note the criticisms of Williamson 2022.

Form and structure

Along with Psalm 1, this psalm forms part of a double introduction to the Psalter (cf. Whiting 2013). This is evident from numerous verbal similarities that link them (see deClaissé-Walford et al. 2014: 65), the most important of which is the use of a beatitude as its close so that this literary structure now forms an inclusion around these psalms. Neither psalm has a title, something unusual within Book 1, where all other psalms apart from 10 and 33 have one. This psalm can be described as a royal psalm in that it is clearly concerned with the king, though as with the 'Torah psalm' this is not always a helpful classification since the royal psalms can usually be placed within other categories. Although we cannot be sure that those compiling the Psalter identified genres along the patterns now widely used, Grant (2004) has noted that Torah and royal psalms are paired at key points in the finished book, providing further evidence for the suggestion that these psalms have been paired. Nevertheless, their pairing does not mean that the meaning of each poem is subsumed into the other. Indeed, as Willgren has noted (2016a: 169), the impulse to treat these psalms as a preface is a relatively modern one, meaning research needs to be focused on how each can be read in the light of the other rather than in seeing them primarily as a combined preface.

In origin, Psalm 2 appears to represent a coronation ritual for an Israelite king, drawing on the background of 2 Samuel 7:1–17. As a ritual, it seems to have had several speakers, at least a priest or prophetic figure and the king himself. Much of the psalm is notionally addressed to nations that do not submit to Yahweh and his anointed, but like the oracles against the nations in the prophets (e.g. Amos 1 – 2) these are words that Israel are meant to overhear and then shape their own life in response.

Although a chiasm can be defended (Becking 1990: 60), the psalm can more simply be structured in four stanzas:

1. The Plans of the Nations (1–3)
2. Yahweh's Response (4–6)
3. Yahweh's Announcement to the King (7–9)
4. Call to Serve Yahweh (10–12)

Comment

1–3. An opening speaker addresses other nations that are presented as seeking to rebel against Yahweh and his anointed. The question 'why' focuses the issue – the assumption is that they should settle under Yahweh and his anointed. The nations are particularly represented by their rulers who have set themselves against Yahweh and his anointed. Why, then, would they be restless and mumbling futile words of rebellion to one another? In purely political terms, this is an 'audacious claim' (Miller 1986: 88), for Israel (and even more so Judah) was never a major political force, even at the height of the Davidic kingdom. From the perspective of the nations, it would make sense to overthrow the claim of any Israelite king. But the psalm makes clear that they are not rebelling against any ordinary king. Rather, Yahweh's anointed – a term that naturally feeds into the messianic hope of the OT – has authority only because Yahweh stands beside him. The nations may imagine that they need offer no fealty to Israel, and in political terms this is coherent. But they are really rebelling against Yahweh, and this is presented as an incoherent strategy. Their plans are futile because of this.

4–6. That Yahweh is the focus is apparent from the fact he is the one who responds to the kings. Where the kings are on earth, Yahweh is seated in heaven. He has a perspective that none of the kings can access. When Yahweh contemplates their plots, he laughs, seeing the futility of their plans and claims. But derision also leads to anger because they have embarked on a futile path, and it is Yahweh's speech that will terrify the kings. But the speech is not about Yahweh's power. Rather, it declares that Yahweh has set his king on his holy mountain, perhaps the point of coronation (so, J. H. Eaton 1976: 112). Just as the opening strophe ended with a quote from the kings, so this second strophe closes with Yahweh's being quoted. And though it may not seem to be the case, the placing of his king on Zion (the area most closely associated with David) is how he terrifies the kings. This may have been politically counterintuitive, but it is fundamental to Yahweh's claim. Zion is not simply a place associated with David. Rather, it is Yahweh's holy mountain. Deities in the ancient east were often associated with mountains, but what distinguished Yahweh's statement was the temple's presence, the visible sign that this was his mountain, the place where a new king could stand and be presented.

7–9. At this point, the king speaks, recounting Yahweh's decree. The use of 'decree' (*ḥōq*) here points to a specific announcement from Yahweh. The announcement is that the king is Yahweh's son, begotten that day. As the king is mature enough to speak, he has clearly not been physically begotten that day (cf. Moenikes 1999; Foster 2019: 19). Rather, the implication is that his enthronement has placed him in a special relationship to Yahweh, the language of sonship drawing on the promise to David (2 Sam. 7:14). At his enthronement the king has entered a new and distinctive relationship with Yahweh, as the one who most truly represents him. Israel's king was not divine, but he did represent Yahweh. This representative role includes the possibility of Yahweh's granting the nations as a heritage to him. This language echoes the promise of the land to Israel in Deuteronomy (e.g. Deut. 4:38), though Israel can also be Yahweh's heritage (Deut. 4:20). The king can thus receive more than Israel while himself being the ideal Israelite, but he receives this gift only by asking. This context means that the king's reign cannot be for himself alone; and when this language is adopted later (Ps. 72:12–14), it is expressed through concern for the poor. In the context of rebellious nations, here the stress is on the king's ability to destroy those who oppose him as he rules with an iron rod, smashing the nations like pieces of pottery. This enables the nations to see the need for submission to Yahweh, since it is his reign expressed through the king.

10–12. Where the position of the nations was a subject for reflection in verses 1–3, they are here addressed directly. The opening 'Now' captures the points made so far and points to the necessary conclusion. The kings need to be wise, though they have also been warned. Both verbs in verse 10, 'be wise' (*śkl*) and 'be warned' (*ysr*), point to the instructional nature of what has been given so far, indicating that all rulers engaged in rebellion need to reconsider. This reconsideration should lead to their seeing that they should serve Yahweh with fear. It is not the king whom they serve but Yahweh. This explains why rebellion is pointless. Serving Yahweh is not an expression of terror but rather of a life shaped by doing his will. Therefore, such service can be matched by rejoicing, even if it can be associated with fearfulness (cf. Ps. 48:6). Yahweh is not to be trifled with, but in serving him there is joy. Only when service is given to Yahweh can the kings also submit to Yahweh's king. The king is Yahweh's representative; they must deal sincerely with him. If not, then the king's anger will be roused, and they will perish on the way. This language echoes Psalm 1:6, placing these kings among those who choose the way of wickedness. Again, it is not said how they perish; what matters is that rebellion against Yahweh is not the way of life. The psalm ends with a beatitude announced for those taking refuge in the king. This echoes Psalm 1:1, showing that the life of blessedness involves the wise course of submission to Yahweh through finding refuge in his king. This is the wise path. Although it may not seem politically astute, it is the way of life.

Explanation

The psalm deals with the coronation of the king, demonstrating that Yahweh stands with his king because he has chosen him, making opposition futile. Obviously, the language is grandiose for the kings of Judah, especially in verse 12. Yet through this we see the development of the hope of the messiah. Because Judah's kings could carry out only in part what is written here, we see foreshadowed the greater king, the messiah. Whether the psalm was intentionally messianic is difficult to say, but it certainly points in that direction, declaring that 'God supports those who submit to divine authority' (Schaefer 2001: 9). Moreover, as Longman (2014: 63–64) makes clear, the NT certainly read the psalm as messianic, and in doing so drew on interpretative traditions that were already present in the OT. Yet alongside this, the psalm also joins with Psalm 1, helping all readers who wrestle with the challenges of a life where many still rebel against God's rule see that the life of blessedness is found in meditation on God's Torah and submitting to his reign expressed in his king. Jesus teaches us to pray 'Your kingdom come' (Matt. 6:10), indicating that the reality of these opening poems in the Psalter continues to shape our hope for the future as we live faithfully in the present.

PSALM 3

Translation

A melody. Davidic, when he fled before Absalom his son.

1 Yahweh, how many are my foes,
  how many are rising against me!
2 Many are saying of me,
  'There is no salvation for him in God!' *Selah*.

3But you, O Yahweh, are a shield about me,
my glory and the lifter of my head.
4With my voice to Yahweh I cry,
and he answered me from his holy mountain. *Selah.*
5I lay down and slept, I awoke,
because Yahweh sustains me.
6I will not fear myriads of people
who set themselves against me all around.

7Arise O Yahweh, save me, O my God,
indeed, break the jaws of all my enemies,
shatter the teeth of the wicked.
8Salvation belongs to Yahweh,
your blessing be upon your people. *Selah.*

Notes on the text

Title: Hebr. *mizmôr* is usually rendered 'psalm' but is a different word from the title of the book. To maintain a distinction, its more basic sense of 'melody' is used throughout. *lědāwid* is often understood as indicating authorship, but the preposition *lě* more likely indicates possession without having to indicate authorship (*WHS* §270). The psalm belongs to David in some way, but the preposition does not resolve how this is understood and needs to be understood in a case-by-case approach. 'Davidic' is used to retain this ambiguity. On David's flight before Absalom, see 'Form and structure'.

2. Hebr. *nepeš* is often translated 'soul' but here represents the whole person. *Selâ* is a word that always stands outside a syntactic relationship. Its meaning is unknown but could indicate a pause in reading.

7. Both *hikîtā* and *šibbartā* are understood as prec. pfs., emphasizing the expectation of the prayer being realized; see W-O §30.4.5.c–d and Stone 2021. Accordingly, *kî* is asseverative; see *WHS* §261.

Form and structure

Psalm 3 is the first psalm to have a title (see Introduction, §4, 'Psalm titles'). Within Book 1 this becomes the norm, with only Psalms 10 and 33 lacking one. This makes the fact that Psalms 1–2 lack a title more remarkable, marking them off from what follows. Psalm 3 thus leads readers into the main part of the 'book of praises' (see Introduction, §1, 'Name'), but it is immediately notable that this is not praise as the modern world typically defines it. It has strong linguistic connections with Psalms 1–2 (Cole 2012: 143–144), meaning it is intended to have this bridging position. This bridge is continued into Psalm 4 (cf. Auffret 1998: 332), which also has linguistic and formal connections to Psalm 3. Both are complaint psalms, though they also introduce an alternating pattern of morning–evening that runs through to Psalm 7 (cf. Waltke 2008: 2). Psalm 8 breaks this pattern (cf. Smith and Domeris 2010), though functioning as a bridge for a collection that runs through to Psalm 14 (cf. Hartenstein 2010). However, this is only a minor break as every titled psalm in Book 1 is Davidic, making this an important marker within this collection.

The title links the psalm to David's flight from Absalom (2 Sam. 15:14). There are some verbal links between the psalm and 2 Samuel 15 – 18, and David there undoubtedly faces numerous enemies, but the connections are relatively general. Moreover, reference to Yahweh's holy mountain (v. 4) suggests that the temple was already associated with Zion, something not true until Solomon. There is also no point at which David shows the sort of confidence expressed in verses 3–6. None of this makes it invalid to read the psalm against this background, and indeed the title encourages readers to understand it via David's experience. These words were appropriate for David at that time of great distress and are also appropriate for all who seek Yahweh's protection, especially those who take refuge in Yahweh and are committed to his Torah (cf. Tournay 1991: 192). This feature makes this a good example of how complaint psalms and songs of trust shade into one another (Firth 2005b: 54), while also making it difficult to identify a specific life setting (similarly, W. S. Prinsloo 1991b: 8).

Key verbal repetitions hold the psalm together, especially the language of 'many' (*rbb*, vv. 1, 2, 6) and 'salvation' (*yš*ʿ, vv. 2, 7, 8). As this latter element creates an inclusion for the whole poem, the suggestion that verse 8 is a gloss (Van der Ploeg 1973: 47) is unnecessary (cf. W. S. Prinsloo 1991b: 23). Structurally, the body of the psalm can be analysed in three stanzas, with the second containing two strophes (Firth 2005b: 56–57):

1. Call to God about enemies (1–2)
2. Statements of confidence (3–6)
   a. Yahweh as protector (3–4)
   b. Confidence before enemies (5–6)
3. Appeal in confidence (7–8)

Comment

Title: See 'Notes on the text' and 'Form and structure'.

1–2. Opening with a direct address to Yahweh, the poet outlines the severity of the situation faced because of many foes. The two parts of verse 1 build on repetition of 'many' (*rbb*), moving from asking Yahweh to note the poet's many foes before observing that they are rising against the psalmist. The word 'foes' (*ṣar*) suggests they in some way constrict the poet. This constriction is developed by pointing out that they are rising up against the poet. Although this may suggest a military context, there is also evidence of a psychological threat as we move into verse 2 with its emphasis on the foes' speech as they declare that the poet has no hope of salvation from God. This too draws on the language of 'many', phrasing picked up in Psalm 4:6. In presenting the actions and words of the foes, the psalmist effectively challenges Yahweh to act. The foes deny that Yahweh is a source of salvation, and it is the conflict between this claim and the poet's confidence that drives the balance of the psalm.

3–4. The second stanza opens by again addressing Yahweh directly, describing him in terms contrary to the claim of the foes. The psalmist needs to be saved from the foes, and as the poet's shield Yahweh can fulfil this function. If Psalms 3–7 form a small group, this may be further evidenced by Psalm 7:10 indicating that the poet's shield is with God, the one who saves the upright, creating clear verbal links with Psalm 3. The shield in both cases is the small shield (*māgēn*) that a soldier might carry into battle, but that this is no ordinary shield is made clear by the observation that Yahweh is a shield about the poet, one that protects at all points in a way a shield would not normally do. The enemies are all about, but Yahweh provides protection wherever they are. Military language is dropped for the balance of this section. Rather, Yahweh is described as the poet's 'glory' and the one who 'lifts' the head. That is, Yahweh is the one who restores the psalmist. Evidence for this is found in the fact that the poet has cried out to Yahweh and been answered before. The phrasing of verse 4 emphasizes the poet's voice, that this was a cry made and heard as Yahweh answered from his holy mountain. Unlike the speech of the foes, the poet's words have been heard and acted on by Yahweh.

5–6. Yahweh's previous actions give the poet confidence, enabling sleep because of Yahweh's sustaining power. Yahweh's sustaining of the psalmist is not a one-off event, but something that endures. Within the poem, such confidence is important because the night is a time of threat when the enemies could have attacked, but this sustenance goes beyond that point. Therefore, the psalmist is not afraid of myriads, a more specific number that builds further on the 'many' in verses 1–2 through repetition of the root *rbb*. They may set themselves against the poet, and they may be all around, but if Yahweh is a shield all around who continually sustains the poet, then there is no need for fear.

7–8. The final stanza also opens with a direct address to Yahweh, summoning him to arise, the verb *qûmâ* (arise) echoing the actions of the foes in verse 1. The link to the opening stanza is strengthened by the call for Yahweh to save the psalmist, because this in turn negates the foes' claim about God's not saving the poet. The appeal matches the enemies' actions quite specifically, including the interchange in divine names from 'Yahweh' to 'God'. The second half of verse 7 asks for specific actions, but with confidence that Yahweh will act (cf. 'Notes on the text'). The central element of threat from the foes was expressed verbally, so the request is that Yahweh act to prevent such threats continuing, striking the enemies on the jaw and shattering their teeth. It is an exact reversal of what they have done, which also demonstrates that Yahweh does save. Notably, the poet does not ask for the ability to enact this personally: retribution is left to Yahweh alone. That is why the psalm closes by declaring that salvation does indeed belong to Yahweh, and those who are so struck are the wicked, the very ones Psalm 1:6 had indicated would perish. If Yahweh does bring salvation, then his blessing would be shown on his people. This blessing differs from that of Psalm 1, which describes a state of blessedness by here wishing for Yahweh to bring his blessing to bear on his people.

Explanation

Psalm 3 brings readers into the body of the Psalter, though this book of praises immediately includes complaint, but complaint that is shaped by confidence. The combination is possible because the poet is presented as one who has understood the need to find refuge in Yahweh and stand apart from the wicked. These elements draw on themes from Psalms 1–2. Psalm 1 had set up a contrast between the many who take the path of wickedness and the few who remain loyal to Yahweh, something that finds an echo here as the psalmist faces myriads of the wicked. But the psalmist also takes refuge in Yahweh, the one who set his king on his holy hill in Psalm 2 and who answers from there in this psalm. Immediately therefore we know that the orientation provided by the opening psalms does not assume an easy path for the faithful but rather that it will be one challenged by the wicked, into which the category of the 'foe', which will be so important for the rest of the Psalter, has here been introduced. And it is in this world of challenge and uncertainty that the faithful can live in confidence. This is not confidence that no challenges will occur, but rather that Yahweh does indeed act for his people and that they can ask him to do so. At the same time, the psalm introduces another key motif in the psalter, which is that even where prayer is offered against the enemies, this prayer must leave any act of retribution to Yahweh alone, with the prayer's content matching the harm inflicted by the foes. Yahweh saves, but he is also just, and prayer is shaped in those terms (Firth 2005b: 61–62). All this was brought out in David's experience as he fled from Absalom (cf. Schroeder 2000: 250).

PSALM 4

Translation

The director's. With stringed instruments. A melody, Davidic.

1When I call, answer me,
O God of my righteousness,
when pressed, grant me space,
be gracious to me and hear my prayer.

2People, how long shall my honour become ignominy,
shall you love worthlessness,
shall you seek falsehood? *Selah.*
3But know that Yahweh has set aside the godly for himself,
Yahweh hears when I call to him.
4Tremble and do not sin,
reflect on your beds and be silent. *Selah.*
5Offer right sacrifices
and trust in Yahweh.

6Many are saying 'Who will show us good?'
Lift up the light of your face upon us Yahweh!
7You have put more joy in my heart
than when their grain and new wine abound.
8In peace I both lie down and sleep,
for you alone O Yahweh make me dwell securely.

Notes on the text

Title: Hebr. *lamnaṣṣēaḥ*, 'the director's', occurs fifty-five times in the Psalter, always in the title. LXX understands it as referring to 'eternity', but more likely it derives from a leadership role, which in 1 Chronicles 15:21 is musical. For *mizmôr* (a melody) and *lĕdāwid* (Davidic), see on the title of Psalm 3.

1. Hebr. *hirḥabtā* (grant space) is understood as a prec. pf. See 'Notes on the text' on Psalm 3:7.

4. Although the verb *'mr* commonly introduces speech, when conducted 'in the heart' (as here) it refers to thought expressed as an internal discourse. Against Kselman (1987), MT is here retained.

6. Reading *nś'* with one MS. Hebr. *nĕsâ* suggests a continuation of the lament, but this is inconsistent with the preposition. Although derived from a different root, LXX seems to read the line similarly.

Form and structure

As noted (see 'Form and structure' on Ps. 3), there are numerous linguistic connections between Psalms 3, 4. Most importantly, the phrase 'many are saying' occurs in both (Pss 3:2; 4:6), while the reference to sleep (v. 8) continues the morning/evening pattern that extends to Psalm 7. They remain distinct poems, but these links suggest that, as with Psalms 1–2, these poems are to be read in the light of each other (cf. Schaefer 2001: 12–13). Given the lack of progress made in various attempts to identify a more specific background to the psalm (ably summarized in deClaissé-Walford et al. 2014: 79–80, probably because the psalm's language is often ambiguous; see Goldingay 2006b), the literary context probably provides a more fruitful path for interpretation (cf. Botha 2018a: 26), especially noting that the pattern of prayer and confidence found in this psalm is present throughout Psalms 3–7. That said, it can be described as a complaint psalm: the attempts to go beyond this have proved unsuccessful.

The title here introduces the 'director', a term usually understood as indicating the psalm was part of a collection associated with more formal worship (see Introduction, §4, 'Psalm titles'). Often, mention of the director is associated with a musical note (though not always; cf. Ps. 11), with this psalm to be performed on stringed instruments.

A notable feature of this poem is the repetition of key words. In particular, the pattern of 'call' (*qr'*) and 'hear' (*šm'*) joins verses 1 and 3, while mention of speech (*'mr*) and the heart (*lēb*) links verses 4, 6, 7. The root *škb*, in both its nominal (v. 4, 'bed') and verbal forms (v. 8, 'lie down'), also binds sections of the poem together. 'Trust' (*bṭḥ*) occurs in verses 5, 8, while 'righteousness' (*ṣdq*) is in verses 1, 5. Beyond the fact of the repetitions, it should be observed that they establish contrasts within the poem between the experience of the poet and the adversaries. Hence, the 'call'/'hear' pattern in verse 1 is the point where the poet petitions Yahweh, while in verse 3 it is a report to the adversaries of what Yahweh has done. The speech in verse 4 is silent since it is in the heart and constitutes behaviour the adversaries should follow, whereas in verse 6 what is reported is their utterance, which the rest of the poem shows is misguided. This is why there is joy in the poet's heart. This makes sleep possible, whereas the adversaries need to spend time in their beds reflecting, as one can trust and the other cannot. This is because Yahweh is the God of the poet's righteousness, whereas they need to offer right sacrifices.

The poem can be analysed in three stanzas, marked off by the change of addressee:

1. Address to God (1)
2. Address to community (2–5)
3. Address to Yahweh and affirmation of trust (6–8)

Comment

Title: See 'Notes on the text' and 'Form and structure'. For 'a melody' and 'Davidic' see on Psalm 3.

1. Although the psalm will predominantly use the divine name Yahweh, the opening appeal uses 'God of my righteousness' instead. The phrase is unique to this psalm, indicating that the poet is in a relationship with Yahweh that enables this appeal to be made. The appeal is not limited to a specific point of time, but rather asks God to respond whenever such a call is made. This would perhaps explain the use of the pf. *hirḥabtā* (grant me space) here. The form assumes that God has previously acted, but when understood as a prec. an appeal is made for further action, albeit an appeal made with confidence. This appeal also plays on the fact that the word for 'distress' (*ṣār*) has the sense of being pressed into somewhere narrow, so that deliverance is the granting of space. The more immediate need is for God to be gracious and hear the poet's prayer. Mention of grace makes clear that although the poet appeals from a position of righteousness, this is understood in general terms only, and that grace is always needed.

2. Attention now switches to a presumed human audience, who are addressed directly and who emerge as adversaries, though the assumption is that God continues to hear. The audience are opposed to the poet, though the psalm now addresses all who encounter it. The question 'how long' presumes that these people have acted against the poet for some time, seeking to turn the psalmist's honour to ignominy. Although elided, the force of 'how long' continues in the second half of the verse, which describes how the people addressed have acted against the psalmist through love of what is worthless and seeking lies. This language could allude to court practices but can also refer to idolatry. Although a specific determination is not possible, the psalmist makes clear that their position is false, something standing in contrast to the poet's position of being right before God.

3–5. These verses are joined through their opening imperatives, all addressed to the adversaries. They are first told to note that Yahweh has set aside the godly for himself. This makes an immediate division between the godly and the wicked, building on the division established in Psalm 1. If Yahweh watches over the way of the righteous (Ps. 1:6), then it makes sense that he has set aside the godly. But that is not simply an abstract truth. Instead, it is applied in the observation that Yahweh hears the psalmist's call. This echoes the opening plea of verse 1, though as noted above, the appeal included confidence that Yahweh hears. This in turn leads to the string of imperatives in verse 4 that summon the people to tremble and ponder. The opening imperative ('tremble') is joined to the prohibition 'do not sin', the clear implication being that their current actions are sinful. As such, they should tremble in fear because Yahweh will act (cf. Ps. 99:1). At the same time, awareness of Yahweh's commitment to the godly should lead to reflection on these matters, expressed here in terms of internal discourse and silence upon their beds at night. Where the psalm will close with the poet sleeping soundly, the adversaries are advised to spend their nights reflecting on Yahweh's character. The gradual build-up of imperatives concludes in verse 5 as the people are told to offer right sacrifices and trust in Yahweh. This implies that they have not been doing so. 'Right sacrifices' (cf. Deut. 33:19; Ps. 51:19; also Zwickel 1995) are sacrifices that come out of a right relationship with Yahweh, which is why such sacrifices cannot be offered apart from trust in Yahweh.

6. The poet now turns once more to address Yahweh directly, though the wider audience continue to overhear. The opening quote picks up the words of various adversaries which appear to deny that the godly will experience any good in life. Note that the quote places the poet in a larger group ('us'), though the assumption is that this is still smaller than the many who are speaking. The wording of the second half of the verse is difficult (see 'Notes on the text'), but it probably summons Yahweh to lift the light of his face towards the godly. The language evokes the priestly blessing (Num. 6:24–26), asking that the good the godly experience be seen in their lived reality because this would silence the many who make this claim.

7–8. The poet's personal testimony is that Yahweh has acted, granting joy that is greater even than when grain and new wine abound. The harvest was a time of celebration, but such joy could be fleeting. It was God's presence that provided greater joy. Because this was true, the poet could both lie down and sleep in peace. The granting of 'peace' (*šālôm*) was also part of the priestly blessing invoked in verse 6, and because of this the poet could dwell securely. This security was an expression of trust in Yahweh that emerges from discovering how his presence sustains the godly.

Explanation

Psalm 4 is closely joined to Psalm 3, continuing to explore the issue of how the godly are to live in a world where those opposed to them are likely to be in the majority, though without denying that there is still a community of the godly. The psalm recognizes that it is possible to live a life that is right with God and so call on him with confidence. Indeed, it suggests that such calls are possible because God has acted in the past for his people, and therefore they can call with confidence. Where it extends the message of Psalm 3 is that it also looks out to the adversaries, addressing them directly so that they too are challenged to consider the claims of a life lived trusting Yahweh. Through this address, a wider audience are also asked to reflect on the issues raised here – if Yahweh does indeed act for the godly, hearing them when they call, then how should they respond to the claims of this God? The response summoned here is essentially one of repentance that is expressed through the move to a life of trust. This trust is demonstrated by the poet who discovers more joy in Yahweh's presence than do others in the harvest with its abundance of grain and wine. It is this presence that leads to a secure life, a life aware of the challenges that exist, but which sees that the joy given by God exceeds all else, something to which Paul may allude (2 Cor. 7:2–5).

PSALM 5

Translation

The director's. For the flutes. A melody, Davidic.

1Give ear to my words O Yahweh,
  consider my groaning,
2attend to the sound of my cry,
  my king and my God,
  for to you do I pray.
3O Yahweh, in the morning you hear my voice,
  in the morning do I lay it out for you and keep watch.
4For you are not a God who delights in wickedness,
  evil may not dwell with you.
5The boastful shall not take their stand before your eyes,
  you hate all workers of iniquity,
6you destroy those speaking what is false;
  a person of bloodshed and rebellion Yahweh abhors.
7But I, in the greatness of your kindness, shall enter your house,
  I shall prostrate myself before your holy temple in reverence of you.

8O Yahweh, lead me in your righteousness
  because of my enemies,
  make your path straight before me.

9For there is nothing dependable in such a one's mouth,
  their inner being is a chasm,
their throat is an open grave,
  with their tongue they flatter.
10Declare them guilty, O God,
  let them fall by their own counsels,
banish them because of the abundance of their transgressions,
  for they have rebelled against you.

[11]But let all who take refuge in you rejoice,
let them ever sing,
and may you cover them
so those who love your name may exalt in you.
[12]For you bless the righteous, O Yahweh,
you cover that one with favour like a shield.

Notes on the text

7. On the translation of 'kindness' for *ḥesed*, see Ziegert 2020.
9. Reading the initial suffix as distributive.

Form and structure

As with Psalms 3–4, the important context for interpreting this psalm is provided by its setting in the Psalter's opening movement. Although attempts have been made to tie this psalm more specifically to the prayers of the accused (see Kraus 1988: 153; Seybold 1996: 40), it is better to regard the language of the prayer as relatively open so that a range of life settings can reasonably be imagined. The more important connections are thus with the larger body of Psalms 1–2 and 3–7 (similarly, Botha 2018b). Within Psalms 3–7, Psalm 5 represents the morning prayer (v. 3) that follows the evening prayer of Psalm 4, continuing the pattern of complaint psalms that run through this section. These psalms are also joined through the language of prayer (*pll*; Pss 4:1; 5:2; cf. Vesco 2006, 1: 117). The psalm also makes numerous linguistic connections with Psalms 1–2, so that it now functions as a prayer that reflects on the orientation established by those poems. With Psalm 1, Psalm 5 draws on the way motif (Pss 1:6; 5:8), while both make a clear distinction between the righteous and the wicked. With Psalm 2, it shares the motif of refuge (Pss 2:12; 5:11). Although in Psalm 2 refuge is sought in Yahweh's king, whereas here Yahweh is king, the reality is that taking refuge in Yahweh's king is taking refuge in Yahweh, so there is an equivalence between these. Although not equivalent, 'groaning' (*hăgîgî*) is possibly cognate to *hgh* (meditate) in Psalm 1:2 and may at least evoke the former term.

The psalm can be analysed in three stanzas, though the first can be subdivided into three strophes:

1. Appeal to Yahweh (1–7)
   a. Initial appeal (1–3)
   b. Observations on Yahweh's character (4–6)
   c. Poet's intention to worship (7)

2. Requests because of the enemies (8–10)
3. Hope for the righteous (11–12)

Comment

Title: For 'the director's' see on Ps. 4. For 'melody' and 'Davidic' see on Ps. 3. As is common with psalms from the director's collection, this one is associated with music, in this case flutes.

1–3. There is an intense pattern of three imperatives with which the initial appeal begins. Each is concerned with Yahweh's awareness of the poet's situation (give ear, consider, attend) and in turn is paired with an expression referring to the utterance to be noted, all of which prepares for Yahweh to hear in the morning. These progress from the more ordered 'words' to the more inchoate 'groaning' before coming together as the sound of the psalmist's cry. Such a cry is thus both ordered and unformed speech, together forming a cry for help. Yahweh should heed this cry (now defined as prayer) because he is the poet's king and God. Although Yahweh's kingship becomes an important theme in the Psalter (Mays 1994a), this is the first point at which the motif occurs. Here, his kingship is patterned on the king's role of hearing those who come before him with some need (e.g. 2 Sam. 14:4–11). Following on from this, verse 3 anticipates Yahweh hearing the poet's voice, though the poet will also lay something out and keep watch. This could refer to arranging a sacrifice and waiting to see if Yahweh responds favourably, though the laying out of the prayer itself may now fulfil this function.

4–6. The psalmist has confidence to pray because of Yahweh's character and how this is expressed in Yahweh's actions. These verses list three things Yahweh does not do and three things he does. Yahweh has no delight in wickedness, does not allow evil to dwell with him, refuses the boastful the right to stand before him. Implicitly, the poet claims that none of these statements are applicable, and that therefore Yahweh will permit this prayer. Some of the language here echoes Psalm 1, forming a negative counterpoint to what is encouraged there, while anticipating that of Psalm 15 which will more directly encourage the faithful to avoid the behaviours noted here (cf. G. T. M. Prinsloo 1998b: 633). Following the three negative statements, we then read three statements about how Yahweh acts towards such people, hating workers of iniquity, destroying those speaking what is false (cf. Ps. 4:2) and abhorring the violent and rebellion. In this case, the first category (workers of iniquity) is probably defined by the two cases that follow since they are more specific. The falsehood here may be false gods or lies about the poet. 'Bloodshed' is more limited in focus, but 'rebellion' may be against Yahweh's reign or wider social structures. If the second and third categories are defining the first, then Yahweh's destruction of the first is consistent with the fate of the wicked in Psalm 1:6.

7. The previous verses had indicated why some could not enter Yahweh's presence. Although not stated directly, the poet has claimed that these categories do not apply. But not falling into the paths that are rejected are not of themselves sufficient. Rather, the psalmist enters the temple based on Yahweh's great 'kindness' (*ḥesed*). This term frequently occurs in covenant contexts, with crucial background being provided by Yahweh's self-designation in Exodus 34:6, where this is central to God's character. There may be human actions that disqualify one from entering the temple, but that entry is still an act of divine grace. It is this that leads the poet to describe the worship there in terms of prostration and awe, the appropriate posture for being in the presence of the divine king.

8–10. Yahweh is again addressed directly as the psalmist's request is made, asking to be led by Yahweh in his righteousness. That is, although the poet has implicitly denied acting in the ways of verses 4–6, there is still a need to live a life marked by righteousness, again evoking the categories of Psalm 1. Such leading is needed because of the adversaries who are like those described in Psalm 1:1, whereas the psalmist wants to be on the way approved by Yahweh (Ps. 1:6). Help is needed because the enemies offer speech that is like that rejected in Psalm 1:1 (cf. Rom. 3:13) that would direct the poet away from Yahweh with words that are really a form of flattery that leads to death because they point to the way Yahweh destroys. Yet, although they represent the way that Yahweh ultimately destroys, the psalmist is also aware that they have not yet been destroyed, which is why there is a prayer for them to be declared guilty. Their guilt is that they lead others to the path of destruction. Nevertheless, as is consistent across the Psalter, the prayer here does not ask for more than they do to be done to them, requesting that they fall by their own counsel (cf. Ps. 1:1), deserving banishment because they have rebelled against Yahweh, thus being among those Yahweh abhors (v. 6). But it is finally Yahweh who must act on this (Goldingay 2006a: 133).

11–12. By contrast, the psalmist anticipates the point where those taking refuge in Yahweh would continually rejoice. Taking refuge evokes Psalm 2:12, except that the focus is directly on Yahweh as the king. The speech of those taking refuge in him contrasts markedly with that of the enemies, being marked with joy. Instead of being on the path of destruction, those taking refuge can anticipate being covered by Yahweh's protection, enabling those who love his name (the name representing his character) to exalt in him. This is possible because Yahweh 'blesses' (*brk*) the righteous, covering them with favour in the same way as a warrior is protected by a shield.

Explanation

This prayer is a serious exploration of the patterns laid out in Psalms 1–2, which builds further on themes already established in Psalms 3–4. As the two preceding psalms have made clear, the life of the righteous is not free of pain and difficulty, something implicit in Psalm 1 but made explicit here. Yet the orientation to life that Psalms 1–2 provide is not to be set aside. Rather, it forms the foundation for prayer. It is the language of these psalms that shapes this prayer, encouraging the faithful to pray about situations in which the type of life described in Psalm 1:1 predominates. As noted, that psalm made clear that those not walking with Yahweh were the majority. But they were not following the way of righteousness, and the way to righteousness is prayer that asks Yahweh to act in the patterns established in Psalm 1. The righteous are also here encouraged to find refuge in Yahweh, conforming to the pattern of Psalm 2. In doing so, they are reminded that the basis for prayer is Yahweh's kindness even as they are also encouraged to shape their own life in response to this reality. Most importantly, the way to righteousness is through prayer that asks to be led by Yahweh and that wickedness be stopped. Such prayer asks those who pray to consider their own life.

PSALM 6

Translation

The director's. With stringed instruments, upon the eighth. A melody, Davidic.

[1]Yahweh, do not rebuke me in your anger,
  and do not discipline me in your wrath.
[2]Be gracious to me, O Yahweh, because I am weak,
  heal me, O Yahweh, because my bones are disturbed.
[3]My life is greatly disturbed,
  but you, O Yahweh, how long?

[4]Turn, O Yahweh, deliver my life,
  save me on account of your kindness,
[5]for there is no remembrance of you in death,
  in Sheol, who shall give thanks to you?
[6]I have grown weary with my sighing,
  I flood my bed every night,
  with my tears I drench my couch,
[7]my eye fails because of vexation,
  it grows weak because of all my foes.

8Turn from me all workers of iniquity,
because Yahweh has heard my weeping.
9Yahweh has heard my supplication,
Yahweh has received my prayer.
10All my enemies shall be greatly ashamed and disturbed,
they shall be turned back, ashamed, in a moment!

Notes on the text

Title: The terms here replicate those of Psalm 4, but with the addition of *'al haššĕmînît*, a term that appears elsewhere in the Psalter only in the title of Psalm 12 (cf. 1 Chr. 15:21). If 'upon the eighth' is to do with an octave, then it may be a note about tuning, but this is uncertain.

3. For *nepeš* as 'life, vitality', see Janowski 2013: 188–194. The traditional rendering 'soul' suggests something purely inward, whereas here the word refers to the whole of the poet's life.

Form and structure

Psalm 6 is the fourth successive complaint psalm within the block of Psalms 3–7. Continuing the morning–evening pattern that runs through this small collection, it provides an evening prayer (note v. 6). As with the previous psalms in this group, a range of settings is possible because of the openness of the language, though there is enough reference to serious illness to think that this is the most likely setting (Seybold 1996: 43). Nevertheless, the language does not have to be restricted to physical illness and can refer to any form of serious distress (cf. McCann 1996: 703). The language's openness is perhaps why it has traditionally been included among the seven penitential psalms (with Pss 32, 38, 51, 102, 130, 143). This grouping can be traced back to at least Cassiodorus (see Vesco 2006, 2: 123) and is used in Lent, though this psalm has no obvious sign of penitence. A broader range of settings for reading the psalm is established by its placement in this small collection since it shares key terms with others here, especially Psalms 4–5. This patterning is already evident in the title, which is close to that of Psalm 4, the other evening psalm in this group. Some points of language overlap are insufficiently distinctive to press further, but other points provide a clear connection. Sometimes, these connections move in a different direction to what has gone before – Psalm 4 had drawn on the bed motif both to admonish the adversaries and to express confidence (Ps. 4:4, 8), whereas here it points to the poet's suffering. However, with Psalm 4 it declares a need for Yahweh's grace (Pss 4:1; 6:2). Where Psalm 4:2 looked for Yahweh to hear the poet's prayer, here there is assurance that Yahweh has indeed heard (v. 9). Hearing prayer is also important in Psalm 5:2–3, but there it was said that he would hear. There is thus a progression with this motif that takes readers from the request that Yahweh hear, to the confidence that he will hear, to a declaration that he has heard.

The psalm can be analysed in three stanzas:

1. Appeal for grace (1–3)
2. Request for deliverance (4–7)
3. Declaration of confidence (8–10)

Comment

Title: See on Psalm 4.

1–3. With Psalm 3, this prayer opens with a voc. addressing Yahweh. But where that psalm points to the problem caused by enemies, the opening here places this psalm in a group that appeals to God for help while also seeing him as part of the problem (cf. Ps. 38:1; Firth 2005a: 57–68). Two prohibitions follow the address, each of which presumably refers to how Yahweh is currently acting towards the psalmist. That is, the prayer assumes that the poet is in some way experiencing God's anger, though there is no reason given for this. Although this anger has a reforming goal (through discipline), the poet asks that this cease. Instead, grace is needed because of the poet's weakness. This weakness is described as having one's bones disturbed, and therefore healing is requested. This request is the positive counterpart to the prohibitions of verse 1. A need for healing is suggestive of illness, even if the disease cannot be diagnosed. However, this sense of disturbance is extended in verse 3, where it now becomes clear that the poet's whole being is experiencing this (cf. 'Notes on the text'). This could mean that the illness is having a wider impact, though it may also mean that the disorder experienced goes beyond illness. But if we cannot diagnose an exact cause, the psalmist has no problem in showing that Yahweh needs to act, turning once more to address him directly and challenge him about how long he has taken. Grace is needed, but the poet, experiencing anger instead, insists that this has not been forthcoming.

4–7. A series of imperatives address Yahweh, asking him to turn, deliver and save the poet. 'Turn' assumes that Yahweh needs to focus once more on the psalmist's needs, while 'deliver' and 'save' are here closely paired expressions of how Yahweh should respond. These two also extend the request for healing, with both verbs suggesting rescue is needed from something too powerful for the poet. The reason initially given for this is Yahweh's kindness (cf. Ps. 5:7), his commitment to his people. The psalmist also insists that if Yahweh fails to act, he will, in effect, lose a worshipper. The reason for this, expressed in verse 5 (cf. Pss

30:9; 88:10–12), is that the dead do not worship. Psalm 139:8 is clear that nowhere is removed from Yahweh's presence, including Sheol (the place of the dead), but within the OT this still does not mean that the dead can worship. Rather, the death of a worshipper is costly to Yahweh (cf. Ps. 116:15). The poet has not yet joined the dead but is suffering in a way that suggests its imminence. This is portrayed through a weakness of the eyes, the place from which tears come, but also the organ that allows the poet to look for signs of grace. Complicating this is the otherwise unexpected mention of foes. Their role here is unclear (unless we are to think along similar lines to Job's friends who used Job's suffering as a reason to condemn him), but they are Yahweh's foes as well as the poet's (Brueggemann and Bellinger 2014: 49).

8–10. A significant shift occurs at this point as the workers of iniquity (cf. Ps. 5:5) are now told to leave because Yahweh has heard the poet's weeping. Where Yahweh was asked to turn towards the poet, they are asked to turn away. That which had pointed to the psalmist's weakness is what Yahweh has heard, though it is then said that Yahweh has also heard the poet's supplication and received the prayer. There is no indication of anything that causes this sudden change in mood. This has often led to attempts to identify an event in the temple that would explain it. But rather than looking outside the Psalter, we need to heed the context established within Psalms 3–7, which showed that Yahweh does hear the prayers and tears of the weak. The act of prayer is here enough for the psalmist to have confidence that Yahweh will act. As such, the enemies will be put to shame and disturbed. Their being put to shame shows that Yahweh has acted for the poet. The poet's earlier experience is now that of the enemies. Where previously the poet's cry 'How long' suggested an extended period of suffering, this is now changed in a moment.

Explanation

The fundamental affirmation of this psalm is that Yahweh hears prayer, and in this fact is hope. This is good news, and consistent with Jesus' teaching on the importance of prayer (e.g. Luke 11:1–11). Nevertheless, this truth is balanced here with the reality that sometimes prayer is a long-term discipline, and prayer may include both words and tears. The point at which God acts for his people may well be in a moment, but the prayer that led to it may have been offered over a long period that included deep suffering, whether illness or the assaults of others. This must be matched to the possibility of divine anger, something that assumes sin is present. The psalm does not mention sin directly, but the fact that grace is the initial request and that Yahweh's kindness is the reason for hope could certainly suggest this is important background. God's anger is not to be set aside, for it continues to be directed against sin (Rom. 1:18). But in prayer, grace can be sought and found, and that reality is attested here in a way that reminds the worshipping community that the experience of one poet is one from which all learn and share (see Achtemeier 1974; da Silva 1992: 221–222).

PSALM 7

Translation

A Shiggaion. Davidic, which he sang to Yahweh concerning the words of Cush the Benjaminite.

1Yahweh my God, in you I take refuge,
  save me from all those pursuing me and deliver me,
2lest he rend my life like a lion
  tearing apart and there is no deliverer.

3Yahweh my God, if I have done this,
  if there is wrongdoing in my hand,
4if I have repaid my friend with harm,
  or despoiled my enemy without cause,
5let the enemy pursue my life and overtake it,
  let that one trample my existence to the ground,
  and lay my honour in the dust. *Selah.*

6Arise, O Yahweh, in your anger,
  lift yourself against the fury of my foes,
  wake up for me – you have ordered justice!
7Let the assembly of the peoples be gathered round you,
  and return on high over it.
8Yahweh requites the peoples,
  judge me O Yahweh, according to my righteousness
  and according to the integrity in me.
9May the evil of the wicked come to an end,
  and may you establish the righteous,
O tester of mind and sentiment,
  O righteous God.
10My shield above is God,
  the saviour of the upright of mind.
11God is a righteous judge
  and an indignant God every day.

12Surely again he sharpens his sword,
  his bow he has bent and readied.

13and he has prepared his implements of death,
he has prepared his fiery arrows.
14Behold, he has conceived harm,
he is pregnant with trouble
and gives birth to falsehood.
15He has hewn a cistern and dug it out,
but he falls into the hole he has made.
16May his trouble return upon his head,
and his violence come down on his forehead.
17I will give thanks to Yahweh according to his righteousness,
yes, I will make melody to the name of Yahweh Most High.

Notes on the text

Title: The meaning of 'Shiggaion' is unknown, though the pl. form occurs also in Habakkuk 3:1. See Sawyer 2011: 294. On 'Davidic', see on Psalm 3.

2. The sg. form here could be distributive and describe each enemy (so e.g. Dahood 1965: 41), but it is also possible that the sg. allows for focus on a ringleader (Firth 2005b: 23).

9. Yahweh is, more literally, tester of 'heart and kidneys'. On the anthropological significance of these terms see Janowski 2013: 155–162.

12. On *šûb* as 'again', see GKC §120d.

Form and structure

The closing poem in the subset of Psalms 3–7, this psalm lacks the expected 'morning' reference after the 'morning–evening' pattern that ran through the previous four psalms. As the closing psalm in the sequence, it concludes the pattern by referring instead to 'every day' (v. 11). The title also marks this psalm out as breaking the cycle as the only one not called a 'melody'. On the other hand, the title shares with Psalm 3 reference to an event in David's life. The event in this case is uncertain (see 'Comment'), but this helps to mark the boundaries of this unit. The strength of this link is also shown in the shared language that joins Psalm 7 with Psalm 3, especially the language of salvation and deliverance as well as some lesser links with Psalms 4–6 (see Smith and Domeris 2010: 374–375).

Of all the psalms in this group, Psalm 7 has the clearest evidence of its background, in this case in the prayers of the accused (Firth 2005b: 20–22). This is most evident from the presentation of a charge before Yahweh (vv. 3–5) and the request to be judged by Yahweh (v. 8). Such prayers probably originated through the temple's role in resolving complex legal disputes (Deut. 17:8–13). However, the Psalter does not record exact processes by which such prayers functioned, instead putting them into a broader context. More immediately, within Psalms 3–7, false accusation now becomes a more particular example of how Yahweh can be expected to respond to the cries of those in need.

The psalm can be analysed in four stanzas:

1. Initial plea (1–2)
2. Declaration of innocence (3–5)
3. Affirmation of Yahweh's authority to judge (6–11)
4. Statement on the assured end of the wicked (12–17)

Comment

Title: David is said to have sung this psalm (cf. Ps. 18) concerning the words of Cush the Benjaminite. Unfortunately, no one by that name is known to us, and it is unlikely to be the Cushite mentioned in 2 Samuel 18:21–32, though one could conceivably read verses 15–16 in the light of Absalom's demise (2 Sam. 18:9–15). Perhaps more probably (but with no certainty), the unknown Cush is regarded as an ally of Saul, since he encouraged support particularly from within Benjamin (1 Sam. 22:7–8). If so, then we would read David's affirmation of innocence against the claim that he had conspired against Saul, even though Saul continually pursued him (cf. Vesco 2006, 2: 128–131; Berger 2014: 281–286).

1–2. As with Psalms 3 and 6, this prayer opens by addressing Yahweh directly, calling him 'my God', repeating the form also occurring at Psalms 3:8; 5:2. More importantly, the poet has taken refuge in Yahweh, as encouraged in Psalm 2:12, while 5:11 has expressed the hope that all taking refuge in Yahweh will rejoice. However, the prayer's content makes clear that the psalmist is not yet rejoicing. Rather, the poet is pursued by unnamed adversaries, needing deliverance. The threat faced is serious, with one enemy singled out as seeking the poet's life in the same way a ravenous lion tears apart its prey. There is no other deliverer, so the psalmist can ask only Yahweh for salvation and deliverance, making real the hope held out to those who take refuge in Yahweh.

3–5. A new direct address to Yahweh, repeating the start of verse 1, then moves into a form of self-curse that is effectively a declaration of innocence. The implication is that the poet has not done anything that would merit the decision permitted in verse 5, while leaving the matter to Yahweh. Verses 3–4 are presented as a series of hypothetical cases for which a charge might have been made, with the first three headed by an 'if' statement (implied in the fourth). It is notable that each 'if' statement lacks specificity. In the first case, 'if I have done this' is open ended, because 'this' is not defined, perhaps enabling each person praying the psalm to indicate what the charge may be. What follows is also open, moving through wrongdoing in general, to mistreatment of a friend and then of an enemy. Again, petitioners may specify these in their own prayer, or it may be left for Yahweh to determine. But if the person is guilty (and we must presume a serious charge), then the enemy could indeed pursue them, with the possibility of the death penalty being applied. What the adversary sought (vv. 1–2) would be valid, though only because Yahweh judges that the person has indeed committed a crime that merits such a penalty.

6–11. Having presented the case to Yahweh, he is now summoned to act as judge. As judge, he is called to arise, though doing so in anger. Yahweh's anger was unwanted in Psalm 6:1, but where that anger works towards justice it can be desired. In this case, the anger is to be directed towards the fury of the foes, to work for the poet. Yahweh has ordered justice, it is meant to define his people, and so the poet wants to see it now. Such justice is also meant to be public, so Yahweh is to be surrounded by an assembly of the peoples, something that shows his justice going beyond Israel. That it is Yahweh's justice which matters is clear from the fact that he rules these peoples. Moreover, he governs the peoples, judging them. Yahweh only judges the peoples, and he also judges individuals among his people, and the poet therefore asks to be judged based on personal righteousness and integrity. The poet does not claim perfection, merely innocence of the particular charge (Kwakkel 2002: 64–65). Such judgement is to be seen within the wider wish of the poet that evil be ended and the righteous established. Yahweh alone can do this because he is the one who tests both mind and sentiment; he knows human plans (cf. Ps. 139:23). He can act this way because he truly is righteous. Because of this, the poet can speak above of God as a shield (cf. Ps. 3:4) and the saviour (as one who rights injustice; cf. Sawyer 2011: 403) of the upright of mind. When Yahweh acts as judge, he can be the saviour for which the psalmist has prayed (v. 2). Crucially, he is saviour because he is judge (similarly, Longman 2014: 77). Acting as judge also means Yahweh is indignant towards those who act in ways contrary to his justice since his justice acts for the innocent and against the oppressor.

12–17. A key issue here is the subject of the verbs in verse 12. No change of subject is marked, and so the reference could be to Yahweh. But this is not decisive since verse 14 refers to the enemy and the change is still unmarked (ESV adds 'the wicked man', but this is a clarifying expansion). It is better to take the oath formula with which verse 12 opens (*'im lō'*) as marking the point where we return to the subject of verse 5, so that the focus is on the adversary. Though awkward, this results in an intelligible text that does not require significant emendation. If so, then having pointed to the fact that Yahweh is a righteous judge who acts for the innocent, the poet points again to the threat posed by the enemy, one where the accusation puts the poet's life at risk. Words have become weapons of war. That the accusation is false is asserted through the association with childbirth in verse 14 that traces the development of the accusation from conception and pregnancy to birth as falsehood (see Grohman 2005). But if Yahweh is a righteous judge, then the poet can draw comfort from elements of the wisdom tradition where the wicked bring back their trouble on to themselves (cf. Prov. 26:27; Eccl. 10:8), here pictured through someone falling into the pit they had dug to trap others. That is, as is true of the law of false accusation (Deut. 19:15–21), a malicious accuser should receive the penalty that would have applied to the crime had it been committed, whether this is simply the outworking of evil or Yahweh's intervention (cf. Hubbard 1982; Charney 2013: 60). Because Yahweh is the righteous judge, the one who acts to defend the innocent, the psalmist can offer praise even though the case has not yet been resolved. It is Yahweh's righteousness that gives hope.

Explanation

The closing prayer in the opening sequence (Pss 3–7), this poem draws together important themes from the previous poems while also providing a clearer context where the hope offered through the previous psalms can be applied. Ritual for dealing with false accusation may well have had its origins in the temple, but this psalm makes the process accessible to a wider range of readers, all of whom have been given an emerging pattern of hope within this small collection. Not all those accused will face situations that threaten their lives, but this psalm reminds them that their hope is in the justice of Yahweh and that Yahweh can be trusted. Finding refuge in Yahweh is still possible, despite extreme threat, and the act of taking refuge is itself a source of encouragement that helps the one who takes refuge remember that Yahweh is indeed a righteous judge, a saviour who works like a defence advocate for those falsely accused (cf. Ps. 1:6). Praise is possible because of Yahweh's commitment to justice.

PSALM 8

Translation

The director's. Upon Gittith. A melody. Davidic.

1Yahweh our lord,
  how majestic is your name in all the earth!
  You have set your splendour above the heavens.

[2]From the mouth of babes and infants,
you have established a stronghold because of your enemies,
to still the enemy and the vengeful.

[3]When I look at your heavens,
the works of your fingers,
the moon and the stars that you have established,
[4]what is a mortal that you remember them,
and a human that you attend to them?
[5]Yet you have made them only a little less than God,
and crown them with glory and honour.
[6]You have made them rule over the works of your hands,
you have put all things under their feet,
[7]all sheep and cattle
and beasts of the field,
[8]the birds of the heavens and the fish of the sea,
that which passes along the paths of the sea.

[9]Yahweh our lord,
how majestic is your name in all the earth!

Notes on the text

Title: *'al haggittît* is obscure, presumably referring to something under the director's control.

1. *'ăšer tĕnâ* is problematic, the problems already visible in the versions. Occasionally *'ăšer* functions as equivalent to *kî* (e.g. 2 Sam. 11:20), 'for, that' and that is plausible here. But the imperative is still difficult, and of the options, following Syr. and reading a pf. here makes most sense unless *tĕnâ* is the inf. const. functioning as equivalent to a pf. For the options, see M. S. Smith (1997) and Keener (2013: 39–40).

4. M. sg. is used through the psalm to describe humans. But as these are representative of all humans, it is better to translate as pl., though this loses the connection to Jesus taken up in the NT (e.g. 1 Cor. 15:20–28; Heb. 2:6–8). Note that Hebr. *'ĕnôš* here has semantic overlap with *'ādām* (Gen. 1:26–27) but is not identical to it, though it is picked up in *uben 'ādām*. More literally 'son of man', the connection to Jesus is understandable, though in the first instance it is an idiomatic way of referring to a person. Since the context in Hebrews makes clear that Jesus is also the representative human, there is an exegetical connection (similarly, Terrien 2003, 2: 133).

5. *'ĕlōhîm* can refer to (at least) God, the gods of the nations or Yahweh's council. All can be defended here, but the glory given to humans suggests that 'God' is the correct translation.

Form and structure

Following the complaint psalms that formed the subunit of Psalms 3–7, there is an immediate and obvious change in tone here. Rather than pointing to the psalmists' enemies, we now encounter Yahweh's, and the clear assurance that Yahweh overcomes them. Yahweh's lordship over all creation is celebrated here along with reflection on the place of humanity within it (cf. Mays 1994c; Maré 2006a). Yet there are also important links between this psalm and the preceding poems. Perhaps most obviously, Psalm 7 ended with a promise to praise Yahweh, and that praise is taken up here. This link is strengthened if we note that Yahweh's name was particularly the focus of that praise (Ps. 7:17; cf. Ps. 5:11), and the praise of Yahweh's name forms an envelope around this psalm. These connections indicate that although this hymn focuses on the wonder of creation and humanity's place within it (in part as a meditation on Gen. 1), it does so within the context established by the preceding poems (cf. Vesco 2006, 2: 136–137). Alongside the connections these links establish, the poem's distinctiveness as the only praise psalm wholly addressed to Yahweh should be noted (Tate 2001: 344). Praise is declared, and it is this that challenges readers to see that the struggles of the preceding psalms (and indeed those that follow) do not have the last word.

Acknowledging that there are multiple structuring devices in this poem (see G. T. M. Prinsloo 1995b; 376–377; Auffret 2002b), we can analyse the psalm in three stanzas:

1. Declaration of Yahweh's lordship (1–2)
2. The Wonder of creation and humanity's place (3–8)
3. Closing declaration of Yahweh's lordship (9)

Comment

Title: See on Psalms 3, 4 plus 'Notes on the text'.

1–2. With Psalms 3, 6 and 7, this poem opens with the voc. 'Yahweh'. But where those poems spoke of Yahweh in terms of the individual who prayed, this psalm is immediately placed in the context of the community, an audience implied in the preceding psalms but now made explicit. Yahweh is 'our lord'. No longer are we dealing with the struggles of individuals but rather joining the worshipping community in celebrating Yahweh's character as lord. That character is summed up by his name, which stands for all Yahweh is. Rather than attempting to define this, the poem moves to express awe at the splendour of Yahweh's name, introducing the interrogative *mâ* (how) which occurs three times in the poem (vv. 1, 4, 9). Here, as in verse 9, it functions as an exclamation of awe at the majesty of Yahweh's name, something seen in all the earth. That is, although 'our lord' is a clearly Israelite statement, Yahweh's splendour is not restricted to Israel. This is closely matched by Psalm 76:4 which also reflects on the majesty of Yahweh's name in the context of heavens and earth. In Psalm 8, this majesty is parallel with Yahweh's splendour, which he has set (cf. 'Notes on the text') above the heavens. Whether one looks to land or sky, Yahweh's majesty is experienced. Like many other rulers, there are those who resist Yahweh's lordship. But where they may use warfare, Yahweh has established his stronghold through the mouths of babes and infants. They would not produce praise in a recognizable form, and indeed are more likely to cry out in need of maternal milk. Babes and infants are helpless, and yet their cries are how Yahweh establishes a stronghold that stills enemy and avenger. That which is weakest in creation is evidence of Yahweh's strength, which overcomes all his foes, whether cosmic or temporal.

3–8. Yahweh's lordship is put into context by consideration of the whole of creation, something already flagged in the earth–heavens parallel in verse 1. Taking one's stand on earth, it is the sky that is easily visible. The psalmist therefore looks to the heavens, noting that they are Yahweh's heavens – however much other peoples might have thought that the sky belonged to another deity, this psalm is clear that they are Yahweh's. They are his because he made them. Where Genesis 1 speaks of Yahweh's creation by word, here the heavens are the work of his fingers, the fine-detail work, which is how the stars would appear when viewed from the earth. The moon is also included with the stars as among Yahweh's works, though it appears to be larger than the stars. Perhaps more importantly, both moon and stars were regarded as deities by many. Yet here they are reduced to the fine-detail work in Yahweh's heavens. But if the wonders of the heavens can be so reduced, what is the place of humankind (cf. 'Notes on the text')? Are humans similarly reduced? The question's phrasing in verse 4 already points to something grander, since Yahweh remembers and attends to them, the very thing those who prayed Psalms 3–7 have sought. That Yahweh remembers someone typically means that he is about to act on their behalf (Childs 1962), and this suggests that although the verb translated 'attend to' (*pqd*) can mean 'punish', its more positive sense is intended here. Yahweh cares for humans, but their status has not yet been addressed. Now it is declared that humans are only slightly less than God, placing them above all else in creation. Humans are crowned with glory and honour, terms that differ from Yahweh's own splendour (v. 1) but that still point to the special status of humans. 'Crowned' suggests that all humans have royal dignity, and therefore can rule. That rule is not itself royal, since Yahweh is the king even if that term is not used, but it is a rule Yahweh has granted over the works of his hands. Creation is here considered phenomenologically, so that the larger items are those most immediately around humans; hence, the work of his hands. All things have also been placed under human feet, again evidence of the royal status afforded to humans since things ruled would be placed under a king's feet (cf. Ps. 110:1). This statement of status is then defined in terms of both domesticated and non-domesticated creatures (cf. Whitekettle 2005: 250–252). Sheep and cattle may more easily be seen under human rule, though the beasts of the field would include non-domesticated animals too. The spread of human rule also includes birds and fish, the latter of which was certainly not domesticated, especially any creature in the paths of the seas, which may include even Leviathan (Ps. 104:26). All this may seem beyond human rule, and yet the psalm is clear in insisting that Yahweh, the Lord, has granted rule over this to humans, marking them out as only slightly less than God.

9. The closing verse repeats the first two lines of verse 1, creating an inclusio for the whole psalm. But it is not simply a repetition. Having explored Yahweh's lordship in creation and its relationship to humankind, we now join the poet in expressing wonder at Yahweh's majesty, a majesty seen in all the earth even where rule has been granted to humans.

Explanation

Psalm 8 is a text that draws on other parts of the OT and creates echoes that run through the whole Bible (see Childs 1969: 24–26; Keener 2013), only a small portion of which is noted here. In its presentation of Yahweh's splendour, we never lose sight of his lordship. This is not lordship that demands and takes. It is lordship that gives, in this instance granting rulership of creation to humans – even though (as creator) all belongs to Yahweh. Yet this key human responsibility remains a devolved task since it is Yahweh who is lord, and human rulership is called to point back to Yahweh. The praise this psalm offers is something humans also do in their rulership. Moreover, humans can exercise this rulership because Yahweh has created a world that is secure, where hostile forces cannot overcome him. The psalm is thus a crucial text for reflections on our responsibility for creation, a point that should not be lost even as we also acknowledge the Christological thrust in the NT. Jesus is indeed the representative human, the one who demonstrates the importance of this psalm, but in doing so also shows the way that believers continue to praise God through their commitment to his creation, to the weak and the vulnerable (cf. A. P. Ross 2011: 298).

PSALM 9

Translation

The director's. According to Muth-labben. A melody. Davidic.

[1]I will give thanks to Yahweh with all my heart,
  I will recount all your wondrous deeds.
[2]I will rejoice and exult in you,
  I will make music to your name, O Most High.
[3]When my enemies turn back,
  they stumble and perish before your presence.
[4]For you have executed my cause and my suit,
  you sat on your throne giving right judgement.
[5]You rebuked the nations,
  you destroyed the wicked,
  you blotted out their name for ever and ever!
[6]The enemy is finished, an enduring ruin,
  you uprooted their cities,
  their very memory perished.

[7]But Yahweh sits for ever,
  he has established his throne for justice.
[8]Yes, he judges the world in righteousness,
  and brings justice for the peoples with equity.
[9]May Yahweh be a stronghold for the oppressed,
  a stronghold in times of distress.
[10]May those who know your name trust in you,
  for you have not forsaken those who seek you O Yahweh.
[11]Make music to Yahweh who dwells in Zion,
  declare his deeds among the peoples,
[12]for he who avenges bloodshed remembers them,
  he does not forget the cry of the afflicted.

[13]Be gracious to me, O Yahweh,
  see my affliction from those who hate me,
  O the one who lifts me from the gates of death,
[14]so that I may recount all your praises,
  in the gates of daughter Zion,
  rejoice in your salvation.
[15]The nations have sunk in the pit they made,
  in the net they hid has their own foot been caught.
[16]Yahweh is known, he has executed justice!
  The wicked are struck down by the deeds of their hands. *Higgaion. Selah.*
[17]The wicked shall return to Sheol,

all nations who forget God.
[18]For the needy shall not be forgotten for ever,
the hope of the poor perishes for ever.
[19]Arise, O Yahweh, let not mortals prevail,
let the nations be judged before you.
[20]Appoint a teacher for them O Yahweh,
let the nations know that they are mortal. *Selah.*

Notes on the text

Title: Reading *'al mût*, though the significance of this remains unclear.

16. As with Psalm 10, *rāšā'* (wicked) is grammatically sg., but distributive, making a pl. rendering appropriate. Normally, *selah* (see note Ps. 3:3) stands alone outside the sentence. Here it is joined with *Higgaion*, the meaning of which is also unknown (but cf. Ps. 92:3).

Form and structure

Almost certainly, Psalms 9 and 10 were originally one poem, and are presented as such in LXX. Although now presented as two psalms in MT, evidence of their original unity has been retained. One easily seen element that points to this is the lack of a title for Psalm 10 – within Book 1, only Psalms 1–2, 10 and 33 lack a title. In this case, the one title covers both psalms, even if the meaning of 'Muth-labben' is uncertain. Likewise, the *selah* with which Psalm 9 now ends is odd, as this is the only place apart from Psalms 24, 46 where it occurs at the end of a psalm – an occurrence in the middle of a poem is normal. Beyond this, several features point to the poem's unity, though they are not visible in translation. The most important of these is an acrostic scheme broadly visible across the poem, with the first half of the alphabet in Psalm 9 and the second in Psalm 10. As the psalms now stand, the acrostic is incomplete, and finding some letters involves reconstructing text or moving words to lines where the fit is awkward. Given the tentative nature of these, the above translation resists such moves, though it should be acknowledged that the text is not always easy (Rendsburg 1990: 19–27 thinks northern dialect may also be involved). But enough of the acrostic is retained to point to the original unity. Beyond this, we can also note the concentrated language of the poor across both psalms as a feature which points to their original unity. Nevertheless, as presented in MT, they are two psalms. The division occurs in the kaph section, which represents the midpoint of the alphabet, but it is notable that with the division each half now focuses on the limitations of humans as opposed to Yahweh, so that human claims to dominion are subjected to Yahweh's. The division of the poem at 9:20 makes this theme prominent and may explain the division, though Goldingay (2006a: 169) also notes that whereas Psalm 9 has a more national focus, Psalm 10 is more individual.

Although distinctive works, they are also linked to the psalms around them. The focus on human limitation uses the word *'ĕnôš*, a term given special prominence in Psalm 8:4 for describing humans. There, that humans are only a little less than God is a point to be celebrated, but this is balanced by the understanding of human limitation here. Yahweh's name is important (Ps. 9:2, 10), again echoing the theme developed in Psalm 8:1, 9. They also initiate another small collection that runs through to Psalm 14, which explores the problems of a society disordered by 'wickedness' (*rāšā'* occurs for the first time here), with the thought that 'There is no God' (Pss 10:4; 14:1) providing a boundary marker. Here, that problem is acknowledged but also mixed with statements of faith that interact with surrounding poems.

One could use the acrostic to analyse the poem but, since it uses multiple structuring devices, it is better to follow the thematic developments in the following pattern in five stanzas:

1. Reasons for thanksgiving (9:1–6)
2. Yahweh as righteous judge (9:7–12)
3. Appeal for grace and justice (9:13–20)
4. Complaints about God and the wicked (10:1–11)
5. Appeal for Yahweh to enact justice (10:12–18)

Comment

Title: 'According to Muth-labben' presumably refers to something under the director's control but is unclear. Different pointing may lead to the translation 'the maidens, the son's', though this is not much of an improvement. On the other terms, see on Psalms 3, 4.

1–6. The poem opens with five first-person verbs that suggest a thanksgiving will follow as the poet expresses an intent to give thanks to Yahweh, recounting his wondrous deeds and rejoicing in him through music. This intent is never set aside completely, and the focus on Yahweh's kingship throughout the poem provides a constant reason for praise. That reign is expressed here in Yahweh's defeat of the poet's enemies, noting that they perish before Yahweh – an echo of Psalm 1:6. The defeat of the enemies is also linked to the theme of Yahweh as the righteous judge, another recurring motif through the poem. Indeed, Yahweh's role as judge is central to each stanza, and is expressed here as one of his wondrous deeds the poet will recount. The poet's cause was just (cf. Ps. 7) and Yahweh has acted in the light of this, following the pattern where a king was expected to provide justice. As such, the motifs of Yahweh's reign and justice are closely interwoven. This also involved the rebuking of nations, suggesting that the enemies are more than just those of an individual, as also seen in the destruction of their cities. Perhaps all possible enemies are caught up here because Yahweh has defeated them all and, whatever the context, thanksgiving is possible.

7–12. Where the opening stanza had largely looked back on what Yahweh had done as the basis for praise, the second stanza is more concerned with Yahweh's current role as king and its implications for others (the motif of his enthronement marks out this stanza). Verse 7 establishes the basis for this, that Yahweh is enthroned for ever, and his throne exists for justice. This justice is not restricted to Israel but is for the world. This is why he can also act against the nations where necessary, doing so with equity. The corollary of this is that Yahweh may also be a stronghold (cf. Ps. 46:7, 11) for the oppressed, for those experiencing distress. Such people need justice, and Yahweh offers this. Indeed, with a brief look back, the poet can state that Yahweh has not forgotten those who seek him. Given this, verse 11 switches to the imperative, summoning worshippers to make music in worship of Yahweh as the one enthroned in Zion. Since the psalm is consistently concerned with the nations, his deeds are not simply to be recounted there but rather among the nations. A key reason for this is his work in avenging bloodshed, remembering the cry of the afflicted. This involves a play on different senses of the verb *drš* – in verse 10 it is the act of seeking Yahweh, whereas here it is Yahweh's seeking out those who shed blood to avenge those acting against the afflicted. Yet this also introduces a key paradox, for though Yahweh acts this way, the wicked are still active and bringing disorder. Yahweh acts to bring justice, but does so in a disordered world where the weak experience violence. But Yahweh's memory of them is a constant reminder that he can be praised because of his commitment to act for them.

13–20. The third stanza then appeals to Yahweh for grace and justice, drawing together the themes of the first two. The poet's own need is foregrounded in the appeal for grace, though since this also involves rescue from enemies, justice is not entirely forgotten. This is because their hatred has placed the poet's life at risk, and Yahweh needs to act to protect it. Such a deliverance is tied to the opening vow of praise (v. 1) as the poet vows to recount Yahweh's praises in the gates of daughter Zion, the place where he is enthroned, while also rejoicing in Yahweh's salvation. That is, the poet looks for a moment where the promises of the first two verses may be expressed. Verses 15–18 then generalize these themes, focusing on the nations and then the wicked more generally. The nations might have been caught in their own traps, just as Psalm 7:14–16 suggests may also happen to wicked individuals. This may simply be a case of evil sowing its own seeds of destruction, but the psalm is clear that this is still an expression of Yahweh's justice, something that makes him known. Therefore, the wicked (both individually and nationally) will ultimately fail, and it is this that gives the needy hope. But the balance between hope and present reality that has been carefully laid out is not forgotten, because the poet still asks that Yahweh arise and prevent mortals from prevailing, calling for the nations to be judged. The hope has not been removed, but the prayer is that its reality be experienced. Humans need to be taught again of their limits, reminded that they are indeed less than God.

Explanation

With the observation that humans need to be reminded of their limitations, the poem is paused, though with hints that it is to continue. Clearly, the poem did not need to be divided at this point, but the MT tradition felt that a pause was needed. Breaking the poem at this point enables a moment of reflection, one that realizes that we live in a world full of opportunities to praise God, but also of experiences contrary to this, where wickedness does indeed seem to be predominant. All of this is centred on the knowledge of God's reign, and it is this that continues to give hope to the afflicted even as humans attempt to exercise the authority that really belongs to God. There is a practical atheism in wickedness that will become explicit in Psalm 10. But here we pause and remember that wickedness does not have the last word, even as we join with believers down the centuries and cry out that God's justice will indeed be seen.

PSALM 10

Translation

[1]Why, O Yahweh, do you stand far off,
  hiding in times of distress?
[2]In arrogance the wicked hotly pursue the afflicted,
  let them be caught in the schemes they have devised!
[3]For the wicked praise the craving of their appetite,
  the greedy for gain curse and renounce Yahweh.
[4]The wicked, by the haughtiness of their face,
  do not seek him,
  only thinking 'There is no God.'
[5]Their ways are firm all the time,
  your judgements are too high for them,
  they scoff at all their foes.
[6]They have thought 'I will not slip,
  through the generations I shall meet no harm.'

7Their mouth is filled with cursing and deceit and oppression,
mischief and iniquity are under their tongue.
8They sit in ambush in settlements,
in hiding places they kill the innocent,
their eyes watch the helpless in secret.
9They lay an ambush in a hiding place like a lion in a lair,
they lay an ambush to seize the afflicted,
they seize the afflicted as they pull in their net.
10The helpless are broken, sink down,
fallen in his might.
11They think, 'God has forgotten,
he has hidden his face; he will never see.'

12Arise, O Yahweh,
O God raise your hand,
do not forget the afflicted.
13Why do the wicked spurn God,
and think 'He will not call to account.'
14You have seen – yes you! – trouble and vexation,
you consider it to take it into your hands;
unto you have the helpless committed themselves,
you yourself have been a helper for the orphan.
15Break the arm of the wicked and evildoer,
call their wickedness to account until you find no more.
16Yahweh is king for ever and ever,
the nations perish from his land.
17The craving of the needy you hear, O Yahweh,
you establish their heart, you incline your ear,
18to grant justice to the orphan and the oppressed,
so a mortal who is of the earth will strike terror no more.

Notes on the text

2. *rāšāʿ* (wicked) is sg., and the subsequent verbs are also sg., but as the noun is a distributive pl., this is more appropriate in English.

3. *brk* is usually 'bless' but as with Job 1:11 it is here a euphemism for 'curse'.

10. The verse is difficult and could have included the missing tsade line. With Q, read *ydkh*; for K, *wdkh*, as it provides a plausible verb.

Form and structure

See on Psalm 9.

Comment

1–11. The issue of theodicy, which has lain in the poem's background to this point, is now foregrounded. Yahweh is a God of justice, and humans need to know their limitations. Why then does he stand far off, seemingly hiding? The opening question finds a close parallel in Habakkuk 1:2–4, which explores similar issues. If the wicked are simply able to satisfy their appetite, where is justice? The poet wants them to be caught in their own devices (cf. Ps. 9:15), because at this point they seek only that which is to their own benefit. This is an expression of practical atheism that finds expression in the thought that there is no God. The attitude is not that God does not exist, but that he does not engage with human activity in a way that makes attention to him matter, finding evidence for this in the security of their own actions, which have not had any divine impediment (cf. Rom. 3:14). This absence is shown by their use of 'God' rather than Yahweh – they think in generic terms, not the reality of Yahweh. Hence, their thoughts can be cited again in verse 6 to show that God will not intervene, and they can be secure in their wickedness. This indeed is made explicit in the third citation of their thoughts in verse 11. While Yahweh stands far off, the wicked are free to think this way and so are still in need of a divinely appointed teacher to show them their limits as humans. Moreover, such thoughts are also the basis for their actions, renouncing Yahweh and attacking the weak, with their various devices in this compared to a lion or hunter that trap the helpless.

12–18. In effect, the poet uses the thoughts of the wicked to frame the issue of theodicy (cf. R. A. Jacobson 2004: 30), providing the foundations for the prayer for justice with which the poem concludes. As in Psalm 9:19, Yahweh is called to arise; that is, to enact justice. Being enthroned is good, but a king also needs to stand and act for the poor. That is why Yahweh needs to raise his hand (standing here for his power), and not forget the afflicted. The wicked may forget Yahweh, but Yahweh may not forget the afflicted. The thoughts of the wicked are again cited, claiming that God will not call them to account, and it is against this that Yahweh must act because he has indeed seen the trouble and vexation experienced by the helpless. This is important because the helpless have committed themselves to Yahweh as the one who previously helped the orphan. The means of justice summoned here is breaking the arm of the wicked, calling them to 'account' (another use of *drš*) until no more wickedness is found. The 'arm' here stands for how the wicked exercise power, and it is their power that is to be broken so wickedness may not continue. Instead, Yahweh's kingship is to dominate. Rather than the wicked receiving the craving of their appetite, Yahweh is to hear the craving of the needy, to heed their desire for justice. In this, as with 9:20, humans are again shown their limitations.

Explanation

Psalm 10 needs to be read along with Psalm 9 since the two form one poem. But it is also presented here as a separate psalm, one that is particularly concerned with the issue of theodicy. This was largely implicit in Psalm 9, but is brought to prominence here, especially through the four citations of the thoughts of the wicked. At heart, the psalm wrestles with similar issues to the book of Habakkuk – how it is that the afflicted can continue hoping in Yahweh if the wicked are able to act with impunity. For this psalm, theodicy is not something to be discussed in abstract. It is not a hypothetical problem but rather one that is experienced. Core to Israel's confession, and the church's faith, is that God is king and his justice is real. Justice is not only something attributed to God: it is to be experienced in life. The psalm knows that there have been times in the past where Yahweh's justice has been seen, and so longs for that to happen now. Because Yahweh is a just king, it is possible to pray for his justice to be seen. This is essential, because without visible justice humans continue to exalt themselves and so fail to understand their limits, and the poor continue to suffer. McCann (1996: 720) helpfully compares this to the reality of the kingdom of God as something we hold both as a present reality and something for which we pray (Luke 17:20–21; 21:29–36). With this psalm, we hold to the reality of God as just even as we pray for his justice to be seen and so be given new opportunities for praise.

PSALM 11

Translation

The director's. Davidic.

1In Yahweh do I take refuge;
  how can you say to me,
  'Flit to your mountain O bird!
2For behold the wicked bend the bow,
  they have set their arrow on the bowstring,
  to shoot in the darkness at the upright of heart.
3For when the foundations are ruined,
  what can the righteous achieve?'

4Yahweh is in his holy temple,
  Yahweh's throne is in heaven,
  his eyes behold,
  his eyelids test humankind.

5Yahweh tests the righteous,
but the wicked and lovers of violence
does he himself hate.
6May he rain down bird-traps upon the wicked,
fire and sulphur and a scorching wind
the portion of their cup.
7For Yahweh is righteous, loving righteous deeds,
the upright shall behold his face.

Notes on the text

1. Read *nûdî* with Q. The pl. suffix of *harkem* is problematic but is taken here as indicating the one addressed is part of a wider group.

6. Many ET (e.g. ESV, NIV) follow the suggestion of emending *paḥîm* to *paḥămê* ('coals'; this reading is found in Sym). This makes for a smoother flow but loses the recurrence of the bird motif. With A. P. Ross (2011: 336), MT is retained as *lectio difficilior.*

7. With the versions, reading *pānāyv* (his face).

Form and structure

Psalm 11 can be recognized as a psalm of trust (albeit one marked with wisdom terminology; Longman 2014: 90; and aspects of lament, Bellinger 1984: 96), though it clearly reflects a situation where trust is challenged. This is clear from the fact that the poet has taken refuge in Yahweh. This has a clear parallel from Psalm 7:1, except that in that case taking refuge was the basis for an appeal to Yahweh. This time, the context is more generally the problem of wickedness, which is destructive of society. In this sense, it continues to explore the problems of wickedness in society laid out in Psalms 9–10. In doing so, it also introduces some contrasts that encourage trust, most obviously presenting as hopeful the upright seeing Yahweh's face (v. 7), whereas such an encounter is destructive for the wicked (Ps. 9:4; cf. Vesco 2006, 2: 157). In addition, both psalms cite the words of others (Pss 10:4, 6, 11; 11:1b–3) as a means of exploring key themes. This literary context is more secure than proposals that involve the poet finding asylum in the temple (Seybold 1996: 60), though this is an example of the type of situation envisaged where trust can be demonstrated.

The poem can be analysed into two stanzas, each closing with a *kî* (here 'for') clause and containing an observation on the experience of the upright:

1. Refuge claimed (1–3)
2. Yahweh as hope for the upright (4–7)

Comment

Title: See on Psalms 3, 4.

1–3. The poem opens by declaring that the poet has taken refuge in Yahweh. Taking refuge is a key motif in the Psalter, established by the beatitude expressed over those taking refuge in Yahweh's anointed (Ps. 2:12), but subsequently expressed as taking refuge in Yahweh himself (Pss 5:11; 7:1). Although this may be expressed by formal action in the sanctuary (cf. 1 Kgs 1:50; 2:28), the only temple mentioned in this psalm is Yahweh's heavenly one, suggesting that taking refuge is not dependent on a specific location. It is Yahweh himself who provides refuge, and this is not geographically limited even if the temple would be an obvious place to claim refuge. Here, claiming refuge provides opportunity to reject the speech of figures who are initially undefined. As with Psalm 10:4, 6, 11, citing the adversaries provides a perspective that will be rejected, something already hinted at in the question that introduces it. A key question, though, revolves around the quote's boundaries. Verse 1b clearly is included, and in theory could represent the whole citation (so Gerstenberger 1988: 77). If so, verses 2–3 would be the poet's own words in response to this. But then the poet would in effect agree with the situation in these verses, something that stands in contrast to the opening 'How?' The quote should therefore finish in verse 3 and represent the words of 'misguided counsellors' (R. A. Jacobson 2004: 32). These counsellors advise the poet to flit to the mountains as a place of security, reasoning that the wicked have overrun the structures of society, something expressed in the image of hunters whose bow is ready to shoot at the upright of heart. The upright of heart are at risk because the foundations of a just society are under attack by the wicked. Hence, they pose the question of verse 3, the implied answer of which is that the righteous cannot achieve anything of substance when the foundations are ruined. Trust under such circumstances seems misplaced.

4–7. Verse 4 is best understood as a series of short declarations that counter the false counsel. Society can be marked by wickedness, and it can seem to be dominant. But this has not removed Yahweh from his temple, and this awareness of Yahweh's presence is the real centre of the poem (G. T. M. Prinsloo 2015: 778–779). Here, we need to note that Hebrew uses the same word for 'temple' and 'palace' and both senses are present here. A temple may be a place of refuge, but a palace is where a throne is kept. The Jerusalem sanctuary is the obvious example of this, but Yahweh's presence is not restricted to this (cf. 1 Kgs 8:27). Rather, from his heavenly throne he beholds humankind, testing them. This testing includes the righteous (cf. Ps. 1:6), but also exposes the wicked and those committed to violence. In the context of this psalm, the violence is not only physical threat, but also structural. Anything that promotes a society contrary to Yahweh's purposes creates violence, and Yahweh's revulsion of this is clear in the declaration that he hates such things. Yahweh's throne may be in heaven, but it does not mean he is remote. Rather, his testing of humans is part of his commitment to creation. Verse 6 could then be either a declaration of what Yahweh is doing or a wish. The juss. here is more likely a wish (though GKC §109k notes they can function like impfs.), one that hopes for them to receive something equivalent to their own actions. Here, the counsellors suggested the poet needed to flee like a bird, but the psalmist wants Yahweh to rain down traps on them, a type of trap often used for a bird. But this verse is not limited to one image alone; it also includes the image of fire and sulphur, a combination that alludes to Sodom and Gomorrah (Gen. 19:24), another society marked by wickedness. The portion of their cup (i.e. their destiny) is not to claim society through violence but rather to experience what they are doing. Trust here is waiting for Yahweh to do this, knowing that even as he hates violence, he loves righteous deeds. The upright can look forward to beholding his face, something they can anticipate with confidence (perhaps anticipating Ps. 17:15), whereas for the wicked this leads to punishment.

Explanation

Taking up the general problem of wickedness in society laid out in Psalms 9–10, this poem explores the response of the righteous. As such, it builds directly on the contrast between the wicked and the righteous in Psalm 1 while demonstrating what the refuge suggested in Psalm 2 can mean. Psalm 1 had allowed that the wicked may be more numerous than the righteous, and under such circumstances there is a strong temptation for the righteous to retreat to secure locations like the mountains. This is particularly so when the wicked seem to undermine the very foundations of society, promoting the structural violence that harms the life of whole communities. Under such circumstances, one can well understand the impulse to flee, to retreat to some place of imagined security. But Psalms 9–10 have also reminded us of the limitations of humankind, pointing back to the reality that Yahweh is lord. That lordship is demonstrated here in the existence of his heavenly temple and commitment to the righteous. Trust is not a matter of fleeing, but rather of staying, knowing that Yahweh exposes the violence of wickedness while providing hope for the righteous. The psalm thus points to the radically countercultural nature of biblical faith when it can assert, 'Blessed are the meek' (Matt. 5:5). When they shall inherit the earth is not made explicit, but the background of Sodom and Gomorrah reminds the faithful that there are times when wickedness is overthrown. Trust involves living in a world of violence while remembering that humans are limited (cf. Kraus 1988:

204), and that Yahweh is finally the one who reigns, even as we may wish to see his acts of justice now.

PSALM 12

Translation

The director's. Upon the eighth. A melody, Davidic.

1Save, O Yahweh, for the faithful have gone,
indeed, the trustworthy have disappeared from among humankind.
2Each speaks what is worthless to their companion,
with flattering lips and double heart do they speak.
3May Yahweh cut off all flattering lips,
the tongue claiming great things,
4when they say 'With our tongue we prevail,
our lips are with us,
who is our lord?'

5'Because of the oppression of the needy, the groaning of the poor,
now I will arise' says Yahweh,
'I will set them in the secure place desired.'
6Yahweh's words are pure words,
silver refined in a furnace on the ground,
refined seven times.
7You, O Yahweh, will keep them,
you will protect this one from this generation and for ever.
8The wicked walk about all around
when worthlessness is exalted among humankind.

Notes on the text

Title: See on Psalms 3, 4, 6.

1. *ḥāsîd* (faithful) is treated here as a collective noun.

5. *yāpîaḥ* read here from *pwḥ* II (*DCH*). The alternative (following Miller 1979b) is to understand this as reference to a witness.

Form and structure

Within the subunit of Psalms 9–14, Psalm 12 continues to explore the effect of wickedness on society (cf. Hab. 1:2–4), most especially the effects of untrustworthy speech in contrast to Yahweh's reliable speech. Psalms

9–10 explored the issue of wickedness in terms of theodicy that looked for Yahweh's justice to be established, while Psalm 11 expressed trust that Yahweh's righteousness would be experienced by the righteous. Psalm 12 then moves to ask that Yahweh act to save the needy since they suffer in the context of oppression and structural violence. Along with these thematic links (and some verbal ones), it is notable that the motif of citing the words of the wicked recurs (v. 4), again using these words as expressing something Yahweh is to reject. As a prayer, it is possible to consider this psalm as among the communal laments, but if so, it should be noted that it includes motifs drawn from wisdom literature in expressing trust as well. Given the variation in speakers within it, the suggestion that these elements come together in a form of liturgy (Broyles 1999: 83) has merit.

The psalm can be analysed in two stanzas, though each could be divided into two strophes:

1. Appeal to be saved (1–4)
2. Assurance of Yahweh's protection (5–8)

Comment

Title: See on Psalms 3, 4, 6.

1–4. Some prayers take time before reaching their appeal, but not this one. Instead, it immediately cries out for Yahweh to save. The verb *yšʿ* is the most general one for salvation in the OT, and predominantly looks for an immediate act to change current circumstances (e.g. Exod. 14:30). Such salvation is needed here because of the disappearance of the faithful and trustworthy from the population. The cause of their absence is not specified, though the reference to the dominance of the wicked in verse 8 suggests that their absence is the fruit of the violence of the wicked. A link between these verses is certainly made by repetition of the phrase *bĕnê 'ādām* (humankind) in both, creating an inclusio in the poem. In the absence of the faithful, society is marked by untrustworthy speech. This speech is not only careless, but malicious, as may be noted by the fact that 'worthless' (*šāwĕ'*) occurs in Exodus 23:1 to describe falsehood that can be linked to malicious testimony, while in Deuteronomy 5:20 it describes someone untrustworthy in court. In both reports of the Decalogue, it is the 'false purpose' for which someone bears Yahweh's name (Exod. 20:7; Deut. 5:11). The speech reported here is the sort of flattery that may be offered, but that comes from a double heart; that is, a mind without concern for consistency or integrity (cf. Jas 1:8). It is because of the damage such speech does to a community that the poet wishes that Yahweh would cut off such lips, boastful tongues. That is, remove those whose speech exalts themselves but damages the basic fabric of the community. As with the citations in Psalm 10:4, 6, 11, the citation of the wicked's speech here moves to a position of practical atheism – it is not that Yahweh's existence is denied, but they claim to have no one greater. Speech is their mechanism for prevailing, but their hubris is also made clear in their question with which verse 4 closes.

5–8. The psalm pivots on verse 5. Up to this point we have heard from the psalmist and the wicked, but now Yahweh speaks, repudiating the claims made by the wicked. That it is Yahweh who speaks, and not the poet, is initially deferred as the speech begins without introduction. Yahweh notes two reasons why he must act – the oppression of the needy and groaning of the poor. Both reflect a situation where society's structure is flawed ('oppression', *šōd*, is often used to describe structural violence; e.g. Amos 3:10), and we may think of the oppression and groaning here in a cause-and-effect relationship. Oppression damages society, the poor lack the resources to change it and so can only groan. But their groan is effective as prayer, and Yahweh now vows to arise, thus doing as had been requested in Psalms 9:20; 10:12. Although the last part of verse 5 is not clear, it seems that Yahweh promises to grant the requested salvation, thus responding also to the plea of verse 1. Yahweh speaks only once in the poem, but those words are enough to change its orientation from need to confidence. This is because (unlike the speech of the wicked) Yahweh's words are pure. The term for 'words' here (*'imrâ*) is often translated 'promise' in Psalm 119, and that sense may be appropriate here given that Yahweh has stated what he is about to do, though a more general observation about the reliability of Yahweh's word is also appropriate. The quality of Yahweh's words, as opposed to the wicked, is like the most highly refined silver, free of impurity. Therefore, because of Yahweh's word, the psalm moves to express confidence that Yahweh will keep the poor. If the switch from pl. to sg. in verse 7b is correct, then it is likely that the poet is noted as one who will be protected. None of this means the situation has yet been resolved, as the wicked walk around when worthlessness is exalted among humans – precisely what the speech of the wicked has been doing. But though it seems they will have the last word, it is Yahweh's word which has declared that this is not how things will always be.

Explanation

Psalm 12 can be read on its own as both a prayer and an expression of hope in Yahweh amid structural violence. But Psalms 9–14 (cf. Botha 2012a) provide a larger context in which to read it, continuing to explore how the righteous are to respond to a society out of step with the ways of God. Yahweh's words not only address the boastful claims of the wicked in this psalm; they also respond to the prayer for him to arise in Psalm 10 while providing an example of the basis for trust expressed in Psalm 11. But this psalm, with its allusions to the Decalogue, also situates itself in a larger scriptural context (note G. T. M. Prinsloo 1998a), noting the damage done to the community through boastful speech that attempts to remove God from our discourse, exalting humans who have failed to note their limitations. If James's reference to the double-minded is an allusion to this psalm, then we may also read his warnings about the tongue (Jas 3:1–12) in the light of it too, warning of the damage our speech can do, recognizing that abusive speech is itself a form of violence. And it is against this that Yahweh promises to act, a promise that continues to give hope. McCann (1996: 725) notes that this hope shaped Jesus' own prayer in John 17, and from this continues to shape our own.

PSALM 13

Translation

The director's. A melody, Davidic.

1How long, O Yahweh, shall you forget me for ever?
   How long shall you hide your face from me?
2How long shall I bear pain within me,
   have sorrow in my heart all day?
   How long shall my enemy be exalted over me?

3Consider and answer me, O Yahweh my God,
   give light to my eyes lest I sleep the sleep of death,
4lest my enemy say, 'I have prevailed over him,'
   my adversaries rejoice because I am shaken.

5But I have myself trusted in your kindness,
   my heart shall rejoice in your salvation.
6I will sing to Yahweh,
   because he has dealt well with me.

Notes on the text

2. *'ēṣôt* is often emended to *'aṣṣebet* (hardship), but with *DCH*, *'ṣb* III is read here, meaning the emendation is unnecessary.

Form and structure

When listing examples of the individual complaint, Hermann Gunkel turned first to Psalm 13 (Gunkel 1998: 19; the German was from 1933).

Since his work, when introductory texts have sought to demonstrate the form and structure of these poems, Psalm 13 has been a common choice (e.g. Jacobson and Jacobson 2012: 39–40). There can be little doubt that it is an excellent example of the genre in that it clearly asks Yahweh to act to change a difficult circumstance. There is a point of need, and Yahweh is petitioned to intervene on the poet's behalf. Nevertheless, Gunkel's exploration of such poems noted a range of settings from which they originate, and this indicates that 'individual complaint' is more of an umbrella category for a range of poems rather than the end point in interpretation. In this case, it should also be noted that this is a psalm that also complains about Yahweh since he has apparently taken too long (in the psalmist's view) to act (cf. Broyles 1989: 37–38).

It is also important to read this psalm within the context of Psalms 9–14. This is especially because of the appeal made to Yahweh in Psalms 9:19–20 and 10:12 and their concern that Yahweh's justice be seen. Psalms 11–12 have explored this in terms of the damage done by the wicked to society, while this poem examines the issue from the perspective of the individual, picking up particularly on the closing verse of Psalm 12, while the fact that the poet has not yet seen God's face echoes with the closing verse of Psalm 11 (cf. Vesco 2006, 2: 165). It is also bound to this collection through the motif of citing the speech of adversaries as something to be rejected, while key elements anticipate Psalm 14 (G. T. M. Prinsloo 2013: 797). Psalm 13 may be the 'prototype' of the individual complaint (Seybold 1996: 65, following Gunkel), but it must be read in its canonical setting.

The psalm can be analysed in three stanzas, though this should not mask the ways in which they interact with one another (cf. Auffret 2011: 45–50). Each is two verses (in English – the last verse in Hebrew is presented as two in English), though this masks the fact that each stanza is a little shorter than its predecessor (cf. Goldingay 2006a: 204):

1. Initial appeal (1–2)
2. Request for action (3–4)
3. Closing affirmation (5–6)

Comment

Title: See on Psalms 3, 4.

1–2. The question 'How long?' (*'ad 'ānâ*) opens the psalm with real urgency, its fourfold repetition unparalleled in Psalms. The question appears elsewhere in English (e.g. Pss 4:2; 6:3), but the wording is different, though in Psalm 6 it is also directed to Yahweh. The implication is that the poet expected Yahweh to act for their well-being and has waited for some time for this to happen. Instead, the psalmist feels forgotten by Yahweh, the very thing Psalm 10:12 had asked Yahweh not to do. Yahweh is also accused of hiding his face from the poet, even though Psalm 11:7 indicated that the righteous would see his face. This might have had a particular meaning in the sanctuary, but the sense here is primarily that Yahweh has not acted beneficially towards the poet (cf. Num. 6:24–26). Although the complaint psalms often raise the issue of enemies, the initial problem here is Yahweh, and whatever the other problems are, this continues to be the case. It is because Yahweh has apparently not acted that the poet has ongoing pain and sorrow while the enemy is exalted over the psalmist. Yahweh needs to note the trouble and vexation caused to the poet (cf. Ps. 10:14) and act promptly since deliverance delayed is no deliverance.

3–4. Psalm 10:14 pointed out that Yahweh notes trouble and vexation, and so he is now asked to do that (repeating the verb *nbṭ*). The poet asks not only that Yahweh consider the situation, but also that he answers – after all, the poet calls him 'my God', language that presumes Yahweh is responsible for his own people. The time delay to this point means that considering is not enough – an answer is also required. The answer required is not words but action, that Yahweh grant light to the psalmist's eyes, an action preventing three possible outcomes should Yahweh not act. The first two of these are introduced by 'lest' (*pen*), but this is implied in the final line of verse 4. In Psalm 19:8, Yahweh's commandment enlightens the eyes within a pattern by which Yahweh's word provides a proper context for life. If this provides any guidance to the expression here, the sense seems to be that the poet wants enlightenment to understand how to make sense of the current distress, though there is also the element of life being restored to something that can be enjoyed. Death is not the only threat, because there is also the possibility that the enemy will believe they have prevailed, and thus not realize their limitation as humans (Ps. 10:18), rejoicing instead at the poet's suffering. Throughout, it is clear that the enemy's ability to act is there only because Yahweh has not acted, and this is why the request focuses only on what Yahweh is to do, with each reason pointing to why it is important that he act.

5–6. In contrast to the adversaries who have seen an opportunity to prevail, the poet's claim is to have trusted Yahweh's kindness. That Yahweh has delayed acting for the psalmist was not a reason to abandon Yahweh. Rather, Yahweh is known for his 'kindness' (*ḥesed*), his commitment to his people. As such, trusting in Yahweh's kindness is not a matter of trusting in this kindness on its own terms, but rather of focusing on this aspect of Yahweh's character as the point that continued to provide hope. Within the psalm, protesting to Yahweh about Yahweh is thus an expression of trust. This is then contrasted with the future focus that develops in verses 5a–6b, where the poet anticipates actions in response to Yahweh's acting. Because of Yahweh's kindness, the poet has a real expectation of deliverance, and so anticipates the point where rejoicing and song will be the natural responses. The closing line of verse 6 could mean that Yahweh has already dealt well with the poet, perhaps because an oracle or some other cultic form of reassurance was given (so Weiser 1962: 163). But this is probably too specific, and subsequent users of the psalm would not have such a word, so it is probably better to see this as an expression of confidence that Yahweh would indeed act for the psalmist's well-being, with the verb anticipating the point where this would have happened.

Explanation

Starting from a sense of God's absence (cf. G. H. Wilson 2002: 283–285; Janowski 2013: 57–59), this psalm challenges Yahweh to act for his people. The questions put to God in the opening stanza are sharp and pointed. There is a real expectation here that Yahweh's kindness is to be experienced, not deferred. He is challenged to act in a way consistent with his character, demonstrating that trust in him is justified. The psalm can thus stand on its own as an important exploration of the importance of complaint, especially of complaint to God about God (cf. Morrow 2007: 57). But it also sits within its immediate context, where such complaint is contextualized by the issue of theodicy that dominates Psalms 9–14. It is Yahweh who is God, and humans need to be shown their limitations. The protest here thus has a specific focus, one in which the limitations of the enemies need to be revealed. Yet, even though protest continues, it is a protest that also trusts in Yahweh's kindness, anticipating the moment of deliverance and so of rejoicing. Protest about Yahweh can be made to Yahweh precisely because there is a real expectation that he will act, and his kindness permits this protest as a valid form of prayer in which we wrestle with God (Coetzee 1998: 550–551). As Brueggemann and Bellinger (2014: 78) state, this pattern is one that continues in Jesus' teaching on prayer (Matt. 7:7).

PSALM 14

Translation

The director's. Davidic.

[1]The fool has said in his heart, 'There is no God.'
  they are corrupt, they do the abominable,
  there is no one doing good.
[2]Yahweh looks down from the heavens upon humankind
  to see if there is anyone prudent,

who seeks God.
[3]All have turned aside,
together they have become corrupt.
There is no one doing good,
there is not even one.

[4]Do all those practising evil not know,
those eating my people as they eat bread?
Yahweh they do not call!
[5]There they tremble with dread,
because God is with the generation of the righteous.
[6]You would shame the plan of the poor,
though Yahweh is their refuge.

[7]O that salvation for Israel
would come from Zion!
When Yahweh restores the fortunes of his people,
Jacob will exult, Israel rejoice.

Notes on the text

3. LXX has an extensive plus, cited in Romans 3:13–18. Paul may be drawing on an existing collection or creating his own, but the absence of this material in the largely parallel Psalm 53 suggests that this is a subsequent addition to LXX (cf. A. P. Ross 2011: 371–372).

6. On concessive *kî*, see *WHS* §448.

7. Desiderative *mî*, see *WHS* §122.

Form and structure

Psalm 14 is almost identical to Psalm 53, with only slight variations other than switching the divine name between 'Yahweh' (Ps. 14) and 'God' (Ps. 53). The almost verbatim repetition of the poem probably points to the Psalter being made up of various smaller collections brought together to form each of its five books before all came together to form the current book of Psalms (similarly, A. A. Anderson 1972, 1: 170). Nevertheless, although the poem is nearly identical each time, the final form of the Psalter has placed each poem in a literary context and allowed those differences to stand, so that each must still be interpreted in its own terms, even though many issues remain common (cf. Botha 2013b). Here, the poem concludes the small collection of Psalms 9–14, most obviously through repetition of the quote from others that 'there is no God' (Pss 10:4; 14:1). The issue of theodicy is addressed particularly sharply in this collection, especially through the practical atheism implied by this citation. Such an attitude leads humans to lose sight of the fact that they are a 'little less than God' (Ps. 8:5), and as a result attempt to rule society for the benefit of the powerful, creating a pattern of structural violence. A different approach will be modelled in Psalm 15:2, where those who dwell with Yahweh speak truth in their heart. Through repetition of the word 'heart' (*lēb*) this psalm both closes the previous section and prepares for what follows as Psalms 15–24 explore a more positive pattern for the life of the community, one rooted in worship expressed through positive relationships with others.

The focus on theodicy, combined with some language more typical of the wisdom tradition, indicates that this poem is intended to provide a formal pattern of instruction, albeit one that includes elements that move towards prayer and prophetic proclamation. Although the various elements merge, and on any reading verse 4 is the pivot, the poem can be analysed in three stanzas (cf. Botha 1995: 19–20):

1. The problem of practical atheism (1–3)
2. Hints of Yahweh's involvement (4–6)
3. Hope for salvation (7)

Comment

Title: See on Psalms 3, 4.

1–3. Where Psalms 9–10 had deferred the citation of practical atheism until the fourth stanza, here it is the starting point. In Psalm 10:4 those who thought 'there is no God' are defined as 'wicked'. Here, those who think this way are called a 'fool' (*nābāl*); cf. Nabal in 1 Sam. 25). This is not the most common term for the fool, but it is linked to a related noun (*nĕbālâ*) that often refers to a disgraceful act (Judg. 19:23; 2 Sam. 13:12), especially one where the powerful abuse the weak. The fool here appears to be one who is assessed in those terms, for fools not only deny the reality of God (at least in terms of his practical engagement with the world), but are also involved in acts that are recognizably corrupt. These actions may echo those that led to the creation being declared corrupt (Gen. 6:11), but they can also be described as an abomination, acts repugnant to Yahweh. That none do good thus stands in marked contrast to Yahweh, whose goodness is repeatedly celebrated in Psalms (e.g. Ps. 136:1). More importantly in this context, those who act as if Yahweh does not act ignore the fact that he does look down from heaven (cf. Ps. 102:19), looking to find those who are prudent. Instead of being like those in Psalm 2:10 who take refuge in Yahweh's king, the situation is closer to that of Psalm 36:3, where the wicked have also ceased to act prudently. Here, the most prudent course of action would be to seek

God; that is, to live in a manner consistent with his ways, a pattern that sends us back to Psalm 1. But this is not the way of the fool, and the one mentioned in verse 1 is representative of a wider problem where no one does good. The phrasing is hyperbolic (since it clearly does not include the audience addressed in v. 4) but is an important part of how the psalm stresses the dangers of those who ignore God (cf. Mays 1994a: 83). All who assume Yahweh is not involved in daily life have become corrupt, as they no longer walk in his way. Anyone who has turned away from Yahweh is, by definition, not doing what is good. That there is not even one who does good stems from the basic orientation of the fool. Once it is assumed that God is not active, then the path laid out by Psalm 1 has been left behind and doing good is no longer possible.

4–6. The question of verse 4 is the pivot around which the psalm moves. The exact sense is not clear as the text is very terse, but the basic point can be seen. Having highlighted the problem of the fool, the poet addresses an audience who can see that those ignoring Yahweh should know better than to act as if he is not involved in the world. Such people act to satisfy themselves without concern for others, and hence they eat people (cf. Mic. 3:1–3) in the same way as they eat bread while continuing to ignore Yahweh. The problem is that although they should know better, they act as if Yahweh is remote and uninvolved, indicating that those described are those who have social power, unlike those addressed here (Botha 1995: 22). Those eaten are called 'my people', showing that the poet is associated with those who are suffering from such oppressors. But the audience are then reassured that those acting apart from Yahweh will not finally triumph. Although the place where these people will tremble with dread is not specified, the important point is that Yahweh is with the generation of the righteous; that is, with those who have committed themselves to him and his ways. Yahweh looks down from the heavens (v. 2), but he does not remain aloof. Rather, he is positively with the righteous for their well-being. Given this fact, the poet then addresses the fools, stressing that their self-interested approach to life seeks to shame the poor, an approach that ignores the reality that Yahweh is their refuge (cf. Ps. 5:11). The fool works on the assumption that Yahweh does not engage with the world, but the psalm makes clear that this approach is fundamentally flawed.

7. Although the psalm has shown that Yahweh does act for those in need, it also recognizes that this is not always the experience of the faithful. Indeed, the problem posed by the fool is raised precisely because some seem to lead successful and prosperous lives by ignoring God. The affirmation of Yahweh's involvement in verses 4–6 does not deny that this is not always what is experienced. Rather, as is consistent with Psalms 9–14, this poem sees that there is evidence of Yahweh's commitment to the poor alongside times where the powerful seem to flourish without him. Hence, the poem closes with a wish, that salvation would come for Israel from Zion. That is, that the truth celebrated in worship at the temple would be experienced throughout Israel as they see Yahweh's commitment to the righteous in all circumstances. The poem also knows that Yahweh will at one point restore the fortunes of his people, at which point they will rejoice because they are living in the blessings Yahweh has for his people. But that is not now, and so the model of faith is to hold to Yahweh's commitment to justice while hoping for that time when it will be fully revealed.

Explanation

Psalm 14 brings the small collection of Psalms 9–14 to a close by reflecting once more on the issue of theodicy, and the problem that practical atheists seem to enjoy success. There is no doubt that this is a problem to be faced in the modern world as also in the ancient one (including that of the NT; cf. Rom. 3:10–12, where this psalm is central to introducing the problem to which the gospel is the solution). The psalm does not deny the success that such people have – how else could they 'eat my people' in the same way as bread? But it insists that this is not the way it will always be, and that already there are ways where Yahweh's commitment to his people is being worked out and can be seen. Seeing these helps the faithful to understand that the success of those ignoring God is not the last word. Nevertheless, the psalm does not allow believers simply to wish away the prosperity of such fools. Their impact on society must be appreciated because they prosper only by feeding on the weak. This is not the society Israel was meant to be, and neither is it the way the kingdom is presented in the NT. For Christians, the reality of the kingdom is that it already belongs to the poor, and those who hunger now will be satisfied (Luke 6:20–21). Every time we utter the Lord's prayer (esp. in its Matthean form, Matt. 6:9–13) we also express a desire that the kingdom come in all its fullness, something close to the wish with which this psalm ends.

PSALM 15

Translation

A melody. Davidic.

[1]Yahweh, who may sojourn in your tent,
  who may reside on your holy mountain?

[2]Those walking with integrity,
  practising what is right,

and speaking the truth within;
3there is no slander on their tongue,
they do not harm their neighbour,
nor take up a taunt against their associates.
4Despised in their eyes are the reprobate,
but they honour those who fear Yahweh.
They swear an oath to their disadvantage
and do not change.
5They do not lend their money with interest,
nor take a bribe against the innocent.

Those doing these things
will never stumble.

Notes on the text

2–5. Although Hebr. here is sg., this is a representative figure, and a pl. translation is more appropriate.

4. LXX reads *lhr'* as referring to a neighbour, but MT is coherent if awkward. *yāmir* is difficult, but LXX already seems to treat it as a by-form of *mrr*.

Form and structure

Just as Psalms 3 and 8 act as bridges between units in Book 1, so Psalm 15 provides a bridge between Psalms 9–14 and 15–24. Where Psalms 9–10 and 14 had reflected on false speech in the heart that denied God any active role in the world, Psalm 15 instead commends those who speak truth in the heart. Although this truthfulness is focused on outward relations, it emerges from a commitment to Yahweh's ways. It picks up language that was central to the structure of Psalms 9–14 but employs it to encourage a commitment to Yahweh. The portrait of the just that it paints thus contrasts strongly with that of the wicked in Psalms 9–14, especially the fool of Psalm 14 (cf. Vesco 2006, 2: 176; Grogan 2008: 60). Having created a bridge from the previous unit, it now introduces a collection that runs to Psalm 24 (cf. W. P. Brown 2010; Futato 2013; Quinn 2023). This unit is bounded by two entrance liturgies (Seybold 1996: 68; cf. Isa. 33:14–16), both of which encourage those who would worship Yahweh to express this in how they relate to others. In this, they provide an antithesis to Psalms 9–14 and their exploration of a world in which God's activity is excluded. If the person who did not take God's engagement with the world seriously can be labelled as a 'fool' in Psalm 14, then both Psalms 15 and 24 encourage those who would rejoice in Yahweh's presence in the sanctuary to reflect that presence in the wider world. At the heart of this collection, Psalms 18–21 provide an integration of devotion to Yahweh's Torah and king, thus providing a point for reflecting on the significance of these themes from Psalms 1–2 while greatly expanding their interest in prayer in responding to enemies (Grant 2004: 118–119). Prayer, as offered by both the king and the wider worshipping community, is central to the whole of the unit Psalms 15–24 as it explores the struggle of faith (cf. Sumpter 2013: 192). Indeed, although it is often treated as an 'entrance liturgy' it should be noted that Psalm 15 opens with what is presented as a brief prayer, preparing for the expansion of this motif through the unit.

The interchange of speakers is a key marker in noting the structure of a poem (cf. W. S. Prinsloo 1991b: 21), where 'aesthetics and semantics flow together' (Miller 1979a: 423). Though there may be other factors at play (Barré 1984), Psalm 15 can be analysed in three stanzas:

1. An opening question (1)
2. A didactic response (2–5b)
3. A closing affirmation (5c)

Comment

Title: See on Psalm 3.

1. The psalm opens with a question addressed to Yahweh that is focused on the possibility of dwelling at the sanctuary. It is likely that these words are modelled on the types of questions worshippers might have asked as they arrived there, though they have been formalized here so that the question also prepares for the answer. In effect, the question now establishes the possibility for the answer provided in the second stanza. This does not mean the question is artificial. The question is real because it is concerned with remaining in Yahweh's presence, a matter of interest to a worshipper. The question speaks of the sanctuary as a 'tent', a term that could evoke the tabernacle from the wilderness period or the tent established by David when he had brought the Ark to Jerusalem (2 Sam. 7:1–2). That the question also refers to a holy mountain probably indicates that Jerusalem, and not earlier sanctuaries such as Shiloh (Josh. 18:1), is intended. Although the initial verb ('sojourn') suggests a short-term residence, the second ('reside') would anticipate an enduring stay. As both verb forms could indicate an enduring residence, it seems that this is the focus. In short, who can remain in Yahweh's presence since it is his tent and mountain? Since no one lived at the sanctuary, it may seem that the question is redundant. Yet this would not prevent the question from being posed.

2–5b. Rather than looking for a particular person who can dwell at the sanctuary, the answer looks at the character such a person should show. Although the answer (which might have been delivered by a second speaker) runs through to verse 5b, there is a distinction between verse 2 and what follows. The response begins with three ptcs. that may be said to describe the general character of such a person (similarly, Vesco 2006, 2: 179; Owens 2013: 44–45), with the move to finite verbs from verse 3 providing examples of each element in verse 2. Hence, verse 2 characterizes the person who remains in Yahweh's presence as one whose conduct is marked by 'integrity' (*tāmîm*), whose acts are typically 'right' (*ṣedeq*), whose thoughts show 'truth' or 'faithfulness' (*'ĕmet*) to others. All three qualifying terms relate to how someone relates to others. To be blameless is to live (lit. 'walk') with integrity towards God (e.g. Gen. 17:1) or others (e.g. Prov. 11:20). Similarly, to do what is right is to live in a way consistent with God's own character, which is why the prayer in Psalm 7:9 looks for Yahweh to establish the righteous while also being righteous himself. 'Truth' includes speaking that which is factually correct but is often a characteristic of those who are reliable (e.g. Neh. 7:2). That such people (lit.) 'speaks truth in his heart' is best understood as meaning that even in their thought life they seek to be faithful towards others. Thus, in commencing the answer, verse 2 has shifted our focus away from the sanctuary and on to relationships with others.

Verses 3–5b then provide examples of this. As such, they are not comprehensive but are representative of this sort of life. The three examples are all presented through negatives, statements of what such people do not do. The first example is an absence of slander on the tongue – something that does not occur if thoughts are faithful towards others. Likewise, acts that cause harm to others, whether in deeds or speech, are excluded. By contrast, verse 4 is made up of two contrasting pairs, which only returns to what is not done at the end of the verse. The first contrast is between the reprobate and those who fear Yahweh. In context, it is clear that the 'reprobate' are those who do not fear Yahweh. They are like the fool of Psalm 14, and the damage such a person does to society is clear there. The thrust of the contrast is found in the verb 'honour' (*kbd*) that closes the clause. Rather than granting importance to those who reject Yahweh, weight is properly given to those who fear him. That is, the person who would dwell in Yahweh's presence does so by focusing on those who put Yahweh first. Although the last part of verse 4 is grammatically awkward, the behaviour commended is where people are faithful to commitments they have made, even when those commitments may be costly to keep. The issue of attitudes is explored in verse 5ab, though without losing sight of the fact that these attitudes are expressed in actions. Not lending at interest represents a choice to avoid making a profit that harms others, as would routinely happen in the ancient world where loans tended to support subsistence needs rather than the development of capital. Taking a bribe against the innocent is another way of profiting by harming others. Whether through actions one may initiate oneself, or offers made by others, profit through harming others is excluded. In short, the answer makes clear that the person who wishes to dwell in Yahweh's presence does not achieve this by retreating to the sanctuary. Rather, it is found in ethical actions that promote the well-being of Yahweh's people.

5c. Having outlined the character of the person who would dwell in Yahweh's presence, the psalm closes with an affirmation addressed to the wider community, declaring that those who act in accord with the answer shall never stumble. This ties back to the motif of 'walking' at the start of verse 2. Anyone on a journey may stumble, but such a person will not stumble on their journey. That is, their concern is to reflect Yahweh's character in their relationships to others. Provided this orientation is retained, they will not stumble in that journey.

Explanation

Psalm 15 moves us from the pattern of complaint that dominates Psalms 9–14 into a new subunit of Book 1 that continues to Psalm 24. Its concern is with the character of those who worship Yahweh (Owens 2013: 21, 35) and is particularly concerned to demonstrate that life in Yahweh's presence is not found by remaining at the sanctuary, as desirable as that may be. Rather, worshippers live in Yahweh's presence by a positive commitment to others, working out Yahweh's own priorities in their life as they relate to others in that community. These priorities involve refraining from thoughts, speech and actions that harm others and engaging instead in practices that honour those who also fear Yahweh, even if that is to their own cost. Ethics, not cultic activity, shows one lives in Yahweh's presence (cf. deClaissé-Walford et al. 2014: 172). Those who begin this journey are assured that they will not stumble. Paul's exposition of the church as those having free access to God in Christ in Ephesians 3 likewise works out the life of the church in Ephesians 4 in our relationship with others.

PSALM 16

Translation

A Miktam. Davidic.

1Guard me O God,
  because I have taken refuge in you.

2I said to Yahweh, 'You are my Lord,
surely my well-being is with you.'
3Concerning the saints who are in the land,
yes, my majestic ones is where all my delight is,
4(those who hasten after another multiply their sorrow,
I will not pour out their drink offerings from their blood,
I will not take up their names on my lips).
5Yahweh is the share of my portion and my cup,
you take hold of my lot.
6The boundaries have fallen for me in pleasant places,
indeed, I have a beautiful heritage.

7I will bless Yahweh who counsels me,
surely at night my conscience corrects me.
8I have set Yahweh continually before me,
yes, my right hand, I will not stumble!
9Therefore my mind rejoices, my being exults,
surely my body dwells securely.
10For you will not abandon me to Sheol,
you will not give over your faithful one to see the pit.
11You make known to me the path of life,
an abundance of joy in your presence,
delights are at your right hand for ever.

Notes on the text

Title: 'Miktam' occurs here, and in the titles of Psalms 56–60. Unless derived from a root meaning 'stained', its meaning is unknown. LXX seems to have read *miktāb* for its rendering *stēlographia* (inscription). On Davidic, see title of Psalm 3.

2. With many MSS, LXX and Syr., here reading *'āmartî*, though with Rendsburg (1990: 29) the same result may be achieved by understanding this as an old Phoenician form of spelling retained in MT. The last part of the verse is often taken as corrupt, but with Craigie and Tate (2004: 155) we can read *bal* as an intensifying particle.

3. The many emendations proposed for this verse, going back to the versions, show this has always been regarded as a difficult verse, but none are especially persuasive. Hence, the above attempts to make sense of MT save for reading *wĕ'addîray* for *wĕ'addîrê*. Liess (2004: 43–45) defends MT as *lectio difficilior* but despite her efforts it is difficult to find a meaningful sense without some emendation. For the view that this verse describes idolatry that is also rejected, see Peels 2000.

7. 'Conscience' is lit. 'kidneys'. See Janowski 2013: 155–162.

8. *hû'* is often inserted but could be implied with Yahweh now described as the poet's right hand.

Form and structure

Although a difficult text at various points (perhaps as an example of northern dialect; so Rendsburg 1990: 29–33), this psalm can be understood primarily as an expression of trust, though it is trust that exists in the face of significant challenges. That is why the psalm opens with a declaration of having taken refuge in Yahweh and a plea for protection. The poet balances the act of taking refuge in Yahweh with the challenges that are being faced, showing that the statement refers not to the claiming of refuge in the sanctuary (against Kraus 1988: 234) but rather of understanding that the pattern of refuge can also be claimed for life in general. If so, then the declaration at the end of verse 8 about not stumbling also provides a link to Psalm 15:6, where the same verb was used to describe those who honoured Yahweh. Psalm 16 thus begins to explore the life of faithfulness outside the sanctuary that Psalm 15 promotes (cf. Vesco 2006, 2: 2:180). Where the worshipper who wanted to dwell in Yahweh's presence in Psalm 15 was encouraged to look to the wider community, Psalm 16 finds the reality of refuge in that community. Refuge is needed because there are challenges, especially from those who follow other gods and from the threat of death, but it is still possible to trust Yahweh under these circumstances and find a life of joy and satisfaction. In that the psalm also draws on elements from wisdom traditions, the elements of prayer here also become an element of teaching for readers who encounter the psalm (cf. Botha 2016b: 66).

Although its divisions are not always clearly marked, it is possible to analyse the psalm in three stanzas (note that tricola point to significant breaks in vv. 4, 11):

1. Taking refuge amid other options (1–4)
2. Yahweh and the psalmist's heritage (5–6)
3. Confidence in Yahweh (7–11)

Comment

Title: See 'Notes on the text'.

1–4. The poem begins with an appeal to God for protection which is rooted in the claim of refuge. Such claims have already appeared (Pss 5:11; 7:1; 11:1) and represent a significant element within the Psalter (see esp. Creach 1996). Here, as in Psalm 7:1, the background appears to be the claiming of sanctuary, something illustrated by Joab's (albeit unsuccessful) act in 1 Kings 2:28. God's protection was claimed by those facing a charge or danger of some sort. The opening thus orients readers towards the expectation that the focus will be on acts that occur in the sanctuary, something seemingly confirmed in the citation of the poet's words to Yahweh in verse 2, though the balance of the psalm looks beyond the sanctuary. Claiming Yahweh as 'Lord' in this context indicates that Yahweh is not only the one who protects but also the one who provides for the poet (cf. Joseph's role in Gen. 45:4–15). But claiming Yahweh as lord is not simply to be asserted. Rather, the psalmist is positively aligned with the saints in the land, those who have aligned themselves to Yahweh's values, perhaps even those outlined in Psalm 15. Evidence for Yahweh's status as the poet's lord is thus found in a commitment to such people that finds delight in them. Such delight is like that of the righteous in Psalm 1:2, except that there it is centred on Yahweh's Torah. However, if Torah is intended to promote a positive view of community, then finding delight in those who embody such values (and can thus be considered the majestic ones of the community) is a natural extension of that delight. But loyalty to Yahweh as lord also means avoiding those who diverge from such patterns, and though the details in verse 4 are not clear, the point seems to be that the poet avoids any association with those who promote other patterns of life and worship (cf. Brueggemann and Bellinger 2014: 86).

5–6. In contrast to those whose ways are not taken, these verses focus on the positive ways Yahweh relates to the poet. The language echoes the land allocation in the book of Joshua, where reference to a 'portion' (*ḥeleq*), 'lot' (*gôrāl*) and 'heritage' (*naḥălâ*) are all relatively common in the allocation of the land (*naḥălâ* occurs fifty times), while Joshua 17:5 speaks of the boundary line of Manasseh 'falling' and hence defining their territory, though 'portion' could also allude to a priestly share of a sacrifice (Lev. 6:17 [MT 6:10]). Where Joshua uses this language to speak of the allocation of land, here the focus is changed to make Yahweh the poet's heritage. This would be consistent with the poet being a Levite since they did not receive an allocation like the other tribes (so, deClaissé-Walford et al. 2014: 176; cf. Num. 18:20), though this is not necessary (cf. Broyles 1999: 97). If so, it would indicate that the poet finds satisfaction in a relationship with Yahweh rather than in possessing the land that would normally have been thought of as providing security and wealth. Yet the word 'cup' (*kôs*) stands out in this context (cf. Ps. 23:5), since it does not occur in Joshua or the texts describing the role of the Levites in Leviticus and Numbers. It functions here to provide a contrast to those things refused in verse 4 – those drink offerings could not be consumed, but Yahweh's provision can be enjoyed. At other points, a 'cup' is mentioned in a liturgical setting (e.g. Ps. 116:13) but situating the term here in language that otherwise evokes receipt of the land moves it away from a more cultic meaning, suggesting that although Yahweh's goodness can be appreciated in liturgy, it is not restricted to that sphere.

7–11. In the final stanza, the poet responds to the points made in the second. The stanza could be subdivided into two strophes marked by repetition of *'ap* (surely) in verses 7 and 9 (Liess 2004: 30–31), but it is better to hold the unit together. Verses 7, 8 use contrasting verbs, looking forward in verse 7 to blessing Yahweh because of his continued counsel for the psalmist while verse 8 looks back to a previous decision to set Yahweh 'before me'. Nevertheless, both point to Yahweh's continued guidance of the psalmist (whether through direct counsel or through a conscience shaped by this) and build to the assurance at the end of verse 8 that the psalmist will not stumble, picking up Psalm 15's conclusion. It is Yahweh's continued presence through all contexts, not just the sanctuary, that provides confidence. This in turn provides the psalmist with reason to rejoice. Such rejoicing is expressed in the whole person, both inwardly and outwardly, and is rooted in confidence that Yahweh will continue to guard the psalmist, keeping the poet from the potentially deadly threat for which refuge was initially claimed. Both 'Sheol' and the 'pit' stand for death, understanding it as a descent to the underworld, a place many would think of as separated from Yahweh (cf. Lindblom 1974: 192; Groenewald 2012: 48). But the psalmist is confident that Yahweh's protection extends through all of life and so he will not permit one faithful to him to suffer an unjust death. Rather, Yahweh will make the path of life known to the poet. The path of life is not only the absence of death. Rather, it is an abundance of joy in Yahweh's presence which discovers that the delights Yahweh grants are not restricted to the heritage already received. These delights are found at Yahweh's right hand, a place of honour for his faithful ones, where they continue for ever. Where verse 8 seems to suggest that Yahweh was the poet's right hand, it is now the poet who is at Yahweh's right hand to enjoy these delights.

Explanation

Developing from Psalm 15 the theme of living in God's presence beyond the sanctuary, this poem takes the motif of claiming refuge in Yahweh and moves it from an act that happened only at the sanctuary and shows that it can be applied to the whole of life. It is an expression of confidence, but one that is given in full awareness of threats that exist against the faithful. These threats may lead one to claim refuge in the sanctuary. But although that is not rejected here, the psalm stresses that the faithful can trust Yahweh in all of life. Yahweh's goodness is not restricted to the sanctuary, so that the good things he has provided are seen in the routine aspects of life too. Just as Yahweh provided the land for Israel in the settlement, so he continues to provide for the faithful. This provision is not simply the basics; rather, Yahweh provides an abundance of joy in his presence, a presence that is not restricted to the sanctuary. This abundance continues to find expression in Paul's description of God's grace as something lavished on believers (Eph. 1:8) as he makes known his way to us through Christ. But alongside this, the psalm also insists that the believer lives in the knowledge that there is only one Lord and that faithfulness to him is also crucial. Confidence in God's keeping power is found most fully in committing oneself faithfully to serve God, and to do so within a culture that does not always value such faithfulness. Acts 2:22–32 (cf. Acts 13:35) expounds this in terms of Jesus' death and resurrection, where Jesus' example most fully bears out the realities to which this psalm attests. In Peter's speech it is presented as evidence of his messiahship (Harriman 2017: 250), while continuing to provide hope for all believers.

PSALM 17

Translation

A prayer. Davidic.

[1]Hear, O Yahweh, a just cause,
  give attention to my cry,
listen to my prayer
  from lips without deceit.
[2]From your presence let my vindication come,
  let your eyes see uprightness.
[3]You have tested my mind, you visited me at night,
  you refined me, you find nothing –
  I determined that my mouth would not transgress.
[4]Concerning human deeds, by the word of your lips,
  I have kept from the paths of the violent,
[5]my steps hold fast to your tracks,
  my feet have not stumbled.

[6]As for me, I call on you because you answer me O God;
  incline your ear to me, hear my utterance!
[7]Wondrously demonstrate your kindness,
  O saviour of those seeking refuge,
  from those rebelling against your right hand.
[8]Keep me as the apple of your eye,
  in the shadow of your wings shelter me,

[9]from the wicked who assail me,
  my deadly enemies who encompass me.
[10]They shut their minds with fat,
  their mouths speak with arrogance.
[11]They have tracked me down,
  now they surround me,
  they set their eyes to cast me to the ground.
[12]He is like a lion eager to tear,
  like a young lion sitting in a hiding place.

[13]Rise up O Yahweh! Confront him! Subdue him!
  Save my life from the wicked by your sword,
[14]from mortals with your hand O Yahweh,
  from mortals whose lifespan and portion are this life.
But for your treasured ones you fill their belly,
  may they be satisfied with children,
  may they settle their residue on their children.
[15]I, in righteousness, will behold your face,
  let me be satisfied on waking with your likeness.

Notes on the text

Title: For 'A prayer', see 'Comment'. On 'Davidic', see title of Psalm 3.

3. The division of the lines here is disputed (cf. *BHS*, which locates *zammōtî* to the end of the previous line; cf. Goldingay 2006a: 235–236), but the MT accentuation can be followed and still be read as a coherent text.

7. With many MSS reading *pl'* for *plh*, though it is possible to consider these as by-forms (cf. A. P. Ross 2011: 416).

10. Reading *ḥēleb libbāmô sāgĕrû*, assuming a haplography (similarly, Kwakkel 2002: 77).

11. Reading *'iššĕrûnî* and retaining K rather than Q.

14. Retaining K (though Q would be similar), but the whole verse is very difficult, as is evident already in the difficulties found in the versions. The above is highly tentative. For reflections on the task of translating a verse like this, see de Villiers 2002.

Form and structure

Psalm 17 (like Ps. 7) shows several features that suggest its origin could lie in prayers of the accused that might have been associated with a temple ritual (so, Delekat 1967: 224; Beyerlin 1970: 107). Most notably, the opening appeal assumes that the psalmist's claim is 'just' (*ṣedeq*), while the 'vindication' requested (*mišpāṭî*) also assumes a legal background (vv. 1–2). In this context, the denial of violence (vv. 3–5) can be understood as a claim of innocence from a major, potentially capital, crime (cf. Kwakkel 2002: 88). Yahweh's role in saving those who seek refuge (v. 7) is consistent with this, while other language can also be understood as having a claim of sanctuary in the background. Yet, although this background in the temple is probably correct, we do not have any direct evidence of what such a ritual looked like, so this psalm (like Ps. 7) needs to be understood more in its canonical setting than in any proposed ritual (Firth 2005b: 27–30). That is, in the process of forming the Psalter, various psalms have been allowed to retain elements that point to their origin, in this case enabling a range of readers who have been accused of something to learn from this prayer, while not tying them to a specific cultic setting. This would be true even if, with Kwakkel (2002: 69; cf. Eaton 1976: 34–35), we understand the original petitioner as the king since the poem's presence in the Psalter opens it to a wider range of readers.

The setting in the book provides important connections to Psalms 15–16, most notably repetition of the language of feet not stumbling (v. 5; cf. Pss 15:6; 16:8). The language of refuge is also important, since the confidence expressed in Psalm 16 derives from an appeal for refuge, while Psalm 17:7 expresses confidence that Yahweh saves those who claim refuge. Further, Psalm 16:7 speaks of correction from Yahweh (via the poet's conscience) at night, while Psalm 17:3 reflects on Yahweh's visiting and testing the psalmist at night. Looking forward to Psalm 18, the declaration of innocence made here (vv. 3–5) prepares for the claim of innocence made there (Ps. 18:20–24). These features all suggest that although the psalm's origins in a cultic procedure for determining innocence in formal legal matters are still visible, the more important context is that provided by its literary setting.

The psalm can be analysed in three stanzas, each containing two strophes that begin with a plea (marked by imp. verbs), though more complex analyses are also possible that stress the place of verse 7 as a pivot within the poem (cf. Auffret 1994; Mosca 2011):

1. Initial appeal for vindication (1–5)
   a. Plea (1–2)
   b. Negative confession (3–5)
2. Request for protection (6–12)
   a. Plea (6–9)
   b. Description of adversaries (10–12)
3. Request for rescue (13–15)
   a. Plea (13–14)
   b. Confidence in Yahweh (15)

Comment

Title: Although the term 'prayer' (*tĕpilâ*) has appeared earlier (Pss 4:2; 6:10), this is the first time it appears as part of a title. It shares this feature with Psalms 86, 90, 102 and 142. Each of these is an appeal to God, suggesting that the term refers to this specific type of prayer rather than being a more generic term. This is also borne out by its use across the Psalter, though Psalm 72:20 could allow a more general sense.

1–2. The urgency of the appeal for vindication is evident in three imperatives with which the prayer commences, each of which urges Yahweh to hear the poet's claim. Initially, Yahweh is called to hear a 'just cause' (*ṣedeq*), a claim that can also imply the psalmist's innocence of a specific charge. The word *ṣedeq* recurs in verse 15 (there, 'righteousness'), forming an inclusio that brackets the poem, while continuing to show that the psalmist can experience Yahweh's presence because of this righteousness. Where the first imperative asks Yahweh to hear a just cause, defining the nature of what he is to hear, the second and third imperatives are followed by terms that indicate how the poet brings this concern to Yahweh. The 'cry' can be one of joy (e.g. Isa. 35:10) or supplication (e.g. 1 Kgs 8:28), though the context here already makes clear that this is an act of supplication, something confirmed by the fact that the third imp. asks Yahweh to hear a prayer, using the same term as in the title. Both the shout and the prayer are expressions of speech, and this leads to the claim that the poet's speech is free from deceit. Yahweh is then summoned to let 'my vindication come forth'; that is, provide some means of demonstrating the legitimacy of the poet's claim. The goal of this is that Yahweh see uprightness because his actions have provided evidence of justice.

3–5. Having made the initial plea, the poet now provides a 'negative confession that functions as a declaration of innocence' (Firth 2005b: 30). The negative confession begins by recounting Yahweh's previous examination of the psalmist, a process of testing, visitation and refining that has found nothing unworthy. If the poet was guilty, then Yahweh would already have discovered this. That nothing has been found demonstrates innocence instead. Having focused on what Yahweh has not found, the negative confession then outlines how the poet has avoided patterns of behaviour that might have led to a guilty verdict. Just as Psalm 15:2 had encouraged positive behaviour that began with thoughts before speech, so also the poet begins with a decision made not to engage in false speech before then noting that, on the basis of Yahweh's word, the paths of the violent have been avoided. Instead, the psalmist has followed Yahweh's tracks without stumbling. That Yahweh has not found anything against the psalmist is thus consistent with this decision and its outworking in the poet's behaviour.

6–9. The request for protection is also commenced with imperatives, though in this case they are withheld until the second part line in verse 6.

God can be approached because he answers, and because of this the poet again asks to be heard. The content of the poet's words is then recounted in verses 7–9, beginning with the request that Yahweh demonstrate his 'kindness' (*ḥesed*) through some wondrous deed. The reason Yahweh should act is that he is the saviour of those seeking refuge, and the opening plea makes clear that this is the psalmist's situation. Something miraculous is needed because of a group who are rebelling against God's right hand, perhaps a reference to the king. It is because of this group that the poet needs to be kept safe (cf. Ps. 16:1), specifically as the 'apple' of Yahweh's eye; that is, as one who receives Yahweh's protection. This can be symbolized by Yahweh's wings as a place of hiding for the poet. In the temple, this would have referred to the wings of the cherubim that extended from the inner sanctuary (1 Kgs 6:23–28), though such language could also be used metaphorically (e.g. Ruth 2:12). This protection was needed because of those assailing the psalmist. They are described here as 'wicked' in contrast to the psalmist's self-presentation as righteous, pointing out that their claims against the poet are false. If they are permitted to continue, the poet's life will be at risk.

10–12. The actions of the opponents are now described, showing why they are wicked. Initially, they are described as a group, but an individual emerges in verse 12. Where the poet's mind can be searched by Yahweh, the wicked have closed theirs off with fat (see 'Notes on the text'). Since 'mind' is more literally 'heart', the image is of closing it off by surrounding it with the fat of the midriff. With a closed mind, they do not evaluate evidence and instead speak with arrogance, showing the sort of behaviour denied in the negative confession. Their thoughts lead to false speech that manifests itself in violence towards the poet, who is portrayed here like prey hunted until it is trapped and cast to the ground. The language switches from pl. to sg. in verse 12, perhaps pointing to a leader who is portrayed as a lion eager for prey, or as a young lion waiting in ambush.

13–14. The poet's life is at risk from such people, and so the psalm now moves to a new plea, calling Yahweh to arise. This time the plea begins with four closely related imperatives, all asking Yahweh to save the poet. The first three form a logical sequence, where Yahweh rises, then confronts the enemy and subdues him (the sg. is retained, so the leader is in focus). The fourth, though still expressed as an imp., brings the preceding three together in asking that Yahweh deliver the psalmist's life. Yahweh's power is greater than that of mortals, which is why the psalmist knows he can deliver from them, especially those who seek satisfaction in what they can achieve and do not look beyond this rather than in what Yahweh provides. Assuming the text of verse 14b is correct (see 'Notes on the text'), then it is likely that the plea contrasts the actions of the wicked with the righteous, who are understood as finding satisfaction in what Yahweh provides.

15. The theme of satisfaction leads into the closing statement. Because the claim is just, then the poet can be confident of seeing Yahweh's face. Although Dahood (1965: 99) believes this is a beatific vision, M. S. Smith (1988: 181) is more likely correct that this is simply a pictorial way of describing Yahweh's presence. Reference to 'awaking' and seeing this likeness could reference a detail of temple ritual, but it now picks up the element of Yahweh's testing the psalmist at night (v. 3), showing that the psalmist can continue as one declared innocent by Yahweh.

Explanation

Perhaps originally a prayer that was part of a temple ritual for determining the innocence of those facing a significant charge (cf. Deut. 17:8–12), this psalm is now more tightly tied to its literary setting through its links to Psalms 15–16 and 18. As such, it picks up on the themes of being in God's presence and refuge that were developed in those psalms in the particular case of those who are wrongly accused. Where Psalm 16 ended with confidence that satisfaction was found in Yahweh's presence, Psalm 17 also expresses confidence that satisfaction is found in Yahweh's presence even though there are threats against the psalmist's life because of enemies who rebel against Yahweh and accuse the poet. The psalm knows that the life of satisfaction is one that can face significant distress, but it is still to be found in the presence of God. That presence can be both testing and comforting, and it would be wrong to assume that one removes the other, but this is the mode of satisfaction that is needed, and which is available to all. Where the psalm might originally have meant only an encounter with God's presence in the temple, the context allows for a broader sense, creating the trajectory that builds to the hope expressed in 1 John 3:2.

PSALM 18

Translation

The director's. For Yahweh's servant. Davidic – when he spoke the words of this song to Yahweh on the day Yahweh delivered him from the grasp of all his enemies and from the control of Saul, he said:

[1]I love you, O Yahweh, my strength.
[2]Yahweh is my crag, my stronghold, my deliverer,
  my God, my rock in whom I take refuge,

my shield, the horn of my salvation, my place of security.
3I call on Yahweh who is worthy to be praised,
and I am saved from my enemies.

4The cords of death encompassed me,
and the torrents of destruction assailed me;
5the cords of Sheol surrounded me,
the snares of death confronted me.
6In my distress I called out to Yahweh,
yes, to my God I cried for help,
he heard my voice from his sanctuary,
yes, my cry to him for help came to his ears.
7The earth reeled and quaked,
and the foundations of the mountains trembled,
and reeled to and fro because he was angry.
8Smoke went up from his nostrils,
and a consuming fire from his mouth,
coals blazed out from him.
9He bent the heavens and came down,
thick darkness was under his feet.
10He rode on a cherub and flew,
he soared upon the wings of the wind.
11He made darkness his hiding place, his covering about him,
dense clouds dark with water.
12His clouds passed on from the brightness before him,
hail and fiery coals.
13Yahweh thundered in the heavens,
and the Most High put forth his voice,
yes, hail and fiery coals.
14He sent forth his arrows and scattered them,
he flashed forth much lightning and confused them.
15The beds of the waters were seen,
the foundations of the world were exposed by your rebuke, O Yahweh,
at the blast of the breath of your nostrils.
16He sent from above, he took me,
he drew me up from many waters.
17He delivered me from my strong enemy,
and from those who hate me when they are too strong for me.
18They confronted me on the day of my distress,
but Yahweh was my support.
19And he brought me out to a broad place,
he rescued me because he delighted in me.

20Yahweh has dealt with me according to my righteousness,
he rewarded me according to the cleanness of my hands.

[21]For I have kept to Yahweh's ways,
I have not become guilty before my God.
[22]For all his rules are before me,
and his statutes I have not put away from me.
[23]I have been blameless with him,
and have kept myself from my iniquity.
[24]So Yahweh has rewarded me according to my righteousness,
according to the cleanness of my hands in his sight.
[25]With the faithful you show yourself kind,
with the blameless person you show yourself one who deals with integrity,
[26]with the clean you show yourself pure,
but with the perverted you show yourself to be astute.
[27]For you save a humble people,
but the eyes of the haughty you bring low.
[28]For you light my lamp,
Yahweh my God enlightens my darkness.
[29]For with you I can run at a troop,
and in my God, I can leap over a wall.
[30]This God, his way is blameless,
the promise of Yahweh is tested,
a shield is he to all who take refuge in him.

[31]For who is God other than Yahweh,
and who is a rock apart from our God?
[32]The God who girds me with valour,
and made my way blameless,
[33]who makes my feet like those of the hind,
and makes me stand upon the heights,
[34]who trains my hands for war,
my arms can bend a bow of bronze.
[35]You gave me the shield of your salvation,
your right hand supported me,
your condescension made me great.
[36]You broaden the place for my feet beneath me,
my ankles have not shaken.
[37]I pursued my enemies and overtook them,
and did not turn back until they were finished.
[38]I shattered them so they can no longer rise,
they fell beneath my feet.
[39]You gird me with valour for war,
you make those who rise against me to bow beneath me.
[40]You gave me the back of my enemies,
and those who hate me I destroyed.
[41]They cried for help but there was no saviour,
unto Yahweh but he did not answer them.

42I beat them as fine as dust before the wind,
  I emptied them out like the mire of the streets.
43You delivered me from contention with people,
  you set me as head of the nations,
  people I do not know serve me.
44When the ear heard, they obeyed me,
  children of foreigners came cringing to me.
45Children of foreigners lose heart,
  and come out trembling from their strongholds.

46Yahweh lives, and blessed be my rock,
  and exalted be the God of my salvation,
47the God who gives me vengeance,
  and subdues peoples under me,
48the one who delivers me from my enemies,
  yes, you exalted me from those who rose against me,
  from the man of violence, you rescued me.
49Therefore will I give thanks to you among the nations, O Yahweh,
  and I will make melody to your name,
50the one who brings great salvation for his king,
  who shows kindness to his anointed,
  to David and his seed for ever.

Notes on the text

Since Psalm 18 is essentially the same poem as 2 Samuel 22 (see 'Form and structure'), it is possible to create a text which is the ancestor of both. However, most variants between them are insignificant, and each has its own textual history (cf. Firth 2009: 515–516). The text in Samuel probably represents an earlier version of the poem since it retains more 'defective' spelling, but the text of Psalm 18 is generally better preserved. Because they each have their own textual history, no attempt is made here to list the variants between them. Only points significant for the interpretation of Psalm 18 are noted. For a more detailed analysis, see Adam 2001: 45–47 and Berry 1993: 26–50.

9. The preposition *bĕ* sometimes means 'from' (*WHS* §251). This is its normal sense in Ugar.

21. Taking the *min* as representative of standpoint (*WHS* §323c).

34. Lack of concord in gender and number between verb (*wĕniḥatâ*) and subject is explicable (GKC §145o).

50. Reading *magdîl* with Q.

Form and structure

As mentioned above, Psalm 18 is almost identical to 2 Samuel 22, and the two are indisputably variants on the one poem. But it is still important to note that we have two versions of the poem (as e.g. with Pss 14, 53) and each needs to be understood in its own context. For 2 Samuel 22, this is primarily its place within the Samuel Conclusion and then to the rest of Samuel (cf. Firth 2009: 511–523), whereas here it needs to be understood most immediately within its setting in Psalms 15–24 and then in relation to the rest of the Psalter. Read this way, it is important to note that it both picks up elements from Psalm 17 and prepares for Psalm 19. A royal psalm, it also has connections with Psalms 20–21. This is not to deny that the poem had a literary function outside either setting where we now find it, and we must also note that its meaning cannot be reduced to its current context. But it is to affirm that those literary contexts in which we now find it are important for its interpretation.

As noted, Psalm 17 can be classified among the prayers of the accused (see 'Form and structure' there). Although Psalm 18 is a royal thanksgiving song (one that shares much with Ps. 144), it also includes elements that are more typical of the prayers of the accused. To be clear, Psalm 18 is not a prayer of the accused, but the declaration that Yahweh has dealt with the psalmist 'according to my righteousness' (v. 20) finds a close parallel to Psalm 7:8. What is here a point of thanksgiving is there a point of appeal, one closely linked to Psalm 17:1, 15. Such an appeal to Yahweh is reported at verse 6, while the thanksgiving in verse 30 returns once again to the theme of refuge. Similarly, the declaration in Psalm 17:4 about the psalmist keeping away from the paths of the violent finds a positive affirmation in Psalm 18:21. All this suggests that although Psalm 18 celebrates the victory Yahweh has given, it also assumes that a prayer not dissimilar to Psalm 17 was also prayed before it, especially if the desire for God's presence in Psalm 17:15 is linked to the theophany described in verses 7–15. Psalm 18 thus becomes evidence that Yahweh does indeed answer such prayers. It should be acknowledged that the place of verses 20–29 (where these motifs are most pronounced) has often been treated as an addition to the basic poem (e.g. Adam 2001: 128–144), but Kwakkel (2002: 262–271) has demonstrated the coherence of the final text and as such it is appropriate to read it as a whole (cf. Kuntz 1983: 19–21).

Psalm 18 refers to Yahweh's 'ways', a more general term for obedience, as well as his 'rules' (*mišpaṭ*) and 'statutes' (*ḥuqot*). These terms are more typically at home in the so-called Torah psalms (e.g. Ps. 1). However, Grant (2004: 71–119) has shown that (esp. in Book 1) there is a clear correlation of royal and Torah psalms. Within the slightly larger unit of Psalms 15–24, Psalms 18–21 form a particular block consisting of:

Psalm 18: Royal psalm with elements of Torah
Psalm 19: Torah psalm
Psalms 20–21: Paired royal psalms

Considering this progression, Psalm 18 simultaneously initiates this sequence and emerges from the preceding psalms. None of this should distract us from seeing that this is a royal thanksgiving psalm, a poem that acknowledges what Yahweh has done for the king because of the Davidic covenant. The importance of thanksgiving in analysing the poem is evident in the use of elements of thanksgiving in both the opening (vv. 1–3) and close, with these forming an envelope around the whole. Within this, the poem reports on Yahweh's actions for the king. Accordingly, it can be analysed in five stanzas as follows:

1. Opening praise (1–3)
2. Theophany (4–19)
   a. Initial distress (4–6)
   b. Report of theophany (7–15)
   c. Deliverance in theophany (16–19)
3. Yahweh's reliability (20–30)
   a. Reasons for deliverance (20–24)
   b. Reflection on Yahweh's character (25–30)
4. Report of Yahweh's actions for David (31–45)
   a. Yahweh the equipper (31–34)
   b. Address to Yahweh (35–36)
   c. Victory reports (37–45)
5. Closing praise (46–50)

Comment

Title: On 'the director's', see on Psalm 4. 'For Yahweh's Servant' and 'Davidic' occur elsewhere in the title of Psalm 36. On 'Davidic' see on Psalm 3. 'Yahweh's servant' does not occur in the parallel in 2 Samuel 22:1, making this an important addition to the psalm, enhancing its messianic dimension. David is said to have spoken the words of this song on the day Yahweh delivered him from all his enemies and Saul. There is no point in Samuel that matches this description; instead, the song reflects on Yahweh's faithfulness through time (though for possible connections, see V. L. Johnson 2009: 115–121). As David is named in both the title and the closing verse, which includes more messianic terms, it seems likely that he is presented here as taking up an existing song, albeit one we are to read in the light of his experience. Nevertheless, more than in most other cases, this is a psalm that is to be read through David's experience (cf. Berry 1993: 132).

1–3. Verse 1 has no parallel in 2 Samuel 22. Declaring 'love' for Yahweh is rare in the OT, and the verb used here (*rḥm*) refers to Yahweh's love for his people in its other occurrences in Psalms. A different verb (*'hb*) is used when people are called to love Yahweh (e.g. Deut. 6:5). David's love for Yahweh is grounded in Yahweh's character and his responsiveness. Having described Yahweh as his strength, verse 2 provides a range of terms that explore this theme. Several of these are related to the metaphor of Yahweh as 'rock' – here 'crag' and 'stronghold' associate Yahweh with a cliff, a place that is high and thus secure (cf. Fernandes 2013: 91–92). This is defensive language, but the statement that Yahweh is David's deliverer presents God in more active terms while still allowing that deliverance may come through defence. Yahweh is also David's God, emphasizing the importance of a relationship with him. That relationship allows David to use the more general term 'rock' to describe Yahweh, the term here again referring to the security Yahweh grants, which is why David can take refuge in him. The final part of verse 2 then develops this security by portraying Yahweh as a shield (cf. Pss 3:4; 7:11), another defensive metaphor, before describing him as the 'horn of my salvation'. Although 'horn' could be understood as something offensive, here it is more likely to refer to Yahweh's power, declaring that he has the power to save David from his enemies, and is hence a place of security. Verse 3 then shifts in focus to note that part of Yahweh's praiseworthy character is that he responds to David's call, saving him from his enemies. Again, David's posture is defensive, a position consistent with the title.

4–6. The psalm now moves from general declarations about Yahweh to recount points where he has acted for David through the second stanza. However, since the title encourages us to read the psalm against much of David's life, we must be careful about making connections to specific events. The descriptions of distress to which Yahweh responded are generalized, often drawing on elements familiar from ANE mythology (cf. Berry 1993: 70–75; Shnider 2006). Nevertheless, as verses 4–5 make clear, these were real threats to David's life from which he could not have delivered himself. Much of David's ascent to the throne in Samuel (1 Sam. 16:1 – 2 Sam. 5:5) is a story of his life being at risk from Saul and various Philistines. He was on the run from Saul, and even though he at points took shelter with the Philistines it is clear they did not trust him (1 Sam. 29). Yet a consistent theme of these stories is that Yahweh was with David, and it was because of Yahweh that he survived various attempts on his life, whether from people he had helped (1 Sam. 23:1–14) or at points where Saul had almost caught him (1 Sam. 23:20–29). Such accounts represent the sorts of situations to which verses 4–5 refer, even if a specific connection cannot be made. This strophe is also bounded by references to David's calling on Yahweh and being saved because Yahweh has heard David's cry, all of which demonstrates why it commences with the note that Yahweh is worthy of praise. That Yahweh has heard from his temple is probably a reference to the heavenly temple (cf. Ps. 1:4), since it is also from here that he acted to save David.

7–15. Where the first strophe of the stanza outlines its central theme – that Yahweh saved David – the second focuses on how Yahweh was experienced, here drawing on themes of theophany from elsewhere in the OT. This draws on the encounter with Yahweh at Mount Sinai (Exod. 19; cf. Niehaus 1995: 302–304), though here there are also close connections to Habakkuk 3:1–16. The language draws on the awesome encounter at Sinai to explain how Yahweh was also present to David. As Gray (2014) has made clear for the whole of this psalm, the various metaphors here are strongly pictorial – as readers we are meant to see them. The language of verses 7–8 evokes both an earthquake and a volcanic eruption, closely matching the experience at Sinai. The shaking of the ground and the volcanic material prepares for the point where Yahweh is said to have bent the heavens and come down. That is, Yahweh has not remained aloof in the heavenly sanctuary but has come to his creation. As Yahweh comes, he remains an awesome figure, with thick darkness under his feet that prevents him being seen directly even as he flies on a cherub. Within the temple, the wings of cherubs came out of the inner sanctuary (1 Kgs 6:23–28), similarly representative of Yahweh's presence. Yet even as Yahweh is manifest, he is also hidden by darkness and thick clouds. These elements are also typical of volcanic activity, though they can also indicate storm activity, and it is a storm that becomes the dominant motif from verse 12 onwards with its reference to hail and lightning generating a sense of awe (cf. Wiggins 2014: 102). Although these can be natural meteoric elements, here they are pointers to Yahweh's speaking. Yahweh's voice is like thunder, both awesome and powerful, with hail and lightning the expressions of his voice. In their overwhelming power, they have confused those forces that brought David close to death. Yahweh's speech is a powerful rebuke of the forces that threatened David, a rebuke which shows that Yahweh's breath is more powerful than any other force within creation as the blast from Yahweh's nostrils exposes the world's foundations. Yahweh has come, and he has come in the power that was seen at Sinai, to save David.

16–19. Where the account of the theophany has emphasized Yahweh's power in coming to David, this third strophe describes his various acts in delivering David. The language of verse 16 picks up elements from verses 4–5, all of which described the movement towards death as a downward event. But from on high Yahweh has drawn David back up from many waters, reversing the direction of travel. This involved delivering David from a strong enemy, and those who hated him who were stronger than him. Just as the title mentions

Saul and all David's enemies, so here we have a strong individual enemy and a group of those who hated David and were more powerful than him. All this explains why the report of the theophany was so important in demonstrating that Yahweh's power is greater than any other. When confronted by his enemies on the day of distress, Yahweh was David's support. More than that, he had brought David to a broad place (v. 19). This links back to verse 6 where the term for 'distress' (*ṣar*; a different word is used in v. 18) can also mean a place that is particularly narrow. Being in a broad space is a place of freedom and hence a release from distress. Yahweh had done this for David because he had delighted in him, perhaps a reference to the promise to David in 2 Samuel 7:1–17.

20–24. The second stanza has closed by reporting on Yahweh's deliverance of David, but it has not explained why he delighted in David and thus rescued him. The third stanza thus moves from a report of deliverance (which we may expect from the title to be the whole poem) to explore why Yahweh has acted this way. In its first strophe, the psalm responds to the statement that Yahweh has delighted in David, with which the first stanza closed. The basic point is made in the opening statement, that Yahweh has dealt with David according to his righteousness, language picked up again in verse 24, forming an envelope around this strophe. Readers of 2 Samuel 10 – 20 may be surprised by this since those chapters recount aspects of David's reign that would hardly provide an assessment of him as righteous or as someone with clean hands (cf. Ps. 24:4). There, he is a murderer and adulterer who is unable to deal wisely with his family. It is certainly true that Samuel paints a complex picture of David, one that shows him capable of acts of cruelty and the abuse of power. But here the background of the prayers of the accused provided by Psalm 17 (and through it Ps. 7) becomes important. Those psalms also claim righteousness, but that righteousness is not absolute. Rather, it refers to a specific charge, and David here claims to be innocent of that charge. All this is explored in verses 21–23, which outline various ways in which David has not only been innocent of a particular charge but explain that he has also walked in Yahweh's ways, faithful to his law, with blamelessness consistent with Psalm 15:2. That is, he is not guilty of a specific charge and his whole life can be assessed as one of faithfulness to Yahweh's teaching. It is not clear that we can identify the specific charge, and the prayers of the accused never specify one, but in this case the title may provide a clue. Much of David's early life had been spent on the run from Saul, yet even though Saul sought his death, David twice refused to kill him (1 Sam. 24, 26). As king, David was expected to understand that power could be given only by Yahweh, not claimed for his own ends. On this charge, which was seemingly reported among Saul's supporters (cf. 2 Sam. 16:5–14), David could claim innocence. That he was ultimately delivered from Saul by

Yahweh provides a basis both for this song of thanksgiving and for the more specific claims made here. Nevertheless, as Kwakkel (2002: 282) has noted, the larger goal of this stanza is to stress Yahweh's reliability, a reliability that leads to praise. David's claim of innocence remains ironic in terms of what we know of the whole of his reign, but what is stressed here does provide a reason for praising Yahweh, and indeed declaring David's love for him (v. 1).

25–30. That the main goal of this third stanza is to declare Yahweh's reliability becomes clear in this second strophe. This is developed through a pattern in verses 25–26a where an adjective that describes a person is matched with a cognate verb that affirms Yahweh's acts. But in verse 26b this pattern changes, so that when dealing with the perverted Yahweh is shown to be astute. This demonstrates that Yahweh responds positively to those who live in a way consistent with his ways, but also that he is not taken in by appearances. Faithfulness, blamelessness and purity are not to be feigned simply to receive good from Yahweh. He recognizes when such things are feigned and responds appropriately to these people too. David's righteousness therefore could not be feigned. This leads into verses 27–29, each of which begins with *kî* (for), explaining something fundamental about Yahweh's character. In verse 27 these statements are more general, focusing on Yahweh's saving of the humble and bringing down the haughty, but in verse 28 this is now applied to David, noting that Yahweh had illumined David's lamp, enlightening his darkness. The point is that David had been in a position of weakness compared to Saul, but Yahweh had raised him up and given him a place of prominence. David was thus able to take on marauders or overcome defensive barriers like walls. The important shift in verse 29 is that David now speaks in terms of his relationship with Yahweh – it is not that David on his own could do these things but rather that they could be done through relationship with Yahweh. Verse 30 then brings the stanza to a close with a reflective tricolon. Where the preceding verses are addressed directly to Yahweh, now an audience are addressed and encouraged to learn about Yahweh's character, through drawing on language from earlier in the psalm. Hence, Yahweh's way is 'blameless' (*tāmîm*), repeating a term David had used of himself (v. 24) and in the general description of Yahweh's character (v. 26). This leads into the affirmation that Yahweh's promise is tested, an image that echoes Psalm 17:3, where Yahweh had tested the psalmist. Here, the point is that Yahweh's promise is not only trustworthy as a general statement, but also that it had been shown to be true. Reference to Yahweh as a shield for all who take refuge in him shows that what he had previously been for David (v. 2) can now be applied to all who take refuge in him. The climax of the stanza is thus to declare that what had been true for David can now be experienced by all who align themselves with Yahweh.

31–34. Having linked David's experience to that of others, the fourth stanza explores the significance of this for the wider community. After the opening verse, the focus is on what Yahweh has done for David, but, as verse 31 opens with questions aimed at the wider audience, it becomes clear that the goal is to show that David's experience of Yahweh provides a pattern for others. The starting point is recognizing that there is no God but Yahweh, nor any rock but Israel's God. Again, the language evokes verse 2. There David could refer to Yahweh as 'my God' and 'my rock'. These terms can now be claimed by the wider community for whom they can also be true. David's own example can then be recounted in verses 32–34. Yahweh has equipped David with valour (cf. v. 39) and made his way blameless, echoing verse 23. Here, there is an important paradox in which David's ability to walk in Yahweh's way is both a commitment David makes and something Yahweh enables. Echoing Habakkuk 3:19, David speaks of being given feet like a hind and being enabled to walk on the heights. The image reflects the ability of hinds to walk on very steep hillsides and remain secure. This defensive image is balanced by the offensive element in describing how Yahweh has taught him to bend a bronze bow as preparation for war.

35–36. The poem shifts from addressing a wider audience to speaking directly to Yahweh, though the wider audience overhear. Here, David emphasizes that his successes are due to Yahweh, who has protected him as a shield, whose right hand has upheld him and whose condescension has made him great. Once again, language of Yahweh as a shield of salvation echoes verse 2, providing examples of how the general statements there have worked out in David's life. Similarly, reference to Yahweh's creating a wide space for his steps draws on the statement in verse 19. David's address to Yahweh here thus invites readers to see how all the elements of the first stanza have worked out as expressions of Yahweh's condescension towards David.

37–45. David continues to address Yahweh in the victory reports provided here, each of which continues to be overheard by a wider audience. Throughout this strophe, there is a balance between David's achievements and the things Yahweh has done. David has been successful, but his successes have occurred because of what Yahweh has done. If Yahweh has provided David with secure footing, then this is why he can pursue his enemies and overtake them, continuing battle until victory is complete so that they are now destroyed and under his feet. The reason this was possible was because Yahweh had enabled him while also causing those who rose against David either to bow down before him or to flee, presenting their backs to him. Those who hated David were destroyed even if they cried out because apart from Yahweh there could be no saviour, and because he was with David, he was not with those opposed to him. The tension between David's achievements and the reality of what Yahweh has done for him is especially clear in verses

42–43. On the one hand, David can claim to have beaten his enemies, so they are like dust before the wind, but on the other he also acknowledges that Yahweh delivered him from contention with others while granting him an exalted status as head over various nations, perhaps reflecting the victories reported in 2 Samuel 8:1–14. It was because of Yahweh that foreigners left their own places of security and became David's servants, including those David had not previously known. Yahweh continued to be David's place of security, but (considering what Yahweh had done for David) his enemies would abandon theirs.

46–50. It is because David's achievements ultimately depend on Yahweh that the closing stanza focuses on praising Yahweh. The stanza's opening intentionally echoes the psalm's beginning, blessing Yahweh as the living God who is David's rock and source of salvation (cf. v. 2), statements for which the rest of the psalm has provided evidence. Verse 47 then echoes verses 31, 34, the boundaries of the opening strophe of the fourth stanza through its declaration about what God has done, reporting this in verse 48. Unlike the victory reports with which the previous stanza closed, here the focus is on what Yahweh has done in subduing peoples, delivering David from his enemies and exalting him from those who rose against him, most notably from the 'man of violence'. Given the heading, this could be a reference to Saul, though it can also refer to all the opponents. Characterizing them this way makes clear that the vengeance David gained is what was needed to defeat violence. All this leads to David's promising to praise Yahweh among the nations. This praise was initiated in verse 1, but is now to be shared among the nations because Yahweh has led these nations to submit to David. This is because it is Yahweh who brings great salvation for his king, who shows kindness to his anointed; that is, to David and his descendants for ever. The closing verse joins with the title in referring to David in the third person, but in so doing adds the titles 'king' and 'anointed' to him in addition to the title 'Yahweh's servant' from the title. By stressing that these aspects of Yahweh's commitment to David continue, the psalm takes on a messianic cast, anticipating that Yahweh will demonstrate this again. Moreover, the community who have celebrated Yahweh's victories through David and who know that Yahweh has shown himself to be greater than all the foes David faced are reassured that Yahweh continues to work for his servant. Although this is challenged in Psalm 89 (cf. Broyles 1999: 107), this is the pattern finally affirmed by the Psalter.

Explanation

Psalm 18 is a long and complex poem that contains a range of elements. As well as being important as a poem itself, it also plays an important role within the collection of poems that is Psalms 18–24. This means that although it is essentially the same poem as occurs in 2 Samuel 22, we must still read it in its current literary setting and allow each to control our reading (cf. Beuken 2020: 105). This is strongly shaped by connections to Psalms 17, 19, but even more so by the title, which indicates that it represents words sung by David at a point of significant victory. The title does not have to mean that David is the poem's author – it perhaps means that David took up an existing text. If so, we do not need to find an exact match between David's experience and every element of the poem so much as look for general points of coherence. Read this way, there are significant points of contact that can be noted between David's experience in Samuel (1 Chronicles does not seem to form a literary background) that match what is described here. But the literary presentation of David is not restricted to Samuel here as the connections with Psalm 17 (also a 'Davidic' psalm) provide a framework for reading at least the third stanza of this poem since the poet in Psalm 17 looks to be cleared of a charge, and David here celebrates a positive judgement from Yahweh.

Most importantly, Psalm 18 commences with a rare declaration of love for Yahweh, so that the rest of the psalm then explains the reasons for that love. What emerges through the subsequent stanzas is that David outlines reasons for this love, all of which is grounded in the security Yahweh has provided. Each of the following stanzas reflects on these opening themes. The second stanza demonstrates this through a theophany report, which shows the power of Yahweh that has saved David from his enemies. The third stanza then brings in Yahweh's statutes and judgement to show that he has ultimately affirmed David, while the fourth then demonstrates that whatever victories David has won were achieved because of Yahweh's presence with him. In this stanza, the audience who encounter this psalm are encouraged to see the truth of these matters for themselves. The final stanza, with important links back to the first then praises Yahweh for his continued work, not only for David but also for his descendants. This final stanza makes clear the messianic cast of the final poem as it looks beyond David's own experiences to anticipate points where Yahweh would overcome foes and provide security for those descendants. David's own experience provides a pattern that looks forward to those times when God will again do such things for a descendant of David (cf. Gerstenberger 1988: 100, though without the composition as late as he suggests). As the Psalter was likely edited after the exile when there was no king, this further accentuates this element in the poem. This hope lies behind Zechariah's words (Luke 1:69), but also leads into Psalm 19, which continues to encourage faithfulness to Yahweh's word while waiting for the messianic reign to come. Paul also takes up this psalm (Rom. 15:9), seeing the promise of praise among the nations finding its hope in Jesus (cf. Longman 2014: 117).

PSALM 19

Translation

The director's. A melody. Davidic.

1The heavens recount the glory of God,
  the firmament declares the works of his hands.
2Day to day pours out speech,
  night to night announces knowledge.
3There is neither speech nor words,
  whose voice is not heard.
4Their measuring line has gone out into all the earth,
  their words to the ends of the world.
For the sun, he pitched a tent in them,
  5and it is a like a bridegroom coming forth from his chamber,
  it exults like a warrior to run the race.
6It goes forth from one end of the heavens,
  and its circuit is to their end,
  nothing is hidden from its heat.

7The Torah of Yahweh is perfect,
  reviving life,
the testimony of Yahweh is trustworthy,
  making the simple wise.
8The precepts of Yahweh are upright,
  making the heart glad,
the commandment of Yahweh is pure,
  enlightening the eyes.
9The fear of Yahweh is clean,
  enduring for ever,
the ordinances of Yahweh are true,
  they are altogether righteous.
10They are more desirable than gold,
  than much pure gold,
they are sweeter than honey,
  even flowing honey in the comb.
11Indeed, your servant is instructed by them,
  in keeping them is great reward.

12Errors, who can discern?
  Acquit me from hidden faults!
13Also, restrain the insolent from your servant,
  may they not rule over me.
Then I shall be blameless

and innocent of great transgression.
[14]May the words of my mouth
and the meditations of my heart
be pleasing to you
Yahweh, my rock and my redeemer.

Notes on the text

3. *bělî* can be a negation (esp. for a pass. ptc.), but at other points implies a restriction. Many EVV (e.g. ESV) translate as a negative, but this seems to create an unnecessary tension with the previous lines. Similarly, Goldingay (2006a: 288).

Form and structure

Psalm 19 stands at the centre of Psalms 15–24. Indeed, if the paired royal psalms that follow (20–21) are treated together, a chiasm can be noted (see Sumpter 2013: 186). Even if this larger structure is not accepted, the relationship between it and Psalms 18 and 20–21 is clear. The pattern of linking royal psalms with Torah is an important one in the Psalter, and Grant (2004: 112) has noted an extensive range of textual links that join these psalms. We have already noted some of the associations with the motif of Torah in Psalm 18 (see 'Form and structure' on Ps. 18), largely because these were unexpected in a royal psalm. Conversely, the motif of Yahweh as the psalmist's rock (v. 14) is unique in a Torah psalm, yet here it functions as a key theme in the closing prayer. Its place near the beginning of Psalm 18 (v. 2) and its placement at the end of this psalm forms an envelope around this pair. Perhaps more importantly, given the importance of prayer as a key theme for the whole of 15–24, it ties together the themes of kingship, Torah and prayer at the concluding point of this psalm while preparing for the prayers about kingship that follow in Psalms 20–21. In addition, the title of Psalm 18 refers to David as Yahweh's servant, while the poet here twice uses the self-description of 'your servant' (vv. 11, 13). The request for acquittal (v. 12) also links this poem with Psalm 17 through Psalm 18.

Psalm 19's inclusion among the Torah psalms is not disputed, though in fact the term *tôrâ* (law) occurs only once (v. 7). Rather like Psalm 119 (which seems to use it as a template; cf. Firth 2015b: 72), it uses a series of synonyms in verses 7–9, exploring the range of what Yahweh's instruction looks like. Whichever term is used, Yahweh's instruction is shown to be lifegiving, consistent with the picture in Psalm 1:3. Nevertheless, the Torah theme is not introduced until verse 7. Verses 1–6 can be understood as a creation hymn, one that speaks of God (*'ělōhîm*), whereas in verses 7–14 the name Yahweh is used. Also, verses 12–14 are clearly a prayer. Form-critical analysis may suggest that these components are all separate, leading Seybold (1996: 85) to observe that the central problem in this psalm's interpretation is the question of its unity.

The solution to this issue is to note that even though Psalm 19 is a Torah psalm, this category is defined more by the presence of certain vocabulary than structure, whereas the other elements are recognizable by their form (and hence one can note wisdom motifs here too; see Cheung 2015: 164–176). Once we recognize that both the creation hymn and the meditation on Torah build to the closing petitions, with solar imagery throughout, it becomes clear that the whole poem is a prayer (J. R. Wagner 1999). Both creation and Torah provide the poet with a means of understanding Yahweh and the appropriate way of living before him. It is this knowledge that leads to the closing petitions. It remains possible that the poet has drawn on existing components (so, Kraus 1988: 269), but if so, they have all been shaped to form a coherent prayer with key linguistic connections across the components (W. P. Brown 2002: 83).

Accordingly, the poem can be analysed in three stanzas:

1. God speaks through creation (1–6)
2. God speaks through his word (7–11)
3. Prayer of response (12–14)

Comment

Title: On 'The director's', see on Psalm 4. For 'A melody. Davidic', see on Psalm 3.

1–6. The poem opens by introducing the key theme that runs through the first two stanzas, that of divine speech. In this first stanza, the more generic 'God' is used rather than the covenant name 'Yahweh'. While this may reflect original source material, in the final form it maintains an important distinction between the more general forms of speech outlined in this stanza compared with the covenant-specific language of Torah in the second stanza. Yet even without access to Torah, the psalm stresses the abundance of divine speech. Creation points to God's glory, with the ptcs. in verse 1 emphasizing the enduring nature of this announcement. This is confirmed in verse 2, where the poem shifts to impf. verbs alongside references to both day and night. There is an internal connection between these verses in that the heavens also mark day and night. If all this points to the glory of God, then it is also the knowledge that is announced. Creation's speech is not abstract but rather about God's glory. Verse 3 poses a challenge to interpretation, especially as commonly translated, since it suggests that this abundant speech is not heard, though verse 4 seems to indicate it is. As translated here (cf. 'Notes on the text'), the point is that all speech can be heard, and that indeed the measuring line of speech from creation about God's glory has reached the ends of the earth (cf. Rom. 10:18). There has been abundance of speech, but to this point there is no evidence of a response, perhaps because, although the poem describes speech, everything in creation is experienced visually (Klouda 2000; W. P. Brown 2002: 84). Indeed, all knowledge within the psalm is essentially embodied, related to lived experience (Coetzee 2009a). Having moved from the heavens to the earth in verses 1–4b, in verse 4c we return once more to the heavens to track the movement of the sun. Just as speech about God's glory reaches the earth, so also the heat from the sun. The presentation of the sun here knows, but resists, the common mythologies of the time (cf. Vesco 2006, 2: 207–208) that treated the sun as a deity of justice. Instead, it is a phenomenon of the heavens under God's control – it has a tent in which to spend the night because God has pitched it in the heavens. Its daily rising and setting are like divine speech going out with the eagerness of a bridegroom going to his wedding or a champion stepping out to battle, though its circuit brings it nightly back to its tent. As such, its daily circuit is another means by which the heavens declare God's glory. Yet in spite of the sun's importance, key elements in the balance of the poem show that its role has been taken over by Yahweh's word (cf. W. P. Brown 2002: 92–94).

7–11. An abrupt change in poetic form occurs here even as the theme of divine speech continues to dominate. A series of six synonyms introduces a series of short lines in verses 7–9, each pointing to the written word. As the terms used are all relevant to the covenant, they are all followed by the name Yahweh and then a word describing them. The second part line is then two words describing how the relevant term is lifegiving. Although it is possible to distinguish the various terms, each of Torah, testimony, precepts, commandment and ordinances are probably intended as broadly synonymous, pointing to all the ways Yahweh's written word is understood. As such, the 'fear of Yahweh' stands out, as it elsewhere reflects an attitude towards Yahweh rather than his word. But here the statement that it endures for ever is odd if it is only a human attitude towards Yahweh. Perhaps here it is to be understood as the point where Yahweh's word and human response engage one another and, in that, Yahweh continues to speak. Irrespective of the term used, Yahweh's word does what humans cannot, perhaps why many of the elements here have a parallel in Psalm 18 in describing what Yahweh himself does. Here, Yahweh's word not only revives life – it also gives shape to life through the provision of skills needed to flourish; perhaps why the synonym list is bound by reference to its perfection and trustworthiness. In every way it achieves more than the speech of creation. Creation's speech enabled the knowledge of God, but the written word permits knowledge of Yahweh's will (cf. Sommer 2015). It is this that makes Yahweh's word so desirable, whether thought of in terms of an abundance of wealth or pleasures like fine honey – note the similarity in colour for gold and honey that may suggest this comparison. All this is then applied in the life of the poet, who closes this stanza by pointing out that the claims made in verses 7–9 are borne out in personal experience, indicating that the experiences described there are the reward that has been experienced.

12–14. A further transition occurs here as the focus shifts from divine to human speech. Creation tells about God, and in his word Yahweh has spoken. But humans are not always fully self-aware, and so the poet begins by noting that anyone may unintentionally act in ways inconsistent with Torah. That is why Yahweh needs to acquit the poet from hidden faults. Where verse 12 looks inward to note problems hidden from us, verse 13 considers the possible effects of others, asking that the insolent not rule over the poet since this would be inconsistent with a life shaped by Torah. Yahweh's power enables the poet to live a blameless life, one marked by appropriate speech, and thus one consistent with Torah itself. This kind of life was anticipated in Psalm 15:2. The means to such a life begins with human speech, whether words physically uttered or thought about, which, like a sacrifice (cf. Lev. 1:3) are pleasing to Yahweh. If Yahweh is the poet's rock and redeemer, then he is the one who provides security and restoration. The poet's desire is thus to live in a manner pleasing to Yahweh. Hence, the closing prayer, the aim of the whole psalm, is that Yahweh enable the poet's speech to fulfil that goal.

Explanation

Speech is central to this psalm. It begins by observing that all creation continually speaks of God's glory. This speech is helpful, but although it reaches all the earth, it has limits. Those limits do not affect Yahweh's written word, whichever term for Torah is used. Rather, this word itself provides nourishment and sustenance, much as was already suggested by Psalm 1. Through this word it is possible to live a life pleasing to Yahweh. Nevertheless, although it is important to take nourishment from this word, it is still Yahweh himself who enables the poet to live the life that pleases him, a life that also begins with human speech, whether uttered or not. Humans can therefore learn much by studying creation, and this should ultimately point us to the glory of God. But more important still is to live a life in relationship to God, one shaped by his written word and that asks God to shape us, so we please him (cf. Cook 2018: 100–101). Wealth and luxury goods do not compensate for this. Rather, we can understand who we are only in relation to God, living to please God by asking him to enable this. As McCann (1996: 753) points out, this is the antithesis of the creed of autonomy of modern society, one that sends us back to live by the word of God alone (Matt. 4:4). The psalm assures us that such a life is truly worth living.

PSALM 20

Translation

The director's. A melody. Davidic.

1May Yahweh answer you in the day of distress,
may the name of the God of Jacob set you securely on high.
2May he send you help from the sanctuary
and from Zion may he sustain you.
3May he remember all your offerings
and your burnt offerings may he find acceptable. *Selah*.
4May he grant your heart's desire,
may he fulfil all your plans.
5May we cry aloud at your victory,
in the name of our God may we set up a banner.
May Yahweh fulfil all your requests.

6Now I know that Yahweh saves his anointed,
he answers him from his holy heavens
in the saving might of his right hand.
7Some acknowledge their chariots, and some their horses,
but we will acknowledge the name of Yahweh our God.
8They shall bow down and fall
but we shall rise and be restored!
9Save the king, Yahweh!
Answer us on the day we call!

Notes on the text

5. LXX (cf. NEB) presumes *ngdl* for MT *ndgl*, but MT is retained as *lectio difficilior*.

9. Moving *atnach* to *hamelek* and reading (with Tg and LXX) *w'nnv* for *y'nnv*. For a defence of MT, see deClaissé-Walford et al. 2014: 219.

Form and structure

Psalm 20 is rightly classified as a royal psalm, again one with some messianic significance. The term *měšîaḥ* occurs in verse 6 (cf. Pss 2:2; 18:50), though the immediate point of reference is clearly the king prayed for. As always with royal psalms, the designation emerges from language associated with the king, and all the royal psalms could be classified in other ways. In this case, the bulk of the psalm is a prayer for Yahweh's blessing on the king. The king must always face the trouble of battle, but the prayer reminds him that Yahweh is his source of salvation. The context of a coming battle seems likely (though Weiser [1962: 205–206] links it instead to his proposed New Year's festival), but the Psalter's inclusion of the psalm opens this prayer up to any believer (so, deClaissé-Walford et al. 2014: 215). Nevertheless, reference to so many cultic activities demonstrates that the psalm is to be read first against a cultic background, concerned with the king's military needs. Within the structure of the Psalter, though, it is now paired with Psalm 21, which is a thanksgiving for the sort of victory requested here.

As a royal psalm, it naturally shares important vocabulary with Psalm 18 while also anticipating Psalm 21. As well as use of *mĕšîaḥ*, Yahweh is said in Psalms 18:36 and 20:6 to support the king, while enemies falling before the king is also a shared motif (Pss 18:39; 20:8). There are less direct links to Psalm 19, though of course it ends with a prayer while Psalm 20 commences with one. Nevertheless, it should be noted that Psalm 19:15 asked for a heart pleasing to Yahweh while Psalm 20:4 asks that Yahweh grant the desire of the king's heart, linking the prayers (cf. Vesco 2006, 2: 213).

The structure is relatively straightforward. Reference to Yahweh's answering provides an inclusio that can otherwise be analysed into two stanzas, each concluding with a petition:

1. Prayer for Yahweh's blessing (1–5)
2. Confidence in Yahweh's protection (6–9)

Comment

Title: Identical to Psalms 19, 21, a further mechanism linking these psalms. For 'The director's', see on Psalm 4. For 'A melody. Davidic', see on Psalm 3.

1–5. The first stanza commences with a series of jussives (though Brueggemann and Bellinger 2014: 104, are open to the possibility that they are impfs.), each of which expresses a wish that Yahweh act for an initially unnamed 'you'. These wishes pivot around the *selah* at the end of verse 3, moving from a focus on acts of worship to points where victory is given. The opening wish is that Yahweh respond to prayers offered on the day of distress (cf. 1 Sam. 7:7–9), an item later bookended with the community's own prayer (v. 9). A day of distress need not refer to battle, but the larger context indicates that this is the intent. It is the 'name' of the God of Jacob that is to place this person in a high and secure place. 'Name' here stands for God, while also preparing for the community's own acknowledgement of Yahweh's name (vv. 5, 7). 'God of Jacob' occurs elsewhere in psalms with a focus on Jerusalem (e.g. Pss 46:7, 11; 76:6;

81:1), and this is consistent with the request that God send help from the sanctuary. Although *qōdeš* is not a common term for the sanctuary, this sense occurs elsewhere in Psalms (Pss 24:3; 63:2; 68:24), and the parallel with Zion makes clear that the temple is meant. It is from there that God should provide support, especially as this is where the various offerings, grain and animal, will have been presented. As God cannot be manipulated, these are not automatically accepted, which is why the prayer asks that they be accepted (cf. Broyles 1999: 111). From verse 4 the stanza moves to focus on what is desired for the person relative to others. The desires of the heart and plans would presumably be included in prayers Yahweh was to answer (v. 1) but, as verse 5 makes clear, they are for victory that Yahweh will grant, demonstrating that the day of distress in verse 1 was the day of battle. Verse 5 also shifts from wishes about what Yahweh will do for this person to what the community may do as they cry aloud at the victory. Such a cry can be in distress (Lam. 2:19), but here is clearly joyful. Raising a banner reflects a military tradition (Exod. 17:15) that marked a victory, so both shout and banner celebrate victory. That the banner is set up in 'the name of our God' points back to the mention of God's name in verse 1, while also making clear that Yahweh has given the victory, and in doing so granted the person's requests.

6–9. An individual speaker now emerges and makes clear that the one prayed for in the first stanza is the king. Just as reference to God's name bookends the first stanza, mention of the king bookends the second. Here, the king is initially called Yahweh's 'anointed'. This can refer to other figures chosen by Yahweh such as a priest (Exod. 28:11) or prophet (1 Kgs 19:16), though in Psalms it is always the king, apart from Psalm 105:15, where it is Israel. The speaker's identity is unclear. The larger context, with its reference to cultic activities, may suggest a priest, though Grogan (2008: 70) thinks it could be the king. Whoever it is, the opening declaration indicates that some piece of new knowledge has been achieved, seeing that Yahweh has answered the king's prayers. 'Answer' is thus not only used to bookend the poem overall; it is also a pivot around which it turns. Yahweh's 'saving' the king also employs a verb (*yš'*) cognate to the noun 'victory'. This is achieved with his saving right hand (again from *yš'*), indicating the place of honour given to the king (cf. Ps. 110:1). In contrast therefore to other nations who may find their hope in advanced military equipment (horses and chariots), the community announce that they will place their trust in the name of Yahweh their God (cf. Deut. 20:1–4; Cornell 2020: 137), again highlighting the 'name' motif. The verb *zkr* here is unusual for the theme of 'trust' as commonly translated (e.g. ESV) since it is most associated with remembering, but it is chosen because it echoes the request in verse 3. Israel expresses its trust by reminding itself of Yahweh's name. It is through his work that their enemies shall bow and fall whereas they will rise and be restored. Yet one victory is not the end of conflict for the nation, and so the psalm closes with an urgent prayer that Yahweh save the king, echoing the language of victory in verses 6–7. Each new day of distress requires Yahweh's intervention because only then can they continue to remember him. Beyond this, the people ask that Yahweh continue to answer when they call. Yahweh is not only to answer the king. He is to answer all the people because all are to remember him, even as he remembers their commitment to him. God answers prayer, and in that there is hope.

Explanation

The idea of a hymn before battle may sound strange to us, unless we identify our nation with Israel in the OT, a move the NT would discourage. More fundamentally, we need to note that the central point is that God's people trust him, not weapons (cf. Eph. 6:10–20). Understood in those terms, the prayer has a wider applicability, especially when prayed through Christ's victory. The final analysis reminds us that God is indeed a warrior on behalf of his people, and force is his prerogative, not ours. We are also reminded that God is active on behalf of his people, and final victory is his. Unlike the people of Israel, we do not need to pray for Christ's victory (Kraus 1988: 282). However, we are challenged by a prayer like this. We may have the level of insight reached here through a relationship with Jesus, and if so are called to live in the light of his victory and to allow this to shape our prayer.

PSALM 21

Translation

The director's. A melody. Davidic.

1Yahweh, in your strength the king rejoices,
  and in your victory how greatly he rejoices.
2The desire of his heart you have granted to him
  and the request of his lips you have not refused. *Selah.*
3Because you met him with blessings of goodness,
  and placed a crown of pure gold on his head.
4Life he asked of you; you gave it to him,
  length of days for ever and ever.
5Great is his glory in your victory,
  splendour and majesty have you bestowed on him,
6for you give him eternal blessings,
  you make him rejoice in the gladness of your presence.

[7]For the king trusts in Yahweh,
and by the kindness of the Most High he will not stumble.

[8]Your hand will find out all your enemies,
your right hand will find those who hate you.
[9]You shall make them like a fiery furnace
at the time of your appearing.
In his wrath Yahweh will swallow them,
fire will consume them.
[10]You will destroy their fruit from the earth,
and their seed from humankind.
[11]When they stretch out evil against you,
when they devise a wicked scheme, they shall not prevail.
[12]For you will make them turn their back
when you set your bow at them.

[13]Be exalted, Yahweh, in your strength,
let us sing and make melody in your might.

Notes on the text

1. Reading *yāgel* with Q and many MSS.

10. *BHS* sets 'Yahweh' as a voc. at the end of the previous line. Although this is metrically more regular, it makes more sense as the subject of verse 9b.

12. *mêtār* is lit. 'bowstring' but here stands for the whole bow.

Form and structure

Psalm 21 is a royal psalm paired with Psalm 20 (cf. Quinn 2023: 137–142). The former prays for a king before a battle, anticipating victory, whereas Psalm 21 is a thanksgiving for victory. Psalm 20 asks Yahweh for victory, and now Yahweh is thanked for it. As such, there is also important vocabulary shared that joins these psalms, notably mention of Yahweh's right hand (Pss 20:6; 21:8) and 'might' (*gĕbûrâ*; Pss 20:6; 21:13) and emphasis on the fact that the victory is Yahweh's (Pss 20:5; 21:1, 5). These psalms are also joined to Psalm 19 by their shared title, and through it also connect to Psalm 18, with which Psalm 21 has shared themes since both are royal thanksgivings. How this might have been performed has led to numerous proposals about links with various festivals. Although many remain plausible (e.g. Terrien 2003, 2: 220–223), it is better to attend to the context provided by Psalms 15–24 and read this as a thanksgiving that demonstrates the validity of prayers such as Psalm 20.

Psalm 21 is bounded by reference to Yahweh's 'strength' ('ōz; vv. 1, 13), while the motif of joy appears at key points through the poem (vv. 1, 6). Though more complex analyses are possible (cf. Auffret 1990), the poem can be analysed into two stanzas, each of which contains two strophes. In each, the first strophe contains six bicola while the second is a single bicolon, though the bicola are shorter in the second stanza. This leads to the following:

1. Rejoicing in Yahweh's victory (1–7)
   a. Victory won by Yahweh (1–6)
   b. Royal trust (7)
2. Assurance of future victory (8–13)
   a. Destruction of enemies (8–12)
   b. National celebration (13)

Comment

Title: Identical to Psalms 19, 20. On 'The director's', see on Psalm 4. For 'A melody. Davidic', see on Psalm 3.

1–6. The first stanza focuses on what Yahweh has achieved for the king, something emphasized through the opening voc. Yahweh is addressed because he has won the victory. The king therefore cannot rejoice in his own strength but only in Yahweh's. Knowledge of Yahweh's strength can give confidence before the battle, but, as is made clear in verse 1b, the victory is Yahweh's, and it is this that is a source of joy. Verse 2 can thus look back to earlier prayers, both those wished and those spoken, and note that Yahweh has responded. The *selah* at the end of verse 2 provides a suitable moment of pause before noting ways Yahweh has acted for the king in verses 3–4. The verbs here could refer to Yahweh's provision at a specific battle, in which case mention of blessings and the crown are both ways of pointing to the victory Yahweh has given the king. If a festal background is appropriate, they could refer to various ways Yahweh acts for the king. But since verse 4 seems to refer to a specific prayer for life, a natural request before battle, we should probably read verse 3 as describing the victory, with the blessings of goodness being the victory itself, while the crown would point to the king's status. Such a reading then flows in verse 5, which makes clear that the king's glory in victory is great, but all of this is because it is Yahweh's victory, and the king's splendour and majesty have been bestowed on him by Yahweh. Just as the king asked for enduring life, so the blessings Yahweh gives are not restricted to the battle, but look also beyond that point, enabling the king to rejoice in Yahweh's presence.

7. Both stanzas conclude with a reflective statement. Since this stanza is focused on Yahweh's victory for the king, this verse notes that the king trusts in Yahweh. Such trust is an extension of the community's announcement in Psalm 20:7. Although there is a change in the verb to *bṭḥ* (*zkr* in Ps. 20:7), there is a clear thematic link because this victory was not won through horses or other forms of military might but through Yahweh. Because of this trust, Israel can be confident that the king will not stumble, because of the power of Yahweh's kindness. The king's not stumbling evokes Psalms 15:5, 16:8 and 17:5, showing that the king's trust demonstrates the kind of life commended by Psalm 15. That the king will not stumble because of Yahweh's kindness also prepares for the assurances given in the second stanza, making this verse a bridge between the stanzas.

8–12. The second stanza addresses an undefined 'you' who could be Yahweh (thus continuing the pattern of stanza 1; so de Suva 1995: 54–55) or the king. Although there is no initial marker, that Yahweh is spoken of in the third person in verse 9b means it is more likely that the king is addressed. The verbs here are most probably focused on the future, offering assurance that Yahweh continues to act for the king. Mention of Yahweh means that although the king hears a message of assurance, he is reminded that it is ultimately Yahweh who enables these things. As such, although the king's hand will find out his enemies, the enemies found also need to be Yahweh's adversaries. This makes sense of the prayer for victory in Psalm 20 – the king still needs to have found favour with Yahweh for him to act. But if that condition is met, then the assurance is not only that he will find his enemies, but also that Yahweh will destroy them. This is portrayed in verse 9 through a pair of bicola, both of which work with the image of fire, a point that brings together the king's actions with Yahweh's. Together, the elements of verse 9 stress that Yahweh's presence with the king, something for which the poet prayed in Psalm 17:15, is the point where his enemies are destroyed. Such destruction is comprehensive, though hyperbolic (cf. deClaissé-Walford et al. 2014: 225), their 'fruit' here referring to their influence while their 'seed' not only picks up the image of fruit but also refers to their descendants. The king's enemies may therefore plot against him, but they cannot prevail, because Yahweh stands with his king when his people are attacked. As Goldingay (2006a: 317) points out, this means Yahweh's commitment is only defensive. Because of this, the enemies flee before him when they see the king's bow aimed at them.

13. The second stanza responds to the message of assurance by asking that Yahweh be exalted, raised on high, a term principally used for worship in Psalms. Indeed, apart from Psalm 74:3, the imperative of *rûm* (be exalted) is always directed towards Yahweh's exaltation, often in the context of victories won (cf. Ps. 99:5, 9). Here, it is Yahweh's strength, employed to grant the king victory, that provides the context for exaltation. It is Yahweh's strength, not the king's, which makes the difference (cf. McCann 1996: 757). The proper response to this is worship, which is why the community commits themselves to making music to praise Yahweh's might, linking this assurance to that requested in Psalm 20:6.

Explanation

Following the prayer for the king's victory in Psalm 20, Psalm 21 offers thanksgiving for granting just such a victory. It provides a liturgical reminder of the fact that Yahweh answers prayer and an opportunity to voice this in thanksgiving that is ultimately taken up by the whole community. The thanksgiving also instructs the king and the community about continuing to trust Yahweh to provide victories for his king. But at this point, the psalm's placement along with Psalm 20 is particularly important. Psalm 20 prays that Yahweh will accept the king and grant victory, showing that the king cannot presume upon it. It creates important conditions through which the assurances of Psalm 21 are also to be read, reminding the king and the community that these assurances are in the context of a right relationship with Yahweh, one where the king submits to Yahweh's reign (Mays 1994b: 103). If this condition is met, the community can follow the pattern of the king and trust Yahweh while anticipating times when they will be those giving thanks. Contemporary leaders may not have the king's authority, but this continues to provide an appropriate pattern to be followed.

Christian reading of the psalm will naturally focus on the victory Jesus has won in his death and resurrection. It is his victory – the point where God's great power was most obviously evident (Eph. 1:20) – that assures us that God's power continues to be available to believers today since this same power is at work in us (Eph. 3:20).

PSALM 22

Translation

The director's. According to the doe of the morning. A melody. Davidic.

[1]My God, my God – why have you forsaken me,
  far from saving me, from the words I roar?
[2]My God, I call by day, but you do not answer,
  at night and I have no rest.
[3]But you are holy,
  enthroned on the praises of Israel.
[4]Our ancestors trusted you,
  they trusted and you delivered them!

5 To you they cried and were delivered,
in you they trusted and were not put to shame.

6 But I am a grub and not a human,
the reproach of humankind and despised by people.
7 Everyone who sees me mocks me,
they deride with the lip; they wag the head.
8 'Commit to Yahweh! Let him deliver him,
let him rescue him because he delights in him.'
9 Yet you are the one who brought me forth from the belly,
making me trust you at my mother's breasts.
10 On you was I cast from the womb,
from my mother's belly you are my God.

11 Do not be far from me because distress is near,
no one helps.
12 Many bulls surround me,
mighty ones from Bashan encircle me.
13 They open their mouths against me,
a lion tearing and roaring.
14 I am poured out like waters,
all my bones are dislocated,
my heart is like wax,
it has melted within my bowels.
15 My strength is dried up like a potsherd,
my tongue clings to my palate,
you have laid me down in the dust of death.
16 For dogs surround me,
an assembly of evildoers encompasses me,
they have pierced my hands and my feet.
17 I can count all my bones,
they gloat, they stare at me.
18 They divide my garments for themselves,
and they cast the lot for my clothing.
19 But you, O Yahweh, do not be far,
O my strength, make haste to help me.
20 Rescue my life from the sword,
my only life from the power of a dog.
21 Save me from the mouth of a lion,
from the horns of the wild ox answer me.

22 I will recount your name to my kin,
in the midst of the assembly, I shall praise you.
23 Those who fear Yahweh, praise him,
honour him, all seed of Jacob,

stand in awe of him, all seed of Israel!
24 For he has not despised
nor has he spurned the lament of the weak,
He has not hidden his face from him.
and heard when he cried to him.
25 From you is my praise in the great assembly,
my vows shall I fulfil before those who fear him.

26 The afflicted shall eat and be satisfied,
those who seek Yahweh shall praise him,
may your heart live for ever!
27 All the ends of the earth shall remember and return to Yahweh,
yes, all the clans of the nations shall worship before you,
28 for the kingdom is Yahweh's,
and dominion in the nations.
29 The desirable of the earth shall eat and worship,
all those going down to the dust shall kneel before him,
even the one who could not stay alive.
30 Posterity shall serve him,
a coming generation will be told of the Lord.
31 They will come and speak of his righteousness,
To a people unborn, that 'He has acted.'

Notes on the text

8. Tg suggests *gal* (cf. Matt. 27:43). MT is retained, but the text is difficult.

16. With some MSS, read *k'rw* for *k'ry*, though even with this the text remains difficult. See A. P. Ross 2011: 523–524. The verb *k'r* means 'to dig', so 'pierced' is just possible, though *k'r* Vg (in *DCH*) suggests 'shrivel' (cf. NRSV).

21. Reading *'ănîtānî* as a prec. pf. See W-O §30.4.5.c–d, Armitage 2010 and Andrason 2013: 10.

Form and structure

With its opening words quoted by Jesus on the cross (Mark 15:34), this is perhaps the best-known complaint psalm, especially one that complains about God. Its significance for Jesus himself and for understanding his death cannot be overstated in Christian theology, a fact that becomes clearer when we note the extent to which this psalm has been woven into the whole account of Jesus' death by the evangelists. Staying only with Mark, it is possible to trace allusions to this psalm in Mark 9:12, 15:24, 29 as well as the direct citation at 15:34. Nevertheless, our first task is to understand the psalm in its immediate context within the Psalter because until this is done, we cannot understand the use made of it by the NT writers (cf. Pierce 2008: 259–260). Our primary task here is interpreting the psalm within the Psalter, though some brief comments on its reception in the NT can be offered. In passing, it should be noted that *Midrash Tehellim* identifies this psalm as Esther's prayer when about to risk her life for her people (Esth. 4; cf. Menn 2000: 317–327).

The poem follows two royal psalms, both of which stressed that Israel's king is ultimately subservient to Yahweh. Although Israel asks that Yahweh save the king (Ps. 20:9), they also know that Yahweh is to be exalted (Ps. 21:13). This complaint takes this theme seriously, showing that Yahweh is seated on Israel's praises, and is thus Israel's ultimate king (Ps. 22:3), a point stressed in the declaration that the kingdom is Yahweh's (Ps. 22:29). The language of the kingdom of God may be more familiar from the NT, but finds a clear antecedent here. The place where Yahweh is seated is where the psalmist's own praises will be recounted (v. 22). Such praises do not belong only to the powerful (such as a king) but are something that even the afflicted can offer. Such language could be spoken by the king, but the possibility of prayer and praise is also democratized by this psalm. As such, connections with Psalm 17 should also be noted, especially in the motif of being surrounded by enemies (Pss 17:8–10; 22:12–13, 16). These links matter because these poems have similar structural positions within the block of Psalms 15–24 (W. P. Brown 2010). Without excluding the king, the psalm thus shows that Yahweh's acts of deliverance are also accessible to a wider audience precisely because Yahweh is Israel's ultimate king (cf. Vesco 2006, 2: 221).

Critical discussion has also focused on the psalm's unity, principally the possibility that verses 22–31 are secondary to the original poem (for a summary, see Broyles 1989: 187–189). There are good reasons to think that verses 1–21 might indeed have been an original poem in that they assume deliverance is needed, while verses 22–31 give thanks because deliverance has been provided (similarly, Goldingay 2006a: 323–324). However, there are clear connections across the entire psalm, so even if someone has added to an existing poem, it has been done in a manner consistent with what has gone before. In doing so, the contrasting situations have been allowed to stand, but in a way that also demonstrates the realities earlier psalms in this collection have stressed – that Yahweh does indeed respond to the prayers of his people.

Structurally, there is a clear division at the end of verse 21 in the shift from complaint to thanksgiving, indicating that there are two main stanzas (cf. Patterson 2004: 216–217), though each can be subdivided further. A simplified analysis would suggest the following structure:

1. *Complaint*: request to be saved (1–21)
   a. Experience of divine absence (1–5)

   b. Contrast between human taunts and experience of Yahweh (6–10)
   c. Appeal for divine nearness (11–21)
2. *Thanksgiving*: testimony to others (22–31)
   a. Vow of praise (22–25)
   b. Hope of universal worship (26–31)

Comment

Title: On 'The director's', see on Psalm 4. For 'A melody. Davidic' see on Psalm 3. The 'doe of the morning' may be a tune or refer to some ritual activity (Sawyer 2011: 297). It is not mentioned elsewhere. However, the 'doe' picks up an important term from Psalm 18:33, while anticipating Psalm 29:8.

1–5. The opening is dramatic. The repeated 'My God' has no direct parallel in the Psalter. There is a sharp contrast between the fact that the poet speaks of 'my God' and yet asserts divine abandonment. The psalmist has 'roared' (*šʾg*) a complaint of divine distance but has not been saved. The verb *šʾg* establishes the intensity of the psalmist's cries while also introducing the lion motif (cf. v. 13), which is linked to wider animal imagery through the appeal. More typical terms for calling to God are used in verse 2, but where verse 1 points to their intensity, now the focus is on their persistence. Day and night the poet has called (cf. Ps. 88:1), but there has been no answer, leaving the poet without rest. All of this is contrary to the psalmist's expectations. These expectations have been shaped around God's holiness as the one who received Israel's praises. That God is seated on these praises could be understood as enthronement (so e.g. ESV), though the more neutral 'seated' can also be retained since the specific language of God's kingship is made explicit only in the second stanza. That God is holy is the basis of Israel's worship, something worked out in the experience of previous generations who had trusted him and been delivered. Their cries had been heard and so they were not ashamed. But this is not the poet's experience. The one who had delivered others has abandoned the psalmist. Indeed, like Psalm 6, the claim is that God is the problem.

6–10. Instead of deliverance, the psalm now describes the experience of mockery from others that seemingly contradicts the faith passed on since birth. The opening 'But I' marks a contrast between what the poet has experienced and what was expected. The poet's self-description of being a 'grub and not a human' is not an objective statement but rather a deeply subjective one. As a human, the psalmist expects that God would have acted, but that this has not happened suggests comparative insignificance (cf. G. T. M. Prinsloo 1995a: 70). Reproach from others, not deliverance, is the experience to this point. We cannot know what that reproach was. However, Psalm 15:3 had indicated that the righteous do not engage in such practices, making clear that this experience here was unjustified. For reasons now unclear, others saw the psalmist as someone to be mocked and sneered at, with wagging the head also indicating scorn. The reproaches of others are summarized in the unmarked quote attributed to them. Sarcastically, they suggest that the poet commit (literally 'roll') to Yahweh so that he can deliver the poet. Their expectation, though, is that this will not happen. The problem for the poet, though, is that if God remains distant, then these reproaches, though offered sarcastically, summarize what is happening, reinforcing the conflict between received faith and experience. This faith has been the poet's since birth, a birth where God was active in enabling a safe delivery and in encouraging trust in him even while a suckling. From birth, the psalmist has had no other God.

11–21. A long third strophe now begins the process of bringing together experience and faith, even if it ends without reaching resolution. The opening appeal that God be not far from the psalmist anticipates an appeal that will be made more fully in verses 19–21. Divine distance was introduced as a problem in verse 1, so the statement that there was no helper near continues the theme of divine absence. Where God was distant, distress was near. It is the distress that dominates verses 12–18. Its emphasis on animal imagery portrays the psalmist as someone hunted down by various animals (with possible mythic overtones), though these represent the people previously hurling abuse. All these animals represent a threat. So, the bulls are threatening because of their strength and especially their horns. That they represent humans is perhaps evident in the description of the bulls opening their mouths against the poet, something that indicates the mockery that has been received. But this mockery is not simply verbal since it is also compared to the acts of a roaring lion seeking prey. The poet faces verbal abuse and a threat to life. The threat posed is debilitating, with verses 14–15 providing a series of metaphors showing this. In verse 14 these metaphors take what is normally solid (bones, the heart) and treats them as liquids. By contrast, verse 15 uses the image of things that have been dried up – a broken potsherd is something fired in a kiln and so lacking moisture, while the tongue cleaves to the palate due to thirst. All this leads to the accusation directed to God that he has laid the poet in the dust of death. Life's vibrancy is lost in all that is dry and desiccated, and God has placed the poet in this position. Although some enemies are described as a pack of dogs surrounding the poet, God is ultimately responsible for the psalmist's suffering. The enemies are still dangerous and have perhaps already wounded the poet. Along with their threat, that the poet can 'count all my bones' may indicate that illness is an issue, though it could also be a more general reference to suffering while being stared at by gloating foes. From the perspective of the foes, the psalmist is already as good as dead, which is why they can gamble for the poet's clothes. It is because the root of the problem sits with Yahweh that the poet appeals directly to him in verses 19–21. The enemies are a threat precisely because Yahweh is seemingly distant, and so the appeal is made for Yahweh to be closer; indeed, as the source of the poet's strength, Yahweh needs to make haste and help. A distant and remote deity is not what is needed. The psalmist's life is under threat, and it is Yahweh who needs to rescue it, whether that threat is conceived of as a sword, a dog, or a lion. Hence, along with these forms of threat we also have a clustering of salvation terms (help, rescue, save), all of which look for Yahweh to do what has so far not happened. The final verb in verse 22 has been variously understood, but if it is a prec. (see 'Notes on the text') then it emphasizes the poet's expectation of an answer and hence prepares for what follows in the second stanza.

22–25. Emerging from the poet's confidence that Yahweh will answer the prayer of the first stanza, the second opens with a vow of praise that assumes the deliverance has happened. Where previously the poet could speak of counting bones (v. 17), now the promise is to recount Yahweh's name – here standing for his character – in praise offered in the assembly. Indeed, the language of praise dominates verses 22–23 as the poet's praise is picked up by those who reverence Yahweh and then taken up by all Israel who honour Yahweh and stand in awe of him. Such a response assumes that the requested salvation has occurred. This is confirmed by the verbs in verse 24 that look back to a prior act of deliverance. In form, the verse notes three things Yahweh has *not* done – he has not despised or spurned the lament of the weak, nor hidden his face from them. Rather, he has heard their cry for help. Although these lines describe Yahweh's actions for the needy in general, they also refer to the poet's own experience. This is clear from the psalmist's observation that it is Yahweh who enables praise in the great assembly, while also providing a reason for the poet to fulfil any vows before those who fear Yahweh. The language of praise, the assembly and those who fear Yahweh repeats terms from earlier in the strophe, creating a boundary around the first strophe in this stanza.

26–31. The second strophe moves beyond the praise of the poet and the community of Israel to anticipate universal praise grounded in Yahweh's kingship. Admittedly, the translation is uncertain at key points, but the general trend is clear enough. In this stanza's first strophe, praise was traced outwards from the psalmist to the rest of Israel. In this second strophe, praise is traced outwards to the rest of the world. The starting point of this is Yahweh's commitment to the afflicted that will lead to the afflicted eating and being satisfied, while those who seek Yahweh will praise him. The afflicted and those seeking Yahweh could still be Israelites but, as the psalm progresses, a wider community are drawn to worship. This may already be anticipated in the closing line of verse 26 where the wish for a group's heart to live for ever (perhaps, to remain in understanding) refers to those who seek Yahweh. As we move into verse 27, the community that are to recall and return to Yahweh come from the ends of the earth as all the clans of nations shall worship. Such worship echoes Genesis 12:1–3 (similarly, Longman 2014: 132), anticipating the moment when all the clans shall seek blessing in Abraham. This is possible because the kingdom is Yahweh's, and his kingdom is not restricted to Israel but is over all the nations. The desired of the earth, here understood as the people that would be most admired, will come and worship (an act that includes eating). These were those previously headed for the dust but, unlike the poet's sense in verse 15, there is now the hope of life from Yahweh. Although there is no expectation of resurrection here, verse 30 does anticipate future generations who will serve Yahweh as they are told about him. The language of verse 30 picks up on the motif of recounting from verse 22 except that this is now the act of future generations, even those not yet born, who can speak of Yahweh's righteousness and that he does indeed act. Where the psalm opens with Yahweh's seeming absence from the poet, it closes with universal acknowledgement of Yahweh's presence and deeds. Rather than abandonment, the psalm closes with a declaration that Yahweh has acted.

Explanation

Psalm 22 provides a prayer from the depths, one where the poet has a profound sense of being abandoned by God. This abandonment stands in contrast to the faith of Israel with its emphasis on the nearness of God. For the poet, this is not an abstract discussion of theology but a very real matter of life and death. In addition to the deep sense of abandonment, the psalmist claims to have been laid in the dust of death by Yahweh. Rather than Yahweh's being the giver of life, the psalmist's experience of him is one of death. Such an experience contrasts markedly with what Yahweh has given the king in Psalm 21, a seeming contradiction to all that has been learned about God to this point. Yet, while the psalm sees Yahweh very much as the problem, it also presents him as the solution. Yahweh's coming near to the psalmist will enable life to be lived once more, but he must act quickly. All this stands in marked contrast to the second stanza with its emphasis on giving thanks to Yahweh, with the poet's thanksgiving spreading first to Israel and then to the ends of the earth as Yahweh's kingdom is declared among the nations and to generations unborn. It is an astonishing change, but pivotal to understanding this psalm. Psalms 20–21 laid a foundation for understanding the kingdom as Yahweh's. Even if the king is the individual through whom Yahweh's enemies are destroyed (Ps. 21:8–12), it is still Yahweh who does this. Those enemies are also Yahweh's enemies, and therefore it is not only the king but all the people who can trust him (Ps. 20:8). This reality is crucial here and enables the psalmist as a representative Israelite to trust that Yahweh will be true to his character and intervene. If Yahweh intervenes to save his people, then this is something to be proclaimed in praise, and the nature of that praise cannot be restricted but must reach the ends of the earth. Starting from the depths of abandonment, Psalm 22 sees that Yahweh will be true to his character and so anticipates the point where his kingdom is seen by all (cf. Davis 1992a).

This provides important background to Jesus' use of the psalm, and indeed its wider use in the NT. The psalm assumes that the one who suffers does so unjustly (partly through the link to Ps. 17). Although claims of unjust suffering in the Psalms do not assume sinlessness on the part of the one who prays, this is certainly a feature of the passion narrative. Jesus is the one whose suffering has no basis in justice and yet who suffers for others. Of course, nothing makes this clearer than the fact that Jesus cites the psalm while on the cross. We cannot know if he cites the whole psalm or just the opening verses (cf. Janowski 2013: 337–338), but the way the psalm is woven into the narrative suggests that we are to read the account in the light of all of it. The resurrection will show that Jesus was not ultimately abandoned (cf. Heb. 2:11–12). Rather, the resurrection is the great demonstration of the kingdom of God, and in the Matthean and Lukan accounts leads to the commission to share the good news with all the world (Matt. 28:16–20; Luke 24:44–49), precisely what the second stanza of the psalm has already anticipated. That all will ultimately recount this good news reminds us that this psalm does not end with Jesus' use of it but rather that his use reminds us all how we may continue to cry out (against Schaefer 2001: 57).

PSALM 23

Translation

A melody. Davidic.

1Yahweh is my shepherd,
  I shall not be in want.
2He grants me repose in green meadows,
  he guides me unto waters of rest.
3He refreshes my life,
  he leads me on right tracks
  for his name's sake.
4Even when I go through the valley of death's shadow,
  I fear no harm,

for you are with me,
  your rod and your staff
  they comfort me.

[5]You lay a table for me
  before my enemies,
you anoint my head with oil,
  my cup is well filled.
[6]Surely goodness and kindness shall pursue me
  all the days of my life,
and I shall return to the house of Yahweh
  endless days.

Notes on the text

4. Hebr. *ṣalmawet* is split into two words (*ṣel mawet*) to produce the traditional 'valley of the shadow of death'. The word is difficult and may mean 'darkest shadow'.

6. The common rendering 'I shall dwell in the house of Yahweh' involves emending *šabtî* to *šibtî* (cf. Ps. 27:4). But MT should stand. See also Knauf 2001.

Form and structure

Psalm 23 is perhaps the Psalter's best-known poem, a text that provides pictures of trusting Yahweh that have resonated with many through the ages. Despite this, disputes about its interpretation are legion, perhaps because the highly metaphorical language throughout means it can be read across a range of backgrounds – whether cultic, royal or individual (for the options, see A. P. Ross 2011: 555–556). Its life setting may be difficult to determine, but it can be read as a psalm of confidence (Miller 1986: 112–119) because this motif does not depend on any one life setting. Once again, its setting within the Psalter provides clearer guidance on its interpretation. Within the structure of Psalms 15–24, it provides an important balance to Psalm 16, a poem also primarily an expression of trust. That psalm followed an entrance liturgy that focused on encouraging those who would dwell in Yahweh's presence to work this out in relationships with others. Psalm 23 is an expression of trust that leads into Psalm 24, another entrance liturgy that likewise encourages positive relationships with others. The closing reference to the temple here is an important bridge to what follows. This bridge also draws on Psalm 22, which emphasizes Yahweh's kingship (Ps. 22:28), a motif also evident in Psalm 24:8. Although the language of kingship does not occur in Psalm 23, its two central metaphors (Yahweh as shepherd and host) both draw on common kingship motifs across the ANE (cf. Böckle 2021: 198–200). The confidence expressed in Psalm 23 also has its roots in the turning point of Psalm 22:21, where the closing verb could simultaneously appeal to Yahweh and express confidence. Psalm 22:1–21 describes an experience that could well be described as 'the valley of death's shadow' before coming to a point of confidence, and that turn continues here. Hence, the psalm's confidence is contextualized by the psalms around it, especially if the feast in verse 5 echoes the hope of Psalm 22:26.

Although complex structural features operate across the psalm (cf. Tappy 1995: 256–259), it can be analysed in two stanzas based on the dominant metaphor at each point:

1. Yahweh as shepherd (1–4)
2. Yahweh as host (5–6)

Comment

Title: For 'A melody. Davidic', see on Psalm 3.

1–4. The psalm's opening line is widely recognized perhaps because the personal nature of faith is clearly expressed here. It is crucial to note that referring to Yahweh as shepherd is principally to speak of him as king, a metaphor occurring elsewhere in Psalms (e.g. Pss 28, 80, 100) and the OT more generally (e.g. Jer. 23:1–8; cf. Vos 2020: 637). But where kings can be distant, Yahweh is a shepherd close to the psalmist, caring as a shepherd should for the flock. Yahweh is not a shepherd who rules to his own advantage, something elsewhere condemned (Ezek. 34:1–10). Rather, he exercises care to provide for and protect his flock. That provision is expressed in the simple declaration that 'I shall not be in want.' This does not suggest any excess of provision but rather that what is needed is there even if the nature of that provision is not made explicit. Provision certainly includes sufficient food and drink, which is evident in the green meadows and waters of rest, both of which indicate giving what is needed for sustenance. But the life lived with Yahweh is not only about the basics. The grassy meadows are also a place where Yahweh grants repose and the waters are a place of rest. Both terms indicate that Yahweh's care for his flock includes the provision of security since 'rest' is often experienced through the absence of external threat (e.g. 2 Sam. 7:1). Yahweh as shepherd provides sustenance and security. The poet can thus testify that Yahweh 'refreshes my life'. As shepherd-king, Yahweh provides a context where life can thrive. But this thriving is not an end in itself. Instead, Yahweh leads on right tracks (cf. Ps. 17:5). These tracks can be understood as safe paths that can be walked, but they are also the way that is consistent with his character (cf. deClaissé-Walford et al. 2014: 242; Abernethy 2015b). They are right because the sheep do not get lost, whether that is understood as the classic problem of leading sheep from one place to another or at the level of ethical and theological faithfulness to Yahweh, suggesting also a connection here with the wisdom literature (Botha 2015). This is why Yahweh leads his flock for his name's sake – the flock need to be kept safe, but the flock are themselves also to reflect his character. Yahweh's goodness and provision for his people are seen most clearly when his people walk on his tracks rather than on their own. To this point, it is possible to imagine that Yahweh's shepherding means the flock endures no threat. But as David's experience makes clear, this is not true of the experience of any shepherd (1 Sam. 17:34–37) since they are responsible for protecting the flock in the face of threat. Likewise, Yahweh's protection of the flock is not only in the absence of threat but also in the most difficult of places, here described as the valley of death's shadow. A narrow and dark valley could be a place of threat for a flock where particular vigilance was needed, and Yahweh continues to protect even in these places. Fear of harm was unnecessary, even in such places, because of Yahweh's presence. At this point of greatest threat the poem moves from speaking about Yahweh, perhaps spoken to other worshippers, to address him directly, suggesting that the intimacy with Yahweh hinted at in verse 1 is particularly experienced in times of threat. At this point, Yahweh's rod and staff are a source of comfort. These are the shepherd's tools of the trade, something to fight off threats and help with walking. But the rod can also be a royal sceptre (Pss 2:9; 45:6), while 2 Kings 18:21 could suggest that the staff may also be a royal symbol. Comfort is found, even in the face of threat, because Yahweh is shepherd and king.

5–6. The direct address to Yahweh introduced in verse 4b continues here, ensuring that there is a clear link between the two metaphors. Yahweh is no longer a shepherd. Instead, he is a banquet host. Nel (2005: 99–100) places the metaphor of the host within the domain of the shepherd, but it is better to see both metaphors as pointing to the dominant claim that Yahweh is king. Although anyone could (in theory) host a banquet, they were particularly associated with royalty since they demonstrated the king's power and wealth (e.g. Esth. 1:3–9). This feast happens in Yahweh's house, the temple, which was also his palace. Such a feast could emerge from Israel's worship, though the feast here could still be a metaphor. Just as Yahweh had protected in the valley of death's shadow, so he protects here even as he lays on a feast since the feast is laid on a table before the poet's enemies. The valley of death's shadow speaks of Yahweh's protection in a metaphorical key, but to speak of enemies is to make the threat even more real. Yet even in this context, Yahweh continues to provide generously, anointing the psalmist's head with oil. The image here does not attribute royalty to the poet since the verb for 'anointing' here is *dšn* rather than *mšḥ*, one not associated with royalty. It provides another image of Yahweh's providing refreshment since the oil would be refreshing in a warm and dry climate. The banquet is also generous so that the poet's cup is well filled. There is no lack, so even in the presence of enemies, the psalmist continues to experience provision and protection. This leads to the declaration of verse 6 (again, addressing others) that goodness and kindness would continually pursue the poet. The traditional 'follow' here is far too weak. Instead, goodness and kindness are personified, chasing the poet down so that the poet can never get away from them (even if such should be desired). A life marked by Yahweh's provision and protection experiences goodness and kindness, something greater than any enemies. For this reason, the poet will always return to Yahweh's house. It may not be the place of permanent dwelling (though it is permissible to desire such a thing; cf. Ps. 27:4), but it is always the poet's home base since this is the place where one is always reminded of Yahweh's provision and protection. This return also prepares for the entrance to the temple in Psalm 24.

Explanation

Yahweh is king, and he is the one who both provides for and protects his people. This is the good news celebrated by this psalm. As those under his care, goodness and kindness will pursue his people ensuring provision and protection, and this reminds us that worship is at the heart of what it means to be God's people. None of this means that believers avoid challenge and struggle. But Yahweh journeys with his people in places of great threat: he is present and providing even in the presence of enemies. No human king ever matched this standard, and Israel's kings were often condemned for failing to understand how Yahweh's kingship was expressed. Readers coming from Psalm 22 have been reminded of the possibility of continuing to hope in Yahweh as king, and this is confirmed here, even as it anticipates further reflection on this motif in Psalm 24. Yahweh's kingship provides no easy answers, but it does provide hope.

Israel's kings did not live out what it meant to shepherd their people like this (cf. 1 Kgs 22:17), but Jesus takes up the language of this psalm in describing himself (John 10:1–18). In describing himself as the good shepherd he shows that he is the one who truly protects his flock, even though it involves his own death, and through this he also provides for them. Likewise, in Mark 6:30–44, he is the shepherd who provides for his people. Here, again is good news of a God who provides for the needs of his flock and protects them.

PSALM 24

Translation

Davidic. A melody.

1 The earth and all its fullness is Yahweh's,
  the world and those dwelling on it.
2 For he founded it upon the waters,
  and upon the rivers he established it.

3 Who may ascend Yahweh's mountain,
  who may stand in his holy place?
4 The clean of hand and the pure of heart,
  who do not lift themselves to what is false,
  nor swear deceitfully.
5 They shall obtain a blessing from Yahweh,
  and righteousness from the God of their salvation.
6 This is the generation of those who seek him,
  who seek your face Jacob. *Selah.*

7 Lift up your heads, O gates,
  and lift yourselves O ancient doors,
  that the glorious king may come in.
8 Who is this glorious king?
  Yahweh, powerful and mighty,
  Yahweh, mighty in battle
9 Lift up your heads, O gates,
  and lift up O ancient doors,
  that the glorious king may come in.
10 Who is he, this glorious king?
  Yahweh of Hosts,
  he is the glorious king. *Selah.*

Notes on the text

4. With many MSS, read *napšō* for L's *napšî.*

6. Read with Q, *dōrĕšāyb*. Most EVV follow LXX and read 'the face of the God of Jacob' (see ESV) rather than 'your face Jacob'. For a defence of this option, see Owens 2013: 63–64. The early variants are probably attempts to understand MT (cf. Duke 2011: 221). As MT explains the existence of the others, it is retained. See Sumpter 2015: 79–82.

Form and structure

Balancing Psalm 15, the opening psalm of the unit Psalms 15–24, this poem is another entrance liturgy, one that again stresses the ethical life of those who would worship at the temple. Like Psalm 15, it uses a question-and-answer format, but unlike Psalm 15 deploys this across the second and third stanzas. The tone of these questions, especially in a context focused on access to the temple, gives a clearly liturgical feel to the poem. Attempts to go beyond this and identify a particular liturgical occasion that gave rise to it (outlined in Owens 2013: 66–67) have been less successful, perhaps because liturgy is meant to be applicable in a range of circumstances. As Botha (2009: 549–551) argues, the psalm now functions to challenge readers to consider what it means to be a worshipper of Yahweh while also highlighting Yahweh's power. In recognizing this, the absence of the question-and-answer form in the first stanza is important because it establishes the context from which the subsequent material is to be interpreted.

As well as appreciating its liturgical form, the literary context is important for interpretation. Readers coming from Psalm 23:6 have seen the importance of returning to the temple, and the 'right tracks' (Ps. 23:3) would include a life ethically committed to Yahweh. This life is exemplified in the second stanza here with its focus on clean hands and pure hearts. There are clear links between this pattern of life and that encouraged in Psalm 15:2–5. As such, Psalm 24 provides a close to the block that began at Psalm 15. Yet, just as Psalm 15 was also joined to Psalm 14, so also introduction of the 'heart' motif here prepares for its prominence in the following poems (25:17; 28:3; 31:24). As a liturgy, it both prepares for those who come to the temple for worship and sends them out to live according to Yahweh's values.

Various attempts have been made to separate the psalm into discrete parts – Seybold (1996: 103–104) believes it consists of three relatively independent parts. However, as the whole poem is centred on the theme of entering Yahweh's presence, it seems better to see it as a unity built around three stanzas:

1. Declaration: Yahweh is creator (1–2)
2. Questions about entering Yahweh's presence (3–6)
3. Questions about Yahweh's character (7–10)

Comment

Title: The title reverses the elements from Psalm 23. For the elements, see on Psalm 3.

1–2. The psalm opens with an emphatic statement – the earth and everything in it belongs to Yahweh. This is not restricted to physical objects since anything or anyone who lives in the world also belongs to Yahweh. Yahweh's ownership of all is stressed by the word order, which begins (lit.) 'To Yahweh is the earth'. Verse 2 then points to Yahweh's work in creation as the basis for this. Although the verbs here are about Yahweh's 'founding' (*ysd*) and 'establishing' (*kwn*) the world rather than the more common verbs for creating (*br'*, *'śh*), they have semantic overlap (Kumpmann 2016: 48–50) and work well with the concept of the world being founded on the waters. Mention of the waters and rivers here is representative of the world view that saw the earth as being between the waters above and the waters below the expanse (Gen. 1:7). Both 'Sea' and 'River' were venerated as deities in Canaanite tradition, but are stripped of that status here, simply describing the place where Yahweh established the earth. As Yahweh has established the earth, it is not floating on these waters but firmly held in place. Yahweh has created a world that can be inhabited and filled. Although 'founded' represents a past act, the final verb in verse 2 would suggest his continued involvement with creation. All belongs to Yahweh because he is the creator who continues to engage with his creation. That is why Paul can encourage believers to enjoy all foods, even engaging in meals with non-believers, because nothing can change the fact that all ultimately belongs to God (1 Cor. 10:26).

3–6. If all the world belongs to Yahweh, then access to his temple is a special privilege. Hence, the second stanza reflects on who can go there. Verse 3 thus poses a double question, though in focus they come to a single point. As with Psalm 15, the question of 'who' does not seek to identify a specific individual. Rather, it provides a context to explore the character of those who would enter the temple by ascending that part of Mount Zion where the temple was found and then entering it. The character of that person is then defined in verse 4 by making two positive statements which are then defined by two negatives. The positive statements are that this person must have clean hands and a pure heart. These body parts reflect on both an outward and inward dimension of the person. Their hands stand for their acts, and these are to be clean. The adjective 'clean' (*nāqî*) does not refer to ritual cleanness but rather indicates that the hands of this person are exempt from actions that would trigger guilt with reference to others. For example, Psalm 15:5 indicates that those who enter Yahweh's presence do not take a bribe against the 'innocent' (*nāqî*), creating another link between these psalms. Those coming into Yahweh's presence have not acted in ways that harm others. Alongside this, they have demonstrated purity of heart. The 'heart' often points to human volition and in Psalm 15:2 is the place where those entering Yahweh's presence speak truth about others. Both Psalms 15 and 24 thus focus on the outward and inward dimension of the character of those entering the sanctuary. These positive statements are balanced by two negations that focus on the person's relationship with Yahweh. Not lifting themselves to what is 'false' (*šāwĕ'*) probably alludes to Exodus 20:7 and the prohibition on bearing Yahweh's name falsely (cf. Imes 2018). Those who bear Yahweh's name are meant to act in a manner consistent with this status, which is why treacherous oaths are also forbidden, again echoing Psalm 15:2. Where such people have not 'lifted' (*nś'*) themselves to what is false, they now 'obtain' (*nś'*) a blessing from Yahweh. The content of the blessing is not outlined unless it is a declaration of righteousness from God (a very Pauline note, well before Paul! Cf. Broyles 1999: 130). If so, it would represent the right to be in Yahweh's presence in the sanctuary (cf. Owens 2013: 76–81). This would be consistent with the reference to Yahweh as the God of their salvation – it is Yahweh who enables those who live for him to be with him. Verse 6 then generalizes this so that the 'who' of verse 4 can be understood as a generation of those who seek Yahweh. Nevertheless, we need to note that MT speaks of those who 'seek your face Jacob'. But once we understand that 'Jacob' is here parallel to 'generation', we can see that those who seek Yahweh are defined as 'Jacob' and thus the true people of Yahweh (cf. Botha 2009: 539–540).

7–10. A new set of (possibly antiphonal) liturgical questions occurs in this final stanza, though now instead of focusing on the worshipper's character attention is given to Yahweh's. Taking up the key word 'lift' (*nś'*) from the second stanza, this stanza initially addresses the gates. From the context, these are the temple gates. They need to lift their heads so that the glorious king may enter. Since ancient gates did not go up, a physical description of the gates' movement is unlikely unless there is an expectation of the lintels being lifted. But lifting the head could also be an idiom that tells another to take courage (cf. Judg. 8:28, where an inability to lift one's head points to a loss of courage). Likewise, the ancient doors of the temple need to open to enable this king's entry, though a lifted head would also enable these gates to see the king in his procession. The glorious king is not initially identified, though given that he needs to be admitted the assumption is that he is outside the sanctuary. Leaving the glorious king unidentified enables the question of verse 8. Only now is the king identified as Yahweh, though he is then defined in terms of his military capacity – Yahweh is strong and mighty, mighty in battle. The striking assumption here is that Yahweh is outside the sanctuary, whereas the second stanza had assumed that one encountered Yahweh in the temple. This is why we need the context established by the first stanza – if all the world is Yahweh's, then there is no limit to where he can be encountered even if it is possible to think of special ways in which he may be encountered. Verse 9 is almost a repetition of verse 7, again addressing the gates and doors that they may open for the glorious king's entry. Verse 10 is likewise almost a repetition of verse 8, except that this time the title is Yahweh of Hosts; that is, the one in charge of the heavenly armies. Hence, it is not only the inhabited world and the waters beneath that belong to Yahweh. Everything in the heavens belongs to him too, which is why he truly is the glorious king of all creation.

Explanation

Yahweh is king of all, and therefore no other can claim his authority. This is the decisive claim of this psalm. Throughout their history, Israel encountered others who would deny this, whether an invading king like Sennacherib (2 Kgs 18 – 19) or association with deities worshipped by others. The temptation was always to permit Yahweh's glory and authority to be shared with others. But this psalm resists this, insisting instead that those who gain access to worship Yahweh live in ways that reflect his character as they engage with others. Worshippers may be tempted to look inward but, rather than ritual, this psalm joins with Psalm 15 in insisting that ethics is the most effective form of worship. This does not mean the psalm sees no place for worship at the sanctuary because it is there that the worshipping community most truly see what it means to know that Yahweh is the glorious king of all creation. Worshippers today face similar challenges as politicians, armies and cultured despisers of Christian faith encourage us to look elsewhere for authority. But this psalm will not let us do so. Rather, as those who live in the now and not yet that is the kingdom of God as initiated by Jesus, we are called to practise the justice of the kingdom in our relationships with others even as we glimpse the glorious king in our own times of gathered worship. And in naming Jesus as Lord, we declare with this psalm that no other can be. If so, and the world is his, then this calls us to act as stewards of his world (Mott 2018).

PSALM 25

Translation

Davidic.

1To you, O Yahweh, I lift myself.
2O my God, I trust in you,
  let me not be put to shame,
  let not my enemies exult over me.
3Indeed, may all who wait for you not be put to shame,

may those who act treacherously without cause be put to shame.
4Show me your ways O Yahweh,
teach me your paths.
5Lead me in your truth and teach me,
for you are the God of my salvation,
for you do I wait all day long.
6Remember your compassion O Yahweh, and your kindness,
for they are from of old.
7Do not remember the sins of my youth or my transgressions,
according to your kindness remember me,
for the sake of your goodness O Yahweh.

8Good and upright is Yahweh,
therefore, he instructs sinners in the way.
9He leads the afflicted in the way of justice,
and teaches the afflicted his way.
10All the paths of Yahweh are kindness and truth,
for those who keep his covenant and testimonies.
11For the sake of your name, O Yahweh,
pardon my iniquity for it is great.
12Who is the one who fears Yahweh?
he will instruct that one in the way to choose.
13That one shall abide in what is good,
and their seed shall possess the land.
14Yahweh's counsel is for those who fear him,
he makes known his covenant to them.

15My eyes are continually towards Yahweh,
for he brings my feet out from the net.
16Turn to me and be gracious to me,
for I am lonely and afflicted.
17The distresses of my heart are enlarged,
bring me out from my distresses!
18See my affliction and my trouble,
and forgive all my sins.
19See my enemies, for they are many,
that they hate me with violent enmity.
20Guard my life and deliver me!
Let me not be put to shame because I have taken refuge in you.
21May integrity and uprightness preserve me,
because I hope in you.

22Redeem Israel, O God,
from all its distresses.

Notes on the text

5. Some MSS add an expected *wĕ* at the start of the final part line of the verse.

18. The absence of a qoph at this point has led to proposals to reconstruct one, but none are persuasive. It is highly likely that this acrostic would have had a *q* line, but we have no certain evidence to reconstruct it.

Form and structure

Psalm 25 commences a new block within Book 1 that continues to Psalm 34. As with Psalm 15, which introduced Psalms 15–24, this is a bridge poem that has links to what has gone before while also introducing this section. The block is bounded by acrostic poems (Pss 25, 34), both of which have the idiosyncrasy of an additional pe line at the end of the poem, something not evident in the Psalter's other acrostics (Pss 9–10 [partial], 37, 111, 112, 119, 145). The block is centred on Psalm 29 and gives special emphasis to the temple (Vesco 2006, 2: 257; Botha and Weber 2019: 20–22). Such an emphasis was already in evidence in Psalms 15–24 with its boundary-marking entrance liturgies (Pss 15, 24). However, those psalms emphasized movement away from the temple through ethical engagement, a theme less evident in this block.

As a bridge psalm (Robertson [2015a: 227–228] does note this but sees the structural role of this psalm differently), there are important connections with Psalm 24. Notably, both psalms use rhetorical questions (24:3, 8, 10; 25:11), though there are also important points of shared vocabulary. Both speak of Yahweh as the 'God of [one's] salvation' (Ps. 24:5; 25:4) and use the idiom of 'lifting oneself' (24:4; 25:1). These connections, especially when combined with the frequent requests for instruction, suggest that this poem can be read as a request to learn how to live in the pattern established in Psalm 24.

An acrostic, one of several wisdom influences (cf. Human 1996), Psalm 25 commences each verse with the successive letters of the Hebrew alphabet save for the presence of two *r* lines (vv. 18–19) and no *q* line where it would be expected (v. 18; see 'Notes on the text'). The *w* line (v. 5c) is also textually uncertain (see 'Notes on the text'), while the *b* line is achieved through a slight adjustment to the colometry (following LXX). There is also the additional *p* line (v. 22), which stands outside the main structure. The missing letters from the alphabet may simply be evidence of textual corruption, but the additional *p* line is clearly an intentional addition to the structure. As an acrostic, it may be thought that the poem would have no other structuring device than the alphabet, but it does show broad development and can be analysed in four stanzas:

1. Prayer for guidance (1–7)
2. The character of Yahweh (8–14)
3. Prayer for personal deliverance and forgiveness (15–21)
4. Prayer for national deliverance (22)

Comment

Title: For 'Davidic', see on Psalm 3.

1–7. Although not exact, the first stanza is broadly in the first person, whereas the second is in the third. The third stanza returns to the first-person emphasis. So, the poem commences with the poet turning to Yahweh. To 'lift up' one's 'being' (*nepeš*) is to present oneself to Yahweh as an act of commitment (cf. Pss 86:4; 143:8). This is made clear by the declaration of having trusted in Yahweh in verse 2. But it becomes clear that the reason for reporting this is that the poet faces a threat of some sort. That is why the poet immediately asks not to be put to shame. 'Shame' is a key word in verses 2–3. Since it is contrasted with enemies exulting over the poet, it is evident that shame would be caused should Yahweh fail to act for the psalmist. At the same time the poet asks that all those hoping in Yahweh not be put to shame. Instead, those who act treacherously, seeking their own goals, are the ones who should be put to shame. Shame occurs either when Yahweh does not act for those who are faithful to him or when those who ignore his ways discover him working against them. The poet desires to live as one faithful to Yahweh, but there are two potential barriers to this – either lack of awareness of Yahweh's ways, or sin which is a barrier between the poet and Yahweh. The balance of this stanza thus addresses these two issues. First, verses 4–5 ask that Yahweh instruct the poet in his ways. The 'way' metaphor is a common one in the Psalter, having been clearly established in Psalm 1. As with that psalm, the assumption here is that there are two ways – Yahweh's or the way of the wicked (the enemies who would exult over the psalmist). Nevertheless, knowledge alone is insufficient. Hence, although verse 4 asks for instruction, verse 5 extends this by asking that Yahweh lead the poet in his truth along with teaching. This is grounded in the fact that Yahweh is 'the God of my salvation', and thus the one in whom it is right that the poet should hope. The poet acknowledges that whoever the enemies are, they can be overcome only through Yahweh, but fundamental to that is Yahweh's teaching and leading. The other barrier (sin), points to where the poet has not walked in Yahweh's ways and so needs forgiveness. For these to be addressed, Yahweh needs to engage in an act of remembering and of not forgetting. The act of remembering is to remember his compassion and kindness, since these are fundamental to his character. In remembering these, the poet then asks that Yahweh not remember the poet's sins. This is grounded in Yahweh's character as one who is good. This part of the prayer also echoes Exodus 34:6–7 and Yahweh's self-disclosure as one who is gracious and compassionate, forgiving sin and iniquity. The request is that previous sin not disqualify the poet from a secure relationship with Yahweh, and that Yahweh take this forward by leading the psalmist in his ways.

8–14. Aspects of Yahweh's character gradually came to the fore through the first stanza, so this second stanza is principally concerned with exploring this in the light of the prayer focus of the first while also preparing for the third. There are important verbal links that join all three stanzas, and that is immediately apparent here. The first stanza ended by mentioning Yahweh's 'goodness' (*ṭûb*), while the second opens by declaring that Yahweh is 'good' (*ṭôb*) and upright, which is also why he teaches sinners in the way. Likewise, the act of teaching and leading the afflicted is both something for which the poet has prayed, and a fundamental of Yahweh's character. The important addition here is that his leading of the afflicted is in the way of justice, though this is here closely aligned with the truth in the earlier request (v. 5), as Yahweh's ways are also said to be those of 'kindness' (*ḥesed*) and truth for those who keep his covenant and testimonies. That is, there is a proper shape to a relationship with Yahweh, which is defined by covenant, most probably a reference to the Sinai covenant given the allusions to Exodus 34. The predominant shape of this second stanza is punctuated by verse 11, very much the midpoint of the poem (Doyle 2001), as a return to the request for forgiveness, this time asking that Yahweh pardon the poet's iniquity. The shift back to the first person gives particular focus to this request, while use of the verb 'pardon' (*slḥ*) makes clear that this is something only Yahweh can do. Having referred to the events of Exodus 34, the poet has made clear that such acts of pardon are fundamental to Yahweh's character (represented by Yahweh's name), so even though this first-person request breaks the pattern of the stanza, it is still integrated into it. This prepares for the description of those who fear Yahweh in verses 12–14. The question that opens verse 12 is essentially rhetorical, like those of Psalm 24. The poet is the one who fears Yahweh and therefore can expect to be taught the way to choose, a way that permits abiding in what is good. The 'good' here is principally a positive relationship with Yahweh and thus one that does not involve shame, evidence for which is the possession of the land. Moreover, such a person receives more than simple teaching, since Yahweh's counsel is also provided, the subtler guidance needed in working out how life in covenant is to be lived.

15–21. The third stanza is predominantly in the first person and is again a prayer, one that moves from the poet to the nation, even as it continues to focus on themes of forgiveness. Just as the first stanza opened by focusing on the poet's commitment to Yahweh, so also the third commences by noting that the psalmist's eyes are continually on

Yahweh. In this instance, the reason is that Yahweh brings the psalmist's feet out from a net; that is, acts that protect the poet from the acts of enemies. At the same time, there is also a need for Yahweh to turn to the poet and be gracious, a request that echoes the priestly blessing (Num. 6:24–26). The poet needs an alignment with Yahweh because, in a setting of affliction, it is Yahweh who can act (cf. v. 9), and such an act is one of grace. The distress that the poet experiences is both external and internal. The presence of a net points to enemies, but in verse 17 the psalmist also admits to distress of heart, a will that struggles to remain in alignment with Yahweh. Just as Yahweh has brought the poet's feet out from the net, so also Yahweh needs to bring the poet out from this distress. As the text now stands, both verses 18, 19 commence with a request for Yahweh to look on the experience of the poet (see 'Notes on the text'). In verse 18, it is the internal problems Yahweh needs to consider, the affliction and trouble experienced being capable of remedy through forgiveness, again alluding to Exodus 34:6–7. In verse 19, the focus is more on the attitudes and actions of the psalmist's many enemies who approach the poet with violent enmity, leading to the plea in verse 20 that Yahweh guard and deliver the poet, thus avoiding shame (cf. vv. 2–3) because the psalmist has taken refuge in Yahweh, a concept that here fits with the wisdom elements found in the poem (Creach 1996: 68). In verse 21, this becomes a wish that the poet be preserved by integrity and uprightness because of hope placed in Yahweh. Such hope has already been mentioned (vv. 3, 5), again providing a link between the end of this third stanza and the first. The integrity and uprightness that are to preserve the poet are a personification of key aspects of Yahweh's character (cf. v. 8). Here, it may be another way of speaking of Yahweh's continued involvement, though given the prayer to walk in Yahweh's ways it can also be an effect of the poet living out Yahweh's instruction and counsel. Most likely, both elements are intended, as the poet continues to hope in Yahweh.

22. The final verse, like verse 11, is clearly marked by the fact that it breaks the pattern of what is around it. We have already had a *p* verse at the appropriate point (v. 16) so adding this here is unnecessary in terms of the acrostic structure. Nevertheless, it is an apt addition to the form, taking up the language that has been applied to the individual who has prayed in the first and third stanzas and applying it to Israel as a whole. Just as the individual needed Yahweh, so also Yahweh needed to act to redeem the nation from its distresses.

Explanation

This acrostic poem introduces a new block of psalms that runs through to Psalm 34 even as it extends motifs from Psalm 24, the closing psalm in the unit Psalms 15–24. Psalm 24 had reported that those who could approach Yahweh were those clean of hand and pure of heart. But who will always live up to that standard? This psalm understands that all fall short of this (as Paul would say, Rom. 3:23), and that therefore there is always a need for grace. Complicating this is pressure from others that encourages something other than trust in God, especially if their claims or threats lead to shame because faith and experience do not line up with one another. So, this psalm looks to bring faith and experience together, grounding faith in what God has previously revealed about himself in the Sinai covenant, and especially that he is a God who forgives those who seek him, something Psalm 24 has also encouraged. That seeking of God is here described as fearing him, a relationship of trust that seeks to live out God's ways despite the challenges life generates, challenges that can come from our own sinfulness or the acts of others. Hence, we need guidance, and so the poet prays that just as Yahweh previously revealed his will, so he will continue to teach the psalmist (cf. Abernethy 2015a). That is, there is an important balance to be struck between knowing God's will at a general level and how it is to be worked out in a specific circumstance. The psalm knows that believers will often fail in this, but also that as we continue to seek God's instruction it is possible to hope in him. Moreover, the experience of the individual is also matched by God's people, which is why the prayer now looks to the nation too. As the A–Z of prayer, it continues to model a pattern of reflection on Scripture and experience that shapes prayer, trusting that we know a God rich in mercy (Eph. 2:4).

PSALM 26

Translation

Davidic.

1Judge me, O Yahweh,
  because I have walked in my integrity,
and in Yahweh have I trusted,
  never slipping.
2Examine me, O Yahweh, and try me,
  test my mind and sentiment.
3For your kindness is before my eyes,
  and I have walked in your truth.

4I have not sat with people of falsehood,
  I do not engage with dissemblers.
5I hate the assembly of evildoers,

I do not sit with the wicked.
6I wash my palms in innocence,
I go around your altar, O Yahweh,
7proclaiming thanksgiving aloud,
recounting all your wondrous deeds.
8O Yahweh, I love the habitation of your house,
the place where your glory dwells.
9Do not gather me with sinners,
my life with the bloodthirsty
10who have evil devices in their hands,
their right hands are filled with bribes.

11As for me, I shall walk in my integrity,
redeem me and be gracious to me.
12My foot stands on a level place,
in the great assembly I will bless Yahweh.

Notes on the text

2. With Q, read *ṣorpâ*. On 'mind and sentiment', see 'Notes on the text' on Psalm 7:9.

6. The cohort. *wa'ăsōbĕbâ* could indicate purpose (*WHS* §187) but, with Kwakkel (2002: 117), it is better to see this as an instance where its use is equivalent to an impf., perhaps pointing to repeated action.

7. Parsing *lašmiaʿ* as a hiph. infin. const.

Form and structure

As with Psalms 7, 17, Psalm 26 is best understood as a prayer of innocence (with Bellinger 1993: 456; cf. 'Form and structure', Ps. 7). This is particularly evident when we note the close links in vocabulary with Psalm 7, including the appeal to be judged by Yahweh (Pss 7:8; 26:1) and the request that Yahweh test the poet's mind and sentiment (Pss 7:9; 26:2). There may be a hint of a ritual that those claiming innocence followed in verse 6, but it is unwise to make too much of this. Indeed, a key feature of the Psalter is that whatever rituals were involved in demonstrating someone's guilt or evidence have not been preserved, and poems such as this are therefore open to a wider range of applications. This can also be seen in the important connections between this poem and Psalm 25. There, Yahweh's paths are 'kindness and truth' (Ps. 25:10), while the poet here claims to have walked in Yahweh's truth while following his kindness (v. 2). Moreover, the prayer in Psalm 25:21 is that the poet's integrity will preserve him, and here integrity is presented as the basis for Yahweh's assessing the psalmist positively (vv. 1, 11), echoing Psalm 7:8. As such, although a background in the prayers of innocence remains visible and is an important component of its interpretation, we also need to read this psalm as a prayer that takes up the petition of the previous psalm.

Structurally, the psalm contains three stanzas, with the third closely echoing the first (Auffret 2002a). The second stanza could be divided into strophes (cf. Mosca 1985: 225–227, though he analyses only at one level), but for our purposes analysis to the stanza level is sufficient, yielding the following:

1. Opening appeal (1–3)
2. Affirmations of innocence (4–10)
3. Closing vows (11–12)

Comment

Title: For 'Davidic', see on Psalm 3.

1–3. The opening appeal is that Yahweh judge the psalmist. Although the verb *špṭ* can mean 'vindicate' (so NRSV), and vindication is the poet's goal, this vindication depends on the poet's innocence being established. Yahweh must judge the poet before vindication can be achieved. Nevertheless, just as Psalm 25:21 allowed that integrity (NIV's 'blameless life' is too strong) could preserve those who waited on Yahweh, so the poet here presents personal integrity as the foundational element that leads to vindication. Within the prayers of innocence, claims of integrity are not general statements of righteousness but rather refer to the specific issue for which the psalmist is to be judged. We cannot know the specific charge because these prayers are open to a range of users, but the general thrust here appears to relate to the suggestion that someone has been unfaithful to Yahweh. That would explain the ways in which the balance of verse 1 focuses on the poet's enduring trust in Yahweh. This would then explain the imperatives in verse 2 which asks for a more specific evaluation of the psalmist's mind and sentiment. The concern is not so much with actions as attitudes, though these attitudes have also been expressed in the psalmist's actions, which is why verse 3 draws on the way metaphor to stress that the poet has walked in Yahweh's truth. In judging the psalmist, Yahweh should see someone who has been committed to him in attitude and action, someone guided by Yahweh's kindness.

4–10. The second stanza is more focused on the evidence that demonstrates the poet's innocence. If Yahweh is to judge the psalmist and reach a favourable verdict, then evidence is needed. In verses 4–5, the focus is primarily on what the poet has not done, whereas verses 6–8 provide positive evidence. All these climax in the appeal of verses 9–10. The opening of verse 4 is reminiscent of Psalm 1:1; indeed, the transition from 'walk' (v. 3) to 'sit' (v. 4) follows the pattern there. The 'people of falsehood' here are like the 'scoffers' there, though if Exodus 23:1 provides some background to this verse, then they are also those who make false reports about others. The word 'falsehood' (*šāwĕ'*) also refers to a false approach to bearing Yahweh's name (Exod. 20:7). This too is probably in the background here, so these people are false in both their attitude to Yahweh and how this works out in relation to others. Verses 1–3 have shown that these points do not apply to the poet, but the point is reinforced in verse 3b in noting that the psalmist does not deal with dissemblers, those who hide their real purposes. Verse 5 reinforces these points by way of negation. The poet claims to hate the assembly of evildoers, a claim of innocence by not associating with those who do evil, something confirmed by the refusal to sit with the wicked. By contrast, verses 6–8 provide more positive evidence for a favourable judgement. It is possible that verse 6 refers to a ritual where someone who was accused washed their hands in the temple while walking around the altar to signify their innocence (cf. Ps. 73:13; Matt. 27:24), with this accompanied by proclamations of thanksgiving and a recounting of Yahweh's wondrous deeds, perhaps focused on events such as the exodus. Nevertheless, within the psalm this is addressed to Yahweh and the focus is on reporting this as part of the prayer rather than describing a ritual. It also finds its conclusion in the confession of the poet's love of the temple, here understood as the dwelling place of Yahweh's glory, echoing events in 1 Kings 8:11. As one who loves the place where Yahweh is worshipped, we have further evidence of the psalmist's innocence of a charge of disloyalty to Yahweh. This then prepares for the requests in verses 9–10. As judge, Yahweh is tasked with taking sinners and removing them from the company of his people. These sinners are defined as those who practise bloodshed, whose hands are involved in work damaging to the community in both the plans they make and the ways they act against the weak in receiving bribes. These points could indicate the nature of the charge of disloyalty to Yahweh involved here. If so, it is notable that, like Psalms 15, 24, the focus is on the damage done to the vulnerable in the community. Even if we cannot be so specific about the charge, it still indicates that a key measure of faithfulness to Yahweh is how one relates to the most vulnerable. Within the psalm, the point is that the psalmist has in fact engaged more positively with the community, and therefore can appeal to Yahweh not to be included with those found guilty of such actions.

11–12. The closing vows draw together themes from the previous stanzas. The promise to continue walking in integrity points to the basis for Yahweh's judgement of the poet stated in verse 1, except that where the opening statement points to prior acts, this time the focus is on the future. Yet this future still requires Yahweh to act for the psalmist; hence, the requests for redemption and grace. The forces that led to the poet needing to make an affirmation of innocence are presumably still active, and it is Yahweh who can change that. Redemption could imply the payment of a ransom, though here it is perhaps simply part of the language of salvation. That such redemption also requires grace indicates that the poet is not claiming to be faultless. A future of integrity still requires grace. The psalm closes with the poet claiming to stand in uprightness. Although the term *mîšôr* can refer to a 'level place' (cf. ESV) it is also related to the word for 'upright' (*yšr*), a term that often has ethical overtones. Both elements are probably present if the poet is imagined as being in the temple, though the 'great assembly' can be other contexts for worship. Whatever the worship context, the poet closes by promising to bless Yahweh (cf. Ps. 103:1), publicly affirming what Yahweh has done.

Explanation

A prayer of innocence, Psalm 26 takes the claims of Psalm 1 seriously. It knows, as the psalms that have come since Psalm 1 have made clear, that this is a world in which there is violence and bloodshed, in which the righteous are often a minority. But it holds to the affirmation of Psalm 1 that walking with Yahweh is the way of blessedness. In addition, it remembers the affirmation there that the wicked shall not rise in the judgement, and so calls on Yahweh to judge the psalmist and issue a decree of 'innocent'. To sustain this, it points to a life structured around integrity, one that is patterned on Yahweh's kindness and truth. All this gains particular importance in the light of Psalm 25 and its prayer that integrity will sustain the poet. No enemies are named in this poem, but the denials made in sustaining the poet's innocence make clear that they are present. It is against their implied charges that the psalmist needs to be found innocent by Yahweh. The claims of integrity here are not therefore a denial of any failure on the part of the poet, only that the pattern of the poet's life is dedicated to Yahweh along the lines outlined in Psalms 15, 24. On this basis, it is possible to ask for vindication from Yahweh. Moreover, as an application of the patterns of Psalms 15, 24 it continues to challenge readers to wholehearted service of God alone (Botha 2011; cf. Matt 6:24).

PSALM 27

Translation

Davidic.

[1]Yahweh is my light and my salvation,
  whom shall I fear?

Yahweh is the stronghold of my life,
whom shall I dread?
2When evildoers draw near me
to consume my flesh,
my adversaries and foes against me,
they stumble and fall.
3If an army should encamp against me,
my heart will not fear.
If battle should arise against me,
in this I will trust.
4One thing have I asked from Yahweh,
this do I seek:
to dwell in the house of Yahweh
all the days of my life,
to gaze on the beauty of Yahweh,
to enquire in his temple.
5For he will hide me in a shelter on the day of distress,
he will conceal me in the protection of his tent,
on a crag shall he lift me high.
6And now my head is lifted up
above my enemies who surround me,
and I will offer resounding sacrifices in his tent.
I will sing and make melody to Yahweh!

7Hear, O Yahweh, my voice as I call out,
and be gracious to me and answer me.
8To you has my heart said, 'Seek my face.'
Your face, O Yahweh, do I seek.
9Do not hide your face from me,
do not turn aside your servant in wrath,
you have been my help!
Do not abandon me and forsake me,
O God of my salvation!
10Though my father and my mother abandon me,
yet Yahweh will take me in.
11Teach me your way, O Yahweh,
and lead me in a level path,
on account of my enemies.
12Do not give me over to the purpose of my adversaries,
for false witnesses rise up against me,
yes, witnesses of violence.

13Indeed, I believe I will look on to the goodness of Yahweh,
in the land of the living.
14Wait for Yahweh,

be strong and let your heart take courage.
Wait for Yahweh!

Notes on the text

4. Levenson (1985) argues for a technical sense of *nʿm* as related to augury, but this seems overly specific given the desire to 'gaze' on Yahweh's beauty.

8. Often emended as corrupt (cf. *BHS*), but variations in the versions suggest that they are attempting to resolve a difficult text, in which case it is better to retain MT.

12. Hebr. *wîpēaḥ* has traditionally been derived from a root *ypḥ*, meaning 'to breathe'. But Ugar. evidence suggests that 'witness' is also plausible, and it makes more sense here. See Pardee 1978, 2013.

13. *lûlē'* is difficult. Commonly, it means 'unless'. Given this sense, it would here introduce an aposiopesis, though an inverted conditional sentence is also possible (Niehaus 1979). But in context, it seems better to take it as an asseveration.

Form and structure

Psalm 27 is a poem that has proved problematic for form critics (cf. Firth 2005b: 61–65). This is because it contains material that is quite disparate. Verses 1–6 express trust whereas verses 7–14 are more obviously aligned with the complaint psalms. Because of this, it is often treated as two distinct poems that can be treated separately (e.g. A. A. Anderson 1972, 2: 219; Van der Ploeg 1973: 180). Yet, it is also apparent that the two parts of the poem contain significant words that occur in both parts (Craigie and Tate 2004: 231) and that can be shown to relate to one another (Coetzee 1986: 106–108). If the two parts of the psalm had a separate origin, then at least one of them was presumably composed with knowledge of the other. The more likely option is that verses 7–14 were composed second, with the psalmist using the song of trust as a key device in which to situate the prayer for protection that follows. If so, then the complaint section never existed apart from the song of trust and was always intended to be read with it. The psalm thus has a compositional integrity that requires it to be read as a unit.

There are also important links with the surrounding psalms which suggest that its present literary setting is intentional (Botha and Weber 2019). For example, we can note that the psalmist wishes to be led on a level 'path' (*mîšôr*) in verse 11, echoing the experience of Psalm 26:12, drawing on a key term that occurs in only three other places in the Psalter. The appeal for grace in verse 7 echoes the similar appeal in 26:11. Despite these links, there is not enough evidence here to suggest that this too is a prayer of the accused (against Kraus 1988: 333; Seybold 1996: 115). Use of the 'way metaphor' here also connects to Psalm 25:4, while the motif of seeking Yahweh's face echoes Psalm 24:6. Finally, the motif of dwelling in the temple (v. 4) matches Psalm 23:6.

Despite the frequent division into two parts, it can be analysed in three stanzas, with the first two also containing two strophes, and each stanza closing with a three-part line (cf. Sommer 2023: 114):

1. Song of Confidence (1–6)
   a. Confidence in threat (1–3)
   b. Yahweh's shelter (4–6)
2. Prayer (7–12)
   a. Plea for protection (7–9)
   b. Plea for leading (10–12)
3. Closing admonition to trust Yahweh (13–14)

Comment

Title: For 'Davidic', see on Psalm 3.

1–3. The psalm opens with confident declarations of Yahweh's relationship with the poet. That Yahweh is the psalmist's light is unique to this psalm, though 'light' is always positive in Psalms (e.g. Ps. 36:10). That Yahweh is the psalmist's salvation takes a motif from Psalm 2:5, the one for whom the poet must wait, a theme that now prepares for the admonition in verse 14. These declarations prepare for the rhetorical question about fear, the implication being that fear is unnecessary. This is confirmed by the further declaration that Yahweh is the poet's stronghold, which leads to a similar rhetorical question. These statements are not abstract expressions but rather provide reassurance in the face of challenges. One form of those challenges is attack by adversaries, but in verse 2 such evildoers are said to stumble and fall (cf. Ps. 20:8). That these evildoers will stumble then provides a context for trusting that even if such an assault against the poet were to be made by an army, the poet's heart would not fear. Rather, knowing that Yahweh is the psalmist's light and salvation, continues to encourage trust even in battle.

4–6. Where the first strophe focused on Yahweh's attributes as reasons for confidence, the second looks back to an earlier prayer and in particular a request to dwell at the temple, a prayer that continues to define the psalmist's desire. Strictly, no one dwelled permanently in the temple but, as with Psalms 15, 24, the request here reflects a desire to be in Yahweh's presence, and nothing expressed this more than the temple since this was the obvious place to experience the beauty of Yahweh's presence and to enquire of him. Yahweh's presence was both his means of protection and the expression of his justice (Erbele-Küster 2016: 48–50), neither of which was necessarily restricted to the temple since this protection could be in a temporary 'shelter' (*sōk*) or a tent. Admittedly, the temple can be described as a 'tent' (Ps. 15:1), but the parallelism here suggests that its more typical sense is intended here, though by verse 6 it will once again stand for the temple. Temporary residences would not normally provide security in battle, but they become places of safety because of Yahweh's presence, a security that is then pictured in more traditional terms as being lifted high on to a crag. Where verse 5 has anticipated a point where Yahweh lifts the psalmist in a time of conflict, verse 6 brings that back to the poet's present experience. Prayer in the past has given assurance for the future, and this gives confidence in the present. That Yahweh provides for the poet is ample reason to worship him with both noisy sacrifices (perhaps joyful shouts) and songs of praise.

7–9. There is a clear shift in mood at this point. Instead of confidence, the text now reports desperate pleas for Yahweh to act. At the heart of these pleas is a desire for Yahweh's presence, the very thing that was celebrated in the first stanza. The absence of what otherwise seemed assured now drives the prayer. Rather than gazing at Yahweh's beauty, the psalmist now entreats him through three rapid imperatives to hear, be gracious and answer. It is Yahweh who must act for the poet, and that as a matter of grace. Verse 8 then provides a reason for Yahweh to view the psalmist positively, though the detail is uncertain. If we are right to retain MT (see 'Notes on the text'), then we need to understand the opening of verse 8 as quoting Yahweh's words back to him (cf. Goldingay 2006a: 396). The pl. imp. 'seek' (*baqqšû*) cannot refer only to the poet's self-direction (which would be sg.), but if taken as a citation of Yahweh's call to his people means that the psalmist is then claiming in verse 8b to have done the very thing Yahweh has summoned. If the poet has done as Yahweh has said, then this provides reasons for Yahweh to hear. Yet, the opening appeal of verse 9 suggests that Yahweh's presence is not being experienced; hence, the request that Yahweh not hide it from the poet. Indeed, the parallel suggests not only that Yahweh has hidden his presence, but also that he has acted in wrath against one of his servants in turning the poet aside, even though he has previously been the psalmist's help. All this is brought together in the closing appeal that Yahweh neither abandon nor forsake the poet, a prayer without direct parallel in the Psalter. That Yahweh is indeed the God of the poet's salvation (echoing v. 1) provides the key reason why Yahweh should hear this prayer.

10–12. The context that led to the pleas becomes more apparent here, though the details are not always clear. We can take the opening conj. *kî* (though) with concessive force here, meaning that it describes a possible case, not actual abandonment by the psalmist's parents. They are mentioned as the ultimate example of humans whom we might expect always to stay with the poet. It can be admitted that even parents may abandon their children, but Yahweh instead gathers his people to himself. This picks up on the key word 'abandon' (*'zb*) from the previous verse, making clear that even if the psalmist feels abandoned by Yahweh, this is not what is happening. Being gathered in by Yahweh is not simply to a place of security but now provides a context where Yahweh can teach and lead the poet to a place of security because of the enemies. Ultimately, the poet needs to be protected from them, and not to be given over to them even though they demonstrate violence as they testify falsely. Yahweh's presence will be experienced as he does not permit the enemies to overcome the poet.

13–14. The third stanza begins with a fresh statement of confidence that acknowledges the current threat. There is confidence that Yahweh's goodness will be experienced in life, and thus that the violence of the enemies will not triumph. This confidence can then be offered to another, as verse 14 is expressly didactic (cf. Mandolfo 2002: 62), encouraging someone (perhaps including the poet) to wait for Yahweh (cf. Ps. 25:5). The admonition to be strong and let one's heart take courage evokes Yahweh's message to Joshua (Josh. 1:5), while also picking up the heart motif from verse 8. It is this that enables the psalm to conclude by repeating the admonition to wait for Yahweh.

Explanation

At heart, Psalm 27 wrestles with understanding faith and its opposite, which here is fear, not doubt (cf. Matt. 8:26, where Jesus makes the same distinction). The psalmist opens with what seems like an untroubled faith, one that is confident Yahweh will provide the protection needed. Yet as we progress, we come to a clearly troubled faith, one that holds to Yahweh in prayer even as it pleads for him to act. The importance of faith is then evident in the final stanza as the poet recalls both what has been believed and encourages another to wait for Yahweh, adopting a hopeful attitude to the future because of Yahweh. Nothing within the psalm has yet changed and yet by its close all has changed, so that others can be encouraged to wait. This is a faith tested by challenge, which has moved beyond naivete, and continues to encourage both self and others because it knows Yahweh is the one who ultimately provides the protection his people need, even in times when it does not feel that way.

PSALM 28

Translation

Davidic.

1To you, O Yahweh, do I call,
O my crag, do not be deaf to me,
lest you be silent to me,
and I be like those going down to the pit.
2Hear the sound of my plea for grace
as my cry to you for help,
as I lift my hand
to your holy inner sanctuary.
3Do not drag me off with the wicked
nor with those working evil,
those speaking peace with their neighbour,
when evil is in their mind.
4Give to them according to their work,
and according to the evil of their deeds,
according to the work of their hands give to them,
return their recompense to them!
5Because they did not consider the deeds of Yahweh,
nor the works of his hands,
he will tear them down
and not rebuild them.

6Blessed be Yahweh,
for he has heard the sound of my plea for grace.
7Yahweh is my strength and my shield,
my heart trusted in him.
I was helped and my heart exults,
and with my song I give thanks to him.
8Yahweh is the strength of his people,
he is the saving stronghold of his anointed.
9Save your people and bless your heritage!
Yes, shepherd them and bear them for ever.

Notes on the text

8. With several MSS, LXX and Syr. read *lĕʿammô*.

Form and structure

As with Psalm 27, form-critical discussion here has been less than helpful as the psalm contains elements of complaint (vv. 1–5) and thanksgiving (vv. 6–9), while mention of Yahweh's anointed could also associate the poem with the royal psalms. Again, it is the integration of these elements that matters most. Where Psalm 27 moves from confidence to complaint, Psalm 28 moves from complaint to thanksgiving before closing with an appeal to Yahweh. Perhaps it is enough (with Kraus 1988: 339) to describe the psalm as a prayer and recognize that although prayers frequently follow standard forms, not all do.

The psalm is also linked to those around it (cf. Vesco 2006, 2: 278; Fernandes 2013: 147–151). It is the closing poem in a run of four since Psalm 25 that have borne the simple title 'Davidic'. It joins Psalm 27 in having a focus on the temple (Pss 27:4; 28:2). The motif of the 'crag' as a symbol of protection also recurs (Pss 27:5; 28:1), except that now Yahweh is the crag (cf. Ps. 18:2), though both also point to Yahweh as a stronghold (Pss 27:1; 28:8) and as the source of salvation (Pss 27:1, 9; 28:8–9). The 'heart' motif (vv. 3, 7) also links it to both Psalms 26 and 27 (26:2; 27:3, 8, 14). These features, along with its structural reversal of Psalm 27, suggest that these poems stand in a particularly close relationship.

The psalm can be analysed in two stanzas, with the motif of the plea for grace linking them:

1. Plea for grace (1–5)
2. Thanksgiving and prayer (6–9)

Comment

Title: For 'Davidic', see on Psalm 3.

1–5. As with many prayers, this one opens with an intense appeal to Yahweh. The psalmist's appeal addresses Yahweh as 'my crag', a term that points to Yahweh as a place of personal security. Yet this reality is put at risk if Yahweh should not hear ('be deaf', *ḥrš*) or be unresponsive ('be silent', *ḥšh*). Instead of being placed high on a crag, the poet would be like those on a downward journey to the pit, a symbol of death (cf. Ps. 30:3). Rather than being deaf, Yahweh needs to heed the sound of the plea for grace as the psalmist cries out for help, cries matched with hands lifted towards the innermost part of the temple, the place where the Ark was kept and that thus symbolized Yahweh's enthronement (1 Kgs 6:19). This is both verbal and physical prayer, with the content of the prayer outlined in verses 3–5, with verse 3 outlining what is not wanted and verses 4–5 what is. Negatively, the psalmist asks not to be dragged off with the wicked and workers of evil. Although the 'wicked' (*rĕšāʿîm*) can be understood broadly as those not aligned with Yahweh, as in Psalm 1 (and by Mowinckel [1962, 1: 1–8] regarded as the 'workers of evil' [*pōʿălê ʾāwen*], magicians), here it is best to understand these groups as defined by verse 3b as those whose speech is peaceable but who are really thinking about harm for others. This puts them outside the pattern established in Psalm 15:2, where consistency between thought and speech was a marker of those who were in Yahweh's presence. If these people were outside Yahweh's presence, then the psalmist expects they would be dragged off by Yahweh to a place of punishment. In verse 4 the psalmist then asks for the desired punishment of these people, which is that they should receive from Yahweh what they have done to others. Where Psalm 15 encouraged a view of righteousness as positive practice towards others, here we see the other side of that coin. Wickedness is understood as practices that damage the life of others, and Yahweh is asked to provide a punishment that matches this. This follows the pattern established in Psalm 3, that the punishment Yahweh gives should match the harm done by the wicked; so the recompense Yahweh returns on the wicked is simply what they have done to others. As is typical of the Psalter, it is Yahweh and not the poet who must do this, though the psalm does provide additional reasons for this punishment in verse 5, noting that their failure to recognize that Yahweh is indeed active has led them to a sort of practical atheism (as in Ps. 14), and this is what leads to their destruction. Although verse 5 speaks about Yahweh rather than addressing him (as before), it is also joined to verses 1–4 and so is read here as a continuation of the prayer, though one that moves towards certainty that Yahweh will act.

6–9. There is an abrupt change in tone at this point as the poet blesses Yahweh for having heard the plea for grace, linking verse 6 to the appeal in verse 2. It is not implausible that someone praying this psalm in the temple would have received a word of encouragement after verse 5, and this would explain this change (Schaefer 2001: 70). But the poem is not dependent on a temple setting even if it references it in verse 2. Rather, the psalm now serves as a further reminder to those who pray it that Yahweh does answer prayer. In that the psalmist needed protection from the wicked, the affirmation that Yahweh is the poet's strength (cf. Ps. 118:4) and shield (cf. Pss 3:4; 18:2) is tied to the idea of Yahweh as the poet's crag (v. 1) since all these terms function to indicate Yahweh's protective action in the Psalter. Here, the point is that these are not abstract claims but rather the basis for the poet's trust, trust that was repaid when Yahweh provided help. That Yahweh has acted means that the psalmist's heart exults, leading to worship in song. Verse 8 then takes the experience of the one who prays and puts it into a wider context. The poet could assert that Yahweh is 'my strength' because Yahweh is the strength of his people. That is, the poet's experience is not distinctive but typical. Moreover, Yahweh was also the saving stronghold of his anointed; that is, the king. The statement is here further evidence of Yahweh's concern for all his people. One might expect that a deity would protect his king, but the psalmist's experience matches that of the king, showing Yahweh's concern for all his people. It is because Yahweh's protection is for all his people that the psalm can close with the appeal that Yahweh save his people and bless his heritage. 'Save' (*yš'*) implies that they need to be rescued as the poet has been, whereas 'bless' (*brk*) looks for Yahweh to enrich the experience of his people, here called his 'heritage'. Beyond this, the prayer looks to Yahweh to shepherd the nation, taking the metaphor from Psalm 23, where it had been applied to an individual and now asking that this continue to be true for the nation. Yahweh's saving power had been shown to the individual who prayed, and it can now be shown to the nation in perpetuity.

Explanation

At heart, Psalm 28 is a cry for justice. Where Psalm 26 looked for justice for one accused, Psalm 28 looks for justice that is also grace. It makes clear that it is Yahweh who needs to respond to the psalmist's cry for help so that his strength is not simply something asserted. Rather, Yahweh's strength needs to be demonstrated so that the workers of evil who damage both the individual and the community of God's people receive a punishment equivalent to the harm they have done. Punishment of the evildoers is Yahweh's task, for he is the one who enacts justice that protects the weak and yet also tears down those who damage his people. Confidence in this was also central to Psalm 27, a poem with which this one is closely matched. Such prayer continues to be important for many today, following the pattern of Jesus' promise that justice will indeed be given (Luke 18:1–8; cf. Kidner 1975, 1: 123). As with this psalm, such prayer needs to be both individual and communal.

PSALM 29

Translation

A melody. Davidic.

1Ascribe to Yahweh heavenly beings,
ascribe to Yahweh glory and strength,
2ascribe to Yahweh the glory of his name,
worship Yahweh in holy attire.

3The voice of Yahweh is over the waters,
the God of glory thunders,
Yahweh is over many waters.
4The voice of Yahweh is powerful,
the voice of Yahweh is majestic,
5the voice of Yahweh breaks cedars,
yes, Yahweh shatters the cedars of Lebanon,
6and makes Lebanon skip like a calf,
and Sirion like a young wild ox.
7The voice of Yahweh divides flames of fire.
8The voice of Yahweh makes wilderness tremble,
Yahweh makes the wilderness of Kadesh tremble.
9The voice of Yahweh sends the deer into labour
and strips the forest bare,
and in his temple all say, 'Glory!'

10Yahweh sits upon the flood,
yes, Yahweh sits as king for ever.
11May Yahweh give strength to his people,
may Yahweh bless his people with peace.

Notes on the text

6. With Craigie and Tate (2004: 243), read the ending of *wayyarqîdēm* as an enclitic particle.

7. The verse breaks the rhythm of the section, leading to the proposal (cf. *BHS*) to move verse 3b here. Kraus (1988: 345) is sympathetic, but ultimately retains the text. Some dislocation is possible, but the evidence is insufficient to make this emendation.

9. The pl. *yĕʿārôt* is anomalous since the pl. is usually m. Rendsburg (1990: 36) believes this may indicate a northern origin. There is no need to revocalize *ʾāyyalôt* to *ʾêlôt* (cf. Seybold 1996: 121) solely because of parallelism.

Form and structure

Psalm 29 stands at the heart of the subcollection of Psalms 25–34. Each of 25–28 has the simple title 'Davidic' but that is varied here, distinguishing this psalm from those before. More importantly it brings together key themes from the preceding poems while also preparing for those that follow. Psalms 26–28 all focus on human voices heard by God (Pss 26:7; 27:7; 28:2, 6), but here the focus is on how all creation encounters Yahweh's voice. This voice is noted for its power, while

Yahweh himself is associated with strength (vv. 1, 11), a motif that forms an inclusio in the poem. The inclusio also provides a link to 28:9, which had prayed for Yahweh's blessing on his people, a blessing that is now the provision of peace (29:11). The ability to provide this is linked with Yahweh's kingship, something evident to all in the temple (29:9), thus picking up mention of the temple in Psalms 26:6, 27:4 and 28:2. But where this psalm goes beyond the others is in its stress on Yahweh's kingship in creation. It thus shows that the confidence in Yahweh seen in the temple in the preceding psalms is well placed, but also that confidence in Yahweh's power is not restricted to the temple.

For some time, Psalm 29 has been noted as having originated in Israel's north since the geographic terms are focused there. But significant connections with Ugar. texts have been noted too, and these also point to a northern origin (see Rendsburg 1990: 35–38, though the older suggestion that this is a reworked Baal hymn is difficult to sustain; see Wagner 1996). Although these links are retained, the psalm also references the temple (v. 9), bringing these northern motifs to the south. The most important point of these northern connections is that the psalm draws on the mythology of the region, only to point to Yahweh and not Canaanite deities as the source of all power (cf. Pardee and Pardee 2009: 122–124). Whether or not this can be called 'polemic' (cf. Diehl et al. 1999 and Kynes 2011: 297–300) may be debated, but the superiority of Yahweh to Baal is made clear. All of this explains why Yahweh alone can bless his people.

The poem can be analysed in three stanzas:

1. A summons to worship (1–2)
2. Yahweh's powerful voice (3–9)
3. Wishes from the enthroned king (10–11)

Comment

Title: For the title, see on Psalm 3.

1–2. The opening imp. 'ascribe' (*hābû*) is unusual in psalms (cf. Deut. 32:3), yet occurs three times here, something matched only by Psalm 96:7–8, another poem that subverts the language of mythology in demonstrating Yahweh's kingship. The identity of the 'heavenly beings' is ambiguous. Rather than the more common *bĕnê 'ĕlōhîm* (cf. Job 1:6), the psalm uses *bĕnê 'ēlîm*, a phrase that occurs elsewhere only in Psalm 89:6. The parallel in Exodus 15:6 indicates that *'ēlîm* can refer to other deities, though there too the point is Yahweh's incomparability. The most likely interpretation is that this is a reference to beings in Yahweh's heavenly court. If so, it draws on the idea of such a court in Ugar. mythology, especially that of Baal, whose 'voice' is also important (Pardee and Pardee 2009: 122), while also insisting that whatever heavenly beings may exist, their task is to ascribe glory and strength to Yahweh. Yahweh's glory was a critical element of Psalm 24:7–10, while the temple was the place of his glory (Ps. 26:8). Although the temple was where humans recognized Yahweh's glory, there is also a heavenly court where it is recognized. This glory was associated with his name, with the name standing for his reputation. Just as human priests were dressed appropriately for worship, so also these heavenly beings have holy attire for worship. If these beings worship Yahweh, how much more should humans?

3–9. Yahweh's voice is central to this stanza, occurring seven times in these verses (cf. Rev. 10:3). As a storm deity, Baal was noted for his voice, but Yahweh's voice is stressed here. In rejecting Baal, the psalm retains storm imagery through these verses, tracing a storm that begins in the far north and following it to the far south, while insisting that it is Yahweh's voice that thunders (cf. Wiggins 2014: 57–61). Despite the stress on Yahweh's voice, the final voice heard in the stanza is human, the cry of 'Glory' in the temple matching that of the heavenly beings, the only possible response to experiencing the power of Yahweh's voice. Indeed, this glory is established at the outset where Yahweh is described as the 'God of glory'. Just as Yahweh's strength forms an inclusio for the whole poem, his glory forms an inclusio for this stanza. Yahweh's voice is initially said to be over the waters, the place where Baal's voice may be expected. But it is Yahweh who is the God of glory who thunders, not Baal. Where verse 3 focuses on the reality of Yahweh's voice, verses 4–9a consider its character. In verse 4, this is achieved by considering its attributes, noting that it is powerful and majestic. Verses 5–9a then demonstrate the reality of this assertion by reporting what Yahweh's voice does. In verses 5–6, the focus is on the effect of Yahweh's voice in the south Lebanon range. The famous Lebanon cedars growing there can reach as high as 140 feet (43 m), but Yahweh's voice breaks them; indeed, Yahweh shatters these cedars. This area is also noted for its mountains, massively greater in size than the cedars, and yet Yahweh's voice makes them skip like a calf, the poem describing the sensation of those in the mountains during a thunderstorm. Sirion, an alternative name for Mount Hermon (Deut. 3:8–9) is the highest mountain there, rising to over 9,200 feet (2,804 m). But in Ugar. mythology (as Mount Zaphon) it is also Baal's abode. If it skips at Yahweh's voice like a young wild ox, then we once again see the great power of Yahweh's voice. Yahweh's voice dividing the flames of fire may also refer to lightning forks, another reference to a storm that responds to Yahweh. Where the references in verses 5–6 were northern, it is likely that the wilderness which shakes in verse 8 is now in the south, especially if the Kadesh mentioned here is Kadesh-Barnea, a place Numbers 13 indicates is on the southern boundary of Canaan. There is another Kadesh in Syria, on the Orontes (A. P. Ross 2011: 66, prefers it), but reference to the wilderness here makes the southern site more likely. The power of Yahweh's voice also causes the deer to writhe like the wilderness, though now the sense is probably that the deer gives birth while the forests are stripped bare. In response, those in the temple cry 'Glory!' Where focus on Yahweh's voice was on its power, the focus is now on actual speech, a coherent response in the temple. Given that the heavenly beings were to ascribe to Yahweh, this could be those in the heavenly temple (Goldingay 2006a: 419). But since the storm has passed over the temple in Jerusalem, there is no reason it could not be those there who also cry out there.

10–11. Yahweh's kingship has been implicit in the psalm to this point, but it is now made explicit. As king, he is enthroned over the floods (cf. Gen. 6 – 9), the chaotic waters that may threaten others but do not threaten him. Indeed, Yahweh is seated as king for ever. Because Yahweh is king, all creation is under his authority. This suggests that his enthronement here is in the heavenly sanctuary, though the earthly one continues to represent it. As king, Yahweh can also give strength to his people. The heavenly beings need to worship him and recognize his strength, but it is to his people that he may give strength. The verbs in verse 11 could be read as impfs., so that these become statements. However, in the light of the psalm to this point, it is more likely that his people now express a wish for his strength and the blessing of peace. Strength is not needed for war, but rather for peace, though this is a gift for which Yahweh's people hope.

Explanation

In his famous book *The Lion, the Witch and the Wardrobe*, C. S. Lewis famously denies that the lion Aslan is tame. His point is that God is not someone we can domesticate. This psalm insists that is true. To say that our God is an awesome God is a potentially terrifying statement, but only potentially. Because the good news is that this awesome God brings peace, something Baal could not do. Indeed, to look to Baal or any other power to provide for us is to miss the point. The power to change things, to make them better through peace, is found in Yahweh alone (cf. McCann 1996: 792). In NT terms, we understand this as the peace of God that guards us in Christ (Phil. 4:7).

PSALM 30

Translation

A melody. A song of dedication of the house. Davidic.

1 I will exalt you Yahweh because you have drawn me up
and you have not let my enemies exult over me.

2 Yahweh my God, I cried to you for help
and you healed me.
3 Yahweh, you raised me up from Sheol,
you restored my life from those going down to the pit.

4 Sing praises to Yahweh his saints,
give thanks for his holy renown.
5 For his anger lasts but a moment,
his favour is for life.
Weeping may lodge for the evening,
but a cry of joy in the morning!

6 As for me, I had said in my ease
'I shall never stumble.'
7 Yahweh, in your favour you made my mountain stand strong,
when you covered your face, I was dismayed.

8 I was crying out to you, Yahweh,
and pleading for grace to the Lord.
9 'What profit is there in my blood,
In my going down to the pit?
Shall the dust give you thanks?
Shall it declare your faithfulness?
10 Hear, Yahweh, and be gracious to me.
Yahweh! Be my helper!'

11 You have turned my mourning into dancing,
you have removed my sackcloth and dressed me with gladness.
12 Therefore my glory shall sing your praise and not be silent.
Yahweh, my God, I shall give you thanks for ever.

Notes on the text

3. Read *mîyôrĕdê* with Q, many MSS and the main versions. For a defence of K, see Craigie and Tate 2004: 251.

4. *zēker* is lit. 'memorial' but here stands for Yahweh's character (cf. Ps. 97:12).

7. LXX's reading (which presumes *lahădārî*) is a plausible correction to an obscure expression.

12. With LXX, read *kĕbēdî*.

Form and structure

This psalm fits the general category of individual thanksgiving psalms (Seybold 1996: 124) or, perhaps better, prayers of 'new orientation' in Brueggemann's (1984) typology. Yet, as deClaissé-Walford et al. (2014: 289) point out, the poem uses multiple forms of praise, so form criticism is not finally determinative. Since the psalm shows parallels with Hezekiah's prayer (Isa. 38:10–20; cf. Grogan 2008: 82) there is still virtue in considering the psalm as at least rooted in individual thanksgiving. This could be for recovery from illness (so, Croft 1987: 140) as the language of healing is present, but it is also possible to imagine healing more broadly as some form of restoration that does not necessitate serious illness. Nevertheless, recovery from illness forms at least one plausible context against which to read the psalm, and even if a more general approach is adopted (cf. Goldingay 2006a: 433), it is still the pattern through which it is understood. As is typical of such poems, it shifts between addressing Yahweh and a congregation (Firth 1999), encouraging all to be involved in praise.

The psalm is also carefully integrated into its context within the subcollection of Psalms 25–34. Within the chiastic structure of this unit, it has close parallels to Psalm 28, notably reference to going down to the pit (Pss 28:1; 30:3), except that Psalm 28 asks not to be among those going down, whereas Psalm 30 gives thanks for being brought back from it. Likewise, Psalm 28:2, 6 referred to a plea for grace, a motif repeated here (v. 8) in the report of prior prayer. Psalm 28:7 also reports giving thanks with song, a theme repeated here (v. 12). There are also more immediate connections to Psalm 29, notably the unusual use of 'glory' (v. 12), which picks up on a key term there (Ps. 29:1, 2, 3, 9). This is not to say that Psalm 30 was originally a thanksgiving responding to Psalm 28 (the prayer report in verse 9 also has close connections with Pss 6:5; 88:10–12). Rather, in this literary context it now serves to provide evidence of the power of the God of glory celebrated in Psalm 29 to respond to the type of prayer found in Psalm 28, showing that the confidence there is not misplaced. This may also explain (in part) the association with the dedication of the house in the title. This is most likely a reference to the rededication of the temple in 165 BC after the Maccabean revolt (note that the Talmud, *b. Sop.* 18.3 assigns this psalm for reading at Hannukah). The psalm itself seems to be more the report of an individual's restoration, but just as it provides a pattern of individual thanksgiving within this literary context, so it also now provides a pattern for the nation to see its restoration (cf. Loader 2003). This becomes more probable when we note the prevalence of references to the temple across this subcollection (Pss 26:6; 27:4; 28:2; 29:9). This is a reapplication of the psalm, but one that is consistent with this section of the Psalter.

The psalm can be analysed in three stanzas, the first two of which also contain two strophes:

1. Thanksgiving and praise (1–5)
   a. Individual thanksgiving (1–3)
   b. Exhortation to praise (4–5)
2. Report of previous experience (6–10)
   a. Misplaced confidence (6–7)
   b. Prayer report (8–10)
3. Promise of thanksgiving (11–12)

Comment

Title: For 'melody' and 'Davidic', see on Psalm 3. Reference to dedication of the house is unique. 'Dedication' (*ḥanukâ*) occurs also in Ezekiel 6:16–17 (there in Aram.), referring to the dedication of the second temple (also called a 'house' there). This is a possible reference here, but given the link to Hannukah, rededication after the Maccabean revolt is more likely. But on either reading, this is a reapplication of the psalm to the nation, so that an individual's experience of restoration provides a pattern for the nation.

1–3. The opening words of praise are directed to Yahweh. Having been brought back up by Yahweh, the psalmist vows to exalt him. There is clear spatial language here since exalting means raising Yahweh high, and this corresponds to Yahweh's act in drawing the poet up, the latter verb elsewhere referring to bringing a bucket back up (Exod. 2:6, 19). There was also apparently a threat from enemies, but in restoring the poet Yahweh prevented them from exulting over the poet. That Yahweh is the focus of praise is stressed by the vocs. in verses 2–3. These declare that Yahweh is the psalmist's God, who has responded to a prior cry for help and healed the poet. The threat was apparently serious since Yahweh has raised the psalmist from Sheol, the place of the dead. Death is portrayed as a downward movement (hence, the 'pit'), but Yahweh has brought the psalmist up from this. Yahweh has brought the poet up; the promise of praise now looks to exalt Yahweh.

4–5. The psalmist now shifts to address a wider audience of those committed to Yahweh (the *ḥāsîd*, 'righteous') who have heard the poet's thanksgiving, encouraging them to join in praise. Where the poet's praise comes from personal experience, the congregation are instead encouraged to see this testimony in the light of Yahweh's holy character (*zēker*; see 'Notes on the text'). They are called to sing and give thanks, mapping their experience to that of the psalmist. At this point it is possible to see how the title lets later audiences see the nation's restoration as another expression of Yahweh's holy character, providing a setting not only for sung praise but also thanksgiving for their own experience of grace. The reason for this is that Yahweh's anger is momentary, whereas his favour lasts a lifetime. Therefore, though one may weep through the evening, joy awaits in the morning. Applied to the poet's life, this probably means that the previous experience was understood as divine discipline (Weiser 1962: 270) that has ended, and the audience can now apply this to their own experience.

6–7. Where the opening stanza is concerned with praise because of what Yahweh has done, the second focuses on the circumstances that led up to his intervention. This commences with the poet's confession of a previously misplaced confidence. A previous period of ease had led to what was effectively a boast, 'I shall never stumble.' This reflects on the promise of Psalm 15:6, but without the ethical commitment expected there, and so functions as a confession of sin, close to the use of the same phrase in Psalm 10:6 (R. A. Jacobson 2004: 62). Rather than a life rooted in Yahweh's values, the psalmist had assumed that a period of ease was a sign of Yahweh's blessing. But such prosperity theology was misplaced. The meaning of Yahweh's making the poet's 'mountain stand strong' is obscure. In context, it seems to equate the poet's period of prosperity with a mountain, something vast and secure (something Ps. 29 challenges!). If this reading is correct, the psalmist is acknowledging that the period of ease had been Yahweh's gift. But by focusing on the gift rather than the giver, the poet had misconstrued this to mean that stumbling could not happen. This misunderstanding was revealed through a period where Yahweh's presence was hidden, causing dismay.

8–10. The dismay reported in verse 7 led to a period of prayer. The impf. verbs in verse 9 indicate that this happened over some time, seeking grace from Yahweh. The content of that plea is reported in verses 8–9. Though a plea for grace, it is also prepared to challenge Yahweh in a manner similar to Psalms 6:5 and 88:10–12. So, verse 9 challenges Yahweh to realize that the poet's death would have been costly. Reference to descent to the pit echoes the psalm's opening (v. 3). But the language here pushes Yahweh to see that the poet's death was unjust, since 'profit' (*beṣa'*) is typically unjust gain (cf. Exod. 18:21; Judg. 5:19; Mic. 4:13). If the poet's death would not have given Yahweh even unjust gain, why should Yahweh have permitted it? Yahweh had lost a worshipper, the dust that would be left could not replace him. As such, the psalmist had urged Yahweh to hear the plea for grace and therefore help.

11–12. The psalm's opening makes clear that Yahweh responded to this plea for grace. This is confirmed in verse 11, which reports that Yahweh has changed the dismay of verse 7 to joy. It is Yahweh and not the poet who has wrought this change. Yahweh has indeed helped the poet. The effect of this change is described through two metaphors of transformation, both of which reflect a change from mourning to joy. First, mourning is changed to dancing, two things elsewhere expressed as polar opposites (Eccles. 3:4, though with a different verb for dancing). A similar contrast is evident in the clothing metaphor, with sackcloth a rough cloth typically worn while mourning (Gen. 37:34; 2 Kgs 6:30). Yahweh has removed this and instead clothed the poet with gladness. Yahweh prevented the enemies from rejoicing over the psalmist and has now clothed the poet with joy. That is, Yahweh has moved the poet from a condition of mourning to joy. Therefore, the psalmist promises to sing praise to Yahweh, giving thanks for ever. The psalmist speaks of 'my glory' singing praise. This is more than a circumlocution for 'I'. It is the best of who the poet is that gives praise and thanks.

Explanation

This psalm speaks of the discovery of grace as the antidote to self-sufficiency. The psalmist discovered that self-sufficiency was a sin, a factor made clear through suffering, perhaps illness. It was at this time of weakness that Yahweh's grace was discovered, grace that summons all to praise. Though the psalm is one person's testimony, it provides a pattern on which a whole community can draw, a pattern that after the Maccabean revolt might have been especially important, so that experience of one becomes a paradigm for all. Both individually and corporately, gratitude expressed in praise is the appropriate response to grace. As worshippers take up this psalm today, they too become the 'I' who speaks and responds to God's grace (cf. J. T. James 2017: 28).

PSALM 31

Translation

The director's. A melody. Davidic.

1In you, O Yahweh, do I take refuge,
  let me never be put to shame,
  in your righteousness, deliver me!
2Incline your ear to me,
  rescue me quickly!
Be my crag of security,
  a secure fastness to save me.
3For you are my crag and fastness,
  for your name's sake, you lead me and guide me.
4You bring me out from the net they have hidden for me,
  for you are my secure fastness.

5Into your hand do I commit my spirit;
you have redeemed me, O Yahweh, God of truth.
6I hate those holding to vain idols,
but for me, I trust in Yahweh.
7Let me exult and rejoice in your kindness,
because you have seen my affliction,
you know my life's distress,
8and you have not delivered me over into the enemy's hand,
you made my feet stand in a spacious place.

9Be gracious to me Yahweh because I am in distress,
my eye wastes away with grief,
my throat and inner organs.
10For my life is spent with sorrow,
and my years with a sigh.
My strength stumbles because of my iniquity,
my bones waste away.
11Because of all my foes I have become a reproach,
more so to my neighbours;
an object of dread to my acquaintances.
Those who see me on the street
flee from me.
12I am forgotten, like the dead gone from the mind,
I have become like a broken vessel.
13For I hear many whispering,
'Terror on every side'
as they conspire together against me,
they plan to take my life.

14But as for me, I trust you, O Yahweh,
I say, 'You are my God.'
15My times are in your hand,
deliver me from the hand of my enemies and persecutors.
16Make your face shine upon your servant,
save me by your kindness.
17O Yahweh, let me not be put to shame
Because I call on you.
Let the wicked be put to shame,
let them be still in Sheol.
18Let deceptive lips be silent,
those speaking insolently against the righteous,
with arrogance and contempt.

19How great is your goodness which you store up for those who fear you,
that you perform for those taking refuge in you,

in the sight of humankind.
20You hide them in the shelter of your presence,
from human intrigues,
You store them in a shelter,
from the contention of tongues.
21Blessed be Yahweh,
for he has wondrously demonstrated his kindness towards me
in a besieged city.
22As for me, I had said in my haste,
'I am cut off from before your eyes.'
But you heard my plea for grace,
when I cried to you for help.

23Love Yahweh, all his saints!
Yahweh keeps the faithful,
but he repays abundantly the one who acts in arrogance.
24Be strong and let your heart take courage,
all who hope in Yahweh.

Notes on the text

9. Hebr. *ʿšš* (cf. Ps. 6:7) is uncertain, but context suggests something like 'waste away'. Cf. Seybold 1996: 131.

10. NRSV is typical of those following Gk, resulting in 'misery' rather than 'iniquity'. But MT is supported by the Naḥal ḥever MS and should be retained (see Flint 2000: 165).

Form and structure

There is no one obvious way to classify this psalm (cf. Fernandes 2013: 153–154) since it includes elements of thanksgiving (vv. 5–8, 21–22) and points of petition that ask Yahweh to act for the psalmist as would be typical of the complaint psalms (vv. 1–2, 9–13). These elements are mixed with addresses to a congregation encouraging trust (vv. 22–23) and expressions of trust in Yahweh (vv. 14–15a), while the force of other parts of the psalm depends on how we construe the verbs. The view developed here is that the psalm is intentionally structured to reach its concluding verses, exhorting a wider community to be encouraged by placing their hope in Yahweh. In doing so, it does repeat itself so that we twice go through the phase of petition and thanksgiving in establishing a context for continued trust. In that it would therefore have a clearly didactic goal, we could consider it as a wisdom text, though, if so, it is very different from other texts that may be classified in such terms (see

Cheung 2015; Stocks 2016) since in this case the individual's experience is presented as a pattern for others.

Though the psalm's form is disputed, its context within Psalms 25–34 is clearer. Within this unit, it balances Psalm 27, and there is a clear connection as both psalms conclude with an admonition to hope in Yahweh, the main difference being that here the admonition is pl. Apart from this, both psalms also speak of Yahweh as a 'crag', *ṣûr* (Pss 27:5; 31:2) and as a 'place of security' (*mā'ôz*; Pss 27:1; 31:2), yet also offer pleas for grace (Pss 27:7; 31:9). There are also connections with Psalm 30, the most important of which are the presence of a report of earlier speech that is no longer representative of the poet's perspective (Pss 30:6; 31:22) and the call to the direct address to the 'saints' (Pss 30:4; 31:23). These, and other connections to this unit (cf. Vesco 2006, 2: 292–293) show that the poem is well integrated in this context.

The poem's structure is also disputed. Though differing on key points, there is much to learn from Potgieter's analysis (2012: 118–121). However, if we understand the rhetorical goal to be reached in the closing verses, then the following three-stanza analysis is possible:

1. First complaint and thanksgiving (1–8)
   a. Prayer for rescue (1–4)
   b. Thanksgiving (5–8)
2. Second complaint and thanksgiving (9–22)
   a. Prayer for grace (9–13)
   b. Trust and petition (14–18)
   c. Thanksgiving (19–22)
3. Admonition to hope in Yahweh (23–24)

Comment

Title: On 'The director's', see on Psalm 4. For 'A melody. Davidic', see on Psalm 3.

1–4. The opening prayer starts from the posture of relationship with Yahweh, seeing him as the poet's point of refuge (cf. Basson 2005). On this basis, the poet asks not to be put to shame. This is not just due to an immediate threat, but rather is something enduring. If Yahweh is the place of refuge, then he needs to deliver the psalmist from an unspecified threat because this would express Yahweh's own righteousness. The language of rescue and sanctuary remains in focus as we move through verse 2. Attending to the poet's appeal, Yahweh is summoned to rescue and help the poet, reflecting the need for deliverance. As the poet's sanctuary, he is also to be a crag of security, a place of security because it is inaccessible to others. The reason for this is that just as Yahweh is the poet's place of refuge, so also, he is the needed secure place. All this is reminiscent of Psalm 18:2, but themes from there are now linked with the motif of Yahweh's leading the poet, drawing on Psalms 2:3 and 27:11. Especially given the links to Psalm 27, it is likely that the appeal to be led and guided by Yahweh here is to be read in the light of the earlier appeal, though this leading is now expanded by the request to be guided, the latter also echoing Psalm 23:2. Such leading is needed because of the actions of enemies who are pictured as hunters who have previously spread a net to catch the poet. The hunters fail because Yahweh brings the poet out of the net. This echoes Psalm 25:15, which was confident that Yahweh would indeed act this way. So here, it can be presented as further evidence of what it means to say that Yahweh is the place of security. If this is how Yahweh acts, then the poet desires that it happen once more.

5–8. The opening of verse 5 picks up the theme of petition from the opening strophe to provide a context for thanksgiving. Placing one's spirit in Yahweh's hand is trusting one's life to his care (when taken up in the NT [Luke 23:46; Acts 7:59] it looks to God's care beyond death, and so goes beyond the sense here, though is entirely appropriate in a Christian context), and this is what Yahweh has done in redeeming the poet, demonstrating that he is the God of truth. Hebr. *'emet* can mean 'truth', though the meaning can also shade into 'faithfulness' (cf. Exod. 34:6), and both these elements can be seen here. In effect, naming Yahweh as 'God of truth' here affirms that he truly is the place of refuge. This validates the psalmist for having trusted Yahweh rather than joining those holding to vain idols (cf. Pss 24:4; 26:4) and provides a basis for the psalmist to exult and rejoice in Yahweh's kindness (perhaps alluding to Exod. 34:6). The key point for the psalmist is that discussion of Yahweh's kindness is not theoretical but rather something experienced since Yahweh acted by not shutting up the poet in the hand of an enemy. Instead, Yahweh placed the psalmist's feet in a spacious place, the opposite of a place of distress. Thus, Yahweh has acted for the psalmist, validating the affirmations made about him.

9–13. Where the first complaint sought rescue from enemies, the second seeks grace, again connecting to Psalm 27 (v. 9). Foes are still present, but the need this time is more focused on the effect of personal iniquity on the poet's life. Although mention of the iniquity is deferred until verse 10b, it is the cause of the physical distress that is described. Mention of iniquity evokes the plea for pardon in Psalm 25:11, while also anticipating the celebration of receiving in Psalm 32:1–2. The distress this causes affects the psalmist outwardly through tears and inwardly through the 'throat' (*nepeš*) to the inner organs. This also has an impact on the whole lived experience, which is marked by sorrow and sighing. Where iniquity is the problem, grace is needed. Yet the impact of foes is not forgotten, even if they are contextualized by the confession of iniquity. Since foes are often associated with other aspects of suffering (cf. Ps. 6), it is not surprising that they are also mentioned here. As well as internal distress, the poet suffers a sense of alienation from others. Being a reproach to one's foes is no surprise (cf. Pss 22:7; 109:25), but this sense of alienation is now found in relationship to neighbours and friends, so that people seeing the poet on the streets flee. Rather than being part of a vital community, the psalmist experiences being forgotten, just as the dead recede from the mind, and is instead like a broken vessel. This sense of social alienation matches the internal suffering. Where it goes further is in hearing these acquaintances plotting against the psalmist's life, seeing the poet as a source of terror to the community (cf. Jer. 20:10, where similar language is applied to Jeremiah). Although the foes (esp.) threaten the psalmist, the request here is still for grace, stressing the impact of iniquity.

14–18. Where the first complaint moved straight to thanksgiving, the second complaint pauses to declare the poet's trust in Yahweh, though retaining links to the first stanza (v. 7) and moving to petition. Trust in Yahweh is a key element in Psalms 25–34 (Pss 25:2; 26:1; 27:3; 28:7; 32:10; 33:21). Here, it introduces the psalmist's attitude in contrast to the actions of the foes, affirming that Yahweh is the poet's God, and therefore the poet's times are in Yahweh's hand. But as one who trusts Yahweh, the poet can also ask him to act; hence, the declaration of trust leads to a request to be delivered from enemies and persecutors. But the request also asks that Yahweh cause his face to shine on the poet, echoing the priestly blessing (Num. 6:24–26). This is, in effect, a further request for grace, asking for a restored relationship with Yahweh, which is why Yahweh is also asked to save the poet in his kindness (echoing v. 7). When the poet again asks not to be put to shame (cf. v. 1), it is thus a request to show that the psalmist's trust, expressed through calling on Yahweh, has been well placed. By contrast, the wicked (a new category in this psalm) should be put to shame, though in their case this includes the possibility of death, the very thing the foes had plotted against the psalmist. These people have spoken against the psalmist, defined as among the righteous as one who trusts in Yahweh, and therefore the punishment of the wicked needs to match their prior actions, losing the ability to speak because of the harm it has done. As is typical in the Psalter, the penalty sought in prayer matches the harm that has been done.

19–22. The stanza now turns to thanksgiving, which is focused on the theme of refuge, another key motif in Psalms 25–34 (Pss 25:20; 34:8, 22), though the more immediate link here is to verse 1. The opening focuses on Yahweh's goodness to those who fear him, something that has been publicly demonstrated for those who take refuge in him. This is demonstrated in the provision of shelter, protecting those taking refuge from human plots. The opening comments are general statements about

Yahweh's actions for those taking refuge, though with obvious connections to earlier parts of the prayer (cf. v. 13). But in verses 21–22 these themes are applied to the poet's experience. They are no longer just general affirmations: these statements describe what Yahweh has done for the poet. That Yahweh has 'acted wondrously' (*pl'*) for the poet points to an act that is beyond what a human could achieve (e.g. Exod. 3:20; 34:10; Josh. 3:5), which is why the poet here blesses Yahweh. The kindness of Yahweh celebrated in verse 7 has therefore been experienced. The report of previous speech in verse 23 (as with Ps. 30:6) uses the form *'ănî 'āmartî* (As for me, I had said) to introduce a statement that the poet no longer regards as true. In haste, the poet claimed to be cut off from Yahweh's sight, but now it is clear that Yahweh has heard the plea for grace (v. 9). Thus, the poet recognizes a misplaced period of doubt that has now been resolved so that trust can continue in the context of thanksgiving.

23–24. The poem's conclusion draws on patterns in Psalms 27, 30. The opening address, summoning the saints to love Yahweh is like Psalm 30:4, moving from an individual's thanksgiving to address a wider audience (the 'saints') who are now told to love Yahweh, the only time in the OT where an imp. is used to direct love for Yahweh. If Deuteronomy 6:4–5 lies in the background here, we should understand this love as an act of covenant loyalty. This would be consistent with Yahweh's own covenant loyalty in his preserving of the faithful while also repaying the arrogant. That is, Yahweh continues to act in loyalty to his people, and they should respond by being loyal to him. The closing verse is then very similar to Psalm 27:14, except that rather than addressing an individual it is now addressed to a community. The experience of the individual in the previous petitions and thanksgivings provides a pattern for the wider community, assuring them that they too can be encouraged as they hope in Yahweh. The poet's experience indicates that there will be times when holding to this hope is challenged, but there is good reason to continue in hope. Encouragement in the face of challenge is thus entirely possible.

Explanation

Trusting Yahweh is a core motif in this psalm as it takes up themes from elsewhere in Psalms 25–34 (esp. Ps. 27) and reflects on them through a cycle of petition and thanksgiving. Where these elements are more typically separated, in this psalm they are brought together and in so doing indicate that there is not necessarily one point at which all challenges faced are resolved. Rather, in prayer we move through requests for rescue or grace to thanksgiving and back once more to request. In that respect, this psalm reflects the wider pattern of the Psalter. Crucially, periods of struggle and threat are not in themselves reasons to lose trust. Rather, it is possible to move between such times where trust is a challenge to times of thanksgiving and praise. All this is thus applied in the closing admonition, which reminds believers that there are always reasons to hope in Yahweh. And, as Paul reminds us, such hope does not disappoint (Rom. 5:5).

PSALM 32

Translation

Davidic. A Maskil.

1Oh the blessedness of the one whose transgression is forgiven,
whose guilt is covered.
2Oh the blessedness of the person against whom Yahweh does not reckon iniquity,
and in whose spirit is no treachery.

3When I was silent, my bones wasted away,
through my screaming all day long.
4For day and night your hand was heavy upon me,
my vitality was changed as by the heat of summer. *Selah.*
5I acknowledged my guilt to you,
and I did not cover my iniquity.
I said, 'I will confess against myself
my transgressions to Yahweh,'
and you forgave the iniquity of my guilt. *Selah.*
6Therefore, let all the saints offer prayer to you
at a time when you may be found.
Surely in the flood of great waters
they shall not reach him.
7You are my hiding place,
you preserve me from trouble,
you surround me with songs of deliverance. *Selah.*

8I will instruct you and teach you in the way you should walk,
I will counsel you with my eye upon you.
9Do not be like horse or mule which have no understanding,
which must be curbed with a bit and bridle,
or it will not stay near to you.
10Many are the sorrows of the wicked
but the one who trusts in Yahweh,
kindness shall surround him.
11Rejoice in Yahweh and be glad, O righteous ones,
and give a ringing shout all the upright of heart!

Notes on the text

2. Gk has 'in his mouth' for 'spirit', whereas Syr. has 'in his heart'. As neither is an obvious improvement, MT is retained.

4. Hebr. *lĕšadî* is uncertain. In Numbers 11:8 it appears to be a cake baked with oil. It is understood here as something vital (like sap). The range of textual options suggests the difficulty was felt early and does not encourage adopting any as an emendation.

5. With deClaissé-Walford et al. 2014: 307, retaining 'against myself' in translation.

Form and structure

As with Psalm 31, this poem represents a mixture of the main genres (cf. Seybold 1996: 134). The opening beatitudes (vv. 1–2) are more typical of wisdom texts. This is also true of the admonition to the audience (v. 9), where there is a warning against lacking understanding, the didacticism of which is also typical of this genre (cf. Cheung 2015: 28–50). Yet other parts of the poem are more typical of thanksgivings, including the recounting of previous failures (vv. 3–4) and recognition of how Yahweh has acted for the poet (v. 7). Inclusion of these testimonial features is common in thanksgivings, though testimony is not restricted to thanksgiving psalms (e.g. Ps. 73). A common feature of testimonial psalms is that they address multiple audiences (Firth 1999), something evident here as the poet addresses both a congregation (e.g. v. 8) and Yahweh (e.g. v. 7). It seems best therefore to understand the poem as mixing various elements, but with the didactic and thanksgiving elements integrated into the testimony offered as a teaching device (similarly, Botha 2014; Potgieter 2014), encouraging its community to see that trusting Yahweh was the appropriate strategy (Botha 2019).

Though the poem plays with various generic elements, it is more securely integrated into its literary context. Most importantly, it takes up the confession of iniquity (Ps. 31:10) and now reflects on the experience of one who is forgiven. This connection is strengthened by the reference to 'spirit' – in Psalm 31:5 the poet's spirit is committed to Yahweh, whereas here (v. 6) a state of blessedness is noted for those whose spirit lacks deceit. This in turn prepares for the assurance that Yahweh is near those crushed in spirit (Ps. 34:18). Beatitudes also join Psalms 32–34 (32:1–2; 33:12; 34:8). Psalm 31:9–10 spoke of bodily distress, including bones wasting away, and that is taken up here (vv. 3–4). The first thanksgiving in Psalm 31:7 rejoiced in Yahweh's kindness, something all the saints are here encouraged to do (vv. 10–11; cf. 31:24), an acclamation that also echoes Psalm 26:12.

Taking the didactic shape of the testimony as key to its structure, the psalm can be analysed in three stanzas, with the whole poem pivoting around verse 5:

1. Opening beatitudes (1–2)
2. Testimony (3–7)
3. Admonitions (8–11)

Comment

Title: On 'Davidic', see on Psalm 3. This is the first of thirteen psalms to include 'Maskil' in the title (42, 44, 45, 52, 53, 54, 55, 74, 78, 88, 89, 142). The word also appears in Psalm 47:7, where it is a form of praise melody. If derived from a root meaning 'prudent', this would be consistent with the didactic form of this poem (cf. v. 8), though this would not fit as well with other psalms with this title. It may also represent a type of instructional musical text employed with complex antiphony (Amzallag and Yona 2016), though it is difficult to establish this on the Psalter's evidence alone.

1–2. The opening beatitudes echo Psalm 1:1. There are twenty-six beatitudes in the Psalter, though pairs occur elsewhere only in Psalms 119:1–2, 128:1–2, 137:8–9 and 144:15, making this the only pair outside Book 5. The pairing here anticipates the beatitudes coming in Psalms 33 and 34 and emphasizes the state of blessedness of those who are forgiven. Though beatitudes often stress a counterintuitive point (cf. Ps. 1:1; Matt. 5:3–10), the point here is clearly positive. The first beatitude speaks of the blessedness of the one whose transgression is forgiven and whose sin is covered. This beatitude introduces two of the three key roots for sin in Hebrew, with the third (iniquity) coming in the second, with all three repeated in verse 5. These three occur elsewhere only in Psalms 51, 59, 103, creating a close link between these poems. In whatever way sin is conceived, anyone who knows Yahweh has forgiven them is in a state of blessedness. There is a slight change in the form of the two beatitudes (hence, 'the one' and 'the person'), and these mark important developments between them. In verse 1, what is celebrated is the state of forgiveness, whereas in the second it is explicitly stated that such a person is one against whom Yahweh does not reckon iniquity. In this case, we move from a condition of forgiveness to one of right standing before Yahweh, a theme developed in the final line's observation about the lack of deceit in the person's spirit. This would not be a claim of perfection, but rather (as consistently in the Psalter) a claim of living generally for Yahweh. If this psalm is paired with Psalm 26 within the chiastic structure of Psalms 25–34, then this interpretation becomes more likely since that is the status requested there. However, it is also related to the confession in verse 5, in which case the reckoning of no deceit is also the fact that the poet has confessed the relevant sin. Blessedness is thus a state of forgiveness because confession has been made.

3–7. Although it is possible to treat this stanza in three strophes (Snyman 2003: 513), each bounded by *selah*, there is also value in keeping it together, while noting the progression that comes through each stage. Verses 3–4 describe the psalmist's experience before confession. This was a time of suffering, marked by inner failings (bones wasting away), that was paired with screams of distress. Though many EVV render *šĕʿāgâ* as 'groaning' (e.g. ESV), this is too weak for a term that elsewhere refers to the roar of a lion (Isa. 5:29). It is a cry of distress, but it is something screamed, consistent with the sense of internal decay. The reason for this is that while sin was unconfessed, Yahweh's hand was heavy on the poet (cf. Ps. 38:4), leaving a feeling of being drained like something wilting in the heat of summer (cf. Prov. 28:13). The crucial change occurs with the confession of guilt in verse 5. The poet's attempt to cover iniquity had been part of the problem. Where reference to prior speech in Psalm 31:22 pointed to misguided thinking, this time the report of speech introduces the point where the psalmist recognized the need to confess transgression to Yahweh. It was because of this that Yahweh forgave the psalmist's sin and iniquity. The poet's testimony thus provides a reason for all the saints to pray. Exactly what the time is when Yahweh may be found is unclear, but in context may be understood as the point where someone realizes the need to confess, before sin brings punishment. This would be consistent with the floodwaters not reaching them if those waters are understood as an expression of punishment. Being kept from the floodwaters is also consistent with the declaration that Yahweh is the poet's hiding place, the one who protects the poet. Rather than being surrounded by foes, the poet is thus surrounded by songs of deliverance, further evidence of the blessedness described in verses 1–2.

8–11. In the final stanza, an audience are now addressed. Goldingay (2006a: 458) suggests that Yahweh is the speaker, but it is more likely the poet since such shifts are common in testimony and Yahweh is mentioned in the third person in verse 10. Alternatively, with A. P. Ross (2011: 717; cf. Hildebrandt 2020: 207–209), we could understand the poet to be citing an oracle received from Yahweh. This section opens with the promise to instruct and teach this audience in the path to be followed. The verb 'instruct' comes from the same root as 'Maskil', providing further evidence that such poems can have an intentionally didactic purpose. Certainly, the combination of instruction, teaching and counsel is consistent with a wisdom background to the poem, the assumption here being that the psalmist functions as a mentor for this audience. Just as verse 5 outlined the problems caused by the poet's failure to confess, so the admonition begins with what should not be done, warning against lacking insight like a horse or mule, since they must be led by bit and bridle. Such means are unpleasant and to be avoided. So also, the wicked (as those who have not confessed) suffer many pains (by implication from Yahweh), whereas those who trust in Yahweh are surrounded by his kindness, this kindness here paralleling the songs of deliverance in verse 7. Given Yahweh's kindness, the righteous (as a group – the 'you' in v. 8 is sg.) are summoned to rejoice and exult in Yahweh, with ringing shouts from the upright of heart, those who are aligned with Yahweh, something taken up in Psalm 33:1.

Explanation

Integrating other forms into a testimony, the psalm reflects on the blessedness of forgiveness. It looks back to life before sin was confessed and when the poet sought to hide it. This was a time of suffering, of alienation from Yahweh. But when Yahweh forgives, he truly covers sin, and this is a state of blessedness. This is the life the psalmist missed when sin was unconfessed, and so the poem closes by advising those who encounter this testimony that they too need to trust in Yahweh rather than suffer the pains of separation from him. Such trust in this psalm includes confession and can be made because of Yahweh's kindness, and leads in turn to worship. Such forgiveness is a central theme in the Bible as a whole, drawing on Yahweh's self-declaration of his character (Exod. 34:7, a passage also important in Ps. 31) and reaching through to Paul's celebration of forgiveness (Rom. 4:7–8; cf. 1 John 1:9). The psalm makes clear that forgiveness is utterly desirable, and that the experience of it can lead only to testimony and joyful worship.

PSALM 33

Translation

Give a ringing shout, O righteous, in Yahweh,
  praise is fitting for the upright.
2Give thanks to Yahweh on the lyre,
  on the ten-stringed harp make melody to him.
3Sing to him, sing a new song,
  play skilfully with shouts.

4For Yahweh's word is upright,
  and his every deed is done in faithfulness.

5A lover of righteousness and justice,
Yahweh's kindness fills the earth!
6By Yahweh's word were the heavens made,
and by the breath of his mouth all their host,
7gathering the waters of the sea like a dam,
placing the watery deeps in storehouses.

8Let all the earth fear Yahweh,
let all the inhabitants of the world stand in awe of him.
9For he spoke, and it came to be,
he commanded, and it stood.
10Yahweh negates the counsel of the nations,
He frustrates the plans of the peoples.
11Yahweh's counsel stands for ever,
the plans of his heart are from generation to generation.
12Oh the blessedness of the nation whose God is Yahweh,
the people he has chosen as his heritage.
13Yahweh looks out from heaven,
he sees all humankind.
14From his dwelling place he regards
all the inhabitants of the earth,
15the one who fashioned their heart together,
discerning all their works.

16No king is saved by the greatness of an army,
nor a warrior rescued by the greatness of might.
17A horse is a false hope for salvation,
by the greatness of its might it does not deliver.
18Behold, the eyes of Yahweh are on those who fear him,
to those hoping in his kindness,
19to rescue their life from death,
and to keep them alive in famine.

20Our being waits for Yahweh,
our shield and our help is he!
21For in him does our heart rejoice,
for in his holy name have we trusted.
22Let your kindness be upon us O Yahweh,
even as we hope in you.

Notes on the text

18. With one MS, Gk and Syr. reading *'ēnê*.

Form and structure

Psalm 33 is distinctive within Book 1 in lacking a Davidic superscription. Although one occurs in Gk, this is typical of its pattern of adding such titles. Within Book 1, only Psalms 1–2 and 10 lack a title, with all others 'Davidic'. In Book 1 (and Book 2; cf. Ps. 43) absence of a title is a mechanism for linking a psalm to its predecessor (cf. Wilson 1985b). With Psalms 1–2, this was achieved by creating an inclusio through the beatitudes found there, while Psalm 10 continues the acrostic initiated in Psalm 9. Here, absence of the title allows readers to go straight from the summons to give a ringing shout with which Psalm 32 closes to its initiation here (Snyman 2003: 509–11). Indeed, so close is the relationship between these psalms that some MSS join them. Hence, the hymn of praise requested by Psalm 32 for the righteous is provided here, enabling those who trust Yahweh to give voice to this praise.

As well as the smooth transition from Psalm 32:11 to 33:1, there are numerous other links between these poems. The motif of trust in Yahweh from 32:10 recurs in 33:21, while the hope of Yahweh's kindness (32:10) becomes part of the closing prayer here (33:22). Yahweh's ability to protect from the waters those who trust him (32:6) links also to his control of the waters here, verse 7. The beatitudes in Psalm 32:1–2 focus on the individual, but by the psalm's close this becomes advice given to the community, and this is taken further by the beatitude here (v. 12), which now looks to the nation. We may also note the continuation of the language of counsel (Ps. 32:8), with the focus now on the enduring nature of Yahweh's counsel as opposed to that of the nations (v. 10).

A typical hymn (though with variations in the final stanza), the psalm can be analysed in three stanzas, with the second stanza divided into three strophes, the first two marked off by participial phrases and the third by infins. (cf. Witte 2002: 523–525, who develops a chiasm on a similar analysis). On this basis, the outline would be:

1. Summons to praise (1–3)
2. Reasons for praise (4–19)
   a. An ordered creation (4–7)
   b. Reasons to fear Yahweh (8–15)
   c. Yahweh as only saviour (16–19)
3. Waiting on Yahweh (20–22)

Comment

1–3. Opening where Psalm 32 closed, the psalm commences with a call for the righteous to raise a ringing shout to Yahweh, making clear that such a shout is an act of praise. Psalm 32:11 spoke of the upright of heart, here echoed by mention of the upright as those for whom praise is fitting. The link with Psalm 32 makes clear that the upright are those who have accepted Yahweh's grace. This praise becomes explicitly musical in verses 2–3, with thanksgiving offered on lyre and harp, while a new song is sung along with skilful playing and shouts. The theme of a new song is developed more fully in Psalms 40, 96, 98, 144, 149 (see Patterson 2007), but here it is probably best understood as a more freeform expression of musical praise, perhaps pointing to the 'constantly new and renewed sung testimony of God's people' (deClaissé-Walford et al. 2014: 314). Not all praise is musical, but the Psalter recognizes that praise and music often come together.

4–7. As is typical of hymns, the opening summons to praise is followed by reasons for praise. But rather than focusing on Yahweh's character (e.g. Ps. 113:4–9b), initial attention here is given to Yahweh's word and acts before turning to his 'kindness' (*ḥesed*). The 'upright' (*yāšār*) character of Yahweh's wordplays with the sound of 'song' (*šîr*) in the previous verse, while its description is also appropriate for the upright, for whom praise is fitting (v. 1). For the upright, the upright nature of Yahweh's word is itself a reason for praise. Yahweh's word here is related to the written word, meaning this psalm draws on elements more typically associated with Torah psalms (with Botha and Potgieter 2010), but paralleling it with Yahweh's every deed broadens the focus so his speech and acts can be understood as reliable. This in turn prepares for the note in verse 5 that is now focused on Yahweh's character as one who loves righteousness and justice, further emphasizing his reliability, before celebrating the fact that his kindness fills the earth. Creation has not been central to the psalm before this point but is now the dominant motif in the strophe. Creation is also tied to Yahweh's word, so that it can be affirmed that Yahweh made the heavens by his word, connecting this statement back to the strophe's opening. The hosts made by the breath of his mouth are here the heavenly bodies. That they too were made by the breath of his mouth links them to Yahweh's word, though use of 'breath' (*rûaḥ*) links this to mention of the 'Spirit' (*rûaḥ*) in Genesis 1:1. As the ptcs. in verse 7 are understood here, they expand on Yahweh's creative acts in further dialogue with Genesis 1:1. There Yahweh's Spirit hovered above the 'watery deep' (*tĕhôm*). Here, the watery deeps are gathered along with the sea (with both watery deep and sea understood as potential sources of chaos or even deities within ANE mythology) and placed in storehouses. They are no longer chaotic forces that place creation under threat (cf. Gen. 7:11). Rather, the heavenly host and the waters are under Yahweh's control (cf. Exod. 15:8; Josh. 3:13), evidence of the dependability of his word and deeds.

8–15. The second strophe is centred on the beatitude of verse 12. Verses 8–11 build towards it, opening with the hope that all the earth will fear Yahweh, thus beginning to focus on humans, a point made explicit in verse 8b as it refers to the world's inhabitants. The reason for their standing in awe of Yahweh is focused on the combination of his word and deed, as can be seen in the fact that verse 9 includes two verbs of speech ('spoke' and 'commanded') both of which result in the existence and stability of creation. Creation is reliable because Yahweh stands behind it. But human activity is also a key source of disorder within creation, especially as humans reach beyond the role assigned for them in Genesis 1. Where a nation's counsel or plans are contrary to his purposes, Yahweh thwarts such counsel or plans. This is possible because it is Yahweh's counsel and plans that stand. That his counsel (another example of Yahweh's word) stands places it in a place equal to his command, which also stands. Yahweh can frustrate the peoples' plans, but his endures. Yahweh's word can thus be trusted, and his creation is thus secure. In this context, therefore, a state of blessedness exists in being the nation that has Yahweh as its God, the people he has chosen as his heritage. Both 'nation' and 'people' here echo key terms from verse 10, except that now we speak of a people who are aligned with Yahweh's purposes. Where verse 8 had hoped for all to fear him, and thus considers human response to Yahweh, here the focus is Yahweh's choice in determining the people who are his heritage. Within the psalm, those who stand in this state of blessedness are those who fear Yahweh and thus desire to live in harmony with his word since, as in Psalm 1, this is where blessedness is found. The blessedness of this nation is then placed in context by verses 13–15. From heaven, Yahweh looks out to all humankind. As we progress through these verses, there is a gradual intensification in his act of looking. In verse 13 this is a more general act of looking, observing all humankind. In verse 14, this is now 'regarding' (*hišgîaḥ*), a rarer verb that seems to involve a more focused look (cf. Song 2:9). This is brought to its conclusion through the ptcs. in verse 15, which are here understood as qualifying the preceding statements and showing that Yahweh as creator has special insight into humans. As the one who formed them, he understands their 'heart', which here probably stands for both human thought and volition, while also discerning their works. Yahweh's word and works are secure and trustworthy, but that is not always true of humans, and Yahweh understands this.

16–19. The third strophe emerges from the first two, with verses 16–17 showing wrong human choices and contrasting them with Yahweh's dependability. Human counsel is attracted to visible forms of might, and hence a king would seek a powerful army. But if Yahweh thwarts the counsel of the nations, then there is no reason to think that a powerful army is really the means of victory. No king is saved that way (cf. 2 Chr. 20), and neither is a warrior rescued simply by his great might (cf. 1 Sam. 17). The folly of trusting horses for victory has already been highlighted in Psalm 20:7, but now such trust is explicitly stated to be false, for although a horse may have great strength, this is insufficient to deliver.

Rather, Yahweh's eyes are on those who fear him. Mention of Yahweh's eyes picks up the motif of his looking in verses 13–15, while mention of those who fear Yahweh links back to verse 8, enabling this third strophe to tie together key themes across the whole of the second stanza. This is further emphasized through the note that these people hope in Yahweh's kindness, tying this stanza's close to the first (v. 5) while also preparing for the third (v. 22), a connection also made through repetition of the motif of hope (v. 22). That Yahweh can rescue from death, especially those hoping in him from famine, could suggest that this was the background to the psalm, a context in which a reminder of the stability of creation would be particularly important.

20–22. Where the previous stanza has discussed Yahweh's relationship to humans in general terms, the final stanza shifts to the experience of the praying community. Yahweh can deliver those who hope in him, and so the community now declare that they wait hopefully on Yahweh, affirming that he is their shield and help. This combination occurs elsewhere only in Psalm 115:9–11, though there it occurs three times, always in the context of trusting Yahweh. Indeed, these are the only two psalms that speak of Yahweh as his people's help. However, there is also a close link with Psalm 28:7, which also describes Yahweh as 'shield' and affirms that he 'helped' the poet. Within the subunit of Psalms 25–34, this provides an evidential basis for the affirmation made here, a point of testimony that explains why the community can see Yahweh in these terms. This provides a context for the declaration of trust in verse 21, though trust is linked to rejoicing. Trust is here in Yahweh's holy name, another way of stressing his dependable character as the one unlike the gods of the nations. Understanding that Yahweh can be trusted, and that he does help his people, the psalm closes by expressing the wish that his kindness will be upon them as they hope in him; that is, that they may experience the deliverance spoken of in verses 16–19. Praise has been key, but it is still applied to the people's need.

Explanation

Building on the blessedness of forgiveness in Psalm 32, Psalm 33 invites all who have found this joy to participate in praising Yahweh. Throughout, there is a focus on the interplay between Yahweh's word and creation, both of which can be trusted, providing a secure basis for people to hope in Yahweh. The praise offered here engages with the mythological concerns of the ancient world when it considered creation, though it also addresses the modern world and the challenges it faces (cf. Firth 2014: 109–112), continuing to stress the dependability of both Yahweh's word and the creation in which we live. Praise as those forgiven leads to an awareness of the world God has created, a creation that the NT insists is through Jesus Christ (Col. 1:15–20; Heb. 1:1–3), and that continues to be upheld through him. In our world too, the closing wish to experience God's kindness even as we hope in him continues to be important. By grounding our hope in praise we remind ourselves that it is God alone who holds this world, and it is in him that we hope.

PSALM 34

Translation

Davidic. When he altered his behaviour before Abimelech, and he banished him, and he left.

1I will bless Yahweh at all times,
his praise shall continually be in my mouth.
2In Yahweh shall my being boast,
let the afflicted hear and be glad.
3Magnify Yahweh with me,
and let us exalt his name together.

4I sought Yahweh and he answered me,
and from all my terrors he rescued me.
5Look to him and be radiant,
and your faces shall not be put to shame.
6This poor one called out, and Yahweh heard,
and from all his straits he saved this one.
7Yahweh's messenger camps around those who fear him,
and he delivers them.

8Taste and see that Yahweh is good,
Oh the blessedness of one who takes refuge in him!
9Fear Yahweh O his saints,
for there is no lack for those who fear him.
10Young lions may be in want and hungry,
But those who seek Yahweh lack no good thing.
11Come children, listen to me,
I shall teach you the fear of Yahweh.
12Who is the one who delights in life,
who loves daily to see good?
13Keep your tongue from evil,
and your lips from speaking deceit.
14Turn from evil and do good,
seek peace and pursue it.

15Yahweh's eyes are on the righteous,
his ears are turned towards their cry for help.
16Yahweh's face is against those who do evil,
to cut off their memory from the earth.
17The righteous cry out and Yahweh hears,
and from all their straits he delivers them.
18Yahweh is near to the broken hearted,
and the crushed of spirit he saves.
19Many are the troubles of the righteous,
but Yahweh rescues them from them all,
20protecting all their bones,
not one of them is broken.
21Affliction kills the wicked,
and those who hate the righteous will be condemned.

22Yahweh redeems the life of his servant,
and will not condemn any taking refuge in him.

Notes on the text

5. With Gk, reading the opening verbs as imperatives and then the second-person pr. suff. for 'your faces'.

11. Gk (cf. Syr.) reads *plousioi*, suggesting *kĕbēdîm* for *kĕpîrîm*. In a consonantal text, this is only a *p–b* interchange. Both senses work well, but as MT is slightly more difficult it is retained. Cf. Roberts 1973.

18. With Gk, adding 'the righteous'.

Form and structure

Along with Psalm 25, Psalm 34 provides an acrostic psalm that forms a boundary to the subunit of Psalms 25–34. These two psalms are linked by more than their acrostic structure (cf. Maloney 2008: 69–73), with the verses starting with the successive letters of the Hebrew alphabet, since both include an additional *p* verse to close the poem (and both using the verb *pdh* for this). The resulting poem contains twenty-two verses, matching the number of letters in the Hebrew alphabet, by omitting a verse commencing with *w*, perhaps because so few words begin with this letter (unless we find it *en passant* in v. 5b). The alphabet here features not only as a structuring device, but also as a central element to the psalm's teaching (cf. Ceresko 1985). As a boundary marker, it is also notable that where Psalm 25 draws more on the complaint tradition, Psalm 34 features more elements that are typical of thanksgiving psalms, joining Psalms 32, 33 in integrating these with wisdom elements and allusions to Deuteronomy (cf. Owens 2013: 105–106). This subunit, with its pivot around Psalm 29 and its celebration of Yahweh's power, has an initial focus on complaint (Pss 25–28), but as we move to its conclusion it increasingly emphasizes thanksgiving.

Given these points, it is not surprising that the poem is well integrated into its literary context. The beatitude of verse 8 is part of a string of beatitudes that hold together Psalms 32–34 (32:1–2; 33:12; 34:8). Direct addresses to a congregation also occur in Psalms 30:4–5, 31:23–24, 32:11 and 33:1–3, a feature only marginally present in Psalms 25–28 (cf. Ps. 27:14). More immediately, verse 15 picks up on the motif of Yahweh's eyes being on the righteous in Psalm 33:18, while both refer positively to those who fear Yahweh (Pss 33:8; 34:7, 9). As a balancing item to Psalm 25, where the poet asks not to be put to shame (Ps. 25:2), here there is the declaration that those looking to Yahweh will not be put to shame (v. 5). In sum, the wisdom-tinged observations of this psalm now serve to conclude this subunit, showing that the power of Yahweh celebrated in Psalm 29 can indeed address the concerns raised in Psalms 25–28, and so bring those supplicants to a position of thanksgiving through Psalms 30–33.

Although the acrostic controls the form of the poem, its use of elements from thanksgiving poems means it is possible to trace a structure that emerges from these elements that also makes clear the poem's didactic intent (cf. Owens 2013: 96):

1. Poet as fellow worshipper (1–10)
   a. Call to praise (1–3)
   b. Testimony leading to praise (4–7)
   c. Encouragement to take refuge in Yahweh (8–10)
2. Poet as teacher (11–21)
   a. Instruction on the fear of Yahweh (11–14)
   b. Yahweh's relationship to the righteous and the wicked (15–21)
3. Closing summary (22)

Comment

Title: On 'Davidic', see on Psalm 3. Apart from this poem, Psalms 3, 18 are the only examples in Book 1 of psalms tied to events in David's life. In this case, it appears to refer to David's feigning of madness in 1 Samuel 21:10–15, though the king's name there is Achish. Craigie and Tate (2004: 278) suggest that Abimelech (my father is king) could have been a dynastic name, possibly also evoking the king of Genesis 20:26 (so, Goldingay 2006a: 478). By evoking these stories, we read this psalm from the perspective of someone who needs to understand that whatever else happened in a time of crisis, it was still finally Yahweh who had been at work.

1–3. The psalm commences with a promise to bless Yahweh (cf. Ps. 16:7). Blessing Yahweh is a close synonym for praise, though the more common term 'praise' then follows. Yahweh's praise will continually be in the poet's mouth, pointing to spoken praise, though such praise may be joyful shouts or more carefully formed speech. 'Praise' (*tĕhillâ*) and 'boast' (*hll*) are related words, making clear that the boast is not bragging but rather a positive report of Yahweh, one that the afflicted can hear and so be glad. This statement makes clear that the promise of praise is itself intended to be instructive, which is why a congregation is now asked to join the poet in magnifying Yahweh and exalting his name, both forms of praise that aim to demonstrate Yahweh's greatness.

4–7. Having invited the congregation to participate in praise, the poet now recounts an experience of Yahweh's responsiveness to the call of his people. These verses alternate between testimony (vv. 4, 6) and assurances that others can experience something similar (vv. 5, 7). The poet reports a time of seeking Yahweh, presumably in prayer. Yahweh answered by delivering the psalmist from the terrors that had triggered this. This experience is applied to the congregation, who are told to look to Yahweh and so be radiant (i.e. joyful), since looking to Yahweh in this way avoids the experience of shame. Verse 6 then reverts to the poet's experience and is closely patterned on verse 4. The reference to the poet in the third person is necessitated by the acrostic structure, but it also allows space for others to step into this experience and perhaps see themselves as one of the poor who have needed to cry out to Yahweh knowing that he hears. Evidence that Yahweh heard is then provided in the note that he saved the poet from all the terrors that triggered the prayer. This move to the third person is continued in the advice in verse 7 that now speaks of those who fear Yahweh rather than directly addressing the congregation, as in verse 5. Mention of Yahweh's messenger introduces a new figure into the poem, though in context it also prepares for the dual mention of the messenger in Psalm 35:5–6. There, the hope is that the messenger will act against enemies, whereas here the assurance is that the messenger camps around those who fear Yahweh and rescues them. White's analysis (1999) of narrative references to the messenger concludes that this language functions as a euphemism for God, and such a conclusion is likely here too since the reverence the psalm seeks is directed to Yahweh and not to the messenger (cf. v. 9). This leaves open the possibility that Yahweh's actions may be seen through others and are not necessarily miraculous. The point thus is that just as Yahweh responded to the poet's cry, so also those who fear Yahweh may be confident that he has a means of delivering them, though the poem does not specify the means.

8–10. Having shared testimony, the congregation is again addressed. Verse 8 opens with two imperatives, 'taste and see' that Yahweh is good (cf. 1 Peter 2:3), before a beatitude that points to the desirability of taking refuge in him. Both imperatives point to the experience of Yahweh's goodness, stressing that it is something experienced, perhaps rooted in meals celebrated in the sanctuary (cf. Deut. 14:23–29; deClaissé-Walford et al. 2014: 326). This goodness can then be understood through taking refuge in Yahweh; that is, finding him as the place of protection. Verse 10 then commences with another imp., urging the fear of Yahweh by his saints (cf. Josh. 24:14; 1 Sam. 12:24) since those who fear him lack nothing. By contrast, even predators like young lions may experience lack, but those who seek Yahweh lack no good thing. This statement points back to the testimony in verse 4 since the poet has sought Yahweh, and so this provides additional support for the directive to fear Yahweh.

11–14. Since the fear of Yahweh is so important, the audience are invited to come and listen to the poet so it may be taught this fear. The fear of Yahweh is not a terror, since Yahweh has delivered the poet from these (v. 4), but rather a way of orienting one's life before Yahweh. Hence, the summons to come and learn does not initially explain the content of this fear. Rather (echoing Pss 15:1; 24:3), it poses a question to the congregation, asking who delights in life and longs to see good. This is something anyone would want, though by picking up on the key word 'good' it ties this question to verses 8, 10. As such, 'good' is given a specific content in terms of a relationship with Yahweh, and the fear of Yahweh is a 'good' that gives life value. The means of accessing this is the fear of Yahweh, and the means of experiencing this is outlined in verses 13–14. As with Psalms 15, 24, the way this relationship with Yahweh is worked out is first in relation to others, initially through control of speech, which now avoids speaking evil or deceit. This is then developed in verse 14 as turning from evil and doing good. Hence, we move from speech that is negative towards others to actions more generally. Doing 'good' here must refer to that which is consistent with Yahweh's will, though, as it is developed as 'seeking' (*baqqēš*) peace, it also means promoting positive relationships with others (cf. Heb. 12:14). The fear of Yahweh is an embodied ethic that refrains from destructive speech and acts, positively seeking the well-being of others.

15–21. Having taught the fear of Yahweh, the poem now explores Yahweh's relationship with the righteous and the wicked to provide further encouragement for people to fear Yahweh. This is established by an immediate contrast in verses 15–16. That Yahweh's eyes and ears are with the righteous points to his care for them and response to their cry, as already seen in the poet's testimony. By contrast, his face is against those doing evil, to cut off even the memory of them in the earth. Cutting off memory of someone makes it as if they had never been. Verses 17–18 then provide further evidence of Yahweh's concern for the righteous, responding to their cry by rescuing them from their straits, echoing the poet's experience (v. 6). Though the righteous may lack no good thing, the psalm also recognizes that the righteous can go through periods of suffering (cf. the poet's self-description in v. 6). But Yahweh is near them when they suffer, saving them in times of distress. All this is summarized in verse 19's observation that though the righteous have many troubles, Yahweh rescues them from them all. In doing so, he guards them so that even though they may be broken of heart, not one bone is broken. By contrast, the wicked are killed by affliction, while those who hate the righteous will be condemned. Like Psalm 1, the poem refrains from declaring that Yahweh will do this, seeing that it is also possible that the actions of such people may also contain the seeds of their own destruction.

22. The final verse functions like a coda to the poem. In terms of its content, one could see it as a continuation of the second stanza, but by standing outside the acrostic pattern it is marked as distinct while also echoing Psalm 25:22. Although this verse now speaks of Yahweh's servants, they are clearly those who fear Yahweh who can trust that he redeems their life. That he will not condemn those who take refuge in him echoes the beatitude of verse 8 and indicates that they too are those who fear him and can therefore be confident that he will not find them guilty but grant continued refuge.

Explanation

As the conclusion to the subunit of Psalms 25–34, this poem offers a word of testimony that the situations of complaint that dominated Psalms 25–28 were not the last word. Rather, following the pattern of thanksgiving that emerges in Psalms 30–33 we see that the power of Yahweh celebrated in Psalm 29 is not just general statements but rather something that can be experienced. That is why it is important to note that the thanksgiving element of the poem is also reporting experience. In doing this, it recognizes the reality of times of distress in the life of the faithful but also offers clear evidence that this is not necessarily the way it must be, though (with Ps. 73) it refrains from providing a simple answer to the complex realities faced by believers. Testimony through thanksgiving is then applied to more direct teaching, encouraging an audience to engage with the fear of Yahweh in the face of challenges (cf. Botha 1997: 189). In doing so, it encourages readers to understand that the fear of Yahweh is not simply privatized piety. Rather, joining with Psalms 15, 24 (the boundaries of the previous subunit) it encourages believers to see that the fear of Yahweh is expressed most fully in developing positive relationships with others, seeking peace (cf. Matt. 5:9) as a genuine response to having experienced God's goodness (Botha 2012b: 75). Discovering God's goodness is thus a basis for continued praise, testimony and trust that seeks to work this out in developing the community of which we are a part (cf. 1 Peter 3:10–18). We do not make joy our goal, yet in seeking such a community we discover it as a gift of God.

PSALM 35

Translation

Davidic.

1Dispute, O Yahweh, with those who dispute with me,
fight against those who fight me!
2Grasp shield and buckler
and rise in my assistance.
3Draw out spear and javelin to confront those who pursue me,
say to me, 'I am your salvation.'
4Let those seeking my life be ashamed and confounded,
let them be turned back and abashed,
who devise evil against me.
5May they be like chaff before the wind,
with Yahweh's messenger driving it.
6May their path be dark and slippery,
with Yahweh's messenger pursuing them.
7For without cause, they concealed their net as a trap for me,
without cause, they scouted out my life.
8May destruction take him unawares,
and may the net he concealed capture him,
as devastation, let him fall in it.
9So may my being rejoice in Yahweh,
may it exult in his salvation.
10All my bones shall say, 'O Yahweh, who is like you,
delivering the afflicted from those stronger than them,
the afflicted and needy from those who rob them?'

11Violent witnesses have arisen,
what I do not know, they ask me.
12They recompense me evil for good,
bereavement to my being.
13As for me, when they were ill, I wore sackcloth,
I afflicted myself with fasting,
and my prayer turned on my chest.
14I went about as for my friend or brother,
as one laments a mother, I was bowed down and mourning.
15They rejoiced and gathered when I stumbled,

they gathered against me,
wretches that I did not know,
they tore and were not still,
16like a circle of godless mockers
gnashing their teeth against me.
17O Lord, how long will you look on?
Restore my life from their ravages,
my precious life from the young lions.
18I will give you thanks in the great congregation,
in the throngs of people, I will praise you.

19Do not let those who are my foes for no reason rejoice over me,
nor let those who hate me without cause wink the eye.
20For they do not speak peace,
but against the quiet of the land
they devise words of treachery.
21They open wide their mouths against me,
they say, 'Aha! Aha!
Our eyes have seen!'
22You have seen, O Yahweh, do not be silent,
O Lord do not be far from me.
23Wake up! Rouse yourself for my claim for justice,
My God and my Lord, for my dispute.
24Judge me according to your righteousness, O Yahweh my God,
and do not let them rejoice over me.
25Do not let them think, 'Aha, we have our desire.'
Do not let them say, 'We have swallowed him up.'
26Let those rejoicing at my harm be ashamed and abashed together,
let them be clothed with shame and ignominy,
those who magnify themselves against me.
27Let those who take pleasure in my righteousness shout and rejoice,
let them say continually, 'Yahweh is great,
the one who delights in his servant's well-being.'
28So shall my tongue speak of your righteousness,
your praise all day.

Notes on the text

7. *ḥpr* is commonly 'dig', leading to the assumption that a pit is dug (cf. Syr.). But in Job 39:29 it refers to scouting for something, and that meaning is adopted here.

16. MT here is very difficult. Many follow LXX, but it is difficult to see this text emerging if it is original. Here, the initial *bĕ* is read as *beth essentiae* (*WHS* §249), and *mā'ôg* as 'circle' (cf. *DCH*).

Form and structure

The diverse forms of language found in this psalm make it difficult to assign it to a particular *Sitz im Leben*. Depending on which elements are said to be literal and which metaphorical, it is possible to claim that the psalm represents the prayer of a king facing battle (e.g. Eaton 1976: 41–42) or someone facing false accusation (e.g. Delekat 1967: 114–116), though elements suggesting illness are also present. Because of these motifs, Beuken (2020: 25) suggests that an earlier poem might have been expanded to include the various elements. While not impossible, it is perhaps more plausible to consider the psalm as intentionally metaphorical throughout, allowing each element to speak in its own terms, but which the final shape of the Psalter leaves open so that, apart from the general plea for protection, no one motif can dominate (Firth 2005b: 69–71).

Psalm 35 introduces the final main section of Book 1, running through to its close with Psalm 41. As Beuken (2020: 83–93; cf. Simango 2022: 443–448) has shown, this collection is arranged in two largely parallel panels, Psalms 35–37 and 38–41, with all now functioning as supplications of David in affliction (P. C. W. Ho 2019: 335). As the first psalm in a new unit, it functions as a bridge from the previous unit, so that the enduring praise promised in Psalm 34:1 is taken up by the closing affirmation here (v. 28). Mention of the 'young lions' also provides a key word that joins these poems (Pss 34:10; 35:17), as does reference to Yahweh's messenger (Pss 34:7; 35:5–6). More generally, Psalm 34:15–21 assured the righteous that Yahweh delivers them from their afflictions, and this psalm takes up that point in asking that Yahweh act to deliver the poet. These features show that the collections within Book 1 are not absolutely distinct, but the stronger connections are still with the psalms that follow, such as the existence of those contending with the psalmist (Pss 35:1–3; 36:2–4) and the expectation of their defeat (Pss 35:8; 36:12.

The main metaphors also shape the psalm's structure in three stanzas, with each closing with the hope of praise:

1. Protection in a military context (1–10)
   a. Appeal to Yahweh (1–3)
   b. Prayer for protection (4–8)
   c. Hope of praise (9–10)
2. Protection in a legal context (11–18)
   a. Prayer for protection (11–17)
   b. Hope of praise (18)
3. Prayer against enemies (19–28)
   a. Prevention of enemy activity (19–26)
   b. Hope of praise (27–28)

Comment

Title: On 'Davidic', see on Psalm 3.

1–3. The psalm's opening appeal provides the context for the whole poem and not just the first stanza. The opening imp. *rîbâ* can describe both military and legal conflict (note the cognate noun in v. 23), and so initiates the appeal that Yahweh act against those acting against the psalmist in the mode in which they act. As the appeal continues, the language becomes progressively more military. It is notable that Yahweh is not first called to take up weapons. Rather, a small and large shield are to be taken up to aid the psalmist, with Yahweh's acting as the poet's armour-bearer (cf. Sutton 2018). Nevertheless, if Yahweh is to fight these battles, then some weapons are required, and these become the focus in verse 3. The spear is easily recognized, though the 'javelin' is less certain. What matters is that Yahweh use these weapons to confront those pursuing the poet while also reassuring the psalmist that Yahweh is the needed source of salvation.

4–8. In the prayer for protection, the poet focuses on how Yahweh is to thwart the adversaries. The threat against the poet is severe, potentially fatal, and so the prayer asks for actions that offset those, though without asking for the death of these opponents. They have been seeking to harm the poet, so the request is that they be turned back, having first been shamed and confounded. The assumption is that the futility of their choice of seeking the psalmist's life will be made clear. As the prayer progresses, we hear echoes of Psalm 1:4 in the request that the enemies may be like chaff driven by the wind, a status that would clearly confirm them as wicked and therefore liable to Yahweh's judgement. This is confirmed by the action of Yahweh's messenger, who is to drive them. Mention of the messenger could simply be another way of speaking of Yahweh, though perhaps leaving open how Yahweh will act. Not only are the enemies to be turned back, but their path is to be dark and slippery as the messenger now pursues them instead of their pursuing the psalmist. The reason for this is that they have acted against the poet without cause, laying traps (a net) and scouting out other ways to act against the psalmist. They are thus clearly identified as the wicked against whom Yahweh should act. Although the enemies have been spoken of as a group to this point, in verse 8 there is a shift to the sg. This could indicate focus on a ringleader, though the sense could also be 'each one'. However, the punishment requested is still intended to match the harm that has been sought against the psalmist, even to the extent of being caught in the net laid for the poet. As is common in the Psalms, the punishment requested against the enemies is equal to the harm sought, but not more (cf. Firth 2005b: 73).

9–10. The opening stanza closes with an anticipation of praise, with the language here echoing terms from the appeal and prayer. Yahweh is to be the poet's help and salvation, and so the hope expressed here anticipates the moment of rejoicing in Yahweh because of his salvation. This praise is expressed through the psalmist's bones, indicating that praise is a whole-body experience as Yahweh's incomparability is initially raised. The question 'Who is like you' is like Exodus 15:3, 11 (cf. Mic. 7:18), with the implied answer that 'No one is like Yahweh.' It is because Yahweh has no equal that he delivers the afflicted and needy from those who are more powerful than them and who would rob them. In this way, he offers the hope that the weak need, providing encouragement for them to live the life of the righteous encouraged by Psalm 1.

11–17. Where the first stanza drew more on military language, the second prefers the language of the courtroom. There is no opening appeal here; the appeal in verses 1–3 continues to lay the foundation for what follows. Rather than the language of pursuit, we are now told of violent witnesses who have arisen against the poet, the implication being that their testimony is false as they seek the psalmist's harm. As witnesses, they are also prosecutors, requesting responses to questions the poet cannot provide. Such actions are contrary to the earlier relationship that existed: where the poet had acted for their well-being, they now bring harm and bereavement. Evidence for the poet's positive actions for the enemies is then recounted in verses 13–14, describing actions of solidarity in prayer and fasting with them during periods of illness, treating them as if they were close family members (note the increasing levels of intimacy here; cf. Janzen 1995: 60). This is then contrasted with their response to a point when the psalmist stumbled in verses 15–16. Where the psalmist acted in solidarity, the enemies saw the poet's time of weakness as a chance to take advantage of the situation, attacking the psalmist yet more, drawing in others to join the assault (cf. 'Notes on the text'). If the legal context introduced in verse 11 provides the background here, then the implication is that the poet has been suffering from continued legal assaults rather than physical attack, though the latter is certainly a plausible outcome from such a setting. Thus, the poet asks Yahweh how long he will look on, the implication being that Yahweh should have acted before now. Since the legal threat places the poet's life at risk, the plea is that his life be restored. Since these enemies are now characterized as young lions, they clearly fit the category of those too powerful for the psalmist (v. 10), showing that this is a point at which Yahweh should act.

18. The second stanza also closes with the hope of praise, with thanksgiving to be given in the great congregation. The poet showed solidarity with the needy even though they have not reciprocated. Similarly, communal solidarity is expected in the giving of thanks and sharing praise since this is the appropriate context for sharing how Yahweh has acted to restore life that was under threat.

19–26. The psalmist's foes may be military or legal, and these categories could also stand for others. As such, the third stanza now asks Yahweh to act more generally against the enemies, though in doing so it reuses important terms from the first two stanzas. The enemies' goal is to rejoice over the psalmist, claiming victory through some form of conspiracy (winking the eye), but the poet asks Yahweh to prevent this since their hatred has no cause. Their actions against the psalmist are representative of wider actions against the land since instead of speech that promotes peace, they speak in ways destructive of quiet in the land, promoting treachery. But this is still focused on the poet as they open their mouths and claim to have seen things, presumably the false testimony from the second stanza. What they claim to have seen is immediately contrasted with what Yahweh has seen, and Yahweh's own status as a witness means that he cannot be silent. Yahweh has seen and therefore needs to be near the poet. The first element in this involves Yahweh's rousing himself. The suggestion is that Yahweh has been sleeping on the job; but if justice is to be served, then this cannot continue. Yahweh needs to awake and act for the poet in this dispute. Yet although we may expect the psalmist to ask that Yahweh judge the enemies, instead the request is that Yahweh judge the poet according to his righteousness. This is different from the prayers of the accused where the psalmists ask for their own righteousness (i.e. innocence) to provide the basis (e.g. Pss 7:8; 26:1). Rather, Yahweh's righteousness is the basis for judgement, since this will show that the poet needs him to act and thus prevent the enemies from rejoicing over the psalmist. Their desire is expressed in the thought noted in verse 25, that they would have destroyed the poet. Instead, the request is that those who would rejoice at the psalmist's harm would be ashamed and abashed, echoing the prayer from verse 4. They have sought to magnify themselves unjustly, and so the request is that they be clothed instead with shame and ignominy. Once again, there are careful limits in this prayer, with the punishment requested not exceeding the harm sought.

27–28. The closing hope of praise also draws together elements from preceding prayer. Rather than the joyful shouts of triumph anticipated by the enemies, the psalm instead looks forward to such shouts from those who have recognized the poet's righteousness. It was this that was threatened by the violent witnesses, but it must be Yahweh who resolves this. Where the enemies magnified themselves, now Yahweh's greatness is continually declared by those who respond to his delight in the well-being of his servants, showing that Yahweh is the opposite of the enemies (v. 20). Thus, the poet will join with those speaking (cf. Ps. 1:2) of Yahweh's righteousness and praise because Yahweh will have wrought justice.

Explanation

Beginning a new subunit in Book 1, Psalm 35 places its focus clearly on supplication. Here, the poet stresses that enemies have acted without cause (vv. 7, 19) while also emphasizing that it is Yahweh who needs to act for the psalmist's deliverance. Indeed, it is Yahweh, and not the poet, who must confront the enemies. The psalmist needs instead to submit the often-passionate desire for justice that is expressed here and leave it with Yahweh. Having expressed this desire, it is left for Yahweh to act. The psalm does not close off the conditions that led to this prayer for protection, leaving a range of circumstances available. Rather, it is now open to a range of contexts in which believers may take up the language of this prayer as they face various forms of oppression without reason. In so doing, we follow the pattern of Jesus (John 15:25) who was also hated without cause, while we take seriously the fact that he taught us to pray 'deliver us from evil' (Matt. 6:13; cf. McCann 1996: 820).

PSALM 36

Translation

The director's. For Yahweh's Servant. Davidic.

1An oracle by transgression to the wicked one is within my heart,
  'There is no dread of God before his eyes,
2because he deceives himself in his eyes
  about finding his iniquity to hate it.
3The words of his mouth are trouble and deceit,
  he refrains from acting wisely and doing good.
4He plots injustice upon his bed,
  he sets himself on a path that is not good,
  evil he does not reject.'

5Yahweh, your kindness is unto the heavens,
  your faithfulness to the clouds,
6your righteousness is like the mightiest mountains,
  your justice is like the great deep,
  you save human and beast, O Yahweh.
7How precious is your kindness,
  heavenly beings and human children
  take shelter in the shadow of your wings.
8They are filled from the abundance of your house,
  you give them drink from the river of your delights,

[9]because with you is the fountain of life,
  in your light we see light.

[10]Spread out your kindness for those who know you,
  and your righteousness for the upright of heart.
[11]Do not let the foot of the arrogant approach me,
  and do not let the hand of the wicked make me wander as a fugitive.
[12]There the workers of evil fall:
  they are thrust down and are no longer able to rise.

Notes on the text

1. The opening is very difficult, with numerous options (cf. *BHS*). LXX is smoother, but as deClaissé-Walford et al. note (2014: 339), is anachronistic and therefore unlikely. *peša'* is here understood as a subjective genitive, and thus personified as one speaking. 'My heart' is often changed to 'his heart' (with Syr.), but if David is understood as the speaker, then MT can be retained, with the utterance then reported.

7. Often scanned as a bicolon, it is here read as a tricolon (see Introduction, §3.1.1, 'Psalms as poetry'). Although the first line could end with a voc. 'O God', commencing the second line with the conj. *wĕ* is odd. But placing *'ĕlōhîm* as the first part of the middle line and understanding it as part of the demythologizing pattern of the stanza provides a workable solution without emendation.

Form and structure

Like Psalm 35, Psalm 36 appears to bring together discrete elements while still integrating them into a single poem. Thus, it opens with one of only two oracles in the Psalter (cf. Ps. 110:1), though in this case the oracle sounds rather like a wisdom saying. This is followed by praise of Yahweh's character and then a concluding prayer that Yahweh's kindness will see the fall of the wicked. If we take the prayer as the life setting, then we could classify the psalm as a prayer for protection. If so, then both the oracle and the praise unit find their goal in this prayer as it draws on themes from both, notably in the interplay between Yahweh's kindness and the fate of the wicked (cf. Seybold 1996: 150), though the integration of these parts means we can also see elements of the Song of Confidence (so, Longman 2014: 175).

There are important links with Psalm 35. Both psalms reflect on those who contend with the psalmist (Pss 35:1–3; 36:2–4). Both also have the motif of speech in the heart (Pss 35:25; 36:1) as well as the expectation that the wicked will fall (Pss 35:8; 36:12). Where Yahweh's messenger drives the adversaries (Ps. 35:5), the prayer here asks that the poet not be driven away (Ps. 36:12). Both psalms also interact with Psalms 1–2 as they explore how Yahweh engages with the wicked.

As with Psalm 35, this poem can be analysed through its component parts in three stanzas (cf. Auffret 1988), with the last picking up themes from the previous two:

1. Oracle about the wicked (1–4)
2. The reality of Yahweh's kindness (5–9)
3. Plea to experience Yahweh's kindness (10–12)

Comment

Title: On 'The director's', see on Psalm 4. For 'Davidic' see on Psalm 3. 'Yahweh's Servant' here would include David (cf. Ps. 18), but could here refer also to other supplicants, picking up on Psalm 35:27.

1–4. The exact sense of verse 1 is uncertain (cf. 'Notes on the text') but is here understood as an oracle delivered by a personified transgression. If so, there is something deeply ironic in its nature. We would normally expect an oracle to be delivered by a prophetic figure, which in 2 Samuel 23:1 includes David, but here that role is taken on by transgression. The 'wicked one' may here also be a personification rather than a particular person, perhaps drawing on the pattern of the wicked in Psalm 1. The poet claims to have internalized this oracle, so that even though it comes from an unexpected source, it can be remembered because even transgression can recognize the problem of wickedness. The oracle, which is cast more as a wisdom saying, is then reported from verse 1b to the end of the stanza. The oracle opens by defining the wicked one as someone who has no dread of God. Such dread can be terror, but here is more likely expressing the lack of willingness to be shaped by the knowledge of God (cf. Ps. 119:161; Rom. 3:18). That is, the wicked one lives as if God does not matter, someone shaped by self-deception who does not recognize the effects of iniquity as something to be spurned. In all, the wicked ones do not shape their life in relation to God, and it is this fundamental failure that marks their life as wicked. Nevertheless, this orientation expresses itself in actions that are damaging towards others, creating trouble and deceit in speech, and refraining from actions that may contribute to the well-being of others, something that shows a lack of wisdom. All this finds its focus in verse 4, where the wicked one is pictured as plotting injustice while in bed. Once God is functionally removed from the scene, the values he gives to society are removed from people's actions. This path is here described as 'not good', as something that fails to reject evil, because the framework for so doing has been removed. In all, the wicked one here is very much like the fool in Psalm 14 who rejects God.

5–9. The second stanza addresses Yahweh directly, focusing immediately on his kindness and faithfulness. Locating them in the heavens and clouds (cf. Ps. 57:10) suggests that they are in position to affect all the earth as they are above the physical world. As key characteristics of Yahweh, they also contrast immediately with the presentation of the evil one since Yahweh's kindness and faithfulness are expressed positively towards others. The wicked plan for their own benefit while ignoring God, but Yahweh expresses himself in his commitment to others. Yahweh's kindness and faithfulness are matched with his righteousness and justice, the greatness of which is seen in the comparison to the highest and lowest points of the physical creation. The 'mightiest mountains' are literally 'the mountains of God [*'ēl*]', while the 'great deep' are the waters thought to be below the earth (Gen. 1:1). The language here takes up the mythological themes of the region while yet demythologizing them since these too are under Yahweh. More importantly, all creation points to Yahweh's commitment to righteousness and justice, something demonstrated in his saving of both human and beast. This is carried through into verse 7, where the poet ponders the precious nature of Yahweh's 'kindness', perhaps seeing this term as the summary of those covered in the previous verses. So precious is it that both heavenly beings and humans take refuge under Yahweh's wings, alluding to the cherubs' wings in the inner sanctuary of the temple (1 Kgs 6:23–28), a place where refuge could be claimed (cf. Ruth 2:12). Yahweh not only saves human and beast, but also provides a place of refuge for the whole cosmos. Reference to the temple becomes more explicit in the stanza's closing verses, where mention of Yahweh's 'house' refers to the temple. Here, Yahweh provides abundantly for those who have taken refuge, providing food and drink that echo that of Eden, perhaps because the temple was itself meant in some ways to represent Eden (cf. Botha 2004c: 512). Where the wicked think only of themselves, Yahweh provides for all who take refuge in him, demonstrating that the fountain of life is with him, perhaps another allusion to Eden (Gen. 2:10) and Ezekiel's river flowing from the new temple (Ezek. 47:1–12; cf. Rev. 22:1). The temple here represents the whole of creation, showing it belongs to Yahweh. This is brought together in the closing affirmation that we see light only because of Yahweh's light.

10–12. The closing plea draws on themes from the first two stanzas. It begins with the imp. 'stretch out', asking that Yahweh extend his kindness to those who know him, his righteousness to the upright of heart. Both 'kindness' and 'righteousness' were key terms in defining Yahweh's character in the second stanza, while the 'upright of heart' here contrast with the wicked in stanza 1. That these elements are to be stretched out indicates that they are already experienced, but that the poet seeks an extension of them among the community of the faithful. This is personalized in verse 11, where the poet asks to be kept from the effects of the foot of the arrogant and the hand of the wicked. 'Foot' and 'hand' here stand for the ways in which such people may act against the poet, picking up on the wicked one's plans in the first stanza. If Yahweh's justice is to be shown, then it is those who work evil who must fall, unable to rise because Yahweh's kindness and righteousness have worked for the poet.

Explanation

Psalm 36 is deeply rooted in the OT's world and worship, yet its themes continue to be relevant. It recognizes that the way of wickedness is most simply life that fails to heed the reality of God. Once this move has been made, then it is all too easy to be self-deceived and imagine that one's own goals are good, even those that harm others. Yahweh, by contrast, is shown to be one whose kindness, righteousness and justice work for the well-being of all who take refuge in him, as well as overcoming all forces in creation. For Israel, this was modelled in the structures of the temple. In the NT, these themes are taken up in the person of Jesus. He is the light of the world (John 8:29), the true temple (John 2:18–22), the one in whom we see life (John 1:4), the source of the water of life (John 7:37–38). On that basis, believers may continue to pray for the extension of God's kindness through him.

PSALM 37

Translation

Davidic.

1Do not be vexed about evildoers,
  do not be envious of those practising injustice,
2because they will wilt quickly like grass,
  wither like a green herb.
3Trust in Yahweh and do good,
  dwell in the land and shepherd faithfulness,
4delight yourself in Yahweh,
  and he will grant your heart's petitions.
5Commit your way to Yahweh,
  yes, trust in him and he will act,
6and he will bring forth your righteousness like the light,
  your justice like the noonday.

7Be silent before Yahweh and wait patiently for him,
do not be vexed when the way prospers
of those who enact evil plots.
8Hold back from anger, forsake wrath,
do not be vexed; it leads to evil;
9because evildoers will be cut off,
but those who hope in Yahweh shall possess the land.
10Yet a little while and the wicked will be no more,
when you give close attention to their place, then it shall be no more,
11but the afflicted shall possess the land,
and delight themselves in great prosperity.

12The wicked devise evil against the righteous,
and gnash their teeth against them;
13the Lord laughs at them,
for he sees that their day is coming.
14The wicked have drawn the sword,
and have bent the bow,
to bring down the afflicted and the needy,
to slay those whose way is upright;
15their sword shall pierce their heart,
and their bows shall be broken.
16Better a little that belongs to the righteous
than the abundance of many wicked,
17because the arms of the wicked shall be broken,
but Yahweh will uphold the righteous.
18Yahweh knows the days of the blameless,
and their heritage shall endure for ever,
19they shall not be put to shame in the time of difficulty,
and in the days of famine, they shall be satisfied.
20Indeed, the wicked will perish,
Yahweh's enemies are like the glory of the meadows,
they vanish; they vanish like smoke.
21The wicked borrow but do not repay,
but the righteous are generous and giving,
22for those Yahweh blesses shall possess the land,
but those he belittles shall be cut off.

23From Yahweh are one's steps established,
and he delights in their way;
24though they stumble they shall not be cast down,
because Yahweh upholds them with his hand.
25I was young and now am old,
but I have not seen the righteous forsaken,
nor their children begging for bread,

26 they are always gracious and lending,
  and their children become a blessing.
27 Turn from evil and do good
  and dwell for ever,
28 for Yahweh loves justice,
  and will not forsake his saints.
They are protected for ever,
  but the children of the wicked will be cut off.
29 The righteous shall possess the land
  and shall dwell for ever upon it.
30 The mouth of the righteous utters wisdom,
  and their tongue speaks justice,
31 the Torah of their God is in their heart,
  their steps do not slip.

32 The wicked lie in wait for the righteous,
  seeking to kill them;
33 Yahweh does not abandon them to their hand,
  nor let them be condemned when brought to trial.
34 Wait for Yahweh and keep to his way,
  and he will exalt you to possess the land;
  you will see when the wicked are cut off.
35 I have seen the wicked who act ruthlessly,
  spreading like a luxuriant native tree,
36 but he passed on and was not,
  though I sought him, he was not found.
37 Note the blameless and see the upright,
  there is a future for a person of peace,
38 but transgressors shall be destroyed all together,
  the future for the wicked will be cut off.
39 The deliverance of the righteous is from Yahweh,
  their refuge in a time of distress,
40 and Yahweh will help them and deliver them,
  he will deliver them from the wicked,
  save them because they have taken refuge in him.

Notes on the text

10. Hebr. is sg., but the figure is representative, so pl. is used in translation, both here and throughout the psalm.

35. Hebr. *mitʻāreh* is difficult, and Gk would suggest a very different text. The verb would typically mean 'to expose oneself as naked' but as applied to a tree could be understood as 'spreading oneself'. If so, MT is retained as *lectio difficilior*.

Form and structure

Psalm 37 is perhaps the classic example of a 'wisdom psalm'. Although the presence of this category has been widely debated (see Cheung 2015: 1–21), the clearly didactic nature of this poem, which addresses itself to its audience in a manner similar to Proverbs 1–9, indicates that it is at home in this context. Along with this, it is also arranged as an extensive acrostic that (mostly) allots two verses to each letter of the Hebrew alphabet. The letters *d*, *k* and *q* receive only one verse each, while the verse division does not recognize the letter ayin, starting it at verse 28b, resulting in our forty-verse form.

In context, the poem addresses the problem of the prosperity of the wicked. This picks up on the presentation of the wicked in Psalm 36:1–4, while encouraging those troubled by their continued prosperity to trust that the conclusion reached in Psalm 36:12 will ultimately be realized, and that the hope of the upright of heart (Ps. 36:10) will be seen. The whole poem responds to an issue raised in the previous psalm, though in doing this there are also more specific links such as the motif of Yahweh as the source of light (Pss 36:9; 37:6) and salvation (Pss 36:6; 37:39–40). As such, although the psalm addresses any audience troubled by the issue of the prosperity of the wicked, it particularly does so by engaging with texts around it.

Although the acrostic is the poem's most obvious structural device, resulting in its sometimes feeling more like a mosaic of images viewed through a kaleidoscope, especially through repetition of key terms and sounds (cf. Lehmann and Levine 2021), some structure which can still be recognized:

1. Encouragements to the faithful (1–11)
2. Observations on the wicked (12–22)
3. The life of the faithful (23–31)
4. The future of the righteous and the wicked (32–40)

Comment

Title: On 'Davidic', see on Psalm 3.

1–11. That the prosperity of the wicked is a fundamental problem is immediately flagged by the opening prohibitions against being vexed or being envious of evildoers (cf. Prov. 24:19). The concern is with those who prosper, even though their actions are contrary to Yahweh's ways, something that may cause the faithful to be concerned about the validity of their faith. Verse 2 then follows this up with what is effectively a theme statement for the psalm, asserting that they will wither like plants with insufficient water. They are the opposite of the righteous person in Psalm

1:3. Where verse 1 warned against negative behaviour, verse 3 encourages a positive alternative, trust in Yahweh, which is expressed in doing good. That is, the wicked are marked in verse 1 by behaviours contrary to trust in Yahweh, while those who trust Yahweh demonstrate this through doing good and encouraging faithfulness. All this can be understood as finding an abiding satisfaction in a relationship with Yahweh, who will then grant the petitions the righteous make to him. The pattern of verses 3–4 is largely repeated in verses 5–6, where committing one's way to Yahweh is a further expression of trust in him, confident that he acts for the faithful, making the righteousness and justice of the faithful visible, like something brought out into the light at noon. Verse 7 then explores what this commitment to Yahweh looks like in practice. It encourages silence, not as an absence of prayer but rather of activism (cf. Ps. 62:5), so that those who trust Yahweh wait hopefully on him, not being vexed over the continued prosperity of those enacting evil plots. This approach to trust is extended in verses 8–9, encouraging the faithful to refrain from anger and forsake wrath, both of which could lead to further vexation, because this leads only to further evil. Instead, the faithful acknowledge that evildoers will ultimately be cut off and that those who hope in Yahweh will possess the land. Thus, verse 9 brings together the two main strands of the argument, stressing that the prosperity of the wicked is temporary, whereas those who hope in Yahweh ultimately prosper. This, though, raises the question of when this reversal will take place, making this the main issue in verses 10–11. Here, it is stressed that the dominance of the wicked is time limited, that they will not endure, and when the faithful look for them they will no longer be there. Although 'a little while' may suggest that their demise was imminent (cf. Jer. 51:33; Hos. 1:4), within the overall movement of the psalm it is more likely that this is intended as a contrast with the enduring experience of the faithful in possessing the land and taking great delight in their abundant prosperity. Rather than fretting over the temporary successes of the wicked, the faithful are assured of a hope that both endures and exceeds the success of the evildoers.

12–22. Where the first stanza encouraged the faithful to continue trusting in Yahweh, the second focuses on the character of the wicked. Here, the central theme is that although the wicked act against the faithful, Yahweh will ultimately act for the faithful. Although verses 10–11 have looked forward to the great prosperity, it is important to understand that this is future and that until then the faithful will experience the wicked acting against them but not finally triumphing. In verses 11–12, this is pictured as the wicked plotting against the righteous, finding ways to threaten them ('gnashing their teeth'), but the Lord laughs at them, responding to them just as Yahweh had done to rebellious nations (Ps. 2:4). Yahweh can see what they cannot, that they have a day of judgement coming and that their plots cannot finally succeed. This does not change the fact that the wicked choose to act with violence against the faithful, with the upright of heart here also classified as poor and needy, in that they lack the resources to resist on their own. The wicked are portrayed in verses 13–14 as ranging various weapons against the poor in order to slay them; but where they intended to harm the faithful, it is the wicked who will be injured by their own weapons. Although Yahweh is not mentioned here, the implication is that he either acts directly against the wicked or creates a context where the violence of the wicked brings about their own end, with their weapons broken. As such, verses 16–17 stress that it is better to be satisfied with the apparently lesser prosperity of the righteous than to desire the great wealth of the wicked, since although the wicked seemingly have strength on their side that will be broken, Yahweh shall sustain the righteous. This hope is grounded in Yahweh's knowledge of the blameless (cf. Ps. 1:6), something that grants them an enduring heritage. Further, this hope means they will not be put to shame in a time of difficulty, nor suffer hunger in time of famine. By contrast, verse 20, again echoing Psalm 1:6, stresses that the wicked shall perish, being as transient as beautiful flowers in a meadow or smoke that simply vanishes. The goal of the stanza is reached in verses 21–22 in the contrast here between the righteous and the wicked. The righteous act in ways that enable others, but the wicked act in ways that enable only themselves. Those who look to the well-being of others are those blessed by Yahweh, and can anticipate possession of the land as the mark of enduring well-being, while the wicked are those belittled by Yahweh and so cut off, excluded from this life of blessing.

23–31. Verse 22 is a pivot point within the psalm. Having outlined the end for those blessed by Yahweh and those disdained by him, the third stanza then focuses on the life of the faithful as those blessed by Yahweh. Although verse 23's opening may suggest that a person's steps are established by Yahweh, it quickly becomes clear that since this is the path in which Yahweh delights (cf. Ps. 1:2), it is the way of the righteous. Therefore, a moment of stumbling does not lead to a complete fall since Yahweh upholds them. This leads to a moment where the poet's experience is presented as evidence for this in verses 25–26. The psalmist has not seen the righteous forsaken or their children begging for bread. It is important to note that this is not a guarantee. It is a testimony, something that has convinced the poet. It is not denied that the faithful will have times of challenge but rather that there is no point at which they were completely destitute. Even in challenging times, they were showing grace and lending to those in need, living out the model of verse 21, a pattern of blessing continued in their children. If so, then the faithful are called (vv. 27–28a) to turn from evil and do good, expressing trust in Yahweh (cf. v. 3), with this enabling them to dwell in the land for ever. The implication is then that this is not the hope of the wicked. Hope is grounded in Yahweh's love of justice, meaning that provision for his saints is itself a just act and hence he does not abandon them. Not only will Yahweh not abandon the faithful, but verses 28b–29 declare they are kept for ever, whereas the children of the wicked are cut off. That is why it is the righteous who will possess the land and dwell in it for ever. As Yahweh has delighted in the way of the faithful, so also the righteous here are defined by their commitment to Yahweh, again in terms like Psalm 1:2–3. There, the righteous speak of Yahweh's Torah, whereas here it is wisdom and justice, though since God's Torah is in the heart of the righteous, there is a close correlation between Torah, justice and wisdom. Because of this, their steps will not slip.

32–40. An immediate contrast is made between the righteous and the wicked in the final stanza, a contrast established in verses 32–33. Rather than speaking of justice, the wicked lie in ambush, looking to kill the righteous. The ambushes are not necessarily literal and could include attempts to have the righteous condemned through the court, but because Yahweh does not abandon the righteous, the wicked will not succeed in their actions against them. Given this, verse 34 encourages hopeful waiting in Yahweh, something that involves a commitment to his way, with the assurance that Yahweh will exalt them to possess the land. By contrast, the righteous will see the wicked cut off. This leads back to a further point of testimony in verses 35–36, this time focused on the wicked. The poet has seen instances where the wicked, marked by their ruthless behaviour towards others, have seemed to flourish, like a tree in suitable soil. But this was transient, because the point at which Yahweh passed by removed them so that even though the poet had sought for them, they could not be found. Drawing on this, verses 37–38 contrast the two futures of the righteous and the wicked while encouraging the audience to choose the right way. Hence, they are to consider the life of the blameless (cf. Kselman 1997: 253–254) and the upright because they have a future, unlike transgressors who will be destroyed, leaving the wicked cut off from a meaningful future. The implications of this are outlined in verses 39–40, which stress that Yahweh is the one who delivers the righteous and provides them with a place of security in times of distress. It is Yahweh who helps the righteous, delivering them from the wicked, saving them because they have taken refuge in him. Psalm 2:12 has declared that any who take refuge in Yahweh are blessed, so Psalm 37 encourages the faithful to do that.

Explanation

Taking up the problem of the wicked from Psalm 36, and in dialogue with Psalms 1–2, this poem provides a pastoral approach to an important issue. Granted that we live in a world where the wicked (i.e. those who do not order their lives around God) often seem to thrive, does this undermine the validity of the claims of faith in God? The issues addressed here are not unique to the ancient world and continue to vex believers today, and as such this psalm is an important word of encouragement to continue trusting in God, to understand that as believers we take refuge in him. The act of taking refuge acknowledges that this is not a world in which there are simple resolutions to this problem, and as much of the world continues to believe that might is right, we know that the posture of trust encouraged here is no easier today than in the ancient world. Yet such trust is still important. It is the starting point that leads us towards living the very different demands of the gospel, demands that continue to show the validity of faith. Taking this psalm seriously is not to propose a simplistic but inadequate ethic (so Maré 2010), but rather following the pattern Jesus also adopted when citing verse 11 in his beatitudes (Matt. 5:5), recognizing that this is an eschatological reality to which we commit ourselves now. In taking up this psalm we express the hope of the better world to come even as we honestly face the world as it is (cf. Stocks 2016).

PSALM 38

Translation

A melody. Davidic. For commemoration.

[1]O Yahweh, do not rebuke me in your anger,
  nor chastise me in your wrath,
[2]for your arrows have pierced me,
  and your hand has descended on me.
[3]There is no soundness in my flesh because of your indignation,
  there is no wholeness in my bones because of my guilt.
[4]For my iniquities have passed over my head,
  like a heavy burden, they are too heavy for me.
[5]My wounds stink, they fester,
  because of my folly.
[6]I am twisted, sharply bent over,
  I go about mourning all day,
[7]for my loins are filled with contempt,
  and there is no soundness in my flesh.
[8]I have become numb and utterly crushed,
  I roar because of the groaning of my heart.

[9]O Lord, all my longing is before you,
  and my sighing is not hidden from you.
[10]My heart throbs, my strength has abandoned me,

and the light of my eyes is also no longer with me.
11My friends and companions stand apart from my affliction,
and my close associates stand far off.
12So those seeking my life have laid snares,
and those looking for my harm speak threats,
they utter treachery all day.
13But I am like a deaf person, I do not hear,
like a mute who does not open his mouth.
14And I have become like one who does not hear,
in whose mouth there are no rebukes.
15Because in you, O Yahweh, have I hoped,
you yourself shall answer me, O Lord my God.
16For I had said, 'Let them not rejoice over me,
who boast over me when my feet slip.'

17For I am ready to stumble,
and my pain is continually before me.
18For I declare my iniquity,
I am concerned about my guilt.
19Yet the foes of my life are numerous,
and those who hate me falsely are many,
20and those who would repay me evil in place of good,
they accuse me though I seek good.
21Do not forsake me, O Yahweh,
O my God do not be far from me.
22Make haste to help me,
O Lord of my salvation.

Notes on the text

6. *qdr* can refer to 'being dark', but by extension can also refer to 'mourning' (cf. Job 30:28; Ps. 35:14; Jer. 8:21).

Form and structure

There is broad agreement that illness is a major factor in this poem (cf. Seybold 1996: 159; A. P. Ross 2011: 821), though whether its language requires illness as its background is a slightly different matter. If we set aside royal or national interpretations that understand the psalm in terms of national conflict (for a survey, see Firth 2005b: 115–118), it is evident that much of the poem uses the language of illness (vv. 3, 5–8, 10, 17). Those who read this literally classify this as a psalm of sickness. Along with the language of illness, there are also several references to sin (vv. 3–5, 18), all of which occur near a mention of illness, a factor that has contributed to the poem's inclusion in the 'seven penitential psalms' typically read in Lent (Pss 6, 32, 38, 51, 102, 130, 143). It should be noted that although sin is mentioned, there is no penitence as such in this psalm (against Goldingay 2006a: 550), though there is confession. Sickness and sin are closely linked, and verses 3–4 suggest that Yahweh has caused the illness due to sin. Lindström (1994: 239–241) rejects this, but only by arguing that certain verses are secondary. Even if we granted this possibility, it would not change the fact that the connection is now present. This does not mean that there is an automatic connection between sickness and sin, but this psalm allows it as a possibility. Some of the language can also be understood as describing suffering more broadly, so although sickness may have been the trigger for the psalm's composition, it is written in a way that allows those who suffer in a range of ways to find their experience voiced here (cf. McCann 1996: 833).

Although Psalm 38 initiates the second half of the unit Psalms 35–41 (cf. Beuken 2020: 87–93), it still has important connections to the preceding psalms. Several of these elements exist by way of contrast. Most obviously, the psalmist has sought to do good (v. 20), thus picking a key theme from Psalm 37:3, 27, but has experienced suffering. As such, the poet here asks specifically that affirmations about Yahweh's not abandoning the faithful (Ps. 37:25–26, 28, 33) should now be found true in experience (v. 21).

Although the details of the poem's structure are not agreed, it should be noted that there is a close relationship between the opening (vv. 1–2) and close (vv. 21–22), with both marked by negative pleas, asking Yahweh not to act in a particular way, while the close also gathers divine epithets that emerge through the poem. Beyond this, we can analyse the psalm in three stanzas:

1. Plea for Yahweh to relent (1–8)
2. Description of suffering (9–16)
3. Confession and prayer (17–22)

Comment

Title: For 'A Melody. Davidic', see on Psalm 3. 'For commemoration' occurs only here and for Psalm 70, with both psalms concluding with an appeal for urgent action (cf. Waltke et al. 2014: 136). It could be a genre label, referring to prayers of petition, though of course other prayers include petition but do not have this label, and the term can elsewhere include praise (e.g. Ps. 20:7).

1–8. The psalm begins and closes with requests that Yahweh not act against the poet's well-being (cf. Ps. 6:1). Verses 1–2 suggest that the poet's suffering is experienced as Yahweh's discipline. It is not that Yahweh is never to rebuke or chastise the poet, but that rather the current experience has reached a point where it needs to cease. This is clear from the fact that Yahweh's arrows have pierced the poet. The arrows are metaphoric, referring to an unspecified form of discipline that has affected the psalmist physically, as becomes evident in the various descriptions of bodily ill-health that follow. Reference to Yahweh's hand is not comforting since it has descended on the psalmist, indicating that some form of restraint is experienced. As a result, the psalmist describes an acute absence of health. The cause of this is twofold, though the elements are closely related. The poet points to Yahweh's indignation as the cause, before linking this to personal guilt. It quickly becomes clear in verse 4 that the trigger for Yahweh's indignation is the psalmist's iniquities. Exactly what they were is left undefined, the focus instead being on their extent. This is clear from the images used to describe them, first treating them like something that passed over the poet's head (perhaps like waters) and then as a heavy burden, one too heavy to carry. However it is described, iniquity is something the poet cannot manage as it causes significant physical distress, with symptoms described in verses 5–8, the root cause of which is said to be folly. Such folly is often condemned in Proverbs, pointing to a life not centred on living with Yahweh (e.g. Prov. 19:3; 24:9). The connection here between folly and sin is consistent with this pattern, as is the association with illness. Yet even though we have a range of symptoms seemingly described, it is unlikely that they guide to a particular diagnosis, describing instead a life not lived within the blessedness encouraged by Psalm 1, which Psalm 37 has reaffirmed. Rather, the point is to be seen in the total impact of the sin/folly nexus and the damage it does to all aspects of bodily life (cf. Coetzee 2000: 518–520). The results of this are expressed in verse 8, where the description of being numb and crushed describes more the condition of a life not lived with Yahweh than a particular illness, though pain from it leads to the poet roaring out because of the anguish this causes. It is because of this that Yahweh needs to relent.

9–16. Like the first stanza, the second commences with a direct address to God, this time addressed as 'Lord', a title that also closes this stanza. Having asked Yahweh to relent in the first stanza, the focus of the second is primarily to outline the poet's sufferings, even though Yahweh is aware of them. The poet has described the experience of suffering in the first stanza, and the second opens by noting that none of this has been hidden from Yahweh. But along with the elements already noted, verse 10 adds further elements of physical suffering, each of which reflects a loss of physical vitality. Verses 11–12 then describe increasing levels of social alienation. This starts with those closest to the poet socially distancing themselves because of the psalmist's affliction before noting that adversaries have sought to act against the poet. Particular attention is given to malicious speech. Such speech is associated in Proverbs with the wicked (e.g. Prov. 12:5; 26:24), and is itself associated with folly (Prov. 14:8). That they utter treachery is also the antithesis of Psalm 1:2. There, the verb *hgh* refers to reflection on Yahweh's Torah (and in Ps. 37:30 it is wisdom), whereas here the enemies are focused on treachery, and are thus aligned with the nations opposed to Yahweh's anointed in Psalm 2:1: Despite their verbal threats, the poet has become like the deaf, not hearing their speech, or a mute who does not speak, and so unable to respond in kind. The reason for this is that the poet has hoped in Yahweh, and thus it is up to Yahweh to respond to these people and demonstrate the appropriateness of the poet hoping in him. This hope has remained even as the poet faces the possibility of slipping (v. 16), presumably reference to the folly that led to the psalmist's iniquity, though even then the psalmist had prayed that Yahweh will prevent the triumph of the enemies. This would confirm the advice of Psalm 37, showing instead that Yahweh triumphs (cf. R. A. Jacobson 2004: 69).

17–22. Where the second stanza began by noting that the poet's longing was before God, the third begins by observing that pain is before the poet, making stumbling a real possibility. The poet will not allow unconfessed sin to be the cause of this, with iniquity confessed along with the uncertainties caused by guilt, linking the final stanza to the first (cf. vv. 3–4). Stumbling could also be caused by the numerous enemies (vv. 19–20), linking this stanza to the second (cf. v. 12), as they repay the poet's good with evil. The poet's pain is potentially life-threatening, whether it is caused by sin or the actions of enemies. But no matter the source of the threat, Yahweh is the one who needs to act. Yahweh is not to forsake the poet, demonstrating the truth of the observations in Psalm 37:25, 28, 33. Yahweh is expected to act justly for the faithful. Though the poet confesses sin, at no point does the psalm indicate a turning from Yahweh. As such, although the poet's friends have distanced themselves, Yahweh is asked not to do so, demonstrating that he remains close to the faithful. Yahweh is the one who must help (cf. Ps. 35:2) and do so quickly, demonstrating that he is indeed Lord of the poet's salvation, just as Psalm 37:39 indicated.

Explanation

Following the encouragements of Psalm 37 to remain faithful to Yahweh, Psalm 38 now explores this theme from the perspective of those who are conscious of sin in their life and who understand their current suffering to be a result of divine discipline because of this sin. Initiated by Yahweh, this suffering is extended by the actions of others who act against the poet. If people are conscious that they have no right to claim Yahweh's deliverance because of their own righteousness, will he indeed act as their saviour simply because they turn to him? In exploring this, it is important to note that the psalm does not assume a necessary link between sin and suffering. Like Job, the Psalter knows that suffering derives from a range of sources, so we cannot claim that all suffering is caused by sin. But by including poems such as this, it allows that at least some suffering may be. In this case, it raises the stakes – the present suffering is (at least in part) a result of sin, so will Yahweh prove faithful and answer the supplicant? In this psalm we do not have a final answer beyond the closing note that Yahweh is still the psalmist's saviour. In this, we see a hint that Yahweh will save, and in the use of nearly the same language in Psalm 40:13 the Psalter also points to this hope. Salvation is ultimately an act of grace towards the supplicant, a theme that finds clear echoes in the NT (cf. Eph. 2:8–19). Moreover, as Brueggemann and Bellinger note (2014: 189–190), Jesus also clearly recognizes a link between healing and forgiveness (Mark 2:1–12), providing an embodied example of a prayer like this finding its answer.

PSALM 39

Translation

The director's. Jeduthun's. A melody. Davidic.

1 I said, 'I will guard my ways from sin with my tongue,
  I will guard my mouth with a muzzle,
  while the wicked are before me.'
2 I was mute in silence,
  I kept silent without benefit,
  and my pain was increased.
3 My heart grew hot within me,
  in my musing a fire burned.

I spoke with my tongue,
4 'Make known to me, O Yahweh, my end,
  what the measure of my days is,
  that I may know how fleeting I am.
5 Behold, you have made my days a few handbreadths,
  and my lifespan is as nothing before you,
  surely all humankind vanishes like vapour.' *Selah*.
6 Surely, one goes about as a shadow,
  surely, they bustle about like a vapour,
  one heaps up but does not know who will gather.

7 But now, what have I hoped for O Lord?
  My hope is in you.

8Deliver me from all my transgressions,
do not make me into a fool's reproach.
9I was mute, I did not open my mouth,
for you have acted.
10Remove your affliction from me,
from the stroke of your hand am I finished.
11You discipline someone with rebukes for iniquity,
and you consume their desire like a moth,
surely all humankind is vapour. *Selah*.

12Hear my prayer, O Yahweh,
give ear to my cry for help:
be not deaf to my tears,
for I am an alien with you,
a sojourner like all my ancestors.
13Look away from me that I may be cheerful,
before I go and am no more.

Notes on the text

1. With Gk, read *'āšîmâ*.

4. With several MSS, Gk and Syr., reading *we'ēdĕ'â*.

5. With most MSS, omit the first *kol* as dittography. Following *DCH*, *niṣab* is understood as *nṣb* III, 'vanish', rather than *nṣb* I, 'stand'.

Form and structure

With Psalm 38, this psalm integrates the motifs of sin and discipline by Yahweh, though without explicit connection to illness (against Seybold 1996: 162). The closing prayer makes clear that the psalmist believes that the sin which led to this has been recognized and confessed, and that Yahweh should now act to improve the poet's life, even if it may only be brief. These elements are consistent with treating the poem as a complaint psalm, but like Psalm 38 there are also elements here more at home in the wisdom tradition. The refrain-like statements about humans being 'vapour' (vv. 5, 11) echo various comments of Qoheleth (e.g. Eccl. 1:2, 14; 2:11). The psalm also contains testimonial fragments (e.g. vv. 1, 3c–5). Attempts to tie this poem to a single category therefore seem destined to fail, and its function as a prayer is found in its integration of complaint, wisdom and testimony.

As noted, there are important links with Psalm 38 (cf. Waltke et al. 2014: 160), though through it there are also connections with Psalm 37. That is because Psalms 38, 39 engage in different ways with Psalm 37.

Psalm 37's encouragement to the faithful tends to assume that Yahweh will respond to them in this life, whereas Psalm 39 allows for the possibility that because human life is brief, it may not be experienced in the life of a particular petitioner (cf. Botha 2017a: 241). But with Psalm 38, it explores this issue from the perspective of one who is conscious of sin's effects. Psalm 38 has shown that Yahweh does respond to the penitent sinner, but it allows that human transience may limit the human ability to enjoy this fully. The perspective of Psalm 37 is not denied, but cases it does not address are thus provided to give more context to it. As will be seen, Psalm 40 will then provide a more hopeful perspective (cf. Beuken 2020: 88–90), so that both the more hopeful stance of Psalm 37 and the more cautious one of Psalms 38–39 provide internal limits within the Psalter to ensure that no one psalm has the final say. Rather, a dialogue between these poems is encouraged, the petitioners thus needing wisdom to determine the one most appropriate to their circumstances.

The combination of various elements makes an analysis of the poem difficult. But if the observation on human transience is valid, then it provides a structural clue (cf. Raabe 1990: 165), though as this draws on the wisdom elements it cannot provide the whole analysis. Once we recognize the element of testimony in verses 1, 3c, these too become important, while the petition in verses 12–13 also draws on the complaint elements. Taken together, the psalm can be analysed as follows:

1. Testimony of suffering (1–3b)
2. Testimony of prayer and wisdom observation (3c–6)
3. Testimony of hope and wisdom observation (7–11)
4. Prayer for help

Comment

Title: For 'The director's', see on Psalm 4. For 'A melody. Davidic', see on Psalm 3. 'Jeduthun' may mean 'one who confesses'. This would not have to mean confession of sin, though Achan is someone who did this (Josh. 7:19) and reference to the poet's pain becoming 'worse' (*neʿkār*) could also allude to Achan (cf. Josh. 7:25–26). A Jeduthun is also mentioned in 1 Chronicles 25:1–6 as a Levitical musician, perhaps further associating this psalm with the temple. He is also mentioned in the titles of Psalms 62, 77, and Terrien (2003, 1: 458) highlights important similarities in these three poems.

1–3b. Uniquely, this psalm opens with a report of a previous statement, presumably one offered as a vow. The poet reports a promise to avoid sin through speech, an important motif in a psalm where speech and silence are key themes. The opening element is unexpected. In that the poet's 'ways' were to be guarded against sin with the tongue, we might expect that words would be the issue (cf. Kraus 1988: 416). However, this statement can now sit alongside the frequent use of the 'way' metaphor in Psalm 37 (vv. 5, 7, 14, 23), especially given its concern with the wicked. If the psalmist was one whose way was committed to Yahweh (Ps. 37:5), then care with speech in the presence of the wicked mattered, perhaps because it is easy to be drawn into negative speech or such speech might have harmed others (cf. Ps. 73:15). Verses 2–3 then report that although the poet remained silent, the outcome was not positive. Silence not only led to an absence of good; it also saw the poet's pain increase. The nature of the pain is not outlined but, given the presence of the wicked, it is likely to be the intellectual distress caused by their continued presence. This can be seen in the reference to the poet's heart growing hot, since the heart is often the seat of cognitive processes in the OT (e.g. Gen. 17:17; 24:45; Exod. 36:2), while the poet's musings also refer to matters of reflection, and these too became so heated they were like an emotional fire.

3c–6. The second stanza also begins with a report of prior speech, though there is a change of verb, perhaps indicating that this did not contradict the previous vow (cf. Broyles 1989: 199). Where the first speech reports a vow, this reports a prayer, the content of which carries through to the end of verse 5 before the accompanying wisdom observation in verse 6. The prayer asks Yahweh to show that the psalmist's life is brief, asking to know its end (cf. Job 6:11; Kynes 2012: 130–132), placing it in the context of human transience, though this is also shaped by the present suffering. The theme of transience is especially developed in verse 5, noting especially the difference between Yahweh and humans since even a long human life is as nothing before Yahweh. Hence, just as vapour quickly vanishes, human life is fleeting, a theme with close parallels in Ecclesiastes. Although the prayer could conceivably continue into verse 6, it is likely that the *selah* at the end of verse 5 marks its conclusion, so that the repeated 'surely' (*'ak*; v. 6) introduces an observation made to the audience, who encounter the report of the prayer. The point of the prayer has been to bring the psalmist to the point of accepting this reality of human life, not to bring about something new. As such, the audience are also now to accept this reality, seeing all human life as having as much substance as a shadow and the durability of vapour, one where humans strive in various ways but cannot know what will become of what is accumulated (cf. Eccl. 2:17–23).

7–11. Where the second stanza reported a previous prayer, Yahweh is now addressed in a prayer that runs through to verse 11b, with the wisdom observation then closing the stanza in verse 11c. Rather than placing hope in transient humans, the prayer now focuses on God as the source of hope, the one in whom the poet has already hoped. This hope is needed because of the psalmist's own failings and the deeds of others. Hence, the poet asks both to be delivered 'from all my transgressions' and not to become the reproach of fools. The implication is that the psalmist is aware of sin as a barrier to God, but that enemies are also active. The reproach the enemies make is apparently claiming that the psalmist's current suffering indicates that the psalmist is not in a good relationship with God. The psalmist has not responded to this claim because at least some suffering is understood as having been brought about by God. Therefore, the psalmist cannot respond to the claims of the enemies, but ask only that God remove his affliction. That is, the current suffering is understood to be a stroke from God that is bringing the psalmist close to death. God therefore needs to remove this and thus prevent the psalmist from becoming a reproach of fools who do not see that God disciplines those who have committed iniquity. However, if the consuming of their desire (as a moth consumes a cloth) is about ending practices leading away from God, then this discipline is restorative. Nevertheless, as the final wisdom observation makes clear, the transience of all humans needs to be recognized so that God's purposes are the ones that remain.

12–13. Where the first two stanzas primarily reported previous speech, the closing prayer is very much in the present, building on the 'But now' of verse 7. The poet knows that human life is transient, and that it therefore cannot be assumed that the challenges will be resolved during one's life. But it is still possible to ask Yahweh to respond more immediately. Further, though the psalmist's mouth was previously muzzled, now Yahweh is urged to hear. What Yahweh is to hear is a 'prayer' and a 'cry for help'. The former may be considered a more structured appeal, while the latter can also be less formal. It is notable that Psalm 40:1 indicates that Yahweh has heard a cry for help. But Yahweh is also asked not to be deaf to the poet's tears, an even less structured appeal. Where the psalm opened with the poet functionally mute, now Yahweh is not to be deaf. The reason why Yahweh is to be attentive is striking – the poet does not claim to be an Israelite, but rather a resident foreigner, one of a line of such people who have come before Yahweh (cf. 1 Chr. 29:15). One may think these would be reasons to disqualify someone from Yahweh's mercy, but here it is another reason why he should act. Just as Rahab could be included within Israel (Josh. 6:25), unlike Achan who was excluded, so this poet also claims that a relationship with Yahweh is a sufficient basis for him to act. But that action may also include Yahweh's ceasing to discipline the psalmist for sin, a matter of particular importance given the brevity of life, leaving the possibility of some joy. This sudden close allows the psalm to keep despair and hope together (McCann 1996: 839).

Explanation

With Psalm 38, this poem forms an important response to Psalm 37, one that allows petitioners struggling with suffering to examine it from a range of perspectives. Psalm 37 may be described as the most optimistic of these poems, encouraging trust and reassuring believers that they will inherit the land. But it has addressed the issue from only one perspective, and Psalm 38 takes it up from the perspective of one who has suffered because of sin. Despite this, it still shows that Yahweh will be faithful to his people. Psalm 39 may then be classified as the least optimistic as, in addition to the issue of sin, it also considers those who may not have a direct claim on Yahweh through kinship within Israel. Like Ecclesiastes, it presumes that not every situation will be resolved within the lifetime of any one petitioner. Although it accepts that human life is brief, it does not move into resignation. Instead, it asks Yahweh to act, responding to both articulate and inarticulate cries for help. In doing so, it moves from silence to speech, asking that Yahweh bring some joy to life now. Its language is taken up in 1 Peter 2:11 (cf. Heb. 11:13) to describe Christian communities who might likewise not have had a claim on God through kinship to Israel, but who may now do so through Jesus Christ. There, Peter also recognizes that suffering may be believers' reality but points us to Jesus' own suffering, reminding us that he has also shown us the way to hold fast to God in this life even as we hope for something better.

PSALM 40

Translation

The director's. Davidic. A melody.

[1]I waited eagerly for Yahweh,
  and he inclined to me and heard my cry for help.
[2]He brought me up from the pit of destruction,
  from the miry clay,
and lifted my feet up on a cliff,
  he made my steps secure.
[3]He placed a new song in my mouth,
  praise to our God.
Many shall see and fear,
  and they shall trust in Yahweh.

[4]Oh the blessedness of the one
  who sets one's trust on Yahweh,

who has not turned to the proud,
  to those going astray after falsehood.

5You have multiplied, O Yahweh my God,
  your wonders and your thoughts towards us,
  they cannot be arranged before you.
I will declare and I will speak –
  they are too numerous for me!
6Sacrifice and offering you have not desired,
  you have dug out ears for me,
  burnt offering and sin offering you have not requested.
7Then I said, 'See, I have come,
  in the scroll of the book it is written about me.
8I delight to do what pleases you O my God,
  and your Torah is in my viscera.
9I have announced the good news of righteousness in the great assembly,
  my lips I have not restrained,
  as you know O Yahweh.
10I have not concealed your righteousness in my heart,
  I have spoken of your faithfulness and salvation,
  I have not hidden your kindness and truth from the great assembly.'

11Do not restrain your compassion from me, O Yahweh,
  may your kindness and truth continually preserve me.
12For evils beyond number have surrounded me,
  my iniquities have overtaken me and I cannot see,
they number more than the hairs of my head
  and my heart has failed me.

13Be pleased, O Yahweh, to deliver me,
  O Yahweh, make haste to help me.
14Let them be ashamed and abashed together,
  those who seek to snatch away my life,
let them be turned back and confounded,
  those who delight in my harm.
15Let them be appalled because of their shame,
  those who say to me, 'Aha! Aha!'
16Let all who seek you rejoice and be glad in you,
  let them say continually 'Great is Yahweh,'
  those who love your salvation.

17Though I am poor and needy,
  may the Lord consider me.
You are my help and deliverer,
  O my God, do not delay.

Notes on the text

1. *qwh* could either be 'to hope, wait' or 'to cry out'. Although 'to cry out' fits with the 'cry for help', 'hope, wait' is preferable due to the emphasis on this theme within Psalms 35–41, while also allowing the content of the waiting to be revealed in the second half of the line.

6. LXX renders *krh* (dug) with *katartizō* (mend). The Hebrew idiom is odd, so Gk is probably interpretative rather than suggesting a different text.

Form and structure

Previous discussion on this psalm has been shaped by the fact that verses 13–17 are repeated almost exactly as Psalm 70. Inevitably, this has led to discussion about the psalm's integrity, especially when form criticism identifies two different types, with verses 1–12 primarily a song of thanksgiving, whereas verses 13–17 a complaint. The most common assumption has been that Psalm 40 is a combination of two discrete parts, and that these can be treated separately. Kraus (1988: 424) accordingly declines to comment on verses 13–17, deferring the discussion until his treatment of Psalm 70. Yet as Beuken (2020: 68) has noted, this approach fails to deal with the current text. While acknowledging that verses 13–17 might originally have been a discrete text, it is possible (with Villanueva 2007: 109–111) to see that verses 11–12 have been shaped as a bridge between verses 1–10 and verses 13–17, indicating that the finished psalm is an intentional unit (cf. Naudé 2000: 116–122), one that moves from thanksgiving to complaint.

Although the move from thanksgiving to complaint is unusual, it may best be understood through awareness of the context created by its placement within Psalms 35–41. Here, Psalm 40 provides a more hopeful response to the situation of Psalms 38–39. The psalm opens by reporting hopeful waiting on Yahweh that resulted in delivery (40:1–2), demonstrating that the hope reported in Psalm 39:7 was justified. Rather than the silence of Psalm 39:1–3 (cf. 38:13), now the poet can speak with unrestrained lips (40:9–10). Nevertheless, with Psalm 38:22, the psalm still desires Yahweh to make haste and help (40:13). In this way, the validity of the two previous complaint psalms is upheld, especially as all three poems show awareness of sin (38:4, 18; 39:11; 40:12), showing that Yahweh does respond to sinners, therefore allowing further requests to be made as new challenges arise.

The psalm can be analysed as follows:

1. Thanksgiving (1–10)
   a. Report of deliverance (1–3)

   b. Benediction (4)
   c. Speech of praise (5–10)
2. Transition (11–12)
3. Prayer for deliverance (13–17)
   a. Appeal (13–16)
   b. Declaration (17)

Comment

Title: For 'The director's', see on Psalm 4. For 'A melody. Davidic', see on Psalm 3.

1–3. The psalm opens with testimony of previous waiting on Yahweh where he responded to the poet's cry for help (cf. Ps. 39:12). This anticipates the psalm's close, which summons Yahweh to respond quickly to the poet, avoiding a lengthy wait. Where the two previous psalms call out to Yahweh, this reports Yahweh's positive response. The circumstances implied in verses 2–3 are difficult to determine since the language is stylized, but the pit of destruction suggests a serious threat to life, something the poet could not have resolved because of the lack of somewhere firm to stand, whereas now Yahweh has provided a secure place. Where Psalms 18:2, 31:2 characterize Yahweh as a cliff, and thus a place of security, here Yahweh has placed the poet on a cliff, out of reach of threatening forces, allowing freedom. Along with this, Yahweh has placed a new song in the poet's mouth. The 'new song' is a concept that emerges through the Psalter (see on Ps. 33:3), and here is individual praise for Yahweh's saving acts that becomes a testimony that encourages others to trust Yahweh, building on Psalm 37:3, 5.

4. Thanksgiving now becomes beatitude, suggesting to others that they too can experience this desirable state. On the form, see on Psalm 1:1. The beatitude here plays on the cognate word for 'steps' (v. 2), while reflecting on the desirability of a life based on trusting Yahweh rather than turning either to the proud or falsehood. It is desirable because Yahweh does hear and respond. The 'proud' (*rĕhābîm*) here could refer to the insolent generally, but the word can also refer to a sea monster (Isa. 51:9; Ps. 89:11) or serve as a name for Egypt ('Rahab', Isa. 30:7; Ps. 87:4). Likewise, 'falsehood' could be a lie (Ps. 62:9) or false gods (Amos 2:4). The terms are deliberately open because there are numerous false paths, but what they have in common is that they do not respond as Yahweh does.

5–10. The speech of praise locates itself within the wider context of what Yahweh has done for 'us', with the language evoking the exodus traditions. The poet's deliverance fits into this wider pattern of Yahweh's multiplying his wonders and thoughts for his people, though this is not a pattern that can be organized into a system. The poet is compelled to speak of them, though just as they cannot be arranged, so also it is ultimately impossible to speak of them all. Though they cannot all be uttered, there is one central point to be made; sacrifice and offering are not what Yahweh has desired (cf. 1 Sam. 15:21–23). This statement fits with observations such as those of Psalm 50:7–15, Amos 5:22 and Micah 6:6–8, all of which also downplay the sacrificial system. These statements need to be read carefully because none are absolute rejections of this system, only of the use of sacrifice alone as the means of approaching Yahweh. Rather, Yahweh has enabled the poet to understand that there is something more important than the whole of the sacrificial system. Obedience to Yahweh matters more, and it is only in this context that sacrifice has any meaning. Hence, the poet comes as the sort of worshipper sought in Torah, one whose delight is doing Yahweh's will. Yahweh did not delight in sacrifice as an end in itself, but the psalmist can delight in doing Yahweh's will, embodying the sorts of practices mentioned in Psalms 15, 24. Hence, the Torah can be experienced viscerally, embodying the hope mentioned in Jeremiah 31:31–34. This means that there is good news to be proclaimed in the great assembly, perhaps the audience anticipated in verse 3, and the poet has already announced this. Yahweh has placed a new song in the poet's mouth, and now Yahweh knows that the psalmist's lips have not been restrained. Rather, the psalmist has freely announced Yahweh's faithfulness and salvation, making clear his kindness and truth. This truth makes clear that the blessedness declared in verse 4 is available to all.

11–12. The poet has not hidden Yahweh's kindness and truth, but the transition to the complaint recognizes that Yahweh may yet restrain his compassion. The reason for this becomes evident only in the confession of sin that emerges in verse 12, but before that the themes of kindness and truth are brought to the foreground, the psalmist asking that they will continue to preserve him. The psalm has downplayed the role of sacrifice, so if sin is to be addressed it must be through Yahweh's kindness and truth. Sin here is set in the context of evils surrounding the psalmist, suggesting forces external to the poet, whereas the numerous iniquities are internal. Both external and internal forces can lead to someone going astray after falsehood (v. 3), and both can be debilitating, which is why Yahweh's kindness and truth are needed.

13–16. The prayer commences with words similar to Psalm 38:22, indicating that deliverance is needed quickly. Yahweh has not desired sacrifices, but can be pleased to act for the psalmist. Although iniquity was confessed in verse 12b, the focus now is on the external factors that brought harm to the psalmist, their desire for harm being an expression of the uncountable evils of verse 12a. By contrast, iniquity has been confessed with no request for forgiveness unless this is seen in Yahweh's also being pleased to act against those who have sought the poet's harm. A contrast is drawn between those who have sought the poet's harm and those who rejoice in Yahweh. The request is that those who seek the poet's harm be turned back and suffer shame because of their actions. Shame was something deeply felt, a loss of fundamental honour. Nevertheless, although dimensions of shame are developed here, the psalmist does not ask Yahweh to do otherwise than turn the enemies back – shame at their failure is the result of this. They have sought to bring shame to the psalmist (in their cry 'Aha! Aha!'), but that situation is to be inverted by Yahweh's delivering of the poet. By contrast, those who seek Yahweh and love his salvation are not among those seeking the poet's harm. The poet asks that they be able to rejoice in Yahweh even as they confess his greatness. In this, they will act as the poet has already done (vv. 1–3), and they too may sing Yahweh's praise.

17. The closing declaration accepts that the poet has no intrinsic claim on Yahweh. Describing oneself as 'poor and needy' may not be a statement of the poet's economic well-being (though it is not excluded). Rather, it accepts that the psalmist does not have the ability to overcome these evils. However, Yahweh is the poet's help (cf. v. 13) and deliverance, and so the one who can assist. Hence, just as the prayer began by asking that Yahweh act quickly, it ends by asking that he not delay.

Explanation

Where many complaint psalms move from complaint to confidence, this moves in the opposite direction. It begins by reflecting on a previous experience of deliverance even as this prepares for the complaint with which the psalm concludes. These elements are shaped by the placement of this psalm as it develops motifs from Psalms 38–39, especially as they wrestle with the question of how Yahweh deals with those who recognize themselves as sinners. Here, we begin to hear good news that God accepts and works with sinners, and that he does so because of his kindness and truth, not sacrifice and offering. The psalm then imagines the one who comes into the assembly as an idealized personification of the worshipper sought by the Torah, a move taken to its logical conclusion in Hebrews 10:5–7, which sees Jesus as the one who truly is this worshipper. The writer to the Hebrews goes on to stress that final forgiveness is found in Jesus, so that he becomes the one who is the final answer to the question of how God may deal with sinners that has been central to Psalms 38–40. Within that framework, the persistent prayer encouraged by this psalm remains important.

PSALM 41

Translation

The director's. A melody. Davidic.

1Oh the blessedness of the one who ponders the weak!
On the day of trouble Yahweh will rescue that one.
2Yahweh will keep and preserve that one's life,
so that one will be called blessed in the land;
you do not give that one up into the desire of their enemies.
3Yahweh will sustain that one on a sickbed,
and you change the couch where that one lies suffering.

4I had said, 'O Yahweh, be gracious to me,
heal me, for I have sinned against you.'
5My enemies talk maliciously of me,
'How long until he dies so his name perishes?'
6When people come to see,
their heart speaks worthlessness,
they gather wickedness to themselves,
when they go outside, they speak.
7All those who hate me whisper against me,
they devise trouble against me.
8'A matter of destruction is poured out against him,
when he has lain down, he will not rise again.'
9Indeed, even my close companion whom I trusted,
one who ate my food,
has raised his heel against me.
10But you, O Yahweh, be gracious to me and raise me up,
that I might restore them.

11By this I know that you delight in me,
that my enemy does not shout in triumph over me.
12As for me, in my integrity you have upheld me,
you have placed me before you for ever.
13Blessed be Yahweh the God of Israel,
from everlasting to everlasting!
Amen and Amen!

Notes on the text

6. Hebr. sg. is distributive, making pl. the appropriate translation.

8. Hebr. *dĕbar bĕlîya'al* is ambiguous, perhaps intentionally. The root *dbr* could refer to 'words' or a 'thing', while a repointing would suggest a 'plague'.

10. Pi. of *šlm* has a range of possible senses (Terrien 2003, 2: 346, thinks it is ambiguous). Often translated 'requite' (so RSV), this would suggest paying back those who have harmed another (e.g. Ps. 137:8). But 'restore' is also possible (cf. Job 8:6) and, because of the play on words with 'companion' (also from *šlm*), is more likely. Goldingay (2006a: 587) points out that *Midrash Tehellim* already proposed this.

Form and structure

Psalm 41 closes both the collection Psalms 35–41 and Book 1. This latter point is marked by the opening beatitude, matching the opening of Psalm 1 so that these two psalms form bookends for Book 1. In addition, this psalm closes with a doxology (v. 13), establishing a pattern where each book other than Book 5 closes with a similar doxology (Pss 72:19; 89:52; 106:48). These features suggest that Book 1 has an intentional shape, that it is intended to be read as a unit. Connections to Psalms 35–41 are also important. Notably, the motifs of sin and sickness, which have been prominent in this collection (38:4, 18; 39:11; 40:12), are brought together here (v. 4), though there is also a direct link between the close of Psalm 40 and the opening of Psalm 41. The beatitude that opens this psalm also links to Psalm 40:5. In addition, just as Psalm 37 closed the first subunit of the collection with a direct instruction, this psalm closes the second subunit (cf. Beuken 2020: 83), with both psalms noting the prominent place in the land given to the righteous (Pss 37:11; 41:2). In short, Psalm 41 is given a place of prominence within both the collection and Book 1.

But what sort of psalm is it? It includes features considered typical of a range of different psalm types, including the beatitude (v. 1), a prayer for grace (vv. 4, 10), evidence of illness (vv. 3, 4–5, 8) and a declaration of integrity (v. 12). Depending on how we construe verses 4–10, they can be understood as either a testimony, which suggests thanksgiving, or as present distress. As with Psalm 40, it is best to read the poem as integrating a range of types, and with Kraus (1988: 430) to treat it simply as a prayer, recognizing that prayer can take diverse forms. It is possible that verse 13 has been added to the psalm to close Book 1, though in this case the doxology has a close enough relationship with the psalm that it can be read as integral to it (cf. Barbiero 2019).

The psalm can be analysed in three stanzas, each notable for its distinct form, with the second stanza bookended with pleas for grace:

1. Benediction (1–3)
2. Report (4–10)
3. Praise (11–13)

Comment

Title: The title is identical to Psalm 40, joining these psalms. For 'The director's', see on Psalm 4. For 'A melody. Davidic', see on Psalm 3.

1–3. The opening beatitude echoes Psalm 1 since along with that in Psalm 32 these are the only beatitudes that open a psalm in Book 1. On the form of the beatitude, see on Psalm 1:1. The blessed person here is noted for pondering of the weak. This can be seen as an application of the reflection on Torah that was central to Psalm 1. The term used for 'the weak' here (*dal*) is not particularly common, though the Torah does express concern for them (Exod. 23:3; 30:15; Lev. 14:21; 19:15). But seen as a representative term for the poor more generally, the concern referred to here can be understood as pointing to a widespread concern for the poor in the Torah. This possibility becomes stronger when we note that Psalm 40:17 ends with two other terms for the poor, so that, taken together, a wider view of the poor is provided. In Psalm 40, the plea is for Yahweh to save one who is poor, but here the beatitude declares that a desirable life is lived by one who ponders the weak. Such a person is in a state of blessedness because Yahweh rescues such on the day of trouble. Although it is possible that the one rescued is the weak (so Barbiero 2019: 326–328), it is more likely that the reference is to the one on whom the beatitude is pronounced since this is why their life is considered desirable. Indeed, Yahweh will keep and preserve such a person, and this leads to their being recognized as living in a state of blessedness. That this state is recognized in the land aligns this beatitude with Psalm 37:11. This state is not one that is a condition of simple bliss – that Yahweh needs to deliver such people from the day of trouble and protect them from enemies makes clear that this state is recognized within the conflicts of life and the challenges of serious illness. In all cases, Yahweh responds to a concern for the weak, perhaps because such a concern mirrors his own commitment to the needy.

4–10. A central question in interpreting these verses is whether they are a report of prior or present suffering. Central to resolving this is the opening statement *'ănî 'āmartî*, which could be either a report of present speech ('I say') or a statement of what was previously said (for the alternative, see Longman 2014: 190–192). Overall, usage of this phrase in Psalms points to previous speech, which no longer points to current circumstances (Pss 30:6; 31:22; 82:6; 116:11), and that is probably to be preferred here. As such, these verses prepare to give thanks to Yahweh because this is no longer the psalmist's condition, indicating that the deliverance mentioned in verse 1 has been experienced (cf. Weiser 1962: 343). Grace both opens and closes this section, drawing on the language of the grace formula (Exod. 34:6–7). The psalmist called out for grace, seeing a need for healing. Here, the poet assumes a link between the sickness and sin, a feature of Psalms 38–41. The statement does not indicate a definite causal link between sickness and sin, but does allow that sin can lead to illness. As is common in psalms that mention illness, enemies are also involved (cf. Ps. 6:7), speaking maliciously and openly seeking the poet's death. These people were not always enemies, but their visits to the psalmist increased his sense of isolation, speaking only what was worthless with the poet. But their other speech found fresh ways to devise trouble. Their speech also shows signs of hubris in verse 8, as they are sure that the psalmist is suffering from something terminal. The nature of this is not specified, and the verse can be read in various ways, but the overall sense is clear – they are waiting for the poet's death. In verse 9 we discover that one of the enemies had been a close friend, someone trusted by the poet. Yet even this person had lifted the heel against the poet, roughly equivalent to the English idiom of turning one's back on one in need, a betrayal of someone close with whom the poet had shared table fellowship (cf. John 13:18). Although many translations look for the chance to repay the enemies, suggesting vengeance, it is preferable to note that the former friend was (more literally) a 'man of my well-being' and that the verb here joins this in using the root *šlm* (cf. 'Notes on the text'). Given the contrast established, it seems more likely that the poet has therefore asked for restoration of this relationship, despite the strains placed on it.

11–13. Having reported the previous circumstances, the psalm moves to praise. Evidence of receiving requested graces is seen in the fact that the enemies' speech is no longer one of triumph over the poet. Yahweh has been gracious, and indeed delights in the psalmist. It is ultimately Yahweh who has done this, having responded to the psalmist's integrity. Claims of integrity in Psalms are not claims of perfection. Rather, they point to commitment to Yahweh (cf. Ps. 26). The poet was committed to Yahweh and has therefore been placed in Yahweh's presence. Yahweh has been gracious, and as such the poet can utter a doxology that 'blesses' (*brk*) Yahweh as the God of Israel. This declaration of praise affirms that Yahweh is always worthy of praise, with the closing 'Amen, amen' giving others the opportunity to affirm this praise and make it their own.

Explanation

Psalm 41 provides a conclusion to Book 1, creating a frame with Psalm 1. Together, these psalms encourage love of God and love of neighbour (McCann 1996: 848). In this case, the desirable life is one that is prepared to learn from the weak, reflecting on God's concern for them, a consistent motif in Book 1. If God is at work for the weak, then the blessed life adopts the same principle (Matt. 5:7). This psalmist also looks back and sees God at work in personal healing, despite the twin realities of personal sin and pressure from enemies, including former friends. The psalmist has discovered the joy of being in God's presence because God has not allowed enemies to triumph. The key is continued trust in God, and this in turn leads to a declaration of perpetual praise. The psalm thus encourages us to reread not only Psalms 35–41, the collection of which it is part, but also the whole of Book 1 and so to praise God even as we too ask how we can consider the weak.

BOOK 2

PSALM 42

Translation

The director's. A Maskil. Korahite.

1As the deer craves channels of water,
so my being craves you, O God.
2My being thirsts for God, the living God!
When shall I come and see God?
3My tears have been my food day and night,
as they continually say to me, 'Where is your God?'
4These things I recall
while I pour out my being within me,
how I would go with the throng
lead them in procession to the house of God,
with the sound of joyful shouts and praise,
a multitude keeping festival.
5Why are you downcast, O my being,
and why moan within me?
Hope in God, for I will yet praise him,
the help of my countenance and my God.

6My being is downcast within me,
therefore, I remember you,
from the land of the Jordan and Hermon,
from Mount Mizar.
7Deep calls to deep,
at the sound of your waterfalls,
All your breakers and waves,
have passed over me.
8By day has Yahweh commanded his kindness,
by night is his song with me,
a prayer to the living God.
9I say to God my rock,
'Why have you forgotten me?
Why do I go mourning
because of the oppression of the enemy?'
10With a deadly wound in my bones
while my adversaries reproach me
as they continually say to me, 'Where is your God?'
11Why are you downcast, O my being,
and why moan within me?
Hope in God, for I will yet praise him,
the help of my countenance and my God.

Notes on the text

2. With several MSS vocalize the verb as qal rather than niph. MT may attempt to avoid the possibility of seeing God (33:20); but the point is, being in God's presence.

3. With several MSS and Syr., reading *bĕʾāmĕrām*.

5. The refrain is here harmonized to verse 11 and 43:5. Misplacement of the conjunction before *ʾĕlōhê* so it becomes a suffix on *pānay* has triggered this, resulting in a displacement of the start of the verse.

9. With many MSS, read *ḥay*.

Form and structure

The first psalm in Book 2, Psalm 42 also introduces two other important collections: the Korahite psalms and the Elohistic Psalter. The Korahite psalms cover Psalms 42–49, 84–85, 86–87, and are placed at or near major seams in the Psalter across Books 2 (Pss 42–72) and 3 (Pss 73–89) and are marked by repeating vocabulary and themes (cf. Vesco 2006, 1: 390). The Korahites probably trace themselves back to the Korah mentioned in 1 Chronicles 6:22 and formed a musical group in the temple (1 Chr.

6:33), while 1 Chronicles 9:19 indicates that such a group was active after the exile (on the group more broadly, see J. Smith 2012: 54–81; Steiner 2017). At least some of these psalms may well have a northern origin (Goulder 1982: 13–14; Rendsburg 1990: 51–59), moving to Jerusalem after the northern kingdom's fall in 722 BC. However, attempts to define an original northern festival through them (Goulder 1982: 1–22) are too speculative to be persuasive and evidence for a northern origin is far from uniform. The Elohistic Psalter covers Psalms 42–83 (for the minority view that this classification should be extended to Psalm 89, see Wardlaw 2015: 60–61), again crossing the seam between Books 2 and 3. These psalms have this label because of the strong preference for 'Elohim' as the name for God rather than 'Yahweh', for which the rest of the Psalter has a strong preference, though other unifying elements are present (see C.-W. Kim 2021). It should be noted that the block of Korahite psalms in Book 3 falls out of the Elohistic Psalter, so that though they commence the Elohistic Psalter, they are also the point at which the Psalter returns to Yahweh as the dominant divine name (for possible reasons behind this collection, see Joffe 2002; Hossfeld and Zenger 2003; Burnett 2006).

Many MSS treat Psalms 42 and 43 as a single psalm, and there is certainly good reason for treating them as a single poem – note the repeating refrain at 42:5, 11 and 43:5 (cf. Alonso-Schökel 1976; and Raabe 1990: 40–42, who also notes two minor refrains). In addition, Psalm 43 lacks a title (though Gk provides one), a feature it shares with only Psalm 71 in Book 2, something that leads to its being read in the light of what has gone before (cf. Pss 10, 33). So, as with Psalms 9–10, we have here the phenomenon of one poem being presented as two psalms. Although both psalms can be classified as complaints, it should be noted that in Psalm 42 the poet's 'being' (*nepeš*) is addressed, while in Psalm 43 God is addressed (cf. deClaissé-Walford et al. 2014: 404). The division into two psalms highlights this distinction so that it is now a psalm in its own right rather than the poem's closing stanza.

Psalm 42 can be analysed in two stanzas, each marked by the refrain:

1. Craving God (1–5)
   a. Desiring God in conflict (1–4)
   b. Refrain (5)
2. Separation from God (6–11)
   a. Remembering God from a distance (6–10)
   b. Refrain (11)

Comment

Title: For 'The director's', see on Psalm 4. For 'Maskil', see on Psalm 32. For 'Korahite', see above, 'Form and structure', and Firth 2008: 26–27.

1–4. The psalm opens with the powerful simile of a deer in the wilderness desperately craving streambeds to find water. This image points to a lack of water, though in the second stanza the problem is its excess. The image of the deer is then applied to the poet, who likewise thirsts, but not for water. Rather, the poet craves God's presence. For reasons not outlined, the psalmist is unable to attend the sanctuary and there see God. The language of 'seeing God' draws conceptually on Psalms 11:7 and 17:15 (among others), which speak of seeing God as an expression of being in God's presence. Although a different verb is used (*ḥzh* in those psalms; *r'h* here), they have enough semantic overlap for this basic point to hold. It is separation from God, expressed through attending the sanctuary, that is the issue. Rather than drinking water, tears have fed the psalmist while unnamed enemies have mocked, asking 'Where is your God?' The implication is that God is not with the poet, and that claims of God's faithfulness are unfounded. Despite such mocking questions, the psalmist recalls earlier times of worship, his joining with the crowds who went to the temple in the festivals, events marked by joyful cries of praise. Memory of these joyful shouts sustains the poet in the face of mocking questions about God's presence.

5. This memory leads into the poem's refrain, repeated at verse 11 and Psalm 43:5. In a soliloquy, the poet asks why such a sense of absence, and the pain that goes with it, should continue. Memory of previous times of worship shows that future worship is possible. Waiting hopefully for God is thus required, the assumption being that God will allow the psalmist once more to praise him since he is the one who helps and who can be known as the psalmist's God. The refrain's first occurrence thus rejects the question of the adversaries. God is not restricted to the sanctuary; but this is certainly a place where he can be praised, and so the psalmist has hope.

6–10. Although the refrain points to a resolution, the challenge to the psalmist remains, as is shown by the repetition of the verb 'downcast' (*šḥh*) in verse 6. Knowing an answer does not mean the poet's circumstances have changed. However, this now allows the psalmist not only to remember previous times of worship, but to remember God. Such a memory here is not only recollection of fact but rather a point of reorientation. The place of remembering God seems, however, to be a long way from the sanctuary if reference to the land of the Jordan, Hermon range, and Mount Mizar are all indicators of a northern site, perhaps north of Lake Huleh, around the Jordan's headwaters (though Mount Mizar is otherwise unknown). Such a location is consistent with the reference to the 'deep', which normally refers to subterranean waters, though it can also simply mean deep waters generally. Here, these waters are personified, with one deep calling to another at the sound of God's waterfalls. All this points to an abundance of water, which is here troubling to the poet as it is now characterized as God's breakers and waves passing overhead, a terrifying experience for a non-swimmer (cf. Pss 69:1–2; 88:7). This experience is contrary to the faith affirmed in verse 8, which notes that Yahweh (the only occurrence of this name in the poem) has commanded his kindness by day and that his song is with the psalmist at night, a prayer to the living God. This is an affirmation of what faith should be, but the poet's declaration in verse 9 makes clear that this is not how God is being experienced. Where the psalmist has remembered both prior worship and God himself, the poet asks God why he has 'forgotten me'. God is meant to be the poet's crag, a place where the poet can be secure (cf. Pss 18:2; 31:3). Instead, God has allowed the psalmist to be oppressed by enemies, and the poet therefore mourns. This mourning is experienced as a deadly wound from the reproaches thrown by the enemies who ask, 'Where is your God?', repeating the question from verse 4. Again, the question assumes God's absence or inability to assist the psalmist.

11. But the question returns the poet to the refrain. The present experience is not desired, and the psalmist's own observations have made clear that the orthodox statement of verse 8 is not being experienced. But that does not make it untrue. Pain may currently be experienced, but the poet's soliloquy makes clear that it does not have to continue that way. Hopeful waiting on God anticipates a time when worship will again be possible, and praise can be offered in God's presence.

Explanation

Although it finds its completion as a poem only in Psalm 43, Psalm 42 stands as a distinct psalm. Its well-known opening simile expresses a deep desire for communion with God, something the poet currently finds impossible. But the reality of these challenges does not remove the desire. The psalmist faces pressure from adversaries who effectively deny that God can be expected to act. That the poet's experience can be construed this way is recognized here too in the contrast between the orthodox affirmation of verse 8 and the descriptions of experience that surround it. Both opponents and experience therefore seem to suggest that the communion with God that the psalmist craves cannot happen. And yet the psalm's refrain constantly suggests an alternative. Orthodox affirmations are not devoid of meaning even when they are not experienced. Rather, they point to a truth for which the psalmist waits, because it is God who is himself the salvation the poet needs, and it is God who will enable rejoining the community where praise is given in his presence. In the NT, we see that free access to God's presence is no longer bound to one place but rather to the person of Jesus (Eph.

3:11–12), but this psalm will continue to speak to those who are unable to access fellowship with other believers, and perhaps we would do well to remember that Jesus himself echoes these words in Gethsemane (John 12:27).

PSALM 43

Translation

1Vindicate me, O God, and contend my case
  from an impious people,
  from the deceitful and unjust one deliver me.
2Because you are my God, my stronghold:
  why have you rejected me?
Why must I go about mourning,
  because of the oppression of the enemy?
3Send forth your light and your truth,
  let them lead me,
let them bring me to your holy mountain,
  and to your sanctuary.
4Then I will go to the altar of God,
  to the God of the gladness of my rejoicing,
I will praise you with a lyre
  O God, my God.
5Why are you downcast, O my being,
  and why moan within me?
Hope in God, for I will yet praise him,
  the help of my countenance and my God.

Notes on the text

3. Lit. 'sanctuaries', but with this understood as a pl. of respect (*WHS* §9).

Form and structure

See on Psalm 42.

Psalm 43 can be analysed on a similar pattern to Psalms 42–43:

1. Returning to the sanctuary (1–4)
2. Refrain (5)

Comment

1–4. As noted (see 'Form and structure'), Psalm 43 poetically continues Psalm 42. However, it is marked off as a separate psalm to highlight the shift in address. Direct address to God has been anticipated in Psalm 42 (esp. v. 8), but in these verses God rather than the poet's self is the object of address. The language of verse 1 speaks to God in legal terms, 'vindicate' (*špṭ*) indicating a judgement issued by God in the psalmist's favour. However, although God is also asked to contend for the poet's case, these terms are here more likely metaphors for God's action in favour of the psalmist than references to an actual legal case. Faced with questions that suggest divine absence, God is instead to act and deliver the psalmist from the enemies here described as impious and deceitful, clear indications of their opposition to God's purposes. Such an action would be consistent with the idea of God as the poet's stronghold, one who is in a personal relationship with the psalmist. This summons is then contrasted with the series of questions in verse 2b. Failure to act would make it seem that God has rejected the psalmist, leading to a continuation of the life of mourning because of the enemy's oppression (cf. Ps. 42:9). Instead, Yahweh was to send forth his light and truth, with these divine attributes personified so that they might lead the psalmist. Such leading is not only on the right path (cf. Pss 23:3; 27:11; 31:4) as a way of life, but also to the place of worship. The psalmist has longed to be in God's presence, and the experience of the divine attributes allows once again for the possibility of entering the sanctuary. Because of this, the psalmist now anticipates the joy of time at God's altar since this is the place of joy that is marked with music.

5. The closing verse returns to the refrain. But this time it is not in response to taunts from adversaries. Instead, it is a reflection on the hope expressed in this psalm, hope that now anticipates God's action for the psalmist. The poet's circumstances have not yet changed, but the way they are viewed has. If God will indeed vindicate the psalmist, then hopeful waiting on him is what is needed, because praise will again be offered to God as the reality of his salvation is demonstrated.

Explanation

A continuation of Psalm 42, Psalm 43 turns from addressing the poet's inmost self and instead addresses God. It is this shift that enables the poet to reframe present experience. What is needed is that God act, vindicating the poet so the enemies can see the reality of God as one who acts, that he is indeed the psalmist's place of security. God's action should also lead the poet back to the sanctuary, leaving the mountains of the north and coming instead to God's holy mountain, the place of the temple, where praise will occur in the context of a community of praise. As part of the longer poem, it closes with the refrain from Psalm 42, but this time emerges from reflection on how God acts and not taunts from enemies. As such, it provides a more hopeful way of understanding present experience, a reminder of the importance of hopeful waiting on God.

PSALM 44

Translation

The director's. Korahite. A Maskil.

1O God, with our ears we have heard,
  our forebears have told us,
the deeds you performed in their days
  in days of yore.
2You, with your own hand, drove out nations and planted them,
  you afflicted peoples but set them free.
3For they did not possess the land by their sword,
  and their arm did not save them,
rather, your right hand and your arm,
  and the light of your face,
  because you delighted in them.

4You are my king, O God,
  command the deliverances of Jacob!
5Through you we thrust down our foes,
  in your name we tread down those who oppose us.
6For not in my bow do I trust,
  and my sword does not save me.
7For you save us from our foes,
  you put to shame those who hate us.
8In God we have boasted continually,
  and your name we praise for ever. *Selah.*

9How then have you spurned us and humiliated us,
  and do not go out with our armies?
10You have turned us back from the foe,
  and those who hate us have got spoil.
11You have made us like sheep, as food,
  you have scattered us among the nations.
12You have sold your people for no value,
  you have not made a profit from their price.
13You have made us a reproach to our neighbours,
  an object of mockery and derision to those around us.

14You have made us a byword among the nations,
a shaking of the head among the peoples.
15My disgrace is before me all the day,
my face's shame has covered me,
16at the sound of the taunter and reviler,
from the presence of the enemy and the avenger.

17You have brought all this upon us
though we have not forgotten you
and not been false to your covenant.
18We have not drawn our heart back,
our steps have not turned from your path.
19Yet you have crushed us at the place of jackals,
and covered us with death's shadow.
20If we had forgotten the name of our God,
or spread our hands to a strange god,
21would not God have discovered this,
since he knows the hidden things of the heart?
22Yet for your sake we are killed continually,
we are considered as sheep for the slaughter.

23Rouse yourself! Why should you sleep my Lord?
Wake up, do not spurn in perpetuity!
24Why do you hide your face,
forget our affliction and oppression?
25For our being sinks down to the dust,
our belly clings to the earth.
26Arise, be our help!
Yes, redeem us for the sake of your kindness.

Notes on the text

4. MT is often emended on basis of Gk (e.g. Kraus 1988: 444), but with A. P. Ross (2013: 38) is retained.

9. Though *'ap* is often a conjunction, Job 9:14 shows it can mark a rhetorical question.

14. Here following numerous MSS rather than L. See Waltke et al. 2014: 184.

Form and structure

The second poem but third psalm in the first Korahite collection, Psalm 44 is also the Psalter's first generally recognized communal complaint (cf.

Bouzard 1997: 102), one in which a community gives voice to pain. In this case, although the 'we' form dominates in the complaint, in verses 4, 6 and 15–16 we also hear from an individual, either as a personification of the community or the voice of a worship leader (cf. Kwakkel 2002: 218). Although this allows for a distinctive voice to emerge within the poem, its reflections are consistent with those of the bulk of the psalm. As a complaint psalm, it is also consistent with prayers such as Psalm 6 in accusing God of failing to act as he should, a feature not widely present in the communal complaints (Rom-Shiloni 2008: 685). The presence of enemies is acknowledged here, but though they are the problem in many complaint psalms, this time it is God who is the problem. This becomes particularly evident in the complaint proper (vv. 9–18) which consistently focuses on God's perceived failings, which led to the nation's defeat in battle. Complaint about God is also evident in Psalm 88, the last Korahite psalm, though the motif is also evident in Psalm 42:9. There, God is accused of having forgotten the psalmist, whereas here the community insist that they have not forgotten God (vv. 17, 20). This is one of several linguistic links between these poems (cf. Vesco 2006: 2:401–402), beginning with the titles, which contain the same elements (albeit in a different order; cf. Firth 2020: 29–34). We might also note that the refrain from Psalms 42–43 finds an immediate echo in the community's self-description in verse 25. These connections indicate that we should read Psalm 44 as expressing communally what was said individually in Psalms 42–43, with the sense of personal rejection by God finding an immediate echo in the communal experience here. As there, the community here longs for their relationship to be restored so that faith and experience line up.

The psalm can be analysed in three stanzas (Crow 1992: 394, using broadly the same divisions, identifies a loose chiasm):

1. Celebration of God's prior acts (1–8)
    a. Past reports (1–3)
    b. Current trust (5–8)
2. Accusations about God's failures (9–22)
    a. Spurned by God (9–16)
    b. Affirmation of loyalty (17–22)
3. Appeal for God to act (23–26)

Comment

Title: For 'The director's', see on Psalm 4. For 'Korahite', see on Psalm 42. For 'Maskil', see on Psalm 32.

1–3. The psalm's opening could suggest a praise poem, but like Psalm 89 the opening affirmations of what God has done in the past will be turned to complaint that he is not acting in the same way now. The possibility for such a turn here is established in the opening verse, which situates God's mighty acts in a distant past – something recounted to the current generation by their forebears but not necessarily their experience. The recounting of the past focused on Israel's entry to the land under Joshua (cf. Ps. 47:3–4) as Israel was planted in the land (cf. Ps. 80:8–15), though verse 2b then goes backwards in time in referring to the exodus. The land's occupation is the focus of verse 3, which stresses, as does Joshua 10 – 11, that God fought the battle for them – it was not a matter of Israel's military might (Josh. 24:12). They had received God's favour (cf. Deut. 10:15), echoing the blessing of Numbers 6:24–26. Yet whereas the past generation experienced the light of God's face, it is now hidden from them (v. 24).

4–8. The second strophe moves from past to present. The psalmist's loyalty to God is affirmed, calling him 'my king'. As such, God has his people's loyalty, and so is also responsible for them. Hence, the poet asks that God command salvation for Jacob, a first indication of the nation's distress. Nevertheless, before focusing on the present need the psalmist affirms that the current generation have also seen success because of God's actions for them. Like their forebears, they have trusted God rather than sword or bow (cf. Josh. 24:12), and through God have thrust down their foes. This generation knows that it is trusting God, not the sword, that saves. Hence, they too have experienced times when God has saved them from their foes. As a result, they have boasted in God's name, and so are confident of offering continued praise to him.

9–16. The praise anticipated at the close of verse 8 never comes. Instead, there is a sharp turn, albeit one that picks up hints in the first stanza. Instead of praise, there is accusation. Verse 9 uses three verbs, all accusing God of acting against his people, while each of verses 10–14 opens with a verb accusing him. Verse 9's rhetorical question asks God to justify himself – given that the psalmist speaks for God's people, why should he have rejected and disgraced them, not going out with their armies (cf. Ps. 60:1, 10)? The failure to go out with the army makes clear that the rejection and disgrace come from military defeat. Such defeat is not unknown, even in Israel's conquest traditions (Josh. 7), but in Joshua a reason was given in response to Joshua's prayer (Josh. 7:6–15). God is thus challenged to provide a reason for his inaction here, inaction that on its own leads to the charges in verses 10–14 since each of these points to Israel's inability to succeed militarily without God's involvement. Had God gone out with the army, none of these things would be true, but because he has not gone out with them, Israel is forced to turn back and become the spoil of their foes. Rather than gaining spoil themselves, they have become the food of their enemies, a people sold and scattered among the nations who now show them no respect. The type of victory anticipated through Deuteronomy 32:30 is far from them as they become a source of mockery. This pain is not just experienced communally. In verses 15–16 we hear the solo voice again, a voice that moves away from generalized description, allowing this pain to be personalized. That God's people are shamed brings shame on God (cf. Maré 2014: 3–7), and thus challenges him to act.

17–22. A shift occurs at this point as the poem anticipates a divine defence like that after Israel's defeat at Ai (Josh. 7). There, Yahweh points out that Israel broke the covenant (Josh. 7:11), explaining that their defeat was not a matter of his failure but of theirs. But that possibility is now excluded. Israel has not forgotten God or been false to the covenant. God still needs to answer the charge initiated at verse 10 but, before he can do so, the most likely divine defence (human sin) is denied. God has brought Israel to a place of unmerited suffering. Rather than leading them safely through the deadly shadow (cf. Ps. 23:4), God has covered them with it. The poet accepts that such an experience would have been valid had they forgotten God or worshipped other deities but insists that this has not happened. Indeed, had they done so, then God would have discovered it since he knows even secret thoughts. But God has brought no such charge against them, a responsibility that would fall on him under the covenant. So, Israel is left bereft, treated as sheep destined for the slaughter as their forces are killed (cf. Rom. 8:36). God stands accused of abandoning Israel without reason, leaving them at the mercy of their foes.

23–26. The final stanza turns to God as the solution to Israel's problem. God may be the problem, but he is also the solution. The appeal is bounded by paired imperatives in verses 23, 26 that ask God to act. Both verses offer less than flattering portrayals of God, though that is consistent with the rest of the poem. That God is called to awake is not metaphoric – the assumption is that God has indeed been sleeping on the job since the nation's condition is not the result of sin. Many ancient gods were thought to sleep (cf. Batto 2013: 139–157), so Israel's God is treated in similar terms, needing to rouse himself and so act for Israel. For him to sleep would leave him barely distinguishable from other deities. Only by rousing himself can God ensure that he does not spurn Israel and once more be Israel's divine warrior (cf. K. N. Jacobson 2014: 136; Waltman 2018: 213). These imperatives lead to the questions of verse 24, both of which pick up on themes from earlier in the psalm while still accusing him of failing to attend to his people's suffering (v. 25). Hence, the psalm closes with a final pair of imperatives, asking God to arise, and thus show that he truly is Israel's help by redeeming them as an example of his kindness. The nation might have been sold, but Yahweh can redeem them by acting as the covenant indicates he should.

Explanation

Where the opening verses of this psalm feel comforting, much of what follows comes as a shock. Rather than the Bible's dominant portrayal of God as a shepherd-king who cares for his people and is faithful to his promises, this psalm insists that God has failed to remember his covenant. It insists that the people have not breached covenant by serving other gods, creating a basis for punishment. Rather, it insists that despite the ancient stories that have been passed down that stress God's fidelity, God has treated Israel unjustly. Remarkably, there are no notes to suggest that the psalmists have a faulty perspective. God has been charged, and must rouse himself to demonstrate his kindness, his covenant commitment to his people.

These words may be grating, but they have a raw authenticity that the Psalter is content to leave without offering immediate amelioration. Even Paul's appropriation of it (Rom. 8:36; cf. Stewart 2013) understands that Christian believers may also experience similar suffering, though in context arguing that nothing separates believers from God's love. Paul's argument picks up on the motif of God's kindness with which the psalm ends. Yet, the pain of the psalm is increased when read alongside Psalms 42–43, where we read of an individual who feels alienated from God, whereas here it is the community. Read together, we understand that such prayers are perfectly acceptable. But there are also mechanisms by which the Psalter creates some boundaries about how such a prayer is appropriated even if the absence of specific historical reference (cf. Human 1998: 577–578) opens this psalm to repeated use (for which 2 Chr. 20 may provide at least one contextual model). Allusions to Joshua 7 remind us that even when such prayers are honestly prayed, it remains possible that the fault is with our perspective, though even there it is precisely because a prayer like this is offered that the truth is revealed. Beyond this, we also note that Psalm 45 begins a process of exploring how God might achieve victory for his people – we need to hear Psalm 44 as a witness in its own terms (along with Pss 42–43), but we also see that this is not the last word, and other ways of seeing God at work must also be explored (cf. Firth 2020: 35–36).

PSALM 45

Translation

The director's. According to Lilies. Korahite. A Maskil. A song of love.

1My heart is stirred with a pleasing word,
  I address my opus to the king,
  my tongue is the pen of a ready scribe.

2You are the fairest of humans,
grace is poured out on your lips,
therefore God has blessed you for ever.
3Gird your sword upon your thigh, O warrior,
your splendour and your majesty!
4Yes, your majesty – ride out victoriously
for the cause of truth and humility of righteousness
and may your right hand teach you awesome deeds.
5Your arrows are sharp,
peoples fall beneath you
in the midst of the king's enemies.
6Your throne, O God, is for ever and ever,
a sceptre of rectitude is the sceptre of your kingdom.
7You love righteousness and hate wickedness,
therefore God, your God, has anointed you
with the oil of gladness beyond your companions.
8Myrrh and aloes, cassia – all are in your robes,
from the ivory palace, stringed instruments make you glad.
9Daughters of kings are in your retinue,
the queen stands at your right hand with gold of Ophir.

10Hear, O daughter and see, and incline your ear,
and forget your people and your father's house,
11and the king shall desire your beauty,
because he is your lord bow down to him.
12Daughter Tyre shall seek your presence with a gift,
the rich ones of the people.
13All glorious is the king's daughter in the harem,
her clothing is brighter than settings of gold.
14With embroidered garments she is led to the king,
the young women behind her, her companions,
are brought to her.
15They are led with joy and gladness,
they enter the king's palace.

16Your children shall be in place of your forebears,
you shall appoint them as princes in all the earth.
17I will cause your name to be remembered in all generations,
therefore the peoples will praise you for ever and ever.

Notes on the text

2. *yāpěyāpîtâ* intensifies through reduplication, so emendation is unnecessary (contra Riede 2022: 28).

7. The translation of this verse is much debated, but as Harris (1984) has shown, the most straightforward translation (followed here) is also the most likely.

13. *pĕnîmâ* refers to something inward, mostly within a building (cf. Riede 2022: 47; though, as he notes later (243), its meaning is not altogether clear). It is understood here as representing the harem as those who live within the palace.

14. With two MSS, reading *lāh*.

Form and structure

Although clearly recognizable as a royal psalm because of its concern with the king, Psalm 45 is unique within the Psalter as the only one to praise a human. Its title mentions a 'song of love' that links to the poem's content since it is addressed to a royal couple on their wedding day. Unusually, it addresses both the king and his bride, albeit in idealized terms, encouraging them to fulfil their respective royal roles. By general consent (contra Postell 2019, who argues it was intentionally messianic), it was written for a royal wedding and its associated celebrations, but it lacks details that would allow identification with a particular wedding (cf. Starbuck 1999: 114). This is somewhat ironic given the composer's vow to ensure the king's name is remembered perpetually, but that promise does not depend on this poem alone.

Though its historical setting is difficult to determine, and attempts to define a ritual in which it played a part (e.g. Goulder 1982: 121–122) are overly speculative, its place within the first Korahite collection provides a literary context against which to read it. Its uniqueness remains, but it has striking connections to the surrounding poems such that it begins the process of addressing the unresolved complaints of Psalms 42–44. Where God as king is presented as having failed to keep covenant in those psalms, here the king is addressed as 'God' (see 'Comment') and encouraged to go forth in his victories (45:4), indicating that the king is one means by which God achieves victories for his people, though God's direct action will be seen in Psalm 46.

The psalm can be analysed in two main stanzas based on the person addressed, while comments from the poet also form an inclusion for the whole (cf. Schroeder 1996: 420):

1. Poet's declaration (1)
2. Message for the king (2–9)
3. Message for the bride and groom (10–15)
4. Poet's declaration (16–17)

Comment

Title: For 'The director's', see on Psalm 4. 'According to Lilies' recurs in the titles of Psalm 69, and with a slight change, Psalm 80, with a related title at Psalm 60. The meaning is unclear, but as part of the director's collection could refer to a tune – a more probable option than Goulder's (1982: 124) suggestion that it refers to the throne site at Tel Dan. For 'Korahite', see on Psalm 42. For 'Maskil', see on Psalm 32; note that each poem in Psalms 42–45 is called a 'maskil' but this term does not occur elsewhere in the Korahite psalms other than Psalm 88, suggesting we are to read them as a small collection. 'A song of love' is unique to Psalm 45, though it joins with Psalms 46, 48 in the first Korahite collection in being a song.

1. The psalm's distinctiveness is seen in the poet's opening declaration, which is addressed to the wider audience. Courtly language makes clear the poet's pleasure in presenting this psalm, reporting that this opus is addressed to the king. Although a message will be given to the queen, the psalm is always addressed to the king. The poem is presented as an oral piece, with the poet's tongue taking the part of a stylus a scribe would use. Despite this oral background, we have the psalm as a written piece, something subsequent performers could use.

2–9. The message to the king, presented here in an idealized form, focuses upon his excellence in all things (using motifs widespread in the OT and ANE, richly documented in Riede 2022: 78–202). The king is superior to all others because of his special relationship with God. This is initially presented in terms of his appearance, which is said to be fairer than any other. This is combined with fairness of speech as evidence of God's enduring blessing on the king. These external signs of divine blessing provide a context in which the king can confidently enter battle. Indeed, the king equipped for battle is evidence of his majesty, and as such the king can ride out victoriously, knowing the justice of his cause. Engaging in battle enables the king to learn awesome deeds through his victory, deeds which let him know that God is with him. The king's equipment, symbolized by his sharp arrows, is also superior, such that his enemies fall beneath him. The statements to this point have been hyperbolic, but the hyperbole reaches a new level in verse 6, where the king is addressed as 'God' when he is assured that his throne endures for ever. Although Israel recognized only one God, the word translated 'God' (*'ĕlōhîm*) can be flexible in meaning. Here, it perhaps indicates that God stands so closely with the king because of the Davidic covenant (cf. 2 Sam. 7:1–17), and as one appointed by God, that he can be addressed as God (cf. Exod. 7:1; 21:6; 22:8–9, 28; Ps. 138:1; cf. Cheung 2016: 330). God's throne is genuinely eternal, so the endurance of the king's reign reflects this. Moreover, that God is the one whose reign is marked by righteousness indicates that the king's reign should be modelled on

God's reign. To the extent that the king's reign demonstrates a love of righteousness and rejection of wickedness, the king truly reigns as God's representative and so can be addressed this way. But that the king is ultimately not God is made clear by the statement in verse 7 that God has anointed the king (cf. A. P. Ross 2013: 63). The king was addressed as God, but there is one who stands above him who is truly God, and the king reigns because God has anointed him (cf. Ps. 2:7). Hence, even as the psalm borrows the courtly language of its time, it limits its implications in a manner distinctive to Israel. Nevertheless, as the one anointed by God, the king enjoys wealth and comfort, symbolized by superior garments, luxury goods such as ivory and musical instruments, all natural elements of a wedding party ultimately focused on the queen (perhaps the queen mother, not the bride; cf. Schroeder 1996: 428), who stands with her own signs of wealth.

10–15. At this point, the poem addresses the bride, though from verse 13 it is perhaps more accurate to say she is spoken about so that the king and the bride are addressed. Before pointing to her beauty, the poet first counsels her to forget her own people, indicating that she is a foreign princess. This was important advice since returning home would be very difficult, but it would also show her commitment to the king, while he would desire her beauty. Her commitment is further shown by her bowing down to him, showing that she regards him as her lord. This indicates that this is a marriage of diplomacy, not the sort of relationship anticipated by Genesis 2:24. Her place beside such an exalted king would also see neighbouring peoples bringing gifts to her, rather like the Queen of Sheba with Solomon (1 Kgs 10:10). Mention of Tyre (in Phoenicia) may indicate she is herself Tyrian, but they may be mentioned because they were noted for their wealth (though mention of Tyre is consistent with the poem's northern linguistic features; cf. Patterson 1985: 34). The bride will also be recognized within the harem as the one whose beauty stands out among the others, including her attendants who follow her in their luxury garments, finding joy in coming into the king's presence.

16–17. The address switches back to the king, anticipating the birth of children who will continue the royal line and themselves take on important roles in other lands. The poem closes with a second declaration from the poet (Hildebrandt [2020: 210] wishes to leave room for God to be the speaker), again addressing the king, and promising to make his name remembered through all generations so that the praise given in this poem will continue. Remarkably, that praise will come from the peoples.

Explanation

As the only poem of praise addressed to a human, Psalm 45 is an oddity. Its distinctiveness, however, is clearly framed by its place within the Psalter. In this setting, which has already established that the king reigns only as God's representative (Ps. 2) it is appropriate to praise the king. But this praise also carefully guides the king, reminding him that as God's representative his reign is to be marked by the commitment to justice and the needy that God also demonstrates. Even as the king is praised, the psalm offers a careful critique, indicating that the reign that matters is one that serves God and not self-interest (a point that begins to address the concerns of Bowen [2003]). Through such a king, this psalm also begins to resolve the hurt left unresolved in Psalms 42–44. There is a way in which God's people may see him going out with their armies, and that is with a king who is committed to God's purposes. This is not the end of this matter, and Psalm 46 will take it further, but it shows that the idealized language about the king is not mere flattery – it is also a statement about the pattern of politics that should mark God's people. Beyond this, Hebrews 1:8–9 cites verses 6–7 when referring to Jesus since he is the one who truly embodied these principles, the one who can be addressed as God without qualification. If Jesus fully embodies this psalm, then those who follow him are also called to live in the light of his reign, serving the cause of truth and righteousness with him.

PSALM 46

Translation

The director's. Korahite. According to Maidens. A Song.

[1]God is our shelter and refuge,
a very present help in distresses.
[2]Therefore we will not fear when the earth is changed
and the mountains slip into the heart of the sea,
[3]its waters roar, they foam,
the mountains quake at its swelling. *Selah.*

[4]A river! Its streams gladden the city of God,
the holy dwelling place of the Most High.
[5]God is in her midst – she shall not totter!
God is her help when morning comes.
[6]The nations roar, kingdoms totter,
he puts forth his voice, the earth melts.
[7]Yahweh of Hosts is with us,
the God of Jacob is our refuge. *Selah.*

[8]Come, see Yahweh's deeds
how he set desolations in the earth,

9causing wars to cease to the ends of the earth,
the bow he shatters and the spear he has cut in two,
the war-carts he burns with fire.
10Stop, and know that I am God,
I will be exalted in the nations,
I will be exalted in the earth.
11Yahweh of Hosts is with us,
the God of Jacob is our refuge. *Selah*.

Notes on the text

Title: 'Maidens' is often simply transliterated as 'Alamoth', but its meaning is clear so it is translated here. It occurs only here in the titles.

3. *BHS* suggests inserting the refrain from verses 7, 11 prior to the *selah* (similarly, Raabe 1990: 53–54). It is possible that the refrain was lost early in transmission, and it would fit well here but the absence of MS evidence must be held against it, as is the fact that refrains in the Psalter are seldom regular (cf. Goldingay 2007: 66).

Form and structure

Psalm 46 develops themes initiated in Psalm 45, extending its response to the challenges posed by Psalms 42–44. Where God's kingship was challenged in the opening Korahite psalms, Psalm 45 began to offer an alternative perspective in which God's reign could be seen in his king. Yet, Psalm 45 remains a theological outlier because of its willingness to praise the king. Psalm 46 addresses this by pointing readers back to God, Yahweh of Hosts, as the one who provides hope for Israel and decisively wins battles. It is Yahweh who provides hope for Israel and, with this point established, each of the remaining psalms in the first Korahite collection explores the implications of this. Psalm 46 is thus at the heart of the first Korahite collection (cf. Firth 2020), allowing both praise (Pss 47–48) and reflection (Ps. 49).

Psalm 46 is commonly regarded as a 'Song of Zion' (e.g. Kraus 1988: 459; cf. Ravasi 1985a: 821–824), poems that celebrate Yahweh's presence with his people there. Although much in the poem is consistent with this, and various elements within the poem can point towards Jerusalem (though others are more northern; cf. Rendsburg 1990: 52), it is notable that neither Jerusalem nor Zion is mentioned in the poem (similarly, Craigie and Tate 2004: 342; Kelly's [1970] otherwise helpful essay is weakened by its failure to note this). Rather, the various descriptions of God's actions can be seen in a more universal light, consistent with the need to address the sense of absence felt when geographically removed from the sanctuary in Psalms 42–43. This is continued into Psalm 47, which is also universal in focus, so that Zion is explicitly named only in Psalm 48. This is not to deny the value of seeing the poem within this category, but to note that it cannot constrain all features of its interpretation. Since it reflects confidence in God's reign, we can also consider it as a song of trust (cf. Longman 2014: 204).

The psalm can be analysed in three stanzas, marked by the three occurrences of *selah*, though with key vocabulary recurring across them. Their presence sometimes also leads to a twofold analysis (cf. R. A. Jacobson 2020: 312–314 for summary and critique). While Amzallag (2015) suggests a far more complex structure, the threefold structure sits more obviously with the poem's surface form and rhetorical goals (cf. Cook 2017):

1. The certainty of God's help (1–3)
2. The encouragement of God's presence (4–7)
3. Reflections on God's works (8–11)

Comment

Title: For 'The director's', see on Psalm 4. 'According to Maidens' is unclear, but as part of the director's collection could refer to a tune, or a mode of singing (cf. 1 Chr. 15:20–21). For 'Korahite', see on Psalm 42. Like Psalm 45, this is a song.

1–3. In stark contrast to the uncertainty that marked Psalm 44, this poem opens with a confident declaration. Rather than needing to be roused (Ps. 44:23), this poem confidently asserts that God is indeed the community's shelter and refuge. Psalm 14:6 has already noted that Yahweh is the refuge of the poor, while the poet will also in Psalm 62:8 claim God as refuge and strength. Yahweh was earlier declared to be the strength of both the king (Ps. 21:1) and his people (Ps. 28:8), so the declaration here is consistent with other parts of the Psalter. Where it goes beyond earlier references is in noting that God is a very 'present' (*nimṣā'*) help in distress. The verb here suggests that God is found through his presence in distress (cf. Wardlaw 2015: 79–80). Distress is not avoided, but the reality of God's help is found in it. It is God's help in distress that leads to the conclusion voiced in verses 2–3. Because God is such a reliable help in times of distress, even the worst that can be imagined, where the earth changes and mountains fall into the heart of the sea and other mountains tremble (perhaps pointing to an earthquake; cf. Bang 2017), does not lead to fear. The experience of God's help in the past means fear is unnecessary even in the face of cosmic collapse, though such language can also refer to military crises (e.g. Judg. 5:4–5; cf. A. P. Ross 2013: 90).

4–7. In contrast to the unpredictable seas, God's city (presumably Jerusalem, but unnamed) has a river, perhaps the Gihon spring, though now imagined as something much greater via Genesis 2:10 (and perhaps Ezek. 47:1–12; cf. Vesco 2006, 2: 425), which makes it glad. A spring that produces a stream is not only pleasant on a warm day, but helpful in case of a siege as it ensures a continuous water supply. The city not only has a river, but is also the Most High's holy dwelling place. The epithet 'Most High' has occurred previously (e.g. Pss 7:18; 9:2) but, perhaps more importantly, it prepares for the assertion in Psalm 47:2 that Yahweh, the Most High, is to be feared. Cosmic collapse need not generate fear because of God's presence, but God is to be feared (in the sense of giving reverence). The city is where this God is present (cf. Gen. 14:18) and the city is therefore secure, helping it when morning dawns since this is the time when attacks were most likely (cf. Exod. 14:27). The consistent help mentioned in verse 1 will be experienced at such a time. So, although the nations may roar like the seas and kingdoms may be insecure, it is God's voice that brings change to the earth (cf. Ps. 29). It is God who controls the world; it is his voice, not forces of chaos like the sea, that brings real change. Where the more generic 'God' has been used to this point, the psalm now introduces its refrain, declaring that this God is Yahweh of Hosts and he is with the community. The one who commands the hosts of heaven (cf. Ps. 24) is present, but he is also the God of Jacob, the one who has promised his presence to Israel. As both the source of power and the one who is committed to his people, Yahweh is the source of his people's security.

8–11. The final stanza addresses the audience, inviting them to come and see Yahweh's deeds. The psalm does not reference particular examples of what is to be seen (though perhaps Pss 47–48 also give examples), so readers are asked to identify examples through their own experience or the wider witness of the Bible; for example, the deliverance of Jerusalem recounted in 2 Kings 18 – 19. Those addressed could be the city's inhabitants or invading armies, but the inhabitants are more likely since they are the ones who encounter the psalm. Although described as 'desolations'; they are positive for the community since they all reflect ways in which Yahweh ends violence through his interventions. His involvement is not just for the city since he causes wars to cease to the ends of the earth, destroying the weapons of war like the bow and spear, as well as the carts associated with war. Having been invited to come and see, the audience is now addressed by Yahweh, who tells them to stop and know that he is God. What is required here is not some sense of stillness but rather that they cease what they are doing (cf. 1 Sam. 15:16). The suggestion is that the community has been looking for their own source of security and in so doing have forgotten that Yahweh is the one who provides this. They have been reminded of what Yahweh does and must therefore remember that he is God, the one who will be exalted in the nations, across the earth. As any nation attacks the city, they discover the reality that the psalm affirms (and stresses through the refrain in v. 11), that Yahweh is with them and so provides their security. Adversaries cannot succeed against Yahweh and through this he is exalted in the earth.

Explanation

In the face of massive challenges, Psalm 46 encourages believers, reminding them that they can trust in God because he 'is with us'. The psalmist here imagines a 'worst-case scenario' (McCann 1996: 865) of the world in cosmic collapse, perhaps familiar as the twenty-first century struggles with climate change. Yet the otherwise counterintuitive conclusion reached is that 'We shall not fear.' Such a view is counter-intuitive until we recognize the central affirmation of the psalm: God is with us. Scripture has a rich theology of God's presence (see Duvall and Hays 2019), though it finds its final focus in Jesus as Immanuel, the one who can promise to be with us always (Matt. 1:22–23; 28:16–20) in anticipation of the new heavens and earth (Rev. 21 – 22). God's presence is no longer localized to a particular city, though even in the psalm the city is described in terms that transcend any historical location and point to ways in which God's presence provides security for his people where they are. If God is present, then those who rely on this presence are also called to commit themselves to the patterns God demonstrates here. The language of 'Yahweh of Hosts' has a background in warfare (1 Sam. 4:4), but it is notable here that Yahweh acts to end war. Trusting in God as present among us is also seeing what he does and committing ourselves to the same goals.

PSALM 47

Translation

The director's. Korahite. A melody.

1Clap hands, all peoples!
  Shout to God with the sound of a joyful cry!
2Because Yahweh Most High is awesome,
  the great king over all the earth.
3He subdues peoples under him,
  and nations under our feet.
4He chose our heritage for us,
  the majesty of Jacob whom he loves. *Selah.*

5God has gone up with a shout,
Yahweh with the sound of the horn.

6Make music to God, make music!
make music to our king, make music!
7Because God is king of all the earth,
make music with instruction.
8God reigns over the nations,
God is seated upon his holy throne.
9The princes of the peoples gather,
O people of the God of Abraham,
for the shields of the earth are God's,
he is highly exalted.

Notes on the text

3. Taking hiph. *yadbēr* from *dbr* II, 'destroy, subdue'.

6. Taking the *lĕ* as doing double duty.

7. *maśkîl* is elsewhere part of a psalm title.

9. Craigie and Tate (2004: 347) support the view that there is a haplography (based on Gk), but it is more probable that its *meta* is already attempting to expand on an elliptical text. Similarly, Schapfer 1994: 262. The proposal of Bodner (2003), that the phrase be read as a voc., allows MT to be retained.

Form and structure

Where Psalm 46:8 had summoned its audience to 'come and see' Yahweh's works, this psalm begins to outline at least some of them through recognizable allusions to his great acts of the past, most obviously in the references to Israel's entry into the land in verses 3–4, though other parts of the psalm envisage Yahweh's acts more specifically through liturgy. We should not, however, separate these elements since both history and liturgy can demonstrate the acts the audience is called to see, and they are clearly integrated here.

Psalm 47 is commonly regarded as an enthronement psalm that celebrates Yahweh's kingship over the nations. Although the others are gathered in Book 4 (Pss 93, 96–99), the motif of his kingship was made clear in Psalm 29:10. Psalm 46:6 also joined Psalm 29 in celebrating the power of God's voice, suggesting a wider range of connections between Psalm 29 and the Korahite psalms. As is common with the enthronement psalms, Yahweh's reign is presented as a reason for praise.

Unlike Psalm 46, the *selah* does not mark the main divisions (Terrien [2003, 2: 377] thinks it marks the point where a horn was sounded). Rather, the psalm contains two stanzas, each of which begins with imperatives summoning praise before providing reasons for this. The stanzas also reflect the distinction between Yahweh's kingship being predominantly celebrated in history and in liturgy, though they are also linked through plays on the root *'lh* (cf. Steiner 2014: 163–164, though Sibinga [1988] points to numerous other links). This leads to the following analysis:

1. Yahweh's reign in Israel's history (1–5)
2. Yahweh's reign in Israel's liturgy (6–9)

Comment

Title: For 'The director's', see on Psalm 4. For 'Korahite', see on Psalm 42. For 'a melody', see on Psalm 3. This is the first of three psalms with 'a melody' in its title, a mechanism for joining Psalms 47–49 as the conclusion to this first Korahite collection.

1–5. Imperatives dominate verse 1, with the audience told both to 'clap' and 'shout'. Nevertheless, the poet varies the expected word order, so that 'all peoples' opens the psalm, emphasizing the poem's worldwide focus. It is not only Israel who must come and see what Yahweh has done. Rather, all peoples must come to praise God as they see what he has done, with praise expressed through clapping hands and celebratory shouts. The psalm is clear that these peoples are praising Israel's God since his mighty works have shown that he is worthy of praise. That praise is rooted in God's identity and his actions for Israel, though it is God's identity that explains why he can act for Israel. Yahweh, as Most High, is awesome, a term that indicates that he is to be revered. The epithet 'Most High' picks up on its occurrence in Psalm 46:4, also helping to link these two poems. Elsewhere in the Korahite psalms, it occurs only in Psalm 87:5, though again with a focus on Jerusalem, where the title seems to have been of particular importance. But Yahweh is not only associated with Jerusalem. Instead, he is king over all the earth, and so deserving of the praise of all peoples, a bold claim considering the claims of Assyrian kings (cf. 2 Kgs 18:19). As king of all the earth, Yahweh has also acted for Israel, subduing peoples and setting nations under Israel's feet. The reference here is to Israel's entry to the land under Joshua (though allusions to David's victories are also possible), a theme that receives considerably less attention in Psalms than does the exodus. That this is the reference, rather than more general references to victories is evident from the mention of his having chosen Israel's heritage, drawing on a key term in Joshua (e.g. Josh.

13:6–7; 14:2; 19:51). Israel has not chosen its land for itself but rather is an inheritance from Yahweh. It is God's gift to them, a sign of his love, and therefore a source of delight to the nation. Yahweh's kingship is thus a source of praise because of what he has done for Israel in its past. Mention of God's ascent with a shout and the blast of a trumpet most probably refers to the Ark of the Covenant (the presence of which is hinted at in Ps. 46) being taken up to Zion to the temple, rather like David had managed when he first brought the Ark to Jerusalem (2 Sam. 6; Goldingay [2007: 79] also points to the Jericho story in Josh. 6). The Ark would symbolize God's presence among his people and also point to his reign, thus maintaining the emphasis on God's kingship that is prominent in this stanza.

6–9. God's praise is rooted in liturgy in this second stanza, though it is not possible to reconstruct its details beyond a broad outline (cf. Broyles 1999: 213). The audience is addressed three times, commanded to make music in praise of 'God' 'our king'. Yahweh is Israel's king, but he is still king over all the earth, and this gives reason for musical praise. This praise has content, with music that instructs those who offer it. Israel's praise was to have content that enabled the congregation to understand Yahweh's identity as a means of shaping their world view (cf. Brueggemann 1988: 6–11; Hutchinson 2005: 89–90). Here, that praise instructed as it explored the reality of Yahweh's reign. It is notable that whereas verses 3, 7, 8 had focused on Yahweh's kingship, the slight shift in verse 9 is that we now have verbs describing his reign. Although the verb can be taken as referring to the beginning of Yahweh's reign (cf. Mowinckel 1962, 1: 222–224), the earlier references to the reality of his kingship mean it is more likely that the verbs here refer to its enduring nature. There is an ongoing dynamic to his reign as something that began in the past, continues to be experienced and is demonstrated by his being seated on his holy throne, probably another allusion to the Ark (Broyles 2005: 149–150). Israel's worship helps construct their world view through both its affirmations and liturgical practice. That Yahweh is king of all is expressed in the gathering of the princes of the people, who can now be understood as joined with the people of the God of Abraham. This reference points back to Genesis 12:1–3, which makes clear that Yahweh's call of Abraham was to bring blessing to all the clans of the earth, and this gathering (perhaps imaginatively represented in the liturgy) demonstrates this. That Yahweh is exalted in this provides a further link to Psalm 46, which insisted he would be exalted among the nations (v. 10), an exaltation here demonstrated (cf. Vesco 2006, 2: 429). The princes worship Yahweh because the shields of the earth, symbols of power, belong to God. The one who waged peace in Psalm 46 has the power the princes lack and so they gather because God alone is highly exalted.

Explanation

Psalm 47 picks up on the summons to 'come and see' in Psalm 46:8, providing evidence that the claims of God's kingship can be seen. They are seen in both history and liturgy. Historically, they are evidenced by Israel's presence in the land, a heritage Yahweh granted them. Liturgically, it is seen in the celebration of God's reign, a reality that brings the peoples to his worship. God alone is therefore the great king – no human king can make this claim. Indeed, the resources kings claimed as proving their might actually belongs to God. History and liturgy here mutually inform one another – history shapes liturgy and liturgy points to the theological truth that history on its own may not fully discern in declaring God's reign. Liturgy also transcends history, pointing to the greater reality of God's reign, which we see glimpsed in the heavenly liturgy in Revelation 4:9–11, and that is already seen in celebration of the Lord's Supper. For similar reasons, this psalm is also often read at Ascension, linking Jesus' reign and exaltation with that described in the psalm.

PSALM 48

Translation

A melody. A Song. Korahite.

1Great is Yahweh and highly praiseworthy,
in the city of our God, his holy mountain,
2beautiful of elevation, the joy of all the earth,
Mount Zion, remotest part of the north,
city of the great king.
3God is in her citadels,
he is made known as a refuge.

4For behold the kings assembled,
they passed on together.
5When they saw, they froze with fear,
they were horrified, they fled.
6Trembling seized them there,
anguish like a woman giving birth.
7By the east wind,
you shatter the ships of Tarshish.
8Just as we have heard so we have seen,
in the city of Yahweh of Hosts,
in the city of our God,
God will establish her for ever! *Selah*.

9We have pondered your kindness O God,
in the midst of your temple.
10As is your name, O God, so is your praise
to the ends of the earth,
your right hand is filled with justice.
11Let Mount Zion rejoice,
let the daughters of Judah exult,
because of your judgements.

12Go about Zion and circle round her,
count her towers!
13Set your mind to her outer wall,
pass through her citadels,
that you may recount them to the next generation.
14Because this is God,
our God for ever and ever,
he will lead us unto death.

Notes on the text

1. *BHS* suggests having 'his holy mountain' commence the following verse. But the Masoretic structure is defensible and can be explained as enjambment.

3. Taking the niph. *nôdaʿ* as tolerative (*WHS* §138).

13. *passĕgu* is of uncertain derivation but from the context is translated 'pass through'.

14. *ʿal mût* is a notorious crux. Gk's *eis tous aiōnas* is likely an emendation. The same consonants (pointed differently) are part of Psalm 46's title and could allude to it. However, Syr. and Vg support MT's vocalization. The phrase is here taken as both a link to Psalm 49 and an explanation of how God is with his people for ever (cf. A. P. Ross 2013: 119).

Form and structure

As with Psalms 46–47, Psalm 48 is particularly concerned with God's kingship as it is exercised from Zion. Where Psalm 46 had alluded to Jerusalem without mentioning it, Zion is named here. Psalm 48 joins with Psalm 46 in noting that God is known as a refuge (Pss 46:7, 11; 48:3), continuing to insist that Yahweh defeats Zion's foes (Pss 46:6, 9; 48:4). Like Psalm 47, it declares that Yahweh's reign (and therefore his praise) reaches all the earth (Pss 47:6–7; 48:10). These links (cf. Auffret 1991; Schäder 2010), plus repeated elements in the titles (cf. Firth 2020:

29–34), demonstrate the close integration of these psalms where the themes announced in Psalm 46 are developed in Psalms 47–48. This remains true even if, with Steiner (2012), one supposes the poem has gone through multiple editions.

In form-critical terms, Psalm 48 can be considered as a Song of Zion, though this designation is not necessarily entirely separate from other classifications. Psalm 47 may also be considered as a Song of Zion save for the form of the reference to Yahweh's kingship, which leads to its being treated as an enthronement psalm. In reality, these classifications bleed into one another. Psalm 49 is clearly different from the cluster of Psalms 46–48 but the close to Psalm 48 seems to prepare for the meditation on death that is at Psalm 49's heart. As such, we also need to read that psalm within the context of God's kingship such that even death is subject to him. Indeed, this is consistent with elements within Psalm 48 that allude to different aspects of ANE mythology, demonstrating that Yahweh is king over all realms. Its various liturgical elements have also been used to suggest links to various festivals, for which Mowinckel's (1962, 1: 106–192) suggestion of Tabernacles is most probable, but certainty is impossible (though note the scepticism of Kidner [1975, 1: 180]).

The psalm can be analysed in four stanzas, which can be recognized both by content and also the way in which the four cardinal points are placed in the text (cf. Palmer 1965):

1. Great is Yahweh! (1–3)
2. The defeat of the kings (4–8)
3. A lesson learnt (9–11)
4. Enduring security (12–14)

Comment

Title: With Psalms 45, 46, this psalm is a song. For 'A melody', see on Psalm 3. For 'Korahite', see on Psalm 42.

1–3. Continuing the motif of praise from Psalm 47, the opening stanza reaffirms Yahweh's greatness and kingship, moving from the local to the universal (cf. Barré 1988). Yahweh's greatness is itself the basis for praise in his city and on his holy mountain, Zion. Yahweh is specifically 'our God', a term that becomes more significant as the psalm progresses and undermines the claims of other deities known in the region. However, the city becomes the focus in verse 2, noted for the beauty of its elevation and that it is the joy of all the earth. The reasons for this are then explained by connecting Mount Zion with Mount Zaphon, the mountain known in various Ugaritic texts as Baal's abode. Because of its location, Zaphon also became a standard Hebrew term for 'north' (cf. Ps. 89:12). The term is used here both as the mountain and as the cardinal point. Geographically, Zion is far from Zaphon, which stands near the mouth of the Orontes. Zion is neither in the north, nor does it occupy the physical space of Zaphon, but the claim here is theological, not geographical. Whatever may be claimed for Zaphon as the home of Baal really belongs to Yahweh, and if Mount Zion is the location of his city, then it is truly the city of the great king. Yahweh, not Baal, is God, and he is the great king, and it is Yahweh's presence that makes an otherwise unremarkable mountain so important. That he is the great king uses a different word for 'great' (*rab*) to verse 1, but the point is that Yahweh is the one who exceeds all other kings. All other claims to authority are placed under those of Yahweh, and he is the one who can be known as 'our God'. This God is present in the city and has made himself known as the refuge for his people, echoing the claim of Psalm 46:7, 11.

4–8. Having declared Yahweh's greatness, the second stanza provides reasons for it. The focus here is on reporting his protection of the city from attacking forces, confirming the claim of verse 3. The assembly of these kings echoes Psalm 2:1, though here they have crossed over to attack the city rather than resisting Yahweh's anointed. The act of seeing the city was sufficient to thwart their plans so that they were frozen with fear, fleeing in horror. Indeed, rather than being mighty warriors, they were seized with trembling like a woman's birth pains. Although the battle was centred on Zion, Yahweh also used the east wind (cf. Exod. 14:21, and note, a second cardinal point) to destroy the ships of Tarshish (typically regarded as the westernmost point to which one could sail; cf. Jon. 1, and so requiring the most powerful ships; cf. Ezek. 27:25). The ships must be on the sea, but as with the reference to Zaphon, geography matters less here than affirming Yahweh's power to thwart all invaders. Allusion to the exodus and defeat of Pharaoh is consistent with this, so although it is difficult to link the description here to any one battle, it is still grounded in history, even if that history is now generalized. The conclusion is then reached in verse 8 as the community pauses to reflect and acknowledge that the events heard of from the past continued to be true. Most importantly, the city is now said to belong to Yahweh of Hosts, echoing the use of that title in Psalm 46:7, 11. And this mighty God can again be described as 'our God', the one who establishes the city for ever.

9–11. God's commitment to the city leads to reflection on his character. As God is now directly addressed, the community notes that it has pondered God's kindness within his temple, the building that was also God's palace as king. Such reflection leads to awareness of the consistency of God's character (represented by his name), which again leads to praise, this time to the ends of the earth, while God's right hand is filled with justice. Justice is again typical of God's character and is a further reason for his praise. The 'right hand' is also a term for 'south'

(Israelites oriented themselves by the sunrise to the east) as well as a sign of favour. More importantly, that Yahweh's acts of justice could be considered is further reason for Mount Zion to rejoice and the inhabitants of the region to exult.

12–14. The final stanza addresses pilgrims who came to the city, directing them to walk around it and count its towers, to set their mind on the outer wall and pass through its citadels. All this involves making the geography real – rather than an abstract discussion of the city, its features can be imprinted on the memory of those who have come so they can repeat this process without actually being in the city. This imprinting on memory is important if later generations are to know the wonders of the city and therefore those who have counted the towers are also to recount to the next generation. The term translated 'next' can also mean 'west', thus completing the cardinal points within the psalm, while also introducing the motif of time that is then developed in the final verse, which insists that the God celebrated in this psalm is (again) 'our God' for ever. God's reign covers all directions, is greater than all earthly and spiritual powers and therefore can be understood as continuing with his people even unto death.

Explanation

Through praise that extends motifs from Psalms 46 to 47, Psalm 48 asks us to redraw our maps of the world. It puts Jerusalem at the centre, though in a way Israel knew was not geographically true (even if the *Mappa Mundi* attempts this). What mattered was that whether you go north, east, south or west, you end up praising God because he is at the centre of everything.

It also asks us to redraw our political maps, the ones portraying how the world works. That map is typically structured around the idea that power we can see is what matters. But praise focused on God's character sees we need a different way of mapping the world, one that recognizes the importance of his kindness and protection.

For Israel, there was another map, a map of the myths that the world around them told, where Baal and Mot (Death) were the powerful gods, one above the mountain, and another in the depths below. But that map was also flawed, because once you knew Yahweh there was no place for any other God. The modern world has its own myths that we use, seeking to displace God through the power of wealth and the like. The maps we need to redraw are perhaps not the same, but the issues stay the same. As we do so, we orient ourselves to Jesus as the one who dwells with us and is our security.

PSALM 49

Translation

The director's. Korahite. A melody.

1Hear this all peoples,
  give ear all inhabitants of the world,
2both low and high,
  rich and poor together.
3My mouth shall utter wisdom,
  and the musing of my mind understanding.
4I will incline my ear to a proverb,
  I will expound my riddle with a lyre.
5Why should I be afraid in troubling days
  when iniquity surrounds me at my heels,
6those who trust in their wealth,
  and boast in their great riches?

7Surely, no one can redeem another,
  nor give their own ransom to God.
8For the redemption price of their life is costly,
  it is never enough,
9that one may live for ever
  and not see the pit.
10For one can see that the wise die,
  the fool and the stupid alike perish,
  and leave their wealth to those after them.
11Their grave is their home for ever,
  their dwelling place from generation to generation –
  yet they called lands by their own names!
12A human shall not endure in honour,
  is destroyed just like the beasts.

13This is their way, their folly,
  and those after them who approve of their boasts. *Selah.*
14Like sheep, they are designated for Sheol,
  death shall shepherd them.
But the upright shall rule over them in the morning,
  their form shall be consumed in Sheol,
  without a dwelling place.
15Surely, God will redeem my life from the power of Sheol,
  yes, he will take me. *Selah.*

16Do not fear when someone gains riches,

when the glory of their house increases,
17for they take none of it in death,
their glory does not follow them down.
18For while they live, they reckon themselves blessed,
(and they praise you when you do well for yourself),
19they shall go to the generation of their ancestors,
those who shall never again see the light.
20A human with honour but without understanding
like the beasts is destroyed.

Notes on the text

The text of this psalm has numerous problems, and only key points are noted here.

4. *ḥokmôt* is understood here as an abstract pl., though Keefer's (2016) observations that phonic features are also at work is plausible.

8. *'āḥ* is often emended with some MSS to *'ak*. This is a simpler reading, but MT may have the object first (with Raabe 1990: 71; A. P. Ross 2013: 134). Although *'āḥ* is often 'brother', it can be understood as another human.

11. With Gk, Syr. and Tg, reading *qibrām*.

12. Gk suggests *yābîn* rather than *yālîn*, thus conforming this verse to verse 20. Though understandable, it is difficult to explain MT's text, which is retained.

14. With Q and most MSS, read *wĕṣûrām*.

19. *tābô'* is problematic. Often parsed as 2 m. sg., it could be 3 f. sg. if *nepeš* is taken as the subject. As the sg. in these verses is distributive, pl. forms are used in translation. This can also explain the shift to the pl. in *yir'û*.

Form and structure

The closing poem in the first Korahite collection, this psalm retains important links with the preceding poems while retaining its own distinctiveness. It is joined to Psalms 47–48 by the shared note in the title that it is 'a melody'. Beyond this, it offers the sort of instructive music noted in Psalm 47:7, while addressing the issue of death noted in Psalm 48:14. Further, the 'mind' (*lēb*) that had considered Jerusalem's ramparts to understand the enduring security Yahweh gave to Zion must now consider how the same theme can be applied to the experience of someone confronted by the problem of the prosperity of the wicked and the reality of death (Ps. 49:3; cf. Vesco 2006, 2: 443). Moreover, where Psalms 44–48 all focused on the community, Psalms 42–43 and 49 focus more on the individual, bringing the themes of the collection together, though its emphasis on the universality of death is also applicable to the communal emphases of Psalms 44–48 (cf. Cheung 2015: 79).

Understood in its own terms, Psalm 49 can be understood as a wisdom psalm (similarly, Longman 2014: 213), one that engages in a sustained reflection on the issue of death. Beyond the subject matter, it also makes use of a good deal of language associated with the wisdom traditions (esp. vv. 3–4). It makes clear that death is a universal experience, one that cannot be avoided by the accumulation of wealth, and neither can wealth make death more comfortable. The central contrast is established in verse 15, and though its meaning is much debated (see 'Comment') it is clear that this is intended to assist the poem's audience address the issue of death. All this can be closely linked with Ecclesiastes, though whether this means we have to treat them as contemporaries (Spangenberg 2007) is uncertain.

The psalm moves between points where the audience is addressed directly and observations on human life in the face of death. Taking references to fear (vv. 5, 16) as marking key units within the poem in conjunction with the near refrain (vv. 12, 20) results in a four-stanza analysis, though with the whole linked by numerous repetitions and verbal associations (Estes 2004), the presence of which probably renders unnecessary Witte's (2000: 544) more complex analysis:

1. The riddle of death propounded (1–6)
2. The certainty of death (7–12)
3. Hope for the upright (13–15)
4. The riddle resolved (16–20)

Comment

Title: For 'The director's', see on Psalm 4. For 'Korahite', see on Psalm 42. For 'a melody', see on Psalm 3.

1–6. The opening stanza is structured to climax with the question posed in verses 5–6, pointing to an issue but not disclosing its content until that point. Although the riddle outlined there has particular importance within Israel, the psalm's opening (vv. 1–2) makes clear that it is raising an issue of universal concern as all peoples, all the world's inhabitants, are summoned to hear. As a universal matter, all people, irrespective of their social status or wealth encounter this issue, even if the implications that will be drawn from it differ. No one can avoid it, even if its detail is not yet introduced. In verses 3–4 the poet addresses this audience, promising to speak what is wise and offer reflections that promote understanding, achieving this by listening to a proverb and expounding a riddle with a lyre (suggesting a possible link with the cult; see Dell 2004).

The psalmist knows that this is a complex issue which requires personal attention while reassuring the audience that the issue will be addressed with musical accompaniment, indicating that this poem will provide the sort of instructive music noted in Psalm 47:7. The poet uses a range of terms drawn from the wisdom traditions, indicating that the discussion to follow engages with a real issue of lived experience. To speak of the issue as a proverb does not necessarily mean a short statement (as often in Proverbs) since the term here can also refer to longer comparisons or discourses (cf. Job 27:1; 29:1) or even derisory comments (Ps. 44:15). That a complex issue is to be discussed is evident from the use of 'riddle' since this term can refer to that which is difficult to understand (Dan. 8:23; cf. Perdue 1974: 533–538). This pair of terms recurs in Psalm 78:2, another extended reflection on complex themes. The poet's musings are thus deeply reflective ones that can help all peoples. All of this is brought to its point of focus in verses 5–6. Rather than a direct statement, the poet raises the issue through a question of personal experience, though one that the audience should make their own. Troubling days are a potential source of fear, though the ones considered here are defined by verses 5b–6. That is, it is not difficulty itself but rather those difficulties caused for the righteous who are surrounded by iniquity, something here marked by those who trust in wealth and boast of their riches. Such people are iniquitous because they are no longer focused on Yahweh's reign, the central theme of Psalms 46–48, but rather on what they have accumulated for themselves. Troubling days are here understood as a life that trusts in human sufficiency, thus ignoring God's reign. These people are like the fool of Psalm 14:1 (cf. 53:1) who assert that God has no practical engagement with life, so it is troubling when such people come to dominate.

7–12. Troubling days may exist, but all people must face the challenge of death, and death becomes the central motif here. In particular, the focus is on the inability of wealth to change this reality. People may boast in their riches, but no matter the amount, they cannot prevent death, and no payment can be made to God to prevent it. Even if it were possible to calculate a redemption price, no amount of money would suffice to cover it and permit life to continue. Rather, the 'pit' (as the place of the dead; cf. Job 33:18; Pss 16:10; 30:9) is the destiny of all. Wealth cannot prevent this reality. Rather, as is then made clear (vv. 9–10), death is a universal reality (cf. Eccl. 9:1–6). The wise and the fool both die and leave their wealth to others (an issue that troubles Qoheleth, Eccl. 2:18–23), meaning that the value of riches is strictly time limited. The wealthy may own lands they can name after themselves, but their ultimate home is the grave, and it is that which endures. These observations prepare for the observation of verse 12, which forms a near-refrain with verse 20. Humans with wealth are impressive, but the honour of such life does not endure. Rather, echoing Ecclesiastes

9:4, the poet declares that these people are like the beasts in that all are destroyed.

13–15. An alternative perspective now begins to emerge. If concentration on wealth promotes wickedness, what alternative is there? These verses are central to the poem, pointing first to the folly of those who trust in riches and then to the hope of the upright. Verses 13–14a describe the folly of those who trust in wealth or are impressed by it. Their folly is that they ignore the reality of death, assuming their wealth is enough. But the universal reality is that they too are destined to die, with Sheol as their abode, and death (perhaps echoing Canaanite mythology, which considered Death as a deity) will shepherd them towards that destination. But a contrast is introduced in verse 14b with its declaration of a better outcome for the upright, here those who do not trust in wealth. 'Sheol' often seems to represent the place of the dead without distinction, but this is a point where Johnston's observation about it as predominantly the destination of the ungodly (2002: 81) has merit. Having introduced the better hope for the upright, the balance of verse 14 then considers the fate of those who have trusted in wealth. Even their form is consumed in Sheol, leaving them without the sort of dwelling place the wealthy imagine is theirs, having been effectively destroyed in Sheol. By contrast, the hint of something better for the upright becomes more vivid in verse 15 with its declaration that God will redeem the poet from Sheol, showing that God is greater than Death and indeed Death is merely doing God's bidding (cf. Kraus 1988: 483). This has been understood as a reference to eternal life or even resurrection (see J. Smith 2012: 127–129), though Goldingay (2007: 104–105) denies this possibility, arguing that the reference is to rescue from troubles in this world. There is more to be said for the latter view, especially if Sheol is here understood as an undesirable place for the dead. If so, redemption is from the undesired outcomes just described rather than death itself (similarly, Raabe 1990: 78), but the language is sufficiently open that the psalmist could be understood as somehow being in God's presence (cf. Gen. 5:24; 2 Kgs 2:9–12).

16–20. The possibility of being taken to God contrasts with the fate of the wealthy, who cannot take their wealth with them to death. The glory of the wealthy's house may increase, but it is of no value after death, and cannot be taken with them. This is why the poet returns to the theme of fear, advising the audience not to fear. The psalmist does not fear, and the wider audience can now reach the same conclusion. The wealthy can indeed reckon themselves blessed while alive, perhaps because they regard wealth as the sign of blessing. Accordingly, they also praise others who prosper materially. But they have still failed to consider death even though this reality is clearly evidenced in the experience of their forebears. Verse 20 can thus slightly modify verse 12, making clear that though humans may accumulate honour, their outcome is the same as that of the beasts. Indeed, the lack of understanding makes them like the beasts. They lack understanding because wealth accumulation has been their goal and they have not seen the need to look instead to God.

Explanation

Where earlier poems in the first Korahite collection provided Israel with encouragement in the face of threatening powers, Psalm 49 joins with Psalm 42 in addressing the concerns faced by individuals both ancient and modern. Craigie and Tate (2004: 361) helpfully note that this poem addresses two major fears: the threat faced by foes in times of trial, and that the wealthy have an advantage over others. Both these fears, though widely felt, are misplaced. Wealth and power do often threaten the weak, as the earlier psalms in this collection also demonstrate, but do not provide ultimate protection. Rather, hope is provided by trusting God, who, Psalms 42–43 have also shown, can be accessed even when he previously seemed remote. Death remains an important reality, but those who trust in God can hope for a better death than those who trust in wealth instead. By addressing this to all peoples, Psalm 49 joins with the preceding psalms in declaring that the hope provided by Israel's God is a hope for all people (cf. McCann 1996: 876), all of whom may therefore know that not even death can separate us from the love of God (Rom. 8:38–39). Jesus declares that he has given his life as a ransom for many (Mark 10:45), acting as the ransom anticipated here, though he was also aware of the folly of wealth (Luke 12:16–21).

PSALM 50

Translation

A melody. Asaphic.

[1]God, God, Yahweh, has spoken and summoned the earth,
  from the rising of the sun to its setting.
[2]From Zion the perfection of beauty,
  God shines forth.
[3]Our God comes and will not be silent;
  fire consumes before him
  and a raging tempest surrounds him.
[4]He calls to the heavens above,
  and to the earth to judge his people.

5‘Gather to me my loyal ones,
those who made a covenant with me by sacrifice.’
6The heavens shall declare his righteousness
because God himself is judge. *Selah.*

7‘Hear, my people, and I will speak,
and I will testify against you O Israel:
I am God, your God.
8I do not rebuke you for your sacrifices,
and your burnt offerings are continually before me.
9I do not need a bull from your house,
goats from your folds.
10For every creature of the forest is mine,
the cattle on a thousand hills.
11I know every bird of the hills,
the insects of the fields are with me.
12If I was hungry I would not tell you,
because the world and its fullness is mine.
13Do I eat the flesh of bulls,
or drink the blood of goats?
14Make a sacrifice of thanksgiving to God,
fulfil your vows to the Most High,
15and call on me in the day of distress,
I will deliver you and you will glorify me.’

16But to the wicked God says,
‘What right do you have to recite my statutes,
or take up my covenant on your lips?
17You hate discipline,
and have cast my words behind you.
18If you see a thief you run with him,
and your portion is with those committing adultery.
19You let loose your mouth with evil,
and your tongue frames deceit.
20You sit, you speak against your compatriot,
you allege fault against your mother’s son.
21These things you have done and I was silent,
you imagined that I was like you,
I rebuke you and lay out the case before you.

22Consider this, those who forget God,
lest I tear apart and there be none to deliver.
23The one who makes a sacrifice of thanksgiving honours me,
who sets out the way,
I will show that one the salvation of God.’

Notes on the text

1. *'ēl 'ĕlōhîm* could represent two absolute forms of 'God' or be read as a superlative 'The God of Gods'.

11. *zîz* is uncertain, but appears to refer to moving things, and in context is understood as 'insects'. See Whitekettle 2005 for a more precise taxonomy.

18. Reading *wattārāṣ* with Gk.

Form and structure

Psalm 50 introduces Asaph, a new figure to the titles. Psalm 50 stands apart from the rest of the Asaphic psalms, all of which are found in Book 3 (Pss 73–83). Despite the move into Book 3 for the other Asaphic psalms, all are still part of the so-called Elohistic Psalter (see 'Form and structure' on Ps. 42), though Psalm 50 is also distinctive in not having the significant focus on Israel's past stressed by K. N. Jacobson (2017). Asaph is most likely to be identified with the music leader mentioned in 1 Chronicles 6:24 who was also involved with bringing the Ark to the temple (2 Chr. 5:12). Members of a guild associated with Asaph were also involved in the dedication of the second temple (Ezra 3:10), so it is most likely that the historical Asaph initiated a process of composition and collection of psalms that continued over several centuries (against Goulder 1996: 28). Indeed, it seems that the exile was the trigger for the composition of several of the Asaphic psalms (Firth 2008: 25), indicating that Asaph himself remains the figurehead for this collection rather than being their author.

The introduction of a new name in the title means that there is a clear break from the Korahite psalms that have featured so far in Book 2, with Psalm 50 then marked off from the Davidic psalms that follow. Although it may be thought that this leads to its being interpreted with little reference to the surrounding poems, it is better to think of its serving as a bridge between the two main collections in Book 2. In part, it offers a contrast to Psalm 49's address to all peoples (Ps. 49:1) by recounting an address to Israel (Ps. 50:7), though both are united in rejecting hypocrisy (49:13; 50:16). The beauty of Zion also joins this poem with Psalm 48 (Pss 48:2; 50:2). But as a bridge, its downplaying of sacrifice also prepares for Psalm 51 (Pss 50:7–15; 51:15–17).

Psalm 50 is also distinctive in terms of genre. With C. B. Jones (2009: 117), it is perhaps best to see it as 'a prophetic psalm that does include an oracle from God to the people'. As such, it sits outside the standard form-critical classifications, though as a prophetic text it is also directly didactic, albeit in a very different mode from Psalm 49. One important motif found here is a group of allusions to the Decalogue (v. 18). The combination of prophetic speech and allusions to the Decalogue recur in Psalm 81, distinctive features of the Asaphic poems. Beyond the Decalogue, Psalm 50 alludes to numerous OT texts (cf. Kilchör and Weber 2014), only some of which can be noted here.

The structure of the psalm is relatively straightforward, though with important repetitions across the stanzas (Allen 1984: 20–21 finds a chiasm, but this is probably more than can be sustained) and can be outlined in four stanzas:

1. Introductory summons (1–6)
2. Testimony about sacrifice (7–15)
3. Words to the wicked (16–21)
4. Epilogue (22–23)

Comment

Title: For 'A melody', see on Psalm 3. For 'Asaphic', see above, 'Form and structure'.

1–6. The psalm opens with a sonorous declaration of the one who speaks, moving from the most generic form of 'God' (*'ēl*) to the more commonly used form in Israel (*'ĕlōhîm*) and finally to the covenant name 'Yahweh' (cf. Josh. 22:22). Although much of the psalm will be directed to Israel, the opening is addressed to all the earth, from east to west (cf. Ps. 113:3; Mal. 1:11; though Craigie and Tate [2004: 365] suggest this also refers to a whole day). God's message is for the earth, but it is grounded in Zion, the beauty of which evokes Psalm 48:2. The verb 'shine forth' (*yp'*) plays with the sound of the word for 'beauty' (*yŏpî*), bringing Zion and God together. It is also typical of theophany (Deut. 33:2), and Psalm 80:1 will invite God to shine forth again. God's arrival here demonstrates his power. That he is not silent is evidenced by the signs of his presence, consuming fire (cf. Ps. 97:3) and raging tempest, both full of sound that evokes Sinai (Exod. 19). But like the heavens in Psalm 19:1–6, this is not intelligible speech. Therefore, the poet points to God's speech in verse 4, addressing the heavens above and the earth (hence, all visible creation) with the purpose of judging his people. That is, creation is to witness what Yahweh has to say about his people because God has come in power, and his power is focused on calling his people to account. These people are then formally summoned as God speaks in verse 5. The verb 'gather' (*'ispû*) is from the same root as 'Asaph', perhaps an internal allusion to the collection. More importantly, this speech indicates those who are to be gathered as those who are loyal to God, here defined by having made (lit. 'cut'; cf. Gen. 15:7–21) a covenant by sacrifice. The covenant is not named, but the allusion to Deuteronomy 33:2 would suggest that Sinai is in mind. Although the sacrifice here could refer to a foundational act (e.g. Exod. 24:3–8), it is probably better to think of sacrifice here standing in a tradition of practice. Those who are loyal to Yahweh continue to show their commitment to the covenant through sacrifice. The status of the loyal ones is left aside for a moment, so verse 6 can affirm that the heavens not only witness to God's calling of his people to account, but also declare his righteousness, though we may also think of this in terms of his justice since the two are closely related (note the complaint in Isa. 1:21). This characteristic is particularly important given that he has come as judge, preparing for the legal language that follows.

7–15. This stanza consists of an extended prophetic speech (cf. Hilber 2005: 162–166), in this case recognizable in that it reports speech from God, presumably delivered by a temple functionary (cf. A. R. Johnson 1979: 22–30; Tournay 1991: 144). The first stanza has prepared for the language of the law court, and legal language now dominates as God testifies to them about sacrifice. In speaking, God testifies against Israel, indicating that they have a flawed view of sacrifice. Nevertheless, Israel is spoken of as 'my people', while God is 'your God', language typical of a covenant relationship. Within that covenant, Israel was expected to serve God, and sacrifice was central to this. But Israel's understanding of sacrifice needs to be challenged. God's testimony initially notes an area where he does not rebuke Israel, apparently their basic practice in which sacrifices and burnt offerings (cf. Lev. 1 – 3) are continually before him. As such, there is no need for God to take livestock from their home or fold, not least because all animals are God's anyway. This includes both wild and domesticated animals, and as such God can claim the cattle on a thousand hills as well as every bird and insect. As such, God has no need to request sacrifices as if they fed him (unlike other ANE deities) since everything is his, the world and its fullness (cf. Ps. 24:1). He is, in effect, being treated like an idol rather than the creator of all (cf. Bos 1982: 73). The question posed in verse 13 brings the testimony to its point of focus. Although some believed that their sacrifices fed the gods, God makes clear that animal sacrifices are not a food source for him. God does not require animal sacrifices for nutrition. Rather, sacrifice was meant to sustain a covenant relationship. The most appropriate means for this is then outlined in verse 14, which directs Israel to make a thank offering (Lev. 7:11–18) and fulfil their vows to the Most High. Such offerings are about maintaining a relationship with God, whereas the other sacrifices may be thought of as a means of gaining favour with God. The priority of relationship over sacrifice finds its goal in verse 15, which directs Israel to call on God in the time of distress with the assurance that he will deliver them and that they will glorify him. The sacrifice that matters is one that comes out of a committed relationship, and in this is the promise of God's deliverance and the opportunity for further worship where God is given the honour appropriate to him.

16–21. A new introduction in verse 16 indicates a shift away from those whose understanding of sacrifice was flawed but still wished to keep covenant, as God now speaks to the wicked. The defining characteristics that make this audience 'the wicked' are defined by their breaches of covenant, especially the Decalogue (cf. Wenham 2005: 185–186). These breaches mean that although they recite God's statutes or claim to be in covenant, their actions show that this is untrue. The error of their actions is summarized in verse 17, which reports that they hate Yahweh's discipline and cast his words behind them. 'Discipline' (*mûsār*) occurs nowhere else in Psalms, being much more frequent in Proverbs (e.g. Prov. 1:3, where it helps set the theme for the book; Seidl [2012: 82] regards Prov. 12:1 as a key reference), where it often refers to discipline intended to instruct. God has thus provided a means for the wicked to live in covenant and indeed to restore them, but they have instead chosen their own path. Evidence for this is provided in verses 18–20. Starting with association with a thief or adulterers shows that they live outside the basic elements of the Decalogue (Exod. 20:14–15). The remaining charges are concerned with speech that encourages evil (contrast. Ps. 15:2), or speaks falsely against kin, an extension of the commandment against false witness (Exod. 20:16). God's previous silence (cf. v. 3) meant the wicked had erroneously believed he would accept them. But now the legal case announced in the first stanza has been presented and the wicked rebuked.

22–23. Although the wicked have been particularly rebuked, the wider community has not escaped God's scrutiny. The closing stanza is thus addressed to them all, though with a particular focus on the wicked. They need to learn from the rebuke that has just been delivered rather than rejecting discipline as has happened to date. God's previous silence was neither approval nor evidence that he would not act (cf. Ps. 10:4, 11) but rather evidence of forbearance. But this will not continue indefinitely. As such, those who have lived as if God will not be involved with the world (functionally forgetting; cf. Ps. 14:1 and preparing for 53:1) need to understand that he will act against the wicked; and if God acts, there is none who can deliver. Verse 23 then makes clear what is required from all – worship that seeks to honour God through thanksgiving rather than seeing animal sacrifices as a means to obtain rewards from God, and a life shaped by the requirements of covenant. Such a person will be shown God's salvation, a life that enjoys the covenant with him.

Explanation

What does it mean to worship God? At heart, that is the concern of this Psalm. Shaped as a prophetic address from God, it makes clear that worship is grounded in a covenant relationship with God. All else flows from this. But Israel's worship was shaped by the patterns and practices of its culture, something that marks all worship. In their case, animal sacrifice was a widespread practice, but one that Israel interpreted differently. Yet precisely because this was a common cultural feature, it was easy for them to equate their practices with those of the nations around them, imagining that animal sacrifice fed God and was thus how he was satisfied with them, and so would bless them. But this misrepresents the place of sacrifice. It was meant to enable Israel to live in thankful fellowship with God. Even worse, some imagined that sacrifice on its own meant it was possible to live contrary to covenant but have that covered by sacrifice. The prophetic speech here is clear that this is a fundamentally flawed view. God wanted a life shaped by commitment to covenant because only then did sacrifice make sense (cf. Weiser 1962: 393). God here rebukes those who live such a life, warning that should he act against them none will deliver. What God desires is thanksgiving that emerges from a life organized by commitment to covenant. It is this that leads the book of Hebrews to encourage Christians to offer a continual thanksgiving of praise from a life committed to God (Heb. 13:15–16). Such concerns likewise shape Paul's discussion of the Lord's Supper (1 Cor. 11:17–34), where he rebukes those whose worship demeans the poor among the community, because such an approach has failed to live out the hope of the new covenant, where God's requirements are written on the heart (Jer. 31:31–34).

PSALM 51

Translation

The director's. A melody. Davidic. When Nathan the prophet came to him after he had gone in to Bathsheba.

1Be gracious to me O God according to your kindness,
  according to your abundant mercies,
  blot out my transgressions.
2Wash me thoroughly from my iniquity
  and cleanse me from my sin.
3For I know my transgressions
  and my sin is continually before me.
4Against you, and you alone, have I sinned
  and done evil in your eyes.
So that you are right when you speak,
  blameless when you judge.
5Behold, in iniquity was I brought forth,
  and in sin my mother conceived me.
6Behold, you delight in truth within
  and teach me wisdom in the secret parts.

[7]Purify me with hyssop so I shall be clean,
  wash me and I shall be whiter than snow.
[8]Make me hear joy and gladness,
  let the bones you crushed rejoice.
[9]Hide your face from sins,
  and blot out all my iniquities.
[10]Create a clean heart in me O God,
  and renew a steadfast spirit within me.
[11]Do not cast me away from your presence,
  and do not take your holy spirit from me.
[12]Restore to me the joy of your deliverance,
  and let a willing spirit support me.

[13]I will teach transgressors your ways,
  and sinners will return to you.
[14]Deliver me from bloodshed O God,
  O God of my deliverance,
  my tongue shall cry aloud of your righteousness.
[15]Lord, open my lips,
  and my mouth will declare your praise!
[16]For you do not delight in sacrifice, else I would give it,
  nor are you pleased with burnt offerings.
[17]The sacrifices of God are a broken spirit,
  a broken and contrite heart, O God, you will not despise.

[18]By your favour do good to Zion,
  build up the walls of Jerusalem.
[19]Then you will delight in right sacrifices,
  burnt offerings and whole offerings,
  then they will offer up young bulls on your altar.

Notes on the text

11. Reading the construct *rûaḥ qādōšĕkā* as attributive (*WHS* §41). For the options, see Marlowe 1998: 30–34.

12. *tismĕkēnî* could be parsed as 3 f. sg. and refer to the spirit, or 2 m. sg. and be addressed to God.

Form and structure

This is one of the Psalter's best-known poems and a powerful example of confession. It is the fullest of the seven 'penitential psalms' (see on Ps. 6), and the only one for which penitence is the central issue.

Usually classified as a complaint, it is distinct in that the psalmist is also the source of the trouble from which deliverance is needed, whereas the complaints more commonly point to enemies as the source of affliction. It is also the first 'Davidic' psalm of Book 2, introducing a run that continues unbroken until Psalm 65, and then resumes for Psalms 68–70. These psalms are notable for the connections made by many of their titles to events in the books of Samuel (Pss 51–54, 56–57, 59–60, 63), while various technical terms (such as 'Miktam'; Pss 56–60) also point to subunits within this collection. As Goulder (1990: 21) notes, there are also recurring linguistic connections across this collection. Reference to events in Samuel have occurred previously (Pss 3, 7, 18, 34), recurring in Psalm 142. But gathering so many psalms with this feature encourages us to read these psalms against specific events in David's life. These events are not presented in their chronological sequence from Samuel, meaning that this collection begins with a focus on David as a penitent sinner. As well as establishing patterns for the psalms that follow, the poem also exemplifies Psalm 50's call for thanksgiving rather than sacrifice (Hossfeld and Zenger 2006: 24; Sutton 2021b: 341–343).

Should we therefore read these psalms as having been written by David at the time mentioned? This is possible, but the label 'Davidic' is sufficiently flexible in meaning that we might simply be asked to read Psalm 51 against the background of David's encounter with Nathan after his sexual encounter with Bathsheba and murder of Uriah (among other deaths) in 2 Samuel 11 – 12. This context sets the prayer against the darkest of backgrounds while pointing to the possibility of forgiveness for all (cf. V. L. Johnson 2009: 39). Such forgiveness is an act of grace.

The psalm has been variously analysed but is probably best read as consisting of four stanzas (on the unity of the poem, see Ross 2019), all joined by key terms repeated across it. The opening stanza containing two strophes:

1. Opening (1–6)
   a. Invocation (1–2)
   b. Confession (3–6)
2. Request for forgiveness (7–12)
3. Vow of praise (13–17)
4. National prayer (18–19)

Comment

Title: For 'The director's', see on Psalm 4. For 'a melody', see on Psalm 3. For 'Davidic', see on Psalm 3. For the historical reference, see above, 'Form and structure'. 'Go into' is sometimes a euphemism for sexual intercourse and is used in that sense to describe David's relationship with Bathsheba.

1–2. The poem opens with a series of imperatives, each of which asks for God's forgiveness. The initial appeal is for God to act with grace towards the poet, an expression which makes clear that the request is not based on personal merit. Rather, it is God's 'kindness' (*ḥesed*; see on Ps. 5:8) and abundant mercy (probably alluding to Exod. 34:6–8; cf. Goldingay 2007: 126) that provides hope. Different verbs for forgiveness are used (blot out, wash, cleanse) all of which are concerned with sin's removal, though each is rooted in grace. Along with this, the psalm uses different words for sin (transgression, iniquity, sin), reflecting the full range of Israel's vocabulary for it (cf. Ps. 32:1–2, 5). Although distinctions between them can be developed (Dalglish 1962: 91–93), the point here is that however sin is understood, forgiveness needs to come from God's grace.

3–6. The psalmist is continually aware of his sin, making the need for forgiveness acute. Within the OT it is normal to regard sin as ultimately against God (see Tate 1990: 17), and this frames the shape of the confession as being against God alone (modern readers, aware of the title, may feel that Uriah the Hittite – at least – has a claim to having been sinned against but that reflects a different cultural perspective). The focus on sin as being against God sets up the contrast developed in verse 4b, as the poet points out that God is blameless in his judgement, something that cannot be said of the psalmist. This leads to two declarations ('behold') in verses 5–6 that establish a further contrast between God and the psalmist. Although verse 5 has often been read as teaching original sin as something passed on through childbirth, deClaissé-Walford (2014: 456) is surely right to insist that this is a misinterpretation. The point is, rather, to highlight sin's all-pervasive effects. Human life is marked by sin, and this is unlike God's delight in truth within us, something he enables by teaching us wisdom even in those parts of our bodies normally invisible. Sin is a destructive power that shapes all human life. But God not only delights in something better; he provides a means for us to understand it.

7–12. The opening appeal makes clear that forgiveness is the poet's primary need, and it is forgiveness that is central to this stanza. Where imperatives were used in the opening, we now find jussives (though Kidner [1975, 1: 191] reads them as futures), expressing a wish for what God should do. In a play on words, the first verb is the pi. of the root *ḥṭ'*. This root as a noun means 'sin' and in qal means 'to sin', but in pi. means 'to remove sin' (Dahood [1968: 5] suggests 'de-sin'). The appeal thus asks that God address the psalmist's enduring experience of sin. Mention of hyssop suggests a cultic background (Exod. 12:22; Lev. 14:4, 52; Num. 19:6, 18) but here it is essentially a metaphor that prepares for sin to be replaced by purity, as clean as fresh snow (against

Goulder [1990: 57], who detects a purgatory rite). 'When a man [*sic*], however sinful, is cleansed by God, he is clean indeed' (A. A. Anderson 1972, 1: 397). This cleansing is expressed in terms of the whole person, starting with more outward elements, but moving to the inner person, as even the bones God has metaphorically broken also rejoice in this restoration. The request takes a slightly different tack in verse 9, as God is asked to overlook the sin, removing it from his presence and blotting it out, presumably from a book. However, the net effect is much the same. As well as forgiveness, the psalmist desires renewal. The use of 'create' is bold, looking for God to do something fresh, though its parallel with renewal (v. 10b) makes clear that God is working with the existing person. Asking for a renewed heart is not seeking emotional restoration but rather for a mind and will focused on doing God's will. 'Heart' and 'spirit' here refer to the whole of human volition, with both needing to be aligned to God's purposes, so that someone is not removed from God's presence. Verse 11 speaks instead of God's Spirit, which here is understood as a sign of his enduring presence with the poet. It is doubtful that the psalmist understands 'Holy Spirit' in the same terms as the NT (unless understood as referring to the poet's spirit; cf. Estes 2011: 132), but this statement is not inconsistent with it (cf. Maré 2008). Rather, the psalmist knows that God's presence is necessary if one is to live in a way that pleases God, so that human and divine spirit come together.

13–17. The third stanza vows to praise God, most notably by making his ways known to others. Something like this vow lies behind Psalm 32:6–9, where sinners are instructed in Yahweh's ways by the forgiven poet. Those to be instructed (so they may return to God) are here called both 'transgressors' and 'sinners', drawing on two of the three terms for sin used to describe the psalmist (vv. 1–2). In this situation, the psalmist still wishes to be delivered from bloodshed. Such deliverance will permit the psalmist's tongue to cry aloud of God's righteousness. Reference to bloodshed would be consistent with David's actions in 2 Samuel 11, where he was responsible for numerous deaths, though here the reference could also be to future moments of violence. In either case, it is Yahweh's righteousness that is to be announced. Mention of the tongue is then developed in verse 15, where God is asked to enable the psalmist's lips to be opened with the vow that 'my mouth will declare your praise'. Although praise is often offered to God, in this case the praise is declared to the sinners who need to know God's ways, a mechanism by which they may return to God. It is the praise of God to others, and not sacrifice, that will restore the psalmist's relationship with God. Israel's sacrificial system did not provide for deliberate acts of sin, which is why this psalm is a prayer for grace. But it does recognize that there needs to be genuine contrition for the sin, which is why the acceptable sacrifices here are described as a broken spirit and a broken and contrite heart.

Both the spirit and the heart here point to human volition, something that must be submitted to God. With such submission, sacrifice may again be effective.

18–19. The prayer's primary focus to this point has been the psalmist, though the third stanza has begun to look outwards. That outwards move continues in this final stanza (making it more than an 'Appendix'; contra Terrien 2003, 2: 401), which asks that God act for Jerusalem's well-being, building up its walls. The city represents the centre of national life, and the assumption at this point is that its walls are insufficient, needing to be built. Superficially, this contrasts with the language of Psalm 48 and its confidence in the security God provides; but since it is God who must act with favour to build the walls, this request is better understood as asking him to provide a particular mode of security. The restoration of Jerusalem's walls also enables right sacrifices to be offered since the altar is there. The offering of those sacrifices, which must be understood as 'right' both in intent and form, becomes a further witness to God's grace, something expanded through the psalm from the poet to the community and then Jerusalem as a whole.

Explanation

This is a powerful psalm of confession. It reminds us that we are all a part of the pattern of sin, and we all need God's forgiveness – something graphically demonstrated as we move from sin and that which does not give God pleasure to that which does. The possibility of this depends on God's grace. But the psalmist's vow also recognizes that forgiveness is not the end of the matter. Rather, forgiveness not only leads to the restoration of the one forgiven; it also leads to the proclamation and service of the God who in his grace forgives. Who may claim such forgiveness? By situating this psalm so it is read in the light of David's sin and subsequent encounter with Nathan (2 Sam. 11 – 12), it makes clear that even the most heinous sins can be forgiven. With Psalm 50, it knows this cannot be achieved simply through sacrifice alone. Although sacrifice was a good gift, it was not a mechanism for manipulating God. Rather, what was needed was grace, and we can be thankful that God gives it lavishly (Eph. 1:7–8).

PSALM 52

Translation

The director's. A Maskil. Davidic. When Doeg the Edomite came and reported to Saul and told him, 'David came to the house of Ahimelech.'

[1]Why do you boast about evil, O mighty one?
God's kindness endures!
[2]Your tongue plans destruction,
like a sharpened knife working treachery.
[3]You love evil more than good,
falsehood more than speaking what is right. *Selah.*
[4]You love all words that devour,
O treacherous tongue.
[5]Yet God will pull you down for ever,
he will knock you down and tear you away from your tent,
and root you out from the land of the living. *Selah.*

[6]The righteous will see and fear,
and shall mock that one,
[7]'Look, the strong one who did not make God his stronghold
but trusted in the abundance of his wealth,
and sought refuge in his own desire.'

[8]But I am like a luxuriant olive tree in the house of God,
I trust in God's kindness for ever and ever.
[9]I will give you thanks for ever because you have acted,
and I will hope in your name for it is good,
in the presence of your saints.

Notes on the text

1. The range of textual options here shows that the difficulty is longstanding. MT is retained here, understood as an exclamation that contrasts with the acts of the mighty one (similarly, Hossfeld and Zenger 2006: 26).

7. *DCH* suggests four possible roots for *hawwâ*, two of which are plausible: either 'desire' or 'destruction'. Although many EVV opt for 'destruction' (e.g. ESV), it is unlikely that this person seeks refuge there. 'Desire' is thus more likely, but the psalm plays with the two possible senses so that the 'desire' is 'destruction'.

Form and structure

Where most complaint psalms are addressed to God, this one moves between a direct address to an enemy and to a congregation. God is not addressed until the final verse. This element, along with motifs such as the luxuriant tree (v. 8), which at least in part echoes the presentation of the righteous in Psalm 1, may suggest that there is also a background in the wisdom literature (cf. Botha 2013a). That does not ignore the clear element of complaint that runs through the opening verses, which informs the psalm's instruction, but rather indicates that the psalm draws on multiple traditions. Comparison with Psalm 1 is also instructive in showing that this psalm also draws on the two-ways motif, contrasting the righteous and the wicked while demonstrating the better life of the righteous. As with Psalm 1, the better alternative is presented but it is left for readers to determine their response.

Along with Psalm 51, this psalm's title associates it with an event in David's life. Where Psalm 51 is associated with David's time as king, this psalm initiates a time where the historical references that occur (Pss 54, 56, 59) point to David's time on the run from Saul that ends only in Psalm 60. This enables us to move from David in his strength, but needing to repent, to David in a position of weakness and needing to trust God. Psalm 52's presentation of this very theme makes it an appropriate beginning of this subunit. Psalms 52–59 themselves can be divided into two main units: Psalms 52–55, each of which is a 'Maskil' and Psalms 56–59, each of which is a 'Miktam'. Psalm 60, the last 'Miktam' is a bridge into the next unit, marked by a return to David as king. As Botha (2018b: 114–117) has demonstrated, Psalms 52–55 are also joined by a significant range of key words. Psalm 52 is also presented as an immediate example of the instructing of transgressors promised in Psalm 51:13 (deClaissé-Walford et al. 2014: 459).

Although multiple structuring elements can be observed, it is simplest to analyse the poem in three stanzas, marked by the shift in the pronouns from second person to third and finally first:

1. Warning to the mighty one (1–5)
2. Actions of the righteous (6–7)
3. Exemplary individual (8–9)

Comment

Title: For 'The director's', see on Psalm 4. For 'Maskil', see on Psalm 32. For 'Davidic', see on Psalm 3. Reference to Doeg the Edomite brings together the time when he had seen David at the sanctuary in 1 Samuel 21: 1–10 and later reported this in a way that maximized any potential wrongdoing by Ahimelech in 1 Samuel 22:6–10, suggesting he had enquired of Yahweh for him, something not reported in the earlier passage. We are to read the psalm against that background, making Goulder's attempt to read it against Absalom's rebellion (1990: 74–75) unnecessary.

1–5. This stanza is spoken to the mighty one. The opening verse establishes an immediate contrast between the misplaced boasting of the mighty one in evil, understood against the background of Doeg as one who has acted out of self-interest. Such an approach is flawed because God's kindness is what endures. Boasting in evil is misplaced because it is focused on oneself and not on God. It is speech that especially defines the mighty one's evil. Although Doeg would go on to murder almost all the priests at Nob (1 Sam. 21:18–19), the psalm does not focus on the actions so much as the speech. The destruction was planned through speech, here likened to a sharpened knife engaging in treachery, and this finds an echo in the events at Nob. Speech as the primary problem is also evident in verses 3–4, verses joined by the opening 'You love'. The opening of verse 3 may be thought to generalize the evil of the mighty one, but is immediately clarified as speaking falsehood rather than what is right. This falsehood can then be understood as speech that devours others, demonstrating the treachery of the mighty one's tongue. Yet the mighty one will not endure, and the tricolon at verse 5 declares that God will act. Rather than enduring success, the mighty one will be pulled down for ever, unable to continue speaking treacherously. Indeed, a series of verbs point to the mighty one's destruction, culminating in death. Boasting in evil is misplaced because God's enduring kindness will not allow such boasting to continue indefinitely.

6–7. The second stanza addresses an audience hearing the psalm, though speech remains a central focus. The righteous, those who have committed themselves to God's kindness, will see the end of the mighty one and thus fear. The verbs 'see' (*wĕyir'û*) and 'fear' (*wĕyîrā'û*) are similar in sound, while 'righteous' (*ṣadîqîm*) and 'mock' (*yiśḥāqû*) play with sibilants, so that verse 6 is full of wordplays save for the point that refers to the mighty one, effectively isolating this figure (cf. Potgieter 2013: 3). This figure is linguistically isolated, and this isolation is driven home in the mocking speech of the righteous, who regard this one's end as pointing to the outcome of those who have trusted in the abundance of their wealth rather than making God their stronghold. Instead, their refuge (a word related to 'stronghold') is their own desires, and the outcome of those desires is destruction (cf. 'Notes on the text').

8–9. The final stanza is spoken as a form of testimony. The mighty one will be destroyed, but the poet is instead like a luxuriant olive tree in God's house. The mighty one was uprooted from the land of the living, but a luxuriant tree has strong roots, and those roots are the psalmist's trust in God's kindness. This kindness was ignored by the mighty one who will be destroyed, but the psalmist's testimony is that trusting in God's kindness rather than wealth is the way to a flourishing life. Testimony turns to prayer in the final verse as the poet promises enduring thanksgiving because of what God has done. It is this speech, shared in the presence of God's saints, that is worth uttering. That God has acted does not mean the mighty one has yet been brought down, but the poet is certain that this will happen, and so continues to hope in God's good name, a pointer to the reliability of his character.

Explanation

The power of malign speech is well known in the psalms and continues into the NT – James 3:1–12 vividly illustrates the sorts of issues shown here. But when malign speech is aligned with social power (whether through wealth or prestige), its effects can be magnified, something easily recognized among 'influencers' on various social-media platforms. Such speech can easily be boastful and when it focuses on self-achievement can also boast in evil. The fundamental problem with such speech is that it ignores God; but although it seems to offer success, it will not finally succeed. God may be ignored by the powerful, but he does not ignore them, and they will finally be brought down, rather like the rich fool in Jesus' parable (Luke 12:13–21). Rather than being drawn in by deceptive words, appropriate speech gives thanks to God and continues to hope in him because this is the life that ultimately leads to flourishing. Boastfulness, whether personified in someone like Doeg, who was more concerned about self-advancement irrespective of what that involved, or numerous others through history, is not the way to flourish. This psalm thus lays the choice before readers to decide the life they will live, but (like Ps. 1) it clearly believes there is only one real choice.

PSALM 53

Translation

The director's. According to Mahalath. A Maskil. Davidic.

1The fool has said in his heart, 'There is no God.'
  they are corrupt, they do abominable evil,
  there is no one doing good.
2God looks down from the heavens upon humankind
  to see if there is anyone prudent,
  who seeks God.
3All of them are disloyal,
  together they have become corrupt.
There is no one doing good,
  there is not even one.

4Do not those practising evil know,
  those eating my people as they eat bread?

They do not call on God!
[5]There they will tremble with dread,
where there was no dread
because God has scattered the bones of those who encamp against you,
you have shamed them because God has rejected them.

[6]O that salvation for Israel
would come from Zion!
When God restores the fortunes of his people,
Jacob will exult, Israel rejoice.

Notes on the text

5. Understanding the closing suffix as doing double duty for the whole line.

6. Desiderative *mî*; see *WHS* §122.

Form and structure

For the most part, Psalm 53 is the same poem as Psalm 14 (see 'Form and structure' there). There are some minor variants (see Botha 2013b: 585–586), but the most important changes are that where Psalm 14 uses the name 'Yahweh', Psalm 53 uses 'God' throughout. The abominable acts of verse 1 are now specified as 'evil', a different verb is used in verse 3a while verse 5b is also distinctive and the title is expanded. It is theoretically possible to reconstruct the original poem by comparing these elements, but it is better to recognize that one poem could be adapted to different contexts, and that just as Psalm 14 is integrated into Psalms 9–14, so also Psalm 53 is integrated into Psalms 52–55, each of which is a 'Maskil'. Here, the 'mighty one' of Psalm 52 whose speech had done such harm can be characterized as a fool. But where the speech of that psalm was overt, here it is expressed in the heart, thought rather than said outright. The statement 'There is no God' now summarizes the attitude of the mighty one, though this can be classified as folly, an explicit wisdom motif that reflects the wisdom elements also notable in Psalm 52. It is also notable that this poem is not related to a specific event in David's life, whereas Psalm 54 is. Although we cannot be certain, it is possible that this indicates we are to read this poem against the same background as Psalm 52, while Psalm 55 (also not tied to a specific event) is joined with Psalm 54. This divides Psalms 52–55 into two parts; Psalms 52–53, which draw on wisdom motifs via prophetic speech forms, and Psalms 54 – 55.

Although its various elements merge, the poem can be analysed in three stanzas:

1. The problem of practical atheism (1–3)
2. Hints of Yahweh's involvement (4–5)
3. Hope for salvation (6)

Comment

Title: For 'The director's', see on Psalm 4. For 'Maskil', see on Psalm 32. 'According to Mahalath' is uncertain, but as part of the director's collection could be a musical notation. It recurs in Psalm 88's title. For 'Davidic', see on Psalm 3.

1–3. Although the statement 'there is no God' could be construed as philosophical atheism, when read against the background of Psalm 52 it is better understood as practical atheism. That is, the fool does not deny God's existence, but thinks that God does not act and so can be ignored by the powerful. The fool who is cited here is not a lone figure, but rather recognizable as any who is corrupt, someone who practises evil. The evil mentioned here is particularly notable among traders, who engage in various forms of sharp practice (cf. Lev. 19:35; Ezek. 28:18) as well as in judicial abuse (Lev. 19:15). It is enacted by the powerful against the weak and so is inconsistent with Yahweh's character (Deut. 32:4). The Psalms consistently point to God's goodness, so repeated affirmation that no one does good shows the extent to which practical atheism has developed. The fool may think there is no God, but the reality is that God does look down from heaven, examining humankind, to identify the 'prudent' (*maśkîl*), those who seek God. The poem thus embraces the two-ways pattern also hinted at in Psalm 52, defining them as the ways of folly and prudence. Yet, thought of in totality, all fools have demonstrated their disloyalty and corruption by denying that God can be significant in their lives, with not even one of them doing good. Although the language of verse 3 may be taken as universal (cf. Rom. 3:10–12), it is really a hyperbolic description of the fool understood collectively since those addressed by the poem are to be understood as the prudent whom God seeks.

4–5. The problem with practical atheism is initially explored by means of a rhetorical question. The implication is these people really should know that though they are prepared to devour the poet's people, God stands behind his people. Their fundamental error is that they do not call on God. Their basic orientation of self-sufficiency leads them in the wrong direction, and as they encounter God this problem is exposed. The language of these verses is very terse, but the basic sense is clear enough. Once they encounter God, evildoers are faced with great terror when previously there was none. The reason for this is that they now encounter evidence of God's presence in defending his people, scattering the bones of those who have encamped against them – perhaps reference to a recent moment of deliverance. As a result, it is the audience who hear the psalm who have put these people to shame by their continued trust in God, though only because God has rejected the evildoers. Here is the irony of practical atheism – it assumes God is of no relevance to life but actually such people are rejected by God.

6. An element of complaint is retained through the closing prayer that looks for the time when God will act. That is, the problem of practical atheism continues until those points when God acts decisively for his people. Psalm 52 also waited for God to act against the 'mighty one' and that hopeful waiting here becomes a prayer that anticipates future joy.

Explanation

Although largely a repeat of Psalm 14, Psalm 53 needs to be read on its own terms (against Kraus 1988: 513). The small changes made to the poem and its placement within this collection of Davidic prayers all shape how it is to be read. This psalm's audience may well be reflecting on a recent deliverance and so see evidence of God's actions for them. The psalm now points to some act of God's on their behalf, showing that through this those who have trusted in God have put to shame the fools who believe God will not act. Such fools are evident from their willingness to act against others in the mistaken belief that God will not act against them. But this psalm, though it longs for the joy to come when God's act of salvation is more decisively demonstrated, insists that fools will not remain for ever. Alongside Psalm 52, it suggests we look back to the story of Doeg the Edomite and his association with Saul as evidence of this sort of fool. Reading the psalm in the light of David's subsequent accession reminds readers that although the fool looked powerful, as if he could indeed destroy God's people, this was not the end. In his commitment to David, God had shown that he did indeed act for his people. The only wise course is to wait on God and cry out for his salvation.

PSALM 54

Translation

The director's. With stringed instruments. A Maskil. Davidic. When the Ziphites came and said to Saul, 'Is not David hiding himself with us?'

[1]O God, by your name, save me,
  and by your might vindicate me.
[2]O God, hear my prayer,
  give ear to the words of my mouth.
[3]For strangers have risen against me,
  tyrants seek my life,
  they do not place God before themselves. *Selah.*

[4]Behold, God is the one helping me,
  the Lord is the one sustaining my life.
[5]He will return harm to my enemies,
  in your faithfulness destroy them.

[6]I will sacrifice to you with a free-will offering,
  I will give thanks to your name, O Yahweh, because it is good.
[7]For he has delivered me from every distress,
  and my eye has looked upon my enemy.

Notes on the text

3. Some MSS (and Tg) read the orthographically similar *zēdîm* (proud), perhaps influenced by the otherwise very similar Psalm 86:14. Support for this is strong, but *zārîm* is retained as a more difficult reading.

4. The pl. const. ptc. *bĕsōmĕkê* is understood as a pl. of majesty with the prep. as the beth of identity (*WHS* §249).

5. With Q and many MSS, reading *yāšîb*, understanding God as the subject. Dahood (1968: 42, followed by NIV) has argued that 'enemies' is more specifically 'slanderers'. For a rebuttal, see Firth 1998.

Form and structure

The third of four successive poems entitled a 'Maskil', this poem shares a reference in the title to a moment in David's life with Psalm 52, the first of the four. Psalm 55, the closing Maskil, is joined to this poem by this shared-genre label and the fact that both are performed 'with stringed instruments'. The reference to the enemies as people who do not set God before themselves means that they embody the perspective of the fool from Psalm 53, further joining these poems.

The background provided by the title here refers to the events in 1 Samuel 23:15–24 and 1 Samuel 26, where the inhabitants of the wilderness of Ziph offered to give David over to Saul (see also V. L. Johnson 2009: 49–59). As the wording here is a citation of their speech in 1 Samuel 23:19 (though note also 1 Sam. 26:1), it is probable that the

Psalter's compilers had access to something approaching our book of Samuel. It is not necessary that David composed the psalm at this time (though neither is it impossible), but the compilers are suggesting that we read it in the light of this account.

This poem is a classic example of the individual lament, its three stanzas working through the form, with reference to God's name at the start of each stanza also creating an envelope construction for the whole (reinforced through plays on sound; cf. Botha 2000: 509):

1. Request for deliverance (1–3)
2. Declaration of confidence (4–5)
3. Vow of praise (6–7)

Comment

Title: For 'The director's', see on Psalm 4. 'With stringed instruments' occurs in the title of six psalms (Pss 4, 6, 54, 55, 61, 67, 76, with a similar phrase in Psalm 61's title), all belonging to the director's collection. It also occurs in the closing note to Habakkuk's psalm (Hab. 3:19). For 'Maskil', see on Psalm 32. For 'Davidic', see on Psalm 3. For the background, see 'Form and structure'.

1–3. The psalm opens with paired verses, addressing God directly. Verse 1 asks that he save the poet by his 'name'. It is not that God's name itself has any power but rather mention of God's name points to his character as one who is just and good, anticipating the reference to his name once more in verse 6. Because God is good, those in need can call on him. The salvation needed may have a judicial background if we understand the verb *dîn* (vindicate) in a specifically legal sense (cf. Kraus 1988: 514), but the fact that God is to vindicate the psalmist through his might suggests that rescue more generally is needed. Verse 2 balances verse 1 by also opening with the voc. 'God', but the request this time is that he heed the poet's prayer. Together, these verses indicate the urgency of the psalmist's need, though the need is outlined only in verse 3. Unlike the preceding verses, this one is a tricolon that opens with a conjunction, explaining why the poet is in need, something reinforced by the change in poetic form. The identity of the strangers who have arisen against the poet is unclear within the psalm itself; but when read against the background in 1 Samuel 23, they can be identified as the Ziphites since they are not part of David's clan. More broadly, such strangers can be hostile because of wickedness (Ps. 58:4), something consistent here with their being regarded as ruthless in their seeking of the poet's life (cf. 1 Sam. 23: 15), though this does not require a background in warfare (as suggested by Goulder [1990: 93]). But what defines them most is their failure to set God before themselves, showing that they live like the fool rejected by Psalm 53.

4–5. The second stanza addresses a wider audience while returning to a direct address to God in the final line. The opening 'behold' invites an audience to adopt the psalmist's perspective. When they do, they see that God is active in assisting the poet – it is not just that God is the psalmist's helper. The ptcs. here stress that he is active in helping and sustaining the poet, meaning that the strangers cannot achieve their goal of taking the psalmist's life. The strangers fail to set God before themselves, and so ignore the reason they cannot succeed in their attack of the poet. Indeed, the poet is confident that God will turn back the harm intended by the enemies, but still asks that God destroy the enemies. Consistent with what we also observe in Psalm 55, this request is effectively an application of the *lex talionis*, asking that what the enemies have sought to do to the psalmist is what God should do to them. Nevertheless, as is also the case in Psalm 55, the psalmist does not specify the means by which God should act and neither is there a request for permission to execute this punishment. Rather, the poet looks to God's faithfulness to ensure that the punishment fits the crime but without seeking the right to carry it out. If God is to vindicate the psalmist, then this is consistent with the legal dimension of the plea from verse 1.

6–7. Rather than acting personally against the enemies, the psalmist looks instead to acts of worship that express thanks to God. The poet anticipates making a free-will offering, most probably a whole burnt offering given in thanksgiving (Lev. 22:17–19). Such an offering is not required but would demonstrate the worshipper's commitment to God. This is linked here with giving thanks to God's name, here specified as Yahweh, because his name is good. This goodness comes from God's faithfulness to his people, so that giving thanks to his name is another way of giving thanks because of his character. Verse 7 then extends this by reporting that Yahweh has delivered the poet from every distress (cf. 1 Sam. 26:24), not just the current one (while perhaps anticipating future deliverance), so that the promised thanksgiving relates to a life that has experienced God's faithfulness. It is God's faithfulness, not the poet's own achievements, that allows the psalmist to look on the enemies. It is God's faithfulness, not human vindictiveness, that has the last word (against Weiser 1962: 417).

Explanation

Psalm 54 is initially to be read against David's experience of the Ziphites' betrayal while Saul sought his life. That Yahweh delivered David from Saul even at the very point where it seemed flight was no longer possible (1 Sam. 23:24–29) provides a powerful illustration of this poem's central theme – that Yahweh's character is good and that his faithfulness means he can be trusted to vindicate his people. Beyond the background in Samuel, it is also to be read in its literary context in Psalms 52–55. Here, we see it as a first example of the wisdom themes of the two preceding psalms that had stressed God's dependability, even in the face of powerful foes. The faithful know that there are powerful foes who deny the reality of God, and they are evident here, but God's faithfulness continues to provide a basis for confidence. Together, these psalms recognize both that believers face continued opposition and that they can continue to trust God to vindicate them. This vindication comes from God alone – it is not the place of believers to enact or even ask for the right to act against foes themselves. Rather, just as Jesus entrusted himself to the Father but was ultimately vindicated by the Spirit (1 Tim. 3:16), so also believers trust and wait for vindication.

PSALM 55

Translation

The director's. With stringed instruments. A Maskil. Davidic.

[1]Give ear, O God, to my prayer,
  do not hide yourself from my supplication.
[2]Listen to me and answer me,
  I am troubled in my complaint
  and I am disquieted
[3]from the sound of the enemy,
  from the clamour of the wicked,
for they bring down misfortune on me,
  and in anger they are hostile towards me.

[4]My heart writhes within me,
  deathly terrors fall on me.
[5]Fear and quaking have come into me,
  shuddering overwhelms me.
[6]And I say, 'O that I had wings like a bird,
  I would fly away and be at rest.
[7]Behold, I would flee far away,
  I would lodge in the wilderness. *Selah*.
[8]I would hurry to my place of refuge,
  from the winnowing wind, from the tempest.'

[9]Destroy, O Lord,
  divide their tongue,

for I see violence and strife in the city.
10Day and night they go around it upon its walls,
but misfortune and trouble are within it.
11Destruction is in its midst,
and oppression and deceit does not cease from its marketplace.

12For it is not an enemy who taunts me –
that I would bear –
it is not one who hates me who acts insolently against me –
then I would hide from him,
13but it is you, someone of the same value,
my close companion and friend.
14We who took sweet counsel together,
we walked in the house of God among the crowd.

15Let death beguile them,
let them go down to Sheol alive,
because evil is in their dwelling place, within them.

16As for me, I call out to God,
and Yahweh will save me.
17Evening, morning and noon I complain and murmur,
and he hears my voice.
18He redeems my life in peace from the battle that is against me,
when many are arranged against me.
19God will hear and afflict them,
yes, the one who is enthroned from of old. *Selah*.
Because they do not change,
and do not fear God.

20He has sent forth his hand against his friends,
he has violated his covenant.
21The buttery speech of his mouth was slippery,
but battle was in his heart,
his words were smoother than oil,
but they were drawn swords.

22Cast your burden on Yahweh,
and he will sustain you,
he will never let the righteous stumble.
23But you, O God, will bring them down to the pit of destruction,
mortals of bloodshed and deceit shall not live half of their days,
but as for me, I will trust in you.

Notes on the text

2. The meaning of *'ārîd* is uncertain (cf. Firth 2005b: 82), though some sense of trouble is implied. The cohort. *'āhîmâ* is also awkward but is understood here as an impf. with paragogic he.

3. Hebr. *'āqat* could be 'stare' or 'oppression' as well as 'clamour'. All fit contextually, but 'clamour' is adopted here because of its continuation of the sound motif of the first part of the line.

6. Desiderative *mî*; see *WHS* §122.

9. Taking *balla'* as 'destroy'. The more basic meaning is 'swallow' but destruction is the intended outcome.

14. The second half of the verse is textually uncertain, but none of the proposed emendations is persuasive. The best sense is obtained by understanding *regeš* as a reference to a crowd, but it is uncertain.

15. Reading with Q and many MSS, *yaššî māwet*.

19. *wĕya'ănēm* could also be 'and answer them' (cf. Hossfeld and Zenger 2006: 51), but with Gk it is best understood as 'afflict'. A deliberate play on these senses cannot be ruled out.

Form and structure

This psalm has long posed numerous interpretative problems (cf. Human 1997a: 245–250). It is a difficult text whose 'jagged, hectic character' (J. H. Eaton 1976: 74) raises significant questions because of the high number of rare words and difficult syntactic structures. As such, the 'Notes on the text' above address only the most important for translation, and it is readily apparent from a comparison of the major translations that points of debate are plentiful. Dahood (1968: 30) was an apparent outlier in this discussion since he felt that the poem could be adequately explained from comparative Ugaritic materials, but his suggestions have not aged well, and indeed he later felt the need to make alternative explanations (Dahood 1979, 1982).

The textual difficulties have led to the suggestion that the present poem is a composite, with the parts needing to be interpreted differently. Briggs and Briggs (1907: 19–20) divided it into two discrete poems, both of which were overwritten by numerous glosses. Kraus (1988: 519–520), building on Gunkel, opts for a simpler division with two basic psalms made up of verses 1–18a and 18b–23. Here, the main evidence is the apparent sense of closure in verse 18a, from which it is concluded that we have moved to a completely different poem, which has been placed here by accident. One cannot rule out the possibility that the psalm is made up of different pieces, but the presence of consistent stylistic devices across the proposed division suggests a need for caution in making such divisions (with Hossfeld and Zenger 2006: 53). Indeed, the presence of these features may suggest that a better approach is to understand the psalm as a unified piece (however formed) that has been composed to allow the reader to experience something of the poet's 'emotional roller coaster' (deClaissé-Walford et al. 2014: 473). This means we journey with the poet through the plea for protection until finally reaching the expression of trust with which the psalm closes.

The varied elements within the poem make it suitable as the closing psalm in the subunit of Psalms 52–55. It is most immediately joined to Psalm 54 by a repetition of the technical elements of the title, while the absence of a reference to David's experience again suggests that we read it first against the experiences in 1 Samuel 23 and 26 (see above, 'Form and structure' on Ps. 54). These connections are confirmed by the close similarity of verse 2 with Psalm 54. In addition, where Psalm 54:3 reported strangers who sought the poet's life, while the psalm also declared that God would act, we here have a report of God's redeeming the psalmist's life (v. 18). These links also point back to Psalms 52–53, notably through the syntactic similarity of verse 6 to 53:6, while the close friend turned adversary here is now like the fool of Psalm 53, a fool who was in turn the embodiment of the mighty man of Psalm 52. The closing note of trust here is thus not only relevant to this psalm; it also sums up the various forms of opposition described in the earlier parts of this subunit.

Granted the unity of the final piece, the text is still difficult to analyse. Human (1997b) regards it as among the most difficult to analyse, especially as it frequently makes sudden unmarked changes. Although it is an oversimplification (cf. Hardmeier 2016: 2–9), the psalm is here analysed in three stanzas (cf. Van Uchelen 1977: 103–104):

1. Opening plea (1–8)
    a. Call for hearing (1–3)
    b. Description of suffering (4–8)
2. Appeal for action (9–15)
    a. Summons to God (9–11)
    b. Complaint about friend (12–14)
    c. Appeal (15)
3. Trust and uncertainty (16–23)
    a. Statement of trust (16–19)
    b. Complaint about friend (20–21)
    c. Statement of trust (22–23)

Comment

Title: The technical items replicate the title of Psalm 54. See 'Comment' there for details.

1–3. The call for hearing is initially marked by a rush of imperatives, supplemented by the negation that asks God not to hide himself. There is an urgent need for God to hear and answer. God is to hear the psalmist's prayer, with the difficulty of the situation emphasized by the report of the poet's current suffering. The prayer is also called a 'supplication' and 'complaint', indicating both that the psalmist is aware of the need for God's grace and that the prayer emerges from a time of pain that leaves the poet disquieted. The reasons for this emerge in verse 3, which insists that this has been brought about by an enemy. Although a specific enemy emerges later in the poem, it is probable at this point that the enemy is a more generalized figure – note the pl. verbs in the second half of the verse. Although the details are obscure (cf. 'Notes on the text'), it seems likely that the enemy is attacking the psalmist through speech, building pressure through it. Psychological threat is experienced, including the suggestion that yet more misfortune may be brought down on the psalmist, while the adversaries' anger continues to demonstrate hostility. It is because of this pressure that God needs to hear and answer.

4–8. The effects of the psychological pressure are described through their physical manifestations on the poet. The use of first-person forms through this strophe marks it out as a distinct unit, with first-person forms occurring in every part line except for verse 8b, which allows for the move from this strophe into the second stanza. Verses 4–5 emphasize the immediate effect on the poet. Because the 'heart' often points to the psalmist's thought world (cf. Janowski 2013: 155–162), the writhing of the heart probably points to disquieted thoughts, something matched by the deathly terrors that are the fears caused by the pressure from the enemies. These psychological pressures then manifest physically in fear and quaking along with shuddering. That these have been brought about by enemy action is clear from the fact that, other than the writhing heart, all of these effects have come on the poet from elsewhere. Because of this, in verses 6–8 the poet expresses a desire to escape from these pressures, wishing to have wings like a bird and fly to a remote place, and so be able to rest, away from these pressures (cf. Jer. 9:1–3). Separation from the enemy is the way the psalmist sees as enabling rest rather than being caught in the continued tempest of current experience. Yet although the poet wishes for this, the reality is that this is impossible. However desirable it may be to fly away and be at rest, this is simply not an option. The tempest continues to blow.

9–11. As we move into the second stanza, the poem returns to the imp. Fleeing is not possible, but Yahweh is the one who can bring about deliverance. Since speech has been central to the activity of the enemy, the psalmist asks for the 'Lord' (*'ădōnāy*) to destroy, to divide their tongue. Their speech has brought about the psalmist's suffering, and God is to act against this so that their punishment fits the crime. A new element is also introduced here as we discover that the psalmist can observe 'violence and strife' (*ḥāmās wĕrîb*) in the city. The poet has experienced suffering because of the enemy, but it seems that this is part of a wider pattern of social unrest brought about by the wicked. This is demonstrated by the presence of the enemies constantly going around the walls, bringing about misfortune and trouble. Rather than being a sign of security, the walls are now a source of trouble. Earlier, the enemy was said to bring misfortune on the psalmist, so mention of this once more indicates that the poet's experience is in many ways typical of the wider community. Rather than being guards on the city walls, they are the ones who bring the threat into the city. So, where the psalmist has experienced deathly terrors, the city experiences destruction, oppression and deceit, with the marketplace a key example of this (cf. Amos 8:4–6).

12–14. As with the first stanza, the second moves from a direct address to God to the first-person experience in the second strophe. But where verses 4–8 focused more on the effects of the suffering, this time the primary concern is with identifying the source of the suffering. Here, the poem indicates two parallel conditions the poet might have tolerated before pointing to what makes the current situation so difficult. Had it been an enemy or one who hated the psalmist, then this might have been borne, or at least the psalmist might have found a means of hiding from it. Of course, numerous psalms complain to God about the acts of enemies, so we cannot assume that their assaults would simply have been tolerated. But what makes the suffering so difficult is that it comes from one the psalmist has previously regarded as a close friend. Indeed, the psalmist imaginatively speaks directly to the former friend in verses 13–14. The exact sense of verse 13a is not entirely clear, but it seems likely that the sense of the psalmist's description of the former friend as (lit.) 'a human of my valuation' is that they have a shared value, that is, that they are social equals (cf. ESV). As social equals, they were also close friends who had previously worshipped together. The expectation is that such a person would remain loyal rather than taunt and act insolently against the psalmist (though cf. Ps. 41:9 for another false friend). That this person is the source of the psalmist's suffering is what makes it so shocking.

15. The second stanza closes with a wish. Whereas the summons to God in verses 9–11 directly requested action, this time it is expressed as an outcome that is desired rather than something directly sought. It is a wish, but perhaps not something the poet can request directly. The text here returns to speaking of the enemies in the pl., indicating that the former friend is part of a wider pattern of abusive behaviour, something consistent with the description of structural violence in verses 9–11. Indeed, verses 4–5 report that the enemies caused the psalmist to experience 'deathly terrors', so, although the wish is forceful, it is also shaped (at least in part) by the *lex talionis*; thus the punishment hoped for is equivalent to the harm wrought by the enemies (Firth 2005b: 85).

They have brought death into the experience of both the psalmist and the wider community, and the hope is that they should experience this themselves (cf. Num. 16:30–31). Nevertheless, it is notable that although this hope is presented to God in the prayer, the psalmist does not ask for the right to act – only God can deal with this.

16–19. The third stanza also begins with an address to God, though this time by reporting extended examples of crying out to him. Where earlier points in the psalm had mentioned either 'God' or 'the Lord', this time the psalmist uses 'Yahweh'. It is Yahweh who will save the poet and, if so, it is Yahweh alone who can determine what will be done to the enemies. For the psalmist, there is simply a regular pattern of crying out to God throughout the day (evening being when the day was considered to begin), ensuring that the psalmist's complaint is presented to him. But where the opening appeal (v. 1) asked God to 'give ear' to the poet, this time confidence is expressed – God will hear the poet's voice, even if those earlier points were no more than a murmur. God's hearing is fundamental, for the one who hears is the one who redeems the poet's life, creating well-being in the face of conflict. It is this that provides hope, even though many are arrayed against the psalmist. Hence, verse 19 can affirm not only that God hears, but also that he acts against the enemies. The reason for this is that God is enthroned from of old. It is God who reigns, and this provides hope for the psalmist, hope that the enemies cannot have because they are locked into patterns of behaviour that cause harm. All this can be traced to their failure to fear God, meaning that they act like the fool of Psalm 53:1.

20–21. The change of topic here is abrupt. Nevertheless, the nature of the actions described is consistent with the description of the former friend and so they are best interpreted this way. As such, they are what we expect of one who does not fear God and so are contrary to God's own actions. Thus, whereas God redeems 'in peace' (v. 18), the enemy acts against his friend, though the term for 'friend' here is *šālôm*. So, the enemy may also be thought to be acting against his own well-being in violating a covenant. Although covenant may be understood in terms of God's covenant with Israel, it is more likely here that the reference is to the close relationship with the psalmist that has now been violated. Similarly, where God redeems from battle, the enemy's seemingly pleasant words conceal battle in his heart, with words that may seem gentle really being drawn swords. The enemy is thus not only the psalmist's adversary: his actions show that he is God's enemy too.

22–23. If God hears and acts against those who are his enemies, then those who have aligned themselves with God can be confident that he will ultimately act for them. Hence, the psalmist now addresses a wider audience, advising them to learn from the experiences outlined in this poem. Although the Hebr. here is in the sg., the 'you' here is representative of all who have heard this psalm. Just as the psalmist can affirm Yahweh's redemption from suffering, so those addressed here are told to cast their burden on Yahweh because he will sustain them (cf. Ps. 37:5). As is clear from this psalm, this does not mean that suffering will not be experienced but rather that the proper response is to trust Yahweh because of his enduring commitment to the righteous (cf. Ps. 15:6). Verse 23, then, addresses God, though the clear intention is that this point should be overheard by the audience as the psalmist declares that God will bring these enemies down to the pit of destruction; that is, that they shall not survive. These enemies of God are marked by bloodshed and deceit, as shown by their impact on the city, and though they may appear to be successful, the psalmist is confident that they will not continue. Those who survive through violence will also die through it. On its own, this observation may be thought to be at home in the wisdom world of Psalm 37. But here, it is both wisdom and faith, trust in the midst of conflict, trust confirmed by the closing declaration. The circumstances might not yet have changed, but the psalmist can affirm enduring trust in Yahweh, and this provides an example for the audience.

Explanation

Perhaps more than most, Psalm 55 demonstrates the limitations of too tight a focus on the main form-critical categories, in that it is both a complaint psalm and a declaration of trust. It is essential in reading this psalm that these elements are held together. In doing this, we can appreciate that complaint and trust are not opposites. Rather, they are to be held together in faith that complaint can be brought to God in the face of challenges that seem to overwhelm us – whether that is structural violence brought about by the wicked or an act of betrayal by a formerly close friend. We may complain to God because he is also the one we can trust. The psalm's closing note of trust is thus vital. But this note also looks beyond the experience recounted in this poem to the subunit of which it is a part, Psalms 52–55. Read in context, we note Psalm 52:8 was also a closing note of trust, while each psalm in this subunit has in various ways assured us of God's commitment to his people. This psalm's conclusion is thus not only appropriate to it as a poem; it is also appropriate to this subunit. It is no surprise, then, that 1 Peter 5:7 takes up this same theme for Christians who were suffering in the Roman Empire since they too lived in a world (as do many today) where it seems that the powerful triumph, with structures of violence becoming entrenched. Such a world needs to be faced honestly, but the encouragement of this psalm is that we continue to cast our burden on the Lord and discover his sustaining power.

PSALM 56

Translation

The director's. According to the silent dove of the distant ones. Davidic. A Miktam. When the Philistines seized him in Gath.

1Be gracious to me, O God, for mortals have crushed me,
fighting throughout the day they oppress me.
2My foes have crushed me throughout the day,
for many are those fighting proudly against me.

3The day I fear,
I trust in you.
4In God, whose word I praise,
in God shall I trust – I will not fear,
what can flesh do to me?

5Throughout the day they twist my words,
all their thoughts concerning me are for harm.
6They attack, they hide,
they watch my heels,
while they waited for my life.

7Because of wickedness, is there delivery for them?
In wrath bring down the peoples, O God!
8You have considered my grief,
put my tears in your bottle,
are they not in your scroll?
9Then shall my enemies turn back on the day I call,
this I know because God is for me.

10In God, whose word I praise,
in Yahweh, whose word I praise,
11In God I trust and will not fear,
what can a human do to me?

12My vows to you are my responsibility, O God,
I will complete thank offerings to you,
13for you have delivered my life from death.
Have you not delivered my feet from stumbling,
to walk before God,
in the light of the living?

Notes on the text

Title: *'ēlem* is often emended to *'ēlîm* (cf. Begg 1988a), resulting in 'dove of the distant oaks'. But MT can stand.

1. Treating *'ĕnōš* as a collective noun.

7. *'āwen* is difficult and often emended (cf. *BHS*). Kraus (1988: 525), for example, declares 'the text is meaningless' (cf. Seybold 1996: 226), though the proposed emendations do not offer much improvement. Although Goldingay (2007: 182) regards reading the first half-line as a question as 'arbitrary', it is possible for questions to be unmarked (*WHS* §542).

8. *nōdî* could be 'my wandering' (cf. Driver 1970), but it is better to understand it as a reference to grief (cf. Ps. 69:20).

10. Understanding the suff. from verse 4 to have carried over in the refrain.

Form and structure

As with Psalm 55, this prayer also mixes elements of complaint and trust, and is closely linked to Psalm 55 through this combination, especially the declarations of trust (vv. 4, 11; cf. Ps. 55:23). However, there is good reason for seeing Psalm 55 as the close of the subunit of Psalms 52–55 (each a 'Maskil'), while Psalm 56 initiates a new subunit that runs to Psalm 60 (each a 'Miktam'; see on Ps. 16). The motif of trust is a bridge that joins these subunits, but the more important connections are with the psalms that follow. It is notable that this psalm includes refrain-like material in verses 4, 10–11, and that the same is true of Psalms 57, 59, while Psalms 58, 60 include cited material, a pattern that could provide a clue to the meaning of the otherwise obscure 'Miktam' in the title (cf. Raabe 1990: 92, who builds on observations from Franz Delitzsch [1996, repr.]: 388) to suggest the term could point to an 'inscription'; cf. *DCH*).

The combination of elements within this psalm also leads to dispute over the form-critical categorization (cf. Firth 2005b: 87–89), and once again too-rigid an application of these is to be avoided. Rather, we can read this as a poem that offers a prayer for protection which includes expressions of trust within it.

The refrain-like material in verses 4, 10–11 and its movement between the trust declared there and the need for protection elsewhere in the psalm provides its main structuring element. Taking this as our main point of division, we can analyse the poem in three stanzas:

1. Appeal and trust (1–4)
   a. Appeal (1–2)
   b. Trust (3–4)

2. Second appeal and trust (5–11)
   a. Enemy activities (5–6)
   b. Evidence of God's faithfulness (7–9)
   c. Trust (10–11)
3. Thanksgiving (12–13)

Comment

Title: For 'The director's', see on Psalm 4. 'According to' seems to indicate the title of a tune, which is likely here. For 'Davidic', see on Psalm 3. For 'Miktam', see on Psalm 16. The historical note here probably refers to 1 Samuel 21:10–15 when David feigned madness after being brought to Achish. See also the title of Psalm 34. Goulder (1990: 109–110) links it to David's flight from Olivet, but this means creating an entirely new background to the one provided by the title.

1–2. The psalm opens with an appeal for grace. Such appeals are relatively common in Psalms, but only this poem and Psalms 51, 57 commence with this appeal, all three then addressing God directly. This suggests an urgency in the appeal – there is no call for God to hear the poet's voice. Instead, we move immediately to the call for grace. The reason for this need is laid out in the balance of the strophe, drawing on militaristic language to describe the activities of the enemies. There is surely a contrast here between God as the one who can offer grace and the mortals who crush and oppress the poet. Establishing this contrast between God and humans prepares for the declarations of faith that make this contrast explicit. But the contrast does not change the urgency of the appeal since it is twice said that the poet is being crushed by these people. Their constant fighting against the psalmist happens throughout the 'day' and thus establishes a key word for the poem.

3–4. Although the foes have placed the psalmist under great pressure, the psalm here moves to the first declaration of trust. Although 'the day' here essentially means 'whenever', it is retained in translation to highlight the link to the 'day' motif running through the poem. The psalmist does not deny the reality of fear generated by others. Such fear is a real emotion, but is here recontextualized through trust in God. This recontextualization is developed in verse 4b, which picks up key terms from verse 3. Where fear precedes trust in verse 3, in verse 4b the reality of trust means fear is no longer required. This change has happened because of the reliability of God's word, something that provides a context for trust. Trust is not an end in itself. Rather, it is shaped by that which God has said, and it is this that provides the setting for fear to be transformed. In the light of this, the poet closes the first occurrence of the refrain-like section with a rhetorical question. Where God's word has been given, it is possible to trust God and know that flesh, a term that by definition excludes God, cannot triumph. The opening strophe makes clear that opposition happens, but the second strophe closes the stanza with the certain hope that however vigorous such opposition might be, when set against God's word, it cannot succeed.

5–6. The second stanza also begins by focusing on the activities of the enemies, picking up on the key term 'word' from the affirmation of trust while continuing the 'day' motif. But where the psalmist focused on God's word, the enemies are concerned with the words of the poet. The exact sense of their mistreatment of these words is uncertain since the root *'ṣb* can mean either 'harm' (cf. ESV) or 'twist'. The former, however, is too general, and it is better to see a more explicit statement here, with the psalmist's words twisted into unintended meanings. This is consistent with their general concern with the psalmist's harm. This intention for harm can take numerous forms, whether covert (hiding, perhaps in the sense of a metaphorical attempt to ambush the psalmist) or overt in direct attack. Whatever form it takes, the goal is to take the psalmist's life. So, the threat is very real.

7–9. The move to trust is more complex in this stanza, opening with what appears to be another question (cf. 'Notes on the text'). The context for it is developed in this strophe as it again addresses God, even if this is initially somewhat oblique. The thrust of the opening question is to indicate that those just described should not be able to act with impunity. They cannot realistically expect deliverance given the effects of their actions. The appeal in verse 7b emerges from this, with the enemies personified as nations (A. A. Anderson 1972, 1: 423), while also introducing another key motif for this subunit, asking that they be brought down. That is, they should not be able to continue as they are; hence, losing the power to act. God is to act against the enemies, but also for the psalmist. God has noted the psalmist's grief, so is therefore summoned to place the poet's tears in a bottle, presumably as an enduring reminder of the suffering caused by the enemies. A further question drives this point home – the poet's suffering is in God's scroll (a noun cognate to the verb for 'consider'). As such, God already has the information needed to act. Given this, the psalmist knows the enemies will be turned back at the point God is summoned because of God's commitment.

10–11. The near-refrain is reintroduced at this point. Again, focus is on God's word as the basis for hope, but there is a subtle development. Not only does the psalmist speak of God, but this time the covenant name of 'Yahweh' is introduced. The one whose word is praised is not any deity. It is Israel's covenant God. So, when the psalmist again announces trust in God as the antidote to fear, we know it is an antidote shaped by God's word and his covenant commitment to his people.

Hence, this strophe can also close with a rhetorical question, this time making explicit what was implied before in the word 'flesh' (v. 4), that 'humans' (*'ādām*) cannot triumph over God.

12–13. If God is committed to the psalmist (cf. Rom. 8:37–39), then the poet should also be committed to God. Hence, the psalmist accepts the need to fulfil vows made to God. Such vows represent the psalmist's words to God and if God's words are a basis for trusting God, then God should be able to trust the psalmist's words too. Thank offerings are associated with the fellowship offering (Lev. 7:11–18), so the vows here may anticipate restored relationships with others. But whatever the content of the vows, the psalmist accepts (again through a rhetorical question) that if God has prevented death and enabled the possibility of living before him, then it is right to fulfil the vows made and give thanks to God.

Explanation

The title suggests reading this psalm against the background of David's experience in 1 Samuel 21:10–15. There, he was seized by the Philistines and had to feign madness to be released. Strikingly, there is no mention of God there, so linking this psalm with that context creates a new framework for reading that story while also informing our reading of this psalm. The psalm itself closely integrates the motifs of fear and trust, recognizing that these are not necessarily opposites. Rather, it is perfectly possible for believers to have real times of fear even if they can also be balanced with trust in God's protection. The key to this trust is God's word, something left undefined within the psalm, and that could include Scripture; though, if we take David's background seriously, it is more likely to be some form of prophetic word. We would search in vain in Samuel for a particular word here apart from David's anointing by Samuel (1 Sam. 16:1–13). There, David was assured that Yahweh had a purpose for him, and therefore when we read this psalm, we understand it as trust based on a word that shaped David's life. Because of this he could trust God even if being seized by the Philistines was also a legitimate reason for fear. This framework guides further reading of the psalm, suggesting that believers cannot claim any word as the basis for not being afraid (there are still legitimate times for fear!), but rather they should ask how any situation fits with those promises of God that can be known through Scripture. It is these that enable believers to know that God will never leave nor forsake his people (Heb. 13:5) and that enable trust (cf. C. B. Jones 2018: 22), even in those times when fear is real, so that we may walk in the light of life (cf. John 8:12).

PSALM 57

Translation

The director's. Do Not Destroy. Davidic. A Miktam. When he fled from Saul into the cave.

[1]Be gracious to me, O God, be gracious to me,
for in you do I take refuge,
and in the shadow of your wings will I take refuge,
until destruction passes by.
[2]I call out to God Most High,
to the God who completes his purposes for me.
[3]He will send from heaven and rescue me,
he will reproach the one who pursues me. *Selah.*
God will send forth his kindness and faithfulness,
[4]and rescue me.
I lie down amid lions, ravenous ones,
humans whose teeth are spears and arrows,
whose tongues are sharp swords.
[5]Be exalted above the heavens, O God,
your glory above all the earth.

[6]A net have they set out for my steps,
my whole being is bowed down. *Selah.*
they dug out a pit before me,
they have fallen into the midst of it!
[7]My heart is steadfast, O God, my heart is steadfast,
I will sing and make melody.
[8]Awake, O my glory,
awake, O harp and lyre,
I will awaken the dawn.
[9]I will give thanks to you among the peoples, O Lord,
I will make melody to you among the peoples.
[10]For your kindness is great to the heavens,
and your faithfulness to the clouds.
[11]Be exalted above the heavens, O God,
your glory above all the earth.

Notes on the text

3–4. With Gk and Syr., reading *wĕyôša‘* before *napšî*, creating a balancing colon to the end of verse 3, the second occurrence of the verb perhaps missed because of its use in verse 3a (unless with Goldingay [2007: 195] we assume it is implied from v. 3a – but the effect is the same). Verse 4 is analysed differently, though on any reading *lōhăṭîm* is difficult. It is taken here to mean 'ravenous' rather than the more common 'blazing'. It is not directly connected to either the lions or humans, so read here as placed as a bridge between the part lines, covering both (cf. Raabe 1990: 117).

10. Redividing the closing words and reading *bal'ummîm*.

Form and structure

As with the preceding psalm, this one is linked to an event in David's life. Reference to 'the cave' could mean either his time in Adullam (1 Sam. 22:1–5) or while he was in the wilderness of En-gedi (1 Sam. 24). Both are possible. Repetition of the opening line from Psalm 56 points to a particularly close link between these two psalms; and, since we read them sequentially, preference should be given to Adullam as the time that followed David's time in Gath, referenced in Psalm 56's title, though V. L. Johnson (2009: 93) suggests that repetition of the word *kānāp* ('wing'; 1 Sam. 24:5, 12; Ps. 57:1) makes 1 Samuel 24 preferable. But since both share the context of his being on the run from Saul, a choice is not essential. Both settings make clear that David needed deliverance from one who pursued him, a rescue clearly needed in this poem. As with Psalm 56, when read against this background it provides a theological focus otherwise absent from the Samuel material.

As the second Miktam in Psalms 56–60, this poem also includes wider links with Psalm 56. As well as the opening appeal for grace, it is notable that this psalm also includes a refrain (vv. 5, 11), though this time the refrain is more exact. The 'peoples' motif introduced there (Ps. 56:7) also finds an echo here, as the peoples now become the context in which thanksgiving to God is to be declared. The enemies in both psalms are also portrayed as laying ambush to the poet, focusing on their steps (Ps. 56:6; 57:6). Although the verb 'trust' does not recur from the previous psalm, elements of trust are also evident, especially in verses 2–3. So, although the psalm is generally treated as a complaint (e.g. Sabourin 2010: 247–248), it is not just a complaint. With small variations, verses 7–11 are repeated as Psalm 108:1–5.

The refrain here plays a central structural role, making it possible to analyse the psalm in two stanzas:

1. Appeal for grace (1–5)
2. Steadfastness under pressure (6–11)

Comment

Title: For 'The director's', see on Psalm 4. 'Do Not Destroy' is a new element in the titles, recurring in Psalms 58, 59, 75. It may be the name of a tune. Most importantly, it provides a means of further linking Psalms 57, 58 and 59. For 'Davidic', see on Psalm 3. For 'Miktam', see on Psalm 16. As noted above, the historical note could refer either to 1 Samuel 22:1–5 or 1 Samuel 24. Mention of a cave recurs in the title of Psalm 142.

1–5. As with Psalm 56, this poem opens with an appeal for grace, addressing God directly, though most of the stanza addresses an audience. In doing so, it repeats the request for grace, initiating a pattern of verbal repetitions that occur across the psalm (cf. vv. 7–8). Grace is claimed because the psalmist has taken refuge in God (cf. Ps. 7:1) and because the poet cannot overcome the opposing forces. Read against the background of 1 Samuel 22 or 24, claiming refuge is metaphorical, though within the temple it was possible to claim refuge by taking hold of the altar (cf. Exod. 21:12–14). Of course, both God (Ps. 46:1) and the king (Ps. 2:12) could also be a source of refuge, so it does not have to be tied to the temple. However, reference to the shadow of God's wings may refer to the wings of the cherubim in the inner sanctuary, so this at least provides a possible background to the statement (cf. Broyles 1999: 243–244). The poet need not be in the sanctuary but knowledge of it helps explain the nature of the claim of refuge, and that God is to provide protection until the destruction threatening the poet has passed by. Of course, the imagery can also work if we think of a bird hovering over its young (cf. Hossfeld and Zenger 2006: 71), and it is perhaps unnecessary to choose between these ways of understanding the image. The psalmist is experiencing threat, but having claimed refuge can express confidence. God has been summoned, and as the Most High (Ps. 46:4) is the one who is over all opposing forces and can be relied on to act for the psalmist, avenging the wrongs done. The psalm holds a similar tension to Solomon's dedicatory prayer for the temple (1 Kgs 8:22–53), which allows for both God's presence in the temple and that the heavens are his abode. So, irrespective of where the psalmist is, God can indeed send from heaven and rescue the poet, overcoming the one who is attacking. Not only will God act, but he will send forth his kindness and faithfulness as the means of rescue. As with Psalm 23:6, where God's goodness and faithfulness pursue the psalmist, these characteristics of God are here personified, though ultimately it is still God who acts. The forces facing the psalmist are clearly dangerous, likened to a ravenous lion, though in reality they are humans whose speech is clearly dangerous since it functions like dangerous weapons. The psalmist 'lies down' among these foes, something that may also be taken as a sign of trust. The element of trust leads to the initial occurrence of the refrain, asking that God be exalted above the heavens. It is from the heavens that he is to send and rescue the psalmist, but there he is to be exalted, perhaps through heavenly worship. Alongside this, God's glory is to be over all the earth, meaning that all the earth can join this worship, bringing heaven and earth together just as the psalmist also anticipates God's act of deliverance bringing heaven and earth together. All this points to God's status as king of all creation, summoning him therefore to bring justice.

6–11. The second stanza begins by returning to military, or perhaps hunting, imagery for the enemies. They are said to use various strategies to capture the psalmist, including laying a net while leaving the poet under great pressure. The poet acknowledges the reality of the threat from the enemies, but alongside this points to the pit they were digging as where they fell. What they set out against the poet has trapped them instead. Because of this, the psalmist again expresses confidence, the 'steadfast heart' pointing to an assured conviction that God is for the poet, an assurance that contrasts with the misplaced confidence of the enemies in their net. Because of this conviction, and perhaps initial evidence that the enemies cannot succeed, the psalmist desires to join the worship indicated in the refrain's initial occurrence. The psalmist will sing and asks therefore to be fully enlivened ('my glory' is a circumlocution for 'me' in worship) to join this musical worship, not only joining in with harp and lyre but with music so rousing it awakens the dawn. In this context, the psalmist will give thanks to God among the peoples. God's glory is over all the earth, so all the earth is to worship him, and giving thanks among the peoples is a means of joining this universal worship. This emerges from God's prior sending of his kindness and faithfulness, both of which are now said to reach to the heavens (the clouds being in the heavens; cf. Ps. 36:5). The refrain's recurrence brings this together – God can be trusted to act for his people in their distress, and in so doing inaugurates worship that reaches all creation. It is this the psalmist intends to join, and the psalm encourages all to participate because this worship points to God's glory over all creation.

Explanation

The compilers of the Psalter indicate that this psalm is to be read against the background of David's time in the wilderness while he was under threat from Saul. Such a setting provides a rich context in which to understand the psalm's combination of cries for mercy and trust. David was in need, and yet could continue to trust that God would deliver him. The psalm is also given a literary context through its position next to Psalm 56, enabling an intensification of the themes of complaint and trust developed there. In particular, this psalm expresses trust through worship that sees all creation as belonging to God. Thus, although the poet suffers major threats, especially through the speech of enemies, the psalmist's own speech is finally focused on worship. This worship holds together the reality that the enemies continue to threaten and yet God is also active, meaning that the enemies' plots backfire. The tongues of the enemies may threaten (cf. Jas 3:1–12), but the speech of the faithful can still be worshipful because God is king above all creation, and so we pray for this to be seen.

PSALM 58

Translation

The director's. Do Not Destroy. Davidic. A Miktam.

1Do you indeed decree what is right, mighty ones,
  do you judge humankind with equity?
2Surely, in your heart you devise injustice,
  your hands weigh out violence in the land.

3The wicked are estranged from the womb,
  they have strayed from birth, speaking lies.
4Their venom is like a serpent's venom,
  like a deaf horned viper, its ear stopped up,
5which does not hearken to the voice of charmers,
  the charms of a trained charmer.

6O God, break their teeth in their mouth,
  smash the jaws of the young lions, O Yahweh!
7Let them vanish like waters that run away,
  when he aims his arrows, let them fall short,
8like a snail melting away as it goes,
  a woman's aborted foetus, not seeing the sun.
9Before your pots can discern the thorns,
  whether fresh or burning, may he sweep them away.

10May the righteous rejoice when they see redress,
  they will bathe their feet in the blood of the wicked.
11Then humankind will say, 'Surely, there is fruit for the righteous,
  surely there is a God who judges on earth.'

Notes on the text

1. With Tate (1990: 82), reading *'ēlîm* rather than *'ēlem*. Given the range of northern features in the psalm, it is conceivable (similarly, van

Gemeren 2008: 466) that this is in fact the sense of the consonantal text without emendation, in which case the psalm has retained defective spelling, which then masks the long vowel. Begg's proposal (1988b: 401–404) that we should read *'ĕlōhîm* probably goes a step too far. For a defence of MT, see Hamilton 2021: 1:544–545. Hossfeld and Zenger (2006: 77–78) also retain MT, but more from a lack of confidence in the alternatives. 'Humankind' could also be a voc. (as in LXX), leading to 'do you humans judge with equity?'

7. With Q, reading *ḥiṣṣāyw*.

8. If, with Rendsburg (1990: 65–66) we understand the psalm's language as representing a northern dialect, there is no need to emend the otherwise unusual *'ēšet*, despite Kraus's claim that this form is 'impossible' (1988: 534).

9. This verse is so difficult that Dahood (1968: 57) declines to offer a translation! But see Althann 1983.

10. Taking *ṣaddîq* as a collective, so translating in pl.

Form and structure

The third Miktam in the subunit Psalms 56–60, this poem is also joined to Psalms 57, 59 through the element 'Do Not Destroy' in the title. However, where both Psalms 57, 59 are linked to episodes in David's life, no such connection is provided here, perhaps meaning that we continue to read this psalm against the background of Psalm 57. Other features indicate that this poem needs to be read alongside Psalm 57. The animal imagery for the enemies in Psalm 57:4 finds an echo in verses 4–6 (which might have contributed to the shape of the imprecation; cf. Miglio 2015), while the arrows of verse 8 are probably once more damaging speech aimed at the poet. The request for their teeth to be broken (v. 6) is consistent with this damaging speech, and it is notable that across all three psalms there is an emphasis on the harm caused through speech, a motif that continues in Psalm 59 before being contrasted with God's speech in Psalm 60.

Where Psalms 56–57 mix both complaint and trust, with a greater emphasis on trust, this poem is better understood as a complaint psalm, one particularly concerned with the effects of injustice brought about by malicious speech. It does in verse 11 express a degree of trust, but is primarily a prayer for justice expressed in the form of a wish. The wish does seem to show some wisdom influences, so the psalm mixes forms. One can also read the psalm as a form of a court case, one where the 'mighty ones' are addressed because of their failure to stop the wicked, so that Yahweh instead is to bring about justice. On that model, it can be analysed in four short stanzas:

1. Address to the powerful (1–2)
2. The problem of the wicked (3–5)
3. Prayer for vengeance (6–9)
4. Hope for the righteous (10–11)

Comment

Title: For 'The director's', see on Psalm 4. For 'Do Not Destroy', see on Psalm 57. For 'Davidic', see on Psalm 3. For 'Miktam', see on Psalm 16.

1–2. Where the two preceding psalms begin by addressing God, this poem (like Ps. 82) begins by addressing figures who are meant to provide justice. Their exact identity is uncertain, especially if we retain MT, which would result in a translation such as 'Do you really speak what is right when silent?' (LEB), leaving the identity of those addressed unstated. But this reading makes awkward syntactic connections, and it is better to accept an emendation resulting in the reading above with the 'mighty ones'. But who are these mighty ones? Our reading here may also be shaped by how we interpret the second part of verse 1. If we are correct in seeing 'humankind' as the object of the verb 'judge' at this point, then the opening verse challenges the mighty ones about their practice of justice as humans experience it, setting up a contrast with what Yahweh is to do in the final stanza. That is, Yahweh is unlike the mighty ones. But how? The word *'ēlîm* could be translated 'gods' (so NRSV), in which case the parallel with Psalm 82 is closer and we could therefore assume that the psalm draws on a mythological background. But it is also possible for the word to describe those who hold a position of authority (so, deClaissé-Walford et al. 2014: 492), in which case the reference is to human judges. Perhaps we should allow the term's ambiguity to stand, and allow that both options are possible, and an ancient audience might not have separated these possibilities. However an ancient audience conceived of those responsible for delivering justice, the psalm opens by challenging them because rather than enabling humans to experience justice, they were bringing about injustice. In the place of justice, they were ensuring that humans experienced the structural violence of entrenched injustice.

3–5. What does this injustice and violence look like? This stanza addresses this issue by looking at the life of the wicked, a group who can be understood as those who do not orient themselves to serve Yahweh (cf. Pss 1:4–5; 36:1–4). If the mighty ones are meant to ensure justice, then the wicked should not triumph, the expectation being that their actions would be limited. But the opening stanza has made clear that there is no such limit on the wicked, and so they can live in a manner contrary to Yahweh's will. Indeed, their whole life is marked by this pattern, resulting in their speaking lies. False speech is the particular problem noted here, with its effects compared to deadly snake venom. What makes them dangerous is that they ignore attempts to limit their actions, so that they can be compared to a snake which is not only deaf, but has blocked its ears so it cannot even recognize the work of a highly skilful charmer. The wicked orient themselves so as to ignore God, living the life of practical atheism rejected in Psalm 53. It is this that allows violence to flourish, resulting in the absence of justice.

6–9. Only at this point does the psalm address God. In a poem that has a possible mythological background, that God is addressed in verse 6 both as 'God' and 'Yahweh' is important. All other deities or spiritual beings are excluded. It is Israel's covenant God who is to bring about change. The language used here is forceful, but also carefully tied to the damage done by the wicked. The damage done by the wicked is compared to the venom injected by a snake. So, asking God to break their teeth in their mouth is thus specific to the means by which the wicked enable harm (cf. Ps. 3:7). That is, God is asked to destroy that which causes the spread of injustice and violence. This is continued in the image of the young lions having their jawbones broken, again focusing on the means by which harm is inflicted on society (cf. Ps. 17:12). Both these requests are concerned with the mouth, the site from which lies are spoken. Although the details are not always clear, this line of interpretation is borne out by the further requests in verses 7–8, all of which are concerned with the removal of the possibility of the wicked inflicting harm through their actions. How their actions are prevented from inflicting harm varies – they may vanish, their efforts may simply fail, they may die or never get the chance to act. Although the imagery in verse 9 is even more unclear, the sense seems to be that the poet longs for the wicked to be removed, and thus be unable to act. In this case, it seems that the wicked are again addressed, with the wish that God will deal with them quickly.

10–12. When God acts, it is possible to see justice. For the righteous, those who shape their lives in accordance with God's will (Ps. 1:2–3), it will be possible to rejoice when they see God's redress (cf. Goldingay 2007: 208). Such redress is not unlimited, but within the context of the psalm is specific to those things that perpetuate injustice and violence. The righteous can rejoice when they see God's justice enacted, an integral part of their lived experience. The language is vigorous, especially when speaking of the righteous as 'bathing their feet in the blood of the wicked', but this is hyperbole for God's complete victory over wickedness (cf. A. A. Anderson 1972, 1: 434). Most importantly, God, and not the righteous, is the one who brings this about (cf. Day 2005: 55). This is reinforced by the closing declaration. Instead of the powerful assuming they can do as they wish, because they have the power, humankind can know there is a reward (lit. a 'fruit') for righteousness, a life shaped by conformity to God's will. More importantly, when God brings about redress it will make clear that there is a God who judges on the earth. The mighty ones, whoever they are, do not have the final say.

Explanation

Continuing from Psalms 56–57 the motif of the damage done through speech, this psalm looks for God to demonstrate his justice on earth, ending the structural violence brought about by powerful figures who not only permit injustice but benefit from it. We can read this against the background of David's flight from Saul when he knew that Saul was wrongly claiming that David was his enemy. Saul's misrepresentation of David put David's life at risk, and he longed for God's redress. But the psalm is also to be read in its literary context as the third Miktam. Here, it becomes a powerful prayer for the afflicted who see the ways in which the powerful manipulate circumstances to their own ends, crying out for God to demonstrate his justice by preventing such people from flourishing and demonstrating his justice instead. Such a cry means leaving redress to God alone since it is not ours to enact, perhaps also involving self-examination to determine whether we may also be part of the problem (cf. Maré 2003: 328–330). But with Abraham (Gen. 18:25) we too may look for the judge of all the earth to enact his justice, a hope we express every time we pray 'may your kingdom come'.

PSALM 59

Translation

The director's. Do Not Destroy. Davidic. A Miktam. When Saul sent and they guarded the house to kill him.

1Deliver me from my enemies, O my God,
  secure me from those rising up against me.
2Deliver me from those who work injustice,
  and save me from those who shed blood.
3For look, they lie in ambush for my life,
  mighty ones stir up strife against me,
  for no transgression or sin of mine, O Yahweh.
4Without iniquity of mine they run and prepare themselves,
  stir yourself to meet me and see.
5And you, Yahweh God of Hosts, God of Israel,
  rouse yourself to punish all the nations,
  do not be gracious to all those treacherously enacting evil. *Selah.*

6They return at evening,
they growl like a dog,
as they prowl around the city.
7Look, they pour out with their mouths,
swords in their lips,
'For, who will hear?'

8But you, O Yahweh, laugh at them,
you hold all the nations in derision.
9O my strength, I watch for you,
for you, O God, are my secure refuge.
10My kind God will meet me,
God will let me look on my foes.
11Do not kill them lest my people forget,
make them wander by your might and bring them down,
O Lord, our shield.
12The sin of their mouth, the word of their lips,
let them be caught by their pride,
because of the curses and lies they declare.
13Destroy in anger, destroy so they are no more,
and let them know that God rules in Jacob,
to the ends of the earth. *Selah.*

14They return at evening,
they growl like a dog
as they prowl around the city.
15They wander about for food,
they growl when they are not satisfied.

16But as for me, I will sing of your strength,
and I will cry aloud of your kindness in the morning,
for you are my secure refuge,
and my refuge on the day of trouble.
17O my strength, I will make melody to you,
because God is my secure refuge,
my kind God.

Notes on the text

9. With some MSS and Gk, reading *'uzzî*. Cf. verse 17.
10. With many MSS and Q, reading *ḥasdî*.
15. With Gk, read *wĕyallînû*.

Form and structure

The fourth Miktam in the subunit of Psalms 56–60, this one is also closely aligned to Psalms 57–58 in that each includes 'Do Not Destroy' in the title. Again, it is a prayer from one in need, though it also integrates elements of trust. Beyond this, the psalm also continues other key motifs that run through the subunit, including the 'nations' (v. 8; cf. Pss 56:7; 57:9), portrayal of enemies through animal imagery (vv. 6, 14; cf. 57:4; 58:4), the threat of ambush from the adversaries (v. 3; cf. 56:6; 57:6) and the presence of threatening speech (v. 7; cf. Pss 57:4; 58:3). With Psalm 58:11, there is also a desire that God's rule will be seen and recognized beyond Israel (v. 13). There is also a refrain (vv. 6, 14, and a near refrain in vv. 10, 17; cf. Raabe 1990: 132–133; Forti 2018: 37–39), continuing the pattern seen in Psalms 56–57. However, the title's historical reference now moves to before David's time on the run in the wilderness of Judea, pointing instead to 1 Samuel 19:11 when Saul's messengers were waiting to kill him, but Michal warned him, and he escaped. Goulder (1990: 131) again situates this prayer in David's flight from Absalom (2 Sam. 15:13–37), but this seems determined more by his overriding theory than the text's own evidence.

As well as the refrain, the poem is marked by repeated phrases and key terms that hold it together. There is a small inclusio for the psalm through repetition of the root *śgb* ('secure'; vv. 1, 17), initially occurring as a verb and then as a noun. The noun also occurs in verses 9, 16. The psalm also emphasizes God's 'kindness' (*ḥesed*; vv. 10, 16, 17) and 'strength' (*'ōz*; vv. 9, 16, 17, contrasted with the foes, v. 3). Distribution of these terms and the refrain suggests the following five-stanza structure, one not requiring Seybold's extensive surgery (1996: 235):

1. Appeal for rescue (1–5)
2. Refrain (6–7)
3. Prayer against enemies (8–13)
4. Refrain (14–15)
5. Waiting for Yahweh (16–17)

Comment

Title: For 'The director's', see on Psalm 4. For 'Do Not Destroy', see on Psalm 57. For 'Davidic', see on Psalm 3. For 'Miktam', see on Psalm 16. In 1 Samuel 19:11, Saul decided to kill David after his attempt to have him killed by the Philistines failed. However, though Saul sent troops, David was warned by Michal, who assisted him in escaping, initiating the wilderness period referenced in Psalms 52, 54, 56, 57.

1–5. Prayers for deliverance are relatively common in Psalms (e.g. Pss 7:1; 51:14; 143:9), but only here is it the psalm's opening. The urgency of this need is emphasized by the repetition of the plea in verse 2. The connections between the opening verses go beyond repetition of the appeal, since the two share the same structure, with the appeal in the first part line (including a direct address to God in v. 1) and then a description of the enemies, who are those rising against the poet and shedding blood. These people are not merely seeking to gain an advantage. When they rise against the psalmist, their goal is death. This is described in military terms in verse 3, using the image of an ambush that aims at the psalmist's death. These opponents are noted for their strength and willingness to generate strife for the poet. Unlike Psalm 51, where the poet confesses sin, transgression and iniquity (Ps. 51:3–5), that is denied here. Contextually, this is not a denial of any sin, but rather of any that might legitimately lead to pursuit of the psalmist (e.g. murder). Although the opponents have no basis for their actions, they prepare to act against the poet. The poet's negative confession here is similar to the national statement in Psalm 44:17–22, laying out that there is no basis for God to stand aloof. As there (Ps. 44:23), God is asked to rouse himself and act for the poet's well-being. Notably, the psalmist refers to God by his full covenant name, emphasizing his commitment to Israel and his power to act. It is Yahweh who can change the poet's situation, just as he can change national ones. The prayer is not so much concerned with the nations but rather that if God can bring down nations, then he should withhold grace from those who choose the practice of treachery.

6–7. Within this psalm, the refrain is preceded each time by *selah*. Although this mysterious word's function is unclear, here it seems to provide a structural marker, pointing to a break within the poem. The refrain compares the enemies to dogs (perhaps a contemptuous reference; so Doyle 2004) which come out after dark, prowling around the city, growling at those who get in their way. They are a threat to those who encounter them. Just as the dog's mouth is a source of threat, so also the enemies' mouths create danger, pouring it out with lips that can be likened to swords because of their threats. Although the exact sense of verse 7c is uncertain, it seems to be a summary of their thoughts (cf. R. A. Jacobson 2004: 34). If so, they demonstrate the sort of practical atheism rejected in Psalm 53.

8–13. Practical atheism is also rejected in verse 8, drawing on language that reflects Yahweh's response to the nations in Psalm 2:4. Where Psalm 2 used this language when speaking about Yahweh, here he is directly addressed, reminding him of his role, with the expectation that the enemies should experience this derision. By contrast, the poet watches for Yahweh, seeing him as the place of security. Because of this, the poet expresses confidence in verse 10, anticipating an encounter with the kindly God who will enable the psalmist to look on the adversaries. Nevertheless, in verses 11–13 we encounter requests for God to act against the enemies. This request needs to be understood in the light of the negative confession in verses 1–2. The psalmist is not guilty of an action justifying the death penalty, but those pursuing the poet without a just cause are. This does not require that this psalm be one of the prayers of the accused (see on Ps. 7), but this may still form part of the background. In this case, the psalmist can refer to the 'sin of their mouth' as providing a basis for Yahweh's judgement, though this forms part of a wider pattern of sinful speech. The psalmist wants an appropriate penalty for the crime, though initially it is not death. The reason for this appears to be that it would not witness to God's justice, leading to others forgetting about this aspect of God's character. Rather, some form of exile seems to be imagined, and certainly a loss of the power they have deployed. This should be appropriate to the crime, one where they will be caught out by the things they have said and done. In effect, what they have attempted to inflict on others should be done to them (cf. Deut. 19:16–20). Verse 13 sits in some tension with this since it now asks for their destruction, but in this case the concern has shifted from what Israel may forget to what the world must know. Israel needs a mechanism to remember that God is just, while the world needs to know it. The tension of whether to destroy or not is left to God to resolve, though perhaps verse 13 looks to the ultimate outcome whereas verse 11 is concerned with the short term (cf. Longman 2014: 238).

14–15. The refrain recurs here, effectively pointing God once more to observe the actions of the enemies. However, although the canine imagery in verse 14 is the same as verse 6, there is a shift in verse 15 that now focuses on the image of food. In effect, people like the psalmist are under threat of destruction by the enemies, just as food is destroyed in the act of eating. The growling of the dogs returns to the theme of what comes out of their mouth, pointing to the abiding threat they pose.

16–17. The enemies' words are threatening, but by contrast the psalmist's words offer worship that affirms the truth of God's identity. The enemies may threaten, but God is strong, and his strength is matched to his kindness. All this the psalmist declares in song, even in times of distress. The morning is the appropriate time for this because the dogs who come in the evening have failed. This praise is possible because God is the one who provides security, a place of refuge in distress. Melodic praise can be offered because God is strong, a place of security, and kind. The psalm closes with speech which affirms the hope that Yahweh gives, a hope Israel needs to remember, and the world needs to know.

Explanation

Read against the background of 1 Samuel 19:11, the psalm provides additional perspectives to those in Samuel (cf. V. L. Johnson 2009: 41). Most importantly, where Samuel stresses Michal's involvement, the psalm makes clear that it was Yahweh who acted for David. These are not contradictory – God can and does work through people. But where Samuel reflects on the human dimension, the psalm points to the divine. Within the subunit of Psalms 56–60, this psalm provides a further example of the combination of petition and trust, a passionate desire that God should act, and a firm resolve that he does. It now wants those elements brought together. It knows that the faithful may suffer unwarranted attacks, but also insists that God alone is our security, and it is God's kindness that makes his security available to us (cf. Vosloo 1987: 233). We pray urgently that God will act against those forces that act against his justice so that all the ends of the world will know of his reign, again asking that God's kingdom comes.

PSALM 60

Translation

The director's. According to Shushan-Eduth. A Miktam. Davidic. To teach. When he struggled with Aram-Naharaim and Aram-Zobah, and Joab turned and struck twelve thousand Edomites in Salt Valley.

1O God, you have rejected us, you have breached us,
you have been angry – may you restore us!
2You shook the earth, you split it open,
heal its fissures because it sways.
3You have made your people see hard things,
you made us drink wine that intoxicates.
4Grant those who fear you a banner where they can flee,
from before the bow. *Selah.*
5So that your beloved ones may be delivered,
save by your right hand and answer me.

6God has spoken in his holiness,
'I will triumph, I will apportion Shechem,
and the valley of Sukkoth I will measure off.
7Gilead is mine and Manasseh is mine,
while Ephraim is my head's protection,
Judah is my commander's sceptre.
8Moab is my wash pot,
over Edom I cast my shoe,
unto me, O Philistia, shout in triumph.'

9Who will conduct me to the fortified city,
who will bring me to Edom?

[10]Have not you, O God, rejected us?
You do not go out, O God, with our armies!
[11]Grant us help from the foe,
for human deliverance is worthless.
[12]With God we can do valiantly,
and he himself could trample down our foes.

Notes on the text

Title: 'Shushan-Eduth' could be the Lily of Testimony (cf. the similar title of Ps. 80). Gk has David's 'burning' rather fighting these sites.

4. With Hossfeld and Zenger (2006: 93) understanding *nātatâ* as a prec. pf. (see W-O §30.4.5.c–d).

5. *lĕmaʿan* could conclude the previous verse, but the *selah* suggests it introduces a new clause, the completion of which is found in verse 5b. With many MSS and Q, read *waʿănēnî* (cf. Ps. 108:6). The sg. here is unexpected, making this *lectio difficilior*.

8. Often emended (with one MS and Syr., with Ps. 108:9) to *'etrôʿāʿ*, but we need to allow for the distinct concerns of each poem, and MT is plausible.

12. With Tate (1990: 84), reading the verbs modally.

Form and structure

The final Miktam in the subunit of Psalms 56–60, this poem brings the 'nations' motif to a climax through its focus on peoples in Israel's vicinity (cf. Vesco 2006, 2: 532–533). There is also an immediate connection with Psalm 59:5, where Yahweh is the God of hosts (i.e. armies) and here is asked to go out with Israel's armies (v. 10). Yet it also marks a decisive shift in that where the preceding psalms were individual laments with some corporate elements, this is a communal lament with some individual elements. Yet, just as Psalm 55 was a bridge between Psalms 52–55 and 56–60, so also Psalm 60 is a bridge into the next subunit, Psalms 61–64. Perhaps the most important connection is that the individual who appears here (vv. 5, 9) is probably best understood as the king, a figure of particular concern in what follows (Pss 61:6; 63:11).

As a communal complaint it joins with prayers such as Psalm 44 (cf. Pss 44:9; 60:1), which not only ask God to resolve a conflict, but also place the blame for the situation on him (see Broyles 1989: 144–149). This complaint is particularly concerned with military threats faced by the nation, but the possibility of the victory Yahweh might win is illustrated by the victory mentioned in the title. The exact reference, though, is unclear, as it seems to draw together elements from 2 Samuel

8:3, 13–14 and 10:9–13. Perhaps the intent is to point to a range of prior victories, all of which make the current situation more challenging. With only minor variations, verses 5–12 are repeated in Psalm 108:6–13. In that Psalm 108:1–5 is basically Psalm 57:7–11, it most likely borrows from this poem.

The poem can be analysed into three stanzas. The *selah* could support dividing the first into two strophes, but this is not essential, though it also allows verse 5 to act as a bridge between the stanzas:

1. Opening appeals and complaint (1–5)
2. Divine oracle (6–8)
3. Closing prayer (9–12)

Comment

Title: For 'The director's', see on Psalm 4. 'Shushan-Eduth' (cf. 'Notes on the text') is unique to this psalm, though Psalm 80's title is similar. For 'Davidic', see on Psalm 3. For 'Miktam', see on Psalm 16. 'To teach' is also unique to this psalm, though Goldingay (2007: 226) notes the similarity to 2 Samuel 1:18. The historical reference makes this the Psalter's longest title. On the setting implied, see 'Form and structure' above.

1–5. Unlike Psalm 44, which opens by presenting a record of the good things God has done, this psalm opens with accusations against God. Two verbs point to the evidence for this, noting that God has spurned and breached the nation, leading to the third, which explains this – God is angry with them. Yet no reason is given for this. As with Psalm 44, the community cannot understand why they are suffering, and so appeal to God for restoration. That is, they wish once more to be in a right relationship with him and to be complete. Yet this wish faces immediate challenges, which are outlined in verses 2–3. The breaches God made in the nation are replicated in the land, which is also split open. The shaking of the earth could refer to an earthquake, though a metaphorical reading is also possible. On either reading, the land needs healing. The breaches, both national and physical, are a challenge for the people to see (likened to the time of the Exodus, Exod. 1:14) and are attributed to God through the image of God's making the nation drink intoxicating wine. As with Psalm 75:8 this wine is an act of judgement that, through its intoxication (literally 'wine of reeling'), caused the defeat. The appeal to God becomes more direct in verses 4–5. First, verse 4 considers the context of battle, asking for a banner to which the defeated can flee and find safety. This probably draws on Exodus 17:14–15 (cf. Isa. 11:10–12), where the banner is a symbol of Yahweh's victory and perhaps a link to his throne. Yet this security is not for all; rather, it is those who fear God who should be able to access this. If so, then the second request (on behalf of God's beloved) is also concerned that those who relate appropriately to God be delivered. Here, the psalm unexpectedly introduces an individual figure whose deliverance will point to the people's deliverance. God needs to save through his right hand; that is, visibly act; and this finds its focus in this individual. As the psalm was prayed in liturgy, this might have been a worship leader, but the king is the one whose deliverance could represent the nation, making the latter the most likely candidate. God is summoned to save the king and, through this, demonstrate hope for all who fear God.

6–8. A further unexpected element is introduced with the second stanza through the citation (shifting to tricola) of a divine oracle (cf. Ps. 50). C. E. Anderson (2015: 317) argues the oracle continues to verse 9 (cf. Ogden 1985: 84), but this seems to confuse the linking of the oracle to the rest of the poem with the oracle itself. The citation's function is debated (see R. A. Jacobson 2004: 114–118). It could be a salvation oracle (e.g. Miller 1994: 172), an interpretation strengthened if we understand 'in holiness' as 'in the sanctuary' and so interpret it as a word of assurance given by a prophet there. Yet, we might expect to move into a statement of confidence in what follows if this were the case, but the third stanza instead returns to an appeal. If so, it seems more likely that the poet cites an earlier message from God (which, as Hilber 2005: 194–202, argues, is still an oracle) to convince God to act. That God has spoken in his holiness is evidence that it is trustworthy, and therefore words that provide the basis for an appeal. Fundamentally, the oracle asserts God's control over all territories, something achieved by moving from Israelite-controlled areas to other peoples. God's triumph is certain, and evidence for this is seen in his sovereignty over land and peoples. Shechem, a town in Israel's central highlands (about 40 miles [64 km] north of Jerusalem), is perhaps mentioned first because it was the place where Yahweh had appeared to Abraham and promised the land (Gen. 12:6–7). The valley of Sukkoth is east of the Jordan, north of the Jabbok and where Jacob built a house before heading to Shechem (Gen. 33:17–18). Hence, God controls and allots land both inside and outside the territory initially promised to Abraham. Gilead is also east of the Jordan, while Manasseh is a bridge-tribe, with territory on either side of the Jordan, and both belong to God. Ephraim, in the central highlands and the tribe to which Shechem was allotted, was the dominant northern tribe, while Judah was dominant in the south. Both serve the divine warrior. God's reign goes beyond his own people, so that Moab and Edom (both east of the Jordan) and Philistia (to the south-west) are also subject to his reign, even if they do not recognize it and have much more subservient positions.

9–12. Given God's sovereignty, the third stanza returns to an appeal, initially through two rhetorical questions. Faced with military conflict, the poet asks about being led to a fortified city or Edom. Neither is immediately accessible but mention of Edom in the oracle means that it should be possible to enter. God can bring the psalmist to these places. But the second rhetorical question challenges this. The promise of the oracle is not being realized, and indeed God does not go out with Israel's armies. Victory cannot be won under those circumstances. Neither can God's help be replaced by any human forces. Only God's help is sufficient, and with God's help victory can be won. Indeed, it is God, not the king or Israel's army, that wins.

Explanation

As the only psalm 'for teaching' this poem has a special function. The background against which the title encourages us to read it stresses that David won victories only because Yahweh had given them. Even Israel's greatest king did not win because of his might or military skill. This background is fundamental to how the psalm is read, reminding all readers that only through God is victory won by God's people (cf. Brueggemann and Bellinger 2014: 267). This poem also challenges God to act on his word, even when he seems to have spurned his people, though the prayer for healing may acknowledge a need on their part to turn back to God. By ending with hope, this psalm brings the nation into line with the individuals in Psalms 56–59 who retain hope even in complaint. Here, hope exists as people and God realign themselves in their covenant faithfulness to each other, a hope that takes particular shape today when we see God's covenant commitment in the cross.

PSALM 61

Translation

The director's. On stringed instruments. Davidic.

[1]Hear, O God, my shout,
  attend to my prayer.
[2]I cry to you from the end of the earth,
  while my heart is faint,
  O lead me to the rock that is higher than I!
[3]For you have been my refuge,
  a strong tower in the presence of the enemy.
[4]May I sojourn for ever in your tent,
  may I find refuge in the shelter of your wings. *Selah.*

[5]For you, O God, have heard my vows,
you gave me the heritage of those who fear your name.
[6]May you add days to the king's days,
his years as generation to generation.
[7]May he dwell for ever before God,
appoint kindness and truth that they may guard him.
[8]So may I make melody to your name for ever,
fulfilling my vows daily.

Notes on the text

4, 8. The cohort. verbs could point to a settled resolve ('I will sojourn'), but a wish (*WHS* §184a) seems more probable. For the alternative view, see Goldingay 2007: 238–239.

Form and structure

Psalm 61's title immediately marks it out as distinct from the preceding psalms, the last five of which were a 'Miktam', while the four before were each a 'Maskil'. As such, it initiates a new subunit that runs through to Psalm 64, with this subunit bounded by the 'refuge' motif with which this psalm opens and Psalm 64 closes (Pss 61:1–4; 64:10). Psalms 61 and 64 also open with an appeal for God to 'Hear' the psalmist. These psalms continue the pattern of appeal and confidence that marks the whole of Psalms 52–60, so that the closing advice of Psalm 64:10 can then generalize this for all worshippers (cf. Ps. 62:8), though this subunit is also marked by a longing for God (Hamilton 2021, 1: 560).

Although it can be read as a complaint psalm, this is another example of a poem breaking the boundaries of form criticism as it moves from an initial appeal to a reflection on a point where God has acted for the poet, and then a further appeal for the king. Read through the figure of David, the royal appellant speaks of his reign in the third person, though these words are now a prayer that can be taken up by all worshippers (though Weber [1993] attempts to link them to Hezekiah).

Bellinger (1999; cf. Auffret 1997: 39–44) has demonstrated that different interpretative approaches to the psalm can lead to differing structures. However, it is sufficient here to analyse the psalm in two stanzas, pivoting on the *selah*:

1. Appeal for refuge (1–4)
2. Prayer for the king (5–8)

Comment

Title: For 'The director's', see on Psalm 4. 'On stringed instruments' is a slight variation on the title of Psalms 4, 6, 54, 55, 67, 76, 77. For 'Davidic', see on Psalm 3.

1–4. The psalm opens with an urgent appeal for God to hear and attend to the poet. There is an urgency expressed here to which God must respond, though the cause is never stated. The 'shout' can be an act of worship (e.g. Pss 42:4; 47:1) but when combined with 'prayer' here is clearly a cry for help since the 'prayer' is more typically a call for divine aid (e.g. 1 Kgs 8:38; Ps. 102:17; Jon. 2:8). The reason for the psalmist's prayer being a shout is that it comes from a remote place, 'the end of the earth' being hyperbole (likewise, A. P. Ross 2013: 353) for somewhere far from the sanctuary. In this place, the psalmist admits to a faint heart, best understood as a loss of general vitality. The heart can refer to the place of thought (e.g. Ps. 14:1; Isa. 47:10), but can also speak of emotions, especially of suffering (e.g. Pss 38:9; 55:4). Remote from God and support, the poet asks to be led to the higher rock; that is, into God's presence. The image of God as rock is often linked to the idea of refuge (e.g. Ps. 18:2) because to be high on a rock was to be away from enemies (Fernandes 2013: 202). Just as a soldier high on a cliff is away from enemies, so also the psalmist desires to be in a place of security with God. The image of refuge is further developed with another defensive image, comparing God to a strong tower in the presence of the enemy, making this a place where one cannot be reached (Judg. 9:51–52). Nevertheless, as verse 4 makes clear, the refuge the psalmist desires is found in the sanctuary. Although the sanctuary was not an obvious place of military security (though its location at Mount Zion was militarily secure) in that it was not fortified, it was the ultimate place of security because it pointed to God's presence among his people (cf. 1 Kgs 8:27–30). Hence, the psalmist asks to sojourn in the sanctuary (here described as a tent) because this means being in God's presence (cf. Ps. 27:4). Being under God's wings can be a general metaphor, though it may also refer to the wings of the cherubim in the heart of the temple (1 Kgs 6:27) as the place where sanctuary was claimed (cf. Pss 17:8; 36:7; 57:1; 91:4). One need not choose between these options, as the sanctuary may represent the model of refuge, but that refuge can be given even at the ends of the earth.

5–8. Where God was asked to hear in the first stanza, the second begins by noting that God has previously heard the psalmist. The poet previously made vows God heard because he responded by granting the psalmist a share in the heritage of those who fear God. Elsewhere, that heritage is typically land (e.g. Deut. 2:5; Josh. 12:6–7), but a relationship with God is more in focus here. That God previously heard the psalmist leads to a request for an extended life for the king before requesting that he dwell in God's presence for ever. The psalmist's own hope has been to sojourn, but the king should be able to dwell in God's presence. These verbs echo Psalm 15:1, where they are broadly synonymous, and the same is probably true here. But where the prayer for the king goes beyond the psalmist's own wish is that God is also asked to appoint kindness and truth that they may guard the king. These characteristics are central to God's self-description (Exod. 34:6–7) and his way of relating to his people. At one level, the request is simply that God will act as he has said he will, but that God is asked to 'appoint' these elements of his character indicates a request that asks for this in special measure. Moreover, as God works for the well-being of the king, so this will create a context for the psalmist to engage in continued worship, both through music and continued fulfilment of vows. If the king can dwell securely in God's presence, then this is also possible for the psalmist.

Explanation

Initiating a new subunit that covers Psalms 61–64, this psalm starts from a position of distance from both God and the sanctuary while urgently desiring to be in God's presence there. To be with God is to be secure. As such, it could be the prayer of a pilgrim heading to the temple (Broyles 1999: 256), though if so, it is a pilgrim who knows that being away from God's presence represents a danger that is not experienced with him. Yet, this worshipper also knows that God has heard previous prayers, so the journey towards God can be made with hope. What is remarkable is that this prayer is united to a prayer for the king, one that asks for a special measure of God's presence to be with him. This recognizes that the king was a key means of God's bringing blessing to his people, even though the psalm also acknowledges that this is not the only way God works. The prayer for the king is here especially stressed because the psalmist desires to continue offering praise to God. God's goodness can be encountered directly in the poet's experience, but it may also be mediated through the king. After the exile, a prayer such as this took on a more obviously messianic dimension (though this is already present), asking for God's promise to be realized in the life of his people. The NT makes clear that this king has come in Jesus, and that through him God's people may continually enter his presence (Heb. 10:19–25).

PSALM 62

Translation

The director's. Upon Jeduthun. A melody. Davidic.

1 In God alone is my being's satisfaction,
my salvation is from him.
2 He alone is my rock and my salvation,
my high refuge – I will not be shaken greatly.

3 How long will you threaten someone,
permitting murder, all of you,
like a leaning wall,
a tottering fence?
4 They plan only to thrust someone down from their high position,
they take pleasure in lies,
with the mouth they bless,
but within themselves they revile. *Selah.*

5 Wait calmly for God alone, O my being,
for my hope is from him.
6 He alone is my rock and my salvation,
my high refuge – I will not be shaken.
7 On God is my salvation and my glory,
my mighty rock, my refuge is in God.

8 Trust in him at all times, O people,
pour out your heart before him,
God is our refuge. *Selah.*
9 Humans are a mere breath,
mortals a lie,
going up on the scales,
together they are merely a breath.
10 Do not trust in extortion,
do not put vain hope in robbery.
Wealth? When it bears fruit,
do not set your mind on it.

11 One thing God has spoken,
two things have I heard,
that might belongs to God,
12 and kindness belongs to you, O Lord,
for you repay mortals according to their deeds.

Notes on the text

1. *dûmîyâ* is typically understood as 'silence' and extrapolated to silent waiting (aligning this with the similar v. 5), but *DCH* notes *dûmîyâ* II can mean 'response, satisfaction', which is more coherent here.

3. *hût* occurs nowhere else, but an Arabic cognate means 'to shout at'. With some MSS, treating *rṣḥ* as pi. rather than pu., but the phrase remains awkward and is here understood as tolerative (*WHS* §142).

9. NIV is representative of translations that assume a contrast between 'lowborn' and 'highborn' (cf. Ps. 49:1), but it is difficult to find examples where the terms mean this, and a synonymous sense is preferable (cf. NET). The *min* is understood here as explicative (*WHS* §326).

Form and structure

Psalm 62 develops several key motifs established in Psalm 61, most importantly the understanding of God as rock (Pss 61:2; 62:2, 6–7), security (Pss 61:3; 62:6) and refuge (Pss 61:3; 62:7). Slightly less obviously, the statement that God is a 'strong' tower (Ps. 61:3) finds an echo in the closing assertion of God's might (Ps. 62:11). This combination of elements provides strong links between these two poems. Though the royal element of Psalm 61 is omitted here, along with a focus on the sanctuary, both recur in Psalm 63.

Once again, this is a poem that breaks the boundaries of the standard form-critical categories. Certainly, elements of complaint are strongly present (vv. 3–4), but alongside this are declarations of trust (vv. 1–2, 5–7), while admonitions to an audience (vv. 8–10) and a closing affirmation of faith (vv. 11–12) show at least some association with wisdom traditions. How and why these various elements come together is much discussed. Kraus (1989: 13), for example, emphasizes complaint and so assigns this psalm to the prayers of the accused (cf. Seybold 1996: 244). If so, we no longer have access to all the elements of the ritual. Hossfeld and Zenger (2006: 112–113; cf. A. P. Ross 2013: 364–365) prefer to emphasize trust. They see the Song of Confidence as having emerged from the complaint, so that the presence of complaint motifs is not unsurprising. The wisdom elements would then encourage a wider audience to share the psalmist's confidence. Perhaps we should think of the psalm as a public meditation in which an audience is invited to place itself in a position of waiting on God in the face of difficulties before being challenged to focus primarily on God (similarly, Broyles 1999: 258). Such a reading puts the primary focus on the wisdom elements (or 'near wisdom', Tate 1990: 120), an approach that may be strengthened when we note that God is not addressed before verse 12, while the rest addresses an audience. This approach still allows for the elements of complaint and trust but sees them as serving the wisdom elements with which the psalm concludes. Botha (2018c) sees this as most appropriate to the post-exilic period, but the poem's themes are applicable across a range of settings.

The psalm uses a range of rhetorical devices, the most notable of which is the use of *'ak* (surely, alone) to open verses 1–2, 4–6 and 9, though other repetitions are present, including a near-refrain (vv. 1–2, 5–6) and the motifs noted above in common with Psalm 61. These elements result in a complex range of structuring devices, but it is still possible to analyse the psalm in two stanzas, with three strophes in the first and two in the second:

1. Trust and complaint (1–7)
   a. Trust in face of threat (1–2)
   b. Threat outlined (3–4)
   c. Reaffirmation of trust (5–7)
2. Admonitions and affirmations (8–12)
   a. Admonitions about trust (8–10)
   b. Affirmation of God's power (11–12)

Comment

Title: For 'The director's', see on Psalm 4. For 'Jeduthun', see on Psalm 39, though the preposition here differs, and could suggest 'according to Jeduthun's style'. For 'a melody' and 'Davidic', see on Psalm 3.

1–2. The opening verses are marked by the paired *'ak* (alone) with which each begins, with both pointing to God as the poet's sole focus. Verse 1's declaration of finding satisfaction in God alone plays with the verb at the start of verse 5 with its emphasis on waiting calmly (or perhaps silently) and is often translated that way – there may be intentional ambiguity here. That God alone is the psalmist's focus enables a listing of what God means for the worshipper as the source of salvation and security. Salvation here refers to deliverance from contemporary threats, something achieved through the security God provides as 'rock', a secure place out of the reach of threatening forces (cf. Fernandes 2013: 31). This is why the psalmist is sure that life will not be seriously disturbed.

3–4. The confidence expressed in the opening verses is not an abstract truth. Rather, it is expressed in a setting of threat against the community. This is made clear as those who may disturb the faithful are addressed in verse 3 (the verb is pl.). The opening 'how long' indicates that these people have been active for some time, representing a significant challenge to the faithful, especially as they act corporately against an individual in their threats while also enabling more significant expressions of violence (even murder). The second half of verse 3 is obscure, but the sense could be that their actions leave the righteous vulnerable to falling in some way. Verse 5 returns to *'ak* (alone) while now speaking to the audience about the violent. Where the poet was focused on God alone, they are focused only on finding ways of bringing people down, using lies and deceitful speech to do so. This is not mere opportunism, for they 'plan' such actions, indicating the presence of structural violence that might today be called 'organized crime'.

5–7. Despite the threat outlined, the poet continues to wait calmly. Verses 5–6 are close to verses 1–2, though this time the imp. verb allows the poet to provide a self-directive. Threats exist, but God alone needs to be the psalmist's focus. A further development from the opening is the declaration that God is also the psalmist's 'hope'. God is the one who provides the possibility of a meaningful future in a world of threat. This is why verse 6 can largely replicate verse 1, but with the removal of 'greatly'. Where the opening allowed for the possibility of some shaking, even this is now removed because of the security God provides. All this is summarized in verse 7 (while anticipating vv. 8–12; so McCann 1996: 923), again with developments. God not only provides salvation; he is also the psalmist's 'glory', the one who provides dignity in life. God is not only a 'rock'; he is a 'mighty' rock, one that cannot be overcome by the violent. As a refuge, God is thus secure.

8–10. The address to the audience now takes on an admonitory tone, encouraging them to learn from the poet's statements. In the presence of violence, it is easy to be drawn to violence as the means of resistance. Instead, they are told that just as the poet has waited on God alone, so they are always to trust in God. This admonition is at home in Proverbs (e.g. Prov. 3:5–6), and echoes Psalm 37:3. The congregation are to acknowledge very real threats, but to look to God as their source of security. In pouring out their hearts before him, they bring before God their experience of threat, knowing that God is their refuge (cf. Ps. 46:1). By contrast, human hope is 'vapid' (*hebel*; often translated 'vanity' in Ecclesiastes; e.g. Eccl. 1:2). Their value is no more than that of a single breath and is often deceptive, so that when humans are placed on a set of scales (cf. Isa. 40:15) they weigh no more than a 'breath' (*hebel*). Others are no help, and equally adopting the methods of the powerful is to be avoided since placing trust in extortion and robbery is also 'vapid' (the adjective from *hbl*). That these methods may seem to offer some benefit is not denied, but the psalmist suggests that thought is not to be given to them because this is simply replicating the source of the problems.

11–12. The number pattern of x, x + 1 is also at home in the wisdom literature (e.g. Prov. 30:18–19; cf. Roth 1962), though its use across Amos 1:3 – 2:16 shows it can be used more broadly. Amos uses a 3, 4 pattern, mostly reporting only one item rather than three or four, though the cited item is the crucial example. Likewise, the 1, 2 pattern here indicates that God has often spoken, but the psalmist will recount only the one that matters most (unless the colon runs to v. 12a) – in this case that might belongs to God. This provides hope for the wider community, the very thing for which the psalmist has waited. This is reported to the community, but in verse 12 the psalmist turns to address God (though the community still hears) and confesses God's 'kindness' (*ḥesed*). It is this kindness that is manifested in his repaying of humans for their deeds, whether good or evil. In a world where violence can easily be perpetuated, this psalm asserts instead that trusting God and confessing his power is how violence is ended, most especially because God's might is shaped by his kindness.

Explanation

Developing themes from Psalm 61, this poem asks a congregation to reflect on the challenge of living faithfully in a world filled with violence. It asks believers to focus on God alone and to understand that their hope is in him alone. Yet it also understands the temptation to respond to violence with violence, either our own or by associating with others who continue it. But it helps us to work through that temptation and so understand that God alone is our hope and that, however attractive some form of human support may be, it is of no ultimate value. God's might is great, yet is also shaped by kindness in a way that no human approach ever is. Hope is trusting God to respond, something Paul understood both in general (Rom. 2:6) and also in his personal experience (2 Tim. 4:14), demonstrating that the NT also understands the important ways a psalm like this breaks cycles of violence (see also K.-S. Kim 2011).

PSALM 63

Translation

A melody. Davidic. When he was in the wilderness of Judah.

1 O God, you are my God, I long for you,
  my being thirsts for you,
my flesh yearns for you,
  in a dry and weary land without water.
2 For in the sanctuary I have beheld you,
  seeing your might and glory.
3 Because your kindness is better than life
  my lips shall laud you.

4So shall I bless you through my life,
in your name shall I lift my hands.

5My being shall be satisfied with fine and rich food,
with exultant lips my mouth shall praise.
6I remember you upon my bed,
in the watches of the night, I meditate on you.
7Because you have been my helper,
and in the shadow of your wings, I shout out.

8My being clings to you,
your right hand upholds me.
9But those seeking my being's ruin,
shall go to the lowest places of the earth,
10they shall be delivered over to the power of the sword,
they shall be a portion for jackals.

11But the king shall rejoice in God,
all who swear an oath by him shall boast,
when the mouth of those speaking falsehood is stopped.

Notes on the text

1. Some MSS read *k* for *b*, but if *b* is beth of identity (*WHS* §249) then the result is the same.

10. Though Gk and Syr. both suggest a hoph. (*yuggĕrû*), the hiph. is retained. The suffix is distributive (W-O §7.2.3), indicating that each one will experience this.

Form and structure

The third poem in the subunit of Psalms 61–64, this poem extends the motif of confidence developed in Psalm 62. Confidence there was expressed in a context of threat, though that element is largely left behind here. Most importantly, the declaration that God has been the poet's helper (v. 7) now confirms the exhortations to trust in Psalm 62, except this is now expressed to God rather to than an audience. The motif of God's might is now tied to the experience of worship in the sanctuary (v. 2, but without this needing to be linked to the claiming of asylum; so Seybold 1996: 248), but this closely echoes the references to this theme in Psalms 61:3 and 62:11. The links with Psalm 61 are also developed through reference to the king, again in the third person (Pss 61:6–7; 63:11), and the motif of shelter under God's wings (Pss 61:4;

63:7), though where the earlier reference was in the context of refuge, now it is a place to shout praise. The shout in Psalm 61:1 was a prayer of need, but now it is praise. And unlike those who blessed outwardly but really reviled (Ps. 62:4), this poet can look forward to a life of blessing God (Ps. 63:4). This psalm not only extends the confidence motif from Psalm 62; it also shows that the prayer of Psalm 61 is answered.

The poem itself is predominantly an expression of confidence in God, a demonstration of the trust encouraged in Psalm 62. Elements of threat are not strongly present this time, though the opening image of being in a dry land presumes that not all have the same desire for God as the poet. Likewise, that the poet clings to God acknowledges that there are real threats. That there are at least some who seek the psalmist's life is also noted, though even this is in an expression of confidence (vv. 9–10). Rather, the psalm focuses on the poet's longing for God and anticipation of future times when God will again help.

The poem can be analysed in four stanzas. The first three are marked by focus on the psalmist's 'being' (*nepeš*; traditionally 'soul', though this is rather misleading) before switching to the king in a closing verse. There are also numerous wordplays across these units:

1. Longing for God (1–4)
2. Satisfied by God (5–7)
3. Clinging to God (8–10)
4. King's rejoicing (11)

Comment

Title: For 'a melody' and 'Davidic', see on Psalm 3. David was in the wilderness of Judah while on the run from Saul (1 Sam. 22 – 26), though it could also refer to when he fled from Absalom and prepared to cross the Jordan (2 Sam. 16:14). Consistent with his model, Goulder (1990: 163) places the psalm slightly later, in the siege of Mahanaim, but the connections there are slight.

1–4. Psalm 54:1 also opens with a voc. (O God) but whereas that is a complaint, this one immediately moves in a different direction. Israel's world was one where many deities were known, but the psalmist here confesses that Israel's God alone was to be served. This was not simply a matter of naming the deity to which one was attached. Rather, the poet expresses a deep longing for relationship with God that is compared to thirst and hunger in a dry land. Finding food and drink under those circumstances is challenging and leads to a deep desire for them, and the poet's desire for God is like that (cf. Pss 42:1–2; 84:2; see Zieba 2010: 160–200). This longing is contrasted with previous experiences in the sanctuary where God's might and glory have been visible in some way, perhaps as a vision. Recalling this reminds the poet of God's 'kindness' (*ḥesed*). This kindness is better than life (perhaps in the sense of that which sustains life; so Goldingay 2007: 258), leading the psalmist to report that this leads to ongoing worship. This worship is fully embodied, just as the desire for God was embodied in verses 1–2. Praise is embodied through the activity of lips in speaking praise, blessing God throughout life, and by hands lifted up at God's name. The lips and hands here speak of the whole person's engagement in worship so that the valued life is a worshipful life (cf. van Rooy 2021: 136).

5–7. Embodied experience continues through the second stanza, with this one bounded by references to the psalmist's shouts of praise. There is also an important contrast with the first stanza. There, the poet speaks of a longing for God when seemingly separated in some way from him. By contrast, this stanza anticipates the point when the poet will be satisfied by God, an experience likened to having feasted on the finest foods (cf. Lev. 7:15–16) and that would lead to the poet's lips engaging in shouts of praise. This is not yet the poet's experience, which means that memory of previous encounters with God guides the psalmist. This too is embodied, as memory happens through the watches of the night (i.e. the point where guards would change) during which the poet meditates on God. There is an echo here of Psalm 1:2, where the righteous meditate on God's Torah, marking the poet here as among the righteous. However, this meditation goes beyond that of Psalm 1 and makes God himself the focal point. Such meditation allows the psalmist to recall points where God has indeed been the poet's helper, and that being in the shadow of God's wings (understood both as a reference to the temple and more generally to God's protection; see above on Ps. 61:4) continues to create a context for shouts of praise. That the recollection alone leads to praise makes it less likely that there is a reference here to a formal vigil in the sanctuary (see Ceresko 1980) since the intent would be for some sign from God were that the case.

8–10. Only in the third stanza are the psalmist's enemies introduced, though there is no complaint made against them. Rather, the sense of embodiment that has run through the first two stanzas recurs, this time covering the psalmist and God while demonstrating the implications of God's help on the adversaries. The psalmist's life is one that clings to God, just as a married couple cling to one another (Gen. 2:24) or Ruth clings to Naomi (Ruth 1:14). Elsewhere in Psalms, the verb 'cling' (*dbq*) refers to things a psalmist would set aside (Pss 101:3; 119:125), though it can also represent a commitment to remain faithful (Ps. 119:31). The force of this clinging is emphasized by the fact that the psalmist (literally) clings 'after you'. The phrase here points to a determination to stay on God's path, as did Caleb (Num. 14:24; Josh. 14:8–9), even in challenging circumstances. The poet's dedication is matched by God's faithfulness, his right hand sustaining the psalmist. Mention of the right hand points to the favourable way God has acted (cf. Gen. 48:13–18; Ps. 45:5; Isa. 41:13). That God acts favourably towards the psalmist (as one committed to him) means that the adversaries have excluded themselves from God's favour because they are, in effect, acting against God. Even though they seek the psalmist's life, they cannot succeed and so will be destroyed, led to the lowest parts of the underworld. This will not be an untroubled end, as they are not only handed over to the power of the sword, but also become food for jackals. The allusion is probably to those left unburied following a military defeat.

11. As with Psalm 61:6–7, the experience of the faithful individual is linked to that of the king. The king, unlike the psalmist's enemies, can rejoice in God. Alongside the king, all who swear an oath 'by him' can 'boast' (*hll* often has the sense of praise, and this is not misplaced bragging). But who is the 'him' in this case, as it could refer either to the king or to God? As God's designate, it could be that people swear their oath by the king, though in this case the value of such an oath is still given by God. More likely, then, these people swear by God, committing themselves in the same way as was expected for the king (even if not always followed). Their boasts, therefore, are that they are sustained just as God sustains the king. This boasting is not abstract but again embodied, this time by the mouth of those speaking falsehood being stopped up. The poet anticipates speech that offers praise, and the basis for that praise will be evident when speech that misrepresents both God and the world is stopped.

Explanation

Whether on the run from Saul or Absalom, David's life was often under threat. The accounts in Samuel do not reflect at length on David's relationship with God, and that gap is filled here. In both of those times he was in a dry and weary land, and in both it was God who ultimately sustained him. That sustenance, and the worship that follows from it, is notable for its fully embodied nature. Human longing for God is not simply a matter of cultivating an inner life; rather, desire for God and the satisfaction he gives are experienced in the whole of our being. The worship that emerges in response to this is likewise fully embodied, integrating reflection and expression. All this emerges from the knowledge that God's kindness is better than life, something Paul shows he understands in Philippians 1:21 (cf. Terrien 2003, 2: 464). Paul there can face the possibility of death with confidence because he knows what God has done in Christ. Although not demonstrating the hope of resurrection that Paul does, the psalm also encourages the faithful that they can continue to trust God in the face of adversity that addresses the whole of their being. For Christians, reflection on the king leads us to consider Jesus as the one who rejoices and who ultimately defeats all that is false.

PSALM 64

Translation

The director's. A melody. Davidic.

1Hear, O God, my voice in my complaint,
guard my life from the dread of the enemy.
2Hide me from the scheme of evildoers,
from the throng of those enacting injustice.

3Because they sharpen their tongue like a sword,
they draw their arrow of bitter speech!
4Shooting the blameless from hiding places,
they shoot suddenly and do not fear.
5They harden themselves with an evil word,
they talk about hidden snares,
they say, 'Who will see them?'
6They plot perversities,
'We have completed a well-planned plot.'
Both someone's inner person and thought is unfathomable.

7But God will shoot them,
with a sudden arrow they are wounded.
8So those who would make another stumble – their tongue is against them!
All who look on them will shudder.
9Then shall all people fear,
and they shall declare the deeds of God,
and they shall ponder his work.

10The righteous shall rejoice in Yahweh and take refuge in him,
and all the upright of heart shall exult.

Notes on the text

3. Normally, one draws (lit. 'treads') the bow, but the expression here is elliptical, so emendation is unnecessary (see Emerton 1976).

5. NRSV reads, 'Who can see us?', but Syr. is an insufficient basis for the change.

6. The citation is unmarked but the accentuation divides the part line, and the parallel with the end of verse 5 indicates that this too represents words attributed to the evildoers. Hossfeld and Zenger (2006: 128) argue the citation goes to the end of the verse, but it is equally plausible for this to be the psalmist's own observation.

7. NIV, ESV and NRSV change the accentuation to make God's shooting sudden, but MT's accentuation can be retained. The verbs here are understood as expressions of confidence (GKC §111w).

8. The first half of the verse is obscure. The translation attempts to make sense of MT in the absence of a persuasive alternative – Barré's (1996) otherwise attractive proposal fails because of the need to introduce the name Yahweh here. Rather than 'shudder' (from *nwd*), BDB proposes 'flee' (from *ndd*). This is not attested in hithpol. Given the verb's low frequency, this is not determinate, but preference is given to the attested form.

Form and structure

Psalm 64 closes the subunit of Psalms 61–64, its closing inclusion of the 'refuge' motif tying it to Psalm 61:1–3. Although slightly cryptic here (v. 6), it also picks up on the contrast between the inner and outer person from Psalm 62:4. That God protects life here (v. 1) also echoes the statement in Psalm 63:5 about God's kindness being better than life. The interaction between king and people that has featured across the subunit also comes to its conclusion in verse 10, where the righteous now share the king's rejoicing (Ps. 63:10). Similarly, the earlier prayer (Ps. 61:7) asked God to protect the king, but that prayer can now be made by the one offering this prayer. Admittedly, Mowinckel (1962, 2: 220) argues that the speaker here is the king, but this depends on the view that all enemies are foreign powers. Even Eaton, who is much more open to royal interpretation than most, denies the speaker is the king (1976: 86; cf. Croft 1987: 144). Slightly more broadly, Hossfeld and Zenger (2006: 131) also point to close links to Psalms 52–53, further evidence that Psalms 52–64 are a larger unit.

The bulk of the psalm can be understood as a prayer for protection from enemies who primarily attack the poet through speech. Delekat (1967: 67–69) places it among the prayers of the accused, but there is little to support so specific an interpretation, and the fact that there is no appeal for judgement argues against this (Firth 2005b: 94–96). Again, the psalm includes elements of complaint and trust, while the closing verses also draw on elements from the wisdom tradition. The psalm allows the complaint to be heard but frames it in a wisdom setting where God acts against the wicked (or where their own actions backfire). The confidence emerging from this enables the closing affirmation, which provides encouragement to the audience who hear the psalm.

The psalm can be analysed in two short stanzas, each with two strophes, all of which are joined by repetition of key terms:

1. The appeal to God (1–6)
   a. Appeal for protection (1–2)
   b. The enemies' actions (3–6)
2. Confidence in God (7–10)
   a. God's actions (7–9)
   b. Closing affirmation (10)

Comment

Title: For 'The director's', see on Psalm 4. For 'Davidic' and 'a melody', see on Psalm 3.

1–2. The opening appeal is direct, asking God to hear the psalmist's voice in complaint. Often in Psalms, it is sufficient simply to ask God to hear the poet's voice, but here that voice is specifically defined as plaintive (cf. Ps. 55:17). The poet is in need, and God must act because the situation is life-threatening, offering protection from the dread caused by the enemy's threats. Although verse 1 speaks only of a single 'enemy' it quickly becomes apparent that the term is collective because the psalmist is threatened by the scheming of the evildoers, who are part of a larger group enacting injustice. The request to be hidden from this is another request for protection.

3–6. The actions of the enemies are primarily expressed in their speech, though the imagery associates it with hunting. The righteous are here hunted by the evildoers, and speech is the primary mechanism. That speech can be particularly damaging is made clear through the images associated with it here. The nature of their speech is immediately evident from the comparison of their tongues to swords, and their words to arrows. That the speech is bitter could also allude to poison sometimes put on an arrow, though it could also refer to its general effects. Hunting with a bow and arrow continues to inform the imagery in verse 4, where they are portrayed as shooting at the blameless (cf. Ps. 15:2), the people who should be in God's presence. Just as a hunter hides to shoot at birds or animals, or soldiers from an ambush, so the evildoers shoot at the blameless. They have no fear, not just because they take the blameless by surprise, but perhaps also lacking fear of God even though the blameless are the objects of his care. Should a thought arise on this matter, they can harden themselves (as Pharaoh did, Exod. 7:13, 22; 8:15) with an 'evil word'. Such speech is evil because it promotes what is contrary to God's purposes while reassuring the speakers that they have plenty of snares set and are confident no one will see the snares – nor those who set them. Indeed, they continue to plot perversities, things recognizably contrary to God's will, encouraging themselves to believe that they have a well-planned plot. That is, they are secure in their plans, using speech not only to attack others, but also to encourage themselves in their perversity. To this, the psalmist can only reflect that understanding such people is impossible, because although we can see their outer actions, the thoughts and motivations that drive them are unfathomable (cf. Jer. 17:9).

7–9. The evildoers have plotted evil, their speech likened to arrows shot from a hide. But now there is an important reversal, as it emerges that God is the one who shoots them. A sudden, unexpected arrow from God is enough to wound them. Psalm 38:2 reports that God has wounded the psalmist, the arrows being evidence of divine discipline. Here, that discipline is sudden, catching the evildoers by surprise much as a hunter seeks to catch prey by surprise. The idea here is that the evildoers receive back what they have done to others, so that their punishment is appropriate to their crimes. Although the exact sense of verse 8 is difficult, the general sense seems to be that the evildoers had used speech to bring down others, but their own speech is now what brings them down. Such thinking is at home in the wisdom traditions (e.g. Prov. 11:2–3), and that may influence the formulation here, but it does not have to be limited to them. Nevertheless, it is another example of the punishment fitting the crime. A balance is struck concerning how the evildoers are stopped – Yahweh may act against them, or their own actions may self-destruct, but the psalmist is confident that evil will not triumph. More importantly, both possible outcomes witness to God's involvement with the world and lead to a response from all who see. They may shudder at the fall of the evildoers, but the more important reaction is demonstrated in verse 9, where all people fear, declare God's deeds and ponder them. The element of 'fear' (*yr'*) is also central to the wisdom material (cf. Job 28:28, Prov. 1:7, Eccles. 12:13), again tying this confidence to those traditions. Likewise, 'pondering' (*śkl*) has roots in wisdom (e.g. Job 34:27; Prov. 1:3; Dan. 9:22), though it occurs across a range of other texts. That God acts becomes a source of reflection for those who fear him; such reflection also means declaring his works in all their diversity.

10. An audience is now addressed with a key point of learning it can take into its own experience. In Psalms, the righteous are those who have oriented their lives to the will of God, and so are the objects of his care (Ps. 1:6). The righteous see points where God (here named as Israel's covenant God, Yahweh) acts against evil and this leads to rejoicing. Yahweh's acts demonstrate that even though evil is often manifest, God continues to work in this world. The righteous have good grounds for continuing to take refuge in him. The righteous here are also the upright of heart, those who orient their lives to doing what is right. Knowing

God's commitment, all people can continue to exult, announcing God's work with excitement. In this state, they are now equal to the king in Psalm 63, showing once again the close relationship between king and people in this subunit.

Explanation

Although we naturally read any poem from beginning to end, there is value in this case in starting at the closing verse, since this is the psalm's goal. It assures the righteous that they will rejoice and exult in God while also inviting them to do so. The reasons for this have been developed through the combination of complaint, confidence and wisdom that are woven through the psalm. The psalm accepts that the life of the faithful is one that faces real challenges, not least from those opposed to such a life. But even in this there is good news, because this is something that can be brought before God. Even as we face major challenges from those who imagine that easily gained wealth and power matter more, the psalm reassures us that this is not the end. God is the one who finally overcomes, disciplining the evildoers so that they receive back what they have done. Each time we see this, we have a further basis for rejoicing and praise; and as we bear witness to this, so others are invited to join this praise. Nowhere do we see this more clearly than in Jesus' resurrection, the knowledge of which continues to invite reflection, proclamation and celebration.

PSALM 65

Translation

The director's. A melody. Davidic. A Song.

1To you, silence is praise, O God in Zion,
  and to you shall a vow be fulfilled,
2O hearer of prayer,
  unto you all flesh comes.
3Iniquitous words prevail over me,
  you atone for our transgressions.
4Oh the blessedness of the one you choose and bring near,
  who dwells in your courts,
we are satisfied by the good things of your house,
  the holiness of your temple.

5With awesome deeds you answer us in righteousness,
  O God of our salvation,

the confidence of all the ends of the earth,
  and the distant sea,
6who establishes the mountains in his strength,
  girded with might,
7who calms the noise of the seas,
  the noise of their rollers,
  and the roar of the peoples,
8so the inhabitants of the remote places are in awe of your signs,
  you make the appearing of morning and evening shout out.

9You visit the earth and water it,
  you enrich it greatly!
The channel of God is full of water,
  you provide their grain,
  because you have prepared it,
10making its furrows drink abundantly,
  flattening its clods,
softening it with copious showers,
  you bless its growth.
11You crown the year with your bounty,
  your paths overflow with abundance.
12The pastures of the wilderness overflow,
  the hills gird themselves with joy.
13The meadows are clothed with flocks,
  and the valleys cover themselves in grain,
  they shout for joy; indeed, they sing!

Notes on the text

1. 'Silence' is often emended on basis of Gk (and Syr.) to 'is fitting', but MT should stand (cf. Hossfeld and Zenger 2006: 138). For a defence of Gk, see van Gemeren 2008: 497.

3. *dābār* can be 'things' (cf. ESV, NET). This sense should not be excluded, but the psalm's move from silence to sound suggests 'words' is slightly preferable.

4. The cohort. here indicates confidence.

10. Parsing the first two verbs as infin. abs.

Form and structure

Psalm 65 initiates a new subunit that runs through to Psalm 68, with each psalm entitled as a 'song'. As the opening poem, it picks up on the close of Psalm 64, which had anticipated the righteous in heart 'exulting' (*hll*) by announcing that 'praise' (from *hll*) belongs to God. Indeed, God's praise is a central theme that runs through this subunit, recurring in each psalm (e.g. Pss 66:8, 67:3, 5 each use *hll*, while Ps. 68 has a range of terms for 'praise'). These psalms also focus in various ways on God's reign over the nations (e.g. Pss 65:5, 8; 66:1–4; 67:2–5; 68:32), a motif woven into his provision in creation and redemption (e.g. Pss 65:9–10; 66:12; 67:6; 68:7–10).

This poem can (broadly) be considered as a hymn of praise addressed to God that integrates wisdom motifs through reflections on God's care of creation. As is typical of hymns, the psalm includes ptcs. that describe God's actions, demonstrating that these are his characteristic mode of dealing with creation. God's dealing with creation is closely related to his care for humans, all of which leads to praise. The diverse sources of praise here are striking, starting paradoxically with silence before considering both humans and the wider created order as a source of praise. This is matched by the increasing volume of the sound of praise in contrast to other forms of noise, both the threatening words of others (v. 3) and troubling sounds within creation (v. 7), so that in the end creation shouts and sings (v. 13). This praise is experienced through an abundant harvest, suggesting that the psalm might have originated in Israel's harvest festivals (Exod. 23:14–17; cf. Weiser 1962: 461), though it is not limited to any of these.

We can analyse the psalm in three stanzas, each of which closes by drawing a conclusion relevant to the stanza (cf. Schaefer 2001: 156):

1. Approaching the atoning God (1–4)
2. God's awesome deeds (5–8)
3. God's provision for all the earth (9–13)

Comment

Title: For 'The director's', see on Psalm 4. For 'a melody' and 'Davidic', see on Psalm 3. As a 'song' it has a sung lyric, consistent with use of this title in Psalms 30, 45 and 46, though how that differs from 'melody' is not clear.

1–4. The poem opens with a paradox that goes immediately to the heart of praise. Addressing God directly, it challenges the basic understanding of praise. Rather than assuming that praise is only that which is sounded, the psalm commences by declaring that silence (cf. 'Notes on the text') is praise to God (cf. Ps. 62:1). That God is located in Zion associates this psalm with the temple, anticipating its mention in verses 3–4. In this case, it is not that anyone is consciously giving praise. Rather, that there is order and therefore no clamour, which is for God praise. Nevertheless, alongside silence we also encounter speech, starting with vows made to God that are to be fulfilled (cf. Ps. 50:14; Eccl. 5:4–7). God not only receives praise in silence and vows; he also hears prayers. These vows and prayers can indicate a world that is out of order and needs God's intervention, though they may also be expressions of praise. Whatever their origin, they all come to God, anticipating the final movement of all flesh; here, initially all people, but given the psalm's close, all life. Among these sounds are also iniquities, both deeds and words (cf. 'Notes on the text'), that are too powerful for the poet; though, even with these, there is the good news that God atones for the community's transgressions. God overcomes that which causes disorder, leading to verse 4's declaration of the blessedness of the one God chooses to bring near and dwell in his courts, the temple. The blessedness of this one, the only beatitude in Book 2, echoes the righteous in Psalm 1:1–3, while the possibility of life in the temple draws on the hopes of Psalms 15, 24. That this possibility exists allows the community to be satisfied with its experience of the good things of God's house, his holy temple.

5–8. Where the first stanza notes ways in which sound creates disorder for humans, the second focuses more on the experience of creation, though without ignoring humans. God's awesome deeds done in righteousness respond to the cries of the community, demonstrating that he is the God of their salvation. But God cannot be restricted to Israel, for he is the source of confidence (cf. Pss 40:4; 71:5) for the ends of the earth, a phrase that covers both humans and the wider creation, as is evident by mention of the distant seas. Just as God responds to human need, so he also sustains and cares for the creation's needs. The mountains are not mighty because of their height; they are mighty because they are established in God's strength. No other deity can lay claim to the mountains, because they are under God's control, as also is the sea. Indeed, much of the sea's noise is threatening, especially to a nation not especially involved in nautical trade. But like threatening sounds from people, God calms these, removing disorienting sound (cf. Mark 4:39). Such awesome acts by God can be regarded as signs, powerful demonstrations of his work, and they leave even inhabitants of remote places in awe of him. Such awe is not necessarily silent, though it may be. But the noise God does create is that which praises him, so that as he brings out morning and evening, they shout out about him. Morning and evening covers movement from east to west and the rhythm of time, so that whether creation is considered temporally or spatially, it issues in praise.

9–13. The final stanza considers creation alone, allowing it to voice praise in response to God's provision. Humans play only a small role here. Farmers routinely prepare their ground for a crop, but this passes without comment here. God's provision of rain (envisioned here as coming from a heavenly ocean down God's canal to the earth), especially in deep winter rains, enriches the earth and enables the harvest. It is God who provides what is needed, so that although humans receive their grain, it all comes about because of what God has done. The balance between time and space hinted at in verse 8 continues here as God not only waters the ground; he also crowns the year with his bounty. The abundance that emerges is not only in the prepared ground; it is found also in the wilderness pastures. Humans do not prepare these lands, but God's provision in creation is there. As a result, all creation is transformed by God's involvement. The hills are girded with joy; that is, transformed into a fertile landscape, something seen also in the meadows being covered with flocks and the valleys in grain. The result of this is not (in this instance) human praise but rather shouts and the song from creation itself. Threatening noise has been removed, and all creation sings the song of God's goodness.

Explanation

Psalm 65 is both an affirmation of the importance of praise and a disorienting text that forces us to rethink its basic contours. It affirms the importance of praise, most probably linking it to the harvest, something not always guaranteed in Israel, while allowing the harvest to point to a wider reality. Indeed, the provision of the harvest in an often-challenging land is further evidence of God's sovereignty over all creation (Wardlaw 2015: 105). God's provision, seen in atonement, in his care of creation and his provision for all the earth, draws forth praise. Such praise exceeds our own experience and looks to the rest of the earth, anticipating the day (with Isa. 66:18–24) when all will acknowledge God's reign. Indeed, this psalm is radically theocentric, refusing to allow any but God alone to receive praise. In this, it prepares for these themes throughout Psalms 65–68. But it also reorients us in our understanding of praise. Its opening line forces us to rethink the nature of praise by announcing that God may experience praise in silence. And indeed, although the psalm closes with noisy imagery such as shouting meadows, in reality these are silent. They have voice only when we appreciate that a bounteous harvest and thriving flocks are themselves praise to God (though see H. N. Wallace 2001: 62–64). This does not supplant human praise for God, but forces us to ponder the breadth of praise, so that the creation is not only sustained by God; it gives praise to him even as we are sustained by God and so give praise.

PSALM 66

Translation

The director's. A song. A melody.

1Shout to God all the earth,
  2make melody to the glory of his name
  set forth his praise gloriously.
3Say to God, 'How awesome are your works,
  in the greatness of your power your enemies submit before you.'
4All the earth worships you,
  makes melody to you,
  makes melody your name. *Selah.*

5Come and see God's acts,
  awesome of deed toward humankind.
6He turned the sea to dry land,
  they passed through the river on foot,
  there we rejoiced in him,
7who rules in his might for ever,
  whose eyes keep watch on the nations –
  let not the rebellious exalt themselves. *Selah.*

8Bless, O peoples, our God,
  let the sound of his praise be heard,
9who kept us among the living,
  and has not let our foot slip.
10For you have examined us, O God,
  you have tried us as silver is tried.
11You have brought us in the net,
  you laid a heavy burden upon our loins,
12you let people ride over our heads,
  we went through fire and water,
  but you led us out to a place of satiation.

13I will enter your house with burnt offerings,
  I will fulfil my vows to you;
14which my lips uttered,
  and my mouth spoke during my distress.
15Burnt offerings of fatlings I will offer up to you,
  with the smoke of rams,
  I will offer cattle and goats. *Selah.*

16Come, hear, and I will recount,

(all those who fear God),
what he has done for me.
17 With my mouth I cried out to him
and he was with my tongue.
18 If I had regarded wickedness in my heart,
the Lord would not have heard.
19 But in fact God has heard,
he has attended to the sound of my prayer.
20 Blessed be God
who has not rejected my prayer,
or removed his kindness from me.

Notes on the text

2. Reading the second *kābôd* adverbially (cf. Tate 1990: 144).

3. The rare meaning 'submit' for *kḥš* may also occur in Psalm 81:15.

5. For *'al* as advantage, see *WHS* §295.

11. *mĕṣûdâ* as 'net' is tentative, and could also refer to a 'mountain stronghold'. The hapax legomenon *mû'āqâ* seems to refer to some form of burden.

Form and structure

Psalm 66 follows immediately on from Psalm 65. Where the previous psalm closed by reporting creation shouting its praise to God, Psalm 66 opens by summoning all the earth to shout his praise (v. 1). God's awesome works were noted in Psalm 65:5 and are again noted here (v. 5). However, where the awesome works of Psalm 65 were God's answers to prayer, here they refer more to his great acts of redemption. The motif of God's answering prayer also recurs in verse 19, so that the testimony of the individual voice that speaks at this point confirms the declaration of the previous psalm. The motif of the harvest strongly present in Psalm 65:9–13 is less marked here, though it is hinted at in verse 12. However, it joins Psalm 65:5–8 in maintaining a focus on all the earth, with all of it summoned to worship God (vv. 1–2, 8). In form, it is notable that both psalms mix an individual voice (Pss 65:3; 66:13–20) with more corporate forms.

The psalm could be considered as a thanksgiving (so, A. P. Ross 2013: 428) in that it reports previous acts God has carried out both for his people in general (vv. 6, 12b) and for the psalmist (vv. 17–20). Yet although thanksgiving is present, it also includes hymnic elements (v. 7) along with more general calls to worship (vv. 1–3, 8), and reports of individual worship (13–15). Seybold (1996: 256) attempts to integrate the elements, suggesting they are an extract from a liturgy for a thanksgiving vow. This accounts for the individual components but struggles with the corporate elements. A doxological hybrid, Psalm 66 bursts the bounds of form so that the key context is its literary setting within Psalms 65–68.

The division between corporate and individual sections provides the division into the stanzas, with each then divided further into strophes. In the first stanza, the strophes are introduced by imperatives summoning worship, while they again introduce the second strophe in the second stanza. A *selah* closes each strophe within a stanza, each time following a tricolon. The psalm can be analysed as follows:

1. Corporate praise (1–12)
   a. Shout to God (1–4)
   b. Come and see (5–7)
   c. Bless, O peoples (8–12)
2. Individual thanksgiving (13–20)
   a. Fulfilled vows (13–15)
   b. Come, hear (16–20)

Comment

Title: This is the first non-Davidic psalm since Psalm 51, a feature it shares with Psalm 67. However, it is integrated into its subunit by sharing 'The director's' (see on Ps. 4), 'a song' (see on Ps. 65) and 'a melody' (see on Ps. 3) with each of these psalms.

1–4. The opening summons to shout to God follows directly on from Psalm 65. Where creation in that psalm called out its praise, 'all the earth' here refers primarily to humans, as becomes clearer in the subsequent strophes. Throughout, God is the subject of praise, whether through shouts or melody, and praise is directed to him. All praise is conducted gloriously, so that its form matches its content. The psalm directs worshippers to make melody about the glory of God's name, with 'name' here standing for his character. That character is explored in the balance of the psalm as the audience in various ways reflects on God's deeds. The audience are thus summoned to recount to God the awesome things he has done, though at this point this account is kept fairly general, noting only that the greatness of God's power led his enemies to submit (cf. 'Notes on the text'). Nevertheless, this leads to the point of reflection in verse 4, which is also addressed to God, concluding that, in the light of his deeds, all the earth shall worship him and make melody to him. The latter point is emphasized through repetition that also draws on mention both of making melody and God's name from verse 2.

5–7. The second strophe returns to opening imperatives, inviting the audience to come and see God's works (cf. Ps. 46:8), here described as 'awesome'. Those works are for the benefit of humankind. Where God's works in the first strophe were general, here they build on his acts in redemption. The turning of the sea to dry land refers to the crossing of the sea in the exodus (Exod. 14:21–25), while passing through the river looks back to Joshua 3 – 4. It is often suggested that the 'river' here is an alternative term for the 'sea' (following Dahood 1968: 120–121), so only the exodus is in view. But this would more typically require the pl. 'rivers' (cf. Ps. 93:3–4), and although the Jordan is not elsewhere called 'the river' it is better to assume both crossings are in view. This compressed account thus covers everything from the exodus through to Israel's entry to the land. The psalm also moves from 'they' to 'we' once it describes the rejoicing after the crossing of the Jordan, indicating that those who worship now are heirs of that story of redemption, with their worship rooted in a history not only of redemption but also of adoration. Just as the worship by the Jordan was for all the earth (Josh. 4:21–24), so also Israel's continued recounting of the story was received by later generations whose worship was also a witness to the peoples. God's actions in Israel's redemption were for the benefit of all peoples. Moreover, the God to whom Israel bears witness in its worship is also the one who rules in his might for ever, keeping watch on the nations because he alone can do so. As with the first strophe, the second closes with an implication emerging from this – given both the reasons for God's actions and his power, no one should exalt themselves against him as Pharaoh had in the exodus (cf. Brueggemann and Bellinger 2014: 287). Rather, praise should be given to God.

8–12. The third strophe also begins with imperatives, directing the audience to bless God (here, a synonym for praise), letting the sound of God's praise be heard. Israel has announced what God has done, but that task is now shared with the peoples. He is Israel's God, but his worship is not restricted to them. Reasons for praise are again rooted in God's deeds, but this time describe a period of testing. Numerous suggestions exist for the time mentioned, but there is insufficient detail to decide, and it is better to regard it as summarizing Israel's relationship with God (Goldingay 2007: 291). Through all their times of suffering it was God who had kept them alive, preventing them from stumbling. That period of suffering can also be attributed to God's examining them like a smelter who determines the purity of silver (cf. Pss 17:3; 26:2). This indicates a period of considerable pain, something probably supported by verse 11, though uncertainty about the translation prevents anything further being added. But if those observations lead into verse 12, then we have further images pointing to trial brought about by other nations dominating Israel, an experience likened to passing through fire and water (cf. Isa. 43:2). Yet, at the end of this, God had brought the nation to a place of satiation (cf. Ps. 23:5), once more living the blessing of covenant life.

13–15. The psalm shifts in the second stanza to a report from an individual. This figure speaks of personal experience, though this is now a microcosm of the national experience already described. The poet begins the worship summoned in the first stanza while also fulfilling previous vows. By addressing this strophe to God, the psalmist enacts what was summoned in verses 1–3. The worship will happen in the temple with burnt offerings (cf. Lev. 1), which might also have been the content of the vows, though need not be restricted to them. The concern here is to ensure that vows made in a time of distress (which could match the national experience from vv. 9–12) be fulfilled. Hence, the psalmist will make extravagant offerings. 'Fatlings' would normally be the best of the flock or herd given in burnt offerings, with the smoke from the rams indicating that the animal is wholly given over to God, who will also receive cattle and goats.

16–20. After the introduction from the individual, the second strophe returns to pl. imperatives, directing all who fear God to come and hear what he has done. The poet's testimony now forms part of the mighty acts recounted in verses 5–7. In verses 17–18, this means reporting a previous time when it was necessary to call out to God, the implication being that God needed to assist the psalmist. The poet notes that the presence of wickedness would have impeded this, suggesting a possible link with the prayers of the accused (see on Ps. 7). That is, if there was a formal charge of which the psalmist was guilty, then God could validly have refused the psalmist's request. The poet is not therefore making a general claim of innocence, but rather innocence of a particular crime. The psalmist's innocence is demonstrated by God's responding to the prayer uttered at that time. The implication drawn here is from the poet's own experience – God is blessed (cf. v. 8) because he has demonstrated that he is one who answers prayer and who can be trusted to keep his kindness with his people. Yet, although this is the poet's own conclusion, it is presented here so all can see how this may be true of their experience too. The formula 'blessed be' (*bārûk*) points to answered prayer (cf. Hossfeld and Zenger 2006: 147), and all are thus encouraged to turn to God in prayer.

Explanation

Psalm 66 speaks about the nature of worship by speaking about God. It reminds us that our own story of God's goodness is part of a larger story, one that is tied to the story of redemption. That story does not belong to us alone: all the earth is invited to hear that story and, more importantly, to discover God through it. It is not a story that ends with the past, a testimony where the full stop has been placed and nothing more is said. Indeed, that is fundamental to the Christian claim of God's continued mighty acts in Jesus, not least the resurrection. By linking the individual's story to the national one, it points to the reality of God's continued acts of salvation. The great acts are not merely those of the past, because God continues to act (cf. Morales 2020). Sometimes that will be in testing, but the purpose is salvific. Appreciating this means we move from praise that is simplistic. Praise that is real faces the complexities of lived experience and invites all the world to be part of it (cf. Sutton 2021a: 8).

PSALM 67

Translation

The director's. On stringed instruments. A melody. A song.

1May God be gracious to us and bless us,
  may he cause his face to shine among us. *Selah.*
2that your way be known in the earth,
  your salvation in all the nations.

3May the peoples confess you, O God,
  may all the peoples confess you.
4May the nations rejoice and shout,
  because you judge the peoples with equity,
  and you guide the nations in the earth. *Selah.*
5May the peoples confess you, O God,
  may all the peoples confess you.

6The earth gives its produce,
  may God, our God, bless us.
7May God bless us,
  that all the ends of the earth may fear him.

Notes on the text

Title: A few MSS make this psalm Davidic.

1–7. The translation of the verbs through this psalm is fundamental to its interpretation (see esp. Talstra and Bosma 2001). Apart from the one pf. verb (v. 6) the rest can be impf. or juss. Context is usually the only means of distinguishing these other than the hiphs. in verses 1, 3, 5, which are undoubtedly juss. A juss. may be recognized in the address to a superior (W-O §34.3.b), clearly the case here, while placing these verbs at the start of a clause may also indicate a juss.

3, 5. Hebr. (cf. deClaissé-Walford et al. 2014: 60) *ydh* can mean 'give thanks' or 'confess'. The former includes thanksgiving and praise (e.g. Gen. 29:35). But at other points 'confess' (in the sense of recognize) is more appropriate (e.g. Job 40:14). Here, both elements are ultimately present (cf. Ps. 43:4; 44:8) but, in that the peoples must acknowledge God before consciously offering praise, 'confess' is the more appropriate translation.

6. Kraus (1988: 39) translates the pf. as a prec., but his comments treat it duratively. A prec. here seems unlikely.

Form and structure

Just as Psalm 66 follows closely on Psalm 65, so also Psalm 67 follows closely on Psalm 66, which closed by declaring God 'blessed' (*bārûk*; Ps. 66:20); and that same verb is taken up in the opening of Psalm 67 in its desire that God be gracious and 'bless' (*brk*) Israel. As with both Psalms 65 and 66, Psalm 67 is concerned with the relationship between God and the nations, desiring that all the nations will come to acknowledge God (Pss 65:2, 5; 66:1–7), something particularly stressed in the refrain (vv. 3, 5). The motif of the harvest (Ps. 65:9–13) is again prominent here (Ps. 67:6). Where creation sang God's praises there, here Psalm 67 develops the theme of the harvest as providing the basis for the nations to fear God. Psalm 66:16 speaks of 'all who fear God' and Psalm 67:7 extends that by expressing the hope that all the ends of the earth might fear God. This is consistent with the nations rejoicing and shouting (v. 4), picking up on Psalm 66:1–4.

The interpretation of this poem is heavily dependent on translation choices, most of which cannot be expressed with certainty. As developed here (cf. 'Notes on the text'), the bulk of the psalm is a wish-prayer (cf. NRSV), though it could also be a thanksgiving for a harvest that has come in (cf. CSB) or a series of confident statements about what will be (cf. NJPS). As Tanner suggests (deClaissé-Walford et al. 2014: 538), it is entirely possible that, depending on the context in which it was read, any of these may be correct. Accordingly, priority is given to the poem's own form rather than to a proposed background (with W. S. Prinsloo 1994b). However, when read in the literary setting of Psalms 65–68 with their concern for all the nations to worship God, there is a slight preference for understanding Psalm 67 primarily as a wish-prayer that looks to all the nations coming to worship God since in this it extends the earlier summonses to worship (similarly, Botha 2004b).

The presence of the refrain (vv. 3, 5) is structurally significant, though in this case by creating an inclusion around the central stanza. A more important structural marker is provided by noting the goal of the wish-prayer, and this leads to a three-part analysis:

1. Wish for grace (1–2)
2. Wish for the nations (3–5)
3. Wish for extension of blessing (6–7)

Comment

Title: For 'The director's' and 'On stringed instruments', see on Psalm 4. For 'A melody', see on Psalm 3. For 'A song', see on Psalm 65.

1–2. The opening creatively adapts and reorders the Aaronic blessing (Num. 6:24–26; cf. Fletcher 2018: 86–88), substituting 'God' for 'Yahweh' and making it into a wish-prayer. The change in divine name may simply be a feature of the Elohistic Psalter, but it is also plausible that a prayer that ultimately focuses on the nations could use the more generic term precisely because it is open to them. The blessing asks for God's continued grace (granting what is not earned) and blessing (giving something additional that enhances life). That is, the wish starts from the posture of a supplicant. This supplication desires that God cause his face to shine among the people. The wish here is for God's beneficence, his shining face indicating his positive attention towards them (cf. Pss 4:6; 31:16; 80:3, 7, 19). The *selah* here may suggest a short pause that encourages reflection on the blessing while preparing for the purpose of this blessing to be shown in verse 2. The wish for divine beneficence is not an end in itself. Rather, the goal is that God's way may be known in the earth, echoing the call of the previous psalm, particularly that his salvation be known among the nations. 'Salvation', a new motif within Psalms 65–68, anticipates the declaration of God's character in Psalm 68:20. Here, 'salvation' is understood as God's continued gracious blessing of his people, though this is an extension of the exodus given its goal of entry into the land (cf. Ps. 66:6). However, as God's way is known among the nations, so they can see this as an example of salvation.

3–5. The hope is now expressed that the peoples will confess God (cf. 'Notes on the text'). This confession includes praise but is not limited to this as it is also the result of their coming to know God's way. Verse 3b makes clear that this hope is not simply for some peoples. Rather, and consistent with the desire that God's way be known in all the earth, this is a hope for all peoples. That their confession moves into praise is made explicit by verse 4, where they rejoice and shout, taking up this motif from Psalm 66:1–4. Three different terms for 'peoples' and 'nations' are used in the psalm (*gôyim*, v. 2; *'ammîm* and *lĕ'ummîm*, vv. 3–5). In theory, one can distinguish between these terms, but they are fundamentally synonyms here, indicating in effect that however one construes a people or nation, the hope is that all will confess Israel's God in joyful worship, a point reiterated through the repetition of the refrain (v. 6). The reason for their joyful worship is that they discover the reality of God's active presence among them. The statement that God judges the nations could have a future sense, though this is not excluded if we understand it as describing what God is already doing. His judging of the nations is not here one of punishment. Rather, it points to his just rule of the nations, something indicated also by his guidance of them. What Israel has received as a blessing before (Pss 23:3; 31:3) is something God is already doing among the nations even though they do not yet confess him. They now need to confess God and so come to worship him.

6–7. A significant change is introduced by the shift to a pf. verb in verse 6. Emphasis is placed on the earth (here situated at the start of the sentence), whereas the more standard word order would commence with the verb, noting that the earth gives its produce. This could refer to a particular harvest (so ESV), but the word order is better understood duratively – the earth regularly gives its produce. If so, then each harvest would be evidence of this, and not just one harvest alone. Yet, although the earth provides the harvest, this depends upon God's continued blessing of the nation, which is why a wish for God's blessing is once more expressed. Moreover, God is now 'our God', stressing that it is not any deity that has acted but only Israel's God. Thus, the poem closes with a further wish for God's blessing, but, as with the opening wish (v. 1), one that is directed to the rest of the world. God's blessing is not for Israel alone. God's blessing of Israel is that all the ends of the earth may fear him, so that they too may come and hear what God has done (Ps. 66:16–20).

Explanation

In adapting the Aaronic blessing, Goldingay (2007: 304) notes that the psalm takes something that otherwise requires the priest and makes it something with which the congregation may bless each other. In a sense, this blessing has therefore already begun to demonstrate the heart of the wish-prayer in this psalm. The desire is that the blessing of God Israel experienced move beyond them to all the nations, continuing a pattern already evident in Abram's call (Gen. 12:1–3). Just as not everyone could access the temple to be blessed by a priest, so not everyone could come to Israel and worship Israel's God. But this God is not to be constrained, and the blessing he gives to his people is to be shared with and for all peoples. Although rare, wish-prayers also occur in the NT (e.g. 1 Thess. 3:11–13), so this is a mode of prayer that continues to have a valid and important place in patterns of prayer. The NT also looks to the point when all the nations will sing the praise of God because they have experienced his salvation (Rev. 7:9–10).

PSALM 68

Translation

The director's. Davidic. A melody. A song.

1God arises, his enemies scatter,
and those who hate him flee from his presence.
2As smoke is driven off, you drive them off,
as wax melts before a fire,
the wicked perish before God.
3But the righteous shall be glad,
they shall exult before God,
they shall rejoice with joy!
4Sing to God, make melody to his name,
exalt the one who rides in the clouds – his name is Yah,
and exult before him.

5Father of the fatherless and defender of widows,
is God in his holy habitation.
6God settles the lonely in a home,
brings out the prisoners in prosperity,
while the rebellious dwell in a scorched land.

7O God, when you come forth before your people,
when you march forth in the desert, *selah*,
8the earth shakes, yes, the heavens drip,
before God, this one of Sinai,
before God, the God of Israel.
9Rain of abundance, O God, you cause to fall,
your inheritance, as it languished, you sustained.
10Your community live in it,
you secure the needy with your good things, O God.

11The Lord gives a command,
the women announcing good news are a great host,
12'The kings of armies flee, they flee!
At the entrance of the house, you divide the spoil.
13When you lie down among the sheepfolds,
the wings of a dove are covered in silver,
its pinions with shimmering gold.

[14]When Shaddai scatters kings there,
it snows on Zalmon.
[15]A mountain of God is the mountain of Bashan,
a mountain of peaks is the mountain of Bashan.
[16]Why do you stealthily watch, O mountain of peaks,
the mountain God has desired for his dwelling?
Yes, Yahweh lives there for ever!
[17]The chariots of God are twice ten thousand,
thousands twice told,
the Lord is among them, Sinai is the sanctuary.
[18]You ascended on high, you led captive the captives,
you received tribute among humankind,
even the rebellious, for Yah God to dwell there.'

[19]Blessed be the Lord,
day by day he carries us,
God is our salvation. *Selah.*
[20]Our God is a God of salvation,
and the departure to death belongs to Yahweh the Lord.
[21]Surely, God strikes the head of his enemies,
the hairy scalp of the one who walks about in guilt.
[22]The Lord says 'I will bring back from Bashan,
I will bring back from the depths of the sea,
[23]so you may strike your feet in their blood,
the tongue of your dogs receiving their share from the enemies.'

[24]They see your processions, O God,
the processions of my God, my king, into the sanctuary.
[25]The singers go first, the string players after them,
young women beating hand-drums in their midst.
[26]In the assemblies, bless God,
Yahweh from the fountain of Israel.
[27]There is little Benjamin leading them,
the princes of Judah their throng,
the princes of Zebulun, the princes of Naphtali.
[28]Your God has summoned your strength;
show yourself strong, O God,
when you act for us.

[29]Because your temple is over Jerusalem,
kings will bring a gift to you.
[30]Rebuke the beasts of the reeds,
the assembly of the mighty in the calves of the peoples,
each one trampling on pieces of silver;
he scatters peoples who delight in battles.

31They come with bronzeware from Egypt,
Cush hastens to stretch out its hands to God.

32Sing to God, O kingdoms of the earth,
make melody to the Lord, *selah*,
33to the one who rides in the heavens, the ancient heavens;
behold, he gives forth his voice, a mighty voice.
34Yield strength to God,
his eminence over Israel,
and his strength in the clouds.
35Awesome is God from your sanctuaries,
the God of Israel who gives strength and might to the people,
blessed be God!

Notes on the text

1. Many EVV (e.g. NIV) treat the verbs here as jussives, but this fails to recognize that this is an adaptation, not quotation, of Numbers 10:35.

4. Hebr. *ʿărābôt* can also be 'steppe' (or 'wilderness'; e.g. ESV) but is here understood as a homonym meaning 'clouds'. Of course, the term here may be intentionally ambiguous, so readers recognize the sense only by the poem's end (cf. Vincent 2001: 24; Müller 2005: 210–211; Grogan 2008: 125). Gk and Syr. seem to have read *kî Yah*, but though interchange between *b* and *k* is easily explained, MT can be retained as beth of identity (*WHS* §249).

10. The meaning of *ḥayyâ* is uncertain. With BDB, it is here taken as a rare term meaning 'community' rather than the more common 'wild animals'.

13. Hebr. *šĕpattayim* is uncertain. An allusion to Judges 5:16 is possible, though *mišpĕtayim* there is not much clearer. So, emending does not assist translation.

17. Hebr. *šin'ān* is a hapax and of uncertain meaning.

20. With Goldingay (2007: 307), it is better to understand *tôṣāʾôt* as 'departure' rather than 'escape' since this meaning is not otherwise attested.

27. Hebr. *rigĕmâ* is uncertain. Probably from *rgm* (to stone) it appears to mean a 'heap of stones' and by extension a large mass of people (throng).

30. The meaning of *mitrappēs* can be regarded only as a surmise. The sg. ptc. is here understood as distributive.

34. With Tate (1990: 170), translating *ntn* as 'yield'.

Form and structure

Although much is uncertain in the interpretation of this psalm (though Kraus 1989: 47 is probably too pessimistic), we can be reasonably confident that it closes the subunit of Psalms 65–68 since it shares the label 'song' with the others in the group, while repeating key themes with these poems (see 'Form and structure' on Ps. 65, and Vesco 2006, 2: 586). Beyond that, almost everything is debated, something not helped by a difficult text with numerous rare words and unusual syntactical constructions, only the most important of which are noted above. However, with the rest of this subunit it stresses the reality of God's power, something experienced in Israel but not restricted to them since the nations come in worship, singing praise to God (vv. 31–33). Such praise was the hope of Psalm 67. It is notable that this psalm also joins Psalm 67 by opening with an adaptation of a liturgical line from Numbers (Num. 10:35).

The poem itself is highly complex, and there is a great deal of uncertainty about its form since it does not really conform to the standard categories (though, with Goldingay 2007: 310, we can broadly describe it as a praise psalm). Although many backgrounds or original forms have been proposed (e.g. Seybold [1996: 262–263] reconstructs an acrostic, while Goulder [1990: 191] links it to David's defeat of Absalom in 2 Sam. 18), the poem itself must remain the primary focus of research (with Vincent 2001). It has in various ways adapted elements of the Baal-myth to Yahwism and the Jerusalem temple (cf. Knohl 2013: 3–5). This is particularly evident in verse 4, where the label 'one who rides in the clouds', which would traditionally have been ascribed to Baal, is now given to Yahweh. In a literary context concerned with the worship of the nations, this represents an important shift, taking up the language used by the nations, only to reframe it to relate to Yahweh. This motif is taken up again in verses 33–34, where God's eminence is experienced in Israel. The reframing of characteristics associated with Baal so they are aligned with Yahweh is also a major feature of Hosea (cf. Hos. 2:16) and may suggest that the poem has a northern origin. If so, then one goal of the poem is to encourage its audience to see that it is Yahweh and not Baal who truly is God and who sustains his people. Since the nations are also addressed, the concern is not merely to ensure that Israel does not make the mistake of trusting Baal but rather that the nations see the truth of Yahweh's provision as reason for all to worship Yahweh. Although the details are often unclear, at least some of that worship is described here.

The poem's structure is also a matter of considerable debate. Hossfeld proposes a complex inner and outer shape (Hossfeld and Zenger 2006: 161–164), but at points this seems to mix observations on the development of the poem and its current shape, though the links between the poem's opening and conclusion that they note are important. Without claiming anything definitive, a three-stanza structure is adopted here (cf. deClaissé-Walford et al. 2014: 543):

1. Yah as the God to worship (1–6)
   a. The righteous rejoice (1–4)
   b. Yah as god of the poor (5–6)
2. Theophany and worship (7–28)
   a. Provision of rain (7–10)
   b. The Lord and his power (11–18)
   c. Praise of the Lord (19–23)
   d. Witness of worship (24–28)
3. Worship from all (29–35)
   a. Gifts for God (29–31)
   b. Universal praise (32–35)

Comment

Title: Apart from the exchange of 'Davidic' for 'On stringed instruments' the title is identical to Psalm 67. Reintroduction of 'Davidic' joins it to Psalm 65, the other Davidic poem in this subunit. For 'The director's', see on Psalm 4. For 'Davidic' and 'A melody', see on Psalm 3. For 'A song', see on Psalm 65.

1–4. The poem's opening adapts Numbers 10:35, the words Moses was to use when the Ark was moved in Israel's wilderness wandering. Rather than being a wish, here it becomes a statement of fact about Yahweh's enemies being routinely scattered. This scattering is compared to smoke before a wind or wax melting before a fire; his enemies encounter a force they cannot resist, a motif developed through the psalm. Hence, the wicked perish, echoing Psalm 1:6. The contrast with the righteous (v. 3) extends the echo of Psalm 1, as their rejoicing is reported. As with Psalm 1, the righteous and the wicked are not ethical evaluations. Rather, the concern is with whether someone worships Yahweh. This worship is here expressed in song and music as God is exalted, again echoing the language of Psalms 65–67. The decisive change is introduced in verse 4 where we are told that the one they worship rides in the clouds, terminology typically applied to Baal, before declaring that the name of this deity is Yah (cf. v. 18). The joyful worship of the righteous finds its focus in Israel's God.

5–6. Baal was primarily known as the storm god, his provision coming through rain. That element is picked up later in the poem and applied to God, but before that a second strophe pauses to reflect on Yah's character. God is particularly known as a father of the fatherless and defender of the widow, picking up the common concern for these people found in Israel's law (e.g. Exod. 22:24–27; Deut. 10:18). This characteristic of

God is established in his holy habitation, which the psalm will gradually demonstrate is the temple, not Mount Hermon where Baal was thought to dwell. Beyond his care for the fatherless and the widow, God also settles the lonely and brings out the prisoner to a place of prosperity, both motifs that draw on the exodus and anticipate themes that emerge in the second stanza. By contrast, the rebellious dwell in a scorched land, away from the provision God grants to the righteous.

7–10. Where God has been discussed to this point, he is now addressed (cf. vv. 9–10, 24, 28), though most of the psalm continues to discuss him. These direct addresses to God all occur at structurally significant points. These vocs. provide the boundaries for this stanza and also the opening and closing strophes within it. The opening voc. here enables the poet to declare God's mighty acts in the exodus, while allowing the audience to give their assent. Reference to God's coming forth before his people evokes the exodus traditions, especially from the wilderness. Nevertheless, it points to more than just these traditions, starting with an unusual word for 'wilderness' (*yĕšîmôn*), a term found only three times outside Psalms (Deut. 32:10; Isa. 43:19–20). The unusually placed *selah* (here, mid-sentence) may also suggest that readers should pause before moving on to the next verse to note this. Verses 8–9 then report a shaken earth and abundant rain. Deborah's Song makes a similar statement about an earthquake (Judg. 5:4), but there the setting is more explicitly a theophany rather than the exodus. As there is no report of a shaking earth in the Pentateuch's reports of the exodus and wilderness traditions, nor of such abundant rain, it seems that the psalm here deliberately joins theophanic traditions with those of the exodus, with the latter reintroduced through reference to Sinai. The point is that the God who saved Israel in the exodus is the one who rules all creation and continues to provide for his people's need. This provision can be traced back to the exodus and is still experienced by his people, now portrayed as God's own community, those among whom God continues to demonstrate his concern for the needy.

11–18. The second strophe introduces a new term for God, 'the Lord' (*'ădōnāy*). The central concern through this strophe is the power of God's word, both through his own command and the message he announces through others; here, the many women who speak for him. Whether direct or mediated, God's speech is powerful. A citation is begun in verse 12, though its boundaries are far from clear. On the basis that verse 19 commences a new strophe, which has its own citations, verses 12–18 are here understood as the citation, though it may plausibly be only verse 12. The women who bear good news announce that kings flee, presumably foes who attack the nation. Because of this, at the entry to the houses God divides the spoil that has been provided. Accordingly, when the nation lies down among the sheepfolds, even there they find rich treasures, with bird carvings overlaid with silver and gold (unless, with Tate [1990: 179], we understand the doves as the messengers). The defeat of the kings is picked up again in verse 14, referencing Mount Zalmon, a peak otherwise known only from Judges 9:46–49. The details are uncertain, but the defeat is associated with an apparently unexpected snowfall, with God this time called 'Shaddai'. This epithet occurs forty-one times in the OT, but only here and Psalm 91:1 in Psalms, and is generally thought to refer to God's almighty power (Gk takes it this way). In context, the point appears to be that all kings are weak before Israel's God, and were defeated at Mount Zalmon. Mountains were often thought of as places where a deity would be encountered, so the psalm turns to consider a mountain in Bashan, a region east of the Jordan. Bashan runs up to Mount Hermon in the north, a mountain possibly associated with Baal. One might therefore think of it as a mountain of God within its range, but it is not the crucial mountain. For all the claims made for it, this mountain can only look on stealthily at the mountain God has desired, the one that Israel's covenant God Yahweh has chosen as his enduring abode. These mountains look on, desiring grandeur, but only one mountain deserves this, and it is because Yahweh has made it his dwelling place. Zion, a physically unimpressive mountain, is the place where Yahweh dwells, and his power is evident there in the heavenly army present with him. Indeed, Sinai itself can be said to be in the sanctuary (the only time Sinai and Zion are textually joined), again joining exodus and theophany. God's power in the sanctuary is also evident in the gifts he receives there, even from the rebellious who find themselves unable to resist, since the sanctuary is the place where he receives gifts from all people, including those who have otherwise resisted him. Paul will give this a cosmic twist when describing Jesus' work (Eph. 4:8).

19-23. Because of God's power, the third strophe makes worship its central call. Rather than being the unwilling rebels, it is better to choose worship. Thus, the opening observation notes that God is to be blessed because of his continued deliverance of his people. Indeed, the Lord can be described as a 'God of salvation'. This point is repeated in verse 20, but then contrasted with the fate of those who oppose him since they depart to death (possibly alluding to Mot, the god of death), a point extended in verse 21 with its report of the destruction of his enemies. Again, the point is to encourage the worship of Yahweh since this is evidence of his salvation of Israel. This finds its focus in the citation of God's speech in verses 22–23. God not only defeats his foes; he also brings his people back to him wherever they are, whether the heights of Bashan (which, if an allusion to Mount Hermon is included, means the highest point known to Israel) through to the depths of the sea. Given that the 'sea' was also regarded as the deity Yam, the comparison may also have mythological overtones, where God restores his people from all places and forces that may be ranged against him. This allows them to join in the victory he has won, with even their dogs claiming a share of the spoil.

24–28. Israel's worship is now viewed by others who observe processions honouring God. Israel's God is here also 'my God, my king', as a representative individual speaks, describing the procession. The identity of this figure is not clear but is someone who can speak for the people in describing the worship procession as it enters the sanctuary. The procession initially consists of singers and musicians, with the young women beating hand-drums in their midst (cf. Exod. 15:20; 1 Sam. 18:5). Verse 26 is conceivably the song of the musicians, though it now summons all to bless God (cf. Judg. 5:2, 9), and to do so in the temple, here conceived of as the 'fountain of Israel' unless with Goldingay (2007: 329) this is a further description of Yahweh. But since the temple is Yahweh's abode, perhaps both can be seen as the fountain, the means by which provision is made for Israel. Description of the procession resumes in verse 27, starting with Benjamin and Judah, representing the southern tribes that related to Jerusalem, and then Zebulun and Naphtali representing the northern tribes. The whole nation is encompassed by these tribes, who are reminded that God has summoned their strength while also asking that he continue to show his strength while working for his people.

29–31. The final stanza draws some conclusions from the first two, pointing once more to God's power and the importance of the sanctuary. The temple's importance is immediately noted, especially because of its prominence in Jerusalem. Perhaps more importantly, it is God's temple and, because of this, kings bring their gifts to him there. Kings have been shown to be powerless before God through the psalm, and here have become willing worshippers. God is also opposed (in mythological terms) by other deities, even if the psalm has shown them to be of no power or threat. Nevertheless, the psalm also looks for God to show his victory over such forces. These forces are embodied here in powerful animals, perhaps a hippopotamus representing Egypt and its power and deities. Such an interpretation seems more likely when we note that 'mighty ones' are presented as Egyptian foes defeated by Yahweh in Jeremiah 46:15. The dominant note of the psalm has been to show the inability of Baal (best known to Israel's north) to save Israel, but Egypt too is powerless before God. They may seem powerful when trampling pieces of silver, but God scatters them. Hence, Egypt and nearby Cush will also bring their valuables in the worship of God.

32–35. Given that all will worship God, the final strophe directs the kingdoms of the earth to sing his praises. He is the one who rides in the heavens, whose voice is mighty in its thunder (cf. Ps. 29). Israel's God is the only one worthy of worship because only he is God. Rather than claiming power for themselves, they need to yield strength to God, the one whose eminence is over Israel and whose strength is visible to all in the clouds. Hence, the conclusion that all need to draw is stated in verse 36 – God is awesome in his sanctuary, and the God of Israel (and no other) is the one who gives strength to the people. Because all strength belongs to God, the various patterns of human violence traced through the psalm are shown to be pointless, and the only real option is to join the worship of God. This God is blessed, and thus to be worshipped by all.

Explanation

Psalm 68 is a complex text that integrates numerous elements. It draws on Israel's historical traditions, especially those from the exodus and Judges 5, bringing them together in worship in the temple. This worship declares that the God who acted in the past continues to work among his people. Yet the text also daringly engages with the mythological world of the nations around Israel to declare that Israel's God, Yahweh, is the only one worthy of worship. It is not Baal, the gods of Egypt, Yam (the sea god), or any other, who have power. The only one to have real power is the God worshipped in the temple on Zion, the mountain that not only represents the great moments from Israel's past at Sinai but also holds together anything of value that other peoples might claim belong to their deities. This interaction is vital because the goal of this psalm is to persuade both Israel and the kingdoms of the earth that Yahweh is the only one worthy of worship. All this explains why Paul applies this psalm so specifically to the worship of Jesus as the one in whom God is now most fully made known (see Greever 2020).

PSALM 69

Translation

The director's. According to Lilies. Davidic.

[1]Save me, O God,
  because the waters have come up to my neck.
[2]I sink in deep mire
  and there is no foothold:
I have entered deep waters,
  and the torrent overwhelms me.
[3]I am weary with my calling out,
  my throat is hoarse:
my eyes fail,
  waiting for my God.

4More numerous than the hairs on my head
are those who hate me without cause:
those who would destroy me – my false enemies – are mighty,
what I did not steal I must then restore.
5O God, you know my foolishness,
and my guilt is not hidden from you.

6Let not those who wait on you,
O Lord Yahweh of Hosts, be put to shame because of me:
let not those who seek you be confounded because of me,
O God of Israel.
7For I bear reproach on account of you,
disgrace has covered my face.
8I am estranged from my kin,
and a foreigner to my mother's children.
9For zeal for your house consumed me,
and the reproaches of those who reproach you fell upon me.
10When I wept with fasting of my appetite,
it brought me reproaches.
11When I changed my clothing to sackcloth,
then I became a byword to them.
12Those sitting in the gate gossip about me,
even the mocking songs of those taking strong drink!

13But as for me, my prayer is to you O Yahweh,
for a time of favour:
O God, in the greatness of your kindness,
answer me with your faithful salvation.
14Deliver me from the mud
that I may not sink:
let me be delivered from those who hate me,
and from the deep waters.
15Let not the torrent of waters overwhelm me,
and let not the deep swallow me,
nor let the pit close its mouth over me.
16Answer me, O Yahweh, because your kindness is good,
according to your great compassion turn to me.
17Do not hide your face from your servant,
because of my distress answer me quickly.
18Draw near me and redeem me,
ransom me because of my enemies.

19You know my reproach, my shame and my disgrace,
all my adversaries are before you.
20Reproach has broken my heart, and I am sick,

though I hoped for sympathy there was none,
and for comforters but found none.
21 They put poison in my food,
and for my thirst they gave me vinegar to drink.

22 May their table be a trap before them,
and a snare for their friends.
23 May their eyes grow dim from looking,
and make their hips shake continually.
24 Pour out your indignation upon them,
and let your burning anger overtake them.
25 May their encampment be desolate,
may no one dwell in their tents,
26 because they persecute the one you struck,
and they recount the pain of the ones you have pierced.
27 Add punishment on their punishment,
and do not let them enter your righteousness.
28 Let them be blotted out from the book of the living,
and do not let them be recorded with the righteous.
29 But I am afflicted and in pain,
may your salvation grant me security.

30 I will praise the name of God in song,
and I will magnify it with thanksgiving.
31 This will please Yahweh more than an ox,
than a bull with horns and divided hoofs.
32 The oppressed see, they will rejoice!
O those seeking God, let your heart live!
33 For Yahweh hearkens to the afflicted,
and does not despise his prisoners.

34 Let the heavens and the earth praise him,
the waters and all that moves in them.
35 For God will save Zion,
will build the cities of Judah,
they shall live there and possess it,
36 the seed of his servants shall inherit it,
those who love his name shall dwell in it.

Notes on the text

4. The last line is often taken as a question, but if so, it is unmarked as such.

10. Retaining MT. For *nepeš* as 'appetite', see Job 6:7; Eccl. 6:9.

11. For *nĕgînâ* as a mocking song, see Lamentations 3:63.

22. Tg suggests *wĕšalmêhem*; hence, 'sacrificial feasts' (so, Kraus 1988: 58). As this merely repoints the text, it is a plausible reading, but MT's pointing also makes sense, and both readings offer a plausible parallelism.

Form and structure

Psalm 69 initiates the closing movement of Book 2. The label 'song', which unites Psalms 65–68, along with themes of universal worship, is dropped here. This final subunit is bound more loosely than previous subunits in the collection Psalms 51–72, lacking a unifying element in the titles, and without any historical references to David in Samuel. However, there are still elements holding these psalms together (see also Choi 2021: 165–167), notably concern for the poor who call out to God (Pss 69:29–33; 70:5; 72:2–4, 12–14). Each of Psalms 69–71 also speaks of enemies seeking the psalmist's life (Pss 69:4; 70:2; 71:4, 10) and of the need for God to hasten to deliver the poet (69:17; 70:1; 71:12). Psalm 72 is clearly distinct but is still thematically joined to the others in the subunit as the king becomes God's vehicle for providing deliverance. As the close of Psalms 51–72, both Psalms 69 and 72 provide important links to Psalm 51. Psalm 69 shares the link of the building up of Jerusalem (Pss 51:18; 69:35), while Psalm 72's Solomonic title joins Psalm 51's title in pointing to the events of 2 Samuel 11 – 12. As is common for a psalm that bridges one subunit to another, there are also important connections to Psalm 68 (cf. Vesco 2006, 2: 602). The most obvious of these is that where Psalm 68 anticipates the destruction of God's enemies (Ps. 68:1, 21–23), Psalm 69 now asks for this to occur in the poet's experience (Ps. 69:4, 14), while God's concern for the prisoner (Ps. 68:6) also finds expression here (Ps. 69:33).

The poem itself can be classified as a complaint psalm (cf. Firth 2005b: 125–129), though it is difficult to be more specific than that. It has been understood as a royal prayer before battle (Croft 1987: 44), and verse 25 could support this position. Goulder (1990: 217) also sees it as royal, linking it to Sheba's rebellion against David (2 Sam. 20), though the hints he claims point to this are not particularly substantial, and again seem more determined by his thesis than the evidence. Beyond this, the concluding verses seem to point to Jerusalem as needing to be rebuilt, something that would be more consistent with this being an exilic or post-exilic prayer. In the absence of a king, an individual is more likely, though such an individual could still be representative in some way. The exact circumstances faced are difficult to pin down, since as well as the military language the psalmist also reports threats from enemies (v. 4), estrangement from kin (v. 8), reproach for attempting to be faithful (v.

9) and illness (v. 20) as well as national challenges (vv. 35–36). Although Kraus (1989: 60) interprets verse 5 as indicating it should be included among the prayers of the accused (see on Ps. 7), the poet's confession of guilt there is hardly consistent with this. The breadth of elements noted here indicate that we should not attempt to tie the psalm to any one element. Rather, as with Psalm 38, we see a combination of elements, showing that distress could come from multiple sources. As such, we should allow that the psalm integrates the various sources of distress into a single prayer, making it available to a wide range of readers.

In terms of structure, there is an obvious change at verse 30 as the poem shifts from complaint to a vow of praise, a change that is more marked than in many other psalms. Leaving aside approaches that delete various sections of the poem (e.g. Briggs and Briggs 1906, 1: 112–113; Lindström 1994: 327–330), we need to see this as a major point of division within the poem. This would not deny (with Groenewald 2003: 176–290) that much of this could have emerged through reworking of older material, but it also allows for coherence in the finished piece that is more important. Working with this, Allen (1986: 588) has argued that verses 1–30 are made up of two largely parallel panels, pivoting at verse 13. In this pattern, verses 13c–18 fit awkwardly, unless with Coetzee (1986: 170) we see this as a plea for rescue with links to both verse 1 and verses 30–36. This model allows more for the various relationships within the poem than Groenewald's complex approach (2003: 36–175). Integrating Allen and Coetzee's insights, we emerge with a two-stanza pattern, with the first containing five strophes (cf. Firth 2005b: 131–132):

1. Complaint (1–29)
   a. Opening plea (1–5)
   b. Description of circumstances (6–12)
   c. Petition for rescue (13–18)
   d. Description of circumstances (19–21)
   e. Prayer against enemies (22–29)
2. Vow of praise (30–36)
   a. Personal vow (30–33)
   b. Call for universal praise (34–36)

Comment

Title: For 'The director's', see on Psalm 4. For 'According to Lilies', see on Psalm 45. For 'Davidic', see on Psalm 3.

1–5. The psalm opens with an urgent appeal for salvation, with this motif marking the boundaries of the first stanza. The reason given is that the waters have risen to the poet's neck. Imagery of water is also plentiful in the psalm, and it is consistently threatening (cf. vv. 14–15).

Closely linked to this is the image of sinking into thick mud, where it is impossible to gain a foothold and get free. The torrent of waters thus threatens the poet's life, and there is no means of saving himself. Only God can save, but the poet is also weary from calling out. So, despite the abundant water, the psalmist's throat is hoarse from calling out. Faced with overwhelming pressures, the poet sees life failing, marked by a loss of sight, something that creates further threat when under such pressure. Yet, as verse 4 makes clear, the threat facing the poet is not being caught in a swollen stream but rather human enemies, enemies who are so numerous they are effectively uncountable. Making this worse is the fact that their actions towards the psalmist are apparently baseless, but they still use their great power in ways contrary to justice to force the psalmist to act. Under Israelite law, a thief should return what was stolen (along with a fine, Exod. 22:1–4), but the psalmist is forced to return what was not stolen. The psalmist acknowledges both folly and some guilt, but the appeal assumes that the enemies lack any valid reason. Rather, like an overwhelming flood they use their power to manipulate processes meant to ensure justice.

6–12. Where the opening strophe focuses more on how the poet experienced injustice, the second looks more at its expression. Central to the prayer is that God must act and bring about justice. Most importantly, God needs to be seen to act justly for the psalmist because this is a witness to others that he is just. Strikingly (esp. in the so-called Elohistic Psalter), the psalmist here refers to God as 'Lord Yahweh of Hosts', a unique combination in Psalms, stressing God's rule, covenant relationship to Israel and ability to act for his people. That he is also referred to here as 'God of Israel' further emphasizes the covenant relationship between God and his people, and therefore why he needs to act to prevent others being confounded, by drawing wrong conclusions about what it means to seek God. This is particularly important as the psalmist claims to bear reproach on God's behalf (cf. Jer. 15:15), and the current disgrace both impairs the poet's life and raises questions about God's justice. The poet's disgrace starts at the level of family, being estranged from them and treated like a 'foreigner' (*nokrî*) by even close family members. The implication is that they act as if the psalmist has no right to claim justice under Israel's law. The paradox is that the poet experiences an overwhelming zeal for the temple and all it represents, even accepting reproaches aimed at God. These reproaches are outlined in verses 10–12. Rather than fasting and tears being regarded as evidence of piety, it brought reproach. Wearing sackcloth was typically a sign of sorrow or repentance (e.g. 1 Kgs 19:2; Jon. 3:8) but instead of this being seen as a sign of commitment to God, it made the poet a byword, an example of folly. Rather than the poet's zeal being seen as evidence of a life to emulate, he is now a source of gossip, the topic of drunken songs.

13–18. Much of this strophe replicates material from the first one, but it represents a development of the prayer. Having outlined both the impact of the enemies on the psalmist and the fact that the psalmist is in fact a loyal worshipper of Yahweh, it reintroduces the effect of this on the psalmist to stress why God must act. Verse 13 is thus crucial in advancing the argument, insisting that the prayer is directed to God, and asking for action in a favourable time. Repetition of the motifs of flood-waters and mud from the first strophe insist however that this favourable time should not be delayed, because the psalmist lacks the resources to continue standing. Indeed, the waters here are even more threatening than before as they are likened to the deep and the pit, images of death that will consume the poet. The poet calls on God to answer because of the goodness of God's 'kindness' (*ḥesed*), a key marker of his covenant faithfulness to his people (Exod. 34:6–8). This kindness is matched by God's compassion, and together these mean God needs to turn to the psalmist, to act in deliverance. The alternative would be for God to hide his face (a sign of disfavour, Ps. 30:6–7); that is, not to act for the poet. But the level of distress makes this unacceptable, meaning that God needs to act quickly. As with the first strophe, this returns to the issue of the enemies, making clear that they are the ones who threaten the psalmist. God must rescue the poet from them by coming near, entering the psalmist's experience.

19–21. The prayer for deliverance is again focused on how the psalmist experienced injustice, and again followed by its expression of this injustice. This time, rather than describing the reproach (along with the shame and disgrace), the psalmist insists that God already knows it. Likewise, the foes are before God, so are known to him. God already knows, but the psalmist reports the effect of the reproach as illness of some sort. The breaking of the heart would include grief (cf. Jer. 8:18), but also a loss of strength (for the heart as the location of strength, see Ps. 27:14). As with verses 9–12, this experience is contrary to expectations – a period of distress should lead to comfort (as Job's friends at least intended), but instead there was neither sympathy nor comfort. Rather, the enemies have exacerbated the psalmist's suffering, adding poison to food and giving vinegar to drink. These are probably metaphors for their actions in bringing distress to the poet, but expressing it in these terms allows for the deep impact of the enemies to be made clear.

22–29. The final strophe in this first stanza now introduces new material as the psalmist presents an imprecation before God. The language here is forceful, but is all shaped by the actions of the enemies against the psalmist. The psalmist seeks justice where the punishment fits the crime, and the requests are matched to the reproaches experienced. The language is carefully linked to what has been done so that the punishment matches the crime (cf. Firth 2005b: 135–136). Asking that their table become a trap for the enemies and their friends reflects their attempts to poison the psalmist (v. 21). Loss of eyesight and bodily vigour links to the poet's suffering (vv. 3, 20). Indeed, the whole of verses 22–25 can be understood as an expression of the illness caused by the many who have attacked the poet, though now to be given to them by God as opposed to their bringing it on to the psalmist. All this finds its focus in verse 26, which indicates that the punishment requested emerges from their persecution of the poet and their engagement in the gossip mentioned in verse 12. The enemies have also falsely accused the psalmist (v. 3), and so verses 27–28 ask that they receive the punishment of those who have made such accusations, not least as one who is apparently also disciplined by God in some way (cf. Ps. 38:1–2). The enemies' goal was the poet's destruction, so the request is now that they receive what they sought, most obviously by not being included with God's righteous ones, whether that is understood as being part of the assembly in worship or in the book of life, where he records his people (cf. Exod. 32:32–33; Mal. 3:16). Revelation 3:5 points to those who will not be blotted out of the book of the living, providing an important counterpoint to this psalm. But here the point is that as they have sought the poet's death, so death is the punishment sought for them because of the condition of pain in which they have left the poet. Yet it is important to note that the poet leaves all this with God and, as is typical with such imprecations, does not ask for the right to enact the punishment himself. The psalmist needs justice from God, and therefore God must enact justice with the enemies. For the poet, God's salvation, not vengeance, needs to be the source of security.

30–33. The second stanza represents a marked change in tone. Rather than distress, the psalmist now vows praise. The assumption within the poem is that having presented the case to God, a resolution can be assumed, making praise possible. The psalmist promises to praise God's name, with God's name again representing his character. This praise is offered in 'song' (*šîr*) along with thanksgiving that magnifies God's name; that is, demonstrates its greatness. The psalm then joins Psalms 40, 50, 51 in indicating that such heartfelt worship is more pleasing to God than animal sacrifices (including an 'ox', *šôr*, playing on 'song'), even though these are obviously costly. Indeed, as Longman (2014: 266) points out, this is particularly good news for the poor because they could not afford such animals. Therefore, such heartfelt worship would be seen by the afflicted and lead them to rejoice. The earlier request was that others not be put to shame because of the psalmist's suffering, but now the expectation is that heartfelt and joyful worship will be seen, encouraging others to let their hearts live, finding full life through being those who seek God. All of this comes back to Yahweh as one who attends to the afflicted, not despising prisoners. Again, the psalm uses 'Yahweh' to stress that this is the God who is in covenant with his people, and that such concerns are inherent to his character, something most obviously seen in the exodus.

34–36. Not only does the psalmist vow praise, but praise from all creation is now summoned, whether heaven or earth or anything in the seas. This time, it is because of the assurance that God will save Zion, bringing the salvation motif of the first stanza into the second. This salvation is not only deliverance from a specific threat but also the building up of Judah's cities, so that its people may live there and possess it. This may suggest a background in the exile (cf. Groenewald 2003: 235–239, though Kidner 1975, 1: 249, thinks of the time when Sennacherib besieged Jerusalem). More important than the specific background is that the deliverance of the one has now become a pattern for all. God saves the individual in distress, and he also saves his people, providing them with security in their land.

Explanation

Introducing the final subunit of Book 2, Psalm 69 is an individual complaint that anticipates widescale praise. Yet this praise is hard won, emerging from deep distress and suffering, and challenges God to demonstrate the reality of his justice; yet, having done so, surrenders to God the right of doing more. It also demonstrates that the life of discipleship can be one where the attempt to be faithful leads to further suffering even as the hope of salvation remains. But it also understands that what God does in and through one person can point to his larger work for all so that evidence of his saving work for one is evidence of his wider faithfulness to his people. For these reasons, it is no surprise that this psalm is of such importance in the NT's exploration of Jesus' life and ministry. Staying just with John, we see that, like the psalmist, zeal for God's house consumed him (John 2:17). Like the psalmist, he could tell his disciples that he was hated without reason (John 15:18). Like the psalmist, they gave him vinegar to drink (John 19:29). And yet he could cry, 'Father forgive'. Jesus lived the life that is prayed here, and he is the one who helps us understand what salvation looks like. It is Jesus who continues to accompany us and who promises to respond when we cry out that we too are in over our heads.

PSALM 70

Translation

The director's. Davidic. For commemoration.

1 O God, deliver me,
  O Yahweh, make haste to help me.

[2]Let them be ashamed and abashed,
those who seek my life:
let them be turned back and confounded,
those who delight in my harm.
[3]Let them turn back because of their shame,
those who say, 'Aha! Aha!'
[4]Let them rejoice and be glad in you,
all those who seek you:
let them say continually, 'God is great,'
those who love your salvation.

[5]Though I am poor and needy,
O God hasten to me.
You are my help and my deliverer.
O Yahweh, do not delay.

Notes on the text

1. Psalm 40 includes *rṣh*, and it could be included here if the following is an infin. expecting a main verb (cf. NRSV). It is also possible that 'make haste' has been elided to the second part line, with the one verb covering both part lines (cf. ESV). But this may also be a rare instance of the pi. imp. with an emphatic lamed (W-O §11.2.10i; so deClaissé-Walford et al. 2014: 564).

Form and structure

Psalm 70 is closely related to Psalm 40:13–17. Considerable debate has focused on the issue of which is the original poem, though without clear resolution. Hence, Kraus (1988: 67) considers it the original poem and provides full comment, whereas Seybold (1996: 271) notes the textual variants and redactional issues, but then directs readers back to his comments on Psalm 40. However, as with Psalms 14 and 53, the more important questions arise from the placement of this poem at this point within the Psalter and also how it functions as an independent poem irrespective of its possible relationship to Psalm 40 (though see 'Form and structure' there). Accordingly, the text-critical notes above do not use evidence from Psalm 40 to reconstruct a potentially original poem. Rather, each now needs to be understood on its own terms (Firth 2022). However, it should be noted that although the texts are very similar, there are some important differences. As is typical in the Elohistic Psalter, most instances of 'Yahweh' from Psalm 40 are here 'God', though one instance of 'Yahweh' remains in verse 1. Yet remarkably, the one instance of 'God' in Ps. 40:17 is now 'Yahweh' (v. 5). There are also important changes of verb in verses 3 and 5. In verse 3 (Ps. 40:15), *šwb* (turn back) is found rather than *šmm* (appalled), while in verse 5 the motif of 'haste' (*ḥwš*) occurs rather than 'consider' (*ḥšb*). These could be copyists' errors, but when placed alongside the fact that Psalm 70 is a consistently shorter text (two verbs from Ps. 40:13–14 are also absent from vv. 1–2), it seems more likely that both poems have been edited to fit their present location. Given the importance of the haste motif for Psalms 69–71, the fact that this poem now opens and closes with this language indicates its importance for the current setting. Likewise, where 'salvation' was a key theme in Psalm 69 (vv. 1, 29, 35), it is here the hope of those who seek God (v. 5). Finally, we should note that where Psalm 69:6–10, 19–20 ask for an absence of shame for the righteous, this psalm (vv. 2–3) looks for the enemies to be shamed. For other links, including those with Psalm 38, see Tate 1990: 204–205.

Taken as a complete poem in its own right (irrespective of its origin), we can treat this as a complaint psalm, though it lacks the characteristic vow of praise, a feature that is particularly striking after the extended vow in Psalm 69. The haste motif now forms an inclusion for the poem (Hossfeld and Zenger 2006: 188–189 find a chiasm), but we can otherwise see the same structure as the third stanza of Psalm 40, analysing this poem in two main stanzas:

1. Appeal (1–4)
2. Declaration (5)

Comment

Title: The title differs from Psalm 40 by omitting 'A melody' and including 'For commemoration'. For 'The director's', see on Psalm 4. For 'For commemoration', see on Psalm 38. For 'Davidic', see on Psalm 3.

1–4. Like Psalm 69, Psalm 70 opens with an appeal for rescue, though the verb now is 'deliver' (*nṣl*). The appeal indicates its urgency in the second part of verse 1, where Yahweh is urged to make haste to help the poet. Along with 'haste' and the repetition of 'Yahweh', 'help' also recurs in verse 5, creating an inclusion for the whole poem. Verses 2–3 then express wishes about the enemies from whom deliverance is needed while also indicating the threat the psalmist faces. The language is shaped by concern with honour, or in this case that those who have sought the psalmist's life should experience shame. These verses are analysed here as three bicola, with each commencing with a wish for the shaming of the enemies in the first part line, while the second part line uses a ptc. to characterize the enemies' actions. Verse 2a opens with two terms indicating loss of honour because they seek the poet's life. Verse

2b also has two verbs, both of which are again concerned with loss of honour, because they delight in the poet's harm. These elements come together in verse 3 which asks for the foes to be turned back because of their shame, while reporting their mocking speech. Although one could argue for a decline in the intensity of the enemy actions across these verses, it is probable that we should see the verses as broadly equivalent. Most importantly, the shame Yahweh brings is what turns them back. Verse 4 then contains two bicola that express a wish for those aligned with the poet, contrasting with the enemies, with the second part line also shaped by ptcs. Again, two verbs are in parallel in verse 4a, looking for joy for these people. Where the enemies have sought the poet's life, these people have sought God. This climaxes in verse 4b, which anticipates the speech of these people as offering continued praise as those who love God's salvation. Use of speech here provides a further contrast with the enemies – in verse 3 their speech mocks, while here speech praises God.

5. The closing verse returns to the psalmist's need. The psalmist's self-description as 'poor and needy' does not necessarily indicate physical poverty, as it could simply mean the poet lacks the resources to overcome the adversaries, though poverty cannot be ruled out. Certainly, in context it explains why God must hasten to the psalmist. Since God can 'help' (v. 1) the psalmist now declares that he is 'my help and my deliverer', tying the appeal to verse 1. The urgency of this is emphasized with the request that Yahweh not delay. Haste is needed, not delay, and it is Yahweh who can help and rescue.

Explanation

Jerome Creach (2006: 66) helpfully notes that 'Ps. 70 reminds us that praise, when properly framed, emerges from the depths of life.' This short poem is offered from the depths, and all of it is offered as an urgent plea to God for deliverance. Its urgency joins with that of Psalm 69:1–29, though it does not reach the vow of praise found there. The absence of the vow of praise, so typical of the complaint psalms, is important, joining this prayer to Psalm 88. Strikingly, both absences occur in the closing segment of their book, as indeed is the case with Psalm 40:13–17, with which this prayer shares most of its content. Each of the Psalter's first three books approaches its close with the possibility of struggle affirmed. Although Psalm 70 also runs into Psalm 71 (see there on 'Form and structure'), where the hope of praise returns, it remains here as a brief reminder that sometimes all that can be offered in prayer are words from the depths. Praise will come, but sometimes we need to be content to allow the call from the depths to stand in its brief urgency.

PSALM 71

Translation

1In you, O Yahweh, have I taken refuge,
  let me never be put to shame.
2In your righteousness deliver me and rescue me,
  incline your ear to me and save me.
3Be to me a rock of dwelling to which I may continually come,
  command my salvation,
  for you are my crag and mountain stronghold.

4O my God, rescue me from the hand of the wicked,
  from the power of the unjust and oppressive.
5For you are my hope,
  O Lord Yahweh, my confidence from my youth.
6Upon you have I leant from birth,
  from my mother's womb you are my sustainer,
  my praise is continually of you.
7I have become a wonder to many,
  but you are my strong refuge.
8My mouth is filled with your praise,
  your glory all day.

9Do not cast me off at a time of old age,
  do not forsake me when my vitality ends.
10For my enemies talk about me,
  and those watching my life take counsel together,
11saying 'God has forsaken him,
  chase and seize him,
  for there is no one to deliver.'
12O God, do not be far from me,
  O my God, make haste to help me.
13Let those who persecute me be ashamed, perish,
  may they be covered in reproach and ignominy,
  those who seek my harm.

14But I wait continually,
  that I may add to all your praise.
15My mouth shall recount your righteousness,
  your salvation all day,
  though I know not its number.
16I enter into the mighty deeds of the Lord Yahweh,
  I will make your righteousness known, yours alone.

[17]O God, from my youth you have taught me,
and still I proclaim your wondrous acts.
[18]So even unto old age and grey hair,
O God do not forsake me,
until I proclaim your power to a generation,
your strength to all those to come.
[19]And your righteousness, O God, is to the height;
because you have done great things,
O God, who is like you?
[20]You who have shown me many troubles and evils,
you shall again revive me,
and from the depths of the earth
you shall again bring me up.
[21]May you increase my greatness,
and comfort me again.

[22]As for me, I will give you thanks with a stringed instrument,
your faithfulness O my God!
I will make melody to you with a lyre,
O Holy One of Israel.
[23]My lips will cry out as I make melody to you,
yes, my very self that you have redeemed.
[24]My tongue also shall tell of your righteousness all day,
because they have been shamed, abashed,
those who seek my harm.

Notes on the text

3. For *mā'ôn*, many MSS read the orthographically similar *mā'ôz* ('refuge'; cf. Ps. 31:2). This is a plausible reading (esp. given the close links to Ps. 31:1–3), though *mā'ôn*, when understood as an abode in God's presence, may also be understood as a secure place, and may also echo Psalm 68:5. *ṣiwwîtî* is understood as a prec. (cf. NIV).

6. *gôzî* is awkward and often emended on the assumption that it is derived from the root *gzh*, meaning 'to cut' (unless, with Goulder 1990: 234) we understand this as God's cutting the umbilical cord (Claasens 2007 explores the theological potential of this possibility). But *gwz* is also possible, and though it often refers to 'flight', we can understand it is sustaining flight. See Obinwa 2006: 59–61.

12. With Q, read *ḥûšâ*.

19. For *'ăšer* as causal, see *WHS* §468.

20. *'ăšer* is often deleted, but as an independent relative (*WHS* §463b) can be retained, and echoes the second part of the previous verse. With Q, many MSS and most versions, read *hir'îtanî* and *tĕḥayyînî*.

Form and structure

Psalm 71 follows closely on to Psalm 70, with verse 12b taking up the language of Psalm 70:5. The lack of a title also encourages reading these psalms particularly closely. Within Book 2, Psalm 43 is the only other poem to lack a title, and it is closely tied to Psalm 42. This follows the pattern of Book 1, which also used the absence of a title to show the close links between Psalms 9–10 and 32–33. Psalms 1–2, also untitled, are read together. Each psalm remains a discrete text within the collection, but light is shed on it by reading it in dialogue with the previous text. Indeed, several MSS treat Psalms 70–71 as a single text, and this approach is followed by some scholars (e.g. Vesco [2006, 2: 616] claims that Pss 70:2, 71:13, 24 are a refrain, justifying treating them together). The pressure to join these texts was apparently felt by Gk, which includes a Davidic title here, ensuring the poems are still seen as discrete works. In that Psalm 71 introduces some distinctive elements and lacks the urgency of Psalm 70, it is best to see it as a separate work while also appreciating that it is particularly close to Psalm 70. Intriguingly, in 4QPs[a] it immediately follows Psalm 38, another poem with which it has much in common, so other options were clearly available for its placement. It also has numerous links to Psalms 22, 31, 35, making it a composition deeply grounded in the wider traditions of the Psalter (cf. Tate 1990: 211; Obinwa 2006: 27–35).

As with Psalm 70, we can treat Psalm 71 as a complaint psalm, though this time the anticipation of praise notably absent from Psalm 70 is present, especially in verses 14–24. The exact circumstances that initiated the complaint cannot be determined with certainty beyond the fact that the psalmist seeks rescue from adversaries, having taken refuge with Yahweh (see Obinwa 2006: 41–48). This is consistent with Psalm 70, where the poet also seeks rescue from adversaries. The issue of honour and shame, strongly present in Psalm 70, continues here. Perhaps more strikingly, both psalms also include the speech of adversaries (Pss 70:3; 71:11) and the image of God as helper (Pss 70:1; 71:12). Although we cannot determine the circumstances that gave rise to the psalm, its placement alongside Psalm 70 creates a context in which to read it.

The poem does not show strong structural markers. However, it can be analysed as containing two stanzas, each containing three strophes:

1. Appeal for rescue (1–13)
   a. Yahweh as refuge (1–3)
   b. Request for rescue (4–8)
   c. Request not to be forsaken (9–13)
2. Waiting and anticipating praise (14–24)
   a. Waiting to praise (14–16)
   b. God's keeping of the psalmist (17–21)
   c. Praise promised (22–24)

Comment

1–3. Where Psalm 70 is all urgent appeal, Psalm 71 gradually builds to this. It starts instead by focusing on Yahweh as the one in whom the poet has taken refuge. Such a claim could mean the poet has come to the temple, but it is a metaphor here. Having taken refuge, the psalmist asks not to be put to shame, evoking the 'shame' motif from Psalm 70. Shame would be incurred should Yahweh fail to deliver the psalmist, so verse 2 asks for Yahweh to deliver and rescue the poet 'in his righteousness'. If refuge is understood to be in the temple, then this could refer to the prayers of the accused, with Yahweh's acting as the divine judge. But a more general sense is probably intended, so that Yahweh's righteousness points to his character in general as one who helps the needy. There is a sense of increased urgency by the appeal of verse 2b, where the psalmist asks to be heard and saved, leading to the further request of verse 3. Here, the poet again uses imagery of refuge, asking that Yahweh be the psalmist's point of refuge. If Yahweh is the secure place, then the psalmist can always go there, unlike the temple, which would always require a journey. The image of Yahweh as a rock or crag again draws on the idea of being on a high and inaccessible place and so secure (Fernandes 2013: 212–217). It is from there that Yahweh can command the salvation the psalmist desires. The psalmist has claimed refuge in Yahweh, but that refuge needs to be demonstrated.

4–8. The means by which Yahweh demonstrates that he is a refuge is by rescuing those in need. Addressing him as 'my God' and thus insisting on a close personal bond, the psalmist now asks to be rescued from the hand of the wicked, further defined as the unjust and oppressive. The psalmist is in some way under their power, and it is God who must deliver. This would demonstrate that a lifetime of hoping in God has been an appropriate choice. Calling God 'Lord Yahweh' makes clear that the poet's God is Israel's God, who has the power to change things. We cannot know the psalmist's age at this point, but the implication of verse 5 is that the poet has trusted God for some time. This element of trust is developed in verse 6, which insists that the psalmist's hope is not passive. Rather, the poet has leant on Yahweh throughout life, finding God to be a sustainer worthy of all praise. This life has made the psalmist a sign to many, indicating that this faith has been lived out in public, and this God has been a strong refuge. Experience encourages the poet to believe that God remains as a strong refuge. Such experience means the psalmist's mouth is filled with praise so that God's glory is always set forth.

9–13. The third strophe again appeals to God, starting with what the poet does not want to happen and concluding with what is wanted concerning the enemies. Through this, God will demonstrate that he is indeed the psalmist's refuge. Verse 9 contains a pair of negative wishes, things the psalmist does not want God to do. It is not necessary that the poet has now reached old age or lost vitality (against Blackburn 1991), but rather is concerned that God may not stand with one for whom this is the case. The point is that the psalmist never wishes to be separated from God, especially if he is always the poet's refuge. The reason this concern is raised is because of the speech of the adversaries, which is prepared to suggest that God has done exactly this. They have been watching for the psalmist's life, and taking counsel, deeming this is the appropriate time to act and seize the psalmist. They argue that God has abandoned the psalmist, who therefore cannot have a deliverer. Only now in verse 12 does the appeal become urgent, asking that God not stand far off but rather hasten to help. The poet can be saved only by God's involvement. The psalmist did not wish to be put to shame, so now asks that the enemies be put to shame, an outcome that will demonstrate that God is indeed the psalmist's refuge. The enemies have persecuted the poet, so now they are to experience the shame and ignominy the poet would have experienced were Yahweh not a true refuge.

14–16. The second stanza commences by noting a contrast – the poet has taken refuge in Yahweh, but now waits. This waiting, typically a hopeful act, anticipates adding to God's praise. In verse 2 the psalmist had pointed to Yahweh's righteousness as the reason he should save the poet, and this righteousness is to be central to the praise offered. The poet anticipates this salvation as evidence of Yahweh's righteousness and this forms the core of the anticipated praise, though the psalmist also admits to ignorance of all God's acts. Nevertheless, when the poet enters the assembly for praise, his mouth will utter the mighty acts of the Lord Yahweh, the one who has power and who is in covenant with his people. Yahweh's acts alone will constitute the content of the praise.

17–21. The voc. at verse 17 marks the commencement of the second strophe. God's role as the poet's teacher from youth is affirmed so that the psalmist has been able to proclaim God's wonders to this point. God has sustained the poet through teaching, and now the poet asks for this to continue through all life. It is not that the poet has reached old age and fears being forsaken but rather hopes for the close relationship with God to continue. The goal is that the psalmist will continue to proclaim God's might to subsequent generations so that they too will offer God praise. Mention of praise returns to the theme of God's righteousness, which has run like a thread through the poem, this time emphasizing that it reaches to the heights, presumably the heavens. This is evidenced by the great things God has done, leading to the rhetorical question about his incomparability (cf. Exod. 15:11). This declaration about God does not stand in isolation. Instead, it is applied to the challenges facing the psalmist since it is also God who has caused the poet to see many troubles and evils. But God's incomparability and power also mean he will revive the psalmist. These challenges, even when they seem to bring the poet to the realm of death in the underworld, cannot triumph, because of God's righteousness. Yet, because the challenges remain, the psalmist asks for increased greatness (here in the sense of complete restoration) and that God may again provide comfort.

22–24. The final strophe focuses on the anticipated praise, moving beyond the testimony anticipated earlier into musical worship. God's faithfulness and status as the Holy One of Israel merit praise, though since 'thanksgiving' is introduced here it is clear that this praise begins with anticipation of the poet's restoration. God will have proved to be a refuge, and this demonstrates his faithfulness. The praise offered is fully embodied, drawing on the psalmist's lips and tongue ('mouth' in v. 15, creating an inclusion within the stanza), though the playing of instruments would also include other body parts. All of this is because God will have redeemed the psalmist, leading to continued speech about God's righteousness, which is evidenced by those who have sought the psalmist's harm, suffering shame rather than the poet, with these motifs drawing on verse 1 and forming an inclusion for the whole poem.

Explanation

God's righteousness and God as refuge run through this psalm as key themes. Within the Psalter, there are immediate links to Psalm 70, providing both continuity and difference for reading this poem. It joins Psalm 70 in asking God to act urgently, but it is also content to follow a slightly more leisurely path in getting there because it already knows that God is a refuge for the believer. One can simultaneously live with an urgent desire for deliverance and have an enduring hope that God will act. All this is grounded in a deep knowledge of the traditions of the Psalter, which are brought together here, and that make clear what it means to assert that God is a refuge, continuing to be one throughout life. God as refuge is shaped by the declaration of God's righteousness. This is not used in the Pauline sense of a righteousness given by God, but rather the fact that because righteousness defines God's character, we can wait hopefully for him to save his people, something that remains true through all life. It is this that also enables praise to shape all of life.

PSALM 72

Translation

Solomonic.

1O God, give your just decisions to the king
  and your righteousness to the king's son.

2May he judge your people with righteousness,
and your afflicted ones with justice.
3May the mountains bear well-being for the people
and the hills righteousness.
4May he act justly for the afflicted of the people,
save the children of the needy,
and crush the oppressor.
5May he endure long with the sun,
and the presence of the moon,
generation to generation.
6May he descend like rain on the mown field,
like the showers that water the earth.
7May what is right sprout in his days,
and well-being abound
until the moon is no more.
8May he rule from sea to sea,
and from the river to the ends of the earth.
9May the desert dwellers bow down before him,
and may his enemies lick up the dust.
10May the kings of Tarshish and the coastlands render tribute,
the kings of Sheba and Seba draw near with gifts.
11May all the kings do obeisance to him,
may all the nations serve him.

12For he delivers the needy who cry for help,
both the afflicted and the one with no helper.
13He has pity for the weak and the needy,
and the lives of the needy he saves.
14From injury and from violence,
he redeems their lives,
and their blood is precious in his sight.
15So may he live, and may gold from Sheba be given to him,
and may prayer be continually offered for him,
and may blessing be invoked for him all day.
16May there be an abundance of grain in the land,
on the tops of the mountains,
may his fruit be plentiful like Lebanon,
and may those from the town blossom like the grass of the field.
17May his name endure for ever,
may his name be propagated before the sun:
may all nations find blessing through him,
and may they declare his blessedness.

18Blessed be Yahweh God, the God of Israel,
who alone does wondrous deeds!

[19]And blessed be his glorious name for ever,
and may his glory fill all the earth.
Amen and amen!

[20]The prayers of David ben Jesse are finished.

Notes on the text

5. With Gk, read *wĕya'ărîk*. NET defends MT.

16. Both *pissat* and *r'š* are uncertain but context suggests both are related to fruitfulness.

17. With many MSS and Q, read *yinnôq*.

Form and structure

Psalm 72, a royal psalm, has a threefold closing function, completing each of Book 2 (Pss 42–72), the prayers of David (Pss 51–72) and its final subunit (Pss 69–72). The final subunit has been marked by a concern for God to act for the needy (Pss 69:33; 70:5; then typified through the one who prays in Ps. 71), evidenced by God's being their help (Pss 70:1, 5–6; 71:12). Although God may do this in other ways, this psalm expects the king to provide this help (v. 12), while also being one who delivers the needy (vv. 2, 4, 12–14). The psalm also develops the universalism of Psalms 65–68 by anticipating the king being the focus for the worship of the nations (vv. 9–11, 17). The Solomonic title of this psalm provides an important link to Psalm 51 since that psalm's title refers to the background of Solomon's birth. More explicitly, verse 20 reports the close of the prayers of David, providing a title for the collection. The closing doxology, in this case probably an addition to the core poem, marks the end of Book 2. Beyond the closing functions, the doxology also provides an important link to Psalms 1–2 through its allusion to the beatitude with which Psalm 1 begins (v. 18), while the wider psalm, in its development of the themes of the Davidic covenant, alludes to Psalm 2. In all, it marks a significant break within the Psalter, a point to reread the first two psalms as an orientation to the Psalter to this point, while also taking up their themes as readers move into Book 3. Yet it also advances these elements through its allusion to the Abrahamic covenant (v. 17), linking these covenants in God's work through Israel while anticipating the further joining of the covenants in Psalms 105–106 as they bring Book 4 to a close (see Hensley 2018: 185–195).

The analysis of the verbs in verses 2–11 is fundamental to the poem's interpretation. Most can be analysed as either impfs. or jussives, though some are definitely impfs. If read as impfs. (cf. NET, NIV 1984), then the psalm declares what the king will do in the light of the initial prayer (v. 1). If jussives (so NRSV, NIV 2011), then these verses are an extended form of wish-prayer. On balance, the latter is more likely since the king described here clearly goes beyond any one king in Israel's story. In that even the definite impfs. depend on the initial imp., they too have at least some of the character of the juss. This means the prayer is rooted in Israel's past while being more explicitly eschatological in its messianic hope than any other psalm. Christians, of course, confess that in Jesus we know this king, 'Great David's greater Son' as the hymnwriter James Montgomery puts it ('Hail to the Lord's Anointed'). Nevertheless, as the psalm's use in Advent reminds us, it remains a prayer with an eschatological dimension even now. Like Psalm 2, an earlier form of the poem might have played a part in the coronation of kings in Jerusalem, reminding each descendant of David of the task they were to carry out, even if none fully embodied it.

The change in verb forms at verse 11 marks a significant change in the poem, creating the limit of the opening stanza. Likewise, verses 18–20 stand apart from the rest of it as a coda, though one carefully joined to what precedes (on the poem's integrity, see Barbiero 2008). The return to jussives at verse 15 also introduces a new section (though Kselman [1975: 77] makes v. 15 a closing verse). We may therefore analyse the psalm in three stanzas plus the coda, though subdividing the first:

1. Prayer for well-being through the king (1–11)
   a. Focus on the king (1)
   b. Prayer for justice (2–4)
   c. Prayer for the king's Life (5–7)
   d. Prayer for dominion (8–11)
2. The basis for and hope of dominion (12–14)
3. Prayer for prosperity (15–17)
4. Coda (18–20)
   a. Doxology (18–19)
   b. Editorial note (20)

Comment

Title: 'Solomonic' (elsewhere only in the title of Ps. 127) functions rather like 'Davidic' (see on Ps. 3) in that it can be variously understood. If we understand the closing note in verse 20 about the finishing of the Prayers of David to mean David wrote Psalms 51–71, then the inclusion of this psalm in this collection would also imply he also wrote this one. But that would mean that although the grammatical form of 'Solomonic' and 'Davidic' is the same, we interpret them differently even though consistent interpretation is preferable. Understanding Solomon as the author is also possible but, if so, why is it part of the 'Prayers of David'? The coda suggests that a different sense is required. The title is best understood as a dedication to Solomon as the first king after David, the one through whom the messianic line is developed (similarly, Vesco 2006, 2: 628).

1. The opening verse introduces an extended prayer for the king that runs through to verse 11. This verse is especially closely integrated with verses 2–4 through the extension of the justice motif. But it also stands apart grammatically as the one verse to name the king as the one God is to enable, while also extending this to include the king's son, and thus the messianic line. It also uses an imp., whereas the rest of the prayer uses the juss. to return to the king. The request is that the king receive and demonstrate God's justice and righteousness, enabling his reign to represent the models of justice God desired for his people. God, not the king, is the source of justice.

2–4. This strophe develops the theme of justice from verse 1 but changes the form of the verbs so that the prayer becomes an extended wish for the king (cf. Mays 1994b: 237). If the king receives God's justice, then it is essential that he judge with righteousness and justice since this combination is evidence of God's presence (cf. Amos 5:24). The king, however, remains as God's regent, since the people (and the afflicted in particular) are God's: they do not belong to the king. A society founded on divine justice is one that can flourish, and this is portrayed in verse 3 through the image of the mountains bearing 'well-being' (*šālôm*), while the hills bear 'righteousness'. Although not evident in English, there is an alternation in the Hebrew terms for 'righteousness', with the term in verses 1, 3 more typically referring to specific acts and that in verse 2 to the overall practice, though the distinction is not to be pushed. However righteousness might be conceived, it needs to be evident in the king's reign, not only in the legal process but in the whole society. But its most immediate manifestation is in the promotion of justice for the poor and action against oppressors who thus work against justice. The poor had least access to justice (cf. Amos 2:6–8; 5:10–13), making it essential that the king work for and promote justice.

5–7. Although less evident, the motif of justice continues here, though it is linked to the prayer for the king's life. This is evident from the unusually phrased opening to verse 5. The prep. *'im* is often construed to mean something like 'as long as' but this is not really an established meaning for it. Most commonly it is rendered 'with' – though exactly how one is 'with' another varies considerably. However, one possibility is for this to mean 'in the presence of' (cf. Exod. 34:28). The request here is not that the king live as long as the sun but more likely live (for an admittedly extended life) in the sun's presence. It is important to note that the sun was commonly regarded as the justice god Shamash (Hebr. for 'sun' is *šemeš*). The sun god is here demythologized, now simply put in parallel with moon, and with his role in promoting justice taken over by God but passed to the king. In this, the psalm joins with Psalm 104 in its integration of solar imagery that also draws on Genesis 1:14–18, which, while not necessarily polemical, insists that Israel's God alone is the one who promotes justice (see also Taylor 1993: 226–234). Long life alone is insufficient; it should also be marked by justice. A life marked by justice bears fruit for the people and is here compared to rain on a freshly mown field or showers sprinkled on the ground, which enable growth. Such well-watered ground creates the setting for righteousness to sprout and well-being to abound as long as there is a moon. The heavenly lights form an inclusion for this strophe, while also pointing to the hope of enduring well-being brought through the king.

8–11. The previous strophe developed elements of its predecessor, and this one picks up on elements of verses 5–7. Most notably, the opening verb (*rdh*) plays with the sound of 'may he come down' (*yrd*) in verse 6 while transitioning to the theme of the king's dominion. 'From sea to sea' could have a restricted sense, moving from the Dead Sea to the Mediterranean, but considering the parallel 'from the river [probably the Euphrates] to the ends of the earth' a more universal sense is intended. Israel's king, if granted God's justice, was the king the world needed. If so, then all peoples needed to come before him and accept his rule, even barely known peoples from the wilderness. This king's enemies would also lick the dust before him, an image of prostration. Likewise, kings from remote places like Tarshish (typically regarded as the westernmost location; cf. Jon. 1:3) or the distant coastlands would render tribute. Sheba (in southern Arabia, and home of the Queen of Sheba, 1 Kgs 10:1–13) and Seba (possibly in the region of Ethiopia (cf. Isa. 43:3) are also included. The point is not achieved through geographic specificity. Rather, the psalm considers places as remote from Jerusalem as can be imagined and sees them bringing their tribute to the king, a vision that climaxes in the image of all kings doing obeisance before the king, symbolizing all the nations serving him.

12–14. A new stanza begins here as we move away from the jussives that dominated since verse 2. Much has been asked for the king, but now we are told why. The nations need a king who exercises God's justice. Such a king rescues the needy when they cry out, along with the afflicted and those without help. This king inhabits God's justice, providing the help God was asked to provide in Psalm 70. Beyond this, the king is marked by pity, a commitment to the needs of those who lack the resources to change their circumstances. Salvation for the poor here is therefore expressly experienced in this world as they receive the justice they cannot otherwise achieve because of their lack of resources. The concentration of language about the poor here is notable and exceeded only by Psalm 82. The king's actions for these people continues in verse 14 where he redeems the life of the poor from injury and violence. The verb 'redeem' (*g'l*) is elsewhere used for the kinsperson who restores those who have had to sell their property, or even themselves, due to poverty (e.g. Lev. 25:25, 47–49), or who were otherwise unable to support themselves (e.g. Ruth 3:13). The king takes on this role for the poor, considering their lives as precious in his sight.

15–17. The third stanza returns to wish-prayers for the king. Where the first stanza was concerned with how the king would govern, this stanza is focused on the king's own lived experience. This experience emerges from the type of reign described in the second stanza, bringing together elements from earlier in the poem. The opening of verse 15 is often taken as a request for long life (e.g. ESV; cf. 1 Sam. 10:24), and that may be present here. But the use of the conj. to open the verse suggests a link to what has gone before, making a summary link with the previous stanza (see W-O §33.2.1.d). The balance of verse 15 then has three impersonal verbs that look for the result of this life in which the king receives gold from Sheba (cf. 1 Kgs 10:1–13), prayer is made continually for him and the people bless him. In effect, the request is for a wider community to continue the content of this prayer. This is extended in verse 16 with the request that fruitfulness be extended across the land, with mountains and hills full of grain, while the king's fruitfulness is likened to Lebanon, perhaps because of its famous cedars. The king's fruitfulness would specifically include his descendants, linking this request to mention of the king's son in verse 1. But the fruitfulness is also expressed in the king's positive impact on all people, so that urban inhabitants might likewise flourish. Verse 17 closes the stanza with three more wishes. The first is still concerned with the king, asking that his name (his renown) might endure for ever before the sun. This may again echo the motif of the king's justice (vv. 2–4) while also picking up the mention of the sun in verse 5. The king's renown as a practitioner of justice needs to be public and enduring. The king's name is then the link to the second request here, but this now moves beyond the king himself to consider the relationship between the king and the nations. The king's name is to be propagated; that is, sown like a seed, with the goal that the nations invoke blessing on themselves through him. They wish to be blessed in the same way his people are blessed, the language here evoking the Abrahamic blessing and the desire of the nations to find the same blessing God was giving through Abraham (Gen. 12:3; 22:18). The universal dominion of the second stanza becomes something nations desire so that all nations may pronounce his blessedness. In this, the closing wishes join this prayer to Psalms 1–2, with the king the ultimate representative of the blessed one of Psalm 1 and the one to whom the nations from Psalm 2 should submit.

18–19. Although the coda has been added to the poem, it still functions as part of the psalm and needs to be read with it (see Davage 2021). Each book in the Psalter ends with a doxology (though in Book 5 that is Pss

146–150; see also Introduction, §3.2.2, 'Structure of the Psalter'). These doxologies have certain commonalities (all are based on the verb *brk*, 'bless'), but each is also distinct, with this the fullest. Here, Yahweh God is initially blessed, a comparatively rare form in the Psalter (Ps. 84:11 is the nearest parallel) and a form that is especially important within the Elohistic Psalter. Moreover, this God is Israel's God, evidence for which is provided by the fact that he alone does wondrous things. Where the prayer asked for peoples to find blessing through the king's name, here it can be affirmed that Yahweh's glorious name is blessed for ever and indeed his glory fills all the earth. However much the people pray for the king, it always remains within the context of Yahweh's reign. The doubled 'Amen' is, then, how all who take up this prayer affirm it.

20. A closing editorial note is added here. In that there are further Davidic prayers after this (e.g. Ps. 86), it is unlikely to mean that there are no more Davidic prayers in the Psalter. But neither is it a frozen editorial remark from Book 2 alone (against Willgren 2016b). Rather, it most probably refers to the collection Psalms 51–72, which constitute 'The Prayers of David'. Psalm 72 is Solomonic, but this note ensures we continue to read it within the collection rather than seeing it as standing alone.

Explanation

Psalm 72 closes Book 2 with a glorious vision of a kingdom marked by justice. In doing so, it immediately sets Israel's view of kingship apart by insisting that it is God, not the king, who initiates justice. The king's role is to administer what God has given. The psalm is a prayer for a king who will act this way, prioritizing care for the poor. That such a prayer was needed makes clear that none of Israel's kings measured up to this standard (Wilson 2002: 990), but its presence here in the Psalter remains an important mechanism for challenging those in power within Israel (Houston 1999: 359–360; W. S. Prinsloo 1999a) and by which believers continue to challenge those in government (Human 2002: 673–675). Moreover, this king was assessed by his care for the poor, something deeply countercultural in Israel's world. As this king ignores the things typically thought to bring power, such as massive buildings or conquest programmes, so he gains the real power that matters (Broyles 1999: 297). As Israel's king administered God's justice, so God's reign was spread throughout the world. The psalm joins the Davidic covenant to the Abrahamic, pointing to how all the nations will come to know the blessing of Yahweh. Its placement and links to other parts of the Psalter mean it is also a point at which readers may pause and reflect on how the whole Psalter to this point shows the way of blessedness, a way that has included much suffering as well as praise. The psalm asks readers to look back, yet also to look forward through the messianic framework (against Carrière 1991: 69 there is no need to think of this in a limited sense) developed here, awaiting the king who will fully embody this vision of God's kingdom. The allusions to the psalm in the visit of the Magi (Matt. 2:1–12) make clear that Jesus is this king, but as with all the royal psalms, believers continue to await the time when all will be fully revealed.

BOOK 3

PSALM 73

Translation

A melody. Asaphic.

1Surely God is good to Israel,
to the pure in heart.

2But as for me, my feet had almost stumbled,
my steps nearly slipped,
3because I was envious of the boastful,
I saw the well-being of the wicked.

4For they have no pains up to their death,
and their body is fat.
5They do not have the troubles of mortals,
they do not suffer the diseases of humanity.
6Therefore pride is their necklace,
a garment of violence encloses them.
7Their eyes bulge with fatness,
the conceits of their hearts cross over.

[8]They mock and they speak maliciously of brutality,
they speak from on high.
[9]They set their mouth against heaven,
and their tongue walks on the earth.
[10]Therefore his people turn there,
and abundant waters are drained by them.
[11]And they say 'How can God know?
Is their knowledge with the Most High?'

[12]Behold, these are the wicked,
and always at ease they increase influence.

[13]Surely in vain have I kept my heart pure,
and washed my hands in innocence.
[14]And I was stricken all day,
rebuked every morning.
[15]If I had said 'I shall recount this,'
behold, I would have betrayed a generation of your children.
[16]When I thought to understand this,
it was burdensome in my eyes,
[17]until I entered God's sanctuary,
and I understood their end.

[18]Surely you set them in slippery places,
you make them fall for deceptions.
[19]How they become a desolation in a moment –
they are finished, consumed, by terrors.
[20]Like a dream when one awakes,
Lord, you shall despise their image when aroused.

[21]For my mind was embittered,
and I was pierced emotionally.
[22]For I was a brute, and I did not know,
I was like a beast with you.
[23]But I am always with you,
you hold my right hand.
[24]You lead me with your counsel,
and afterwards you take me to glory.
[25]Whom do I have in heaven?
And with you, there is nothing I desire on earth!
[26]My flesh and my heart end,
but God is the rock of my heart and my portion for ever.
[27]For behold, those who are far from you shall perish,
you destroy those prostituting themselves from you.
[28]As for me, the nearness of God is for my good,

I have made the Lord Yahweh my refuge,
to recount all your works.

Notes on the text

1. Often emended to 'good to the upright' (cf. NRSV). But the text is coherent and supported by the versions, so MT is retained.

2. With Q and many MSS, read *nāṭāyw*.

5. Often emended by dividing *lĕmôtām*, but, as with verse 1, MT is coherent and supported by the versions.

8. *mwq* is a hapax legomenon.

10. With Q and many MSS, read *yāšûb*.

12. *šālēw* is uncertain. Hebr. *ḥāyil* can refer to wealth or power, and 'influence' attempts to bring these elements together.

16. With Q and many MSS, read *hû'*.

17. The pl. *miqdāšîm* is understood as a pl. of extension (*WHS* §11) because the temple consists of several areas.

18. 'Deceptions' could also be 'ruins' (cf. Ps. 74:3). These involve different roots (*š'h* or *nš'*), the determination of which is uncertain. Plausibly (since the poet is not bound by etymology) we can understand the deceptions as causing ruin.

20. With Gk, read *bĕûrĕkā*.

Form and structure

Book 2 ended by simultaneously encouraging readers to look both backwards and forwards. They look back to Psalms 1–2 to understand the orientation these texts provide for prayer and praise, while also looking forwards to the king who would embody the vision of the kingdom in Psalm 72. Book 3 opens on a much more confused note, something that prepares readers for the wider conflict of faith and experience that dominates this book (cf. Foster 2019: 83). This poem reintroduces the Asaphic psalms from Psalm 50 (see 'Form and structure' there), a collection that continues through to Psalm 83. The connection to Psalm 50 points to links with Book 2 more broadly, the most important of which is the continuation of the Elohistic Psalter through to the end of the Asaphic collection. More immediately, Psalm 73 reflects on a world where the application of justice through the king announced in Psalm 72 is not yet experienced (see esp. Cole 2000: 15–17). God's justice will ultimately be applied, but it is not yet a reality. Psalm 73 wrestles with this disjuncture. It also enables these themes to be explored at a corporate level in Psalms 74–78, something also evident through repetition of key terms and themes (see S. J. Smith 2021, though he treats

Ps. 73 both as part of the subunit and as a programmatic introduction). The struggle to see God's justice is, indeed, a central theme throughout Psalms 73–83 (with S. J. Smith 2022).

The poem has been variously assessed in terms of the main categories but does not really fit any, crossing various proposed genres (Cheung 2015: 101–102), while joining Psalms 37 and 49 in addressing the issue of the prosperity of the wicked as a general theological problem (Goulder [1996: 52–61] ties it specifically to the Assyrians). It is clearly a didactic text, though to some extent this is true of the whole Psalter (cf. McCann 1993; Firth 2005c). A better approach is thus to ask how a given text teaches (similarly, Wendland 1998: 130–132). In this case, we can point to testimony as the mechanism. Testimony occurs across a range of the main types (Firth 1999), not just 'wisdom' psalms, and is marked by speakers recounting their own experience. Testimony allows an audience to see a connection between the sort of hope to which a poem like Psalm 72 points but without claiming that this experience is universal. Rather, the audience is asked to reflect on its own experience. This explains why the poet closes with a personal affirmation but without promising more. As with the poem's form, discussion of the identity of the psalm's speaker has not led to any clear resolution. Tournay's proposal (1991: 148) of a Levite is plausible given the reference to the sanctuary and the idea of God as the poet's heritage (cf. Josh. 21), but it is preferable to see this as something also left intentionally open so readers from other settings are not excluded.

Structurally, the poem seems to turn on the three occurrences of *'ak* (surely), with these marking the main stanzas (cf. McCann 1996: 968), though there is also an inclusio focused on the goodness of God for the whole poem (Wong 2016). We can analyse it in three stanzas:

1. The prosperity of the wicked (1–12)
   a. Declaration (1)
   b. Psalmist's envy (2–3)
   c. Way of the wicked (4–11)
   d. Declaration (12)
2. Torment caused by their prosperity (13–17)
3. Resolution: God's nearness (18–28)
   a. The end of the wicked (18–20)
   b. God and the psalmist (21–28)

Comment

Title: For 'A melody', see on Psalm 4. For 'Asaphic', see on Psalm 50.

1. The psalm commences with its characteristic 'Surely'. The term typically indicates something self-evidently true (e.g. Gen. 26:9; Ps.

58:11), though even that will be challenged in the first two stanzas, if only to reformulate it. God's goodness is a core affirmation of the Psalter (Pss 34:8; 100:5; 135:3; 145:9), especially to his servants. They are here defined as 'Israel' and the 'pure in heart'. Mention of Israel here is surprising in that this is an individual's testimony, but it prepares for the corporate focus present in the Asaphic psalms, allowing this poem to introduce this collection. Purity of heart introduces a key motif for this psalm, as the 'heart' becomes a key term throughout (vv. 1, 7, 13, 21, 26). As a declaration, this stands alone, a point with which a worshipping audience would agree, but it will be challenged as the testimony continues.

2–3. The poet now recounts the steps that led to this declaration being troublesome, admitting that envy of the wicked led to a crisis of faith, though the 'almost' makes clear that it was limited. The OT often uses the image of life as a journey (e.g. Ps. 1; cf. Kartje 2014: 101), and mention of the poet's steps here takes up this metaphor, explaining how the psalmist almost fell from the path. There may be a play on the beatitude form of Psalm 1 here as the word 'steps' (*'ăšurāy*) is close to 'blessed' (*'ăšrê*), indicating how close the poet was to moving out of the blessed life. This was caused by the poet being envious of the boastful (against which Ps. 37 counselled), of people whose praise is not directed to God. Most importantly, the poet saw the well-being of the wicked, the people who should not thrive (cf. Ps. 37:1–2, 10–13).

4–11. Having pointed to the well-being of the wicked, the psalmist then explains why this struggle occurred by describing the way of the wicked. Verses 4–5 note what is missing in their lives. Because of their wealth, they do not appear to suffer the problems and illnesses that are the common lot of humanity. These people eventually die, but even their deaths are more comfortable! Verses 6–11 then point to their actions and their effects on society. According to verse 6, it is because of their apparent comfort that they can clothe themselves (a metaphor for their way of life, Grogan 2008: 134) with violence, being a part of structures that oppress the righteous. Verses 7–8 develop this, showing they live comfortably at the expense of others. The image of the 'bulging' eye here is understood as evidence of their ambition to take from others, with their conceits unbounded by societal norms and matched by speech that mocks others. This ultimately applies to their view of God in verses 9–11, though verse 10 is difficult. Their attitude's climax is seen in setting themselves against heaven in verse 9, an expression of 'unbounded hubris' (Kraus 1989: 88) that applies their attitude to other people to God. In the flow of thought, verse 10 is problematic. A literal rendering is given in the translation. The sense is perhaps that the righteous are so impressed by the wicked that they turn and become like them (Tate 1990: 229). Alternatively, we could we follow NIV (cf. van Gemeren 2008: 562), suggesting that their success makes even sin seem attractive. The thought is similar in either case, so it is wise to stay with the MT. The height of the wicked's arrogance is seen in the rhetorical question of verse 11. God's existence is not denied, but the question assumes (with Pss 14, 53) that it makes no practical difference. The suggestion is that God is too high to be bothered!

12. The stanza closes with another declaration, but this time it is not a routine affirmation of faith. Rather, it asserts that the people described are representative of the wicked, allowing the audience to give their assent through their experience too.

13–17. The second stanza also begins with 'surely', taking up the language of Psalm 24:3–4. Again, this will be challenged. Given the psalmist's testimony so far, striving for purity of heart (cf. v. 1) may seem pointless. Extending this, verse 14 seems to indicate that the psalmist had even become ill from envy of the wicked. Yet verse 15 begins to offer a counter-narrative, and as the middle verse it is also a pivot within the poem (similarly, Hamilton 2021, 2: 9). A resolution is withheld here but the poet perceives that to have spoken of the well-being of the wicked in the same terms as verses 4–11 would have been a denial of his faith that would have damaged the whole community. Speech like that was not possible, but verse 16 indicates that reflection on it was a source of torment. It could not be spoken of, but neither could it be ignored. All this begins to change in verse 17, which indicates that a moment of understanding occurred in worship (the sanctuary could be the temple referred to metaphorically, but the point remains the same). What triggered this is not stated (despite speculation on it; cf. A. A. Anderson 1972, 1: 533–534), and this silence is an important element in the text. Testimony needs to leave space for an audience to fill this gap, so, beyond the importance of worship, we do not know what happened.

18–20. The third stanza also commences with 'surely' – except this time it introduces a point the poet can affirm. This stanza, apart from verse 28, is addressed directly to God, so it is overheard by an audience. God would not allow the wicked to continue unchallenged. Where the psalmist's feet had almost slipped, the wicked are placed in slippery places by God and do fall. It may be that they fall for deceptions (in this case the pursuit of wickedness), but these deceptions are also their ruin (cf. 'Notes on the text'). They have brought pain to many, but suddenly become desolate, consumed by terrors. When God is roused, he acts against the wicked. What the wicked deny in verse 11 is answered, though doing so creates space for further reflection on verse 1. There is indeed knowledge with God, and he is good to the pure in heart.

21–28. The psalmist's relationship with God is now central, contrasting the previous state with the current through a series of wordplays (Allen 1982: 104). Verses 21–22 describe the poet before the discovery in the sanctuary, reflecting on the torment caused by the well-being of the wicked as something that attacks both mind (heart) and emotion (kidneys). Thinking in those terms left the poet more like an animal, unable to understand the subtlety of God's interaction with the world. The past is contrasted with the present in verse 23, where the psalmist recognizes God's enduring presence, holding the psalmist's right hand so that something that would otherwise be understood as a royal prerogative (cf. Fernandes 2013: 233) is made available to an ordinary worshipper. God is thus always leading, ultimately taking the psalmist to glory. Whether glory is to be understood here as an eschatological reference or not is disputed. Against it is the fact that the idea occurs directly nowhere else in Psalms (Tate 1990: 236 rejects the possibility). However, the possibility of a novel insight cannot be discounted, so the psalmist could be moving towards an eschatological hope, though glory may also be experienced in this life. The phrasing's ambiguity makes a definite conclusion impossible (cf. Estes 2019: 37), and that may be intended. But God's presence reminds the psalmist that nothing more is needed in heaven or earth. There is no need to be envious of the wicked because God provides security as the psalmist's rock, and even death cannot change this. By contrast, the wicked have no hope and will perish (cf. Ps. 1:6). They have sought their well-being away from God and so are finally destroyed, even if no timescale can be described. Rather than being far from God, the poet understands that nearness to God is truly good. The Lord Yahweh, Israel's covenant God, is the refuge (cf. Ps. 2:12) the psalmist needs in a world of thriving wickedness, and from there all God's wondrous works can be recounted so others may also learn to live with the challenges of this world.

Explanation

This psalm is a moving testimony of experience, an experience that is simultaneously individual and representative (against Ray [2020: 70], who misses the representative element). Within Book 3, Psalm 73 addresses the individual and the nation, summoning them to faithfulness, even when experience seemed to deny God's goodness, or rather a simplistic understanding of it (cf. Hossfeld and Zenger 2006: 225). It also provides the opportunity to reflect further on Psalm 1 and the choices noted there. In Psalm 1, the way of the righteous is a minority choice, made in the knowledge that the seductions of alternatives will always be there. In presenting the way of blessedness, it does not explore what happens when the wicked seem to flourish. This psalm makes clear that this possibility must be acknowledged, not ignored, but confessed in a way that enables others to work through the challenges posed. The central claims of Psalm 1, and indeed the whole of Books 1 and 2, are reaffirmed as we enter Book 3 (cf. Brueggemann 1991b; Brueggemann and Miller 1996; Clayton 2006: 124–126), but reaffirmed from the perspective that this does not make the life of faith straightforward and pain free. Doubt needs to find a place in worship because only in worship is it truly addressed, as there we are we reminded of God's enduring presence.

PSALM 74

Translation

A Maskil. Asaphic.

1Why, O God, do you reject us for ever,
does your anger smoke against the sheep of your pasture?
2Remember your congregation that you acquired long ago,
you redeemed the tribe of your inheritance,
this Mount Zion where you dwell.
3Lift your steps to the enduring ruins,
all the damage the enemy has done in the sanctuary.

4Your adversaries roared within your appointed place,
they set up their signs as signs.
5It seems like one has lifted up
axes in a forest of trees.
6And now all its carved works,
they have struck down with an axe and crowbars.
7They burnt your sanctuary with fire,
they have defiled your dwelling place of your name to the ground.
8They thought to themselves, 'We will utterly oppress them,'
they burned all God's appointed places in the land.
9We do not see our signs,
there is no longer a prophet,
and no one with us knows how long.

10How long, O God, will the adversary taunt,
shall the enemy spurn your name for ever?
11Why do you turn back your hand, your right hand?
From your bosom, destroy!

12But God is my king from of old,
achieving victories in the midst of the earth.
13You yourself divided the sea by your might,
you shattered the heads of the sea monster on the waters.
14You yourself crushed the heads of Leviathan,
you gave him as food to the inhabitants of the wilderness.

[15]You yourself broke open spring and stream,
you yourself dried up the perennial rivers.
[16]The day is yours, the night also is yours,
you yourself established the luminary and sun.
[17]You yourself established all the boundaries of the earth,
summer and winter you yourself formed.

[18]Remember this, O Yahweh, the enemy taunts,
and a senseless people reviles your name.
[19]Do not give the life of your turtledove to the beasts,
do not forget the life of your afflicted ones for ever.
[20]Have regard for the covenant,
for the land's hiding places are full,
habitations of violence.
[21]Do not let the oppressed return humiliated,
let the needy and the poor praise your name.
[22]Rise up, O God, contend your cause,
remember how the fool reproaches you all the day.
[23]Do not forget the sound of your adversaries,
the din of those who rise against you going up continually.

Notes on the text

1. 'Us' is understood from the context, though the identity of those spurned is elided until the second half-line of this verse.

2. A. P. Ross (2013: 579) argues for *qnh* II (create) rather than 'acquire'. But the connection to the exodus suggests that *qnh* I is correct.

5. *yiwwāda'* is often emended, but, if understood in a derived sense as 'it seems like' (with Tate 1990: 242), can be sustained, though it remains very difficult. Alternatively, Rendsburg (1990: 69) suggests that there the root *yd'* could mean 'smite' in Israelite (northern) Hebr.

6. With Q, read *wĕ'attâ*.

11. With Q, many MSS and the versions, read *ḥêḥĕkā*.

14. Hebr. *lĕṣîyim* is uncertain and the translation is tentative. The proposed emendation in *BHS* requires too many changes to be plausible.

Form and structure

Psalm 74 introduces a run of three communal psalms that move through a process similar to Psalm 73, from grief at the destruction wrought by Yahweh's enemies to confidence in God as the one who works for his people. Psalm 74 is a communal lament that responds to the destruction of the sanctuary. Psalm 75 is a communal thanksgiving that understands that God will indeed judge, while Psalm 76 celebrates God as the one to be feared. Although each of these poems must first be interpreted as a work distinct in itself, we can also see that Psalm 74 matches Psalm 73 up to the point of the poet's entry to the sanctuary (Ps. 73:17), while Psalm 75 matches the poet's insights in Psalm 73:18–26 and Psalm 76 joins with the affirmations of Psalm 73:27–28. More directly, Psalm 74 takes up an unresolved issue from Psalm 73 – the psalmist's insights there emerged in the sanctuary, but the community lives in a time when the sanctuary has been destroyed (vv. 4–8). How is the community to approach God? The answer is to place the current crisis in an enduring conflict that reaches back to creation and in which God's victories can be seen, creating a continued basis for appeal (Michael 2019: 27–29). This can then be extended in Psalms 77–78 to Israel's own story, so their history is part of the longer demonstration of God's acts of salvation. Further, Psalm 73:7 pointed to the malicious thoughts in the hearts of the wicked, and those thoughts are reported here in verse 8; and the 'ruins' (v. 3) at least plays on the 'deceptions' of Psalm 73:18 as the only two occurrences of this word. Approaching God through Psalm 73, the community looks for God to act against the wicked who are attacking them, though without yet reaching a resolution.

References to the destruction of the sanctuary suggest a background after the Babylonians captured Jerusalem. This is not easy to match with evidence of northern dialect in the poem (Rendsburg 1990: 69–71). Goulder (1996: 63) argues that it originally referred to the destruction of the sanctuary in Bethel but was subsequently brought south (cf. Weber 2000: 523–528), yet much of this depends on his proposed festival using the Asaph psalms, which is not otherwise convincing. Even if he was correct, the final form of the psalm is still found in a collection that otherwise focuses on the exile, making this the most likely background against which to read this prayer (alternative suggestions include the times of Rehoboam [so Hamilton 2021, 2: 19] or the Maccabees). It might have drawn on existing materials; hence, the northern elements. But the final composition is exilic and reference to Zion (v. 2) is certainly indicative of a concern with Jerusalem (Wardlaw 2015: 123).

The poem can be analysed in three stanzas, with the first further divided by the changing verb forms:

1. Why, O God? (1–11)
    a. An extended relationship (1–3)
    b. Destruction of the sanctuary (4–9)
    c. How long? (10–11)
2. God as divine king (12–17)
3. Appeal for Yahweh to remember (18–23)

Comment

Title: For 'A Maskil', see on Psalm 32. For 'Asaphic', see on Psalm 50.

1–3. The psalm commences with an abrupt question (cf. Gerstenberger 2001: 78). It cannot deny the nation's experience, but needs to know why. Although the sanctuary's destruction will emerge as a key issue, it is placed in a secondary position. What matters here is to know why God has acted against his people. The assumption is that God's anger means they are rejected in perpetuity, even though they are the sheep of his pasture. This introduces the shepherd motif, a key element through this collection (Pss 77:20; 78:72; 79:13; 80:1), one that both describes God's relationship to his people and provides a basis for appeal since a shepherd was meant to care for the sheep (Broyles 1989: 152). Because they are God's people, the community appeals for him to remember that he acquired them in the past, perhaps an allusion to the exodus (Exod. 15:13–17). Asking God to remember does not assume he has forgotten but rather asks him to act in terms of his commitment to them (cf. Gen. 8:1; Exod. 2:24). This commitment emerges from his redemption of the nation, primarily a reference to the exodus, where he entered a special relationship with Israel, along with his commitment to Mount Zion, an appeal linked with the Davidic covenant. The appeal to remember is thus rooted in the covenant traditions of the OT, while anticipating the third stanza. Yet all of this seems undermined by the temple's destruction, and so God is summoned to come and inspect the damage wrought by the unnamed enemy. Perhaps then God can answer the question 'why'.

4–9. The second strophe is marked by pf. verbs that report the enemy's activity and is bounded by reference to signs at the sanctuary. While some details are difficult to interpret, the picture is one of total destruction. An important shift here is that the enemies become 'your adversaries'. They are unnamed, but the community makes clear that those who have done this are God's enemies. Some of the terminology here is unusual; for example, calling the temple an 'appointed place' (*mô'ēd*; elsewhere only Lam. 2:6), anticipating some allusions to Genesis 1 in the second stanza. The enemies are portrayed as having engaged in wanton violence, roaring like animals and replacing with their own the signs that announced Israel's God. God's enemies attacked the sanctuary with various tools, wantonly damaging its carved works and sending fire on it as if they were cutting wood in a forest. Burning it not only damaged the building; it also defiled the dwelling place of God's name. The sanctuary announced the God of the whole earth, but this is removed with its destruction. The psalmist even cites the enemy's thoughts in verse 8, noting their desire to utterly oppress the community while destroying any place where God may be worshipped. This comes to its conclusion in verse 9 as the community summarizes its experience. They cannot see their signs, those things that point to God's presence, and neither do they have a prophet they trust (cf. Roberts 1977: 481) to tell them how long all this will continue. Everything that helped them interpret their situation is gone, and the 'why' of verse 1 remains unanswered.

10–11. With the question of 'why' unanswered, the community turns to 'how long', a question that recurs in various forms through Book 3 (Pss 79:5; 80:4; 82:2; 89:46), picking up on the uncertainty reported in verse 9. Where verses 1–3 were concerned with God's anger, the question is now about the enemy. They taunt and spurn God's name, seemingly without end, thus matching the community's sense of God's anger. But this brings the community back to the question of 'why' – given what God can do, why does he pull back his hand, even his right hand? The community knows God can act but are perplexed that he does not. Rather than having his hand pulled back to his chest, they want him to bring it out and destroy. The questions have not been answered, but the community knows what they want God to do.

12–17. An individual speaker appears in the second stanza, though like the poet in Psalm 73 this is a representative individual, one who articulates the community's hope. The speaker affirms God's kingship as something that has been experienced from of old, linking this statement to verse 2. As king, God has wrought victories on the earth. The victories include the exodus, but the balance of the stanza concerns God's victories in creation, not only its origin but also its sustenance. These victories engage the mythological views of the region (see also Ps. 82). They do not affirm those myths but use them to demonstrate God's kingship and authority over all creation, however it may be conceived, so that God defeats all his enemies (Tsumura 2015). The stanza is also marked by the repeating form 'you yourself' (using a pr. and verb, though the Hebr. verb contains a pr.). The point is emphatically made that God is the one who has acted and overcome forces that anyone would have considered too powerful, and therefore can overcome the enemy. Ugar. sources speak of the sea as a deity, and also chaos monsters that existed because of the chaotic threat of the sea, and these stories provide important background here (Day 1985: 21–25; cf. Psa. 89:9–14). So, God's dividing the sea refers to his defeat of a force that might be thought to oppose him in creation, though of course he also divided the sea in the exodus (Exod. 14:21). God also shattered the heads of the sea monster (which he created, Gen. 1:21), creatures that ultimately praise him (Ps. 148:7). Even the terrifying monster Leviathan (a seven-headed creature at Ugarit; see Greene 2017: 95) was crushed and given as food. In context, the spring and stream are probably other waters thought of as resisting God but which he overcame. But God's provision of water in the exodus (Exod. 17:5–6) shows that he continues to reign over creation. That is why we have a change at verse 16, which effectively declares that all creation, starting with day and night and thus the most basic division of Genesis 1:3–5, belongs to God. This division has an impact on all time, as marked by the two great lights in Genesis 1:14–18. Here, the sun is named, but the other is the 'luminary', presumably the moon, but here simply a light. Reference to these lights enables the psalm to move to time as it is now experienced in a world whose boundaries God has fixed and where time is ordered through the division between summer and winter. However creation is understood, God has overcome any forces that might have opposed him, and has continued to do so. He is not only the speaker's king: he reigns over everything.

18–23. The final stanza therefore also returns to verse 2 as it asks God to remember. But rather than the community, the concern now is with the enemy. Because of his commitment, Yahweh needs to act against a taunting enemy (cf. 1 Sam. 17:10; 2 Kgs 19:4). Use of the name 'Yahweh' reminds God of his covenant commitment to his people and shows the folly of those reviling his name. Parallel to remembering the enemy, God is also asked not to give the life of his turtledove to the beasts. According to Leviticus 5:7, the turtledove was a bird the poor might offer to Yahweh, and the bird here stands for them, which is why Yahweh is not to forget the afflicted for ever. Remembering the enemy means not forgetting the needy who belong to him. This finds its focus in the covenant that exists with Israel, the formal relationship where God commits himself to his people, allusion to which runs through the psalm, though the links with creation also suggest an allusion to the Noahic covenant (Gen. 9:1–17) as well as Davidic elements (Human 1995a). This is urgent because violence dominates the land, even in hiding places that might have been thought too dark for the enemy. The oppressed and needy must return to worship, so God is asked to prevent their humiliation and to allow them to return to praise. But this is not something the community can do. It is God who has to rise up and contend for them, fighting his own cause rather than allowing the fool to continue reproaching him. Until then, the noise of the enemies continues, and God is asked not to forget that they continue to rise against him. They are his enemies, and therefore God needs to act.

Explanation

Unanswered questions run through this psalm's first stanza – 'why' and 'how long' are asked about the community's suffering, but no answer is forthcoming. Indeed, there is almost an oxymoron in the opening verses – God is the people's shepherd, the one who cares for, guides and protects his people. But now they experience only the pain of his anger, an anger for which it seems there is no end. This anger has allowed an enemy to devastate the sanctuary, the place that declared God's majesty and reign as well as being the centre of Israel's worship. The enemy that has acted seems unstoppable. Yet, the second stanza insists that God remains king. However much the temple's devastation may hurt, God's reign has not ended. Indeed, God has defeated foes far greater than these enemies in the past (see Baumann 2006: 426–427). What the community needs is that God remember his covenant, and therefore act for his people. Importantly, the tension between what God can do and what he has done to date in no way undermines his kingship. But God is asked to remember that he is king in a covenant relationship and thus needs to act. In the psalm, the people never admit to any wrongdoing (perhaps because that would begin to answer the 'why' question), and neither do we have a resolution where God acts. Rather, the psalm is content to allow its readers to live in that point of unresolved faith that knows God will act and calls urgently on him to do so while leaving to him when that will happen. 'How long' is therefore also unanswered, but when read after Psalm 73 we know it is not, in fact, for ever. More than that cannot be said until we come to Psalm 75.

PSALM 75

Translation

The director's. Do Not Destroy. A melody. Asaphic. A song.

1We gave thanks to you, O God,
we gave thanks and your name is near,
your wondrous acts were recounted.

2'When I set an appointed time,
I judge equitably.
3The earth and all its inhabitants are melting away,
I set its pillars in order.' *Selah*.

4I say to the boastful, 'Do not boast,'
and to the wicked, 'Do not raise a horn.
5Do not raise your horn up high,
or speak with an arrogant neck.'
6For not from east nor west,
nor from the wilderness is the lifting up.
7For God is judge,
he brings one low and another he lifts up.
8For a cup is in Yahweh's hand,
foaming wine and fully spiced;
and he pours from it,
surely they drain, they drink its dregs,
all the wicked of the land.

[9]But as for me, I will proclaim for ever,
I will make melody to the God of Jacob.
[10]All the horns of the wicked I will cut down,
but the horns of the righteous shall be lifted up.

Notes on the text

1. *sippĕrû* is understood as an impersonal verb (*WHS* §160), making emendation based on Gk unnecessary.

5. The negative *'al* is elided for the second line but understood from context.

7. *hārîm* could be either the noun 'mountains' or the hiph. inf. const., the option followed here, but both senses could be intended.

Form and structure

Psalm 74 ends on a point of non-resolution. Psalm 75 begins the movement towards resolution so that the community's experience in Psalms 74–76 matches the representative individual who speaks in Psalm 73 (similarly, Jensen 2001: 418–422). There are also key verbal links between Psalms 74 and 75, most notably the use of *mô'ēd* in verse 3, though here it refers to an appointed time rather than place as in Psalm 74:4, 8. That God is judge (vv. 2, 7) gives hope that he will indeed contend for the community (Ps. 74:22), while the fact that God is the one who secures an unsteady world (v. 3) reflects both the suffering described in Psalm 74:4–9 and his authority over creation (Ps. 74:12–17). Including 'Do Not Destroy' in the title links this psalm to Psalms 57–59. Here, it links to the requests in Psalm 74:19, so the psalm title continues the prayer from there. That God has an appointed time to judge means that the 'how long' question from Psalm 74 is at least partially addressed (with Cole 2000: 38–39), though it is not entirely clear that the statement of verse 7 addresses the 'why' question from there (against Cole 2000: 39).

The poem itself has proved difficult to analyse and cannot be easily fitted into the main categories (cf. Seybold 1996: 291). In part, this is because of the (sometimes unmarked) shifts in the speaker, but more broadly it can be noted that, along with thanksgiving (v. 1), it includes statements of confidence (v. 7), while still including vows that are more common in complaint psalms (vv. 10–11). Assuming verses 2–3 are quoting God through a prophet, we can understand it as liturgically shaped poetic oracle (with A. P. Ross 2013: 595), though this does not resolve all the issues since the boundaries of the citation are unmarked. However, since *selah* (v. 3) often marks points of transition (contra Terrien 2003, 2:545, who continues the oracle to v. 6), we would have a prophetic figure speaking from that point. This figure speaks about God, which is why a division needs to be made at verse 4. The oracle proper would then end with the closing vows in verses 9–10, though the closing vow also appears to quote God. The use of speeches by God is a core technique of the Asaphic psalms (also in Pss 50, 81, 82), so it is important here, especially as God's speech represents the start of God's action in response to the prayer of Psalm 74.

The change of speaker provides the most obvious means of structuring the poem, which contains three stanzas, the last of which includes two strophes:

1. Communal report of thanksgiving (1)
2. Divine oracle (2–3)
3. Prophetic speech (4–10)
   a. Admonition to the boastful (4–8)
   b. Vows (9–10)

Comment

Title: For 'The director's', see on Psalm 4. For 'Do Not Destroy', see on Psalm 57. For 'A melody', see on Psalm 3. For 'Asaphic', see on Psalm 50. For 'A song', see on Psalm 65. Psalms 75, 76, 83 are all 'songs' in the Asaphic collection, with repetition of this element in the title forming another link between Psalms 75, 76.

1. Where Psalm 74 opened with an abrupt complaint, Psalm 75 opens with a report of thanksgiving, though unusually it does not indicate why this is done. Rather, the community twice declares to God that it gives thanks to him, the second time adding that God's name is near. The enemies had defiled the dwelling place of God's name (Ps. 74:7), but the community can still affirm the nearness of it. As God's name points to his character, so also it is possible to report that God's wondrous acts (including Ps. 74:12–17) continue to be recounted. The poet of Psalm 73 wanted to continue recounting these acts, and here the community sees that the nearness of God's name in the act of thanksgiving creates a context where those deeds are recounted.

2–3. Having addressed God, these verses represent an unmarked speech in response by God. That God is the speaker can be determined from the speech's content. It is God who sets the time for judgement, and it is God who alone judges equitably. In context, this statement reassures the community that despite their suffering, God will ensure their case is properly heard. Yet the importance of God's justice is not restricted to the community's immediate need. Rather, the whole earth is pictured as melting away, meaning that chaos threatens the community. In Psalm 45:6, the earth melts at God's voice, but here it seems to melt because of its own injustice, taking its inhabitants with it. But God here sets its pillars (cf. 1 Sam. 2:8) in order, ensuring that the world continues to be a secure place to live. The image, as with Psalm 74:12–17, depends on a mythological world view in which the habitable world was upheld by pillars where removal of those pillars would see the world collapse into the subterranean ocean. But God does not allow this to happen – his commitment to creation (cf. Gen. 8:22) means he continues to secure it and so allows the community the hope of justice.

4–8. A new voice now emerges, someone responding to God's words, drawing important implications from them. God sustains the created order and will bring justice, so those resisting his reign are initially warned in two admonitions. The briefer one tells the boastful not to boast. The boastful are those whose praise is misplaced, attending to themselves rather than God. Praise needs to be directed to God, just as the psalm initially confessed. The second admonition is longer, warning the wicked against raising a horn or speaking with an impudent neck. Both these elements refer to a misplaced sense of authority. A 'horn' is often a symbol of power (e.g. 2 Sam. 2:1, 10), especially political power. Raising a horn means claiming power that really belongs to God since he alone sustains creation. Speaking with an arrogant neck assumes the wicked have attempted to lift their head too high, again claiming authority that is not theirs. Again, this authority belongs to God alone. The two admonitions are then followed by three verses, all of which begin 'For' (*kî*). God's speech has already shown that claims to authority that set him aside are misplaced, but the speaker reinforces this point. The exaltation claimed by humans is misplaced because it is not found geographically, no matter which direction one may turn (though this is phrased rather obliquely). Rather, it is God who can raise someone up, but he can also bring someone down (cf. 1 Sam. 2:6–8). As judge, it is God alone who does this, and his activity as judge is demonstrated by the reference to the cup of spiced wine in his hand, which all the wicked fully drain. The 'cup' can be an image for judgement in the OT (Ps. 11:6; Isa. 51:17, 22; Jer. 25:15; 49:12). Though this may derive from a practice in the sanctuary, the details no longer exist, and it is more commonly a metaphor. So, here it reminds those tempted to claim inappropriate power that they will not finally triumph, because God's judgement is prepared.

9–10. The speaker now offers an alternative approach, which is continued service and worship of the God of Jacob. The community has given thanks, and the speaker now reports an intent to continue by continuing to proclaim and worship God, encouraging them to join in with this. The speaker of the second vow is less clear. It could be the same figure as in verses 4–9, but the nature of the vow is more consistent with God's again speaking (unless, with Goldingay [2007: 439] we assume that the speaker is the king, in which case he speaks as the one who enacts God's justice). If so, then God responds to the vow of praise by taking up its language and vowing to ensure that justice is indeed wrought. The wicked, those who reject God's ways (Ps. 1), will have their horn hewn off, but the horn of the righteous will be exalted. God's promise of justice will continue to be worked out so that God's justice provides hope.

Explanation

Psalm 75 brings together the themes of praise and justice in reassuring the worshipping community that God's justice will eventually be seen. The psalm does not provide clues to a particular setting, but its placement alongside Psalm 74 encourages us to read it against the background of the exile. This reading strategy is enhanced by the links between these psalms. By placing these psalms together, we see this poem as an initial response to the challenge raised towards God in Psalm 74, especially as God speaks directly in this psalm in verses 2–3, 10. What we see there is that God is the one who sustains the world in its totality, even though it is filled with injustice, and that he will bring down the wicked and exalt the righteous. The worshipping community responds to this by committing itself to continued worship, the very act of which continues to announce the reality of God's presence and justice. The psalm emerged in a world where that was challenged, most obviously by Babylonian power in the exile, but continues to insist that God's justice will be worked out according to God's timetable. Therefore, the psalm calls for a decision, one where we do not seek to exalt ourselves but God instead, encouraging continued trust in him (Botha 2002a: 329–331). The hope of God's justice becomes cruciform in the NT, though the psalm's language continues to shape the hope for justice that it articulates (Rev. 14:10).

PSALM 76

Translation

The director's. With stringed instruments. A melody. Asaphic. A song.

[1]God is known in Judah,
his name is great in Israel.
[2]His abode is in Salem,
his dwelling place in Zion.
[3]There he shattered the flame-arrows of the bow,
shield and sword and weapons of war. *Selah*.

[4]Radiant are you, O Majestic One,
from the mountains of prey.
[5]The strong of heart became booty,
they are drowsy with their sleep,
and none of their men of valour could find their hands.
[6]From your rebuke, O God of Jacob,
both rider and horse are stunned.

[7]You, you are awesome,
and who can stand before you
when you are angry?
[8]You announced judgement from the heavens,
the earth feared and was still,
[9]when God arose for judgement,
to save all the poor of the earth. *Selah.*

[10]For human wrath will confess you,
you shall gird yourself with the remnant of the wrath.
[11]Make vows and fulfil them to Yahweh your God,
let all those around him bring a gift
to the One to be Feared,
[12]who humbles the spirit of princes,
the Awesome One before all the kings of the earth.

Notes on the text

3. Hebr. *milḥāmâ*, 'war', by synecdoche stands for the weapons.

10. The verse is difficult (Seybold [1996: 137] reckons even the Masoretes could make no sense of it!) but the above attempts to make sense of MT (NASB is similar), understanding *ḥdr* to include acting on oneself. Hebr. *ydh* can mean 'confess' or 'give thanks'. In that human wrath is brought to see something it previously opposed, 'confess' is the better translation here. For an alternative that attempts to stay with MT, see Emerton 1974b.

12. The meaning of *bṣr* is uncertain, but with HALOT 'humbles' is preferred here to 'cuts off' (so BDB).

Form and structure

Psalm 76 closes the short run that began in Psalm 74, with Psalms 74–76 taking the community through the experience of the individual from Psalm 73. Accordingly, it has important links with the two preceding poems. Notably, the phrase 'God of Jacob' occurs both here (v. 6) and in Psalm 75:9, a divine title that occurs elsewhere in the Asaph psalms in Psalm 81:1, 4. Here, it provides a hinge between these two poems. Verses 8–9 also represent the point where God acts in response to the appeal of Psalm 74:19–21 as God acts to save the poor of the land. As the psalm reflects on God's power in Jerusalem, so also the community is reminded that he continues to sustain them, and that like the poet of Psalm 73 they are to bring their worship to him. As well as the immediate textual setting, the psalm also shows important parallels to Psalms 46–48 (see Hossfeld and Zenger 2006: 261–262), not only in the presentation of God as the 'God of Jacob' (Ps. 46:7, 11), but also in the presentation of God as the one who ends war (v. 3; Ps. 46:9), showing that the psalm draws on a deep well of reflections on Zion.

The links to Psalms 46–48 mean that Psalm 76 is usually classified as a Song of Zion, those poems that celebrate God's choice of Zion and the importance of the temple. This is true to a point, though the psalm is more concerned with the God who is made known there than the city itself (see Leuenberger 2020: 80; Mays 1994b: 250). These differences are important in the current literary context where Psalm 76 becomes the community's proclamation of God's mighty deeds, corresponding to the hope of the poet in Psalm 73:27–28. It is God's deeds in his destruction of the wicked that the community now understands as applying to them and that they recount here.

The psalm is one where the *selah* appears to provide the major divisions, forming three stanzas, though the second can be divided into two strophes:

1. God is known (1–3)
2. God's characteristics (4–9)
   a. The Radiant One (4–6)
   b. The Awesome One (7–9)
3. Worship of God (10–12)

Comment

Title: For 'The director's' and 'With stringed instruments', see on Psalm 4. For 'A melody', see on Psalm 3. For 'Asaphic', see on Psalm 50. For 'A song', see on Psalm 65. Apart from replacing 'Do Not Destroy' with 'with stringed instruments', the title is the same as Psalm 75, providing further evidence of the linking of these two poems.

1–3. The psalm opens with a niph. ptc., with the same grammatical form also introducing its closing line and forming an inclusio for the whole poem, with others introducing the two strophes in the second stanza. Each of these ptcs. declares something about God that is explored in the balance of the segment. Here, it declares that God is known in Judah though the parallel statement about his name makes clear that this knowledge is not restricted to Judah. Nevertheless, as the poem continues, we focus more on Judah by noting that God has an abode in Salem, an ancient name for Jerusalem (Gen. 14:18; Goulder [1996: 86–88] argues for a location near Shechem, but the parallelism here surely equates Salem with Zion) and a dwelling place in Zion. Although Zion can be treated as a synonym for Jerusalem, it is more strictly the area where the temple was situated. Here, it seems that the psalm initially declares that God is known more widely, but then narrows our attention to the temple's location. The temple could be considered God's dwelling place even though it was also accepted that the temple could not contain him (1 Kgs 8:27–30). However, the terms used in verse 2 are unusual, and though both refer to a dwelling place, they can also allude to a lion's hunting place (cf. Ps. 10:9; Jer. 25:38 for *sōk*, 'abode'; and Psalm 104:22, Amos 3:4 for *mĕʿōnâ*, 'dwelling place'). The association with Zion makes the above translation appropriate, but the leonine imagery also prepares for other motifs in the second stanza. Thus, the poem asserts that the temple is God's dwelling place, something that is typically good news, while preparing us to note that it can also be bad news for God's opponents. But in this stanza, the focus is the good news that God has shattered fire arrows, shield, sword and everything else associated with war. The name Salem is related to *šālôm*, and God has brought peace by shattering that which enables war. No particular event can be associated with this, but readers may well think of the events recounted in 2 Kings 18 – 19 (indeed, Gk's title already does this).

4–6. The second stanza attends to God's character, utilizing distinctive divine titles, always addressed to God. The first declares that God is 'radiant' while also calling him the 'Majestic One'. 'Radiant' is related to the word for 'light'. Psalm 74:16 noted that God had established the 'luminary' but now affirms that he is radiant, associating him with the sun. This is linked to his majesty. In Psalm 8:2, 10 it is God's name that is majestic, but that here becomes a divine title, one that is exercised from 'mountains of prey'. This phrase requires readers to recognize the leonine imagery in the first stanza and to understand that the one who dwells in Zion also attacks enemies from there, with those who resist him also his prey. Hence, even warriors who were otherwise strong of heart have become his booty, with their drowsiness probably the sleep of death. Against God as a roaring lion, no one could even find their hands and thus engage in battle. All that was needed to defeat even horse and rider (cf. Exod. 15:21) was God's rebuke, which drove back the waters (Ps. 18:16) and will also trouble the community (Ps. 80:16). The radiant, majestic God is the one who defeats his enemies and cannot be resisted.

7–9. The second strophe of this stanza now reflects on God as the Awesome One, anticipating the use of this as a divine title in the closing verse. Here, the community asserts that God is awesome. The word is from a root (*yr'*) that is often translated 'fear', anticipating the root's use in verse 8. God is to be feared in the sense of revered. As with the previous strophe, this divine characteristic is applied to God's ability to defeat his foes. The point is achieved this time through a rhetorical question, the point of which is that no one can stand up before his anger. God's anger is here directed against injustice, especially against the poor. Hence, God announced judgement from heaven, and the earth feared and was still as he rose to enact justice, here saving the poor of the earth. God's enemies are thus not only military forces arrayed against Judah and Israel; they are all who act against the poor. God is awesome because he acts for the poor.

10–12. The third stanza defers the divine title until its end. As it opens, the psalm still addresses God, though this changes in verses 11–12 as the community is again addressed. The text of verse 10 is exceptionally difficult (cf. 'Notes on the text'), but the sense seems to be that human wrath cannot thwart God's purposes, and that even it will eventually confess God since God can make even human wrath suit his purposes. This being so, the community is then addressed again in verses 11–12, where it is urged to make vows to 'Yahweh your God' and 'fulfil them'. 'Fulfil' (pi. of *šlm*) echoes the name 'Salem' from verse 2. The vows here are signs of commitment to Yahweh, the one who is committed to his people and who deserves the divine titles throughout the poem. However, the worship of Yahweh goes beyond the community, as all those around the one to be feared are summoned to bring their gift too. Just as God ends war (v. 2), so he also humbles the spirit of princes and indeed is the Awesome One before all the kings of the earth. God is known in Judah, but reigns over all.

Explanation

Psalm 76 represents a short pause in the Asaph psalms, the point where the community reminds itself that, like the poet of Psalm 73, it too can recount God's wondrous works. Those works here are centred on God's presence in Zion. This presence is simultaneously a source of hope and a threat. For those who are committed to Yahweh, it is a source of hope because it reminds readers that his power cannot be challenged, and that he uses that power to end war and the oppression of the poor. Yet, by also including leonine imagery, the psalm indicates that this divine presence can be a threat to all who resist God. God's awesome power is also suggested by the divine titles that run through the psalm, all of which emphasize his authority and that the only appropriate responses to him are worship and faithful service. The psalm leaves open the question of how God achieves the victories described here because its concern is rather to encourage readers to commit themselves to the values God demonstrates here – working for peace and justice – and to do so in the setting of worship. The vision of Revelation 5, however, indicates that the Lion of the tribe of Judah has achieved the victory described here through his death and resurrection. As followers of the Lamb that was slain, we too are called to work for God's values.

PSALM 77

Translation

The director's. According to Jeduthun. Asaphic. A melody.

1My voice is before God and I cry out,
  my voice is before God so he will heed me.
2On the day of my distress I sought the Lord,
  my hand was stretched out at night and did not grow weary,
  I refused to be consoled.
3I remember God and I moan,
  I lament, and my spirit grows faint. *Selah.*

4You grasped the guards of my eyes,
  I was troubled and could not speak.
5I contemplate the days of old,
  ancient years.
6I remember my songs in the night,
  with my mind I reflect,
  and my spirit wonders.

7'Shall the Lord reject for ever,
  and never again show favour?
8Has his kindness failed in perpetuity,
  the word offered from generation to generation ended?
9Has God forgotten to be gracious,
  or shut up his compassion in anger?' *Selah.*

10And I said, 'This is my pain,
  the changing of the right hand of the Most High.'
11I remember Yah's deeds,
  yes, I remember your wonders from of old.
12So I reflect on all your deeds,
  and contemplate your acts.
13O God, your way is with the holy –
  what deity is great like God?
14You are the God who does wonders,

you make known your might among the peoples.
[15]With your arm you redeemed your people,
the children of Jacob and Joseph. *Selah.*

[16]The waters saw you, O God,
the waters saw you, they trembled,
surely the deeps shook.
[17]Water poured forth from clouds,
the palls gave voice,
surely your arrows went about.
[18]The voice of your thunder was in the whirlwind,
lightning illuminated the world,
the earth shook and quaked.
[19]Your path was through the sea,
and your track was through many waters,
but your footprints were unknown.
[20]You led your people like a flock,
by the hand of Moses and Aaron.

Notes on the text

Title: With Q and many MSS, reading *yĕdûtûn.*

6. Although *rûaḥ* is more commonly f., it can be m. As such, no emendation is needed here.

10. Deriving *ḥallôtî* from *ḥlh* (sickness) rather than *ḥll* (pierced), though either could lead to the above translation. Hebr. *šĕnôt* could be the noun 'years' (cf. ESV) or inf. const. of *šnh*. The line is cryptic, and the former fits with the various references to time through the poem, but the latter provides a better explanation of the poet's grief. See Weber 1995: 95–108.

11. With Q and many MSS, reading *'ezkôr.*

19. With Q and many MSS, reading *ûšĕbîlĕkā.*

Form and structure

Psalm 77 introduces a new subunit within Psalms 73–78. Psalm 73 drew on a representative individual whose resolution to the problem of the prosperity of the wicked was paralleled in the community's experience in Psalms 74–76. Although these psalms all have an exilic background, they are notable for their use of mythological themes in declaring God's strength. Psalm 77, which with its open conclusion leads into Psalm 78, allows this to be tied more directly to the recognizable history found in Psalm 78. It also creates important links with Psalm 76, such as the shared rhetorical questions about God (Pss 76:7; 77:13) and mention of the human spirit (Pss 76:12; 77:3, 6), ensuring these poems are read together.

The poem's form has been variously assessed. A. A. Anderson (1972, 2: 556) simply says it is 'not clear'. The issue stems from the fact that an individual speaks in verses 1–12, whereas verses 13–20 are formed more like a hymn. Rather than seeking a particular form, we are better to follow Weber (1995: 1–2) and look more closely at the psalm's poetic structures. When we do that, it becomes possible to note repetition in key vocabulary that holds the whole together and the poem's unity should be our starting point. The individual who speaks is a representative figure, something already evident in the questions of verses 7–9, meaning that the psalm is primarily communal, though without losing the importance of the individual. The fusing of the individual and communal in this poem thus matches the form of Psalms 73–76, preparing for the individual who addresses the community in Psalm 78:1, while the pain here takes us back to the experience at Psalm 74. This fusion is developed through a report of present experience and reflection on God's great acts, especially from the exodus (see Kselman 1983; Stevenson 1997), allowing both individual and community to move towards a resolution, even if one is not given in this psalm.

As with Psalm 76, each occurrence of *selah* here appears to mark a division, dividing the poem into four stanzas:

1. Cry to God (1–3)
2. Contemplation and questions (4–9)
   a. Silent pondering (4–6)
   b. Questions raised (7–9)
3. Pain and contemplation (10–15)
4. God led his people (16–20)

Comment

Title: For 'The director's', see on Psalm 4. For 'According to Jeduthun', see on Psalm 39. For 'Asaphic', see on Psalm 50. For 'A melody', see on Psalm 3.

1–3. The psalm opens with a report of an individual's cry to God. The speaker is clearly in distress, but this stanza does not explain the source of that distress, deferring this to the next stanza. Rather, through repetition of 'my voice' it initiates a key term for the psalm, as God's voice returns in verse 18. The appeal is urgent, asking that God heed the poet, though verse 2 also makes clear that the current circumstances are rooted in earlier distress. At that time, the psalmist had sought God, perhaps in the temple, with hands outstretched despite the pain this causes, and had refused to be consoled. The reason for that is not yet clear. Instead, the poem introduces more key terms, reporting that the poet 'remembered' (*zkr*) God and 'reflected' (*śyḥ*; also Weber 1995: 217–220).

4–6. The poet's voice was prominent in the first stanza, but this stanza begins by reporting silence. The image in verse 4 is of God's holding the poet's eyelids (the only point God is addressed before v. 11), presumably preventing sleep since the verb for 'troubled' (*pʿm*) is elsewhere associated with sleeplessness or vivid dreams (Gen. 41:8; Dan. 2:3). The poet was in God's presence, but the agitation caused by this meant there was no speech. Instead, this led to a time of reflection, his thinking about important times in the distant past, introducing the motif of time, which is also important within the poem. These times are not defined here, though they are clearly distant from the poet's own time, suggesting that the exodus is in view. Nevertheless, although this motif is introduced in the final stanza, it is not made explicit here. This distant past is not, however, separate from the psalmist's own experience. Instead, it is tied to the memory of the poet's songs in the night and subsequent reflection on them. These songs are typically mocking (Ps. 69:13; Lam. 3:14, 63; also Ray 2020: 151), and so represent part of the poet's distress rather than praise offered. The poet is faced by a contrast between the stories of the past and present experience, and so reflects on these.

7–9. This second strophe emerges directly from the first but is separated for analysis since it represents the point at which the problem is indicated. It is not formulated in the abstract but rather through a question that wonders if God continues his relationship with the community. The alternative is that he has rejected them, the implication being that exile represents a point of national rejection. Perception of God's rejection can be expressed as the possibility of his not again showing favour, though this formulation already indicates that grace was in some way essential to the relationship with God. If God has rejected them permanently, then this raises the possibility that his 'kindness' (*ḥesed*) has failed, and that his word that was meant to be passed on through the generations (cf. Deut. 6:20–25; 11:18–25) had ended. Posing the question indicates that this should not happen, because God's kindness is meant to abound (Exod. 34:6–8), and his word should be trustworthy. But if the logic of the questions is followed through, then we reach verse 9, which wonders if the gracious and compassionate God of Exodus 34:6–8 has instead closed up his compassion in anger. The community knows it should not be like this, but it is how they are experiencing God. The pain of the individual who speaks is thus the pain of the community.

10–15. The pain, however, is still localized in the speaker even though it is also the community's pain. The perceived cause is the changing of the right hand of the Most High. The right hand is a sign of favour (cf. Exod. 15:6; see *DCH*), while 'Most High' is a name for God often associated with Zion (cf. Pss 46:4; 47:2). The claim is that God has not continued to show favour to his people, and especially the sanctuary. The psalm here turns from 'I' to 'you' (cf. Brueggemann 1988: 137–140), meaning that these points are now put to God (Broyles 1999: 316). The poet's present is set against the memory of Yah's deeds, using the shorter form of the covenant name, evoking the Song of the Sea (Exod. 15:2). For the poet, the concern is to call to mind and think through the implications of God's great acts in the past. These past deeds are rooted in history, but they can also be considered wonders. In these wonders, God has rescued his people from forces greater than themselves. The psalmist ponders these in the light of the apparent change of Yahweh's favour. How can the God whose wonders were so great (cf. Exod. 15:11), who with his arm redeemed his people, showing his power among the nations (Exod. 15:13), leave them so weak? This point is made more acute through the rhetorical question of verse 13. The question stresses God's incomparability, with this emerging from his holiness, that which defines his character. Yah is the God who does wonders, both for Jacob (perhaps referring to the whole of Israel and Judah) and Joseph (here probably standing for the northern tribes who by the time of the exile had been exiled themselves for well over a century). Reflection on the past is both a source of hope and concern – if God has allowed the north to be exiled in perpetuity, might this also result in a permanent change for Judah?

16–20. The crossing of the sea in the exodus continues to provide key background in the final stanza. The poem personifies the waters of the sea, drawing on mythological presentation (perhaps adapting existing material; see van de Meer 1994) while remaining focused on the exodus, as is made clear by the closing reference to Moses and Aaron. Both the waters and the deeps are mentioned here, as in the Song of the Sea (Exod. 15:8); and, though the verbs are different, the concept is similar. The encounter with God brought the creation into a state of turmoil. The visible waters and the waters beneath are matched by reference to the waters pouring down from the clouds along with thunder and lightning. God's presence challenges the creation, so the whole world shook as in an earthquake (cf. Hab. 3:8–11). Because of his authority over creation, God had a path through the sea, a path through many waters, though one that left no visible footprints. This might have seemed inhospitable for his people, yet it was at this time that God had also led his people like a flock, taking up the shepherd motif (cf. Ps. 74:1), with his leadership expressed through Moses and Aaron. But here the psalm ends, like a song without a resolving chord. God's wonders have been seen in the past: they are not simply myths. But what does that mean for the community now?

Explanation

In a sense, Psalm 77 takes readers back to Psalm 74 (see Cole 2000: 54–56) and the pain of the exile as something that is unresolved. Of course, readers who have worked through Psalms 75–76 know this is not the end of the story, but if these psalms reached their present form in the exile, then the community would continue to face challenging questions about God. Psalm 77 is a remarkable composition that addresses the uncertainties exile raised. The individual who speaks in the opening stanzas emerges as a representative figure who speaks for the nation, with personal reflections helping the community to wrestle with complex questions about the faithfulness of God. Most importantly, is the God of the exodus still Israel's God in exile? Remarkably, although this psalm is ultimately a prayer that emerges from distress, it never specifies the source of its distress or asks anything from God. Instead, it presents both an honest report of distress and a series of reflections rooted in God's actions in the past. Some scholars (e.g. Grogan 2008: 139) believe that the psalm concludes with full-hearted praise, but this seems to read too much in the poem's final two stanzas. These instead reflect on the past, presenting this to God. There is at most an implied request for God to act in the same way, whether through miracle or figures such as Moses and Aaron. With Tate (1990: 275–276) it seems better to read these stanzas as part of the ongoing reflection, an unresolved tension with what is known about God and how he seems to be experienced (though some resolution will emerge in Ps. 78). Such a profile suggests an important pattern for prayer that refuses to give up on God and the story of his great acts of deliverance while insisting that present suffering must still be named before him. The psalm, like much prayer, does not result in immediate resolution. Lack of immediate resolution does not lead to abandonment of what is known about God but rather requires deeper reflection on what it means to pray the tradition (cf. C. B. Jones 2009: 82).

PSALM 78

Translation

A Maskil. Asaphic.

1Heed, O my people, my instruction,
  incline your ear to the words of my mouth.
2I will open my mouth with a parable,
  I will pour forth riddles from of old.
3What we have heard and known,

that our ancestors recounted to us.
[4]We will not hide from their children,
to a later generation,
recounting the praises of Yahweh
his might and his wonders that he has performed.

[5]For set up a testimony in Jacob,
and set instruction in Israel,
which he commanded our ancestors
to make known to their children,
[6]so that the next generation might know,
children yet to be born,
would rise and recount to their children,
[7]and set their confidence in God,
and not forget God's deeds,
but keep his commandments,
[8]and not be like their ancestors,
a stubborn and rebellious generation,
a generation that did not make its heart firm,
and whose spirit was not faithful to God.

[9]The Ephraimites, armed with archers,
turned back on the day of battle.
[10]They did not keep God's covenant,
and refused to walk in his instruction.
[11]They forgot his acts,
and his wonders that he had shown them.

[12]He had performed a wonder before their fathers,
in the land of Egypt, the region of Zoan.
[13]He split the sea and brought them across,
and made the waters stand erect like a heap.
[14]He led them in a cloud by day,
and all night by a fiery light.

[15]He split rocks in the wilderness,
and provided drink as abundantly as from the great deeps.
[16]He brought out streams from the crag,
and made waters flow down like rivers.
[17]But they continued to sin against him,
to rebel against the Most High in the desert.
[18]So they put God to the test in their heart
by requesting food for their appetite.
[19]They spoke against God,
they said 'Is God able

to spread a table in the wilderness?
20Sure, he struck a rock,
and the waters flowed, and rivers ran:
is he also able to grant bread,
or provide meat for his people?'
21Surely Yahweh heard,
so he became angry,
and fire was kindled against Jacob,
indeed, wrath went up against Israel,
22because they did not believe God,
they did not trust in his salvation.
23So he commanded the clouds above,
and opened the doors of the heavens,
24and rained down manna upon them to eat,
yes, he gave them the grain of heaven.
25People ate the bread of the mighty ones,
he sent provision to satisfy.

26He made the east wind blow in the heavens,
and drove the south wind by his might,
27and he rained meat on them like dust,
winged birds like the sand of the seas.
28And he made them fall within his camp,
all around his dwelling places.
29So they ate and were well satisfied,
he brought their craving to them.
30They had not turned aside from their craving,
while their food was in their mouth,
31the anger of God came up against them,
and killed their sturdiest ones,
and he threw Israel's youth into misery.

32In all this they sinned yet more,
and did not believe his wondrous deeds.
33So he consumed their days in vanity,
and their years in sudden horror.
34When he killed them, they sought him,
repented and sought God earnestly;
35they remembered that God was their rock,
and God Most High their redeemer.
36So they deceived him with their mouth,
with their tongue they lied to him.
37Their heart was not firm with him,
and they were not faithful to his covenant.
38But he is compassionate,

he atones for their iniquity and does not destroy,
he has often held back his anger,
and not stirring up his wrath.
39So he remembered that they were flesh,
a breath that goes out and does not return.

40How often they rebelled against him in the wilderness,
and caused him pain in the wastelands.
41But they turned back and tested God,
they wounded the Holy One of Israel.
42They did not remember his hand,
the day he redeemed them from the foe,
43when he set his signs in Egypt,
and his wonders in the region of Zoan.
44he turned their Nile streams to blood,
they could drink of their rivulets.
45He sent a swarm against them that devoured them,
and frogs that destroyed them.
46He gave their produce to the grasshopper,
their toil's product to the locust.
47He killed their vines with hail,
and their sycamores with frost.
48He delivered up their cattle to the hail,
their livestock to the lightning bolts.
49He sent his fierce anger against them,
rage and indignation and distress,
a deputation of harmful messengers.
50He cleared a pathway for his anger,
he did not keep them back from death,
but delivered up their life to plague.
51He struck all the firstborn in Egypt,
the first of their virility in the tents of Ham.

52He brought out his people like sheep,
and he led them like a flock in the wilderness.
53He guided them in safety, and they did not dread,
while the sea covered their enemies.
54He brought them to the border of his holy land,
the hill country that his right hand acquired.
55He drove out nations before them,
he allotted an inheritance with a measuring line,
settled the tribes of Israel in their tents.

56But they tested and rebelled against God Most High,
they did not keep his testimonies.

57They were disloyal and treacherous, like their ancestors,
they were unreliable, like a slack bow.
58They provoked him with their high places,
and provoked him to jealousy with their idols.
59God heard and was furious,
he utterly rejected Israel.
60He forsook the dwelling place at Shiloh,
the tent he pitched among humankind.
61He gave over his strength to captivity,
his splendour into the hand of a foe.
62He delivered up his people to the sword,
he was furious with his inheritance.
63Fire consumed his young men,
and his young women had no praises.
64His priests fell by the sword,
and his widows did not weep.

65Then the Lord awoke like one asleep,
like a warrior shouting because of wine.
66He struck his foe behind,
he gave an everlasting disgrace.
67He rejected the tent of Joseph,
and did not choose the tribe of Ephraim.
68But he chose the tribe of Judah,
Mount Zion which he loves.
69He built his sanctuary like the heights,
like the earth, established for ever.
70He chose David his servant,
he took him from the sheepfold.
71He brought him from behind the sucklings,
to shepherd his people Jacob,
and his inheritance Israel.
72He shepherded them according to the integrity of his heart,
and led them with skilful hand.

Notes on the text

18. For Hebr. *nepeš* as 'appetite', see Eccl. 6:9.

28. Gk reads 'their dwelling places', an emendation widely accepted (e.g. NIV). While possible, MT should be retained because this verse asserts God's overall possession of the camp.

47. Hebr. *ḥănāmal* is uncertain beyond being a serious weather event.

Form and structure

Judged purely on the criterion of length, Psalm 78 overshadows all the psalms that have preceded it, while of those that follow only Psalm 119 is longer. The Masoretes have given it a place of special prominence as both midpoint of Book 3's Asaph psalms, with five psalms before it and five after, while also reckoning that verse 36 is the middle verse in the whole Psalter (cf. S. J. Smith 2022: 125–138). As the midpoint of this Asaphic collection, and its affirmation of the Jerusalem sanctuary, it also prepares for the increased level of appeal that marks Psalms 79–83. Given its length and the common features found across the Asaphic psalms, it is not surprising that it has numerous links with the preceding Asaphic psalms, though the density of the links with Psalm 77 should be especially noted (see Cole 2000: 63–67), most obviously because the unresolved ending of Psalm 77 leads directly into the present psalm, establishing its key theme of God's guidance, while also tracing how this moves from Moses and Aaron (Ps. 77:20) to David (Ps. 78:70–72). Although Foster (2019: 91) claims the psalm demonstrates key elements the previous psalm omitted, it is better to read these poems as complementary rather than contradictory.

As well as the Asaphic psalms, Psalm 78 also belongs with the historical psalms (Pss 105–106, 135–136), poems that recount Israel's story. However, although there are obvious similarities of form shared with these poems, Psalm 78 is distinctive in its focus on David. By contrast, although Psalm 106's conclusion makes clear its exilic background, the Asaphic psalms all focus on the exodus and wilderness period. Stinson (2017: 206–220) has also shown that Psalm 78 has a richer interest in the provision of food than the other historical psalms, though concern with food provision is relatively widespread within the Asaph psalms. As a work of history, it is notable that the author calls it a 'parable' (*māšāl*). We should not immediately think here in terms of Jesus' parables in the NT, though there is a connection in that both use a story that has a comparison used to make a point (note how Matt. 13:34–35 draws on vv. 1–2). The obvious difference is that although some of his parables use recognizable historical features, Jesus typically creates fictional stories, whereas this psalm makes its comparison through historical events the audience is meant to recognize. The genre label 'parable' is consistent with this being a work of wisdom, a form of instruction (or, with McMillion 2001: 221, 'catechesis') addressed to an audience rather than God. In this, Psalm 78 differs notably from Psalms 77:13–20 and 79 since these are addressed to God. As Poe Hays (2016) has demonstrated, this integration of wisdom and history is vital to the psalm's goal of helping the community to see new possibilities from past pain, an element undergirded by its poetic form (Estes 2016). In drawing on Israel's story, it is not always possible to determine the exact references intended, and at points several similar accounts seem to be conflated, but with Leonard (2016), the best way of recognizing the sources used is through shared language, especially when it is distinctive or where we have phrases rather than single words, though we cannot rule out other ways of alluding.

Despite various efforts at establishing layers of redaction (e.g. Oded 2017), Campbell's case for the poem's unity (1979: 52–58) remains sound. As a didactic poem, it does not break up into obvious stanzas, though it is possible to divide the psalm based on its content. It should be noted that the history is not recounted in sequence, so the order is more thematic than arbitrary (Hossfeld and Zenger 2006: 286). The following is used to assist the presentation here:

1. Introduction and theme (1–11)
   a. Summons to attend (1–4)
   b. Reasons for passing on the story (5–8)
   c. Ephraim's failure (9–11)
2. From Egypt to the land (12–55)
   a. Crossing the sea (12–14)
   b. Food, drink and rebellion in the wilderness (15–31)
   c. More sin in the wilderness (32–39)
   d. The plagues in Egypt (40–51)
   e. Summary: exodus and eisodus (52–55)
3. Failure and hope in the land (56–72)
   a. Loss of Shiloh (56–64)
   b. Election of David and Zion (65–72)

Comment

Title: For 'Maskil', see on Psalm 32. For 'Asaphic', see on Psalm 50. The title is identical to Psalm 74, providing an additional link between these psalms.

1–4. The psalm's opening makes clear that this is fundamentally a didactic text to which an audience is expected to attend. The speaker is part of the community addressed ('my people'), though sufficiently separate to provide instruction. The language for instruction overlaps with terms for law found in Psalm 119 (see Firth 2015b: 68–75), though here they show more clearly the concern for teaching, especially as the language also draws on terminology more typically associated with wisdom (e.g. parable, riddle; in this case, the riddle involves recognizing how theological themes develop through history; see also Ps. 49:4). The speaker's teaching is thus rooted in a range of pedagogical patterns. These patterns are also associated with information passed on through the generations, so that although the speaker wishes to make fresh applications from Israel's story, it is a story with which the audience is familiar. Yet even a familiar story needs to be passed on, so the community remembers the wonders Yahweh has performed. In this, the psalm shares the pattern of repeating the story of Yahweh's deeds with Deuteronomy 6:20–25. As Witte (2006: 27) notes, the ideal community in this psalm is one that narrates and remembers, as this ensures the story is both told and considered.

5–8. Deuteronomy 6:20–25 insists that recounting the story of God's deliverance will lead to continued faithful practice, a concept shared here. So, the speaker sets out key themes for what follows, placing the more specific elements that will follow in a larger story, the goal of which is that subsequent generations will place their confidence in God and keep his commandments, passing on the story to subsequent generations. This practice is based on what God has done in establishing a 'testimony' in Jacob, paralleled with 'instruction' in Israel. These terms are elsewhere translated as 'stipulation' and 'law', but here are more about the fact that what God has done testifies about him, and that this is a continuing form of instruction, though the law also includes this function, so we cannot separate these elements completely. The important contrast here is that previous generations have not remained faithful to Yahweh, but by passing on the story the hope is that future generations will keep God's commandments. The identity of the previous generations is not clarified, but the contrast between past, present and future is pivotal to the whole poem.

9–11. The introduction closes by mentioning a battle that involved the Ephraimites. Their story is paradigmatic for what follows, failing to keep covenant and forgetting God's acts. Mention of Ephraimites here points to a situation after the entry to the land, whereas verses 12–55 are based on the exodus and wilderness period. The specific battle is not named but could be the loss of Shiloh (vv. 56–66) since it is in Ephraim. Perhaps the audience knew the battle, but the core concern here is that although Ephraim was well equipped with its archers, they turned back when battle approached. This was not because of a lack of military knowledge. Rather, it was because they did not keep covenant; that is, they did not make the relationship with God central, as is made clear by their failure to walk in God's instruction. They were assuredly not living the life encouraged by Psalm 1. This failure was matched by their forgetting of the wonders God had performed, the implication being that a people who fail to remember these things will not live in accordance with the covenant – which is why the story must be told here.

12–14. The crossing of the sea has been an important motif in the Asaphic psalms, even when mixed with references to mythological material (Pss 74:12–17; 77:15–16). Given its importance for Israel's story, it naturally stands first since it clearly demonstrates God's wonders, though it is integrated into the wider range of wonders God performed in the exodus. The point about these wonders is that they happened before the community's ancestors, meaning they were well placed to pass these stories on. 'Egypt' here is paralleled by the region of 'Zoan'. The latter was a city in the Nile Delta, apparently noted for its wisdom (Isa. 19:11–13). Perhaps more importantly, that at least some of the wonders of the exodus were performed there meant they were visible to the exodus generation since the Israelites lived near Goshen (Gen. 45:10; Exod. 8:22; 9:26), from where they set out in the exodus. These wonders will be the focus of verses 40–51, but here attention moves quickly to the crossing of the sea and the fact that it was God who worked and brought the ancestors across. The language here evokes both the prose (Exod. 14:21–31) and poetic (Exod. 15:1–21) accounts of the crossing. The verb 'split' (*bq*ʿ) is found in Exodus 14:21, and both cloud and fire are found in Exodus 14:24, while the waters standing erect like a heap alludes to Exodus 15:8. In the crossing of the sea, the ancestors experienced God's mighty works for themselves. Because of this, they should have lived a life of faithfulness that includes passing on these stories.

15–31. This section of the poem includes several events (water, manna, quail), but they are all linked through the motif of the provision of food and drink (Stinson 2017: 104–149). Because of this linkage, it is better to treat them together as they all demonstrate both God's continued wonders and the failures of the ancestors. The opening of this section repeats the verb 'split' (*bq*ʿ) from verse 13, linking it to the crossing of the sea, while introducing the food motif. There are two possible references to rocks being split in the wilderness (Exod. 17:1–7, Num. 20:1–13). These accounts use different words for 'rock', *ṣûr* (rock) and *sela*ʿ (crag), but since the initial reference is to 'rocks' and both terms are used in the poem, it seems the intention is to bring these accounts together, stressing that God provided abundant water both times. Yet both stories led to further sin and rebellion in the desert. The term used for 'desert' here (*ṣîyâ*) emphasizes that this was dry land, emphasizing the greatness of the miracle and the inexplicable nature of the ancestors' continued sin.

The ancestors' sin in verses 18–25 is related to the provision of manna (Exod. 16). Within the exodus account this precedes the first water miracle, but is placed here to join it more explicitly to the quail story in verses 26–31, joining the food elements and linking them to the manna and quail accounts in both Exodus 16 and Numbers 11:4–31. Unlike the water miracles, where the people's complaint is not mentioned, the manna is here linked to the people testing God. The 'testing' (*nsh*) motif joins the stories of the sweetening of water with the manna in Exodus 15:22 – 16:4, but in those instances these become tests for the people, whereas here it is said that the people tested God. Both accounts are, however, initiated by the people grumbling. The testing motif is absent from the Numbers account, but it is likely that, as with the water miracle, the psalm refers to both manna stories even if the strongest parallels are with the Exodus account. The grumbling in Exodus is less specific than what is recounted here, but one can reasonably understand the people's questions, which are against God (hence, testing or trying him), as a poetic presentation of the complaint from Exodus 16:3. The question implies that, because Israel was in the wilderness, God could not provide sufficient food, even if he had provided abundant water from the rock. The provision of one did not mean that he could provide the other, while the mention of bread and meat here probably alludes to Numbers 11:4–31 since quail play only a minor role in Exodus 16:13. God understood the implication made and became angry because of the people's failure to believe in him. At this point, God's anger does not lead to punishment. Rather, having given the command to open the heavenly resources he 'rained down' (*mṭr*) the manna on them, so that the people ate heavenly bread. Mention of the manna 'raining down' alludes to Exodus 16:4, where the same verb is used to describe the manna's arrival. For the psalm, this was a remarkable provision because it means that humans ate food that otherwise belonged to the mighty ones. This term more commonly refers to powerful humans (e.g. Ps. 76:4) or animals (e.g. Ps. 22:13; Isa. 34:7), but here refers to heavenly beings (cf. Sir. 43:5). God provided his own food in the wilderness so that a people who did not believe he could provide were fully satisfied: indeed, they had an abundance.

Allusion to the wind in verse 26 indicates that we have moved to another miracle since it is not associated with either manna account. It is, however, associated with the provision of quail. As noted, quail are mentioned in both manna accounts, so their presence here is unsurprising. This account is linked to the manna within the psalm by repeating the verb 'rained down'. The quail too are part of God's abundant provision. Here they are so abundant that they are like the dust or the sand of the sea. Neither simile occurs in the quail accounts, but both Exodus 16:13 and Numbers 11:31 speak of the quail coming down in the camp, while Numbers 11:31 also stresses that it was all around the camp. The camp is here noted as God's camp, meaning that he provides for the people wherever they are. The provision of the quail was also abundant, so that everyone was satisfied (a motif subverted by Jesus' adversaries in John 6:31). They had craved meat, and God had brought it to them, even where they did not believe it could be. Nevertheless, consistent with Numbers 11:33, the meat was also a point where God acted in judgement against this generation. Numbers 11:33 indicates that God struck the people with a severe plague, leading to the place being called Kibroth-hattaavah ('Graves of craving'), with 'craving' also a key term here. The anger that arose in verse 21 but not acted on is expressed in verse 31. God has been tested, and though initially this did not lead to punishment, a punishment did come.

32–39. These verses, the middle of both the Book's Asaphic collection and the whole Psalter (see Weber 2009 for insightful reflections on this), pause to reflect on the narrative to date. Rather than pointing to recognizable events in the wilderness period, the speaker provides a summary of key issues. The central concern is introduced in verse 32, which stresses the continued sin of not believing. The rhetorical question of verses 19–20 effectively announced that God could not provide through a miracle. They had received that provision abundantly, but the disbelief of verse 22 continued, leading to further punishment. The tragedy emphasized in verses 35–36 is that it was only when God disciplined them, putting some to death (as e.g. in Num. 16:31–35), that they sought God and turned back to him. At this point, they remembered that God was their rock, that God Most High was their redeemer. The title 'God Most High' links to the Zion traditions, but here stresses that the God known in the sanctuary was the one who had been with the people throughout. However, the problem the speaker notes is that although they remembered this, their service of God was insincere. Although they said the right things, they did not mean them, so their heart was not with God, and the problem of unbelief continued (v. 37). Unbelief here takes a special form, which is unbelief about the covenant, linking the wilderness generation to the Ephraimites (vv. 9–10). These people did not believe God would continue to act in accord with his commitment to his people. The flaw in this is then exposed through the allusion to Exodus 34:6–8 in verse 38 and the comment on their transience in verse 39. The statement in verse 38 avers that God is compassionate, that he atones for iniquity. Therefore, he does not let iniquity lead to destruction. God may be angered by the sin of his people, but he restrains that anger. The reason is that he remembers that humans are flesh. Unlike the people who remembered God but distorted what this should mean, God remembers the true nature of humans, that they are breath which goes out and does not return. These statements represent the turning point of this section of the psalm, reminding the audience about the fundamentals of God's character, explaining why they can continue to trust him.

40–51. This section returns to the plague narrative, events that happened before the exodus proper. However, it does so in the context of the wilderness generation's failure to remember these events. So, although we move back to an earlier period, we do so to continue illustrating the failure of the wilderness generation. There are clear links here with verses 15–31. Verses 40–41 are a bridge from the previous summary, again emphasizing that generation's continued rebellions. These rebellions continue to test God, alluding back to verse 18 and preparing for verse 56 (where this motif recurs for people in the land), while also hurting him. The failure of the people to remember (v. 42) looks back to the triggers for memory in verse 35, creating further links. It is also notable that of the plagues selected, most also allude to food, and though they are also recounted out of chronological sequence, their selection and arrangement point to the speaker's rhetorical purposes (Lee 1990a; Stinson 2017: 159). The location of the plagues (here described as signs and wonders) in the region of Zoan connects this section to the summary about Ephraim (vv. 9–11), pointing to a rebellion that began in the wilderness and continues to have an impact on the community. The account of the plagues proper begins in verse 44 with the turning of water to blood (Exod. 7:14–24), the first plague in Exodus. The waters here are the Nile and its streams (cf. Exod. 7:19) which became undrinkable. The plague account here is thus the opposite of the water miracles in the wilderness, where God provided abundant potable water. This establishes the key contrast with the wilderness provision in that the plagues occurred in a place noted for its plentiful food and water, whereas the wilderness was associated with neither. This contrast is immediately reinforced through verses 45–47, which all refer to processes that damaged Egypt's ability to grow crops. Initially, verse 45 refers to two plagues, the second of which is the plague of frogs (Exod. 8:1, 15). The 'swarms' mentioned first could be either the plagues of gnats (Exod. 8:16–19) or the plague of flies (Exod. 8:20–32). Since the word for 'swarm' occurs in both accounts (Exod. 8:17–18, 20, 25, 27), it is plausible that these accounts are here conflated, just as the feeding miracles were while recounting the wilderness miracles. Both the swarm and the frogs are said to have attacked the Egyptians, though the means is not stated. That is deferred until verses 46–47 which refer to the plagues of locusts (Exod. 10:1–20) and hail (Exod. 9:13–35). Mention of 'frost' (or perhaps some form of flood – the term is a hapax) finds no parallel in the plague narratives but is probably understood as an extension of the hail. The key point is that each of these plagues removed Egypt's crops, so that the order of what is removed represents a contrasting parallel to the provision of bread in the wilderness (vv. 23–25). The plague of hail is also linked to the death of the Egyptian livestock in verse 48, conflating it with plague against the livestock (Exod. 9:1–7). The reason it is introduced at this point is so the inability to eat meat now represents the final element of the plagues, matching the provision of the quail in verses 26–29. Verses 49–51 then provide summary statements about how God acted in judgement on Egypt, while principally alluding to the death of the firstborn (Exod. 11). This, of course, is the final plague, but its placement here (esp. with the emphasis on God's anger) also matches the death of the wilderness generation in verses 30–31. The prime of Egypt's youth were struck, just as happened to Israel's youth. The wilderness generation's question failed to understand God's provision of food and drink, and both suffered the same penalty.

52–55. This section summarizes the wilderness period from the perspective of what God did. Unlike the wilderness generation who forgot God and his covenant, God remained faithful. Accordingly, he led them like a flock, again employing the image of God as the shepherd who led his flock through the wilderness, a place where provision was not easily found. Israel moved in safety, not dreading their enemies. This obviously was not what happened when the spies entered the land (Num. 13), so the reference is rather to the travels up to that point. Further reference to the crossing of the sea here makes this the archetype of God's protection since other enemies were defeated in battle (cf. Exod. 17:8–16). The point here is to move from the early wilderness period to the point where Israel entered the land while continuing to emphasize that they occupied their territory because God had brought them there, that God had acquired the land and driven out the previous inhabitants and allotted the land so that each tribe dwelt in its inheritance. Accordingly, the whole book of Joshua is here summarized in just a handful of verses, stressing that this was what God did. The mighty signs were not restricted to Egypt or the wilderness, but continued as Israel entered the land and dwelt in it.

56–64. Having brought the people into the land, the third major section reflects on the themes previously established, showing how they continued in the land. In doing this, this closing section connects itself to the report about the Ephraimites (vv. 9–11) while also demonstrating that the 'testing' and 'rebellion' motifs continued. Indeed, these terms are placed at the beginning of this section, which notes that the later generation acted in the same way as the ancestors, with reference to the 'slack bow' (v. 57; cf. Hos. 7:16) alluding again to the Ephraimites (vv. 9–11). Nevertheless, the new generation introduced sins not mentioned earlier through their introduction of high places and idolatry, provoking God and placing the people under God's wrath so that he rejected Israel. Although 'Israel' sometimes means the whole people, in this case it means only the northern kingdom since the sins mentioned here are like those mentioned for them in 2 Kings 17:7–21. Further, the closing section makes clear that the north alone was rejected, here permanently exiled, while God continued to act for Judah. God's actions against Israel include forsaking Shiloh, the site of the Tent of Meeting (Josh. 18:1) and delivering his people into captivity. The exact point of Shiloh's fall is uncertain. It was still the site of the sanctuary at the time of Samuel's birth (1 Sam. 1) and where God appeared to him (1 Sam. 1:1 – 4:1a). Mention of giving God's 'strength' and 'splendour' to captivity may then allude to the Ark's capture (1 Sam. 4:1b–22), and this could also be the background to the people being given over to the sword and thus being subject to God's wrath. The key point here is that this generation too placed themselves under God's wrath, with the young men and women who died continuing the pattern of the wilderness generation and the Egyptians. If the Ark's capture is still in the background, then the mention of the priests' death refers to Eli's sons, who died when the Ark was captured (1 Sam. 4:11).

65–72. The rejection of Shiloh was a moment of tragedy, but it was not the end of what God was doing. Verses 65–66 provide a summarizing bridge that moves to God's promise through David. Just as the rebellion in the wilderness did not see God abandon his covenant, so also the sin of Israel did not mean Judah was abandoned. The picture of God's resuming his acts for Judah in verses 65–66 likens him to a warrior who has had too much to drink but finally awakes and acts once more. The image is like the appeal in Psalm 44:23–26, except that this time God does act. Describing God this way represents the people's perception of him, not the reality, since the psalm has been at pains to show his continued involvement in Israel's life. The removal of the age-old reproach could allude to numerous points, but may allude to 1 Samuel 17:26, a text that prepares for David's encounter with Goliath. Although the northern tribes, summarized as Joseph and Ephraim (though technically, Ephraim was half of Joseph with Manasseh), were rejected and thus not chosen, Judah was. More specifically, Zion is the place God loves. Shiloh had been rejected, but at Zion God built a sanctuary that provided real access to heaven ('like the heights' referring to the heights of heaven). This sanctuary was founded like the earth, able to stand in perpetuity. Zion remained as the place where God was worshipped, though the NT indicates that this is now transferred to Jesus. Along with Zion, God has also chosen David, taking him from the sheepfolds. God remains the shepherd, but David was the one through whom he would exercise this role so that David, along with the temple, is God's gift to the nation (Frisch 2009: 194). David was God's servant, an elevated title originally held by Moses (Deut. 34:5) that was later applied to Joshua (Josh. 24:29). All three provide background for the Servant in Isaiah 40 – 55. As God's chosen one, David's role was not limited to Judah, but applied to all the people, a point emphasized through the return to 'Jacob' as the label for them, with the whole nation also described as God's inheritance. David was the one who shepherded the people with integrity of heart and skilful hand; that is, in both intent and deed. The portrayal of David in Samuel does not shy away from his faults, but he remains the pattern for kings in both Kings and Chronicles because of his commitment to Yahweh (1 Kgs 15:3–5). David is the one who does not doubt God nor trigger his wrath. Accordingly, he is the goal of this recounting of Israel's story, the one whose story needs to be told so that subsequent generations set their confidence in God (v. 7). Yet, those subsequent generations will also need to read on into the remaining Asaphic psalms, which develop the themes here (see C. B. Jones 2017: 179).

Explanation

Few psalms are as clear as to their purpose as this one. It recounts Israel's story so that subsequent generations might set their confidence in God. That confidence depends on knowing the story of both the great things God has done and the continued sin of Israel. The key sins here are 'forgetting' and 'not believing', though in reality they are closely linked. Forgetting is not something that slips one's mind. It is a deliberate choice that comes from a failure to put God's covenant into practice. This failure is also a lack of belief or trust. Both stem from a proper understanding of the story. The story does tell us of God's anger at sin, but also pauses to remind us of God's grace, grace that continues despite the people's sin. It is therefore not enough simply to know the history if by that we mean knowing basic facts. That is simply accumulating theological trivia. The psalm insists that knowing the story means knowing the God who has been active throughout. This God has remained faithful, and this is good news to be passed on. The memory the psalm encourages is memory that leads to change because it comes to a deeper understanding of God (cf. Greenstein 1990; Pavan 2014: 280). That faithfulness in the psalm reaches its climax in God's commitment to David, though the NT then extends that to Jesus as the great Son of David. In telling the story, we come now to Jesus, but it is a story we need to know and pass on so that it leads to transformation. In doing so, we must not lose sight of the roots of that story here, one that already shows how God's covenant faithfulness provides a new beginning for his people (see Kim and van Rooy 2003).

PSALM 79

Translation

A melody. Asaphic.

[1]O God, the nations have come into your inheritance,
they have defiled your holy temple,
they have made Jerusalem a heap of ruins.
[2]They gave the corpses of your servants
as food to the birds of the heavens,
the flesh of your loyal ones to the beasts of the earth.
[3]They poured out their blood like water
around Jerusalem
and there was no one to bury them.
[4]We have become an object of disgrace to our neighbours,
derision and mockery to those around us.

[5]How long, O Yahweh?
Will you be angry for ever,
will your anger burn like fire?

6Pour out your wrath on the nations
that do not know you,
and upon the kingdoms
that do not call upon your name.
7For they have consumed Jacob,
and have made his habitation desolate.
8Do not remember our former iniquities against us,
let your compassion meet us quickly,
because we have been brought very low.
9Help us, O God of our salvation,
for the glory of your name,
rescue us and atone for our sins,
for your name's sake.

10Why should the nations say, 'Where is their God?'
Let it be known among the nations in our sight,
the avenging of the outpoured blood of your servants.
11May the groans of the prisoners come before you;
in accordance with the power of your arm,
preserve those facing death.
12Return sevenfold into the breast of our neighbours,
their reproach with which they reproached you, O Lord.
13And we, your people and the sheep of your pasture,
shall give thanks to you for ever,
From generation to generation,
we shall recount your praise.

Notes on the text

7. With many MSS and the versions, reading *'ākĕlû* (cf. Jer. 10:25).
10. With Q and many MSS, read *baggôyim*.

Form and structure

Following Psalm 78:67–72's affirmation of the temple's enduring nature and Israel's status as God's inheritance, Psalm 79 comes as a shock (cf. Schaefer 2001: 194–195). Both are suddenly under threat because of the arrival of invading nations who have defiled the sanctuary as Jerusalem lies in ruins. The contrast between these psalms is acute, but the links are important. Psalm 78 has shown that God's anger because of sin among his people leads to periods of judgement, and this psalm accepts both that God is angry with the community and that they need forgiveness (vv. 5, 9). That is, the exposition of Israel's history in the previous psalm helps the community understand their current suffering. Emerging from this, the community's vow of recounting God's praises (v. 13) means that they are taking seriously the task indicated in Psalm 78:4–6, itself drawing on Psalm 73:28. The exile provides the best background to this prayer (though Bouzard 1997: 185 suggests it is pre-exilic), meaning this psalm is also closely linked to Psalm 74 (cf. Hossfeld and Zenger 2006: 305), with both sharing the image of Israel as God's inheritance (Pss 74:2; 79:1). Both develop the motif of God as shepherd (Pss 74:1; 79:13) and pose the question of 'how long' (Pss 74:10; 79:5). These motifs also prepare for the remaining Asaphic psalms as they continue to plead for restoration from God.

The poem demonstrates an internal coherence, even though many verses draw on other OT passages, most especially from Jeremiah (cf. Botha 2004a: 366–368). This element further ties its composition to Jerusalem's fall even though the events are not narrated directly. Many of its phrases are also drawn from the wider Psalter, suggesting a composer who has 'thoroughly assimilated' it (Goldingay 2007: 519). As a communal lament, it is notable for including a confession of sin (v. 8), not something otherwise typical of these psalms. There is also a notable development within the poem as the community demonstrates its alignment with God, so that although the nations are said to have reproached the community in verse 4, by verse 12 those reproaches are said to be directed against God. The community has recognized its sin and realigned itself with God, and so anticipates future praise.

The poem's anthological nature has led to various schemes for understanding its structure, but a threefold analysis makes sense, with the second and third stanzas initiated by new questions, while the first and third are joined by repetitions of key terms:

1. The arrival of the nations (1–4)
2. How long? (5–9)
3. Why should the nations say? (10–13)

Comment

Title: The title is identical to Psalms 73 and 82, indicating that this title introduces sections within the Asaphic collection. For 'Asaphic', see on Psalm 50. For 'A melody', see on Psalm 3.

1–4. The psalm opens with a voc., addressing God directly. This has not occurred previously in the Asaphic psalms, but recurs in both Psalms 80 and 83, a further link within Psalms 79–83. Having addressed God, the poet then describes the situation that triggered the prayer, reporting the arrival of the nations into God's inheritance, language evoking Psalm 78:71. That the arrival of these nations is troubling is made clear by the note that they have defiled the sanctuary. The verb used here (*ṭm'*, 'defiled') can indicate either that something or someone is ritually unfit for being in God's presence (e.g. Lev. 11:1–8) or morally defiled (e.g. Gen. 34:5; Num. 35:34), though these elements can come together (e.g. Ezek. 36:17). A defiled temple is no longer suited for God's presence. Moreover, the damage was not restricted to the temple since Jerusalem had also been reduced to ruins (cf. Mic. 3:12). The harm inflicted by the nations also affected the people as they suffered the indignity of their dead being unburied, becoming food for the birds and wild animals. The contrast with Psalm 78:21–31, where the birds had been food for Israel, is marked. The community here describes themselves as God's 'servants', taking up the term used for David (Ps. 78:70). But rather than receiving honour, their blood has been poured out, with no one left to bury the dead. The result of this is described in verse 4 as the community is now an object of derision to the peoples around them. Texts such as Obadiah 1 – 14 (cf. Ps. 137:7) suggest that Edom would be among the neighbours who now deride the community, but the psalm is not concerned with listing the neighbours. Rather, we feel the community's pain, and this is what is presented to God.

5–9. The second stanza opens with the question 'How long?', a question repeated in Psalm 89:46. This is the only point in the psalm where the name 'Yahweh' is used, a reminder of the covenant relationship that exists with Israel, which was so important in Psalm 78, while echoing the question of Psalm 74:10. The question's implication is that the suffering has gone on long enough. Nevertheless, the community knows Yahweh's anger may not be spent, wondering if it can continue to burn like a fire indefinitely. The community's blood has previously been poured out (v. 3), so now they ask God to pour out his wrath on the nations who do not know him. It is not that these nations do not know about Yahweh (they have defiled his temple), but rather that they do not acknowledge him; hence, the kingdoms do not call on his name and worship him. Where the community have experienced God's anger, they now ask for it to be directed to the nations that entered the temple. Verse 7 then returns to the community's experience, noting that God's anger has consumed Jacob, leaving it desolate. Although the nations have defiled the temple and destroyed the city, the community accept that this was ultimately God's anger at work. The appeal of verses 8–9 thus looks to address the anger's cause, asking that God no longer remember their former sins and instead speedily bring his compassion to bear. Instead of having his compassion shut up in anger (Ps. 77:9), the community seeks a release of compassion upon them, something that is urgent because of how low they have fallen. The appeal is thus intensified in verse 9, where God is asked to help, rescue and atone for the community. Each of these verbs explores what it means to speak of the 'God of our salvation', creating a context for forgiveness in an enduring relationship. All this is rooted in the glory of God's name, with 'name' here reflecting his fundamental character. God's name points to him as the God of salvation, and acting for the community will demonstrate this.

10–13. The question opening the third stanza raises the status of the nations, assuming that if God does not act, then this will raise questions among them. So long as God refrains from acting, the nations can legitimately ask where he is, implying either that he does not exist or is powerless to act. The community therefore desires that God demonstrate his power, though they also want the avenging of the outpoured blood of his servant to be something they see. The request is linked to the description of the activities of the nations in the first stanza, so that the vengeance is intended to match what the nations have done to God's servants. Rather than allowing continued suffering, verse 11 focuses on particular aspects of suffering among the community, asking God to hear the groans of the prisoners, and with his arm (an expression of his might) rescue those facing death. Following the fall of a city it was common for the leadership to be imprisoned or executed; so, if the exile is the background, this could represent a prayer that included the king. As well as acting for his people, God is asked to act against the nations, returning the reproaches of the neighbours to them sevenfold. This is not a massive increase in the reproaches so much as a complete response to what they have done (cf. Gen. 4:15). By contrast, the community anticipates a time when they will engage in continued praise, with the recounting of God's praise across the generations taking up the challenge of Psalm 78:1–8.

Explanation

Following Psalm 78, this is a poem that brings readers up short. The previous psalm ends in celebration of God's commitment to Jerusalem and the temple, and to the hope of Davidic kings who could follow the pattern of David and shepherd the people with skill. Now, the temple and the city are in ruins, and no king is present – or if he is alluded to, then he is simply another prisoner. Yet we are not asked to choose between these two poems. Rather, they inform one another, especially as Psalm 79 closes with an unexpected anticipation of recounting God's praise, the very thing Psalm 78:1–8 expects God's people to do. In Psalm 78, this is so we may pass on an informed faith to our descendants. Here, the community prays out of the presentation of God in Psalm 78:32–39. They know the invaders were too powerful for them but also that they have sin that needs to be resolved. Yahweh is the only one who can do this, and it needs to be an expression of his compassion and mercy. Doing this renders powerless the nations' question 'Where is their God?', a question Mays (1994b: 260) points out is the theological heart of the psalm. Psalm 78 knows the community must share faith among themselves, but this psalm, even from great suffering, knows this faith must be passed on to others (cf. S. J. Smith 2022: 526), and that will happen when others see God act. This hope has reassured others through time, including the Maccabean revolt (1 Macc. 7:17) and suffering Christians in the first century (Rev. 6:10). In all cases, the desire is that God's justice be seen along with his mercy, a combination that comes together in the cross.

PSALM 80

Translation

The director's. According to Lilies. A testimony. Asaphic. A melody.

1O Shepherd of Israel give ear,
O one who drives Joseph like a flock,
O one seated upon the cherubim, shine forth.
2Before Ephraim, Benjamin and Manasseh,
rouse your strength,
and come for our salvation!
3Restore us, O God,
let your face shine that we may be saved.
4Yahweh, God of Hosts,
how long will you be angry
with the prayer of your people?
5You fed them the bread of tears,
and made them drink tears by third measure.
6You have made us an object of contempt among our neighbours,
our enemies mock us.
7Restore us, O God of Hosts,
let your face shine that we may be saved.
8You moved a vine from Egypt,
you drove out nations and you planted.
9You cleared a space before it,
the root was strong and filled the land.
10The mountains were covered with its shade,
the mighty cedars with its branches.
11It sent its boughs to the sea,
and its shoots to the river.
12Why have you broken down its walls,
so all who pass the way pluck it?
13The boar from the forest eats it away,
the field's insects graze on it.

[14]O God of Hosts, turn!
Consider from heaven and see!
Visit this vine
[15]and the rootstock that your right hand planted,
and the son you strengthened for yourself.
[16]It was burned with fire, cut down;
may they perish at the rebuke from your face!
[17]But let your hand be on the person of your right hand,
upon the human you strengthened for yourself.
[18]We shall not be disloyal to you;
revive us, and we shall call on your name!
[19]Yahweh, God of Hosts, restore us,
let your face shine that we may be saved.

Notes on the text

10. 'Mighty cedars' or 'cedars of God'. It seems likely that *'ēl* is used as a superlative here (*WHS* §80).

13. As with 50:11, *zîz* is uncertain, but appears to refer to moving things, and in context is understood as insects.

Form and structure

Psalm 80 is closely joined to Psalm 79 (see Cole 2000: 88–91). That psalm closed by describing the community as the sheep of God's pasture, while this commences by addressing God as 'Shepherd of Israel'. The shepherd theme is within the Asaphic psalms (see on Ps. 74:1) and is particularly prominent here. As shepherd, God is expected to care for his flock, but the community needs God to act for them. This is because their experience of God's anger continues (v. 4), meaning the question of Psalm 79:5 remains unanswered. Psalm 79 was also concerned with the nations, especially the mockery of the community's neighbours, and that theme continues as the God of salvation (Ps. 79:9) is again called to save the community (v. 2).

As with Psalm 79, the poem itself can be classified as a communal complaint. There is clear evidence of this in that the poem speaks of a community's need for restoration, consistently using the first-person pl. in describing the community (e.g. vv. 2–3), while also pointing to the activities of an undefined 'they' who act against them (v. 16; cf. H.-S. Kim 2014: 106–112). There is also a (near) refrain that occurs in verses 3, 7, 19 (plus a variation on this in v. 14), with each occurrence of the refrain developing the name of God used while consistently asking to be saved. Woven into this is an extended vine metaphor that reflects on the exodus and Israel's entry into the land, showing the community reflecting on its past, just as Psalm 78 has encouraged. From this, the community understands both why it needs to be loyal to God (v. 18) and that this background provides a basis for their appeal to him. As is common with the Asaphic psalms, the poem mentions northern locations and uses northern idioms (Rendsburg 1990: 79), leading to the suggestion that this may be an older poem that was brought to Jerusalem after the northern kingdom fell (see Hossfeld and Zenger 2006: 310–311; cf. Nasuti 1988: 102–108). This is certainly plausible, though its present literary location also encourages us to read it against the background of Jerusalem's fall (cf. G. T. M. Prinsloo 1997), though now extending the geography of Psalm 79 to include the north as well as Jerusalem.

The refrain provides the most important structural clue, meaning that we can analyse the poem in three stanzas, each closed by the refrain:

1. Prayer for restoration (1–3)
2. Complaint against God (4–7)
3. The vine (8–19)
   a. Planted but now ravaged (8–13)
   b. Appeal for the vine (14–19)

Comment

Title: For 'The director's', see on Psalm 4. For 'According to Lilies', see on Psalm 45. Hamilton (2021, 2: 72–73) suggests all the psalms with this have a messianic element, though in the case of Psalm 69 this is more evident in the poem's reception. 'A Testimony' is unique to this psalm, though note Psalm 60's title. Among the Asaphic psalms, the term occurs in Psalms 78:5, 56 and 81:5, so serves as an important link across these poems. More broadly, it is a key 'Torah' synonym in Psalms, and here perhaps anticipates the important references to the Pentateuch throughout, especially in the refrain. For 'Asaphic', see on Psalm 50. For 'A melody', see on Psalm 3.

1–3. The psalm opens with a set of vocs., though unlike Psalm 79, which simply named God, this time they are in the form of three ptcs. that describe God's relationship to the people. The first and third of these are linked to imperatives that point to the community's request. The first and second ptcs. are linked through the shepherd metaphor, the first explicitly naming God as Israel's shepherd, with the second pointing to God's action in driving Joseph like a flock. This image recurs in Psalm 78:52, which uses this language to describe the exodus, a motif probably present here too. So, the community appeals to the God who cares for his people like a shepherd and who continues to lead them as he did in the exodus, to give heed to them. That is, he needs to hear their prayer, suggesting that this is not their current experience, and in context Psalm 79 represents their prayer. The third ptc. changes the metaphor, describing God as being seated upon the cherubim, alluding to the Ark of the Covenant (cf. 1 Sam. 4:4). The allusion points to God's kingship (hence, 'enthroned' in ESV) as well as to the sanctuary as the place where he is worshipped. Of course, 'shepherd' is also a royal image (cf. Ps. 78:72), so the metaphors are closely linked. In this instance, God is asked to 'shine forth'. This picks up on Psalm 50:2, which reported that he 'shone forth' from Zion. The request asks God to do what he did previously. Deuteronomy 33:2 reports God as shining forth in a theophany, coming in great power, and that is the request here. Rather than leave his people suffering, he is to heed their need and come in power. This is developed in verse 2, which asks that God rouse his strength and come to save his people, with this particularly evident among the northern tribes of Ephraim, Benjamin and Manasseh (all Rachel-tribes). The stanza closes with the first instance of the refrain, the shortest form in which it occurs. God needs to restore the community, with his face shining on them so they can be saved. God's shining face (cf. Ps. 67:1) alludes to the priestly blessing (Num. 6:24–26), asking that God's favour be experienced. Through this, salvation from the current distress is possible.

4–7. The second stanza also opens with vocs., but this time employs the name 'Yahweh, God of Hosts'. Within the Elohistic Psalter, such a title is unusual (only in Ps. 59:5), and here stresses that the one addressed through the ptcs. in the first stanza is Israel's covenant God. As with the allusion to the Ark, this title may allude to 1 Samuel 4:4, pointing to God's ability to defeat Israel's enemies (accepting that Israel can become God's enemy). The one who needs to act is covenanted to his people and has the power to save, but this is not experienced. Hence, the question of 'how long', which here accepts that God has the right to be angry with the community (cf. Ps. 74:1). Yet, remarkably, it is the people's prayer that triggers God's anger, something personalized as the poem shifts from 'them' to 'us' in verse 6. The community does not confess sin here (though see Ps. 79:8), but this seems to be implicit. God's anger has seen them fed with the bread of tears, with tears also their drink. That is, suffering has shaped their experience, and the community's shepherd has not led them to green pasture or by restful waters (Ps. 23:2). Instead, they have become an object of contempt among their neighbours (cf. Ps. 79:4). Instead of being a community that leads the nations to praise him, Yahweh has left the community as an object of mockery. The stanza closes with the refrain's second occurrence, this time expanding God's title to 'God of Hosts', stressing that God has the power to act and save the community.

8–13. The third stanza divides into two strophes that pivot on the appeal (based on the refrain) in verse 14. The first strophe introduces the allegory of Israel as a vine that God brought out from Egypt, bringing them into the land where he established them. Verse 8 thus summarizes both the exodus and the opening chapters of Joshua, stressing that the nation's presence in the land was God's work. That he expelled the nations before them points again to God's power and hence his ability to overcome those countries now oppressing the community. Describing the nation as a vine draws on an established metaphor, one based on the widespread experience in viniculture. Isaiah 5:1–7 speaks of Israel as Yahweh's vineyard, while Deuteronomy 32:32 also speaks of other nations as a vine (though there associating them with evil). The metaphor of the vine here clearly describes a vine that far exceeds any normal growth, more like Jack's beanstalk than traditional grapevines (cf. Goldingay 2007: 539). This is evident in verse 10, where the vine provides shade for the mountains and its branches cover the cedars, trees known for their height. The hyperbolic description of the vine stresses that God took a community that would not normally achieve political significance and granted it to them, with their influence running from the sea to the river, perhaps the Dead Sea to the Euphrates. But all this only makes the question of verses 12–13 even more shocking. It is God who has broken down the vineyard's walls, meaning its fruit can be picked by those walking by, or that a boar (known for its damage to agricultural land) will eat it away while insects also infest and damage it. The question is asked, but no answer is given.

14–19. The stanza's second strophe opens with an appeal that is closely related to the refrain. The opening voc. picks up the divine name from the refrain of the previous stanza, while the verb is related to the verb from the refrain but with the key difference that it is now God who is called to turn. As God of hosts, he has the power to save, but because he has not yet acted, he is also summoned to look from heaven and see the community's position. Seeing in this case should lead to action, visiting this vine. God's visitation can be to punish (e.g. Isa. 23:17), to assess (e.g. Ps. 17:3) or to act favourably (e.g. Gen. 21:1; 1 Sam. 2:21), and it is this latter sense that is intended here, though some form of assessment may also be presumed. God's visitation is necessary because he is the one who planted the vine's rootstock with his right hand, signifying its favoured status. The vine is also here called a 'son'. In context, it refers to the community, stressing its special relationship with God, though it also prepares for mention of a particular figure in verse 17. The community can be God's son, but there is also a specific figure who embodies this. Yet between this, verse 16 speaks of somewhere burned with fire, while hoping that an undefined 'they' might perish. It is probably best to assume that the vine has been burned and cut down, but who is to perish? The community or their enemies? The poem avoids defining these people and this ambiguity should be retained. After all, if God visits and assesses, then he, not the poet, will determine those who should perish. Nevertheless, God needs to continue showing favour, strengthening not only the community but also one key figure, most likely the king who, even in exile, remains a potent symbol of God's commitment to the community. As they see God's favour, the community in turn commits itself to remain faithful and that, when revived, they will call on God's name; that is, worship him. As they anticipate calling on God's name, the poem concludes with the refrain's final occurrence, this time addressing God by the fullest title. Yahweh, Israel's covenant God is their God, and he is the one with the power to save. He needs to demonstrate favour to the community because only then will they be saved.

Explanation

Extending the complaint of Psalm 79 to include northern regions of Israel as well, this psalm is a prayer that holds to two fundamental realities, knowing that they must always be held together. First, the community holds to God as the one who is, in covenant, committed to them and who has the power to save. It is God, not the community, who can do this. They know too that their current experience is an expression of God's anger towards them. Holding to the covenant God does not always mean blessing – they must also accept his discipline. Second, the community face their current circumstances with absolute seriousness, refusing to downplay either their suffering or their sense that God has also in some way brought this about. Holding these elements together also means taking seriously the whole of God's relationship with his people, whether how God is represented in the temple or how the story of his work for them is told. Because of this, they can ask God both to restore them and to turn himself. Only as God and community come together is there a future, a future that finds its focus in the king and the memory of what God has previously done. When the psalm is read against the exile, we see a period when the king was a lowly prisoner in Babylon. But even such apparent weakness does not matter because knowing what God has done continues to bring hope. Like Paul, the community here knows its strength is found in coming to terms with its weakness (2 Cor. 12:9–10). The early Christian community knew that it too lived in a place of weakness, but, in seeing eschatological possibilities in both the image of the vine (cf. John 15:1–17) and the royal figure, found in the psalm a hope that stood within a line of Jewish interpreters who read the psalm in a similar way (Streett 2014).

PSALM 81

Translation

The director's. Upon Gittith. Asaphic.

1Shout joyfully to God our strength,
  shout to the God of Jacob.
2Raise a melody and strike the hand-drum,
  the sweet lyre with the harp.
3Give a blast on the ram's horn at the new moon,
  at the full moon, for our festal day,
4because it is a statute for Israel,
  an ordinance of the God of Jacob.
5He established a testimony in Joseph,
  when he went out against the land of Egypt.

  'I was hearing a language I did not acknowledge.
6I removed a burden from his shoulder,
  his hands were freed from the basket.
7In distress you called, and I rescued you,
  I answered you in the secret place of thunder,
  I tested you at the waters of Meribah.' *Selah.*

8'Heed, O my people, and I will testify against you,
  O Israel, if only you would heed me.
9There shall be no strange god among you,
  nor shall you worship a foreign god.
10I am Yahweh your God,
  who brought you up from the land of Egypt:
  open wide your mouth and I will fill it.
11But my people did not heed my voice,
  and Israel did not accede to me.
12So I sent him off in the stubbornness of their heart,
  they walked in their own counsels.
13If only my people would heed me,
  that Israel would walk in my way!
14I would quickly subdue their enemies,
  and rear back my hand against their foes.'

15'Those who hate Yahweh act deceitfully toward him,
  but their time will last for ever.
16But he fed him from the finest wheat,
  and I would satisfy you with honey from the cliff.'

Notes on the text

The psalm is notable for the changes in pronouns in verses 6–7, 11–12, 15–16. Most EVV resolve these into something more consistent, but (with deClaissé-Walford et al. 2014: 636) the translation above follows MT in each case.

5. The spelling of Joseph is unusual, but this is not enough to support de Boer's (1984) proposal that the spelling represents Judean opposition to the house of Joseph. Layton (1988) argues that this is a deliberate inclusion of a theophoric element, which is plausible, but not requiring the late date he suggests.

14. For hiph. *šwb* as 'rear back', see LeMon 2013, especially the iconographic evidence which shows that Yahweh is ready to vanquish foes.

15. For pi. *kḥš* as 'act deceitfully'; cf. Lev. 5:21; 19:11.

Form and structure

Psalm 81 follows on from Psalms 79–80. Where those psalms were communal complaints addressed to God, Psalm 81 records God's complaint to the community. Its use of first-person speech from God means it joins with Psalms 50, 75 in the Asaphic collection in using this technique. It thus provides an important response to the questions raised in those psalms, though without resolving them all. Despite its distinctive form, there are also important linguistic links with the preceding poems. The most notable is the use of 'testimony' (*'ēdût*), a key term from Psalms 78:5, 56 and Psalm 80's title, which recurs here in verse 5. There is also an important connection with Psalm 80 in that both reflect on the exodus. Psalm 80:8–13 does so through the vine allegory, whereas here it is God's reflection (v. 10) as he reminds them of aspects of the Decalogue. The question of 'how long' (Ps. 80:4) receives a possible answer in verse 14 as God declares that he is willing to act quickly against the community's enemies. Cole (2000: 96–97) has also noted important connections with Psalm 84, especially the unusual 'Upon Gittith' in the title. Psalm 84 returns us to Korahite psalms, so Psalm 81 thus serves both as a key unit within the Asaphic psalms and as a bridge to the next segment of Book 3.

Psalm 81 does not fit easily into the standard categories. It shares with Psalms 50, 95 the element of a prophetic oracle, where God speaks to the community after a call to worship. Whether these shared features are enough to define a category of 'festival psalms' (see Hosfeld and Zenger 2006: 320) can be questioned due to the limited evidence. These three psalms should be read in the light of each other, but their distinctiveness also needs to be noted (cf. Nasuti 1988: 102). Psalm 81, for example, is the only one that mentions a festival (v. 3); and, though such a background for the other two is plausible, it is not stated. In this case, we do not know which festival is meant. What matters is that a festival provided the opportunity to remind the community of both the exodus and what God expected from Israel in response, most especially through reflections on the Decalogue (Wenham 2005: 180–181; 2012: 100–101). Although Psalm 50:18 may also allude to the Decalogue, it is more explicit here, so that the whole psalm effectively becomes a call to decision, a choosing of Yahweh's way and its associated blessings.

The move between the call to worship and the divine oracle provides the most important structural clue here, leading to the following analysis:

1. Call to worship (1–5a)
2. God's speech (5b–16)
   a. Removal of burdens (5b–7)
   b. Testimony against the community (8–14)
   c. Possible outcomes (15–16)

Comment

Title: For 'The director's', see on Psalm 4. For 'Upon Gittith', see on Psalm 8. For 'Asaphic', see on Psalm 50.

1–5b. The psalm opens with a flurry of five imperatives (vv. 1–3), each summoning the community to worship. The worship is praise oriented, with the opening shout typically marking joy (Ps. 32:11) while the second verb for 'shout' is associated with royal acclamation (1 Sam. 10:24; Zech. 9:9). Such joyful shouts are directed to God because he is 'our strength', the one who sustains the community. Although the shouts can be musical, the worship becomes expressly musical in verse 2, which calls for melody and playing of a hand-drum along with lyre and harp, though these are probably representative of wider instrumentation (Emanuel 2009: 13). The music is melodic and rhythmic. Along with this there is also a blast on the ram's horn at the new moon, presumably a signal to gather. Numbers 28:11–15 requires offerings at the start of the month, which is marked by the new moon, so the blast on the horn would indicate this. 1 Samuel 20:5 also indicates that families might use the new moon to mark a feast of their own. The full moon is elsewhere mentioned only in Proverbs 7:20. It would mark the midpoint of each month (roughly twenty-nine days each), which in the first month is also the date of Passover and Unleavened Bread (Num. 28:16–17). This is a plausible point for the 'festal day' mentioned here; but as Tabernacles occurs on the fifteenth day of the seventh month (Num. 29:12), it is also possible. Moreover, the Day of Atonement is the only festival associated with a blast on the ram's horn (Lev. 25:9). Psalm 78 was content to conflate various events in Israel's story, and perhaps here too the psalm alludes to several festivals to indicate that these words are appropriate at any festival. The reason for the community's worship is traced back to a statute God has set for Israel, pointing readers to Israel's law. The structure of worship is rooted in what God has established for his people, something based in the events of the exodus when he acted against Egypt. This could also allude to the exodus since the celebration of Passover and Unleavened Bread was mandated at the point where God was about to act against Egypt's firstborn (Exod. 12:14–20). This testimony was established in 'Joseph'; though, since 'Joseph' here is parallel to 'Israel', it is probably a case of one tribe standing for the whole people (with Goldingay 2007: 550).

5b–7. A new speaker enters at this point, reporting hearing an otherwise unknown language. This is perhaps someone who recounts God's speech from verse 6, the otherwise unknown language then being God's words. It is common in prophetic speech for the speaker's identity and God's to merge, and this would account for the fact that God is clearly speaking from verse 7 onwards. The initial reference is clearly to the deliverance from Egypt, though we see here the shift between 'him' and 'you' that recurs later. Here, we could think of 'his' in verse 6 as Israel personified in Egypt, but presented as distinct from the community. It was those in Egypt who experienced God's removing the marks of slavery. But verse 7 then speaks of 'you'. In this case, it is the community, so when they called out in distress, God also rescued them. This might have occurred in a theophany if this is the background to the thunder mentioned here, but it may also be a means of speaking of God's power. The community had cried out in distress, and God had kept them safe when he rescued them. The final part line in verse 7 then links the current community with that of the exodus since God is said to have tested them at Meribah even though they are a later generation than those in the exodus, and the original generation were said to have tested God. Such generational blurring occurs elsewhere (e.g. Josh. 24:2–13; cf. C. L. Eaton 2020: 334–339) and functions to tie the present community to God's acts in the past. The place name Meribah (Contention) occurs in Exodus 17:1–7 and Numbers 20:2–13, both times in the provision of water, though in neither case is God said to have tested Israel. Either miracle could be alluded to here.

8–14. A fresh imperative at the start of verse 8 indicates the start of a new strophe. The people are summoned to heed God so he can testify against them (cf. Ps. 50:7), with 'heed' (*šmʿ*) serving as the key term for the strophe (echoing Deut. 6:4–5). The need for this is implied by verse 8b, where God expresses a wish that Israel will heed him, the implication being that they do not. The previous two psalms saw the community wondering why they still suffered God's anger, and this is the answer. The issue is then addressed in verses 9–10, which refer to the first commandment in the Decalogue. Israel was to have no other gods before

Yahweh (Exod. 20:3), with those gods here described as 'strange' (cf. Ps. 44:20) and foreign. But in case the connection to the Decalogue was missed, verse 10 closely paraphrases Exodus 20:2, the Decalogue's introduction. Israel had been rescued by Yahweh, and therefore should have no other god. Had they done so, they could have opened their mouth and had it filled with food or praise. That is, God would have provided for their needs just as happened at Meribah. The problem is that this was not what they did. Israel did not heed God, choosing not to accede to him. Verse 12 is a tangle of pronouns, with Israel initially personified as an individual sent off by God, but also a group whose heart was stubborn, choosing to conduct themselves by their own counsels rather than God's (cf. Jer. 7:24; Booij 1984: 467–468). The accusation is thus that they have served gods other than Yahweh – God has given them what they wanted, but it turns out not to be what they want. Verses 14–15 then offer an alternative that was possible had the community heeded God, walking in God's ways rather than their own counsels. Had that been the case, then God would quickly have acted for them – 'how long' would no longer be the question as God subdued their enemies.

15–16. The final strophe offers what is in effect a variation of the two-ways model from Psalm 1. Those who hate Yahweh are evident from the fact that they act deceitfully towards him. Hatred here is to claim loyalty but not to demonstrate it in a faithful life. Such people will find their current time continuing. That is, they remain outside God's blessing because they are not loyal. God provided the best for the wilderness generation (again, here 'him'), providing the finest wheat, and he will do the same for the community today. They therefore miss God's offer of providing the food they have longed for, the best of the wheat and honey from the rock (cf. Deut. 32:13–14), the latter pointing to God's provision coming in unexpected ways, like water from a rock.

Explanation

Readers of Psalms 79–80 may wonder how the prophets responded to the community's complaints. Those psalms challenge and probe God, but do not really acknowledge sin beyond the passing note in Psalm 79:8, and even that could assume God was punishing the nation for prior sins rather than something that continued. The Asaphic tradition allows those psalms to remain, accepting that at times this is all we can do in prayer. But here we also have a response, one in which God speaks. The community has gathered for worship as it knows it must, and the shouts and music bespeak joyful celebration. Yet the reason for this gathering is not to celebrate current events. Rather, the community is reminded that God's law has required it. This does not remove the joy (any more than the fact that annual celebration of Christmas makes it joyless), but it places this worship in a context of obedience to God. That obedience, heeding what God has to say, is at the heart of what follows. The community has a history that looks back to what God has done in the past in delivering them. It has a present that seems to lack the desired blessing, though God can point out that this is because of their disloyalty. God has let them experience what they desired because this demonstrates it is not what they want (cf. Rom. 1:24–32). The psalm also offers a future, one where the community truly heeds God, and he truly satisfies them. It is a word of gospel (cf. Weiser 1962: 555; Brueggemann 1984: 93) that finds a close parallel in the celebration of Communion, which also takes us from past to present and the hope of the future.

PSALM 82

Translation

A melody. Asaphic.

1God stations himself in the divine assembly,
he judges amid the gods.
2'How long will you judge unjustly,
and show favouritism to the wicked? *Selah*.
3Give justice to the helpless and orphan,
maintain the right of the afflicted and poor.
4Deliver the helpless and needy,
rescue from the hand of the wicked.
5They do not know, they do not understand,
they go about in darkness:
all the earth's foundations are shaken.'

6"I had said, "You are gods,
and all of you sons of the Most High."
7But you shall die like a human,
and fall like one of the rulers.'

8Rise up, O God, judge the earth,
for you have an inheritance in all the nations.

Notes on the text

1. The psalm's interpretative challenges cluster around the translation of verse 1, though the whole poem is 'ripe with ambiguity' (Mongé-Greer

2023: 45; cf. Handy 1990: 53–54). Much depends on the interpretation of *ba'ădat 'ēl*. The main options for this are as follows:

1. 'Divine assembly', which assumes a Canaanite background, perhaps taken polemically (e.g. NET; cf. van Gemeren 2008: 550).
2. 'Great assembly', thus taking *'ēl* as a superlative (e.g. NIV).
3. God's 'own congregation', assuming that *'ēl* is the shortened form of *'ĕlōhîm* from the line's opening (e.g. NASB), presumably assuming the same reference as Psalm 74:2.

Mongé-Greer (2023: 65) also notes that the initial ptc. (*niṣṣāb*) can be read as sg., thus indicating that the initial *'ĕlōhîm* refers to Israel's God, or distributive and thus cover a plurality of *'ĕlōhîm*. If so, this ambiguity is resolved in the closing verse. Those who replace *'ĕlōhîm* with the Tetragrammaton here (e.g. Kraus 1989: 153–154) resolve this ambiguity, but without actual textual warrant beyond the belief that the Elohistic Psalter has replaced 'Yahweh' with *'ĕlōhîm*, something that is difficult to sustain given that 'Yahweh' does occur at key points in this collection.

The recurrence of *'ĕlōhîm* as the ones among who God judges is also ambiguous, as the term could refer to any deity other than Israel's God, angelic figures (cf. Ps. 8:5) or a human figure appointed by God, perhaps a king or judge (cf. Ps. 45:6). Most commentators try to determine which of these senses is intended, but it seems better to allow that all are possible (similarly, Niehr 1987).

All these issues would be transparent to an ancient audience but tend to be masked for modern readers because English lacks terms with the flexibility exploited by the poet here. The translation above aims to retain as much of the ambiguity as possible while accepting that some points will still be lost.

6. Hebr. *'ănî 'āmartî* is taken by Hossfeld and Zenger (2006: 329) as a pf. of coincidence, rejecting the view that this represents a previous statement or thought no longer held. But this is the sense of the idiom elsewhere in Psalms (30:5; 31:22; 116:11), with only Psalm 41:4 as a possible exception, making this more probable.

Form and structure

Although its language is disorienting through its presentation of a divine assembly (cf. Miller 1986: 120–121) in which other *'ĕlōhîm* are present, there is still an important development here from Psalm 81:9. There, the community was reminded that no 'strange' or 'foreign' god (*'ēl*) should be among them, but now God has stationed himself among the gods (*'ĕlōhîm*; cf. Vesco 2006, 2: 745; Heiser 2008). The identity of these 'gods' (see 'Notes on the text') is ambiguous, perhaps intentionally, to reject any that might claim this title other than Israel's God. This is linked to a deep concern with injustice that disadvantages the poor, something God alone can resolve (v. 7). The concern with justice links Psalm 82 with Psalm 72 except that it looks to God rather than the king to bring this about. Cole (2000: 103) also notes that various forms of 'how long' have peppered the Asaphic psalms (74:10; 79:5; 80:4), always spoken by the community to God. But now it is God who asks the question, this time addressed to those in his assembly. God's speaking in this psalm then prepares for the appeal for further speech in Psalm 83.

It is difficult to align this poem with the standard categories, though verse 8 may suggest complaint (McLellan 2018). It is better to see it instead as a dialogue with the dominant ANE world view, presented through a vision of the divine council. This council occurs elsewhere in the OT (cf. Morgenstern 1939: 40–59; Kee 2009), such as when various figures present themselves before Yahweh in Job 1 – 2. In the OT, other beings who exist in the heavenly realm should serve Yahweh. But peoples around Israel worked with several deities, usually in some form of a hierarchy, and the psalm is initially presented in a way that allows both options to be present (see Mongé-Greer's careful comparison with the Ugar. Epic of Aqhat (2023: 108–113)). In the end, we see that any other heavenly being is subject to Israel's God, and he is the one who is to bring about justice for the poor.

The poem can be analysed in three stanzas, with the second divided further (cf. W. S. Prinsloo 1995a: 222–227):

1. Vision of the divine council (1)
2. Divine speech (2–7)
   a. How long? (2–5)
   b. The death of the *'ĕlōhîm* (6–7)
3. Appeal to God (8)

Comment

Title: Identical to Psalms 73, 79. For 'A melody', see on Psalm 4. For 'Asaphic', see on Psalm 50.

1. As noted above (see 'Notes on the text'), much of this verse is ambiguous, making it difficult to sustain a single line of interpretation. Readers are probably meant to be disoriented about the identity of the various figures mentioned. The verse points to the existence of a divine council, though initially leaving open the question of whether the God who has stationed himself there is Israel's God or those of the nations that surrounded Israel. As such, even the nature of this assembly is initially ambiguous. What is clear, though, is that within an assembly a deity has stationed himself among the others who are there, though the fact that this deity stations (lit. 'stands') may indicate that he is not presiding (normally seated; cf. Trotter 2012: 222–228). But this deity has the authority to judge, though we do not know if those subject to the deity's authority are mortals or those in the assembly. Of course, inclusion of this poem within the Psalter predisposes readers to assume that this deity is Israel's God, but that is not initially resolved.

2–5. Someone now speaks, probably the deity who stationed himself in the assembly, unless with Goldingay (2007: 559) we assume one speaker throughout. The assembly is asked how long they will continue judging unjustly, especially showing favouritism to the wicked. The wicked are a persistent problem within the Psalter, reaching back to Psalm 1, and were also a source of trouble to the poet in Psalm 73, while the closing vow of Psalm 75:9–10 promised to cut them off. Within the assembly, there continued to be those who favoured them, allowing their continued flourishing. But this is contrary to the assembly's role; hence, the question asks how long they will continue to do this. The *selah* at the end of verse 2 may indicate a short pause before the speech switches to imp. mode, directing them to execute justice for the helpless and orphan, maintaining the right of those in need. The imperatives continue into verse 4, demanding deliverance for the helpless and needy, rescuing them from the power of the wicked. Care for the poor is the marker of a commitment to justice (cf. Dickson 1995). Members of the divine assembly should know this, but verse 5 then offers an aside, a comment probably addressed to the psalm's readership about the divine assembly (Ray 2020: 316), its importance marked by being the poem's only tricolon. This assembly is apparently ignorant of its basic responsibilities, their lack of knowledge and insight matched by their wandering around in darkness. But their ignorance not only harms them, since their continued injustice also damages the earth's foundations; the very order of creation is threatened by members of the divine assembly who support the wicked rather than the poor.

6–7. The speaker (presumably God, against Frankle 2018) now looks back to a previously held view, when those addressed were declared to be *'ĕlōhîm*. Much here depends on the word's range of meaning. Those addressed may be considered as 'gods' and perhaps understand their status in those terms. But it can also mean those appointed by God (see 'Notes on the text' on v. 1). This ambiguity is continued when they are described as 'sons of the Most High' since they may be either members of the divine assembly in their own right, or those brought in by the Most High. But irrespective of how they understand their previous status, the speaker now declares that they 'shall die like a human', falling like any other ruler. Whatever previous status might have been assigned to them, they are no more important or powerful than any human.

Anything in the heavenly realm that does not practise God's justice has no claim to any special status, and the same is therefore true for any human who claims to do God's work. Only as they care for the poor can they claim to be involved in God's work. Only one is left who can truly be called God.

8. Only now is God addressed within the poem. By now we know that this can only be Israel's God, because whatever else exists in the divine sphere is subject to this God. The audience knows that only God can bring about the needed justice, and so asks that he rise up and judge the earth. The reason for this is that God has an inheritance in all the nations (cf. Deut. 32:8–9; cf. Tsevat 1970: 132–133). That is, there are those who belong to God in all the nations, and he has a responsibility towards them (esp. the poor) to ensure they receive justice. The nations might also have been thought to belong to the gods, but all that now clearly belongs to God alone (cf. Terrien 2003, 2: 591). The appeal assumes that this is not yet the case, but it knows that God alone can ensure this (cf. Ps. 58:11).

Explanation

Where Psalm 81 admonishes the community for failing to remain true to covenant, Psalm 82 addresses the inhabitants of the divine assembly and admonishes them for failing to maintain justice. Read together, the problem of injustice derives from both the human and the heavenly realm. The community has been told to heed God's voice, and now the heavenly realm is told that it retains God's support only if it practises justice. This is communicated in deeply mythological language, but language that knows God has already announced the death of any among the 'gods' who do not seek justice for the poor. A longstanding debate has focused on whether these 'gods' are spiritual beings or humans who hold office on God's behalf (cf. Morgenstern 1939: 31–33; Heiser 2008: 18–20). Although the majority opinion is now that these 'gods' are spiritual beings who have lost their status, there remains value in noting the alternative (though we should note that Jesus is said to have overcome all the spiritual powers in his death and resurrection; cf. Col. 2:15; Goldingay 2007: 570). Humans who are called to act for God are likewise warned that the measure of their commitment to doing God's work is their commitment to the poor. Knowing this, the community calls on God to arise and act for justice in all the nations, though this community also knows they are called to commitment to the poor if they align themselves with God. In passing, we should note Jesus' citation of verse 6 (John 10:34–36), but his argument here is ad hominem, not an exegesis of the passage (with Longman 2014: 308).

PSALM 83

Translation

A song. A melody. Asaphic.

1O God, do not stay quiet,
  do not be silent and do not be inactive, O God!

2For behold, your enemies make an uproar,
  and those who hate you have lifted their head.
3Against your people they lay crafty plans,
  they conspire together against your treasured ones.
4They say, 'Come, and let us annihilate them so they are not a nation,
  so the name of Israel is remembered no more.'
5For they have conspired together with one mind,
  they have made a covenant against you.

6The tents of Edom and the Ishmaelites,
  Moab and the Hagrites,
7Gebal, Ammon and Amalek,
  Philistia with the inhabitants of Tyre,
8even Assyria is joined with them –
  they are the arm of the children of Lot! *Selah.*

9Do to them what you did to Midian,
  to Sisera and Jabin at the Wadi Kishon –
10they were destroyed at En-dor,
  they became dung for the ground.
11Make their nobles like Oreb and Zeeb,
  all their leaders like Zebah and Zalmunna,
12when they said, 'Let us possess for ourselves,
  the pastures of God.'

13O my God, make them like tumbleweed,
  like chaff before the wind.
14As a fire burns a forest,
  and as a flame sets the mountains ablaze,
15so may you pursue them with your tempest,
  and terrify them with your gale.

16Fill their faces with dishonour,
  so they might seek your name, O Yahweh.
17Let them be ashamed and dismayed for ever,
  let them be confounded and perish.

[18]Let them know that you,
your name alone is Yahweh,
Most High over all the earth.

Notes on the text

1. The presence of both *'ĕlōhîm* and *'ēl* in this verse is a further link to Psalm 82:1.

3. Or 'protected ones' for the ptc. *ṣĕpûneykā*.

10. NEB (cf. *BHS*) has En Harod, an easy emendation that conforms the text to Judg. 7:1, but lack of MS evidence and the possibility of making sense of En-dor makes this unnecessary.

Form and structure

This poem closes both the Asaphic collection and the Elohistic Psalter. The final prayer, that the enemies know Yahweh's name provides a bridge to the rest of the Psalter, which typically prefers the name Yahweh (see 'Form and structure' on Ps. 42). The prayer also has close links with Psalm 82 (cf. Auffret 1993: 57–59). That poem ended with a plea for God to rise up and bring justice in the nations, following a psalm that most probably contains a good deal of speech by God. Just as God spoke in both Psalms 81 and 82, so this psalm pleads with him that he not now remain silent, something necessitated by the speech of the enemies, which is directed against the community. The conspiracies of the nations (vv. 3–4) are reminiscent of Psalm 2:1–3, while the punishments sought in verse 13 classify them with the wicked from Psalm 1:4. It also joins with Psalm 73 in looking for God's justice to be worked out in lived experience (cf. Cole 2000: 112). The poem thus closes the Asaphic collection with reference to the whole of Psalms 73–83 and to Psalms 1–2, so that this appeal is placed in the framework of the whole Psalter.

As with Psalms 74 and 79–80, this is a communal complaint. It is grounded not only in the wider Psalter but also in earlier narratives where Israel was under threat, especially the Gideon narrative (Judg. 6 – 8; see Swale 2021: 94–138). These earlier traditions provide a source of hope for the community while also shaping their prayer. Despite these clear links to other texts, the exact situation faced by the community is non-specific, being open to a range of possible threats. Most importantly, the aim of the enemies is to ensure that Israel's name is remembered no more (v. 4). As the community prays, they ask instead that the enemies seek Yahweh's name (v. 16), and even in defeat come to know the uniqueness of Yahweh's name (v. 18). This last point is stressed through the presence of the poem's only tricolon.

The *selah* at the end of verse 8 marks the major division of the poem into two stanzas, each of which is opened by an appeal, with the first stanza pointing to what God is not to do and the second to what the community desires he should do. This leads to the following analysis:

1. Appeal that God is not silent (1–8)
   a. Appeal (1)
   b. The plans of the nations (2–5)
   c. The extent of the conspiracy (6–8)
2. Appeal that God act (9–18)
   a. Defeat of the nations (9–12)
   b. Terrifying the nations (13–15)
   c. From shame to knowing Yahweh (16–18)

Comment

Title: With Psalms 75–76, this is a 'song', though this is the only place in the Asaphic collection where this term occurs first. For 'song', see on Psalm 65. A 'melody' is a common element in the titles (see on Ps. 4), but here particularly links the psalm to Psalms 73 and 82. For 'Asaphic', see on Psalm 50.

1. God's speech has been prominent in Psalms 81–82, but the community is here concerned with his silence. That the appeal is urgent is evident from the three negative requests here that link silence with inaction. If God is silent (contrast Ps. 50:3), then he might not act. Vocs. bookend the verse, making clear that it is God who must respond.

2–5. Both verses 2, 5 open with *kî*, introducing a reason why God should act. Both thus build on the initial appeal. Although the community has enemies, it is clear these are God's enemies – people who hate God, who have raised their head against him. Mention of the 'head' introduces a run of terms ('mind' in v. 5 is literally 'heart'; 'arm', v. 8) which demonstrate that the enemies are an embodied threat who have set themselves against God, though the phrasing may also allude to Judges 8:28, preparing for later allusions to Judges. This has been done by acting against the community of God's people, those whom he treasures and protects (cf. 'Notes on the text'). Their conspiracy (cf. Ps. 2:1–3) seeks to destroy the community, so that they are no longer even remembered as a nation. With their name gone, it will be as if they never existed. So strong is the conspiracy that they have even made a covenant, the only covenant against people mentioned in the OT. Although the covenant might have been against Israel, that they seek its destruction means it is really against God, closing the strophe by again stressing that these nations are God's enemies.

6–8. The nations conspiring against the community are listed, showing Israel surrounded by enemies. Mention of their 'tents' could refer to a military camp where these groups come together. We know of no conflict in which these nations were all active, though if all were influenced by Assyria it is possible that various conflicts are conflated, making this a representative or symbolic list. Edom lived south-east of Israel, east of the Dead Sea, and were descended from Jacob's brother Esau (Gen. 36:9). They are linked with the Ishmaelites, descendants of Abraham's son Ishmael (Gen. 25:12–17), who lived in the southern wilderness. Moab was east of Israel, north of Edom, and descended from Lot (Gen. 19:30–39). They are linked with the Hagrites, a semi-nomadic group who also lived east of the Jordan (1 Chr. 5:10). Gebal also refers to a people that might have been semi-nomadic, living east of the Jordan (Josh. 13:5; unless it is an alternative name for Byblos in Lebanon), which would also explain their association with Ammon. Ammon too were descended from Lot (Gen. 19:30–39), living east of the Jordan and north of Moab. Ammon is joined to Amalek, another semi-nomadic people, though they are more closely associated with the southern wilderness and were long-term enemies (Exod. 17:8–16). Amalek could also move towards Egypt, so mention of them prepares for the Philistines, a people who lived on Israel's south-western coastal plain. They are linked with Tyre, a major Mediterranean port north of Israel. None of these peoples was a major power, but if Israel was surrounded by enemies, then they lived under constant threat. This threat is then increased by the note that Assyria, the major power in the region from the ninth to seventh centuries BC, had joined them. If Assyria is also the 'arm' of the children of Lot, then the implication is that Assyria was using these nations to destabilize Israel.

9–12. Having outlined the threat, the poet appeals to God to act as before and deliver the nation. Several of the peoples mentioned are closely associated with Judges 4 – 8. Mention of Midian is not restricted to those chapters, but God defeated them through Gideon (Judg. 6:1–2, where they are joined by the Amalekites, 7:19–25). Midian's defeat is joined to the defeat of Sisera, commander of Jabin's army (Judg. 4 – 5), with Sisera famously killed by Jael's tent peg (Judg. (4:17–22), and his forces swept away at the Wadi Kishon (Judg. 5:21). The combination of both the Deborah and Gideon stories here is probably because these were instances where Israel faced seemingly overwhelming forces, but God still gave the victory. Mention of En-dor, however, must either know something not in the Judges account (which does not mention the town) or use the town as an approximation for the site of Gideon's victory. The victory was total, which is why the defeated army is likened to dung on the ground. As well as defeating the enemy nations, verses 11–12 look for the destruction of their leaders, again patterned on Judges 4 – 8. Oreb and Zeeb were captured and killed by Gideon (Judg. 7:25), while

Zebah and Zalmunna were Midianite kings he captured and killed (Judg. 8:4–21), and their experience is the pattern for all the leaders of the enemies. They had sought to attack Israel but were really trying to take what belonged to God, and so were God's enemies.

13–15. A second appeal for God to act against the enemies is grounded in earlier psalms rather than Judges. The relationship between a representative individual and God is stressed before asking that the enemies become like tumbleweed (cf. Isa. 17:12–14), anticipating the development of this theme where they are asked to be made like chaff driven before the wind, echoing Psalm 1:4. The motif of storm winds driving the enemies is continued in verses 14–15, though here merged with the image of a fire consuming huge areas (forests, winds), emphasizing again the size of the nation's enemies and the reality that it is God who must defeat them.

16–18. Although the imagery in the first two parts of the appeal may point to destruction, it becomes clear in the closing part that this language is an expression of complete victory, not necessarily of destruction. Rather, these enemies should be filled with shame, which emerges from their defeat by so small a nation as Israel. Defeat points them to the real victor, to Yahweh, so that they seek his name. Nevertheless, the possibility of resistance to Yahweh remains and, if so, they should remain in shame, ultimately perishing (cf. Judg. 5:31; Pss 1:6; 2:12). What matters is that they know Israel's God, that his name is Yahweh, the Most High over all the earth. The Elohistic Psalter thus closes with a ringing declaration of the name of Yahweh.

Explanation

Taking Psalm 82's call for God to judge the earth and closing the Asaphic collection, this communal lament reflects on Israel's position as a nation among the nations perennially hostile towards it, with local foes joining major powers in seeking to destroy the nation. This psalm insists, though, that to act against Israel is to act against God. The conspiracies of the nations echo the attitude of the nations in Psalm 2, attitudes seen in the period of the judges. Weaving together a dialogue between Psalms 1–2 and Judges 4 – 8, this prayer looks back to previous moments of deliverance to remind the community that God has indeed acted powerfully for them in the past and to insist that the certainty of God's victory in future, as reflected in Psalms 1–2, is grounded in history (cf. Human 1995b: 178). The real suffering of the nation is voiced in the appeal to God to act, an appeal that uses hyperbolic language in asking for total victory while also looking for the time when the nations will recognize Yahweh alone as God. As the conclusion to the Elohistic Psalter (Pss 42–83) Psalm 83 thus presents us with the reality of Israel's lived experience as a threatened people, while making clear that the goal of their existence remained that moment when every people would know God (cf. Rev. 7:9–10).

PSALM 84

Translation

The director's. Upon Gittith. Korahite. A melody.

1How beloved are your dwelling places
O Yahweh of Hosts.
2My whole being longs, indeed yearns,
for the courts of Yahweh,
My heart and my flesh
shout out for the living God.
3Even the bird has found a home,
and the swallow a nest for herself
where she may set her young,
near your altars O Yahweh of Hosts,
my King and my God!
4O the blessedness of those who dwell in your house,
they are ever praising you. *Selah*.

5O the blessedness of the one whose strength is in you,
the temple's ways are in their heart.
6Passing through the Valley of Baca,
they make it a spring;
indeed, the early rain wraps it with blessings.
7They journey from strength to strength,
each appears before God in Zion.

8O Yahweh God of Hosts, hear my prayer,
give ear, O God of Jacob. *Selah*.
9See our shield, O God,
look upon the face of your anointed one.
10For better is one day in your courts than a thousand elsewhere,
I choose to stand at the threshold of the house of my God
rather than to dwell in the tents of wickedness.
11For Yahweh God is a sun and a shield,
Yahweh gives grace and honour,
he withholds no good thing from those who walk with integrity.
12Yahweh of Hosts,
O the blessedness of the one who trusts in you!

Notes on the text

3. 'Altars' does not refer to multiple altars but is part of a consistent use of plurals, *pars pro toto*, to cover the whole of the temple (cf. Jerome 2004: 36).

5. Hebr. *mĕsillôt* is awkward, something already felt in antiquity by Gk. The common sense 'highways' is unlikely here, and one could follow *DCH* in positing 'high praises' as the sense. But with reference to the temple, it can refer to pathways within the temple complex (1 Chr. 26:16, 18; 2 Chr. 9:11) and that sense is plausible here.

6. Hebr. *bĕrākôt* (blessings) is often emended to *bĕrēkôt* (pools) because of the parallelism with spring in the previous line (so NET). This is plausible, but the text may intend both senses since the pools of water would be considered a blessing, and the consonantal text is the same.

7. Taking *yērā'eh* as distributive. Gk suggests 'until the God of Gods is seen'.

9. Y.-K. Kim (2017) argues that 'our shield' is a voc., addressed to God, but the verse's chiastic structure suggests it opens and closes with what is to be seen.

Form and structure

Book 3 opened with Psalm 73, a poem where the psalmist found meaning in the temple. That poem also commenced the main Asaphic collection (Pss 73–83), which concluded with a prayer for the nations to know Yahweh's uniqueness, a prayer that also closes the Elohistic Psalter (Pss 42–83). Psalm 84 commences the second Korahite collection (cf. Pss 42–49) with focus on the temple (cf. Goulder 1982: 37–38). Desire to be in God's presence in the temple marked Psalm 42, a desire also strongly present here, though without the barriers seen there. Psalm 84 thus introduces this new segment of Book 3 by returning to the theme of desire for the temple. Although Psalm 84 introduces a new section within Book 3, it is also connected to the earlier Asaphic psalms, especially Psalms 80–83. With Psalm 80, it includes the form 'of Hosts' (*ṣĕbā'ôt*) four times with the divine name (vv. 1, 3, 8, 12), a frequency not found elsewhere in the Psalter, while it is linked to Psalm 81 through the rare 'Upon Gittith' in the title (elsewhere only Ps. 8). Finally, we can note that this psalm emphasizes the blessedness of being among those who dwell in the temple, something that stands in marked contrast with those dwelling elsewhere in Psalm 83:6–8 (cf. Cole 2000: 115–116). Therefore, God should look on the face of his 'anointed one' (v. 9), in contrast with the faces of his adversaries being covered with shame (Ps. 83:16).

The psalm is probably intended for pilgrims to sing on their journey to the temple, declaring their trust in Yahweh. Such a journey would have been greatly anticipated, reflected in the desire for the temple expressed here. The temple is shown to be the most desirable of places (v. 1), while even the anticipation of it seems to change the countryside as the pilgrims pass through (vv. 5–7). Nevertheless, although the temple is clearly important within the poem, it has importance only as a means of accessing Yahweh. The temple is Yahweh's dwelling place, and when appearing before him there the faithful hope he will hear their prayer (v. 8). It is from the temple that the faithful hope Yahweh will act for his anointed one (v. 9), while continuing to act for those who trust him (v. 12).

The poem is divided into three stanzas. The recurrence of *selah* in verses 4, 8 may suggest that these are the main divisions, but the second occurs midway through a prayer for the king that begins in the previous verse and commences the third stanza. However, these stanzas are linked by important repetitions. In addition to the 'of Hosts' (*ṣĕbā'ôt*) element in the divine names, we should also note the presence of a beatitude in each stanza, closing stanzas 1 and 3 (vv. 4, 12) and opening stanza 2 (v. 5). Accordingly, the psalm can be analysed as follows:

1. The blessedness of dwelling in the temple (1–4)
2. The blessedness of those whose strength is in Yahweh (5–7)
3. The blessedness of those who trust in Yahweh (8–12)

Comment

Title: For 'The director's', see on Psalm 4. For 'Upon Gittith', see on Psalm 8. For 'Korahite', see on Psalm 42. For 'A melody', see on Psalm 3.

1–4. The psalm commences by emphasizing the desirability of Yahweh's dwelling places (cf. Jerome 2004: 94–100). These places are not only desirable; they are 'beloved'. This designation more typically refers to people (e.g. Deut. 30:12; Pss 60:5; 127:2; Isa. 5:1), and only here refers to a place. It thus points to the deep affection held for the temple. The one who dwells there is here called 'Yahweh of Hosts', a title that points to God's power (cf. Ps. 24:7–10) and recurs in verse 12, creating an inclusio for the poem, and as the 'living God', a designation also found in Psalm 42:3. Given that Yahweh's dwelling places are beloved, it is natural that the psalmist should describe a deep longing for the temple since it was Yahweh's own courts. This deep longing takes physical form in the poet's heart and flesh, which cry out for the living God. The 'heart' may here refer to the psalmist's mind and so point to thought processes, whereas the 'flesh' refers to physical existence. We might today speak of mind and body crying out for God. This desire for God exists because of the need to go to the temple, somewhere that even birds have found to be a place of security. The first bird may be generic, though it could also be a sparrow. The second bird is the swallow, a bird possibly associated with release. If so, the swallow finds its freedom in building a nest near Yahweh's altars. These birds are in a desirable position because of their closeness to Yahweh. If this is true of the birds, then how much more desirable is the position of a person who might dwell in God's house (cf. Ps. 65:4) since this would be a place of ongoing praise.

5–7. Having declared a beatitude on those dwelling in the temple, the second stanza opens with a beatitude pronounced on those whose strength is in Yahweh. Such people are close to God, having the temple's own walkways in their heart (cf. 'Notes on the text'). That is, even when away from the temple, these people know its layout because they treasure it. These people journey towards the temple, seemingly bringing the presence of God with them as they travel. The 'Valley of Baca' is unknown, but the fact that they make it a spring as they journey suggests it becomes verdant as they pass through. The valley's name suggests a place where Balsam trees grow, and hence a dry area (cf. Estes 2019: 131), though it may also play with the word for 'weeping'. These would indicate that this is a challenging place, but by bringing Yahweh's presence, these pilgrims see this land become a place of plentiful water, with the 'blessings' perhaps pools of water (cf. 'Notes on the text'), while the early rains suggest they pass through in autumn, perhaps going to celebrate Tabernacles. These pilgrims are also renewed as they journey, moving from 'strength to strength'. This could suggest they move from one secure place to another, from where they receive provision for their journey, so that each may appear before God in Zion.

8–12. Once at the temple, they cry out a prayer, asking Yahweh to hear. The *selah* here seems awkward, but perhaps the intention is to pause before recounting the intercession. The prayer suggests that even though being in God's presence is highly desirable, there is also a need for Yahweh to attend to the wider needs of his people. Hence, he needs to look on the people's 'shield'. The 'shield' here refers to the king as the one who protects the people, with this prayer perhaps being a rather abbreviated version of the one for the king in Psalm 72. Having prayed for the king, the poem returns to the temple and then to Yahweh, the one already declared to be king (v. 3). The reason for this is that although prayer for the king is important, the temple remains the most desirable place to be because it is here that Yahweh is encountered. The poet knows one cannot remain indefinitely in the temple but accepts that a day there, even only at its threshold, is better than a thousand elsewhere. The psalmist prefers to be there because of Yahweh's presence. The king is the nation's shield, but Yahweh is sun and shield, the one who provides justice and protection, sharing his good gifts with those who walk with integrity (cf. Ps. 15:2). Hence, the psalm closes with a final beatitude that reflects on the desirability of the life of those who trust Yahweh.

Explanation

This psalm most probably reflects the journey of pilgrims heading to the temple, and also takes readers on a journey within it. Starting with a desire for the temple as the dwelling place of Yahweh, it closes with the last of its three beatitudes focusing on the blessedness of those who trust Yahweh. Within the poem, readers journey from feeling distant from God's presence to his being experienced as near, each beatitude bringing us nearer to God. Although the psalm localizes God's presence in the temple as the primary way in which his presence is experienced, it also points beyond the temple since the pilgrims also bring God's presence with them as they journey towards the temple. That is, the psalm knows that God was experienced in the temple but does not restrict the experience to the temple alone. The community who worship encounter God. This balance is also reflected in the NT's presentation of Jesus as the new temple (cf. Eph. 2:11–22). In gathering, perhaps most especially around Communion, we encounter him in a special way, but our encounter with him is not restricted to this. By analogy, every time the church gathers it encounters the living God in Jesus through the Spirit, and this psalm gives voice to the desire for this presence that should mark Christian worship. But we also bring the presence of Christ with us wherever we are (cf. 2 Cor. 2:14–17), discovering the continued blessedness of those who trust him.

PSALM 85

Translation

The director's. Korahite. A melody.

1 You favoured your land, O Yahweh,
  you restored the fortunes of Jacob.
2 You forgave your people's iniquity,
  you covered all their sin. *Selah*.
3 You withdrew all your fury,
  you turned back your raging anger.

4 Restore us, O God of our salvation,
  and annul your vexation with us.
5 Should you be angry with us for ever,
  extending your anger from generation to generation?
6 Should you not again revive us,
  that your people may rejoice in you?
7 Show us your kindness, O Yahweh,
  and grant us your salvation.

[8]I will hearken to what God, Yahweh, will say,
for he will speak peace,
to his people, yes to his faithful ones,
but do not let them turn to stupidity.
[9]Surely his salvation is near to those who fear him,
that glory might dwell in our land.
[10]Kindness and faithfulness have met,
righteousness and peace have kissed.
[11]Faithfulness springs up from the ground,
and righteousness looks down from the heavens.
[12]Indeed, Yahweh will give what is good,
and our land will give its produce.
[13]Righteousness goes before him,
and prepares a pathway for his steps.

Notes on the text

1. The sense of the idiom here is unclear, depending on whether the root of *šĕbît* is *šbh* (capture) or *šûb* (turn); cf. K and Q.

4. For *hpr* as 'annul', see Numbers 30:13.

9. Taking the infin. as indicating purpose.

Form and structure

The second Korahite psalm of Book 3 builds on motifs of its predecessor while also acknowledging the reality of suffering among the community. Though Psalm 84 focused on the temple, it closed by announcing a blessing on those who trust in Yahweh. Psalm 85 expresses that trust, something that emerges from the experience of Yahweh's grace while also accepting that he has grounds for present anger against the community. Despite this, they continue to hope for Yahweh's salvation, embodying the trust encouraged by Psalm 84:12. Goulder (1982: 85) suggests that reading this poem against Psalm 44 is better, but though these poems have some similarities this seems driven more by his overall thesis. Moreover, the repetition of the 'glory' motif (Pss 84:11; 85:9) provides a close link between these psalms, especially as in both cases it is linked with God's provision of 'good' for his people (Pss 84:11; 85:12).

The poem contains three stanzas, each with a distinct focus in time. The opening stanza (vv. 1–3) looks back to what Yahweh has done in restoring the nation. By contrast, the second (vv. 4–7) looks at a pressing need in the present, while the third anticipates how Yahweh will act in the future (vv. 8–13). This careful development, along with the shift to the first-person sg. from the pl. at verse 8 (though without ignoring communal elements in this stanza) may suggest that the psalm has its roots in a liturgy. Even if this is the case, the final form is best understood as a prayer for restoration (deClaissé-Walford et al. 2014: 655). The community knows God has acted in the past, and so asks for and anticipates his salvation.

As noted, the psalm can be analysed in three stanzas (similarly, Körting 2020: 145–148):

1. Yahweh's past acts of grace (1–3)
2. Appeal for salvation (4–7)
3. The nearness of Yahweh's salvation (8–13)

Comment

Title: For 'The director's', see on Psalm 4. For 'Korahite', see on Psalm 42. For 'A melody', see on Psalm 3. Apart from 'Upon Gittith' it is identical to Psalm 84, providing a further link between these psalms.

1–3. The verbs of this stanza point to Yahweh's prior acts of grace, though it is not possible to tie them to a specific moment, and future moments could also be anticipated (cf. Hossfeld and Zenger 2006: 362). The end of the exile could be spoken of in these terms (Boda 2009: 412–413; cf. Ps. 126), but the absence of a historic reference probably means the audience is able to identify various points where Yahweh was gracious to them (cf. Mays 1994b: 277). The opening verb (*rṣh*) points to an act of favour, not something the community merited. Mention of the land in verse 1 anticipates the mention of crops in verse 12, though it is also clear that the land stands for the people, as is clear in the reference to the restoration of Jacob's fortunes. The idiom here is ambiguous but introduces the key verb *šwb* (turn, return), which recurs in verse 3 and is also prominent in the second stanza. The key point is that Yahweh has restored the nation, and in verses 2–3 we discover this involves forgiveness. The language of forgiveness in verse 2 echoes that of Psalm 32:1, but this is extended in verse 3 to note Yahweh has withdrawn his anger. The forgiveness experienced is thus one of grace since the presence of Yahweh's anger shows that the nation merited further punishment. But instead, Yahweh showed favour and restored them.

4–7. Yahweh's prior grace provides the foundation for the second stanza's appeal. Just as Yahweh restored the nation in the past, so he is asked to restore them again, being characterized as the 'God of our salvation'. God has already been described in these terms in Psalms 65:5 and 79:9. The epithet demonstrates Yahweh can transform the community's experience. Yet the people also acknowledge that this must be an act of grace since Yahweh also needs to annul his vexation with them. They accept that there are grounds for Yahweh to be vexed, but desire that he should act in grace. Rather than direct appeals, verses 5–6 approach this issue through questions. In verse 5, the implied answer to the question is that Yahweh should not continue his anger indefinitely. Verse 6 then shifts to a question which assumes that Yahweh will agree that he should revive the nation (again, using *šwb*). This language assumes that they are close to death and that only Yahweh can bring them back, though when he does there will be joy. The stanza returns to direct appeal in verse 7, asking that Yahweh show his kindness by granting his salvation. Yahweh is the God of salvation, and his kindness is the basis on which it can again be experienced. As with the first stanza, it is possible to tie this appeal to various moments in Israel's history, but the absence of anything specific here leaves open the possibility that this is something that can be prayed at numerous points.

8–13. An individual voice is heard at verse 8, as a speaker commits to hearing what Yahweh will say (cf. Hab. 2:1). 'Hearing' here represents a commitment to that word, doing and not just hearing (cf. Jas 1:22). The cohort. could also express a desire to hear (so deClaissé-Walford et al. 2014: 656), but since the reality of God's speech here is assumed, it seems better to understand the verb as a strong commitment to hear (cf. W-O, §34.5.1) and be shaped by Yahweh's word. This shaping derives from the fact that Yahweh will speak 'peace' (*šālôm*) to his people, indicating already the form of salvation he will provide. Yahweh's people are here further described as his 'faithful ones', indicating that God's people are those committed to him. Nevertheless, the speaker recognizes that they could again act in ways that trigger Yahweh's anger; hence, the request to prevent their turning (again, *šwb*) to stupidity. Stupidity in this setting would be turning away from faithfulness to Yahweh. That turning away from Yahweh is stupidity is made clear by the declaration of verse 9, that Yahweh's salvation is near to those who fear him. The opening 'surely' recalls the key word from Psalm 73, and affirms that reality of this statement. This salvation is not for everyone, but for those in an appropriate relationship to Yahweh, but it also points beyond them because of Yahweh's intention that glory (evidence of his presence; hence, 'glory' is here personified; similarly, Tate 1990: 366) may dwell in the land. The shape of that glory is developed in verses 10–11. Here, language that may otherwise describe Yahweh (note how v. 10's opening echoes Exod. 34:6; cf. Schnittjer 2021: 877), and with numerous echoes of Isaiah 40 – 66, is now applied to the land's experience of glory. A land in which Yahweh is present experiences his character as kindness and faithfulness meet, while righteousness and peace come closer still as they kiss, marking their close relationship. Faithfulness and righteousness are then developed in verse 11, so that faithfulness sprouts from the ground like the fruit of the harvest, while righteousness looks down from heaven. The pairing of earth and heaven suggests that the whole inhabited world is bounded by Yahweh's character. This is a land where glory is present. A land where glory dwells experiences Yahweh's beneficence, where he gives good and does not express anger, with a bountiful harvest the most obvious expression of this. Although the individual voice probably continues from verse 8, it is notable that it is 'our land', indicating that this one speaks for the community. The poem closes by noting that righteousness goes before Yahweh, marking his presence and creating the way for his footsteps. If this is what a land marked by Yahweh's presence is like, then committing oneself to live in terms of Yahweh's message is the only wise approach.

Explanation

Psalm 84 closed by encouraging continued trust in Yahweh, stressing that those who do so are blessed. That trust is embodied in this psalm. Here, the community pauses to acknowledge Yahweh's grace towards them, grace shown even though divine anger was appropriate. But they also know that a previous experience of grace does not mean they have no further need of grace, and so appeal for Yahweh to restore them. The need may well be a failure of the harvest (cf. Ps. 126; Coetzee 2009b: 556–557), but the language of the appeal is sufficiently open that it can be applied to numerous situations. The good news is that one past act of grace does not exclude a future one, as if grace has a limit. Rather, the community is reminded as they attend to Yahweh's message (perhaps one already known) that the God who was made known as gracious (Exod. 34:6–8) continues to be gracious. God's grace does not run out, even when wrath may seem more appropriate. God's grace does not change the individual alone, it transforms the community and the land as God's own characteristics are manifest. As God's glory dwells in the land, so all is changed and experiences peace. Such a hope is something experienced already but can also be something anticipated in future. This hope is also apparent in Titus 2:11–13, which likewise starts with God's grace (now in Jesus), encourages believers to live in the light of what God will ultimately do and anticipates the appearance of Jesus' glory. Knowing what God will do, understood through what he has done, continues to encourage prayer and a communal life that truly expresses God's peace.

PSALM 86

Translation

A prayer. Davidic.

[1]Incline, O Yahweh, your ear, answer me,
  because I am poor and needy.
[2]Guard my life, because I am loyal,

save your servant (you are my God),
one who trusts in you.
3Be gracious to me, O Lord,
because to you I call all day long.
4Gladden your servant,
because to you, O Lord, I lift myself.
5For you, O Lord, are good and forgiving,
abounding in kindness to all who call on you.
6Heed, O Yahweh, my prayer,
attend to the sound of my supplications.
7On the day of my distress I call to you
because you answer me.

8There is no one like you among the gods O Lord,
nor are there deeds like yours.
9All the nations that you made,
shall come and worship before you O Lord,
they shall glorify your name,
10because you are great and perform wonders:
you alone are God.
11Teach me, O Yahweh, your path,
I will walk in your truth,
unite my heart to fear your name.
12I will give thanks to you, O Lord my God, with all my heart,
and will glorify your name for ever,
13because great is your kindness towards me,
and you have delivered my life from lowest Sheol.

14O God, the presumptuous rise against me,
a terrifying mob seek my life,
they do not set your name before them.
15But you, O Lord, are a gracious and compassionate God,
slow to anger and abounding in kindness and faithfulness.
16Turn to me and be gracious to me,
give your strength to your servant,
and save the son of your maidservant!
17Grant me a sign of bounty,
so those who hate me may fear and be put to shame;
because you O Yahweh, helped and comforted me.

Notes on the text

3, 5, 8, 9, 15. A number of MSS read 'Yahweh rather than *'ădōnāy*. Both readings are plausible, but since 'Yahweh' occurs elsewhere in the poem it is perhaps slightly more likely that scribes have conformed their readings to it.

11. The only instance of pi. *yḥd* probably leads to Gk misreading it as *ḥdh*. Only once the heart is united can the praise of 'all' the poet's heart (v. 12) be achieved.

Form and structure

The only Davidic psalm in Book 3, this poem is placed within the second collection of Korah psalms. This creates a pause within this group of Korahite psalms, though there are also clear links to the poems around it so that key themes continue to develop. As a Davidic poem it is clearly distinct, yet it is also integrated into its context, playing an important structural role within Psalms 84–89 (cf. Loader 2010: 672–677). As a complaint, it emerges out of the expressions of trust in Psalm 84 and the communal appeal in Psalm 85. The Davidic title here points readers to see an individual whose trust in Yahweh is also expressed through appeal to him. It joins Psalm 85 in acknowledging the harm caused by sin and the importance of forgiveness (Pss 85:2–4; 86:5). Both psalms also refer to the revelation of God's graciousness in Exodus 34:6–7 (cf. Ps. 85:10), though it is much more prominent here as it provides the foundation for the appeal for help (vv. 3, 5), as well as the basis for hope (vv. 13, 15). Indeed, as the psalm progresses, so the allusion to this foundational declaration about God becomes more prominent. As such, although the poem draws on the language of numerous earlier poems, it is not simply a repetition of earlier texts but rather a prayer that is strongly shaped by earlier works while still offering its own distinctive perspective (cf. A. A. Anderson 1972, 1: 613). At the same time, the anticipation of the gathering of the nations in worship of Yahweh (v. 9) anticipates that worship in Psalm 87.

Although the poem can be considered a complaint, where the psalmist is aware of his need to walk in Yahweh's ways, it is notable that (unlike most complaints) the anticipated praise of verses 12–13 is not the concluding point. Rather, the psalm returns to complaint in verses 14–17. However, the issue in the initial complaint (vv. 1–7) is the psalmist's own need for grace, whereas in the second complaint the poet's enemies are mentioned for the first time. Here again, grace is the central need (vv. 15–16). All this is held together by the mention of grace in verse 13, which points to the poet's experience of grace and commitment to walk in that grace. Accordingly, we can analyse the poem in three stanzas, each of which has its own structural unity even as each contributes to the poem's development:

1. Plea for Yahweh to hear (1–7)
2. The God who acts for the needy (8–13)
3. Plea for sign of bounty (14–17)

Comment

Title: For 'A prayer', see on Psalm 17. For 'Davidic', see on Psalm 3, though cf. Psalm 72:20.

1–7. As is common for complaint psalms, the prayer commences with an appeal to be heard, though without laying out the underlying circumstances. Rather, verses 1–4 wholly consist of appeals for God to hear and respond to the psalmist's need while providing reasons for his response. Verse 1 contains two appeals, though the second is immediately tied to the declaration of the poet's need as the basis for the appeal. The language here also prepares for the appeal in verse 6 and the reason why the poet appeals in verse 7, creating an inclusio for this stanza. Yahweh needs to hear and answer the psalmist because he alone can resolve the situation. This may involve a threat against the poet's life (v. 2). This is the only anticipation of the role of enemies in this stanza, though it prepares for the third stanza, where this becomes more prominent. Yahweh needs to guard and save because the poet is loyal to Yahweh, his servant, one who trusts him. The poet is loyal to Yahweh, but the basis for the appeal is still grace. Here, the psalm makes its first allusion to Exodus 34:6–8, preparing for the subsequent allusions, which develop as the poem progresses. Yahweh's grace is not only to save; it is also to gladden the psalmist as one who has come before Yahweh (cf. Ps. 25:1). Within this collection of appeals, verse 5 thus stands out as the only verse in the stanza introduced by 'For' (*kî*), making it the only reason for Yahweh to act not directly linked to a specific appeal. Rather, through a direct allusion to Exodus 34:6 it grounds the appeal more directly to Yahweh's self-declaration there, while also adding that he is forgiving (*slḥ*), introducing a word not present there, but that is consistent with it. Moreover, although the poet has been aligned with Yahweh, it is made clear here that Yahweh responds to all who call. With this established, the stanza returns to appeals in verse 6, this time without any reason since Yahweh's response is already established. Yahweh needs to heed the poet, and respond to the supplications, themselves appeals for grace. Verse 7 makes clear that the psalmist is one of those who call to Yahweh and who can therefore expect an answer, while also specifying that the appeal is made in a time of distress. Yahweh is gracious, and in distress, the poet appeals to that grace and asks for deliverance.

8–13. Where the first stanza appeals to Yahweh, the second explores his character as the one who acts for the needy. Central to this is Yahweh's uniqueness: there is none like him among the gods. This statement reflects the wider world view, also seen in Psalm 82, where Israel acknowledged the existence of other divine beings. Again, these beings are marginalized because Yahweh is incomparable in both his being and his deeds. The result is that all the nations shall come and worship Yahweh because he has made them, a theme consistent with the pattern especially evident in Psalms 65–68 (cf. Rev. 15:4; Longman 2014: 317). In worship, they shall glorify his name, with 'name' here reflecting Yahweh's character. This character is explored in verse 10 where he is described as great in his own person and as one who does great deeds, perhaps an allusion to the exodus. As such, although the psalm acknowledges the existence of other divine beings, only Yahweh truly merits the title 'God'. The stanza shifts at verse 11, returning to appeal, perhaps supporting Auffret's (1979) argument for this being the poem's centre. However, this appeal is to enable the psalmist to walk in Yahweh's truth, something that will be enabled through Yahweh's teaching the poet his way. A barrier to this was apparently a lack of faithfulness to Yahweh, which is why the psalmist asks for a united heart. The heart often stands for the mind, and that is the case here. A divided heart is not fully committed to Yahweh, so the poet desires to have that limitation addressed, something that can then lead to wholehearted thanksgiving, with the poet joining the nations in glorifying Yahweh, this time for ever. Verse 13 then notes that Yahweh's great kindness (again, alluding to Exod. 34:6–7) has been experienced by the psalmist, and indeed Yahweh has rescued the poet from Sheol's depths. Yahweh's grace and great works are not generic. Instead, they are central to the poet's own experience.

14–17. The third stanza is once more focused on appeal, making clear that the poet is experiencing threats from enemies. That they are presumptuous and terrifying shows they are not committed to Yahweh and are thus not those who would call on him. These enemies threaten the psalmist's life, bringing an urgency to the appeal that was not so evident in the first stanza. The enemies stand in marked contrast with Yahweh as one who is compassionate and gracious. The statement in verse 15 is the poem's fullest reference to Exodus 34:6. It gives the poet hope in the face of threat, and provides the foundation for the appeal in verse 16, asking that Yahweh turn to the poet. Such a turn is itself an act of grace, as also is the giving of strength to the poet, who is again styled as Yahweh's servant, with this extended in verse 16b to 'the son of your maidservant'. The granting of strength is important, but the psalmist needs to be saved from these enemies. This salvation is also to be marked by a sign that points to God's bounty, and is primarily evidence aimed towards the enemies, leading to their shame. Presumably, this also means they cease acting against the poet. The poet can be confident Yahweh will act because doing so is consistent with his character, something the poet has experienced through previous times of help and comfort. Yahweh's grace is the basis for the appeal and something the poet has experienced.

Explanation

Psalm 86 is deeply rooted in multiple contexts. It is the poet's prayer in a time of distress, one that prioritizes Yahweh's character as gracious. It is knowing Yahweh that provides hope. It is also situated within the second Korahite collection, a rare individual complaint in Book 3, a book where complaints are more typically communal. But through the Davidic association here, the psalm provides an important individual voice that speaks to the national experience. David had experienced grace, and it was grace that was requested in Psalm 51:1. This individual experience is now a model for the community, a matter of particular importance if the exile provides the background to Book 3. More broadly, it is deeply rooted in Israel's wider traditions, showing that the key affirmations made about Yahweh continue to matter, even in times of great struggle (cf. Brueggemann 1984: 63). What matters in this psalm is that these contexts come together. It enables all who read it to see a mirror of their own experience at both the individual and the communal level, while also pointing to the wider biblical context. It demonstrates that prayer is richest when it engages Scripture's traditions and draws them into our own experience and petitions.

PSALM 87

Translation

Korahite. A melody. A song.

1 Its foundation is on the holy mountain –
2 Yahweh loves
the gates of Zion,
more than all the dwelling places of Jacob.
3 Glorious things are spoken of you,
O city of God. *Selah.*

4 'I announce Rahab and Babylon among those who know me,
indeed, Philistia and Tyre with Cush,
this one was born there.'
5 And of Zion it shall be said,
'This one and that were born in her,
and the Most High himself establishes her.'
6 Yahweh writes in the register of the peoples,
'This one was born there.' *Selah.*

7 And those singing while dancing,
'All my springs are in you.'

Notes on the text

The text is extremely difficult and often emended. But as even the ancient versions struggle to make sense of it, it seems more likely that emendations from them simply reflect ancient guesses rather than evidence of textual corruption in MT. As such, the above attempts to stay close to MT. See also Hossfeld and Zenger 2006: 377–378.

1. Reading *harĕrê* as a pl. of respect (*WHS* §8).

2. Taking the opening ptc. as both closing the previous clause and introducing what follows. Cf. Booij 1987: 18. The *miškĕnôt* could also refer to other sanctuaries (e.g. Gilgal; so A. P. Ross 2013: 795).

4. Only 4c is commonly treated as direct discourse (e.g. ESV), but with Hossfeld and Zenger (2006: 378) it is better to read the whole verse as a comment from Yahweh.

6. With many MSS and Gk, here reading *biktāb*.

7. *ḥōlĕlîm* could be a polel ptc. from *ḥwl*, 'dancing', or a qal ptc. from *hll*, 'play the pipe'. Either is possible.

Form and structure

Following the Davidic Psalm 86, we return to the Korahite psalms, though with a rather enigmatic poem, the complexity of which has led to significant debates about its translation and interpretation (for overviews, see Booij 1987; Emerton 2000). Although much remains uncertain, what can be agreed is that it celebrates Zion (though Goulder [1982: 171–172], consistent with his larger thesis, believes it was originally a song about Dan that was transferred to Zion, a view to which Seybold [1996: 341] is drawn), joining earlier Korahite psalms in doing so (esp. Ps. 48 with which it shares key terms: Pss 46–47 also discuss Jerusalem but without naming Zion). Yet, in doing so, it expands the focus of earlier Zion poems by integrating this motif with that of the nations coming to Yahweh. As such, the poem develops the reference to the coming of the nations from Psalm 86:9, so that all nations now find their home in Zion. As Goldingay (2007: 632) has observed, this psalm is simultaneously particularist and universalist. It is particularist because Zion, at the heart of Israel's worship, also becomes part of the point where the nations find life. In this, it joins with some key motifs from the prophets (e.g. Isa. 11:1–10; Mic. 5:1–5). Within Book 3, it also provides an important contrast with Psalm 83. There, the nations were a threat to Israel, consistent with a key element of the Asaphic psalms. But now they are welcomed. Perhaps most surprising is that at least some of the nations welcomed are historic enemies of Israel (cf. Grant 2023). But where Psalm 83 prays out of a moment of threat, Psalm 87 looks beyond that to Yahweh's purpose for the nations, one where old enemies are welcomed to Zion. Zion is where Yahweh's great victories were won (Ps. 48) but also where enemies ultimately become friends.

The poem's terse nature makes the analysis difficult, but it is reasonable to see the two instances of *selah* as marking breaks within it. If so, it can be analysed in three short stanzas:

1. Declarations about Zion (1–3)
2. Zion and the nations (4–6)
3. Rejoicing over Zion (7)

Comment

Title: For 'Korahite', see on Psalm 42. For 'A melody', see on Psalm 3. For 'A song', see on Psalm 65. Although the order of the elements differs, the components are the same as Psalm 48, suggesting a further link between these psalms.

1–3. The psalm opens abruptly with what may seem only a part line, with translations often adding a verb to complete it. But the terseness of verse 1 establishes a key pattern for the whole psalm. Someone has something founded on the holy mountain, with the identity of the one who has done so initially unstated. Nevertheless, the 'holy mountain' (though a common concept in the ANE) can refer only to Zion, something confirmed as the psalm progresses. That the one who has founded it is Yahweh becomes clear in verse 2, where the announcement of his love does double duty, referring both back to what is founded on Zion and its gates. That is, Yahweh loves all that is associated with Zion, with the 'gates' here referring to the whole city as well as the sanctuary. As the place he loves, it is also the place he has chosen. Jacob, standing here for all Israel, has numerous dwelling places, all of which are loved by Yahweh, but his love for Zion exceeds them all. Zion is the site of the city of God, the place of which glorious things are spoken. In that the psalm to this point largely looks back, these glorious things could be the mighty works done there in the past. But as the psalm progresses it also anticipates great future moments, linking this observation with some of the prophetic statements that look towards a renewed Zion as the place to which the peoples will come (e.g. Zech. 8:20–23).

4–6. A first-person voice now emerges, most likely citing Yahweh since he alone can make this declaration, directly addressing Zion. The declaration looks beyond Judah and Israel to announce new peoples who know Yahweh, with the nations mentioned representative of Yahweh's universal purpose. 'Rahab' (not the same in Hebrew as the woman in Josh. 2) refers to Egypt. The term elsewhere can refer to a mythical sea monster defeated by Yahweh (Job 9:13; 26:12; Ps. 89:11; Isa. 51:9), but it is also a mocking term for Egypt (Isa. 30:7). The parallel with Babylon here makes clear that the reference is to Egypt, and the astonishing thing is that these traditional oppressors of Israel are now said to be among those who know Yahweh. Isaiah 19:16–25 anticipates a time when Egypt and Assyria will worship Yahweh, and that text may lie in the background here. If so, it expands it to cover Babylon as the empire that had swallowed up Assyria's. Local states had also pressured Israel in the days of the judges, none more so than the Philistines. They are here joined with Tyre, to the north of Israel's land, and distant Cush (roughly the north of modern Ethiopia; cf. Ps. 68:31). Tyre was also said in Psalm 83:5–8 to have conspired with the Philistines against Israel. These nations too can be declared to have been born 'there', presumably in Zion. Of course, the peoples of these nations were not born there, but by making this declaration Yahweh grants them the same status as those who were, because this is their real home (cf. Booij 1987). They are truly part of God's people, kin to Israel. Verse 5 extends this theme, moving from the nations to individuals also said to be born in Zion, the city that the Most High (a common name for God in the Zion tradition; cf. Ps. 46) has established. Hence, Yahweh himself can prepare the birth register of the peoples, declaring them to have been born in Zion. Zion is where Yahweh not only demonstrates his rule over the nations, but also where he brings them to himself and grants them citizenship.

7. This verse is terse and open to various readings. However, it makes most sense to see it as a joyful response to what Yahweh has declared, marked by singing and dancing. We should probably understand the final line as something voiced by the singers. Reference to the 'springs' could suggest the Gihon (a little below the temple mount), but perhaps we should follow Goldingay (2007: 639) and understand it as a reference to the conception of children (cf. Prov. 5:16). The nations declared to be part of Zion are now those who declare with joy that their origin is also in Zion.

Explanation

Psalm 84 began a group of psalms that gradually approach Zion as the place where God is worshipped. We may think in this context of it as the place where those who already knew Yahweh would want to go. But picking up on the hope of the nations from Psalm 86:9, we now encounter Zion as the place to which all the nations will come and worship. This hope is consistent with the fact that Abraham's call was directed towards all the clans of the earth finding blessing (Gen. 12:1–3), as well as the motif of the gathering of the nations, which is found elsewhere in the prophets and Psalms (see above, 'Form and structure'). This hope continues to find expression in the NT, as we see in Revelation 21:22–27. There, the city is where the glory of the nations comes. Psalm

87 thus joins with a range of texts in asserting God's universal concern. Yet, its place in Book 3 suggests an additional concern. Much of this book emerges from situations where the nations are a threat to Jerusalem (e.g. Pss 74, 79, 80, 83). That the nations who come to Zion in this psalm are traditional oppressors and enemies is not only a word of hope for the future, but also a challenge to a community that suffered to prepare itself to receive even those who had previously been enemies. The wideness to God's mercy means that even those we wish to exclude are included in his purposes. As we pray for those who persecute us (Matt. 5:4–45), we perhaps begin to live out the hope of this psalm.

PSALM 88

Translation

A song. A melody. Korahite. The director's. According to Mahalath Leannoth. A Maskil. Heman the Ezrahite's.

1Yahweh, the God of my salvation,
I cry out by day,
nightly before you.
2May my prayer come before you,
incline your ear to my shout.

3For my being is weary with troubles,
and my life draws near to Sheol.
4I am reckoned with those who go down to the pit,
I am like a warrior without strength,
5set free among the dead,
like the slain lying in the grave,
whom you no longer remember,
for they are cut off from your hand.
6You have placed me at the lowest points of the pit,
in the dark places, in the depths.
7Your wrath rests upon me,
and with all your breakers you afflict me. *Selah*.
8You have removed my friends from me,
you have made me abominable to them;
shut in and I cannot go out,
9my eyes languish because of my affliction.

I called out to you daily, Yahweh,
I spread out my palms to you.
10Do you do wonders for the dead?

Do the Rephaim rise up to give you thanks? *Selah.*
11 Is your kindness recounted in the grave,
your faithfulness in Abaddon?
12 Are your wonders known in the darkness,
your righteousness in the land of oblivion?

13 But I cry out for help to you, Yahweh,
and in the morning my prayer shall meet you.
14 Why do you reject me, Yahweh,
why do you hide your face from me?
15 I have been afflicted and perishing from my youth,
I have borne your terrors, I am powerless.
16 Your outbursts of anger pass over me,
your terrors annihilate me,
17 they surround me like water all day,
they close in on me together.
18 You have removed from me loved one and friend.
My companions – darkness!

Notes on the text

4. Hebr. *'ĕyāl* is a hapax. 'Strength' is contextually appropriate, though an Aram. cognate (cf. BDB) would suggest 'help'. In either case, the point is the poet has no resources to change the situation.

15. Hebr. *'āpûnâ* is a hapax. 'Powerless' (following *DCH*) seems contextually appropriate but is uncertain.

Form and structure

Although typically treated as the gloomiest of the complaint psalms (e.g. Brueggemann 1984: 78), it does not fit the *Gattung* of the complaint particularly well, lacking several elements usually said to define it (W. S. Prinsloo 1992a: 334–336; cf. Howard 2008: 133; Held 2023: 142–147). There is, for example, no obvious appeal for help, and neither is there any vow of praise. Yet, in that it clearly emerges from an extended period of distress, the label 'complaint' is not inappropriate, though this is to adopt a popular understanding of the term rather than the more technical sense in which it is often used. We can adopt Broyles's (1989) distinction between 'complaint' (where a psalmist lodges a complaint against God) and a 'plea' (in which God is asked for help against another threat). Yet even here, Psalm 88 is an outlier, quite different from other psalms. Nevertheless, it is surely important that Psalms 88–89 are both (in Broyles's terms) 'complaint' psalms, and that together they bring

Book 3 to a close through an individual and communal complaint. The two are also joined through their titles, with both linked to an 'Ezrahite'. This means that Book 3 is bound by a combination of individual and communal psalms (Pss 73–74; 88–89; cf. Grogan 2008: 154). Like Psalm 87, it is also a 'song'.

Psalm 88 also has links to the preceding poems. Its dual title is unique, but the Korahite component links it with Psalms 84–85, 86–87. The psalmist's status as one on the edge of death creates a strong contrast with the affirmation of God's goodness for those who trust him (Ps. 84:11), and the central elements of the challenge to God in verses 9b–12 respond to the more positive statements found in Psalms 85 and 87. God could 'announce' (*zkr*) that the nations belong to him (Ps. 87:4), but the psalmist feels like one whom God no longer 'remembers' (*zkr*), while also preparing for the plea to be remembered in Psalm 89:47. There are also important links to Psalm 86, most obviously the repeated appeal for God to incline his ear to the psalmist (Pss 86:1; 88:2), though where God previously delivered the psalmist from Sheol (Ps. 86:13), the poet now draws near to there (Ps. 88:3). This is consistent with the fact that Psalm 86:10 celebrates Yahweh's wondrous 'works' (*pl'*) before the nations, whereas the psalmist here wonders if he will do them for the dead (Ps. 88:10). Psalm 88 is thus both a distinctive poem and yet also a work closely integrated into its context in Book 3 (cf. Cole 2000: 167–176).

Although it does not fit the standard pattern of the complaint psalms, there is broad agreement that the poem can be analysed in four stanzas:

1. Opening petition (1–2)
2. Initial complaint (3–9a)
3. Interrogation of Yahweh (9b–12)
4. Second complaint (13–18)

Comment

Title: For 'A song', see on Psalm 65. For 'A melody', see on Psalm 3. For 'Korahite', see on Psalm 42. For 'The director's', see on Psalm 4. 'Mahalath' also occurs in the title of Psalm 53, but the meaning is uncertain. 'Leannoth' could be derived from a root for singing, though it can also mean 'to answer'. Some form of responsive singing could be intended (so *DCH*), but as Thornhill (2015: 49) observes, it is 'notoriously inscrutable'. For 'Maskil', see on Psalm 32. Heman the Ezrahite was a wise man from the time of Solomon (1 Kgs 4:31). Another Heman is a Levite (1 Chr. 6:33), though these two could be the same (so Longman 2014: 27). If so, then there is no need to regard the first half of this title as being a colophon to Psalm 87.

1–2. Addressing Yahweh as 'God of my salvation' represents a key component of the prayer, even if the rest of it is a relentless exploration of what it may mean to speak of Yahweh in these terms. This foundation guides the rest of the prayer (so Kraus 1989: 193), even as it is also problematized by what follows. It is to Yahweh that the poet cries day and night. Yahweh cannot be unaware of the distress experienced. Yet, the distress is unrelieved; hence, verse 2 contains the prayer's only request – asking that the poet's prayer come before Yahweh, that he attend to the poet's shout. Although such a shout can be joyful (e.g. Prov. 11:10), here it is the shout of those who suffer, one to which Yahweh should respond (cf. Ps. 106:44). The inference is that Yahweh has not responded to prayer, something made explicit in verse 14, but the prayer is grounded in the hope that he will.

3–9a. The opening complaint is linked to the opening petition, explaining (*kî*) why Yahweh needs to show himself as 'the God of the psalmist's salvation' (Schaefer 2001: 215). As verse 3 makes clear, the poet's whole life is filled with troubles, with the psalmist approaching death. 'Sheol' refers to the world of the dead, somewhere dreaded, an underworld especially marked by the presence of those who rejected God's ways (Prov. 5:5). Death's gravity pulls hard on the poet (Schaefer 2001: 215). The language of 'Sheol' (cf. Johnston 2002) is developed by other terms for the underworld since the poet is apparently reckoned among those going down to the 'pit' (vv. 4, 6), somewhere dark and filled with waters. It is a dangerous place, beyond human control. Others apparently already treat the psalmist as one belonging to the world of the dead, anticipating the later accusations against Yahweh concerning the poet's friends. The poet cannot change the situation, but in verse 6 this begins to become a charge against Yahweh. The poet is 'set free' – but among the dead, not to life. Those set free are elsewhere manumitted slaves (Exod. 21:12; Job 3:19), but where those released were meant to be well provisioned (Deut. 15:12–18), the psalmist is set free only among the dead, among the slain in the grave. This is a freedom no one wants. When the psalmist claims that Yahweh remembers such people no more, with their being cut off from his hand, the point is that he does not act for them. Typically, the language of Yahweh 'remembering' (*zkr*) someone indicates a point at which he acts positively for them (e.g. Gen. 8:1). The psalmist believes that Yahweh does not act favourably for those in Sheol. This highlights the challenge faced by the poet, because verse 6 insists that Yahweh has placed the psalmist in the pit, this deep and dark place. It is Yahweh who afflicts the psalmist with his wrath. Since Sheol is often portrayed as watery, the fact that Yahweh's breakers afflict the poet means that the horrors of death already impinge on the psalmist's life. The *selah* offers only a brief pause, moving from how Yahweh has acted directly against the psalmist to how this affects social relations. Yahweh is accused of having removed friends, making the poet an abomination (the antithesis of what is acceptable to Yahweh) to them. The psalmist is isolated, unable to go out, and left only with tears.

9b–12. The second stanza is initiated by verbs that report a history of calling out to Yahweh. This was embodied prayer, engaging the voice in calling and spreading out palms to show submission. Yet, Yahweh has plainly not answered. Therefore, the psalmist switches to sharp rhetorical questions (though not merely rhetorical; see Crüsemann 2003) that expect the answer 'no', supporting the claim that Yahweh does not remember the dead (cf. Pss 6:5; 30:9; 116:3–4). The opening question introduces the motif of God's wonders, miraculous acts that show his power, a motif that also closes the stanza. The point here is that God does his wonders for the living, not the dead. As such, the Rephaim, here understood as those living in Sheol (cf. Isa. 26:14) rather than an ancient race of giants (Deut. 2:20), do not rise to give God thanks. As such, no one recounts God's kindness in the grave or his faithfulness in Abaddon (destruction). If the dead do not experience God's goodness, then in this place of darkness his wonders will not be known. Should the psalmist die, then there would be one more among the dead not acknowledging Yahweh. The questions probe Yahweh, asking him to recognize that he loses a worshipper if he allows the psalmist to die.

13–18. Where the dead do not address Yahweh, the poet does, crying out for help with a prayer that will meet Yahweh. The opening stanza asked for the prayer to come before Yahweh, but the point here is more that it will confront him. The prayer will reach Yahweh, but Yahweh needs to respond. Where the initial complaint moved slowly towards accusing Yahweh, this one quickly reaches that point, beginning with questions and then moving to direct statements. The poet claims to have been spurned by Yahweh, unable to encounter his goodness because of Yahweh's hiding his face. This has resulted in an extended period of distress ('from my youth') during which the poet bore Yahweh's terrors, lacking the power to change anything. Yahweh's outbursts of anger swamp the psalmist. Yahweh is presented as the one who torments, surrounds and pummels the poet, even though he is the one who must provide salvation. The poet is isolated because Yahweh has removed all friends and companions. After these forceful comments, the final part line is terse. Yahweh has removed loved ones and placed the psalmist in the place of darkness, and darkness is all the psalmist has left. Yet even this is a plea, because Yahweh cannot leave things this way (cf. Hossfeld and Zenger 2006: 396).

Explanation

Psalm 88 stands as a challenge to any form of 'health and wealth' gospel. Whether its function is to lead us to the cross (Weiser 1962: 587) is debatable, though the cross is where we begin to see the resolution of the psalmist's problems. But we are not yet in the eschaton, and the reality of life for many is that it is full of pain that often seems meaningless. Even those who believe in God can find that their life contains unrelieved pain (Kidner 1975, 1: 319). This psalm rejects the cheap talk and easy answers we might be tempted to utilize to overcome (by avoiding!) the very real pain of life. Even worse for the psalmist is that there appears to be no basis for the suffering. Rather, Yahweh is seen as the source of this great suffering.

This may not seem to offer any positive assistance to us. And perhaps that is part of why this psalm is in the canon. But it is a prayer, a prayer of faith, even if the psalmist is uncertain of being heard. As a prayer, it knows the language that easily speaks of God's goodness but will not allow it to be uttered without holding God to account for why pain must be experienced. At the same time, there is a remarkable moderation to the language that probes God but is not angry with him (see Watson, forthcoming). As such, it challenges us to consider the nature of prayer. Prayer is wrestling with God, not a shopping list of requests (cf. van Gemeren 2008: 562), asking him to bring forth his blessing. Prayer's foundational reality is simply to be honest before God and to know that he hears our prayer on that basis alone. In the end, these are 'words that are not to be used frequently, but for the limit experiences when words must be honest and not claim too much' (Brueggemann 1984: 81).

PSALM 89

Translation

A Maskil. Ethan the Ezrahite's.

1 I will sing of Yahweh's kind acts for ever,
I will make known to all generations
your faithfulness with my mouth.
2 For I said, 'Kindness shall be built up for ever,
the heavens – you shall establish your faithfulness in them.'
3 'I made a covenant with my chosen one,
I swore an oath to my servant David.
4 I shall establish your descendants for ever,
and build your throne for all generations.' *Selah*.

5 The heavens praise your wonders, O Yahweh,
your faithfulness in the assembly of the holy ones.
6 For who in the sky compares to Yahweh,
or among the heavenly beings is like Yahweh,

7a God greatly feared in the council of the holy ones,
more awesome than all who surround him?
8O Yahweh, God of Hosts,
who is like you, mighty Yah,
with your faithfulness around you?
9You rule the surging of the sea,
when its waves rise, you still them.
10You crushed Rahab like one slain,
with your mighty arm you scattered your enemies.
11The heavens are yours,
yes, the earth is yours,
the world and all that is in them,
you founded them.
12North and south – you created them,
Tabor and Hermon shout out at your name.

13You have a mighty arm,
your hand prevails, your right hand is high.
14Righteousness and justice are the foundation of your throne,
kindness and faithfulness go before you.
15O the blessedness of the people who know the joyful shout,
O Yahweh, in the light of your face do they walk.
16They exult in your name all day,
and in your righteousness, they are exalted.
17For you are the splendour of their strength,
and by your favour our horn is exalted.
18For our shield belongs to Yahweh,
and our king to the Holy One of Israel.

19Previously you spoke in a vision to your godly ones and said,
'I have bestowed help on a mighty one,
I have exalted one chosen from the people.
20I have found David, my servant,
I anointed him with my holy oil,
21with whom my hand shall be firm,
indeed, my arm strengthens him.
22An enemy shall not beguile him,
nor the malicious oppress him.
23But I shall beat down his adversaries before him,
I shall strike down those who hate him.
24My faithfulness and kindness will be with him,
and in my name shall his horn be exalted.
25I shall set his hand on the sea,
and his right hand on the rivers.
26He shall call out to me, 'You are my father,

my God, and the rock of my salvation.'
27Surely, I will make him the firstborn,
the highest of the kings of the earth.
28I will keep my kindness for him for ever,
and my covenant for him will be firm.
29I will establish his descendants for ever,
and his throne like the days of the heavens.
30If his sons forsake my instruction,
and do not walk in my judgements,
31if they defile my statutes,
and do not keep my commandments,
32I will punish their transgression with a rod,
and their iniquity with affliction,
33but I will not remove my kindness from him,
or be false to my faithfulness.
34I will not violate my covenant,
I will not alter what has gone forth from my lips.
35I have sworn once by my holiness,
I will not lie to David.
36His descendants shall endure for ever,
and his throne shall be like the sun before me.
37Like the moon, it shall be established for ever,
and firm as a trustworthy witness in the sky.' *Selah.*

38But you have spurned and rejected,
you have shown yourself to be angry with your anointed one.
39You have repudiated the covenant with your servant,
you have violated his crown in the land.
40You have breached all his walls,
you have made his stronghold a ruin.
41All those passing by plundered him,
he became a reproach to his neighbours.
42You have exalted the right hand of his adversaries,
you have made all his enemies rejoice.
43You even turned back the edge of his sword,
you did not raise him up in the battle.
44You made his splendour cease,
you hurled his throne to the ground.
45You cut short the days of his youth,
you wrapped him in shame. *Selah.*

46How long, O Yahweh?
Will you hide yourself for ever?
Will your anger burn like fire?
47Remember what my lifespan is,

the futility for which you created all humans.
[48]Which person can live and not see death,
or deliver themselves from the power of Sheol? *Selah.*
[49]Where are your former acts of kindness O Lord,
that you swore to David by your faithfulness?
[50]Remember, O Lord, the reproach of your servants,
I bear the insults of many peoples in my breast
[51]by which your enemies reproach, O Yahweh,
by which they reproach the footsteps of your anointed one.

[52]Blessed be Yahweh for ever!
Amen and Amen.

Notes on the text

12. 'North and south' could also be mythological references. See Venter 2005.

17. With many MSS and Q (also Gk, Syr., Tg), reading *tārûm*.

19. Retaining the pl. here as the more difficult reading.

22. The root *nšʾ* could also refer to exacting something, perhaps an oath.

43. Taking *ṣûr* as 'flint' and hence 'edge'.

47. The syntax is jagged, but no emendation is persuasive.

50. Several MSS read the sg. 'servant'. Earlier references were sg., making the pl. the more difficult reading here.

Form and structure

Psalm 89 provides a powerful and challenging close to Book 3. Through links in its title, it creates a concluding pair with Psalm 88, so that Yahweh is challenged to act for both the individual and the community. The links with Psalm 88 also mean it is joined with the Korahite psalms (84–85, 87–88) and through them to earlier parts of Book 3, and then the first Korahite collection (Pss 42–49). It also contrasts sharply with the more positive presentation of the king in Psalms 2 and 72. As such, readers who have reached Psalm 89 are asked to pause and reflect on how they can understand the promise to David and the role of the king. Nevertheless, the psalm does not announce the failure of the Davidic covenant (against Wilson 1985a: 212–214), though it does leave unresolved the question of how it might continue, anticipating the more eschatological perspective of Psalms 110 and 132 (cf. Pohl 2015). The possibility of this more eschatological reading is established through Psalm 90's reframing of how readers are to understand God's perspective on time (cf. Cole 2000: 177) as well as the emphasis on Yahweh's reign through Book 4. But this perspective is introduced in Psalm 89 itself, with the questions in verses 46–49 assuming Yahweh may yet act because of the Davidic covenant. Elements of this possibility were already established by earlier parts of Book 3 (cf. Cole 2000: 198), and here the continued emphasis on Yahweh's kindness and faithfulness grounds this possibility while providing the poem's theological structure (cf. Collins 2022: 454).

The focus on the king, and especially the Davidic covenant (with overtones of Sinai; cf. Fernandes 2013: 279–280), makes it clear that this is a royal psalm. However, since this designation is marked by reference to the king rather than other formal criteria, other classifications are also possible. The close association with Psalm 88 means that we can also consider this as a psalm of complaint, one where Yahweh is both the problem and the means of possible resolution (cf. Broyles 1989: 168–173). Here, military defeat, most probably the exile, raises questions about the future of the Davidic covenant and how Yahweh will honour it. Unlike Psalm 88, which remains individual in focus, Psalm 89 is communal, though there are numerous points where an individual speaks on behalf of the community. This is a feature it shares with Psalm 44, another complaint. That psalm also began with words of praise (Ps. 44:1–8) before moving to the complaint (Ps. 44:9–26). The opening praise there provides the context for the complaint. This pattern is repeated here, the main difference being that the opening praise is much longer (vv. 1–37), but it again provides the context for the complaint (vv. 38–51). As such, Psalm 89 draws on the same literary traditions as Psalm 44, with both poems informed by Israel's praise traditions while ultimately deploying them as the basis for complaint. In addition, in verses 3–4, 19–37 it draws on a feature found otherwise in the Asaph psalms of including an extended citation of speech by God (cf. 'Form and structure' on Ps. 50). It is a poem that draws widely on the psalmic traditions, while its integration of the Davidic material also points to awareness of 2 Samuel 7.

The psalm can be analysed in two stanzas, each of which can be divided into strophes, plus a colophon that acts as the close of Book 3, the latter of which is probably an addition to the basic poem. Nevertheless, the closing doxology is particularly powerful given the preceding complaint:

1. Praise of God's kindness and covenant (1–37)
   a. Vow of praise (1–4)
   b. Yahweh's power in creation (5–12)
   c. Yahweh's power in justice (13–18)
   d. Celebration of the Davidic covenant (19–37)
2. Complaint about God's renouncing the covenant (38–51)

   a. Yahweh as the enemy (38–45)
   b. Appeal for Yahweh to act in kindness (46–51)
3. Colophon (52)

Comment

Title: For 'Maskil', see on Psalm 32. 'Ethan the Ezrahite' is a wise man with whom Solomon was compared (1 Kgs 4:31).

1–4. The opening strophe features an interchange of voices, including citations of previous words by both the 'I' who speaks (probably a representative figure) and Yahweh. It is introduced with an opening vow of sung praise that focuses on Yahweh's kind acts as something to be made known to future generations. Reference here to Yahweh's kindness and faithfulness immediately establishes two key terms that echo through the psalm, while also alluding to Exodus 34:6. This pair returns in verse 49, where they become part of the questions put to Yahweh. At this point, such language is untroubled, and the psalmist recalls an earlier declaration in verse 2 that also draws on these terms, a point of confidence, where Yahweh's kindness and faithfulness are thought to endure. Further evidence for this is then brought forward by quoting Yahweh in verses 3–4 and the promise of a covenant with David, a promise to establish his descendants and throne for ever. Mention of David also prepares for his importance later in the poem in the celebration of this covenant (vv. 19–37) and the challenges that will be put to Yahweh (vv. 38–45). Verse 49 then brings this covenant and Yahweh's kindness and faithfulness together in the appeal. The past has established present praise, though it also prepares for coming challenges.

5–12. Having established the poem's main themes, the second strophe develops the motif of Yahweh's faithfulness through his power in creation. The heavens proclaim Yahweh's wonders, making clear his faithfulness among the holy ones, perhaps angelic figures. The heavens can do this because, as the questions in verses 6–7 make clear, no being can truly be compared to Yahweh, including angelic ones, since he is the one who is revered in the divine council (cf. Ps. 82), and more awesome than any other. The image here depends on a standard ANE portrayal of the chief deity standing in council with other heavenly beings. However, here the point is that whatever such beings may be, they are subservient to Yahweh. His work in creation demonstrates this and points to his faithfulness. The questions from verse 8 extend this by stressing Yahweh's might as greater than any other and most truly surrounded by his faithfulness. As the one who is mighty, Yahweh rules over the sea, perhaps understood here as a god that would rebel against him, as he calms stormy waters. Rahab (not the person in Josh. 2) was a sea monster defeated by Yahweh (Isa. 51:9; elsewhere it can also refer to Egypt; cf. Ps. 87:4; a sense that could also be present here), a victory again celebrated here. The point is that there are no foes within creation able to resist Yahweh. All creation, however defined, belongs to him and is thus under his authority. Yahweh founded and created it, and all is his, so that even mighty mountains like Tabor (about 12 miles [19 km] south-west of the Sea of Galilee) and Hermon (the tallest mountain in the region, on Israel's north-eastern border) cry out to him, even though both might previously have been sites of worship of other deities.

13–18. Yahweh's mighty arm had defeated Rahab (v. 10), and the strength of that arm is again celebrated in this strophe. Although the idiom is different, mention of Yahweh's arm could allude to the exodus since his arm is often mentioned in this context (e.g. Exod. 6:6; 15:16; Deut. 4:34; 5:15). Mention of Yahweh's strong hand is consistent with this allusion, though it need not be restricted to it. Israel has experienced Yahweh's acts of justice in the past, and it is this justice, along with righteousness, that is the foundation of Yahweh's throne. That is, righteousness and justice are how Yahweh's reign is demonstrated, while kindness and faithfulness (cf. v. 1) mark out his presence. This presence means that Yahweh was not simply involved in creation's initiation, but rather that he continues to engage with the world. That is why a beatitude (cf. Ps. 1:1) can be pronounced on the people who worship Yahweh and conduct themselves before him. Yahweh is a God of justice and righteousness, something his people can experience and trust. Such a people exult in his name continually and are themselves exalted in his righteousness. Such an exaltation means they have the same experience as Yahweh's hand (v. 13), something also matched by their 'horn' (v. 17), which is here a symbol for strength (cf. 1 Sam. 2:1; Ps. 75:4–5), its mention here also preparing for mention of the anointed one's horn (v. 24). Any strength the people possess is given by Yahweh. Accordingly, the nation's shield and king really belong to Yahweh. The 'shield' here probably refers to the king (cf. Ps. 84:9). The people's security is thus not found in military resources but rather in understanding that even their king is subservient to Yahweh, here called the 'Holy One of Israel', a term more typically known from Isaiah (twenty-five times), though it occurs also in Psalms 71:22 and 78:41. Whether in the exodus or through Israel's kings, Yahweh's power has been evident and faithfully applied to Israel.

19–37. Mention of David (v. 3) and the king (v. 18) prepare for this strophe which is given over entirely to a celebration of the Davidic covenant, all of it (barring the introduction) citing Yahweh directly in a speech directed to the people, assuring them of Yahweh's commitment to David and his descendants. Although the speech was given in a vision, it is not possible to point to a single text that reports this, though mention of a vision links it to Nathan's oracle to David (2 Sam. 7:1–17). The speech moves around key themes but can be subdivided into three main sections – verses 20–28 are primarily concerned with Yahweh's commitment to David, while verses 29–33 focus on his descendants and verses 34–37 point to Yahweh's enduring commitment to this covenant.

Verses 20–28 open with Yahweh's declaration of having 'found' David, who is here designated as 'my servant', an important honorific David shares with Moses (e.g. Num. 12:7–8; Mal. 4:4), Joshua (Josh. 24:29) and the 'Servant of the Lord' mentioned in Isaiah 40 – 55 (e.g. Isa. 42:1–4). Here, Yahweh claims to have anointed him, perhaps alluding to 1 Samuel 16:1–13, where Samuel was sent to anoint one of Jesse's sons and anointed David, with this marking Yahweh's commitment to sustain and strengthen David. Accordingly, David's enemies could not triumph because Yahweh would defeat them. Yahweh's faithfulness and kindness, central motifs in this poem, were to go with Yahweh as permanent markers of God's presence with David. David's name will be exalted, but only because Yahweh exalts his horn, echoing 1 Samuel 2:10 and the messianic hope there where the horn stands for strength. Yahweh will also place his hand on the sea and the rivers. As both could be construed as forces of chaos opposed to Yahweh (cf. Ps. 24:1–2), the king is here the one through whom Yahweh's reign is established. This is also linked to the close relationship between the king and Yahweh, as the king can speak of Yahweh as his father (cf. 2 Sam. 7:14), God and rock of salvation. The image of God as 'rock' often points to Yahweh as the one who provides security and is linked here to these other images, providing confidence in the face of threat (Fernandes 2013: 283). The king's close relationship to Yahweh is matched with Yahweh's commitment to the king, as the king is treated as Yahweh's firstborn, an adopted status here linked with the king being made the highest of the kings of the earth. The closeness of this relationship means that Yahweh promises to keep his kindness and covenant with the king for ever.

The covenant did not end with David, and verses 29–33 explore the implications of this covenant with his descendants. This is a natural result of the commitment to David enduring, also echoing 2 Samuel 7:12–16. David's descendants and throne would thus continue to receive Yahweh's support. Although 2 Samuel 7:12–16 does not directly mention the requirement for David's sons to remain faithful, it may be implied in the declaration there that Yahweh would discipline them when needed, and this is a common element in later reflections on the Davidic covenant (e.g. 1 Kgs 8:25). Here, the point is made that David's descendants are expected to conduct themselves within the terms of the law (linking this poem to Pss 19, 119) while noting that they will be punished if they do not do so. However, the failure of the sons to remain faithful is not enough to overturn the covenant. Rather, Yahweh's kindness and faithfulness will remain.

Because of this commitment, verses 34–37 then explore Yahweh's enduring commitment to the covenant. It is something he has promised, and therefore he will remain true to it, not altering a word. The reason for this is that Yahweh has sworn by his holiness, by his own nature, that he will not lie to David. Accordingly, David's line of descent will continue, and his throne will stand like the sun and the moon before Yahweh. The principal heavenly lights are thus permanent witnesses before Yahweh and to the congregation of this commitment, witnesses that are an essential element in a covenant (see Mullen 1983: 214–217). Yahweh's commitment is irrevocable.

38–45. A fundamental shift is announced here in the opening 'But you' with which the psalm focuses on the experience of exile. Yahweh's words have been cited, as have the core elements of Israel's theology. Now, as Yahweh is addressed the psalm challenges him about his kindness and faithfulness. The address indeed focuses on Yahweh, repeatedly stressing what he has done, and none of it sounds anything like the wonderful promises that have been cited. Rather than sustaining David, Yahweh has spurned and rejected, showing himself angry with his anointed. This is matched with his repudiation of the covenant, resulting in David's crown being violated in the land. Rather than providing security, it is Yahweh who has broken down the king's walls, leaving his strongholds in ruins, allowing passers-by to plunder the king so that, rather than being a sign of Yahweh's power, the king is instead a reproach to his neighbours. It is the enemies, not the king, who rejoice, contrary to the claims of verses 20–24. Rather than helping the king in battle, Yahweh has acted against him, turning back his sword and not raising him up. Yahweh has caused the king's splendour to cease and hurled his throne to the ground rather than establishing it (v. 29). Rather than long life for the dynasty (v. 36), exile cuts short the king's life, wrapping him in shame rather than honour. It is not foreign powers who have reduced the king (probably Jehoiachin; cf. Tate 1990: 416–417) to this state – the psalm is clear that Yahweh has become the enemy.

46–51. The second strophe of this stanza engages with Yahweh through a mix of questions and admonitions that are introduced with a call for Yahweh to remember. The questions are rhetorical in that they are not really asking for information but are aimed at spurring Yahweh to act positively, ensuring that his faithfulness and kindness are experienced. That is, what the psalmist initially declared would be the content of continued praise is what needs to be evident in the community's lived experience. Only then would such praise make sense. Hence, verse 46 asks 'How long?', a question that assumes the suffering has gone on too long. Yahweh has both hidden himself from his people and allowed his wrath to burn against them and this has gone on too long. Instead, he needs to remember the short lifespan of the speaker, though this individual's transience is like that of humankind overall. They cannot wait for ever. Calling God to remember does not mean that he has previously forgotten. Rather, it indicates that he needs to act positively for people in terms of his previous relationship with them (Childs 1962: 32–34). No human can wait indefinitely, because death is our shared experience, and so the psalm asks God to remember, the implication being that he must act soon. By putting this to Yahweh in questions, the psalm draws him into the conversation, asking him to acknowledge these realities. The *selah* in verse 48 represents a minor break in this strophe, preparing for a new question that focuses specifically on the Davidic covenant (v. 49), integrating this with the motif of Yahweh's kindness and faithfulness. These were meant to be an enduring part of Israel's experience, but if Yahweh has become the enemy, then they are not being experienced. Hence, Yahweh is again asked to remember, this time for the community as a whole because of the mockery, as well as the psalmist who speaks for them and bears a special pain because of the treatment of Yahweh's anointed. The speaker, the community and the king all suffer reproach – each is affected, though each remains discrete (cf. Krusche 2020). Yahweh needs to remember and act once more for all because of the Davidic covenant and the promise made (cf. van Wolde 2019: 524).

52. As the closing verse of Book 3, it is likely that this doxology is an addition to the main poem. It is like those at Psalms 41:13, 72:18–19 and 106:48, each of which ends a book of the Psalter, though this is the briefest. Perhaps in this case, brevity reminds the community of the tenuous nature of their relationship with Yahweh, one that cannot be given up but which at this point is also costly to hold.

Explanation

In closing Book 3, Psalm 89 points to a fundamental paradox. Here, the poet promises to sing of Yahweh's kindness and faithfulness for ever, themes that seemingly lead to praise. As the poem comes towards its close the poet still sings of them, but now questions Yahweh about where they are (cf. Schaefer 2001: 222). Yahweh has promised, but now that promise is turned back on him. The psalmist, and the community, need to know why the horrors of exile have come upon them, why the king is no longer leading the nation in victory. If Yahweh has promised, and that promise can be cited at length, then what is to be done? As the psalm ends, no answer is available. But there is a word of prayer, a word not even uttered until verse 50, but that is the one point of hope to which the psalm clings. Yahweh is asked to remember. Only as Yahweh remembers his covenant commitments, here joining the Sinai covenant with the Davidic, can the nation and the anointed both experience Yahweh's kindness and faithfulness. The psalm is therefore an extraordinary expression of faith. It knows Yahweh is kind and faithful, fundamental characteristics that were shown after the golden calf (Exod. 32) and that Yahweh affirmed were core to his identity (Exod. 34:6–7). But these are not currently being experienced. The psalm will not let go of God, but neither will it let God off. God's kindness and faithfulness remain central to the worship of his people, but they need to experience them too. Words uttered in worship must have meaning in lived experience. This psalm joins with the prayer of the saints who also cry out for Yahweh's justice to be seen on the earth (Rev. 6:10), holding fast to God while pleading for him to act.

BOOK 4

PSALM 90

Translation

A prayer, Mosaic, the man of God.

[1]O Lord, you have been our dwelling place
  from generation to generation,
[2]before the mountains were born,
  and you brought to birth the land and world,
  from everlasting to everlasting,
  you are God.

[3]You make a human return to dust,
  and say, 'Return, O children of Adam.'
[4]For a thousand years in your eyes
  are like yesterday as it passes,
  and the watch of the night.
[5]You overwhelm them, they are asleep,
  like grass renewed in the morning,
[6]in the morning it sprouts and is renewed,
  in the evening it withers and dries.

7For we are destroyed in your anger
  in your wrath are we dismayed.
8You set our iniquities before you,
  our secrets in the light of your presence.
9For all our days decline in your indignation,
  we complete our years like a sigh.
10The days of our years, in them are seventy years,
  perhaps eighty years with strength,
their pride is toil and trouble,
  that passes quickly and we fly away.
11Who knows the strength of your anger,
  that your indignation is like the fear of you?
12So teach us to number our days,
  that we may gain a wise mind.

13Turn, O Yahweh! How long?
  Have compassion on your servants!
14Satisfy us in the morning with your kindness,
  that we may shout out and rejoice through all our days.
15Make us rejoice for as many days as you afflicted us,
  the years we have seen calamity.
16Let your work be visible to your servants,
  and your majesty to their children.
17So may the loveliness of the Lord our God be upon us,
  establish the work of our hands for us,
  yes, the works of our hands, establish it.

Notes on the text

1. Hebr. *mā'ôn* could also be a hiding place or help.

3. Hebr. *dākā'* is lit. 'pulverized material'.

5. The verse is difficult and often emended, but no proposal is persuasive (cf. Tate 1990: 433–434). The verb *zrm* is here understood as 'overwhelm' rather than 'destroy'.

8. Retaining K.

9. Hebr. *pnh* is commonly 'to turn' but this can also refer to the turn of a day, and thus of its decline (cf. Jer. 6:4).

11. Taking the second part line as a verbless clause, but the verse is difficult.

Form and structure

Following the uncertainty with which Book 3 closes, Book 4 opens with the Psalter's only Mosaic prayer. Book 3 closed with questions about

Yahweh's faithfulness to the Davidic covenant, so by introducing a Mosaic prayer at this point readers are pushed back to the earliest period of Israel's life. Indeed, probable allusions to Gen. 2 – 3 take us back to creation. This allows this psalm to place human perceptions of time and the rate at which God works in dialogue with one another so that we see that God's relationship to time is different from ours. What may seem like an impossible situation from a human perspective on time could be entirely resolvable from God's. This does not mean that Psalm 90 provides a quick and easy resolution to the questions of Psalms 88–89. But it does enable those who enter Book 4 with the questions of Book 3 unresolved to have a framework with which to consider these questions. Moreover, the introduction of Moses here also prepares for a significant emphasis on him throughout Book 4 (cf. Pss 99:6; 103:7; 105:26; 106:16, 23, 32), even though he is mentioned only once before in Psalms (77: 21). Moses is a significant figure for Book 4, and his introduction prepares readers for a range of significant themes across the book, so much so that McKelvey (2014: 40) suggests every psalm in this book should, to some extent, be read in the light of Psalm 90.

As well as preparing for what follows, this psalm also has important connections with Psalm 89 (cf. Vesco 2006, 2: 843–844). As noted, it addresses the question of time, a motif introduced in Psalm 89:2, 4, 53, which finds a clear echo here (vv. 1–2, 4, 10, 12, 14–15). Linked to this is the fact that human life is brief (Pss 89:47–48; 90:10), and confronts the reality of death (Ps. 90:3). Human finitude stands in contrast with God's eternity, something seen in his status as creator of the mountains (Pss 89:12; 90:2). Both poems can ask 'How long?' (Pss 89:46; 90:13), though with different perspectives on what that may mean.

Although it has clear links with other psalms, it also needs to be interpreted as a discrete poem. Its exact form has been a matter of debate since it does not really map easily on to the form-critical model. The meditation on time could fit with Israel's wisdom traditions (e.g. Eccl. 3:1–8), as would the observations based on patterns in nature. The importance of wisdom is also prominent in the appeal of verse 12. But the question 'How long?' (v. 13) is more consistent with the complaint psalms, particularly those that hold God responsible (cf. Broyles 1989: 173–177), and this introduces an extended appeal that desires the removal of current suffering and the introduction of fresh stability (vv. 13–17), echoing the opening affirmations about God's previous work (vv. 1–2). Kynes (2018) has demonstrated that wisdom is not wholly discrete from Israel's other literary traditions, and as such we can understand the poem as an integration of these elements. We can analyse the poem in four stanzas, with the opening and closing verses forming an inclusio:

1. God as the eternal dwelling (1–2)
2. Human life as transitory (3–6)

3. Learning through God's power (7–12)
4. Prayer for compassion (13–17)

Comment

Title: The issues surrounding 'Mosaic' in this title are the same as for 'Davidic' elsewhere. On the grammatical issues, see 'Notes on the text' on Psalm 3's title. The title need not mean Moses is the poem's author, but it is to be read in association with Moses, an association strengthened by various allusions to the Pentateuch. 'Man of God' more commonly designates a prophetic figure such as Elijah or Elisha (cf. Petersen 1981: 40–50), though it is used of Moses (Deut. 33:1; Josh. 14:6). Moses is elsewhere Israel's model prophet (Deut. 18:15–22; 34:10–12), though using different terminology, but this background informs the reading of this psalm.

1–2. The psalm opens with the voc. 'O Lord' (*'ādōnay*), a divine name to which the psalm returns in verse 17. The voc. establishes a key feature of the psalm, which is throughout addressed directly to God. Calling him 'Lord' emphasizes his role as one who rules, a key theme for this poem and for addressing the questions with which Book 3 closed. God is not only one who reigns; he has also been the people's dwelling place (cf. Deut. 33:27). This dwelling place can refer to the temple (Ps. 26:8), a place of security to which someone might flee. This background probably informs the usage here, so that God is the one to whom the people can come and find help and security. Most importantly, this was not limited to the time when there was a temple. Rather, God has always been this secure dwelling place, reaching back through all time. This can be traced back to creation, here expressed in the image of God's having given birth to the habitable world. Israel's Lord has always been God, and all creation is under his rule. To assert that he has always been the people's dwelling place is to declare that he is the one who provides security.

3–6. God existed before there was a habitable world, but humans are transitory. Indeed, it is God who returns us to dust. The word for 'dust' here (*dākā'*) differs from that in Genesis 2:7, but it is probable that Genesis 1 – 3 stands behind this stanza's meditation, especially as we are called 'children of Adam' (similarly, Collins 2022: 462). God does not permit humans to live for ever, contrasting our existence with his. This contrast is heightened in verse 4, which insists that what may seem extraordinarily long times for humans are brief for God (cf. 2 Peter 3:8). God perceives time, but does not experience it as we do, so that a thousand years is no different from how humans perceive yesterday or even a watch set by soldiers for a few hours in the night. How verse 5 develops this is uncertain because of translational difficulties, but it perhaps develops an analogy between humans and grass (cf. Ps. 103:14–15; Isa. 40:6–8). Humans are overwhelmed by God and are simply asleep (possibly a euphemism for death; so Estes 2019: 177), perhaps suggesting that compared to God we are dormant. Like grass, which is refreshed by overnight dew, humans have a period in which we flourish. But grass also withers and dries through the heat of the day. God is eternal, but humans are transitory, and even our flourishing is limited when compared to God.

7–12. Grass fades and withers before the heat of the sun, and the human experience before God's wrath is no better. Humans before God's anger are destroyed. The psalm indicates that this anger is appropriate because of human iniquity, the fact that we do not live as God desires, though Psalm 103:3 provides hope on this issue. Humans may hide their iniquity from one another, but God brings our secrets out into the open when we encounter him. Human life is not only transient; it moves through stages of decline, like the sun as it sets, as we experience God's indignation at our iniquity, finally ending with a sigh. This awareness of human sin and mortality does not here lead to fatalism. Rather, the poet reflects on the duration of the human life as something which is relatively short. In modern developed economies, a lifespan of seventy or eighty years is not unusual, but this is only a relatively recent development, and in ancient times such a lifespan would be considered very long. The achievements of such a life (here, its 'pride') are still only toil and trouble, aligning the poet with some of Qoheleth's observations (e.g. Eccl. 1:3). Human achievement is likewise transient, and our life can therefore be compared to a bird that flies away. Human achievement must also be set against God's anger, here still directed against human iniquity, the strength of which is beyond human comprehension. How this relates to the fear of God in verse 11b is uncertain (see 'Notes on the text'), but if the point is to contrast divine indignation at sin with human achievement, then this becomes a further way of noting human finitude. The fear of God can mark a healthy relationship with God (Prov. 1:7), but here the point is perhaps that the presence of the fear of God does not remove God's indignation at sin. Yet the psalm does not leave us without hope. Rather, the petition of verse 12 presents the appropriate response. Humans are limited, but the time we have should be used constructively. Asking that God teach us to number our days is a mechanism for appreciating our limits (and perhaps also for learning from a period of divine anger), and so, fundamental to gaining a wise mind. The petition, as the stanza's goal, reminds us of our limitations while stressing that God provides a means for gaining the needed wisdom by accepting this point.

13–17. A community that has learnt wisdom can, then, pray to experience God's compassion. It is one that has come to terms with its limits and the reality of divine punishment for sin. But it can also ask God to be gracious towards them, to show compassion because of their need (cf. Exod. 32:12–14; Deut. 32:36). Indeed, the opening appeal here assumes that God's anger has fully done its work. The community has recognized its limitations, and so needs God to relent from his anger. The compassion sought wants God to relent from the current punishment, which (from their perspective) now needs to cease. Rather than experiencing anger, the community longs to be satisfied with God's 'kindness' (*ḥesed*), hoping for a time when its life can be marked instead by praise and joy. Human life is still limited, but it can yet be marked with joy. At this point, the community's experience is one of affliction and calamity, but it looks to have this period matched in future by joy. This joy is to be based on evidence of God's work among the people, something they can see, and that also allows their descendants to see God's majesty. Restoration from calamity will thus show all the reality of God's majesty. This will demonstrate that God's loveliness, his favour, is presence among his people. This favour will also mean God establishes the community's works. Their own works will be enjoyed rather than lost to others because God has relented and shown favour to them.

Explanation

As we enter Book 4, we are reminded that time matters. Coming out of the uncertainty with which Book 3 ended, this provides an important point of reference. God's eternity provides an important contrast to human finitude, and this contrast helps us understand that what may seem like extended periods of pain and suffering are, when seen from God's side of things, not extended at all. Further, those periods of suffering may well be justified by human sin that triggers God's wrath. Hence, we need to learn a different approach to time, which faces the reality of what we experience (and can still ask 'How long?'), and yet also sees that God's purposes run to a different schedule from our own. The psalm lets us see that these are both appropriate ways of seeing time. This balance is important, because to emphasize only God's side may treat human pain too lightly. However, seeing only the human side prevents us from seeing that God may well have greater purposes. Read against the background of exile, it allows both the length of exile to be understood and its reasons accepted while also insisting that this does not need to be the end of the matter. God's compassion and kindness remain and can be sought. Such a background makes sense of how this psalm is taken up in 2 Peter 3:8–10, where believers are reminded that Christ's return is a perennial reality while also being something that runs to God's time, not ours.

PSALM 91

Translation

1 One who dwells in the shelter of the Most High,
lodges in the shadow of Shaddai.
2 I say to Yahweh, 'My refuge and my stronghold,
my God in whom I trust.'

3 For he will rescue you from the fowler's snare,
from the pestilence of destruction.
4 He will cover you with his pinions,
under his wings you take refuge,
a shield and a buckler are his constancy.
5 You will not fear the terror of night,
the arrow that flies by day,
6 the pestilence that is abroad in the darkness,
the destruction that ravages at noon.
7 A thousand may fall at your side,
ten thousand at your right hand,
but it will not come near you.
8 You will only look with your eyes,
and see the punishment of the wicked.

9 Truly, you, O Yahweh, are my refuge!
You have made the Most High your dwelling place.
10 No harm will befall you,
no assault shall come near your tent.
11 For he will command his messengers concerning you,
to guard you on all your paths.
12 They shall bear you up on their palms,
lest you strike your foot on a stone.
13 You will tread on lion and adder,
you will trample on the young lion and the serpent.

14 For the one devoted to me I will deliver,
I set that one who knows my name securely on high.
15 This one will call on me and I will answer,
I am with this one in distress,
I will rescue and honour this one.
16 I will satisfy this one with length of days,
and I will show this one my salvation.

Notes on the text

11QPsAp[a] differs at numerous points, but no deviations from MT are required. Six MSS join the first six verses of this psalm to Psalm 90, though this seems to be a case of untitled psalms running into one another rather than being interpretatively significant (against R. E. Wallace 2007: 23–24).

Title: Gk makes the psalm Davidic (as with all untitled psalms in Book 4), but this is probably an addition to the Masoretic tradition.

2. Gk makes the opening verb 3 m. sg. (cf. NIV, Kraus 1989: 220). But MT can be retained.

4. Although *bĕʾbrātô* is sg., it is understood here as collective. Hebr. *sōḥērâ* is a hapax, but points to some form of protection. Given the parallel, a buckler is more likely than NIV's 'rampart', though Hossfeld and Zenger's (2006: 427) 'sheltering wall' is plausible.

9. Reading *kî* as asseverative (*WHS* §449).

Form and structure

Where Psalm 90 encouraged readers to re-evaluate their experience in the light of Yahweh's eternity, Psalm 91 encourages trust in the present. These psalms are particularly linked through the appeal to Yahweh in Psalm 90:12–15 and Yahweh's speech in Psalm 91:14–16. Yahweh was asked to return and have pity on his servants, satisfying them with his kindness, and this is now promised. Beyond this, Psalm 91 explores the opening statement of Psalm 90: 1 about God's being his people's dwelling place, developing this by pointing to him as refuge (vv. 2, 9). Although the brevity of human life remains (Ps. 90: 3, 10), yet Yahweh here still promises long life to those who love him (v. 16). It should be noted, though, that whereas previous untitled psalms (1, 2, 10, 33, 43, 71) were closely tied to the preceding poem, the links here are looser, preparing perhaps for the run of untitled psalms that follows in Psalms 93–97.

The psalm contains several allusions to the temple. These could suggest a liturgical origin, something that might be supported by noting the change in the speaker in each stanza. The first two could also be analysed as an interchange between teacher and student (and there are significant wisdom connections; see Botha 2012c), though Yahweh appears to be the speaker in the third stanza. There is, however, no need to choose between a liturgical and an instructional form, as these can go together, and both encourage trust in all circumstances (cf. W. S. Prinsloo 2003: 408).

Based on the interchange of speakers evident throughout, the psalm can be analysed in three stanzas, the second containing two strophes:

1. Opening affirmation (1–2)
2. Reasons to trust God (3–13)
   a. God saves (3–8)
   b. God protects (9–13)
3. Oracle of promise (14–16)

Comment

1–2. The poem opens with an affirmation of faith, initially in general terms. The reference is to anyone who finds their security in God, here referred to by two ancient titles, Elyon (Most High) and Shaddai. 'Most High' perhaps alludes to Abram's encounter with Melchizedek (Gen. 14:20), though within the Psalter it is also tied to Zion (Pss 46:5; 47:2; 87:5). 'Shaddai' also has roots in the Abraham story (Gen. 17:1), though it is otherwise only in Psalm 68:14. What joins them in Psalms is that both epithets point to God's ability to protect his people and win battles. This sense is also evident in one of Balaam's oracles, where the combination also appears (Num. 24:16). This background is applied here in the image of dwelling under God's protection, language that alludes to the temple as the place where security may be found, much as one might find shelter under the shadow of the cherubim's wings (Pss 17:8; 36:7; 57:1; 63:7). No other psalm speaks of lodging (or spending the night) with God, but the sense of protection is still clear. The language thus alludes to the temple but can also point more widely to God's protection. Verse 2 then makes this specific to the speaker, who makes clear that these ancient epithets belong to Yahweh, and he is the speaker's refuge and stronghold, the one the speaker trusts. The speaker affirms that the general statement of verse 1 is something that can be personally applied, specifically through trusting Yahweh as God. This trust is not abstract. Rather, it is trust that God's protection can be experienced.

3–8. The second stanza addresses a listener directly. The two strophes are thematically close, but the brief shift of speaker in verse 9a marks a break that introduces the second strophe. Here, the speaker helps the listener focus on what trusting Yahweh can mean, emphasizing that Yahweh rescues the listener. Yahweh's protection is from both the fowler's snare and pestilence. The former could refer to an accidental experience, though since elsewhere in Psalms this imagery refers to the actions of enemies (cf. Ps. 124:7), more deliberate acts by adversaries are probably included. Pestilence, though, is more random. The speaker declares that God's protection is found in all types of circumstances. This protection is not restricted to those in the temple even though temple imagery continues to be used in verse 4, though the ornithological imagery could also be more general. Rather, God's constancy (or faithfulness) is protective in all circumstances, like a shield that protects from attack. Because God is like this, the listener need not fear unexpected attacks by enemies or pestilence, whether by day or night. The speaker does not presume that the listener is somehow kept separate from such challenging circumstances, as becomes clear in verses 7–8, which describe the many who do fall in battle. 'Thousand' and 'Ten thousand' are both hyperbolic numbers here, probably meaning 'more than can reasonably be counted'. The point is that these people fall, but the listener will be kept safe from these attacks, even though the listener was present among them. God's protective power will not keep the listener from these threats but will keep the listener safe in them. Instead, it is the wicked who fall, as is clear from the fact that the listener will see punishment of the wicked, suggesting that the protection offered is specifically against them (Collins 2022: 466).

9–13. The opening of verse 9 is difficult but can be understood as an initial response given by the listener, after which the speaker continues to stress Yahweh's protective power (also Tate 1990: 449). If this is correct, then in verse 9a the listener addresses Yahweh, making a personal confession of faith. Describing Yahweh as 'my refuge' is thus consistent with the themes developed by the speaker, though it also ties this psalm to the wider 'Yahweh as refuge' motif that runs through the Psalter (cf. Pss 14:6; 46:1; Creach 1996). In response to the affirmation of faith, the speaker then continues to expound God's protection in the light of the listener's response. Referring to God again as 'Most High' ties this exposition to the opening affirmations of both this psalm and Psalm 90. Here, the listener is assured that God prevents harm from befalling both individuals and their 'tent', the latter standing here for the family. The reason for this is that Yahweh has commanded his messengers to guard the listener, providing protection from a range of ills, all of which are associated with the motif of life as a journey (cf. Brueggemann 1984: 157); hence, each is associated with walking. These include mundane things such as striking one's foot on a stone, or the more deadly threat of treading on a lion or adder. These words are quoted by the devil when tempting Jesus (Matt. 4:5–6), though Jesus' response there makes clear that believers are not to seek out situations like this. The imagery is also fantastic in that one can imagine someone treading on a snake, but this is less likely with a lion. The point is that God's protection covers all possibilities, from the trivial to the highly threatening.

14–16. Though unmarked (NIV expands for clarification), there is a shift of speaker here as a divine oracle is cited. Here, God responds to the listener's affirmation of faith in verse 9a, promising both to deliver and protect the listener as one who knows his name, with the 'name' here standing for God's character. The assurance seems, however, to be given to the speaker, confirming the speaker's role in teaching about God this way. God's deliverance here implies a situation where the threat has become real, suggesting that the secure place is one reached amid threat, not being kept from it. This is confirmed by verse 15, which promises that God will respond when the listener cries out in times of distress. It is from distress that God rescues and glorifies the listener as one who trusts in him. Human life, as Psalm 90:10, makes clear is limited and can be full of trouble, but for the one who trusts in God it can also be satisfying (cf. Ps. 90:14) as God shows such a person his salvation.

Explanation

This psalm encourages readers to know that God delights to share with those committed to him, to save and protect in all life's circumstances. It knows there will be times of great challenge for all believers, and in the light of Psalm 90 it also knows that the mere fact of commitment to God is insufficient to claim that believers never experience pain or loss. But in a world where it is all too easy to focus on those points of difficulty, it encourages us to trust God and perhaps see the numerous ways he saves and protects us. We will not always appreciate it has happened, not least because we will not always know when we have trodden on something dangerous. What matters is putting our trust in God alone and discovering all he does for us. The encouragement of this psalm needs to be tempered by the wider testimony of the Psalter since so many complaint psalms wrestle with pain and uncertainty. But neither can we ignore the encouragement it offers as it insists God journeys with those who trust him (cf. Rom. 8:29–31).

PSALM 92

Translation

A melody. A song. For the Sabbath day

1It is good to give thanks to Yahweh,
  and to make music to your name, O Most High,
2to declare your kindness in the morning,
  and your faithfulness in the night-time,
3upon the ten string and the harp,
  with a tune on the lyre.
4For you have made me glad, O Yahweh, in your deeds,
  at the work of your hands I raise a shout.

5How great are your works, O Yahweh,
  how very deep are your thoughts.
6An obtuse person does not know,

and a fool cannot discern this:
7when the wicked sprout like grass,
and evildoers flourish,
it is so they can be destroyed for ever,
8but you, O Yahweh, are the exalted one for ever.

9For behold your enemies, O Yahweh,
for behold your enemies shall perish,
all evildoers shall be scattered.
10But you exalt my horn like a wild ox,
I am covered with fresh oil.
11My eyes look triumphantly on my enemies,
my ears hear the wicked who rise against me.

12The righteous shall sprout like a palm tree,
and shall grow great like a cedar in Lebanon.
13Planted in the house of Yahweh,
they flourish in the courts of our God,
14they still bear fruit in old age,
they are full of sap and fresh,
15to declare that Yahweh is upright,
my rock, and there is no injustice in him.

Notes on the text

7–8. MT accents these verses as tricolon plus monocolon, but they are read here as two bicola. Futato (2009: 300) shows how verse 8 is the poem's literary and theological centre, but this remains even without treating it as a monocolon.

10. Hebr. *ballōtî* is often emended on basis of Syr. to *ballōtanî*, resulting in 'I am anointed' (cf. *BHS*). But *bll* (usually 'mix') can be understood here as covering the poet (cf. NET), though it remains awkward. Compare Booij 1988a.

13. The verb *prḥ* appears in qal in verses 7, 12 and is rendered sprout, but the switch to hiph. here suggests a development; hence, 'flourish'.

16. With Q, read *'awlātâ*.

Form and structure

Psalm 92 develops the themes of Psalm 91 by exploring more clearly the identity of those who know Yahweh's protection as those committed to him and his worship. The poems are linked by referring to God as 'Most High' (Pss 91:1, 9; 92:1) as well as the references to both day and night and focus on God's name. But where Psalm 92 points to possible threats from which God protects (Ps. 91:5), here they are the times when the faithful celebrate God's kindness and faithfulness (v. 2). They can do so because they now look on to the downfall of their enemies (v. 11), reflecting the assurances given earlier (Ps. 91:7–8). Those who enjoy God's protection in Psalm 91 give thanks because they have come to appreciate the reality of his protection. In addition, the satisfied long life spoken of in Psalm 91:16 finds expression in those who remain fruitful even in old age in the temple courts (v. 13). Like Psalm 90, this psalm also has a unique title in its reference to the Sabbath Day. Mention of Sabbath here also ties the psalm to the creation motifs that emerge in Psalm 93 (cf. Fernandes 2013: 300), though it is the only time Sabbath is mentioned in the Psalter (cf. Sarna 1962: 159–165; Tucker 2019: 363–365).

The opening focus on giving thanks suggests that we can treat this as a thanksgiving psalm (so Seybold 1996: 365), though it also has a strongly didactic tone throughout. It should be observed that the psalm reflects on the goodness of thanksgiving rather than giving thanks, while language discussing the fool (v. 6) is also at home in wisdom traditions. Like Psalm 90, it transcends the usual form-critical divisions, merging praise and instruction, so integrating forms. It is perhaps better to think of it as a fusion of thanksgiving and instruction, transcending both to create something that is more than the sum of its parts.

Various analyses of the psalm are possible, especially as it repeats some key terms across the poem. But the most straightforward is to divide it into three stanzas, each opening with a core affirmation, with the second stanza containing two strophes:

1. Giving thanks (1–4)
2. Great works (5–11)
   a. The failures of the stupid (5–8)
   b. Triumph over the enemies (9–11)
3. The flourishing of the righteous (12–15)

Comment

Title: For 'A melody', see on Psalm 3. For 'A song', see on Psalm 65. 'For the Sabbath Day' is unique but suggests a liturgical role. The title opens possible allusions to Genesis 1:1 – 2:3 and the place of Sabbath in creation, anticipating the focus on creation as the place of Yahweh's rule in Psalms 93–100.

1–4. Giving thanks to Yahweh is often summoned (e.g. Ps. 105:1), but here it is the basis of reflection even as the stanza builds to reasons why the psalmist would also give thanks. From the outset the psalm integrates reflective teaching and praise. Thanksgiving, matched with music, is itself a good thing because it focuses on God's name. Both 'Yahweh' and 'Most High' appear here, so God's name here is not just the label by which he is known but a fundamental reflection on his character. That character is explored through the content of the thanksgiving in verse 2 and the musical mode by which it is expressed in verse 3. The thanksgiving focuses on Yahweh's 'kindness' (*ḥesed*) and 'faithfulness' (*'ĕmûnâ*), a combination found elsewhere in Psalms 36:5, 40:10 and 89:1. Mention of God's kindness may also allude to Exodus 34:6–8, where it is fundamental to his character, while God's faithfulness could also point to Deuteronomy 32:4. This verse is also alluded to in verse 15, making this reference an inclusio for the psalm. This thanksgiving happens in the morning (perhaps alluding to Gen. 1:3–5) and the night-time (rather than evening), perhaps as the time when one might particularly feel threats. But together, morning and night-time suggests continuous thanksgiving. The content of thanksgiving is expressed through music, with the three instruments mentioned here probably representing different sizes of harp (cf. Hossfeld and Zenger 2006: 438), perhaps roughly equivalent to bass, baritone and tenor. The appropriateness of such praise is not simply because of Yahweh's character in general. Rather, it is also the poet's own experience, having been gladdened through Yahweh's deeds and so crying out at the work of his hands.

5–8. The poet's own experience in verse 4 is a bridge between the first two stanzas. It provides a personal basis on which the goodness of thanksgiving can be understood and the foundation for the reflection on Yahweh's works in the second stanza (note the repetition of 'works' in vv. 4–5). The first strophe of this stanza opens with a declaration of awe and the greatness of Yahweh's works and the depths of his thoughts. This affirmation is explored through the inability of the obtuse (perhaps 'brutish', *ba'ar*) to know not only the general truth affirmed in verse 5, but also its outworking in those times when the wicked seemingly sprout like grass. That the wicked may sometimes appear dominant is not the final perspective, and the fool cannot understand this. Driven by the immediate, they fail to understand God's great works and deep thoughts, something preparatory to their final destruction. Creation has a built-in moral order, even if not all can see it (Brueggemann and Bellinger 2014: 400; cf. Ps. 73). Only Yahweh remains on high for ever, language that anticipates celebration of his reign in the coming psalms (McKelvey 2014: 55).

9–11. The evildoers mentioned in the first strophe provide the link to the second strophe here, while working out the implication of Yahweh's exalted status in the poet's own experience. As the poem's only tricolon (cf. 'Notes on the text' on vv. 7–8), verse 9 receives particular emphasis. The repetition of 'For behold your enemies' in the first two part lines makes them a point of focus, building to the affirmation that verse 9b closes, that the enemies perish (cf. Judg. 5:31; Ps. 1:6). The enemies are linked with the evildoers who are scattered, another mode of defeat for them. But this is not the poet's experience. Instead, the psalmist's 'horn' (a metaphor for power; cf. 1 Sam. 2:1, 10) has been exalted like a wild ox, a declaration of being given power matched by the presence of refreshing oil. The psalmist has not only been gladdened by Yahweh's works (v. 4). Rather, they have been applied so that the poet looks in triumph on his enemies, safe from those rising up with ill intent.

12–15. The closing stanza draws together the first two. Where the wicked sprout like grass but perish, the righteous flourish like abundant trees. The downfall of the wicked is contrasted with the flourishing of the righteous (cf. Patterson 2009), with the palm noted for its height and dates (cf. Song 7:8–9), while Lebanon's cedars are renowned for their stature (Isa. 2:13; Ezek. 17:23). Both trees were also represented in the temple (Longman 2014: 333). The comparison to the trees extends into verse 13 which imagines the righteous as trees planted in the sanctuary, the place where they flourish as they dwell with God. The arboreal imagery (along with fruitfulness) is connected to Psalm 1:3 (cf. Ps. 52; R. E. Wallace 2007: 27), suggesting that being in the temple is similar in its effect to a life shaped by Yahweh's instruction, while echoing Eden. Even in old age, the righteous continue to bear fruit and show evidence of vigour. The righteous thus have the satisfied old life from Psalm 91:16. This satisfied life finds its goal in declaring the uprightness of Yahweh as rock and as the one without injustice, effectively citing Deuteronomy 32:4. This is the fitting thanksgiving of which the opening stanza speaks.

Explanation

This poem carefully integrates thanksgiving with instruction, bringing these elements together as it closes the opening movement of Book 4 (cf. Tucker and Grant 2018: 366–368). It both affirms the goodness of praise and offers it, while facing some fundamental challenges. Here, it is affirmed that praise (esp. thanksgiving) is a vital element in addressing profound and challenging circumstances (also Tucker 2019). In the psalm itself, this is demonstrated in those times when the wicked appear to dominate, but it insists that there is a greater reality at work so that it is finally the righteous who flourish. Most importantly, it is thanksgiving that enables worshippers to see this. This thanksgiving comes both from personal experience and a deep engagement with Scripture, something particularly seen in the way Deuteronomy 32:4 shapes the poem. Those who know the truth declared there have a secure foundation for facing a challenging world, one that helps them understand personal experience. For the community who prayed the Psalter, it closes Psalms 90–92 by showing how the righteous can indeed flourish, even in times when this seems impossible. The uncertainties of exile with which Book 3 ended are not the final word. Likewise, the saints who suffer continue to sing it as they look to the point when God's reign is fully seen (Rev. 15:2–4). The goodness of praise, grounded in what God has revealed, continues to offer hope while anticipating the coming declaration of God's reign.

PSALM 93

Translation

1Yahweh reigns, he is robed with majesty,
  Yahweh is robed, he has girded himself with strength:
  indeed, the world is established, it shall not be moved.
2Your throne is established from of old,
  you are from everlasting.

3The rivers lifted up, O Yahweh,
  the rivers lifted up their voice,
  the rivers lift up their pounding.
4Greater than the sound of many waters,
  majestic breakers of the sea,
  Yahweh on high is majestic.

5Your testimonies are very trustworthy,
  holiness befits your house,
  O Yahweh for length of days.

Notes on the text

1. Hebr. *yhwh mālāk* could also be 'Yahweh is king' or 'Yahweh has become king'. Compare Psalm 47:8. See Mays 1993: 118. The verb is probably ingressive and durative, suggesting that Yahweh has always been king.

3. Hebr. *dokyām* is a hapax, probably derived from *dk'* (crush).

Form and structure

Psalm 93 commences a new segment of Book 4, which runs through to Psalm 100 (see Howard 1997: 166–183). Its opening affirmation of Yahweh's reign recurs in Psalms 97 and 99, though this motif is also fundamental to Psalm 94. Woven through these psalms are others that summon singing (Ps. 95) and, more specifically, a 'new song' (Pss 96, 98). As the collection progresses, the nations play an increasing role, so that their place at the head of Psalm 100 (itself echoing Ps. 98:4) is the collection's climax as Yahweh's 'faithfulness' (*'ĕmûnâ*) is celebrated. This faithfulness links this collection to Psalm 92, where it provided an inclusio for the poem, building on the reference there to Deuteronomy 32:4. More immediately, Psalm 93:5's reference to Yahweh's house complements the focus on the temple in Psalm 92:12–15. The place where the righteous flourish is adorned by Yahweh's holiness. Similarly, verse 4 notes that Yahweh is on high, linking this poem to Psalm 92:8.

The poem is a hymn of praise, though, as with Psalm 92, the opening is slightly unusual. Here, the change is that verse 1 is a declaration about Yahweh, whereas the rest of the poem addresses Yahweh in the light of the declaration. Rather than Yahweh's works in history, this poem focuses on creation, with language that engages directly with mythological views (cf. Waltke and Houston 2019: 133–134). There are forces within creation that can be understood as chaotic, especially the sea. Both sea and river were also regarded as deities in Ugarit, providing a threat to stability. But the reality of Yahweh's reign is such that creation remains secure (cf. Sylva 2012). Accordingly, he can be worshipped, and life can be built around his testimonies.

The poem can be analysed in three stanzas:

1. Declaring Yahweh's reign (1–2)
2. Evidence of Yahweh's reign (3–4)
3. Responding to Yahweh's reign (5)

Comment

1–2. The psalm opens with a ringing affirmation of Yahweh's kingship. This affirmation has been fundamental to theories of an enthronement festival in ancient Israel (see Mowinckel 1962, 1: 113–114; 2: 222; but cf. Weiser 1962: 617). Such a festival is not impossible, but the evidence is highly inferential. As such, it is better to read the phrase within the psalm and its literary context, especially as the whole of Psalms 93–100 explore the reality of Yahweh's reign (McKelvey 2014: 67). Yahweh's reign here stands against any other claim of rule, whether from human kings or forces of chaos that may seem to oppose him. Fundamentally, the line affirms that Yahweh is king, that he reigns and that he always will. Yahweh's reign is here celebrated through his regalia, all pointing to his royal status. Hence, he is robed with majesty, his garments declaring his power and status. As well as his robes, Yahweh is girded with strength. The image is military, pointing to Yahweh as the warrior ready for battle (cf. 1 Sam. 2:4; Ps. 65:6–7). Yahweh is equipped to overcome his foes. But the foes here are not human kings and nations. Rather, forces in creation seem to resist Yahweh (vv. 3–4). But, because of Yahweh's rule, the world is established and shall not be moved. In verse 1 there is a shift from general affirmation to praise addressed to Yahweh. This praise recognizes that Yahweh's reign is not a recent innovation. Rather, echoing the affirmation of Psalm 90:2, this psalm understands that Yahweh's throne is long established, consistent with his eternal nature. There is neither end nor viable rival to Yahweh's reign.

3–4. Yahweh's reign is clear, but in Israel's world there were obvious challengers. At Ugarit, the sea deity (Yam) is also known as 'River' (cf. Day 1985: 7, 35–37). The rivers, perhaps representing chaotic floodwaters that may otherwise be thought to oppose Yahweh, are here lifting their voices. Israel was used to floodwaters, as most of the rivers ran only in the wet season, and then often in floods that could not be controlled as they ran down the mountains towards the coastal plain or Jordan valley. But these waters are subservient to Yahweh. Indeed, in lifting their voices it is much more likely they now do so in praise (cf. Gillmayr-Bucher 2019: 380). Defeating the waters could also allude to Pharaoh's defeat (cf. Exod. 15:10–11), but creation remains firmly in view. Many waters can create a terrifying noise, as indeed might the majesty of powerful waves breaking in the sea, but, as in Psalm 29:10, Yahweh is above it all, reigning as the majestic one.

5. The closing verse introduces a new motif, though it is founded on the opening stanzas. Because Yahweh's reign is secure, his testimonies are certain. Yahweh's testimonies here are an important synonym for his Torah (cf. Pss 19:7; 78:5; 81:6; 119:88). As king, Yahweh directs his servants, and his directions are 'very trustworthy', something on which to build one's life. Those who depend on Yahweh's testimonies will worship him, and the temple is the focal point for that. As the focal point, holiness (that which is committed to Yahweh) befits his house. Since Yahweh is eternal, the holiness appropriate for that house is likewise something that endures.

Explanation

Yahweh, and only Yahweh, reigns. That is the good news of this psalm as it initiates a collection that explores this theme. Yahweh's reign is central to the message of the Psalter (Mays 1994a: 12–22), though it is important to note that it is never an abstract doctrine. Here, it is applied to the challenge posed by the exile and the uncertainty it provoked, which can be seen in Psalm 89. Psalms 90–92 established once more the value of trusting Yahweh, preparing for the affirmation of Yahweh's reign here. The exile was one threat to that reign, but not the only one. Just as Psalm 90 took Israel back to the Mosaic period to stress that Yahweh's purposes for them had deep roots, so also Psalm 93 goes back, this time to creation itself. In Israel's world, creation – and especially the waters – were a threat. But creation represents no threat to Yahweh because he rules over even the most threatening elements, ensuring that the world itself is stable. A stable world creates the possibility of a stable life, and that life is here shaped by worship in the temple and Yahweh's testimonies, his guidance for that life. Yahweh's reign provides stability in a world that may seem overwhelming. Jesus' announcement of the kingdom builds on this reality, demonstrating his authority over the waters (Mark 4:35–41) and providing the guidance around which life can be lived (John 14:15).

PSALM 94

Translation

1O God of vengeance, Yahweh,
  O God of vengeance, reveal yourself.
2Rise up, O judge of the earth,
  render the recompense due upon the proud.

3How long shall the wicked, O Yahweh,
  how long shall the wicked exult?
4They spout, they utter arrogance,
  all the evildoers boast.
5Your people, O Yahweh, they crush,
  and your heritage they oppress,
6widow and stranger they kill,
  and the orphan they murder.
7For they say, 'Yah does not see,
  and the God of Jacob does not perceive.'

8Perceive, O obtuse ones among my people,
  and fools, how long until you have insight?
9Does not the one who plants the ear hear,
  does not the one who forms the eye see?
10Does not the one who disciplines nations reprove,
  the one who teaches humans knowledge?
11Yahweh knows human thoughts,
  that they are vapid.

12O the blessedness of the one whom you educate, O Yah,
  whom you teach from your Torah,
13to give rest from days of trouble,
  until a pit is dug for the wicked.
14For Yahweh will not abandon his people,

his heritage he will not forsake.
[15]For judgement will return to righteousness,
and all the upright of heart will follow it.

[16]Who rises for me against the wicked,
who takes a stand for me against the evildoers?
[17]If Yahweh had not been my helper,
I would soon have dwelt in silence.
[18]When I thought, 'My foot is slipping,'
your kindness, O Yahweh, sustained me.
[19]When anxious thoughts are many within me,
your consolations gladden me.
[20]Can a throne of destruction be allied with you,
one that devises wrong by statute?
[21]They band together against the life of the righteous,
and condemn innocent blood.

[22]But Yahweh was my stronghold,
and my God my rock of refuge.
[23]He turns back their iniquity against them,
and annihilates them through their evil,
Yahweh our God annihilates them.

Notes on the text

1. Goldingay (2008: 73) reads *hôpiya'* as a pf., but an imp. is possible (GKC §53m) and supported by the later versions, though Gk treats it as a pf. If a pf., it is probably prec. (W-O §30.4.5.c–d).

10. It is possible that a word is missing at the end of this verse (so deClaissé-Walford et al. 2014: 711), but MT can be retained if understood as explanatory of the previous questions (similarly, Ross 2016: 93).

15. Two MSS (cf. Syr.) read *ṣaddîq* for *ṣedeq*. This results in an easier text and is proposed by *BHS*. But MT is intelligible and preferred as *lectio difficilior*.

17, 19. Hebr. *nepeš* here stands for the whole person.

23. The waw consecutive (for *wayyāšem*) occasionally refers to the future, and is so understood here (with Ross 2016: 95).

Form and structure

Following the joyous praise of Psalm 93, this poem may at first be a surprise. If Yahweh's reign is the key to understanding the challenges posed by the exile, we might have expected a further exposition of that reign here. That exposition will come, but first the challenge of the injustice presently experienced needs to be addressed. Yet Psalm 94 still has key elements that develop the theme of Yahweh's kingship (esp. his role in establishing justice in a world where that is lacking). It is because Yahweh is king that he can establish justice and be trusted as the one who does not abandon his people (vv. 14–15). Thematically, therefore, this psalm plays an important role in exploring Yahweh's reign (Howard 1997: 130). Although the links are less evident than in other places, there are also key lexical links with Psalm 93. First, Yahweh is clothed with 'majesty' (*gē'ût*) in Psalm 93:1, reflecting what is fitting for him. But here, he is to oppose the 'proud' (*gē'îm*; v. 2). The words are cognate, showing that Yahweh is to oppose that which claims what belongs to him alone. Second, the 'pounding' in Psalm 93:3 is probably derived from the root *dk'* (crush), which here describes the actions of the evildoers (v. 7). A close connection is also made with Psalm 92:6 as the 'obtuse' and 'fools' are again mentioned together (v. 8). These connections suggest that though this is a distinctive work within this part of the Psalter, it is intentionally placed here.

As with Psalms 90–92, it is difficult to align this poem with the standard categories. Focus on verses 1–7 and their appeal for Yahweh to act may lead to it being regarded as a complaint psalm (so, Howard 1997: 119). But verses 8–15 engage instead with wisdom traditions, calling an audience to come to a new point of understanding. Yet verses 16–23 seem also to offer thanksgiving for previous acts of deliverance, making thanksgiving the main genre (so, Dahood 1968: 346). There is also a shift between first-person sg. and pl. as well as addresses to Yahweh and an audience. But these variations are problematic only if we regard the main types as prescriptive. Yet, as Hossfeld and Zenger argue (2006: 453), with this psalm it is the mixture that is precisely the point. In this case, the variations allow readers to use it to express their uncertainty while being reminded of the reality of God's reign as something that all can trust (similarly, Tate 1990: 487).

The psalm can be analysed in three stanzas, each of which contains two strophes:

1. Complaint (1–7)
   a. Appeal to Yahweh (1–2)
   b. Description of the wicked (3–7)
2. Reflection (8–15)
   a. Appeal for understanding (8–11)
   b. Beatitude (12–15)
3. Thanksgiving (16–23)
   a. Testimony of rescue (16–19)
   b. Assurance (20–23)

Comment

1–2. The complaint's appeal opens by twice addressing Yahweh as the 'God of vengeance' before asking that he reveal himself. 'Vengeance' (*nĕqāmôt* is probably an abstract pl.; cf. *WHS* §7, Ps. 18:47, Seybold 1996: 372) here does not refer to revenge but rather appeals to Yahweh as the one who is to ensure justice (cf. Deut. 32:34–36). Yahweh is the one who acts for his people, and is therefore asked to show himself (lit. 'shine forth'; cf. Ps. 50:2). Yahweh is characterized by justice, and the appeal looks for him to demonstrate this. As judge of the earth (itself an expression of his kingship), Yahweh is asked to rise up and render the recompense due to the proud. The 'proud' are those who have not recognized Yahweh's reign (cf. Ps. 123:4) and who thus act against his people. The recompense they need to receive is one appropriate to their deeds (cf. Ps. 28:4) and hence is an act of justice.

3–7. The need for justice is explored in the second strophe. It opens with another doubled statement, this time asking how long the wicked should exult. The wicked here are the proud, and their exultation reflects their sense of self-determination, rejecting Yahweh's kingship. Yahweh needs to demonstrate his kingship by acting against them because they have rejected his reign for too long. Their actions are then catalogued in verses 4–7, with a focus on their speech in verses 4, 7 and direct actions against others in verses 5–6. The initial complaint about their speech is both that it is continuous, like the water coming from a spring, and that its content is arrogant and marked by boasting. Although their actions against others will be noted, their status as evildoers is founded on their self-serving speech, which works itself out in acts against others. Those whom they crush and afflict are Yahweh's people, his heritage. Those who belong to Yahweh are especially the vulnerable, of whom the widow, stranger and orphan are representative figures. This combination appears frequently as the objects of Yahweh's special concern, which is why Israel made special provision for them (e.g. Deut. 10:17–19; 14:28–29). But the evildoers kill these people, exploiting their vulnerability as those lacking others to defend them. The reason they do so is given in their closing speech, claiming that Yahweh does not see. This speech echoes the claim of the wicked in Psalm 10:4, 11 and the assertion of practical atheism in Psalm 73:11. Yahweh needs to show himself as the God of vengeance, the one who acts for the vulnerable, because this will disprove the claims of the evildoers.

8–11. A clear change in tone occurs here, marked by a shift of address. An audience is addressed rather than Yahweh as the psalm engages with wisdom motifs. It is joined to the previous stanza by repetition of the verb 'perceive' (*byn*). The imp. asks the audience to see immediately that the evildoers' claim is false. Those addressed could include the evildoers, asking them to re-evaluate their claim. The desire for Yahweh to act remains, but the timing of that remains Yahweh's right as king. Those addressed here are called 'obtuse' (*bō'ărîm*) and 'fools' (*kĕsîlîm*). This is not a general comment on their intellectual capacity so much as their ability to recognize how Yahweh acts. Their lack of insight is problematic, holding back the community's ability to appreciate Yahweh's kingship. Their limitations are highlighted through a series of rhetorical questions. Verses 9a and 10a have the same syntactical structure, with variations in 9b and 10b that prepare for the declaration in verse 11 about what Yahweh knows. The questions in verse 9 are linked by their reference to body parts associated with perception, the ear and eye. Yahweh is the one who has granted perception through them (cf. Prov. 20:12). He has given these to humans because he is the one who hears and sees. Claims that Yahweh does not perceive are thus fundamentally flawed. Neither can anyone claim ignorance of Yahweh's just requirements since he is the one who disciplines nations and instructs humankind. Accordingly, the psalmist can insist that Yahweh knows human thoughts. Those thoughts are 'vapid' (*hebel*, a key term for Qoheleth; e.g. Eccl. 1:2; 12:8), lacking substance. Perhaps the most insubstantial thought for this psalm is the idea that Yahweh will not perceive wickedness.

12–15. The second strophe contrasts the way of the evildoers with the way of blessedness (on the form, see on Ps. 1:1). This beatitude is unusual in that it is addressed to Yahweh, though it is no doubt intended to be overheard. The desirable life is not that of the evildoers. Rather, it is a life educated by God, taught from his instruction. There is a clear link here with Psalm 1:1–3, picking up on the allusion to that passage in Psalm 92:12–15. Yahweh instructs all humankind, but there is particular benefit in that teaching coming from his Torah since it provides rest in times of difficulty and awareness that the wicked will not finally triumph. The reason for this is that Yahweh will not abandon his people, who in a link back to verse 5, are also called his heritage. Evildoers can seem to triumph, but the blessed are taught by Yahweh and know this is not the final situation. Although verse 15 is difficult, it appears to suggest something similar, looking forward to the point when Yahweh's justice will be demonstrated for the righteous, leading the upright of heart (those who follow Yahweh) to follow righteousness in their life.

16–19. The third stanza introduces a further shift. Like the first stanza, it opens with a repetition, though this time through two questions about who works for the psalmist against the evildoers, tying these questions back to verse 4. The need for Yahweh to act against them is not simply abstract. Instead, it is rooted in the poet's experience. The questions are not left unanswered. Yahweh is the one who has acted for the poet, confirming the claims made in the second stanza. Yahweh was the one who helped, preventing the psalmist's death ('silence' here stands for death; cf. Ps. 115:17). Even when death seemed inevitable, it was Yahweh's 'kindness' (*ḥesed*) that sustained the poet. This testimony is then applied, providing reassurance in times of anxiety as Yahweh's consolations gladden the poet.

20–23. This reassurance provides a frame of reference for interpreting the actions of the powerful. This is initiated by a further rhetorical question (v. 20), the implication of which is that rulers who enact laws that perpetuate injustice are, by definition, acting against Yahweh's rule. They band together (cf. Ps. 2:1–3), acting against the righteous, but these are the ones for whom Yahweh brings justice. The poet's own experience provides the framework through which all can evaluate such people. Evildoers may band together to act contrary to Yahweh's reign, but Yahweh has continued to be the poet's stronghold and rock of refuge. Such language is fundamental to the Psalter (cf. Pss 9:9; 59:16; 144:2), but the key point here is made by way of testimony. The poet's experience provides evidence that such claims can be experienced while also linking this testimony to the declaration of Psalm 92:15. This provides reassurance that can be shared with the wider community, reassurance that receives emphasis here through being the poem's only tricolon. The actions of the evildoers will be turned back on them so that their own evil becomes the means by which Yahweh annihilates them. The dual mention of this annihilation links this closing affirmation to the dual address of verse 1, and so makes clear that this is an act of divine justice.

Explanation

Yahweh's reign is central to Book 4, especially Psalms 93–100. But what might it be like if Yahweh did not reign, or if his reign was so ineffective that it made no functional difference? This psalm addresses that fundamental question (Brueggemann and Bellinger 2014: 408), and so sits alongside poems such as Psalms 37 and 73 as they wrestle with the prosperity of the wicked, and Psalms 9–10, 14 and 53 as they engage with the issue of practical atheism. Its starting point is the reality that Yahweh reigns, and that it is right for the faithful to ask him to demonstrate that reign, demonstrating justice and care for the vulnerable. Signs of Yahweh's reign are evident among the nations and in personal experience, and failure to see this is simply being obtuse. The poet indeed reports personal experience of Yahweh's reign; so, although the world continues to experience those in power who believe they can act against Yahweh's reign, their power is limited. As the one who reigns, Yahweh will finally destroy them because of his commitment to the vulnerable. Although applied only to individuals, Paul's understanding of God as an avenger (1 Thess. 4:6) is consistent with this, while his statements about all humankind in Romans

1:18–22 also assume that God's instruction is revealed to all and that to live otherwise is rebellion against him. The psalm assumes that God's reign is something both present and future, something simultaneously claimed and prayed for, much as Jesus teaches us to pray 'may your kingdom come' (Luke 11:2).

PSALM 95

Translation

1Come, let us shout to Yahweh,
  let us cry out to the rock of our salvation.
2Let us approach his presence with thanksgiving,
  with songs let us cry out to him.
3For Yahweh is the great God,
  and a great king over all the gods.
4Because the depths of the earth are in his hand,
  and the mountain peaks are his,
5because the sea is his, yes, he made it,
  and his hands formed the dry land.

6Enter in, let us worship and bow down,
  let us kneel before Yahweh our maker.
7For he is our God,
  and we are the people of his pasture,
  and the flock of his hand.

O that today you would hear his voice!
8'Do not harden your heart like at Meribah,
  like the day at Massah in the wilderness.
9where your ancestors tested me,
  they tried me though they had seen my deeds.
10Forty years was I disgusted with that generation,
  and said, "They are a people erring of heart,
  and they do not know my ways."
11So I swore in my wrath,
  "They shall not enter into my rest."'

Notes on the text

4, 5. The opening *'ăšer* of each line is causal (*WHS* §468).
7d. With Howard (1997: 57), reading as optative.
11. The opening *'ăšer* is resultative (*WHS* §465).

Form and structure

Psalm 95 is closely linked to Psalm 94 through repetition of Yahweh as rock (Pss 94:22; 95:1; cf. Fernandes 2013: 337). Yahweh's role as creator is celebrated in both; though, where Psalm 94:9 points to this relative to humans, here it is applied to sea and dry land (v. 5) and humans (v. 6). Crucially, it develops the theme of Yahweh's reign (v. 3), joining this poem to Psalm 93 and anticipating Psalms 96:10; 97:1; 98:6; 99:1, 4. Yahweh's exaltation above the gods was hinted at in Psalm 93:3–4, but that is made explicit here (v. 3), anticipating 96:4; 97:7, 9. The image of his people as sheep (v. 7) anticipates Psalm 100:3 (cf. Tucker 2000). With its emphasis on worship and Yahweh's reign, Psalm 95 is thus at the theological heart of Psalms 93–100.

The psalm probably has its roots in temple worship, as is seen in its summons to enter Yahweh's presence (vv. 2, 6). In this context, it also engages with other texts. It joins Psalms 50:7–23 and 81:6–14 in including a section where God speaks (vv. 7d–11), including shared Pentateuchal references. But the most important Pentateuchal reference is probably Deuteronomy 32 (Howard 1997: 60–61), with which the psalm shares significant points of contact, including the reference to Yahweh as rock (Deut. 32:4; Ps. 95:1). Since Deuteronomy 32 was also significant for Psalm 92 (see 'Form and structure'), it is likely that this reference is also important for linking these two psalms.

Although often analysed in two stanzas, it is better to identify three, while treating the poem as a unit (cf. Girard 1981; W. S. Prinsloo 1995b: 397–406). The first stanza (vv. 1–5) is bounded by a wordplay between 'rock' (*ṣûr*) and 'formed' (*yāṣārû*), with the second introduced by a new imp. Verse 7d forms a bridge between the second and third stanzas but is best aligned with the third. This results in the following analysis:

1. Summons to worship (1–5)
2. Summons to bow down (6–7c)
3. Prophetic oracle (7d–11)

Comment

1–5. The psalm opens with an appeal to worshippers to join a noisy 'journey' (*lĕkû*) to worship Yahweh, possibly at a festival. Only in the second stanza are they called to enter in. The journey has a clear goal, that the community should sing praise to Yahweh as the rock of their salvation, the one who provides security in the face of threat. The verbs in verse 1 about calling out to Yahweh (*nĕrannĕnâ*, *nārîʿâ*) are chosen in part for their similar sound, though in context both suggest joyful shouts. The reason for this is that the community is to enter

Yahweh's presence, approaching him with thanksgiving. The testimony in Psalm 94:16–19 offers one example of thanksgiving, though these thanksgivings are expressed in song. Thanksgiving here is grounded in Yahweh's identity more than personal experience. Yahweh's status as greater than all the gods develops the reference to chaotic forces from Psalm 93:3, which alluded to some ANE deities. But here that is made explicit. Most ancient pantheons had a high god, and that status is here applied to Yahweh, making him the great king above all gods, and hence any human king. This does not yet deny the existence of these deities, though their idols will subsequently be declared to be worthless (Pss 96:5; 97:6). Nevertheless, the value of other deities is questioned by the statements about Yahweh in verses 4–5. Here, the psalm declares that all aspects of creation belong to Yahweh, even those otherwise thought to belong to other deities. The depths could refer to the underworld, a place that usually had its own deities; but here it belongs to Yahweh. Likewise, the mountain peaks were often regarded as a place belonging to gods (e.g. Baal on Mount Zaphon), but both depth and height belong to Yahweh. Rare terms are used here for both the depths and the heights, perhaps to avoid terms that may be more directly associated with such gods. So, whether viewed simply as geography or through the grid of mythology, all belongs to Yahweh. The same is true as we move from a horizontal to a vertical axis. The sea was also regarded as a god (Yam), but now is simply an expanse of water that belongs to Yahweh, as also the dry land. Although the verb 'he formed it' strictly refers only to the dry land, as the close to the affirmations here it covers each element of creation. All is Yahweh's because he formed it.

6–7c. A new imp. (*bō'û*) summons the congregation to enter in. The journey initiated at verse 1 is now to reach its goal by entering the sanctuary. Again, the imp. is followed by a string of three pl. cohorts. that describe what is to happen after entering. All three have the sense of prostrating oneself or bowing down, so are probably intended to emphasize this act (so, deClaissé-Walford et al. 2014: 715). Encountering Yahweh is the goal, and that encounter is expressed in a full-body engagement. Here, Yahweh is described as 'our maker', drawing a parallel between the community and the wider creation. Yahweh is the Creator and this is the reason to worship him, especially since other deities have been shown to have no functional authority. As with the first stanza, the cohorts. lead to a reason for worship introduced with 'for' (*kî*). Here the good news is that Yahweh, the creator of all who is greater than all, is 'our God'. The community belongs to the one who is the great king above all. The people can be likened to his sheep, drawing on the common motif of the king as shepherd of his people. As the sheep of his hand, they are held by the one who alone is king.

7d–11. If Yahweh is king, then the people's fundamental task is to listen to him; that is, to obey him. Yet this has not been the community's consistent practice, and the third stanza commences with a wish that they would heed Yahweh. The need to do so is reinforced by a prophetic speech that cites Yahweh, summoning them to make their worship real, and to do so immediately ('today'). They have come to encounter Yahweh, and he speaks to them, warning against hardening their hearts. 'Hardening' the heart alludes to Pharaoh's decision to reject Yahweh's purposes (Exod. 7:3). The people are not to do so, avoiding the pattern of earlier incidents at Meribah and Massah, where the people put Yahweh to the test. This could refer to events in Exodus 17:1–7 or Numbers 20:2–13, though the Exodus reference is perhaps primary (Tate 1990: 502). Given the allusions to Deuteronomy 32, Deuteronomy 33:8 may lie in the background too. The point is that the worshipping community is not to follow the way of their ancestors who tested Yahweh even though they had seen his works, presumably the exodus. That led to the forty years of wilderness wanderings, though by now we have also reached the response to the spies and the people not entering the land (Num. 14:33; Deut. 1:34), indicating that the divine speech uses the initial references to cover a range of rebellions. These are summed up in Yahweh's assessment of them as a people of erring heart who do not know his ways. It is not that they did not know them intellectually, but rather that they did not obey, so their knowledge had not changed their behaviour. Yahweh had sworn that the earlier generation would not enter his rest; that is, enter the land. But those who have come in worship have the chance to enter that rest – they simply need to choose to obey Yahweh.

Explanation

Psalm 95 builds on the image of God as rock from Psalm 94. As rock, he is the one who protects and saves his people. Yet, in Psalm 94 the issue was largely that Yahweh seemed not to have fulfilled his role as king, and so was summoned to arise and bring justice for his people. The poet there knew from experience that Yahweh could be trusted and that he would bring about justice. With this truth affirmed, Psalm 95 invites a congregation to come and worship Yahweh as king, offering full-throated shouts of praise. This praise can be offered because Yahweh alone is king, a position no other can hold. The people invited to worship are also invited to enter Yahweh's presence, on their knees and celebrating the wonders of his reign as the shepherd of his sheep, itself another royal image. Yet, rather than exuberant praise, what follows is a stunning warning, one so sharp that many liturgical traditions omit it, missing the poem's central message. Here, a prophetic voice declares a warning from Yahweh, warning of the tragic risks of failing to obey his voice, something illustrated through the rebellions at Massah and Meribah. Where Psalm 94 was concerned with Yahweh's perceived failure to act, Psalm 95 now challenges the congregation, warning them against following the pattern of their forebears. Rather, they needed to heed the voice of their shepherd (cf. John 10:1–6) since this was the way towards God's promised rest. For the wilderness generation, that rest had been entry to the land, something at risk for the community addressed here. Yet, there remained for them a fuller rest (see McKelvey 2014: 99), a rest that Hebrews 3 – 4 announces can still be found in Christ.

PSALM 96

Translation

1Sing to Yahweh a new song,
  sing to Yahweh all the earth.
2Sing to Yahweh, bless his name,
  announce his salvation from day to day.
3Recount his glory among the nations,
  his wonderful deeds among all the peoples.
4For Yahweh is great and greatly to be praised,
  awesome above all the gods.
5For all the gods of the peoples are worthless,
  but Yahweh made the heavens.
6Splendour and majesty are before him,
  strength and beauty are in his sanctuary.

7Ascribe to Yahweh, O clans of peoples,
  ascribe to Yahweh glory and strength.
8Ascribe to Yahweh the glory of his name,
  take up an offering and enter his courts.
9Worship Yahweh in holy attire,
  tremble before him all the earth.
10Say among the nations, 'Yahweh reigns!
  Indeed, the world is established, it shall not be shaken,
  he will judge the peoples with equity.'

11Let the heavens be glad and the earth exult,
  let the sea and all that fills it roar.
12Let the fields and everything in them exult,
  let the trees of the forest shout,
13before Yahweh because he comes,
  because he comes to judge the earth.
He will judge the world with righteousness,
  and the peoples in his faithfulness.

Notes on the text

5. Hebr. *'ĕlîlîm* can refer to idols but can also point to their lack of value. See Lynch 2021: 15–16.

9. Dahood (1968: 358) appeals to Ugar. evidence to propose an appearance of Yahweh, but the evidence is weak, depending on a hapax that is of uncertain meaning. Compare Tate 1990: 511.

10. See 'Notes on the text', Psalm 93:1

12. Hebr. *'āz* provides emphasis rather than sequence ('then'), so is untranslated; cf. Waltke and Houston 2019: 166.

13. Reading both instances of *bā'* as ptcs. rather than as pfs.

Form and structure

Psalm 95:2 summoned an audience to come before Yahweh with songs, so Psalm 96 now opens with three imperatives that direct an audience to sing Yahweh's praise (vv. 1–2). Yahweh's reign over all gods was declared there (Ps. 95:3), and that theme is extended here as we are reminded that he is awesome above all gods – the gods of the peoples are worthless whereas Yahweh is the Creator (v. 5). In describing the people as Yahweh's flock, Psalm 95:6–7c emphasized his kingship over them, but that theme is here extended to his reign among all the peoples. Moreover, Yahweh's reign over creation (Ps. 95:4–5) now becomes the foundation for creation itself exulting in Yahweh. Central to this is the declaration of his work as the judge of the earth (vv. 10, 13), with the announcement of his coming as judge responding to the plea for him to judge in Psalm 94:2, while citing Psalm 93:1's declaration about creation. The warning against disobeying Yahweh (Ps. 95:7d–11) is not developed directly here, unless (with McKelvey 2014: 107) this is implied in the note of Yahweh's coming as judge. As well as links with previous psalms, it also establishes key themes that run through Psalms 97–99, most obviously through the interchange between 'sing a new song' and 'Yahweh reigns' (cf. Tate 1990: 508–509; Howard 1997: 142–153).

The poem itself can be considered a hymn of praise in which all are called to worship Yahweh as king. Yahweh's reign is not limited to Israel but is over all peoples and over creation itself. The idol polemic in the psalm is similar to that found in Isaiah 40 – 55 (e.g. Isa. 44:23; 49:13). Kraus (1989: 251) believes it is therefore dependent on Isaiah 40 – 66, but it is more probable that both draw on similar traditions (A. A. Anderson 1972, 1: 681). Most of the psalm also reappears in 1 Chronicles 16:23–33 within the composite poem in 1 Chronicles 16:8–43. The Chronicler may present a reliable tradition about the psalm's use, though it is also possible that this is presented as a sample of the sort of text David used.

However, the festal report there would seem to represent how the poem would have been used in the sanctuary.

Although there is much debate about its structure, it seems reasonable to analyse the psalm in three stanzas, the first two marked by clusters of imperatives and the third by jussives. On that basis, the following is possible:

1. Sing a new song (1–6)
2. Ascribe glory (7–10)
3. Rejoicing at Yahweh's coming (11–13)

Comment

1–6. The psalm opens with a cluster of six imperatives. The first three are 'Sing' (vv. 1–2a), with a development of the singing in what follows. The first imp. indicates that praise is to be sung to Yahweh in the form of a new song. It is only in verse 1b that we learn that those to sing include 'all the earth', here meaning its inhabitants, though in verse 11 it refers to the earth itself. This is developed in verse 2, which, having repeated the command to sing to Yahweh, immediately extends this with the command to announce the good news of his salvation daily. The content of the new song is rooted in praise of Yahweh's identity, with the 'name' here representing his character. A further imp. directs that Yahweh's glory be announced daily among the nations. The background to this new song is probably found in a battle victory won by Yahweh that creates new freedom (Longman and Reid 1995: 45; cf. Ross 2016: 136). This good news is to be announced daily, so that the victory remains fresh in the community's experience. Both the glory and wonders recounted here are rooted in the victories he has won, including events like the crossing of the sea (Exod. 14:21–31). The poem shifts from imperatives to reasons for praise in verses 4–5 (cf. Tucker 2011: 127–128), with both verses commencing with *kî* (for). The reasons given here depend on Yahweh's identity as the true God in contrast to the gods of the nations. Yahweh is great and to be praised, awesome (or to be feared) more than all the gods. Unlike the gods of the peoples, Yahweh is the creator of the heavens, demonstrating that he acts, unlike the gods of the nations, which are worthless (cf. Ps. 97:7). Yahweh's glory is not restricted to the heavens but can be experienced in the sanctuary, where his splendour, majesty, strength and beauty are evident. Beuken (1992: 3) accordingly stresses Yahweh's transcendence and immanence. Those singing Yahweh's praise in the sanctuary evoke the wonders of creation, his authority over the nations and the reality that he alone is worthy of praise.

7–10. The second stanza echoes Psalm 29:1–2, the only other psalm to use 'ascribe' (*yhb*) when summoning praise. There, it was angelic beings who were addressed, but here it is humans. Just as three imperatives summon singing in verses 1–2, so also the imp. 'ascribe' occurs three times in verses 7–8. Here, the clans of the peoples (i.e. the extended families; cf. Gen. 12:3) are to ascribe to Yahweh glory and strength, both elements also ascribed to him in Psalm 29:1–2. The clans can do so because Yahweh's marvellous deeds have been recounted among them (v. 3). The third imp. directs them to ascribe the glory due to Yahweh's name, echoing the mention of Yahweh's name in verse 2, and again pointing to his character. A further imp. directs them to bring an offering to his courts (v. 8), indicating that the peoples are to come to the sanctuary. Not only does all the earth sing Yahweh's praise, but they join with the procession that came in worship in Psalm 95. All the earth is then to worship Yahweh, picking up on the statement from Psalm 95:6. There, the verb 'worship' occurs in a context that suggests kneeling, and that is likely present here too as the peoples are also told to tremble before him, a symbol of being overcome with awe in Yahweh's presence. The striking element is that the peoples are to worship Yahweh in holy attire – this is not something restricted to the priests or Israel alone, but metaphorically available to all. Further, the peoples who have come are now told to announce Yahweh's reign among the nations. This reign is evidenced by the security of creation (cf. Ps. 93:1). The world cannot be moved because Yahweh reigns. His reign also means that he will judge the world, though as a trustworthy monarch he does so with equity.

11–13. If Yahweh rules and so sustains creation, then it is also possible for creation itself to rejoice. Hence, the psalm now moves beyond the peoples to creation itself. Rather than imperatives, the poem shifts to jussives, expressing a desire for creation to rejoice in Yahweh. Mention of heavens and earth echoes Genesis 1:1, and thus covers the entire creation, with all of it to rejoice. Although the verb *rʿm* (roar) can be negative, the sea here is clearly roaring with praise, adding its voice to the full-throated shouts of Psalm 95:1–2. The sea's roaring is matched by the exulting of the fields since both include everything in them (thus life forms from Gen. 1). The fields are joined on dry land by the forest, whose trees also shout out (cf. Isa. 44:23). The exultant noise of creation is because Yahweh is coming to judge. The verb for 'judge' here (*špṭ*) differs from verse 10 (*dyn*), but they are probably used synonymously. Yahweh comes to judge the earth, meaning all creation. This is extended in verse 13b, which indicates that this includes the world and the peoples, though both will be judged fairly, with both 'righteousness' and 'faithfulness' explaining the 'equity' of verse 10. Injustice affects creation and humans, and all creation can anticipate joining in praise when Yahweh comes and brings justice.

Explanation

Psalm 96 responds to the challenge of Psalm 95 with a summons to praise Yahweh as the one who reigns. As Schaefer observes (2001: 239), it is praise that includes everyone and everything except the gods since they are 'mere nothings'. Rather than hardened hearts, this poem calls Israel to sing the new song of Yahweh's victory, announcing this as good news for all. This good news is to be taken up by the peoples, who now join in the worship of Yahweh while themselves proclaiming his reign. This reign is not restricted to Israel but is for all peoples. As Grant notes, this is a psalm replete with missional themes (Tucker and Grant 2018: 412), one which grasps that mission is from everywhere to everywhere. Indeed, all creation is finally to join this praise because all experience Yahweh's justice. This hope is reflected in the new song in Revelation 14:3, which also anticipates the coming of God's justice. The summons to praise here is also a challenge, asking us to consider how our praise proclaims good news to all while pointing to the coming of God's justice for all creation.

PSALM 97

Translation

1Yahweh reigns, let the earth rejoice,
  let the distant coastlands be glad.

2Cloud and thick darkness surround him,
  righteousness and justice are the foundation of his throne.
3Fire goes before him,
  and consumes his enemies all around.
4His lightning bolts light up the world,
  the earth sees and writhes.
5Mountains melt like wax at Yahweh's presence,
  at the presence of the lord of all the earth.
6The heavens declare his righteousness,
  and all the peoples see his glory.

7All who serve graven images are ashamed,
  those who boast in what is worthless –
  worship him all gods!
8Zion hears and is glad,
  and the daughters of Judah rejoice,
  because of your acts of judgement, O Yahweh.
9Because you, O Yahweh,

are Most High over all the earth,
you are highly exalted above all the gods.

10 O those who love Yahweh, hate evil!
The one who protects the lives of his godly ones
delivers them from the hand of the wicked.
11 Light is sown for the righteous,
and joy for the upright of heart.
12 Rejoice, O righteous, in Yahweh,
and give thanks for the remembrance of his holiness.

Notes on the text

1. See 'Notes on the text' on Psalm 93:1.

4–6. Rendering the qat. verbs here is difficult. They could refer to a particular point, perhaps then to a moment in a liturgy. But this is likely to indicate something that continues beyond this point, perhaps something understood to be always true, so they are treated here as constative, integrating the initiation and its continuation (W-O §30.2.3b).

7. The final clause could be 'all the gods worship him' since the form is the same. For a defence of this, see Howard 1997: 70.

10. NRSV follows common emendation, making Yahweh the subject of the initial ptc., but this is unnecessary.

Form and structure

Psalm 97 is closely linked to Psalm 96, with Howard (1997: 141–144) noting that these psalms share more terms in common than any others within 93–100. As is consistent within this group, Yahweh's kingship is again stressed (v. 1), joining Psalm 97 with Psalms 93, 99 in placing this element first, whereas it is centrally placed in Psalm 96:10. It joins Psalm 96:5 in declaring the gods of the nations as worthless (v. 7), pointing to Yahweh's superiority (Pss 96:4; 97:9). Psalm 96:13 looks towards the hope of the coming of Yahweh's justice, while here Yahweh's justice is foundational to his reign (v. 2), and his acts of judgement produce joy (v. 8). The theophanic language of Psalm 97:2 develops the hope of Yahweh's coming in Psalm 96:13, while anticipating similar language in Psalm 99:7, a poem that also emphasizes the importance of Yahweh's justice among the peoples. Connections with Psalm 98 are less developed, perhaps because of its role in joining with Psalm 96 through the 'new song', though once again Yahweh's kingship is central (Ps. 98:6), as is his coming to execute justice (Ps. 98).

As is typical of the kingship-of-Yahweh collection, we can consider this a psalm of descriptive praise (similarly, Estes 2019: 223). The nature of that description is not straightforward because of the challenge in understanding the verbs in verses 4–6. They could be rendered as simple pasts, suggesting that there was a particular point at which the events described happened, perhaps in a temple liturgy or a particular theophany. However, the numerous points of contact with Isaiah 40 – 66 (see Kraus 1989: 257–258), which uses similar language with a more eschatological flavour, suggests it speaks of ways in which Yahweh has previously appeared as a model for his ongoing comings to his people (cf. McKelvey 2014: 121). Alongside this theophanic language, Psalm 97 also joins Psalms 90–92 in drawing on a range of wisdom-like motifs, especially in its contrast between the righteous and the wicked (vv. 10–12), which has close associations here with Psalm 92's presentation of the flourishing of the righteous. With Psalm 96, this poem draws together key elements from across this collection.

The psalm can be analysed in four stanzas (cf. W. S. Prinsloo 1995c: 1090–1100), with the whole poem bounded by references to rejoicing (vv. 1, 12; Schaefer 2001: 240):

1. Affirmation of Yahweh's reign (1)
2. Expression of Yahweh's reign (2–6)
3. Effects of Yahweh's reign (7–9)
4. Implications for the righteous (10–12)

Comment

1. With Psalms 93 and 99, this poem opens with a ringing declaration of Yahweh's reign. It is because Yahweh is king that the world can rejoice. Human kings claimed power but brought loss and pain. Other nations may point to their gods, but they are 'worthless' (v. 7). Yahweh's reign has been shown to be the source of justice and security no other can provide. All the earth can rejoice, including remote coastlands, because Yahweh's reign is good news for all.

2–6. Yahweh's reign is described on the pattern of a theophany (cf. Ps. 18:9–15). As is typical for the OT, this echoes aspects of Yahweh's presentation at Sinai (refracted through Isa. 6 and Hab. 3), though the Sinai themes were already hinted at in the presentation of Yahweh as king at the crossing of the sea (Exod. 15:18; cf. Niehaus 1995: 85). Cloud was present at Sinai (Exod. 19:9; 24:15), as also was the thick darkness (Exod. 20:21; perhaps an impenetrable cloud). Yahweh's coming in the psalm points to Sinai as the place where his reign was evident, and where his giving of the Torah established his patterns of justice and righteousness. Those elements are now the foundations of his throne, the fundamental means by which his reign is expressed. Fire also marks Yahweh's presence at Sinai (Exod. 19:18; 24:17). Lightning bolts point to storm-god imagery, subverting any claims Baal may have (anticipating the third stanza) while also drawing on Sinai (Exod. 19:16). It is Yahweh's lightning bolts that light up the world, not Baal's. This motif reflects the polemic against the gods in this collection without requiring that it adapt Canaanite material (against Seybold 1996: 383). The description of Yahweh's coming has an impact on the world, and from verse 4b the stanza is concerned with describing this impact (cf. Ps. 77:16–18). Lightning bolts can be terrifying, and the earth writhing when they see them reflects a typical human response to the storm, which is extended to creation. Yahweh's presence is awe inspiring, and this is continued into verse 5a, which describes mountains melting like wax (perhaps reflecting a volcanic eruption), imagery that recurs in Micah 1:4 as it too describes a theophany. Such an awesome impact is to be expected because the one who comes is Lord of all the earth, and all creation, animate or inanimate, is ruled by Yahweh. Yet, though he is awe inspiring, Yahweh's reign is not a source of terror since the heavens declare his righteousness, allowing all peoples to see his glory (cf. Ps. 19:1) because of the order he brings. Yahweh's reign is over all creation, and this allows all peoples to see his glory as the one who is powerful and just.

7–9. Effects flow from Yahweh's reign. First, that all creation is under him means no other can meaningfully claim divine status, even if people speak of their gods. To trust these deities is folly, and so those who serve graven images should be ashamed since their praise has been directed to something worthless. The close of verse 7 probably directs such gods to worship Yahweh (though see 'Notes on the text'). By contrast, Zion (where Yahweh was worshipped) and those who worship Yahweh there rejoice because of his acts of justice. What other gods cannot do, Yahweh has done, providing evidence of his justice for his people. The echoes of the exodus suggest that it is the key example of this celebrated in this psalm, and this was celebrated at Zion. Yahweh's identity as the Most High (cf. Ps. 46:4) means his rule is not restricted to Zion but rather is over all the earth and over all the gods. Yahweh reigns, and nothing can challenge him.

10–12. The final strophe teases out some implications of Yahweh's reign, initially addressing readers directly. For those who love Yahweh there is the need to hate evil; that is, to reject all that is contrary to his righteousness. Alongside this can be confidence that Yahweh delivers his godly ones from the power of the wicked. This is developed through verse 11, with its imagery of light being sown for the righteous and joy for the upright of heart. The contrast between the righteous and the wicked reaches back to Psalm 1, though more immediately points to the image of the flourishing of the righteous in Psalm 92:12–15. Here that flourishing is demonstrated through the sowing of light and provision of joy. The image of light being sown is unusual; but if light is a symbol for salvation (e.g. Isa. 9:1), it can be understood as something sown, offering the possibility of a fruitful life. Accordingly, the psalm closes by summoning the righteous to rejoice in Yahweh as the one who reigns and to give thanks to him. Here, the 'remembrance of his holiness' stands for his name (cf. Exod. 3:15) but does so in a way that points specifically to his holiness as something to be recalled. The one who is entirely other and who comes in theophany is also the holy king who comes with justice and is to be remembered.

Explanation

Following the announcement of the coming of Yahweh's justice in Psalm 96, Psalm 97 declares that justice has come. Drawing on the language of Sinai, it declares to a world that believes others reign that Yahweh is the true king, and his reign is marked by justice. The transcendent God described in the theophany is the God who has come to his people, having come in the past and coming continually in liturgy that points to his great coming. Others might have claimed to be king, but only Yahweh has that right – not human kings or worthless idols that also claimed authority but in fact perpetuated injustice. That Yahweh reigns is a source of joy, something expressed spontaneously when his glory is seen, but also commanded, reminding us that joy is not necessarily the emotion humans automatically express. Since Yahweh's reign is founded on justice, those who love him are called also to hate evil such that our own lives point to the reality of Yahweh's reign. Jesus' announcement of the kingdom (Mark 1:14–15) is a summons to live in the light of this reality, with repentance that is not just turning from sin but towards the reality of God's reign, even in a world that so often denies it. In this, is joy.

PSALM 98

Translation

A melody.

[1]Sing to Yahweh a new song,
  for he has done marvellous things,
his right hand has won him victory,
  with his holy arm.
[2]Yahweh has made known his victory,
  in the sight of the nations

he has revealed his righteousness.
3 He has remembered his kindness and faithfulness
for the house of Israel,
all the ends of the earth have seen,
the victory of our God.

4 Shout to Yahweh all the earth,
be jubilant, exult and make melody.
5 Make melody to Yahweh on the lyre,
on the lyre and with the sound of melody,
6 with trumpets and the sound of the horn,
shout before Yahweh the king.

7 Let the sea and all that fills it thunder,
the world and those dwelling on it.
8 Let the rivers clap hands,
the mountains exult together,
9 before Yahweh because he comes to judge the earth.
He will judge the world with righteousness,
and the peoples with equity.

Notes on the text

1. The root *yšʿ* is commonly translated as 'save'. This is certainly valid, but it often reflects victory in battle (e.g. Exod. 14:30; 20:4; Judg. 7:7). Longman (1984) has demonstrated that the psalm reports the victory of Yahweh as the divine warrior, and this is therefore reflected in rendering the verb (and the cognate noun in vv. 2–3) in terms of victory (also Davidson 1998: 322). For the noun as 'victory', compare Psalms 35:3; 140:8; Kidner 1975, 1: 385.

9. Unlike Psalm 96:13, *bāʾ* is here a pf. rather than a ptc. (with Goldingay 2008: 123). However, this does not have to give it a past-time only reference. It is probably constative, integrating the initiation and continuation of Yahweh's coming with justice (W-O §30.2.3b).

Form and structure

As the first psalm with a title since Psalm 92 (in MT – all have titles in Gk), a short break is introduced after Psalm 97 (similarly, Tate 1990: 524). As the opening of Psalms 98–99 match those of Psalms 96–97, one function of the title is to enable these poems to be read as matched pairs within the collection of Psalms 93–100, creating an interplay between the motifs of 'new song' and Yahweh's reign. The psalm has other important connections with poems in the section, notably the emphasis on Yahweh's coming in justice (v. 8), further joining this poem to Psalms 96:13, 97:2 while anticipating the return of this motif in Psalm 99:4. Yahweh's relationship to the nations (vv. 2–3) and creation (vv. 7–8; cf. McCann 2023) also takes up themes from Psalms 96:3, 10, 97:4–6 while anticipating them in Psalm 99:1–3.

Although firmly set in its literary context, the poem also needs to be read in its own terms. It can best be described as a psalm that both summons and offers praise (Davis 1992b: 172). The more particular source of that praise is found in a victory won by Yahweh. Reference to Yahweh's 'right hand' and 'arm' echoes language of holy war (Longman 1984: 269; Davis 1992b: 172), so that the first stanza celebrates his victory as the divine warrior (cf. van Gemeren 2008: 733–737). The 'new song' is thus (as with Ps. 96) a response to the new thing Yahweh has done. What is important is that Yahweh's victory is not only good news for Israel; it is good news for all the earth, both peoples and creation itself. The shouts and music of verses 4–6 have a background in war; though, here (anticipating Ps. 100), they are focused on Yahweh's praise. This praise is not restricted to humans but is extended to creation itself because Yahweh's victory, combined with his role as king, creates the context where his justice is evident.

The psalm, which deploys a range of poetic techniques, can be analysed in three stanzas (cf. W. S. Prinsloo 1994c: 157–162), with the first two marked by initial imperatives and the third with jussives:

1. Sing: victory won (1–3)
2. Shout: Yahweh is king (4–6)
3. Let creation praise the judge (7–9)

Comment

Title: On 'A melody', see on Psalm 3. The title also links to references to melody within the poem (vv. 4–5; cf. Tucker and Grant 2018: 436). This is the only psalm where this is the whole title.

1–3. The identity of those addressed by the opening command to sing is not specified, though 'our God' (v. 3b) indicates it is Israel. It might have been a congregation, but the psalm now addresses all who encounter it, with the reasons for praise then developed through the balance of the stanza. The command repeats that of Psalm 96:1, directing that a new song be sung to Yahweh because of the wonders he has done (cf. Ps. 96:3; Hamilton [2021, 2: 199] also thinks it stands in contrast to the 'old' song from the crossing of the sea). Yahweh's wonders can be battle victories (Josh. 3:5) or miraculous deeds that overcome Israel's enemies (Exod. 3:20). Here, the victory is key, with mention of Yahweh's arm and right hand echoing the crossing of the sea (Exod. 15:6, 16; cf. Isa. 52:10). However, no one victory is mentioned, making the psalm suitable for use in multiple contexts. The central point is that a new experience of Yahweh's salvation is a call for a new song of praise. The victory not only speaks to Israel – it has also revealed Yahweh's righteousness before the nations. Here, Yahweh's righteousness is demonstrated by his covenant commitment to the house of Israel. In remembering his kindness and faithfulness to them, he has acted decisively for Israel because of his commitment to them, enabling all the ends of the earth to see the victory of Israel's God. The victory demonstrates that Yahweh is a God whose commitment to his people can be trusted, something now shown to all.

4–6. Where the first stanza was an imp. followed by reasons for praise, the second consists entirely of imperatives directing praise to Yahweh. The stanza is also bounded by the repeated command to 'shout' (vv. 4, 6). The reasons for praise were given in the first stanza so now it is a matter of filling out the form of the new song. Although the victory is won by Israel's God, this is good news for all the earth. Hence, all are to shout, exult, be jubilant and make melody. This praise is loud and exuberant. It was also profoundly musical, even if, drawing on this list of instruments, not all of it might be regarded as tuneful today. The lyre was a stringed instrument that would have been tuned and so would be appropriate for melodic praise. The trumpet was also part of Israel's worship (Num. 10:1–10) and was a metallic wind instrument. The 'horn' was made from a ram's horn and was associated with aspects of Israel's ritual life (e.g. Lev. 25:9), including perhaps the recognition of kings (1 Kgs 32 – 48). It was more commonly used in military settings (e.g. Josh. 6:4–20; Judg. 3:27) and was probably more noted for the noise it could make than any melody it could sound. However, within a song celebrating Yahweh's victory and kingship, it is an appropriate instrument with which to close the list here as the shout is specified as being directed to Yahweh, the king.

7–9. Because Yahweh's victory is good news for all creation, it is now summoned to join the praise, including forces that might traditionally have been thought to be hostile to Yahweh. The sea could be regarded as hostile to Yahweh (see Day 1985) but now it is part of creation, which uses whatever voice it has to praise him. Not only does the sea roar in praise, but so does all life in it, something matched by the fact that the world and all dwelling on it do the same. The rivers (which could be aligned with the sea) now join with the hills, personified in their praise (cf. Isa. 55:12–13). The reason they do so is because Yahweh comes to judge the earth (echoing Ps. 96:13). His judgement is an act of justice for all creation. The peoples are judged with equity, a key expression of his justice, but all creation experiences this justice. Israel's hope is not restricted to itself, but in Yahweh's reign provides an eschatological hope for all (cf. McKelvey 2014: 134–135).

Explanation

Although similar to Psalm 96, this poem brings its own distinctive emphases even as it joins with that psalm in calling for a new song of praise to Yahweh because of his victory. A new experience of Yahweh's saving power calls forth new expressions of praise. The victory celebrated here is placed within a larger pattern of Yahweh's work that points to him as king. The victory that invites the new song is a witness to Yahweh's faithfulness and kindness to both Israel and all the nations. That is, Yahweh's acts for Israel are not for them alone: they are for all nations. And if they are for all the nations, then they are for all creation. This is because his victorious coming is part of a pattern of his coming in judgement, a pattern in which he establishes his justice for all. Yahweh's coming to judge is good news because he is the king who can be trusted, the one who remembers his commitments. It is this reality that Paul presents as good news in Athens, pointing to the great victory that is Jesus' resurrection (Acts 17:31).

PSALM 99

Translation

1Yahweh reigns, let the peoples tremble,
  enthroned above the cherubim,
  let the earth quake.
2Yahweh is great in Zion,
  and exalted is he,
  over all the peoples.
3Let them give thanks for your name,
  great and awesome,
  holy is he.

4The strength of the king loves justice;
  you have established equity,
justice and righteousness in Jacob
  have you executed.
5Exalt Yahweh our God,
  bow down at his footstool,
  holy is he.

6Moses and Aaron were among his priests,
  Samuel among those who called on his name,
  those who called out to Yahweh, and he answered them.
7In the pillar of cloud he spoke to them,

they kept his testimonies and the statute he gave them.
8Yahweh our God, you answered them,
you were a forgiving God to them,
and an avenger of the things done to them.
9Exalt Yahweh our God,
and bow down at his holy mountain,
because Yahweh our God is holy.

Notes on the text

1. See 'Notes on the text' on Psalm 93:1; compare W. S. Prinsloo 1993a: 622–623. Apart from a possible emendation at Judges 5:4, *nwṭ* is a hapax, but the meaning is secure because of the parallelism and a possible Ugar. cognate.

2. A few MSS have 'gods' rather than 'peoples' (cf. Pss 95:3; 96:4; 97:9), but this is probably because scribes knowing those texts accidentally conformed them.

3. Hebr. *hûʾ* could be 'he' or 'it'. In the latter case, the reference is to Yahweh's name, but if the name stands for Yahweh anyway then 'he' is most appropriate.

4. The noun *ʿōz* could be revocalized as the adjective *ʿaz*. This would be a smoother text (cf. NET; Kraus 1989: 268), but MT is to be retained even though the colometry is uncertain.

8. With Waltke and Houston (2019: 231; cf. Seybold 1996: 390), reading the suff. as an objective gen.

Form and structure

Psalm 99 is paired with Psalm 98, continuing the 'new song'–'Yahweh reigns' pattern also seen in Psalms 96–97. As the final 'Yahweh reigns' psalm it also prepares for the close of this section of Book 4 (Pss 93–100) in the summons to universal worship in Psalm 100. It thus gathers key motifs from the whole of Psalms 93–98, emphasizing Yahweh's universal reign and the justice he brings. As this section's conclusion, it is also notable for the elements not continued. Where earlier poems in this section particularly stressed Yahweh's coming to bring justice (Pss 96:13; 98:9), here we see Yahweh as the one who has established equity (v. 4). Psalm 98 could see the victory won as evidence of Yahweh's coming justice, but here we see examples of how that justice is already present. Justice is the marker of Yahweh's reign, and provides the reason for all to worship him now (cf. McKelvey 2014: 154).

Though brief, the psalm poses numerous difficulties in translation, only some of which can be addressed in the 'Notes on the text'.

Nevertheless, the overall shape of the poem is clear, and it can (like Ps. 97) be classified as a psalm of descriptive praise. Yahweh's holiness is fundamental to this praise, with this motif occurring three times (vv. 3, 5, 9). The emphasis on Yahweh's holiness extends an element from Psalm 97:12, which is developed through Book 4 (cf. Pss 103:1; 105:3; 106:47). Yahweh is the king whom all are to worship, but he is also holy, unlike any other. He is the king who establishes justice and has no rival precisely because he is holy. For this reason, the psalm uses descriptive praise to encourage all to worship Yahweh.

Taking the declarations of holiness as marking the main divisions, we can analyse the psalm in three stanzas:

1. The exalted, holy king (1–3)
2. The just king (4–5)
3. The responding king (6–9)

Comment

1–3. As with Psalm 97:1, the declaration that Yahweh reigns has immediate implications. This time, it is that the peoples should tremble. Such trembling can be from dread (Exod. 15:14) or awe at an encounter with Yahweh (Hab. 3:16). Both themes are probably at work here. Encounters with a king were meant to inspire awe and the reality of Yahweh's reign should provoke this response among the peoples. The one who reigns was also enthroned above the cherubim, probably a reference to the cherubim on the Ark (1 Sam. 4:4; 2 Kgs 19:15; cf. Ps. 80:1) and in the temple's holy of holies (1 Kgs 6:23–28). Yahweh, as king, could be approached in the temple, the place of his throne. The presence of this king not only causes the peoples to tremble, but the earth also quakes. Yahweh is king and this generates awe among the peoples and even the earth itself. Yahweh's greatness can be seen in Zion; though it is not limited to it, because Yahweh's exaltation is over all the peoples. The markers of Yahweh's reign in the temple point to his universal reign. Hence, the hope is that the peoples will give thanks to Yahweh's name, recognizing that it is great and awesome because it represents his character. The crucial element of that character is that Yahweh is holy. The threefold repetition of this motif in the psalm echoes Isaiah 6:3, though the combination of Yahweh's exaltation and holiness also points to Isaiah 57:15. The paradox at the heart of this psalm, and indeed of biblical worship more generally, is that the one who is unapproachably holy is the one who is encountered in worship.

4–5. The text at this point is difficult, but the translation above attempts to make sense of MT. The assumption is that Yahweh is the king, but what does it mean that his 'strength' loves justice? We should probably assume that 'strength' here refers to Yahweh's holiness, that which defines his identity. Yahweh's identity as the holy king is expressed in his love of justice. From this point, the verse moves from a statement about Yahweh as king to address him directly, noting that his love of justice is expressed in things he has done (the 'you' is emphatic). Equity is something he has established, ensuring that all are treated with uprightness. This is described through the word pair 'justice and righteousness' as what he has executed in Jacob; that is, in all Israel and Judah. It is because Yahweh's commitment to justice can be demonstrated that he is to be worshipped. Verse 5 therefore opens with an imp., summoning the audience to exalt Yahweh. The verb here picks up the statement about Yahweh in verse 2, directing the audience to raise Yahweh high; that is, to exalt him in praise. The psalm does not say who is to do this, but the emphasis on Yahweh's universal reign throughout this collection may suggest that the peoples are being called to worship Yahweh, even though they know he is Israel's God. The act of worship, which involves prostrating oneself at Yahweh's footstool (probably the Ark), is contrasted with the exaltation of Yahweh. Yahweh is lifted high in praise, while the worshippers stoop low. In doing so, they encounter the holy one who is for all, not only Israel.

6–9. A brief historical element is now introduced, looking back to Moses and Aaron. Moses is a pivotal figure for Book 4 (see 'Form and structure', Ps. 90), while Aaron is also mentioned in Psalms 105:26; 106:16. The priestly status of both is emphasized. As high priest, this is common for Aaron (cf. Exod. 28), though not for Moses. But as a descendant of Levi (Exod. 6:16–30) he can be considered priestly. It should be noted that the OT sometimes refers to non-Levitical figures as priests (e.g. David's sons, 2 Sam. 8:18), so Moses may also be considered in this broader configuration of priesthood (cf. Exod. 24:6–7; Heb. 3:1–6). Samuel has a clearer priestly heritage (1 Chr. 6:16–30) and moves Israel's story on from the wilderness period to its life in the land, though pausing before there was a human king (cf. 1 Sam. 8:4–22). Samuel was among those who called on Yahweh, that is, who prayed to him, something also true of Moses and Aaron. These three are representative of a wider body who interceded before Yahweh and to whom Yahweh responded, though Samuel here also anticipates the return of Davidic psalms from Psalm 101 (R. E. Wallace 2007: 47). Verse 7 takes the means by which Yahweh responded back to the wilderness, specifically to Yahweh's discussions with Moses (Exod. 33:7), though this is representative of his wider speech. Their response to Yahweh's speech was that they kept his testimonies and the statute he gave. There are numerous incidents in the wilderness (and at Sinai) where this was not the case, but Moses and Samuel at least are generally positive examples; and, though Aaron's record is more mixed, he did at least initiate the tabernacle.

These experiences are then generalized in verse 8, which again points to Yahweh's answering them. The form that answering took was that he forgave them for their own failings and avenged them when others acted against them. In both cases, the emphasis is more on Yahweh's character as one who forgives (cf. Exod. 34:6) and avenges (cf. Ps. 94:1) than on particular actions. Responding to this, verse 9 takes up the language of verse 5. Again, those addressed by the imp. 'exalt' are undefined but would include all who see the truth of this description of Yahweh's character. The site of worship is Zion itself, Yahweh's holy mountain, rather than just his footstool, perhaps anticipating a larger group of worshippers. Yahweh's holiness remains pivotal, with the nature of his holiness demonstrated through the psalm.

Explanation

This psalm demonstrates the paradox of holiness as we find it in the Bible. Yahweh is utterly holy, utterly distinct and separate from us. But as king, Yahweh also involves himself in our experience, dealing with us to establish justice, allowing himself to be found by sinners, and forgiving even as he deals with sin. The paradox in the Bible is that Yahweh is distinct because he is holy, but Yahweh does not separate himself, because his holiness is for his people. Nowhere do we see this with greater clarity than in the cross of Jesus, though the psalm also points back to the exodus and the crossing of the sea (Exod. 15:1–18; cf. McCann 1996: 1075). On the cross, the holy God becomes one with us to die and so bring forgiveness. In Jesus, we see where this psalm, and indeed the whole of Psalms 93–99, leads. God's holiness remains a summons to worship, a summons to tremble before him, but also a declaration of hope because this holy God provides structures of justice and responds when his people call. God's reign means he is exalted, and the only proper response is to bow before him.

PSALM 100

Translation

A melody. For thanksgiving.

[1]Shout to Yahweh all the earth,
[2]serve Yahweh with jubilation,
  come in before him with rejoicing shouts.

[3]Know that Yahweh is God,

he is our maker, we are his,
his people and the sheep of his pasture.

4Enter his gates with thanksgiving,
his courts with praise,
give thanks to him, bless his name!
5Because Yahweh is good,
his kindness endures for ever,
his faithfulness to all generations.

Notes on the text

3. With Q and many MSS, read *wĕlô* rather than K *wĕlō'*. The widespread support for Q suggests that K is a corruption based on a scribe mishearing the text. As Hossfeld and Zenger note (2006: 492–493), the line is based on Psalm 95:6, further supporting Q. For a discussion of other options, see Howard 1997: 92–94.

Form and structure

With Psalm 100, the celebration of Yahweh's kingship that dominates Pss 93–99 reaches its conclusion (cf. W. S. Prinsloo 1991a: 972; Mays 1994b: 317–318). In particular, the focus on the universal worship of Yahweh (e.g. Pss 96:1, 7; 97:1; 98:3) finds its focus in the opening summons for all the earth to shout to Yahweh (Ps. 100:1). Given that the two 'new song' psalms (Pss 96, 98) are probably celebrations of the victory of the divine warrior (see 'Form and structure' for each), it is perhaps unsurprising that much of the language of worship that runs through the psalm can be traced back to earlier use in warfare (Firth 2021). For example, the 'shout' was a battle cry (e.g. Josh. 6:5, 10, 16, 20), but is now an acclamation of Yahweh in worship. Warfare cannot be separated entirely from worship, but it is a striking feature of the psalm that all such language is now transformed to be a celebration of Yahweh's reign. The strong focus on worship frames Psalms 95–99 within the collection, so that worship becomes the proper response to Yahweh's reign (McKelvey 2014: 165–166).

With Psalm 95, it probably has its roots in temple worship, especially as the references to the 'gates' and 'courts' refer to features of the temple, though these could also be features of a royal palace. The psalm is fundamentally a summons to worship. As such, it both directs an audience to offer praise to Yahweh and also explains why such praise is appropriate.

Setting aside Amzallag's (2014: 540–542) more complex analysis, since it requires the title to be part of the poem, the psalm can reasonably be analysed in two or three stanzas, depending on the placement of verse 3. Waltke (Waltke and Houston 2019: 255–256) defends the two-stanza structure (vv. 1–3, 4–5), but the three-stanza structure is slightly better in that it allows worship and reflection a stanza each before bringing these elements together in the third stanza (similarly, Maré 2000: 220–222; Auffret 2007), leading to the following analysis:

1. Worship in action (1–2)
2. Worship in reflection (3)
3. Worship in action and reflection (4–5)

Comment

Title: For 'A melody', see on Psalm 3. 'For thanksgiving' is a unique title for this psalm. 'Thanksgiving' could also refer to the thank offering (Lev. 7:12), but as verse 4 uses the same term with reference to praise, thanksgiving is more likely.

1–2. The stanza is dominated by imperatives that summon worship, with a focus on external actions. The shout of all the earth is, in context, a shout of acclamation of Yahweh as king, the one who has come and brought justice. As well as shouting out to Yahweh, all the earth is to serve him. The language of serving here evokes Psalm 2:11, and again points to Yahweh as the king who reigns, though the language of service also points to worship. Serving a conquering king may feel harsh, but the service here is marked by jubilation (cf. Esth. 8:16), an appropriate response to the experience of Yahweh's reign, though such joy could also be expressed in the festivals (Neh. 8:17). Having been summoned, the final imp. directs all to come in before Yahweh. As with Psalm 95:6, what is described is the act of entering the temple and so coming into Yahweh's presence. Yahweh is awe inspiring, but a people so summoned can come into his presence with shouts of rejoicing. Yahweh is the victorious and just king, and all the earth can experience joy in coming into his presence.

3. The second stanza also opens with an imp., but then transitions to reflections on why it is appropriate to worship Yahweh. Whereas the opening stanza was concerned with acts of worship, this stanza summons reflection on it. The only imp. here is 'know'. The audience needs to understand that there is a reason for this joyful worship. The block of Psalms 93–100 has consistently demonstrated that Yahweh is greater than all the gods (Pss 95:3; 96:4–5; 97:7), rendering the worship of other deities pointless. Here, the stanza modifies Psalm 95:7, so instead of stating that Yahweh is 'our God' (which might allow the possibility that others could worship their gods), now we are simply told that Yahweh is God (cf. 1 Kgs 18:39). The functional monotheism that dominates these psalms thus comes to its natural conclusion. By making this small shift, the repetition of the language from Psalm 95:7 (see 'Comment' there) indicates that all the earth has now been made Yahweh's people, the sheep of his pasture. This is a truth to be understood and experienced. The language of people as sheep is again royal, pointing to Yahweh as king, but clearly now king of all the earth, the one to whom all peoples now belong and become one people, Yahweh's people.

4–5. The third stanza opens with three more imperatives. The first summons people to enter the temple complex, going through its gates and passing through its courts, acts that were to be marked with thanksgiving and praise. The right to come before the one who is God provides a reason for such joy and thanksgiving. The possibility of being in Yahweh's presence leads to a pair of imperatives, directing worshippers to give thanks to Yahweh and bless his name. Thanksgiving is an act that recognizes the good Yahweh has done and responds to it, while blessing his name is a form of praise where words are a gift to Yahweh. As is common in Psalms, Yahweh's 'name' here stands for his character, though in the larger context of this segment of the Psalter it has a focus on his role as king. Verse 5 provides further reason for such praise, declaring that Yahweh is good and that his kindness endures for ever. This affirmation anticipates Psalms 106:1 and 107:1, which take up this declaration before it becomes the refrain of Book 5 (see Jenkins 2021: 174–179). It is also the first time in Book 4 that Yahweh has been declared to be good (R. E. Wallace 2007: 50). Yahweh is marked by his goodness and kindness, the latter of which is linked to his enduring faithfulness. It is also a key element of the two 'new song' psalms (96:13; 98:3), tying this psalm to the theme of Yahweh's victory and the justice he brings. Although each of goodness, kindness and faithfulness can be understood more generally, the context thus makes clear that we are to understand them specifically within the context of Yahweh's reign and as a key reason for praise.

Explanation

This poem is often used in Christian worship as an invitation to worship, summoning the congregation to praise, a practice with deep roots in synagogue and church. In that the psalm summons all the earth to worship Israel's God, this is entirely appropriate. Nevertheless, such use touches only on some of its significance. Transforming military language and rooting it only in worship, points to Yahweh's victory over the nations and their gods, a victory that now provides a reason for all to know and experience the truth that Yahweh is God. If Yahweh alone is God, then he is also the one who reigns as king, thus enabling this psalm to conclude the collection of Psalms 93–100. It is important to stress the radical nature of this good news. Coming after Book 3's close and the uncertainty there, this psalm again points to Yahweh's goodness, tying it to his kindness and faithfulness, themes that point back to his self-disclosure in Exodus 34:6–8. For a people who struggled with doubt, as is clear from the end of Book 3, Psalm 100 is thus a word of reassurance. Even if the form in which it is experienced may remain uncertain, Yahweh's goodness and covenant commitment remain. In pointing to Yahweh's victory, the psalm also asserts that the superpowers of every age and their claims have no enduring value. Read through the perspective of the cross, resurrection and ascension, we see both how God's reign continues to be demonstrated as good news for all and an anticipation of the point when all acknowledge the truth of this God who reigns. Such a life is to be marked by praise to the one who gives it (Brueggemann 1985: 65), with such praise always looking beyond ourselves (Mays 1994a: 68).

PSALM 101

Translation

Davidic. A melody.

[1]Of kindness and justice will I sing,
 to you, O Yahweh, will I make melody.
[2]I will ponder the way of integrity:
 When shall you come to me?
I will conduct myself in the integrity of my heart,
 within my house.
[3]I shall not set before my eyes,
 any worthless thing.
I hate the practice of deviance,
 it will not cling to me.
[4]A perverse heart shall depart from me,
 evil I will not know.

[5]One who slanders their neighbour in secret,
 shall I silence.
The haughty of eyes and arrogant of heart,
 I shall not endure.
[6]My eyes are on the faithful of the land,
 that they may dwell with me.
The one who walks in the way of integrity,
 shall minister to me.

[7]The one who shall not dwell in my house,
  is the one who practises deceit.
The one who speaks lies,
  shall not be established in my presence.
[8]Every morning,
  I will silence all the wicked of the land,
to cut off from the city of Yahweh,
  all workers of iniquity.

Notes on the text

5. With Q and many MSS, reading *melāšĕnî*. Rather than *ṣmt* I, 'ruin', the context points to speech, making *ṣmt* II, 'silence', more probable. Also, verse 8. Allen (2002: 7), points to Ugar. evidence supporting this, though he opts for *ṣmt* I in verse 8.

Form and structure

Psalm 101 commences a new segment of Book 4 that runs through to the end of the book, though it can be further subdivided (e.g. Pss 105–106 are a clear pair). Hence, where previous psalms in Book 4 generally have strong connections to those before them, in this case there are only the most general verbal connections, and these relate to common words (e.g. 'come', *bw'*) that occur in different contexts and are therefore not significant for interpretation. However, in this case one important difference probably matters most – this poem has the first Davidic title of Book 4. Book 3 ended with the community asking questions about the future of the Davidic covenant, while Book 4 to this point has focused on pointing to Yahweh's kingship, especially in Psalms 93–100. But by reintroducing David here, the book places David into the context of Yahweh's kingship. 2 Samuel 7 makes clear that Davidic kingship falls under Yahweh's reign, but the priority of Yahweh's kingship as the source of hope for Israel and the nations has been a central concern in Book 4. David is not forgotten, but it is Yahweh who remains the hope of the people.

Attention to its literary context is important for understanding the form of the poem. It is often classified as a royal psalm (e.g. McKelvey 2014: 170), though in fact it lacks any direct mention of the king, usually regarded as the defining mark of a royal psalm. Starbuck (1999: 118) notes that the speaker is clearly someone with authority, and so is content to assume that it is the prayer of a king of Judah, though without going further. Yet before we reach those elements in verse 8, it is worth noting that the poem draws on a range of wisdom motifs (see Botha 2016a: 5–7). These are particularly evident in the speaker's intent of pondering the 'way of integrity' while also living a life marked by integrity (v. 2). Such a commitment echoes the life desired in Psalm 15:2 (cf. Ps. 18:25, 30). Likewise, the determination to avoid all evil echoes Psalm 1's understanding of righteousness. In all, it seems best to read the psalm as a work infused with elements of wisdom, which provides a grid through which a king may operate under Yahweh's reign. This approach recognizes the royal elements, especially in verse 8, but understands them eschatologically, providing a pattern for how a future Davidic king may embody Yahweh's reign within his own (similarly, McCann 1996: 1081–1082), something far exceeding David's own life (Kidner 1975, 1: 391).

As with its form, there is much debate about the poem's structure. It repeats various terms but without clear evidence that these are structurally significant (though see Schaefer 2001: 248). However, a three-stanza analysis is possible, though without significant variations between them:

1. Reflections on the way of integrity (1–4)
2. Supporting the way of integrity (5–6)
3. Commitments about the wicked (7–8)

Comment

Title: For 'Davidic', see on Psalm 3. For 'A melody', see on Psalm 4.

1–4. The speaker commences with a vow to sing of kindness and justice. Although these can both be general virtues, they are given a particular focus here by the additional note that the speaker will make melody to Yahweh. Both kindness and justice are fundamental aspects of Yahweh's character and define his reign (Ps. 89:15) and should also define integrity before him (Mic. 6:8). In vowing to sing of these, the speaker commits to exalting Yahweh. This vow is linked in verse 2 to a further vow, to ponder the way of integrity. This way is a human response to Yahweh's kindness and justice, a desire to live out Yahweh's priorities. Such a commitment is worked out in Psalm 15, which explores this integrity in terms of positive commitments to other humans, though paradoxically this is what it means to dwell in Yahweh's presence. The commitment to ponder this way sees it as the way of flourishing. Nevertheless, this is not an end in itself, as verse 2b briefly adopts the shape of a complaint psalm, asking when Yahweh will come to the speaker. The point is that real change comes about only when Yahweh has come, perhaps in a mode of revelation (Booij 1988b). But the speaker remains oriented to Yahweh's purposes in the commitment to conduct marked by integrity. This commitment starts in the speaker's house. If we are correct in thinking of this as an idealized king, then the house would refer both to the palace and the royal dynasty (both senses of 'house' in 2 Sam. 7). Integrity is meant to be visible in the relationships in the house and the speaker's wider conduct. This is marked in verse 3 by the speaker avoiding practices inconsistent with integrity, echoing the position of Psalm 1:1–3, where the righteous avoid that which is inconsistent with Torah. Here, the speaker vows to avoid that which is worthless, not even bringing it into view, while hating all acts that seek some way around Yahweh's desires. Clever ways of claiming to meet Yahweh's purposes while avoiding their real intent (cf. Mark 7:9–13) are hated, and so cannot cling to the speaker. Likewise, verse 4 stresses that the speaker will be separate from a perverse heart and evil. The perverse heart refers to a mind and will contrary to the way of integrity and is here paralleled with evil, a summary term for anything inconsistent with integrity.

5–6. The second stanza develops the first but focuses on how the speaker relates to others. The way of integrity is not something only the speaker must follow. Rather, it must be enabled for others. This occurs through preventing that which hinders integrity in verse 5, and by promoting it in others. Secret slander of a neighbour is destructive of community, and so the speaker vows to silence (see 'Notes on the text') those who do so. Misdirected speech was also a key concern of Psalm 15:2–3, and its silencing here addresses the element that causes harm. In such a short statement, the means of doing so is not announced, but the point is that preventative action is consistent with the harm caused. The haughty and the arrogant could allude to Proverbs 16:5, where such a person is an abomination to Yahweh, and hence someone the speaker will not endure. Again, the impact of this is unstated, but the point is that the speaker needs a different set of priorities. Mention of 'eyes' links these verses, but now it is the direction of the speaker's eyes that matters. The speaker's eyes will be on the faithful; that is, the speaker will focus on them and their welfare. The goal of this is that they should dwell with the speaker, meaning the land is like the speaker's house, marked by integrity. Indeed, the motif of integrity closes the stanza, as those who share Yahweh's values minister to the speaker.

7–8. The third stanza provides further commitments about how the speaker will engage with the evil, again contrasting what is not to happen with what will. This develops themes from the previous stanza. Workers of deceit (cf. Ps. 52:2) are those whose practice is inconsistent with integrity. Since the speaker's house is to be marked by integrity, such people cannot be there. Public practice and private piety must align. The deceitful are paired with liars, returning to the theme of speech within the poem, and such people cannot be established since this would undermine the promotion of integrity, especially in the practice of justice. The problem of the wicked is to be addressed daily by silencing them (cf. 'Notes on the text'), ensuring that those whose speech undermines integrity are not established in the land, thus moving beyond the speaker's immediate context to the land as a whole. The goal of silencing the wicked, and hence preventing them from promoting speech that damages the well-being of the community, is to remove those who practise iniquity from the city of Yahweh. All that distracts from integrity is damaging to the community, and so the speaker vows that a context for flourishing will be established.

Explanation

Terrien (2003, 2: 694) notes that this psalm combines 'sapiential ethics with theocentric spirituality'. His summary catches well the tension within the psalm. In it, a Davidic voice is introduced into Book 4, though one that now has a more explicitly messianic focus. No Davidic king in Israel's past measured up to the standards of the royal vow here, but the short prayer in verse 2 makes clear that looking for a human to achieve all this misses the point. Yahweh's reign is fundamental, and Davidic kingship fits within it. Yahweh's kingship (taken up again in Ps. 102:2–17) is the means by which justice and kindness are truly established. But Yahweh also allows Davidic kings to have a role within it, and in that context an ideal king here commits himself to work out the principles of Yahweh's reign. That king, in dependence on Yahweh, vows to work for the way of integrity Yahweh desires, which is also expected of all worshippers (Ps. 15). Living the way of integrity and promoting that within society, this messianic king provides a pattern that points to Yahweh's reign. The psalm thus provides hope of the future Yahweh will bring, while at the same time calling the community to live in the light of that future – not to bring it about, but being a sign of what Yahweh will do. Within the Christian church, we may point similarly to the Lord's Supper as a point at which we commit ourselves to the values of the kingdom while pointing to Jesus 'until he comes' (1 Cor. 11:26).

PSALM 102

Translation

A prayer. For a needy one when faint and pouring out one's complaint before Yahweh.

1O Yahweh, hear my prayer,
  and let my cry for help come to you!
2Do not hide your face from me,

on the day of my distress,
incline your ear to me,
on the day I call answer me speedily!

3For my days end in smoke,
and my bones are scorched like a hearth,
4my heart is struck like grass and withers,
I forget to eat my food,
5due to the sound of my groaning,
my bones stick to my flesh.
6I am like a desert owl,
I have become like a small owl of the desolate places.
7I stay awake,
like a solitary bird on the roof.
8All day my enemies taunt me,
those who mock me swear oaths against me.
9For I eat ashes like food,
and mix my drink with tears,
10because of your indignation and wrath,
for you have lifted me up and thrown me away.
11My days stretch out like a shadow,
and I wither like the grass.

12But you, O Yahweh, are enthroned for ever,
and remembrance of you is from generation to generation.
13You will arise, you will have compassion for Zion,
for it is time to show her favour,
for the appointed time has come.
14For your servants take delight in her stones,
and have pity on her dust.
15The nations shall fear your name, O Yahweh,
and all the kings of the earth your glory.
16For Yahweh built up Zion,
and appeared in glory.
17He attended to the prayer of the destitute,
and did not despise their prayer.

18Let this be written for a subsequent generation,
that a people to be created may praise Yah:
19that he looked down from his holy height.
that Yahweh looked out from heaven to earth,
20to hear the groaning of the prisoner,
to release those doomed to death,
21to tell of the name of Yahweh in Zion,
and his praise in Jerusalem,

22when the peoples are gathered together,
and the kingdoms, to serve Yahweh.

23He has broken my strength on the way,
he has shortened my days.
24I say, 'My God, do not take me away in the midst of my days,
your years are in all the generations.'

25Of old you laid the foundations of the earth,
the heavens are the work of your hands.
26They could perish but you shall endure,
all of them could wear out like a garment,
you would replace them like clothing, and they would pass away.
27But you are the same,
your years have no end.
28Your servants' children shall settle down,
their descendants shall be established before you.

Notes on the text

6. The exact identification of the birds is uncertain, though both are unclean (Lev. 11:17–18).

23. With Q and many MSS, including 4QPs[b], reading *kōḥî*. Gk here revocalizes and produces a more explicitly messianic reading running through to verse 26, but MT is preferable, and the future hope still emerges in verses 27–28 (cf. Kidner 1975, 1: 395–396).

26. Understanding the verbs here as expressing potential (*WHS* §169).

Form and structure

Just as Psalm 101 represents a significant break from Psalms 93–100, so also Psalm 102 represents a break from Psalm 101, its links being much closer to Psalm 103 (see 'Form and structure' there). Nevertheless, Psalms 101–103 are bound together by the presence of titles, especially the fact that Psalms 101, 103 are Davidic. As such, the titles make it possible that Psalms 101–103 are to be read together, though Psalms 103–104 also have significant connections. But even within Psalms 101–103, the title here marks this poem as distinct, since every element apart from 'A prayer' is unique. As such, the suggestion that we should read this poem as 'Davidic' (see McKelvey 2014: 192–193; cf. Witt 2012: 591–596) seems to overread the evidence, though it is certainly placed within a Davidic frame (Hamilton 2021, 2: 217 prefers 'tinge'). If so, its anticipation of Yahweh's future for Zion joins with Psalm 101's hope of the messianic king, but from the posture of one in need while awaiting this future.

As with many poems in Book 4, this one draws on several elements, possibly various existing pieces (e.g. Briggs and Briggs 1907, 1: 317–318; see discussion in Allen 2002: 16–19), though our task is to interpret the poem we now have (cf. Mays 1994b: 323; and, as Goldingay [2008: 149] points out, we have no evidence of the parts existing separately). The first stanza (see below) is largely consistent with the individual complaints save for the vow of praise. But the second stanza draws on the motif of Yahweh's kingship and is focused on hope of restoration for Zion as the place where the peoples gather. Rather than the need of an individual, this element points to the need of a nation, and is perhaps the point where the Davidic frame is most important for interpretation. The individual and the corporate come together in the third stanza, which initially returns to the need of the petitioner before moving to corporate hope in its closing strophe. Although less marked than in Psalm 101, there are some hints of wisdom motifs in the comparisons that run through the first stanza (vv. 3–7, 11; Forti 2018: 72–79). Reflection on the motif of time (cf. deClaissé-Walford et al. 2014: 757) would also suggest a foundation in wisdom. The psalm has traditionally been regarded as one of the seven penitential psalms, though aside from mention of Yahweh's anger in verse 10, penitence is at best a marginal motif.

The psalm can be analysed in three stanzas of somewhat irregular length, each containing two strophes:

1. Complaint (1–11)
   a. Appeal to be heard (1–2)
   b. Descriptions of distress (3–11)
2. Hope (12–22)
   a. Future for Zion (12–17)
   b. A record for future generations (18–22)
3. Complaint and hope (23–28)
   a. Renewed appeal (22–23)
   b. Yahweh as source of hope (24–28)

Comment

Title: For 'A prayer', see on Psalm 17. The rest of the title specifies that this is a prayer that comes out of deep distress. The petitioner lacks the strength to change the circumstances. That the complaint is poured out before Yahweh could suggest a temple setting. Mention of 'complaint' here certainly describes the first stanza and parts of the third, but the term should be distinguished from the form-critical category (against R. E. Wallace 2007: 57).

1–2. The opening appeal (which integrates language from numerous psalms) links immediately to the title by asking that Yahweh hear the prayer, a point reinforced by the request that the poet's cry for help reach Yahweh. Mention of prayer anticipates the declaration in verse 17 about Yahweh's commitment to the prayers of the destitute, though at this point there is simply an appeal to be heard. Yahweh should hear; but, if he were to hide his face (thus, remove his presence), the prayer would not be heard. Hence, the psalmist asks not only that Yahweh not hide his face but that he incline his ear to hear the cry for help. Yahweh needs to be attentive to the petitioner and so answer speedily on the day of distress since this is the point where the need is most acute.

3–11. The distress is now described, making clear that the opening appeal is grounded in current need. The distress moves from a description of the poet's present experience (vv. 3–7), through description of the enemies (v. 8), and then the effects of Yahweh's anger (vv. 9–11). As the climax of the strophe, Yahweh's anger is understood as the primary cause of distress (see Broyles 1989: 210), though it is not separate from the actions of others. The importance of divine anger is why the appeal reaching Yahweh is so important. The description of the poet's experience in verses 4–7 draws on a range of similes, all of which point to the diminished quality of life being experienced, but without pointing to a cause. Hence, the psalmist's days are as transient as smoke, or as damaged as bones burnt in a fire. The poet's heart is struck down, diminishing mental acuity so that even food is forgotten. The results of this are visible in the loss of weight and vitality described in verse 5. Comparison with birds in verse 6 is more difficult because of uncertainty in their identification. However, the theme uniting them is their place in remote locations, pointing to separation from community, something matched by the description of sleeplessness (also linked to a bird) in verse 7. Life is diminished through social isolation. Initially, this may seem to be because of the enemies who taunt the psalmist, but from verse 10 it becomes clear that Yahweh's anger is the principal cause of the distress even if the enemies exacerbate it. The initial reference to the poor food and drink again points to a diminution of life quality, but verse 10 makes clear that Yahweh's anger is the prime cause. No reason for this anger is given, but the result is that the poet has been raised by Yahweh only to be thrown away. Instead of providing a flourishing life, the psalmist expresses divine abandonment, with the result that life itself now fades like a shadow as the sun sets, or grass that is withered by the heat of the day. The subsequent linking of the poet's experience with that of Zion may be the language of exile (Davidson 1998: 332), something consistent with the desire for national restoration that emerges through the poem.

12–17. Human transience is immediately contrasted with divine eternality, echoing Psalm 90 (cf. Wilson 1985a: 218). The petitioner's life feels like it is fading, but Yahweh is eternal. This point is emphasized through direct address to Yahweh which notes that he is enthroned for ever, and that every generation receives remembrance of him it can pass on. The direct address continues in verse 13. The opening verbs here have a future orientation, anticipating a point when Yahweh will arise and have compassion for Zion (perhaps echoing Exod. 34:6), suggesting that Zion's present experience matches that of the petitioner in the first stanza. When that future comes, Yahweh will be gracious to Zion because its moment has come. Yahweh's compassion is matched by the pleasure his servants take even in the city's stones and the pity they have for its dust. The concern with the nations that marked Psalms 93–100 is again evident here as the nations fear Yahweh's name, something defined further through kings responding to his glory. In this case, both 'name' and 'glory' point to Yahweh's essential character, though 'glory' also serves as a catchword with verse 16. The verbs in verses 16–17 can be understood as having a past reference, but it is more likely that they are effectively a projection to the future mentioned in verse 14 (see *WHS* §162). Yahweh will have compassion on Zion and, when he does, he will rebuild Zion (cf. Ps. 51:18) because his glory is seen; likewise, attending to the prayer of the destitute.

18–22. Because Yahweh will act, the petitioner asks for a written record to be created that will enable future generations to praise Yahweh (cf. Ps. 22:30–31). Yahweh's coming compassion on Zion is not simply an experience for one generation. Rather, each moment of Yahweh's action for his people is to be recorded, providing an ongoing basis for praise. The content of the record of Yahweh's action runs through verses 19–22. In essence, it is an extended reflection on verses 16–17, describing how Yahweh looked down from heaven and acted, responding to the cries of those in need, even when those cries had no actual words. Hence, the first people assisted are the prisoners mentioned in verse 20, where Yahweh's response was to note their groans (not even formed cries for help) and then release them from the threat of death. Those released would then recount Yahweh's name in Zion, itself an act of praise that anticipates the praise of the future generation. This praise is not restricted to Zion, because verse 15 anticipated the gathering of the peoples, and their worship is now mentioned in verse 22. The record for the future generations is thus that Yahweh remembers his commitment to the needy and to Zion, so that their praise is linked to that of the nations. This record helps the people in future to have a grasp on history that understands Yahweh's faithfulness as the basis for praise.

23–24. The hope of the second stanza is real, but it is not yet the petitioner's experience. It provides reason for continued prayer even though, as was clear from the first stanza, the poet sees Yahweh as the source of the current distress. Yahweh's anger (v. 10) is not mentioned this time, though it lies in the background, explaining why Yahweh has acted against the psalmist, though without providing a reason for the anger. All the psalmist knows is that life has been greatly reduced, cut off in its prime. Hence, the psalmist reports a prayer asking not to be taken away when life should be full of vitality. The basis of this is the contrast between human transience and divine eternality introduced in verses 11–12, so that the bridge between the first two stanzas provides the entry point to the third. For the petitioner, Yahweh has brought about the distress, and Yahweh is the one who needs to resolve it.

25–28. That Yahweh endures provides continuing hope. The poet notes this by first pointing back to creation (anticipating Ps. 104) as Yahweh's work. The world, earth and heavens standing for all creation, exists only because Yahweh made it. The poet can imagine a point where heavens and earth will perish, wearing out like an old garment. But because creation belongs to Yahweh, he can change it like another piece of clothing even if part of it wears out. Everything in creation can change, but Yahweh remains the same, without end in time. This provides ongoing hope, not only for the petitioner, but also for later descendants who worship Yahweh. Within the context of the psalm, we remember that this includes the nations as they join with Zion and the afflicted in knowing that Yahweh, the eternal God, is the source of hope.

Explanation

Psalm 101 provides a wisdom-inflected hope through a messianic voice. Psalm 102 also provides a wisdom-inflected hope, but this time through the integration of the prayer of a suffering individual with the hope of the nation. The wisdom element here is particularly focused on the issue of time, linking it with Psalm 90, contrasting human transience with Yahweh's eternality. Like Psalms 22, 69, this poem closely integrates the need of the individual with the need of the nation, with both finding their hope in Yahweh's eternality. All else may be subject to change, but Yahweh endures and, as the gracious and compassionate God, he continues to provide hope for all. No other offers this hope and, as the one who reigns, Yahweh also has the ability to bring about his purposes. So important is this that the psalm can even anticipate the future moment when Yahweh's latest act of grace will provide a foundation for praise. Hebrews 1:10–12 (cf. 13:8) takes up verses 25–26, applying them to Jesus (using the variations in Gk, see 'Notes on the text'; cf. Church 2016: 277–285). The writer stresses that Jesus is the one who endures, treating him for the purpose of the writer's argument in the same way as the psalm presents Yahweh, stressing that Jesus remains the source of hope for believers, both as individuals and as part of the wider body of believers.

PSALM 103

Translation

Davidic.

1Bless Yahweh, O my whole self,
and all within me, his holy name.
2Bless Yahweh, O my whole self,
and do not forget all his benefits.
3The one who pardons all your iniquities,
who heals all your diseases,
4who redeems your life from the pit,
who crowns you with kindness and compassion,
5who satisfies your life with good,
who renews your strength like an eagle's.

6Yahweh does righteous acts,
and deeds of justice for all the oppressed.
7He made his ways known to Moses,
his deeds to the children of Israel.
8Yahweh is merciful and gracious,
slow to anger and abounding in kindness.

9He will not contend for ever,
nor will he remain angry for ever.
10He does not deal with us according to our sins,
nor does he repay us as our iniquities warrant.
11For as heaven is high over the earth,
his kindness has prevailed over those who fear him.
12For as far as the east is from the west,
thus far has he removed our transgressions from us.
13As a father has compassion on his children,
Yahweh has compassion on those who fear him,
14for he knows how we were formed,
he remembers that we were dust.
15A human being's days are like grass,
blossoming like the flowers of the field.
16When the wind passes over it, we are nothing,
and their place does not recognize them.
17But the kindness of Yahweh is from eternity,
and to eternity for those who fear him,
his righteousness is for the children's children,
18to those who keep his covenant,
and to those who remember to do his precepts.

[19]Yahweh has established his throne in heaven,
  and his kingdom rules over all.

[20]Bless Yahweh, O his messengers,
  powerful ones who do his word,
  hearkening to the sound of his word.
[21]Bless Yahweh, all his hosts,
  his servants who do his will.
[22]Bless Yahweh, all his works,
  in all places of his rule.
Bless Yahweh, O my whole self.

Notes on the text

1. Hebr. *nephеš* is traditionally 'soul' but here stands for the whole person. On use of the term, see Janowski 2013: 189–198.

5. Hebr. *'edyēk* (lit. 'your ornaments') is difficult. Gk's *epithymia* ('desires'; so NIV, NRSV) is unlikely. With Allen (2002: 26), assume metathesis of the last two consonants, resulting in *'ōdēkî*, 'your existence'. This is consistent with the Aramaizing suffixes in verses 3–5.

Form and structure

The psalm has clear links with both Psalms 102 and 104. Along with Psalm 102, it reflects on the transience of human life in comparison with divine eternity, with both psalms comparing human life to dried grass (Pss 102:12, 25–27; 103:17; cf. Schaefer 2001: 253). Both are also concerned with the hope of the descendants of the current generation (Pss 102:28; 103:17). In both cases, it is Yahweh's reign as king that provides the hope (Pss 102:12; 103:19), tying these psalms to the main themes of Book 4. Psalms 103 and 104 are the only psalms to employ the idiom of self-address, 'Bless Yahweh, O my whole self', with both poems using this phrase as an inclusio, creating a strong link between them. The inclusion of a 'Davidic' title links this poem to Psalm 101 as part of the Davidic frame for Psalms 101–103 (though Fiß [2019: 27–28] suggests the group is Pss 102–106).

The psalm can be classified in various ways – it could be a thanksgiving or a hymn, but includes elements of both in an integrated composition (cf. Allen 2002: 27 or Estes 2019: 262 when trying to use Westermann's [1981] model of descriptive and declarative praise). It is perhaps sufficient to accept that it is a psalm of praise that draws on a range of praise traditions (cf. Foster 2008; Cook 2018: 115), and that while distinctions between them can analytically be helpful, we should not expect poets to be constricted by them. The use of various elements from Israel's praise tradition is consistent with the psalm's allusion to a range of other OT texts. Although it can be read as a coherent unit without awareness of this feature, readers attuned to its references to other texts gain a richer appreciation of its theology, especially its emphasis on grace (cf. Fiß 2019: 26–28).

The psalm employs twenty-two verses, typical of an acrostic, and although it is not one, it may hint at the completeness of that pattern by its frequent use of 'all' (see Hossfeld and Zenger 2011: 37). The movement between individual thanksgiving and hymn provides a clear division for the main units of the psalm, though it should always be noted that the opening and closing lines provide an inclusio for the whole (similarly, Futato 2009: 326). On that basis, the psalm can be analysed in three stanzas (for more complex analyses, see T. M. Willis 1991; Fokkelman 2007), with three strophes in the second:

1. Individual thanksgiving (1–5)
2. Hymn of praise (6–19)
   a. Past grace (6–8)
   b. Ongoing grace (9–18)
   c. Yahweh's reign (19)
3. Call for universal praise (20–22)

Comment

Title: For 'Davidic', see on Psalm 3.

1–5. The psalm opens with a self-exhortation, mirrored in Psalm 104:1. 'Bless' is often rendered 'praise' (e.g. NIV), and there is significant overlap between these terms. But 'bless' (*brk*), perhaps deriving from the act of bending the knee, can be distinguished by noting that to bless Yahweh is a specific form of praise in which human words are a gift to God. The self-exhortation indicates that the poet's whole being is involved in blessing both Yahweh and his holy name, though these terms are here largely equivalent. The self-exhortation is resumed in verse 2 and contrasted with the possibility of forgetting Yahweh's benefits. These benefits are then outlined in verses 3–5 through a series of participial phrases, each of which points to the particular benefit as something Yahweh characteristically does for the psalm's audience (*WHS* §213), for which the poet is the initial example. Although the language of grace is withheld until verses 6–8, Yahweh's benefits can all be classified as examples of grace. The series begins by noting that Yahweh forgives iniquity. The root *slḥ* (forgive) is used only with Yahweh as the subject, making it his gift (cf. Exod. 34:9). Forgiveness is a form of restoration, and this is thus followed by the note that Yahweh heals all the audience's diseases. It is possible that the psalmist has been healed after forgiveness (Brown 1995: 150; cf. Longman 2014: 356), especially as subsequent references to Yahweh's actions can be understood in these terms. However, if there is an element of personal testimony here, it remains undeveloped. Nevertheless, forgiveness and healing are both elements of restoration, and the other acts of Yahweh in verses 4–5 can also be understood restoratively. Redemption of one's life from the pit also implies a time approaching death from which someone has been redeemed, though redemption is not simply restoration to life. Rather, the audience is told that Yahweh crowns them with kindness and compassion, language that prepares for the fuller reference to Exodus 34:6–8 in verses 6–8. Yahweh's restoration is not miserly but rather treats humans with immense respect. Hence, he satisfies the audience with good in its life, so that its youth is renewed like an eagle's (cf. Isa. 40:30–31). This last statement breaks the run of ptcs., and so closes the opening stanza.

6–8. The second stanza also opens with a ptc., making the verse a bridge with the opening stanza (O'Kennedy 1998: 111), which stresses Yahweh's characteristic activity as one who enacts righteous deeds. Yahweh's righteousness is not merely a characteristic to be asserted but something seen in what he does in his acts of justice for the oppressed. The language evokes the exodus, as becomes clear in the statement of verse 7 that he made his ways known to Moses and deeds to the Israelites. These deeds become the basis for praise in Psalm 105:1, but here reflect on the exodus, climaxing in verse 8 with a near citation of the grace formula of Exodus 34:6–8 (on this allusion, see Cook 2018: 122–124). This allusion points back to a time when Israel was forgiven and restored following the incident of the golden calf (Exod. 32). The benefits that the congregation joins the poet in not forgetting are rooted in Israel's story, creating a consciousness of the past that parallels the anticipation of the future in Psalm 102:18–22.

9–18. Having pointed to the definitive moment of Yahweh's grace, the second strophe explores ways in which Yahweh's grace continues to be worked out, again engaging with a range of texts. Verses 9–10 note that Yahweh does not continually contend or maintain his wrath indefinitely. Here, the psalmist joins with the audience addressed, so that the themes are applied to both. That Yahweh does not deal with us as our sins merit or repay us for our iniquity is again a statement of grace, providing a different angle to the simpler statement of verse 3 on forgiveness. How Yahweh does not deal with us according to our sin is then developed through two spatial images in verses 11–12. The first looks up, seeing in the height of the heavens an analogy for the greatness of Yahweh's 'kindness' (*ḥesed*). The second looks on an east–west axis, using the distance between east and west to explain how far Yahweh has removed transgression, introducing a third key term for sin into the poem. Ancient audiences would not have known that there is no limit to how far one can travel east and never go west (unlike north–south), so the image here is more in terms of the distance between sunrise and sunset. But this too, like the distance between earth and the heavens, is a distance beyond imagining. A further metaphor is introduced in verses 13–14, comparing Yahweh to a caring father. The opening of verse 13 is similar in sound to the opening of verse 12, linking these metaphors. Yahweh's compassion on those who fear him is like that of a father on his children, a theme Jesus picks up in the parable of the prodigal (Luke 15:20). Yahweh's children here are those who fear him, those who have committed themselves to him. His compassion is based on his deep knowledge of the human condition. This is rooted in an allusion to Genesis 2:7, which points to Yahweh's forming the man from the dust, and thus that humans are limited. This motif is developed in a different metaphor in verses 15–16, which compares humans to grass that flowers in the field but wilts when the wind blows on it, echoing Isaiah 40:6–8. Humans flourish for a period, but are ultimately transient, and the place we have lived ultimately knows us no more (perhaps echoing Eccl. 1:11; 3:16–22). By contrast, Yahweh's kindness endures, and is therefore always available to those who fear him, continuing through the generations. His kindness is for those who keep his covenant, something evidenced through the carrying out of his precepts in the Torah. The strophe demonstrates that Yahweh's grace was not simply something expressed in the time of Moses, but rather remains as something expressed to Yahweh's people.

19. This verse acts as a hinge between the second and third stanzas (similarly, Waltke and Houston 2019: 271), linking his activity in the heavens and on earth because Yahweh reigns as king. The experiences described to this point are experienced on earth, but occur because of the reality of Yahweh's reign.

20–22. Having expressed both personal and national reasons for praise, the final stanza calls for universal praise in all of creation, including those residing in the heavens. Because Yahweh rules over all creation, he must be praised by all. None are excluded from this pattern, though heavenly beings are the primary reference here. Hence, we have the repeated imp. 'bless' (*brk*) commencing each of these verses as well as the final line. Although the figures referred to in verses 20–21 are clearly angelic, there is no reason to think that the same is true of verse 22. There is probably some development in verses 20–21 in terms of the heavenly figures called to bless Yahweh, though perhaps the more important point is that if angels who hear Yahweh's word are called to bless him, then an even stronger case exists for humans to do so. Even Yahweh's works, which are presumably inanimate, are called to bless Yahweh, joining with the angelic beings. All are called to join in a symphony of praise. Hence, the psalm closes with a final self-exhortation – if all else should bless Yahweh, then the poet can do no less.

Explanation

This psalm is a masterpiece of praise. It reminds us that praise moves in outward circles from the experience of the individual to the covenant community and finally to the breadth of creation, for God is to be praised by all creation. It reminds us that in God's grace, love and compassion, we have reason for such praise because God is prepared to forgive (on forgiveness in Psalms, see van Gemeren 2008: 760–762). This praise has content, even if we cannot locate that content in the experience of a particular individual. We see this in how this psalm incorporates elements from creation, exodus and redemption. It would be anachronistic to speak of this psalm as a meditation on the canon, but it is certainly moving in that direction while continuing to develop the themes of human transience and divine eternality. In doing so, it provides an initial answer to the plea of Psalm 102 and the needs of the exilic community, while preparing us once more to reflect on creation in Psalm 104, and all within the context of God's kingship. Moreover, in the act of praise we also see the need to be conformed to what God desires, to be those who fear him. We do so not out of terror but out of joy at the grace we have received (cf. Rom. 5:1–5).

PSALM 104

Translation

1Bless Yahweh, O my whole self!

Yahweh my God, you are very great,
  you clothe yourself with splendour and majesty,
2covering yourself with light like a cloak,
  stretching out the heavens like a curtain,
3the one who lays the beams of his lofty abode on the waters,
  making the clouds his chariot,
  the one who walks on the wings of the wind,
4making winds his messengers,
  his attendants a flaming fire.

5He set the earth upon its foundations,
  it shall never totter.
6You covered it with the watery deep like a garment,
  waters stood above the mountains.
7They fled from your rebuke,
  they hurried away from the sound of your thunder.
8The mountains rose, the valleys sank,

to the place you have founded for them.
9You set a boundary they shall not pass,
they shall not return to cover the earth.

10The one who sends the springs in the valleys,
they flow between the hills;
11they supply water for every beast of the field;
the wild asses quench their thirst.
12The birds of the heavens dwell beside them,
they give out their voice from the foliage.
13The one who waters the mountains from his lofty abode,
from the fruit of your work the earth is satisfied.
14The one who causes the grass to sprout for the livestock,
and plants for humans to tend,
to bring forth food from the earth,
15and wine to gladden the human heart,
to make faces shine with oil,
and food to sustain the human heart.
16The trees of Yahweh are satisfied,
the cedars of Lebanon that he planted,
17where birds set their nest,
the stork has its nest in the juniper trees.
18The lofty hills are for the ibexes,
the cliffs are a refuge for the rock badgers.

19He made the moon for appointed times,
the sun knows its setting time.
20You bring on darkness and it is night,
all the creatures of the forest prowl in it.
21The young lions roar for their prey,
seeking their food from God.
22The sun shines, they hide away,
and lie down in their dens.
23Humans come out for their work,
to their service until evening.

24How many are your works, O Yahweh,
you have made them all with skill,
the earth is full of your possessions.
25There is the sea, vast and wide of measure,
where creatures without number move,
living things small and great.
26There the ships move,
Leviathan whom you formed to frolic in it!
27All of them look to you,

to provide their food at the right time.
28 You give it to them, they gather up,
you open your hands, they are satisfied with good.
29 You hide your face, they are dismayed,
you take back their breath, they expire,
and return to their dust.
30 You send your Spirit, they are created,
you renew the face of the ground.

31 May the glory of Yahweh endure for ever,
may Yahweh rejoice in his works,
32 the one who looks at the earth and it quakes,
touches the mountains and they smoke.

33 I will sing to Yahweh throughout my life,
I will make melody to my God for ever.

34 May my reflection be pleasing to him,
I will rejoice in Yahweh!
35 Let sinners be removed from the earth,
and let the wicked be no more.

Bless Yahweh O my whole self!
Hallelujah!

Notes on the text

1, 35. See 'Notes on the text' on Psalm 103:1.

4. Gk (cf. Heb. 1:7) resolves the ambiguous language here differently, making 'his messengers winds' (ESV). For defence of this rendering, see Collins 2022: 517.

5. Several traditions continue the ptcs. here, but a finite verb works well to initiate the stanza.

8. The subject of the verbs here is unclear, and it could refer to the waters from the previous two verses.

12. Hebr. *'ŏpā'yim* is a hapax.

23. Hebr. *'ādām* is a collective sg. (*WHS* §2), so represented here by the pl.

35c. Gk places the last line as the start of the next psalm, a plausible location as it would create an inclusio for the poem. However, its place in MT also creates a bridge to Psalm 105.

Form and structure

There is a clear link with Psalm 104 as both share the inclusio 'Bless Yahweh, O my whole self!' since this phrase does not occur outside these two psalms. However, the connections go further than this. Psalm 103 anticipated a point where all Yahweh's works in creation blessed him, while this poem reflects on the wonder of creation in the praise of God. Nevertheless, there is an important balance struck between Psalm 103:10, with its emphasis on Yahweh's forgiveness, and Psalm 104:35, which asks for the removal of the wicked (cf. Vesco 2006, 2: 953). Yahweh is gracious and forgives, but there remain those resistant to his purposes since Yahweh's kindness finds its focus on those who fear him (Ps. 103:17–18), so the prayer here considers those who do not fear Yahweh. Both psalms point to Yahweh's eternality (Pss 103:17; 104:31) and his care for creation, with a move from a prime focus on humans in Psalm 103 to the wider creation in Psalm 104, though humans continue to have an important role here (vv. 14–15, 23). Both psalms also engage with Genesis 1 – 2 as a key intertext, a further element joining them. Psalm 104 also prepares for Psalms 105–106 and their focus on Israel's story (cf. Wilson 1985a: 218–219; Creach 1996: 99; Coetzee 2008), though without mentioning Israel. Psalm 103 pointed to the exodus, a motif not evident here as we go back more strongly to the creation accounts, but doing so then prepares for the move to Psalm 105 with the closing 'Hallelujah' anticipating Psalm 105:45 and its use as an inclusio in Psalm 106. The strongly sapiential tone through the poem (cf. Kraus 1989: 301) also creates a wisdom frame for reading Israel's history.

Along with its connections to Genesis 1 – 2 (and Job 38 – 39, see Frevel 2013; Gottlieb 2016), considerable discussion has focused on possible parallels with Akhenaten's Hymn to Aten (esp. vv. 20–26) and some Ugar. material (for the literature, see Allen 2002: 39–43; McKelvey 2014: 208–209). However, as Walton (1989: 163–165; cf. Craigie 1983: 76–79) points out, there is no evidence for the distribution of Akhenaten's hymn, so at most we can see points of similarity arising from the genre of a hymn praising creation, a pattern also true for the Ugar. parallels. It is more important therefore to analyse the psalm in its own terms. In doing so, we can note that the form is often rather choppy, moving between ptcs. and finite verbs, a feature the translation here attempts to replicate. In reflecting on creation, the poem also moves between reflections on the initial creation (e.g. v. 5) and Yahweh's work in sustaining it (e.g. v. 30). Consideration of creation here is reflection on both its origin and sustenance, with Yahweh responsible for both. Yahweh does so because he is presented throughout as king, even though the word is not used (R. E. Wallace 2007: 70–71).

The uneven style of the poem means there is no clear agreement on its structure beyond noting the inclusio, perhaps offering an 'impressionistic contemplation' (Schaefer 2001: 257), one driven by its joyful response to creation (cf. Gnuse 2021: 6). Other analyses are possible, but the following is used here:

1. Praise exhortation (1a)
2. Yahweh's greatness (1b–4)
3. Creation's security (5–9)
4. Yahweh's provision (10–18)
5. Creation's orderliness (19–23)
6. Creation's breadth (24–30)
7. Creation and eternity (31–35a)
   a. Yahweh's glory (31–32)
   b. Poet's vow (33)
   c. Pleasing Yahweh (34–35a)
8. Praise exhortation (35b)

Comment

1a. Unlike Psalm 103, the exhortation to praise here stands outside the psalm's main movement. Nevertheless, it again represents both the poet's own self-address, and one that readers of the psalm are to make their own, illustrating the point that the psalms are self-involving language that commits readers to certain acts (see Wenham 2013: 31–35). The poet's whole being is to bless Yahweh (see 'Comment' on Ps. 103:1), as also is the audience's.

2–4. Committed to blessing Yahweh, the poet first explores Yahweh's greatness, establishing the foundation for all that follows through theophanic language (cf. Ps. 18:7–15). Where the opening exhortation spoke about Yahweh, Yahweh is now addressed in a personal relationship as 'my God'. This could make the speaker a significant figure in Israel, though the probable exilic background makes it unlikely to be the king. The language can also be understood as stressing the covenant relationship with Yahweh as something experienced by all. Yahweh's greatness is a key theme in Book 4 (Pss 95:3; 96:4; 99:2), always in the context of Yahweh's kingship. Splendour and majesty were also associated with Yahweh's kingship in Psalm 96:6, so although the term 'king' is not used, the declarations still portray Yahweh as king, the one whose greatness is inherent and so clothed in royal raiment. The clothing metaphor is continued into verse 2a, which introduces a set of ptcs., describing Yahweh as covered with light like a cloak. The image perhaps points to the sun as something that cannot be looked at directly, and the same is true of Yahweh's role in stretching out the heavens like a curtain. The heavens, in all their splendour, exist because Yahweh has arranged them. Yahweh's authority over creation is also evident in the establishment of his abode on the waters and his use of clouds and wind for transport. The language evokes patterns associated with Baal in Canaanite traditions, but whatever might have been claimed for Baal actually belongs to Yahweh, who is the true lord. Moreover, Yahweh is no remote king, for he retains means of connecting with creation, even if he cannot be fully understood or observed from earth.

5–9. The second stanza turns from Yahweh's greatness to the security of creation. Unlike many societies around Israel where the gods could not control creation, Yahweh can do so because he founded it. Indeed, he has done it so well that it cannot totter. Creation is secure because Yahweh has made it that way. Alluding to Genesis 1:2, the psalm points to the initial covering of the earth with the primeval waters so that even the mountains were covered by the waters. These waters were regarded as a threat by others, but here they fled from Yahweh's rebuke, running in alarm from his thunder (cf. Ps. 29:3). Accordingly, the mountains and hills rose, and the valleys sank to the places Yahweh had appointed for them, while (perhaps alluding to Gen. 1:9–10) the waters were set in a place they could not pass (cf. Clifford 1981). The earth remains a secure habitat because all is under Yahweh's control, not powerful forces resistant to him.

10–18. Creation is secure, but this is not the end of Yahweh's involvement. Rather, he continues to provide for all life within it. Fundamental to this is the provision of drink and food. The springs Yahweh causes to gush and run as streams in the valleys provide drink for every beast in the field. The reference here is to wild animals rather than livestock, something made clear by the reference to wild asses, non-domesticated donkeys, whose thirst is sated. The birds also dwell with the wild animals, singing from the foliage. All this happens because Yahweh is the one who provides water on the mountains, with the result that the earth is satisfied from the fruit of his deeds. The stanza shifts to consider Yahweh's sustenance of agriculture in verses 14–15, providing the pasture needed for livestock to graze and the plants needed for humans to cultivate. Reflecting the man's role in the garden (Gen. 2:15), humans are to tend the plants provided and so receive their food. There is thus an important difference between humans and animals in that Yahweh provides directly for the animals, while for humans he provides the resources needed. Yahweh's provision for humans is not stinting. Through the work he gives, humans receive both their essential food and also goods that improve the experience of life, through wine that gladdens the heart and oil that could be applied as a form of cosmetic to make the face shine and increase comfort. All this is bounded by reference to food, without which such luxury goods would have no meaning. Although some distinction is thus made for humans, it is a distinction that still fits within Yahweh's provision for the whole creation, so that verses 16–17 point to Yahweh's provision for all the trees, including

Lebanon's magnificent cedars, a place where birds make their nests even as the stork makes its home in the juniper, which, by comparison, is only a small shrub. All are supported by Yahweh, and through them he provides all the birds with a home. That provision also includes animals that live in what humans might consider inaccessible places, including ibexes on the high hills and rock badgers on the cliffs. Yahweh provides food and shelter for all creation, the king who is involved in his creation.

19–23. As well as providing sustenance for all, Yahweh has also structured creation, giving it a recognizable chronological order. Genesis 1:14–15 lies behind the reference to the moon and sun, though where they are the greater and lesser light there, here they are named. In addition, where both mark the seasons there, here it is only the moon, though the sun's role in knowing the time for setting is consistent with the role both have in defining day and night there. The important point for the psalm is that the role of sun and moon in marking off day and night also points to creation's own order, an order Yahweh continues to sustain. In this setting, different creatures can emerge at night, creeping around the forest. The young lions also look for their food around dusk, but even these fierce animals depend on God for their food before returning to their dens when dawn's light flashes across the sky. Dawn then marks the point where humans come out to do their work, labouring until evening, when the cycle begins again. Creation's orderliness creates a context for all life to flourish, and this too is Yahweh's provision.

24–30. The poet now turns from describing Yahweh's role in creation to reflections on it, addressing Yahweh directly for the first time since verses 1, 6. Although various categories of life have been described in the poem, they are only a sample of all that Yahweh has made. The poet looks at the diversity of all Yahweh has created, marvelling at the skill with which it has been made. 'Skill' (*ḥokmâ*) is often rendered 'wisdom', but the parallel here is probably with the craftsmen who constructed the tabernacle, both of whom were filled with Yahweh's Spirit and *ḥokmâ*, there referring to their skill (Exod. 31:1–5; cf. 1 Kgs 7:13–14). Proverbs 3:19–20 also draws on this language for creation, though there the translation 'wisdom' is more appropriate. Both elements of the word's meaning are probably present here, so one might paraphrase that Yahweh has made everything with skill and wisdom, and all in it belongs to him. The sea is a particular example of this, a point that again stands against the Canaanite tradition, where the sea was a god. Here, it is something immeasurably large and filled with countless creatures large and small, all moving about. Ships traverse the sea, a further reference to human activity, though one that again stresses that humans work only within the scope Yahweh provides. The sea is often portrayed in threatening terms, but the greatest threat feared was the huge sea creature (Gen. 1:21) referred to as Litan in Ugar. texts (cf. *KTU* 1.5), which here appears as Leviathan (cf. Job 41). It could be understood simply as a huge creature, or as an ancient monster. But however conceived, Leviathan is no threat here (cf. Ps. 74:13), simply a creature that frolics in the sea. As with the rest of creation, all sea creatures depend on Yahweh for their food at the appropriate time. Yahweh provides it, and each one gathers as appropriate, and is satisfied with good. Yet there are times when Yahweh hides his face and they are terrified; and when Yahweh removes their breath (*rûaḥ*), they die, returning to the dust (cf. Gen. 2:7 Eccl. 12:7). Life exists because Yahweh gives it, but Yahweh is also the one who removes it. However, in an echo of Genesis 1:2, he sends his Spirit (playing on the senses of *rûaḥ*), so again there is life – creation here refers to the continuation of life, not its initiation (cf. Ps. 51:10) – a renewal that affects both animate life and even the ground itself. The wonders of Yahweh's works are seen in all dimensions of creation.

31–32. The final stanza shifts back to address an audience, speaking to them about Yahweh, again using theophanic language. It opens with a wish which asks that Yahweh's glory endure for ever, and that alongside this Yahweh would rejoice in his works. Within the psalm, Yahweh's glory is seen in creation (cf. vv. 1–2), and for this reason he may continue to rejoice in his works, the creation that points to his glory. Yet there remains a profound difference between Yahweh and that creation; for when Yahweh looks at the earth, it trembles, while his touch is enough to make mountains smoke, evoking the image of a volcano. Yet even in this profound difference between Yahweh and his creation, his glory is seen.

33. Accordingly, the psalmist promises to sing continual praise to Yahweh. Creation, Yahweh's works, point to his glory, and the appropriate response is to sing praise. Yahweh's glory endures for ever, but humans are transient (a theme developed in Pss 102–103), so the poet can only vow to sing in praise while life endures. Such a response provides Yahweh with another reason to rejoice in his works.

34–35a. The word rendered 'reflection' (*śîaḥ*) here is 'complaint' in the title of Psalm 102. A more general sense is required here, and Psalm 69:12 suggests it can refer to a point of discussion. The poet has been reflecting on Yahweh through the medium of creation and so desires that this be pleasing to him. Meanwhile, the poet continues rejoicing in Yahweh, demonstrating a degree of reciprocity. Yahweh can be pleased with the reflection, while the psalmist can rejoice in Yahweh. Nevertheless, verse 35 still comes as a shock as it asks for the removal of sinners and the wicked from creation. Yahweh has created a good world, and therefore sin and wickedness, both of which work against his purposes, need to be removed. Creation points to Yahweh's glory; indeed, it is sacred space (Laurence 2022); and so the poet hopes for the removal of all that is contrary to this.

35b. The poem ends with a double praise exhortation, the second forming a bridge to Psalms 105–106. The first exhortation replicates verse 1a, providing an inclusio for the poem. The second introduces 'Hallelujah' to the Psalter. Although the verb 'praise' (*hll*) has been used previously, this is the first time we have the familiar imp. 'Praise Yah' – a phrase that occurs nowhere else within the OT but that has a structuring function for the balance of the Psalter (Robertson 2015b). Apart from Psalm 135:3, the command always stands apart from any other syntactic elements. It commences, ends or forms an inclusio for a psalm (see Hossfeld and Zenger 2011: 39–41). Here, it affirms that everything necessary has been said, and Yahweh is to be praised.

Explanation

Much contemporary discussion focuses on how we are to save the planet. But this psalm suggests we may need to repent of the idea that we save the planet. That is blasphemy, because this is God's creation, not ours. Our repentance leads us to worship, to praise. As we do that, we see that all creation reflects God's skill and wisdom (not just the parts we like). Through that, we see that God's Spirit is already bringing renewal to creation, even as we pray for the completion of that renewal. That does not mean we can abuse the creation, because this ignores the fact that it is God's. Indeed, one way in which the wicked might be no more is if we stopped abusing the creation. Moreover, if the psalm is a further declaration that Yahweh is king, then we respond to his reign by tending that which he has given us. In our tending of creation and our words of praise, we bless Yahweh and offer our praise to the one who continues to sustain creation (cf. Limburg 1994; McCann 1996: 1099–1101). The gracious God of Psalm 103 is also the great God of Psalm 104. Hallelujah!

PSALM 105

Translation

1Give thanks to Yahweh, call on his name,
  make known his deeds among the peoples.
2Sing to him, make melody to him,
  reflect on all his wondrous acts.
3Glory in his holy name,
  let the heart of those who seek Yahweh rejoice.
4Seek Yahweh and his strength,
  seek his face continually.
5Remember his wondrous acts that he performed,
  his signs and the judgements of his mouth.

6O seed of his servant Abraham,
O children of Jacob, his chosen ones,
7he is Yahweh our God,
his acts of justice are in all the earth!

8He remembers his covenant for ever,
the word he commanded for a thousand generations,
9that he made with Abraham,
and his oath to Isaac,
10that he confirmed to Jacob as a statute,
an everlasting covenant for Israel,
11saying, 'To you will I give the land of Canaan,
the portion of your inheritance.'

12When they were people few of number,
very few, and strangers in it,
13and wandered from nation to nation,
from one kingdom to another people,
14he allowed no one to oppress them,
he reproved kings on their behalf:
15'Do not touch my anointed ones,
and do not harm my prophets.'

16Then he summoned a famine in the land,
he broke every staff of bread.
17He sent a man before them,
Joseph who was sold as a slave,
18they bound his feet in fetters,
his neck went into iron.
19until the time of his word came about,
Yahweh's utterance refined him.
20He sent a king who unbound him,
a ruler of peoples freed him.
21He appointed him as master of his house,
and ruler over all he possessed,
22to constrain his officials as he wished,
and make wise his elders.

23Then Israel entered Egypt,
and Jacob sojourned in the land of Ham.
24He made his people very fruitful,
and stronger than their adversaries.
25He turned their heart to hate his people,
to deal deceitfully with his servants.
26He sent Moses, his servant,

Aaron whom he chose,
[27]they set before them explanations of his signs,
and wonders in the land of Ham.
[28]He sent darkness, and made it dark,
and they did not rebel against his word.
[29]He turned their waters to blood,
and killed their fish.
[30]Their land teemed with frogs,
in the chambers of their kings.
[31]He spoke, and swarms of insects came,
gnats within all their territory.
[32]He gave them hail as their rain,
the fire of lightning in their land.
[33]He struck their vines and their fig trees,
and shattered the trees of their territory.
[34]He spoke, and migratory locusts came,
yes, locusts without number,
[35]that ate all the herbage in their land,
and ate all the fruit of their ground.
[36]Then he struck all the firstborn in their land,
the beginning of all their vigour.

[37]Then he brought them out with silver and gold,
and there was no one in his tribes who stumbled.
[38]Egypt rejoiced at their departure,
because dread of them had fallen upon them.
[39]He spread out cloud as a screen,
and fire as a light for night.
[40]He summoned, and quail came,
and with the bread of heaven he satisfied them.
[41]He opened a rock and water gushed forth,
it flowed through the dry region as a river.

[42]For he remembered his holy promise,
to Abraham his servant,
[43]and he brought out his people with exultation,
his chosen ones with a shout.
[44]Then he gave them the lands of the nations,
they possessed the peoples' toil,
[45]that they might observe his statutes,
and keep his instruction.

Hallelujah!

Notes on the text

1. See 'Notes on the text', Psalm 104:35c. Here, and through much of the poem, 11QPs[a] has a variant text. Most are minor, perhaps reflecting the character of that MS. Since none are followed here, they are not reflected in these notes.

18. Though many MSS support Q, here retaining K.

20. With NIV, we could read the king as the subject of the verb here. For this view, see van Gemeren 2008: 778.

22. Gk suggests *lĕyassēr*, a reading that improves the parallelism (see Estes 2019: 289). But with Goldingay (2008: 211), MT should be retained because it establishes a link to a key verb in Genesis 39 – 41.

28. 'Darkness' may here be personified, thus avoiding a tautology (Booij 1989b: 211). NRSV follows Gk and Syr., omitting the negation. But the link to Exodus 10:24 supports MT.

36. Many MSS read 'Egypt' for 'their land' but the sense is the same.

Form and structure

This poem forms part of a dual conclusion to Book 4 (Pss 105–106), with both psalms telling Israel's story, though from contrasting perspectives. Psalm 105 traces the story through to Israel's entry into the land as the place where it was to observe Yahweh's instruction. The story is generally positive, recounting Yahweh's actions in faithfulness to his covenant. Psalm 106 covers a similar period, though reaching to the time of the judges before jumping to the exile. It highlights Israel's failings, through which Yahweh's commitment to the covenant is seen more clearly. Both psalms conclude with 'Hallelujah!', joining them also to Psalm 104:35c. Psalm 105:2 is also linked to Psalm 104:34 through the motif of 'reflection' (*śyḥ*), itself picking up on the same root in Psalm 102's title. The theme of reflection is also closely linked to the references to musical worship in Psalms 104:33 and 105:2, indicating that the reflection is (in part at least) expressed through music. Taken together, Psalms 104–106 move readers from creation to exile, the context in which Israel's life has been lived.

With Psalm 78, Psalm 105 can be seen as a historical recital. Israel's story is told, specifically to highlight key points that can be learnt through the particular lens through which the story is examined. No one telling can reveal all that Israel's story teaches, a point emphasized through the juxtaposition with Psalm 106. For the most part, Psalm 105 draws on material from the Pentateuch and Joshua, drawing them together while shaping a fresh reflection on that story. It is thus a poem that encourages an intertextual approach to its interpretation (see Won 2019: 78–89) even while making its own case about Israel's story (cf. Brueggemann

1991a: 29). A good deal of attention has been devoted to the apparently different order of the plague narrative in the psalm in comparison to Exodus (see Lee 1990b; Brettler 2007; Emanuel 2012: 73–75). But even though the poem seems to reference Exodus it is not necessary for the poet to have the written text to hand during composition, so some variation in order is possible, especially as it enables the recital to build to the declaration of verse 45 (cf. Tucker 2005). Elsewhere, the poem's intertextual possibilities are recognized by the Chronicler, with Psalm 105:1–15 reproduced as 1 Chronicles 16:8–22 in the composite poem of 1 Chronicles 16:8–36 (along with Pss 96:1b–13a; 106:1, 47–48).

The poem can be analysed in seven stanzas:

1. Call to praise (1–7)
2. Covenant with the patriarchs (8–11)
3. Protection of the patriarch (12–15)
4. Deliverance through Joseph (16–22)
5. Israel in Egypt (23–36)
6. The exodus and wilderness (37–41)
7. Yahweh's faithfulness and Israel's purpose (42–45)

Comment

1–7. The psalm opens with a blizzard of imperatives, each summoning a different mode of praise. The initial 'Give thanks' represents a key phrase developed in Book 5 (e.g. Pss 107:1; 118:1), though also developed in Psalm 106:1, which explains that the reason for doing so is that Yahweh is good. Giving thanks can take the form of testimony of what Yahweh has previously done. To call on Yahweh's name is to worship him (e.g. Gen. 12:8; 21:33; Jer. 10:25). Together, thanksgiving and worship lead to the third imp., which is the summons to make known Yahweh's deeds among the peoples, developing the motif of the peoples within Book 4 (e.g. Pss 96:3; 99:1). Worship takes on a musical tone in verse 2 as the opening imperatives summon song and music, though this worship clearly has content since worshippers also reflect on Yahweh's wondrous deeds. As those who have called on Yahweh's name, verse 3 now directs worshippers to glory in his holy name, before breaking the chain of imperatives with a juss. asking that the hearts of those who fear Yahweh may rejoice. The imperatives have all considered worship directed to Yahweh, but the juss. now expresses a wish about the impact this may have on worshippers. Verses 4–5 return to imperatives, with two verbs that both mean to 'seek' (*drš*, *bqš*). The first directs worshippers to seek Yahweh and his strength, while the second directs continued seeking of Yahweh's presence. This is followed by the stanza's final imp., which directs worshippers to remember the wondrous things Yahweh has done, including his speech, with 'remember' here broadly synonymous to 'reflect' in verse 2. Yahweh's wondrous acts, which will be recounted within the psalm, provide a reason for praise, but this requires reflection and memory. This praise is exuberant and informed. Remarkably, it is only at verse 6 that the audience is identified as descendants of Abraham and Jacob. A distinctive element of this psalm, Abraham is singled out as Yahweh's 'servant' (cf. Gen. 26:24), while descendants of Jacob are Yahweh's chosen ones. The Israelite worshippers are reminded of their heritage, establishing a key theme through the psalm. Yahweh is not only their ancestors' God; he is the God of these worshippers, his acts of justice evident in all the earth (cf. Ps. 98:3). Moreover, both 'servant' and 'chosen' are terms elsewhere used of David (e.g. Ps. 89:3, 20, 39), and by using them of Abraham the psalm insists Yahweh's purposes reach much further back in history.

8–11. The opening stanza has summoned to worship, but the reasons for that worship now begin to be explored, establishing the pattern that runs through the balance of the poem. Whereas worshippers were directed to remember Yahweh's wondrous works, the reality of Yahweh's memory is now central. Yahweh remembers his covenant for ever since it is an enduring promise he has made (cf. Luke 1:72–73). That Yahweh remembers means he is committed to working for the well-being of that covenant. Although there are several covenants in the OT, it is the Abrahamic (Gen. 15, 17) that is in view here, a covenant confirmed to Isaac (Gen. 26:2–4) and Jacob (Gen. 28:12–15). This repeated promise can thus be understood as a statute. This term can often refer to a law, but here is parallel to 'covenant' and intended as a synonym that stresses the solemn nature of Yahweh's enduring commitment. Although there are other elements to the Abrahamic covenant, the promise of the land of Canaan (Gen. 15:18–21; 17:8) is central here. This land was Israel's inheritance, something they would possess because of Yahweh's faithfulness to his covenant, and it was the land where they were to show their faithfulness to his statutes (vv. 44–45).

12–15. Yahweh's covenant commitment did not wait for Israel's entry into the land. Rather, it meant he immediately cared for the patriarchs even though they were few in number and thus highly vulnerable as sojourners in someone else's lands (cf. Deut. 26:5). The psalm does not specify the moments Yahweh provided protection, but mentioning people being prevented from touching the patriarchs could allude to Genesis 26:11, where Abimelech warns his people not to touch Isaac, a point affirmed by Abimelech when he meets Isaac again (Gen. 26:28–29). Mention of their status as prophets could allude to Genesis 20:6–7 (which also prohibits touch), where Abraham is designated a prophet, a label here extended to Isaac. Genesis 12 – 50 portrays the patriarchs as nomads, so Yahweh's protection is understood to have been operative through all their travels. It is Yahweh's faithfulness, not what the patriarchs did, that matters and hence why Yahweh is to be praised.

16–22. The record of Yahweh's faithfulness moves forward to the Joseph story, and the famine that eventually saw Israel go down to Egypt. In so doing, this introduces the theme of Yahweh's provision of food, a central element in the psalm (Stinson 2021: 592–595). The famine mentioned here was the subject of Pharaoh's dream that Joseph interpreted (Gen. 41:14–36). That Joseph was sent on ahead of his brothers telescopes his sale as a slave to traders (Gen. 37:25–28) and Joseph's later reflections on how God sent him in advance (Gen. 45:1–8; 50:20; cf. S. Emadi 2022: 104–105). Mention of his being placed in fetters and irons refers to his imprisonment (Gen. 39:20) since it was there that he first interpreted dreams in Egypt, leading to his interpreting Pharaoh's dream (Gen. 40 – 41). His interpretation of Pharaoh's dream is the word that came about since it explained both what God was doing and the appropriate response. That Yahweh's word had refined Joseph suggests that it had also prepared him for his new role in Egypt since we do not see the more pompous behaviour that had led to conflict with his brothers (Gen. 37:2–11). The psalm thus emphasizes Yahweh's preparation of Joseph for his later role during the famine. The king Yahweh sent is presumably the Pharaoh, whose dreams Joseph interprets, who released and promoted him, placing him second only to Pharaoh (Gen. 41:37–45). The psalm also moves beyond the Genesis record to indicate that Joseph was to constrain the officials by ensuring that his guidance was followed, and thus model wisdom to them.

23–36. Verses 23–25 provide a transition between Genesis and Exodus, reporting Israel's arrival and settlement in Egypt (Gen. 46:1 – 47:12; Ham is here an alternative name for Egypt; cf. Gen. 10:6; Ps. 78:51). That they were sojourners there makes clear it was not their permanent home. But, as reported in Exodus 1, Israel there fulfilled God's creational command of being fruitful, itself a sign of God's blessing as promised to Abraham (Gen. 12:1–3). It was Yahweh who made Israel fruitful and hence (by numerical superiority) stronger than their adversaries (itself a wordplay because of its similarity to the word for Egypt). It is because Yahweh made Israel strong that Egypt came to hate them, though Yahweh can still be understood as the primary cause. Because of this, Egypt dealt unfaithfully with Israel, a summary statement that includes both the new Pharaoh, who did not know Joseph, and the subsequent decree for the death of the Egyptian sons (Exod. 1:8–10). But Yahweh did not abandon Israel, and verses 26–36 outline the means of their deliverance. This begins with Yahweh's sending Moses, who here joins Abraham in being called Yahweh's servant (v. 6). The whole nation are also Yahweh's servants (v. 25), but this designation particularly marks Abraham and Moses as key figures through whom Yahweh works. The note in verse 26 abridges Exodus 2 – 4, as it also notes Aaron's presence, one whom Yahweh has chosen, omitting the account of how he came to be with Moses. Here, it is sufficient to note that they were both sent by Yahweh, and both were involved in the plague narrative (Exod. 7 – 12), including announcing the signs (i.e. the plagues). Because the focus is on Yahweh, it is emphasized that the plagues were his signs, with Moses and Aaron his mouthpieces. The account of the plagues here varies from the order in Exodus, though both climax with the death of the firstborn. The comparative order of the plagues can be seen in Table 1.

Table 1: Comparative order of the plagues

Plague	*Verses in Psalm 105*	*Order in Exodus*
Darkness	28	Ninth (9:21–29)
Water to blood	29	First (7:14–25)
Frogs	30	Second (8:1–15)
Flies	31	Fourth (8:20–32)
Gnats	31	Third (8:16–19)
Hail	32–33	Seventh (9:13–35)
Locusts	34–34	Eighth (10:1–20)
Death of firstborn	36	Tenth (12:29–32)
Death of livestock	Omitted	Fifth (9:1–6)
Boils	Omitted	Sixth (9:8–12)

The psalm's presentation is thus selective as well as reordered in comparison with Exodus. As with Psalm 78:44–51, the changes reflect the psalm's rhetorical concerns, here pointing to the reversal of the order of creation in Genesis 1 (Won 2019: 115). Darkness is probably listed first as a portent of death, a theme picked up in the death of the fish, and climaxes in the death of the firstborn. Throughout, the psalm's concern is to show that Yahweh has overcome Israel's adversaries in Egypt. It is also possible that having hail and locusts before the death of the firstborn supports the emphasis on Yahweh's greatness since these are the two where Yahweh states that the plagues are to make him known (Exod. 9:14; 10:2).

37–41. The sixth stanza moves to the exodus itself and the initial period in the wilderness before bypassing Sinai. That Israel left Egypt with silver and gold, while the Egyptians were glad that they had gone, reflects the motif of the plundering of Egypt (Exod. 12:33–36). Again, the emphasis is on Yahweh's actions. Israel did not simply leave; it was Yahweh who brought them out and caused dread of them to fall on Egypt. This is why none of the tribes stumbled. Yahweh's provision continued in the wilderness, with the cloud screening Israel from Egypt in the crossing of the sea (Exod. 14:19), though mention of cloud and fire together also alludes to the more general statement about Yahweh's guidance (Exod. 13:17–22). Yahweh also provided quail and manna (Exod. 16) so they were satisfied. Although the account in Exodus is also critical of Israel, the psalm attends only to Yahweh's provision, a pattern continued in the mention of the water from the rock (Exod. 17:1–7). Israel could not provide food or water in the wilderness, but Yahweh did.

42–45. The seventh stanza brings the psalm to a close with a further reference to Abraham as servant (v. 6), creating an inclusio for the psalm. Yahweh has remembered his covenant (v. 8), and that covenant is again mentioned here as his 'holy promise' given to Abraham. It is the promise to Abraham that drives all Yahweh has done, including bringing his people out of Egypt in the exodus with rejoicing, a motif echoed in new-exodus language (Isa. 51:11; cf. Emanuel 2012: 84). Israel are Yahweh's chosen ones because of his commitment to Abraham, and he has been faithful to that commitment. That faithfulness did not end with the exodus, because the psalm then moves to Joshua by noting that Yahweh gave them the lands of the nations, a place where others had toiled before them. This was Israel's heritage, though this heritage was not an end in itself. Instead, the land was given so Israel had somewhere to keep Yahweh's statutes (cf. v. 10), to comply with his 'instruction' (*tôrâ*). Sinai is unmentioned in the psalm, but that does not mean Yahweh's statutes were irrelevant to this celebration of the Abrahamic covenant. Rather, Sinai was a vital step towards the land as the place where Israel could keep Yahweh's law (cf. McKelvey 2014: 233–234). Both verbs in verse 45 can have the sense of guarding something, and this was part of Israel's role – by living out the statutes they would also guard them, and thus point to Yahweh as the one who stood behind them (cf. Deut. 4:6–8). This statement prepares readers for Psalm 106, which will demonstrate that Israel did not do what verse 45 indicates. But that theme remains unresolved here. Instead, the psalm responds to all that Yahweh has done by once again summoning praise for him. Hallelujah!

Explanation

Building on the theology of creation and God's continued care of it in Psalm 104, this poem traces Israel's story from the patriarchs to Israel's entry into the land under Joshua. The story is carefully presented, omitting points where Israel fails, to emphasize Yahweh's continued faithfulness to his covenant promise to Abraham. This promise is everlasting, an enduring commitment to his people. That it lasts a thousand generations not only emphasizes this point, but also alludes to Exodus 34:6–7, pointing to Yahweh's forgiving grace as something consistent with the enduring commitment to his people. Worshippers encountering this psalm are not only summoned to offer their praise, but are also given an overview of Israel's history, reminding them of

Yahweh's enduring faithfulness. They are given reasons to praise, and those reasons also remind them that what Yahweh has done in the past he can do again. Indeed, his commitment to his people gives a reason to think he will. Israel's story is thus a continued reason for praise, because it is a story of Yahweh's continued covenant faithfulness. The closing note about the Torah is important, asking those who praise to remember that a response is required of them too. Those who have been redeemed have a reason to respond in faithfulness, so that praise is not simply words spoken but also a life lived (cf. Col. 3:1–17). This note also anticipates Psalm 106. But that psalm must wait its turn. At this point we need to be reminded of God's enduring faithfulness to his promise and know this provides continued hope for the future (cf. McMillion 2010: 177–179). Hallelujah!

PSALM 106

Translation

1Hallelujah!
Give thanks to Yahweh for he is good,
  for his kindness endures for ever.
2Who can utter Yahweh's mightiness,
  or proclaim his praise?
3O the blessedness of those who maintain justice,
  the one who always does what is righteous.
4Remember me, O Yahweh, when you show your people favour,
  visit me with your salvation,
5to see the prosperity of your chosen ones,
  to rejoice in your nation's joy,
  to glory with your heritage.

6We and our ancestors have sinned,
  we have acted iniquitously, wickedly.
7Our ancestors in Egypt did not ponder your wondrous deeds,
  they did not remember the abundance of your kindnesses,
  but rebelled by the Sea, the Reed Sea.
8But he saved them for his name's sake,
  to make known his mighty deeds.
9He rebuked the Reed Sea and it became dry,
  and led them through the deeps as through the wilderness.
10He saved them from the hand of one who hated them,
  he redeemed them from the hand of the enemy.
11The waters covered their adversaries,
  not one of them was left.

12Then they believed his words,
  they sang his praise.

13But quickly they forgot his works,
  they did not wait for his counsel.
14They had a wanton craving in the wilderness,
  they tested God in the desert.
15He gave them their request,
  he sent a wasting disease among them.
16They were envious of Moses in the camp,
  of Aaron, the holy one of Yahweh.
17The earth opened up and swallowed Dathan,
  it covered the assembly of Abiram.
18A fire burned in their assembly,
  a flame devoured the wicked.
19They made a young bull at Horeb,
  they worshipped a metal image,
20they exchanged their glory
  for the image of an ox that eats grass.
21They forgot God their saviour,
  who had done great things in Egypt,
22wondrous deeds in the land of Ham,
  awesome deeds at the Reed Sea.
23He decided to destroy them,
  except that Moses his chosen one,
stood in the gap before him
  to turn aside his wrath from destruction.

24They rejected the land of delight,
  they did not believe his promise.
25They murmured in their tents,
  they did not obey Yahweh's voice.
26So he lifted his hand against them,
  to make them fall in the wilderness,
27to make their seed fall among the nations,
  to disperse them in the lands.
28Then they joined themselves to Baal of Peor
  and ate sacrifices of the dead.
29They provoked anger by their deeds,
  and plague broke out upon them.
30But Phinehas stood and interceded,
  and the plague was restrained.
31It was reckoned to him as righteousness,
  from generation to generation and for ever.
32They provoked wrath by the waters of Meribah,

and it was injurious for Moses because of them.
33For they embittered his spirit,
and he spoke rashly with his lips.

34They did not destroy the peoples
as Yahweh had directed them.
35But they mingled with the nations,
and learned their works.
36They served their idols,
and they became a snare to them.
37They sacrificed their sons,
and their daughters to demons,
38they shed innocent blood,
the blood of their sons and their daughters
whom they sacrificed to the idols of Canaan,
and defiled the land with bloodshed.
39They became unclean through their works,
played the harlot through their deeds.
40Yahweh's wrath was kindled against his people,
and he abhorred his heritage.
41He gave them into the hand of nations,
those who hated them ruled over them.
42Their enemies oppressed them,
they were humbled under their hand.
43Many times he delivered them,
but they were rebellious in their plans,
they were brought low in their iniquity.
44But he looked on their distress,
when he heard their cry.
45He remembered his covenant with them,
and relented because of the greatness of his kindness.
46He caused them to be pitied,
before those who held them captive.

47Save us, O Yahweh our God,
and gather us from the nations,
to give thanks to your holy name
to the glory of your praise.

48Blessed be Yahweh the God of Israel,
from everlasting to everlasting,
and all the people say 'Amen'.
Hallelujah!

Notes on the text

2. With deClaissé-Walford et al. (2014: 797), reading *gĕbûrôt* as an abstract pl. (cf. *WHS* §7).

3. Here retaining K.

7. NRSV here emends without MSS evidence, but MT should be retained.

29, 32. In both verses, Gk presumes an object suff., 'him', but this is probably best understood from context.

33. Revocalize to *hēmērû* with two MSS (see Allen 2002: 65). 'His spirit' could refer to either Yahweh (cf. NIV) or Moses but is here understood as Moses, as more consistent with Numbers 20:2–13.

Form and structure

As is now widely recognized, Psalm 106 (with Ps. 105) forms part of a dual conclusion to Book 4 (e.g. Stinson 2021). Although in some ways they are twins, with each recounting Israel's story and summoning praise, they are assuredly not identical. Beyond the observation that they both recount Israel's story, key verbal links provide additional connections. Psalm 106 is bounded by 'Hallelujah', where it ends only Psalm 105, but since this phrase always stands as a discrete element, we can recognize that both psalms commence with a call to give thanks to Yahweh (Pss 105:1; 106:1). The use of 'Hallelujah' also joins these psalms to Psalm 104:35, while 'Give thanks to Yahweh' also anticipates the opening of Book 5 (Ps. 107:1). Both point to the covenant as a key reason for Yahweh's faithfulness (Pss 105:8, 10; 106:45). They also use the comparatively rare hith. of *hll* (Pss 105:3; 106:5) and the designation 'Ham' for Egypt (Pss 105:23, 27; 106:22).

There are thus good reasons for seeing Psalm 106 as a twin of Psalm 105. However, it is also evident that there are important differences, and these are highlighted by having these psalms adjacent to one another. Most importantly, where Psalm 105 is a work of descriptive praise that looks to all Yahweh has done for Israel in protecting them from others, Psalm 106 is better understood as a penitential work. Yahweh is to be thanked for his goodness, but it is a goodness Israel has experienced through its history despite their continued failures. Psalm 105:45's observation that the gift of the land was so Israel could live out Yahweh's statutes is thus explored from the perspective of a people who had not done so, though in fact the failings can be traced back to Israel's beginnings as a nation. Where Psalm 105 carefully avoids mentioning Israel's failings, Psalm 106 consistently highlights them, insisting that the pattern of sin established by previous generations continued to the time of composition (cf. v. 6). Hence, the psalm covers various events that Psalm 105 bypassed in the exodus and wilderness wanderings, while the mention of the failure to destroy the inhabitants of the land traces the story through Joshua and at least on to Judges (vv. 34–46). Yet Yahweh's 'kindness' (*ḥesed*) has been evident through Israel's story and so, when combined with covenant, provides a basis for appeal that he may again act for them, bringing them back from the nations (v. 47). Where Psalm 105 establishes that Yahweh has the power to act, Psalm 106 asks that this power be combined with kindness to restore the nation. As non-identical twins, these psalms thus complement one another, though each needs to be read on its own terms before being placed in dialogue with the other.

Like Psalm 105, it is best to analyse the poem through its content, noting that Yahweh is addressed directly only in the first and last stanzas, with these two forming an inclusio. This results in the following analysis:

1. Call to praise (1–5)
2. Exodus (6–12)
3. Sinai (13–23)
4. The wilderness (24–33)
5. In the land (34–46)
6. A prayer and praise (47–48)

Comment

1–5. The opening 'Hallelujah!' summons praise as the psalm's opening, now building on the close of Psalm 105. It then summons the audience to give thanks to Yahweh but extends the statement from Psalm 105:1 by providing a reason – because he is good (cf. Ps. 100:5). This affirmation will become something of a refrain in Book 5, climaxing in Psalm 136, another poem that recounts Israel's story and then extends and develops this statement throughout the poem. The reason for Yahweh's goodness is here grounded in his enduring 'kindness' (*ḥesed*). This in turn is linked to his mightiness and praise, neither of which can fully be comprehended. Verse 2's question is not asking someone to recount these elements of Yahweh's character but rather to recognize that they are beyond human recounting, though the psalm will at least make a start on the impossible. Yahweh's kindness is here explored through his acts on Israel's behalf, his continued faithfulness to them providing a basis for thanksgiving. Yet before moving to this, the psalm offers a beatitude for those who practise justice and righteousness. This is a state much to be desired, but the psalm will show that this state of blessedness has not been Israel's habitual condition. Before the details of Israel's story can be given, verses 4–5 introduce the voice of an individual who asks to be remembered by Yahweh when he acts favourably for his people, perhaps as their representative (cf. Goldingay 2008: 225). The assumption is that Yahweh will act favourably by saving them from their current circumstances, and so the poet wants to be among those rescued. This salvation will allow the psalmist to see the prosperity of Yahweh's chosen ones, his people, and so rejoice with them and glory with them as Yahweh's heritage. The assumption, though, is that this is not the current situation. Yahweh is to be thanked for his goodness, but that goodness is not now being experienced.

6–12. The historical reflection opens with the exodus, thus bypassing the Abrahamic and plague material central to Psalm 105. This stanza is also headed with a confession of sin that guides the rest of the historical material (cf. Neh. 9:33; Dan. 9:5), linking the poet's own generation with those of their forebears. The psalm accepts that the current generation have joined the ancestors in sin. Although one can point to etymological differences between the three perspectives on sin in verse 6 (sin, iniquity, wickedness) the point is rather to see them as a totality. However sin may be conceived, Israel has done it. The story that follows thus sets Yahweh's goodness against Israel's propensity to sin, demonstrating that Yahweh's goodness both overcomes Israel's sin and Israel's sin means they do not enjoy Yahweh's goodness as they should. The recollection of the exodus begins with the point where Israel left Egypt and reached the Reed Sea. The reference is to the people's complaint when they saw Pharaoh's pursuit, claiming they preferred to continue serving Pharaoh (Exod. 14:10–12). Forgetting Yahweh's wonders in Egypt meant they had no appreciation of how they might pass the Sea. There, Moses told the people to stand firm and see the salvation Yahweh would effect for them. However, the psalmist does not mention Moses, going instead straight to the point where Yahweh acted to save them and so made known his mighty deeds (cf. Exod. 9:16). Mention of Yahweh's rebuking the waters of the Sea probably alludes to the sending of the east wind, which allowed Israel to pass through on dry ground (Exod. 14:21–22). It was thus Yahweh who saved Israel from Pharaoh, here referred to as one who hated them, anticipating those who ruled them under the judges (v. 41). Consistent with the Exodus account, the waters covered the Egyptians, leaving no survivors, so that Israel believed Yahweh (Exod. 14:30–31). Because they saw, the people believed, but the psalm goes on to make clear that this did not continue.

13–23. Following the account of Exodus, the second historical reflection traces events in the wilderness before and after Sinai. Again, a failure of memory is introduced as a key theme, here expressed as rapidly forgetting Yahweh's works and a failure to wait on his counsel. Life in the wilderness meant taking guidance from Yahweh but, because they forgot his works, they did not seek that guidance. This is traced through three main events on the way to Sinai. First, verses 14–15 look back on Israel's craving food in the wilderness and putting God to the test. Mention of the craving is closest to Numbers 11:4, though that could be combined with the grumbling about food in Exodus 16:2–3. These miracles have considerable overlap, so the poet is free to bring them together here. The desire for water in Exodus 17:1–7 was also seen as a point where Israel put Yahweh to the test. Although Yahweh did provide in each of these cases, in Numbers 11:31–35 Israel was also struck with plague. Second, verses 16–18 look back at the rebellions of Korah and of Dathan and Abiram in Numbers 16, something here traced back to their jealousy of Moses and Aaron. The earth opening and swallowing Dathan and Abiram refers to Numbers 16:31–32, while fire was said to have come out and consumed another group of rebels (Num. 16:35), a group here classified as the wicked because they rebelled against Yahweh. Third, verses 19–23 (cf. Deut. 9:7–29) look back to the events around the golden calf (Exod. 32) and Yahweh's expressed intention of destroying Israel and starting again with Moses as a result, a plan averted through Moses' intercession (Exod. 32:7–14; cf. Ezek. 22:30; Kugler 2014: 550). Again, failing to remember is fundamental, including more recent events at the crossing of the Sea as well as the events in Egypt. Forgetting what Yahweh has done meant failing to attend to Yahweh as saviour and placed the nation at risk.

24–33. Focus here shifts to Israel's initial failure to enter the land and its implications for them. In that the rebellions of Korah, Dathan and Abiram also fall into this period, it is clear that the psalm is not attempting to cover everything in a strictly chronological pattern. Verses 24–27 look back on the events of Numbers 13 – 14 where, following the sending of the twelve spies, the people did not go up and take the land. Although memory is not an explicit element in this stanza, the failure to believe Yahweh's promise (v. 24) is tied to the earlier pattern since had they remembered they would have had reason to believe. Instead, they are said to have rejected the land, concluding that taking it was too difficult (Num. 14:31). The psalm ties this to the grumbling motif in the wilderness (cf. Num. 14:2), and so because of this they did not obey Yahweh by taking the land. As a result, Yahweh promised that none of that generation would enter the land. Instead, they would die in the wilderness (Num. 14:26–35). This promise is here expressed through Yahweh's raising his hand, an act that is both the swearing of an oath and an act against that generation, ensuring that generation and their descendants were scattered among the nations. Verses 28–31 then look back to Numbers 25:1–10. There, Israel participated in the worship of other gods. Mention here of the sacrifices of the dead is not entirely clear even if those sacrifices are in view. Such worship could be sacrifices offered to the dead or sacrifices that demanded the death of people (cf. v. 37), but perhaps it is better to think here of them as sacrifices offered to gods who are themselves dead (cf. NIV; Kraus 1989: 320). These sacrifices have no positive value, but turn people from worshipping Yahweh. Whichever is intended, the result there was plague that was only stopped through Phinehas's intervention, an intervention here counted to him as enduring righteousness, aligning him with Abraham (Gen. 15:6). Finally, verses 32–33 reflect on the events at Meribah (Num. 20:2–13), where Moses struck the rock twice and was excluded from entering the land because of his failure to honour Yahweh as holy. In his speech, he claimed that he and Aaron would bring the water from the rock, and hence failed to honour Yahweh. Even Moses, therefore, stands in the history of those who have sinned.

34–46. The final reflection on Israel's past moves into its life in the land, both at the time of Joshua and under the judges. Where events to this point have been relatively specific, now the sins are more generalized, building from the failure to destroy the land's indigenous population. Such a failure is reported at several points in Joshua. Joshua does not always treat this negatively (Firth 2019a: 13–52), though the threat of mingling with those nations remains a key threat within the book when that leads to following their worship (Josh. 23). This concern is developed here, noting that the continued presence of those peoples led to Israel's mixing with them and adopting their worship, even to the point of sacrificing their children to demons. This statement telescopes much of Israel's story, moving from Joshua to 2 Kings 16:3 (provided Ahaz making his son pass through fire is a reference to human sacrifice), but it is rooted in the fact that the continued presence of such worship patterns would entice Israel to follow them. Once they have done so, they can be said to have played the harlot by not remaining loyal to Yahweh. The results of this are explored in verses 40–45. Yahweh's anger with his people led to his handing them over to the nations, a repeated motif in Judges, one that anticipates the exile of the northern kingdom (2 Kgs 17:7–41) and then Judah's exile (2 Kgs 25:8–26). That Yahweh often delivered them alludes to the various judges, though also includes points of deliverance under Samuel, David and other kings after him. These points are not spelled out, because the point is to establish a pattern of behaviour that continued, one that pointed to the iniquity confessed in verse 6. Nevertheless, Yahweh continued to note Israel, and just as he had responded to their cry in Egypt (Exod. 2:23–25), so he also continued to respond to their cry, remembering his covenant with them, acting because of his 'kindness' (*ḥesed*). That Yahweh caused them to be pitied before their captors echoes Hezekiah's letter (2 Chr. 30:6–9), and emphasizes that throughout this history of rebellion, Yahweh has remained faithful.

47–48. In the light of Yahweh's continued faithfulness, the psalm now reaches its appeal, asking Yahweh to save the community and gather them from the nations. The appeal means that this community has remembered what previous generations forgot, which is that Yahweh is their saviour (cf. v. 21). Yahweh previously acted because of his covenant, and so the exiled community can ask that he do so again because he is their God. Moreover, doing so will enable them to give thanks to Yahweh's holy name, fulfilling the opening call to give thanks to Yahweh

(v. 1), and thus provide appropriate praise. Verse 47 thus concludes the body of the poem, as the motif of giving thanks provides an inclusio for it. However, as the final poem of Book 4, it also includes the closing doxology (cf. Pss 41:13; 72:18–19; 89:52). This doxology is particularly close to that of Psalm 41:13, except that it includes the people's response, with their 'Amen' allowing them to confess that they accept the truth of the doxology. To this, the only appropriate response is 'Hallelujah!', something 1 Chronicles 16:35–36 reports in its citation of these verses.

Explanation

A more dismissive approach to history considers it to be simply one more thing after another. Such an approach believes history is nothing more than a series of events. To be sure, there can be no history without understanding what happened, but the crucial matter is to learn from that history. Importantly, as is clear from the parallel arrangement of Psalms 105 and 106, there is no one lesson to be learnt. Rather, different audiences have different things to learn. Here, it is the failure of the exodus generation to ponder Yahweh's acts that is the problem (v. 7). That is, the events were not a matter of ongoing reflection. Without such reflection, the people ceased to remember what Yahweh had done. Once they forgot, they failed to believe. This generation established a pattern that continued through to the exile, a pattern where the failure to believe led to sin and Yahweh's judgement. Yet throughout this, Yahweh remained faithful and responded to the prayers of people like Moses and Phinehas. Futato (2009: 339) points to Romans 5:20 as capturing the heart of this psalm – God's grace abounded even as sin increased. The community addressed here needed to learn more than the facts of Israel's story – they needed to learn the lessons relevant to them. In this, they are close to those represented in the prayers of Nehemiah 9 and Daniel 9, both of whom also look from the experience of exile to see the pattern of sin that led to that point. Yet because Yahweh does remember, because he does respond to prayer, there is hope. That hope comes in the prayer to which this history builds, a prayer that asks Yahweh to save and thus demonstrate again that he remembers even when his people do not, that his kindness is indeed for ever. This is a hope that transcends the experience of the exile and continues to speak to Christians today; as, for example, when Paul looks to Israel's history and notes that these things are also a warning for believers (1 Cor. 10:11). When we note this, we see that this psalm also offers hope for us today, giving us reason to pray and ask for God's kindness to be shown to us in Christ (cf. Ellington 2007; Swale 2019). Perhaps we too can then dare to utter those words of praise with which not only this psalm but the whole of Book 4 ends. So we can all say 'Amen. Hallelujah!'

BOOK 5

PSALM 107

Translation

1Give thanks to Yahweh because he is good,
   for his kindness endures for ever.
2Let the redeemed of Yahweh say so,
   whom he redeemed from the hand of the oppressor,
3whom he gathered from the lands,
   from east and west,
   from north and sea.

4They wandered in the wilderness, in a wasteland,
   the way to a habitable city they could not find.
5Hungry and thirsty,
   their appetite made them grow faint.
6But they cried out to Yahweh in their trouble,
   and he saved them from their distress,
7he led them on a straight way,
   to go to a habitable city.
8Let them thank Yahweh for his kindness,
   and his wondrous deeds for the children of humankind!

9For he satisfied the thirsting throat,
and filled the hungry appetite with good.

10Those sitting in darkness and deep gloom,
prisoners of misery and iron –
11who had rebelled against the words of God,
and spurned the counsel of the Most High –
12he humbled their heart through toil:
they staggered without help.
13But they cried out to Yahweh in their trouble,
and he saved them from their distress.
14He brought them out from darkness and deep gloom,
and snapped their shackles.
15Let them thank Yahweh for his kindness,
and his wondrous deeds for the children of humankind!
16For he shatters the bronze doors,
and hews down the iron bars.

17Fools, because of their transgression,
and because of their iniquities, suffered affliction.
18Their appetite abhorred all food,
and they drew near to the gates of death.
19But they cried out to Yahweh in their trouble,
and he saved them from their distress.
20He sent his word and restored them,
and delivered them from their pits.
21Let them thank Yahweh for his kindness,
and his wondrous deeds for the children of humankind!
22Let them offer sacrifices of thanksgiving,
let them recount his works with a shout!

23Those went down to the sea in ships,
carrying out trade on the great seas.
24They saw Yahweh's works for themselves,
and his wondrous deeds on the deep sea.
25When he spoke a storm wind was raised,
and lifted its waves.
26These rose to the heavens,
they plunged to the depths,
their courage melted away in their misery.
27They staggered and reeled like a drunkard,
and all their skill was confounded.
28But they cried out to Yahweh in their trouble,
and he brought them out from their distress.
29He stilled the storm,

and their waves were still.
30They rejoiced when they were silent,
and he led them to the harbour they desired.
31Let them thank Yahweh for his kindness,
and his wondrous deeds for the children of humankind!
32Let them exalt him in the congregation of the people,
and praise him at the seat of the elders.

33He turns rivers into a wilderness,
gushing waters to thirsty ground,
34a fruitful land to salt,
because of the wickedness of its inhabitants.
35He turns the wilderness to a pool of water.
and a thirsty land to gushing waters.
36He settles the hungry there,
and they establish a habitable city.
37They sow fields and plant vineyards,
they harvest their produce.
38He blesses them, they multiply greatly,
and does not diminish their cattle.
39But when they become few and bowed down,
because of vexation, misery and grief,
40he pours out contempt on princes,
he makes them wander in a trackless waste.
41He sets the needy on high, away from affliction,
and makes clans like a flock.

42The upright see and rejoice,
and all perversity closes its mouth.
43Let whoever is wise heed these things,
and let them consider Yahweh's acts of kindness.

Notes on the text

3. 'Sea' is often emended to 'south' (cf. *BHS*; Kraus 1989: 325) to give the four cardinal points, but the versions support MT and the sea here may be the southern sea, the Gulf of Aqaba. As Hossfeld and Zenger note (2011: 99), the sea is also a primary location of Yahweh's salvation within the psalm.

4. The opening verb is often emended to the ptc. on analogy with verses 10, 23, but in view of the opening verses a finite verb is to be retained.

20. Hebr. *miššĕḥîtôtām* is understood as a deep pit that represents a trap. Cf. Lamentations 4:20, though it should be noted that both are often emended.

21–26, 40. These verses are marked by an inverted *n*, possibly indicating that the Masoretes believed these verses had been misplaced. However, as G. T. M. Prinsloo (2021: 400) notes, if that is the intention here, its function is not clear.

27. The verb *bl'* could be either 'swallow' or 'confuse'. As the only occurrence of the verb in hith., there is no strong linguistic clue to assist with the decision. For 'swallow', see ESV mg.

39–40. Allen (2002: 84) believes these verses should be transposed, but MT can be retained if we see the main verb as deferred.

Form and structure

Where Books 2–4 were each introduced with a psalm clearly distinct from those of the previous book (cf. Foster 2019: 135), Psalm 107 has strong links with Book 4 while also establishing key motifs for Psalm 145 (cf. Zenger 1998: 88–89). The absence of a title assists this since introducing a new key figure in one (e.g. Moses in Ps. 90) creates a break. There is no title here, though it will be followed by three Davidic psalms, softening the break between the books. Moreover, there are strong echoes of Psalms 105–106, most obviously the fact that all three ask for thanksgiving to Yahweh (Pss 105:1; 106:1; 107:1) while stressing his wondrous works (Pss 105:2, 5; 106:7, 22; 107:8, 15, 21, 24, 31). The connection with Psalm 106 is strengthened by the emphasis on Yahweh's goodness (Pss 106:1; 107:1) and enduring 'kindness' (*ḥesed,* Pss 106:1; 107:1). The nation who had asked to be saved so they could praise Yahweh (Ps. 106:47) are now given a range of settings where they may continue to see his saving power (cf. deClaissé-Walford et al. 2014: 812). Beyond these links, it can also be noted that where Psalms 105–106 tell Israel's story through recognizable events from other parts of the OT, Psalm 107 uses type scenes that invite an audience to find their own experience in some way replicated, though it is usually possible to make links with Israel's story, especially the end of the exile. The audience who encounters this psalm are invited not only to offer thanksgiving for Yahweh's works for the nation, but also to find points where their own experience is reflected in the various type scenes recounted (cf. Mays 1994b: 346). These type scenes are open ended, allowing the audience to find themselves in what follows and thus be moved to join with those who give thanks. The closing note, with its call to reflection, makes clear that all who encounter the psalm are to make its themes elements of their ongoing reflection.

The combination of exhortations to thanksgiving and reflection on Yahweh's acts of kindness suggests that we should read the psalm as essentially didactic (similarly, Tucker 2014: 59). This would not prevent it from having functioned liturgically since liturgy can be didactic, but it does mean that focus should fall on its didactic patterns rather than the liturgical ones. This would also allow for the psalm to be understood as a unified composition even though we cannot exclude the possibility that some parts were composed separately (e.g. vv. 33–41, which lack a type scene; see Allen 2002: 84–87 for a summary; Beyerlin 1979). More probably, we should see these statements about Yahweh as an initial reflection that draws together the elements of the type scenes, which then prepares for the closing call to reflection (vv. 42–43).

Structurally, the psalm is bounded by an inclusio through the focus on Yahweh's 'kindness' (*ḥesed*; vv. 1, 43), while there is also significant repeated language; especially in the second stanza, where each strophe is marked by a refrain. On this basis we can analyse the psalm as follows:

1. Opening summons (1–3)
2. Type scenes of Yahweh's salvation (4–32)
   a. Wilderness wanderers (4–9)
   b. Prisoners (10–16)
   c. Fools (17–22)
   d. Sailors (23–32)
3. Yahweh's reversals (33–41)
4. Closing call (42–43)

Comment

1–3. The opening call to give thanks to Yahweh echoes Psalm 106:1, creating strong links to the close of Book 4. Jenkins (2021: 174–177; cf. Vesco 2006, 2: 1035–1036) argues that, when combined with 'Hallelujah!', it also provides an important marker for Book 5's structure, analysing it into three main segments, each commencing with this same summons (Pss 107:1; 118:1; 136:1). The difficulty with his analysis is that Psalms 135–136 seem to be closely linked, while Psalm 118 is more likely closing Book 5's opening section, as it creates an inclusio with Psalm 107 (Crutchfield 2011: 13–14; cf. Snearly 2016: 105–127). But he is certainly correct to note the significant role this refrain plays across Book 5. The community who asked to be gathered by Yahweh at the close of Book 4 are now called to give thanks because of his goodness and enduring kindness (cf. Exod. 34:6–7; Ps. 100:5). The redeemed who offer this thanksgiving are those who have been redeemed and gathered from various lands. Calling these people 'the redeemed' echoes language from Isaiah 35:9, 51:11, 62:12, which uses it to describe those who would return from the exile, though the type scenes in the second stanza allow for the redeemed to be more than just returning exiles (Crutchfield 2011: 20–21). The initial east–west axis suggests a concern with the cardinal points, here tracked by the sun's movement (more literally 'rising and setting'; cf. Isa. 43:5). This is carried into a mention of the 'north', but the pattern is seemingly broken by mention of the 'sea'. 'North' is also Mount Zaphon, a toponym that frequently stands for 'the north', but we do not elsewhere find 'the sea' standing for 'south' (though cf. Isa. 49:12). Assuming we do not need to emend the text (cf. 'Notes on the text'), it is possible that it reflects the move from exile in the east back to the land. A journey there would enter the land from the north, for which the Dead Sea would then be in the south, though 'sea' may then serve multiple purposes since it also prepares for focus on the sea in the type scenes. This would not prevent other symbolism being present (both 'north' and 'sea' can have mythic overtones; cf. Jarick 1997), and the language remains sufficiently open that others who were not themselves part of the return would also have good reason to give thanks.

4–9. The second stanza contains four type scenes, each a strophe within the stanza, and each providing an illustration of Yahweh's goodness, but with important variations in each. Each contains a refrain that mentions the particular group who were redeemed, calling out to Yahweh in their distress (vv. 6, 13, 19, 28) and a description of Yahweh's salvific activity on their behalf before a further call to thanksgiving for Yahweh's wondrous deeds for 'the children of humankind' (vv. 8, 13, 21, 31). The point is that these moments of salvation are representative of a wider range of beneficent acts that merit praise. The opening type scene differs from what follows in commencing with a finite verb rather than a generalizing ptc., but this is probably because of its role in commencing the stanza, and the group described in it remains non-specific. The wilderness wanderers described here are reminiscent of the exodus generation in that they experienced both hunger and thirst, which Yahweh addressed (e.g. Exod. 16:1 – 17:7; cf. Ps. 106:14), with Yahweh said to have led them away from the inhabited areas (Exod. 13:17–18). But the image is more general than this, more closely resembling a caravan that has become lost or has carried insufficient supplies while passing through a remote, arid area, and is thus unable to reach somewhere settled or where they can settle. Like the community at the close of Book 4, these wanderers cried out to Yahweh in their distress and were saved by him, leading them to a habitable city, a place where the needed supplies could be found. The wanderers experienced Yahweh's kindness, and their experience is part of the wider range of wondrous deeds he performs for all humans. The responsibility of those who experienced this salvation is to give thanks, testifying to what Yahweh has done. Such wonders echo those performed against Egypt in the exodus (Exod. 3:20), this time through the provision of food and drink. The closing statement generalizes further in that all who had their thirst slaked and hunger satisfied are called to give thanks, as also are those who have seen this in the experience of others.

10–16. The second type scene focuses on prisoners. These would typically be those captured in war, both combatants and non-combatants, unlike the modern world, which more commonly imprisons those convicted of crimes (though Lev. 24:12 allows for the possibility of short-term custody). Although the prisoners here would more likely have been captives, their captivity is said to have happened because they rebelled against God's words, spurning the Most High's counsel. Such rebellion echoes the exodus generation's failure to enter the land (Deut. 1:26; cf. Ps. 78:17, 40, 56), though scorning God's counsel is more obviously a concern of the wisdom literature (e.g. Prov. 1:30). The words and counsel they rejected could be associated with the Torah, though a broader sense of God's instruction is perhaps meant. These people are prisoners locked in desperate circumstances (both actual and metaphorical), humbled through grievous toil, and stumbling because they lacked any helper. But they too cried out to Yahweh and were saved, brought out from their imprisonment, their chains broken (cf. Isa. 45:2). These prisoners experienced Yahweh's kindness and so they too are to give thanks, testifying to what Yahweh has done, placing their rescue into the larger pattern of Yahweh's wondrous acts for humans. Again, the closing statement generalizes further, so that all who have been released should give thanks, as also are those who have seen this in the experience of others.

17–22. The third type scene refers to fools who have suffered because of their transgression and iniquity. The language is again evocative of wisdom motifs (e.g. Prov. 10:8), which see such folly as producing its own outcomes. But the psalm makes clear that in this case the folly was sinful (transgressions, iniquity), and this triggered their suffering, bringing them close to death (cf. Job 38:17). In this case, their suffering left them abhorring food (as can happen with some illnesses) and so brought them closer to death. But they too cried out to Yahweh and were saved when he sent his word and restored them, delivering them from the pits, which again represent death. They too are to give thanks, testifying to what Yahweh has done in showing his kindness to them. Rather than generalizing this, the fools are called to offer thanksgiving sacrifices (Lev. 3) and recount what Yahweh has done with a shout. Yahweh's kindness can be experienced even by those whose actions merit punishment, and this wondrous fact is to be recounted with joyful shouts.

23–32. The fourth type scene is concerned with sailors, joining the first in being concerned with travellers. Israel's experience of the sea and shipping was not always positive (cf. 1 Kgs 22:48–49; Jon. 1), and that is reflected in the description here (cf. Cho 1997: 81–87). These sailors, like Jonah, went 'down' to the sea, reflecting the fact that many lived in the highlands. Like Solomon, they were engaged in seafaring trade (1 Kgs 9:26–28), though Solomon apparently did not use Israelite sailors. Distinctively, these sailors also saw Yahweh's great works on the sea, a note about Yahweh's power prior to the cry of distress. Mention of the wondrous deeds on the deep sea at this point means that the sea cannot be understood as an enemy of Yahweh's. Rather, as in Psalm 104:24–26, even its most terrifying elements are firmly under his control. Although this will finally mean stilling a stormy sea (cf. Mark 4:35–41), in this case Yahweh commands the wind and brings about a terrifying storm. Unlike the two preceding type scenes, there is no indication of sin among the sailors, showing there is no one source for distress (Broyles 1999: 409). Their experience, however, is terrifying as the waves mount up, with their ship seemingly reaching up as high as the heavens before plunging to the depths between the waves so that the sailors' courage melted. For all their experience on the sea, they were tossed about, looking like drunkards, and lacking the skill to resolve their crisis. But they too cried out to Yahweh, and like the prisoners were 'brought out' (*yṣ'*) from their distress. At that point, Yahweh calmed the wind and stilled the waves. Unsurprisingly, the sailors rejoiced at this, making them the only ones in the type scenes to have an initial response reported, as they not only saw the storm stilled but were brought to the desired harbour. They too were to give thanks, testifying to what Yahweh had done in showing his kindness to them, placing their rescue into the larger pattern of Yahweh's wondrous acts for humans. As the final type scene, there is a final admonition for them to offer their praise among the people more generally, and the elders in particular; indeed, Goldingay (2008: 256) thinks it possible that this thanksgiving might even have been offered in a pagan setting.

33–41. Each type scene includes a reference to the group concerned calling out to Yahweh and experiencing a form of salvation relevant to their need, and in each case the salvation involves a reversal of the previous situation – the lost and hungry are fed and brought to safety, prisoners are released, fools brought close to death are restored to life, and sailors threatened with death on the sea are brought to a secure harbour. This pattern of reversals becomes the focus of the third stanza and as such expands the type scenes into more general statements of Yahweh's work. Not all the reversals are immediately beneficial to humans (just as the sailors did not appreciate the storm), but this is important because it makes clear that all aspects of creation fall under Yahweh's authority. The covenant blessings and curses (Lev. 26; Deut. 28) show that Yahweh can use creation for human weal and woe, and this is possible because all creation belongs to him. This is also true of the second, third and fourth type scenes where Yahweh (either directly or indirectly) brings about the circumstances from which deliverance is needed. As such, the reflection on the reversals here needs to consider reversals that move both ways, starting with the loss of potable water so that rivers become deserts and gushing springs become thirsty, resulting in land that is a salty waste rather than productive. But as was the case in the second and third type scenes, this is because of the wickedness of the land's inhabitants. Yahweh does not remove productivity from the land without reason, echoing the covenant curses. But he is also the one who makes seemingly uninhabitable and unproductive land a place where people can live, providing water and providing a place where the hungry can live, building cities and establishing thriving agriculture that is productive, both with crops and livestock. Such productivity is not simply a further example of the reversal but comes about because of Yahweh's blessing, adding to the goodness of creation. This does not rule out times of trial, as is evident in verses 39–41, which accept that there can be times of suffering. But Yahweh's reversals also mean that he overcomes human rulers who oppress his people. Yahweh thus brings about reversals in creation and history, sending oppressive princes to trackless wastes so that his people multiply like a flock, placed in a high and secure place.

42–43. The psalm's goal is reached in the closing stanza. Yahweh's kindness was central to the community's thanksgiving in verse 1, and we return that 'kindness' (*ḥesed*) here. It is Yahweh's *ḥesed* that has been demonstrated through the type scenes and is explored through reflection on the reversals. The psalm has also shown that Yahweh acts against the wicked. Accordingly, it is the upright who rejoice when they see the demonstrations of Yahweh's kindness, while the wicked remain silent. Thanksgiving is important, but more than that, this thanksgiving is also the basis for enduring reflection. Those who are wise take time to ponder Yahweh's reversals and all other evidence for his kindness (cf. Hos. 14:9). Posing this as a question, the psalm thus asks the audience to choose the path of wisdom. Accordingly, Book 5 commences with a parallel to Book 1 and its encouragement to choose the way of Torah, while ensuring that the error of Psalm 106:7 is not repeated.

Explanation

Thanksgiving, giving 'a verbal account of that for which one is grateful' (Brueggemann and Bellinger 2014: 466), is at the heart of this poem. Thanksgiving is concerned with telling the story of how Yahweh's 'kindness' (*ḥesed*) has been experienced. That experience might have been in the return from the exile, but it cannot be restricted to that one moment. Rather, thanksgiving emerges out of a range of circumstances; and, as instances of Yahweh's kindness in response to prayers offered in distress are recounted, the audience encountering this psalm is invited to see how their own experience may be mirrored in its type scenes, in turn triggering more accounts for which they can express their gratitude to Yahweh. Thanksgiving has an additional element developed in the third stanza as thankful accounts of Yahweh's kindness provide a framework through which the community is to continue learning and reflecting about his involvement with the world, both the creation and human figures in history. Recounting these stories of thanksgiving gives praise to God, but also provides evidence on which believers may continue to reflect, seeing God at work beyond the boundaries of the believing community and reaching all humankind and creation. The wise course of action is therefore to continue reflecting on what God has done and so perceive the breadth of his kindness as something now made known to us in Jesus even as we recognize our continuing need to cry out to God, both in our own distress and for those we see in distress.

PSALM 108

Translation

A song. A melody. Davidic.

1My heart is steadfast, O God,
  I will sing and make melody,
  indeed, my glory!
2Awake, O harp and lyre,
  I will awaken the dawn.
3I will give thanks to you among the peoples, O Yahweh,
  I will make melody to you among the peoples.
4For your kindness is great, beyond the heavens,
  and your faithfulness to the clouds.

5Be exalted above the heavens, O God,
  your glory above all the earth.
6So that your beloved ones may be delivered,
  save by your right hand and answer me.

7God has spoken in his holiness,
  'I will triumph, I will apportion Shechem,
  and the valley of Sukkoth I will measure off.
8Gilead is mine and Manasseh is mine,
  while Ephraim is my head's protection,
  Judah is my commander's sceptre.
9Moab is my wash pot,
  over Edom I cast my shoe,
  over Philistia I will shout in triumph.'

10Who will conduct me to the fortified city,
  who will bring me to Edom?
11Have not you, O God, rejected us?
  You do not go out, O God, with our armies!
12Grant us help from the foe,
  for human deliverance is worthless.
13With God we can do valiantly,
  and he himself could trample down our foes.

Notes on the text

Although drawing on Psalms 57:7–11 and 60:5–12, this psalm needs to be read on its own terms, and variances from those source texts should be allowed to stand.

2. Understanding *'ap* as emphatic.

4. As with Psalm 57:10, redividing the closing words and reading *bal'ummîm*, a reading found in some MSS. Cf. Graham 2023: 74.

13. As with 60:12, reading the verbs modally.

Form and structure

Psalm 108 is (broadly) a combination of Psalms 57:7–11 and 60:5–12, though there are variations in the shared text (cf. Hamilton 2021, 2: 277). We see the phenomenon of shared texts in Psalms 14 and 53, and Psalms 40:12–17 and 70. In each instance, a new work is created that needs to be read in its textual setting in the Psalter and cannot be reduced to simple replication (against Kraus 1989: 333). Other psalms could be composites, drawing multiple poems into a single psalm (e.g. Pss 27, 147), but this is the only indisputable instance of this. We do see the phenomenon of a single poem presented as two psalms elsewhere (Pss 9–10, 42–43), whereas here two previously distinct poetic portions have become one psalm. Clearly, creative use of existing material was an acceptable option, as we also see in 1 Chronicles 16's integration of parts of Psalms 96, 105 and 106.

This is the first of three Davidic psalms focused on the issues of warfare and honour (see Sutton and Human 2017a, 2017b). Along with the shared Davidic element in the title, they are also notable for key shared vocabulary (Sutton 2015: 49–70), the most notable of which is perhaps 'right hand' (*yāmîn*), which is consistently used in relation to the motif of honour (Pss 108:6; 110:6; or its loss in Ps. 109:6). The motif of warfare is also evident here in the statements about Yahweh's need to lead the nation to victory (v. 12), while the messianic figure is promised victory in Psalm 110:1. The language of warfare is individualized in Psalm 109:3, but still present. This collection of Davidic psalms immediately after the opening thanksgiving in Psalm 107 is paralleled by Psalms 138–145, the last Davidic collection, which are then followed by the 'Hallelujah!' poems of Psalms 146–150. Apart from these, Book 5's other Davidic psalms are found in the Songs of the Ascents, providing structural markers for that collection. Psalms 108–109 also reflect on aspects of Yahweh's 'kindness' (*ḥesed*; 108:4; 109:21, 26), picking up on the central motif of Psalm 107 and anticipating the reign of the messianic figure in Psalm 110.

Psalm 108 can be understood as a communal complaint psalm in that it speaks of God's having rejected the community (v. 11), so that they need deliverance. But it also makes use of elements of trust (cf. Crutchfield 2011: 24), especially in the declaration of the greatness of Yahweh's *ḥesed*, while the closing statement also evokes a degree of trust, albeit one that is perhaps uncertain as to the reason for God's apparent rejection of them. In this, it has joined material from an individual complaint (Ps. 57) with a communal one (Ps. 60), beginning the process of transforming the source material. This transformation also leads to a structure that cuts across elements of the source material, especially as the seam where the source material is joined now becomes a strophe in its own right, leading to the following analysis:

1. The God of glory (1–6)
   a. Steadfastness under pressure (1–4)
   b. Appeal for God's exaltation (5–6)
2. Divine oracle (7–9)
3. Closing prayer (10–13)

Comment

Title: For 'A song', see on Psalm 65. For 'A melody' and 'Davidic', see on Psalm 3. The title is much briefer than either source psalm, both of which are linked to specific events in David's life (though Graham [2023: 102–108] claims this briefer superscription initiates an eschatological reading).

1–4. The opening is spoken by an individual who declares his personal commitment to God. Lacking the setting of personal threat from Psalm 57:1–6, it now functions as a model for the wider community, though a declaration of steadfastness could presume there is some threat. This steadfastness is expressed through a vow to sing and make melody, linking the first verse to the title. The closing part line of verse 1 is uncertain, but it could be taken as addressing God as the poet's glory, the one to be praised. If the psalmist is to sing, then accompaniment is also needed, so that the harp and lyre are personified and told to awake in preparation for being played before awakening the dawn, hastening the point when a community might gather for praise (cf. Goldingay 2008: 265), though the mythical elements of dawn might also be present, anticipating their development in Psalm 110:3 (Sutton 2017). For the speaker, singing praise is not only for the community; it is for the nations. The vow to give thanks also extends the call to thanksgiving in Psalm 107 by announcing it is to be among the peoples, while also focusing on Yahweh's kindness and faithfulness. Both the kindness and faithfulness are said to be great, reaching beyond the skies, and thus beyond human reach.

5–6. The second strophe emerges from the first, but now imperatives dominate. First, God is asked to be exalted above the heavens, with his glory above all the earth. All creation is to be overshadowed by God. God's exaltation is ultimately for his beloved's benefit. Those to whom he is committed are to be delivered from affliction through his saving, an act of salvation that will demonstrate God answers this speaker's request.

7–9. God has been called to answer, and an answer is given in this stanza as he speaks. God's speaking in his holiness could be understood as his speaking in the sanctuary (so Allen 2002: 93), but can also be understood as his speaking by what is essential to himself. As with Psalm 60:6–8, we are probably to interpret the oracle as a citation of a message previously given, which is here cited to convince God to act, with the nations mentioned being representative of his universal authority (cf. Tournay 1991: 181). If so, this removes the evidence for a Maccabean dating (Knauf 2000: 61–65). God's earlier declaration asserted that he would come in victory, claiming Israel's territory west and east of the Jordan (Shechem and Sukkoth). From there the whole of the land is given to Israel either side of the river (Gilead is east, Manasseh is a bridge-tribe on both sides, while Ephraim and Judah move south-west of the river). God's authority moves beyond this, being asserted over Moab and Edom (east of the Jordan) and Philistia (west, on the Mediterranean coast). These peoples may not acknowledge God's authority, but the oracle insists they have only subservient positions, however much they may think otherwise.

10–13. Drawing on the oracle, we again hear the individual voice (Goldingay [2008: 270] believes v. 10 continues the oracle, but with Estes [2019: 326] a change of speaker is more probable). The questions of verse 10 are rhetorical, for it is God who must lead the speaker to the fortified city, to Edom. If Edom belongs to God, then reaching there is possible, but this is problematized by a third rhetorical question in verse 11. If God has rejected the community and does not go out with them, how can they succeed? Hence, we return to imperatives as appeals in verse 12 – victory can come only if God grants help against the foe. The community knows that human help offers nothing meaningful. Victory can still be won but happens only if God acts.

Explanation

Sometimes the best way to face a new situation is to go back to the old sources and hear them in the new context. Modern worship music sometimes does this by reworking old hymns, bringing their message to a new audience who may otherwise miss them. Psalm 108 is best understood as an example of this process (Botha 2010: 593), one that helps a community struggling with new challenges (perhaps in the time after the exile) to realize that they stand in a longer tradition of those who have faced foes and even wondered where God was. Hence, the poet of Psalm 108 drew together elements of Psalms 57 and 60, starting with praise rather than complaint, to provide a setting of confidence before turning to the community's complaint. This process of drawing on older material was already evident in Psalm 60, which itself drew on an older oracle from God, and this might have encouraged the composer of Psalm 108 to take the process one step further, reminding a new audience of the continued vitality of God's word to address new circumstances (cf. Heb. 4:12–13). Here, a community who know of God's kindness but wonder how they will experience it are reminded of earlier words on which they can continue to draw as they call out to God, knowing his help alone suffices.

PSALM 109

Translation

The director's. Davidic. A melody.

1O God of my praise, do not be silent!
2For wicked and deceitful mouths were opened against me,
  they spoke to me with a false tongue.
3Words of hatred surrounded me,
  they waged war against me without cause.
4In place of my love they accused me,
  but I am a prayer.
5They have set evil against me in place of good,
  and hate in place of my love.

6Appoint a wicked one against him,
  Let an accuser stand at his right hand.
7Let his wickedness be brought out when he is tried,
  let his prayer be sin!
8May his days be few,
  let another take his goods.
9May his children be fatherless,
  and his wife a widow.
10May his children wander aimlessly and beg,
  yes, beg from their desolate ruins.
11Let a creditor ensnare all that is his,
  and let strangers despoil his property.
12May there not be one extending kindness to him,
  and let there not be one showing grace to his fatherless children.
13May his posterity be cut off,

let their name be blotted out from the next generation.
14Let the iniquity of his fathers be remembered before Yahweh,
let not the sin of his mother be blotted out,
15let them be continually before Yahweh,
that he may cut of their memory from the land,
16because he did not remember to act kindly,
but pursued anyone, the poor and needy,
even the broken-hearted, to kill them.
17For he loved cursing, it entered into him,
and did not delight in blessing –
let it be far from him.
18He clothed himself with cursing as his robe,
it entered his innards like water,
and his bones like oil.
19May it be for him like a garment with which he wraps himself,
and a waistband he girds on continually.

20This is the recompense of my accusers from Yahweh,
and those speaking evil against me.

21But you, O Yahweh, my lord,
deal with me for your name's sake,
because your kindness is good, deliver me.
22For I am poor and needy,
and my heart is pierced within me.
23I am fading like a shadow as it stretches out,
I am shaken off like a locust.
24My knees staggered from fasting,
and my flesh has grown lean, without fat.
25As for me, I have become a reproach to them,
when they see me, they wag their heads.

26Help me, O Yahweh my God,
save me according to your kindness,
27that they might know this is your hand,
you, O Yahweh, have done it.
28They will curse, but you will bless,
they rose, but let them be put to shame,
and your servant will rejoice.
29Let my accusers be clothed with dishonour,
let them be wrapped in their shame like a robe.
30With my mouth I will give great thanks to Yahweh,
and among many I will praise him.
31For he stands at the right hand of the needy,
to save him from those condemning him.

Notes on the text

4. Gk, Tg and Syr. all suggest we should read a verb rather than 'prayer' at this point. But MT can be retained as indicating that the poet embodies prayer (cf. Allen 2002: 99).

8. Hebr. *pĕquddātô* could refer to an office held (cf. Num. 3:36) but given that the following punishments all refer to loss of possession 'goods' seems more probable (cf. Isa. 15:7).

10. Gk suggests we could read *yĕgōrĕšû* (cf. NIV). But *wĕdārašû* provides a better parallel.

20. Hebr. *pĕʿullâ* is difficult but is here understood as an ironic reward given judicially by Yahweh.

Form and structure

The second of three psalms in the small Davidic collection of Psalms 108–110 also contains by far the longest imprecation (a prayer against an enemy) within the Psalter. It is this feature more than any other that has dominated recent scholarly discussion, though earlier generations tended to be more concerned with Peter's citation of it with reference to Judas (Acts 1:20; cf. Hamilton 2021, 2: 285). Alongside this, more recent scholarship has noted its integration into this small subunit, as well as the slightly larger collection of Psalms 107–118 (cf. Crutchfield 2011: 25–30). Most immediately, we can note that verses 30–31 take up the thanksgiving announced in Psalm 108:3. Yahweh's kindness is said to be great (Ps. 108:4), and here provides the basis of the psalmist's appeal for vindication (Ps. 109:21, 26). As a complaint psalm, there are also obvious points of contrast highlighted through similar language, the most important being that Yahweh's right hand is there the means of salvation (Ps. 108:6), anticipating the place of honour in Psalm 110:1, 5. Here, the imprecation asks for an accuser (*śāṭān*) to be at the enemy's right hand (Ps. 109:6), contrasting this with Yahweh's saving presence at the right hand of those in need (Ps. 109:31).

A petitionary psalm (Hossfeld and Zenger 2011: 128), it can also be placed with the prayers of the accused (Firth 2005b: 36–38). These texts originally functioned in the temple for dealing with serious legal charges but are placed into a wider context within the Psalter. False accusation becomes a sample of the circumstances in which Yahweh's kindness is at work, so overcoming of the enemy mentioned here prepares for the defeat of all the psalmist's enemies in Psalm 110. That a legal process, probably dealing with a capital case, lies behind the psalm is supported by the references to accusers that occur at key points throughout (vv. 4, 6, 20, 29) and the fact that death was apparently sought through a legal process (v. 31).

Although this is relatively clear, there is a significant scholarly divide over whether to read the main imprecation (vv. 6–19) as a statement from the psalmist (so, Firth 2005b: 37–38; 2015a: 83) or a citation of the speech of the enemies (most recently, Jenkins 2020b; 2021: 186–190; NRSV makes this interpretation explicit by adding 'They say' at the start of v. 6, though the text does not require this). The issue turns on the switch from pl. to sg. forms, allowing for the possibility that the words of the enemies are quoted as part of the psalmist's defence. This is certainly possible since quotations are not necessarily marked in Hebrew, and the switch is striking. But it is also possible that the psalmist uses the sg. to focus on a ringleader, while the use of such a lengthy unmarked citation is difficult to parallel (cf. Scheffler 2011: 202). An important difficulty for the quotation theory is that verse 20 seems to generalize the imprecation to all the poet's enemies. So, if it is a quote, the generalization suggests it is taken up as the poet's prayer. If so, then it is grammatically easier to assume that the imprecation is the poet's words against the enemy.

The poem's structure is relatively straightforward, with three principal stanzas linked by repeating key words:

1. Appeal for assistance (1–5)
2. Prayer against enemies (6–20)
   a. Imprecation against leader (6–19)
   b. Generalization to other accusers (20)
3. Prayer for deliverance (21–31)
   a. Appeal to God's kindness (21–25)
   b. Appeal for help (26–31)

Comment

Title: For 'The director's', see on Psalm 4. For 'Davidic' and 'A melody', see on Psalm 3.

1–5. The psalm opens with a strong appeal addressed to Yahweh as 'God of my praise'. Yahweh is the recipient of the psalmist's praise, and so has heard the poet speak. Where Yahweh has heard the poet, now he is urged not to be silent (cf. Pss 28:1; 35:22; 39:12; 83:1). Yahweh must speak, and he must speak an authoritative word of judgement. Yahweh's speech is vital because the psalmist is afflicted by malicious speech, words that wage war against the poet without reason, surrounding the poet with hatred. In response to love, the enemies accuse the poet, making the legal context explicit. But where the enemies attack through speech, the psalmist's posture is one of prayer, one that is so all-encompassing that the poet asserts, 'I am a prayer.' The psalmist receives evil for good, hatred for love. Faced with this abuse, Yahweh must not remain silent.

6–19. The psalmist now appeals for Yahweh to act against a specific enemy. Significantly, it is Yahweh who must act, not the psalmist. The m. sg. form running through these verses is most likely the ringleader of those accusing the psalmist, though one could also understand the sg. here as distributive, covering each accuser individually. In making this appeal, care is taken to match the language about the enemy to their acts against the poet. Their speech was wicked, so a wicked person should be appointed against the enemy; they have accused, so an accuser is to be placed at the enemy's right hand. Where the right hand is typically a place of honour, now it becomes the place of threat. Moreover, the enemy's accusations had brought the psalmist to a place of judgement, but now the enemy is to be judged and shown to be wicked. Where the psalmist embodied prayer, the prayer of the enemy is to be regarded as sin, perhaps because a temple ritual would have involved prayers by the accuser, and such prayers would reveal the accuser's guilt. The implications of a guilty verdict against the enemy are then worked out in verses 8–19. The imprecation is extensive, but it is important to read it in the light of the law of false accusation in Deuteronomy 19:16–19, which specifies that a malicious witness should receive the penalty that would have applied to the one accused if they were found guilty. Everything described here can be understood within that framework, so the psalmist is asking for the accuser to receive the full effects of what was sought against the psalmist. Although the process of his court case is clearly irregular, once Naboth was condemned (1 Kgs 21:8–15), Ahab could seize his assets. His case probably indicates that those convicted of capital crimes like this would forfeit their property. As such, the imprecation is an extended reflection on the effects of someone being executed for their crime. Such a person would not live long, and any position they held would pass to another, while his wife would be widowed, and his children left fatherless (vv. 8–9). Having forfeited his property, his family would lose the right to its produce, being reduced to begging. Any creditors would claim that part of the executed person's property necessary to cover outstanding debts, so that even foreigners could despoil the estate. The enemy has failed to show kindness or grace in pursuing the psalmist, and so the request is that the penalty should match the crime, and that just as the enemy's accusations put the psalmist's family at risk, so his family should also receive no pity. Sons in such a family would struggle to marry since there would be no one to arrange the marriage, meaning that the family name would be blotted out. Verse 14 assumes the actions of the accuser are consistent with those of his forebears, so that their iniquity is what should be remembered before Yahweh. Accordingly, he should remove any memory of them from the earth precisely because he always has them in view. Reasons for this are then developed in verses 16–19, which make clear that the accuser's actions against the poet are part of a pattern of behaviour where he failed to show kindness. Operating from a position of power, the accuser pursued the poor and needy, those lacking resources to defend themselves, to kill them. His preferred speech was cursing rather than blessing, and so he should receive curses back. Indeed, he wore cursing like a robe and was so covered by them that they entered his body. In this instance, the image of cursing entering the enemy like water may reflect a ritual such as Numbers 5:11–31 (cf. Kitz 2007). That is, the accuser was completely covered, inside and out, by cursing. Since this was his preferred approach, the psalmist asks that it remain as the garment he wears, like a belt constantly put on. The accuser's life is marked by malicious speech, and so the psalmist asks that this be his experience since it is what he has sought for others.

20. Having prayed against a central figure, the psalmist broadens the imprecation to address all the accusers. The statement is terse, and the meaning is not helped by uncertainty about the meaning of *pĕʿullâ* (cf. 'Notes on the text'). The word could mean 'work' and so be understood as the activity of all the accusers, indicating that they all share the attitudes of the central accuser, but here it seems better to understand it as 'recompense'. Although this can be understood positively (i.e. as pay earned; cf. Lev. 19:13), it is better understood ironically here – this is what they have worked for, so they should receive it from Yahweh. All those who sought the psalmist's life should receive the penalty of the malicious accuser, the penalty they earlier sought against the psalmist.

21–25. The psalmist now addresses Yahweh as Lord, appealing for his help as the one responsible for the psalmist. By calling Yahweh 'Lord' and appealing as one of the 'poor and needy' (i.e. those lacking the power to change circumstances), the text makes clear that the poet is dependent on Yahweh. It is Yahweh who must take responsibility for his own, something indicated by his name, which here points to Yahweh's character. Central to this is his 'kindness' (*ḥesed*). Yahweh's kindness is good, and this goodness should be borne out through the deliverance of the psalmist. The psalmist's need is made clear through the metaphors of weakness in verses 23–25, each of which stresses that the poet's own strength is insufficient to change the situation. A shadow disappears at evening, and the psalmist is like a shadow that the sun's last beams leave vaguely visible. A single locust is easily shaken off, while someone who has fasted for too long (perhaps here involuntarily) will lack the physical strength to bring about change. The psalmist cannot effect change, but the need remains as accusers continue to assail the poet, the wagging of their heads pointing to the scorn they feel towards the poet.

26–31. The prayer returns to imperatives in verse 26, asking that Yahweh help and save the poet. This help is grounded in the fact that Yahweh is the psalmist's God and because he is characterized by 'kindness' (*ḥesed*), picking up on a key term through the psalm. The reason for this is articulated in verse 27, where the psalmist indicates that Yahweh should act so the accusers know that it is Yahweh's hand that has acted, that Yahweh has worked for the psalmist. This point is crucial to understanding the psalm, since it is through this that these malicious accusers know of Yahweh's commitment to the needy. Yahweh's acts counteract those of the accusers, so that where their speech continues to be threatening, Yahweh brings blessing. They have risen against the psalmist to bring shame, but they are the ones who will be shamed; whereas the psalmist can rejoice. Verse 29 then introduces a further imprecation, though in effect it takes up the earlier statements in verses 18–19, asking that all the accusers, not just the ringleader, receive the penalty that fits their actions. Perhaps more importantly verse 30 anticipates giving thanks, so that the poet's speech contrasts with that of the accusers (cf. v. 2). This thanksgiving is within a multitude, offering speech that speaks truly about Yahweh as the one who stands at the right hand of the needy to deliver their life from abuse of the legal system. Thus, the psalm closes with speech that speaks truly and celebrates justice, contrasting it with the malicious speech experienced by the poet.

Explanation

For all its undoubted challenges, Psalm 109 remains a profound reflection on the importance of seeing God's justice in this world. As Goldingay has noted (2008: 288–289), it is based on the principle of divine retribution, a motif that remains in the NT as much as the OT. It falls under the larger motif of God's grace, since the point of forgiveness is that we do not receive what we deserve. But at the same time, the weak must be able to cry out to God for justice. God's kindness is not restricted to forgiveness but may also be applied to deliverance in situations of threat from which the needy cannot save themselves. That help will see God working out the implications of a guilty verdict against those who abuse the weak. Yet, it is also important to observe that the poet's prayer against the enemy is shaped by the Torah. The imprecation is not a request for unlimited judgement. Rather, it is a cry that asks God to apply Torah. Having cried out, there is nothing more the poet can do. The appeal has been made, and it is up to God to decide what happens. This background is informative for reflecting on the use of this psalm in Peter's speech in Acts 1:20, where he treats Judas as the subject of the imprecation in verse 8. It is not that the psalm predicted Judas, but rather the imprecation finds a perfect example in him as the one who has acted against Jesus, David's great descendant.

PSALM 110

Translation

Davidic. A melody.

1An oracle of Yahweh to my lord,
'Sit at my right hand,
until I make your enemies
a footstool for your feet.'
2Your mighty sceptre
shall Yahweh send from Zion,
so that you rule in the midst of your enemies.
3Your people are willing on the day of your power,
in holy majesty from the womb towards dawn,
the dew of your youth is yours.

4Yahweh has sworn and will not relent,
'You are a priest for ever,
according to the pattern of Melchizedek.'
5The Lord at your right hand,
shattered kings on the day of his wrath.
6He executes judgement among the peoples,
filled with corpses,
he shatters heads,
in a vast land.
7He shall drink from the brook on the way,
therefore, he will lift the head.

Notes on the text

2. The imp. *rĕdēh* is a consequence of the imp. (GKC §110c). Vaillancourt (2019: 88) regards it as a further oracle, which is possible but leaves the oracle without introduction.

3. Every clause of this verse is disputed, but MT can (with difficulty!) be retained (against e.g. Kilian 1990). The form *mišḥār* is a hapax. The mem prefix is here taken as indicating motion (W. P. Brown 1998: 93–95; cf. Starbuck 1999: 151).

4. Rather than personal name 'Melchizedek' we could have a 'righteous king' (cf. NRSV mg.), but the history of interpretation, reaching back to Gk and Tg, suggests it should be read as a personal name.

6. The sg. 'head' is collective (cf. LXX; *WHS* §2); hence, pl. in English.

Form and structure

Psalm 110 is generally agreed to be a royal psalm, though beyond that almost everything is debated. The text is often difficult to interpret and frequently emended, whether because of the versions (and Masoretic MSS) or the numerous proposed changes thrown up by the history of exegesis (see the helpful summary in Hossfeld and Zenger 2011: 141–143). Even when MT is followed, as here, there remain obscurities that lead to different interpretations because of uncertainty surrounding the grammatical constructions. Humility in interpretation is always important, but it is especially the case here. Despite these challenges, it is the most frequently referenced Psalm in the NT, especially (but not only) in the epistle to the Hebrews (see Hay 1973; Compton 2015; M. H. Emadi 2022: 147–204).

The psalm is the closing element in the Davidic collections of Psalms 108–110, and is joined with them through repeated elements, especially mention of the right hand as a sign of honour (see 'Form and structure' Ps. 108). It is notable that the right hand forms a link between Psalms 109:31 and 110:1, making the king an exemplar of Yahweh's salvation. As Gillingham (2022: 182) points out, even though these three psalms are very different, they have been brought together in the compilation of the Psalter so they are read together. We might note that Psalms 108 and 110 are joined also by their use of divine oracles (Pss 108:7; 110:1, 4). Where the oracle in Psalm 108 provides a foundation for prayer, here the oracles provide a context for understanding a Davidic king (perhaps on coronation) who is most probably to be understood messianically in that he exceeds the historical experience of David and his descendants. Though, even if this be granted, Wilson (1985a: 221) denies this reading, seeing David as a wise man who heeds Psalm 107:39–42 (cf. Goldingay 2008: 299). Vaillancourt (2019: 85–86) shows that there are significant differences in how it is understood. In both Psalms 108 and 110, Yahweh's prior word provides a basis for hope, a hope here shaped by the focus on the king through patterns that reach back to Melchizedek (Gen. 14:17–20), and thus precede the Davidic monarchy. If Psalms 108–110 are intended as proof of Yahweh's 'kindness' (*ḥesed*) from Psalm 107 (with Hossfeld and Zenger 2011: 146–147), then we can understand the messianic hope as the final evidence for it, albeit a hope grounded in the experience of Davidic kings, especially through links with Psalm 2. It reminds the community that what Yahweh has previously said continues to provide hope for the future. The wise can thus reflect on this hope (Ps. 107:43).

The text's complexities mean there are numerous proposals for the psalm's structure, especially when considering how the oracles are structured, but we can analyse it through the two oracles as containing two stanzas:

1. Oracle of rule (1–3)
2. Oracle of priesthood (4–7)

Comment

Title: For 'Davidic' and 'A melody', see on Psalm 3.

1–3. The psalm begins with an oracle, using *nĕ'um*, a noun that occurs elsewhere in Psalms only at 36:1, itself a difficult text. It could function as a denominative verb (and is often translated by a verb of speech), but there is value in rendering it as a noun even though speech follows, thus marking its status as a particular kind of speech from Yahweh. If the oracle is reported through a prophet (with Hilber 2005: 76–80), then the prophet would speak of the king as 'my lord'. As is common in prophetic oracles, divine and human speech merge, as the king is told to sit at 'my right hand', which in this case is a place of honour with Yahweh (see Sutton 2016). This place of honour anticipates the defeat of the king's enemies, something achieved by Yahweh alone, not the king. This victory anticipates a moment when the enemies become a footstool for the king's feet, pointing to the enemies coming prostrate before the king, acknowledging his rule (and, through him, Yahweh's reign). The implications of this are drawn out in verse 2, where the king is told that Yahweh will extend his mighty sceptre from Zion, establishing the certainty of this reign (cf. Ps. 72:8). The sceptre is a symbol of royal reign (Ps. 45:6, Amos 1:5, 8), while mention of Zion here links this reign both to the promise to David (2 Sam. 7), which followed his capture of Zion (2 Sam. 5:6–10), and to Yahweh's own reign, which is also associated with Zion (e.g. Pss 46–48). The king's reign is sure because of Yahweh's commitment to him. It is Yahweh, not the king, who overcomes the enemies. Nevertheless, a king needs a people, and their place is introduced in verse 3. The king's people willingly join him on the day of his power, the point where he comes to reign. Indeed, the noun here could picture them as free-will offerings (cf. Exod. 35:29; 36:3), emphasizing their voluntary commitment to the king (cf. Judg. 5:2, 9). They are not forced into a place of servitude but give themselves freely. The logic of the balance of the verse is debated, but it seems best to understand mention of the holy array as describing the dress of the king rather than the people (though both are possible), extending the temple imagery of the free-will offerings. The king's holy garments make clear that he represents Yahweh and reigns only because of his commitment to Yahweh, while anticipating the priesthood image of the second oracle. If our understanding of the final part of verse 3b is correct (cf. 'Notes on the text'), then the king is pictured as facing eastwards, the direction of the morning sun. The womb of the dawn would describe the point just before daybreak, a time when dew might be heaviest. Just as the dew would refresh a dry land, so also the king will be refreshed with the dew of his youth. This could point to the king's personal renewal, as if restored to youth, but in the context of the people's commitment is perhaps better understood as the encouragement that comes from the youth committing themselves to him.

4–7. The second oracle is introduced with a new formula, this time pointing to an irrevocable oath, one from which Yahweh will not turn. It combines royal, priestly and military concepts, a combination evident from ancient iconography (Purcell 2020). The oracle itself is the balance of verse 4, which declares that the king is a priest for ever, patterned on Melchizedek. Mention of Melchizedek points back to Genesis 14:17–20, where he is a priest-king at Salem (Jerusalem) in the time of Abraham. This points to well before the time of David or even Aaron, and thus references a different mode of both kingship and priesthood than applied in either the first- or second-temple periods. Much speculation surrounds the figure of Melchizedek (which reaches back to ancient times, as evidenced by 11QMelch), but the point here seems to be that the king will join Melchizedek in being a priest-king. This was not the standard pattern in Israel, though there are points where the possibility exists, such as 2 Samuel 8:18, which notes that David's sons were priests. As priest-king, there is no sense that the king supplants the Aaronic priests in the temple but rather in his reign takes a role in representing the people before God. Following the oracle, we move again to a prophetic figure who explores the significance of the vow. The king is promised that the Lord (here, MT's pointing makes clear that 'Lord' means Yahweh, not the king) is at his right hand. Since the right hand is a metaphor of honour there is no conflict with verse 1 (the change of preposition is also significant), and the point here is that Yahweh stands with the king in times of conflict. Psalm 2:2 anticipated kings resistant to Yahweh's reign through his king, and here it is made clear that Yahweh defeated them on the day of his wrath (cf. Ps. 2:5). The crushing of enemy kings in the past provides assurance to the king that Yahweh's oath can be trusted. Verse 6 takes the king into this future, as it emphasizes that Yahweh executes judgement among the nations, and this includes overcoming all foes no matter how vast the land. Again, it is Yahweh who overcomes, works judgement and crushes opposition, not the king. Verse 7 could form a new stanza, but the contrast between the crushed heads of verse 6 and the raised head (cf. Waltke et al. 2010: 509) here suggests that it should be read within this stanza. It is not clear, though, whether Yahweh or the king is the subject of the verse. It is easier to imagine the king drinking from a brook after his enthronement (so, Vaillancourt 2019: 114–116), perhaps the Gihon (cf. 1 Kgs 1:38–40), and raising his head refreshed from this. But Yahweh was the subject of the previous verbs, and nothing marks a shift here. As such, we should probably read this anthropomorphically, where Yahweh is likened to a human king slaking his thirst after battle (cf. Booij 1989a: 404). The heads of the king's opponents have been crushed, but the one who acts for him has been refreshed and his head is raised, alert to the king's needs.

Explanation

Psalm 110 closes the Davidic trilogy of Psalms 108–110. Psalm 108 had closed in anticipation of victory that could be won when Yahweh fought for his people, while Psalm 109 closed with the assurance that Yahweh stood at the right hand of the needy. Those motifs come together here, as Yahweh stands at the right hand of the king and gains the victory his people need. Although the psalm itself might well have had a coronation in its background (an element that is one of several connections to Ps. 2 taken up in Heb. 1:5–13), its placement within the Psalter is what emphasizes its messianic dimensions (with Vesco 2006, 2: 1052). Yet, in doing this, it joins with Psalm 108 in also looking back to older material in its allusions to the Davidic covenant and especially the use of existing oracles that point to the importance of kings from David's line, while also reaching further back to Melchizedek. The hope of victory Yahweh gives through his king is rooted in Israel's past but is here presented with a look to the future. That victory comes because Yahweh brings it about, while always ensuring this is associated with the king.

The NT takes up the messianic cues from the psalm's context, making clear that this hope finds its focus in Jesus. Indeed, Jesus makes this association himself in his debate with the Pharisees when he points out that the Messiah is greater than David (Mark 12:35–37). This association is taken up elsewhere in the NT. In Peter's Pentecost sermon, he too points to Jesus' superiority to David because of his ascension (Acts 2:34–35; cf. 1 Peter 3:18–22), while Paul also draws on it when pointing to Jesus' ascension and heavenly reign (1 Cor. 15:25). These themes are developed in Hebrews, which uses it to point to Jesus' superiority to the angels (Heb. 1:13), and to his high priestly ministry, which is patterned on Melchizedek and relevant for his heavenly reign and ministry (Heb. 5:5–10; 7:15–25). Lest we think the psalm's significance is exhausted by noting Jesus as fulfilment, we should also note that Paul uses his place at God's right hand as the basis for our own ethical commitment to Jesus (Col. 3:1), reflecting that we are already raised with him (Eph. 2:6). In that believers are called to follow Jesus, we too point to the key political claim of the psalm, which is that all rule and authority are subject to God's reign as now expressed through Jesus.

PSALM 111

Translation

[1]Hallelujah!
I will give thanks to Yahweh with all my heart,
in the council of the upright and the congregation.

[2]Great are the works of Yahweh,
studied by all who delight in them.
[3]Splendour and majesty is his work,
and his righteousness stands for ever.
[4]He has made a memorial for his works,
gracious and compassionate is Yahweh.
[5]He has given food to those who fear him,
he remembers his covenant for ever.
[6]He has declared the power of his works to his people,
giving them the inheritance of the nations.

[7]Truth and justice are the work of his hands,
all his precepts are reliable.
[8]They are established for ever and ever,
done with truth and uprightness.
[9]He has sent redemption to his people,
he has commanded his covenant for ever:
holy and awesome is his name!
[10]The fear of Yahweh is the beginning of wisdom,
good insight belongs to all who do his precepts,
his praise stands for ever.

Notes on the text

10. Taking the pl. suff. on *ʿōśêhem* as referring to the precepts of verse 7 (similarly, Hamilton 2021, 2: 302). Gk and Syr. have sg., which would refer to wisdom. MT is more difficult but can be retained.

Form and structure

Psalm 111 introduces a new segment of Book 5 that runs through to Psalm 118 (cf. Snearly 2016: 105–127). This group is marked by its emphasis on praise, especially its frequent use of 'Hallelujah!' (Pss 111:1; 112:1; 113:1, 9; 115:17, 18; 116:19; 117:2), though this is linked to other terms for praise, notably the return to 'give thanks' (*hōdû*) at Psalm 118:1, which forms an inclusio with Psalm 107. Unlike the previous Davidic trilogy, all these psalms are untitled. Psalms 111–112 are joined particularly closely within this segment, in that each is a twenty-two-line composition (apart from the opening hallelujah), with each line commencing with the successive letters of the Hebrew alphabet. As is typical with acrostics, this form imposes poetic constraints (though these are creatively deployed; cf. Scoralick 1997: 190–191), but both psalms use these constraints to enrich their presentation (which may explain some unusual vocalizations). The connections between these two poems goes further, in that they follow the same structure, with both containing bicola in verses 1–8, but tricola in verses 9–10. Both are also infused with wisdom terminology (e.g. Pss 111:2, 10; 112:1), and have a focus on Torah-related language (Pss 111:7; 112:1; cf. Crutchfield 2011: 34–35), preparing for Psalm 119, a poem that bridges the concerns of Psalms 107–118 and the Songs of the Ascents (Pss 120–134). The connections between Psalms 111 and 112 enable an exploration of the themes of wisdom and Torah from different perspectives. Psalm 111 considers them primarily from the perspective of what this means about understanding Yahweh, whereas Psalm 112 is more concerned with the life of those who commit themselves to Yahweh.

The pared-back acrostic is the controlling structural feature (though with numerous smaller features), with each short part line beginning with the successive letters of the alphabet, but with the twist of a shift from bicola to tricola in verses 9–10. This does not prevent some development in themes, enabling the following analysis:

1. Commitment to praise (1)
2. Yahweh's praiseworthy works (2–6)
3. Yahweh's praiseworthy precepts (7–10)

Comment

1. As is normal, the opening 'Hallelujah!' stands apart from the rest of the verse (see 'Comment', Ps. 104:35b). Here, it addresses a congregation, summoning praise. Following this, an individual voice vows to 'give thanks' (*ydh*), picking up the motif of thanksgiving from Psalm 107 and anticipating its prominence in Psalm 118. The verb can also be a confession (e.g. Prov. 28:13), but here the element of praise is prominent, so the speaker vows wholehearted acclamation of Yahweh. This acclamation is to occur in the council of the upright. This is not only a gathering of those committed to Yahweh's ways, since they are the congregation, but perhaps those who are prepared to give thought to why thanksgiving matters, drawing on the fact the noun *sôd* can refer both to 'council' and 'counsel'. In doing so, it subtly introduces the motif of wisdom into the larger pattern of praise.

2–6. Although the divisions are not absolute, this stanza looks at Yahweh's works, drawing especially on motifs from the exodus and wilderness wanderings. Yahweh's great works are not defined, allowing the audience to see them in both the tradition and their own experience. However, they are studied by those who delight in them, another wisdom element, suggesting that their meaning is not easily exhausted. Yahweh's works reflect his character; hence, they can be defined as splendour and majesty, language that points back to Yahweh's kingship, while they are also evidence of his enduring righteousness. Where the description of the works in verses 2–3 remains general, the balance of the stanza can more easily be associated with the exodus (cf. Broyles 1999: 419). Mention of the remembrance Yahweh has given can be linked to his self-declaration at Exodus 3:15, the revelation of the name Yahweh, suggesting that the works in view are linked to the exodus. This connection is strengthened by the near citation of the grace formula of Exodus 34:6 in verse 4b, so that Yahweh's great works encompass both the exodus and Yahweh's forgiveness of Israel after the sin of the golden calf. Mention of the gift of food could refer to the provision of manna in Exodus 16, though the quail in Numbers 11:4–35 is also possible. That the term for 'food' here is *ṭerep*, elsewhere more often 'prey', could point to a stronger link with the quail (but in later texts this does become a more general term for food; e.g. Mal. 3:10; see Brettler 2009: 65). If the quail is intended, then the celebration of Yahweh's works would follow their canonical order, preparing for the fact that verse 6 reaches Israel's emergence in the land in Joshua 4 – 11, itself a testimony of Yahweh's power for the people after the initial failure of the nation to enter the land following the disappointing report from the spies in Numbers 13 – 14. If this is the intended sequence of reference, then mention of Yahweh's remembering of his covenant is perhaps to be read through the grid of Deuteronomy's emphasis on the covenant, providing a further bridge to Joshua, especially when we note that the provision of food is stressed also there (Josh. 5:10–12). Yahweh's great works are not restricted to the exodus, but this period remains formative for how Israel remembers and studies them, and so shapes its praise as it goes forward, especially after the exile.

7–11. Mention of the covenant enables a shift to a focus on Yahweh's precepts, a key synonym for Torah, anticipating its use in Psalm 119. Prior to that, the psalmist picks up on Yahweh's works, noting that they are characterized by truth and justice. Rather than looking at particular acts, we look now at their character, leading to the statement about the reliability of Yahweh's precepts. This reliability means the faithful can trust them for their own life. The importance of the precepts is evident from the fact that verse 8 continues to reflect on them, noting that they have been established for ever and are performed with truth and uprightness.

Yahweh's precepts are the basis for life, and those who do them are also marked by characteristics otherwise associated with Yahweh. If verse 10 is also concerned with Yahweh's precepts, then we should probably also see the reference to redemption and the covenant in reference to them. Yahweh's precepts came because of his redemption of his people in the exodus, but that redemption continues to be experienced by those who perform his precepts. The precepts are an expression of Yahweh's covenant with his people, the reliability of which is also seen in his holiness. This reaches its conclusion in verse 10, which takes up the motif of the 'fear' (*yr'*, the same root as 'awesome' in v. 9) of Yahweh, which is otherwise particularly prominent in Proverbs (e.g. Prov. 1:7, 29; 2:5). The fear of Yahweh refers to a commitment to his service and is thus a desire to live in accord with covenant. The wise life is shaped by such a commitment and so expressed in the doing of the precepts. The precepts thus point to Yahweh's character and permit the wise to live in a way that reflects that character, being given insight into life's complexities. The net result of this is that Yahweh's praise endures, thus providing a link back to verse 1.

Explanation

Utilizing a stripped-back acrostic, Psalm 111 offers a powerful integration of history, wisdom and Torah in offering informed praise. Wholehearted praise expresses itself through thoughtful reflection on Yahweh's great acts, which culminate in the gifts of land and Torah, both of which are expressions of covenant. Praise is here informed by study that builds a relationship characterized by the fear of Yahweh and thus prepares for the introduction of this motif in Psalm 112:1. But where Psalm 112 will focus on the implications of these elements for the worshipper's life, here Yahweh's holiness, expressed in his works, is central. Reflection on this leads to praise. Paul develops the themes of this psalm in Romans 15:4–7, where he demonstrates such reflection on God's commitment in the past and that its instructional value is fundamental to how Christian community continues to form and welcome all, including those who might otherwise be excluded.

PSALM 112

Translation

[1]Hallelujah!

O the blessedness of the one who fears Yahweh,
who delights greatly in his commandments.

[2]Such a one's seed shall be mighty in the earth,
the generation of the upright shall be blessed.
[3]Wealth and riches are in that one's house,
and that one's righteousness stands for ever.

[4]Light dawns in the darkness for the upright,
who are gracious, merciful and righteous.
[5]Virtuous is the one who is gracious and lends,
who conducts matters with justice.
[6]For this one will never stumble,
the righteous one will be a perpetual remembrance.

[7]This one will not fear grievous tidings,
with a firm heart, trusting in Yahweh.
[8]Steady of heart, this one will not fear,
when looking upon oppressors.
[9]This one has distributed freely, has given to the poor,
this one's righteousness stands for ever,
with a horn exalted in honour.
[10]The wicked one sees and is vexed,
grinding teeth and melting away,
the desire of the wicked will perish.

Notes on the text

5. Hebr. *ṭôb* is often treated adverbially (e.g. ESV), but the setting here points more to the person's character, making an adjectival sense preferable, here a predicative adjective (*WHS* §75).

Form and structure

Psalm 112 forms a pair with Psalm 111 (cf. 'Form and structure' there), sharing its acrostic structure, even as far as the move to a pair of tricola in the final two verses, as well as the opening 'Hallelujah!', which stands outside the acrostic. The two are also linked by the emphasis on the fear of Yahweh, a key wisdom motif, as the close of Psalm 111 is taken up in verse 1 here. The two also share an interest in Yahweh's Torah, with both using synonyms that also appear in Psalm 119 (here *miṣwâ*). Their pairing still allows for distinct emphases, so that where Psalm 111 is more concerned with Yahweh, Psalm 112's interest is in the one who fears Yahweh. Accordingly, it takes terminology applied to Yahweh in Psalm 111 and applies it to the one who fears Yahweh; most obviously in verse 3, which notes that this person's righteousness endures for ever, mirroring the statement about Yahweh in Psalm 111:3. Similarly, the allusion to Exodus 34:6 applies to the one who fears Yahweh (v. 1), whereas in Psalm 111:4 it is applied to Yahweh. Likewise, where Yahweh had provided a memorial (Ps. 111:4), here the righteous will be a memorial (Ps. 112:6). Although Psalm 112 works as a distinct text, its placement alongside Psalm 111 shows how the one who fears Yahweh becomes like Yahweh. Indeed, so close are these connections that it is possible that the poem's author had Psalm 111 available when composing it (cf. G. T. M. Prinsloo 2019).

The emphasis on Torah motifs also connects the psalm to Psalm 119, with this pair of poems and the long psalm providing an envelope around Psalms 113–118 and their close interest in the exodus, stressing that exodus and Torah go together. This link to Psalm 119 also points to connections with other Torah psalms, such as Psalm 19, and perhaps more directly to Psalm 1 (cf. Thomas 1986), with which Psalm 112 also shares important features. Here, it should be noted that both poems begin with a beatitude (Pss 1:1; 112:1, when it is recognized that 'Hallelujah!' stands outside the main structure) and ends with the verb 'perish' (*tō'bēd*), while giving attention to a representative individual who embodies commitment to Yahweh, with both 'delighting' (*ḥpṣ*) in Yahweh's Torah (Pss 1:2; 112:1). Since such people embody a commitment to justice, the assertion that they will not stumble (Ps. 112:6) also echoes Psalm 15:6. In short, Psalm 112 is a deeply learned text, engaging with a range of other texts from the OT, embodying the effects of the study encouraged in Psalm 111:2.

Although closely patterned on Psalm 111, the final structure still works with its own concerns, with three stanzas:

1. The blessed one (1–3)
2. The righteous life (4–6)
3. Contrast: righteous and wicked (7–10)

Comment

1–3. As usual, 'Hallelujah!' stands outside the main structure of the psalm. It addresses an audience, summoning praise. In this case, reason for praise is provided through the description of someone who in many ways echoes the righteous person from Psalm 1. The poem proper begins with a beatitude (on the form, see on Ps. 1:1; cf. Ps. 41:1–3), a declaration that the person described lives a desirable life, one to which readers should aspire (cf. Vesco 2006, 2: 1070). In this case, the person living a desirable life is one who fears Yahweh, connecting this statement with Psalm 111:10, which also emphasizes this theme. This language is at home in a wisdom setting, and here particularly encourages reverence for Yahweh shaped around delighting in his commandments, echoing the Torah motif from Psalm 111 while linking this person to Psalm 1:2. An important development here is that this state of blessedness is not restricted to individuals. Instead, it continues through their descendants, who will be mighty in the earth, a blessed generation, though one that others could join by living in accord with the commandments. The language of blessing in verse 2 is distinct from that of verse 1 since here it uses *brk*. This terminology does not occur in the beatitudes and represents the giving of something extra that makes life more positive, something that emerges from the commandments. Verse 3 returns to the individual who is the focus of the beatitude, affirming that the one who fears Yahweh will also experience wealth, while stressing that it is the person's righteousness that endures for ever, a characteristic which means that this one's character mirrors Yahweh's own (Ps. 111:3).

4–6. The second stanza shifts its focus from describing the one who fears Yahweh to consider more such a person's pattern of life. The language of verse 4 is particularly terse (cf. Hossfeld and Zenger 2011: 168), but we are probably to think of the person here embodying the light that shines in darkness for the righteous (cf. Sherwood 1989: 51–58; Estes 2019: 355), though not necessarily the king, with the righteous as a group marked by grace, mercy and righteousness. These characteristics usually typify Yahweh (e.g. Ps. 111:4), so those who fear Yahweh shine light in darkness through their life. The one who practises grace can be described as 'virtuous' (*ṭôb*), with the granting of loans as a key example of this (cf. Prov. 19:17). Such loans would be interest free (Exod. 22:25; Ezek. 18:8), consistent with the general OT attitude towards them. These loans would also be consistent with the pattern of justice sustained through the person's wider conduct in relation to others. Verse 6 can then conclude that such people will never stumble and hence remain as a perpetual remembrance, their life pointing to what the righteous can achieve that others can recall.

7–10. The closing stanza then contrasts the righteous and the wicked and their experience of life, though as Schaefer notes (2001: 278) the wicked receive only one verse, which is all they need. Verses 7–8 are joined by their reference to the heart of those who fear Yahweh and the absence of fear in their wider experience. The poet thus plays with the senses of 'fear' (*yr'*) – with reference to Yahweh, it is about reverence, but with reference to other life experiences it is closer to the English 'fear'. Grievous tidings, which may even be a malicious report, do not cause fear, because of the person's trust in Yahweh. Likewise, encounters with enemies do not bring about fear, though these observations demonstrate that the righteous person's life is not free from struggle. Such people's conduct is an expression of their trust in Yahweh, and their heart (as a seat of awareness, which represents the person) does not fear. Rather, the one who fears Yahweh looks to the needs of others, distributing 'freely' (*pizzar*) and giving to the poor (here, those who could not repay a loan), an act that points to the person's enduring righteousness. As with Psalm 15, righteousness is evidenced through how one acts towards others, in providing for their needs, though this also means that the person receives honour within that society, with the 'horn' a symbol of authority and respect (cf. 1 Sam. 2:1, 10). This condition stands in contrast to that of the wicked, those who do not revere Yahweh. What they see is unstated but is probably the life of the one who fears Yahweh, something that causes them vexation such that they grind their teeth in frustration and melt away, losing their power to affect others. Their desire perishes, linking them also to the wicked in Psalm 1:6. The closing stanza thus validates the opening beatitude, making clear why the one who fears Yahweh lives such a desirable life.

Explanation

A psalm like this cannot say everything about the happy and contented life. It needs to be read alongside Psalm 111 to ensure we do not make the mistake of thinking righteousness is all about human activity. When we read these psalms together, we see that the blessed life comes from knowing God and delighting to know what he is like, and through this becoming (as much as possible) like him. This means looking to the needs of others, just as he does (cf. 2 Cor. 9:6–10). Nowhere do we see that more clearly than in Jesus' giving himself for us, something we celebrate in Communion. This too is a message that brings us to cry 'Hallelujah!' even as we see the need for our behaviour to be shaped by the pattern God provides (cf. Broyles 1999: 421).

PSALM 113

Translation

1Hallelujah!
Praise, O servants of Yahweh,
  praise the name of Yahweh.
2May the name of Yahweh be blessed,
  from now to for ever.
3From the sun's rising unto its setting,
  the name of Yahweh is to be praised.

4Yahweh is high above all nations,
  his glory is over the heavens.

5 Who is like Yahweh our God,
the one enthroned on high,
6 who stoops low to see,
in the heavens and on earth?

7 He raises the poor from the dust,
raises high the needy from the ashes,
8 to seat them with nobles,
with the nobles of his people.
9 He settles the childless woman of the house
as a joyful mother of children.
Hallelujah!

Notes on the text

3. The ptc. *mĕhullāl* is gerundive, indicating what should be done (*WHS* §216).

5. The hiph. ptc. *hamagbîhî* is probably not causative since otherwise this is contrary to the form of the question, unless Yahweh has raised himself (cf. the eagle in Obad. 4).

5–9. The ptcs. through these verses have an unusual *-î* suff., probably a *hireq compagnis* (GKC §90m), which here serves primarily as poetic adornment (Ayars 2019: 68). Cf. Psalm 114:8.

7. The preceding ptcs. were definite but now are indefinite. There remains a close connection with the preceding verses, but for English it is necessary to note the change by treating it like a finite verb.

9. Gk treats the closing 'Hallelujah!' as the start of Psalm 114.

Form and structure

Although closely connected to Psalms 111–112, especially through the opening 'Hallelujah!' and the concern for the poor (Pss 111:5; 112:9; 113:7), Psalm 113 is more closely connected with Psalms 113–118, a collection known as the Egyptian Hallel (see Hayes 1999), which is used in the celebration of Passover. This label derives from the interest in the exodus in Psalm 114 and the collection's frequent use of 'Hallelujah!'. Within the collection, only Psalms 114 and 118 lack 'Hallelujah!' as either the beginning or close of the psalm (see 'Notes on the text' above). The language of praise in Psalm 118 shifts to 'give thanks' (*ydh*), a move allowing it to close both the Egyptian Hallel and the larger unit that began at Psalm 107. Within the Egyptian Hallel, Psalm 113 provides a more general model of praise that recognizes Yahweh's concern for the weak, preparing for the more specific focus on the exodus in Psalm 114 as the primary example of this.

The psalm can easily be recognized as a hymn, and indeed Westermann (1981: 118–120) sees it as representing the basic form of praise. This may perhaps claim too much, but it is certainly a clear distillation of praise. However, it also stands in a wider tradition of praise, most obviously through the clear connections with Hannah's Song (1 Sam. 2:1–10; cf. J. T. Willis 1973: 152–154; G. T. M. Prinsloo 1996: 468–469; Neef 2016: 253–257). Here, verses 7–9 are particularly close to 1 Samuel 2:7–8a, suggesting a possible literary connection. Mention of the barren woman in the psalm probably takes Hannah as the archetype, making it more likely that her prayer has provided a key source adapted in the psalm's composition. This also means that although the psalm itself does not provide specifics to support its observations leading to praise, the connection with Hannah allows an audience to see examples of the praiseworthy activity mentioned in the psalm through her.

Structurally, the poem develops from an opening summons to praise through a series of ptcs. that describe Yahweh's praiseworthy character and deeds. The ptcs. in verses 5–6 are definite whereas those in verses 7–9 are indefinite, suggesting a minor break. This suggests we can analyse the psalm as containing two stanzas, the second of which contains two strophes:

1. Summons to praise (1–3)
2. Yahweh's praiseworthy character and deeds (4–9)
   a. Yahweh's character (4–6)
   b. Yahweh's deeds (7–9)

Comment

1–3. As usual, the opening 'Hallelujah!' stands outside the body of the poem, summoning an audience to praise. In this case, however, a further summons to praise follows immediately, summoning Yahweh's servants to praise his name (mentioned three times). Yahweh's servants here represent all who worship him (cf. Pss 134:1; 135:1). The summons to praise Yahweh's name is, in effect, another way of calling them to praise Yahweh (cf. Ps. 8:1). But mention of the name, representing the whole of Yahweh's character, also leads into verses 2–3, which ask that Yahweh's name be blessed. The blessing of Yahweh echoes the praise offered in Psalms 103–104, adding here that such praise has no chronological limits, as it is to be offered now and for ever. Likewise, again echoing Psalm 103:12 (cf. Mal. 1:11) in its move from east to west, it indicates that there is no spatial limit to the praise of Yahweh's name (establishing a focus on spatial language for the whole collection (G. T. M. Prinsloo 2006). Yahweh's servants, always and everywhere, are summoned to praise Yahweh because he is worthy of praise.

4–6. Focus on Yahweh's character falls on his exaltation (cf. Human 2004b), with spatial language particularly prominent. Language of exaltation here points to his pre-eminence and authority. Yahweh is high above all the nations, and thus in authority over them. This authority is extended by the observation that his glory, which here stands for Yahweh, is above the heavens, indicating that Yahweh reigns over all creation. This prepares for the question in verses 5–6. Given Yahweh's authority over the nations and creation, who is like him (cf. Exod. 15:11; Mic. 7:18)? The obvious answer is 'no one' (and 'no god'!), and the question could have stopped at verse 5a, especially as the language of 'our God' has already stressed the uniqueness of the community's relationship with Yahweh. But the poet extends it further, continuing to deploy spatial language in verses 5b–6. Yahweh is enthroned on high, confirming the statements of verse 4, but this is extended in verse 6 to note that Yahweh stoops to see in both heavens and earth. Yahweh is exalted above all but remains active in heavens and earth. Hence, the question is not simply one of incomparability, but one concerned to stress Yahweh's authority and activity in the heavens and on earth. Yahweh's incomparability is not an abstract statement. Rather, what makes Yahweh unique is that he is exalted above all and yet comes low to engage with all.

7–9. The implications of Yahweh's character can then be drawn out in the life of the servants who are called to praise him. Yahweh's stooping to look is not merely divine tourism. Yahweh stoops to raise up those who are low, reversing the fortunes of the weak. The spatial experience of his servants maps on to Yahweh's own, as the lowly are raised high. Hence, Yahweh raises the poor from the dust. The first term for 'poor' (*dal*) is related to a word meaning 'be low', so is probably chosen to emphasize the lowliness of the poor, something emphasized by their being in the dust. But Yahweh raises them, exalting the needy, from the ashes. The combination of dust and ashes points to human limitation and weakness (cf. Gen. 18:27; Job 30:19; 42:6), but Yahweh overcomes this for the needy, granting them a status that society does not. Indeed, echoing Hannah's Song (1 Sam. 2:8), Yahweh seats the poor with the nobles. The lowly are raised in both their social status and their access to the community's resources. Alongside the poor, childless women would be granted less status, and so they too are the object of his care, receiving homes to dwell in, rejoicing as they become mothers. The conclusion is then reached with the closing 'Hallelujah!'. This is what Yahweh is like and how he acts, so praise is required.

Explanation

Emerging from the 'Hallelujahs' of Psalms 111–112, Psalm 113 provides a bridge into the Egyptian Hallel. It is bounded by 'Hallelujah!', summoning praise. But where the two preceding psalms offer wisdom reflections shaped by Torah, this time the focus is on Yahweh and his incomparability. Yahweh is shown to be always and everywhere worthy of praise because there is no place not under his authority. This authority is evident in his exaltation. But Yahweh's exaltation does not make him transcendently remote. He is the one who stoops to consider the poor and needy, radically changing their circumstances by also raising them up. He is also the one who grants the childless woman children, a clear allusion to Hannah (1 Sam. 1:1 – 2:10). This allusion demonstrates that these are not abstract claims. Psalms 111–112 make clear that Yahweh's servants are to act as he does, so in that sense Psalm 113 is also an encouragement to believers to demonstrate the same commitment to the poor. But by keeping the focus on Yahweh, the psalm warns us against the assumption that it is all up to us (McCann 1996: 1140). We praise God because he has acted this way and continues to do so. Mary understood this too in her song of praise (Luke 1:46–55), celebrating the lifegiving God who had broken into her experience, thus joining Hannah as a further example of God's gift of life and hope, of his concern for the poor. To this, praise is the only suitable response.

PSALM 114

Translation

[1]When Israel came out from Egypt,
  the house of Jacob from a people of a strange language,
[2]Judah became his sanctuary,
  Israel his dominion.

[3]The sea saw and fled,
  and the Jordan turned back,
[4]The mountains leapt like rams,
  the hills like lambs.

[5]Why, O sea, do you flee,
  O Jordan that you turn back?
[6]O mountains, do you leap like rams,
  O hills, like lambs?

[7]Tremble, O earth, at the presence of the Lord,
  at the presence of the God of Jacob,
[8]the one who turns the crag into a pool of water,
  the flinty ground to a spring of water.

Notes on the text

1. Hebr. *lgz* is a hapax.

2. Hebr. *mamšĕlôt* is probably pl. of excellence (*WHS* §8), though Allen (2002: 138) defends a numerical pl.

7. Often emended, but with Hossfeld and Zenger (2011: 187–188), MT is retained.

8. Several important MSS (including L and A), plus Gk, treat Psalms 114–115 as a single text, an approach that would leave the combined poem ending with 'Hallelujah!'. For an experimental reading of the combined text, see G. T. M. Prinsloo 2003b. The breadth of MSS supporting this means it is not easily dismissed, but it seems likely that the merging of the poems might have been an early attempt to resolve the problem of the lack of the 'Hallelujah!' formula. If so, the formal differences between them should be observed and they can still be treated as distinct (though linked) poems.

Form and structure

Psalm 114 is a distinctive poem in its current setting. Each of Psalms 111–113 is bounded by 'Hallelujah!' and Psalms 115–117 will each close with it. Yet Psalm 114 lacks this feature (but see 'Notes on the text', Psalms 113:9; 114:8). It is also the only poem within the Egyptian Hallel (Pss 113–118) that mentions the exodus (vv. 1–5; cf. Gärtner 2016), though it is also comparatively unusual in also going on to mention the conquest traditions. It is thus a text dense with allusions to other traditions (see Bauer 2001: 302–310). Nevertheless, even though it is distinct as a poem, it now presents the exodus as the key example of Yahweh's commitment to the needy that was central to Psalm 113. Yahweh's authority over the nations (Ps. 113:5) is expressed here as he brings Israel out from Egypt and to the land promised. This authority extends to the creation itself as, in language typical of theophanies (cf. Ps. 29), creation trembles before him. This authority over creation, especially as expressed in verse 8, echoes Psalm 107:35, so that events of the exodus and conquest become a further example of the goodness of Yahweh for which his people give thanks, thus also anticipating Psalm 118.

Although often treated as a hymn, Psalm 114 is distinctive in its form, lacking many of the features associated with this classification (cf. Crutchfield 2011: 41–44). It may also be associated with the historical psalms (Pss 78, 105–106, 135–136; cf. G. T. M. Prinsloo 1998c: 306), though unlike the other examples it does not attempt to place that history in a particular setting. Rather, a setting is now provided by Psalm 113, which encourages reflective praise because of the whole of the exodus–conquest tradition. As Goldingay observes (2008: 321), it encourages its audience to 'take the God of the exodus seriously'. History and praise are fused to enable this.

The poem can be analysed in four short stanzas (which can be arranged as a chiasm, Wilcock 2001, 2: 178; the complex choral arrangement of Amzallag and Avriel [2014] is possible but not necessary), though it is notable that the first two primarily recount the events, whereas the last two address creation:

1. Leaving Egypt (1–2)
2. Entering the land (3–4)
3. Questioning waters and mountains (5–6)
4. Response: tremble, O earth (7–8)

Comment

1–2. A key feature of the psalm is its terse language, and this is immediately apparent here as we enter the exodus story at the point of Israel's departure from Egypt (cf. Exod. 19:1). The plague narrative is presumably known, but no attempt is made to include it. The departure is enough. Egypt is here also called a people of a 'strange', or perhaps 'incomprehensible', language. Egypt was not the people with whom Yahweh worked; Israel was. Verse 2 explores the identity of the house of Jacob, noting that Judah became 'his' sanctuary (cf. Exod. 19:4–6) and Israel 'his' dominion. The identity of the one to whom the sanctuary and dominion belong is not named, and though readers may assume it is Yahweh, this does not become explicit before verse 7 (contra NIV, which introduces God here, while Goldingay [2008: 322] suggests it is the house of Jacob). The poem creates a tension that encourages readers to proceed and discover who this is. Judah's status as the sanctuary perhaps anticipates the temple's construction, but again this is left open. Likewise, Israel's status as 'his dominion' points to a special status, but what that is remains unexplored. Just as we enter the story of the exodus part way through without explanation, so also, we discover the status of Judah and Israel within the context of a larger narrative that is not explained. If, as is possible, the psalm is post-exilic, then 'Judah' and 'Israel' are two ways of speaking of the same people.

3–4. Exodus and eisodus (alluded to in v. 2) are fused here, linking the crossing of the sea (Exod. 14:21–31) with crossing the Jordan (Josh. 3 – 4; cf. Ps. 66:6). This is already evident in Joshua 3 – 4, so the psalm follows an existing exegetical tradition. But consistent with the terse reports of those events, the poem speaks only of the Reed Sea and the Jordan, with each personified. The sea both sees and flees, while the Jordan turns back. Something has caused this, but again we are not told what. In the case of the sea, we are not even told what it saw. We simply know that something caused both to go away. Where the events in verse 3 link to identifiable points in the exodus and eisodus, verse 4 takes this further by speaking of the mountains and hills. Like the waters, the heights are closely paralleled, but with comparisons made to flock animals. Since the mountains are larger, they are compared to rams, while the smaller hills are compared to lambs. Both are said to have leapt about. Such leaping can be celebratory dancing (2 Sam. 6:21; Eccl. 3:4), but if the parallel with the waters continues here, we are probably to think of them being agitated. Sheep can jump about because of excitement of agitation. If the mountains allude to Sinai (Exod. 19), then the theophanic language there may provide some helpful background, perhaps alluding to an earth tremor (cf. Ps. 29:6), though this is not necessary, and we may also think of the heights leaping in celebration at Yahweh's coming (with Hossfeld and Zenger 2011: 196).

5–6. The third stanza takes up the unresolved language about the waters and the heights, addressing each in turn. Given that the sea fled, and the Jordan turned back, why do they do so, especially before fleeing slaves? Likewise, why do the heights leap? Where the previous verse refers to past events, the verbs here seem to describe a present experience, perhaps something replicated in liturgy (Nelson 2009: 172–173). However, the questions still leave unresolved why the waters and heights behaved as they did. Something has triggered their behaviour, but nothing is yet made explicit.

7–8. Only now does the poem introduce a reason for the actions of waters and heights. However, no direct answer is provided to the earlier questions. But a new figure is introduced, the 'Lord' (*'ādôn*), and the land is told to tremble (cf. Hab. 3:10) at his presence. Although *'ereṣ* could mean 'land' (so, Allen 2002: 139), it is more probable that 'earth' is meant since the psalm assumes the land has already been reached. The past has seen waters and heights respond to this Lord, and this is perhaps experienced in the liturgy, but now the land is told to tremble in his presence since he is also the God of Jacob. As God of Jacob, he is also the deity of the house of Jacob, and thus of all Israel and Judah. Moreover, as God this Lord is one who continues to have an impact on creation, turning crags into pools of water. Since such crags are sometimes high cliffs, it is probable that the language here continues to refer to the waters and the heights, a pattern continued into the final part of verse 8, which sees the Lord's transforming even flinty rock into springs, waters that come from beneath the earth (cf. Exod. 17:6; Num. 20:8–13). This is the one who brought Israel out, who caused the waters to turn and the heights to leap, and this is thus the one to be praised as he continues to work.

Explanation

Psalm 114 is distinctive in refraining from naming the one to be praised until its closing stanza. Readers coming from Psalm 113 who have declared 'Hallelujah!' know it is Yahweh, but the poem withholds this information because it intends to explore his kingship before naming the king. The one who reigns, who has Judah and Israel as his dominion and sanctuary, is politically powerful, bringing them out from Egypt. He is also powerful in creation, overcoming the waters, and before whom the heights leap. The great political powers are nothing before this one, and neither are sea, river, mountain or hill, all sites that could be associated with Canaanite worship, as well as powerful representations of creation. Indeed, all the earth, however viewed, is to tremble before this Lord, the God of Jacob. The good news is not just that God's greatness and rule are seen in the past. Rather, he continues to provide, bringing life out of what seems unfruitful. Here is good news for a small and struggling people – the God who acted in the past continues to work and provide because no force in creation or politics is greater than him. John extends this hope to struggling Christian communities (Rev. 20:11). As the risen Christ continues to attest to God's reign, so we too are called to serve this world-changing and world-ruling God (cf. Brueggemann 1984: 142; Davidson 1998: 375).

PSALM 115

Translation

1Not to us, O Yahweh, not to us,
  but to your name give glory,
  because of your kindness, your faithfulness.
2Why should the nations say,
  'Where is their God?'

3For our God is in the heavens,
  he does as he pleases!
4Their idols are silver and gold,
  the work of human hands.
5They have a mouth, but do not speak,
  they have eyes, but do not see,
6they have ears, but do not hear,
  they have a nose, but do not smell,
7their hands do not feel,
  their feet do not walk,
  they do not murmur with their throat.

8Those who make idols shall be like them,
everyone trusting in them.

9O Israel, trust in Yahweh,
he is their help and shield.
10O house of Aaron, trust in Yahweh,
he is their help and shield.
11O those who fear Yahweh, trust in Yahweh,
he is their help and shield.

12Yahweh has remembered us, he blesses,
he blesses the house of Israel,
he blesses the house of Aaron,
13he blesses those who fear Yahweh,
both small and great.
14Yahweh will grant you increase,
you and your children.
15May you be blessed by Yahweh,
the maker of heaven and earth.

16The heavens are Yahweh's heavens,
but the earth he has given to humankind.
17The dead do not praise Yah,
nor do all descending into silence.
18But we, we bless Yah,
from now to for ever!
Hallelujah!

Notes on the text

1. See 'Notes on the text' on Psalm 114:8.

9. Many MSS (and Gk and Syr.) read 'house of Israel'. It is easy to understand *bayit* being missed by a scribe, but this reading may also conform this text to verse 12 (cf. Ps. 135:19), so MT is retained.

12. Several MSS begin a new psalm at this point, reflecting general uncertainty about psalm boundaries at this point. However, the close linguistic connections within the poem make it more probable that the poem continues to verse 18.

Form and structure

Psalm 115 opens by taking up Psalm 113's stress on Yahweh's name (Ps. 113:1–3), extending this by asking for Yahweh to give it glory (v. 1), glory that has previously been said to be above the heavens (Ps. 113:4). Other connections with Psalm 113 emerge from this, notably emphasis on Yahweh's dwelling in the heavens (Pss 113:4; 115:3) and focus on the language of blessing (Pss 113:2; 115:12–13). The closing 'Hallelujah!' (v. 18) links the poem to Psalm 113 and Psalms 116–117. Verbal connections to Psalm 114 are rarer (see Gärtner 2016: 78). However, the spatial language evident in Psalms 113–114 is again evident in Psalm 115 (G. T. M. Prinsloo 2006: 746–748). So, where Psalm 114's movement was on the terrestrial plane, Psalms 113 and 115 move between heaven and earth, with Psalm 115:17 going below the terrestrial to the world of the dead. Exodus and eisodus in Psalm 114 are now placed within the setting of Yahweh's heavenly reign, a reign already experienced in Israel (Ps. 114:2), a reign that offers the hope of future blessing.

Although there are important connections with the surrounding poems, it is also distinct in including polemic against idols (vv. 4–8; cf. 135: 15–18; Deut. 4:28; Isa. 40:18–20; 41:7, 22–24, 28–29; 42:17; 43:9; 44:9–20; 45:16, 20; 46:1–2, 7–9; 48:5, 14; Jer. 10:1–10; Hab. 2:18–19) and exhortations to trust in Yahweh (vv. 9–11). These elements are closely linked. The idols of the nations are attacked to demonstrate that they cannot bless, whereas Yahweh can. The community must trust Yahweh, because such trust is the setting in which Yahweh's blessing is experienced. The interweaving of these elements means we should not abandon the psalm's unity (e.g. Seybold [1996: 450] separates vv. 1–8 and 9–18) but rather see it as a complex piece that integrates diverse material. This material could have functioned liturgically (note the shifts between first and second person), though it could also have been composed as a reflection on other parts of the OT, encouraging trust in Yahweh that leads to praise.

The psalm can be analysed in five stanzas that pivot on the call to trust Yahweh, with key vocabulary linking them. Recognizing that the closing 'Hallelujah!' stands outside the main structure, this leads to the following analysis:

1. Glory to Yahweh's name (1–2)
2. The inability of idols (3–8)
3. Trust in Yahweh! (9–11)
4. Yahweh's ability (12–15)
5. Blessing Yahweh (16–18)

Comment

1–2. The psalm opens with a strong affirmation that glory properly belongs to Yahweh's name alone. It may be possible for humans to claim glory, in the sense of honour, but the psalm insists that true glory belongs only to Yahweh's name. Yahweh's name here stands for his reputation (cf. Skinner 2023). Yahweh is to give glory to his own name, suggesting there are those who deny it. The reason for glory being given to Yahweh's name is because of his 'kindness' (*ḥesed*) and 'faithfulness' (*'emet*). Both terms point to his commitment to his people, suggesting that the way Yahweh gives glory to his name is by acting in faithfulness to his people. The need for this becomes clear in the rhetorical question of verse 2 (cf. Ps. 79:10; Joel 2:17; Mic. 7:10). Enemies are asking where their God is, suggesting that they do not see evidence of his work, though they may also wonder why there is no idol visible. Yahweh's giving glory to his name would remove the grounds for this question.

3–8. The second stanza makes clear that the question is fundamentally flawed in its assumptions. Israel's God is not located in any one place. Rather, he is resident in the heavens and has the power to do as he pleases (cf. Ps. 103:19), acting for his people (Krawelitzki 2014: 438). The contrast with idols is then marked. They may be made with valuable metals such as silver and gold (cf. Hos. 8:4; Swale 2023) but are only the work of human hands. By contrast, Yahweh is maker of heaven and earth (v. 15), so whatever the idol-makers use, it is simply manufactured from what Yahweh has made. The idols are produced with features that suggest they can act and respond to their worshippers, but none of those features make any difference. A manufactured mouth cannot speak, manufactured eyes cannot see, manufactured ears cannot hear, and neither can a manufactured nose smell. The description of the idols' inabilities changes form in verse 7 as the unit moves towards a close, but the point remains the same – their hands cannot touch, feet cannot walk and their throat cannot even mutter. These idols are manufactured to look like they can act, but they cannot. They are mute and immobile, unfeeling and unresponsive. Worse, those who manufacture them become like them, and so does anyone who trusts them. Those who trust in them may be able to respond, but functionally end up doing nothing.

9–11. Trusting in idols is damaging, so the alternative is laid out here in the psalm's turning point. Three groups are addressed in turn (cf. Ps. 118:2–4), each directed to trust in Yahweh. Although they are addressed directly, the statement about Yahweh as help and shield, both core images in Psalms, is expressed in the third person, suggesting that a wider audience hears these affirmations and so realizes that they too can trust Yahweh (cf. A. P. Ross 2016: 417). The three groups addressed are Israel, the house of Aaron and those who fear Yahweh. Israel was Yahweh's dominion in Psalm 114:2, and a similar sense is probably intended here, with Israel as the people where Yahweh's reign is most clearly seen. The house of Aaron refers to the priests as those who lead worship, though of course they are already part of Israel, so there is not an absolute distinction between the first two groups. Those who fear Yahweh live a life of blessedness (Ps. 112:1; cf. Ps. 111:10) and should be found within Israel and the priests. In this case, the possibility exists that such people are found outside Israel's boundaries (cf. Ps. 113:3), but they are primarily found within Israel. Although distinctions can be drawn between the three groups, the boundaries between them are fluid, and it is better to think of them as different ways of describing those who need to trust in Yahweh.

12–15. The idols were incapable of action, but that is not the case with Yahweh. Rather, the community affirms that Yahweh had remembered them, that he has acted for them. This may refer to the return from exile (with Goulder 1998: 168–174), though other points are possible. More importantly, although Yahweh has acted, this is not the end. Rather, the one who has remembered is also the one who blesses, enabling his people's flourishing. Moreover, Yahweh's blessings are for all his people, whether thought of as Israel, the house of Aaron or those who fear him. Yahweh's blessings are not restricted to the powerful either, for he blesses small and great. The form those blessings take is not described here, but the observation that Yahweh blesses then leads to a prayer in verse 14, asking that Yahweh grant increase to both the worshippers and their children, asking for a life filled with his blessing. This prayer is extended through a wish in verse 15 that provides the key reason why Yahweh can bless – because he is the maker of heaven and earth, and therefore all belongs to him. He can therefore do as he pleases within his creation.

16–18. The closing stanza takes up themes from the first. Yahweh resides in the heavens (v. 3), and all the heavens belong to him (v. 16). Where the earth was unmentioned in the first stanza, it is now affirmed that Yahweh has given it to humans. But humans are not the ones to receive glory; Yahweh is. As such, the dead do not praise him. The dead here are also those going down to silence, a poetic way of portraying Sheol. That the dead do not praise Yahweh picks up an important theme within the Psalter (Pss 6:5; 30:9; 88:11–12), reaching its conclusion here. The dead do not praise Yahweh, and thus give him the glory, but the living do. Hence, the community commits itself (the 'we' is emphatic) to the task of blessing Yahweh (cf. Ps. 103:1–2) as a means of giving him glory. With that commitment made, the psalm closes with a charge to its audience – they too are to praise Yahweh.

Explanation

Glory belongs to God alone. But where is that glory seen? For the nations around Israel, the expectation was that it should be in sanctuaries where their idols were kept. But Psalm 114:2 has already made clear that God's people are his sanctuary, a theme Paul develops when he notes that believers (both corporately and individually) are God's temple (1 Cor. 3:16; 6:19). It is among God's people that his glory can be seen, but this also raises the risk that those observing may be confused, attributing glory to the people, not to God alone. Psalm 115 thus extends themes from Psalm 114 to ask that glory be seen in God's people and that those observing it will know the one to whom glory belongs. Doing this will make clear that Israel's God is fundamentally different from the nations' idols. They may be beautifully made, but are inert and lifeless, unable to act. Yet God can do as he pleases, and indeed has acted for his people. As such, they can trust him, knowing he will continue to act for them. The only response to this is to bless and praise God, the one whose glory is made clear for and among his people in Jesus (Col. 1:15–20).

PSALM 116

Translation

[1]I love because Yahweh hears
  my voice and my pleas for grace,
[2]because he has inclined his ear to me,
  so shall I call out all my days.

[3]The cords of death encompassed me,
  the straits of Sheol found me;
  I found distress and grief.
[4]But I called on the name of Yahweh,
  'Ah Yahweh, deliver my life.'
[5]Gracious is Yahweh and righteous,
  our God is compassionate,
[6]Yahweh guards the simple,
  I was low and he saved me.

[7]Return, o my being, to your resting place,
  for Yahweh has dealt bountifully with you,
[8]for you have delivered me from death,
  my eye from tears,
  my foot from stumbling.
[9]I shall walk before Yahweh,
  In the lands of the living.

[10]I believed when I spoke,
  'I am greatly afflicted.'
[11]I had said in my haste,
  'Everyone is a liar.'

[12]What can I return to Yahweh,
  for all his bounty to me?
[13]I will raise the cup of salvation,

and call on the name of Yahweh.
[14]I will fulfil my vows to Yahweh,
in the presence of all his people.

[15]Costly in the eyes of Yahweh
is the death of his saints.
[16]Ah Yahweh, I am your servant,
I am your servant, the son of your maidservant,
you have loosed my bonds!
[17]I shall offer you the sacrifice of thanksgiving,
and call on the name of Yahweh.
[18]I will fulfil my vows to Yahweh,
in the presence of all his people,
[19]in the courts of Yahweh's house,
in your midst, O Jerusalem!
Hallelujah!

Notes on the text

1. Many EVV follow the proposed emendation in *BHS*, transposing 'Yahweh' to follow the opening verb. But the elision is an important poetic device, stressing that Yahweh is 'an active subject' (W. S. Prinsloo 1993b: 76). 'Pleas for grace' follows Hossfeld and Zenger (2011: 214) in linking this term with 'gracious' in verse 5.

3. The verbs are preterite (with Dahood 1970: 145; *WHS* §177b).

9. Versional evidence (Gk, Syr., Tg) suggests sg. 'land' (cf. Pss 27:13; 52:5). But with Ayars (2019: 171), MT is retained.

10. Gk (and Jerome) begins a new psalm at this point.

14. Absent from Gk, but (with Allen 2002: 113) this appears to be an attempt to abbreviate the text due to the similarity with verse 18.

15. For *yqr* as 'costly', see the helpful summary by Gibbs (2023), though compare Pinker 2009.

19. Allen (2002: 152) judges direct address unlikely, interpreting the suff. as a rare form of const. state. But it is consistent with the Aramaizing suffixes in verses 7, 12, making this more probable (the point would hold even if, with Rendsburg [1990: 83–86], we think of this as evidence of northern dialect). Gk has 'Hallelujah!' at the start of Psalm 117, but it should probably be kept here.

Form and structure

Psalm 115 closed with a vow of praise, noting especially that the living, not the dead, praise Yahweh (Ps. 115:17–18). This vow finds immediate expression in Psalm 116 as the psalmist praises Yahweh for deliverance from death (vv. 3–9), promising to fulfil prior vows (vv. 14, 18) within a general context of thanksgiving. As such, the poem's placement here means it immediately models the praise promised in the previous psalm while also anticipating the corporate praise of Psalm 117 and the declaration of hope in Psalm 118:17–18 (cf. Vesco 2006, 2: 1089; Crutchfield 2011: 48) while continuing the spatial language of the rest of Psalms 113–118.

The poem can be analysed as an individual thanksgiving, though, as is typical of the collection in Psalms 113–118, it does not fit easily within that description (see J. T. James 2017: 42–49). In this case, elements of thanksgiving (e.g. vv. 2, 8) are mixed with elements of trust and complaint (e.g. vv. 10–11), a combination that has led to claims of disordered expansions (cf. Seybold 1996: 454). But this seems to be a case of expecting ancient poets to compose within the categories modern exegesis has defined rather than allowing them freedom to adapt forms (Weiser [1962: 719] accordingly speaks of a 'free' use of the form). In this case, as Ayars (2019: 171) observes, the poem is an artful combination of elements (often drawn from other psalms; cf. Potgieter 2019: 403–410) that stress the results of Yahweh's interventions. These interventions are celebrated liturgically in the fulfilment of vows and the raising of the cup of salvation (vv. 12–14), the latter perhaps linked to the bringing of a thank offering (vv. 17–19).

The psalm's structure is much debated (cf. Barré 1990: 62–69), largely because of different assessments of how the various elements come together. Cook (2018: 200–202) also notes that the poetic and rhetorical structures differ. It should be said that overlapping structures are possible, but we can note that there is a movement between narrative, acts of worship and confessions that come together in four stanzas, with the second to fourth open to further division. This yields the following analysis:

1. Opening declaration (1–2)
2. First narrative and confession (3–9)
    a. Report of grace (3–6)
    b. Self-exhortation (7–9)
3. Second narrative and vow (10–14)
    a. Past misunderstanding (10–11)
    b. Fulfilling vows (12–14)
4. Confession and vows (15–19)
    a. Confession (15–16)
    b. Fulfilling vows (17–19)

Comment

1–2. Declarations of love for Yahweh are unusual in the OT, and even here it is an announcement of the possibility of love. Israel can be told to love Yahweh (Deut. 6:5; Ps. 31:23), but personal affirmations such as this are distinctive, with Psalm 18:1 offering the nearest analogy (though with a different verb). The psalmist even defers naming Yahweh here until after the report that Yahweh is the one who hears the poet's pleas for grace. The effect of this is to make clear that the love declared is a proper response to what God has already done and is itself an expression of covenantal commitment (cf. 1 John 4:19). Yahweh has shown his commitment, and the poet responds to this. More particularly, the practice of love is then described as continued calling on Yahweh. That is, love here is an expression of trust that works itself out in dependence on Yahweh throughout life.

3–6. The first narrative offers a brief recounting of a moment of deliverance experienced by the poet, juxtaposing life and death (see Snyman 2022). In some form, the psalmist was threatened by death, here portrayed as a hunter chasing prey. Death had cords to bind the psalmist (cf. Ps. 18:4–5). Sheol, as the place of the dead, similarly met the poet, resulting in the experience of distress and grief. Yet, at that moment the psalmist cried out, asking for deliverance, and Yahweh acted. Before any report of deliverance, the psalmist makes a fundamental assertion about Yahweh as gracious and righteous, before noting that 'our God' is compassionate. The description of Yahweh has clear echoes of Exodus 34:6–7 (Janowski 2013: 283), while referring to him as 'our God' makes clear that Yahweh lives in relationship to his people. Yahweh is righteous and compassionate, but not distant. This is why the psalmist can affirm that Yahweh guards the simple, a group with which the poet identified. The poet had been low, lacking social status, but was saved by Yahweh.

7–9. Yahweh's prior acts provide hope that he shall act again. Hence, the psalmist engages in self-exhortation, insisting on the need to return to Yahweh as the one who provides rest. The reason for this is that Yahweh has acted for the psalmist before. These previous actions can be characterized as 'bountiful', language which makes clear that Yahweh's actions for his people are not stingy. Yahweh's bountiful acts are associated with the provision of life, and hence Yahweh has delivered the poet from death. This deliverance is expressed in terms of body parts, with Yahweh's actions appropriate for that body part, so that the eyes are delivered from tears and the feet from stumbling. Because of this, the psalmist anticipates continued life, pictured as walking before Yahweh in the land of the living (cf. Pss 27:13; 56:13). The psalmist does not anticipate endless life, but rather that a full life can be lived because Yahweh intervened to prevent premature death. This can happen in various ways (hence, '*lands* of the living'), but the important thing is that it is a life lived before God.

10–11. A second narrative now reports previous suffering. This suffering did not limit the psalmist's faith (the parallel with v. 1 indicates that the faith is in Yahweh), even when it could be said the suffering was acute (cf. 2 Cor. 4:13). A second statement is also recalled which is parallel to the first (cf. Booij 1995: 390–392), one that asserted that all people were liars. That this was said in haste may indicate that it is now regarded as hyperbolic. But if the suffering was triggered by malicious speech, then such a statement is easily understood.

12–14. The poet's reconfigured understanding leads back to Yahweh and the need to respond to his benefits. Yahweh has both addressed the affliction and provided new insights into its interpretation. Yahweh's benefits are thus both deliverance from oppression and a mechanism for understanding them. In response to this, the poet poses a rhetorical question about how to respond, the answer being to raise the cup of salvation and call on Yahweh's name. The cup here probably refers to a ritual act in the sanctuary, though, beyond the fact that this is a positive presentation of a cup (cf. Pss 16:5; 23:5; elsewhere, a cup can also be a symbol of judgement, as e.g. in Ps. 75:9; Jer. 51:7; Ezek. 23:33), it is difficult to draw firm conclusions about the ritual. Calling on Yahweh's name could be limited to the cup ritual but could also be an affirmation of what the psalmist will do beyond that point. Along with the cup ritual, the psalmist will also fulfil vows made, presumably during the affliction, doing so in the presence of the people as a public testimony of deliverance. These verses apparently formed the text for the first Christian sermon preached in Australia, though we do not know if the convicts transported so far were particularly thankful!

15–16. Rather than a narrative, the final stanza commences with a confession, one that builds on the two prior narratives before again moving to focus on the fulfilment of vows as public worship. Traditionally, the confession has been translated as indicating that the death of Yahweh's saints is 'precious' in his sight (e.g. ESV). But it is much more probable that *yqr* here in verse 15 has the sense of 'costly' (cf. 'Notes on the text'). The death of any worshipper is costly to Yahweh, both because of his personal commitment to them and because he loses someone who testifies to him. The first narrative pointed to Yahweh's rescuing the poet from death, showing that Yahweh is one who grants life. That life could be impaired by oppression, but Yahweh also rescues from that. This demonstrates that Yahweh does not wish to suffer the loss through the death (esp. premature) of those who honour him. The psalmist's personal confession is based on this. The psalmist is Yahweh's servant and the son of a maidservant, part of a tradition of those loyal to Yahweh. But this is not simply a matter of family descent. The psalmist knows its reality because Yahweh has loosened death's bonds, something consistent with the opening declaration, though the opening 'Ah' (*'ānnâ*) can also suggest continued distress so that further deliverance is needed.

17–19. The psalm closes with a further commitment to the fulfilment of vows, tying this stanza back to the second narrative and vow. The distinctive addition here is the offering of the thanksgiving sacrifice while again calling on Yahweh's name, an element consistent with the lifting of the cup of salvation. This may suggest that the cup was associated with the thanksgiving offering, though they could remain discrete acts. This worship fulfils what were probably private vows in a public setting, within the courts of the sanctuary in Jerusalem, the city here personified through direct address. In response, all are called to cry 'Hallelujah!' and reflect on their own experience.

Explanation

This psalm celebrates the fact that Yahweh values the life of those who are loyal to him, so much so that the death of one is costly to him. The psalmist here recounts a personal story of how that was experienced, but with a clear view of encouraging others to see their own experience reflected in this. Consistently, the telling of the story brings the poet back to worship, and, as the psalm closes with 'Hallelujah!', the congregation that has experienced it is called to worship. Put simply, those who experience God's grace can only give thanks, and encourage others to do the same (see Tucker and Grant 2018: 668). This takes on a fresh perspective when viewed through the lens of the Lord's Supper, where the cup that is drunk reminds us of Jesus' death, which initiated the new covenant, though it is through his death that life is given. Likewise, Sheol's cords could not hold him, as he was raised to new life. If (as is possible) the Passover Seder at the Last Supper included the singing of this psalm, then Jesus presented himself as the one through whom his disciples can now see their own experience and praise the God who gives life.

PSALM 117

Translation

[1]Praise Yahweh all nations,
  laud him all peoples,
[2]for his kindness has prevailed over us,
  and Yahweh's faithfulness endures for ever.
Hallelujah!

Notes on the text

1. Gk places the closing 'Hallelujah!' from Psalm 116 here. On the boundaries of the text, see Snyman 2011b: 112. Some MSS include the whole psalm as a conclusion to Psalm 116, but the material is distinct, and MT should be retained. Hebr. *hā'ummîm* is an Aramaism, so no emendation is needed. A. P. Ross (2016: 435) links this with the verb *sbḥ*, another possible Aramaism, suggesting the poet might have used these terms because of the text's international focus.

2. Hebr. *gbr* is often rendered as 'great' but (with Ps. 103:11) the verb represents spatial language, so that Yahweh's kindness prevails by 'towering' over the community.

Form and structure

The shortest psalm (indeed, the Bible's shortest chapter; by word count, it is even shorter than Esth. 8:9!) continues the focus on praise that began in Psalm 111. Its brevity means that verbal links with the preceding psalm are lacking apart from the closing 'Hallelujah', though it does continue the use of spatial language that typifies Psalms 113–118 (cf. 'Notes on the text'). It does, however, extend the message of Psalm 116 from the individual to the nations. Where Psalm 116 presented the voice of an individual responding to Yahweh's grace with the intent of leading to praise, now all peoples are called to praise Yahweh. In this, it joins Psalm 99 in seeing evidence of Yahweh's work in Israel as a reason for inviting the nations to join in praise. It should also be noted that the reasons for praise (Yahweh's kindness and faithfulness) here join it to Psalm 115:1. This, combined with the closing 'Hallelujah!' and allusions to Exodus 34:6–7 in each, shows that Psalms 115–117 are joined as a unit within Psalms 113–118 (Crutchfield 2011: 50–51). It also provides a bridge into Psalm 118 (Seybold 1996: 456), which develops a different mode of praise, as a doxology that begins to close this collection (with Westermann 1981: 257).

The psalm's brevity means it is possible to see the basics of the imp. hymn with a summons to praise that is grounded in a *kî* (for) clause that provides the reason for the praise (cf. Brueggeman 1984: 159). The closing 'Hallelujah!' is the only supplementary element, though here it now forms an inclusio with the opening 'Praise Yahweh'.

Although one can note the pivot in the psalm at verse 2 and the inclusio formed by the summons to praise (for which Snyman [2011a: 31] suggests a small chiasm), no further analysis is provided as the psalm consists of a single stanza.

Comment

1–2. The opening summons to praise uses the fuller form 'Yahweh', unlike the close which uses the shorter form 'Yah' within 'Hallelujah!'. Unlike the short form, which is almost always an independent unit outside the poem's main structure, this longer form is integrated into the poem. That integration is here shown through the parallel with 'laud him' (*śabbĕḥûhû*). In both instances, it is those beyond Israel who are called to praise. It is doubtful that the nations would have heard this summons since the psalm would have been sung within Israel, but the psalm has an eschatological orientation that anticipates the point when this universal praise would be offered (anticipating the breadth of praise in Pss 148, 150). Since the closing 'Hallelujah!' initially addresses those who were present and directs them to praise Yahweh, their praise anticipates the praise that is to come. The reason for the nations to praise is indicated by verse 2. The language here is striking. It is not simply that Yahweh's kindness is great. Rather, Yahweh has prevailed over his people through his kindness. He has overpowered them with his kindness that has towered over them. This kindness is matched with his enduring faithfulness, the combination of kindness and faithfulness pointing to Exodus 34:6–7. Israel has been overpowered by Yahweh's kindness in a pattern that can be traced back to Sinai, and this experience provides hope for the nations since Israel is there understood to exist for them (Exod. 19:4–6). This points to Yahweh's character as one who redeems and restores, making him one whom the nations also can trust (cf. Rom. 15:11). The 'us' who has experienced this kindness is initially Israel, but the psalm anticipates that as all join in praise, they too will have discovered this truth (cf. Ps. 113:4).

Explanation

Mays (1994b: 372) notes that the praise of God is incomplete 'until all are drawn into its faith and joy'. At heart, that is the message of this psalm, one that packs a huge message into a compact space. The story of the exodus, and the hope it provides, is finally for all nations and peoples. This is the nature of the God of grace made known in Exodus 34:6–7, one who provides the opportunity for Israel to serve as priests towards all nations (Exod. 19:4–6). This God's kindness is what has prevailed! This psalm's hope is taken up in the song of the elders (Rev. 5:9–10) as those who have discovered this reality. It is the hope that continues to shape Christian praise that understands God's purpose has always been that all the families of the earth may find blessing (Gen. 12:1–3).

PSALM 118

Translation

1Give thanks to Yahweh because he is good,
because his kindness endures for ever.
2Let Israel say,
'Because his kindness endures for ever.'
3Let the house of Aaron say,
'Because his kindness endures for ever.'
4Let those who fear Yahweh say,
'Because his kindness endures for ever.'

5From straits I called to Yah,
in a broad place Yah answered me.
6Yahweh is with me, I will not fear,
what can a human do to me?
7Yahweh is with me as one of my helpers,
and I shall look on those who hate me.

8It is better to seek refuge in Yahweh,
than to trust in a human.
9It is better to seek refuge in Yahweh,
than to trust in princes.

10All the nations surrounded me,
in Yahweh's name I indeed drive them back.
11They surrounded me, yes, they surrounded me,
in Yahweh's name I indeed drive them back.
12They surrounded me like bees,
they were extinguished like a fire of thorns,
in Yahweh's name I indeed drive them back.

13You pushed hard to make me fall,
but Yahweh helped me.
14Yah is my strength and song,
and he has become my salvation.

15The sound of shouting and salvation,
is in the tents of the righteous,
'Yahweh's right hand has acted powerfully.
16Yahweh's right hand exalts,
Yahweh's right hand has acted powerfully.'

17I shall not die but live,

and I will recount the deeds of Yah.
18Yah disciplined me severely,
but he did not give me over to death.

19Open for me gates of righteousness,
I will enter and give thanks to Yah.
20This is the gate to Yahweh,
the righteous enter through it.
21I will give thanks to you because you answered me,
and became my salvation.

22The stone the builders rejected,
has become the capstone.
23This has come from Yahweh,
it is marvellous in our eyes.
24This is the day Yahweh has acted,
we will rejoice and be glad in him.

25O Yahweh, please save!
O Yahweh, please grant flourishing!
26Blessed is the one who comes in Yahweh's name,
we bless you from Yahweh's house.
27Yahweh is God and has given us light!
Bind the festival offering with cords,
up to the horns of the altar.

28You are my God, and I give you thanks,
my God, and I exalt you.
29Give thanks to Yahweh because he is good,
because his kindness endures for ever.

Notes on the text

5. Several MSS begin a new psalm here.

10–12. Hiph. *mwl* is uncertain, but here following HALOT (and Gk), though the cautions raised by A. P. Ross (2016: 449) should be noted. LeMon (2015) proposes 'cut to pieces' on the basis of iconographic evidence, a reading that is also plausible.

11. Missing from 4QPs[a] but should be retained.

13. Gk and Syr. suggest a niph. here, but qal can be retained.

14. The citation from Exodus 15:21 (Isa. 12:2 is almost identical) indicates that the text's form is fixed.

24. Traditionally, *'āśâ* has been interpreted with reference to Yahweh's making the day, but in the light of verses 15–16 it is more likely that the reference is to the deeds performed (Dahood 1970: 155; Berlin 1977).

27. Hebr. *ʿăbôt* can refer to either 'cords' or 'branches'. Since binding is involved, 'cords' is more appropriate, meaning that *ḥag* refers to the sacrifice and not just the festival (similarly, Vaillancourt 2019: 139).

Form and structure

Psalm 118 closes the first major division of Book 5. It is bound by an inclusio (vv. 1, 29) that is identical to Psalm 107:1 and anticipates Psalm 136, where the motif of giving thanks to Yahweh runs through the entire poem. It also closes the Egyptian Hallel (Pss 113–118), drawing together key themes and motifs (cf. Crutchfield 2011: 54). Although it makes 'thanks' (*ydh*) its key verb rather than 'praise' (*hll*), which has been central to Psalms 111–117, it is bound to the collection through the repetition of key terminology and themes (Hayes 1999), notably the continued use of spatial language that has characterized the collection (G. T. M. Prinsloo 2006), while the focus on Yahweh's 'kindness' (*ḥesed*) also provides a key link to Psalm 117. The change in the language of praise signals the close of both the larger unit (Pss 107–118) and this smaller collection (Pss 113–118), preparing for Psalm 119. The long psalm's celebration of Torah joins it to Psalms 111–112, making it the capstone of the Book to this point.

There is general agreement that Psalm 118 is a liturgical thanksgiving, but, beyond that, significant differences in interpretation emerge (helpfully summarized in Booij 2015). This is caused (in part at least) by the apparent use of a significant body of material that cites earlier texts, only some of which are known to us. These include Psalms 18:19, 107:1, Exodus 15:2, 6, 11, 12, though Grant (2004: 127–143) also points to significant connections with Deuteronomy. As such, the thanksgiving is embedded in these texts, perhaps as a means of placing it into Israel's larger story. Since the individual who speaks through much of the psalm ties his own experience to the nation's, we should regard this person as a leader of some sort. If the poem is pre-exilic, then this could be the king (so, Eaton 1976: 61–63; Croft 1987: 82–88; Grant 2004: 143–148; though Broyles [1999: 438–439] notes that none of the language is exclusively royal); but if post-exilic, we can still think of a worship leader who gives voice to the nation's need through representative experience. For Vaillancourt (2019: 134, 175–176), the figure is primarily but not exclusively royal, a position that allows the various dimensions of this figure to emerge, especially links to a Mosaic prophet. The psalm also makes use of numerous repetitions (e.g. vv. 1–4, 15–16), suggesting liturgical performance that involved a choir or the worshipping community, with a clear focus on thanksgiving.

As with most elements, the psalm's structure is much debated (see the chart in Potgieter 2003: 392–393), with no clear agreement. Many of these variations depend on assigning elements to various form-critical categories. But this fails to attend to the fact that the psalm deploys existing texts within its own form, and therefore the categorization of the whole will not follow the categories to which we might assign the parts. When read in its own terms, certain elements can be readily recognized, most notably the inclusio formed by the first and last verses, a point that weakens Ravassi's (1985c: 418) otherwise impressive liturgy. If we attend to the repetitions and dominant voice at each stage (e.g. vv. 5–21 use an individual voice), it is then possible to propose the following outline:

1. Theme: Yahweh's kindness (1–4)
2. Confidence in straits (5–14)
   a. Answered cry (5–7)
   b. Yahweh as refuge (8–9)
   c. Surrounded (10–12)
   d. Yahweh helped (13–14)
3. Yahweh as salvation (15–21)
   a. Yahweh's right hand (15–16)
   b. Recounting Yahweh's deeds (17–18)
   c. Righteousness and salvation (19–21)
4. Yahweh's acts (22–27)
   a. The stone (22–24)
   b. Appeal (25)
   c. Blessing shared (26–27)
5. Theme: Yahweh's kindness (28–29)

Comment

1–4. The psalm opens by recalling Psalm 107:1 and its affirmation of Yahweh's goodness and enduring kindness. Indeed, the balance of the psalm is effectively an exposition of what it means to affirm that Yahweh is good and that his kindness endures (W. S. Prinsloo 2003: 421). What is clear is that affirming this is both a truth that is confessed and the basis for continued thanksgiving. After all, if there is no limit to Yahweh's kindness, neither is there any limit that can be placed on thanksgiving. Here, those key themes are taken up by different groups within the worshipping community. The three groups mentioned – Israel, the house of Aaron and those who fear Yahweh – are the same as those who were to trust Yahweh in Psalm 115:9–13. As there, the boundaries between these groups were fluid and, although distinctions can be drawn, it is probably better to think of these labels as reflecting different ways in which Israel could be configured rather than necessarily distinct groups. All could know Yahweh's goodness and enduring kindness and are here called to affirm this for themselves.

5–7. An individual voice now emerges, giving testimony to Yahweh's kindness. In a straitened time (cf. Lam. 1:3), this person called to Yahweh (or even simply called 'Yah'; cf. Goldingay 2008: 356–357) but found Yahweh's response in a broad place, a place of freedom. From this, the individual draws a conclusion about Yahweh's presence that all who have affirmed Yahweh's kindness can also affirm. If Yahweh is present, then human opposition is not to be feared, because humans cannot overcome Yahweh. Yahweh was not the poet's only helper, so human help can be recognized. But Yahweh's help was decisive in enabling the speaker to take a new view of adversaries (cf. Rom. 8:31; Heb. 13:6).

8–9. The lesson from the individual's experience is now applied to the wider audience. If Yahweh responds to those who call, then taking refuge in him is always preferable. Human limitation in general was already pointed out in verse 6, so the opening statement here extends that point. One might still think that more powerful humans, such as princes, offer more benefit, so the initial point is then strengthened through repetition that is now extended to include princes. No human can be trusted more than Yahweh, thus again reaffirming the point from Psalm 115:9–11.

10–12. The straitened circumstances of verses 5–7 were not defined, so it is possible that they are now described here. Again, repetition features as the individual describes a period of being surrounded by the nations, the very people Psalm 117 has called to praise Yahweh. Again, the repetition leads to an intensification of being surrounded on every side, as with bees attacking in a swarm. Yet, in each case the poet can claim to have driven the nations back. Indeed, before the final statement of driving them back, there is an additional note about their being extinguished like a fire of thorns, something that might have glowed quickly, but which equally quickly is extinguished because of the lack of fuel thorns provide.

13–14. The adversaries were not only external. Now, the poet addresses someone from within the community (cf. Botha 2003: 203–204). This person pressed hard against the speaker, but Yahweh's help means the speaker has not fallen. Citing Exodus 15:21 (cf. Isa. 12:2), the speaker affirms that Yahweh is both helper and song, the one who has sustained and become the object of praise. This citation also places the speaker's experience in the wider story of Yahweh's work for Israel, while the reference to help also points back to verse 7.

15–16. The language of salvation becomes a pivot that leads into the third stanza, which opens by affirming that Yahweh's work of salvation is for all the righteous, with the language of righteousness prominent across this stanza. Indeed, 'salvation' and 'righteousness' form an inclusio for this stanza (cf. vv. 19–21). Here, they become the focus for thanksgiving in the tents of the righteous; that is, among those committed to Yahweh. The righteous can shout out their thanksgiving because Yahweh's right hand has acted powerfully for them. Indeed, it is likely that verses 15b–16 are a report of the shout of the righteous, celebrating the powerful work of Yahweh's right hand, based on Exodus 15:6, 12. The right hand itself is a sign of favour, perhaps linking the community to the messianic figure of Psalm 110:1, but the more important point is that even though the individual reports victories achieved in verses 10–12, it is made clear here that Yahweh won the victory.

17–18. In response, the individual again speaks, this time claiming he will not die. We should not understand this as meaning that death will never come so much as that the speaker's death is not imminent because of God's actions. The gift of continued life provides a setting for the speaker to recount Yahweh's deeds, deeds that included a period of discipline, but not discipline to the point of death. This can be read against the background of the exile, in which case the speaker gives voice to the experience of the nation, which, in the return from exile, shows that it continues to live, though a range of other possible settings are possible.

19–21. Since the speaker is not about to die, the appropriate response is to worship Yahweh. The gates of righteousness may be a metaphor, though they may also refer to access to the temple (Seybold 1996: 460) or the city (Hamidović: 2000). Since the psalm could be performed in numerous settings, it is not necessary to choose one option alone, though the temple setting would certainly add to the drama of the language (cf. Pss 15; 24:3–6). The gates of righteousness are so named because they are the point where the righteous come into Yahweh's presence and give thanks. Here, the speaker goes to give thanks to Yahweh because he answered the earlier cry and wrought salvation (cf. Exod. 15:2). The speaker, by entering and giving thanks, becomes the model for the whole community.

22–24. Yahweh's deeds have been a key motif throughout, and they become more prominent in the fourth stanza, spoken in response to the individual. The opening statement about the stone is picked up at key places in the NT (e.g. Matt. 23:29; 1 Peter 2:4) and applied to Jesus, in part because of a pun between the words 'stone' (*'eben*) and 'son' (*bēn*). But the more important connection is that the stone in the psalm is one whose importance was not initially observed, and so was cast away by the builders until they recognized that it was suited to be the capstone, the piece that finished the building (cf. Isa. 28:16; Zech. 4:7). Jesus likewise was not widely recognized in the Gospels but was the one through whom God's work was most completely done. Within the psalm the use of the stone was not foreseen, but what is celebrated here is that Yahweh saw what no one else could, and this was indeed marvellous. The completion of the building (perhaps the second temple; cf. Hossfeld and Zenger 2011: 241–242) means there was a day the congregation could look back on and affirm that Yahweh had indeed acted (cf. 'Notes on the text'). If Yahweh had acted that day when a key building was completed, then the community's task was to rejoice and be glad in his work. Yahweh's goodness had been demonstrated, and his kindness seen in his act that day, just as also occurred in the crossing of the sea (Exod. 15:1–18).

25. That Yahweh had acted at that point did not resolve all the community's challenges. Hence, having stressed that Yahweh is a God of salvation (vv. 14, 15, 21), they now ask for salvation. Their precise need is not expressed, but although they can see that Yahweh has acted, they need a further experience of salvation, an act not restricted to a single moment. Rather, it needs to lead to further flourishing, so that the community may be like the one who meditates on Yahweh's Torah in Psalm 1:2–3, an allusion that also prepares for the great focus on Torah in Psalm 119.

26–27. The psalm's liturgical elements are particularly evident in this strophe. It opens with a declaration of the blessedness of one who comes in Yahweh's name, one who represents him in worship and wishes to enter the gates (v. 19). The identity of this figure is not disclosed, though the person is representative. It is sung by the crowds as Jesus enters Jerusalem at the start of Holy Week (Mark 11:9), though there the appeal for Yahweh to save has become 'Hosanna!'. This transliterates the request for salvation in verse 25, though there it is a form of acclamation because Yahweh is known as one who saves. A group also speaks in verse 26, offering a blessing from the temple for those who come, indicating again that the individual central to the psalm is also a representative figure for all who come in worship. Those announcing this blessing affirm that Yahweh, who alone is God, has shone on them, a sign of his blessing on the community (cf. Num. 6:24–26; Ps. 67:1). In response, those attending the festival are called to bind their festal offering on the altar (cf. 'Notes on the text'), and thus through it express their thanksgiving.

28–29. The closing stanza ties the various elements together, again pointing back to Exodus 15:2 (cf. Isa. 25:1). The individual again speaks, affirming a close relationship with God, a relationship that leads to thanksgiving and exalting him. Yahweh is good, and his kindness endures for ever, and therefore all can be summoned to give thanks.

Explanation

Psalm 118 closes both the 'Hallelujah!' collection of Psalms 111–118 and the first major segment of Book 5. It does so through a poetic liturgy where the community is called to celebrate Yahweh's goodness and kindness, themes that have been developing through Book 5 to this point. Within the psalm, the community's need to acknowledge these themes through thanksgiving finds focus in the voice of a representative figure whose own testimony is carefully linked to Israel's in the exodus, especially the crossing of the sea (Exod. 15:1–21). This individual's testimony of experiencing Yahweh's salvation is of a piece with what Yahweh has done in the past, encouraging the worshipping community to see that the same is true for them, that Yahweh has also acted decisively for them. If the psalm is post-exilic, then the return from exile would represent a key example of this, though it need not be restricted to any one event – there are numerous points where a worshipping community can pause and see the continued pattern of God's salvation. The NT takes this in a strongly Christological manner, tracing this in part to Jesus' own teaching (Matt. 23:29; cf. 1 Peter 2:4) as well as the song of the crowds as he arrived in Jerusalem on Palm Sunday (Mark 11:9). For Christian worship, there is no clearer evidence of the day when God acted (v. 24) than in the resurrection (Schaefer 2001: 291), which through this psalm is tied to the larger story of salvation that runs through the Bible. As with the report of salvation in this psalm, this is a victory that seemed impossible, yet through God's action the impossible became reality.

PSALM 119

Translation

[1]Oh the blessedness of those of the blameless way,
who walk in Yahweh's teaching.
[2]Oh the blessedness of those who keep his testimonies,
they seek him with all their heart.
[3]Indeed, they do no wrong,
they walk in his ways.
[4]You have commanded your precepts,
to be kept diligently.
[5]Oh that my ways were established,
to keep your statutes!
[6]Then I would not be ashamed,
when I consider all your commandments.
[7]I will give you thanks with the upright of heart,
that I may learn your righteous ordinances.
[8]Your statutes will I keep,
do not utterly forsake me!

[9]How can any youth purify their path?
By keeping your word.
[10]With all my heart have I sought you,

do not let me stray from your commandments.
11I have stored up your promise in my heart,
so that I may not sin against you.
12Blessed are you, O Yahweh,
teach me your statutes.
13With my lips have I recounted,
all the ordinances of your mouth.
14In the way of your testimonies have I rejoiced,
as with all wealth.
15On your precepts will I reflect,
and consider your paths.
16In your statutes will I delight,
I will not forget your word.

17Deal generously with your servant that I may live,
and I will keep your word.
18Open my eyes that I may consider,
the wonders of your teaching.
19I was an alien in the land,
do not hide your commandments from me.
20My being is crushed with longing,
for your ordinances all the time.
21You rebuke the insolent, the accursed,
those who stray from your commandments.
22Roll away disgrace and contempt from me,
for I observe your testimonies.
23Even when leaders sit and speak against me,
your servant shall reflect on your statutes.
24Indeed, your statues are my delight,
my counsellor.

25My being clings to the dust,
revive me according to your word.
26I recounted my ways, and you answered,
teach me your statutes.
27Make me understand the way of your precepts,
that I may reflect on your wondrous deeds.
28My being weeps because of grief,
strengthen me according to your word.
29Remove the way of falsehood from me,
and graciously grant me your teaching.
30I have chosen the way of faithfulness,
I regard your ordinances as a ruler.
31I cling to your testimonies,
O Yahweh do not put me to shame.

32I run in the way of your commandments,
for you expand my heart.

33Teach me, O Yahweh, the way of your statutes,
that I may observe them to the end.
34Grant me insight that I may observe your teaching,
and I will keep it with my whole heart.
35Lead me in the path of your commandments,
for I delight in it.
36Turn my heart to your testimonies,
and not to unjust gain.
37Avert my eyes from looking on deceit,
grant me life in your way.
38Establish your promise for your servant,
that you may be revered.
39Remove the disgrace that I fear,
because your ordinances are good.
40Behold, I have longed for your precepts,
revive me in your righteousness.

41May your kindness come to me, O Yahweh,
your salvation according to your promise.
42Then I will answer those who reproach me,
because I trust in your word.
43Do not take the word of your truth utterly from my mouth,
for I hope in your ordinance.
44So I will keep your teaching continually,
for ever and ever.
45Let me walk in freedom,
because I seek your precepts.
46I will speak of your testimonies before kings,
and I will not be ashamed.
47I delight in your commandments,
which I love.
48I will lift my hands to your commandments, which I love,
and I will reflect on your statutes.

49Remember the word to your servant,
in which you have made me hope.
50This is my comfort in my affliction,
that your promise gives me life.
51The insolent greatly deride me,
I did not turn from your teaching.
52I remember your ordinances from of old, O Yahweh,
and I am comforted.

53Rage seizes me because of the wicked,
those who forsake your teaching.
54Your statutes will be songs to me,
in the house of my sojourning.
55I remember your name in the night, O Yahweh,
I will keep your teaching.
56This has been my practice,
for I observe your precepts.

57Yahweh is my portion,
I resolved to keep your words.
58I entreat your favour with all my heart,
be gracious to me according to your promise.
59I considered my ways,
that I might turn my feet to your testimonies.
60I hurried and did not tarry,
to keep your commandments.
61The snares of the wicked surround me,
but I do not forget your teaching.
62I rise in the middle of the night to give thanks to you,
for your righteous ordinances.
63I am a companion for all who fear you,
and to those who keep your precepts.
64Your kindness, O Yahweh, fills the earth,
teach me your statutes.

65You deal well with your servant,
O Yahweh, according to your word.
66Teach me good discernment and knowledge,
for I trust in your commandments.
67I strayed even before I was afflicted,
but now I keep your promise.
68You are good and do good,
teach me your statutes.
69The insolent besmirch me with lies,
I, with a whole heart, observe your precepts.
70Their heart is gross like fat,
but I delight in your teaching.
71It was better for me that I was afflicted,
that I might learn from your statutes.
72The teaching of your mouth is better for me,
than thousands of gold and silver pieces.

73Your hands made me and fashioned me,
grant me insight that I may learn your commandments.

74Those who fear you will see me and be glad,
because I hope in your word.
75I know, O Yahweh, that your ordinances are righteous,
and in faithfulness you afflicted me.
76O may your kindness please comfort me,
according to your promise to your servant.
77Let your compassion come to me that I may live,
because your teaching is my delight.
78Let the insolent be put to shame because they afflicted me with falsehood,
I will reflect on your precepts.
79Let those who fear you turn to me,
those who know your testimonies.
80May my heart be complete in your statutes,
that I may not be put to shame.

81My being longs for your salvation,
I hope in your word.
82My eyes long for your promise,
thinking, 'When will you comfort me?'
83For I have been like a leather bottle in thick smoke,
I have not forgotten your statutes.
84How many are the days of your servant?
When will you enact justice against those who pursue me?
85The insolent dig out traps for me,
that are not according to your teaching.
86All your commandments are trustworthy,
they pursue me falsely – help me!
87They almost destroyed me on the earth,
but I have not forsaken your precepts.
88According to your kindness grant me life,
that I may keep the testimony of your mouth.

89For ever, O Yahweh,
your word stands firm in the heavens.
90Your faithfulness is from generation to generation,
you established the earth, and it stands firm.
91By your ordinances do they stand today,
for everything is your servant's.
92If your teaching was not my delight,
I would have perished in my affliction.
93I will never forget your precepts,
for in them you have given me life.
94I am yours – save me,
for I have sought your precepts.
95The wicked wait for me to destroy me,

I attend to your testimonies.
96I see a limit to all perfection,
but your commandment is very broad.

97How I love your teaching!
It is my reflection all day.
98Your commandment makes me wiser than my enemies,
for it is always with me.
99I have more insight than all my instructors,
because your testimonies are my reflection.
100I have more awareness than my elders,
because I observe your precepts.
101I have restrained my feet from every wrong path,
that I may keep your word.
102I have not turned from your regulations,
because you, you instructed me.
103How pleasant are your promises to my palate,
better than honey in my mouth.
104I gain awareness from your precepts;
therefore, I hate every false path.

105Your word is a lamp to my feet,
and a light for my pathway.
106I have sworn and will be sure,
to keep your righteous ordinances.
107I have been greatly afflicted,
O Yahweh, grant me life according to your word.
108Please accept the free-will offerings of my mouth, O Yahweh,
and teach me your regulations.
109My being is in my hand continually,
but I do not forget your teaching.
110The wicked have laid a trap for me,
but I do not stray from your precepts.
111I have inherited your testimonies for ever,
because they are joy to my heart.
112I have inclined my heart to perform your statutes,
for ever, to the end.

113I hate the double-minded,
but I love your teaching.
114You are my hiding place and shield,
I hope in your word.
115Turn from me O evildoers,
that I may observe the commandments of my God.
116Sustain me according to your promise that I may live,

and do not let me be ashamed because of my hope.
117Uphold me and I will be saved,
that I may continually regard your statutes.
118You discard all who stray from your statutes,
for falsehood is their deceit.
119You destroy the wicked of the earth like dross,
therefore, I love your testimonies.
120My flesh trembles from dread of you,
but I revere your ordinances.

121I have done what is just and right,
do not leave me with my oppressors.
122Stand surety for the well-being of your servant,
do not let the insolent oppress me.
123My eyes long for your salvation,
and for your righteous promise.
124Deal with your servant according to your kindness,
and teach me your statutes.
125I am your servant, grant me understanding,
that I may know your testimonies.
126Time to act, O Yahweh:
they have broken your teaching!
127Therefore, I love your commandments,
more than gold, even refined gold.
128Therefore, I regard all your precepts as upright,
I hate every false path.

129Wondrous are your testimonies,
therefore, my being observes them.
130The unfolding of your words gives light,
granting the simple insight.
131I open my mouth and pant,
because I long for your commandments.
132Turn to me and be gracious to me,
according to your ordinance for those who love your name.
133Establish my footsteps according to your promise,
and do not let any trouble master me.
134Redeem me from human oppression,
that I may keep your precepts.
135Shine your face on your servant,
and teach me your statutes.
136Streams of water run down from my eyes,
because they do not keep your teaching.

137You are righteous, Yahweh,

and your ordinances are upright.
138The testimonies you have commanded are right,
totally trustworthy.
139My zeal consumes me,
when my foes forget your words.
140Your promise is thoroughly refined,
and your servant loves it.
141I am insignificant and despised,
I do not forget your precepts.
142Your righteousness is always right,
and your teaching is truth.
143Hardship and distress have found me,
your commandments are my delight.
144Your testimonies are for ever right,
grant me insight that I may live.

145I called out with all my heart, 'Answer me, O Yahweh,
I will observe your statutes!'
146I called out to you, 'Save me,
and I will keep your testimonies!'
147I arise while it is dark that I may cry for help,
I hope in your word.
148My eyes anticipate the night watches,
to reflect on your promise.
149Hear my voice according to your kindness,
O Yahweh, according to your ordinance grant me life.
150Those who pursue wickedness draw near,
they are far from your teaching.
151You are near, O Yahweh,
and all your commandments are true.
152From of old have I known about your testimonies,
because you founded them for ever.

153See my affliction and rescue me,
for I have not forgotten your teaching.
154Argue my case and redeem me,
grant me life according to your promise.
155Salvation is far from the wicked,
for they do not pursue your teaching.
156Your compassion is great, O Yahweh,
according to your ordinances, grant me life.
157Many are my persecutors and foes,
I have not turned aside from your testimonies.
158I see those who act treacherously and feel loathing,
because they do not keep your promise.

[159]See that I love your precepts,
O Yahweh, according to your kindness, grant me life.
[160]The sum of your word is truth,
and every regulation of your righteousness is for ever.

[161]Princes persecute me without reason,
but my heart is in awe of your word.
[162]I am joyful at your promise,
like one finding much spoil.
[163]I hate and abhor falsehood,
I love your teaching.
[164]Seven times a day shall I praise you,
because of your righteous ordinances.
[165]There is great peace for those who love your teaching,
and they have no stumbling block.
[166]I wait for your salvation, O Yahweh,
and I perform your commandments.
[167]My being keeps your testimonies,
for I love them greatly.
[168]I keep your precepts and testimonies,
because all my ways are before you.

[169]May my shout come before you, O Yahweh,
grant me insight according to your word.
[170]May my supplication come before you,
rescue me according to your promise.
[171]My lips will pour out praise,
because you teach me your statutes.
[172]My tongue will sing of your promise,
because all your commandments are right.
[173]May your hand be my help,
because I have chosen your precepts.
[174]I long for your salvation, O Yahweh,
and your teaching is my delight.
[175]May my being live and praise you,
and may your ordinances help me.
[176]I have strayed like a perishing sheep,
seek your servant,
because I have not forgotten your commandments.

Notes on the text

22. Here, deriving *gal* from *gll*, whereas in verse 18 it is from *glh*.

30. The verb *šwh* is difficult, and Gk seems to be uncertain. *DCH* offers nine possible roots, and for this option points to Psalm 89:20, though that is also uncertain.

38. Hebr. *'ăšer* introduces a result clause (*WHS* §465).

79. Following Q, Gk and several MSS.

91. Though difficult, as evidenced by the textual variants, MT should stand.

98. MT has pl. 'commandments', but revocalized here to sg. with Gk.

103. A few MSS agree with Gk and Tg with the pl. 'promises' here, but the sg. in MT could be collective.

119. 11QPs[a] has 'I regard' (*ḥšbty*), but retain MT.

128. With Gk, read *lĕkol piqqûdêkā.*

158. Hebr. *'ăšer* introduces a result clause (*WHS* §465).

161. With many MSS, Q, Syr. and Tg, read *ûmiddĕbārkā.*

Form and structure

Psalm 119 both stands apart from the poems around it and is closely linked to them. It stands apart because of its size, more than twice the length of any other psalm – indeed, it is nearly twice the combined length of all the Songs of the Ascents (Pss 120–134). Its literary complexity, with its acrostic form devoting eight letters to each letter of the Hebrew alphabet, plus every verse (other than vv. 3, 37, 90, 122) containing at least one of eight synonyms for Yahweh's Torah (vv. 16, 48, 160, 168, 172 have two; note Freedman 1999: 26), immediately indicates the care with which it is composed, even if the synonyms are not distributed on any clear pattern. There are possible nuances of difference between these terms (see van Gemeren 2008: 859–860; Wenham 2012: 86–88), but we can think of them all as expressing Yahweh's revealed instruction in written form, so the focus is much more on what Yahweh's instruction achieves than on distinction between the terms (Burt 2018). Its focus on Yahweh's Torah also links it to other poems (esp., but not only, Pss 1, 19; cf. Firth 2015b), so that although its length is undoubtedly distinctive, its central theme is not. Indeed, its parallels with Psalm 1 led Westermann to suggest that at an earlier stage the Psalter might even have ended with Psalm 119 (1981: 256–257), though this remains supposition. More immediately, within Book 5 we have noted that Psalms 107–118 form a distinctive unit, and the same is true of Psalms 120–134. Psalm 119 is thus both a massive reflection on Torah and a bridge between these two blocks. Looking back to Psalms 107–118, we can note that both Psalms 111 and 112 followed the Davidic triad of Psalms 108–110 with short acrostics that reflected on Torah before the Egyptian Hallel of Psalms 113–118. Grant has noted significant connections between Psalms 118 and 119 (2004: 175–180; cf. Vesco 2006, 2: 1112–1113), while S. S. Ho has also pointed to literary and thematic connections with the Songs of the Ascents (2011: 112–136; though the arrangement in 11QPs[a] differs, showing it could be read in other ways). While Psalm 119 may dominate all around it because of its size, its placement within the Psalter means it plays an important role in Book 5.

Although it can be considered a 'Torah' psalm, attention to its content makes clear that it draws on a range of poetic forms, and 'Torah' is better considered as a central theme than a description of its form. These forms integrate elements of wisdom (e.g. the beatitudes of vv. 1–2; cf. Mensah 2021), confession of sin (e.g. v. 67), complaint and appeal (e.g. v. 25), all leading to the closing appeal of verse 176, the poem's only tricolon. That they work together towards this conclusion indicates that, with Soll (1991: 59–86), we should regard it primarily as a prayer of one who knows the importance of Torah and desires to be shaped by it, even if this has not always been achieved, while asking Yahweh to restore the psalmist to a full life. That it is primarily a prayer, one richly informed by various traditions (cf. Botha 1992; Allen [2002: 181] calls it a 'medley'), is also evident from the fact that apart from verses 1–3, 115, every verse is addressed to Yahweh. Nevertheless, as a prayer we need to recognize it as a work in which the psalmist has consciously chosen to work within the constraints imposed by the acrostic form and the eight instruction terms (Callaham 2009) while also consciously expanding the range of the acrostic (E. T. James 2022).

The poem's acrostic form is its most obvious structural feature, and indeed many do not go beyond commenting on each eight-verse strophe, treating the poem as having no obvious structure beyond this point (e.g. deClaissé-Walford et al. 2014: 870–886). Any structural proposal should start at this point, while also acknowledging that the literary form militates against a clear linear development. This structure can be examined in terms of the distribution of the key terms (Freedman 1999: 57–86), though it is likely that even the decision to use eight verses per Hebrew letter and eight synonyms may also build on the symbolic value of the number, especially in priestly literature (Hossfeld and Zenger 2011: 257–260). Soll (1991: 87–111) has also shown that there is greater coherence than is often observed, and that we can analyse the psalm in six stanzas, with the strophe for each letter of the alphabet forming their constituent parts. Hossfeld and Zenger (2011: 261) also note that each strophe can be divided into two parts of four verses each. Adapting Soll's model slightly (and only as a rough guide), we can thus point to the following overall structure, with an initial stanza of two strophes and then five stanzas of four strophes each:

1. Prologue: orientation (1–16)
2. Initial lament (17–48)
3. Reflecting on the past (49–80)
4. Hope in conflict (81–112)

5. Thematic consolidation (113–144)
6. Conclusion: loyalty and appeal (145–176)

Comment

1–8. The psalm opens by declaring its theme in the aleph strophe, the blessedness of those whose life is lived within the constraints of Yahweh's instruction. This is emphasized by the pair of beatitudes in verses 1–2 (Ps. 32:1–2 is the Psalter's only other example of paired beatitudes). These beatitudes also echo Psalm 1:1–2 and its emphasis on the blessedness of those whose life is shaped by Yahweh's teaching. The beatitudes introduce the first two key words, 'teaching' (*tôrâ*) and 'testimony' (*'ēdût*). The blessed life here is not so much whether someone knows Yahweh's teaching, though appeals for this come later, but whether someone's life is lived in accordance with it by seeking Yahweh. This life is blessed and thus highly desirable. It is also marked by commitment to Yahweh's goals because his 'precepts' (*piqûdîm*) were commanded to be done. This is what is desired, but in verses 5–8 we see that this is not yet the poet's experience. Hence, the psalmist wishes to be established in Yahweh's 'statutes' (*ḥōq*), with this as a means of avoiding shame when linked with time given to consideration of Yahweh's 'commandments' (*miṣwâ*). The benefit of this is that it enables thanksgiving as the psalmist learns Yahweh's 'ordinances' (*mišpaṭ*). The psalmist knows that the blessed life is one that lives out Yahweh's teaching, but this teaching must be learnt, introducing an important motif through the poem as the poet asks twelve times to be taught this instruction (vv. 12, 24, 64, 66, 68, 71, 73, 99, 108, 124, 135, 171). The blessedness of Yahweh's instruction is found by living it, but it must first be taught. The desire to learn is matched by a commitment to keep Yahweh's statutes, though that this is not yet the poet's position is clear from the final appeal not to be abandoned by Yahweh.

9–16. Although there are no further beatitudes, this strophe (beth) continues to develop the pattern of the blessed life as one shaped by Yahweh's instruction. The general focus on the possibilities of a life lived by Yahweh's instruction is established by the rhetorical question of verse 9a and its answer about the keeping of Yahweh's 'word' (*dābār*) in verse 9b. This thought is then developed through the poet's own life in verses 10–12, which focus on the heart as the seat of knowledge (including a focus on Yahweh's 'promise' (*'imrâ*) as well as commitment, which is why this is concluded with the first appeal to be taught Yahweh's statutes. Yahweh's ordinances have been recounted, so the psalmist is not lacking in knowledge in at least some of Yahweh's instruction. In this context, it was possible to find greater joy in Yahweh's testimonies than in wealth. Accordingly, the psalmist promises to 'reflect' (*śyḥ*; cf.

Marlowe and Savelle 2021: 198) on the precepts and 'consider' (*nbṭ*) the paths in which they lead, and also to delight in the statutes and so not forget Yahweh's word.

17–24. Having established the centrality and possibilities of Yahweh's instruction, the second stanza develops the motif of lament hinted at in the opening strophe. Here, the poet accepts the possibilities provided by Yahweh's instruction, but accepts that this is not yet being lived out. This strophe (gimel) opens with an appeal for Yahweh to deal well with his servant, a key self-description of the poet through the psalm (vv. 23, 38, 49, 65, 76, 84, 91, 122, 124, 125, 135, 140, 176). Yahweh's beneficence towards the poet is to grant life, something often under threat (vv. 25, 37, 40, 50, 77, 88, 93, 107, 116, 149, 154, 156, 159, 175). The language of this opening verse of the stanza is closely linked to the poem's closing verses, showing we have now entered the poem's body. It is also joined to the end of the opening stanza by repetition of 'word' (*dābār*) from verse 16. As becomes clear in verses 18–20, the psalmist strongly desires to discover the possibilities that emerge from Yahweh's instruction. The small shift at verse 21 allows the psalmist to accept that Yahweh acts against the insolent (who become the main opponents; cf. vv. 61, 69, 78, 85, 122), defined as those who stray from Yahweh's commandments. This enables a request for Yahweh to remove reproach and contempt, that which the insolent cause, because of the poet's commitment to Yahweh's testimonies. This commitment means that the poet is willing to reflect on Yahweh's statutes even when facing a hostile situation from the powerful, something enabled by the fact that the testimonies are the poet's delight and counsel.

25–32. The opening half (vv. 25–28) of this strophe (daleth) is bound by references to the psalmist's whole 'being' (*nepeš*) and the experience of suffering that needs to be restored in accord with Yahweh's word. The poet is experiencing a diminished life, and longs to be restored in accordance with Yahweh's word. Yahweh has encountered the poet's ways and has answered, but there is more to be done; hence, the appeal to be taught Yahweh's statutes, with his precepts and wonders then a basis for ongoing reflection. But as verse 28 makes clear, the psalmist continues to suffer, needing to be strengthened by Yahweh through his word. The motif of the 'way' then dominates verses 29–32 (cf. v. 26). Initially, the contrast is drawn between the way of falsehood as something the poet rejects in favour of Yahweh's teaching, though needing to be taken from the false way by Yahweh. The preferred option is the way of faithfulness, which the psalmist has chosen with the goal of reflecting on Yahweh's ordinances. But doing this remains challenging, even though the psalmist clings to Yahweh's testimonies. The poet accordingly asks not to be put to shame before promising to run in the path of Yahweh's commandments. As part of the lament, the poet has not yet experienced all the benefits of Yahweh's instruction, but can testify to an expanded heart, here signifying both increased knowledge (cf. 1 Kgs 4:29) and improved life experience.

33–40. The 'way' motif links this strophe (hê) with its predecessor. The first half (vv. 33–36) is bound by imperatives associated with learning, asking Yahweh to 'teach' (v. 33) or 'incline the heart' (and so learn) his instruction. This learning is to be enduring (v. 33) because Yahweh's statutes are their own reward, which is why the psalmist asks to be kept from unjust gain. Within this, the psalmist asks for the ability to focus on Yahweh's teaching as something to be kept with a whole heart, with the commandments also a delightful path in which the psalmist may walk. By contrast, verses 37–40 focus on being turned from that which is contrary to Yahweh's purposes, asking that the poet's eyes be turned away from deceit since Yahweh's word is the means to life. Hence, the poet needs to be established in Yahweh's promise so that Yahweh may be revered. Disgrace also needs to be turned away because Yahweh's ordinances offer something better. The poet has longed for Yahweh's precepts, and so asks to be granted life through Yahweh's righteousness.

41–48. The waw strophe is distinct in that each line begins with the conj. (often 'and') because of a lack of words starting with this letter. The first half (vv. 41–44) builds on the opening appeal for Yahweh's kindness to come to the poet, here defined as Yahweh's salvation in accord with his promise. This would enable the psalmist to provide a word in response to those bringing reproach, a word shaped by trust in Yahweh's word. The word of Yahweh's truth should therefore never be removed from the psalmist's mouth because Yahweh's ordinances are the source of the poet's hope. Hence, the psalmist vows to keep Yahweh's teaching for ever. The second half (vv. 45–48) develops from the desire to walk (i.e. conduct oneself) in a spacious place (and so away from foes) through seeking Yahweh's precepts. Should this happen, the psalmist can speak of Yahweh's testimonies before kings and not be put to shame, finding delight instead in Yahweh's commandments. The poet's commitment to Yahweh is demonstrated by lifting the hands, an act of homage that comes from love for and continued reflection on the statutes.

49–56. The third stanza has a more reflective character. Its opening strophe (zayin) is well suited for this because this is also the first letter for the word 'remember'. Indeed, the strophe's first half (vv. 49–52) is bound by this verb. The first instance is an appeal to Yahweh to remember a word given to the servant, again here 'your servant', which provided hope. Although this could be an independent prophetic word, the context of the psalm makes it more likely that this is concerned with Yahweh's instruction more generally. The psalmist can appropriate this and be given hope. Memory of this word comforts the poet in affliction because Yahweh's promise gives life. The affliction is recalled through the insolent who derided the poet, but this did not lead to a turning aside from Yahweh's teaching. The poet therefore remembers Yahweh's ordinances as something from of old and again finds comfort, their antiquity perhaps pointing to their long-term impact for Yahweh's servants. The second half (vv. 53–56) considers the wicked, contrasting them with the psalmist's attitude to Yahweh's instruction. Their abandoning of Yahweh's teaching creates rage, whereas the statutes have been a metaphorical dwelling place for the psalmist. Hence, the poet can remember Yahweh's name (standing for his character) and commit to keeping his teaching, the opposite to the approach of the wicked. Although the last line (v. 56) is elliptical, it seems to suggest that this has been the psalmist's practice.

57–64. The next strophe (ḥeth) begins (vv. 57–60) with a reflection on the concept of Yahweh as the psalmist's portion. The language of a portion regards Yahweh as an inheritance, and just as someone inheriting an estate would keep it, so the psalmist is to keep Yahweh's words. If Yahweh is the poet's portion, then it is also possible to entreat him for grace, doing so on the basis of his promise. Recollection drives verses 59–60 as the psalmist recalls turning from another way to follow Yahweh's testimonies, hurrying to keep his commandments. The impact of the wicked then shapes verses 61–64. Their snares surrounded the psalmist, but Yahweh's teaching was not forgotten. Unlike the wicked, the psalmist rises to give thanks in the middle of the night because of Yahweh's righteous ordinances. The psalmist is aligned with those who fear Yahweh, those who keep Yahweh's precepts. The good news is that Yahweh's kindness fills the earth (cf. Ps. 33:5), and since this can be understood through Yahweh's statutes, the psalmist asks to be taught these.

65–72. This strophe (teth) is shaped by Yahweh's goodness. The first half (vv. 65–68) is bound by statements about how Yahweh is 'good' (*ṭôb*), preparing for a contrast with the insolent in verses 69–72. Yahweh's goodness is evident in his positive deeds for his servant, consistent with his word. As such, the psalmist asks to be taught good discernment and knowledge as an expression of believing Yahweh's commandments. The psalmist then recalls earlier times where this was not the case but affirms that Yahweh's promise is now kept. This points again to Yahweh as one who is good and does what is good, for which reason the psalmist asks to be taught his statutes. The insolent are unlike this, besmirching the poet with falsehood. By contrast, the poet commits to observing Yahweh's precepts. The insolent are also the wicked, people whose heart is gross with fat, and do not have a mind devoted to Yahweh, whereas Yahweh's teaching is the poet's delight. The poet also realizes that the previous time of affliction also had a 'positive' (*ṭôb*) effect because it led to learning Yahweh's statutes. Hence, Yahweh's teaching is 'better' (*ṭôb*) than an abundance of gold and silver.

73–80. The final strophe (yod) of this stanza opens by referring again to Yahweh's acts, connecting it to the start of the previous strophe.

Yahweh's hands made and fashioned the poet, and therefore the psalmist desires insight through learning Yahweh's commandments. A life lived this way instructs others, so that when those who fear Yahweh see the poet, they will rejoice because of the poet's hope in Yahweh's word. This hope means the psalmist knows that Yahweh's ordinances are righteous. Therefore, although Yahweh previously afflicted the poet, it was an act of faithfulness. What the psalmist therefore desires is to experience Yahweh's kindness as comfort, in accordance with his promise to his servant. Yahweh's acts are again contrasted with the insolent. Yahweh's compassion is needed to grant life because his teaching is the psalmist's delight. The psalmist's desire is that the insolent be put to shame because they afflicted the psalmist through falsehood – there was no good purpose in their deeds, even as the poet vows to continue reflecting on Yahweh's precepts. Rather than the insolent, the psalmist desires to be joined by those who fear Yahweh, those who know his testimonies, while also desiring the chance to engage continually with Yahweh's statutes as a way of avoiding shame.

81–88. The fourth stanza emerges out of the previous two, retaining key motifs from them while turning more towards hope. Its opening strophe (kaph) opens by expressing the psalmist's desire for Yahweh's salvation, something grounded in the poet's hope in Yahweh's word. The poet's experience is still difficult, longing for Yahweh's promise, asking when comfort will be experienced. The difficulties lead to the image of the psalmist as being like a leather bottle in smoke, something shrivelled and unsuited to its purposes, even though the poet has not forgotten Yahweh's statutes. Hence, although there is hope, the first half of the stanza closes with the classic complaint of 'How long?', asking when Yahweh will act justly (according to his ordinance) against those who pursue the psalmist. The troubles caused by the insolent are then the focus of the strophe's second half (vv. 85–88). They have dug traps for the psalmist, acts that show they do not live by Yahweh's teaching. Where Yahweh's commandments are trustworthy, the insolent are marked by falsehood, which is why the psalmist needs help. The psalmist's position is desperate because of their actions, but can appeal to Yahweh because of not forgetting his precepts. But it is Yahweh who provides hope, as he is asked to grant life according to his kindness, while the psalmist will keep Yahweh's testimonies.

89–96. The important shift in this strophe (lamed) is that it introduces a new timeframe, a motif occurring in both halves of the strophe. The enemies are bound by time, but Yahweh is not, which is why his word stands firm in the heavens. This extended temporal framework is extended in verse 90, which focuses on Yahweh's enduring faithfulness, something that means creation itself is secure (cf. Ps. 93:1). Indeed, all stands secure today because of Yahweh's ordinances, which means all things are ultimately his servants. The poet found delight in Yahweh's teaching, accepting that if this had not been the case, then he could possibly have perished. The strophe's second half (vv. 93–96) begins by noting the psalmist's enduring commitment never to forget Yahweh's precepts since life is found in them, even though the psalmist's commitment is bound by time. What matters is that the psalmist belongs to Yahweh, and it is Yahweh who must save the poet as one who seeks Yahweh's precepts. Salvation is needed because the wicked wait to destroy the psalmist. But the psalmist continues attending to Yahweh's precepts. The closing verse again sees the distinction in time, noting that there is a limit to all perfection in human experience, but Yahweh's commandment is exceedingly broad, not constrained like human constructs.

97–104. The benefits of Yahweh's instruction are central to this strophe (mêm). After an opening declaration of love for Yahweh's teaching, itself a mark of devotion to Yahweh, the psalmist also notes that it has provided a basis for continual reflection. Reasons for this are developed through verses 98–100, where each of Yahweh's commandments, testimonies and precepts is shown to give the psalmist a benefit over others, presumably those not attending to Yahweh's instruction. First, the commandments make the psalmist wiser than enemies because they stand outside the limits of human time, connecting this strophe to its predecessor. Perhaps surprisingly, the next two are benefits relative to those within the poet's community. First, Yahweh's testimonies provide more insight than the psalmist's teachers, while observing Yahweh's precepts means more awareness than the community's elders. Even within the community of faith, the psalmist recognizes differences in commitment and therefore the extent to which others benefit from Yahweh's instruction. The strophe's second half (vv. 101–104) is bound by the path motif, anticipating the start of the next strophe. Given the benefits of Yahweh's instruction, the psalmist has committed to hold back from every wrong path in order to keep Yahweh's word; and, accordingly, has not turned from Yahweh's ordinances, since this is what Yahweh has taught. Yahweh's promise can thus be compared to honey, declared to be sweeter to the taste. Given that Yahweh's precepts provide the insight that matters, the poet hates any false way.

105–112. The fourth stanza closes with the nun strophe, one that develops the metaphor of life as a path from the previous strophe while showing how Yahweh guides. This point is affirmed with the opening affirmation that Yahweh's word is a lamp, guiding someone along a pathway, somewhere dangerous without sufficient light. Knowing this, the psalmist has sworn to keep Yahweh's righteous ordinances, a vow reaffirmed here. The psalmist still experiences suffering, and so asks for life according to Yahweh's word, also asking for vows made to please Yahweh, who is in turn to teach the psalmist his ordinances. The strophe's second half (vv. 109–112) begins by accepting that the psalmist is in danger (likely the sense of 'My being is in my hand continually'), but this does not mean Yahweh's teaching was forgotten. Those dangers are evident in the actions of the wicked, who set traps for the poet; but, despite this, the psalmist does not stray from Yahweh's precepts. In contrast with the acts of the wicked, the psalmist has an enduring heritage in Yahweh's testimonies, something that continues giving joy to the heart. Accordingly, the psalmist inclines the heart to perform Yahweh's statutes for ever, without limit.

113–120. The fifth stanza draws together threads from the previous stanzas rather than moving the direction of the poem. As such, elements of complaint and hope continue to emerge. The opening strophe (samek) begins by referring to verse 97, noting the psalmist's love for Yahweh's teaching, whereas the double-minded (cf. Jas 1:5–8) are hated. Hate here refers to a rejection of their pattern of life. The psalmist identifies Yahweh as a hiding place and shield, a place of security, which is experienced through his word in which the psalmist has hope. Evildoers can therefore be directed to turn away so the psalmist can observe the commandments of 'my God', the only point at which Yahweh is referred to this way. Because of the relationship with God, Yahweh is asked to sustain the psalmist in accordance with his promise. This way, the psalmist may live and not be put to shame by a failure of hope. The strophe's second half (vv. 117–120) provides reasons for Yahweh to act for the psalmist. First, upholding the psalmist provides safety, and hence a continued opportunity to regard Yahweh's statutes. This upholding is consistent with Yahweh's pattern of discarding those who stray from his statutes, people who have been drawn into deceit. Indeed, Yahweh regards the wicked in the same way a silversmith regards dross, but the psalmist instead loves his testimonies. The psalmist knows that Yahweh and his word are not identical, for the psalmist is in dread of Yahweh himself (albeit dread that is also awe), but knows it is possible to fear (and thus revere) his ordinances.

121–128. This strophe (ayin) is focused on the poet's loyalty to Yahweh and Yahweh's need to act in response. The first half (vv. 121–124) is bounded by the verb *'śh* (do, make), while the first two verses also reference the poet's oppressors. It opens by pointing to the psalmist's own practice of righteousness and 'justice' (*mišpaṭ*) as why Yahweh needs to act by not allowing the psalmist to be given over to oppressors. This is extended through the metaphor of standing surety for his servant's well-being, providing protection from insolent oppressors. The poet's desire for salvation from the oppression, expressed through the image of the longing of the eyes, is here linked to the desire for Yahweh's righteous promise. Hence, Yahweh is asked to deal kindly with his servant, something at least partially demonstrated in the teaching of his statutes. The second half closes with two 'therefore' statements, which emerge from the poet's status as Yahweh's servant. This status is reinforced in verse 125, explaining why Yahweh should grant the psalmist understanding through his testimonies. This is not to be delayed, as is clear in the urgency of verse 126, which insists that the time for Yahweh to act has come because of breaches of his teaching. But this has not been the psalmist's approach. Rather than breaking Yahweh's teaching, the poet again expresses love for Yahweh's commandments, regarding them as superior to even the best gold. The poet knows Yahweh's precepts are upright, and so avoids false paths, those leading away from Yahweh's instruction.

129–136. The expression 'therefore' (*'al kēn*) provides a link to this strophe (pê). Its first half (vv. 129–132) is concerned with the desirability of Yahweh's instruction. The strophe opens with an affirmation of the wondrous nature of Yahweh's testimonies, and this alone is reason for them to be observed. This is explored in terms of the benefits provided in verses 129–130, where the unfolding of Yahweh's word gives light that enables even the simple to gain insight, while the psalmist's own longing for Yahweh's commandments is like someone who pants, desperately desiring to experience more of them. Yahweh is therefore asked to turn to the psalmist and be gracious in accordance with his ordinance for those who love his name. This stands in contrast to the psalmist's experience in verses 133–136. Yahweh's grace is possible, but the psalmist needs to be able to walk securely in Yahweh's promise, preventing the triumph of any evildoer. The threat of the evildoers is then made clear in that the psalmist faces human oppression (cf. vv. 121–122), from which redemption needs to come from Yahweh, redemption that will allow the psalmist to keep Yahweh's statutes. The request for Yahweh to shine his face on his servant (cf. Num. 6:24) is another request for grace through which Yahweh demonstrates his beneficence towards the psalmist, especially through teaching his statutes. The psalmist's status as Yahweh's servant is demonstrated in the tears shed because of the breach of Yahweh's teaching (tears that echo the waters of Ps. 1:3), providing further reason for Yahweh to act.

137–144. The thematic consolidation closes with this strophe (tsadhe), which has a particular focus on Yahweh's righteousness and therefore the righteousness of that associated with him, with the strophe's opening and closing verses (plus vv. 138, 142) developing this motif. The strophe's first half (vv. 137–140) establishes this central motif from the outset, declaring Yahweh's righteousness is matched by the upright (and thus reliable) nature of his ordinances. This is extended by the note that Yahweh has commanded his righteous testimonies, something entirely trustworthy. Yahweh's righteousness is thus to be carried out by those who know him, and finds expression in the psalmist's zeal for this, unlike the foes who forget Yahweh's word. A wordplay between 'foes' (*ṣārāy*) and 'refined' (*ṣĕʳrûpâ*) joins the closing lines of this half by highlighting the value of Yahweh's promise as something the psalmist loves. The poet thus demonstrates an awareness the foes do not. The strophe's second half (vv. 141–144), though pointing to complaint, points more to the psalmist's loyalty to Yahweh through his word. The poet's self-description is as one who is insignificant and despised, at least as seen by other humans. But the psalmist remains loyal to Yahweh, not forgetting his precepts. The psalmist knows that Yahweh's righteousness is expressed in his teaching. Even as the psalmist experiences hardship, Yahweh's commandments provide delight, and therefore the strophe closes with an appeal for Yahweh to grant insight into his perennially righteous testimonies, thus granting the psalmist life.

145–152. The themes of loyalty and appeal to Yahweh with which the previous strophe close form a bridge into the final stanza in which they become much more prominent. The element of appeal is particularly clear in this strophe (qoph). Its first half (vv. 145–148) opens with two reports of calling out to Yahweh and closes with a further pair of reports of the psalmist's practice. The two reports of calling look back on previous times, where the poet called out wholeheartedly, seeking an answer and requested salvation because of observing Yahweh's statutes and keeping his testimonies. The psalmist is loyal to Yahweh, and for this reason appeals to him. This loyalty is also evident in the psalmist's pattern of devotion, involving rising while it is still dark and crying for deliverance as one hoping in Yahweh's word. This theme is extended through the image of the poet's eyes anticipating the night watches as a chance to reflect on Yahweh's promise. The second half (vv. 149–152) moves to fresh appeals, asking Yahweh, because of his kindness, to hear the psalmist's voice, granting life according to his ordinance. The threat to the poet's life is seen in cunning persecutors who are near the psalmist but far from Yahweh's teaching. But Yahweh is also near, and his commandments are true. The poet has known Yahweh's testimonies from of old since they have been founded for ever. Since Yahweh's instruction expresses his character, he thus needs to hear the psalmist's cry for help.

153–160. The motifs of appeal and loyalty continue into this strophe (resh) – the psalmist has called, so Yahweh must see. The first half (vv. 153–156) extends the element of appeal to Yahweh. It opens with a pair of appeals that ask Yahweh to look on the psalmist's affliction and to argue the poet's case, a legal metaphor. In both cases, Yahweh needs to deliver. In the opening line, this is because the poet has not forgotten Yahweh's teaching and is thus loyal, while the second line extends the notion of rescue by asking that Yahweh grant life in accord with his promise. The poet is contrasted with the wicked, those far from Yahweh's salvation because of their failure to pursue his precepts. The first half closes with a further appeal for life in accord with Yahweh's ordinances, though this time it is because of his great compassion – even the loyal, like the psalmist, know it is finally Yahweh's compassion that leads him to act. The strophe's second half contrasts the poet with the adversaries.

They are numerous and marked by their failure to align themselves with Yahweh's testimonies. Seeing this, the poet is revolted by their failure to keep Yahweh's promises. By contrast, Yahweh can see that the psalmist loves Yahweh's precepts, and so asks for Yahweh to grant life because of his kindness. The strophe closes with two instruction terms, 'word' and 'ordinances', both of which are trustworthy because they point to Yahweh's own righteousness and thus give the poet hope.

161–168. This strophe (sin/shin) has a greater focus on the motif of the psalmist's loyalty to Yahweh. The strophe's first half (vv. 161–164) is concerned with how the poet demonstrates loyalty in a challenging world. As one loyal to Yahweh, the psalmist has faced persecution from those in power, but has continued in awe of Yahweh's word. Indeed, the poet's delight is found in Yahweh's promise, the value of which is compared to the delight of someone who has found great spoil as treasure. As such, the poet hates and abhors falsehood but loves Yahweh's teaching, love that is expressed by rising seven times a day to praise Yahweh because of his righteous ordinances. 'Seven times' probably means a life shaped by praise (similarly, A. P. Ross 2016: 587; against Goulder 1998: 202–203), though it was taken more literally in the monastic tradition. The second half (vv. 165–168) explores the benefits of loyalty to Yahweh through his instruction. It opens with a general statement about the great peace those who love Yahweh's teaching obtain, avoiding stumbling blocks. This explains why the poet has hoped for Yahweh's salvation while performing his commandments. Indeed, the psalmist's whole being has kept Yahweh's testimonies as an expression of great love for them, aligning the poet with those who have great peace. As with the previous strophe, this one also closes by mentioning two instruction terms, 'precepts' and 'testimonies', pointing out that the psalmist has kept them as one aware that all life is lived before Yahweh.

169–176. The closing strophe (taw) draws the elements of loyalty and appeal to climax in the appeal of the final verse, the poem's only tricolon. The first half (vv. 169–172) has two requests followed by two declarations of coming praise. Both requests ask that Yahweh heed the psalmist, attending to both a shout and a supplication seeking grace, granting insight according to his word and rescue according to his promise. The result of this will be praise, with the lips and tongue here standing for the whole person. The lips shall offer praise because Yahweh teaches his statutes, responding to a frequent plea through the psalm (cf. v. 12), while the tongue shall sing of Yahweh's promise, because all his commandments are right, again drawing two instruction terms into one verse. The second half (vv. 173–176) opens and closes with an appeal, the latter particularly marked out because of the change in poetic form. Where the psalmist's lips and tongue offer praise, Yahweh's hand needs to help the psalmist as one who has chosen his precepts, and thus is loyal. This loyalty is expressed in the poet's longing for Yahweh's salvation while finding delight in his teaching. As such, the psalmist asks for the possibility to live a life of continuous praise while being helped by Yahweh's ordinance. This life is needed because although the psalmist has been loyal to Yahweh, this loyalty has not always been maintained. Hence, the psalm closes with the poet acknowledging a failure to live in the way Yahweh has provided, straying like a perishing sheep. In Psalm 1:6 it is the wicked who perish, but here it is the psalmist. Nevertheless, the psalmist can still appeal for Yahweh to seek his servant, because those failures do not mean the psalmist has forgotten Yahweh's commandments. The psalmist belongs to Yahweh, and it is Yahweh who can seek the lost sheep (cf. Luke 15:3–7).

Explanation

Although many modern readers find Psalm 119 rather overwhelming (e.g. Sabourin 2010: 381; but cf. Freedman [1999: 88], who notes that it is not 'to everyone's taste' before offering an enthusiastic exposition), the reality is that it is a carefully crafted piece in which a student expresses a great desire to know and internalize Yahweh's instruction, instruction that is consistently understood as good news (from A–Z, as it were). As Reynolds (2010: 14, 181) has argued, the goal of this is that it be internalized and so shape the poet's character, perhaps also seeing in reflection on this instruction a means for actualizing Yahweh's presence (Persaud 2016: 81). Readers who encounter this poem are encouraged to follow this path for themselves since it is the way of true blessedness, the way that enables someone to live a full and flourishing life. Alongside this, the psalm remains a prayer, one that acknowledges that the one who prays has not fully lived out this, and that despite having sought to be shaped by Yahweh's instruction is still like a perishing sheep that needs to be sought by Yahweh. Moreover, the psalmist also moves between poles of confidence and complaint, sure of Yahweh's care but also facing persecution from foes and aware that such people sometimes seem to flourish. An important element of theodicy is woven through the poem as it works out how to live in this world (cf. Fletcher 2018: 235), one where the possibilities provided by Yahweh's instruction are real but also balanced by the realities faced. In its own way, the psalm adopts an eschatological perspective, looking for the fullness of what Yahweh's instruction can provide, but closing with the appeal for Yahweh's help because that is what we all need until that reality is achieved. This same balance is also evident in John's discussion of the new commandment (1 John 2:7–14), where he alludes to verse 165 while holding both to the possibilities provided by living by the new commandment and the difficulties of doing so in a world of darkness.

PSALM 120

Translation

A Song of the Ascents

[1]To Yahweh in my distress,
I called and he answered me.
[2]O Yahweh, deliver me,
from lying lips,
from a deceitful tongue.

[3]What will he give to you,
and what more give to you,
O deceitful tongue?
[4]A warrior's sharpened arrows,
with glowing coals of a broom tree!

[5]Woe to me that I sojourn in Meshek,
I dwell with the tents of Kedar.
[6]I have dwelt long enough
with those who hate peace.
[7]I am for peace,
but when I speak,
they are for war.

Notes on the text

1. NIV and NRSV treat the verbs as present, but the structure of a pf. followed by waw-consecutive imp. is more suggestive of a past-time reference.

3. Gk has pass. verbs here (cf. ESV), but MT's act. verbs should be followed.

Form and structure

With Psalms 120–134 we enter a new collection, all marked by the title 'A Song of the Ascents' (with a small variation in Ps. 121). These poems are notable for their repeating poetic forms (helpfully examined by Stocks 2012), the brevity of each (apart from Ps. 132, none exceeds nine verses), and certain recurring themes. W. S. Prinsloo (2003: 423) points to trust as a 'golden thread' that runs through the Ascents, while Gillmayr-Bucher (2010) also highlights their use of spatial imagery. Despite this, much remains uncertain, most notably the meaning of the title (cf. Crow 1996: 3–27). It could refer to 'steps', leading to the suggestion that it refers to the steps on the ascent to the temple (already in the Mishnah, *Sukkah* 15b); though, if taken as a pilgrim collection, it could also refer to the ascent to Jerusalem (cf. Ps. 122:4). This is more probable (with Mitchell 1997: 113–114), but lack of certainty means that a particular background should not be imposed on the Ascents, and it is certainly difficult to align some of the poems with pilgrimage. The title indicates that these psalms form a collection, but the Ascents' significance needs to be determined from the features of the poems themselves. Following this approach, we can note Crow's (1996: 182–184) suggestion about the centrality of Zion as the source of blessing providing a theological core, which holds the collection together. Viviers (1994) has also pointed to key wisdom motifs that run through the Ascents, providing further evidence that they are intended to be read together. In such a reading, it also becomes clear that the community that reads these psalms is itself being formed in their theology, developing trust in Yahweh while looking to Zion as the place from which blessing comes (Cousins 2016), while still noting that trust does not exclude lament (Viviers 1992).

Although trust is a key motif across the Ascents, it takes time to emerge. In this psalm, we should probably read the opening verse as a past-time reference that establishes a possibility of trust by reflecting on past distress, but with trust largely deferred for a more immediate focus on current distress. In this instance, distress is caused by the speech of an unnamed enemy, speech representative of the poet's wider experience. This distress is exacerbated by the poet's experience of living among peoples who are opposed to peace (which in various ways links this poem to Psalm 119; cf. Vesco 2006, 2: 1170). The combination of these elements means the debate about whether to regard the poem as a complaint (e.g. deClaissé-Walford et al. 2014: 891) or thanksgiving (e.g. Allen 2002: 147–148) may miss the point, and the psalm is in fact an integration of these elements in an unresolved move towards trust.

The poem's structure is also disputed, depending on the role assigned to verse 2. However, when seen as the introduction of the current distress (cf. Villanueva 2020), we may analyse the psalm in three stanzas:

1. Distress: past and present (1–2)
2. Address to an enemy (3–4)
3. Longing for peace (5–7)

Comment

Title: The first of fifteen poems with this title. See above, 'Form and structure'.

1–2. The slightly unusual word order here stresses Yahweh as the one on whom the psalmist focused in past distress. Yahweh was the one on whom the poet had called, and Yahweh had answered. The answer presumably resolved the previous distress, but the key point is that Yahweh answers in times of distress, making him unlike the idols of the nations (cf. Pss 115:5–7; 135:16). Hossfeld and Zenger (2011: 306) also point to Elijah's conflict with the prophets of Baal in 1 Kings 18; and if this text lies in the background, it may also explain why verse 4 mentions the broom tree (cf. 1 Kgs 19:4–5). That Yahweh answers means a basis for trust is introduced (cf. Psalms 3:5, 138:3), which points to the potential resolution of the present distress, even if it is not resolved in this psalm. Since citations of speech need not be marked, verse 2 could then report the cry from the previous distress. But this would leave the distress in verses 3–4 without any context, so it is better to understand this as a new call for deliverance, one informed by Yahweh's prior actions. That deliverance is needed from lying lips suggests that the psalmist's 'life' (*nepeš*) is under threat because of malicious claims, with lips standing for the speech of the opponents, a point extended by mention of a deceitful tongue. The form of this threat is undefined and need not refer to a legal case because malicious speech can take many forms, but it clearly causes the poet significant problems.

3–4. The psalmist here addresses those using malicious speech, picking up the language of the deceitful tongue from verse 2. Here, the opponents are personified by the deceitful tongue, making malicious speech their defining characteristic. The address is posed in a question to the opponents, asking what Yahweh will do to them, a question that adapts curse formulas from elsewhere in the OT (e.g. 1 Sam. 3:17). Yahweh is unnamed here; but because Yahweh has previously answered, the assumption is that he will answer again. The opponent needs to ponder what Yahweh will do given their abuse of others. An initial answer is provided by verse 4, which imagines Yahweh's using sharpened arrows and glowing coals against the opponent. The tongue is elsewhere compared to something sharp (Pss 52:4; 57:5; 64:4; 140:4), so reception of a warrior's sharp arrows is a fitting return. Cutting words receive a cutting reply. This reply is matched with a second element, glowing coals from a broom tree, a small shrub apparently well suited for making charcoal. The choice of this image may also derive from the matching of the tongue with dangerous heat (Ps. 39:4). Both images suggest that Yahweh's action against the opponents will match the harm done by their speech. In addressing the opponents, the psalmist continues to trust.

5–7. A new motif is introduced in the third stanza, as the psalmist expresses sorrow for sojourning among peoples who do not share the poet's commitment to peace. The language of 'sojourning' could indicate that the psalmist is not living in Israel, but it could also be a metaphor pointing to the poet as one who remains faithful while living among peoples who are not. Dwelling among the tents of Kedar could point to residence among the Ishmaelites (cf. Gen. 25:13) in Arabia; but Meshek is more difficult to identify, as the OT seems to locate them in various places, most commonly to the north (e.g. Ezek. 39:1–2). Perhaps it is enough to note that Genesis 10:2 makes Meshek a descendant of Japheth. Both names would point to peoples who do not embody faithfulness to Yahweh. Although the psalmist could be physically absent from Israel, it is perhaps more likely that these ethnonyms are used to characterize the opponents as living among those not committed to Yahweh. The psalmist's distress is increased by the fact that such people do not expect Yahweh to act against them, and therefore would see no reason to moderate their speech. That their speech harms others shows they have no commitment to their well-being, their hatred of peace a denial of the importance of human flourishing. The poet's distress is thus caused by living among people who see no need to promote peace, their hatred of peace emerging from the fact that stoking up conflict through speech is their means of increasing power. Hence, although the poet has expressed points that provide pointers to hope, the psalm ends on a point of non-resolution – whenever the psalmist speaks, it is for peace, but the opponents seek only war. The psalmist has indicated that Yahweh will act, but no action has yet occurred. Nevertheless, as the Ascents proceed, the possibility of peace will gradually emerge (Pss 122:6–8; 125:5; 128:6).

Explanation

Psalm 120 opens the Songs of the Ascents with a psalm that integrates thanksgiving and lament, while also creating a context for trusting Yahweh. That context will be extended in Psalm 121, while its hope for peace also anticipates Psalm 122. It is thus a carefully chosen commencement to the Ascents. But it is not just a placeholder. Rather, as a bridge from Psalm 119, it extends key themes developed there, especially the conflict experienced between the assurance of God's actions for his people and the reality of current distress. Neither can be allowed to trump the other, and only when this is recognized can real trust emerge. Thus, the psalmist both recalls past deliverance and hopes for a future experience of peace when God acts against the violent. It is an experience that will be recognized by many communities and individuals in their own discipleship, one that anticipates the 'now and not yet' model that comes to particular clarity in Jesus' announcement of the kingdom (Mark 1:14–15), one that assures believers of the kingdom's nearness while acknowledging that disciples must still take up their cross and follow Jesus (Mark 8:34).

PSALM 121

Translation

A song for the Ascents.

1I lift my eyes to the mountains,
from where shall my help come?
2My help is from Yahweh,
maker of heavens and earth.

3He will not permit your foot to stumble,
your protector will not slumber.
4Indeed, he will not slumber,
nor sleep,
Israel's protector.

5Yahweh is your protector,
Yahweh is your shade at your right hand.
6By day the sun will not strike,
nor the moon at night.

7Yahweh will protect you from all harm,
Yahweh will protect your life.
8Yahweh will protect
your going out and your coming in,
both now and for ever.

Notes on the text

Title: A few MSS (including 11QPs[a]) retain the standard title here, but this is probably because of scribal familiarity with it.

1. For the indirect question, see J-M §161g; Allen 2002: 207.

3. The negative *'al* is often associated with the juss., in which case this verse would express a wish (cf. Kidner 1975, 1: 467). But the longer-form verbs here are more likely imps., in which case a statement is preferable.

4, 8. For the 'para-tricola' in these verses, see Stocks 2012: 77–83.

Form and structure

Where Psalm 120 hinted at the possibilities of trust, that motif emerges as a principal theme here. Where the poet in Psalm 120 could point to previously answered prayer as at least a foundation for trust while living in a world of violence, this psalm is focused on how Yahweh provides help for those who trust him (cf. Ps. 91). Central to this motif is the question of verse 1, which receives a direct response in verse 2. However, there appears to be a key shift in verse 3. Previously, the question has been about 'my help' but from this point the psalmist is apparently addressed by someone else. A dizzying array of suggestions have been made to explain this shift, generally based on a reconstructed background for the psalm which identifies the proposed speakers (ably summarized in Hossfeld and Zenger 2011: 317–319). Although none of these can be demonstrated from the text, the proposed explanation usually controls the psalm's interpretation. The poem permits a view that there are two speakers, but it is also possible that the poet reports an internal monologue (cf. Ps. 42:5) as a device to address readers who may find their own concerns also covered by the response. Fortunately, it is sufficient to note the shift at verse 3 without depending on a specific situation.

Structurally, the shift at verse 3 marks the poem's major turning point, resulting in two stanzas, albeit stanzas that are closely linked (Becking 2009: 4–5). However, the second stanza also contains three strophes of two verses each, with each marking a new step in exploring what it means that Yahweh protects his people. This leads to the following analysis:

1. Question and answer (1–2)
2. Yahweh as protector (3–8)
   a. Yahweh's vigilance (3–4)
   b. Yahweh is your protector (5–6)
   c. The range of Yahweh's protecting (7–8)

Comment

Title: This poem differs slightly from the other Songs of the Ascents in being a song 'for' (*la*) the ascents. Perhaps this change derives from the anticipation of going up to the hills in the first stanza. On this group, see on Psalm 120.

1–2. A speaker describes an experience common to many journeys, not just pilgrimages to Jerusalem: lifting eyes to the mountains. Where modern readers may regard looking to the mountains positively because of their beauty, ancient readers might have regarded them with concern since they provided hiding spots for bandits and were the home of dangerous wildlife – though the lifting eyes can also anticipate something positive (cf. Ps. 123:1). Mountains in the ANE were also regarded as the abode of the gods, a potential risk for a Yahweh worshipper (cf. Maré 2006a). The speaker anticipates entering the mountains, and thus the risks they pose. In such a place, help (esp. protection) is needed, leading to the question of verse 1b, which could be understood generally or with the more specific focus of wondering which mountain might provide help. Having asked the question, the poem offers a declaration of trust, affirming that help comes from Yahweh (cf. Ps. 124:8), not from a mountain (cf. Richter 2004). The speaker can claim this help since it is 'my' help. Yahweh can provide this help in facing the challenges of the mountains because he is the creator of heavens and earth (cf. Pss 115:5; 124:8; 134:3). This refers not only to the initial creation, but also to Yahweh's continued involvement with creation, a motif made explicit as the psalm progresses.

3–4. The second stanza explores what it means to declare that Yahweh helps his people. Throughout this stanza, an unidentified individual is addressed. If the psalm was a real dialogue, then a second speaker addresses the first speaker, explaining how this help will be experienced. If it is a poetic technique, then the poet addresses the psalm's audience. In a real dialogue, the first speaker is a representative individual who stands for the psalm's audience, so in either case readers are effectively offered this reassurance as a basis for their own trust in Yahweh. Within this strophe, there is a shift in the negative adverbs in each verse. In verse 3, 'not' represents *'al*, a negation that typically refers to a particular point, whereas in verse 4 it is *lō'*, a form that usually refers to an enduring negation. It should be noted that this distinction is not absolute, but the deliberate shift suggests it is relevant. Verse 3 reassures the audience that an initially unidentified figure will not permit the foot to stumble at this point before noting that 'your protector' will not slumber. This introduces 'protector' (*šōmēr*), a key term that occurs six times in the psalm and evokes the priestly blessing (Num. 6:24–26). Throughout, the term refers to the provision of protection. Having made this affirmation about the protector, verses 4a–b extends the observation of verse 3b to note that the protector neither slumbers nor sleeps. The ANE was familiar with the idea of sleeping deities (cf. 1 Kgs 18:27; McAlpine 1987: 181–199), so this affirmation is particularly important. This protector is not only always vigilant but is immediately distinguished from other ancient gods. Although verse 2 indicated that Yahweh was the speaker's help, it is only in verse 4c that the protector is specified as Israel's protector.

5–6. Having noted that Israel's protector was always vigilant, the second stanza then clarifies that Yahweh is the helper. The addressee thus knows that Yahweh is not simply the nation's God; he is also concerned with the individual. The protection Yahweh offers is explored through the motif of Yahweh as the individual's shade, present as the addressee's right hand. This is the place from which Yahweh acts for his servants (cf. Pss 109:31; 110:5), in this instance offering protection. The motif of shade prepares for mention of the sun and moon in verse 6, though the image of 'shade' (*ṣēl*) can be understood as offering protection more generally (e.g. Pss 17:8; 36:7; 57:1; 63:7). Here, protection is offered from the sun by day and the moon by night, with day and night also meaning 'continually'. This could be understood in purely physical terms as protection from the heat of the sun, while the moon may also be thought to affect someone's behaviour (e.g. in Matt. 4:24, 17:15 epilepsy is understood as being 'moonstruck'). But both sun and moon could be considered as deities from which Yahweh offers protection, something possible precisely because he is the Creator.

7–8. Where the previous strophes explored what it meant to speak of Yahweh as protector, the closing strophe examines how he protects, those things he does in protecting his people. The key shift is from the ptc. 'protector' to the verb 'protect'. Three times Yahweh is said to protect – from all harm, the addressee's life, and the addressee's going out and coming in. Protection from all harm is largely defined by the previous statements, which allows both for physical threats and mythological ones. No other gods (however construed) can affect those protected by Yahweh. This protection is defined further by the statements that follow, noting that Yahweh protects the addressee's life, the experiences of which can be summed up in terms of going out and coming in (cf. 1 Kgs 3:7). As with Psalm 1, this imagines life as a journey, though in this case one that also has a home to which one may return (cf. Crow 1996: 39). Every time one goes out, not just on pilgrimage, there is threat. But Yahweh protects his people. Likewise, even returning home does not automatically provide safety. But again, Yahweh protects. So, all life experiences are lived under Yahweh's protection. The final line then extends this through time. Yahweh not only protects in all kinds of life experiences; he also protects throughout time.

Explanation

Following Psalm 120, this psalm moves into a full-orbed expression of trust. Yahweh is the ever-vigilant one whose protection is a permanent reality since there is no time or place when we are beyond his protection. Like other psalms of trust (e.g. Pss 23, 91), this psalm encourages trust in a world that often seems troubling, a world where there are many threats to be faced that are beyond our own resources. The key point is that help comes from God, and this help is expressed in real protection, much of which will never be known. Jesus seems to draw on it (at least in part) in assuring the disciples of his presence (Matt. 28:20), a presence that points to his protection. This psalm also seems to shape Paul's own understanding of his life, even as he faced his death (2 Tim. 4:18; cf. Rom. 8:39), seeing God's protection in Christ extending into an eschatological reality. There is indeed no point where we are removed from God's unending vigilance and protection.

PSALM 122

Translation

A Song of the Ascents. Davidic.

1I rejoiced when they said to me,
'We will go to the house of Yahweh.'
2Our feet stand,
in your gates O Jerusalem!

3Jerusalem is built
as a city bound together;
4there the tribes ascended,
the tribes of Yah,
a testimony for Israel,
to give thanks to the name of Yahweh.
5For there the thrones for justice sat,
the thrones for the house of David.

6Pray for the well-being of Jerusalem,
may those who love you be at ease.
7May there be well-being in your ramparts,
security in your fortifications.
8For the sake of my kin and friends,
I will utter 'Well-being be in you.'
9For the sake of the house of Yahweh our God,
I will seek good for you.

Notes on the text

Title: 'Davidic' is not attested in Gk and rejected by Briggs and Briggs (1907, 2: 448), but its presence in 11QPs[a] suggests it should be retained.

3. Or 'Our feet were standing'.

4. 11QPs[a] gives a smoother reading, offering 'assembly' rather than 'testimony', but this is likely an emendation rather than the original reading. Note that MT is supported by 4Q522, though compare Booij 2001.

Form and structure

Where Psalm 121 had looked to the mountains, Psalm 122 is a testimony of someone who has gone to the temple, having ascended to Jerusalem.

It is unclear whether the speaker is imagined as having just arrived in Jerusalem or looks back on a previous journey (cf. 'Notes on the text', v. 3), but in either case it is the most obviously 'pilgrim' psalm within the Ascents (with Goldingay 2008: 463). If the psalm is now accessed through its place in the Psalter (rather than attempting to reconstruct the experience of pilgrimage), it is probably better to think of it as encouraging readers to imagine themselves arriving in the city, though those who have been there can also use it to look back on previous visits. The reader is led from the joy of one who has been asked to join those heading to the temple to the experience of awe on arrival at Jerusalem. The city is not only the place of the temple, where Yahweh was praised; it is also where the Davidic kings reigned. Jerusalem is a place of joy (linking this poem to Pss 46, 48, 76, 84, 87), though as the psalm continues, it is also a place of conflict. These themes are developed as the psalm addresses its audience directly throughout, with successive segments of the poem developing these themes. Yahweh is never addressed, though the audience are urged to pray to Yahweh for Jerusalem's peace, looking for the moment when the city will know true prosperity.

The psalm can be analysed in three stanzas (though with McCann (1996: 1183; cf. Hamilton 2021, 2: 386) we should note that it is bounded by reference to Yahweh's house and places, with David's house at its centre:

1. Joy at the journey (1–2)
2. The wonders of Jerusalem (3–5)
3. Prayer for Jerusalem (6–9)

Comment

Title: On 'Song of the Ascents', see on Psalm 120. For 'Davidic', see on Psalm 3. It is notable for mentioning David within the poem as well as the title, though the psalm itself uses 'David' in the sense of the Davidic dynasty.

1–2. The psalm opens with a word of testimony as an individual reports on the gladness experienced through a request to go to the temple. Mention of the 'house of Yahweh' anticipates its mention in verse 9, creating an inclusio for the psalm. The speaker does not report on the size of the group that issued the invitation, focusing instead on the temple as the goal of the journey. The details of the journey are elided, as are the reasons for it, moving instead to report the arrival in Jerusalem. Mention of the 'gates' (standing both for the point of entry and the city as a whole) probably highlights the moment when the city was entered (Crow 1996: 44), and indeed mention of the group's feet standing there emphasizes the point of their arrival. The city itself is addressed in this recollection, imagining it as a living organism that welcomes pilgrims.

3–5. Having addressed the city, a description is now provided, a move that enables readers to visualize it, experiencing it through the speaker's eyes. The city (perhaps both buildings and people) is compact, a necessity given its location at the top of a mountain, though this could also point to what was required for its defence. The initial observations would point to an unprepossessing town, not necessarily one of any grandeur. What distinguishes it is not its architecture but its place in the life of Yahweh's people. It is the place to which Yahweh's people ascend to give thanks to his name. Jerusalem matters because it is the place Yahweh ordained for worship, the place anticipated by Deuteronomy 16:1–17, where Israel would joyfully celebrate its festivals. Reference to the 'testimony' (*'ēdût*) should probably be understood in the light of its twenty-three occurrences in Psalm 119, where it is one of the main synonyms for Yahweh's teaching. Jerusalem matters because it is the site of the temple, the place where Israel is directed to go to give thanks to Yahweh. As often in Psalms, Yahweh's name here points to his character, as one who is praiseworthy. But Jerusalem is also important as the home of the Davidic kings, the place where they were to execute justice. The 'thrones' here stand for the kings as the place from which they reign. Mention of David's house alludes to 2 Samuel 7 and the promise to David given in Jerusalem, which thus places this psalm's interests within the Davidic covenant. However, 2 Samuel 7 also stresses that David was not the one who would build Yahweh's house, language repeated here. Since 2 Samuel 7 stresses that the Davidic kings would reign under Yahweh's authority, a similar point is probably made here. Jerusalem is important as the place where the Davidic kings reigned (itself perhaps a historical memory when this psalm was included in the Ascents), but their importance is found in how they represented Yahweh and his justice (cf. Deut. 16:18 – 17:20; Ps. 72:1–14). Jerusalem matters, then, because it is central to Yahweh's worship, and even his most important servants there are important only when they see their role as the administration of justice.

6–9. The final stanza looks forward, contemplating Jerusalem's future. It is composed with particular care, with numerous plays on words, especially deploying the letters *š*, *l*, *m*, which form the root of *šālôm*, present in the name 'Jerusalem'. This section suggests that Jerusalem was a place of conflict, which is why the community are directed to pray (more lit., 'ask', *š'l*) for the city's well-being (*šālôm*). Jerusalem has often been a site of conflict, so we cannot restrict this prayer to any one time beyond noting that this community knew that the place of thanksgiving, the place of justice, was a place of conflict, so prayer was needed. Yahweh had chosen this city; hence, it was appropriate to ask for its peace. But the city is more than its buildings – it is also its residents. Hence, the prayer also wants those who love Jerusalem (the 'you' is feminine, referring to the city) to be at 'ease' (*šlh*). The well-being needed is for both the city and its inhabitants. The prayer for well-being is continued in verse 7 which extends this to the city ramparts, its defensive boundaries, while those resident in the fortifications will also find security. Verses 8–9 then extend this beyond the city itself. The speaker reports a wish of peace for the city but notes that this is for the sake of both kin and friends, the implication being that well-being for Jerusalem provides benefits for others. That well-being needs to begin with the house of Yahweh – only if there is a centre for worship does anything else matter. Hence, as well as praying for well-being, the speaker personally commits to seek the city's good. The one who prays for the city and its well-being is also one who works for it.

Explanation

Given the conflict that continues to mark Jerusalem, there is good reason for believers to pray for the peace of that city. But as we reflect on this psalm, we may see that the prayer's challenge is somewhat wider than just one city, however important it remains. We do not face the challenges in getting to worship that the psalmist faced, but there are many believers for whom this is an ongoing reality, believers for whom the very act of gathering is a risk. Prayer for the peace and freedom of Jerusalem now transcends any one place as it also looks to the new Jerusalem (Rev. 21:9–27), the place and time when all believers will be in the presence of the Lamb. Those who are free to gather for worship are called to pray for those who lack that freedom, to pray for those who need opportunity. We are changed by worship, by the experience of being gathered to do so, and so we pray for those who need this freedom.

PSALM 123

Translation

A Song of the Ascents

1To you I lift my eyes,
  the one enthroned in the heavens.
2Behold, as the eyes of slaves are to the hand of their masters,
  as the eyes of a maidservant are to the hand of her mistress,
thus are our eyes to Yahweh our God,
  until he is gracious to us.

[3]Be gracious to us, O Yahweh, be gracious to us,
for we have been fully sated with contempt.
[4]Our whole being has been fully sated with the derision of those who are at ease,
the contempt of the arrogant.

Notes on the text

Title: 11QPs[a] seems to include a Davidic note here.
1. For the ending of the ptcs., see J-M §93n.
4. Retaining K.

Form and structure

Where Psalm 122:6–9 hinted at the conflict faced by the worshipping community through its request for prayer for Jerusalem's well-being and flourishing, Psalm 123 is more explicitly a complaint psalm that emerges from affliction, and hence the first prayer in this collection (Mays 1994b: 394). The psalm need not have been composed as an example of the requested prayer, but the placement of this brief poem immediately after Psalm 122 allows readers to experience it as an example of what such a prayer may be like. Moreover, Psalm 122:9 closed by noting that Yahweh was 'our God' and this theme is also central here (v. 2; cf. Vesco 2006, 2: 1185). This also points to a clear contrast between these two psalms, in that Psalm 122 retains its focus on joy at the possibility of being at the temple, whereas this psalm's focus is on the contempt experienced by the community, contempt that Yahweh needs to resolve as their master. That Yahweh should act for his people also emerges from the connection to Psalm 121:1. There, the psalmist's eyes were lifted to the mountains, a place where Yahweh's help was needed because of possible threats. Here, the psalmist's eyes are lifted to Yahweh, looking to him as the one who reigns in the heavens and who therefore needs to act for his people. The reassurances offered in Psalm 121 are claimed here in the appeal for grace.

Structurally, the psalm can be analysed in two stanzas:

1. Approach to Yahweh (1–2)
2. Appeal to Yahweh (3–4)

Comment

Title: See on Psalm 120.

1–2. The opening evokes Psalm 121:1 in the lifting of the eyes, though here it is initially to an unnamed 'you' who is finally revealed to be

Yahweh. This in turn closely matches Psalm 120:1, except there Yahweh was specified as the one addressed. Although this identification is entirely expected, within the poem it is deferred until a clearer explanation of the relationship between Yahweh and the poet is explored (cf. Botha 2001: 191). Lifting the eyes here is a hopeful, trustful moment, though it is also perhaps an act of boldness, with the individual here standing for the community. Rather than naming Yahweh, we are instead told that he is the one enthroned in the heavens (cf. Ps. 2:4). This statement could represent a mild polemic against communities around Israel who might have made such a claim for at least one of their deities, but within the psalm the more important point is that it establishes the important difference between the psalmist as a supplicant and Yahweh as the king who is approached, the one to whom it is right to lift one's eyes because of his exaltation. The difference in status between the psalmist and Yahweh is explored through an extended simile. Just as male and female slaves look to their master or mistress because they are wholly dependent upon them, so also the community attends to Yahweh. Although the act of looking is clearly intended, it is not mentioned. As if the eyes of the slave and the maidservant are fixed on their master or mistress, so also the community's eyes are fixed on Yahweh. They are wholly dependent on him, and their eyes are fixed on him, looking for grace (cf. Exod. 34:6–7; Num. 6:25). The community cannot compel Yahweh to act; but, unlike slaves, they can look to him for grace since the one enthroned in heaven is 'our God'.

3–4. Where Yahweh's name was withheld in the first stanza, the move into the second gives the name new prominence. There is a close link between the end of verse 2 and the start of verse 3, with both naming Yahweh and introducing the key term 'grace'. But now the community moves from watching for grace to asking for it, its urgency evident from its repetition in verse 3a. Grace is needed, and Yahweh must give it because no other can. The reason for this is introduced only in verse 3b, though it is then extended in verse 4a. The community is said to be sated with contempt. In terms of a meal, being sated is a good thing (e.g. Ps. 78:29). But here it is like being force-fed an abundance of contempt, leaving the community unable to take any more. Along with this, they have also been force-fed with derision by those who are at ease (presumably the economically advantaged; cf. Isa. 32:9; Amos 6:1), people also described as the arrogant who express contempt. No reason for this attitude among the oppressors is given. But the community knows that its hope is found only in Yahweh's grace.

Explanation

The motif of trust so central to the Songs of the Ascents is here joined with an appeal to Yahweh to act, one that recognizes that for him to do so is an act of grace. Unlike most complaint psalms, this one includes no hopeful word in anticipation of the requested deliverance. As readers, we are placed in the same position as all who pray but do not know how their cry for help will be received. Within the psalm, Tucker has pointed to two key metaphors: Yahweh as the one enthroned in the heavens, and as head of the household of which we are a part (Tucker and Grant 2018: 756). These metaphors interact to show both Yahweh's authority to respond and the intimacy with which he engages with his people. The interaction of these metaphors means that God has all necessary power but is not remote. On the other hand, as a master he is defined by grace. A slave might look to the master's hand with fear that it might lead to a beating. But here, believers pray knowing that the power in God's hand is grace. The language of the household becomes a standard element in the presentation of the church (e.g. Gal. 4:1–7; 6:10), reminding us that we are now more than slaves and God's children in Christ. We cry out in times of need as members of God's household, knowing we come to the one who truly reigns even if we do not yet know how God's grace will be worked out.

PSALM 124

Translation

A Song of the Ascents. Davidic.

1If Yahweh had not been for us,
  let Israel say,
2If Yahweh had not been for us,
  when people rose against us,
3then they would have swallowed us alive,
  when their anger was kindled against us,
4then the waters would have engulfed us,
  the wadi would have gone over us,
5then would have gone over us,
  the rising waters.

6Blessed be Yahweh,
  who has not made us a prey for their teeth.
7We have escaped like a bird,
  from the snare of the fowlers,
the snare is broken,
  and we have escaped.
8Our help is in the name of Yahweh,
  maker of heaven and earth.

Notes on the text

5. *zêdôn* is a hapax that may be related to a word meaning 'presumptuous'. 'Rising' here suggests the waters have gone above their real station, indicating a degree of anthropomorphizing.

Form and structure

Psalm 123 ended with an unresolved appeal, unlike many complaint psalms that include a closing element of hope, though this is less common with communal complaints. Its juxtaposition with Psalm 124 allows this psalm to be read as an example of the hope that could be held as it looks back on a time when Yahweh acted for his people at a point where it might otherwise have seemed hope had failed (cf. Vesco 2006, 2: 1189). This is particularly so when we note that the first stanza provides a counterfactual reflection on the past, dealing with the outcome the community would have faced had Yahweh not been for them. This stanza emphasizes the level of the community's distress, a level that could be said to exceed the distress of the previous psalm as the community was trapped in a situation from which they had no escape. But although the distress was real, Yahweh had been for the people. The community had discovered the reality an individual had affirmed in Psalm 121:1, that Yahweh was their help. The details of how Yahweh had helped, or even the time when he had, are not mentioned, allowing the psalm to be applied to various points of deliverance, though perhaps the deliverance of Jerusalem from Sennacherib (2 Kgs 18:13 – 19:37; Isa. 36 – 38) could have served as an example. But the lack of specificity here is an important technique that allows the psalm to be applicable in a range of circumstances in which the community needs to give thanks (perhaps recycling elements of the individual thanksgiving; so, Goldingay 2008: 477) to Yahweh.

The psalm can be analysed in two stanzas:

1. If Yahweh had not been for us (1–5)
2. Our help is in the name of Yahweh (6–9)

Comment

Title: For 'Song of the Ascents', see on Psalm 120. For 'Davidic', see on Psalm 3. Taking 'Davidic' as an ascription of authorship, Collins (2022: 616) tentatively suggests 2 Samuel 5:17–25 as a possible background.

1–5. The first stanza is controlled by the opening declaration of verse 1a, which raises the possibility of what would have occurred had

Yahweh not been with the community (cf. Ps. 94:17), a statement so important that the nation is invited to join the individual who initially speaks and also make this statement. The formula 'let Israel say' recurs in Psalm 129:1, a poem with other links to this one. This structure places particular emphasis on the fact that what follows is counterfactual (cf. Allen 2002: 222, who points to 1 Cor. 15:13–19, where Paul employs a similar mode of argument). The 'let Israel say' formula also allows for a delay of the introduction of the threat that had been faced, with this introduced only in verse 2b. The distress had been caused by the rising of an unnamed people against the community. Use of *'ādām* allows for the adversary to be presented generically, an unnamed people or even humankind, though implicit in that is the idea that no human can overcome Yahweh (cf. Kraus 1989: 441). Rising against the community represented an attack on them, one that apparently represented an overwhelming force they could not have resisted. As such, verses 3–5 introduce a series of 'then' (*'ăzî*) statements, each of which explores the implication of the community having to manage without Yahweh's help. The force of the opponents is such that the community would have had no defence, swallowed alive like small prey caught by wild beasts, an image elsewhere applied to Sheol (Prov. 1:12) or the earth itself in the rebellion of Dathan and Abiram (Num. 16:30–34; Ps. 106:17), while Israel's neighbours applied this image to chaos monsters (see G. T. M. Prinsloo 2003a: 803–807). This first metaphor anticipates its return in verse 6, where the alternative is reported. No reason is given for the enemy's anger against the community, but it was enough to place them under serious threat. A second metaphor is introduced in verses 4–5, where the effect of the opponents is likened to a sudden and overwhelming flood. Rain in the wet season can run quickly down the steep hills of the central highlands, rapidly turning dried-up wadis to raging torrents, impossible for anyone caught there to resist. The wadi's waters could be understood as swamping the whole person; but, since *nepeš* can also mean 'throat' or 'neck' (e.g. Ps. 105:19), we could also imagine the waters reaching the neck (cf. Ps. 69:1). The threat faced was complete, describing powerful waters from which escape was impossible and death the expected outcome.

6–8. But the counterfactual was not true. The opponents had risen against the community, but Yahweh had been for them. Hence, the second stanza opens by 'blessing' (*barûk*) Yahweh (on the nature of this act, see on Ps. 103:1). The community offers its words and indeed itself to Yahweh because he has not allowed them to become prey to the teeth of the opponents, resuming the initial metaphor from verse 3. Yahweh has prevented the opponents from using their overwhelming power. The community would have been overwhelmed had Yahweh given them over to the opponent. But Yahweh had been for them and so this had not happened. This does not mean the distress was not acute – to be like a bird caught in a trap is to face a situation where it seems death was the only possible outcome. The image of a bird in a snare seems to have been a standard one (Crow 1996: 53), most famously used by Sennacherib for Hezekiah in his annals when describing his siege of Jerusalem (see Arnold and Beyer 2002: 146–147). Such birds do not routinely escape, but the community did. Indeed, the snare that held them is broken, incapable of again causing distress. This is Yahweh's doing (though no details are provided), and so the community realizes the affirmation of Psalm 121:1 is also true for them. Yahweh, the one they have blessed, is their help, the one who overcomes what seems like insurmountable opposition. This is possible because he is maker of heaven and earth, meaning that all creation remains at his disposal. It is not Yahweh's initial creation that matters here, but rather that he continues to engage with it, and so the community continues to have hope.

Explanation

This psalm does not promise that Yahweh will always act for a people, though it does assume that the community were loyal to Yahweh. But it does affirm that the community's hope in the face of threat is always found in Yahweh's presence and positive commitment for them. Paul poses the question 'If God is for us, who can be against us?' (Rom. 8:31, ESV). His answer, of course, is that none can separate us from God's love. We may be tempted to think this means we will be kept as the people of God from all struggle and pain, but this is not something Scripture ever affirms. However, it does mean God is for his people, and we can go forward confidently, knowing that no matter how hard the circumstances, God is with us. He is our help in Jesus Christ. We need this testimony here, and perhaps can use it to shape our own. It does not promise we cannot go through difficulty or experiences we would not choose, but it reminds us that God is always our help.

PSALM 125

Translation

A Song of the Ascents

1Those who trust in Yahweh,
  are like Mount Zion, which is not shaken:
  it abides for ever.
2Jerusalem, the mountains surround her,

and Yahweh surrounds his people,
from now and for evermore.

[3]Indeed the sceptre of wickedness will not rest,
upon the allotment of the righteous,
so that the righteous do not put forth
their hands in deceit.

[4]Do good, O Yahweh, to the good,
to those who are upright in their hearts.
[5]But those turning aside to their crooked ways,
Yahweh will lead away with those perpetrating injustice –
peace be upon Israel!

Notes on the text

1. Gk (and some MSS) limits the association to Jerusalemites. But, as Jerusalem is not introduced directly until verse 2, it is better to retain MT. The colometry is difficult, and most EVV ignore *atnach*, but the above (following Stocks 2012: 109–110 in seeing this as a para-tricolon) shows that the Masoretic accentuation can be followed.

3. Crow (1996: 55) treats the initial verb as a volitive, but this is counter to the motif of trust. He seems to read *kî* as an asseverative, but here it indicates the certainty of what follows (*WHS* §449).

Form and structure

The motif of trust that developed through the previous songs in this collection comes to immediate focus here. Where those psalms gradually developed a posture of trust, this poem uses wisdom forms to explore the impacts of that trust. This wisdom focus is matched with attention to Mount Zion, anticipating its mention in Psalm 126:1 and linking these psalms. Although Jerusalem was mentioned in Psalm 122 (cf. Ps. 128:5), Zion has hitherto remained unmentioned in this collection. Yet, from here it is noted six times in the Ascents (Pss 126:1; 128:5; 129:5; 132:13; 133:3; 134:3), making Zion a central motif. Zion is associated in Psalms with Yahweh's presence (e.g. Pss 48, 87), reinforcing the point here that those who trust in Yahweh can be likened to Zion, while also preparing for the development of the Zion motif in the rest of the Ascents. In addition, the element of thanksgiving for deliverance in Psalm 124 has provided further reason for continuing to trust. Nevertheless, although trust is emphasized, the psalm also recognizes a present threat to the community. This becomes evident in the closing verses as they appeal to Yahweh to act for the well-being of the good. The implication is that although trust is appropriate, it is trust that looks for continued evidence of the benefits of trust in Yahweh to be seen in the community. As with Psalm 121, the psalm encourages trust but does so while remaining aware of threats to the community.

The themes of trust and appeal provide the psalm's main divisions, which can be analysed in two stanzas, with the first addressed to a congregation and the second primarily to Yahweh:

1. Reasons for trust (1–3)
   a. Security described (1–2)
   b. Security's goal (3)
2. Appeal (4–5)

Comment

Title: For 'Song of the Ascents', see on Psalm 120.

1–2. The psalm opens with an immediate emphasis on trusting Yahweh, focused on the benefits that flow for those who do so. Although the colometry of verse 1 is difficult (cf. 'Notes on the text'), the point seems to be that they can be likened to Mount Zion as a place which is not shaken and so endures. The experience of those trusting Yahweh is the same, and they will not be shaken either. The language here is similar to that of Psalm 15:5 (cf. Ps. 121:3), suggesting that those who express such trust also express it in their relationship with others, while also echoing the statement about God's city in Psalm 46:5. This observation about those who trust Yahweh draws on wisdom language (cf. Prov. 29:25), drawing on a wide range of texts. The allusion to Psalm 46 and God's city prepares for the move to a statement about Jerusalem in verse 2. The statement here draws on the city's geography in the highlands, which means that it is surrounded by other mountains, all of which are a little higher. The poet casts this observation in a way that enables those who know the city to pause and consider this fact before deriving an analogy from it – just as the mountains surround Jerusalem, so also Yahweh surrounds his people.

3. Being surrounded can be threatening (Ps. 3:6). But being surrounded by Yahweh points to his protection of his people, a point already demonstrated in Psalm 124. Where protection in Psalm 124 referred to military deliverance, here it functions to guide the ethical choices of the righteous. The sceptre (a sign of rule; cf. Gen. 49:10; Pss 2:9; 45:7) of wickedness refers to rule that promoted choices contrary to Yahweh's will, whether understood as foreign powers or Israelite kings. The inability of this sceptre to rest (i.e. remain indefinitely) in the allotment of the righteous could refer to the land given to Israel, drawing on the use of 'lot' (*goral*) to refer both to that which was cast for the allotment of land and the allotment itself (e.g. Josh. 15:1; 17:1). However, this allotment can be understood more generally (e.g. Ps. 16:5). Just as Yahweh watches over the way of the righteous while the way of the wicked perishes (Ps. 1:5–6), so also the righteous are here assured Yahweh's protection means their life experience is one that benefits them by preventing the rule of wickedness. The goal of this is introduced in verse 3b – so the righteous do not engage in deceit. The psalm recognizes that the righteous may be tempted to engage in deceitful practices, but doing so means engaging in wickedness. Knowledge of Yahweh's protection provides a reason to engage in the sort of ethically constructive life imagined in Psalms 15 and 24. Trust thus shapes the life of the righteous such that they understand the importance of continuing to live righteously. There may be pressure to choose an alternative path, but the righteous know this is not the way Yahweh will finally allow them to triumph.

4–5. Knowing that Yahweh protects means the righteous have the possibility of living for him, but it does not necessarily mean they will. Hence, the second stanza moves into an appeal for Yahweh to demonstrate the reality of this protection. The categories of the righteous and the wicked continue here, starting with the righteous. Yahweh is asked to do good for them. Unlike Psalm 1, which speaks of the righteous as an individual in contrast to a group, here the good are also viewed as a group. Although some EVV (e.g. ESV) could be read as treating the good and the upright of heart as two groups, it is probably better to understand verse 4b as providing a further definition of the good. The important point is that the good should receive evidence of Yahweh's goodness to them, providing further reason for them to continue in this path. Yahweh is asked to act for the good, but the assumption is that he will lead the wicked away. The image of life as a path recurs here in the description of their turning aside to their own crooked ways, again echoing Psalm 1. Yahweh is not asked to act against these people, because the psalm assumes this is an assured outcome. It is the good, however, who need more evidence of Yahweh's goodness, especially in a world full of conflict. Hence, the psalm closes with a blessing, looking for Yahweh to grant peace upon Israel, peace that will be the clearest example of his granting good to the good.

Explanation

As Bechtel Reynolds (1994) has pointed out, Psalm 125 wrestles with the issue of trusting God in a world filled with injustice. That is, it offers a fresh perspective on the issue of theodicy. It is far from the only psalm to do this (cf. Pss 37, 49, 73), but where other poems tend to offer advice to their audience (e.g. Ps. 37:3–4), this psalm takes a different approach. It does address its human audience in the first stanza, pointing to the security God provides for them, security that can be likened to a mountain or the protection given to Jerusalem. This security is given to those who trust Yahweh, but it is made clear that this is for a particular reason. The prevalence of wickedness may lead the faithful to choices that align more with wickedness than righteousness (cf. Matt. 24:12). Reminding the community of its security in God helps them understand the ethical choices they need to make. The psalm also moves to prayer, one deeply grounded in Psalm 1, because the security God gives needs to be experienced and not simply declared. Paul takes these themes and grounds them in Christ as he references the psalm's closing line (Gal. 6:16), highlighting the important fact that Christian discipleship continues to wrestle with these issues, even as it sees our security in the cross of Christ.

PSALM 126

Translation

A Song of the Ascents.

1When Yahweh restored the captivity of Zion,
we were like dreamers.
2Then our mouth was filled with laughter,
and our tongue with shouts:
then they said among the nations,
'Yahweh has done great things for them.'
3Yahweh has done great things for us,
we were glad.
4Restore our fortunes, O Yahweh,
like channels in the Negeb.
5Those scattering seed with tears,
shall reap with shouts.
6The one who goes forth weeping,
bearing a bag of seed,
shall come in with shouts,
bearing sheaves.

Notes on the text

1. Since the opening infin. is tenseless, we could understand the whole of verses 1–3 as having a future orientation (cf. NJPS), especially because of the imp. verbs in verse 2. But the pf. verbs in verse 1, 3 suggest that the

imps. of verse 2 describe events within a past-time reference (similarly, G. T. M. Prinsloo 1992: 233; Crow 1996: 60), meaning it must be referring to a prior event. The sense of the idiom *šûb . . . šîbat* is much debated. Drawing on Gk and a handful of MSS, the word *šîbat* has often been understood as an error for *šĕbût* (cf. *BHS*, Pss 14:7; 85:7). Although the derivation is uncertain, MT can be retained. Dahood (1970: 218) points to an Aram. parallel from the eighth century BC, which indicates the idiom was known then. Here, it seems best to derive the noun from *šbh*, 'captivity', while recognizing a play on the similar 'restoration', such that the idiom's meaning transcends its etymology (cf. Bracke 1985; A. P. Ross 2016: 661–662). 'Like dreamers' is also widely emended (cf. NIV mg.), following Gk, which could perhaps have understood the root as the possible *ḥlm* II, 'be healthy', rather than *ḥlm* I, 'dream'. But despite A. P. Ross's (2016: 661–662) argument to the contrary (and the possible support of 4QPs[a], which could be read as the required pass., though 4QPs[a] cannot), van Gemeren (2008: 909) is probably right to say that the evidence for the alternative is weak.

4. Retaining K here allows for a slight shift from verse 1. Admittedly, Q, which aligns this verse with verse 1, has significant textual support in the MS tradition, but as it is easier to imagine scribes aligning the idiom, K is retained as the more difficult reading.

Form and structure

The combination of trust and appeal that marked Psalm 125 finds particular focus in this psalm. Psalm 125:3 expressed confidence that the sceptre of wickedness would not rest upon the land before asking that Yahweh do good for the upright, closing with a wish for 'well-being' (*šālôm*) to be upon the nation. Reasons for that prayer and wish become clear in this communal lament, albeit one that retains considerable hope. Here, the community reflects on a previous experience of restoration by Yahweh before asking for fresh restoration. The focus is especially on Zion (v. 1), and so develops the trust motif from Psalm 125:1. If those who trust are to be like Zion, then Zion also needs to flourish. Although the psalm works well as an independent composition, its placement within the Songs of the Ascents particularly accents the importance of Zion's flourishing.

Taking the shift in time between verses 1, 4 as pivotal (cf. 'Notes on the text'), the psalm can be analysed in two stanzas, an analysis that highlights the close links between memory and the prayer, a pattern not dissimilar to Psalm 85:

1. Memory of restoration (1–3)
2. Prayer for restoration (4–6)

Comment

Title: For 'Song of the Ascents', see on Psalm 120.

1–3. The psalm opens with a reflection on a past event (cf. 'Notes on the text'), most likely referring initially to the end of the exile, though the reference is sufficiently open ended that it can also point to any moment of restoration (similarly, Longman 2014: 423). If we are correct in understanding this as restoration from some form of captivity, then the exile provides the main paradigm against which to understand the restoration. However, because the idiom is relatively widespread, and its meaning transcends its etymology, we cannot be specific as to the event that lies in the background here. What is clear, is that it represents a point from which the community could not have restored itself and as such represents an extension of the deliverance in Psalm 124:7. In that instance, captivity was avoided because of Yahweh's help, whereas this time captivity did occur but has now been reversed because of Yahweh's action. The Songs of the Ascents are open to Yahweh's saving help being experienced in a range of ways. The focus here is not on how Yahweh restored the community but rather its effect on them, a theme developed through verses 1b–2. Here, the community compares itself to dreamers. Unlike English usage, where 'dreams' may reflect personal hopes (even Isa. 29:7–8, which moves in this direction, still assumes an actual dream), the OT does not have this sense. Instead, it regards many dreams as something given by God (e.g. Gen. 28:12), though they may also be claimed by a false prophet (e.g. Deut. 13:6), and some dreams could be considered insubstantial (cf. Ps. 73:20). The sense here seems to be that the community understood itself as having had an experience similar to that of a true prophet who had foreseen that Yahweh would restore them (cf. Joel. 2:28–32). They had experienced something that could only have been conceived through Yahweh's intervention. As a result, their mouths were filled with laughter and tongues with shouts of excitement. Here, the mouth stands for the whole person, the mouth being the body part where such excitement is expressed. Along with the community, people scattered through the nations also use speech to express their response by noting that Yahweh has done great things for them, overcoming whatever forces previously prevented them from flourishing. The community's laughter and shouts (cf. Isa. 51:11) become articulate in verse 3. It aligns itself to what was said among the nations as it realizes Yahweh has indeed done great things for them, which brought joy.

4–6. Whatever happened in the past, the community now faces new challenges. Given the agricultural imagery here, it is most likely that they face significant shortages of food, perhaps famine (cf. Hag. 1:7–11). The prior restoration was a source of joy, but the community cannot survive on memories alone. Those memories, however, do shape their prayer for restoration. The need is urgent, as is clear from the opening reference to the channels in the Negeb, watercourses that would usually be dry, but would fill very quickly when the rains came. Similar speed is needed here. But the community is also confident that just as Yahweh restored them before, so he will restore them again. However, although Yahweh's involvement needed to be rapid, it would not relieve the community from the slow and hard work of preparing for a harvest (cf. Kidner 1975, 1: 475). Rather than those sowing seed going forth with tears, always a risk since no one knew if the crop would grow, they shall now come in with shouts, making them like those who returned in verse 2. The joy experienced in the previous restoration can now be experienced in a new setting as a significant harvest becomes possible, with the reapers shouting out in joy as they reap and then bring in the sheaves. Memory of the past provides a basis for appeal to Yahweh and shape for the hope expressed – that the one who restored the community from captivity will also provide the needed harvest.

Explanation

Psalm 126 can be summarized as joy remembered and joy anticipated (Mays 1994b: 399). The community remembers what Yahweh has done in an earlier restoration, and that memory provides hope that a future restoration can be experienced. Both memory and anticipation are filled with joy, even though the need for restoration means it is also a time of sorrow. This combination probably lies behind the beatitude of Luke 6:21, which seems to allude to this psalm. There, Jesus recognizes that the disciples may experience hunger and tears but looks beyond to a moment of future joy. Within the psalm's own horizon, it is also clear that the community is nourished by the memory of past restoration, but not held prisoner by it. Rather, knowing that God has acted to restore in the past provides hope that he shall do so again. Memory provides hope and so anticipates joy.

PSALM 127

Translation

A song of the Ascents. Solomonic.

[1]Unless Yahweh builds the house,
  in vain have its builders toiled on it;
unless Yahweh guards the city,
  in vain has the guard kept watch.
[2]In vain do you rise early,

refraining from lying down,
eating the bread of anxious toil;
indeed, he gives sleep to his beloved.

3 See, children are a heritage from Yahweh,
the fruit of the womb a reward.
4 Like arrows in in a warrior's hand,
so are the children of youth!
5 O the blessedness of the one
who fills his quiver with them!
They shall not be put to shame,
when they contend with enemies in the gate.

Notes on the text

2. The meaning of *kēn* is uncertain. It most frequently means 'thus', but there is limited evidence that it could mean 'indeed' or 'surely' (HALOT, *kēn* I), and it is possible that the two MSS that read *kî* instead (cf. NIV, NRSV) have understood it this way. The final ʾ on the end of *šēnāʾ* is unusual – we would normally expect *h*. But this could arise from Aram. influence on the spelling (GKC §80c), as well as a desire to represent this in an orthographically similar way to *šāwĕʾ* (similarly, Seybold 1996: 488), consistent with other wordplays in the poem (cf. Miller 1986: 131–132). For an alternative sense, see Emerton 1974a. The term is here understood as the object of the verb, but an adverbial accusative suggesting that God gives to his beloved while sleeping is possible (cf. NRSV mg.)

5. Dahood (1970: 325; cf. Crow 1996: 67) argues that *dbr* here means 'drive back' rather than 'speak'. Although accepted by HALOT (*DCH* is tentative), the sense of defence that he believes is needed is still evident in the more traditional rendering, though 'contend' (NJPS) captures both elements. The verb is pl. because the blessed one is representative.

Form and structure

Following the emphasis on Zion and trust in Psalms 125–126, the collection pauses for the first of a pair of psalms strongly infused with wisdom motifs (cf. Human 2010a: 523–524), a theme accented by the Solomonic title here. Most notably, Psalms 127 and 128 are joined by their shared beatitudes (Pss 127:5; 128:1–2) which form a primary link, one developed by reflections on the blessings of children (Pss 127:3–5; 128:3, 6) and the nature of work (Pss 127:2; 128:2). There is not an absolute break with Psalms 125–126 since the word 'house' here is multivalent, and (as in 2 Sam. 7:3–16) can be understood both as an individual's home and family or refer to the temple (cf. Vesco 2006, 2: 1205), a building closely associated with Zion. The main links look forward to Psalm 128, meaning we are to read these two poems (to some extent) as twin psalms. It also points to a developing wisdom motif in this collection, as Psalm 133 can be considered as a wisdom composition. As is often the case with psalms with wisdom influence, these psalms are addressed to a human audience rather than God, providing direct instruction that arises from experience to that audience (cf. Stocks 2016: 196).

The poem can be analysed in two stanzas, with the first marked by instruction concerned with vanity and the second offering a positive portrayal of children, though both are concerned with family and security (cf. Schaefer 2001: 307):

1. Unless Yahweh . . . (1–2)
2. A heritage from Yahweh (3–5)

Comment

Title: For 'Song of the Ascents', see on Psalm 120. For 'Solomonic', see on Psalm 72. Here, the numerous allusions to Solomon and the wisdom literature strongly suggest we read the psalm in the light of him rather than this being a claim of authorship. German (2012) extends this to the wider Davidic dynasty.

1–2. The psalm opens with a core affirmation about the house that would be at home in Proverbs (cf. Berlin 2023: 34), such as its observations about a man's wife being a gift from Yahweh (Prov. 18:22; 19:14). Such a marriage can flourish because it has come about through Yahweh's involvement. Here, 'house' can refer to the wider family (cf. Deut. 25:4; Josh. 2:12; Ruth 4:12; 1 Sam. 1:21) and the building where they dwelt (cf. 1 Sam. 25:1; 1 Kgs 1:34). Both can be built. Building a dwelling or some other construction would have been fairly routine (e.g. Gen. 4:17; 1 Chr. 22:19; 2 Chr. 17:12; Hos. 8:14), but the idea of building a family or people through children is also evidenced (Ruth 4:11; Ps. 28:5). Yet whatever mode of building is followed, it would flourish only through Yahweh's presence; hence, the people's prayer in Ruth 4:11–12. The theology underlying that prayer finds expression here in this declaration, insisting that toil on building a house cannot flourish unless Yahweh is simultaneously involved. There is no denial of the value of human work; indeed, it is assumed. But human work achieves the house's desired flourishing only when Yahweh also builds. The pattern for the house is repeated in the image of the city watch. Again, this language would be at home in Proverbs (e.g. Prov. 2:8; 3:26), which sees Yahweh as the source of security for his people (Prov. 18:10). As with building, the observation does not discount the role of the guards on the watch, but stresses they succeed only when Yahweh works with them. Mention of the city could allude in this context to Jerusalem, and as such the 'house' could also be the temple; though, given the primacy of familial language through the psalm, this would be only a secondary meaning. More immediately, the city would represent the larger area where a family dwelt, reminding them that their flourishing and security depended on Yahweh. There is a shift in verse 2 that brings the language of what is 'vain' (*šāwĕ'*) to the beginning of the verse, as the audience is addressed directly. Where verse 1 looked at more specific elements of work (even if building refers to more than work), this verse is more concerned with a general description of an agricultural worker's life. Although Yahweh is unnamed in this verse, repetition of 'in vain' makes clear that his involvement is understood to continue. Mention of rising early and staying up late would describe the experience of many agricultural workers, and the language here is probably intended to refer to the totality of their experience. Their labour does involve anxious toil (cf. Gen. 3:17–19), as seen in the tears of those sowing grain (Ps. 126:6). But as with both the builders and the guards, the life of agricultural workers flourishes only if Yahweh is with them. Such will still work hard, but already receive a sign of Yahweh's presence in the gift of sleep. Sleep is a sign that these people are beloved (cf. 1 Sam. 12:24–25), perhaps because they rest rather than fretting continually over their toil (cf. Eccl. 5:12)

3–5. The second stanza extends the first by reflecting on at least one way Yahweh might build a house, the opening 'See' inviting the audience to reflect on what is about to be said. Language of a 'heritage' elsewhere refers to the land allotted to Israel's clans (e.g. Num. 36:7; Deut. 19:14; Josh. 11:23; 24:30; though it can also refer to other nations), but here finds a particular focus in children. This image may draw on the portrayal of Israel as Yahweh's heritage (e.g. Deut. 4:20; Isa. 65:17), the continued existence of the nation functioning as his inheritance. Children would inherit the territory possessed by a family, and thus become the family's heritage. But, as part of Israel, can also be part of Yahweh's heritage, and Yahweh is the one who enables the family to flourish. Yahweh's work enables the mother to conceive, the idea of this being a 'reward' (*śākār*); perhaps alluding to Issachar (Gen. 30:14–18), whose name plays on this word and whose birth is enabled by God (though, cf. Gen. 15:1). The importance of children is developed in verse 4, which compares the children of one's youth with arrows in a quiver. Having children young meant the family would enjoy their benefit and blessing longer, something of great importance when people were older and unable to contribute to physical work themselves, and were thus dependent on children. This may explain the comparison to arrows. Just as arrows provide protection against threats in battle, so children provide protection against the threats of old age as they honour their parents

(Exod. 20:12) and continue to honour them in the long term (cf. Estes 1991). These threats could be experienced through inability to work but might also be experienced in the threat of legal action (carried out in the city gate; Ruth 4:1–6; Amos 5:15). The one who filled their quiver with such arrows could be confident that others would not take advantage of them, meaning that children both continued to provide for parents when they became economically inactive and protected them from threats. Such people were blessed.

Explanation

With Psalm 127 we reach the central poem in the Ascents. If pilgrimage to Jerusalem lies in the background to the whole collection, then that may provide a clue to the meaning of the 'house' and 'city' mentioned, though in so doing the poem's focus on the routine elements of Israel's life should not be missed. In essence, the psalm reflects on the question of how Yahweh's blessing is expressed. Perhaps surprisingly, it does not look to the temple. Instead, it grounds blessedness in a notably ordinary life. Blessing is found in family and work. Blessing is also found in a world where there is constant threat from enemies, not to mention the struggles of most who lived as subsistence farmers. The psalm commends a commitment to regular life, farming and having children, but also makes clear that the community does not flourish simply by these practices. Rather, they flourish because Yahweh is active with them (cf. Futato 2009: 387). Those who come to the temple to worship can be reminded that the temple is not the only place where God is encountered. Rather, he is encountered in the routines of life, providing security through the regular practices of life, and blessing is found in embracing his involvement in all of it (Brueggemann and Bellinger 2014: 544; cf. John 15:5).

PSALM 128

Translation

A Song of the Ascents.

1O the blessedness of all who fear Yahweh,
  whoever walks in his ways.
2The produce of your hands you shall indeed eat –
  O your blessedness, as it goes well for you.
3Your wife shall be like a fruitful vine,
  within your house,

your children shall be like olive tree shoots,
  surrounding your table.

[4]See, thus shall one indeed be blessed,
  who fears Yahweh.
[5]May Yahweh bless you from Zion,
  so you see the well-being of Jerusalem,
all the days of your life,
[6]so you see your children's children.
Peace be upon Israel!

Notes on the text

2, 4. Reading *kî* as asseverative (*WHS* §449).

3. Seybold (1996: 489) understands the verb to be juss. This is grammatically possible, but following the beatitude, it is more likely an imp. (similarly, Hossfeld and Zenger 2011: 397).

5. Taking the imperatives as resulting from the opening juss. (with Crow 1996: 74).

Form and structure

Psalm 128 is paired with Psalm 127, a second wisdom poem within the Ascents. As noted above (see 'Form and structure' on Ps. 127), the two are joined by repeating language and themes. It too can be recognized as a wisdom text through its address to a human audience rather than offering prayer or praise to God. Cheung (2015: 128–137) rightly notes that it does not push particularly far into the sort of intellectual concerns we find in poems like Psalms 37, 49, 73. However, this may mean only that it is not part of a more formal wisdom movement. Since wisdom represents a spectrum of intellectual concerns, there is no need for all exemplars to work the same way. In terms of the Ascents, we should also note that the closing wish for peace matches that of Psalm 125:5, while there is probably a close parallel between the opening reference there to those who trust Yahweh and here those who fear him.

The psalm demonstrates a shift between two kinds of blessedness, something not especially clear in more traditional English renderings. However, the first stanza builds on the beatitudes of verses 1–2 (using *'ašrê*; on the form see on Ps. 1:1), a model that presents the desirability of something in life, and thus already good. But the second moves to blessing God adds to 'experience' (*brk*), with this expressed as a wish and thus consistent with the priestly blessing (Num. 6:24–26; cf. deClaissé-Walford et al. 2014: 921), especially as it combines the wish for blessing with the wish for peace. Within this, verse 4 is a hinge in that it looks back on what can already be expected in the desired life, while introducing the new language of 'blessing' (*brk*) of the second stanza (cf. Stocks 2012: 141–142). This movement is joined by a transition between third-person language in verses 1, 4, and second-person language in verses 2–3, 5–6a, with verse 6b returning to the third person. Drawing these elements together, and acknowledging that verse 4 can be joined to either stanza, we can propose a two-part analysis:

1. Beatitudes on fearing Yahweh (1–3)
2. Priestly hopes for blessing (4–6)

Comment

Title: For 'Song of the Ascents', see on Psalm 120.

1–3. The psalm joins with Psalms 32 and 119 in opening with a pair of beatitudes, though Psalm 84:4–5 (cf. Ps. 84:12) also includes paired beatitudes within the body of the psalm and Psalm 137 concludes with a further pair. It is typical that beatitudes in the Psalter are placed in structurally important parts of the poem, with Psalms 89:15, 94:12, and perhaps 146:5, as the only exceptions. The opening beatitude highlights the blessedness of all who fear Yahweh (cf. Ps. 112:1), with this fear defined as walking in his ways. Both the beatitude and the use of the 'way' metaphor evoke Psalm 1, even if the blessed one there is defined by *not* walking in ways contrary to Yahweh. The blessed life here is one where reverence for Yahweh is demonstrated in the whole of life, and not simply in cultic activity. The blessedness of such persons is evidenced in their ability to eat the harvest of their work, though the shift to the second person means that rather than speaking in general terms, the audience is addressed directly. The juxtaposition with Psalm 127 indicates that this person's work has flourished because of Yahweh's involvement with it. The second beatitude reinforces this point by continuing to address its audience. This makes this beatitude unique within Psalms as the only one applied directly to the audience rather than being discussed in general terms. When people live such a desirable life, it shows that their labour is not in vain and Yahweh allows it to flourish; hence, the expectation is that life will go well. The definition of things going well are then outlined in verse 3. One living a blessed life can expect to have children, with both wife and children compared to bountiful plants within the household. This language echoes the presentation of the house in Psalm 127:1, linking this one to the one considered blessed there (Ps. 127:5), while also inverting the curses from Deuteronomy 28:38–40 (Berlin 2023: 41–42). These children are a gift from Yahweh, as he has built the house.

4–6. As noted, verse 4 is a hinge, a verse that simultaneously closes the first stanza and introduces the second. Its opening seems to summarize the first stanza, especially as it focuses on the one who fears Yahweh, confident that what has been described is how this person will be blessed. But it also introduces new language, with the 'blessing' (now *brk*) something additional Yahweh will do. Introduction of this verb prepares for the priestly language of verses 5–6a, which ask that Yahweh will bring further blessings from Zion, the key place for these to emerge (cf. Viviers 2019: 434–437). Such blessing points to the temple, but the important point is that such blessings are to go beyond the experience of the one mentioned in the beatitudes. Rather, the wish that Yahweh bring blessing is to enable the person to see the well-being of Jerusalem. Such blessing is not restricted to the individual but looks instead to the flourishing of the whole community. The hope is that the person might receive the additional blessings of long life and descendants, including grandchildren, but with this placed in the context of the whole community. Both the individual and the community of Jerusalem need to experience well-being (cf. v. 2), and the hope is that this can be for the longer term. Hence, the closing wish for peace for Israel is an extension of the initial wish, so the hope for both the individual and the community of Jerusalem can be extended to all Israel.

Explanation

The link with Psalm 127 is particularly important for understanding this poem. Psalm 127 starts out from the perspective of routine life without God at the centre, finding it to be vain. By contrast, Psalm 128 starts from the perspective of those who put their relationship with God at the centre. Rather than being divergent (so van Niekerk 1995), these psalms complement each other by exploring different starting points for understanding the blessed life (cf. W. S. Prinsloo 2003: 427). Here, the person centred on Yahweh lives a blessed life, one that others can see and desire. The desirability of this life mattered in the ancient world, where there was no certainty of food or children. Trusting God, fearing him in the whole of life, means we are no longer looking at the vain life of people who try to live as functional atheists. God needs to build the house, and the starting point of this is a life oriented towards him. This life has the blessedness that others desire. Care must be taken at this point because this blessedness is not achieved mechanistically, as if we do certain things and blessing automatically follows. The close connection with Psalm 125 makes this clear, and there we note a prayer for well-being for those who live as God desires (Ps. 125:4). But the psalm does encourage a life lived around faithfulness to God and sees this as central to a life of blessedness. Such blessedness for an individual is not the final goal, for the closing wish for blessing makes clear that the blessedness of one makes sense only in the context of the blessing of all. Believers form a community, one where blessing is always to be shared (cf. Acts 2:42–47; 4:32–37).

PSALM 129

Translation

A Song of the Ascents.

1 'Often have they attacked me from my youth,'
let Israel say,
2 'Often have they attacked me from my youth,
though they have not prevailed over me.
3 The ploughers have ploughed my back,
they made their furrows long.'

4 Yahweh is righteous,
he has cut off the cord of the wicked.

5 May they be put to shame and turned back,
all who hate Zion.
6 May they be like rooftop grass,
that withers before it is pulled up,
7 which does not fill the reaper's hand,
the garment fold of the gatherer,
8 so those who pass by will not say,
'The blessing of Yahweh be upon you,
we bless you in Yahweh's name.'

Notes on the text

3. 11QPs[a] and LXX have 'wicked' for 'ploughers', but this is likely because the play on the sound of the words has led to this verse being brought into agreement with the wicked in verse 4. Read 'furrows' with K and many MSS.

4. Dahood (1970: 231) treats the verb as a prec. pf., but a past-time reference fits well.

5–6. Reading the verbs here as jussives. They could also be imps. (so e.g. Allen 2002: 186; Goldingay [2008: 514–515] retains both options), making what follows a statement of confidence, but the clause-initial placement of the verbs makes a juss. more probable.

8. Plausibly, the final line could be understood as a priestly blessing offered to the worshipping community, with the negation ending at verse 8b (so, Allen 2002: 250). But it is simpler to assume the negation continues to the end of the verse.

Form and structure

Psalm 129 continues the focus on Zion and blessing from Psalm 128. Although important verbal links between the poems emphasize this development (cf. Pss 128:4–5; 129:5, 8), it should be noted that they approach these themes from very different perspectives (also, Schaefer 2001: 309). In this respect, we should also note that there was a strong shift of perspective between Psalms 127 and 128, with one reflecting on life without Yahweh at the centre and the other where Yahweh was at the centre. Here, the important shift focuses on Zion as the place of blessing. In Psalm 128, one could wish for Yahweh's blessing to come from Zion on those who fear Yahweh, whereas here the wish is that those who hate Zion should not be the recipients of Yahweh's blessing. Although there is no significant verbal link with Psalm 127, it seems likely we are to read these three psalms as providing different perspectives on the nature of Yahweh's blessing. The psalm also shows strong links with Psalms 124–126. With Psalm 124:1, it uses the form 'let Israel say' following a speech citation (cf. Ps. 118:2), which is then repeated, while both Psalms 125 and 126 also have a strong focus on Zion and what it may mean for Yahweh to do good for it.

The poem's form can be variously understood, depending on how the verbs in verses 5–6 are understood (cf. 'Notes on the text'). Taken as jussives, we can understand the poem as the community's desire that Yahweh act against those who have attacked it, expressing his righteousness by acting against those who have prevented the community from flourishing. As Yahweh is never addressed, it is not really a prayer; though Yahweh is clearly meant to hear the desire, a desire influenced by wisdom motifs. Read this way, we can analyse it in two stanzas, with direct speech forming an inclusio (Botha 2002b: 1404):

1. Communal and individual affirmations (1–4)
   a. Account of affliction (1–3)
   b. Affirmation of Yahweh's righteousness (4)
2. Imprecatory wishes (5–8)

Comment

Title: For 'Song of the Ascents', see on Psalm 120.

1–3. The psalm opens with a speaker addressing an audience with a word of testimony that reports significant attacks in the past. The speaker's identity is not made clear, though the subsequent invitation to Israel in verse 1b suggests a worship leader. The point of the report is not to separate the speaker from the community but rather to indicate that the speaker's experience is representative of that of the whole community. They have all experienced significant assaults in the past. That these are 'from my youth' suggests they happened over an extended period, probably reaching back to the exodus. Although mention of 'youth' would be more applicable to the worship leader, language that may be literal for this person also works well as a metaphor for the community. Yet the good news is also expressed in verse 2b, which is that despite the extent of the assaults, the opponents have not prevailed. Their assaults have been powerful and painful (possibly including sexual as well as military assault; so, E. T. James 2017), as is evident in the image of ploughers running their ploughs along the speaker's back, and indeed extending their furrows. But these assaults, which also point to the effect of the lash, have not prevailed. The speaker and community have continued to exist.

4. Adversaries have long afflicted both the speaker and the community, but against this stands the reality of Yahweh. Yahweh is declared to be righteous, and hence one who is committed to justice. This commitment to justice is already evident in the fact that he has cut the cord of the wicked. The exact sense of the 'cord' here is uncertain. It could refer to ropes with which something or someone was bound (e.g. Judg. 15:14; 16:12; cf. Ps. 2:3), in which case the image points to the wicked restricting people through their behaviour. By extension, it could also refer to a yoke since this was held in place by a cord, meaning it is not only restriction that is in view but rather that the wicked seek to control others – much as an ox is controlled through the yoke in ploughing (cf. Hossfeld and Zenger 2011: 413–416). But whether the point is restriction or coercion, Yahweh has cut the cord. His commitment to justice has freed the community to live for him, removing the barriers of structural violence.

5–8. Yahweh has removed the power of the wicked to act against the community, but the closing stanza goes further, expressing the wish that they should lose the capacity to do so again. These verses are presented as a wish rather than a prayer, though the hope is clearly that Yahweh should act. The fundamentals of the wish are outlined in verses 5–6, as the community wants the wicked (defined as those who hate Zion and who are thus opposed to the flourishing of Yahweh's community) to be put to shame and turned back. As such, they lose the social standing that may bring others to support them and are removed from a position where they may act against Zion. This is extended in verse 6, which desires them to be like grass that grows in the wet season on the roof of a house in patches of soil there (cf. 2 Kgs 19:26). The 'withering' (*yābēš*) creates a wordplay with 'put to shame' (*yēbōšû*), with these terms creating an inclusio for these verses. Such grass will not flourish, because it lacks depth (cf. Mark 4:16–17) and therefore withers under the sun's heat rather than reaching maturity. Such grass, even if it were a grain, would be of no value and would thus be ignored by harvesters (though in reality it would be treated as a weed to remove to avoid damage to the roof). Hence, the community hopes the wicked will flourish no more, removing the threat of structural violence. This wish is extended further in verse 8 in the hope that no passer-by will again bless them in Yahweh's name. Yahweh's blessing is only for those who fear him, whose house he has built. Not only should the wicked not flourish, but the context where they can flourish should not happen, removing them from the blessings the community share among themselves (cf. Ruth 2:4). Yahweh has cut the cord, and such people should not be blessed in his name.

Explanation

Building on the theme of blessing from Psalm 128, this psalm reflects on those who should not receive Yahweh's blessing. This reflection emerges from a long history of affliction, one where the community looks back and recalls a long history of oppression and suffering. This suffering is not to be spiritualized, because they can in various ways see its scars on their bodies. But the oppressors have never triumphed, because Yahweh has shown himself righteous. The difficulties have been real, but so is the God who has overcome. Emerging from this, we encounter the community's wish that the oppressors never again be able to flourish. They know God's righteousness and wish for a future where that would evidently triumph. For this to happen, blessing cannot sit with those prepared to act violently against them. The psalm, in its own setting, joins with the prayer 'may your kingdom come' (Luke 11:1), the desire that the eschatological reality of God's reign may be manifest in our own world despite those times and places where violence in all its forms seems triumphant.

PSALM 130

Translation

[1]A Song of the Ascents.
From the depths I call to you, O Yahweh,
[2]O Lord, hear my voice!
May your ears be attentive,
  to the sound of my plea for grace!

[3]If you retained iniquities, O Yah,
  O Lord, who could stand?

[4]But with you is forgiveness,
so that you may be feared.

[5]I hope in Yahweh,
my whole being hopes,
and for his word I wait.
[6]My whole being waits for the Lord,
more than those watching for the morning,
than those watching for the morning.

[7]Wait, O Israel, on Yahweh,
because with Yahweh is kindness,
and with him is abundant redemption.
[8]Yes, he will redeem Israel,
from all their iniquities.

Notes on the text

4. An adversative *kî* typically follows a negative (*WHS* §447), in this case noting that *'im* (v. 3) fulfils this function. Some Gk versions presume 'Torah' rather than reverence here, but this is likely confusion between similar sounding words (cf. Sedlmeier 1992: 474–475). NIV adds 'serve' to this verse, but the reason for this is 'enigmatic' (Longman 2014: 431).

5. With Stocks (2012: 152) scanning this verse as a para-tricolon.

Form and structure

Where Psalm 129 offered an alternative perspective on blessing to Psalm 128, Psalm 130 offers a different perspective to Psalm 129 on the potential sources of affliction within Israel. Where the sources of suffering in Psalm 129 are almost certainly those external to the community, this psalm recognizes the possibility of disruption coming from within because of sin (with McCann 1996: 1204). Yet hope remains because Yahweh is gracious. Because of this, there remains the possibility of forgiveness. Not everyone who afflicts the community is necessarily to be included among those who 'hate Zion' (Ps. 129:5). For these people the possibility of forgiveness remains, though the goal of such forgiveness is that Yahweh be feared, thus restoring such worshippers to the state of blessedness announced in Psalm 128:1. As with Psalm 129, individual and community are brought together, so that the experience of the individual can also be the experience of the community. This is achieved through an admonition to the community in verses 7–8. An admonition such as this may be more at home in a wisdom setting (for which note the many links between this poem and Ps. 111), whereas the rest of the psalm is a prayer that includes elements of complaint and thanksgiving. Attempts to reduce it to one of the main categories must inevitably diminish one part of the psalm, and it is better to recognize that it integrates elements in a public prayer that also offers instruction. We therefore do not need to consider it as bringing disparate textual elements together (against Crow 1996: 89–90), even if we recognize that the poet freely employs traditional forms.

The shift from the individual to the pl. provides an important guide to the poem's structure, though it should also be noted that verses 1–4 are addressed to Yahweh, while verses 5–8 are addressed to an audience. All sections are linked through repeated vocabulary that points to the poem's unity (cf. Schaefer 2001: 310; Goldingay 2008: 523–524). We can therefore analyse the poem in two stanzas, each of which contains two strophes (similarly, G. T. M. Prinsloo 2002: 455–457):

1. Prayer (1–4)
    a. Cry for grace (1–2)
    b. Reflection on forgiveness (3–4)
2. Address (5–8)
    a. Testimony (5–6)
    b. Admonition (7–8)

Comment

Title: For 'Song of the Ascents', see on Psalm 120.

1–2. The opening strophe has the speaker addressing Yahweh from the 'depths'. The depths elsewhere are waters (Isa. 51:10), though they can also be a figurative means of speaking about distress (Ps. 69:2, 14). Nevertheless, the literal sense informs the perception of the poet's distress, indicating an overwhelming power (a 'sea of troubles', Allen 2002: 255) that cannot be controlled. It is a place from which only Yahweh can deliver (as evidenced by the use of the vocs. 'Yahweh' and 'Lord'); hence, the urgency of the call for him to hear the psalmist's voice. That hearing is intended to be favourable, which becomes clear as the appeal is for Yahweh to hear the sound (more lit. 'voice', extending the opening appeal) of the call for grace. Psalm 116:1 indicates that Yahweh has heard appeals for grace, so there is reason to think he may hear this one too; but the key fact remains that this is a situation over which the psalmist has no control.

3–4. The opening strophe made clear the poet's need, but without indicating what that need was. Forgiveness will emerge as the key need, but the request for this is offered only indirectly. Rather, again addressing God with a pair of vocs. ('Yah' and 'Lord'), the poet briefly ponders a counterfactual possibility. What would happen if Yahweh stored up iniquities such that they could never be addressed? Such a storing up assumes Yahweh continues to hold these iniquities, an action that would apparently prevent forgiveness, leaving no one able to stand. Left unforgiven, human life is unable to flourish. But, echoing the grace formula of Exodus 34:6–7, the poet points to the alternative. Forgiveness is something Yahweh grants, and indeed the language for 'forgiveness' (*sĕlîḥâ*) here is something unique to Yahweh (cf. Neh. 9:17; Dan. 9:9). Forgiveness is not, however, an end in itself. The goal of forgiveness is restoration, reintegration into the community of Yahweh's people, and the renewal of a life that honours him (cf. Miller 1986: 142). Forgiveness is something Yahweh grants so he may be feared, restoring those forgiven to the state of blessedness in Psalm 128:1 (cf. Ps. 111:10). We do not fear God to be forgiven. God forgives that we may fear him.

5–6. The psalmist speaks in testimony as one who hopes in Yahweh (once again adding 'Lord' in verse 6, retaining the pairing of these terms from the previous strophes), waiting for his word. 'Hope' (*qwh*) and 'wait' (*yḥl*) often occur together and are broadly synonymous (Zimmerli 1971: 1–11; Bullock 2023: 131–137), both pointing to hopeful anticipation. 'Wait' (*qwh*) is repeated in verse 5, emphasizing this element in a poetic mode typical of the Ascents, before introducing 'hope' (*yḥl*) at the end, meaning this motif forms an inclusio for the verse. The element of waiting is directed towards Yahweh as the one who must act to provide forgiveness and is presented as all consuming, while hope is for Yahweh's word. Although 'word' (*dābār*) is often a synonym for Torah (see Firth 2015b), in this case it is more likely that a message announcing forgiveness is intended. How this word would be delivered is not indicated. Within the temple we could imagine a priest announcing this, but these psalms also function outside the temple, so the 'word' could be some other indication that forgiveness had been granted. But in this strophe, it has not yet been given, as is clear from the comparison with the night watch. There is no verb in verse 6, so we need to assume that 'wait' is carried over from the end of verse 5. Here, we see that the waiting is ultimately for the Lord since it is God who must grant this word of forgiveness. The psalmist's desire for God to respond is likened to the desire of sentries on the night watch for the coming of morning and the relative safety of daylight, repeating the motif to stress its importance.

7–8. Having shared personal experience, the audience is directly addressed in the closing strophe. As 'Israel', the community is defined as those who truly belong to Yahweh and therefore need to wait on him. This strophe is unique in using only the divine name, perhaps emphasizing the importance of the covenant relationship between Israel and Yahweh. The imp. directs the audience to join the psalmist in waiting on Yahweh, adopting a posture of hopeful anticipation. Two reasons are given for this – Yahweh's 'kindness' (*ḥesed*) and abundant redemption.

Mention of Yahweh's 'kindness' could allude to Exodus 34:6–7 since that text is foundational to presentation of his forgiveness, and the term for forgiveness in verse 4 is cognate to another there. Matching this with abundant 'redemption' (*pĕdût*; elsewhere only Psalm 111:9) is probably an alternative way of speaking of forgiveness, though again with the possibility of living a life pleasing to God. The noun 'redemption' closes verse 7, anticipating use of the cognate verb (*pdh*) at the start of verse 8, this time with an emphatic pr. which stresses that Yahweh is the one who redeems Israel from all their iniquities. Use of this term ties the closing verse to verse 3, making clear that the possibility of forgiveness is something available to both individual and community.

Explanation

One of the traditional 'seven penitential psalms' (see Gillingham 2022: 310–315), forgiveness here creates a virtuous circle. Those who are forgiven discover that forgiveness not only restores our relationship with God; it also begins to restore our relationship to others. One person's testimony becomes a word of encouragement to others. The psalm encourages its readers to become part of this virtuous circle, celebrating the fact that it is in the character of God that he forgives, and he forgives that he may be revered, restoring those forgiven to a place where they can live for him. This final affirmation finds its goal in the naming of Jesus (Matt. 1:21) since the angel's message there is that he will save his people from all their sins, showing that God's forgiving character finds its central focus in Jesus.

PSALM 131

Translation

A Song of the Ascents. Davidic.

1O Yahweh, my heart is not arrogant,
  my eyes are not haughty,
nor do I engage with things too great,
  or too marvellous for me.
2Rather, I have calmed and quieted my being,
  like a weaned child with its mother,
  my being is like a weaned child within me.

3Wait, O Israel, on Yahweh,
  now and for evermore.

Notes on the text

2. For *'im lō'* as a positive declaration, see *WHS* §456. With Hossfeld and Zenger (2011: 444–446), MT is to be retained, despite its clear difficulties.

Form and structure

As with many of the Songs of the Ascents, this brief poem does not really fit with any of the main categories, a feature that leads Crow (1996: 94) to wonder if it is a fragment retained from a larger poem. Yet, even if this were the case, whoever chose this fragment treated it as a functional unit (cf. Robinson 1998: 194–195). But if this was possible, then it is equally possible that the composition aimed only for a brief reflection, one that contrasted the poet's humility with Israel's need to wait on Yahweh. As is often the case, it is more productive to note how this psalm develops patterns from previous poems. Here, we may note that, as with Psalms 129–130, this poem relates the experience of an individual to the nation. This connection is especially strong when we note that verse 3a here repeats Psalm 130:7a. The comparison between the individual and the weaned child can be considered as a species of wisdom, so this poem joins Psalms 127–130, all of which have drawn on wisdom themes to some extent, while its Davidic title also links it to Psalms 122, 124, both of which have a Davidic title, anticipating David's mention in Psalm 132 and the Davidic title of Psalm 133. These motifs combine to present a psalm which is itself an expression of the hopeful waiting it encourages. This hopeful waiting is placed more broadly within the Songs of the Ascents as hope grounded in Yahweh as the one who forgives, one who provides hope through the promise to David that is especially developed in Psalm 132.

A 'jewel of simplicity' (Gerstenberger 2001: 359), we can analyse the poem in two brief stanzas:

1. Declarations of dependence (1–2)
2. Admonition to wait (3)

Comment

Title: For 'Song of the Ascents', see on Psalm 120. For 'Davidic', see on Psalm 3.

1–2. Where the prayer in Psalm 130 opened by placing the petitioner in the depths, this one begins by making clear that the psalmist is not self-exalting. The opening address to Yahweh makes clear that the psalmist has neither an arrogant heart (cf. Hezekiah in 2 Chr. 32, 25) nor haughty eyes. Both 'arrogant' and 'haughty' refer to raising oneself above what is appropriate (rather than this being an 'egocentric display of humility'; so, Terrien 2003, 2: 843). The heart here refers to the orientation to life that is taken, seeing the heart as symbolic of both the things about which one may think and the choices that emerge from this (cf. Gen. 6:5; Pss 7:9; 12:3). The reference to the eyes is linked to this as they point to the direction in which one may look, and hence the choices made (cf. Ezek. 20:24). This is, therefore, also a way of thinking about the person as whole, both internally and externally, and how dispositions are formed. As such, both 'heart' and 'eyes' also point to the whole person, showing that dispositions are fully embodied. The result of this proper understanding of one's standing before Yahweh is expressed in the psalmist's conduct, thinking of life as a path that may be walked. The poet has not only refrained from setting dispositions too high but has also refrained from engaging in matters too great or wondrous. The testimony of dependence closes by introducing the first point, expressed positively, that the psalmist has accepted that there are matters beyond him. The point is that some matters belong properly to Yahweh alone (cf. Pss 71:19; 86:10; 145:5–6; similarly, deClaissé-Walford et al. 2014: 931), and the poet recognizes this. Hence, the psalmist now introduces a strong counter-affirmation. If they have not aimed too high, what have they done? The answer is that they have calmed and quietened themselves, accepting that some matters belong to Yahweh. This acceptance is compared twice (in a repetition typical of the Songs of the Ascents) with a weaned child, who can settle on the mother without needing to struggle, and so be at rest. A younger child would seek the breast for feeding. The nature of this comparison means it is often thought the poet here (or at least the speaking voice) is a woman (e.g. McCann 1996: 1208), though in principle a man could also have observed this (cf. Knowles 2006: 389. But the weaned child loses this urge, and such a child may rest on the mother without struggle. Alternatively, the image could point to a child who has been satisfied by a feed (cf. van Gemeren 2008: 924), though the result is still that the child is calmed. The poet has reached a point of calm, no longer struggling with what cannot be grasped.

3. The individual's experience is applied to the community that heard the prayer. As with Psalm 130:7, Israel is to wait on Yahweh, adopting a posture of hopeful anticipation for what Yahweh will do. This language is the same as the previous psalm, which focused on coming redemption. That redemption is not necessarily absent here. But given the affirmations in the prayer and their concern with accepting that which is beyond human understanding, the concern here is more that the community needs to adopt this same posture. Its hope is found in Yahweh because Yahweh is the one who understands those things beyond them. Such hopeful waiting accepts that Yahweh stands in a different relationship to time to humans, meaning that hopeful waiting on Yahweh is not constrained by human experiences of time. The community might well have been going through a time of struggle, but they could learn that some things are beyond their control. Once this is understood, hopeful waiting on Yahweh from a posture of humility becomes the way forward.

Explanation

Psalm 130 called upon those who knew God's forgiveness to wait on Yahweh. But what might such a hopeful waiting look like? Although Psalm 131 is so brief it cannot explore all the options, it highlights one. In it, the psalmist's testimony is of humility that has been learned. The dispositions of heart and eyes have found their place. This is because the psalmist is now settled, like a weaned child with its mother, relating to God in the same way. Instead of the restless desire to sort out what God is doing in the world, which is really hubris, the psalmist instead has realized that some things simply need to be left to God. Endlessly trying to resolve complex issues does not help, even if it is the direction in which Western culture may push us. We might note that Jesus' admonitions against worry (Matt. 6:25–34) work in the same way as the psalm, especially since worry about such things will not help. That there are matters about which one may worry is not here denied, but there is a point where we learn that such worry is pointless. The psalmist's discovery is here a gift to the community, showing that one person's experience is a point of learning from which all may learn, and indeed from which Paul might have learned in being content in all circumstances (Phil. 4:11–13).

PSALM 132

Translation

A Song of the Ascents.

[1]Remember, O Yahweh, for David's sake,
all his afflictions
[2]how he swore to Yahweh,
vowed to the Mighty One of Jacob,
[3]'I will neither enter my family tent,
nor get up on to my bed cushion,
[4]nor give sleep to my eyes,
slumber to my eyelids,
[5]until I find a place for Yahweh,
a dwelling place for the Mighty One of Jacob.'

6Behold, we heard it in Ephrathah,
we found it in the fields of Jaar,
7'Let us enter his dwelling place,
let us worship at his footstool.'

8Arise, O Yahweh, to your resting place,
you and the Ark of your might!
9May your priests be clothed with righteousness,
your holy ones shout.
10For the sake of David, your servant,
do not turn away from the face of your anointed one.

11Yahweh has sworn to David,
truly he will not turn away from him,
'One from the fruit of your body,
shall I set on your throne.
12If your sons keep my covenant,
my testimony that I shall teach them,
their sons also for evermore,
shall sit upon your throne.'

13For Yahweh has chosen Zion,
he has desired her for his habitation.
14'This is my resting place for ever and ever,
I will reside here because I have desired it.
15I will surely bless her provisions,
her poor I will satisfy with food
16I will clothe her priests with salvation,
and her holy ones will surely shout.
17There will I cause a horn to thrive for David,
I have prepared a lamp for my anointed one.
18His enemies I will clothe with shame,
but his diadem will flourish upon him.'

Notes on the text

2, 5. Crow (1996: 98) suggests a small repointing to yield 'bull of Jacob' as a divine title. Jeroboam later uses this symbol (1 Kgs 12:25–33), and its parallel with Aaron on Sinai (Exod. 32:1–10) indicates that the idea of representing Yahweh through a bull is not unknown. But the terminology is different, and the phrasing here is a standard title for Yahweh (Gen. 49:24; Isa. 49:26; 60:16), making this emendation unnecessary.

3. Hebr. *bayit* is commonly 'house' but it can stand for the family. Given the background in 2 Samuel 7:1–17, this sense is likely.

5, 7. Hebr. *miškānôt* is understood as a pl. of intensity (*WHS* §8; cf. Pss 43:3; 84:2).

18. The verb *ṣwṣ* can mean 'gleam' but is also related more widely to flowers blooming (e.g. Num. 17:23), but when applied to people refers to their flourishing (e.g. Pss 92:8; 103:15). If the crown here stands for the Davidic house, then flourishing is the more likely sense.

Form and structure

Simply because of its length, Psalm 132 stands out within the Ascents, being about double the length of the next longest psalms within the collection. But it is also distinctive in being the only clearly royal psalm within the Ascents (it is also a Zion song – the categories are not mutually exclusive; similarly, Berlin 2015: 66), an element reinforced by its being bounded by two Davidic poems (Pss 131, 133). Royal elements have occurred elsewhere (e.g. Ps. 122:6), but this is the only psalm in the collection entirely focused on the Davidic promise of 2 Samuel 7:1–17, a text alluded to at key points. Despite its distinctiveness, it is also closely embedded in its context, as David here becomes the ideal expression of the humility affirmed in Psalm 131:2 (Vesco 2006, 2: 1233) as he embodies the desired humility as Yahweh's servant (v. 10), language that alludes to 2 Samuel 7:5, and through this also to passages such as Isaiah 42:1–4. David's election here is also closely linked to Yahweh's choice of Zion (v. 13), pointing to Yahweh's enduring commitment to his people through the sanctuary there, again tying this psalm to 2 Samuel 7:1–17. However, it also looks beyond David's time and experience to explore the implications of the promise for the people, especially the poor. By retaining the strong focus on David, and referring to him twice as Yahweh's anointed, the psalm also fosters a messianic dimension (Allen 2002: 270). Yahweh's need to remember David with favour is not simply a matter of historical recall but rather points to the community's need for Yahweh to act favourably towards the people through the promise to David. Mention of the Ark (v. 8) also alludes to David's moving it to Zion (2 Sam. 6) and the Song of the Ark (Num. 10:35), pointing further to both the importance of the promise to David and the reality of Yahweh's power to achieve his purposes. The integration of these features at a point near the end of the collection, combined with the poem's length, means it is given a place of prominence within it.

The psalm is structured around the references to David (vv. 1, 10, 11, 17–18), and can be understood as containing two stanzas, each of which mentions David to create an inclusio. This and other elements argue against the need to trace a process of development (e.g. Seybold 1996: 497), though it does clearly use older materials (cf. Starbuck 1999: 123–127; R. A. Jacobson 2004: 98–101). Rather, although it could have developed over time (Schreiner 2018; cf. Laato 1992, 1999; Patton 1995), it now has a compositional unity that is primary (with Fretheim 1967: 299–300). Within each stanza, reports of events and speeches form the strophes, though with key language and techniques shared across the whole poem (see Barbiero 2013: 240–242; Human 2017: 78), leading to the following analysis:

1. Prayer for David (1–10)
   a. David's vow (1–5)
   b. Discovery in Ephrathah (6–7)
   c. Summons to Yahweh (8–10)
2. Yahweh's oath to David (11–18)
   a. Content of vow (11–12)
   b. Yahweh's choice of Zion (13–18)

Comment

Title: For 'Song of the Ascents', see on Psalm 120.

1–5. The focus on David is immediate, asking Yahweh to remember his afflictions. Yahweh's remembering of someone is a sign of his favour (e.g. Gen. 8:1), but the request here extends this by mention of David's afflictions. The content of these afflictions is not outlined here. Given it is 'all his afflictions', we cannot restrict this to one event in David's life (though 1 Chr. 22:14 is possible). The language could also associate David with Yahweh's 'servant' (Isa. 53:4). This connection becomes more probable when we note the allusions to 2 Samuel 7:1–17, which also use this language (2 Sam. 7:5), and the explicit mention of David as Yahweh's 'servant' in verse 10. Yahweh's remembering of David is rooted in the oath he swore to Yahweh, here also called 'the Mighty One of Jacob' (cf. 'Notes on the text'). The content of this vow is outlined in verses 3–5, as David vows to deny himself the physical comforts of his own dwelling and rest until he has found a place for Yahweh, defined as a dwelling for the Mighty One of Jacob. Although the vow is hyperbolic (sleep cannot be deferred indefinitely; similarly, A. P. Ross 2016: 734) and cannot be matched to anything David is elsewhere reported as saying, the association is clearly with 2 Samuel 6, where David brought the Ark to Zion and his expressed desire to build a temple (2 Sam. 7:1–3). Crucially, David had sought to prioritize the worship of Yahweh, fulfilling a key role for an Israelite king.

6–7. The community now speaks of its own experience in which it made a discovery in Ephrathah, apparently an alternative name for Bethlehem (Gen. 36:16, 19; Mic. 5:2; Ruth 4:11), a town closely associated with David (1 Sam. 16:1–13). The discovery was in the 'fields of Jaar', apparently the area of Kiriath Jearim, where the Ark was kept with Abinidab (1 Sam. 6:21 – 7:1). The community speaks of itself as if they lived when David was alive, perhaps because as descendants of those earlier people they were present in their ancestors who both 'heard' and 'found' it there (similarly, Goldingay 2008: 549). But what was this 'it'? At this point it is unnamed, but since the Ark will be mentioned in verse 8 this is probably an initial allusion to it, along with its resting place. Against this, we should note that the Ark is typically treated as a m. noun, whereas the references here are f., perhaps why NIV has it refer to David's vow. However, it is treated as f. in 1 Samuel 4:17 and 2 Chronicles 8:11, so this is not an insurmountable problem, especially if the fields of Jaar also allude to the story of the Ark (1 Sam. 4:1b – 7:1). As the community blurs the time difference between themselves and their ancestors, they now express a desire to go to the temple so they can worship there (the footstool perhaps also alluding to the Ark; cf. Ps. 99:5), continuing the pattern David himself established.

8–10. Yahweh is addressed again in language that evokes Numbers 10:35, language that referred to points where Israel was to set out on its journeys in the wilderness, and taken up in Solomon's dedicatory prayer (2 Chr. 6:41–42). Here, the reference is probably to when the Ark needed to move from Kiriath Jearim (following its return from the Philistines) to Zion. Such a move would enable authentic and joyous worship, with the priests clothed with righteousness (embodying what it is to serve Yahweh, unless we follow NJPS and read 'triumph' to align with v. 16), while the people loyal to Yahweh could shout out their praise, knowing that Yahweh was among them. Yahweh is asked to act for David's sake, tying the end of this stanza to its opening, while also pointing to David as both Yahweh's servant and his anointed one, albeit someone embodied in his descendants.

11–12. Where the first stanza worked out the implications of David's oath to Yahweh, the second explores Yahweh's oath to David. Where verse 10 asked Yahweh not to turn back from his anointed, now we are assured that he will not turn back from his oath. The words of the oath, which are clearly dependent on 2 Samuel 7:12–16, are a poetic summary of the earlier promise. The swearing of the oath means Yahweh will not turn from David, though its content allows for the possibility that David's descendants may not be so faithful. Yahweh can be trusted, even if David's descendants cannot. The wording of the oath begins in verse 11b with the declaration that Yahweh will place one of David's sons on the throne. Although initially an oblique reference to Solomon, here the son will include any descendant whom Yahweh enthrones (cf. Ps. 2:7). There is, however, a condition for David's descendants, which is that their enduring experience of the promise requires them to keep Yahweh's covenant, further defined as the testimony Yahweh will teach them. That Yahweh will teach them means they always had the opportunity to know what was required, and hence could retain the throne. The element of conditionality here is important – Yahweh can be trusted, but the kings always need to learn obedience.

13–18. There is a close association between David and Yahweh's choice of Zion as the place for his temple, an association is explored here. Mention of the choice of Zion probably goes beyond David's capture of it (2 Sam. 5:6–10) and includes Yahweh's approval of the temple Solomon built there (1 Kgs 9:2–3; cf. 1 Kgs 8:44). The language of choice here is strengthened by mention of Yahweh's desire, a term that points to a strong wish for something. The combination points to Yahweh's commitment to David and its outworking through the temple on Zion. Indeed, verse 14 shifts from a comment from the poet to the beginning of a speech from Yahweh that Zion is indeed his permanent resting place and that he will dwell there because of his desire. Mention of Yahweh's dwelling there alludes back to 1 Kings 8 and the temple's dedication as well as Yahweh's commitment to it in 1 Kings 9:1–10. That commitment will be expressed in practical terms through the blessing of Zion's provisions, such that even the needy will be satisfied with food. Where the earlier prayer asked for the priests to be clothed with righteousness, now they are to be clothed with salvation, though those committed to Yahweh will continue to shout their praise. The shift in the language of priestly clothing suggests there will be a time when the salvation the community desires will again be experienced, so the shouts here are responding to this. The salvation is linked to a messianic understanding of David. The thriving horn is a symbol for power (e.g. Deut. 33:17; Ps. 22:22; cf. Zech. 3:8; 6:12) and may here also allude back to Hannah's prayer (1 Sam. 2:10), which also looks to Yahweh's exalting the horn of his anointed one. Along with this, mention of Yahweh's preparing a lamp for his anointed one probably alludes to 2 Samuel 23:17 (cf. 1 Kgs 11:36), where David is also described as a lamp. In working for a now-messianic David, Yahweh promises that whereas the priests were clothed in salvation, the king's enemies will be clothed with shame. The royal crown will flourish, pointing to the victory Yahweh will grant.

Explanation

Presenting David as an exemplar of the humility identified in Psalm 131, this poem offers the most extended theological reflection of the Ascents. At heart, it is built around the relationship between David's vow and Yahweh's oath. These elements are integrated to address the suffering of a later community that looks back on David while also holding in hope to Yahweh and his oath to David. The psalm assumes knowledge of 2 Samuel 6 – 7 to fill in key details. Perhaps most importantly, although David there expressed his desire to build a temple for Yahweh, it was Yahweh who promised to build a house for David. Although David's desire to honour Yahweh could be recognized, it is Yahweh who gave the promise to David. The community that prays this psalm continues in the sure hope that Yahweh's promise to see both Zion and David flourish is one that has continued significance for them. The NT makes clear that Jesus is the descendant of David in whom we see fulfilment of this psalm's hope (cf. Luke 1:69; Acts 2:30), though like the ancient worshippers the church continues to pray in hope as it awaits the fullness of God's kingdom in Jesus, prayer joined with hope every time the Lord's Supper is celebrated.

PSALM 133

Translation

A Song of the Ascents. Davidic.

1Behold, how good and how pleasant,
  for kin to dwell together in unity.
2Like fine oil on the head,
  coming down upon the beard, Aaron's beard,
  that comes down upon the edge of his garments.
3Like the dew of Hermon,
  that comes down upon the mountains of Zion.
For there has Yahweh commanded the blessing,
  life for ever more.

Notes on the text

2, 3. Hebr. *peh* (lit. 'mouth') could refer either to the collar or perhaps lower hem (so Tg). 'Edge' aims to retain this ambiguity.

3. Both 11QPs[a] and 11QPs[b] add an additional line at the end of the poem ('peace be upon Israel') but these seem to be liturgical elements since both place the psalm outside the Ascents (cf. Gillingham 2022: 333).

Form and structure

As with Psalms 127–131, this poem is heavily influenced by wisdom traditions, providing teaching that draws on family experience. Yet this family experience is mediated through Israel's legal traditions and linked to its liturgical ones. Along with the wisdom motifs, the poem is also integrated into its current setting through its Davidic title, linking it to Psalm 131, with these psalms also forming an inclusio around Psalm 132, where David is a central figure. It is also joined to Psalm 131 in its use of familial imagery, while linking to Psalm 132:15's focus on Yahweh's blessing as something experienced within the routines of life, here emerging from the model of kin living in unity. The introduction of Aaron picks up on allusions to the temple in Psalm 132 while anticipating the mention of those who serve there in Psalm 134:1 and the prayer for blessing in Psalm 134:3, also anticipating mention of the house of Aaron in Psalm 135:19. Finally, the concern with Zion (v. 3), which picks up Yahweh's choice of Zion for the temple (Ps. 132:13), should be noted. These points suggest it has been carefully placed to prepare for the close of the Ascents in Psalm 134 while gathering up elements from earlier poems.

Despite its brevity, its structure is relatively complex, containing three segments within a single stanza that can be analysed as follows:

1. Opening declaration (1)
2. Two similes (2–3a)
3. The blessing (3b)

Comment

Title: Identical to Psalm 131. For 'Song of the Ascents', see on Psalm 120. For 'Davidic', see on Psalm 3.

1. The opening 'Behold' (*hinnēh*) introduces an observation that is (at least conceptually) accessible to the psalm's audience. This interjection is relatively common in the Ascents, with seven in the collection (Pss 121:4; 123:2; 127:3; 128:4; 132:6; 133:1; 134:1). Apart from Psalm 132:6, where it introduces an account of the Ark, its use to this point in the Ascents presents something to the audience as something with which they can agree. This element is again present here, as an audience is asked to think about how good and how pleasant (a standard word pair; cf. Gen. 49:15; Ps. 147:1; Prov. 24:25) it is when kin live together in unity. The element of the kin is held to the end of the verse, so that the audience are first asked to think about that which is good and pleasant before making clear that the reference is to kin. Great complexity lies behind this seemingly simple observation. It could simply refer to the desirable situation of a family that is not quarrelling with each other (cf. Gen. 13:6; 36:7). But the language also echoes the law of levirate marriage (Deut. 25:5–10), understanding *'āḥ* more literally as 'brothers'). That law recognizes that families do not always work well together, so it is good and pleasant when family members take responsibility for one another. But across large parts of Deuteronomy, though often translated as 'brother', *'āḥ* is really using kinship language to describe all Israelites as an extended family (cf. Seybold 1996: 500), so the psalm leaves open the particular kin in view (cf. Dobbs-Allsopp 2008: 7). The benefits of unity can be seen, irrespective of how kinship is understood. The observation does not admonish the community to seek such unity, but presents this as something desirable, leaving the community to realize that this is something for which they should strive.

2–3a. The desirability of such positive kin relationships is explored through two similes (with Tsumura 1980), oil and dew, each of which depend on an understanding of Jerusalem's climate. In both instances, the simile points to something refreshing, likening positive kin relationships to something renewing in the heat. The first simile likens these kin relationships to oil poured on the head, though it is then extended to Aaron, introducing a priestly motif. That the oil is 'fine' (*ṭôb*) picks up on the language of 'good' in the previous verse, though now indicating the oil's quality. Such oil, from pressed olives, has a variety of uses within the OT, including associations with joy (e.g. Ps. 45:7) or signifying prosperity (e.g. Job 29:6). Perhaps the nearest association here would be Psalm 23:6 (cf. Ps. 92:11; Mic. 6:15), where the psalmist's head is smeared with oil, providing refreshment for someone whose skin is dry and dirty from heat. Given that the oil runs down, it is clearly abundant. This use of oil would be broadly applicable, but the image is extended through reference to its running down Aaron's head and beard, the double mention of Aaron's beard employing the repetition typical of the Ascents. This adds a priestly dimension, reflecting the use of oil in priestly ordination (e.g. Exod. 29:7; Lev. 8:10). The introduction of Aaron at this point probably refers to the fact that he wore special garments at his ordination (Exod. 28:6–14; 29:1–9), and through these garments represented all the people before Yahweh. Aaron would be an integrating figure, representing the unity of the people in worship, and this unity is good and pleasant. The second simile also joins refreshment with unity in worship. The dew falling on the Hermon range provides refreshment in the heat. This dew would not, in fact, fall on Zion (it is about 120 miles [193 km] north), but this dew can here be imagined as falling on Zion. Hermon was renowned as a mountain that remained green with vegetation even in the dry season, receiving constant watering because of the dew, and so with abundant waters (cf. Ps. 42:6–7). This dew is imagined as falling on Zion, with this place name used because of its association with the temple. The unity of the worshipping community is a means for restoration and renewal.

3b. The similes find their application in the closing announcement of the blessing Yahweh has commanded. This blessing is at the mountains of Zion and is specifically said to be life for evermore. The NT sense of the phrase should not be applied here (though Dahood 1970: 253 moves in this direction), though it is almost certainly key background to it. Given the focus on building community, the sense here is that a community renewed in worship endures and hence experiences the richness of life Yahweh intends for it. Its unity builds community, and this community finds its focus in worship that endures, a setting where the community can endure, even in the face of real challenges. This is the blessing Yahweh commands.

Explanation

The psalm holds blessing before us. It insists that this life is something now available. It is a life rooted in what God has done in providing forgiveness, moving to the hope centred on Zion. For Christians, both similes find their fulfilment in the person of Jesus. He is the one through whom forgiveness is offered, who brings us before God, who refreshes us like dew on a hot dry day. Jesus said he had come to bring us life to the full (John 10:10), which is what this psalm explores. Moreover, he also prayed for unity in his church (John 17). Although the NT is clear that there is an eschatological dimension to this, it is one with this psalm in refusing to push this entirely into the future. It calls God's people to live together and overcome the challenges to their unity, for, in doing this, we begin to experience the reality of true life now. Remarkably, the psalm sees no need to exhort its audience towards unity – simply showing it is enough to encourage us to see its value and so pursue it.

PSALM 134

Translation

A Song of the Ascents.

1Behold, bless Yahweh,
all servants of Yahweh,
who stand by night in the house of Yahweh.
2Raise your hands towards the sanctuary,
and bless Yahweh.

3May Yahweh bless you from Zion,
the maker of heaven and earth.

Notes on the text

1. The opening *hinnēh* is often translated as 'come', reflecting what appears to be a unique usage (Allen 2002: 281). This works better for English style, but throughout the Ascents this particle is used to call attention to a point being made (W-O §16.3.5b). 'Behold' is clumsy but retains this link, though 'now' (NJPS; cf. Seybold 1996: 501) is possible.

2. Gk is much longer at this point, seemingly strongly influenced by Psalm 135:2. The shorter MT is preferred (with Crow 1996: 121).

Form and structure

This brief poem brings the Ascents to their close, though its clear links to Psalm 135 means it also serves as a bridge into Psalms 135–136, most obviously through the mention of those who 'stand' in the temple (Pss 134:1; 135:2). There is also a progression in the language of praise, moving from 'bless' (*brk*, Ps. 134) to 'praise' (*hll*, Ps. 135) and 'give thanks' (*ydh*, Ps. 136), which moves from the temple to Israel's story. As the close to the Ascents, it takes up the themes of blessing (Pss 132:15; 133:4) and Zion (Pss 132:13; 133:2; cf. Vesco 2006, 2: 1251–1253). As the collection's close, reference to Yahweh as maker of heaven and earth takes up another core theme across the Ascents (Pss 121:2; 124:8).

As with many of the Ascents, it does not really fall into any of the main categories. The opening verses may suggest something hymnic, but it is broken off because no reason for praise is given where it might otherwise be expected. Verse 3 then introduces a priestly blessing, which is distinct yet also integrated into the poem through repetition of the verb 'bless' (*brk*). Where the opening verses were pl., the 'you' of verse 3 is sg., again marking this verse as distinct. Accordingly, we can analyse the poem in two brief stanzas (with Auffret 1989):

1. Address to Yahweh's servants (1–2)
2. Closing blessing (3)

Comment

Title: For 'Song of the Ascents', see on Psalm 120.

1–2. The opening 'behold' draws the audience's attention to what follows while forming a particularly close link to Psalm 133:1, which also opens with this interjection. Earlier uses were more consistent with a wisdom ethos, whereas here it functions liturgically; though we should not press this distinction since these areas of Israel's life overlapped. What matters most, though, is that Yahweh's servants should bless him, an act of praise where human words and acts are given to Yahweh (see on Ps. 103:1), though this verb is probably also chosen because of the blessing given in verse 3. Although Yahweh's servants earlier in Book 5 could refer to a wider body of his worshippers (Ps. 113:1), the reference here is more likely to figures who serve in the sanctuary since they are those who stand by night in Yahweh's house (against Allen 2002: 283). According to 1 Chronicles 9:33 (cf. Isa. 30:29), there were Levitical singers who served day and night, and they may be the primary reference here, though 1 Samuel 3:2–3 also presents the young Samuel as being on duty overnight. Admittedly, these servants are said to 'stand' whereas he was lying down, but 'stand' (*'md*) can also have the sense of take on a particular role (e.g. Gen. 41:46; 1 Sam. 16:21–22; Dan. 1:19). That a group is mentioned here means preference should be given to the Levitical singers, but others who might serve or be present would be included. These figures were routinely there (the pl. *lêlôt* suggesting 'each night' [cf. NJPS, REB], unless here it means 'all night'), and they are here called to bless Yahweh. The means of doing this was by lifting their hands to the sanctuary. There may be a play here on the fact that the root *brk* can also refer to kneeling (2 Chr. 6:13), so that those who kneel also raise their hands. If so, then the point is that the praise of Yahweh involves the whole body, and thus the presenting of the whole self to Yahweh. Elsewhere in Psalms, it is either Yahweh who raises his hand (Pss 10:12; 106:26) or a worshipper in supplication (Pss 28:2; 141:2), though there are close parallels in Psalms 63:4; 119:48. Here, the hand is raised towards the sanctuary as a sign of worship, so that Yahweh is indeed blessed, perhaps paralleling Aaron (Lev. 9:22).

3. We might have expected a *kî* (because) clause at this point, introducing a reason for praise (cf. Ps. 135:5), though perhaps Goldingay (2008: 571) is right that the previous poems in the collection have provided enough reason (similarly, Ps. 150). Instead, the focus shifts to a wish that Yahweh bless an individual from Zion, itself a reference to the location of the sanctuary as well as a key term in the Ascents. One can imagine the psalm as a dialogue between an individual who addresses those in the sanctuary speaking in verses 1–2, with verse 3 a response from them expressing the hope of a blessing. If the Ascents was originally a pilgrimage collection where worshippers came to Jerusalem to worship, this would form an appropriate conclusion as each worshipper addressed those in the sanctuary and they responded with the wish of a blessing on the worshipper (drawing on Num. 6:24–26; cf. Ps. 129:5). But as we do not actually know how the collection was used, it is more important to read the psalm in its literary setting where it now addresses any worshipper. Whether or not one journeys to Zion, a blessing is offered, one that draws on the fact that Yahweh is maker of heaven and earth (cf. Pss 121:2; 124:8) and thus able to bless every worshipper.

Explanation

This brief poem brings the Ascents to a close with a close focus on some of the collection's key themes: blessing, Yahweh as creator and Zion.

All this is brought together in a poem that stresses key paradoxes and mutuality. The obvious paradox is that Yahweh's blessing is rooted in Zion, and yet he is the creator of heaven and earth. Although Yahweh's blessing is thus universally available, it is also rooted in his revelation of himself at Zion. Zion was also the centre of Israel's worship, but this worship here is fundamentally mutual – the community calls those at the sanctuary to bless Yahweh and they in turn bless the worshippers. Worship and blessing are bound up in one another even as we also see God in both his local revelation and universal power. Worship and blessing are mutual because Yahweh is known in the sanctuary and yet able to be experienced everywhere. The Gospels make clear that the same is true of Jesus as the one known in his death and resurrection, and yet who is everywhere with his servants (Matt. 28). This also informs Paul's understanding of his relationship with the Roman church, where he hopes both to bring a blessing and in turn to be blessed by them (Rom. 1:11–12).

PSALM 135

Translation

1Hallelujah!

Praise the name of Yahweh,
 praise, O servants of Yahweh,
2who stand in the house of Yahweh,
 in the courts of the house of our God.
3Hallelujah – for Yahweh is good,
 make melody to his name for it is pleasant.
4For Yah has chosen Jacob for himself,
 Israel as his prized possession.

5For I myself know that Yahweh is great,
 and our Lord is greater than all gods.
6All that Yahweh desires, he does,
 in the heavens and on earth,
 in the waters and all the deeps.
7Raising clouds from the ends of the earth,
 he makes lightning strokes for the rain,
 bringing forth wind from his storehouses.

8The one who struck the firstborn of Egypt,
 both human and beast,
9he sent signs and wonders in your midst, O Egypt,

against Pharaoh and all his servants.
10 The one who struck many nations,
and slew mighty kings,
11 Sihon king of the Amorites,
and Og king of Bashan,
and all the kingdoms of Canaan,
12 and gave their land as an inheritance,
an inheritance for Israel his people.
13 Yahweh, your name, endures for ever,
remembrance of you is from generation to generation.
14 For Yahweh executes justice for his people,
and has compassion on his servants.

15 The idols of the nations are silver and gold,
the work of human hands.
16 They have a mouth, but do not speak,
they have eyes but do not see,
17 they have ears, but do not hear,
indeed, there is no breath in their mouth.
18 Those who make them will be like them,
all who trust in them!

19 O house of Israel, bless Yahweh,
O house of Aaron, bless Yahweh,
20 O house of Levi, bless Yahweh,
those who fear Yahweh, bless Yahweh!
21 Blessed be Yahweh from Zion,
the one who dwells in Jerusalem!

Hallelujah!

Notes on the text

17. Hebr. *'ap* could also be 'nose' (cf. Ps. 115:6), but here is without the parallel phrase, and so serves as an interjection.

Form and structure

Following the completion of the Ascents, Psalm 135 introduces a run of untitled psalms through to Psalm 137. These three poems form a bridge between the Ascents and the last Davidic collection (Pss 138–145; see Todd 2015: 99–126; deClaissé-Walford 2019). As a bridge, there are elements that tie this poem to the end of the Ascents, especially the close focus on Yahweh's servants standing in the temple (Pss 134:1–2; 135:1–2). Although the principal verb for 'praise' changes from 'bless' (*brk*) to 'praise' (*hll*), as Psalm 135 closes, it returns to 'bless' (vv. 19–21). This enables it to pick up the motif of 'blessing' from Psalms 132–134 along with their focus on Zion. This suggests that Psalm 135 has been placed to initiate the bridge to the last Davidic collection. This bridge then runs into Psalm 136, which shares Psalm 135's focus on Israel's story, with numerous repeated motifs as both reflect on the exodus and movement to the land (Pss 135:8–12; 136:10–21), while also shifting the language of praise to 'give thanks' (*ydh*). But Psalm 135 also links to earlier psalms in Psalms 113–118, especially Psalm 115 and its idol polemic (Pss 115:4–8; 135:15–18) and the direct address to the houses of Israel and Aaron along with those who fear Yahweh (Pss 115:9–11; 135:19–20), while its use of an opening and closing 'hallelujah' recalls Psalms 111–113 and 117. Its pairing with Psalm 136, with both recounting an abbreviated version of Israel's story, is also parallel to Psalms 105–106 (the latter of which is also bounded with 'hallelujah'), and again these parallel accounts emphasize different themes. Although both point to Yahweh as creator, in Psalm 135 the concern is more with his ongoing work within the creation (vv. 5–7), whereas Psalm 136 is more concerned with the initial creation (Ps. 136:5–9), though this is what enables Yahweh to act as he chooses within creation.

Unlike most of the Ascents that did not fit well with the main categories, Psalm 135 can be analysed as a hymn (with Allen 2002: 287–288). The opening summons to praise (vv. 1–4) is followed by 'for' (*kî*; vv. 3–4), introducing reasons for praise through to verse 14. The poem then introduces the idol polemic (vv. 15–18) and the exhortation to various groups to bless Yahweh (vv. 19–21). But the idol polemic primarily serves to contrast the gods of the nations with Yahweh, providing further reasons for Yahweh to be praised. As well as other psalms, this poem references other passages from across the OT, drawing especially on Exodus and Deuteronomy, most obviously verse 5, which is a close adaptation of Exodus 18:11, and verse 14, which cites Deuteronomy 32:36. It is a hymn that works on its own (with Emanuel 2012: 172), but is enriched by its numerous allusions to other events and texts across the OT. Readers who recognize these textual and historical associations are thereby provided with yet more reasons to praise Yahweh.

In addition to its 'Hallelujah!' frame, the poem can be analysed as containing five principal stanzas, which can be seen as forming a chiasm (A–B–C–B–A; so, Broyles 1999: 476), though I will present it in seven stanzas in sequence:

1. Hallelujah! (1a)
2. Call to praise Yahweh (1b–4)
3. Yahweh's greatness (5–7)

4. Yahweh's deeds in history (8–14)
5. The weakness of idols (15–18)
6. Call to bless Yahweh (19–21a)
7. Hallelujah! (21b)

Comment

1a. As usual, 'Hallelujah!' stands outside the body of the poem, summoning the poem's audience to praise Yahweh (see on Ps. 104:35b).

1b–4. Building on the 'Hallelujah!' frame, servants of Yahweh serving in the temple courts are called to praise him. The praise is directed to Yahweh's 'name' (*šēm*), anticipating the focus on the name in verse 13. As with Psalm 113:1 (cf. Ps. 8:1), mention of the name is fundamentally a means of asking those addressed to focus on Yahweh (for wider reflections on Yahweh's name in Psalms, see van Gemeren 2008: 135–136). Those called to offer praise are Yahweh's servants. As with Psalm 134:1, these servants are standing in the house of Yahweh, though that is now explained as the 'courts' of Israel's God. Since the courts covers the wider area of the sanctuary where worshippers could gather (1 Kgs 7:12; Ps. 100:4), Yahweh's servants here represent a wider group than the priestly or Levitical figures in Psalm 134:1–2. This anticipates the summons to a variety of groups to bless Yahweh in verses 19–21a. Somewhat unusually, the 'hallelujah' in verse 3 occurs within the body of the poem, a striking usage that makes it stand out and perhaps gives it additional emphasis, almost as if the poem were starting again (Goldingay 2008: 579). Where the initial call to praise focused on the one to praise, this time the psalm picks up the declaration of Yahweh's goodness, anticipating Psalm 136:1, while also looking back to Psalm 107:1. Yahweh's goodness provides the reason for praise, which is to be expressed through melody made to his 'name' (*šēm*), tying this praise back to that summoned in verses 1b–2. Such melodic praise, perhaps because it truly understands who Yahweh is, can be described as pleasant. The combination of 'good' and 'pleasant' here ties this psalm to Psalm 133:1 (cf. Ps. 147:1). Praise here is like kin dwelling in unity, a source of pleasure for the community, with both honouring Yahweh. Further reasons for praise are provided in verse 4, which notes that Yahweh has chosen Israel, making them his prized possession (cf. Exod. 19:4–6; Deut. 7:6) in his covenant relationship with them. Praise is pleasant for Israel, the appropriate response to Yahweh's choice of them.

5–7. This stanza opens with a further *kî* (for) clause, this one marked off by the introduction of an individual who speaks and close dependence on Exodus 18:11 (cf. Ps. 86:8). The speaker probably speaks for the community, and in confessing Yahweh's greatness and that

Israel's Lord is greater than all the gods, gives voice to the confession of all. The first-person speech here is probably because of the citation from Exodus 18:11 (though the 'I' here is emphatic, unlike the source), where it is Jethro's point when speaking to Moses, perhaps a mechanism by which the psalm points to its use of other materials while also allowing a non-Israelite to make this confession. Yahweh's greatness is a key motif across the psalms, while the comparison with other gods also prepares for the idol polemic (vv. 15–18). The citation is thus sufficiently different that its source from elsewhere can be noted while still being integrated into the psalm. That Yahweh is great also explains why he can do as he desires (cf. Ps. 115:3) in all points of creation. The boundaries of creation are traced from the heavens through the earth and then to the waters and the watery deeps, effectively tracing creation from its highest point to its lowest. Though people may think there are other deities in these places, the psalm is clear that it is Yahweh who acts there as he wants. Since Yahweh is also affirmed to be good, then what Yahweh does is also good, something that finds its focus in his provision of water – and since he is greater than the gods, it is Yahweh, not Baal, who provides it. Hence, he causes the clouds to form from the ends of the earth, language that now traces creation on the horizontal plane of life on the land, with these clouds bringing the rains that come in the storms (cf. Jer. 10:13). Even these storms are under Yahweh's control, since the wind is here pictured as something he has stored up, bringing it out when needed.

8–14. The third stanza is introduced with a minor shift, this time through the relative pr. *šě* at both verses 8 and 10, and by the concern with events in Israel's story, especially the exodus, wilderness wandering and settlement in the land. Throughout, the focus is on those acts Yahweh has performed that demonstrate the claim of verse 6. Although unnamed in verse 8, the relative pr. means we know it is Yahweh who struck down the firstborn of Egypt, both human and beast, alluding to Exodus 11:5, while also sending signs and wonders into Egypt (cf. Exod. 11:9). It is Yahweh who has acted – there is no glorification of anything done by Israel since only Yahweh can be just in such cases. Egypt is addressed directly here, perhaps as a mechanism of imagining their responding to these declarations and affirming them to be true. If Yahweh does as he pleases, then a power like Egypt cannot prevent his acting for his people. Pharaoh and his servants are powerless before Yahweh, whereas Yahweh's servants can trust him. This reality is extended by noting the defeat of many nations and kings who opposed him, the key example being Sihon and Og (Num. 21:21–35), the last kings mentioned in the wilderness traditions. As such, their mention along with that of Egypt places Yahweh's actions within the context of the exodus and wilderness period, though those traditions do not mention the many kings referred to here. But mention of many kings anticipates mention of the gift of the land to Israel in Joshua and its extended list of defeated kings (Josh. 12). This land is now the inheritance of his people, again drawing on language from Joshua, though there may also be a more immediate allusion to Psalm 111:6. That Yahweh has acted for his people in overcoming powerful forces raised against them and given them the land as an inheritance leads to a further reflection on his name, which is here declared to endure for ever. In this instance, given the parallel with his enduring remembrance (here alluding to Exod. 3:15b), Yahweh's name stands for his reputation, with its enduring remembrance providing an ongoing reason for praise (similarly, Todd 2015: 27). Nevertheless, Yahweh's renown is not only rooted in the past. Rather, verse 14 closes this stanza by pointing to his continuing work of executing justice for his people, having compassion on his servants by responding to their needs. Citing Deuteronomy 32:36a, the stanza closes with anticipation of Yahweh's continued work for his people (Schaefer 2001: 318), so the enduring praise will also be linked to Yahweh's continued work.

15–18. This stanza is closely modelled on Psalm 115:4–8. As such, it retains the concern there of noting that although the nation's idols were made in a way that suggested the deities they represented were capable of work, in reality none of them could do anything. They were simply the work of human hands, and incapable of action – mute, blind and deaf. Since they lack breath, they have no life. More immediately, such deities could not execute justice for their worshippers, whereas awareness of Israel's story reminds the audience that Yahweh does speak, see and hear. Yahweh is greater than the gods (v. 5) because he can and does act. He is to be praised since this is real worship, whereas those worshipping idols become like them, unable to make a difference.

19–21a. Building on the idol polemic, this stanza also takes up elements from Psalm 115:9–11. Nevertheless, it is developed in a distinctive form here through the addition of the house of Levi before mention of those who fear Yahweh. Fundamentally, the stanza summons all Israel to 'bless' (*brk*; see on Ps. 103:1) Yahweh. Here, the house of Israel and those who fear Yahweh reference the whole community, with the house of Aaron and house of Levi referring to the priestly community. It recognizes a distinction between them, with Aaron pointing to the priests while Levi includes those who worked with them (cf. Num. 3:6–9). Mention of those who fear Yahweh also allows for those who worshipped him but were not born as Israelites, suggesting that the true community transcends ethnicity (against Weiser 1962: 788). The community is called to bless Yahweh, while Yahweh remains as the one who is 'blessed' (*bārûk*) from Zion, the one whose residence was in Jerusalem in the temple.

21b. The closing 'Hallelujah!' provides a frame for the poem, but is also the appropriate response to the psalm. Given what has been declared, Yahweh is indeed to be praised.

Explanation

Although standing outside the Ascents, this psalm is closely tied to them. It develops key themes (including Yahweh as creator) from that collection and integrates them into Israel's story in the exodus and eisodus. Throughout, it points to Yahweh's supremacy over all other powers, whether other deities or kings and their armies. Yahweh is to be praised because he does what he desires, and what he desires is good. He has demonstrated this in his faithfulness to his people in the past, and continues to do so as he executes justice for them in future. Accordingly, trusting anyone other than Yahweh is simply foolish, choosing death rather than life. Yahweh is therefore the one to be praised, with the option to praise available to all peoples since all may enter his courts and all may fear him. These themes are developed through a careful curation of other OT texts, so that almost every line in the poem either cites or references another text. Audiences encountering this psalm are thus asked both to praise Yahweh and to reflect on why such praise matters by drawing together the scriptural references woven through it, a pattern taken up in Revelation 19:5, which draws on this psalm both to report and encourage praise. Indeed, this psalm clearly demonstrates that theology is 'best done in the context of doxology' (Limburg 2000: 461).

PSALM 136

Translation

1Give thanks to Yahweh for he is good,
  for his kindness endures for ever.
2Give thanks to the God of gods,
  for his kindness endures for ever.
3Give thanks to the Lord of lords,
  for his kindness endures for ever.

4To the one who alone does great wonders,
  for his kindness endures for ever,
5to the one who by understanding made the heavens,
  for his kindness endures for ever,
6to the one who spread the earth upon the waters,
  for his kindness endures for ever,

7to the one who made the great lights,
  for his kindness endures for ever,
8the sun to rule over the day,
  for his kindness endures for ever,
9the moon and the stars to rule over the night,
  for his kindness endures for ever.

10To the one who struck Egypt by their firstborn,
  for his kindness endures for ever,
11and brought Israel out from their midst,
  for his kindness endures for ever,
12with a mighty hand and an outstretched arm,
  for his kindness endures for ever,
13to the one who divided the Sea of Reeds in two,
  for his kindness endures for ever,
14and brought Israel through the midst of it,
  for his kindness endures for ever,
15and tossed Pharaoh and his army into the Sea of Reeds,
  for his kindness endures for ever.

16To the one who led his people through the wilderness,
  for his kindness endures for ever,
17to the one who struck down great kings,
  for his kindness endures for ever,
18and killed mighty kings,
  for his kindness endures for ever,
19Sihon, king of the Amorites,
  for his kindness endures for ever,
20and Og, king of Bashan,
  for his kindness endures for ever,
21and gave their land as a heritage,
  for his kindness endures for ever,
22a heritage for Israel his servant,
  for his kindness endures for ever.

23He has remembered us in our humiliation,
  for his kindness endures for ever,
24and rescued us from our foes,
  for his kindness endures for ever,
25giving food to all flesh,
  for his kindness endures for ever.

26Give thanks to the God of heaven,
  for his kindness endures for ever.

Notes on the text

4. The ptcs. that begin from verse 4 are all dependent on the imp. 'Give thanks', so one may represent the whole psalm until verse 23 as one continuous sentence. But there are also subject breaks and some points that change the grammatical structure and mark divisions within the content. For the sake of English usage, these verses are treated as if they commenced a new sentence.

10. Many EVV make the firstborn the object of the verb, but the prep. (*bĕ*) on the firstborn indicates that they are how Yahweh struck Egypt.

Form and structure

Within the Psalter, Psalm 136 is unique (though 11QPs[a] presents Ps. 145 similarly). It is the only poem to demonstrate such a clear antiphonal pattern, retaining the one response through every verse. This suggests a liturgical performance where a cantor might speak the first part line of each verse with the congregation (or a choir) responding. Yet even though such a background is probable, the more immediate information for its interpretation is provided in its pairing with Psalm 135 (see Mays 1994b: 415). Both are descriptive hymns that praise Yahweh through reflection on his work for Israel through its history. The verb for praise here shifts from 'praise' (*hll*) to 'give thanks' (*ydh*), but there is otherwise a significant overlap between them, with both recounting the striking of the firstborn in Egypt (Pss 135:8–9; 136:10) and the defeat of other kings that culminates in the memory of Sihon and Og (Pss 135:10–11; 136:17–20), culminating in the gift of the land to Israel as its heritage (Pss 135:12; 136:21–22). However, Psalm 136 also introduces a range of motifs not addressed in Psalm 135, providing a fuller reflection on that story. This is because the recounting of history in Psalm 135 is only part of its larger goal of pointing to Yahweh's supremacy, whereas for Psalm 136 the larger story is told because it provides a reason for thanksgiving and understanding Yahweh's enduring 'kindness' (*ḥesed*). Its placement after Psalm 135 reminds readers of Yahweh's supremacy and therefore why he could act as he did, even as it summons thanksgiving to him. It also joins with Psalm 135 in reporting that all acts against Israel's adversaries were carried out by Yahweh, not Israel, preparing for the closing beatitudes in Psalm 137:8–9.

Like Psalm 135, this poem also has links to numerous other poems in the Psalter. The summons to give thanks here joins these two psalms to Psalms 105–106, both of which also reflect on Israel's story while calling on the community to give thanks. The connection with Psalm 106 is stronger since, apart from its opening 'Hallelujah!', its first verse is identical to the opening verse here. The transition from 'praise' (*hll*) to 'give thanks' (*ydh*) is also evident in Psalms 113–118, with Psalm 118:1, 29 identical to the opening verse here. Along with the allusions to other psalms, the poem is replete with references to other texts across the Pentateuch and Joshua (though Hossfeld and Zenger [2011: 504] find only the Pentateuch, while Brettler [2013] limits it to Deut. 10:17 – 11:5), all of which contribute to its call to thanksgiving. Beyond this, the poem's refrain is also found in other post-exilic texts (1 Chr. 16:34; 2 Chr. 20:21; Ezra 3:11). As with Psalm 135, this poem is internally complete and yet also enriched by its interaction with other texts.

Calls to thanksgiving provide an inclusio for the poem, with the bulk of the poem effectively one long sentence (cf. 'Notes on the text'). However, changes in grammatical structure also mark changes in subject, and these provide the basis for the following outline as the story is traced from creation through to the post-exilic community (cf. Auffret 1977):

1. Call to thanksgiving (1–3)
2. Evidence of Yahweh's kindness (4–25)
   a. The creator (4–9)
   b. The redeemer (10–16)
   c. The heritage provider (17–22)
   d. The remembering rescuer (23–25)
3. Call to thanksgiving (26)

Comment

1–3. The opening call to thanksgiving is identical to Psalm 107:1, language that functions as a refrain for Book 5, which provides an important structural marker for the book (Jenkins 2021: 174). No specific audience is mentioned, and it could be universal (so, tentatively, Brueggemann and Bellinger 2014: 569), though it is probably the community that finally emerges in verse 23. Thanksgiving is a form of praise that responds either to something Yahweh has done or to an aspect of his character. In this psalm, these elements are joined as the psalm's refrain stresses the enduring nature of Yahweh's 'kindness' (*ḥesed*), but apart from the opening and closing calls to thanksgiving, always in response to what Yahweh has done. Weaving these elements together enables an audience to see that Yahweh's kindness is not an abstract concept: it is expressed in concrete acts that demonstrate his covenantal commitment to his people. However, before moving to outline these elements, the opening call to thanksgiving explores Yahweh's identity as both 'God of gods' and 'Lord of lords'. Both are instances of the superlative (*WHS* §80), indicating that Yahweh is the greatest one in the class of both 'god' and 'lord'. Both 'god' and 'lord' here probably refer to the deities of the peoples around Israel, offering a potential polemic (Human 2005: 1215), though 'lord' could have a broader reference to human masters. The superlative is used here to stress that however these classes are conceived, Yahweh stands above them all and is the only one to whom such thanksgiving should be given.

4–9. The second stanza offers evidence of Yahweh's kindness through history, interacting with a range of other passages. Its first strophe is concerned with creation. However, before describing creation, the poem insists that Yahweh alone performs great wonders (v. 4), a statement that is a bridge from the opening summons into the report of Yahweh's deeds, which demonstrate his kindness. Indeed, the statement that Yahweh alone performs great wonders makes clear that he is also different in kind from the gods and lords while also setting a framework for the acts then recounted. Yahweh's wonders are elsewhere presented as a basis for thanksgiving (Ps. 107:8). The balance of the strophe is concerned with his work in creation, with a particular emphasis on the sky, perhaps because the nations around Israel viewed heavenly bodies as deities. The strophe is strongly influenced by Genesis 1, though the opening declaration is rooted in wisdom traditions such as Proverbs 3:19, which also emphasizes Yahweh's insight in creating, as well as Jeremiah 10:12; 51:15. The statement draws together various elements of the OT, encouraging readers who are aware of the connections to draw on them in understanding Yahweh's enduring kindness. The opening statement is concerned only with the heavens, with the earth deferred until verse 6. The order of heavens and earth here follows that of Genesis 1:1, though the ptc. used for the spreading of the earth on the 'waters' (*rq'*) is striking because the same root is used in Genesis 1:6–8 for the 'firmament' that forms the sky. Connections with Genesis 1:14–18 are evident in mention of the making of the great lights. The sun and moon are unnamed in Genesis but are named here along with the stars, which are named there. Links with the Genesis account are strengthened by mentioning sun and moon's ruling over day and night, a motif unique to these texts. Yahweh's kindness is eternal because it was present before creation and is seen in creation.

10–16. As well as creation, Yahweh's kindness is seen in redemption. That he is creator means he has freedom to act within creation, and that freedom is seen in his covenant commitment to Israel as demonstrated in the exodus and crossing of the Reed Sea. As with the previous strophe, this one also begins with a ptc. describing Yahweh's acts. That Yahweh 'struck' (*nkh*) Egypt with their firstborn describes his defeat of the nation, with the blow that convinced Pharaoh to release Israel coming through the slaying of the firstborn (Exod. 12:29–32), so that he could lead Israel out from Egypt. That this involved overcoming Egypt is evident from Yahweh's 'mighty hand' and 'outstretched arm', language that also draws from the exodus (Exod. 6:6), though the allusion here may be to Deuteronomy, which often uses this language (Deut. 4:34; 5:15;

7:19; 26:8). Allusion to the exodus continues into the wilderness period through reference to the crossing of the Reed Sea (Exod. 14:21–31) in verses 13–16. This reference is continued in the mention of Pharaoh and his army being tossed into the sea, pointing to Exodus 14:27. Yahweh's kindness is seen in his covenant commitment, demonstrated in bringing Israel out.

17–22. A new strophe is introduced with the same ptc. as at verse 10. Yahweh's acts in the exodus continued to show his enduring kindness in overcoming mighty kings in the wilderness period and the giving of the land to Israel. The great kings Yahweh defeated are not initially specified so one may think of all foes from this period (e.g. Amalek, Exod. 17:8–13), with the key point being that they were both great and mighty. Israel could not defeat them through military skill but rather needed Yahweh to overcome them. Even if the victories may be thought of in more general terms at first, mention of Sihon and Og means the victories in the Transjordan (Num. 21:21–35) are given prominence. However, the wider reference in verses 17–18 means that Yahweh's victories can be seen more generally, and this would include victory over the kings in the land summarized in Joshua 12:7–24. The land taken from the kings is given to Israel, and this broader term suggests that although the Transjordan could be considered a heritage for the eastern tribes (Reuben, Gad, East Manasseh; cf. Num. 32:19), it is more likely that the reference is to the whole of Israel's territory (Josh. 11:23; 13:6). Yahweh's enduring kindness was thus demonstrated in bringing the people through the wilderness and in the gift of the land.

23–25. The final strophe in this stanza is marked by the relative pr., indicating a shift in focus from the previous material. Here, the community's own state is recalled, probably moving down to the period of the exile or after. Yahweh's enduring kindness was not simply something seen in the past that lacked relevance to the community when the psalm was composed. Rather, they are reminded that Yahweh remembered them, and indeed had rescued them from their foes. The humiliation in which he remembered them is not specified, though it clearly represents a low point for them. The exile is certainly possible, but the psalm is non-specific, making it possible for numerous communities through time to see their own experience represented in Yahweh's acts of rescue and provision mentioned here. Yahweh's kindness endures for ever. It is not lost through times of humiliation and suffering, and is something evidenced by his continued provision of food for all, an act that in its simplicity remains one of his wonders.

26. The psalm closes with a further summons to thanksgiving to Yahweh as the God of heaven, a unique title in Psalms (though cf. Ezra 1:2; Neh. 1:4). This links Yahweh with the focus on the heavens in the celebration of creation (vv. 4–9), while again emphasizing his uniqueness.

Yahweh continues to show his kindness because it is fundamental to his character, and so thanksgiving is again summoned.

Explanation

Those who have experienced Yahweh's kindness in creation and history owe him a special service (Human 2004a: 86), and in this psalm that service is thanksgiving, gratitude. This service of thanksgiving emerges because we realize Yahweh's kindness endures for ever. But 'kindness' (*ḥesed*), rather like the NT's 'love' (*agapē*), has often taken a life of its own divorced from any particular text. What matters here is that Yahweh's kindness is not an abstract attribute. It is something for which Israel can give thanks because it has been expressed in creation, in their story from the exodus to the entry to the land, and continued to be expressed in even the provision of food as he remembered a struggling community after the exile. Yahweh's kindness was not restricted to events others might have considered as marvels in the past but continued in his provision for the community in its struggles even as he provided food for all creation. In the Christian tradition, the celebration of Communion has a similar function, reminding the worshipping community of God's extraordinary kindness in Jesus' death, in his presence among his people and the promise of the future even as we give thanks for his continued provision for us, while baptism continues to announce the experience of God's goodness.

PSALM 137

Translation

1By the rivers of Babylon,
  there we sat and wept,
  as we remembered Zion.
2Upon the poplars within her,
  we hung our harps,
3because there our captors asked us,
  for words of song, our mockers for joy,
  'Sing us a Song of Zion!'
4How can we sing Yahweh's song,
  upon foreign ground?

5If I forget you Jerusalem,
  may my right hand wither,
6may my tongue stick to my palate,

if I do not remember you,
if I do not raise up Jerusalem
as my chief joy.

7Remember, O Yahweh, against the sons of Edom,
the day of Jerusalem,
how they said 'Raze it, raze it,
as far as its foundation.'
8Daughter Babylon, doomed to destruction,
O the blessedness of the one who repays you,
for the deed you enacted against us.
9O the blessedness of the one who seizes and shatters,
your children against the rock.

Notes on the text

3. Deriving the hapax *tôlālênû* from *yll*, 'to mock' (see Allen 2002: 302), though more from context than etymology. Dahood (1970: 270) describes it as 'one of the most recalcitrant *hapax legomena* of the Psalter'.

5. The verb *škḥ* (usually 'forget') is often emended to *šḥk* ('wither'; e.g. Kraus 1989: 501). But *DCH* now proposes *škḥ* II with the sense of 'wither, droop', a sense Dahood (1970: 271), possibly stretching the evidence, traces back to the Ugar. *tḫt*. Though not agreed, there are sufficient examples to mean MT remains plausible, even if the sense is the same as the emendation. In both cases there is a wordplay, either through different senses of the one root or through two closely related in sound that simply reverse two consonants.

8. The pass. ptc. *haššdûdâ* is difficult. Following some Gk traditions (plus Syr., Tg), it is often emended to the act. ptc. *haššôdĕdâ*. But the ptc. can refer to an imminent event (*WHS* §214), and as such can stand.

Form and structure

Few psalms generate as strong an emotional response as Psalm 137. Its closing beatitude retains the power to shock even on numerous encounters, something not helped by some Jewish and Christian worship traditions finding ways to omit the closing stanza from regular public reading (see Hays 2005: 35–37; Berlin 2023: 100). But since the closing stanza represents the poem's climax, we cannot omit these verses. They must instead be understood in their context as a plea for Yahweh's justice to be enacted on those who devastated Jerusalem and who continued to mock those who suffered in exile. This background suggests that this psalm, though lacking many significant lexical links (though see Todd 2015: 93–98), has been intentionally placed after Psalms 135–136 since they both included elements of encouragement for the post-exilic community, words that find a particular focus here. Thus, Psalm 135:5–7 could reassure the community that Yahweh could do as he desired, while verse 14 reassured them that Yahweh would vindicate his servants. After tracing evidence of Yahweh's 'kindness' (*ḥesed*), Psalm 136:23–25 pointed to Yahweh's remembering the community's humiliation. Nothing therefore hindered Yahweh from acting for the community, and they already had evidence that he had 'remembered' (*zkr*) them. In Psalm 137:6, the community wants Yahweh to 'remember' (*zkr*) what Edom did to their forebears, a remembering that should lead to action against Babylon too. It should be noted that although Psalms 135–136 recounted military acts, in every instance it was Yahweh, not Israel, who acted. The community's praise and thanksgiving are directed to Yahweh as the one who overcomes enemies too powerful for them. At no point do these psalms report Israel's acting. Psalm 137, dealing with the rage that comes from the exile and reflection on other OT texts about Babylon, leaves the desired vengeance with Yahweh, knowing that he can act if needed (cf. B. Johnson 2019; Boyle 2022). Importantly, it does not request permission to enact violence. But, as Tucker and Grant observe (2018: 902), if we leave things there, then we may reduce this to little more than a therapeutic act (though not one to be ignored). So, it is important to note that this submission of rage to God is in fact a declaration of faith in his reign, accepting that it is his role to act against oppressors, and knowing that there are important instances in the past when he has. These are words that those who have suffered deeply pour out to God (cf. Bellinger 2005: 17–20).

The psalm is probably to be dated shortly after the end of the exile (e.g. Mays 1994b: 421) since the poet remembers the experience 'there', suggesting that it is no longer the community's location. However, there remains a significant minority who place the psalm in the exile itself (e.g. Kidner 1975, 1: 459; Ahn 2008: 273–274). In either case, the experience of exile remains vivid. Although events from Jerusalem's fall are also remembered, these are less personal, suggesting they were part of the communal memory passed down among the exiles. Nevertheless, memory remains a key motif that runs through the poem, both joining it to Psalms 135–136 and providing the key link that joins the psalm's stanzas. As with the uncertainty about its date, scholars have struggled to assign it to any of the major categories (cf. Ahn 2008: 271–272). Some see it as a lament (e.g. A. A. Anderson 1972, 1: 897); though, if so, it joins Psalm 88 in being given this label while lacking many of the features associated with this category (cf. Simango 2018: 229–231). Others associate it with the Songs of Zion (albeit in a modified form; e.g. Allen 2002: 303). Becking (2010: 272) prefers to move outside the standard categories and treat it as a 'topical song', a genre that operates in the sphere of folk music. The benefit of this approach is that it recognizes the distinctiveness of this psalm within the OT, while noting that there are analogies that can be drawn from a range of settings.

The poem's structure has also been approached from a range of perspectives. But allowing for the fact that verse 4 functions as a hinge that joins verses 1–3 (cf. deClaissé-Walford et al. 2014: 953) with verses 5–6 and could be assigned to either stanza, the following three-stanza structure can be observed (though this masks a range of structuring devices evident throughout; see Ravasi 1985c: 757–760), one that moves from past through present to future:

1. Memory of Babylon (1–4)
2. Not forgetting Jerusalem (5–6)
3. Yahweh to remember (7–9)

Comment

1–4. The psalm opens with vivid memories of Babylon. The memory is initially pictorial, recalling times when the community sat by the city's waters. These were most likely the canal system that brought water into the city (cf. Jer. 51:13), though the Tigris and Euphrates could be in mind. We know many Jews lived by the Chebar canal in the exile (Ezek. 1:1; 3:15). It was by these waters, places that might otherwise have been thought beautiful (esp. for a people from a dry climate), that they sat and wept. The reason for this was their memory of Zion. Memory of Zion would include the area of Jerusalem where the temple was located, though it might also have included the promises associated with it. Even within the Psalter, Zion is often a theological symbol that points to Yahweh's promise to Israel (e.g. Ps. 48) and beyond (e.g. Ps. 87). The weeping-inducing memory is probably a complex of factors, but is grounded in the experience of living in exile. Weeping and songs of praise did not cohere, and as a result the captives had hung their harps on the poplars that lined the banks. It is only in verse 3 that we are given a reason for the weeping, which was the demand of the community's captors that they sing words that would otherwise be associated with joy (cf. Ps. 122). This is summed up in their mocking demand that they sing them some of the Songs of Zion. Such songs (as with Pss 48, 87) focused on Zion as a symbol of joy and hope, as a place where Yahweh's covenant commitment would be worked out. But as this community remembers these mocking demands, it also reflects, asking how it can sing Yahweh's song on foreign ground. It is not that the praise of Yahweh cannot be offered outside Israel, but this is foreign ground because the intent was to mock Yahweh. This was a land that claimed Babylon's god (Marduk) had defeated Yahweh, and the demand for song was an extension of this claim. The community that wept at the memory of Zion could not offer praise if it was really a mockery of Yahweh.

5–6. The second stanza moves from Israel's memory to its present, recognizing the importance of remembering Jerusalem. If the psalm emerges from the early years after the exile, then the city still lay in ruins, a shadow of its former self, lacking a temple. Absence of the temple may explain the shift from 'Zion' to 'Jerusalem' in this stanza, though it could also be a stylistic variation. Here, the problem is not one of remembering the past but the danger of forgetting in the present. Hence, this stanza is expressed in a form of an embodied self-curse where an individual speaks on behalf of the community, directly addressing Jerusalem, outlining the negative things to happen should the city be forgotten. The elements of the self-curse are closely tied to the earlier request from the captors since a withered right hand would make it impossible to play the harp and a tongue stuck to the palate would make singing impossible. Should this individual forget Jerusalem, then it would be impossible to sing the Songs of Zion. Remembering Jerusalem was not only about a particular place. It was also a commitment to doing that which truly honoured Yahweh above all else, though expressed through commitment to Jerusalem as the city at the heart of his worship. The psalm recognizes that many things could provide joy but, for this community, Jerusalem (as the place where Yahweh was worshipped) was the greatest source of joy.

7–9. The final stanza is concerned with the need for Yahweh to remember, and thus looks to the future, to points where Yahweh's memory will lead him to act. Yahweh's remembering is initially directed towards Edom, pointing to their glee at Jerusalem's fall ('the day of Jerusalem'), desiring the city to be razed to the ground. The polemic against Edom elsewhere (Jer. 49:7–22; Obad. 10 – 14) probably also draws on Edom's role in Jerusalem's fall to Babylon (cf. Ezek. 35). Such texts lead to an expectation that Yahweh will act against Edom, and in asking him to 'remember' the community is asking that Edom's punishment begin. In verses 8–9 attention is turned to Babylon as it too is addressed directly, linking it to Jerusalem in verses 5–6. As is common in the prophetic literature, the city is addressed as 'daughter' as a means of personifying it. But Daughter Babylon is doomed to destruction because her punishment is certain, simply waiting to be enacted. Babylon has this status because it was not destroyed when it fell. For this community, justice has not yet been fully done. Strikingly, in verse 8 the psalm employs the first of two beatitudes, celebrating the blessedness of the one who does to Babylon what they have done to the community. The intent is clearly that the penalty should match the crime exactly. Many are content with this as a general principle of justice until they see the vigour with which it is expressed here. The first beatitude makes clear, however, that Babylon's punishment must fit their crimes and not exceed them. The second beatitude shocks more, but within the context of the first can refer only to an action that matches Babylon's actions at

Jerusalem. That is, the community declares that the one who seizes and dashes the Babylonian infants on a rock is blessed because of providing a punishment that is an appropriate match to what they did. Indeed, Isaiah 13:16, 14:21 would suggest that there was already an expectation of Yahweh's acting against Babylon in a way similar to what is described here, even though rocks to use for this were hard to find at Babylon. Indeed, that Yahweh was expected to act in this oracle makes clear that he is the one whose blessedness is celebrated here. Yahweh must act and ensure justice is done, just as was celebrated in Israel's story in Psalms 135–136. No individuals have the right to take up this action themselves – only Yahweh can act to bring about this justice.

Explanation

For many, words as angry as these seem somehow beneath us, words that cannot be a relevant part of the life of prayer and worship. John Bright (1975: 234–241) perhaps speaks for many in seeing them as something that need to be brought to Christ. It is true that the gospel encourages us to love our enemies and to pray for our persecutors. But perhaps we also need to sit with those who have suffered the loss of home and sustenance in war or similar oppression to allow the pain behind these words to be experienced and understood (cf. Firth 2015a: 86–89). We should first read this psalm in the context provided for it by the Psalter. When we do this, we may appreciate that it understands the need for such prayers to be uttered, while also modelling a pattern where it is Yahweh alone who can bring about such justice. It is to Yahweh, the one who reigns, that the Psalter looks to bring justice within the murkiness of this world (cf. Day 2005: 66–72). In giving over to God the desire and rage that lead to a psalm such as this, we both affirm the reality of his reign while also surrendering the right to continue the cycles of violence (cf. Zenger 1996: 48). A prayer like this may be a means of breaking such cycles, perhaps (paradoxically) preparing us for those who are blessed because they are peacemakers (Matt. 5:9), even as we continue to pray for all continuing manifestations of Babylon to end (Rev. 18).

PSALM 138

Translation

Davidic

1 I will give thanks to you with all my heart,
  I will make melody to you before the gods.

[2]I will bow down towards your holy temple,
I will give thanks for your name,
because of your kindness and faithfulness,
for you have magnified your name above all – your promise.
[3]On the day I called you answered me,
you encouraged me with strength through my being.

[4]All the kings of the earth shall give you thanks, O Yahweh,
when they hear the promises of your mouth.
[5]They shall sing of Yahweh's ways,
because Yahweh's glory is great.
[6]Though Yahweh is exalted, yet he sees the lowly,
but the haughty he knows from afar.

[7]When I walk amid adversity, you preserve my life,
you send forth your hand against the anger of my enemies.
Your right hand rescues me
[8]may Yahweh complete his purpose for me!
O Yahweh, your kindness endures for ever,
do not forsake the works of your hands.

Notes on the text

1. 11QPs[a] includes a voc. 'Yahweh' in the opening line (cf. NRSV), but this is expansionary, missing the intentional deferring of the name. Gk has 'angels' but this is clearly a theologically motivated change. 'Before' (*neged*) could be understood as a competitive challenge to the gods, but this is uncertain. The psalm reflects a world where many gods vied for attention (Creach 2021: 349).

2. The final line is difficult. Gk can be understood as an attempt to understand the same text as MT. Many insert the conj. 'and' to read, 'you have magnified your name and promise above all'. While smoother, we should note that the accents suggest a break before 'your promise'. MT can then be understood as placing these terms in apposition, with Yahweh's promise understood as another way of conceiving his name. Goldingay (2008: 615) offers a similar solution, deleting the second *maqqef* to create a more balanced line.

8. The meaning of the rare verb *yigmōr* is uncertain. The meaning 'avenge' has been proposed (cf. *DCH*, *gmr* II), but the evidence is uncertain. 'Complete' (in the sense of reaching a goal) can also be found in Psalm 57:3.

Form and structure

Psalm 138 commences a collection of Davidic psalms that runs through to Psalm 145. The opening and closing psalms in this unit are marked by a significant body of shared vocabulary (cf. Buysch 2009: 63–64, who also notes key vocabulary links across the collection), moving beyond what may be expected simply because both are praise psalms. Psalms 139–143 can all be understood as complaints (with other elements), while Psalm 144 includes elements of praise and complaint. As a unit, it is bounded with praise while also providing important reflections on Davidic kingship. These elements suggest this final Davidic group is an intentional collection, one marked by key words that connect each poem within it. As its opening poem, Psalm 138 is also connected to the preceding Psalms 135–137. Most notably, where Psalm 137 reflected on the impossibility of singing Yahweh's song on foreign ground, territory associated with another deity, this psalm commences by vowing to sing Yahweh's praise before the gods. Where Psalms 135–136 primarily celebrated Yahweh's reign over the nations by looking back to the exodus and conquest, and Psalm 137 looked for him to express his reign over Babylon in the events around the end of the exile, Psalm 138 anticipates seeing Yahweh's reign over the kings of the earth as they recognize his ways (vv. 4–6). In this, it joins with Psalm 145:10–13, which also looks to Yahweh's universal reign as Yahweh's 'holy ones' (*ḥăsîdekā*) speak of his kingdom so all may know. Thus, the final Davidic collection, though rooted in Yahweh's promise to David, also offers an eschatological focus.

The psalm itself can be understood as a thanksgiving (whether individual or communal) in only the most general of terms (cf. Buysch 2009: 24). It certainly opens with thanksgiving, as the poet gives thanks for Yahweh's response to an earlier appeal (v. 3). However, it also includes elements of the Song of Confidence (vv. 7–8), perhaps consistent with the anticipated praise from the kings of the earth (vv. 4–6), though the expression of confidence also includes an appeal for Yahweh to act further. As such, although thanksgiving is clearly central, it cannot be reduced to this. Rather, thanksgiving is here applied to future challenges, providing reasons for continued trust.

Structurally, the poem can be analysed in three stanzas, each of which develops a different dimension:

1. Promise of thanksgiving (1–3)
2. Hope of wider thanksgiving (4–6)
3. Confidence and plea (7–8)

Comment

Title: For 'Davidic', see on Psalm 3.

1–3. The opening promise of thanksgiving functions within the psalm as its introduction, though it also picks up on the call to thanksgiving in Psalm 136:1–3, especially as Yahweh's 'kindness' (*ḥesed*) is the reason for thanksgiving in both psalms. Where Yahweh's kindness in Psalm 136 was largely a matter of his prior acts for the nation, here his kindness has been experienced by an individual. The thanksgiving promised here is wholehearted, indicating the poet's commitment to this mode of praise. Strikingly, it is to be offered before the 'gods'. If we imagine the thanksgiving as emerging from a time where the psalmist was wrongly accused, then 'gods' could refer to the judges who declared the poet innocent if this sense of *'ĕlōhîm* is granted for Exodus 21:5; 22:6 (cf. Tg). But the psalm's universal interest would suggest that this is too narrow a reading, so it is better to understand the 'gods' as either the divine council (see on Ps. 82:1) or the gods of the nations. Reference to Yahweh's superiority over the gods (Pss 135:5; 136:2–3) plus the universal implications of his reign within this psalm suggest the gods of the nations are in view. The poet's imagined situation is one where the gods of the nations are visible, perhaps why it is possible to promise to bow down towards Yahweh's holy temple and give thanks to his name. Offering praise before the gods of the nations testifies to them of the reality of Yahweh's kindness and faithfulness, both of which are fundamental to his character (cf. Exod. 34:6–7). In the light of the preceding psalms, it becomes clear that Yahweh has acted for the psalmist, doing what the gods of the nations could not (cf. Ps. 135:15–18). Hence, Yahweh is reported to have magnified his name above all. Although the final clause is difficult (cf. 'Notes on the text'), it seems best to understand the promise here as explaining Yahweh's name. That is, Yahweh's character (represented by his name) is demonstrated by his faithfulness to his promise. This is what Yahweh did on the day the psalmist called out, granting life and encouragement with strength through the psalmist's 'being' (*nepeš*).

4–6. Rather than describing the previous distress where Yahweh acted, the second stanza looks to a more universal thanksgiving, as the kings of the earth also give thanks (cf. Ps. 72:11). The name 'Yahweh' has been withheld to this point (cf. 'Notes on the text', v. 1) to emphasize this universal dimension, though doing so also sharpens the political dimension that undermines all other claims of power (cf. Tucker 2014: 125–128). The psalmist offering thanksgiving before the gods is unusual, but the kings of the earth giving thanks to Yahweh is also remarkable. All would be expected to have their own gods, but Yahweh is now the one they thank. This thanksgiving will come about when they hear Yahweh's promise, picking up a key term from the first stanza. What the poet saw as evidence that confirmed Israel's understanding of Yahweh's character becomes reason for the kings to offer thanks. Indeed, they will sing of Yahweh's ways because of the greatness of his glory. It is possible to understand verse 6b as quoting the words of their song of praise (so Hossfeld and Zenger 2011: 526). On balance, it is more probable that Yahweh's glory provides a reason for their thanksgiving, as this would mean that verses 5–6 are paralleled (each begins with a *kî* clause) in providing reasons for thanksgiving. The second reason emerges from recognition of Yahweh's glory, a motif that points to his exaltation in verse 6. Though Yahweh is exalted, he has regard for the lowly, modelling the pattern kings were meant to demonstrate, while not giving the haughty the attention they might expect (cf. Ps. 113:4–9; Isa. 2:12–17). Yahweh's response to the poet is evidence of this, a further reason for the kings to give thanks.

7–8. The final stanza integrates confidence that echoes Psalm 23:4. The confidence is expressed in verse 7, where the poet speaks in terms of a journey amid adversity, though the journey here is probably a metaphor for life more generally. The adversity is clearly serious since Yahweh's action is to preserve life. The need for protection is also clear in the mention of the enemies' anger directed at the poet. Yet in this threatening situation, Yahweh puts forth his hand, saving with his right hand. Though the situation is hypothetical, the psalmist is confident that the one who has responded before will continue to demonstrate his kindness and faithfulness. The psalmist also knows there are other challenges, and so the psalm ends with a plea. Although the opening part of verse 8 could be a further statement of confidence (cf. NIV), the final appeal that Yahweh not abandon the works of his hands makes it more likely that we should read this as a wish. This wish is grounded in Yahweh's enduring kindness, echoing the refrain from Psalm 136. It is precisely because Yahweh is marked by enduring kindness that the psalmist can make this appeal, something that will be further evidence to the kings.

Explanation

Where the community in Psalm 137 could not sing Yahweh's song, Yahweh's praise is now sung before the gods, and thus to all the nations. Yahweh has acted and thanksgiving is needed. This thanksgiving testifies to the gods of the nations, pointing to Yahweh's faithfulness, character and promise. That this message can be proclaimed in praise before the gods also means the psalm anticipates the time where the kings of the earth also give Yahweh praise, seeing in him the model of what their own rule should be. That Yahweh has acted also means that the psalmist can be confident in future times of struggle. Yahweh's character has been demonstrated, and though this does not mean there can no longer be times of struggle, it is possible to face those times with confidence.

Writing to the Philippians from prison, Paul could express this same confidence for himself (Phil. 1:6), while also encouraging the congregation to live without anxiety in their own struggles (Phil. 4:6).

PSALM 139

Translation

The director's. Davidic. A melody.

1Yahweh, you have searched me and you know!
2You know when I sit and when I rise,
  you discern my thoughts from afar,
3you sift out my wandering and my lying down,
  you are familiar with all my ways,
4for a word is not on my tongue,
  yet you know all of it, Yahweh!
5You confine me from behind and ahead,
  you have placed your palms upon me.
6Such knowledge is too wonderful for me,
  it is exalted, I cannot attain to it.

7Where can I go from your Spirit,
  and where can I flee from your presence?
8If I ascend to the heavens, you are there,
  if I lay down in Sheol, there you would be!
9If I rose on the wings of the dawn,
  and settled on the far side of the sea,
10even there your hand would guide me,
  your right hand would take hold of me.
11I said, 'Surely the darkness will grip me,
  and the light become night around me,'
12but even the darkness is not dark for you,
  the night will shine like the day,
  as is the darkness so the light.

13For you made my inmost being,
  you wove me together in my mother's womb,
14I confess you because fearfully have I been set apart,
  wonderful are your works,
  truly I know it!
15My bones were not hidden from you
  when I was made in the secret place,
  woven together in the deepest parts of the earth.

[16]Your eyes saw my embryo,
  and in your book were they all written,
days that were ordained,
  before one of them was.
[17]How precious are your thoughts to me, God,
  how vast is their sum!
[18]If I were to count them all they would be more than the grains of sand,
  when I awake, I am still with you.

[19]If only you would slay the wicked, God!
  People of bloodshed, turn away from me!
[20]They speak of you deceptively,
  lifting you up with vanity against you.
[21]Do I not hate those who hate you, O Yahweh,
  and loathe those who rebel against you?
[22]I hate them with a perfect hatred,
  they have become my enemies.

[23]Search me, O God, and know my heart,
  examine me and know my anxious thoughts,
[24]and see if the way of idolatry is in me
  and guide me in the perpetual way.

Notes on the text

11. Many versions follow Sym (*episkepasei mē*) and read 'cover' (e.g. ESV), but MT is coherent and the changes required to explain the variation too extensive to be persuasive (similarly, A. P. Ross 2016: 813).

14. Hebr. *niplêtî* is often understood as a reference to God's making of the poet but is better understood here to mean 'seen as distinct', hence set apart.

20. The second half of the verse is difficult. 'Your cities' is usually emended in modern translations, but the versions did not find it troubling. This could be because of an Aramaizing root meaning 'your foes', but this is not entirely clear, and even though the psalm has a number of Aramaisms, it is better to work with known meanings. However, a number of MSS read 'against you' (a very small change in Hebrew) and this is tentatively followed here in the sense of opposition. There is versional support for understanding *nāśu'* as a defective form of *nāśĕ'û*, yielding the above translation. For the possibility that this may also allude to idolatry, see Holman 2007.

24. Hebr. *'ōṣeb* difficult. Gk already shows the difficulty, treating it as 'lawlessness' (*anomia*), though this could be a paraphrase rather than a different text. Elsewhere, it refers to 'pain' (Isa. 14:3), so could be rendered 'painful way'. But Tg already reads it as 'idol' (similarly, Jerome), a sense seen in Isaiah 48:5 (and possibly Hos. 10:6), and that sense works better here. If so, then (with Allen 2002: 318; Goldingay 2008: 639) we could understand *'ôlām* as 'ancient' (cf. Jer. 6:16; 18:15), but this loses sight of the fact that the psalmist anticipates this ancient path as also leading forward; so, 'perpetual' attempts to capture the past and present (cf. Buysch 2009: 75).

Form and structure

Psalm 138:6 pointed to Yahweh's knowledge of all people, and that knowledge is now applied much more specifically to an individual speaker in this psalm, where this knowledge is intensified (vv. 2–4, 7–12). That knowledge expressed itself in his right hand delivering the poet in Psalm 138:7, and it is Yahweh's right hand that grasps the speaker here, even in places otherwise thought to be away from Yahweh's control (vv. 7–12). The opening of Psalm 138 also invited thanksgiving, and that is offered here (v. 14; note that 'confess' is the same verb as 'give thanks' in Ps. 138:1–2, 4). Although these psalms are clearly distinct in many ways, these thematic and linguistic links suggest they have been intentionally placed together (cf. Vesco 2006, 2: 1290).

As with Psalm 138, questions of Psalm 139's literary form are far from settled (cf. Gerstenberger 2001: 405), largely because it draws on a wide range of elements. Reflections on creation and Yahweh's enduring presence would certainly be at home in a wisdom setting (Schüngel-Straumann 1973), though it is perhaps insufficient to classify this as a wisdom poem. The focal point in this process has been to determine the relationship of verses 1–18, 23–24 with verses 19–22. It is, of course, perfectly possible to move from verse 18 to verse 23 without any sense of loss, something encouraged by some lectionaries that recommend the omission of these verses. But setting aside suggestions of multiple psalms having been brought together (e.g. Briggs and Briggs 1907, 1: 491), it is better to ask how we read the psalm as a unit. It should be noted that its only imperatives occur after the imprecation in verses 19–22, suggesting that it has created the setting from which Yahweh should search the psalmist. If so, Yahweh is searching to see if the imprecation represents the psalmist's real loyalty, though the doxological material has already shown that there is no time or place where the psalmist can hide from Yahweh. If this test is failed, then the effect of the imprecation is that Yahweh should slay the poet. That is, the psalmist should only live if found to be fully loyal to Yahweh, a loyalty apparently in question as the issue of idolatry is raised in the closing appeal. If so, we can read the psalm with the prayers of the accused (see on Ps. 7; similarly, Seybold 1996: 515). One can therefore make a technical case for its being a complaint psalm (Firth 2005b: 43–45), though in fact it lacks many features typical of the form. However, a background in the prayers of the accused would also account for the deep vein of ambiguity that runs through the poem (Firth 2019b; cf. Buysch 2009: 76–77), where many elements of God's presence could be comforting or troubling, with their impact dependent on how the one who prays the psalm stands before Yahweh on the question of loyalty.

Despite attempts to see the psalm as composite, the text is best read as a unity (cf. Dannell 1951: 22), albeit one with complex linkages across the whole (see Holman 1971). It is commonly divided into four stanzas (e.g. Rice 1980: 63–67; A. Wagner 2007), though given the major caesura at verse 18 it is better to see it containing two stanzas, the first containing three strophes. There is also an inclusio between verse 1 and verses 23–24 on the theme of Yahweh's searching of the poet. I therefore analyse the poem as follows:

1. Yahweh and the poet (1–18)
   a. Yahweh's knowledge of the poet (1–6)
   b. Yahweh's presence with the poet (7–12)
   c. Yahweh's formation of the poet (13–18)
2. Appeal to Yahweh (19–24)
   a. Imprecation (19–22)
   b. Appeal (23–24)

Comment

Title: For 'The director's', see on Psalm 4. For 'Davidic' and 'A melody', see on Psalm 3. In Book 5, both 'The director's' and 'A melody' occur only in the Davidic psalms.

1–6. The psalm opens with a strophe focused on how Yahweh has known the poet. Following the opening address to Yahweh, the strophe opens with verbs that point to how Yahweh has engaged with the poet in the past. Although a pf. verb in Hebrew does not have to refer to the past, in a narrative it typically does, and the fact that it is followed by a converted imp. strongly suggests a reference to the past. The poet is pointing to what Yahweh has done and therefore already knows. Yahweh has searched the poet and knows. What Yahweh knows is not initially stated, but the same verb is taken up in verse 2 to indicate that Yahweh knows when the poet sits or rises, verbs that here stand for the whole of life's experiences. That is, Yahweh knows all the psalmist does. More than this, Yahweh also knows the psalmist's thoughts from afar, a term related to Yahweh's response to the haughty in Psalm 138:6. Yahweh's knowledge of the poet is thus intimate and practical. For the innocent, this is undoubtedly good news, but less so for the guilty. This pattern continues in the balance of the strophe, as Yahweh sifts out the places where the psalmist both wanders and lies down, a form of knowledge that implies assessment (the verb is elsewhere used of sifting wheat (Ruth 3:2), before noting that his knowledge of the poet's thoughts means Yahweh knows what will be said even before the word has reached the tongue. This leads to the poet's first reflection in verses 5–6. First, Yahweh is said to hem in the psalmist on all sides, laying his hand on the poet. From the perspective of protection, this is good news, but the verb here can also point to oppression. The effect of Yahweh's knowledge depends on the nature of the poet's relationship to Yahweh. It is then observed that Yahweh's knowledge transcends anything the psalmist can truly grasp. Yahweh's knowledge is beyond human comprehension, so there are dimensions of Yahweh's knowledge humans can never grasp, even if some can be understood. Yahweh knows all about the psalmist, but the psalmist can never know all about Yahweh.

7–12. The second strophe builds on the reflection in the first. Given that Yahweh hems the poet in, is it possible to flee from Yahweh's presence (cf. Amos 9:2–4)? This is raised as a hypothetical question in verse 7, with Yahweh's Spirit and presence understood as largely equivalent (Grant 2011). Possible destinations for fleeing from Yahweh are then noted, consistently discovering that one cannot flee from Yahweh. These possibilities are all explored in terms of opposites to show that in whatever direction one flees, Yahweh is always present. The first opposites occur in verse 8, contrasting the heavens (here referring to the skies more than Yahweh's dwelling place) and Sheol. One is as high as possible, and the other the lowest place, but in both the psalmist will encounter Yahweh, even though Sheol is more typically thought of as somewhere separate from Yahweh (e.g. Ps. 6:5; though Tromp [1969: 199–200] misses the rhetorical goal of the passage in claiming a theological problem of Yahweh's presence here, since Yahweh is not prohibited from Sheol; cf. Goldingay 2008: 632). Verses 9–10 then contrast the east with the west, with the wings of the dawn a poetic reference to morning and the east (cf. Ps. 57:8), while the far side of the sea would refer to the distant west. One cannot escape Yahweh on a vertical axis, and the same is true of the horizontal. No matter where the poet goes, Yahweh's hand guides, his right hand grasps. The final contrast is light and darkness in verses 11–12. Here, the psalmist contemplates the possibility of being gripped by the darkness, suggesting it may keep Yahweh away, or that the dark of night may at least allow the poet to remain hidden. But this too is impossible. Light and dark have an impact on humans, but are no barrier to Yahweh. Separation from Yahweh is impossible, and hence his knowledge of the poet cannot be limited.

13–18. If there is no place where Yahweh has not known the poet, is there a time when this may be the case? The options here are more limited since Yahweh has perfect knowledge of the psalmist's life; so instead, the poem turns to a time before the psalmist was born. Here again, there is no limit to Yahweh's knowledge since Yahweh formed the psalmist's inmost being (lit. 'kidneys'), weaving all together in the womb. Thus, Yahweh is confessed, a confession here that includes thanksgiving, but that also recognizes Yahweh's continued interaction with the poet. This interaction recognizes the poet's own distinctiveness, a distinctiveness evident in all Yahweh's works, something the poet knows. Yahweh knew the poet in the womb, and though this was a secret place in the ancient world, it was not secret from Yahweh. Remarkably, the womb is here described as the deepest parts of the earth, perhaps because it was as inaccessible to the ancients as those places. That time is central to this strophe is then shown in verse 16. Yahweh's eyes saw both the poet's embryo in the womb and all the days of the poet's life even before they were written down. That is, Yahweh knew the embryo before birth and granted all the days the poet would live even before they happened. Time is thus no barrier to Yahweh either. Because of this, the psalmist ponders the wonder of Yahweh's thoughts, treating them like an algorithm with a massive answer. Yet there is a key ambiguity here in that such thoughts could be either precious or costly, though this is perhaps clearer for the cognate noun. Yahweh's perennial knowledge of the psalmist could be costly for those who know they have lacked loyalty, though it is a source of encouragement for the loyal. Even if there were a time when Yahweh's thoughts could be counted (an act here clearly impossible), the poet would still be in his presence. Hence, the first stanza shows that there is no time or place where one is beyond Yahweh's knowledge and presence, and the one who has searched and known the psalmist continues to do so.

19–22. The second stanza opens with a strophe that is crucial to the poem. Given that the psalmist has never been separate from Yahweh and beyond his knowledge, the wish that Yahweh might slay the wicked, here defined as those who enact bloodshed, is effectively a self-curse. Within the psalms, the wicked are defined in various ways (starting, of course, in the contrast with the righteous in Ps. 1), but they are fundamentally those who have set themselves against Yahweh. That the wicked here are 'people of bloodshed' does not mean that they are literally killers, though the fact that opposing Yahweh is the path to death means they are moving in that direction. That they have set themselves against Yahweh is evident in their speech since it speaks deceptively of Yahweh. The language here is evocative of the Decalogue (Deut. 5:11) as they promote deceptive claims about Yahweh. Death is not the only possibility for these people since they are also told to turn aside from the psalmist. The poet is not to be associated with them. Hence, in verses 21–22 the psalmist identifies absolutely with Yahweh, hating with perfect hatred those who hate Yahweh, loathing those who rebel against him. The language is forceful. It is essential that the psalmist be distinguished from the wicked, and this distinction rather than any emotion is crucial (Schaefer 2001: 328; cf. Peels 2008). Hence, the wicked have also become the poet's enemies. The psalmist, being entirely separate from the wicked, identifies with Yahweh alone.

23–24. Here we reach the final appeal, the prayer presented to Yahweh. Yahweh has already searched the psalmist (v. 1), but in the light of all that has been said, the poet asks to be searched again. The request is that the psalmist be shown to be loyal to Yahweh as Yahweh knows the heart, testing anxious thoughts. Here, the 'heart' refers to the poet's will and commitment. Yahweh is to search and know that the poet's desire is to be loyal. But this is extended by the note that Yahweh is to test the psalmist (cf. Ps. 7:9) and know even anxious thoughts (or possibly doubts). Are even the poet's weakest points loyal to Yahweh? This is to be tested. The focus of this is made clear in verse 24, where the possibility of idolatry emerges. If the psalm is a prayer of the accused, then idolatry is the charge, and this also explains why loyalty to Yahweh is so important. Wickedness and idolatry go together, and the psalmist wants Yahweh to see if idolatry is present. The assumption of the prayer is that it is not, but this further test will declare the psalmist's innocence, which is why the closing request is that the psalmist be led in the right way (echoing Ps. 1:6), the way that always was and always will be right.

Explanation

In 2 Corinthians 6:14, Paul asks whether light and darkness can have fellowship. The answer there is clearly that they cannot. A similar theme runs through this psalm (even if it uses the metaphor of light and darkness differently from Paul), though it is important that it is not reduced to abstracted theological motifs (Wallace 2006: 182). Throughout, the psalm considers Yahweh in terms of how he relates to the psalmist. The truths about Yahweh affirmed here – his knowledge, his presence with his people, that he is unbounded by time – are applied to the desire of the poet to be shown to be innocent of a charge of disloyalty. Most importantly, the psalm wants Yahweh to act upon the intimate knowledge he has and declare the psalmist as one loyal to him while accepting that however loyal he has been in the past, there is always more to be done. The psalmist, in Paul's terms, wants only to live in the light and for this to be affirmed by God. The psalm may well derive from the prayers of the accused, but the need to live as one loyal to God is not here restricted to a ritual in the temple. Rather, the psalm continues to challenge all who pray it to understand the call to be searched by God is at the same time a call to live wholly for him, a life in which there is light and no darkness as all of it is lived before God.

PSALM 140

Translation

The director's. A melody. Davidic.

1Rescue me, O Yahweh, from evil people,
protect me from violent folk,
2who plan evil things in the heart,
they stir up conflicts continually.
3They sharpen their tongue like a serpent,
a viper's venom is behind their lips. *Selah*.

4Guard me, O Yahweh, from the hands of the wicked,
protect me from violent folk,
who plan to trip my steps.
5The arrogant laid out a trap for me, with cords,
they spread a net by the side of the path,
they have set a snare for me. *Selah*.

6I said to Yahweh, 'You are my God,
listen favourably to the sound of my supplications.
7Yahweh, my Lord, the strength of my salvation,
you covered my head on the day of battle.
8Do not grant the desires of the wicked, O Yahweh,
do not enable their plan – they will be exalted! *Selah*.

9The heads of those who surround me –
may the trouble of their lips cover them.
10Let burning coals drop on them with fire,
let it throw them into the bottomless pit, they shall not rise.
11Let not the slanderer be established in the land,
let evil forcefully hunt down the violent.'

12I know that Yahweh enacts judgement for the afflicted,
justice for the poor.
13Surely, the righteous shall give thanks to your name,
the upright dwell in your presence.

Notes on the text

1. Hebr. *mēʾîš ḥămāsîm* is a compound pl. (*WHS* §14).
2. Reading *gwr* II, 'Attack, show hostility'.
9. Following Q and several MSS.

11. Hebr. *madḥēmâ* is a hapax.
12. With many MSS following Q.

Form and structure

Where Psalm 139 contained only some elements of the complaint psalm, this poem is a much clearer example of the category. Despite this variation, these two psalms share an identical title save for the change in order of 'The director's' and 'Davidic', suggesting a close link. This is confirmed by the fact that the wicked of Psalm 139:19 continue to threaten the psalmist (v. 5; Buysch [2009: 157] regards this as a terminological bridge between them), which is why Yahweh is asked not to grant their desires (v. 8). Although not using identical terms, the 'people of bloodshed' (Ps. 139:19) can be identified here with the violent (vv. 1, 4, 11). If we are correct in reading Psalm 139 in the context of an appeal for a judgement of innocence, then the closing affirmation of Yahweh's justice here (v. 12) could provide additional affirmation of this. Although not directly related to the previous psalm, the three occurrences of *selah* in this poem (vv. 3, 5, 8) also point to the place of this psalm within the final David collection (Pss 138–145). All but three (Hab. 3:3, 9, 13) of seventy-four occurrences of this term are in Psalms, but the last one was Psalm 89:45. However, the three here are joined by one in Psalm 143:6. Given the absence of *selah* in Book 4 and through Book 5 to this point, it seems significant that we should have a further cluster here. Whether it has any significance beyond this point is difficult to say, but it is a linguistic clue that the final David collection has a unity of its own.

As noted, Psalm 140 can be understood as a complaint (introducing a run that continues to Ps. 143), as evident from the appeals to Yahweh in verses 1, 3, as well as the prayer against the wicked (v. 8). Unlike some complaints, the circumstances are not evident (despite attempts to link the emphasis on speech to the prayers of the accused; see Beyerlin 1970: 33; van Gemeren 2008: 965), being concerned with the wicked more generally, perhaps explaining why it also introduces some deviations. As such, there are some echoes of Psalm 1 and its contrast between the righteous and the wicked (cf. Estes 2019: 563), suggesting some awareness of wisdom themes (cf. Hossfeld and Zenger 2011: 551). This could receive further support from the deed–consequence pattern and mention of burning coals (vv. 9–11), although such motifs also occur across the psalms (e.g. Ps. 7:15); so, we cannot place such patterns into a specific setting.

The poem employs key words (e.g. evil, violent, plan, wicked, lips) across the whole, while verses 1b and 5b are identical. Hunting imagery is also used across the poem. The three occurrences of *selah* are structurally significant, though the first separates the two appeals, while the third divides the report of what has previously been said to Yahweh. It thus consistently provides a break, but not always at the same level. Rather, the timing of speech within the poem provides its main division, with verses 1–5, 12–13 reporting present speech and verses 6–11 past speech. Although there is some evidence of a chiastic arrangement (Allen 2002: 335, who also notes that poems can have multiple structures), it can be analysed in three stanzas, the first two each containing two strophes:

1. Appeals to Yahweh (1–5)
   a. Appeal for deliverance (1–3)
   b. Appeal for protection (4–5)
2. Prior speech to Yahweh (6–11)
   a. Confidence and requests (6–8)
   b. Deeds and consequences (9–11)
3. Enduring confidence (12–13)

Comment

Title: For 'The director's', see on Psalm 4. For 'A melody' and 'Davidic', see on Psalm 3.

1–3. The psalm opens with an immediate and forceful plea for rescue by Yahweh. The opening verse is structured as a chiasm save for the voc. 'O Yahweh', so verbs for rescue open and close the initial appeal. This also accents the voc., making clear that Yahweh is the one to rescue and protect the poet from evil people, those marked by violence. They are further defined in verse 2 as those who devise harm, stirring up conflict. This involves both their inward disposition (their thoughts) and their actions. This is not necessarily directed against the psalmist but rather describes their general attitudes and deeds. However, one aspect of their evil is defined in verse 3 as damaging speech. The sharpening of their tongue 'like a serpent' compares their speech to a serpent's fang, preparing for mention of venom beneath their lips (cf. Rom. 3:13). The warfare they provoke is marked by speech that is damaging and potentially deadly. As such, they pose a serious threat to the social order, which is why Yahweh is asked to rescue and protect the psalmist.

4–5. The second appeal develops themes from the first. Verse 4a is structured the same way as verse 1, with a chiasm save for the voc. 'O Yahweh', while verses 1b and 4b are identical. There is development from the first appeal in that both verbs this time are protective, and the evil people are now the wicked. As before, a relative clause defines the wicked, this time as those planning to make the psalmist stumble. The generalized threat of the opening strophe is now directed at the poet. The mention of 'steps' prepares for the 'way' metaphor in verse 5. Although the exact details are not altogether clear, the general thought is that they lay traps beside the path, catching the poet in a net or snare, making the psalmist their prey. The path here refers to the poet's way of life, but this is a vivid expression of how the wicked organize themselves in socially destructive ways, acting against those who live out the faithfulness desired in Psalm 139. If the faithful live for Yahweh, then he is the one who needs to protect them against such attacks.

6–9. The second stanza moves from the present appeal to a report of something the poet has previously said to Yahweh (though Goldingay [2008: 647] suggests we read the verb as a present declaration), the recalling of which gives grounds for the confidence with which the psalm ends. This previous statement covers the whole stanza (though R. A. Jacobson 2004: 23 accepts either 'You are my God' or to the end of v. 8), though it is divided into two parts by the *selah*. It is possible to take this in the present tense (so ESV), but the introduction of a pf. verb at this point makes the past tense more probable. As such, these verses report a previous prayer, one that provides additional reason for Yahweh to act. The report begins with the poet's previous declaration of loyalty, one consistent with Psalm 139:19–22, even if phrased very differently. Yahweh is confessed as God, and therefore was asked to listen favourably to the poet's supplications, a term which indicates that these are appeals for grace. The confession of the relationship with Yahweh continues into verse 7, where Yahweh is described both as 'my Lord' and 'the strength of my salvation'. As Lord, Yahweh is responsible to those who serve him, and he is the one who has the strength to save from those who attack in various ways. This was previously demonstrated when he protected the poet in conflict, but this pattern of protection needs to be continued in future, with Yahweh's neither granting the wicked their desires nor enabling their plans. Although the final verb of verse 8 is awkward, the sense seems to be that a failure to do so would see them exalted.

10–11. Following the *selah*, the second strophe picks up on the request of verse 9. Admittedly, these verses are difficult to construe exactly, but they probably represent a series of requests that develop the implication of verse 9. If Yahweh is not to grant the desires of the wicked, then they should receive back what they have done. The imprecation is thus calibrated to request a punishment that fits the crime, with the damage done by their speech highlighted by further mention of their lips. What they have spoken should come back on them. The details of verse 10 are much disputed, but the burning coals here are probably to be understood as standing for shame (cf. Prov. 25:22; Rom. 12:20; similarly, Collins 2022: 664). Such shame is like being cast into a deep pit, one from which they cannot rise. The damage done by such speech is again addressed in verse 11, which asks that the 'slanderer' (lit. 'man of tongue') not be established in the land, while evil itself is to hunt down the violent. That is, the damage such people do is itself to come back against them, meaning that those who have suffered do not themselves enact retribution.

12–13. Reflection on the earlier prayer provides enduring confidence. That was a prayer Yahweh heard, and therefore the poet moves to declare what is now known – that Yahweh executes justice for those in need. The implication is that the wicked (from whom protection is needed) are the socially powerful, but if Yahweh does not let the wicked achieve their ambitions, then the poor may have continued hope. The present threat against the poor needs to be set in the context of what is known about Yahweh. Hence, the psalm closes with the assurance that the righteous will give thanks to Yahweh's name, while the upright will dwell before him.

Explanation

The possibilities and perils of speech lie at the heart of this psalm. The poet is threatened by malicious speech and so cries out to Yahweh for rescue and protection. But having done so, the psalm turns to earlier speech, a prayer that confessed Yahweh as God and asked him to work in ways that brought justice against the wicked because of the social damage they do. The psalm then closes with words of confidence, certain that Yahweh acts for the needy and that the righteous shall give thanks to him and dwell before him. In short, the psalm recognizes the ways speech can destabilize the hope of the righteous set out in Psalm 1, but also remembers that prayer is speech that calls on Yahweh to bring about the stability that is needed, continuing to provide hope for the poor. The possibilities and perils of speech are worked out further in James 3:1–12, joining with this psalm in encouraging believers to offer speech to one another that is consistent with the speech we offer to and about God, while also tying this to a concern for the poor (Jas 1:26–27).

PSALM 141

Translation

A melody. Davidic.

[1]O Yahweh, I call on you, hasten to me,
listen favourably to my voice when I cry to you!
[2]Let my prayer be established, incense before you,
the lifting of my hands the evening offering.

[3]Set a guard, O Yahweh, on my mouth,
keep watch over the door of my lips.
[4]Do not incline my mind to an evil word,

to the practice of wantonness in wickedness,
with those who practise injustice,
may I not taste their delicacies.

5Let the righteous strike me in kindness,
and let one rebuke me,
it is fine oil, let my head not refuse it,
for my prayer is still against their evil deeds.
6Their judges are thrown on the sides of the crag,
and they will hear my utterances because they are pleasant.

7Like when the earth is ploughed and split,
our bones are scattered at the mouth of Sheol.
8For my eyes are towards you, O Yahweh my Lord,
in you have I sought refuge,
do not pour out my life.
9Guard me from the control of the trap they have laid out for me,
and the snares of those who practise injustice.
10Let the wicked fall into their own nets,
while I utterly pass by.

Notes on the text

5. The verse (indeed all of vv. 5–6) is rightly described by deClaissé-Walford (2014: 973) as 'cryptic'. This may partly be caused by the retention of northern idioms (Rendsburg 1990: 99–102). Weiser (1962: 811) does not even offer a translation of verses 6–7. The above attempts to make sense of MT, largely because proposed emendations (see e.g. Kraus 1989: 525) do not offer anything obviously superior and MT is supported by 11QPs[a]. Note that there is a play on the meaning of *rōʾš*, with the initial meaning of 'superior, fine' (with Allen 2002: 339–340) and the second referring to the head.

6. For *yād* as 'side', see 1 Samuel 4:18; Proverbs 8:23.

9. Hebr. *yād* here picks up on verse 6, but this time in the sense of being in the power of something, though also the flaps on a trap's side that hold the prey.

Form and structure

The second in the sequence of complaints (Pss 140–143), this psalm also includes numerous verbal links to Psalm 140, including the contrast between the righteous and the wicked (Pss 140:4, 8, 13; 141:4, 5, 10; with the 'wicked' here continuing the terminological bridge from Ps.

139). Along with this, the emphasis on speech in Psalm 140:3, 6 recurs in Psalm 141:3, 6, while the hunting imagery from Psalm 140:5 is picked up in Psalm 141:9–10. Importantly, Yahweh is asked in both psalms to protect the poet (Pss 140:1, 4; 141:9), and they also share the theological conviction that Yahweh should ensure that the deeds of the wicked rebound on them. As such, these two psalms seem to have been placed together. Since the connections with Psalms 142–143, though still present, are weaker (while those psalms also share significant links), we can perhaps assume that these four complaints are presented as two pairs, with the distinctive title of Psalm 142 marking it off from Psalms 140–141.

Psalm 141 is clearly a complaint psalm, which continues the wisdom overtones noted in Psalm 141 (Hossfeld and Zenger 2011: 557–558; Longman 2014: 458–459). Although primarily the prayer of an individual, a communal aspect emerges in verse 7. Where Psalm 140 had a significant focus on the effects of speech of others, this time there is a greater focus on the effects of wanton acts that may emerge from the poet's speech. Speech and act clearly go together, and the poet wishes to be kept from such things because they lead to injustice. The main threat comes from what the poet may do, for which restraint is needed from Yahweh (cf. Buysch 2009: 210–211).

The psalm uses a range of structuring devices, and as with Psalm 141 it is possible to analyse it in several ways (see Allen 2002: 342–343), something not helped by the obscurity of parts of verses 5–7. However, it can be analysed in three strophes, the second containing two strophes:

1. Opening appeal (1–2)
2. Petitions (3–6)
   a. Prayer for self-limitation (3–4)
   b. Prayer for righteous reproof (5–6)
3. Confidence (7–10)

Comment

Title: For 'A melody' and 'Davidic', see on Psalm 3.

1–2. The appeal begins by addressing Yahweh, noting that he is the one to whom the psalmist calls. The first verse is bound by this observation into which the content of the appeal is presented. The call contains two imperatives, asking Yahweh to come quickly to the psalmist and to listen favourably to the appeal. Requests for Yahweh to come swiftly have previously occurred in Psalms 22:19; 40:13; 70:1, 5; 71:12. In those instances, the threat was external to the psalmist, but in this case the threat is internal, though that will not become clear until the petitions. Rather, the imperatives point to the speaker's urgent need for Yahweh to respond favourably. This need is explored in verse 2 through images which ask that prayer be treated in the same way as cultic acts, making the prayer equivalent to the offering of incense (or perhaps the smoke of the burnt offering) before Yahweh, the hands lifted in prayer the same as the evening sacrifice (cf. Num. 28:3–8; Ps. 134:2). As Mays (1994b: 431) has noted, prayer, incense and the evening offering are joined elsewhere (e.g. Ezra 9:5), so there is no setting of prayer against these acts of worship (against Weiser 1962: 811). Rather, the request is that prayer be seen as a sincere act of worship to which Yahweh should respond.

3–4. The opening petition indicates the key need. Yahweh is asked to guard the psalmist's mouth and lips. The language here evokes the requests of Psalm 141:4, but with the important shift now towards what the psalmist may say. The protective guard that Yahweh is to set will prevent damaging speech from proceeding from the psalmist, with sealed lips likened to a closed door. But speech does not exist in isolation, so this is extended in verse 4 with a request that Yahweh guide the poet's thought life, with the mind (lit. 'heart') to be kept from anything evil. Here, the semantic breadth of the word *dābār* is deployed, since it can mean 'word' or 'thing'. The earlier references to speech suggest it should mean 'word' here, but the subsequent references are to the wanton acts from which the poet wants to be kept, so 'thing' is also possible (cf. Booij 2005: 98). That is, the poet recognizes that wrong thought can lead to wrong acts. Such acts are commonly with a group (cf. Prov. 24:1), so the request also implies that the poet should be kept from such association, even to the extent of not tasting their delicacies since these would themselves be the fruit of injustice.

5–6. The second petition is difficult because of the uncertainty about aspects of the text (cf. 'Notes on the text'). However, we should probably understand it to offer a parallel to the first petition except that where Yahweh was asked to prevent the psalmist from inappropriate speech and acts, now a righteous person is to strike the psalmist, itself an act of 'kindness' (*ḥesed*). The thought is similar to Proverbs 27:6, with the righteous person striking the petitioner so that they might not join with the wicked, as also clear from the fact that they are to offer a rebuke. The righteous person here is to act for Yahweh, so there is no contrast with the initial petition but rather acceptance that it could be fulfilled in multiple ways. Such striking or a rebuke would, for the petitioner, be a desirable outcome, like fine oil placed on the head, because it would match the fact that the prayer is still against the deeds of the wicked. The wicked apparently have their own judges, perhaps those who justify their choices rather than necessarily being judicial officers, though of course many judicial matters were resolved locally. These judges are imagined as being thrown on the sides of a crag, presumably losing their place of security and authority while still hearing what the psalmist says. This speech is distinguished from the malicious speech because it is pleasant. Judges aligned with the wicked (whether in formal positions or not) may not appreciate such speech if it prevents their designs, but from the poet's perspective such speech is pleasant because it aligns with Yahweh's purposes.

7–10. There remains an urgent need for Yahweh to act because the poet's own group (the righteous) are shown as suffering, with their bones at Sheol's mouth (unless, with A. P. Ross [2016: 852] we understand the speaker here to be the judges who have gone down the crag), nearly in the place of the dead, scattered around like ploughed up soil. The temptation to join the wicked is strong because of the suffering of the righteous, making it urgent that Yahweh act to prevent the poet from joining them. Although the final stanza includes appeals, these are within a context of confidence. The threat comes from the temptation to join the wicked, and the psalmist's eyes are directed to Yahweh, who is also called 'Lord', to avoid this. As 'Lord', Yahweh needs to act for his people, and this is why the poet has come to him to find refuge. As the one who provides refuge, Yahweh is also asked not to pour out the psalmist's life. As well as guarding the psalmist's mouth, Yahweh is also to provide protection from the 'hands' of the trap laid out for the poet. The 'hands' here are the sides of the trap that spring up around the prey, but also point to the control the trap then has of the one caught. Yahweh needs to guard the poet from this trap, a trap laid by the hunters who are here those who practise injustice, the people from whom the poet needed to be kept in verse 4. Rather than taking control of the psalmist, the request is that the wicked fall into the nets they have laid out, catching them in their own traps. By contrast, the psalmist will confidently pass by, secure in the knowledge of Yahweh's guarding presence (cf. Ps. 1:6).

Explanation

For many psalms, the threat to righteousness comes from others. But this prayer is among that rarer group which reflects on the possibility that the threat to righteousness comes from within. Although details within the psalm mean that certainty on all points is impossible, there is enough that makes this clear. Its pairing with Psalm 140 also means that we encounter the threat of dangerous speech from others (Ps. 140) and then the threat of speech (as a manifestation of a life not committed to righteousness) that comes from within. There is often social pressure that leads in this direction (cf. 1 Cor. 15:33). This prayer also asks to be kept from concluding that the righteous should join the wicked simply because the latter appear to prevail (cf. McCann 1996: 1243). Here, then, is a reflective prayer that not only asks not to be led into temptation, but seeks the greater righteousness Jesus encouraged (Matt. 5:20).

PSALM 142

Translation

A Maskil. Davidic. When he was in the cave. A prayer.

1With my voice I cry out to Yahweh,
with my voice I seek favour from Yahweh.
2I pour out my plaint before him,
I declare my distress before him.
3When my spirit becomes faint within me,
you know my path:
on the way that I walk,
they have laid out a trap for me.
4Look to the right and see,
there is none who acknowledge me,
flight has perished from me,
there is no one looking out for me.

5I cry out to you, O Yahweh,
I said, 'You are my refuge,
my portion in the land of the living.'

6Attend to my shout
for I have been brought very low.
Rescue me from my persecutors,
for they are stronger than me.
7Bring me out from prison
to give thanks to your name,
The righteous shall surround me,
for you deal bountifully with me.

Notes on the text

7. Taking the verb as *ktr* II, 'surround'.

Form and structure

This prayer continues the pattern of complaint psalms within the final Davidic collection that began at Psalm 140. Although not as strong as the links with the preceding psalms, the call for Yahweh to hear the psalmist picks up the motif of attending to the poet's voice (Pss 141:1; 142:1), while the motif of the trap also recurs (Pss 141:9; 142:3;

cf. 140:5). Perhaps more generally, the fact that the prayer is called a 'Maskil' may suggest a more reflective piece, building on the wisdom inflections evident in Psalms 140–141. However, within the group of Psalms 140–143 the title here marks a small disjunction, as the note that it is 'Davidic' is the only element it shares with the rest of this small group. Rather, the title serves to direct readers to two possible settings in 1 Samuel (see below, 'Comment').

That this is a complaint psalm is again evident from the opening plea (vv. 1–2) and the references to the adversaries who act against the psalmist (v. 6), leading to the request for rescue (vv. 6b–7). Yet, although not as marked as Psalms 140–141, there is also a wisdom inflection within the poem, one that again evokes elements of Psalm 1. This is most obvious in the reference to the psalmist's path as one that Yahweh knows, evoking Psalm 1:6 (though the word for the path differs). As with the two preceding poems, this is a complaint psalm that is also reflective, a factor perhaps also supported by the fact that the 'plaint' (*śîaḥ*) the poet pours out (v. 2) is a 'meditation' in Psalm 104:34.

The poem is structured around the central confession of faith, in three stanzas:

1. Appeal to Yahweh (1–4)
2. Confession (5)
3. Request for rescue (6–7)

Comment

Title: For 'A Maskil', see on Psalm 32. For 'Davidic', see on Psalm 3. Mention of the time David was in a cave (cf. Ps. 57's title) could allude to either 1 Samuel 22:1–2 or 1 Samuel 24:3–4. Since David is under threat in both, it is impossible to determine which is intended here. For both, David was threatened by Saul and his forces, a group that was apparently stronger than him, so we can reasonably consider both as appropriate background (cf. V. L. Johnson 2009: 99–101). For 'A prayer', see on Psalm 17.

1–4. Where Psalms 140 and 141 both quickly move to a voc. in addressing Yahweh, the appeal here begins with language that describes the process of the appeal before moving to address Yahweh directly only in verses 3–4. The opening is concerned to report more generally that the psalmist cries out to Yahweh, seeking his favour; though if we understand the verbs as a future, then they could announce the prayer that begins in verse 3 (so, Goldingay 2008: 142). The psalmist has done what is right in the light of the previous psalms and called out to Yahweh, making sure that Yahweh knows the need and the distress. Yahweh is addressed directly in verse 3, establishing the pattern followed for the balance of the psalm. However, rather than reporting the distress, we instead have a confession of faith. Yahweh knows the path the poet takes, echoing Psalm 1:6. But this knowledge is immediately challenged by the struggles the psalmist faces since previously unnamed enemies have laid out traps on that path. If Yahweh knows the path, he needs to attend to this. This need is accentuated by the absence of others who acknowledge the psalmist, meaning Yahweh is the one who needs to act, especially since other means of flight have perished (cf. Amos 2:14). The psalmist is 'on the way', and Yahweh needs to demonstrate that he watches over the way of those who are his by responding to the threats being faced.

5. The poem here pauses briefly to report the psalmist's confession of faith. It is a confession made in the midst of distress, but that (like Ps. 140:6) looks back to something said before. The psalmist's confession is made here to remind Yahweh what was said before, desiring that Yahweh act in a manner consistent with the confession. Yahweh was confessed as the poet's refuge, the one who should provide the protection apparently absent in verse 4. That Yahweh is the poet's portion in the land of the living (adapting the language of land allocation in Josh 13 – 19; cf. Ps. 73:26) means Yahweh needs to act now, since it is within life that protection is needed.

6–7. The poet now moves to a more specific appeal. Yahweh knows the psalmist's way and has been confessed as his refuge. As such, he needs to attend to the poet's shout because has been brought too low to escape without help. Moreover, Yahweh needs to rescue (cf. Ps. 140:1) the poet from the unnamed persecutors since they are too strong to resist. As noted, both possible settings in 1 Samuel would be consistent with this while David was on the run from Saul, though if David is here a representative figure, then others may also see the extent of the threat for which appeal may be made. Mention of prison in verse 7 is difficult to align directly with David's experience, though if understood metaphorically (with Buysch 2009: 237; for a literal reading cf. Kraus 1989: 532) as a restriction on freedom of movement, then a correlation is possible, though it could also refer to Sheol (Tromp 1969: 156). Prison, however, extends the metaphor from verse 6 since persecutors could be those who pursue someone, but prison implies capture. The request is that Yahweh bring the poet out from prison so thanksgiving can be given to Yahweh, thanksgiving that will be shared by others as they gather round when they see how bountifully Yahweh has dealt with the psalmist. Being brought out from prison will demonstrate that the psalmist is among the righteous and they, recognizing the truth affirmed in Psalm 1:6, will join in thanksgiving, thus removing the isolation expressed in verse 4.

Explanation

Continuing the pattern of laments within the final Davidic collection, this psalm strengthens its Davidic association with the first reference since Psalm 63 to David's experience on the run from Saul, even if we cannot be sure which time in the cave is meant. David becomes an important figure through which to read the psalm, his time on the run from Saul illustrating the sense of isolation and need expressed here. Although David would gather a group who joined him, he was initially isolated and under threat from Saul. Nevertheless, the psalm remains sufficiently open that we cannot reconstruct David's experiences from it. Rather, his experience provides a template for believers who experience isolation and threat to recall the promise of God as their heritage in the land of the living while anticipating the point where the community joins the one who prays in thanksgiving to God. Isolation is ended when the community sees God at work, recognizing that the claims of his watching over the way of the righteous is true, joining with the one who was previously isolated but now surrounded by those who join in praise. In this, the psalm anticipates the time people from everywhere join such praise (Rev. 7:9).

PSALM 143

Translation

A melody. Davidic.

1O Yahweh, hear my prayer,
listen favourably to my supplications,
in your faithfulness answer me, and in your righteousness.
2Do not enter into judgement with your servant,
for no one living is righteous before you.

3For the enemy pursues me,
crushes my life to the ground,
makes me dwell in dark places,
like those long dead.
4My spirit faints within me,
my heart is appalled inside me.

5I remember days of old,
I meditate on all your deeds,
I reflect on the work of your hands.
6I spread out my hands to you,
my life is like parched ground before you. *Selah*.

[7]Hurry, answer me, O Yahweh,
  my spirit fails,
do not hide your face from me,
  or I will be like those going down to the pit.
[8]Let me hear of your kindness in the morning,
  for I have trusted in you,
Let me know the way where I should walk,
  for I lift myself to you.

[9]Rescue me from my enemies, O Yahweh,
  I have fled to you.
[10]Teach me to do your will,
  because you are my God,
may your good Spirit guide me,
  on level ground.
[11]For the sake of your name, O Yahweh, keep me alive,
  in your righteousness bring me out from distress,
[12]and in your kindness ruin my enemies,
  destroy those acting hostilely towards me,
  because I am your servant.

Notes on the text

6. The final part line is verbless. A verb like 'thirsts' (so ESV) or 'longs' (so NASB) is often supplied, but the verb 'to be' is simpler.

8. With Gk (and one MS), read *nastî*, assuming possible confusion between *n* and *k* (not dissimilar in Hebr.) to produce MT *kissitî* (I am covered) which makes little sense in context (though defended by Hossfeld and Zenger 2011: 570). Similarly, Waltke et al. 2010: 268.

9b–11. Buysch (2009: 260) notes the shift in syntax here, preferring to see these verses as descriptive of a point where Yahweh's protection is maintained rather than requested (similarly, Futato 2009: 422). The syntactical observation is important, but although there is a structural shift, the verbs are better understood as jussives that continue the impact of the imperatives in verses 8–9a.

Form and structure

The last complaint in this collection, and indeed the Psalter's last complaint, this prayer is closely linked to the immediately preceding complaints (Pss 140–142), though it is most closely linked with Psalm 142. The most obvious connection is in the reference to the psalmist's fainting spirit (Pss 142:3; 143:4), a theme extended (v. 7) and contrasted with the work of Yahweh's Spirit (v. 10). In both cases, the poet seeks Yahweh's mercy (Pss 142:1; 143:1), and both also engage in practices of reflection and meditation (Pss 142:2; 143:5). Both also draw on the 'way' metaphor, with it under threat in one (Ps. 142:2) and the direction where Yahweh must lead in the other (Ps. 143:8). The shifts in the language of the Spirit and way between these poems also points to development between them.

Although containing standard elements of a complaint psalm, including an address to Yahweh (vv. 1–2), a description of distress (vv. 3–5) and a request for deliverance (vv. 6–11), there are also elements that are not traditionally part of such psalms, notably reflection on the past in verse 5 and request for instruction in verse 9. However, Psalm 27:1–3 also includes reflection on the past within a complaint, while it and the request for instruction in verse 8 are consistent with the wisdom motif that runs through Psalms 140–143. A consistent feature of these prayers is their integration of elements that transcend a more restrictive understanding of the complaint, allowing us to read this as a prayer for protection against enemies that threaten the psalmist's life (Firth 2005b: 102–104). Although this has sometimes been interpreted against the background of the prayers of the accused (so, Kraus 1989: 535–536; cf. Ps. 7), the fact that the psalmist admits to general guilt in verse 2 means we should not press the legal imagery.

Variance from standard elements of the complaint has led to different attempts to divide this into multiple sources (for a summary, see Firth 2005b: 104–106), but the presence of repeated vocabulary across the whole poem (Coetzee 1986: 247–248), plus the use of Yahweh's righteousness and the poet's status as Yahweh's servant to form an inclusio (vv. 1–2, 11), strongly suggests the poem's unity. Noting the inclusio and the *selah* (v. 6) that seems to divide it, we can analyse the poem in two stanzas, each containing further strophes:

1. Request for deliverance (1–6)
   a. Initial appeal (1–2)
   b. Description of enemies (3–4)
   c. Reflections on the past (5–6)
2. Petitions for help (7–12)
   a. Appeal for deliverance (7–8)
   b. Petitions for instruction (9–12)

Comment

Title: For 'A melody' and 'Davidic', see on Psalm 3. The title is identical to Psalm 141, possibly indicating further links between these two poems.

1–2. As with Psalm 141, the prayer opens with a voc. Yahweh is asked to hear the poet's prayer, a term typically indicating a prayer of complaint.

This is reinforced through the parallel, which asks for the supplications to be heard favourably. The opening appeal's language picks up elements from Psalm 141:1–2, but then adds an appeal to be answered, an element also introduced near the beginning of the second stanza (v. 7). The answer is to be grounded in Yahweh's faithfulness and righteousness, terms that emphasize the relationship between Yahweh and the psalmist. 'Faithfulness' is often used in terms of dependability in relationships, but 'righteousness' can also have this same sense – 1 Samuel 26:23 also uses these terms relationally. However, the addition of righteousness means that justice is expressed in this faithfulness. The psalmist also recognizes that justice cannot control everything, which is why verse 2 also asks that Yahweh not enter into judgement with his servant on the basis that no one is right before him (cf. Rom. 3:20; Gal. 2:16), a general truth unlike the claims to innocence that occur elsewhere and are specific to particular charges (e.g. Ps. 26). Yahweh's righteousness exceeds that of humans, which is why the request can also be called 'supplications' since these are an appeal for grace, a point that can be extended if there is an allusion to Exodus 34:6–7. The poet's self-designation of 'servant' also points to a close relationship with Yahweh, who, as Lord, should work for his servant's well-being, a point to which the poem returns in verse 12.

3–4. Yahweh needs to act because of an enemy's threat. This could be an individual figure, though it is perhaps more likely that the sg. is used in verse 3 collectively since the pl. occurs in verse 9 (A. A. Anderson 1972, 1: 979). Although the more explicit hunting language of Psalms 141–142 is lacking, the pursuers here act like hunters as they crush the psalmist's life to the ground. The psalmist is forced to dwell in dark places, like the dead. This could suggest being in a pit or similar, but it is perhaps more likely that the statements in verse 3 point to the severity of the enemy's actions rather than specific deeds. Their effect, however, is marked, as the poet's spirit fails (cf. Ps. 142:3) and heart is appalled. Both images point to a loss of vitality consistent with being forced to dwell in darkness like those long dead (cf. Lam. 3:6).

5–6. In contrast to the present experience of suffering, the psalmist remembers days from of old. Although this could point back to a much earlier time, it needs only to precede the current distress. This memory is not simply the recall of past facts. Rather, it is the basis of reflective consideration on Yahweh's previous acts (cf. Ps. 77:6, 10–12). This recollection provides the basis for prayer, as reflected in the spreading out of the palms, an act symbolizing supplicatory prayer. The prayer comes from a place of distress, with the psalmist's whole being now resembling a parched land. Such a land lacks the means to sustain life, indicating the extent of the poet's suffering. Yet, it is before Yahweh, meaning he can see it and respond.

7–8. The second stanza also opens with an appeal for Yahweh to answer the poet, this time preceded by a request that he hasten to do this, indicating the urgency behind the appeal. As with the first stanza, the poet's spirit is struggling. This time it is failing, suggesting that death may be more imminent. To avoid this, the poet needs Yahweh's presence; hence, the request that he not hide his face, since doing so would be the equivalent of being moved closer to death, which is the pit mentioned here. Where Yahweh was initially asked to hear the poet (v. 1), now the request is that Yahweh cause the poet to hear of Yahweh's kindness in the morning. The night is a time of struggle, but the hope needed with morning is the experience of Yahweh's 'kindness' (*ḥesed*), an experience consistent with the poet's previous trust in Yahweh. Nevertheless, the need is not merely a resolution of the current distress. Rather, the poet needs to know the path that should be taken going forward. This makes it possible to live for Yahweh, taking the path that pleases him (Ps. 1:6), something consistent with the poet's dedication to Yahweh.

9–12. A way forward is needed, but the immediate crisis still needs to be addressed on the basis of the relationship between Yahweh and the poet. Rescue (cf. Ps. 142:6) from the enemies is needed. If we are correct in reading verse 9 as the poet having fled to Yahweh (cf. 'Notes on the text'), then there is an effective claim of asylum. This could have happened in the temple, but a metaphor is also possible. As with the previous strophe, rescue is also associated with instruction as Yahweh is asked to teach the psalmist to do his will. Such acts could also be understood as living a life acceptable to Yahweh rather than suggesting guidance on particular decisions. Again, this is to be based on the relationship between Yahweh and the poet since Yahweh is affirmed as the poet's God. Where the poet's 'spirit' (*rûaḥ*) is failing (vv. 4, 7), Yahweh's good 'Spirit' (*rûaḥ*; cf. Neh. 9:20) can guide the poet on level ground; that is, in places where it is possible to live faithfully. Although much of the psalm has concerned the poet's relationship with Yahweh, a broader perspective is introduced in verse 11, where Yahweh is urged to act for the sake of his name, here his wider reputation, and restore the psalmist to life. Such a restoration moves against the evidence for the loss of vitality that has been presented to this point. This is also marked by bringing the psalmist out from the current distress, language that evokes the exodus. As with the appeal in verse 1, this is to be marked by Yahweh's righteousness. Mention of Yahweh's 'kindness' (*ḥesed*) in verse 12 creates an inclusio for the second stanza. It is this kindness the poet wants to experience. Yahweh's kindness is to be experienced by the ruin of the enemies, the destruction of those acting hostilely. This imprecation is similar to that of Psalm 140:9–11 in being expressed through wishes. These wishes are forceful, but it should be noted that the request is that the enemies receive what they have attempted against the poet, so the retribution requested is relative to the harm attempted. Further, it is left to Yahweh to carry out, and indeed the fact that the psalm closes with the psalmist's confession of being Yahweh's servant means that the authority to act is left with Yahweh alone. Only Yahweh can truly be just; hence, the emphasis on his righteousness. So, the psalmist leaves the resolution to him (Firth 2005b: 109–110).

Explanation

The Psalter's final complaint psalm joins the others in Psalms 140–143 in integrating wisdom motifs so that complaint becomes a reflective process that integrates memory of Yahweh's character and works as they are known through Israel's wider story and personal experience. These elements provide a frame in which to pray and ask for grace. Only grace is sufficient because no one is righteous before God. This point becomes a key element in Paul's exposition of justification (Rom. 3:20; Gal. 2:16), though his argument probably depends on the psalm as a whole and not just verse 2 (which he cites). The grace Paul expounds is also what is sought here, even if the poet does not express this in Christological terms. It is also clear that the receipt of grace is not to permit the petitioner to remain in sin. Instead, like Paul's rejection of the idea that continued sin permits grace to abound (Rom. 6:1), the psalmist desires to be led by Yahweh's Spirit, anticipating another Pauline motif (Rom. 8:14–17; Gal. 5:18). This does not mean that wickedness is removed from the world, but it does mean that those who pray this psalm may also trust God to be the one who addresses this, since he alone can do so in a way that is both just and gracious. Unlike many complaints, there is no closing vow of praise, but that is coming in the rest of the Psalter.

PSALM 144

Translation

Davidic.

[1]Blessed be Yahweh, my rock,
  who instructs my hands for battle,
  my fingers for war.
[2]my source of kindness and my stronghold,
  my refuge and my deliverer,
my shield in whom I take refuge,
  who subdues peoples under me.

[3]O Yahweh, what is humankind that you notice them,
  mortals that you consider them?

4Humankind are like vapour,
their days like a shadow passing by.

5O Yahweh, bend your heavens and come down,
touch the mountains so they smoke.
6Flash forth lightning and scatter them,
send your arrows and rout them.
7Send your hands from the height,
free and rescue me from many waters,
from the hand of foreigners,
8whose mouth spoke deceit,
and whose right hand is the right hand of falsehood.

9O God, I will sing a new song to you,
with a ten-string harp I will make melody to you,
10who gives victory to kings,
who frees his servant David,
from the dangerous sword.
11Free and rescue me from the hand of foreigners,
whose mouth spoke deceit,
and whose right hand is the right hand of falsehood.

12Then our sons can be like plants,
full grown in their youth,
our daughters like cornerstones,
carved like the pattern of a palace,
13our granaries filled,
providing produce of all kinds,
our flocks bringing forth thousands,
tens of thousands in our fields,
14our cattle laden,
with no breach or loss,
and no outcry in our streets.

15O the blessedness of the people for whom this is so,
O the blessedness of the people whose God is Yahweh.

Notes on the text

2. With many MSS, including 11QPs[a], reading 'peoples' rather than 'my people'.

12. For *'ăšer* introducing a purpose clause, see *WHS* §466. *BHS* suggests emending to form a beatitude, but this is unnecessary, though this relatively unusual use of the pr. could anticipate the beatitude in verse 15.

14. The sense of this verse is uncertain. For a good summary of the issues, see Makujina 2011.

Form and structure

In Psalm 143:2, 12, the poet adopted the position of Yahweh's servant, whereas here David is declared to be the servant (v. 10). David is here like the petitioner in Psalm 143:9 since he too needs deliverance and rescue (v. 10), anticipating the further request of the poet here also for rescue (v. 11). In both poems, Yahweh's 'kindness' (*ḥesed*) is central to his relationship with his people (Pss 143:8, 12; 144:2). Yahweh was asked to teach the petitioner his ways (Ps. 143:10), and here he teaches the psalmist battle (v. 1). Although there is clearly a shift in tone away from complaint, that shift still leaves links between these poems. Moreover, Psalm 144 also introduces themes that are relevant for Psalm 145 (Futato 2009: 425; see 'Form and structure' there), as these two psalms close the final Davidic collection and transition to the Final Hallel (Pss 146–150) with which the Psalter closes.

This poem is generally reckoned to be a royal psalm even though it does not directly reference Israel's king. But since David is apparently distinguished from the speaker in verses 10–11, we can reasonably assume that his name here represents the kings of his line, and that is sufficient to make this a royal psalm. Since royal psalms are typically defined by royal content rather than form, it is no surprise to note that this poem also integrates a range of wisdom features, such as the reflection on the nature of humankind (vv. 3–4) and the use of the beatitudes in verse 15, while also including elements more typical of a complaint. Much of the poem can also be understood as a reworking of Psalm 18 (or 2 Sam. 22), so much so that verse 10 can even be linked to the title of Psalm 18. But this occurs amid a range of other associations (see Table 2):

Table 2: Links between Psalm 144 and other psalms

Psalm 144	*Associated Psalms*
1–2	18:1–2, 34, 46–47
3	8:4
4	39:5–6
5	18:9; 104:32
6	18:14
7	18:16, 44–45
9	33:2–3; 96:1; 98:1
10	18:0 (title)
11	18:16, 44–45
15	33:12

Although the density of adaptations in Psalm 144 is higher than elsewhere, it should be noted that Psalm 143 also adapts language from elsewhere in the Psalter. To some extent these are compositions by poets who have been saturated in the language of Psalms and who express themselves in its idiom, yet create their own distinctive works. It is not a mere pastiche of earlier works but rather a creative adaptation (cf. Brettler 1993: 152) that integrates the wisdom themes central to the final Davidic collection with motifs drawn from across the Psalter. The 'Comment' section will not develop these links further because our goal is to understand the poem we now have, not its sources.

The poem can be analysed in two strophes through the move from 'I' (vv. 1–11) to 'we' (vv. 12–15). Allowing for developments within each stanza, the following structure emerges:

1. Royal prayer (1–11)
   a. Blessing of Yahweh (1–2)
   b. Reflection on humankind (3–4)
   c. Plea for rescue (5–8)
   d. Promise of praise (9–11)
2. Communal blessedness (12–15)
   a. Results of rescue (12–14)
   b. Beatitudes (15)

Comment

Title: For 'Davidic', see on Psalm 3.

1–2. The psalm opens with a declaration that blesses Yahweh (on blessing Yahweh, see on Ps. 103) as the one who prepares the speaker for battle. For a king, divine aid in battle was essential. Yahweh is first blessed as rock, language that points to him as the provider of security and protection. That is, the initial emphasis is defensive. However, this is supplemented by noting that Yahweh is also the one who provides the training the speaker needs for battle. The king was not therefore an intrinsically powerful warrior but was effective only because of Yahweh's work for him. The emphasis on defensive capability is especially evident in verses 2a–c where every element is defensive (cf. Ps. 3:4). Mention of 'my kindness [*ḥesed*]' is perhaps less self-evidently defensive, but it points to the fundamental relationship with Yahweh that enables the other elements of defence to be noted, all leading to the note that the speaker takes refuge in Yahweh. Psalm 2:12 pointed to the blessedness of all who took refuge in Yahweh's king, but here the king takes refuge in Yahweh. Given the prominent location of these two poems, it is likely they are to be read in the light of each other. In the final shape of the

Psalter, we realize the king can be a source of refuge for others only because he takes refuge in Yahweh. Moreover, the king can reign only because Yahweh has subdued peoples under him (or, if we retain MT, 'my people'). The king can rule his people effectively only because of what Yahweh does for him.

3–4. This understanding of the king prepares for reflection on humankind. The king is human and therefore has the weaknesses common to all humans (cf. Job 7:17–18). Hyperbolic language can be used about the king (e.g. Ps. 45), but the human reality is not to be forgotten. At one level, therefore, the human mentioned here could simply be the king, with these verses pointing to the king's weakness, but also the wonder of the fact that Yahweh notices him. But the language is more open ended, placing the king into the wider human setting as one who is limited, as substantial as breath (cf. Eccl. 1:12) and subject to death. A king will not, even if trained for battle, be the nation's source of rescue.

5–8. Following the reflection, the speaker again addresses Yahweh directly, asking for rescue. The language here is theophanic, evoking the experience of Sinai (Exod. 19; cf. Hab. 3). The perspective adopted is the same as being at the foot of the mountain, as Yahweh is asked to bow his heavens and come down, and so enter the earthly realm. Touching the mountains so they smoke evokes the experience of a volcano but is also consistent with Yahweh's coming to Sinai (Exod. 19:18), as were the flashes of lightning (Exod. 19:16), which can also here be compared to arrows fired by Yahweh, who routs unnamed adversaries. Yahweh's theophanic power is to be applied from on high to the speaker's need, rescuing the king both from forces of chaos (many waters) and threatening foreigners. Whatever force opposes the king, it is Yahweh who needs to rescue him. The foreigners were also deceptive, misrepresenting themselves (cf. Ps. 139:20) to the king, suggesting that the king was unable to recognize this.

9–11. A new voc. here ('O God', unusual for Book 5, for which 'O Yahweh' is normal) introduces a new strophe. Now, the king promises to sing a new song of thanksgiving, making use of a ten-string harp. As elsewhere (Pss 33, 96, 98), the new song emerges because of the victory Yahweh has won. The musical language is relatively standard, but it also prepares for David's introduction to the psalm since he was known as a musician and singer (2 Sam. 23:1), even if his ability on the ten-string harp is not otherwise noted. The new song needs to be sung because Yahweh is the one who gives victory to any king, and who freed David from a dangerous sword. The LXX seems to have understood this in terms of Goliath since its expanded title includes mention of this, but the thought here is probably more general (even if the Goliath story is a good illustration of the point), especially as David there declares it would be Yahweh who gave him victory (1 Sam. 17:46). However, it seems the speaker is not David since we now have a further petition for rescue that repeats the language of verses 7–8. What Yahweh has done for David he needs to do again for subsequent kings.

12–14. The second strophe builds on the first to explore the impact of the king's rescue for the community, recognizing that the king's rule was meant to benefit the community rather than enriching him. It may be that the hope expressed here indicates that this was not the community's experience at the time, but it is also possible that such hopes could be expressed as something continuous. Importantly, the goal of rescue looks beyond the current generation to consider those who follow, so its sons and daughters live full lives. The full-grown plants could evoke those of Psalm 92:12–15 (cf. Ps. 127:3–5), suggesting the sons are like those in the temple. The daughters are here likened to valuable items in the palace (possibly the temple), pointing to their being valued. Beyond the community's descendants, the expectation is that Yahweh's victory will lead to abundant provision, with overflowing granaries and stores filled with various kinds of produce. Likewise, the flocks would breed abundantly so there would be plenty of meat and wool. Mention of the cattle is often taken to mean bearing numerous children without mishap (so ESV) but (with Goldingay 2008: 690) the language is m., so it is more likely they are laden because of abundant goods needing to be carried without loss (so NIV).

15. Having opened by blessing Yahweh, the psalm closes with two beatitudes (on the form, see on Ps. 1). Blessing Yahweh is a form of praise for him, whereas a beatitude describes a state in which the best possible life is lived. As always, it is presented to its audience with the intention that they will accept it and shape their own life around it. The desirable life is for those for whom the blessings described in verses 12–14 occur. The means of experiencing this is made clear in the second beatitude – blessedness is the state in which the nation who has Yahweh as God lives. Hope comes from Yahweh, and if there is a king, that hope occurs only because he lives as one who understands his own limitations and lives under Yahweh, modelling for the nation what it means to have Yahweh as God.

Explanation

Where were Israel to find their hope and security? One answer might have been through their king, especially given the promises made to David. But although the Psalms have, at various points, reflected on those promises, this psalm suggests the king alone is not sufficient. The promises to David are not to be ignored, and indeed by its creative reuse of earlier psalms this poem affirms their importance. But it also brings us back to Psalm 2, where the Davidic king was Yahweh's king. A Davidic king mattered only when it was also accepted that any human king was fallible and weak. It was Yahweh, not David, who provided rescue. The Davidic king needed was one who recognized this and whose rule was thus a channel through which Yahweh worked and brought about the blessedness that was desired. The heavenly elders recognize this when they sing their new song (Rev. 5:9–10) and acknowledge it is through his death that the Lamb brought about a kingdom in which all peoples may serve God.

PSALM 145

Translation

An anthem. Davidic.

1I will exalt you, my God the king,
  I will bless your name for ever and ever.
2I will bless you every day,
  and praise your name for ever and ever.

3Great is Yahweh and most praiseworthy,
  his greatness is unsearchable.
4Let generation to generation laud your works,
  declare your powerful deeds.
5On the splendour of the glory of your majesty,
  and the words of your wondrous deeds shall I ponder.
6Let them tell of the strength of your awesome deeds,
  your greatness will I recount.
7Let them utter the memory of your abundant goodness,
  shout out of your righteousness.

8Yahweh is gracious and compassionate,
  slow to anger and abounding in kindness.
9Yahweh is good to all,
  and his compassion is over all his works.

10Let all your works give thanks to you, O Yahweh,
  and your faithful ones bless you.
11Let them tell of the glory of your kingdom,
  and speak of your power,
12to make known his powerful deeds to humankind,
  and the glorious splendour of his kingdom.
13Your kingdom is an everlasting kingdom,
  and your dominion endures from generation to generation.

[Yahweh is faithful in all his deeds,
  and kind in all his works.]
14Yahweh upholds all who are falling,
  and raises up all who are bowed down.
15The eyes of all wait for you,
  and you give them their food in its season,
16opening your hands,
  and satisfying the desire of every living creature.
17Yahweh is righteous in all his ways,
  kind in all his works.
18Yahweh is near to all who call on him,
  to all who call on him in truth.
19He effects the desire of those who fear him,
  he hears their cry for help and rescues them.
20Yahweh protects all who love him,
  but shall destroy all the wicked.

21Let my mouth speak the praise of Yahweh,
  and all flesh bless his holy name,
  for ever and ever!

Notes on the text

Title: 11QPs[a] has the orthographically similar 'A prayer'. But the uniqueness of MT's title supports it.

4–7, 10–11. The verbs here could be juss. or impf. Juss. is marginally preferable in that the psalmist's own vow of praise is then set alongside that which a wider community shall also do.

13. The second colon provides the otherwise missing nun verse. This reading is found in one MS, Gk and Syr., but is absent from all other Masoretic MSS, though a close variant is found in 11QPs[a]. It is difficult to explain the loss of the nun verse from an alphabetic acrostic, especially in Book 5 which follows the now standard form of the alphabet more closely than in Book 1. This colon is also very close to verse 17, possibly suggesting that it was composed to fill the gap. Both these factors could point to retaining MT as *lectio difficilior*, as could the fact that 11QPs[a] includes a liturgical refrain, so it is clearly an edited text. However, the independent witness of Qumran and Gk (Syr. could depend on Gk) narrowly tip the balance in favour of its inclusion, as may some structural elements (Lindars 1989). Note that some EVV (e.g. NEB) list this bicolon as the start of verse 14, whereas most have it as part of verse 13.

Form and structure

The final Davidic collection (Pss 138–145) ends with an alphabetic acrostic that links key themes from across this collection (cf. Buysch 2009: 319–323) while also providing a bridge into the Final Hallel (Pss 146–150; see 'Form and structure' on Ps. 146; Booij [2012: 636–637] believes it could have been composed for this function). This latter group is made up of praise psalms, which all begin and end 'Hallelujah!'. This exclamation of praise is built on the root *hll* (praise), which is also fundamental to this psalm's title (see 'Comment' below), the opening vow of praise (v. 2) and the closing summons to praise (v. 21), and so leads into the praise of the Final Hallel. It also builds on themes from the preceding psalms through its concentration on Yahweh's reign as king. Psalm 144 focused on the Davidic king but made clear that a human king was inherently limited, a passing shadow (Ps. 144:3). By contrast, Yahweh's kingdom is everlasting because Yahweh lacks the limits of any human king (Ps. 145:13). Further evidence for this is seen in the fact that Psalm 138:7 anticipated Yahweh's rescue amid trouble, something celebrated here (Ps. 145:19). Yahweh is also said to be near to those who call on him (v. 18), responding to the psalmist's plea in Psalm 141:1, while his protection of those who love him (v. 20) also responds to earlier pleas (Pss 140:4; 141:9). The psalm is composed in an anthological style that alludes to numerous earlier psalms (esp. Pss 103–104, 111–112, but considerably more besides; cf. Vesco 2006, 2: 1340), though, as with Psalm 144, our concern here is with how the language is used within the psalm rather than its sources.

As with the rest of the final Davidic collection, this psalm does not easily fit into the main categories, drawing on various elements in a wisdom-infused text. The acrostic form is often associated with wisdom, but quite apart from the wider question of whether we can speak of wisdom as a particular literary type (as opposed to a key motif), the poet has clearly not been constrained by the literary features of the acrostic as the poem develops a clear structure across its stanzas. If we are correct in reading many of the verbs as jussives (see 'Notes on the text'), then we can also consider it to be a prayer that praise be offered to Yahweh, though we should also note that the poet's own position is better understood as a vow of praise (esp. vv. 1–2). The central section (vv. 8–13a) may be better understood as a confession of faith, albeit one that provides reason for praise. There is no reason these elements may not be combined so that we can understand the psalm as a text that integrates wisdom elements with both a vow to praise and a prayer that praise be more broadly given.

As noted, the acrostic form does not seem to have limited the poet, and we can analyse it in six stanzas, though it should also be noted that it uses multiple structuring devices to support its rhetorical goals (deClaissé-Walford 2012: 61–65). We can also note that the opening and closing stanzas form an inclusio for the poem, while the first, fourth and sixth stanza all use the verb *brk* (bless) in the second part line of the opening colon:

1. Individual vow of praise (1–2)
2. Prayer for human praise (3–7)
3. Affirmations about Yahweh (8–9)
4. Prayer for Yahweh's works to instruct (10–13a)
5. Affirmations of Yahweh's faithfulness and goodness (13b–20)
6. Closing prayer (21)

Comment

Title: 'An anthem' is unique to this psalm. The term refers specifically to an act of praise, and so anticipates the theme of praise that runs through the psalm, climaxing in use of the same word in verse 21. On 'Davidic', see on Psalm 3.

1–2. Language of praise dominates the opening stanza, drawing on patterns of praise that have emerged throughout the Psalter. Here, the verbs are all first-person sg. as the psalmist vows to God to offer praise. The praise begins by exalting God, an act that recognizes his superiority as something that can be spatially expressed. This exaltation is linked to the fact that the psalmist's God is also the king, one who is therefore above all others. Following this, praise moves to forms of speech about God with the vow to bless God's name for ever (on 'blessing God', see on Ps. 103:1–5). The psalmist wishes to speak positively about God, with the name standing for the whole of the divine character. This vow is then extended through time in the promise to bless God's name daily and then to praise God's name for ever. Both blessing and praise will be offered for ever, anticipating the psalm's closing verse. Beyond this, the psalmist's vow is also presented as a model for others, so that they too can commit to praise.

3–7. Although God has been addressed and vows made about praising his name, only now is the name Yahweh introduced. Yahweh's greatness is affirmed (cf. Ps. 48:1), making him highly praiseworthy and thus connecting this stanza with the first. Although many things may be considered great, Yahweh's greatness is distinct in being unsearchable (cf. Ps. 139:1, 23; Eph. 3:8), and thus beyond human comprehension. As such, and as the one who is highly praiseworthy, the rest of this stanza expresses hope that Yahweh will continue to be praised, using wishes that are effectively prayers. So, verse 4 wants subsequent generations to laud Yahweh's works, giving verbal affirmations about them to others while also declaring his powerful deeds. That is, what Yahweh has done provides an enduring basis for praise. In verse 5 the psalmist's voice again emerges with a fresh vow to ponder Yahweh's majesty and mighty deeds. The mighty deeds here are referred to in terms of their 'words' – a slightly curious phrase that perhaps points both to the deeds themselves and how they are discussed. After the psalmist's intervention, verses 6–7 return to wishes that an unnamed group, presumably the generations mentioned in verse 4, would tell of the strength of Yahweh's awesome deeds alongside the psalmist's own declarations of his greatness. In a sense, the psalmist and the wider community become a choir offering praise, but a choir that also has a soloist. The wish is extended in verse 7 with reference to the wider group pouring forth praise (like a spring that pours forth water) that recalls Yahweh's goodness while also shouting out his righteousness, elements that provide the foundations for the group's relationship with him.

8–9. The wishes for praise pause as the poet introduces an adaptation of the grace formula (Exod. 34:6–7) as part of a series of affirmations about Yahweh. The context in Exodus follows the golden-calf incident (Exod. 32) and celebrates Yahweh's character as one who forgives and restores. In that much of the final Davidic collection assumes a level of suffering, these words provide reassurance about Yahweh through the evocation of the wider story while reinforcing key claims about Yahweh as the one who deals with people with grace, compassion and delayed anger. The consistent emphasis in these terms is that Yahweh does not deal with people as they necessarily deserve. Instead, his abundant kindness continues to provide hope. This is explored through Yahweh's goodness to all, his compassion on all his works. Because of the consistent emphasis on Yahweh as creator (reinforced through the allusion to Ps. 104 in vv. 15–16), his goodness to and compassion on all his works effectively repeat the one point: there is no one to whom Yahweh will not act with compassion.

10–13. In the light of these affirmations, the poem returns to wishes for praise to be given to Yahweh. As with the interchange of 'praise' between the first and second stanzas, so here Yahweh's works provide a key hinge with the preceding stanza, while 'bless' links it to the first and last stanzas. Yahweh has compassion on all his works, so the wish is that they would give thanks to him, responding to his goodness to them. Within Yahweh's works there are also those who are faithful to Yahweh, and the hope is that they would bless him. The blessing could be words spoken to Yahweh, but the blessing here could also be their telling of the glory of his kingdom while speaking of his power. The wonders of Yahweh's kingdom are to be spoken of so that humankind may know of his powerful deeds and the majestic glory of his kingdom. Verses 11–12 are formed around a small chiasm built around the glory of the kingdom and centred on his power. The concern is with the kingdom, a kingdom not limited by time like all human kingdoms (cf. Dan. 4:3), so that

Yahweh's dominion endures through all generations. Again, mention of endless time links this stanza with the first and last, making this stanza the poem's theological heart, even if attempts to make it the structural one (see the summary in Allen 2002: 370) are less persuasive.

13b–20. The fifth stanza is again concerned to make affirmations about Yahweh that prepare for the final vow (v. 21), with all the affirmations consistent with Yahweh's status as king. As noted above (see 'Notes on the text'), the place of verse 13b is far from secure, but included here. If it is excluded, we would lose part of the acrostic, but it is otherwise not dissimilar from other elements in this stanza. Assuming it belongs, we may note that it introduces several verses that commence with ptcs. describing Yahweh's activity. Here, we affirm Yahweh's faithfulness in his works and kindness in his deeds, picking up language from elsewhere in the poem. But in verse 14 the affirmations develop new perspectives, pointing to Yahweh's support for the falling, for the bowed down. Yahweh is not only powerful over all creation; he is also concerned for those who struggle and are afflicted. This is why the eyes of all look to him, waiting hopefully for his provision at the appropriate time (cf. Matt. 6:11), satisfying the desire of all living through the opening of his hands. The language of verses 15–16 is similar to Psalm 104:27–28, but here is applied to the needs of those who particularly need Yahweh's provision as an expression of his goodness. Verse 17 then provides a more direct statement about Yahweh's righteousness in all his ways and faithfulness in all his works. Thus, Yahweh's goodness is not simply something that is generally true but rather can be seen in his actions. These actions matter for those who fear him, those who have set themselves to serve him and whose calling on him emerges from a true relationship, because they will discover that Yahweh is near to them. The motif of those who fear Yahweh is picked up in verse 19 as it affirms that Yahweh effects their desire. This is not a general statement of their receiving anything but rather seen in the fact that he hears their cry for help and rescues them. This theme is extended in verse 20 with its affirmation of Yahweh's protective care for those who love him, another term for those who fear him. By contrast, the wicked, those who do not love Yahweh, are destroyed. This use of the two-ways pattern creates a link to Psalm 1, which also affirms Yahweh's care of the righteous, while the wicked perish. But where Psalm 1:6 does not state that it is Yahweh who makes the wicked perish, this time it is clear that he destroys them. Yahweh is good to all, but that goodness does not mean that the wicked are not punished.

21. Given these affirmations about Yahweh, the psalm closes with a final wish – the psalmist wants to speak Yahweh's praise, joining with all flesh as they bless his holy name. The solo and communal voices here match that of verse 6, except that this time the solo voice is mentioned first. Mention of Yahweh's name provides an additional link to verses

1–2. The additional note that his name is holy joins this affirmation to Psalm 138:1–2, where giving thanks to Yahweh's name is associated with his holy temple. Holiness and Yahweh's name provide the boundaries for the final Davidic collection, while also moving beyond it with the hope of praise that endures for ever and ultimately comes from all that has breath (Ps. 150:6).

Explanation

This psalm is 'the overture to the final movement of the Psalter' (Mays 1994b: 339). Its closing call for praise anticipates the flood of praise with which the Psalter closes. But since it anticipates praise that transcends the generations, we cannot restrict its invocation of praise only to the rest of the Psalter, even if that provides the primary evidence of what that praise looks like. By calling all flesh to join in praise it anticipates the universal praise of God from every people, tribe and language (Rev. 7:9). That praise, which is modelled through the individual who speaks in this psalm, finds its expression in recalling God's grace at Sinai and celebrating his kingdom. Praise here is also comprehensive, running through the A–Z (as it were) of praise, its comprehensiveness further emphasized by its seventeen uses of the Hebrew word for 'all'. It is also unbound by time, transcending the generations as each recounts the good news and grace of the kingdom and so invites subsequent generations among all flesh to know Yahweh's goodness, greatness and graciousness, and so to join the psalmist in praise for ever.

PSALM 146

Translation

1 Hallelujah!

Praise Yahweh, O my being!
2 I will praise Yahweh as long as I live,
  I will make melody to my God as long as I exist.

3 Do not trust in princes,
  in humankind with whom there is no rescue.
4 Their breath leaves and they return to the ground,
  their thoughts perish on that day.

5 Oh the blessedness of one whose help is the God of Jacob,
  whose hope is on Yahweh their God,

[6]the maker of heaven and earth,
the sea and all that is in them,
who remains faithful for ever,
[7]enacting justice for the oppressed,
giving food to the hungry.

Yahweh sets the imprisoned free.
[8]Yahweh opens the eyes of the blind,
Yahweh raises up those who are bowed down,
Yahweh loves the righteous.
[9]Yahweh protects the sojourners,
the fatherless and the widow he upholds,
but the way of the wicked he brings to ruin.

[10]Yahweh reigns for ever,
your God, O Zion, from generation to generation.
Hallelujah!

Notes on the text

4. The Hebrew uses sg., but, as this is distributive, pl. is appropriate.

9–10. 11QPs[a] could suggest an additional bicolon at this point, though it is imperfectly preserved. However, Gk is consistent with MT and the addition would also break the psalm's structure. Given the expansions elsewhere in 11QPs[a], we should retain MT.

Form and structure

This psalm commences the Final Hallel (Pss 146–150), the cavalcade of praise with which the Psalter ends. Each psalm within this group is focused on praise and bound by the praise exclamation 'Hallelujah!'. There are close links between them, though their different locations in 11QPs[a] indicates they did not have to be read together. There is a strong emphasis on Yahweh's role as creator, either as creation's initiator or as the one who controls it (Pss 146:6; 147:4, 8; 148:6; 149:2). Because of this, he is also able to express his concern for the weak (Pss 146:7–9; 147:3, 6). Despite these similarities, each is also distinct, offering its own perspective on praise and leading to the closing call of Psalm 150:6 for everything that has breath to praise Yahweh. Yahweh's role as creator was already noted in Psalm 145:9, as was his concern for the weak (Ps. 145:14–16). Most importantly, Psalm 145:21 reported the poet's vow to praise Yahweh and the wish for all flesh to praise him, and these psalms provide exemplars of that praise. It is also notable that Psalm

145 celebrated Yahweh's status as king (vv. 1, 11–13), a theme picked up here in the closing affirmation of Yahweh's enduring reign (v. 10). Although slightly less direct, the warning against trusting human princes (vv. 3–4) is also consistent with this, with reflection on their limitations also evocative of Psalm 144:3–4. If Psalm 145 provides the bridge into the Final Hallel, Psalm 146 is the link road to the rest.

The 'Hallelujah!' frame makes clear that this is a praise psalm. Reasons for praise run through the whole poem. Yet, as was typical of the prayers in the final Davidic collection (Pss 138–145), the psalm also makes use of various wisdom motifs (cf. Kselman 1998: 590–591), as can be seen in the admonition against trusting princes (vv. 3–4), the beatitude in verse 5 (the last one in the Psalter) and the observation on the fate of the wicked (v. 9). We may therefore observe that this is reflective praise, praise richly informed by other parts of the OT (though lacking direct quotations, with Brodersen 2018: 234), integrating praise and reflection. This praise, rooted in Yahweh's reign as king, is closely tied to lived experience.

The psalm uses a 'Hallelujah!' frame (vv. 1a, 10c), with 'hallelujah' typically standing outside any sentences or stanzas. For convenience, I include them in the nearest stanza, resulting in four stanzas, the third of which contains two strophes noted by the move of 'Yahweh' to the head of the relevant clauses. The leads to the following analysis:

1. Summons and vow to praise (1–2)
2. Admonition against princes (3–4)
3. Blessedness of having Yahweh's help (5–9)
   a. Creator and faithful (5–7b)
   b. Concern for the weak (7c–9)
4. Yahweh's reign (10)

Comment

1–2. The psalm opens with the cry 'Hallelujah!'. Strictly, an imp. to praise Yahweh addressed to others, it is here matched with an imp. to the self to praise Yahweh (cf. Pss 103:1; 104:1, 33). The poet's whole being is to engage in praise, leading into a vow of praise in verse 2. This vow promises to praise Yahweh through the whole of life, though, like the vow of praise in Psalm 145:1–2, it is also presented as a model to the wider community. They have been called to praise, and that praise is modelled through the speaker. The form of praise has not been defined, and so in verse 2b the verb changes to making melody. Praise cannot be reduced to music, especially if it comes from the whole being, but in the ancient world music was (and is in the modern world too) an important mode for expressing praise. An important development here is that

Yahweh is now called 'my God'. Yahweh is not simply Israel's God, but one who can be known and praised throughout an individual's life.

3–4. After the exuberance of the opening verses, this admonition against trusting princes may seem odd. However, it addresses the important temptation of claiming to serve Yahweh while really putting one's trust in resources that can be assembled. The most important of these was the idea that a human ruler provided the desired security, a temptation with roots in ancient Israel, as seen in the elders' request through Samuel for a king (1 Sam. 8:4–22; cf. Ps. 118:8–9). Kings on their own had never been enough for Israel, and so a people who praised Yahweh with all their being needed to recognize this temptation for what it was, to accept that any human ruler was limited (cf. Ps. 144:3–4), incapable of providing the rescue desired (perhaps hinting at the political situation at the time of composition; so Seybold 1996: 536). Rulers, like any other human, are unexceptional; and, when their breath leaves, they die (cf. Eccl. 12:7) and return to the earth (here, a wordplay between 'human' [*'ādām*] and 'earth' [*'ădāmâ*]; cf. Gen. 3:19). Whatever thoughts or plans they may have will at that point perish with them.

5–7b. The third strophe establishes a contrast with human rulers by looking instead at what Yahweh provides. The colometry can be arranged in other ways (e.g. Auffret 2005: 52–54), but the stanza is here understood as two strophes, each made up of two bicola plus a closing tricolon. However, they are linked because each strophe explores the implications of the beatitude in verse 5. The beatitude marks the clear contrast Yahweh provides with human rulers, because all who have Yahweh as their helper can be considered to live in a truly desirable state (on the form of the beatitude, see on Ps. 1). Those who have Yahweh as helper have their hope fixed upon him as their God, meaning that they join the poet in this relationship with him (v. 2). This blessedness is explored through a series of participial statements about Yahweh that demonstrate how he helps, and therefore why hope should be placed in him. Yahweh is the maker of heaven and earth as well as the sea and all that is in them (cf. Exod. 20:11). The language is similar to Psalm 121:2, but mention of the seas and all that is in them goes beyond that point. The development is at least partially spatial – the heavens are above the earth, the earth is where humans live and the sea is beneath. But it also suggests that all dimensions of creation belong to Yahweh and are thus his to control. Within this context, Yahweh can be characterized by his own faithfulness as one who remains perpetually faithful. Unlike human leaders, his protection remains constant. A particular expression of this is seen in his provision of justice for the oppressed and food for the hungry.

7c–9. A shift marking the second strophe occurs here as the main clauses are now introduced with the name Yahweh. Nevertheless, there is clear continuity with the preceding strophe in the continued use of ptcs. to describe Yahweh's acts, continuing to emphasize his care for the weak. So, Yahweh sets the imprisoned free, since they cannot do this themselves. In the ancient world, people were typically held as political or military prisoners (note Jeremiah's imprisonment in Jer. 37:11 – 38:13), meaning they had in some way offended a human ruler. Since Yahweh is greater than these rulers, he releases them, providing the chance to establish themselves once more. The opening of prisons is matched by Yahweh's opening of the eyes of the blind. Blindness was particularly challenging in that society (cf. Lev. 19:14), though with Goldingay (2008: 712) it is perhaps more likely that the eyes opened are those of the imprisoned as they leave the darkness of prison behind. The imprisoned and blind cannot change their circumstances themselves. By contrast, people can be bowed down for a range of reasons, both internal and external. Yet however that happens, they operate from a position of weakness, and it is here that they find Yahweh raising them up. The 'bowed down' are perhaps also the righteous, who are also the objects of Yahweh's love. The righteous here are humans who follow Yahweh's pattern and commit themselves to the weak (Brueggemann and Bellinger 2014: 607). Yahweh's help is brought to its conclusion in the statement of his care for sojourners, widows and fatherless, a standard trio in the OT (e.g. Deut. 10:18; 14:29), a group united by its lack of access to land. All evidence of Yahweh's help in this psalm is also consistent with expectations placed on Israel in the Torah. The means of Yahweh's help could therefore be through his people, though it could also be more direct (most obviously if the blind are those with visual impairment). Through all this, the blessedness of those who know Yahweh's help can be celebrated. A contrast is then drawn with the way of the wicked, those who do not join Yahweh's work for the weak, whom Yahweh brings to ruin. The image here is of Yahweh's making their way crooked (cf. Eccl. 7:13) such that it comes to a point of destruction (cf. Ps. 1:6).

10. The closing stanza returns to the theme of Yahweh's reign. Unlike humans who could be classified only as 'princes', Yahweh reigns as king, and he does so for ever (cf. Exod. 15:18). Unlike human leaders, who remain transient, Yahweh endures, his reign unending. At this point, the psalmist addresses Zion, declaring that its God endures through all generations. Yahweh was the psalmist's God in verse 1, but he now speaks of Yahweh as Zion's God. Zion here points to the site of the temple, and hence the location where Yahweh's people worshipped him. That Yahweh reigns means he can provide the help described in this psalm, something beyond any human ruler. That he can do so means he should be praised, and so the poem closes by returning to its opening – Hallelujah!

Explanation

Vesco (2006, 2: 1350) observes that this is a psalm of good news for all who suffer injustice – perhaps because it again affirms that God helps those who cannot help themselves (Broyles 1999: 510). Its praise looks to Yahweh as the king who practises all that a king is meant to do, committing himself to care for the weak and opposing those who seek to benefit from keeping the weak down. Beyond this, it is also instructive praise, so that all who offer this praise are themselves encouraged by how Yahweh acts and are challenged to embody this concern themselves. In such praise, we are formed and transformed into the likeness of God, because to know and praise him as our God, as the one who works like this, is to know what we are called to be. The acts of God recounted here find a clear echo in Luke 7:22, where Jesus reports the effects of his own ministry to John's messengers, demonstrating that the kingdom of God was indeed breaking in through him. Paul also shows an awareness of it in Galatians 2:10 when emphasizing his own concern for the poor. In Jesus, we see how God's reign proclaimed here finds fulfilment even as we continue to understand that this is also a call for believers to commit themselves to this same pattern. Jesus' beatitudes (Matt. 5:3–10) also point to the reality that blessedness lies in our relationship to God and not in the accumulation of the resources of power and wealth that dominate our world.

PSALM 147

Translation

1Hallelujah!

Yes, it is good to make melody to our God,
  yes, it is pleasant, praise is fitting.
2Yahweh builds up Jerusalem,
  he gathers the scattered of Israel,
3the one who heals the broken hearted,
  and binds their wounds,
4the one who counts the number of the stars,
  he gives names to them all.
5Great is our Lord, and vast of power,
  there is no quantifying his understanding.
6Yahweh upholds the afflicted,
  bringing the wicked down to the ground.

7Sing to Yahweh with thanksgiving,
  make melody to our God with a lyre,

[8]the one who covers the heavens with clouds,
who prepares rain for the earth,
who makes grass grow on mountains,
[9]who gives the beasts their food,
to the young ravens who cry out.
[10]He does not delight in the strength of a horse,
he takes no pleasure in human legs.
[11]Yahweh takes pleasure in those who fear him,
those who wait for his kindness.

[12]Laud Yahweh, O Jerusalem,
praise your God, O Zion,
[13]for he has strengthened the bars of your gates,
he has blessed your children within you,
[14]the one who establishes peace in your territory,
he satisfies you with the finest of wheat,
[15]the one who sends his promise to the earth,
his word runs swiftly,
[16]who gives snow like wool,
he scatters hoarfrost like dust,
[17]the one who casts his ice like breadcrumbs,
who can stand before his cold?
[18]He sends out his word and melts them,
he exhales his breath, the waters flow,
[19]the one who declares his words to Jacob,
his statutes and his righteous ordinances to Israel.
[20]He has not done this for any other nation,
and they do not know his righteous ordinances.

Hallelujah!

Notes on the text

1. Reading the adjectives as referring to praise, though they could refer to God (van Gemeren 2008: 997; cf. NRSV).

19. With many MSS and Q, reading pl. 'words'.

Form and structure

Psalm 147 is the second poem of the Final Hallel, the Psalter's closing collection of praise psalms, all having a 'Hallelujah!' frame. In some respects, it can be considered a further reflection on the beatitude of Psalm 146:5, and themes are shared between these poems. Perhaps the most distinctive is the use of the rare verb 'uphold' ('*wd*) in Psalms 146:9 and 147:6, both times pointing to Yahweh's concern for the weak. There are also extensions in theme, as for example in Yahweh's provision of food for animals (v. 9), whereas in Psalm 146:7 it was given to the hungry, though provision for humans is also mentioned here (v. 14). The unquantifiable nature of Yahweh's understanding as an expression of his greatness (v. 5) also connects this Psalm to Psalm 145:3. Since the Final Hallel emerges from the commitment to praise there (Ps. 145:21), the opening observations (v. 1) about the appropriateness of praise provides a further link. Psalm 145:21 also anticipated 'all flesh' giving praise, but that is transcended here as all creation contributes to praise. As deClaissé-Walford observes (deClaissé-Walford et al. 2014: 999), there is a movement from individual praise in Psalm 145 to communal praise in Psalm 146 and then all creation in praise in Psalm 147, establishing the pattern that then runs through Psalms 148–150.

The above connections presume that we can read this poem as a unit. But many have followed the lead of Gk (and Vg) in regarding this as two separate psalms, treating verses 1–11 and 12–21 as separate poems (cf. Seybold 1996: 538–539; Brueggemann and Bellinger [2014: 610] suggest it might have been three separate poems). There is certainly evidence supporting this, most obviously the fact that Jerusalem is discussed in the third person in verse 2 but addressed directly in verses 12–14. At this point, the imp. verbs shift from the m. pl. of 'Hallelujah!' (addressed to the community) to f. sg., consistent with making Jerusalem the object addressed. In addition, the theme of Yahweh's word (through Torah synonyms) is strongly present in verses 12–21 but absent in verses 1–11. Verses 1–11 are dense with allusions to other biblical texts, whereas these are very limited in verses 12–20 (cf. the table in Hossfeld and Zenger 2011: 621). There is no fundamental problem with bringing two separate poems together to form a single poem, as is evident in the case of Psalm 108 (see 'Form and structure' there), nor of taking one poem to make two psalms, as is evident in the case of Psalms 9–10 (see 'Form and structure' there). Therefore, irrespective of its putative textual history, our main task is to interpret the psalm before us. But this task is greatly enabled by a range of features that also bring these parts together (cf. Schwartz 2018: 319–320). The 'Hallelujah!' frame certainly assists, and while the approach to Jerusalem varies, the city is a central motif, with a second-level frame of 'Israel' (vv. 2, 19). The concern with creation, though particularly prominent in the final stanza, is already evident in verses 4–5, material that provides a context for Yahweh's wider work with creation in verses 15–18. Although it may be considered a standard element of the hymn (the category with which the psalm most easily fits, though as with much of the last Davidic collection [Pss 138–145] and Psalm 146, there are also strong wisdom elements in the reflections on creation), it should also be noted that the text moves between participial clauses and finite verbs in both parts. Where the first stanza begins by reflecting on praise, the next two employ introductory imperatives followed by participial clauses and concluding finite verbs. These features suggest that care has been taken to bring these elements together, so that, irrespective of its prehistory, the text is presented in MT as a unit, a unit that can reasonably be interpreted as a whole (similarly, Brodersen 2018: 201–204).

In the light of what has been observed, we can analyse the psalm in three stanzas (for convenience again attaching the 'Hallelujah!' frame to the nearest stanza), each with broadly similar poetic forms, even if there are also thematic variances:

1. The goodness of praise (1–6)
2. Sing to Yahweh (7–11)
3. Laud Yahweh, O Jerusalem (12–20)

Comment

1–6. As with Psalm 146, the 'Hallelujah!' stands outside the body of each stanza, serving as an independent summons to praise. However, that call to praise is closely woven into the text here as it immediately moves to reflect on the goodness of praise (cf. Ps. 92:1), with verse 1 ending with the key word 'praise'. The goodness of praise can be expressed in melody to our God, indicating that Yahweh is not a remote deity but one the community knows as its own. The praise of God is good in that it is both pleasant and fitting, something that can be enjoyed by the community and is also appropriate because of Yahweh's character and works. His character and works, justifying the goodness of praise, are developed through participial clauses in verses 2–4, pointing to his support for the whole community, especially the weak. Verse 2 stands out in that it commences with a ptc. that describes Yahweh's building Jerusalem while moving to a finite verb, reporting that he gathers the scattered of Israel (cf. Isa. 56:8). This verse sets the scene (perhaps alluding to events under Nehemiah) the remaining participial clauses explore as to how he does these things: healing the broken hearted, binding of their wounds (cf. Isa. 61:1), counting of the stars and giving them names, placing them under his authority. Yahweh's provision for Jerusalem and its weak is expressed by meeting the needs of the weak and through his awareness of the whole cosmos (cf. Isa. 40:26). No detail is beyond Yahweh, the verb 'calling' breaking the participial sequence and closing the subunit and emphasizing this factor. Accordingly, Yahweh's greatness can be affirmed along with his abundant power. Here, the one who has been shown to have this authority and relationship with all can also be called 'our Lord', again stressing that this unimaginably great one is the community's lord. So great is Yahweh that his own understanding is incapable of being quantified. Yet, he is also the one committed to the weak, with verse 6 closing the stanza with further participial clauses that emphasize both his upholding of the weak and bringing down of the wicked. As becomes clear in the second stanza, the wicked are those who do not fear Yahweh, not orienting their lives around his will. Although not the main point here, it also prepares for the focus on Yahweh's word as the guide for the faithful in verse 19, while his upholding of the afflicted is again consistent with his care of the weak.

7–11. The second stanza also opens with a focus on music as a means of expressing praise, except this time singing is expressly summoned and combined with making melody (here with a lyre as accompaniment), echoing verse 1. Yahweh is again 'our God', another instance of the emphasis on the close relationship between God and people in this psalm. Since this singing is focused on praise, he is here to be lauded with thanksgiving, reflecting on how he has engaged with the community in the past. Reasons for this are developed in a series of participial clauses in verses 8–9 that, as with verse 4, close by using 'cry' (*qr'*) as a finite verb. Verse 8 stands out as a tricolon that focuses on Yahweh's provision for creation (extended with an extra part line in Gk, though possibly redactional there). Here, focus is on the provision of rain, moving from clouds forming and then being a store for rain that, when it falls, causes the grass to grow (cf. Ps. 104:14). Although provision for all the beasts is not solely through water, this is fundamental to how all receive their food from Yahweh. We again see Yahweh's attention even to the seemingly insignificant by providing for the young ravens (cf. Luke 12:24). They are carrion eaters, making them unclean (Lev. 11:15), but still not beyond Yahweh's provision. All elements are provided for by Yahweh, each in their own way. But Yahweh does more than simply provide for all creation – he finds sources of pleasure in that creation. This is initially expressed negatively, noting his lack of delight in the strength of a horse or pleasure in human legs. Both elements point to possible military strength, items towards which humans may be drawn. Rather, Yahweh finds pleasure in those who fear him (cf. Ps. 33:16–18). 'Fear' here has its common meaning of worshipful commitment to him, though it receives additional definition by pointing to those who watch for his 'kindness' (*ḥesed*). Such watchfulness is a hopeful anticipation, a fear that looks to Yahweh, not military power, to provide. If Yahweh is the one who builds Jerusalem and whose power and understanding cannot be measured, then the wise response is to look hopefully to him for Jerusalem's continued restoration.

12–20. Yahweh's delight in hopeful waiting on him provides a link into the final stanza. Now, Jerusalem is personified and told to laud Yahweh, praising him as Zion's own God. Again, the language about Yahweh is relational, with a shift to the second person rather than 'our' (as in vv.

1, 5, 7) because of Jerusalem's personification. Here, the city represents God's people and, as they accept what has already been said of Yahweh, they have reason to praise him. Those reasons are extended in verse 13, which uses two pf. verbs to describe what Yahweh has done in strengthening the bars of city gates and blessing Jerusalem's children. The gate bars point to the security Yahweh has provided (exceeding the work in Neh. 3:3–14), while his blessing of the children means a context for their flourishing has been created. The blessing is then developed in verses 14–18, each of which opens with a ptc. in the opening part line and a finite verb in the second, with the verb providing an explanation of the ptc. So, Yahweh sets 'peace' (or 'prosperity'; *šālôm*) within Jerusalem's territory, evidenced through satisfying the city with the finest wheat. This satisfaction means Yahweh's provision for the city is like that of the beasts, though to a higher degree. Yahweh sends his promise to the land (echoing key terminology from Psalm 119; cf. Firth 2015b; Deut. 4:1–8), with this word running swiftly, reaching without delay those who need it. Yahweh's word is thus a further means of satisfying Jerusalem's needs. In verses 16–17 the focus shifts to what may be deemed the less desirable elements of creation, at least for a subsistence society, by noting the sending of elements associated with winter (snow, hoarfrost, ice), building to the question of who can stand before his cold. Crucially, even these elements, which may seem undesirable, belong to Yahweh, and humans again need to recognize their limitations before him. This reaches an initial climax in verse 18, which sets aside the ptcs. to link the themes of Yahweh's word and the cold. Yahweh's word is also powerful against the cold, melting the winter chills, with the simple act of his exhaling enough to make the waters flow again. Mention of Yahweh's 'breath' and the waters echoes Genesis 1:2 (cf. Ps. 33:6), suggesting that *rûaḥ* here could also be understood as Yahweh's Spirit. Yahweh's word is thus powerful, and this prepares for the final reflection in verses 20–21, which celebrates Yahweh's declaration of his word to Israel. Again, the language echoes Psalm 119, here pointing to Israel's immense privilege in having received this word, something no other people have received. Yahweh is building Jerusalem, and his word is central to how he does this. This is good news that can only result in praise – Hallelujah!

Explanation

The reasons for praise in Psalm 146 are extended here with a particular emphasis on Yahweh's deeds (Brodersen 2018: 174). This was already evident in Psalm 146 but is developed here. Those deeds provide reason for praise as he builds up Jerusalem from its earlier weakness, doing so within a context that celebrates his power over all creation. Yahweh is both supreme over all creation and yet intimately involved with all of it. Jerusalem, in its weakness, stands at the centre of this, experiencing his provision. That provision is not only in food and security, but also a means to live that honours Yahweh through the gift of his word. In this, the community knows that their life can please Yahweh. They do not fear him in order to please him but rather discover that they can respond to his provision and so please him, the one they can call 'our God'. The report of Jesus' ministry in Acts 10:36 shows clear parallels with the presentation of Yahweh here, showing that he is the one who continues this work, a work Paul also notes is revealed to all (Acts 14:17). Where this psalm encourages praise from the weak in Jerusalem, its reception in the NT points to the fact that all can now discover how good it is to offer such praise.

PSALM 148

Translation

1Hallelujah!

Praise Yahweh from the heavens,
   praise him in the heights.
2Praise him, all his messengers,
   praise him, all his hosts.
3Praise him, sun and moon,
   praise him all shining stars.
4Praise him, highest of the heavens,
   and the waters over the heavens.
5Let them praise the name of Yahweh,
   because he commanded and they were created,
6he stationed them for ever and ever,
   he gave a statute, and it shall not pass away.

7Praise Yahweh from the earth,
   sea monsters and all deeps,
8fire and hail, snow and smoke,
   stormy wind enacting his word,
9mountains and all hills,
   fruit trees and all cedars,
10wild animals and all livestock,
   creeping thing and winged bird,
11kings of the earth and all nations,
   princes and all judges of the earth,
12young men and women alike,
   elders along with youths.

13Let them praise the name of Yahweh,
because his name alone is exalted,
his splendour is over earth and heavens.
14He has raised up a horn for his people,
praise for all his faithful ones,
for the children of Israel, the people near him.

Hallelujah!

Notes on the text

2. With many mss, following Q.

8. Hebr. *qîṭôr* could be either smoke or fog. If emphasis is placed on fire (unless lightning is meant here; so Futato 2009: 435), then 'smoke' is probable, but if hail and snow are emphasized, then fog is probable. This may be an intentional ambiguity.

Form and structure

The third psalm of the Final Hallel extends themes from the preceding two. Again, it is marked by the 'Hallelujah!' frame that stands outside the main body of the poem, a pattern continued into the remaining psalms. Its emphasis on praise naturally continues elements from the preceding two, picking up both creational and Torah elements even as it develops them. The meteorological interests from Psalm 147:8, 15–18 are taken up here, except that now they are summoned to join the chorus of praise (v. 8), whereas there they were shown to be under Yahweh's authority. Yahweh's word as something that orders creation can be seen alongside the meteorological elements in Psalm 147:15–18, and that is also evident here (v. 8), though there is an additional note about Yahweh's statute ordering creation (v. 6). Finally, apart from the verb 'praise' (which occurs twelve times here) we should also note that the noun (*tĕhillâ*) appears in Psalms 147:1 and 148:14. The psalms are thus closely linked. But there are also important changes. There is a notable reduction in the vocabulary of praise from the four verbs in Psalm 147 (*hll*, *'nh*, *zmr*, *šbḥ*) to just one, *hll*. Further, where Psalm 147 focuses more on what Yahweh does that makes him worthy of praise, the main focus here is on who should offer praise. Although reasons for praise are still offered (vv. 5–6, 13–14), the greater concern is to summon praise, anticipating a further shift in this direction in Psalms 149–150. As with other poems in the Final Hallel, this psalm shows awareness of a range of other texts (notably Gen. 1 and Pss 103–104), but these are well integrated and the poem works even if readers do not recognize them, though their reading is enriched when they do.

The frequent use of the verb 'praise' (*hll*) means there is little debate that this is a psalm of praise, even if its extensive use of imperatives summoning praise is unusual. The creational emphases evident in it mean that there is also a wisdom overtone here, especially in the awareness of the taxonomies presented, though claims of a background in Egyptian wisdom are overstated (Hillers 1978: 329–334). Questions have been raised about the place of verses 13–14b (e.g. Gerstenberger 2001: 447–451), but with W. S. Prinsloo (1992b: 51–53) we can read the psalm as a coherent whole.

We can analyse the psalm in two stanzas, each containing two strophes, again placing the 'Hallelujah!' frame for convenience into the nearest stanza. The second strophe of each is marked by use of a juss. that leads into the reasons for praise:

1. Praise from the heavens (1–6)
   a. Praise commanded (1–4)
   b. Reasons for praise (5–6)
2. Praise from the earth (7–14)
   a. Praise commanded (7–12)
   b. Reasons for praise (13–14)

Comment

1–4. As with Psalms 146–147, the 'Hallelujah!' stands outside the body of each stanza, providing an independent summons to praise. Whereas Psalm 147 took up that summons by reflecting on the goodness of praise, here the concern is to identify all those in the heavens that should praise Yahweh. Hence, immediately following the 'Hallelujah!' (or 'Praise Yah!') the psalm uses the longer form 'Praise Yahweh!' before indicating that this praise is to come from the heavens. Each of verses 1b–4 then use 'praise him' in addressing the heavens, though 1b also forms a hinge to what follows by calling for praise in the heights, here equivalent to the heavens. Praise is to emerge from the heavens but should also be found there. Those who are to praise are listed in the rest of the strophe, personifying at least some aspects of creation. But before any personifications, verse 2 speaks of Yahweh's messengers and hosts, probably his heavenly court. If so, the 'messengers' and 'hosts' are angelic beings. This is consistent with Psalm 103:20–21, where they are also called to offer praise before the call for praise from all Yahweh's works. The rest of this strophe effectively identifies those works that are to praise Yahweh, works that can be drawn from Genesis 1 and Psalm 104. Sun and moon, along with the stars, are to offer praise, treating them simply as bearers of light (Gen. 1:13–16; Ps. 104:19), not gods as was widely believed. By shining, each praises Yahweh from the heavens and in the heights. The heavens themselves are personified in verse 4 as they too are to give praise. The 'highest of the heavens' (a superlative, lit. 'heavens of the heavens'; cf. Deut. 10:14; 1 Kgs 8:27) does not have to mean that there were multiple heavens (cf. 2 Cor. 12:2) but is rather to be understood spatially (even if does allow for the plurality). That which is most excellent in the heavens is to give praise because Yahweh is superior to all. If the spatial sense of 'highest heaven' is correct, then there is a further ascent to the waters above the heavens held there by the expanse in Genesis 1:6–8. All the heavens are to praise Yahweh.

5–6. The strophe shifts to a juss., explaining why all the heavens should praise Yahweh's name, phrasing paralleled in verse 13. Praising Yahweh's name here means praising him. The heavens are to praise because Yahweh commanded, and they were created. None of the heavens exists apart from Yahweh's command (cf. Ps. 33:9). Further, their place is determined by Yahweh and ratified by his statute, which ensures their enduring position (cf. Job 28:26–27). The statute here is specific to the creation, though given the emphasis on Yahweh's word in the surrounding poems it here is also linked to Torah. Hence, Yahweh organizes heavens and earth by his decree.

7–12. The second stanza resumes the call to praise. Here, the longer-form imp. 'Praise Yahweh' recurs from verse 1; but, instead of praise from the heavens, it is now from the earth. Unlike the first stanza, the imp. 'praise' is elided through the rest of this stanza. Instead, we work through various groups that are to praise Yahweh. The opening item, the sea monsters and the deeps, takes up the theme of water from verse 4, with language that echoes Genesis 1:2, 21. However terrifying these were for the ancient world, they were now to praise Yahweh. Both fire and the various meteorological items in verse 8, with their close links to Psalm 147, are also elements that may be regarded as undesirable by subsistence farmers, but these elements too are to praise Yahweh. Indeed, even wind storms were simply following Yahweh's word. Like the elements in the heavens that are governed by Yahweh's statute, so also the wind storm is simply performing Yahweh's word. Mountains and hills were places where people thought they were more likely to encounter the gods, but now they are simply to praise Yahweh, along with fruit trees (cf. Gen. 11 – 12) and cedars. These trees have different functions, one cultivated, one not (Berlin [2023: 162] thinks this is another merism, consistent with the other pairs), but now they simply need to praise. More mobile forms of life are then addressed in verse 10, so that both wild and domestic animals are to join creeping creatures and birds in offering praise (cf. Gen. 1:20–25). Just as humans are presented as the climax of creation in Genesis 1:26–28, so also humans are the climax of the call to praise here. The call to praise looks beyond Israel by calling kings of the nations, along with princes and all judges of the earth, to praise. Praise may seem to be Israel's responsibility, but the universal dimensions hinted at in Psalm 147:19–20 now become explicit. This universal praise comes not only from rulers, but from all dimensions of society, young men and women, elders and youths. The summons to praise is unconstrained by political borders and social boundaries. The high point of human existence is found in the praise of Yahweh, praise in which all are equal before him.

13–14. As with the first stanza, the second strophe is marked by a juss. verb which asks that those noted on earth be able to praise Yahweh's name. The statement about the name is extended here by noting that it is uniquely exalted, so his name also points back to the heavens. Indeed, his splendour is said to be over earth and heavens, providing a focal point for all praise, no matter whether it is from heaven or earth. Yet although all peoples are invited to praise, the psalm closes by noting that Yahweh has acted in a special manner for Israel, by exalting a 'horn' for them as his people (cf. 1 Sam. 2:10). The horn is a symbol of strength, an almost paradoxical statement if this psalm emerges from the post-exilic period, but one that points to their continued importance to Yahweh (cf. Schmutzer and Gauthier 2009). As well as raising up a horn for them, he has raised up praise for his loyal ones. 'Praise' here could be renown they experience from others (cf. NJPS; Allen 2002: 389–390), but within the Final Hallel it is more probable that praise has been raised up for them to offer to Yahweh. Here, his people are defined as his 'faithful ones' (*ḥasîd*), meaning that those who are to offer praise are committed to Yahweh. They do not need a specific command (though they are included in vv. 11–12), but rather receive praise as a gift from Yahweh that they offer back to him. The people who offer praise are finally defined as the 'children of Israel', a group recognized as near to Yahweh. Israel thus has a special opportunity within the nations to lead in offering praise, to align themselves with those in heaven who also do so, and thus lead all nations in offering praise – Hallelujah!

Explanation

Celebrating creation (see esp. Estes 2014, though note the cautions of Viviers 2004) as something both initiated and ordered by Yahweh, Psalm 148 asks all creation to join in praising Yahweh. Two choirs are involved in offering praise, one from heaven and one from earth, but together they are to announce Yahweh's praise. This praise is not limited to things that have a voice, so the praise here goes even beyond that of Psalm 150. Instead, even the inanimate praises him as the one who is truly exalted, whose splendour is over heaven and earth. But among these choirs a special place is held for his people. The Israel addressed in this psalm, probably a weak remnant after the exile, might have seemed politically insignificant. Yet they were at the heart of this praise, leading the nations in offering praise, declaring the word to them they had not previously known (Ps. 147:19–20) in the act of praise. Israel's significance is found in offering praise, a pattern that continues into the NT, where the praise of Jesus continues to testify of his splendour to all (Eph. 3:10; 1 Tim. 3:16; Rev. 5:9–10).

PSALM 149

Translation

1Hallelujah!
Sing to Yahweh a new song,
his praise in the assembly of the faithful.
2Let Israel be glad in his works,
let the children of Zion rejoice in their king.
3Let them praise his name in dance,
with hand-drum and lyre let them make melody to him.
4For Yahweh takes pleasure in his people,
he will adorn the afflicted with salvation.

5Let the faithful exult in glory,
let them shout upon their beds.
6The exaltation of God is in their throats,
it is a two-edged sword in their hand,
7to execute vengeance on the nations,
punishments of the peoples,
8to bind their kings in bonds,
and their honoured ones in iron fetters,
9to execute against them the written judgement,
an honour for all his faithful ones.
Hallelujah!

Notes on the text

6. Reading the waw on 'sword' as explicative (*WHS* §434). Brodersen (2018: 104) rejects this possibility because of its comparative rarity. But frequency points only to general patterns, not the specifics of this text. In this psalm, those who act are the afflicted, lacking military resources, and this makes the explicative more probable (similarly, Creach 2021: 376).

7. Codex L contains an error at this point (as at Pss 44:15; 57:10; 108:4), and should read *balĕʾummîm* (cf. 11QPs[a]; Codex A). Brodersen (2018: 104–105) defends L at this point as *lectio difficilior*, reading 'non-peoples', but as this is a consistent feature of the MS, the emendation should be followed, though with Barbiero and Pavan (2012) we should allow that the scribe of L might have wanted to highlight multiple reading possibilities.

Form and structure

The Final Hallel continues with a fourth psalm that employs the 'Hallelujah!' frame (vv. 1, 9). It also develops close links with Psalm 148, picking up the language of 'praise' (Pss 148:14; 149:1) and focus on the faithful (Pss 148:14; 149:2). More broadly, mention of singing a 'new song' points back to Psalm 144:9, and through it to Psalms 96:1; 98:1 (cf. Ps. 33:3). Nevertheless, there is a different attitude to the nations here, so that where Psalm 148:11–14 anticipates the point where all peoples (including kings) praise Yahweh, this time the concern is with how the faithful are to serve as instruments of Yahweh's vengeance on those same nations, including their kings (vv. 5–9). That vengeance, however, is determined by Yahweh, not the faithful.

As with the rest of the Final Hallel, the 'Hallelujah!' frame shows this is a praise psalm. It summons the faithful both to praise and to participation in seeing Yahweh's justice being brought into being through praise; though, unlike the previous three, it lacks obvious wisdom overtones. Its emphasis on judgement on the nations is also distinctive, giving it an eschatological cast (cf. Seybold 1996: 544). The treatment of the nations must be understood as a desire for justice that transcends the current reasons for praise; though, consistent with wider themes in the Psalter, this justice is wrought by Yahweh, not the faithful themselves (similarly, Hossfeld and Zenger 2011: 646). In demonstrating this, the psalm draws on a range of other texts, especially Isaiah 61 (Allen 2002: 397–398).

Apart from the 'Hallelujah!' frame, other notable repetitions within the poem point to its cohesion (W. S. Prinsloo 1999b: 399). Yahweh's faithful ones are mentioned in verses 1, 5, 9, all structurally significant. Also important is the contrast between Yahweh as the faithful's king (v. 2) and the vengeance on the kings (v. 8). The poem appears to pivot on the mention of the faithful ones in verse 5, and we can therefore analyse it in two stanzas:

1. New song (1–4)
2. Exulting in Yahweh (5–9)

Comment

1–4. As usual, 'Hallelujah!' stands outside the main body of the poem, though it also orients readers towards praise. In this case, we initially move into the form praise is to take as the community addressed is called to sing a new song to Yahweh. The language here evokes Psalms 96:1, 98:1, though in the immediate context it also echoes the vow to sing such a song in Psalm 144:9. The 'new song' in Psalms 96, 98 is a celebration of Yahweh's victory, which may lie in the background here (cf. Isa. 42:10–12; Rev. 5:9; 14:3; Ceresko [1986: 180] proposes the exodus, but, if so, only a type is used). As we move into the second stanza, there is a greater concern with a coming victory, but it remains possible both to reflect on a prior victory and anticipate a coming one. The new song is a song of praise, one that the faithful sing in the assembly. Verses 2–3 switch to jussives, concerned with a wider audience than the faithful in the assembly, desiring Israel to be glad in Yahweh's works, the children of Zion, in their king. The faithful do this as they sing their new song of praise, but the wider community still need to discover this, and so praise Yahweh's name with dance, making melody to him with hand-drum (cf. Exod. 15:20; Judg. 11:34; 1 Sam. 18:6) and lyre. The worship imagined here is fully embodied, with action and music. Verse 4 introduces the reason for such praise with two contrasting points of focus. First, attention is given to Yahweh, observing that Yahweh takes pleasure in his people (cf. Ps. 147:10–11). Although praise may please Yahweh, the concern here is simply his concern with his people, making praise the appropriate response. Second, praise is appropriate because Yahweh will adorn the afflicted with salvation. The afflicted could be the faithful alone, but the whole people are probably in view, looking to a time when he acts decisively for them. Yahweh's pleasure in his people is thus reflected in his coming improvement of their situation, and this provides reason for praise.

5–9. Attention returns to the faithful who are now to exult in glory, here probably their status as those adorned with salvation, and to shout out on their beds. Mention of beds contrasts with the assembly in verse 1, suggesting that praise is offered, and joy experienced and expressed, both in public and in private. The form joy takes is expressed in verse 6, a verse notable as the only one without a verb in the psalm. The faithful's means of exulting is to have God's high praises in their throats. As with praise, joy is also expressed in a wholly embodied manner. If mention of their bed points to the private expression of joy, then it is unlikely that the sword is intended literally. The extolling of God is their weapon (similarly, Broyles 1999: 518), and it is through this that we are to understand verses 7–9. Each of these opens with an infin., expressing the purpose (*WHS* §197) of their extolling God. The community has suffered at the hands of the nations, and although Yahweh has acted for them, there is more to be done if justice is to be restored. That justice is worked out through the worship of the faithful, itself bringing vengeance on the nations and punishment of the peoples. The psalm does not explain how this happens, but we are perhaps to imagine praise and joy in Yahweh as the force which brings nations to change their previous patterns of behaviour that afflicted the faithful (cf. 2 Chr. 20, where Israel's praise leads to victory without their participation in battle). This change in the nations is expressed in the change of status of their kings and honoured ones, who now become prisoners, previously the condition of the exiles. This is summed up in the opening of verse 9 in the statement that this is executing the written judgement against them, perhaps reflecting on texts such as Isaiah 13 – 23, Jeremiah 46:1 – 51:58 or Ezekiel 25 – 32 that announce Yahweh's judgement on various nations, though without being tied to one text. It cannot be the community's vengeance, but only what Yahweh has decreed. The second part of verse 9 is ambiguous. The honour of the faithful ones could be the carrying out of these things through their praise (as in the translation above) or Yahweh himself (W. S. Prinsloo 1999b: 404). In either case, the faithful stand in a special place in Yahweh's purposes, and through their worship become agents of change who bring about justice. Psalm 148:13 anticipates praise for Yahweh from the nations, but we are reminded here that this also involves the establishment of justice in places that have worked against the afflicted. The offering of praise is one way this happens – Hallelujah!

Explanation

Where Psalm 148 looked to the nations praising Yahweh, Psalm 149 looks to his justice being established among them, justice that stands with and for the afflicted who anticipate the time when they will be fully adorned with salvation, even as they are already glad in what he has done for them. Yahweh alone is king, and the kings of the earth must bow before him. This community, in its praise, becomes like the infants of Psalm 8:2 whose praise stills the enemy and avenger (Schaefer 2001: 344). Vesco (2006, 2: 1371) points to the fact that Psalms 1 and 2 look for Yahweh's judgement on the wicked (Ps. 1:6), and for the nations to serve him (Ps. 2:7–12). The Psalter is thus bound (apart from Ps. 150 as a closing invitation to praise) with the hope of God's justice in a world where it is often in short supply, a world where the righteous suffer and yet hope for the final victory that is to come. That justice, which God has decreed, is in various ways already announced and effected through the praise offered by his people. That God's word is powerful enough to achieve such things is implied by Hebrews 4:12, and so continues to encourage the faithful to exult in God, remembering the victory already won and announcing that which is to come.

PSALM 150

Translation

[1]Hallelujah!
Praise God in his sanctuary,
praise him in the firmament of his strength.
[2]Praise him for his mighty deeds,
praise him according to his abundant greatness.

[3]Praise him with the blast of a horn,
praise him with harp and lyre.
[4]Praise him with hand-drum and dance,
praise him with strings and pipe.
[5]Praise him with loud cymbals,
praise him with resounding cymbals.

[6]Let all breath praise Yah!
Hallelujah!

Notes on the text

2. A few MSS conform the prep. on the second part line to the rest of the psalm with *bĕ* rather than *kĕ*, a small orthographic change. But MT is to be retained since this small shift marks the end of the opening stanza (cf. Brodersen 2018: 33).

Form and structure

The Psalter closes with unadulterated praise. As we reach its conclusion, doxology is all that remains. Brueggemann (1988: 92–93) is suspicious of this psalm because it offers praise without reason, a valid concern if we extract it from the Psalter. But if the Psalter is a work meant to be worked through in sequence, then this concern can be addressed. In Psalm 149 (see 'Explanation') we noted elements that point to an inclusio with Psalms 1–2. If so, then the reasons for praise have reached their conclusion, and all that remains is praise, the weapon there that proclaimed Yahweh's kingship. In addition, we may note that some reasons for praise are indicated in verse 2, so even taken on its own there is some reason for praise. But the more significant reason for praise has been provided by the whole of the Psalter, though of course the rest of the Final Hallel (Pss 146–149) has provided good reason for praise. This point is further emphasized by the repetition of some of the forms of praise from Psalm 149, notably the use of both the hand-drum and dance (Pss 149:3; 150:4). The psalm is also joined to the rest of the Final Hallel (Pss 146–150) through use of the 'Hallelujah!' frame.

Since every part line in the psalm includes the verb 'praise' (*hll*), we can clearly classify this poem as a psalm of praise, though perhaps it would be more accurate to describe it as an invitation to praise. Consistent with a move towards universal praise that develops through the Final Hallel, it is finally a summons to all breath to praise Yahweh. This emphasis means that as readers finish this psalm, they also finish the Psalter, making it indeed the book of 'praises' (with Hossfeld and Zenger 2011: 657; cf. Introduction, §1, 'Name').

Although brief, the psalm contains clear points of movement. It can be analysed in three stanzas through these shifts in poetic form and content, though Ceresko's proposal (2006: 42–44) of an alphabetic form seems to exceed the evidence. As with the rest of the Final Hallel, the 'Hallelujah!' frame is incorporated into the nearest stanza for convenience:

1. The where and why of praise (1–2)
2. The how of praise (3–5)
3. Universal summons to praise (6)

Comment

1–2. Again, the 'Hallelujah!' stands outside the body of the poem but makes clear that those who engage with this psalm do so from a perspective of praise. The body of the psalm immediately takes up the imp. verb 'praise' (*hll*) from the frame, but now says to 'Praise God [*'el*]'. Use of the short form of this divine name links this call to the frame. Given the emphasis on the name 'Yahweh' in the Final Hallel (Pss 148:13; 149:3), this name is unexpected, though within this setting there is no doubt as to the God meant. Moreover, the short form could also allude to the Canaanite high deity even if only to show that the one who truly is over all is Yahweh (cf. Human 2010b: 5). God is to be praised in two places – his sanctuary and the firmament of his strength. The sanctuary could be the heavenly temple where the heavenly hosts offer praise (Ps. 148:1–2), though it is more likely the Jerusalem temple where the faithful gather for worship (cf. Ps. 134:2). The 'firmament of his strength' however clearly points to the heavens, possibly alluding to Genesis 1:6–8. The firmament is a marker of God's strength since it is how he separates the waters above and below from the earth. The firmament is also where he has placed the sun, moon and stars (Gen. 1:14–18), treating what others regarded as deities simply as bearers of light, showing his authority over them. The firmament is thus a marker that all powers in creation are subservient to God. That he is to be praised there indicates that the heavenly host are also to engage in praise. If so, then the two choirs that offered praise in Psalm 148 (from the heavens, Ps. 148:1–6; from the earth, Ps. 148:7–14) are again praising God. Both choirs are given reason for praise in verse 2, where God is to be praised for his mighty deeds and abundant greatness. Neither statement is defined here, but the context in the Final Hallel would point to things such as creation, various acts of redemption and the provision of hope that transcends the community's current experience.

3–5. Having called for praise, the second stanza outlines some means of praise. The list is representative rather than comprehensive (notably, there is nothing vocal here), but is fully embodied. Most means of praise here are musical, though not necessarily tuneful or even associated with the temple. On the different instruments that comprise the band here, see van Gemeren 2008: 1010–1011; we might also compare 2 Samuel 6:1–19 for a range of instruments and dance. The emphasis is on bringing in a range of sounds to praise God. The horn here is a ram's horn, something blown for a range of reasons (cf. Josh. 6:16 [battle], 1 Kgs 1:34 [announcing a coronation], Exod. 19:19 [a theophany]), though here it is probably intended simply as part of a sort of temple orchestra (cf. Ps. 81:3; 98:6). Alongside this, with the harp and lyre we have two tuneful instruments, both plucked-string instruments. Tuneful instruments return in verse 4b with mention of strings and pipe, though these are less specific and perhaps refer to a class of instrument, one plucked, and one blown. Between them we also have the hand-drum and dance, recalling Ps. 149:3 and a range of other OT texts that typically refer to women in worship (cf. Exod. 15:20; Judg. 11:34; 1 Sam. 18:6; Mathys 2000: 335–336). Again, worship is fully embodied, though here it is also filled with sound, only some of which is tuneful. The final instruments, two types of cymbals (the main feature of which seems to be that they were loud), again point to the volume of sound rather than tune, though perhaps, like modern orchestral music, the cymbals would be used to mark a musical climax in the praise. Whatever sounds can be produced, they are joined with bodily action to offer exuberant praise, praise that can be offered anywhere.

6. Whereas each line to this point commenced with the verb 'praise' (*hll*), the final stanza delays it, switching to a juss. rather than the previous imperatives. Only after affirming that all breath is involved, do we return to the verb. That 'all breath' should praise Yah would certainly include all humans (cf. Gen. 2:7), but like 'all flesh' (Ps. 145:21) could look beyond humans to include all animate life (Kidner [1975, 1: 529] points to Psalm 148:7–12 in defence of this; cf. Gen. 7:22). Praise may be structured and symphonic, or chaotic and cacophonous; but, however done, anything alive is invited to praise Yah. The only response to this is 'Hallelujah!', the 'Hallelujah!' frame now providing a response to the preceding monocolon.

Explanation

Breath was a gift God gave to all life in creation, and the appropriate response is to give that breath back to God in praise. The praise summoned here brings the Psalter to a fitting close, one that recognizes we exist and find our fullness in the praise of God (similarly, McCann 1996: 1297). The grounds of that praise have been established in all that has come before, meaning that praise has also acknowledged pain and hurt, times when God seems distant and even where his faithfulness to the covenant seems uncertain. But it also remembers his faithfulness, forbearance and forgiveness. It confesses that God alone is king, and that in his kingdom we finally see how our earthly existence comes together with the reality of heaven. As the conclusion to both the Final Hallel and the whole Psalter, Psalm 150 gathers all this together as the choirs of heaven and earth come together in the praise of God, and in doing so invite all that lives to give praise. Every time we pray, 'May your kingdom come,' we anticipate that time when all breath will indeed give praise.

BIBLIOGRAPHY

COMMENTARIES ON PSALMS

Allen, L. C. (2002), *Psalms 101–150*, rev. edn, Nashville: Thomas Nelson.

Anderson, A. A. (1972), *Psalms*, 2 vols., Grand Rapids: Eerdmans.

Berlin, A. (2023), *Psalms 120–150*, Philadelphia: JPS.

Briggs, C. A., and E. G. Briggs (1906, 1907), *A Critical and Exegetical Commentary on the Book of Psalms*, 2 vols., Edinburgh: T. & T. Clark.

Broyles, C. C. (1999), *Psalms*, Peabody: Hendrickson.

Brueggemann, W. (1984), *The Message of the Psalms: A Theological Commentary*, Minneapolis: Augsburg.

Brueggemann, W., and W. H. Bellinger Jr. (2014), *Psalms*, Cambridge: Cambridge University Press.

Collins, C. J. (2022), 'Psalms', in I. M. Duguid, J. M. Hamilton Jr. and J. Sklar (eds.), *ESV Expository Commentary*, vol. 5, Wheaton: Crossway, 21–696.

Craigie, P. C., and M. E. Tate (2004), *Psalms 1–50*, Nashville: Thomas Nelson.

Creach, J. F. D. (2021), *Reading Psalms: A Literary and Theological Commentary*, Macon: Smyth & Helwys.

Curtis, A. H. W. (2005), *Psalms*, Norwich: Epworth.

Dahood, M. J. (1965), *Psalms I:1–50, Introduction, Translation and Notes*, Garden City: Doubleday.

—— (1968), *Psalms II:51–100, Introduction, Translation and Notes*, Garden City: Doubleday.

—— (1970), *Psalms III:101–150, Introduction, Translation and Notes*, Garden City: Doubleday.

Davidson, R. (1998), *The Vitality of Worship: A Commentary on the Book of Psalms*, Grand Rapids: Eerdmans.

deClaissé-Walford, N., R. A. Jacobson and B. LaNeel Tanner (2014), *The Book of Psalms*, Grand Rapids: Eerdmans.

Delitzsch, F. (1996, repr.), *Commentary on the Old Testament: Psalms*, Peabody: Hendrickson.

Emanuel, D. (2022), *An Intertextual Commentary to the Psalter: Juxtaposition and Allusion in Book 1*, Eugene: Pickwick.

Estes, D. J. (2019), *Psalms 73–150*, Nashville: B. & H. Academic.

Futato, M. D. (2009), 'Psalms', in P. W. Comfort (ed.), *Cornerstone Bible Commentary*, vol. 7, Carol Stream: Tyndale House, 1–450.

Gemeren, W. van (2008), 'Psalms', in T. Longman III and D. E. Garland (eds.), *The Expositor's Bible*, vol. 5, Grand Rapids: Zondervan.

Gerstenberger, E. S. (1988), *Psalms, Part I: With an Introduction to Cultic Poetry*, Grand Rapids: Eerdmans.
—— (2001), *Psalms, Part II, and Lamentations*, Grand Rapids: Eerdmans.
Gillingham, S. E. (2008), *Psalms Through the Centuries Volume One*, Oxford: Blackwell.
—— (2018), *Psalms Through the Centuries Volume Two: A Reception History Commentary on Psalms 1–72*, Oxford: Wiley Blackwell.
—— (2022), *Psalms Through the Centuries Volume Three: A Reception History Commentary on Psalms 73–151*, Oxford: Wiley Blackwell.
Goldingay, J. (2006a), *Psalms, Volume 1: Psalms 1–41*, Grand Rapids: Baker Academic.
—— (2007), *Psalms, Volume 2: Psalms 42–89*, Grand Rapids: Baker Academic.
—— (2008), *Psalms, Volume 3: Psalms 90–150*, Grand Rapids: Baker Academic.
Grogan, G. W. (2008), *Psalms*, Grand Rapids: Zondervan.
Hamilton Jr., J. M. (2021), *Psalms*, 2 vols., Bellingham: Lexham Academic.
Hossfeld, F.-L., and E. Zenger (2006), *Psalms 51–100*, Minneapolis: Fortress.
—— (2011), *Psalms 101–150*, Minneapolis: Fortress.
Kidner, D. (1975), *Psalms*, 2 vols., London: Inter-Varsity Press, 1975.
Kraus, H.-J. (1988), *Psalms 1–59: A Commentary*, Minneapolis: Augsburg.
—— (1989), *Psalms 60–150: A Commentary*, Minneapolis: Augsburg.
Limburg, J. (2000), *Psalms*, Louisville: Westminster John Knox.
Longman III, T. (2014), *Psalms: An Introduction and Commentary*, Nottingham: Inter-Varsity Press.
McCann Jr., J. C. (1996), 'The Book of Psalms', in L. E. Keck (ed.), *The New Interpreter's Bible*, vol. 4, Nashville: Abingdon, 639–1280.
Marlowe, W. C., and C. H. Savelle Jr. (2021), *Psalms: Volume 1. The Wisdom Psalms*, Grand Rapids: Kregel Ministry.
Mays, J. L. (1994b), *Psalms*, Louisville: Westminster John Knox.
Prinsloo, W. S. (2003), 'Psalms', in J. Rogerson and J. D. G. Dunn, *Eerdmans Commentary on the Bible*, Grand Rapids: Eerdmans, 364–436.
Ravasi, G. (1985a), *Il Libro dei Salmi: Vol I (1–50)*, Bologna: Edizioni Dehoniane.
—— (1985b), *Il Libro dei Salmi: Vol II (51–100)*, Bologna: Edizioni Dehoniane.
—— (1985c), *Il Libro dei Salmi: Vol III (101–150)*, Bologna: Edizioni Dehoniane.
Ross, A. P. (2011), *A Commentary on the Psalms: Volume 1 (1–41)*, Grand Rapids: Kregel.
—— (2013), *A Commentary on the Psalms: Volume 2 (42–89)*, Grand Rapids: Kregel.
—— (2016), *A Commentary on the Psalms: Volume 3 (90–150)*, Grand Rapids: Kregel.
Schaefer, K. (2001), *Psalms*, Collegeville: Liturgical Press.
Seybold, K. (1996), *Die Psalmen*, Tübingen: Mohr Siebeck.
Tate, M. E. (1990), *Psalms 51–100*, Dallas: Word.

Terrien, S. (2003), *The Psalms: Strophic Structure and Theological Commentary*, 2 vols., Grand Rapids: Eerdmans.

Tucker Jr., W. D., and J. A. Grant (2018), *The NIV Application Commentary: Psalms Volume 2*, Grand Rapids: Zondervan.

Van der Ploeg, J. P. M. (1973), *Psalmen I*, Roermond: J. J. Romen & Zonen.

Van Uchelen, N. A. (1971), *Psalmen I*, Nijkerk: G. F. Callenbach.

—— (1977), *Psalmen II*, Nijkerk: G. F. Callenbach.

Vesco, J.-L. (2006), *Le psautier de David: traduit et commenté*, 2 vols., Paris: Cerf.

Weiser, A. (1962), *The Psalms: A Commentary*, London: SCM.

Wilcock, M. (2001), *The Message of the Psalms: Songs for the People of God*, 2 vols., Leicester: Inter-Varsity Press.

Wilson, G. H. (2002), *The NIV Application Commentary: Psalms Volume 1*, Grand Rapids: Zondervan.

OTHER WORKS

Abernethy, A. T. (2015a), 'God as Teacher in Psalm 25', *VT* 65:339–351.

—— (2015b), '"Right Paths" and/or "Paths of Righteousness"? Examining Psalm 23.3b Within the Psalter', *JSOT* 39:299–318.

Achtemeier, E. (1974), 'Overcoming the World: An Exposition of Psalm 6', *Int* 28:75–88.

Adam, K.-P. (2001), *Der önigliche Held: Die Entsprechung von kämpfendem Gott und kämpfendem König in Psalm 18*, Neukirchner: Neukirchner Verlag.

Ahn, J. (2008), 'Psalm 137: Complex Communal Laments', *JBL* 127:267–289.

Allen, L. C. (1982), 'Psalm 73: An Analysis', *TynB* 33:93–118.

—— (1984), 'Structure and Meaning in Psalm 50', *VE* 14:17–37.

—— (1986), 'The Value of Rhetorical Criticism in Psalm 69', *JBL* 105:577–598.

Alonso-Schökel, L. (1976), 'The Poetic Structure of Psalm 42–43', *JSOT* 1:4–11.

Alter, R. (1985), *The Art of Biblical Poetry*, New York: Basic.

Althann, R. (1983), 'Ps 58,10 in Light of Ebla', *Bib* 64:122–124.

Amzallag, N. (2014), 'The Meaning of *Todah* in the Title of Psalm 100', *ZAW* 126:535–545.

—— (2015), 'The Cryptic Theme of Psalm 46 and the Theology of the Korahites', *RB* 122:26–45.

Amzallag, N., and M. Avriel (2014), 'The Canonic Responsa Reading of Psalm 114 and Its Theological Significance', *OTE* 24:303–323.

Amzallag, N., and S. Yona (2016), 'What Does "Maskil" in the Heading of a Psalm Mean?', *ANES* 53:41–57.

Anderson, C. E. (2015), 'The Politics of Psalmody: Psalm 60 and the Rise and Fall of Judean Independence', *JBL* 134:313–332.

Andrason, A. (2013), 'An Optative Indicative? A Real Factual Past? Toward a

Cognitive-Typological Approach to the Precative Qatal', *JHS* 13, art. 4, 41 pages, DOI:10.5508/jhs.2013.v13.a4.

Armitage, D. A. (2010), 'Rescued Already? The Significance of עניתני in Psalm 22,22', *Bib* 91:335–347.

Arnold, B. T., and B. E. Beyer (2002), *Readings from the Ancient Near East*, Grand Rapids: Baker.

Auffret, P. (1977), 'Note sur la structure littéraire du Psaume CXXXVI', *VT* 27:1–12.

—— (1979), 'Essai sur la structure littéraire du Psaume LXXXVI', *VT* 29:385–402.

—— (1988), '"Yahvé, qu(elle nous est), chère, ta loyauté!" Étude structurelle du Ps 36', *ScEs* 40:57–73.

—— (1989), 'Note on the Literary Structure of Psalm 134', *JSOT* 45:87–89.

—— (1990), '"Dans ta force se réjouit le roi": Étude structurelle du Psaume xxi', *VT* 40:385–410.

—— (1991), 'L'ensemble des trois psaumes 46, 47 et 48: Étude structurelle', *ScEs* 43:339–348.

—— (1993), 'Qu'ils sachent que toi, ton nom est Yhwh! Étude structurelle du Psaume 83', *ScEs* 45:41–59.

—— (1994), '"Je serai rassasié de ton image": Étude structurelle du Psaume 17', *ZAW* 106:446–458.

—— (1997), 'L'étude structurelle des Psaumes: Réponses et compléments II (Pss. 61, 77, 82, 100, 138, 147)', *ScEs* 50:39–61.

—— (1998), 'Sur ton peuple ta bénédiction!: Étude structurelle du Psaume 3', *ScEs* 49:315–334.

—— (2002a), 'Dans les assemblées je bénirai Yhwh: Nouvelle étude structurelle du Psaume xxvi', *VT* 56:303–312.

—— (2002b), 'Qu'est-ce que l'homme, que tu t'en souviennes? Étude structurelle du psaume 8', *ScEs* 54:25–35.

—— (2005), 'YHWH aimant les justes: Étude structurelle du Psaume 146', *ScEs* 57:49–57.

—— (2007), 'Venez à ses portails! Etude structurelle du Psaume 100', *ZAW* 119:236–240.

—— (2011), 'Nouvelle étude structurelle des psaumes 12 et 13', *ScEs* 63:37–50.

Ayars, M. I. (2019), *The Shape of Hebrew Poetry: Exploring the Discourse Function of Linguistic Parallelism in the Egyptian Hallel*, Leiden: Brill, 2019.

Bang, K.-M. (2017), 'A Missing Key to Understanding Psalm 46: Revisiting the Chaoskampf', *Conversations with the Biblical World* 37:68–89.

Barbiero, G. (2008), 'The Risks of a Fragmented Reading of the Psalms: Psalm 72 as a Case in Point', *ZAW* 120:67–91.

—— (2013), 'Psalm 132: A Prayer of "Solomon"', *CBQ* 75:239–258.

—— (2019), 'Psalm 41:14, or the Unity of the Masoretic Psalm 41', *OTE* 32:317–342.

Barbiero, G., and M. Pavan (2012), ‘Psalm 44:15, 57:10, 108:4, 149:7 – בלאמים or בל־אמים*’, *ZAW* 124:598–605.

Barré, M. L. (1984), ‘Recovering the Literary Structure of Psalm xv’, *VT* 34:207–211.

—— (1988), ‘The Seven Epithets of Zion in Ps 48,2–3’, *Bib* 69:557–563.

—— (1990), ‘Psalm 116: Its Structure and Its Enigmas’, *JBL* 109:61–78.

—— (1996), ‘A Proposal on the Crux of Psalm LXIV 9a’, *VT* 46:115–119.

Basson, A. (2005), ‘“You Are My Rock and Fortress”. Refuge Metaphors in Psalm 31. A Perspective from Cognitive Metaphor Theory’, *AcT* (25):2:1–17.

Batto, B. F. (2013), *In the Beginning: Essays on Creation Motifs in the Ancient Near East and the Bible*, Winona Lake: Eisenbrauns.

Bauer, U. F. W. (2001), ‘Eine Literarische Analyse von Psalm CXIV’, *VT* 51:289–311.

Baumann, G. (2006), ‘Psalm 74: Myth as the Source of Hope in Times of Devastation’, *Verbum et Ecclesia* 27:416–430.

Bechtel Reynolds, C. (1994), ‘Psalm 125’, *Int* 48:272–275.

Becking, B. (1990), ‘“Wie Töpfe Sollst Du Sie Zersehm eißen” Mesopotamische Parallelen zu Psalm 2,9b*’, *VT* 102:59–79.

—— (2009), ‘God-Talk for a Disillusioned Pilgrim in Psalm 121’, *JHS* 9, art. 15.

—— (2010), ‘Exilische Identiteit als post-exilische Ideologie: Psalm 137 opnieuw gelezen’, *NTT* 64:269–282.

Becking, B., and E. Peels (2007), *Psalms and Prayers: Papers Read at the Joint Meeting of the Society of Old Testament Study and Het Oudtestamentisch Werkgezelschap in Nederland en België, Apeldoorn August 2006*, Leiden: Brill, 109–118.

Begg, C. T. (1988a), ‘“Dove” and “God(s)” in Ps 56,1’, *ETL* 64:393–396.

—— (1988b), ‘Ps 52a: A *Forschungsbericht* and a Proposal’, *ETL* 64:397–404.

Bellinger Jr., W. H. (1984), ‘The Interpretation of Psalm 11’, *EvQ* 56:95–101.

—— (1993), ‘Psalm XXVI: A Test of Method’, *VT* 48:452–461.

—— (1999), ‘Psalm 61: A Rhetorical Analysis’, *PRS* 26:379–388.

—— (2005), ‘Psalm 137: Memory and Poetry’, *HBT* 27:5–20.

—— (2012), *Psalms: Reading and Studying the Book of Praises*, 2nd edn, Grand Rapids: Baker Academic.

Berger, Y. (2014), ‘The David–Benjaminite Conflict and the Intertextual Field of Psalm 7’, *JSOT* 38:279–296.

Berlin, A. (1977), ‘Psalm 118:24’, *JBL* 96:567–568.

—— (1985), *The Dynamics of Biblical Parallelism*, Bloomington: Indiana University Press.

—— (2015), ‘Psalm 132: A Prayer for the Restoration of Judah’, in S. Yonah, E. L. Greenstein, M. I. Gruber, P. Machinist and S. M. Paul (eds.), *Marbeh Hokmah: Studies in the Bible and the Ancient Near East in Loving Memory of Victor Avigdor Hurowitz*, Winona Lake: Eisenbrauns, 65–72.

Berry, D. K. (1993), *The Psalms and Their Readers: Interpretative Strategies for Psalm 18*, Sheffield: JSOT Press.

Beuken, W. A. M. (1992), 'Psalm 96: Israel en de volken', *SK* 13:1–10.

—— (2020), *From Servant of YHWH to Being Considerate of the Wretched: The Figure of David in the Reading Perspective of Psalms 35–41 MT*, Leuven: Peeters.

Beyerlin, W. (1970), *Die Rettung der Bedrängten in den Feindpsalmen der Einzelnen auf institutionelle zusammenhänge Untersucht*, Göttingen: Vandenhoeck & Ruprecht.

—— (1979), *Werden und Wesen des 107. Psalms*, Berlin: de Gruyter.

Blackburn, B. (1991), 'Psalm 71', *RevExp* 88:241–245.

Böckle, J. (2021), '"Der Herr ist mein Hirte" – Konzeptuelle Metapher als Lebenswirklichkeit', *OTE* 34:189–217.

Boda, M. J. (2009), *A Severe Mercy: Sin and Its Remedy in the Old Testament*, Winona Lake: Eisenbrauns.

Bodner, K. (2003), 'The "Embarrassing Syntax" of Ps. 47:10: A (Pro)Vocative Option', *JTS* 54:570–576.

Boer, P. A. H. de (1984), 'Psalm 81:6a – Observations on Translation and Meaning of One Hebrew Line', in W. B. Barrick and J. R. Spencer (eds.), *In the Shelter of Elyon: Essays on Ancient Palestinian Life and Literature in Honour of G. W. Ahlström*, Sheffield: JSOT Press, 67–80.

Booij, T. (1984), 'The Background of the Oracle in Psalm 81', *Bib* 65:465–475.

—— (1987), 'Some Observations on Psalm LXXXVII', *VT* 37:16–25.

—— (1988a), 'The Hebrew Text of Psalm XCII 11', *VT* 38:210–214.

—— (1988b), 'Psalm CI 2 – "When Wilt Thou Come to Me?"', *VT* 38:458–462.

—— (1989a), 'Psalm CX: "Rule in the Midst of Your Foes!"', *VT* 41:396–407.

—— (1989b), 'The Role of Darkness in Psalm CV 28', *VT* 39:209–214.

—— (1995), 'Psalm 116,10–11: The Account of an Inner Crisis', *Bib* 76:388–395.

—— (2001), 'Psalm CXXII 4: Text and Meaning', *VT* 51:262–266.

—— (2005), 'Psalm 141 – a Prayer for Discipline and Protection', *Bib* 86:97–106.

—— (2012), 'Psalm CXLV: David's Song of Praise', *VT* 58:633–637.

—— (2015), 'Psalm 118 and Form Criticism', *Bib* 96:351–374.

Bos, J. H. W. (1982), 'Oh, When the Saints: A Consideration of the Meaning of Psalm 50', *JSOT* 24:65–77.

Botha, P. J. (1992), 'The Function of the Polarity Between the Pious and the Enemies in Psalm 119', *OTE* 5:252–263.

—— (1995), 'Ironie as Sleutel tot die Verstaan van Psalm 14', *SK* 16:16–27.

—— (1997), 'The Social Setting and Strategy of Psalm 34', *OTE* 10:178–197.

—— (2000), 'Psalm 54: The Power of Positive Patterning', *SK* 21:507–516.

—— (2001), 'Social Values and the Interpretation of Psalm 123', *OTE* 14:189–198.

—— (2002a), '"The Honour of the Righteous Will Be Restored": Psalm 75 in Its Social Context', *OTE* 15:320–334.

—— (2002b), 'A Social-Scientific Reading of Psalm 129', *HTS* 58:1401–1414.
—— (2003), 'Psalm 118 and Social Values in Ancient Israel', *OTE* 16:195–215.
—— (2004a), 'The Poetic Structure and Strategy of Psalm 79', *VeE* 25:357–377.
—— (2004b), 'Psalm 67 in Its Literary and Ideological Context', *OTE* 17:365–379.
—— (2004c), 'The Textual Strategy and Ideology of Psalm 36', *OTE* 17:506–520.
—— (2005a), 'The Ideological Interface Between Psalm 1 and Psalm 2', *OTE* 18:189–203.
—— (2005b), 'Intertextuality and the Interpretation of Psalm 1', *OTE* 18:503–520.
—— (2009), 'Answers Disguised as Questions: Rhetoric and Reasoning in Psalm 24', *OTE* 22:535–553.
—— (2010), 'Psalm 108 and the Quest for Closure to the Exile', *OTE* 23:574–596.
—— (2011), 'Poetry and Perlocution in Psalm 26', *OTE* 24:30–48.
—— (2012a), 'Pride and the Suffering of the Poor in the Persian Period: Psalm 12 in Its Post-Exilic Context', *OTE* 25:40–56.
—— (2012b), 'Psalm 34 and the Ethics of the Hebrew Psalter', in Human, *Psalmody and Poetry*, 56–75.
—— (2012c), 'Psalm 91 and Its Wisdom Connections', *OTE* 25:260–276.
—— (2013a), '"I Am Like a Green Olive Tree": The Wisdom Context of Psalm 52', *HTS Teologiese Studies / Theological Studies* 69 (1), art. 1962, http://dx.doi.org/10.4102/ hts.v69i1.1962.
—— (2013b), 'Psalm 53 in Canonical Perspective', *OTE* 26:583–606.
—— (2014), 'Psalm 32 as a Wisdom Intertext', *HTS Teologiese Studies / Theological Studies* 70 (1), art. 2710, http:// dx.doi.org/10.4102/hts.v70i1.2710.
—— (2015), 'Following the "Tracks of Righteousness" of Psalm 23', *OTE* 28:283–300.
—— (2016a), 'Psalm 101: A Supplication for the Restoration of Society in the Late Post-Exilic Age', *HTS Teologiese Studies / Theological Studies* 72 (4), art. 3389, http://dx.doi. org/10.4102/hts.v72i4.3389.
—— (2016b), 'True Happiness in the Presence of YHWH: The Literary and Theological Context for Understanding Psalm 16', *OTE* 29:61–84.
—— (2017a), 'Psalm 39 and Its Place in the Development of a Doctrine of Retribution in the Hebrew Bible', *OTE* 30:240–264.
—— (2017b), 'Psalm 55 Interpreted in View of Its Textual, Metatextual and Intertextual Connections', *SJOT* 31:118–141.
—— (2018a), 'Psalm 4 and the Poor in the Post-Exilic Province of Judah: A Textual and Contextual Reading', *JNSL* 44:23–39.
—— (2018b), 'Psalm 5 and the Polarity Between Those Who May Stand Before Yahweh and Those Who May Not', *HTS Teologiese Studies / Theological Studies* 74 (1), art. 5087, https://doi.org/ 10.4102/hts.v74i1.5087.

—— (2018c), 'Psalm 62: Prayer, Accusation, Declaration of Innocence, Self-Motivation, Sermon, or All of These?', *AcT* 38:32–48.

—— (2019), 'Psalm 32: A Social-Scientific Investigation', *OTE* 32:12–31.

Botha, P. J., and J. H. Potgieter (2010), '"The Word of Yahweh Is Right": Psalm 33 as a Torah Psalm', *VeE* 31 (1), art. 431, DOI: 10.4102/ve.v31i1.431.

Botha, P. J., and B. Weber (2019), '"The Lord Is My Light and My Salvation . . ." (Ps 27:1): Psalm 27 in the Literary Context of Psalms 25–34', *JNSL* 45:19–50.

Bouzard Jr., W. C. (1997), *We Have Heard with Our Ears, O God: Sources of the Communal Laments in the Psalms*, Atlanta: Scholars Press.

Bowen, N. R. (2003), 'A Fairy Tale Wedding? A Feminist Intertextual Reading of Psalm 45', in Strawn and Bowen, *God So Near*, 53–72.

Boyle, G. R. (2022), 'The Imprecatory Psalms as Means of Mercy and Wellness', *CTQ* 86:193–214.

Bracke, J. M. (1985), '*šûb š*^{e}*bût*: A Reappraisal', *ZAW* 97:233–244.

Brettler, M. Z. (1989), *God Is King: Understanding an Israelite Metaphor*, Sheffield: JSOT Press, 1989.

—— (1993), 'Images of Yahweh the Warrior in Psalms', *Semeia* 61:135–165.

—— (2007), 'The Poet as Historian: The Plague Tradition in Psalm 105', in K. F. Kravitz and D. M. Sharon (eds.), *Bringing the Hidden to Light: The Process of Interpretation. Essays in Honor of Stephen A. Geller*, Winona Lake: Eisenbrauns, 19–28.

—— (2009), 'The Riddle of Psalm 111', in D. A. Green and L. A. Lieber (eds.), *Scriptural Exegesis: The Shapes of Culture and the Religious Imagination. Essays in Honour of Michael Fishbane*, Oxford: Oxford University Press, 62–73.

—— (2013), 'Psalm 136 as an Interpretive Text', *HeBAI* 2:373–395.

Bright, J. (1975), *The Authority of the Old Testament*, Grand Rapids: Baker.

Brodersen, A. (2018), *The End of the Psalter: Psalms 146–150 in the Masoretic Text, the Dead Sea Scrolls and the Septuagint*, Waco: Baylor University Press.

Brown, M. L. (1995), *Israel's Divine Healer*, Grand Rapids: Zondervan.

Brown, W. P. (1998), 'A Royal Performance: Critical Notes on Psalm 110 3ay-b', *JBL* 117:93–96.

—— (2002), *Seeing the Psalms: A Theology of Metaphor*, Louisville: Westminster John Knox.

—— (2010), '"Here Comes the Sun!": The Metaphorical Theology of Psalms 15–24", in Zenger, *Composition*, 259–278.

Broyles, C. C. (1989), *The Conflict of Faith and Experience in the Psalms: A Form-Critical and Theological Study*, Sheffield: JSOT Press.

—— (2005), 'The Psalms and Cult Symbolism: The Case of the Cherubim-Ark', in Johnston and Firth, *Interpreting*, 139–156.

Brueggemann, W. (1984), *The Message of the Psalms: A Theological Commentary*, Minneapolis: Augsburg.

—— (1985), 'Psalm 100', *Int* 39:65–69.

—— (1988), *Israel's Praise: Doxology Against Idolatry and Ideology*, Philadelphia: Fortress.

—— (1991a), *Abiding Astonishment: Psalms, Modernity, and the Making of History*, Louisville: Westminster John Knox.

—— (1991b), 'Bounded by Obedience and Praise', *JSOT* 50:63–92.

Brueggemann, W., and P. D. Miller (1996), 'Psalm 73 as a Canonical Marker', *JSOT* 72:45–56.

Bullock, C. H. (2023), *Theology from the Psalms: The Story of God's Steadfast Love*, Grand Rapids: Baker Academic.

Burnett, J. S. (2006), 'Forty-Two Songs for Elohim: An Ancient Near Eastern Organizing Principle in the Shaping of the Elohistic Psalter', *JSOT* 31:81–101.

Burnett, J. S., W. H. Bellinger Jr. and W. Dennis Tucker Jr. (eds.) (2007), *Diachronic and Synchronic. Reading the Psalms in Real Time: Proceedings on the Baylor Symposium on the Book of Psalms*, London: T. & T. Clark.

Burt, S. (2018), '"Your Torah Is My Delight": Repetition and the Poetics of Immanence in Psalm 119', *JBL* 137:685–700.

Buysch, C. (2009), *De letze Davidpsalter: Interpretation, Komposition und Funktion der Psalmenruppe Ps 138–145*, Stuttgart: Katholisches Bibelwerk.

Callaham, S. N. (2009), 'An Evaluation of Psalm 119 as Constrained Writing', *HS* 50:121–128.

Campbell, A. F. (1979), 'Psalm 78: A Contribution to the Theology of Tenth Century Israel', *CBQ* 41:51–79.

Campbell, S. D., R. G. Rohlfing Jr. and R. S. Briggs (2023), *A New Song: Biblical Hebrew Poetry as Jewish and Christian Scripture*, Bellingham: Lexham Academic.

Carrière, J.-M. (1991), 'Le Ps 72 est-il un psaume messianique?', *Bib* 72:49–69.

Ceresko, A. R. (1980), 'A Note on Psalm 63: A Psalm of Vigil', *ZAW* 92:435–436.

—— (1985), 'The ABCs of Wisdom in Psalm XXXIV', *VT* 35:99–104.

—— (1986), 'Psalm 149: Poetry, Themes (Exodus and Conquest), and Societal Function', *Bib* 67:177–194.

—— (2006), 'Endings and Beginnings: Alphabetic Thinking and the Shaping of Psalms 106 and 150', *CBQ* 68:32–46.

Charlesworth, J. H. (2018), *Has Psalm 156 Been Found?*, Eugene: Cascade.

Charney, D. (2013), 'Maintaining Innocence Before a Divine Hearer: Deliberative Rhetoric in Psalm 22, Psalm 17, and Psalm 7', *BibInt* 21:33–63.

—— (2015), *Persuading God: Rhetorical Studies of First-Person Psalms*, Sheffield: Sheffield Phoenix Press.

Cheung, S. C. (2015), *Wisdom Intoned: A Reappraisal of the Genre 'Wisdom Psalms'*, London: T. & T. Clark.

—— (2016), '"Forget Your People and Your Father's House": The Core Theological Message of Psalm 45 and Its Canonical Position in the Hebrew Psalter', *BBR* 26:325–340.
—— (2022), 'Wisdom Psalms', in K. J. Dell, S. R. Millar and A. J. Keefer (eds.), *Cambridge Companion to Biblical Wisdom Literature*, Cambridge: Cambridge University Press, 219–238.
Childs, B. S. (1962), *Memory and Tradition in Israel*, London: SCM.
—— (1969), 'Psalm 8 in the Context of the Christian Canon', *Int* 23:20–31.
—— (1979), *An Introduction to the Old Testament as Scripture*, Philadelphia: Fortress.
Cho, P. K.-K. (1997), 'The Sea as Everyday Space (Psalms 104 and 107)', *LTQ* 49:79–106.
Choi, Y. H. (2021), *Patterns of Movement in the Hebrew Psalter: A Holistic Thematic Approach with an Exemplar, Psalms 69–87*, New York: Peter Lang.
Church, P. (2016), 'Hebrews 1:10–12 and the Renewal of the Cosmos', *TynB* 67:269–286.
Claasens, L. J. (2007), 'Praying from the Depths of the Deep: Remembering the Image of God as Midwife in Psalm 71', *RevExp* 104:761–775.
Clayton, J. N. (2006), 'An Examination of Holy Space in Psalm 73: Is Wisdom's Path Infused with an Eschatologically Oriented Hope?', *TJ* 27:117–142.
Clifford, R. J. (1981), 'A Note on Ps 104:5–9', *JBL* 100:87–89.
Coetzee, J. H. (1986), 'Die Spanning tussen God se "verborge wees" en Sy "ingrype om te red". 'n Eksegetiese Ondersoek na 'n Aantal Klaagpsalms', DD thesis, University of Pretoria.
—— (1998), 'Worstel met God: Argumenteringstrategiee en hul sosio-retoriese Funksie in Psalm 13', *SK* 19:544–553.
—— (2000), 'Liggaamsimbolisering in Psalm 38', *SK* 23:517–529.
—— (2008), 'Psalm 104: A Bodily Interpretation of "Yahweh's History"', *OTE* 21:298–309.
—— (2009a), 'Listen to the Silent Voice of the Heavens and Taste the Sweetness of Torah: Reading Psalm 19 from a "Body Phenomenological" and an "Embodied Understanding" Perspective', *OTE* 22:281–301.
—— (2009b), 'Psalm 85: Yearning for the Restoration of the Whole Body', *OTE* 22:554–563.
Cole, R. L. (2000), *The Shape and Message of Book III (Psalms 73–89)*, Sheffield: Sheffield Academic Press.
—— (2012), *Psalms 1–2: Gateway to the Psalter*, Sheffield: Sheffield Phoenix.
Compton, J. (2015), *Psalm 110 and the Logic of Hebrews*, London: T. & T. Clark.
Cook, R. J. (2017), 'Prayers That Form Us: Rhetoric and Psalms Interpretation', *JSOT* 39:451–467.
—— (2018), *Rhetoric of Praise: Prayer and Persuasion in the Psalms*, Wilmore: Glossa House.

Cornell, C. (2020), *Divine Aggression in Psalms and Inscriptions: Vengeful Gods and Loyal Kings*, Cambridge: Cambridge University Press.

Cousins, M. (2016), 'Pilgrim Theology: Worldmaking Through Enactment of the Psalms of Ascents (Psalms 120–134)', PhD diss., Charles Sturt University.

Craigie, P. C. (1983), *Ugarit and the Old Testament*, Grand Rapids: Eerdmans.

Creach, J. F. D. (1996), *Yahweh as Refuge and the Editing of the Hebrew Psalter*, Sheffield: Sheffield Academic Press.

—— (2006), 'Psalm 70', *Int* 60:64–66.

—— (2020), *Discovering Psalms: Content, Interpretation, Reception*, Grand Rapids: Eerdmans.

—— (2024), '"Happy Are All Who Take Refuge in Him": The Theological Shape of the Psalter', *Int* 78:120–130.

Crenshaw, J. (2001), *The Psalms: An Introduction*, Grand Rapids: Eerdmans.

Croft, S. J. L. (1987), *The Identity of the Individual in the Psalms*, Sheffield: JSOT Press.

Crow, L. D. (1992), 'The Rhetoric of Psalm 44', *ZAW* 104:394–401.

—— (1996), *The Songs of Ascents (Psalms 120–134): Their Place in Israelite History and Religion*, Atlanta: Scholars Press.

Crüsemann, F. (2003), 'Rhetorische Fragen!? Eine Aufkündigung des Konsenses über Psalm 88:11–13 und seine Bedeutung für das Alttestamentliche Reden von Gott und Tod', *BibInt* 11:345–360.

Crutchfield, J. C. (2011), *Psalms in Their Context: An Interpretation of Psalms 107–118*, Milton Keynes: Paternoster.

Dahood, M. J. (1979), '"A Sea of Troubles": Notes on Psalms 55:3–4 and 140:10–11', *CBQ* 41:604–607.

—— (1982), 'Philological Observations on Five Biblical Texts', *Bib* 63:390–394.

Dalglish, E. R. (1962), *Psalm Fifty-One in the Light of Ancient Near East Patternism*, Leiden: Brill.

Dannell, G. A. (1951), *Psalm 139*, Uppsala: Almqvist Wiksells Boktryckeri.

Davage, D. (2021), 'Paratextual Framings of Psalm 72 and the Shaping of Interpretive Possibilities', *AcT* 32:357–379.

Davis, E. F. (1992a), 'Exploding the Limits: Form and Function in Psalm 22', *JSOT* 53:93–105.

—— (1992b), 'Psalm 98', *Int* 46:171–175.

Day, J. (1985), *God's Conflict with the Dragon and the Sea: Echoes of a Canaanite Myth in the Old Testament*, Cambridge: Cambridge University Press.

—— (1990), *Psalms: Old Testament Guides*, Sheffield: JSOT Press.

Day, J. N. (2005), *Crying for Justice: What the Psalms Teach Us About Mercy and Vengeance in an Age of Terrorism*, Grand Rapids: Kregel.

deClaissé-Walford, N. L. (1997), *Reading from the Beginning: The Shaping of the Hebrew Psalter*, Macon: Mercer University Press.

—— (2012), 'Psalm 145: All Flesh Will Bless God's Holy Name', *CBQ* 74:56–66.

—— (2019), 'The Role of Psalms 135–137 in the Shape and Shaping of Book V of the Hebrew Psalter', *OTE* 32:669–686.
—— (ed.) (2014), *The Shape and Shaping of the Book of Psalms: The Current State of Scholarship*, Atlanta: SBL Press.
Delekat, L. (1967), *Asylie und Schutzorakel am Zionheiligtum: Eine Untersuchung zu den privaten Feindpsalmen*, Leiden: Brill.
Dell, K. J. (2004), '"I Will Solve My Riddle to the Music of the Lyre" (Psalm XLIX 4 [5]): A Cultic Setting for Wisdom Psalms?', *VT* 54:445–458.
Dickson, C. R. (1995), 'The Hebrew Terminology for the Poor in Psalm 82', *HTS* 14:1029–1045.
Diehl, J. F., A. A. Diesel and A. Wagner (1999), 'Von der Grammatik zum Kerygma: Neue grammatische Erkenntnisse und ihre Bedeutung für das Verständnis der Form und des Gehalts von Psalm xxix', *VT* 49:462–486.
Dobbs-Allsop, F. W. (2008), 'Psalm 133: A (Close), Reading', *JHS* 8, art. 20.
Doyle, B. (2001), 'Just You, and I, Waiting – the Poetry of Psalm 25', *OTE* 14:199–213.
—— (2004), 'Howling Like Dogs: Metaphorical Language in Psalm LIX', *VT* 54:61–82.
Driver, G. R. (1970), 'Psalm LVI. 9 "Thou Tellest My Wanderings"', *JTS* 21:402–403.
Duke, R. K. (2011), 'Form and Meaning: Multi-layered Balanced Thought Structures in Psalm 24:4', *TynB* 62:215–232.
Duvall, J. S., and J. D. Hays (2019), *God's Relational Presence: The Cohesive Center of Biblical Theology*, Grand Rapids: Baker Academic.
Eaton, C. L. (2020), 'Joshua 24 and Psalm 81 as Intertexts', in D. I. Block (ed.), *Write That They Might Read: Studies in Literacy and Textualization in the Ancient Near East and Hebrew Scriptures. Essays in Honour of Allan Millard*, Eugene: Pickwick, 330–345.
Eaton, J. H. (1976), *Kingship and the Psalms*, London: SCM.
—— (1995), *Psalms of the Way and the Kingdom: A Conference with the Commentators*, Sheffield: Sheffield Academic Press.
Ellington, S. (2007), 'The Reciprocal Reshaping of History and Experience in the Psalms: Interactions with Pentecostal Testimony', *JPT* 16:18–31.
Ellison, S. D. (2021), 'Old Testament Hope: Psalm 2, the Psalter, and the Anointed One', *Them* 46:534–545.
Emadi, M. H. (2022), *The Royal Priest: Psalm 110 in Biblical Theology*, London: Apollos.
Emadi, S. (2022), *From Prisoner to Prince: The Joseph Story in Biblical Theology*, London: Apollos.
Emanuel, D. (2009), 'An Unrecognized Voice: Intra-Textual and Intertextual Perspectives on Psalm 81', *HS* 50:7–42.
—— (2012), *From Bards to Exegetes: A Close Reading and Intertextual Analysis of Selected Exodus Psalms*, Eugene: Pickwick.
—— (2013), 'The Diachronic Order of Psalms 134–136', *HS* 54:79–92.

Emerton, J. A. (1974a), 'The Meaning of *šēnā'* in Psalm CXXVII 2', *VT* 24:1–18.
—— (1974b), 'A Neglected Solution of a Problem in Psalm LXXVI 11', *VT* 24:136–146.
—— (1976), 'The Translation of Psalm LXIV 4', *JTS* 27:391–392.
—— (2000), 'The Problem of Psalm LXXXVII', *VT* 50:183–199.
Erbele-Küster, D. (2016), 'Poetics and Ethics: Psalm 27 as an Exemplary Reading', *C&C* 10:39–55.
Eriksson, L. O. (1991), *'Come, Children, Listen to Me!' Psalm 34 in the Hebrew Bible and in Early Christian Writings*, Stockholm: Almqvist & Wiksell.
Estes, D. J. (1991), 'Like Arrows in the Hand of a Warrior (Psalm CXXVII)', *VT* 41:304–311.
—— (2004), 'Poetic Artistry in the Expression of Fear in Psalm 49', *BSac* 161:55–71.
—— (2011), 'Spirit and the Psalmist in Psalm 51', in Firth and Wegner, *Presence, Power, Promise*, 122–134.
—— (2014), 'Creation Theology in Psalm 148', *BSac* 171:30–41.
—— (2016), 'Psalm 78:1–8 as a Musical Intertext of Torah and Wisdom', *BSac* 173:297–314.
Fernandes, S. (2013), *God as Rock in the Psalter*, Frankfurt am Main: Peter Lang.
Ferris, P. W. Jr. (1992), *The Genre of Communal Lament in the Bible and the Ancient Near East*, Atlanta: Scholars Press.
Firth, D. G. (1998), 'A Note on the Meaning of שרר in the Psalms', *OTE* 11:40–49.
—— (1999), 'Psalms of Testimony', *OTE* 12:440–454.
—— (2005a), *Hear, O Lord: A Spirituality of the Psalms*, Calver: Cliff College Publishing.
—— (2005b), *Surrendering Retribution in the Psalms: Responses to Violence in the Individual Complaints*, Carlisle: Paternoster.
—— (2005c), 'The Teaching of the Psalms', in Johnston and Firth, *Interpreting*, 159–174.
—— (2008), 'Asaph and Sons of Korah', in Peter Enns and Tremper Longman III (eds.), *Dictionary of the Old Testament: Wisdom, Poetry and Writings*, Downers Grove: IVP Academic, 24–27.
—— (2009), *1 and 2 Samuel*, Nottingham: Apollos.
—— (2014), 'The Spirit and the Renewal of Creation: An Old Testament Perspective', in Moo and Routledge, *Earth Endures*, 107–124.
—— (2015a), 'Cries of the Oppressed: Prayer and Violence in the Psalms', in M. D. Carroll R. and J. B. Wilgus (eds.), *Wrestling with the Violence of God: Soundings in the Old Testament*, Winona Lake: Eisenbrauns, 75–90.
—— (2015b), 'More than Just Torah: God's Instruction in the Psalms', *STR* 6:63–82.

—— (2019a), *Including the Stranger: Foreigners in the Former Prophets*, London: Apollos.

—— (2019b), 'Psalm 139: A Study in Ambiguity', *OTE* 32:491–510.

—— (2020), 'Reading Psalm 46 in Its Canonical Context: An Initial Exploration in Harmonies Consonant and Dissonant', *BBR* 30:22–40.

—— (2021), 'Transformation of War Language in the Worship of all the Earth in Psalm 100', *AcT* 32:320–331.

—— (2022), 'A Poem in Two Contexts: Psalm 40:14–18 and Psalm 70 in Their Canonical Setting', *JSem* 31, https://doi.org/10.25159/2663–6573/12042.

Firth, D. G., and B. N. Melton (2022), 'In a World Without God: Reading Esther Alongside Psalms', in D. G. Firth and B. N. Melton (eds.), *Reading Esther Intertextually*, London: T. & T. Clark, 99–108.

Firth, D. G., and P. D. Wegner (2011), *Presence, Power, Promise: The Role of the Spirit of God in the Old Testament*, Nottingham: Apollos.

Firth, D. G., and L. Wilson (2016), *Exploring Old Testament Wisdom: Literature and Themes*, London: Apollos.

Fiß, A.-C. (2019), *'Lobe den Herrn, meine Seele!' Psalm 103 in seinen Kontexten*, Göttingen: Vandenhoeck & Ruprecht.

Fletcher, D. H. (2018), *Psalms of Christ: The Messiah in Non-Messianic Psalms*, Eugene: Wipf & Stock.

Flint, P. W. (2000), '5/6 Ḥev Psalms', in J. H. Charlesworth, H. Cotton and P. W. Flint (eds.), *Miscellaneous Texts from the Judean Desert*, Oxford: Clarendon, 141–172.

—— (2013), 'The Dead Sea Psalm Scrolls: Psalms Manuscripts, Editions, and the *Oxford Hebrew Bible*', in Susan Gillingham (ed.), *Jewish and Christian Approaches to the Psalms: Conflict and Convergence*, Oxford: Oxford University Press, 11–34.

—— (2014), 'Appendix II: Contents of the Psalms Scrolls and Related Manuscripts', in W. P. Brown, *Oxford Handbook to the Psalms*, Oxford: Oxford University Press, 631–638.

Fokkelman, J. (2007), 'Psalm 103: Design, Boundaries and Mergers', in Becking and Peels, *Psalms and Prayers*, 109–118.

Forti, T. L. (2018), *'Like a Lone Bird on a Roof': Animal Imagery and the Structure of Psalms*, University Park: Eisenbrauns.

Foster, R. L. (2008), '*Topoi* of Praise in the Call to Praise Psalms: Toward a Theology of the Book of Psalms', in Foster and Howard, *'My Words Are Lovely'*, 75–88.

—— (2019), *We Have Heard, O Lord: An Introduction to the Theology of the Psalter*, Lanham: Lexington / Fortress.

Foster, R. L., and D. M. Howard Jr. (2008), *'My Words Are Lovely': Studies in the Rhetoric of the Psalms*, London: T. & T. Clark.

Frankle, D. (2018), 'El as the Speaking Voice in Psalm 82:6–8', *JHS* 10, art. 16, https://doi.org/10.5508/jhs.2010.v10.a16.

Freedman, D. N. (1999), *Psalm 119: The Exaltation of Torah*, Winona Lake: Eisenbrauns.

Fretheim, T. E. (1967), 'Psalm 132: A Form-Critical Study', *JBL* 86:289–300.
Frevel, C. (2013), 'Telling the Secrets of Wisdom: The Use of Psalm 104 in the Book of Job', in K. Dell and W. Kynes (eds.), *Reading Job Intertextually*, London: Bloomsbury, 157–168.
Frisch, A. (2009), 'Ephraim and Treachery, Loyalty and (the House of), David: The Meaning of a Structural Parallel in Psalm 78', *VT* 59:190–198.
Futato, M. D. (2007), *Interpreting the Psalms: An Exegetical Handbook*, Grand Rapids: Kregel, 2007.
—— (2013), 'Psalms 16, 23: Confidence in a Cup', in Schmutzer and Howard, *Psalms*, 231–236.
Gärtner, J. (2016), 'Exodus Psalm 114 – the Hermeneutical Centre of the So-Called Egyptian Hallel?', in J. Gärtner and B. Schmitz (eds.), *Exodus: Rezeptionen in deuterokanonischer und frühjüdischer Literatur*, Berlin: de Gruyter, 71–88.
German, B. T. (2012), 'Contexts for Hearing: Reevaluating the Superscription of Psalm 127', *JSOT* 37:185–199.
Gibbs, G. (2023), 'Precious or Costly? What Is the Death of His People in God's Sight? (Psalm 116:15)', *CJ* 49:7–11.
Gillingham, S. E. (1994), *The Poems and Psalms of the Hebrew Bible*, Oxford: Oxford University Press.
—— (ed.) (2013), *Jewish and Christian Approaches to the Psalms: Conflict and Convergence*, Oxford: Oxford University Press.
Gillmayr-Bucher, S. (2010), '"Like Olive Shoots Around Your Table": Images of Space in the Psalms of the Ascents', in Zenger, *Composition*, 489–500.
—— (2019), '"The Rivers Have Lifted up Their Voice": Imagining the Mighty Waters in Psalm 93', *OTE* 32:378–397.
Girard, M. (1981), 'Analyse structurelle du Psaume 95', *ScEs* 33:179–189.
Gnuse, R. (2021), 'Psalm 104: The Panorama of Life', *BTB* 51:4–14.
Goh, S. T. S. (2017), *The Basics of Hebrew Poetry: Theory and Practice*, Eugene: Cascade.
Goldingay, J. (2006b), 'Psalm 4: Ambiguity and Resolution', *TynB* 57:161–172.
—— (2016), *An Introduction to the Old Testament: Exploring Text, Approaches and Issues*, London: SPCK.
Gottlieb, F. (2016), 'The Creation Theme in Genesis 1, Psalm 104 and Job 38–42', *JQR* 44:29–36.
Goulder, M. D. (1982), *The Psalms of the Sons of Korah*, Sheffield: JSOT Press.
—— (1990), *The Prayers of David (Psalms 51–72)*, Sheffield: JSOT Press.
—— (1996), *The Psalms of Asaph and the Pentateuch*, Sheffield: Sheffield Academic Press.
—— (1998), *The Psalms of the Return (Book V, Psalms 1–7–150)*, Sheffield: Sheffield Academic Press.
Graham, W. A. (2023), *The Promised Davidic King: Psalm 108's Canonical Placement and Use of Earlier Psalms*, Bellingham: Lexham Academic.

Grant, J. A. (2004), *The King as Exemplar: The Function of Deuteronomy's Kingship Law in the Shaping of the Book of Psalms*, Atlanta: SBL Press; Leiden: Brill.

—— (2011), 'The Spirit and Presence in Psalm 139', in Firth and Wegner, *Presence, Power, Promise*, 135–146.

—— (2023), 'Psalm 87 and the Promise of Inclusion', in Howard and Schmutzer, *Reading the Psalms Theologically*, 207–221.

—— (2024), 'The Psalms', in H. H. Hardy II and M. Daniel Carroll R., *The State of Old Testament Studies: A Survey of Recent Research*, Grand Rapids: Baker Academic, 231–243.

Gray, A. R. (2014), *Psalm 18 in Words and Pictures: A Reading Through Metaphor*, Leiden: Brill.

Greene, N. E. (2017), 'Creation, Destruction, and a Psalmist's Plea: Rethinking the Poetic Structure of Psalm 74', *JBL* 136:85–101.

Greenstein, E. L. (1990), 'Mixing Memory and Design: Reading Psalm 78', *Proof* 10:197–218.

Greever, J. M. (2020), 'The Typological Expectation of Psalm 68 and Its Application in Ephesians 4:8', *TynB* 71:253–279.

Groenewald, A. (2003), *Psalm 69: Its Structure, Redaction and Composition*, Münster: Verlag Münster.

—— (2012), 'The Ethical "Way" of Psalm 16', in Human, *Psalmody and Poetry*, 45–55.

Grogan, G. W. (2001), *Prayer, Praise and Prophecy: A Theology of Psalms*, Fearn: Christian Focus.

Grohman, M. (2005), 'Ambivalent Images of Birth in Psalm vii 15', *VT* 55:439–449.

Gunkel, H. (1998), *Introduction to Psalms: The Genres of the Religious Lyric of Israel*, tr. J. D. Nogalski, Macon: Mercer University Press.

Hamidović, D. (2000), '"Les portes de justice" et "la porte de YHWH" dans le Psaume 118,120', *Bib* 81:542–550.

Handy, L. K. (1990), 'Sounds, Words and Meanings in Psalm 82', *JSOT* 47:51–66.

—— (2009), *Psalm 29 Through Time and Tradition*, Cambridge: James Clarke.

Hardmeier, C. (2016), 'Leserhermeneutische Sinnerschließung von Psalm 55', in A. Ruwe (ed.), *Du aber bist es, ein Mensch meinesgleichen (Psalm 55,14): Ein Gespräch über Psalm 55 und seine Parallelen*, Neukirchen-Vluyn: Neukirchener Theologie, 1–82.

Harriman, K. R. (2017), '"For David Said Concerning Him": Foundations of Hope in Psalm 16 and Acts 2', *JTI* 11:239–257.

Harris, M. J. (1984), 'The Translation of Elohim in Psalm 45:7–8', *TynB* 35:65–89.

Hartenstein, F. (2010), '"Schaffe mir Recht, JHWH!" (Psalm 7, 9): Zum theologischen und anthropologischen Profil der Teilkomposition Psalm 3–14', in Zenger, *Composition*, 229–258.

Hay, D. M. (1973), *Glory at the Right Hand: Psalm 110 in Early Christianity*, Nashville: Abingdon.
Hayes, E. (1999), 'The Unity of the Egyptian Hallel: Psalms 113–18', *BBR* 9:145–156.
Hays, C. B. (2005), 'How Shall We Sing? Psalm 137 in Historical and Canonical Context', *HBT* 27:35–55.
Heiser, M. S. (2008), 'Monotheism, Polytheism, Monolatry, or Henotheism? Toward an Assessment of Divine Plurality in the Hebrew Bible', *BBR* 18:1–30.
Held, S. (2023), '"With Fists Flailing at the Gates of Heaven": Wrestling with Psalm 88, A Psalm for Chronic Illness', in Campbell, Rohlfing and Briggs, *New Song*, 142–155.
Hensley, A. D. (2018), *Covenant Relationships and the Editing of the Hebrew Psalter*, London: T. & T. Clark.
Hiehr, H. (1987), 'Götter oder Menschen – eine falsche Alternative: Bemerkungen zu Ps 82', *ZAW* 99:94–98.
Hilber, J. W. (2005), *Cultic Prophecy in the Psalms*, Berlin: de Gruyter.
Hildebrandt, S. (2020), 'Whose Voice Is Heard? Speaker Ambiguity in the Psalms', *CBQ* 82:197–213.
Hillers, D. R. (1978), 'A Study of Psalm 148', *CBQ* 40:323–334.
Ho, P. C. W. (2019), *The Design of the Psalter: A Macrostructural Analysis*, Eugene: Pickwick.
Ho, S. S. (2011), *Wisdom, Prayer for Life and Restoration of Zion: A Compositional Study of Psalm 119 and the Songs of the Ascents (Pss 120–134)*, Saarbrücken: LAP Lambert Academic.
Holman, J. (1971), 'The Structure of Psalm CXXXXIX', *VT* 21:298–310.
—— (2007), 'Are Idols Hiding in Psalm 139:20?', in Becking and Peels, *Psalms and Prayers*, 119–128.
Hossfeld, F.-L., and E. Zenger (2003), 'The So-Called Elohistic Psalter: A New Solution for an Old Problem', in Strawn and Bowen, *God So Near*, 35–52.
Hossfeld, F.-L., J. Bremer and T. M. Steiner (eds.) (2017), *Trägerkreise in den Psalmen*, Göttingen: V. & R. Academic.
Houston, W. J. (1999), 'The King's Preferential Option for the Poor: Rhetoric, Ideology and Ethics in Psalm 72', *BibInt* 7:342–367.
Howard Jr., D. M. (1997), *The Structure of Psalms 93–100*, Winona Lake: Eisenbrauns.
—— (2008), 'Psalm 88 and the Rhetoric of Lament', in Foster and Howard, *'My Words Are Lovely'*, 132–146.
Howard Jr., D. M., and A. Schmutzer (eds.) (2023), *Reading the Psalms Theologically*, Bellingham: Lexham.
Hubbard, R. L. (1982), 'Dynamistic and Legal Processes in Psalm 7', *ZAW* 94:267–279.
Human, D. J. (1995a), '*Bᵉrît* in Psalm 74', *SK* 16:57–66.
—— (1995b), 'Enkele Tradisie-Historiese Perspektiewe op Psalm 83', *HTS* 51:175–188.

—— (1996), 'The Tradition-Historical Setting of Psalm 25: How Wisdom Motives Contribute to Its Understanding', *SK* 17:76–88.
—— (1997a), 'Psalms en Hulle Sitz(e) im Leben. 'n Analise aan die Hand van Psalm 55 en 74', *SK* 19:242–260.
—— (1997b), 'A Tradition-Historical Analysis of Psalm 55', *SK* 18:267–279.
—— (1998), 'Psalm 44: "Why Do You Hide Your Face, O God?!"', *SK* 19:568–583.
—— (2002), 'An Ideal for Leadership – Psalm 72: The (Wise), King – Royal Mediation of God's Universal Reign', *VeE* 23:658–677.
—— (2004a), 'Psalm 136: A Liturgy with Reference to Creation and History', in D. J. Human and C. J. A. Vos (eds.), *Psalms and Liturgy*, London: T. & T. Clark, 73–88.
—— (2004b), 'Yahweh, the Israelite High God Bends Down to Uplift the Downtrodden: Perspectives on the Incomparability of Yahweh in Psalm 113', *JNSL* 30:41–64.
—— (2005), 'Psalm 136: 'n Liturgie as Herinnering en Herbelewenis van God se Krag in die Skepping en in die Geskiedenis', *HTS* 61:1209–1226.
—— (2010a), '"From Exile to Zion": Ethical Perspectives in the *šîrê hama'alôt*. Psalm 127', in Zenger, *Composition*, 523–535.
—— (2010b), '"Praise Beyond Words": Psalm 150 as Grand Finale of the Crescendo in the Psalter', *HTS* 67, art. 917, 10 pages, DOI: 10.4102/hts.v67i1.917.
—— (2017), 'Psalm 132 and Its Compositional Context(s)', *Scrip* 116:75–92.
—— (ed.) (2007), *Psalms and Mythology*, London: T. & T. Clark.
—— (2012), *Psalmody and Poetry in Old Testament Ethics*, London: T. & T. Clark.
Hunter, A. G. (2008), *An Introduction to the Psalms*, London: T. & T. Clark.
Hutchinson, J. H. (2005), 'The Psalms and Praise', in Johnston and Firth, *Interpreting*, 85–100.
Imes, C. J. (2018), *Bearing YHWH's Name at Sinai: A Reexamination of the Name Command of the Decalogue*, Winona Lake: Eisenbrauns.
Jacobson, K. N. (2014), 'Perhaps YHWH Is Sleeping: "Awake" and "Contend" in the Book of Psalms', in N. deClaissé-Walford (ed.), *The Shape and Shaping of the Book of Psalms: The Current State of Scholarship*, Atlanta: SBL Press, 129–146.
—— (2017), *Memories of Asaph: Mnemohistory and the Psalms of Asaph*, Minneapolis: Fortress.
Jacobson, R. A. (2004), *'Many Are Saying': The Function of Direct Discourse in the Hebrew Psalter*, London: T. & T. Clark.
—— (2020), 'Psalm 46: Translation, Structure, and Theology', *WW* 40:308–320.
—— (ed.) (2011), *Soundings in the Theology of the Psalms: Perspectives and Methods in Contemporary Scholarship*, Minneapolis: Fortress.
Jacobson, R. A., and K. N. Jacobson (2012), *Invitation to the Psalms: A Reader's Guide for Discovery and Engagement*, Grand Rapids: Baker Academic.

James, E. T. (2017), '"The Plowers Plowed": The Violated Body in Psalm 129', *BibInt* 25:172–189.

—— (2022), 'The Aesthetics of Biblical Acrostics', *JSOT* 46:319–338.

James, J. T. (2017), *The Storied Ethics of the Thanksgiving Psalms*, London: T. & T. Clark.

Janowski, B. (2010), 'Ein Tempel aus Worten: Zur Theologischen Architektur des Psalters', in Zenger, *Composition*, 279–308.

—— (2013), *Arguing with God: A Theological Anthropology of the Psalms*, Louisville: Westminster John Knox.

Janzen, J. G. (1995), 'The Root *škl* and the Soul Bereaved in Psalm 35', *JSOT* 65:55–69.

Jarick, J. (1997), 'The Four Corners of Psalm 107', *CBQ* 59:270–287.

Jenkins, S. G. (2020a), 'The Antiquity of Psalter Shape Efforts', *TynB* 71:161–180.

—— (2020b), 'A Quotation in Psalm 109 as Defence Exhibit A', *TynB* 71:115–136.

—— (2021), *Imprecations in the Psalms: Love for Enemies in Hard Places*, Eugene: Pickwick.

Jensen, J. E. (2001), 'Psalm 75: Its Poetic Context and Structure', *CBQ* 63:416–429.

Jerome, O. M. (2004), *'How Lovely Is Your Dwelling Place': The Desire for God's House in Psalm 84*, St. Ottilien: EOS Verlag.

Joffe, L. (2002), 'The Answer to the Meaning of Life, the Universe and the Elohistic Psalter', *JSOT* 27:223–235.

Johnson, A. R. (1979), *The Cultic Prophet and Israel's Psalmody*, Cardiff: University of Wales Press.

Johnson, B. (2019), 'Moving from Rage to Praise: How the Imprecatory Ps 137 Can Guide Hearts to Trust God and Process Pain', *TJ* 40:65–82.

Johnson, V. L. (2009), *David in Distress: His Portrait Through the Historical Psalms*, London: T. & T. Clark.

Johnston, P. S. (2002), *Shades of Sheol: Death and the Afterlife in the Old Testament*, Leicester: Apollos.

Johnston, P. S., and D. G. Firth (2005), *Interpreting the Psalms: Issues and Approaches*, Nottingham: Apollos.

Jones, C. B. (2009), 'The Psalms of Asaph: A Study of the Function of a Psalm Collection', PhD diss., Baylor University.

—— (2017), 'Lessons Learned: Applying a Hermeneutic of Curiosity to Psalm 78', *PRSt* 44:173–183.

—— (2018), 'When I Am Afraid: Fear in the Book of Psalms', *RevExp* 115:15–25.

Jones, S. C. (2016), 'Psalm 1 and the Hermeneutics of Torah', *Bib* 97:537–551.

Kartje, J. (2014), *Wisdom Epistemology in the Psalter: A Study of Psalms 1, 73, 90 and 107*, Berlin: de Gruyter.

Kee, M. S. (2009), 'The Heavenly Council and Its Type-Scene', *JSOT* 31:259–273.

Keefer, A. (2016), 'A Phonic Explanation for *Hâkmôt*', *ZAW* 128:695–700.

Keener, H. J. (2013), *A Canonical Exegesis of the Eighth Psalm: Yhwh's Maintenance of the Created Order Through Divine Reversal*, Winona Lake: Eisenbrauns.

Kelly, S. (1970), 'Psalm 46: A Study in Imagery', *JBL* 89:305–312.

Kilchör, B., and B. Weber (2014), '"Unser Gott kommt . . . !" (Ps 50,3): Psalm 50 und sein Setting im Lichte aufgenommener Überlieferungen', *OTE* 27:1084–1111.

Kilian, R. (1990), 'Der "Tau" in Ps 110,3 – ein Mißverständnis?', *ZAW* 102:417–419.

Kim, C.-W. (2021), 'Psalms of Communal Lament as a Relic of Transgenerational Trauma', *JBL* 140:531–556.

Kim, H.-S. (2014), 'A Critique Against God? Reading Psalm 80 in the Context of Vindication', in L. Snow Flesher, C. J. Dempsey and M. J. Boda (eds.), *Why?. . . How Long? Studies of Voice(s), of Lamentation Rooted in Biblical Hebrew Poetry*, London: Bloomsbury T. & T. Clark, 100–114.

Kim, K.-S. (2011), *God Will Judge Each One According to Works: Judgment According to Works and Psalm 62 in Early Judaism and the New Testament*, Berlin: de Gruyter.

Kim, Y., and H. F. van Rooy (2003), 'Reading Psalm 78 Multidimensionally: The Authorial Dimension', *Scrip* 84:468–484.

Kim, Y.-K. (2017), 'The Referent of "Our Shield" in Psalm 84,10', *Bib* 98:10–24.

Kitz, A. M. (2007), 'Effective Simile and Effective Act: Psalm 109, Numbers 5, and KUB 26', *CBQ* 69:440–456.

Klouda, S. L. (2000), 'The Dialectical Interplay of Seeing and Hearing in Psalm 19 and Its Connection to Wisdom', *BBR* 10:181–195.

Knauf, E. A. (2000), 'Psalm LX und Psalm CVIII', *VT* 50:55–65.

—— (2001), 'Psalm xxiii 6', *VT* 51:556.

Knohl, I. (2013), 'Psalm 68: Structure, Composition and Geography', *JHS* 12, art. 15, 21 pages, DOI:10.5508/jhs.2012.v12.a15.

Knowles, M. D. (2006), 'A Woman at Prayer: A Critical Note on Psalm 131:2b', *JBL* 125:385–391.

Koorevaar, H. (2010), 'The Psalter as a Structured Theological Story with the Aid of Subscripts and Superscripts', in Zenger, *Composition*, 579–592.

Körting, C. (2020), 'Utopie und Wirklichkeit im Lande Jhwhs: Eine Analysis von Psalm 85', in C. Körting and R. G. Kratz (eds.), *Fromme und Frevler: Studien zu Psalmen und Weisheit. Festschrift für Hermann Spieckermann zum 70. Geburtstag*, Tübingen: Mohr Siebeck, 143–158.

Kraus, H.-J. (1992), *Theology of the Psalms*, Minneapolis: Fortress.

Krawelitzki, J. (2014), 'God the Almighty? Observations in the Psalms', *VT* 64:434–444.

Krusche, M. (2020), 'A Collective Anointed? David and the People in Psalm 89', *JBL* 139:87–105.

Kselman, J. S. (1975), 'Psalm 72: Some Observations on Structure', *BASOR* 220:77–81.

—— (1983), 'Psalm 77 and the Book of Exodus', *JANES* 15:51–58.
—— (1987), 'A Note on Psalm 4,5', *Bib* 68:103–105.
—— (1997), 'Two Notes on Psalm 37', *Bib* 78:252–254.
—— (1998), 'Psalm 146 in Its Context', *CBQ* 50:587–599.
Kugel, J. L. (1981), *The Idea of Biblical Poetry: Parallelism and Its History*, New Haven: Yale University Press.
Kugler, G. (2014), 'The Dual Rule of Historiography in Psalm 106: Justifying the Present Distress and Demonstrating the Individual's Potential Contribution', *ZAW* 126:546–553.
Kumpmann, C. (2016), *Schöpfen, Schlagen, Schützen: Eine semantische, thematische und theologische Untersuchung des Handelns Gottes in den Psalmen*, Göttingen: V. & R. Academic.
Kuntz, J. K. (1983), 'Psalm 18: A Rhetorical-Critical Analysis', *JSOT* 26:3–31.
Kwakkel, G. (2002), *'According to My Righteousness': Upright Behaviour as Grounds for Deliverance in Psalms 7, 17, 18, 26, and 44*, Leiden: Brill.
Kynes, W. (2011), 'Beat Your Parodies into Swords, and Your Parodied Books into Spears: A New Paradigm for Parody in the Hebrew Bible', *BibInt* 19:276–310.
—— (2012), *My Psalm Has Turned to Weeping: Job's Dialogue with the Psalms*, Berlin: de Gruyter.
—— (2018), *An Obituary for 'Wisdom Literature': The Birth, Death, and Intertextual Reintegration of a Biblical Corpus*, Oxford: Oxford University Press.
Laato, A. (1992), 'Psalm 132 and the Development of the Jerusalemite/Israelite Royal Ideology', *CBQ* 54:49–66.
—— (1999), 'Psalm 132: A Case Study in Methodology', *CBQ* 61:24–32.
Lam, J. (2014), 'Psalm 2 and the Disinheritance of Earthly Rulers: New Light from the Ugaritic Legal Text RS 94.2168', *VT* 64:34–46.
Lasater, P. M. (2015), 'Law for What Ails the Heart: Moral Frailty in Psalm 86', *ZAW* 127:652–668.
Laurence, T. (2022), '"Let Sinners Be Consumed": The Curious Conclusion of Psalm 104', in T. Laurence and H. Paynter (eds.), *Violent Biblical Texts: New Approaches*, Sheffield: Sheffield Phoenix, 141–162.
Layton, S. C. (1988), 'Jehoseph in Ps 81,6', *Bib* 69:406–411.
Lee, A. C. C. (1990a), 'The Context and Function of the Plagues Tradition in Psalm 78', *JSOT* 48:83–89.
—— (1990b), 'Genesis 1 and the Plagues Tradition in Psalm CV', *VT* 40:257–263.
Lefebvre, M. (2016), '"On His Law He Meditates": What Is Psalm 1 Introducing?', *JSOT* 40:439–450.
Lehmann, M. H., and N. Levine (2021), 'An Alliterative-Typographical Device in Psalm 37: Divine Destruction of the Wicked, Enacted in Real Time', *JSOT* 45:407–421.
LeMon, J. (2013), 'Yhwh's Hand and the Iconography of the Blow in Psalm 81:14–16', *JBL* 132:865–882.

—— (2015), 'Cutting the Enemy to Pieces: Ps 118,10–12 and the Iconography of Disarticulation', *ZAW* 126:59–75.

Leonard, J. L. (2016), 'Identifying Inner-Biblical Allusions: Psalm 78 as a Test Case', *JBL* 127:241–265.

Leuenberger, M. (2020), 'Eine zionstheologische Fortschreibung in Psalm 46, 48 und 76: Intertextuelle Befunde und redaktionsgeschichtliche Auswertungen', in A. Brodersen, F. Neumann and D. Willgren (eds.), *Intertextualität und Entstehung des Psalters,* Tübingen: Mohr Siebeck, 75–92.

Levenson, J. D. (1985), 'A Technical Meaning for *n'm* in the Hebrew Bible' *JBL* 35:61–67.

Levine, H. J. (1995), *Sing unto God a New Song: A Contemporary Reading of the Psalms*, Indianapolis: Indiana University Press.

Liess, K. (2004), *Der Weg des Lebens: Psalm 16 und das Lebens- und Todesverständnis der Individualpsalmen*, Tübingen: Mohr Siebeck.

Limburg, J. (1994), 'Down-to-Earth Theology: Psalm 104 and the Environment', *CurrTM* 21:340–346.

Lindars, B. (1989), 'The Structure of Psalm CXLV', *VT* 29:23–30.

Lindblom, J. (1974), 'Erwägungen zu Psalm xvi', *VT* 44:187–195.

Lindström, F. (1994), *Suffering and Sin: Interpretations of Illness in the Individual Complaint Psalms*, Stockholm: Almqvist & Wiksell.

Loader, J. A. (2003), 'Psalm 30 Read Twice', *OTE* 16:291–308.

—— (2010), 'Levels of Contextual Synergy in the Korah Psalms: The Example of Psalm 86', *OTE* 23:666–680.

Longman III, T. (1984), 'Psalm 98: A Divine Warrior Victory Song', *JETS* 27:267–274.

—— (2024), *The Old Testament as Literature: Foundations for Christian Interpretation*, Grand Rapids: Baker Academic.

Longman III, T., and D. G. Reid (1995), *God Is a Warrior*, Grand Rapids: Zondervan.

Lynch, M. J. (2021), *First Isaiah and the Disappearance of the Gods*, University Park: Eisenbrauns.

McAlpine, T. H. (1987), *Sleep, Divine & Human in the Old Testament*, Sheffield: JSOT Press.

McCann Jr., J. C. (1993), *A Theological Introduction to the Book of Psalms: The Psalms as Torah*, Nashville: Abingdon.

—— (2023), 'Reclaiming Divine Sovereignty in the Anthropocene: Psalms 93–100 and the Convergence of Theology and Ecology', in Howard and Schmutzer, *Reading the Psalms Theologically*, 246–256.

McCann Jr., J. C., and J. C. Howell (2001), *Preaching the Psalms*, Nashville: Abingdon.

McKelvey, M. G. (2014), *Moses, David and the High Kingship of Yahweh: A Canonical Study of Book IV of the Psalter*, Piscataway: Gorgias.

McLellan, D. (2018), 'The Hebrew Terminology for the Poor in Psalm 82', *JBL* 137:833–851.

McMillion, P. (2001), 'Psalm 78: Teaching the Next Generation', *ResQ* 43:219–228.

—— (2010), 'Psalm 105: History with a Purpose', *ResQ* 52, 167–179.

Makujina, J. (2011), 'The Interpretation of Ps 144,14: Applying a Pluralistic Approach to a Manifold Difficulty', *Bib* 92:481–502.

Maloney, L. D. (2008), *A Word Fitly Spoken: Poetic Artistry in the First Four Acrostics of the Hebrew Psalter*, New York: Peter Lang.

Mandolfo, C. (2002), *God in the Dock: Dialogical Tension in the Psalms of Lament*, Sheffield: Sheffield Academic Press.

Maré, L. P. (2000), 'Psalm 100 – Uitbundige Lof oor die Godheid, Goedheid en Grootheid van Jahwe', *OTE* 13:218–234.

—— (2003), 'Psalm 58: A Prayer for Vengeance', *OTE* 16:322–331.

—— (2006a), 'Psalm 8: God's Glory and Humanity's Reflected Glory', *OTE* 19:926–938.

—— (2006b), 'Psalm 121: Yahweh's Protection Against Mythological Powers', *OTE* 19:712–722.

—— (2008), 'Psalm 51: "Take Not Your Holy Spirit Away from Me"', *AcT* 28:93–104.

—— (2010), 'The Ethics of Retribution in Psalm 37', *Ekklesiastikos Pharos* 92, https://hdl.handle.net/10520/EJC33049.

—— (2014), 'Honour and Shame in Psalm 44', *Scrip* 113:1–12.

Marlowe, W. C. (1998), '"Spirit of Your Holiness" (רוּחַ קָדְשְׁךָ), in Psalm 51:13', *TJ* 19:29–49.

Mathys, H. L. (2000), 'Psalm xl', *VT* 50:329–344.

Mays, J. L. (1993), 'The Language of the Reign of God', *Int* 47:117–126.

—— (1994a), *The Lord Reigns: A Theological Handbook to the Psalms*, Louisville: Westminster John Knox.

—— (1994c), 'What Is a Human Being? Reflections on Psalm 8', *ThTo* 50:511–520.

—— (2006), *Preaching and Teaching the Psalms*, Louisville: Westminster John Knox.

Meer, W. van de (1994), 'Psalm 77,17–19: Hymnisches Fragment oder Aktualisierung?', *ETL* 70:105–111.

Menn, E. M. (2000), 'No Ordinary Lament: Relecture and the Identity of the Distressed in Psalm 22', *HTR* 93:301–341.

Mensah, M. K. (2021), 'Making Meaning of Wisdom in Psalm 119 and in Contemporary African Contexts', *OTE* 34:165–188.

Michael, G. J. L. (2019), 'The Works of God's Salvation: The Rhetorical Use of Creation Imagery in Psalm 74', *STR* 10:5–29.

Michel, W. L. (1984), 'ṢLMWT, "Deep Darkness" or "Shadow of Death"?', *BBR* 29:5–20.

Miglio, A. E. (2015), 'Imagery and Analogy in Psalm 58:4–9', *VT* 65:114–135.

Miller Jr., P. D. (1979a), 'Poetic Ambiguity and Balance in Psalm xv', *VT* 29:416–424.

—— (1979b), '*Yapiah* in Psalm xii 6', *VT* 29:495–501.
—— (1986), *Interpreting the Psalms*, Philadelphia: Fortress.
—— (1994), *They Cried to the Lord: The Form and Theology of Biblical Prayer*, Minneapolis: Fortress.
Mitchell, D. C. (1997), *The Message of the Psalter: An Eschatological Programme in the Book of Psalms*, Sheffield: Sheffield Academic Press.
Moenikes, A. (1999), 'Psalm 2,7b und die Göttlichkeit des israelitischen Königs', *ZAW* 111:619–621.
Mongé-Greer, E. (2023), *Divine Council, Resistance and Ethics in Psalm 82*, Eugene: Pickwick.
Moo, J., and R. Routledge (eds.) (2014), *As Long as the Earth Endures: The Bible, Creation and the Environment*, Nottingham: Apollos.
Morales, L. M. (2020), *Exodus Old and New: A Biblical Theology of Redemption*, Downers Grove: IVP Academic.
Morgenstern, J. (1939), 'The Mythological Background of Psalm 82', *HUCA* 14:29–126.
Morrow, W. S. (2007), *Protest Against God: The Eclipse of a Biblical Tradition*, Sheffield: Sheffield Phoenix.
Mosca, P. G. (1985), 'Psalm 26: Poetic Structure and the Form-Critical Task', *CBQ* 47:212–237.
—— (2011), 'A Note on Psalm 17:7', *VT* 61:388–392.
Mott, W. (2018), *The Earth Is the Lord's: Nothing Is Secular*, Eugene: Wipf & Stock.
Mowinckel, S. (1962), *The Psalms in Israel's Worship*, 2 vols., Oxford: Blackwell; Nashville: Abingdon.
Mullen Jr., E. T. (1983), 'The Divine Witness and the Davidic Royal Grant: Ps 89:37–38', *JBL* 102:207–218.
Müller, H.-P. (2005), 'Zur Grammatik und zum religionsgeschichtlichen Hintergrund von Ps 68,5', *ZAW* 117:206–216.
Nasuti, H. P. (1988), *Tradition History and the Psalms of Asaph*, Atlanta: Scholars Press.
Naudé, E. (2000), 'Psalm 40: Één of Twee Psalms?', *SK* 21:115–134.
Neef, H. D. (2016), 'Der unvergleichliche Gott – Psalm 113 im Spiegel vom Sam 2:1–10', *VT* 66:245–260.
Nel, P. J. (2005), 'Yahweh Is a Shepherd: Conceptual Metaphor in Psalm 23', *HBT* 27:79–103.
Nelson, R. D. (2009), 'Psalm 114', *Int* 63:172–174.
Niehaus, J. J. (1979), 'The Use of *Lûle* In Psalm 27', *JBL* 98:88–89.
—— (1995), *God at Sinai: Covenant and Theophany in the Bible and Ancient Near East*, Grand Rapids: Zondervan.
Niekerk, M. J. H. van (1995), 'Psalms 127 and 128: Examples of Divergent Wisdom Views on Life', *OTE* 8:414–424.
Niehr, H. (1987), 'Götter oder Menschen – eine falsche Alternative: Bemerkungen zu Ps 82', *ZAW* 99:94–98.
O'Connor, M. (1997), *Hebrew Verse Structure*, Winona Lake: Eisenbrauns.

O'Kennedy, D. F. (1998), 'The Relationship Between Justice and Forgiveness in Psalm 103', *Scrip* 65:109–121.

Obinwa, I. M. C. (2006), *Yahweh My Refuge: A Critical Analysis of Psalm 71*, Frankfurt am Main: Peter Lang.

Oded, T. (2017), 'Psalm 78: A Case Study in Redaction as Propaganda', *CBQ* 79:205–221.

Ogden, G. S. (1985), 'Psalm 60: Its Rhetoric, Form, and Function', *JSOT* 31:83–94.

Owens, D. C. (2013), *Portraits of the Righteous in the Psalms: An Exploration of the Ethics of Book 1*, Eugene: Pickwick.

Palmer, M. (1965), 'Cardinal Points in Psalm 48', *Bib* 46:357–358.

Pardee, D. (1978), '*ypḥ* "*Witness*" in Hebrew and Ugaritic', *VT* 28:204–213.

—— (2013), '*ypḥ* "*Witness*" in Hebrew and Ugaritic', *VT* 63:99–108.

Pardee, D., and N. Pardee (2009), 'Gods of Glory Ought to Thunder: The Canaanite Matrix of Psalm 29', in L. K. Handy (ed.), *Psalm 29 Through Time and Tradition*, Cambridge: James Clarke, 115–125.

Patterson, R. D. (1985), 'A Multiplex Approach to Psalm 45', *GTJ* 6:29–48.

—— (2004), 'Psalm 22: From Trial to Triumph', *JETS* 47:213–233.

—— (2007), 'Singing the New Song: An Examination of Psalms 33, 96, 98, and 149', *BSac* 1646:416–434.

—— (2009), 'Psalm 92:12–15: The Flourishing of the Righteous', *BSac* 164:271–288.

Patton, C. L. (1995), 'Psalm 132: A Methodological Inquiry', *CBQ* 57:643–654.

Pavan, M. (2014), *'He Remembered that They were but Flesh, a Breath that Passes and Does Not Return' (Ps 78.39): The Theme of Memory and Forgetting in the Third Book of the Psalter (Pss 73–89)*, Frankfurt am Main: Peter Lang.

Peels, H. G. L. (2000), 'Sanctorum Communio vel Idolorum Repudiado? A Reconsideration of Psalm 16,3', *ZAW* 112:239–251.

—— (2008), '"I Hate Them with Perfect Hatred" (Psalm 139:21–22)', *TynB* 59:35–51.

Perdue, L. G. (1974), 'The Riddles of Psalm 49', *JBL* 93:533–542.

Persaud, A. J. E. (2016), *Praying the Language of Enmity in the Psalter: A Study of Psalms 110, 119, 129, 137, 139 and 149*, Eugene: Wipf & Stock.

Petersen, D. L. (1981), *The Roles of Israel's Prophets*, Sheffield: JSOT Press.

Pierce, T. M. (2008), *Enthroned on Our Praise: An Old Testament Theology of Worship*, Nashville: B. & H. Academic.

Pinker, A. (2009), 'Psalm 116,15: Death of the Saints?', *ZAW* 121:529–539.

Pleins, D. (1993), *The Psalms: Songs of Tragedy, Hope, and Justice*, Maryknoll: Orbis.

Poe Hays, R. W. (2016), 'Trauma, Remembrance, and Healing: The Meeting of Wisdom and History in Psalm 78', *JSOT* 41:183–204.

Pohl IV, W. C. (2015), 'A Messianic Reading of Psalm 89: A Canonical and Intertextual Study', *JETS* 58:507–525.

Postell, S. D. (2019), 'A Literary, Compositional, and Intertextual Analysis of Psalm 45', *BSac* 176:146–163.
Potgieter, J. H. (2003), 'The Structure and Intent of Psalm 118', *OTE* 16:389–400.
—— (2012), '"David" in Consultation with the Prophets: The Intertextual Relationship of Psalm 31 with the Books of Jonah and Jeremiah', *OTE* 25:115–126.
—— (2013), 'The Profile of the Rich Antagonist and the Pious Protagonist in Psalm 52', *HTS Teologiese Studies / Theological Studies* 69 (1), art. 1963, 7 pages, http://dx.doi.org/10.4102/hts.v69i1.1963.
—— (2014), 'The Structure and Homogeneity of Psalm 32', *HTS Teologiese Studies / Theological Studies* 70 (1), art. 2725, 6 pages, http://dx.doi.org/10.4102/hts.v70i1.2725.
—— (2019), '"I Love Yahweh and I Believe in Him – Therefore I Shall Proclaim His Name": How Psalm 116 Integrated and Reinterpreted Its Constituent Parts', *OTE* 32:398–411.
Prinsloo, G. T. M. (1992), 'Analysing Old Testament Poetry: An Experiment in Methodology with Reference to Psalm 126', *OTE* 5:225–251.
—— (1995a), 'Hope Against Hope – a Theological Reflection on Psalm 22', *OTE* 8:61–85.
—— (1995b), 'Polarity as Dominant Textual Strategy in Psalm 8', *OTE* 8:370–387.
—— (1996), 'Yahweh and the Poor in Psalm 113: Literary Motif and/or Theological Reality?', *OTE* 9:465–485.
—— (1997), 'Shepherd, Vine-Grower, Father – Divine Metaphor and Existential Reality in a Community Lament (Psalm 80)', *OTE* 10:279–302.
—— (1998a), 'Man's Word – God's Word: A Theology of Antithesis in Psalm 12', *ZAW* 110:390–402.
—— (1998b), 'Psalm 5: A Theology of Tension and Reconciliation', *SK* 19:628–643.
—— (1998c), 'Tremble Before the Lord: Myth and History in Psalm 114', *OTE* 11:306–325.
—— (2002), 'Psalm 130: Poetic Patterns and Social Significance', *OTE* 15:453–469.
—— (2003a), 'Historical Reality and Mythological Metaphor in Psalm 124?', *OTE* 18:790–810.
—— (2003b), 'Psalms 114 and 115: One or Two Poems?', *OTE* 16:668–689.
—— (2006), '*Šeʾôl → Yerûšālayim ← Šāmayim*: Spatial Orientation in the Egyptian Hallel (Psalms 113–118)', *OTE* 19:739–760.
—— (2013), 'Suffering Bodies – Divine Absence: Towards a Spatial Reading of Ancient Near Eastern Laments with Reference to Psalm 13 and an Assyrian Elegy (K 890)', *OTE* 26:773–803.
—— (2015), 'Suffering as Separation: Towards a Spatial Reading of Psalm 11', *OTE* 28:777–806.

—— (2019), 'Reading Psalm 112 as a "Midrash" on Psalm 111', *OTE* 32:636–668.
—— (2021), 'From Desperation to Adoration: Reading Psalm 107 as a Transforming Spatial Journey', *AcT* 32:392–425.
Prinsloo, W. S. (1991a), 'Psalm 100: 'n Poëties Minderwaardige en Saamgeflansde Teks?', *HTS* 47:968–982.
—— (1991b), *Die Psalms Leef!*, Pretoria: NGKB.
—— (1992a), 'Psalm 88: The Gloomiest Psalm?', *OTE* 5:332–345.
—— (1992b), 'Structure and Cohesion of Psalm 148', *OTE* 5:46–63.
—— (1993a), 'Psalm 99: Die Here, ons God, Is Heilig', *HTS* 49:621–636.
—— (1993b), 'Psalm 116: Disconnected Text or Symmetrical Whole?', *Bib* 74:71–82.
—— (1994a), 'A Comprehensive Semiostructural Exegetical Approach', *OTE* 7:78–83.
—— (1994b), 'Psalm 67: Harvest Thanksgiving Psalm, (Eschatological), Hymn, Communal Prayer, Communal Lament or . . .?', *OTE* 2:231–246.
—— (1994c), 'Psalm 98: Sing 'n Nuwe Lied tot Lof van die Koning, Jahwe', *HTS* 50:155–168.
—— (1995a), 'Psalm 82: Once Again, Gods or Men?', *Bib* 76:219–228.
—— (1995b), 'Psalm 95: If Only You Will Listen to His Voice!', in M. D. Carroll R., D. J. A. Clines and P. R. Davies (eds.), *The Bible in Human Society: Essays in Honour of John Rogerson*, Sheffield: JSOT Press, 393–410.
—— (1995c), 'Psalm 97: Almal Moet Bly Wees, want Jahwe Is Koning', *HTS* 51:1088–1113.
—— (1999a), 'Psalm 72: 'n Verskuiwing van die Mistieke na die Politieke?', *OTE* 12:536–554.
—— (1999b), 'Psalm 149: Praise Yahweh with Tambourine and Two-Edged Sword', *ZAW* 12:395–407.
Purcell, R. A. (2020), 'The King as Priest: Royal Imagery in Psalm 110 and Ancient Near Eastern Iconography', *JBL* 139:275–300.
Quinn, C. (2023), *The Arrival of the King: The Shape and Story of Psalms 15–24*, Bellingham: Lexham Academic.
Raabe, P. (1990), *Psalm Structures: A Study of Psalms with Refrains*, Sheffield: Sheffield Academic Press.
Ray, D. C. (2020), 'Conflict and Enmity in the Asaph Psalms', PhD diss., Australian College of Theology.
Rendsburg, G. A. (1990), *Linguistic Evidence for the Northern Origin of Selected Psalms*, Atlanta: Scholars Press.
Reynolds, K. A. (2010), *Torah as Teacher: The Exemplary Student in Psalm 119*, Leiden: Brill.
Rice, G. (1980), 'Psalm 139: A Diary of the Inward Odyssey', *JRT* 37:63–67.
Richter, H.-F. (2004), 'Von den Bergen kommt keine Hilfe. Zu Psalm 121', *ZAW* 116:406–408.
Riede, P. (2022), *Zwischen Mensch und Gott: Psalm 45 und die Bedeutung von*

König und Königen im Rahmen der judäischen Herrschaftstheologie, Göttingen: Vandenhoeck & Ruprecht.

Roberts, J. J. M. (1973), 'The Young Lions of Psalm 34,11', *Bib* 54:17–267.

—— (1977), 'Of Signs, Prophets, and Time Limits: A Note on Psalm 74:9', *CBQ* 39:474–481.

Robertson, O. P. (2015a), 'The Alphabetic Acrostic in Book I of the Psalms: An Overlooked Element of Psalter Structure', *JSOT* 40:225–238.

—— (2015b), 'The Strategic Placement of The "*Hallelu-Yah*" Psalms Within the Psalter', *JETS* 58:265–268.

Robinson, B. P. (1998), 'Form and Meaning in Psalm 131', *Bib* 79:180–197.

Rom-Shiloni, D. (2008), 'Psalm 44: The Powers of Protest', *CBQ* 70:683–698.

Rooy, H. F. van (2021), 'Life in the Psalms', in A. J. Coetsee and F. J. Viljoen (eds.), *Biblical Theology of Life in the Old Testament*, Cape Town: AOSIS, 129–142.

Ross, W. A. (2019), 'David's Spiritual Walls and Conceptual Blending in Psalm 51', *JSOT* 43:607–626.

Roth, W. M. (1962), 'The Numerical Sequence x: x + 1 in the Old Testament', *VT* 12:300–311.

Ruwe, A. (ed.) (2016), *Du aber bist es, ein Mensch meinesgleichen (Psalm 55,14): Ein Gespräch über Psalm 55 und seine Parallelen*, Neukirchen-Vluyn: Neukirchener Verlag.

Sabottka, L. (2006), 'Ps 2,11 "Küsst den Sohn!"?', *Bib* 87:96–97.

Sabourin, L. (2010), *The Psalms: Their Origin and Meaning*, Eugene: Wipf & Stock.

Sarna, N. M. (1962), 'The Psalm for the Sabbath Day (Ps 92)', *JBL* 81:155–168.

Sawyer, J. F. A. (2011), *Sacred Texts and Sacred Meanings: Studies in Biblical Language and Literature*, Sheffield: Sheffield Phoenix.

Schäder, J.-M. (2010), 'Understanding (the Lack of), Space in Psalm 47:6 in Light of Its Neighbouring Psalms: A Spatial Reading of Psalms 46–48', *OTE* 23:139–160.

Schapfer, J. (1994), 'Psalm 47 und sein "Sitz im Leben"', *ZAW* 106:262–275.

Scheffler, E. (2011), 'Pleading Poverty (or Identifying with the Poor for Selfish Reasons): On the Ideology of Psalm 109', *OTE* 24:192–207.

Schmutzer, A. J., and R. X. Gauthier (2009), 'The Identity of "Horn" in Psalm 148:14a: An Exegetical Investigation in the MT and LXX Versions', *BBR* 19:161–183.

Schmutzer, A. J., and D. M. Howard Jr. (eds.) (2013), *The Psalms: Language for All Seasons of the Soul*, Chicago: Moody.

Schnittjer, G. E. (2021), *Old Testament Use of Old Testament: A Book-by-Book Guide*, Grand Rapids: Zondervan Academic.

Schreiner, D. B. (2018), 'Double Entendre, Disguised Verbal Resistance, and the Composition of Psalm 132', *BBR* 28:20–33.

Schroeder, C. (1996), '"A Love Song": Psalm 45 in the Light of Ancient Near Eastern Marriage Texts', *CBQ* 58:417–432.

—— (2000), 'Psalm 3 und das Traumorakel des von Feinden bedrängten Beters', *Bib* 81:243–251.

Schüngel-Straumann, H. (1973), 'Zur Gattung und Theologie des 139. Psalms', *BZ* 17:39–51.

Schwartz, S. (2018), 'Bridge Over Troubled Waters: Psalm 147', *JSOT* 42:317–339.

Scoralick, R. (1997), 'Psalm 111 – Bauplan und Gedankengang', *Bib* 78:190–205.

Seale, M. E. (2023), 'Polemicizing the Past: Psalm 115 and Hosea 8', *JETS* 66:481–494.

Sedlmeier, F. (1992), '"Bei dir, da ist die Vergebung, damit du gefürehtet werdest". Überlegungen zu Psalm 130', *Bib* 43:473–495.

Seidl, T. (2012), 'Who Stands Behind the רשׁע in Psalm 50:16a? The Ethical Testimony of Psalm 50:16–22', in Human, *Psalmody and Poetry*, 76–92.

Seow, C. L. (2013), 'An Exquisitely Poetic Introduction to the Psalter', *JBL* 132:275–293.

Sherwood, S. (1989), 'Psalm 112 – A Royal Wisdom Psalm?', *CBQ* 51:50–64.

Shnider, S. (2006), 'Psalm xviii: Theophany, Epiphany Empowerment', *VT* 56:387–398.

Sibinga, J. S. (1988), 'Some Observations on the Composition of Psalm XLVII', *VT* 38:474–480.

Silva, A. A. da (1992), ''n Poetiese Analise van Psalm 6', *OTE* 5:206–224.

Simango, D. (2018), 'A Comprehensive Reading of Psalm 137', *OTE* 31:217–242.

—— (2022), 'A Canonical Reading of Psalm 35', *OTE* 35:433–452.

Skinner, J. (2023), 'A Theology of Glory: Divine Sanctum and Service in the Psalter', in Howard and Schmutzer, *Reading the Psalms Theologically*, 257–270.

Smith, H. C. (2022), 'Worship as Social Creativity: Social Identity and the Form of Psalm 49', *JSOT* 46:516–529.

Smith, J. (2012), *Dust or Dew: Immortality in the Ancient Near East and Psalm 49*, Edinburgh: James Clarke.

Smith, K. S., and W. R. Domeris (2010), 'The Arrangement of Psalms 3–8', *OTE* 23:367–377.

Smith, M. S. (1988), '"Seeing God" in the Psalms: The Background to the Beatific Vision in the Hebrew Bible', *CBQ* 50:171–183.

—— (1997), 'Psalm 8:2b–3: New Proposals for Old Problems', *CBQ* 59:637–641.

Smith, S. J. (2021), 'The Shape and Message of Psalms 73–78', *CBQ* 83:18–37.

—— (2022), *The Conflict Between Faith and Experience, and the Shape of Psalms 73–83*, London: T. & T. Clark Bloomsbury.

Snearly, M. K. (2016), *The Return of the King: Messianic Expectation in Book V of the Psalter*, London: T. & T. Clark Bloomsbury.

Snyman, S. D. (2003), 'Psalm 32 – 'n Eksegeties-Teologiese Verkenning: Sondebelydenis Is Sondevergifnis!', *Dutch Reformed Theological Journal* 44:507–517.

—— (2011a), ''n Ondersoek na die Teologiese Boodskap en Prediking van Psalm 117', *IdS* 45:25–37.

—— (2011b), 'Reading Psalm 117 Against an Exilic Context', *VT* 61:109–118.

—— (2022), 'Juxtaposition as Literary Feature in Psalm 116', *IdS* 56 (1), art. 2873, 7 pages, https://doi.org/10.4102/ids.v56i1.2873.

Soll, W. (1991), *Psalm 119: Matrix, Form and Setting*, Washington: Catholic Biblical Association.

Sommer, B. D. (2015), 'Nature, Revelation, and Grace in Psalm 19: Towards a Theological Reading of Scripture', *HTR* 108:376–401.

—— (2023), 'Prosody and Preaching: Poetic Form and Religious Function in Biblical Verse', in Campbell, Rohlfing and Briggs, *New Song*, 106–141.

Southwood, K., and H. Morse (eds.) (2022), *Psalms and the Use of the Critical Imagination: Essays in Honour of Professor Susan Gillingham*, London: T. & T. Clark.

Spangenberg, I. J. J. (2007), 'Constructing a Historical Context for Psalm 49', *OTE* 20:201–214.

Starbuck, S. R. A. (1999), *Court Oracles in the Psalms: The So-Called Royal Psalms in Their Ancient Near Eastern Context*, Atlanta: Scholars Press.

Steiner, T. M. (2012), 'Perceived and Narrated Space in Psalm 48', *OTE* 25:685–704.

—— (2014), '"Gott stieg hinauf . . ." (Ps 47,6), – wohin? Psalm 47 als exilische Hoffnung auf Restitution', *Bib* 95:161–178.

—— (2017), 'Die Korachiten', in F.-L. Hossfeld, J. Bremer and T. M. Steiner (eds.), *Trägerkreise in den Psalmen*, Göttingen: V. & R. Academic, 133–160.

Stevenson, G. M. (1997), 'Communal Imagery and the Individual Lament: Exodus Typology in Psalm 77', *ResQ* 39:215–229.

Stewart, T. A. (2013), 'The Cry of Victory: A Cruciform Reading of Psalm 44:22 in Romans 8:36', *Journal for the Study of Paul and His Letters* 3:25–45.

Stinson, M. A. (2017), '"A Table in the Wilderness?": The Rhetorical Function of Food Language in Psalm 78', PhD diss., University of Bristol / Trinity College Bristol.

—— (2021), 'Turning Tables in Israel's History: Food Language and Reversals in Psalms 105 and 106', *CBQ* 83:588–598.

Stocks, S. P. (2012), *The Form and Function of the Tricolon in the Psalms of the Ascents: Introducing a New Paradigm for Hebrew Poetic Line-form*, Eugene: Pickwick.

—— (2016), '"Children, Listen to Me": The Voicing of Wisdom in the Psalms', in D. G. Firth and L. Wilson (eds.), *Exploring Old Testament Wisdom: Literature and Themes*, London: Apollos, 194–204.

Stone, M. P. (2021), '(More), on the Precative Qatal in Lamentations 3:56–61: Updating the Argument', *JSOT* 45:493–514.

Strawn, B. A., and N. R. Bowen (eds.) (2003), *A God So Near: Essays on Old Testament Theology in Honor of Patrick D. Miller*, Winona Lake: Eisenbrauns.

Streett, A. (2014), *The Vine and the Son of Man: Eschatological Interpretation of Psalm 80 in Early Judaism*, Minneapolis: Fortress.

Sumpter, P. (2013), 'The Coherence of Psalms 15–24', *Bib* 94:186–209.

—— (2015), *The Substance of Psalm 24: An Attempt to Read Scripture After Brevard S. Childs*, London: T. & T. Clark Bloomsbury.

Sutton, L. (2015), 'A Trilogy of War and Renewed Honour? Psalms 108, 109 and 110 as a Literary Composition', PhD diss., University of Pretoria.

—— (2016), '"A Footstool of War, Honour and Shame?" Perspectives Induced by Psalm 110:1', *JSem* 25:51–71.

—— (2017), 'The Dawn of Two Dawns: The Mythical, Royal and Temporal Implications of Dawn for Psalms 108 and 110', *HTS Teologiese Studies / Theological Studies* 73 (3), art. 4463, 7 pages, https://doi.org/10.4102/hts.v73i3.4463.

—— (2018), 'A Position of Honour or Shame? Yhwh as an Armour Bearer in Psalm 35:1–3', *AcT* Supplement 26:268–285.

—— (2021a), 'Practising Piety in a (Post-) Pandemic Time: A Spatial Reading of Piety in Psalm 66 from the Perspectives of Memory and Bodily Imagery', *HTS Teologiese Studies / Theological Studies* 77 (4), art. 6883, 9 pages, https://doi.org/10.4102/hts.v77i4.6883.

—— (2021b), 'A Transforming Body: A Post-Exilic Reading of Psalms 50 and 51 in the Light of Social Norms Communicated Through the Leviticus Sacrificial System and Body Imagery', *AcT* Supplement 32:326–356.

Sutton, L., and D. J. Human (2017a), '"Off with Their Heads!" The Imagery of the Head in the Trilogy of Psalms 108–110 (Part 1)', *STJ* 3:391–410.

—— (2017b), '"Off with Their Heads!" The Imagery of the Head in the Trilogy of Psalms 108–110 (Part 2)', *STJ* 3:411–428.

Suva, A. A. de (1995), 'Psalm 21 – a Poem of Association and Dissociation', *OTE* 8:48–60.

Swale, M. E. (2019), 'Structure, Allusion, Theology, and Contemporary Address in Psalm 106', *BSac* 176:400–419.

—— (2021), 'From Recollection to Recommitment: The Rhetorical Function of Allusions to Judges in Psalms 68, 83, and 106', PhD diss., Midwestern Baptist Theological Seminary.

—— (2023), 'Polemicizing the Past: Psalm 115 and Hosea 8', *JETS* 66:481–494.

Sylva, D. (2012), 'The Rising נהרות of Psalm 93: Chaotic Order', *JSOT* 36:471–482.

Talstra, E., and C. J. Bosma (2001), 'Psalm 67: Blessing, Harvest and History: A Proposal for Exegetical Methodology', *CTJ* 36:290–313.

Tappy, R. (1995), 'Psalm 23: Symbolism and Structure', *CBQ* 57:255–280.

Tate, M. E. (2001), 'An Exposition of Psalm 8', *PRSt* 28:343–359.

Taylor, J. G. (1993), *Yahweh and the Sun: Biblical and Archaeological Evidence for Sun Worship in Ancient Israel*, Sheffield: JSOT Press.

Thomas, M. E. (1986), 'Psalms 1 and 112 as a Paradigm for the Comparison of Wisdom Motifs in the Psalms', *JETS* 29:15–24.

Thornhill, A. C. (2015), 'A Theology of Psalm 88', *EvQ* 87:45–57.

Todd III, J. M. (2015), *Remember, O Yahweh: The Poetry and Context of Psalms 135–137*, Eugene: Wipf & Stock.
Toorn, K. van der (1988), 'Ordeal Procedures in the Psalms and the Passover Meal', *VT* 38:427–445.
Tournay, R. J. (1991), *Seeing and Hearing God with the Psalms*, Sheffield: JSOT Press.
Tromp, N. (1969), *Primitive Conceptions of Death and the Nether World in the Old Testament*, Rome: Pontifical Biblical Institute.
Trotter, J. M. (2012), 'Death of the אלהים in Psalm 82', *JBL* 131:221–239.
Tsevat, M. (1970), 'God and the Gods in Assembly: An Interpretation of Psalm 82', *HUCA* 41:123–137.
Tsumura, D. T. (1980), 'Sorites in Psalm 133,2–3a', *Bib* 61:416–417.
—— (2015), 'The Creation Motif in Psalm 74:12–14? A Reappraisal of the Dragon Myth', *JBL* 134:547–555.
Tucker Jr., W. D. (2000), 'Psalm 95; Text, Context, and Intertext', *Bib* 81:533–541.
—— (2005), 'Revisiting the Plagues in Psalm CV', *VT* 55:401–411.
—— (2011), 'Hortatory Discourse and Psalm 96', *VT* 61:119–132.
—— (2014), *Constructing and Deconstructing Power in Psalms 107–150*, Atlanta: SBL Press.
—— (2019), 'The Ordered World of Psalm 92', *OTE* 33:358–377.
Vaillancourt, I. J. (2019), *The Multifaceted Saviour of Psalms 110 and 118: A Canonical Exegesis*, Sheffield: Sheffield Phoenix.
Venter, P. M. (2005), 'The Translation of Psalm 89:13 and Its Implications', *HTS* 61:531–544.
Villanueva, F. (2007), 'The "Uncertainty of a Hearing": A Study of the Sudden Change of Mood in the Individual Lament Psalms', PhD diss., University of Bristol.
—— (2020), 'From Thanksgiving to Lament: The Shape of Psalm 120', *VT* 70:479–497.
Villiers, F. T. de (2002), 'Psalm 17:14: Tekskritiek as Kritieke Eerste Stap tot Bybelvertaling', *STJ* 43:39–47.
Vincent, M. A. (2001), 'From Sinai to Jerusalem: A Study of the Hebrew Text of Psalm 68', PhD diss., University of Durham.
Viviers, H. J. (1992), 'Trust and Lament in the *ma'ălôt* Psalms (Pss 120–134)', *OTE* 5:64–77.
—— (1994), 'The Coherence of the *ma'ălôt* Psalms (Pss 120–134)', *ZAW* 106:275–289.
—— (2004), ''n Eko-billike Beoordeling van Psalm 148', *HTS* 60:815–830.
—— (2019), 'The Psychology of Place Attachment and Psalm 128', *OTE* 32:426–443.
Vos, C. J. A. (2020), 'The Lord Is My Shepherd in Suffering', *OTE* 33:634–648.
Vosloo, W. (1987), 'Die Troue God Is My Beskermer: Psalm 59', *SK* 8:223–234.
Wagner, A. (1996), 'Ist Ps 29 die Bearbeitung eines Baal-Hymnus?', *Bib* 77:538–539.

—— (2007), 'Permutatio Religionis – Ps. CXXXIX und der Wandel der Israelitischen Religion zur Bekenntnisreligion', *VT* 57:91–113.

Wagner, J. R. (1999), 'From the Heavens to the Heart: The Dynamics of Psalm 19 as Prayer', *CBQ* 61:245–261.

Wallace, H. N. (2001), '*Jubilate Deo Omnis Terra*: God and Earth in Psalm 65', in N. Habel (ed.), *The Earth Story in the Psalms and the Prophets*, Sheffield: Sheffield Academic Press, 51–64.

—— (2006), *Words to God, Word from God: The Psalms in the Prayer and Preaching of the Church*, Aldershot: Ashgate.

Wallace, R. E. (2007), *The Narrative Effect of Book IV of the Hebrew Psalter*, New York: Peter Lang.

Waltke, B. K. (2008), 'Psalm 3: A Fugitive King's Morning Prayer', *Crux* 44:2–13.

Waltke, B. K., and J. M. Houston (2019), *The Psalms as Christian Praise: A Historical Commentary*, Grand Rapids: Eerdmans.

Waltke, B. K., J. M. Houston and E. Moore (2010), *The Psalms as Christian Worship: A Historical Commentary*, Grand Rapids: Eerdmans.

—— (2014), *The Psalms as Christian Lament: A Historical Commentary*, Grand Rapids: Eerdmans.

Waltman, J. C. (2018), 'Psalms of Lament and God's Silence: Features of Petition not Yet Answered', *EvQ* 89:209–221.

Walton, J. H. (1989), *Ancient Israelite Literature in Its Cultural Context: A Survey of Parallels Between Biblical and Ancient Near Eastern Texts*, Grand Rapids: Zondervan Academic.

Wardlaw Jr., T. R. (2015), *Elohim Within the Psalms: Petitioning the Creator to Order Chaos in Oral-Derived Literature*, London: T. & T. Clark.

Watson, R. S. (forthcoming), 'Psalm 88: A Psalm Without Hope?', in . . . Sheffield: Sheffield Phoenix, xx–xx.

Watson, W. G. E. (1986), *Classical Hebrew Poetry*, 2nd edn, Sheffield: JSOT Press.

Weber, B. (1993), 'Psalm LXI – Versuch einer hiskianischen Situierung', *VT* 4:265–268.

—— (1995), *Psalm 95 und sein Umfeld: Eine poetologische Studie*, Weinheim: Beltz Athenäum.

—— (2000), 'Zur Datierung der Asaph-Psalmen 74 und 79', *Bib* 81:521–532.

—— (2006), 'Psalm 1 and Its Function as a Directive into the Psalter and Towards a Biblical Theology', *OTE* 19:237–260.

—— (2009), 'Psalm 78 als "Mitte" des Psalters? – ein Versuch', *Bib* 88:305–325.

Wendland, E. (1998), 'Introit "into the Sanctuary of God" (Psalm 73:17): Entering the Theological "Heart" of the Psalm at the Centre of the Psalter', *OTE* 11:128–153.

Wenham, G. J. (2005), 'The Ethics of the Psalms', in Johnston and Firth, *Interpreting*, 175–194.

—— (2012), *Psalms as Torah: Reading Biblical Song Ethically*, Grand Rapids: Baker.

—— (2013), *The Psalter Reclaimed: Praying and Praising with the Psalms*, Wheaton: Crossway.

Westermann, C. (1981), *Praise and Lament in the Psalms*, Edinburgh: T. & T. Clark.

White, S. N. (1999), 'Angel of the Lord: Messenger or Euphemism?', *TynB* 50:299–305.

Whitekettle, R. (2005), 'Bugs, Bunny or Boars? Identifying the *Zîz* Animals of Psalms 50 and 80', *CBQ* 67:250–264.

—— (2006), 'Taming the Shrew, Shrike, and Shrimp: The Form and Function of Zoological Classification in Psalm 8', *JBL* 125:749–765.

Whiting, M. J. (2013), 'Psalms 1 and 2 as a Hermeneutical Lens for Reading the Psalter', *EvQ* 85:246–262.

Whybray, N. (1996), *Reading the Psalms as a Book*, Sheffield: Sheffield Academic Press.

Wiggins, S. N. (2014), *Weathering the Psalms: A Meteorological Survey*, Eugene: Cascade.

Willgren, D. (2016a), *The Formation of the 'Book' of Psalms: Reconsidering the Transmission and Canonization of Psalmody in Light of Material Culture and the Poetics of Anthologies*, Tübingen: Mohr Siebeck.

—— (2016b), 'Psalm 72:20: A Frozen Colophon?', *JBL* 135:49–60.

Williamson, H. G. M. (2022), 'Who's Kissing Who? Reflections on Psalm 2:11–12', in Southwood and Morse, *Psalms*, 25–41.

Willis, J. T. (1973), 'The Song of Hannah and Psalm 113', *CBQ* 34:139–154.

Willis, T. M. (1991), '"So Great Is His Steadfast Love": A Rhetorical Analysis of Psalm 103', *Bib* 72:525–537.

Wilson, G. H. (1985a), *The Editing of the Hebrew Psalter*, Chico: Scholars Press.

—— (1985b), 'The Use of "Untitled" Psalms in the Hebrew Psalter', *ZAW* 97:404–413.

Witherington III, B. (2017), *Psalms Old and New: Exegesis, Intertextuality and Hermeneutics*, Minneapolis: Fortress.

Witt, A. (2012), 'Hearing Psalm 102 Within the Context of the Hebrew Psalter', *VT* 62:582–606.

Witte, M. (2000), '"Aber Gott wird Meine Seele Erlosen": Tod und Leben Nach Psalm XLIX', *VT* 50:540–560.

—— (2002), 'Das neue Lied – Beobachtungen zum Zeitverständnis von Psalm 33', *ZAW* 114:522–541.

—— (2006), 'From Exodus to David – History and Historiography in Psalm 78', in N. Calduch-Benages and J. Liesen (eds.), *History and Identity: How Israel's Later Authors Viewed Its Earlier History: Deuterocanonical and Cognate Literature Yearbook 2006*, Berlin: de Gruyter, 21–42.

Wolde, E. van (2019), 'Accusing Yhwh of Fickleness: A Study of Psalm 89,47–52', *Bib* 100:506–526.

Won, Y.-S. (2019), *Remembering the Covenants in Song: An Intertextual Study of the Abrahamic and Mosaic Covenants in Psalm 105*, Eugene: Wipf & Stock.

Wong, G. T. K. (2016), 'Psalm 73 as Ring Composition', *Bib* 97:16–40.

Zenger, E. (1996), *A God of Vengeance? Understanding the Psalms of Divine Wrath*, Louisville: Westminster John Knox.

—— (1998), 'The Composition and Theology of the Fifth Book of Psalms, Psalms 107–145', *JSOT* 80:77–102.

—— (ed.) (2010a), *The Composition of the Book of Psalms*, Leuven: Peeters.

—— (2010b), 'Psalmenexegese und Psalterexegese: Eine Forschungsskizze', in Zenger, *Composition*, 17–67.

Zieba, Z. (2010), 'Psalm 63: A Study of Its Imagery and Theology in the Context of the Psalter', PhD diss., University of Durham.

Ziegert, C. (2020), 'What is חֶסֶד? A Frame-Semantic Approach', *JSOT* 44:711–732.

Zimmerli, W. (1971), *Man and His Hope in the Old Testament*, London: SCM.

Zwickel, W. (1995), '"Opfer der Gerechtigkeit" (Dtn. XXXIII 19; Ps. IV 6, LI 21)', *VT* 45:386–391.

INDEX OF BIBLICAL AND ANCIENT TEXTS

Leviticus

Numbers

INDEX OF AUTHORS

INDEX OF SUBJECTS